E 175.5 .A2 C45 1994

Chalfant, Edward

Better in darkness

COSUMNES RIVER COLLEGE

D0215429

.IBRARY

Date Due

PRINTED IN U.S.A.   CAT. NO. 24 161   BRO DART

Better in Darkness

Better in Darkness

A BIOGRAPHY OF
HENRY ADAMS
HIS SECOND LIFE
1862–1891

EDWARD CHALFANT

Archon Books

1994

© 1994 Edward Chalfant. All rights reserved.
First published 1994 by Archon Books,
an imprint of The Shoe String Press, Inc.
Hamden, Connecticut 06514.

This is volume two of a trilogy of the life
of Henry Adams. Volume one, *Both Sides of the Ocean:
A Biography of Henry Adams—His First Life,
1838–1862* by Edward Chalfant, was published in 1982.

The paper used in this publication meets the minimum
requirements of American National Standard for Information
Sciences—Permanence of Paper for Printed Library Materials.
ANSI Z39.48-1984. ⊗

Printed in the United States of America

Library of Congress Cataloging-in-Publication Data

Better in darkness : a biography of Henry Adams :
his second life, 1862–1891
Edward Chalfant.
p.   cm.
Continues: Both sides of the ocean.
Includes bibliographical references and index.
1. Adams, Henry, 1838–1918.
2. Historians—United States—Biography.
I. Title.
E175.5.A2C45   1993   973'.07202—dc20   93-10202
ISBN 0-208-02041-1

in memory
for Louisa Hooper Thoron

Contents

PART THREE

PREFACE

This book tells a complete story and is meant to be read by itself. It is also the middle book of a trilogy.

Secretly, when almost twenty-four, Henry Adams started over in life because already successful. Openly, when fifty-four, he again started over. When he died at eighty, he had completed three lives.

Each life took the form of a coherent, important story. His biography accordingly should have the form of three books, each readable by itself, the three to be readable in any order, yet form a whole. The catch for the biographer is that Adams improved. In his first life, he reached a high level of achievement. In his second and third, he set himself harder tasks and reached still higher levels. A theoretical consequence is that a fitting biography of Adams would be a trilogy in which the second book is better than the first and the third improves on the second. The theory is all very well, but the biographer has to try to live up to it.

The first book of the present trilogy, *Both Sides of the Ocean*, was published in 1982. It recounts an astounding adventure and moves fast along a road that is mostly straight but becomes exceedingly dangerous.

This middle book, *Better in Darkness*, may qualify as a tragedy, provided it is kept in mind that some Greek and Shakespearean tragedies have light, even happy, endings. One of Adams's qualities was willingness in a given situation to make whatever effort was required, no matter how difficult or prolonged. This quality did not cause tragedies, but it permitted him to surmount them.

It must be said as well that *Better in Darkness* begins as a biography but becomes in part a history of a marriage. Marian (or Clover) Hooper and Henry Adams treated each other as equals and thought, felt, and acted jointly. Wife and husband cannot fairly be separated. They are understood together, or not at all.

The biography also becomes in part a history of an epic

ix

history. Adams's writings during his second life were numerous. *Better in Darkness* touches all of them, including writings that till now have been neglected or not known to have been his. It especially concerns his *History of the United States*, which sooner or later will be recognized as our nation's epic—the one work by an American that rightly bears comparison with Milton's *Paradise Lost* and Homer's *Iliad*.

To summarize, the matters at issue are a man, a marriage, and an epic. These matters require the telling of an extraordinary story that has a wrenched, yet satisfactory, outline. The story begins by telling what Adams was able to do while still unmarried. It continues by telling what he and Clover were able to do in unison, till the morning of her death; and it ends by telling how he succeeded in the work he and she had been wanting him to do, the completion of his *History*. It ends also by going with him to the South Seas and around the world. Thus it shares his personal odyssey.

Acknowledgments

E ven more than is generally realized, biographies owe their leading qualities to the evidence on which they rest. Interpretation and analysis, in my view, should accord with the evidence unfailingly. The premise is one I share with Adams.

The present trilogy—of which this book is the middle volume—is the first biography of Henry Adams developed in its entirety since the opening of the Adams Papers at the Massachusetts Historical Society in 1955; the first to be developed since the finding in the 1960s of a great cache of letters *to* Adams in the Theodore Dwight Papers at the Massachusetts Historical Society; the first to be developed since the preparation of Stephen T. Riley's *Microfilms of the Henry Adams Papers*, published by the Society in 36 reels in 1979; the first to be developed with the support of the new evidence assembled by the editors of *The Letters of Henry Adams*, published by the Harvard University Press in six volumes in 1982 and 1988; the first to draw upon the entire array of evidence relating to Henry and Marian Adams collected by Ward and Louisa Hooper Thoron; and the only one that reflects the full evidence available to Aileen Tone, Adams's companion in his last years. The trilogy rests in addition on a wide range of previously unknown, unavailable, or neglected lesser sources, including some not traced till recent months. In short, it rests on incomparably improved evidence—which, as will be seen, requires a shift from received but mistaken visions of Adams to a different, wholly credible vision: one that till now could not readily be made available in books, but that was more or less familiar to the few persons who knew him well in life.

This middle book was written in two stages. Between 1955 and 1988, I made many efforts to plan, draft, and complete it; and several times I reached the point of believing I was succeeding. In May 1988, intending to do no more than make some changes in

the first chapters, I found myself writing a better, more explanatory version—the book as it now stands.

During the first stage, I was greatly assisted in obtaining
evidence by Aileen Tone; by members of the Adams family, most
notably Henry Adams II, Abigail Adams Homans, and Thomas
Boylston Adams; by relatives of Mrs. Henry Adams, most notably
Louisa Hooper Thoron, Ellen Hooper Potter, and Faith Thoron
Knapp; by directors, librarians, and editors at the Massachusetts
Historical Society, most notably Stephen T. Riley, Lyman Butter-
field, Malcolm Freiberg, Louis Tucker, Peter Drummey, Richard
Ryerson, and Celeste Walker; by three editors of *The Letters of Henry
Adams*, J. C. Levenson, Charles Vandersee, and Viola Hopkins
Winner; by the staffs of the Houghton Library, the University
Archives, and the Law School Library at Harvard University; by
the staff of the John Hay Library at Brown University; by the staffs
of the Newspaper Division and the Rare Books and Manuscripts
Division of the New York Public Library; by the staffs of the Boston
Athenaeum, Boston Public Library, Columbia University Library,
the Library of Congress, the National Archives, the Society Library
in New York, the Department of Manuscripts and the Newspaper
Division of the British Library, and the library of University College
London. I was much assisted in obtaining evidence by fellow
researchers, notably Martin Anthony Brunor, Harold Dean Cater,
Leon Edel, William Jordy, and Arlene Boucher Tehan; also by a
leading book dealer, Stephen Weissman; and further by generous
individuals, most notably Mrs. George M. Grinnell, Mrs. Henry
Adams La Farge; Mr. and Mrs. Harold Landon, Mr. Samuel Reber,
and Mr. and Mrs. Henry S. Sherman.

During the second stage, my main problem was better development of the narrative and notes, but at critical junctures I
needed and was given special assistance relating to evidence. In
this respect, I am especially indebted to a fellow scholar, Richard
Stone; to a leading dealer in manuscripts, Paul C. Richards; to
Jennifer B. Lee at the John Hay Library; to Kenneth D. Ackerman,
the historian of the 1869 gold conspiracy; and to John D. Stinson
and other manuscript specialists at the New York Public Library.
Two friends, Frederick M. Keener and Marilyn Hertling, helpfully
read and responded to drafts of the beginning chapters. Linton S.
Thorn closely read the entire manuscript and offered invaluable
criticisms. As always, my wife, Eleni (or Helen) Chalfant, read and
suggested changes in every draft of the book's chapters and attendant notes. The publisher, James Thorpe III, studied the work

repeatedly, made innumerable discerning suggestions, and gave me timely information, needed advice, and saving encouragement.

All extracts from materials in the Adams Papers appear by permission of the Adams Manuscript Trust and the Massachusetts Historical Society. All the following extracts likewise appear by permission of the Massachusetts Historical Society: those from the collections of the papers of Henry Adams; those from the *Microfilms of the Henry Adams Papers*; those from *The Letters of Henry Adams*; those from the Charles Francis Adams, Jr., Atkinson, Bancroft, Barlow, Cater, Dwight, Elizabeth Cameron, Endicott, Lodge, Morse, Parkman, Shattuck, and Winsor papers; those from materials in the Henry Adams Library; and those from other materials cited as owned by the Society.

All the following extracts appear by permission of Faith Thoron Knapp and Gray Thoron: those from writings by Marian Hooper Adams—born Marian (or Clover) Hooper; those from writings by Ward Thoron and Louisa Hooper Thoron; and those from other materials cited as formerly or presently in the Faith Thoron Knapp Papers.

All the following extracts appear by permission of the Houghton Library, Harvard University: those from the *Microfilms of the Henry Adams Papers*, Harvard reels; those from *The Letters of Henry Adams* that are dependent on Houghton Library holdings; those from papers by Charles Francis Adams III, Louisa Johnson Adams, Elizabeth Sherman Cameron, Marian (Clover) Hooper, William Jones Hoppin, Rebecca Dodge Rae, and Louisa Hooper Thoron owned by the Houghton Library; and those from the E. L. Godkin and the James Family papers.

All the following extracts appear by permission of the John Hay Library, Brown University: those from the *Microfilms of the Henry Adams Papers*, Brown reel; those from *The Letters of Henry Adams* that are dependent on John Hay Library holdings; and those from letters by Clarence King in the John Hay Papers.

All extracts from the John Bigelow Papers, the Worthington C. Ford Papers, and Miscellaneous Personal Manuscripts by Henry Adams appear by permission of the Rare Books and Manuscripts Division, the New York Public Library, Astor, Lenox and Tilden Foundations.

All extracts from the unpublished journal of Benjamin Moran appear through the assistance of the Manuscript Division of the Library of Congress. Adams's letter to Frederick W. Seward, May 4, 1877, appears through the assistance of the National Archives. St.

Gaudens's notes in his scrapbook appear by permission of the Dartmouth College Library.

All extracts from the John Bright Papers appear by permission of the Department of Manuscripts of the British Library. The extract from the letter, John Bright to his wife, June 26, 1867, appears by permission of the library of University College London. The extracts from the letters by Prime Minister Palmerston, June 10, 1862; Foreign Secretary Russell, June 14, 1862; and U. S. Minister C. F. Adams, June 20, 1862, appear by permission of the Trustees of the Broadlands Archives.

PART ONE

1

THE *TRENT* VOLCANO

In mid-January 1862 in London, persons wishing to visit the United States Legation were directed to a house a few steps west of Portland Place at 5 Mansfield Street. Owned by Seymour Fitzgerald, a Conservative member of Parliament, the house was rented temporarily to Minister Charles Francis Adams for use both as a residence for him, his wife, and three of their children and as the Legation's place of business. The house was handsomely furnished and acceptably large, but the minister disliked it. The windows admitted too little sun, and the portraits were antipathetic. The show-piece was "a full length of Napoleon the Great in his robes by Gerrand."[1] Others displayed Nell Gwynne, Lady Jane Grey, Mary Queen of Scots, and assorted male Europeans whom the minister scorned as "decapitated heroes."[2]

A Massachusetts Republican, C. F. Adams could seem a politician much like other American politicians. Yet, in a way that attracted continual notice, he stood apart from all others. His grandfather and father had both been presidents. It chanced too that John Adams and John Quincy Adams had reached the presidency for the most part through success as diplomats. It further chanced that John Adams had served as the first American minister to England, following the War of Independence, and John Quincy Adams likewise had been minister to England, following the War of 1812. These old truths considered, the question had to be asked whether C. F. Adams too might be president.

Most callers at the Legation were ushered to a small room by the entrance and spoke with one or the other of two officials, the secretary of legation, Charles Lush Wilson, and the assistant secretary, Benjamin Moran. As much as the minister, each of the secretaries was a politician. Wilson, an Illinois Republican, had asked the Lincoln administration for a postal appointment in Chicago. He instead was tendered the first secretaryship in the

English mission. He took it but once in London showed little willingness to perform any duties. Moran, a Pennsylvania Democrat, was a holdover from the Buchanan administration. Capable, experienced, and hard-working, he valued his reappointment and nourished dreams of rising in the foreign service.

Callers permitted access to the floor above found themselves in a room the full width of the building. There they encountered Minister Adams and another aide.[3] Had the truth been told, C. F. Adams would have been happier if the official secretaries downstairs had not been commissioned. The only assistant he wanted was his third son. The son's baptismal name was Henry Brooks Adams. His title and function, communicated to the State Department while father and son were still in Boston, was "private Secretary."[4]

The two Adamses worked face to face in near proximity. Similar in physique, they differed in energy and in mental and emotional makeup. C. F. Adams stood about five feet three. Aged fifty-four, he spoke and wrote with cultivated deliberateness. He could be sociable when asked to be, but he much preferred staying home without company. Work permitting, he collected coins and took solitary walks.

On his next birthday, February 16, 1862, H. B. Adams—as he usually signed his name—would be twenty-four. He looked older.[5] His manner was informal, his voice pleasant, his expressions trenchant and humorous, his energy quiet but incessant.[6] Honest to a fault, he tended to be forthright; that is, when candor was possible and not likely to injure the persons he spoke or wrote to. Yet no resource served him better or more often than selective silence. Knowing much, he commonly and without hesitation would say or write a mere fraction of what he knew.[7]

Silence shaded into secrecy. Ambitious from early boyhood, Henry had revealed a few elements of his ambition—enough to camouflage its principal components. For a year, since January 1861, he had carried secrecy to such lengths that no one in England, not his father or other relations, still less the official secretaries, had anything approaching an accurate idea of what his choices had led to. That Henry went beyond ordinary extremes was nothing against him. It instead was a sign that tasks were urgent and he wished to perform them. Also it was an augury that, of the members of America's most noted family, he might in time emerge as the most deserving of attention.

❖ ❖ ❖

Born in 1838 in Boston, Henry was the fourth of seven children. Eldest was Louisa Catherine Adams II, known as Loo. The first and second sons were John Quincy Adams II and Charles Francis Adams, Jr. Henry came next and was followed by much-liked Arthur, who died in early boyhood. The last born were Mary and Brooks.

The children were raised in contrasting environments. During colder months, they lived at their parents' winter house in Boston, near the top of Beacon Hill. During warmer months, they lived near or in the Old House, the Adamses' chief residence, situated on a large property in Quincy, a country town on the Atlantic seven miles south of Boston. The property had attractions. Its high point, President's Hill, afforded open views of the ocean, Boston Harbor, and arriving and departing ships.

More or less from babyhood, third son Henry differed from his siblings in being exceptionally purposive and in allying himself with his father's mother.[8] Louisa Catherine Johnson was born in 1775 in London, the eldest daughter of an American father from Maryland, Joshua Johnson, and an English mother, Catherine Nuth. She passed all her youth abroad. In London in 1797, she married John Quincy Adams, then a rising diplomat. She and the future president lived long, rewarding, difficult lives, partly in Europe, mostly in America; but three of their four children died at early ages, leaving only Charles Francis.

Louisa Catherine Adams and her grandson Henry bore each other a strong facial resemblance.[9] In the 1840s, during long summers together in Quincy, she gave him her unqualified sympathy and approbation. He responded by feeling they were counterparts. When she died, in Washington in 1852, he was fourteen. Then or soon after, her death brought on an extreme response: he felt that she and he were a single being. One can say that Henry *lived* this idea. He saw to it that her life would find its continuation and male variant in his life.[10]

The importance of this linkage can be seen in the characteristic fact that, in Henry's extant papers written before he was thirty-one, Louisa Adams is never mentioned. His sharer of self is everywhere implicit. Yet she nowhere appears.

Two other Adamses with whom Henry especially linked himself were John Adams, his long-deceased great-grandfather, whose life and writings he early began to study, and his grandfather, John Quincy Adams, whom he knew well and freely talked with till late in the summer of 1847, the last season they were together.[11]

For all his involvements with older Adamses, the sole designer of Henry's life was Henry, who was nothing if not a learner, and learned first to become a planner. In his middle teens, secretly, he completed a plan for his future. The plan had four aspects. He meant to be the leading American politician of his time. He aspired to become a great writer. He expected to live in Washington, eventually as renter or even owner of a house. And he hoped to travel over much of the globe.

That the plan was adapted to its maker would appear in his never having to replace it. Its aspects could seem divergent but in practice were mutually supportive. Its extreme ambitiousness was in fact not extreme. It was tailored to comport with his never-failing energy, large prospective pecuniary means, positive talent for practical management, and exceptional powers of imagination, mind, and feeling.[12]

In one way, the plan was timid. It misjudged how rapidly an Adams could succeed. Henry placed an article in the *Harvard Magazine* in 1855 when a freshman. As a senior, he was elected class orator, the highest distinction a class could assign to one of its members. Soon after graduating, he escaped to Europe, worked hard at acquiring languages, and traveled. In the spring of 1860, he made a journey to Italy and wrote a small book of letters about the journey for publication in the Boston press.[13] After a two-year absence, he came home a speaker of fluent German, good French, and a beginning of Italian.

His father was about to start a second term as a Republican congressman. In November 1860 in Quincy, C. F. Adams invited Henry to serve in Washington through the winter as private secretary. Henry responded in two ways. He delightedly assented. Also he sought what could seem a mere small added assignment as a correspondent. Secretly, but with his father's knowledge and consent, he arranged to supply unpaid anonymous news reports from Washington to the most widely circulated newspaper in New England, the *Boston Daily Advertiser*.

The full meaning of this arrangement could be seen only if one considered Henry's aspirations. In the United States in 1860, the line separating newspapers from politics had no existence. A reporter or correspondent, simply by writing for publication, either signed or anonymous, could be an effective politician. No one realized this better than the third son of Congressman Adams; and no Adams—and no American—wanted more to be a powerful politician. These things considered, the two aspects of Henry's new situation had different weights. In one measure, by assenting to serve as private secretary, he became the visible aide of a congress-man, his father. In a much greater measure, by becoming a correspondent of a leading newspaper, he became an invisible independent politician.[14]

Five Adamses—parents, Henry, and the two youngest children, Mary and Brooks—traveled to the capital just when South Carolina and its companion "cotton states" were preparing to secede from the Union. Henry mailed nineteen reports to the *Advertiser* while the secession crisis worsened.[15] He saw seventeen published, un-signed.[16] But something quite unnoticed happened along the way. In January 1861 in Washington, practically without the knowledge of his relations, he allied himself with a stranger, just arrived in the capital, "who came to view the field for the *New York Times*, and . . . was a man of the world." The stranger was Henry Jarvis Ray-mond.[17]

Raymond had co-founded the *New York Times*, with George Jones and E. B. Wesley, in 1851. In 1861, he was one of the newspaper's owners, its editor, and a prominent Republican politi-cian. It can be assumed that he learned directly from Henry that none other than he, young Adams, was writing the Washington reports appearing in the *Boston Advertiser*. The disclosure pointed towards possible future arrangements.[18]

When his stint with the *Advertiser* ended, in mid-February 1861, Henry started work on a secret project all his own. He began to draft a political article of permanent value, to be titled "The Great Secession Winter of 1860–61."[19] The vehicle for which he planned the article was the *Atlantic Monthly*, published in Boston and edited by one of his Harvard teachers, James Russell Lowell.

While busily writing his article, Henry returned to Massachu-setts, ceased being private secretary, and took a role entirely separate from his father by becoming a law clerk in Boston.[20] This new beginning was immediately interrupted. Senator William Henry Seward of New York had been nominated and confirmed to serve under President Lincoln as secretary of state. As a result of urgings by Seward, Lincoln chose C. F. Adams to be minister to England. On learning the news of his appointment, the elder Adams *ordered* Henry to accompany him to London. Henry had no desire to comply. Indeed he strongly wished not to comply. When protests did not avail, he agreed to go, but he imposed conditions. He said that he would go only as "an independent and free citizen" and would serve at the Legation only as "private Secretary." As understood by him, the latter phrase meant that his secretaryship would be wholly unofficial.[21]

Henry prepared to sail for England with his parents and the younger children; but first, in deepest secrecy, this time without his father's knowledge, he arranged to act as paid, regular, anonymous London correspondent of the *New York Times*, a newspaper second to no other in the Union.[22] Dangerous in itself, the arrangement was a mere part, albeit the central part, of a scheme that was dangerous beyond description.[23] He planned to contact *English* editors and publish anonymously in their journals also.

He did not scheme alone. He enlisted as a partner the younger of his elder brothers, C. F. Adams, Jr.[24] As Henry saw it, their enterprise was indispensable. It reflected the fact that their father, although in some ways adept as a politician, was incapable of forming even minimum relations with the American and foreign press.[25]

Minister Adams did not immediately start for London to begin his duties. Instead he waited in Boston to attend the marriage of his eldest son, John Quincy Adams II.

The elder Adams could not have chosen a worse time for a delay. On April 12, 1861, gunfire in the harbor of Charleston, South Carolina, announced the start of a vast rebellion. The United States of America were engulfed in civil war.

The five Adamses who earlier had gone to Washington sailed at last from Boston and landed at Liverpool. They reached London on May 13. Henry resumed his visible old work as private secretary and concurrently began his totally invisible new work as anonymous correspondent of the *New York Times*. The third son seemed to have the faculty of arriving at a place at the moment when his efforts would most be needed. He began his work in London at the instant when relations between the United States and England were revealed to have become exceedingly disturbed. Rapidly his weekly despatches in the *Times* won their unnamed author a leading place in the Union press.[26] In less extraordinary circumstances, he might have contented himself with this single gain. As things were, he brilliantly foresaw that a crisis was in the making. In the belief that he should make every effort he could, he sustained his *Times* despatches and simultaneously visited Manchester in quest of data about the cotton trade. He obtained the data and, despite interruptions, secretly wrote an article for anonymous publication in the *Atlantic Monthly*. As soon as possible, he mailed the article to his brother Charles, who would act as agent.[27]

By then, the *Trent* affair had burst on an astonished world. A strange upheaval, the affair seemed to expand the American Civil War into a vast embroilment ranging what was left of the United

States against England, France, and the Confederacy all at once. Week after week, several North Atlantic powers seemed in process of lapsing into general war.

Henry had feared the expanded war. Even more, he had been wanting to avert it. The *Trent* affair found him so positioned that he could write despatches for the *New York Times* that would affect both the Union government and the public throughout the North. It could seem he was afforded a splendid opportunity. It would be more accurate to say he was placed in mortal danger. No plan, dream, or nightmare could have posed a task more perilous and more exacting than having to write for so strategic a newspaper during a crisis so appalling with the purpose of guiding events to a peaceful outcome. The son was exposed to every risk of acting wrongly. And he had to act alone.

It should not be supposed that Henry performed his task without repeated strain and nearly insurmountable difficulty. Yet he more than performed it. He did not merely *report* the crisis. On the contrary, by great effort, he managed to be one of the half-dozen persons, American and European, who most effectually worked to end it.[28]

The detailed story of young Adams's effort in London in 1861 and the first days of 1862 has been told in the opening book of this trilogy: *Both Sides of the Ocean*. Being already told, it should not be repeated. Before proceeding, it none the less is necessary to look again at what he did. The reason is that events that have important meanings when studied under the lamp of biography can have still more important meanings when reexamined under the lamp of history.

In this instance, the subject, Henry Adams, when not yet twenty-four, won for himself a most unusual, indeed a contradictory gain: a *secret* place in history. The gain considered, his biographers cannot escape the duty of presenting him historically. When this is done, it becomes possible to see from his own point of view exactly what he did in youth that was historic.

As might be expected, reexamination of his feat requires attention to actual wars that were fought between the Americans and the English. Also it requires attention to the means by which the wars were ended.

War first broke out between the Americans and the English in 1775. On the American side, the war was conducted by a Continental Congress and an army led by a farmer-soldier from Virginia,

George Washington. One of the witnesses of the war was an eight-year-old boy in Massachusetts, John Quincy Adams. From a high point near his home, the boy had a deeply exciting experience: he descried in the far distance the battle of Bunker Hill.

In the later judgment of J. Q. Adams, George Washington proved a leader of unexampled ability.[29] Still later, when a small boy, Henry Adams was told his grandfather's appraisal of the great Virginian. Henry took the appraisal to heart, became a close student of Washington's life and character, and in 1875 anonymously published *his* opinion of the Virginian's management of the War of Independence. He wrote: "Every reperusal of this familiar story brings to notice only fresh causes for admiring the combination of prudence with daring, patience with energy, and military skill with political foresight, which distinguishes Washington from all other generals of whatever time or nation. . . ."[30]

In 1781, the Continental Congress named five commissioners to negotiate a treaty of peace. One of the five, Benjamin Franklin, then in Paris, contacted an agent of the English government. A second, John Jay, advised by Franklin that the English were anxious to negotiate, joined him in Paris; and a third, John Adams, hearing from Jay that the English would "conclude a peace or truce with commissioners of the thirteen *United States of America*," likewise appeared in Paris.

The three commissioners negotiated a treaty on terms stunningly favorable to the United States. In the opinion of Henry Adams, published anonymously in 1875, the Treaty of Paris was really one man's work and deserved acknowledgment as the "most brilliant part of Franklin's brilliant career."[31]

For the Americans of the time, the events of 1775–1783 were unforgettable experiences of *war, negotiation, and a treaty*. A generation later, the pattern was repeated. In June 1812, President Madison took the risk of thrusting the United States into a war with England. The vicissitudes of the conflict were mixed. Several captains of American frigates distinguished themselves in sea fights; a young American general, Winfield Scott, won renown in the battles of Chippawa and Lundy's Lane; a British army briefly occupied the newbuilt city of Washington and burned the Capitol, the White House, and other buildings; but the fighting was indecisive.

In May 1813, the secretary of the treasury, Albert Gallatin, was sent with James A. Bayard to Russia in the hope that the English might consent to mediation by Czar Alexander. The mission of Gallatin and Bayard had resulted from conversations in 1812 between the czar and the U. S. minister at St. Petersburg, John Quincy Adams.[32] It developed that the English would *not* consent. The mission proved abortive.

A new mission being necessary, the Senate in January 1814 empowered J. Q. Adams, James A. Bayard, Henry Clay, and Jonathan Russell to act as peace commissioners, meet in Europe, and treat with England. Gallatin, who had stayed abroad, was shortly added as a fifth commissioner.

Apprised of his new appointment, Adams traveled to Holland. Thinking he would return to Russia, he left his wife Louisa and their son Charles Francis, a boy of seven, at St. Petersburg. At the cost of six months of discussions, ending at Christmas, 1814, the American commissioners and their English opposites negotiated the Treaty of Ghent. As a matter of words, the new treaty put the countries where they had been when hostilities started; but, as a matter of practical advantage, it immensely favored the Great Republic, better securing its independence.

After the negotiation, J. Q. Adams wrote to Louisa in St. Petersburg, directing her to join him in Paris. Accompanied by Charles, she traveled nine hundred miles by carriage from the Russian capital to the French in the dead of winter.[33] Mother and son arrived in time for Napoleon's Hundred Days, and impressionable Charles once saw the hated emperor greet a crowd from a window of the Tuileries.[34]

A generation later, Henry Adams was told the story of the journey from St. Petersburg to Paris by the travelers who had made it.[35] Or rather Henry was told many stories; and he listened in such a spirit that his conduct thereafter was that of a person who loved, lived, learned, felt, thought, acted, worked, wrote, and spoke historically.[36]

Especially Louisa Catherine Adams, John Quincy Adams, and Charles Francis Adams stamped on Henry's mind two stories of war, negotiation, and a treaty. As the boy understood the stories, it was no detraction from the first that the leading negotiator of the Treaty of Paris was a Pennsylvanian born in Boston, Benjamin Franklin, nor a detraction from the second that the leading negotiator of the Treaty of Ghent was Albert Gallatin, a Pennsylvanian born in Switzerland. Though a loyal Adams, Henry showed no tendency to confine himself to Adams family interests and New England enthusiasms. He liked to grow. His talents disposed him to feel heroic stories as incitements to that generous kind of rivalry that delights in others' achievements, builds on that delight, and becomes unlimited.

In the boy's universe, great Americans were many. George Washington stood astronomically high.[37] Other males were near-equals. One was John Adams, of whom Henry when a man would sometimes feel himself the representative.[38] Another was John Quincy Adams, alive and not averse to a grandson's constantly intruding in his study.[39] And names could be multiplied.

The peculiarity of the case was Henry's applying his highest evaluation to a woman. Louisa Catherine Adams affected her favorite grandson as most superior, yet continuous with himself. Henry therefore understood that among Americans, he—as much as she—stood first.

Henry's behavior thereafter was erected on that extremely positive assumption. He took it as settled that his future should be given to silent labor. He would "Toil and Trust"—the motto of her Johnson forebears.[40] By that means, in the natural course of things, he would outdo all American rivals, dead or living, not excluding George Washington.[41]

In the crisis of 1861, the historic pattern of war, negotiation, and a treaty was not repeated. England and the United States moved to the verge of war and were expected to fight, but a different pattern was introduced. Indeed the pattern was so different that the American Unionists found it hard to welcome. Put in simple terms, the different pattern was *negotiation first and war avoided*.

No new crisis would have arisen, had England's leaders disregarded events in America. If anything, they over-attended to a cascade of American impingements: first the emergence of a powerful political party, the Republicans, opposed to slavery; next the defeat of the Republicans in the election of 1856; then their victory in 1860; the prospect that Abraham Lincoln, an inexperienced Illinois lawyer, would be installed as president; the resulting secession of the states of the Lower South; their joining to form an attempted nation, the Confederate States of America; assurances that Lincoln would be a figurehead and that William H. Seward, an experienced New Yorker, would lead the diminished Union as "premier" in Lincoln's Cabinet; claims that the "border states," Virginia being chief, would loyally remain in the United States; counter-claims that the border states would join the Confederacy; repeated warnings that Seward, when secretary of state, would foment a *foreign* war, probably with England, in the hopes that such a conflict would renew patriotic feeling and permit his reconstructing the broken Union; news that Lincoln had been inaugurated and Seward's stewardship launched; confirmation that most of the border states were choosing the Confederate side; reports that rebel emissaries, trying to negotiate a peaceful separation of South and North, were given solemn commitments by Seward which he treacherously broke; fearful news that Southern authorities had resorted to arms, beginning with cannon fire against Fort Sumter in Charleston Harbor on April 12, 1861; news that Federal authorities were meeting force with force; announcements that the Confederacy would attack Union merchant ships with privateers; and official statements that the Union government would blockade the rebels' coast.

The English by and large did not have pro-slavery feelings. They had abolished slavery in their empire, and they would hardly have sympathized with a new nation in America composed exclusively of the cotton states of the Lower South. But the English had tired of the bragging of Americans about their Great Republic. Moreover, the English recognized that American bragging had a basis: the vaunted Republic was growing rapidly and might soon be very great. Hence a large majority in England, rather fearing the growth of the Union across the sea, observed its bifurcation with relief and a certain pleasure. Besides, when watching a contest, the English liked to cheer the weaker contestant; and the Confederates, even after gaining most of the counties of Virginia, were patently weaker than the Federals. Then, too, the English felt a tie between themselves and the established families of Virginia, whom they saw as heirs of an Elizabethan—not puritan—founding of English plantations in America. More particularly, the English remembered an English choice. In 1660, a large majority of the English had rejected their puritan-republicans, epitomized by Cromwell, and had restored the monarchy, even at the cost of showing fealty to Charles II, with all his faults. To English minds, the rejection of 1660 found a parallel in 1861 in Virginia's rejection of America's puritan-republicans, epitomized by Seward and Lincoln. Accordingly, when confirmation arrived that the Virginians for the most part had joined the Confederacy, a preponderance of the English felt somewhat warmly *for* the South and very coldly *against* the Union.

This combination of tepid sympathy and frigid antipathy made the English easy gulls for rebel propagandists. The result was mistaken certitudes. It was rootedly established in England that Lincoln was a backwoodsman devoid of civilized qualities and that

Seward was not a gentleman and thus was incapable of honest dealings. The one's barbarity and the other's treachery *were* the American problem, to England's perfect knowledge. Yet the American problem was clearly not of the highest importance. The separation across the sea was known to be irreversible. It followed that peace would soon begin.[42]

So things stood in mid-May 1861, when C. F. Adams and H. B. Adams appeared in London.[43] Yet, month after month, civil war in America continued unabated. Its unlooked-for persistence bred confusion in Europe, a mixture of hope and doubt.[44]

On November 8, Charles Wilkes, captain of the *San Jacinto*, a Union sloop-of-war, directed his vessel to intercept an unarmed English mail ship, the *Trent*, in the Old Bahama Channel off Cuba. By ordering that cannon shots be fired in its path, he brought the ship to a stop. A party headed by Lieutenant Fairfax boarded the *Trent* and wrested two Confederate diplomats and two secretaries from its decks. The captives were shifted to the *San Jacinto*, which gained speed and steered towards Washington or New York.

The news of Wilkes's act reached Washington on November 15. First in the government offices, then everywhere in the Union, his seizure of the rebel diplomats was greeted with ecstasies, as if the captain had seized, not James M. Mason, John Slidell, and their secretaries, but half the South. Seward witnessed the delirium and may have taken some share in it, but the experienced New Yorker occupied a unique point of vantage. Foreign affairs were being treated by President Lincoln as Secretary Seward's business, to be dealt with as much as possible by Seward alone. In the present instance, the secretary expected that a message from England's Foreign Office would soon be placed on his desk for his reply.

The news of the removal of Confederate envoys from an English mail ship was learned in Europe on November 27, at Southampton. Intermixed with the news was a third-hand report, via Lieutenant Fairfax and an English officer to whom he spoke on the *Trent*, that Captain Wilkes had acted on his own initiative. The assertion was published in the English press but also was scoffed at and disbelieved. In its place, the English coined new certitudes: that Wilkes acted in conformity with orders sent by Seward and that the shots fired to stop the *Trent* were Seward's commencement of foreign war.[45]

Without waiting for additional news, the Liberal Ministry placed England on a war-time footing. Each day brought its lists of emergency measures. Troops were sent to Canada; warships sailed for American waters; sales of munitions to the Union were halted;

arsenals worked day and night; and an ultimatum demanding the
return of the captives and an apology for their seizure was borne
by the Cunard steamer *Europa* towards the authorities in Washington.[46]

Two leading Unionists, abroad at Seward's urging, had newly
disembarked at Cherbourg and gone to Paris. One was aged
Lieutenant General Winfield Scott, the ranking officer of the
Union army. The other was elderly Thurlow Weed, the Republican
boss of New York and editor-owner of the *Albany Evening Journal*.
From Paris on December 2, Weed wrote to Seward, "You are in a
'tight place,' and I pray that you may be imbued with the wisdom
the emergency requires." The wisdom recommended was the
return of the captives to English hands. Weed's missive suggesting
their return was a mere private letter, yet possibly was decisive.
Weed and Seward for a generation had worked politically as the
lobes of a single brain. What either urged, in a critical situation,
the other would certainly consider and might well attempt to do.[47]

That same day, December 2, Weed rushed to London, partly
with the object of conferring with C. F. Adams. He appeared at the
Legation and became acquainted with H. B. Adams. The son
proved helpful concerning a matter most interesting to Weed, the
posture of the English press.[48] Crisis was not the word for the
bedlam astir in the British Isles. It was agreed on all hands that
Seward would reject the Ministry's ultimatum.[49] Sufficient proof
could be seen in news from Paris that General Scott was returning
to New York. For any who wished to think so, the old general's
counter-voyage revealed that he would command the Union forces
in the greater war now assuredly set ablaze.

The ultimatum reached the British Legation in Washington at
midnight on December 18. Weed's letter to Seward had arrived or
would arrive in a matter of hours. A week of tension followed. At
the White House on Christmas Day, December 25, and again on
December 26, Lincoln, the Cabinet, and Senator Charles Sumner
of Massachusetts, chairman of the Senate committee on foreign
relations, met to decide how the Union might best respond to
England's demands. Seward had drafted a long reply. Gradually
he won the assent of all present to its adoption. His answer
returned the Confederate captives to English custody.[50]

In retrospect, the secretary's act of persuasion might seem not
difficult. In the doing, it was barely possible. Seward performed it
in the face of overwhelming sentiment throughout the Union
urging the *retention* of the captives. He effected their release by the
narrowest of margins and with the help of few persons. One was

Weed, whose letter Seward may have kept unmentioned during the White House meetings.[51] Another was the anonymous London correspondent of the *New York Times*. His despatches had been appearing in Raymond's newspaper since June 3. They had revealed their author to be an older Unionist accustomed to Europe, who, prior to moving to London, had been in Paris. Seward had not learned the writer's identity; neither had other readers; but the despatches from London mattered, and never so much as on December 25–26 and during the fortnight thereafter, while the Unionists and their government reluctantly adjusted to the sanity and propriety of handing back what Wilkes had seized.[52]

In part, the London despatches mattered because their writer had shown a gift for anticipating events and suggesting what they could lead to. His twenty-seventh despatch had been sent on November 16, eleven days before the news of the rebel diplomats' capture was learned in Europe. The despatch was published in New York on November 30, when jubilance concerning Wilkes's act was flaring to high intensities. It said that a Union warship, the *James Adger*, recently arrived in English waters, was expected by the Admiralty to intercept an English mail ship then overdue from America and delayed by storms, supposedly with Mason and Slidell on board. It added that the purpose of the expected interception would be "to take those gentlemen out of her and to carry them to New York." It emphasized that the *James Adger* was purportedly being watched by "one of Her Majesty's frigates."[53]

This picture of a Union warship being watched by an English warship affected the sensibilities of Union readers, editors, and politicians. Charles wrote privately to Henry that his report about the *James Adger* "created a good deal of uneasiness."[54] Soon after, Charles could have said with justice that Henry's despatch had been clairvoyant. It had given the Unionists a strong, timely warning that England's response to the seizure of Mason and Slidell from *any* English mail ship in *any* waters by sailors from *any* Union warship would be a leap to a war-time footing and the sending of an ultimatum backed by English might.

By the same token, the warning served to advise intelligent Unionists that once a week they should interrupt their raptures and give attention to further despatches from Raymond's correspondent. Henry's subsequent reports were fateful. They brought his countrymen forward from English anxiety about the mission of the *James Adger* to English glee and misconduct following the arrival in Southampton of a Confederate paddle-steamer, the *Nashville*; next to English tumult on learning of the removal of

Mason, Slidell, and their secretaries from the *Trent*; and at last to the English ultimatum and the Ministry's instant readying for still a third war against the United States.

Metaphors can be assistants to clarity. While traveling in Italy in June 1860, Henry had climbed Vesuvius, then mildly erupting. Two years later, in March 1862, he would remember the English during the *Trent* affair as "innocently smiling and dancing" on the slopes of a "volcano."[55] The expression was not too strong; for the affair, though shortly ended, was perilous beyond calculation. The peril was *American*.[56] It was the whirl-around of the Unionists on being told that England's response to Wilkes's act was instant readying for war against the United States.[57] In Union minds, what had been anti-Confederate ecstacy changed to anti-British fury, and the fury grew mountainous and volcanic because it had behind it remembered hatreds of England deeply felt in America during the War of Independence and the War of 1812.[58]

In the days when Seward induced the Unionists to return the captives to English custody, Union fury knew no bounds. What Seward most needed was the support of voices which could affect not only his colleagues in the government but also the Union's newspapers and thus the public. For such support, no voice was more established, trusted, well-informed, and to the point than the voice of the Unionist writing from London to Raymond's *Times*. And if it was true that the writer's despatches had furnished much of the data which had transformed Union jubilance to boiling wrath, it was true as well that his thirtieth despatch, published in the early morning of December 25, 1861, the morning when it could most alter Northern opinion and sway the deliberation in the White House, said in italics, ". . . *the four Confederates should be released and given up to the custody of Great Britain*."[59]

The struggle among the Unionists about the best response to British ultimatum was just that: a struggle by Unionists with other Unionists. Yet it amounted to a negotiation and a treaty, only different from the Treaty of Paris and the Treaty of Ghent in *averting* a war with England.

Admittedly the Unionists and the English showed no disposition to view what happened as a negotiation, still less a treaty. Instead, in both England and the United States, people wished to categorize the furor about the captives as an "affair"—a passing occurrence. Also, during the next three and a half years, the Americans on one side of a civil war would become so intent on crushing the Americans on the other side that the victors would come away from their success with a different pattern etched on their minds: *a great Rebellion, ending in unconditional surrender.*[60]

One can add that the *Trent* affair was seldom mentioned by American Unionists after it ended. Noise yielded to silence. Yet, in a way that Henry Adams was among the first to become aware of, the affair did not end. It persisted in Union hearts in the form of a mostly hidden emotion Henry once called "our bitter state of feeling."[61] The bitter feeling was real and dangerous. Beginning in December 1861, and continuing year after year, innumerable Yankees concealedly wanted war with England and wanted it as revenge.[62]

Rules have exceptions. One young Unionist remained marked by the pattern here summarized as *negotiation first and war avoided.*[63] That was Henry Adams, and the reason was an unspeakable experience. In November 1861, while pressing forward in his despatches for the *Times*, he had realized he was beginning to serve, not just helpfully as a private secretary, and not just importantly as an anonymous correspondent, but instead momentously as a supporting negotiator—an uncommissioned American peace commissioner.[64]

This development was public: the London correspondent's despatches were read throughout the Union. Equally it was secret: his identity was not guessed. And decidedly it was strange. What was strangest for Seward, Weed, Henry Adams, and other Unionists most active and influential on the side of peace with England was their having to negotiate, not so much with the angered English, who could be checked and paralyzed by the return of the captives, but instead with maddened Unionists who were hurtling towards a war with the Confederacy *and* England, not to mention France, which the already-embattled Union could perhaps try to wage but could not sanely expect to win.[65]

There is such a thing as a role that, once and for all, validates a person's attitudes and lines of conduct. Mindful of his own history, the history of his family, and the history of his country, Henry Adams became so deeply engaged in the *Trent* affair as supporting negotiator and uncommissioned peace commissioner that his entire future would be sustained and guided by the experience.

In outline, he would say so. He would give his greatest book, *The Education of Henry Adams*, the form of a third-person narrative. The book's protagonist would be a highly fictional but readily imaginable American named "Henry Adams." A dextrous feature of the book would be a paragraph about the *Trent* affair. The paragraph would say about the fictional Adams that the affair worked "one or two results personal to him which left no trace on the Legation records." The paragraph would not specify the "results."[66] For the Adams of actual life, however, the result that mattered was his forced transformation from correspondent to negotiator and his secret success in the role.

Success occasionally is so large and won at so early an age that the winner has no alternative but to seek the safety of a new beginning. Just so, Adams's *Times* despatches became a success hugely large extremely soon. The despatches helped avert an expanded war disastrous for the Union. They confirmed their author in his sense of unrivaled standing among his fellow Americans. And forcefully they enjoined a halt. Because effective, they brought him to the end of one life and required that he start a second.[67]

Success also required that he *not descend*. He would base his second life at the high level to which old stories, new exigencies, and his own talents and efforts had secretly lifted him.[68]

Success required as well that his second life should have as one of its objects the counteraction of every danger that embittered Americans would start the war with England which they had been induced to forego in December 1861.[69]

Success last required that he go forward on a footing of silence and secrecy continued. His first life he would have to bury. Especially he would have to bury his relation with a newspaper in New York. It still is buried. His despatches have been listed; the story of his writing them has been told and something of their influence has been suggested; but they are yet to be reprinted.[70] Laboriously they can be searched for in microfilms in better-funded libraries; but they can be read with ease only by privileged inquirers permitted to search old bound volumes—priceless "runs"—of Raymond's *Times*.[71] This being the case, their full texts remain the next thing to unknown.

2

CONQUERORS

For four generations, male Adamses had been lawyers. John
Adams began as a lawyer; J. Q. Adams trained in law and
sometimes practiced; C. F. Adams trained also; young John and
Charles did the same; and Henry meant to train in a Boston office
but in 1858 interposed a stay in Europe to acquire modern languages. One delay led to another: his winter in Washington, from
December 1860 to March 1861. He then began a Boston clerkship
but lost it by consenting to go to England. Thus his first life,
though in one perspective sheer victory, could be seen in another
as sheer postponement. It failed to add him to the parade of
Adams lawyers.[1]

In the 1860s, two Adams males imagined the family to be
governed by a rule which extended the right to be a politician only
to the eldest surviving son. The males who imagined the rule to
exist and to be in force were those the rule could seem to favor:
the Chief, as Henry had come to call his father, and first son John.[2]

Under the imagined rule, second son Charles was free to try to
practice law. Charles was trying and failing. The second son's lone
client was Henry, who, before going to England, asked his brother
to oversee his money affairs in Boston.

Charles had not consented to the imagined rule and paradoxically, in a small way, had succeeded as a politician. He had
published unsigned political pieces in Boston newspapers and a
signed full-length political article in the April 1861 issue of the
Atlantic Monthly.[3] But again he had a problem. With respect to
political writing and publication, third son Henry tended to get
ahead of him. The sorest rub was that independently, in February
1861, from Washington, Henry had proposed to write a political
article for the *Atlantic Monthly*. It did not help that he had voiced
his proposal in a letter to Charles *after* Charles in Massachusetts
had already stated to editor James Russell Lowell his own wish to

contribute an article. Neither did it help that Henry went ahead with his article—titled "The Great Secession Winter of 1860–1861"—and made Charles a gift of the manuscript.⁴ Charles reacted defensively. He mentally reserved the *Atlantic Monthly* as political ground allotted to himself. He in addition fell silent. He did not tell Henry that he wanted no intrudings.

The Chief's becoming minister to England seemed to settle Henry's fate. The role the Adamses thought best assigned to the third son was all-purpose servant. Family discussions of Henry's future were vague with respect to how long he would have to stay abroad but clear about his duties. He would be sole confidential aide to his father, general aide to his mother, tutor of Mary, and part-time overseer of Brooks. As courier, he would make all travel arrangements. As housing agent, he would find quarters and effect needed moves. As master of revels, he would try to assure the success of his parents' entertainments.⁵

Henry assumed that he and Charles could cooperate. While still in Boston, he told his brother the fearful secret of his arrangement with Raymond and suggested that they work together as writer-politicians. Charles later went along with the suggestion to the extent of collecting Henry's pay from Raymond and sending political pieces to Henry for English publication. None the less, Charles disliked Henry's *Times* arrangement and wanted it dropped or changed. His stated objection was that Henry did not publish openly—was not *signing* his productions.⁶

On December 10, 1861, in Boston, Charles received from London the manuscript of an article that Henry had secretly written for anonymous inclusion in the December *Atlantic Monthly*. The article was titled "A Visit to Manchester: Extracts from a Private Diary." Delayed in the making, it arrived too late for the December issue. Had his fear for himself been less, Charles might have urged Lowell to accept the article for the January 1862 issue. Instead Charles offered the manuscript to the *Boston Courier*, a comparatively insignificant newspaper to which he had sent some travel letters of Henry's in the spring of 1860.

George Lunt, the *Courier's* editor, published the windfall on the front page of his issue for December 16. On the editorial page, he added a note which said in part: "The interesting Diary at Manchester, on the outside of to-day's COURIER, we feel at liberty to say, is written by Mr. Henry Adams, the son of our Minister to Great Britain. This accomplished young gentleman has been for some time abroad."

Charles privately sent Henry the issue of the *Courier* and

explained that his giving Lunt the article had been a "mistake."[7] Henry accepted the explanation as an apology, but the "mistake" had an all-too-obvious meaning. The offer of Henry's work to the *Courier* and the statements by Lunt in his note were proofs that an older Adams had ruled. Older Charles had ruled that younger Henry would not appear in the *Atlantic Monthly* and that, if he was to appear in a Boston publication, it would be in a minor journal. In the same domineering spirit, Charles told the *Courier* what to say. He arranged that three things—Henry's authorship of "A Visit to Manchester," his being a son of the minister, and his being abroad—should be revealed.[8]

The news that the *Trent* affair had ended was published in Europe on January 8, 1862. Two mornings later, evidence that Henry had authored a political article in the *Boston Courier* was conveyed to C. F. Adams, Wilson, and Moran in the form of a leader in *The Times* of London ridiculing a young American, "Mr. H. Adams," and an article he had written for an American newspaper.[9] The Chief ascertained that *two* sons had been involved. Henry had written a political article, and Charles had arranged its publication with a statement revealing the authorship. The father accordingly wrote to Charles to urge desistance from blunders. Turning about, he extracted from Henry a solemn vow not to publish again on a political topic while they remained at the Legation.[10]

"A Visit to Manchester" was the least of Henry's crimes. An extra effort, the article did not remotely approach in importance his still-appearing, still-unattributed despatches in the *New York Times*. Yet, from the moment it reached the British Isles, the article in the *Boston Courier* elicited a mighty noise. On successive days, the *Manchester Daily Examiner and Times* printed extracts; the *Manchester Guardian* printed extracts and added a commentary; *The Times* smote the author with heavy English ridicule; and the *London Examiner*—to use Henry's expression—scalped him with "considerable savageness."[11]

These occurrences were not ones that Henry could think astonishing. They repeated an old phenomenon. He knew by heart, had known from boyhood, that actions and writings *if by him* were scrutinized and made famous or notorious from the instant his being the originator was disclosed. It seemed the world awaited his efforts.[12]

In the present instance, old knowledge and English noise combined to play him a ferocious trick. Beginning on January 10, he suffered secret agonies of terror that his despatches to the *New York Times* were in process of being unmasked as well. Were that to happen—but it would not happen; Raymond would not betray him; and Charles would not betray him more than he already had—Henry's best options would be two. He could try to flee unrecognized to the Continent or to Canada. He could kill himself.[13]

For several days, in terror, Henry contemplated the wintry vistas of self-removal. His terror was intensified by a new development. Lunt's note in the *Courier* had divulged that the author of "A Visit to Manchester" was a son of Minister Adams and was abroad. It had not divulged that Henry was residing at the Legation at Mansfield Street and serving as his father's private secretary. An English busybody in London, Joe Parkes, hastened to tell the omitted particulars to *The Times*. He then came to Henry and told him about the telling.[14]

The stage was set for new, heavier public punishings of "H. Adams." He waited, but nothing happened. Presumably because English newspapers looked down on private secretaries as near menials, no added blows were struck.[15]

Terror made a permanent difference. Henceforward Henry would labor to keep aware that, being who he was, with relations such as his, he could afford no errors. Errors being avoidable, he would try to improve his management till perfect. Most of all, he would try to be unfailingly vigilant and resourceful with respect to publication and the withholding or disclosure of authorship.[16]

Arriving issues of the *New York Times* meanwhile showed him that his success as uncommissioned peace commissioner and supporting negotiator had been complete. Hence his despatches were also complete and their authorship was more than ever to be concealed. He waited till January 24 and sent Raymond a private letter saying his despatches could not continue.[17] All was changed. Yet all was well.

Work as all-purpose servant kept Henry in close association with his mother. Abigail Brooks Adams—known as Abby—had been rich from birth. Small, stout, and nervous, she at her best was practical and intelligent. Within the family, she was decreasingly at her best. Likely to speak her mind and prone to change it, she could be difficult to deal with. Henry understood her and was her favorite child, but her upsets were putting him off and thrusting him into complicities with the younger children.[18]

Mary, seventeen, dark-haired, and good-looking, came nearer

to averageness than was usual in the family. For her, living in England meant continual lack of friends.[19] Till such persons could be found, she was relying for company on Henry, whom she admired.

Brooks, almost fourteen, had been sent to boarding school but returned on weekends and holidays. He and Henry shared rooms on the top floor. The ten-year difference in their ages did not estrange them. Henry liked to say they should join in brotherly projects.[20]

Following the *Trent* affair, London enjoyed a calm that could pass for normalcy. Henry felt entitled to a vacation and planned to take it. He wrote to Charles, "I shall go over to Paris towards March for a little run, and shall indulge in all the vices and follies possible."[21]

In Paris, Henry would stay with Samuel Franklin Emmons, a lifelong next door neighbor in Quincy. Emmons was studying geology at the École des Mines. The subject interested Henry. As a Harvard senior, he had attended informal lectures by Professor Louis Agassiz. The Swiss geologist had told of his discoveries of enormous ancient glaciers; and listening Henry, to his own surprise, had become a convert to geology and kindred sciences.[22]

In connection with his Paris jaunt, Henry also mentioned, ". . . I am going [to] . . . the carnival with Theodore."[23] The person meant, Theodore Chase, was a friend of Henry's sister Louisa, was musically inclined, and something of a drifter.

Henry's wish to get away was strengthened by loneliness. The few times he had seen young Americans in London, they had either been rushing from Paris to America or from America to Paris. H. H. Richardson, a Louisianan he had known at Harvard, was studying architecture in Paris at the École des Beaux Arts. Some weeks back, intending a visit to America, Richardson had appeared in London, then vanished to board a steamer. Similarly a Bostonian, George Sohier, newly arrived from a steamer, dined twice at Mansfield Street and vanished towards Paris, leaving Henry to exclaim in a letter, ". . . the trouble about London is that no one ever stays here. . . ."[24]

The only male American friend whom Henry had seen much of was old Thurlow Weed. A large, plain man, the Albany editor had proved unexpectedly sympathetic.[25] His appearing at the Legation, both the event and its timing, could seem providential. There had never been an American politician quite like him. Keeping clear of usual methods, he exerted great political influence without holding office. The best example of his influence was his present mission to England and France. He had come abroad as one of four unofficial envoys and in pretence had no authority. Yet he was everywhere recognized as the weightiest Union representative currently in Europe.

Off and on for eight weeks, Henry had been watching Weed extend his sway in London. It seems likely, too, that he took minor shares in some of the old magician's unfollowable operations.[26] The editor's mission, however, was merely temporary and already well advanced. A day would come when Weed too would vanish towards a steamer.

The one friend of Henry's who would not leave was a new friend, a married woman. It chanced that four older Americans, Russell Sturgis, George Peabody, Joshua Bates, and J. S. Morgan, were distinguished London bankers. All had links with the Legation. Sturgis, a partner in Baring Brothers, an important English bank, was domiciled in two sumptuous dwellings: a corner townhouse on Park Crescent, facing Regent's Park at 5 Upper Portland Place, and Mount Felix, a country house in easily accessible Walton-on-Thames. The mistress of both dwellings was his third wife, a Bostonian of forty, born Julia Overing Boit.

For three weeks, beginning at Christmas 1861, Henry had been the guest of the Sturgises at Mount Felix. At the end of each week, he had returned to the Legation for a stint of work.[27] Rapidly, during the other days, he had become Julia Sturgis's special friend. He must have told her a good deal about himself, for she made an extraordinary accommodation. Without display or comment, she gave him absolute free rein under both her roofs. She thus supplied him two things he greatly wanted: a guarantee of affectionate company, and the opportunity to be with or away from his parents somewhat at his own convenience.[28]

In Henry's view, the easiest road to success in politics was continual hospitality centering in good meals.[29] Unfortunately the Chief had inherited a staff of English servants from his ministerial predecessor. Charles Light, the butler-messenger, seemed capable; but, in Henry's words, the cook, Mrs. Hollidge, did not know "anything about cooking." Minister Adams compounded the anomaly by declaring her honest, hence impossible to discharge. Meals at the Legation were thus dependably poor, and the fault could appear to lie with Henry, whose duties as all-purpose servant extended to culinary matters.

His best consolation was that everything was wrong. The Legation was not yet in order. Much-needed improvements—a finer and larger house, better servants, appropriate china, and a long list of comparable necessities—had till then been postponed and not attempted.

Henry was himself presentable. When he started for Paris on February 23, he was dressed as was required in London's privileged classes. He wore a black silk top hat—the compulsory London "tile"—and well-fitting clothes consistent with it in appearance and quality.[30]

His clothes were correct, but his doings in Paris were relaxed. He returned on March 5 and shortly sent Charles an account of his holiday. He had stayed with Frank Emmons and a new acquaintance named Storrow, "both of whom I did my best to debauch, but . . . it wasn't very gay." He had sensible talks with George Sohier and talks as well with classmate Joe Bradlee, who, it developed, had taken a mistress. His worst sins apparently were to witness the more public follies of others and give ear to their tales. He went one night to a masked ball at the Grand Opera and saw that no one there was enjoying it. ". . . suddenly Theodore appeared. . . ." Chase was unhappy and a little angry. ". . . [we] rambled through the Theatre and tried to amuse ourselves with the swarms of flaming whores and the ridiculous masques, but it was no use; so we left the ball and retired to a beer-shop where he poured into my attentive ears a sort of song full of wailing and cursing against Paris and all that was in it."

Immediately following his return, Henry initiated two activities relating to money. He started to save, watching every sixpence. During odd hours, usually late at night, he began a campaign of reading by studying financial theories.[31]

His reason for starting to save was hope of expanding a baby fortune into a fortune big enough to support a bachelor without his having to work for pay. On coming of age in 1859, he had inherited $10,600 from his maternal grandfather, Peter Chardon Brooks. How much his capital had appreciated is unknown, but his current total income is known. Made up partly of earnings from capital, partly of allowances paid to him as son-and-servant, it stood at $2,500.[32] Since he also was receiving free room and board, he could expect to save large amounts.

For Henry, the idea of living entirely on private income was a new idea. He had long had the different idea that he should work for several years as a lawyer. His acting on the new idea did not mean he had dropped the old. He was strongly imbued with both.[33]

A son's ideas were one thing, paternal authority quite another. In C. F. Adams's household, younger sons were *required* to train in law, if only as a means of acquiring what the father would consider sound business habits.[34] Thus, when he worked for three days the previous March in a Boston law office, Henry had presented a picture of filial obedience. Ironically, his father's appointment as minister stopped the obedience; and now, a year later, Henry was performing mandatory duties as all-purpose servant in London at the cost of not resuming his legal training—also mandatory—in distant Boston.

When the matter came up for discussion, his parents supposed an exchange was possible: Henry could return to Boston, and Charles could come to London. A point in favor of the suggestion was that Charles remained unmarried. For the present, however, the suggestion was unworkable. Charles had joined the army. Sworn in as a first lieutenant in the First Massachusetts Volunteer Cavalry, he would have to remain with his unit as long as it was kept in service. He thus could take Henry's place in London only after the Union armies had thoroughly crushed the Confederacy.

An alternative means of freeing Henry to resume his clerkship was the Chief's retirement. To hear him talk, an outsider would have supposed that C. F. Adams was leaving public life. He repeatedly declared that his retirement was near at hand.[35] The avowals were sincere in the way that officeholder's pronouncements were often sincere: he had no awareness that he did not mean them.

Henry was confident of becoming a lawyer, but he based his confidence on the imminent triumph of Union arms. He believed the odds in favor of early victory were very high. His optimism seemed justified. Union armies were closing in on the South. While a large army under General McClellan was readying to seize the Confederate capital at Richmond, other forces were being brought to bear in western Virginia, Kentucky, and Missouri, along several rivers, and along the Atlantic seaboard. Transported by sea, Union soldiers had seized and were holding Port Royal in South Carolina. Lieutenant Adams had been sent there and was expecting to participate in the capture of Charleston.

Just when Henry got back from Paris, news arrived that a Union army commanded by Major General Ulysses S. Grant had crossed from Kentucky into Tennessee, advanced against rebel strongpoints at Fort Henry and Fort Donelson, overrun the first, precipitated the surrender of the second, and taken 15,000 prisoners! Grant's successes were almost too exciting. The Unionists in England were borne up in dizzying elation. "I feel like a King . . . ," Henry exclaimed to Charles. "I assert my nationality with a quiet pugnacity that tells."

The younger brother said he could see "no reason why [Jefferson] Davis and his whole army shouldn't be shut up and forced to capitulate in Virginia." To lend the prospect added joy, he told the lieutenant what a scare the news from America was giving to Europeans. ". . . as our swarm of armies strike deeper and deeper into the South, the contest is beginning to take to Europeans proportions of grandeur and perfection like nothing of which they ever heard or read. They call us insane to attempt what, when achieved, they are almost afraid to appreciate. . . . The English . . . seem to think our dozen armies are already over the St[.] Lawrence and at the gates of Quebec."

The earliest extant writings to and by Henry indicate that he was a precocious writer; also a precocious reader.[36] There is no evidence that he became a writer out of mere wishful hopes. All evidence points instead to his becoming a writer because inhabited from boyhood by a powerful impulse which, in addition to making him a writer as long as he lived, would make him the writer of particular books.

In 1859, writing to Charles from Europe, Henry glancingly wondered whether he might possibly "write a history . . . or a novel."[37] The words were charged with meaning. They were signs that even then he was trying to plan his future history and future novel. At a guess, in 1859 the novel was political and had a setting, the city of Washington, but very blankly lacked a plot.

His history was never a blank. Two years earlier, in the *Harvard Magazine*, he had used a phrase, "the history of these United States as a nation."[38] While not so used in context, the phrase defined what any large-scale history by Henry Adams would be about. For what would a latter-day Adams who aspired to be a great writer most certainly attempt? The question answered itself. He would attempt a history of the nation his forebears had helped to lead and unite.[39]

In May 1860, reading a guidebook in Rome, Henry had come upon a quoted passage by Edward Gibbon telling how he conceived his *Decline and Fall of the Roman Empire*. For Henry, Gibbon's passage had been a summons to work. Last doubts evaporated. He knew he would *have* to write a history of the United States comparable in scale and excellence to the Englishman's history of Rome. He knew he had reached his own beginning: the moment after which every year would *have* to be a year in which he advanced towards completing his own great history.[40]

The passage Henry came upon in the guidebook was taken,

not from Gibbon's *Decline and Fall*, but from his *Memoirs of My Life*. Mulling the passage in 1860, Henry experienced a divination concerning another book, beyond his novel and beyond his history.

For the most part, this divination arose from within. His being a writer was caused by a single impulse so powerful and so channeled that in time he would complete *three* imperishable books: an ambitious political novel, a great history of the United States, and a masterly something else. The different-but-interrelated forms and substances of the three books were inherent in the powerful but channeled impulse. The third book was the last conceived and the least defined. It would not be memoirs. Yet it would somehow concern himself.[41]

Then and later, Henry did not inform the other Adamses that he had the awkward problem of being a great writer of such an age that he was only germinating his greater works. His relations knew, however, that the third son was always writing, liked writing letters, and tended to write varied sorts of articles. At the Legation in March 1862, he told his parents and the younger children that he was anxious to write a non-political article.

The plan was one he was happy to talk about. The previous October, he had visited the Reading Room of the British Museum. Speaking to one of the keepers, Thomas Watts, he had explained that, in America, he had been advised by the historian John Gorham Palfrey, a friend of his father's in Boston, that a familiar episode of Virginia history, Princess Pocahontas's last-minute rescue of Captain John Smith from execution by Indian captors, was a lie, a mere imposture. According to Palfrey, the lie had first appeared in Smith's books early in the seventeenth century and probably was the fault less of Smith than of his London publishers. No one in America had shown conclusively that the rescue had not occurred; but, in Palfrey's opinion, evidence to prove that the captain's rescue was an imposture could be found in books and manuscripts in the possession of the British Museum; and he, Henry, had come to find the evidence.

The October search, guided by Watts, did not lead to the proposed result. Such evidence as Watts and Henry brought to light seemed to prove that Smith's rescue by the Indian princess did occur. Henry accordingly stopped the search and reported to Palfrey. In reply, the historian insisted that Smith's tale was false and urged further inquiry. Henry was too taken up by other concerns to respond to the new injunction. When he finally did so, in March 1862, he was in a different situation, in an altered frame of mind.

After much study of reports in American papers and attendant scrutiny of maps, he had formed a very high opinion of General Grant, who, he wrote, had conducted "a short campaign of ten days or a fortnight, rivalling in its vigor and results those of Napoleon." Simultaneously, he had studied his own case. Duties were consuming all his time. An especially time-taking duty was necessary copying of diplomatic documents. He complained to Charles: "My work is enough to occupy me every day[,] so that I can do little or nothing for myself, or for any really permanent object. . . . Here I am, more dry-nurse than ever, dabbling a little, a very little in society; reading a little; copying a great deal; writing nothing, and not advancing an inch."

The contrast between Grant and himself left him no option but to act. He asked the Chief for time to revisit the British Museum. The Chief consented, and Henry for several days went back to the Reading Room. He came away bearing sheaves of evidence copied from old books of exploration and colonial enterprise. To his mind, the newfound evidence showed that Smith's rescue by Pocahontas was indeed a tall story, and spun by the captain only, in his last years in London.

When brought abreast of the renewed investigation, Palfrey might assume it was his urging that put Henry back to work. Yet for the most part Henry's labor was occasioned by the Napoleonic feat of a Union general in Tennessee. In the privacy of Henry's mind, a rivalry had started. He was vying with a man sixteen years his senior, a military genius whose name, U. H. Grant, had been changed by accident at West Point, suggestively becoming U. S. Grant.

It could be objected, of course, that rivalry was impossible and comparison out of the question. U. S. Grant was a general winning battles. H. B. Adams was a would-be historian who had done a few hours' research. But Henry Adams was a writer. He had to write. He thought a seventeenth-century lie might qualify as a non-political topic, and he correctly understood that his intended article would touch sensitive nerves, even vital organs.

There remained a problem relating to credit. The discovery that Smith's story might be false had been made, as Henry knew, not by John Gorham Palfrey, but by a friend of his named Deane. In London, Henry had found what he thought decisive evidence confirming Deane's discovery, and he was burning to write his proof. Yet Deane had been first in the field.[42] So, to get around the problem, on March 20, Henry appealed to Palfrey: "Perhaps you will be good enough to inform me who Mr[.] Deane is. If I decide to publish anything, his original claim must be acknowledged. . . ."

Charles Deane was a well-to-do Boston businessman who collected old books on America and read them with attention.[43] Far from wishing to protect his claim, he would feel that any credit an Adams might win by exposing Smith's imposture would be that much credit gained by serious historians as a body. But meanwhile Henry confronted a further problem: a choice of courses. He could write his article in a "plain, businesslike, and purely critical way" and send it to Boston for Palfrey and Deane to consider privately, or he could adapt it to popular tastes, place it in a *British* magazine, and look on while copies filtered through the Union blockade and detonated in Virginia.

The second course was attractive but might incur a penalty. The matters hanging in the balance included the interests of persons who would wish Smith's story to be forever true. Belief that Pocahontas rescued Smith from imminent execution by Indian captors was a pillar of the temple of Southern romantic piety. It lent particular support to Virginia's vaunted aristocracy. Were an interloper to enter the temple bearing explosives culled from the holdings of the British Museum and were he identified as an Adams, he could anticipate undying execration as a sacrilegious wrecker and Yankee vandal.

Like rolling dice, the intended article showed changing values. It could be held to be literary and historical, thus permitted. It could be described as through and through political, hence forbidden. In his excitement, Henry judged it part-military and re-permitted. He wrote to Palfrey: "I hardly know whether I ought not to be ashamed of myself for devoting myself to a literary toy like this, in these times, when I ought to be helping or trying to help the great cause. But my pen is forced to keep away from political matters. . . . So perhaps the thing is excusable, especially as it is in some sort a flank, or rather a rear attack, on the Virginia aristocracy, who will be utterly gravelled by it if it is successful."

Prime Minister Palmerston's London residence was Cambridge House in Piccadilly. During the evening of March 22, 1862, accompanied by his wife and his aides, Minister Adams appeared at Lady Palmerston's At Home. Henry and Moran had not previously been to her gatherings. Wilson and Moran arrived separately, moments ahead of the Adamses. Seeing that the latter were arriving, Wilson left Moran and greeted Henry, with whom he was friendly. Next day in his private journal, Moran recorded that he ascended the

stairs alone. ". . . seeing Lady Palmerston[,] I introduced myself.
. . . As Mr. Wilson came up[,] I passed on & was received by Lord
Palmerston. . . . He asked me how I was [and] . . . went to receive
Wilson & Henry B. Adams. By this time many others had arrived,
and the brilliantly lighted Drawing Rooms began to assume an
animated and even gorgeous appearance. . . ."[44]

Lady Palmerston's At Home could be counted as Henry's
entrance into English society. It coincided with startling news
relating to iron warships. The latest American newspapers contained reports of naval actions on Chesapeake Bay. A Confederate
vessel, the *Virginia*, originally the wooden frigate *Merrimac*, rebuilt
as a floating iron fortress, emerged from its lair on the south shore
of Hampton Roads, approached several wooden Union warships,
and destroyed two, the *Cumberland* and the *Congress*. Opportunely,
a Union vessel, the *Monitor*, an iron contrivance of weird design,
able to operate almost submerged, and armed with a heavy gun in
a turret, steamed into sight, opened fire, and drove the *Virginia* to
its harbor.

Disturbing in themselves, the American reports were concurrent with reports in the English press that the *Warrior*, the royal
navy's experimental armored battleship, had proved in tests to be
incapable of withstanding the projectiles of modern cannon. For
Europeans, the clash of iron vessels on Hampton Roads and the
revealed deficiency of the *Warrior* posed an extremely alarming
question. Were the Americans outracing the world in the invention
of armored warships? The question evoked a din of comment.
Moran recorded, "Nothing in modern times ever created such
excitement in Europe."[45]

While the din continued, Seymour Fitzgerald notified C. F.
Adams that his departure from 5 Mansfield Street was urgently
required. In the pinch, the U. S. minister was offered a much
better building. The Sturgises proposed to vacate their splendid
townhouse, freeing it for use by the Adamses and the official
secretaries. The Chief welcomed the offer, and preparations were
begun for an early move.

Prior to the move, on April 5, 1862, the elder Adamses and
Mary took Henry's path and went to Paris. The father had not
been to the Continent since adolescence. Mrs. Adams and Mary
were new to Europe and were making their first venture out of
England.

Henry stayed at Mansfield Street, hating the cook, but pleased
with the international prospect. His optimism had broadened to
enclose the fates of many nations. He reasoned that if wooden

warships were now "useless, rather a weakness than a strength," and if the *Warrior* could be holed and sunk with the latest cannon, then sea powers like England would count for less; land powers like France and Russia would count for more; and a mended United States could flourish unthreatened.

On April 10, a Thursday, the Chief left Mrs. Adams and Mary in Paris and returned to London. He thus was present during the Saturday sending of the weekly despatch bag to Seward in Washington. Henry slipped a letter into the bag for forwarding to Charles. Rather than explain his Smith-Pocahontas project, he told his brother, "I occupy myself in writing, reading and studying up history, as I propose soon to publish a book upon the history and products of the moon. . . ." What he mainly wished to mention was the news about the warships.

> . . . I think I see a thing or two. And one of those things is that the military power of France is nearly doubled by having the seas free; and that our good country the United States is left to a career that is positively unlimited except by the powers of the imagination. And for England there is still greatness and safety, if she will draw her colonies round her, and turn her hegemony into a Confederation of British nations.
>
> You may think all this nonsense, but I tell you these are great times. Man has mounted science, and is now run away with. I firmly believe that before many centuries more, science will be the master of man. The engines he will have invented will be beyond his strength to control. Some day science may have the existence of mankind in its power, and the human race [may] commit suicide, by blowing up the world.

The Chief and Henry had apparently agreed that one of them should be always present at the Legation. On Sunday, Henry and Brooks went to Paris. There Henry escorted Mary to a dentist and was informed that she would have to make several visits. He advised the Chief that the party would be detained. He frankly added that he did not enjoy having to act as substitute head of a family.

In London, the Chief remarked in a letter to Charles that Henry was "a little too much disposed to inertia."[46] The remark showed how little the father was apprised of Henry's activities. Albeit quietly, the third son had been active. The visible evidence was the Sturgises' house at 5 Upper Portland Place. The one strong link connecting the Adams and Sturgis families was the new-made friendship of Henry Adams and Julia Sturgis. That he and she had secretly engineered the yielding of the house to the Chief was more than a conjecture. It was an inescapable supposition.[47]

Just as real, but quite invisible, was Henry's first experience of

sexual relations. He had never been in love but was much attracted
to women. Beginning at an unstated time, he got himself into
"scrapes," meaning encounters with women he paid for sexual
favors.[48] He later wrote to Brooks that his "first experience" made
him wretched for "two months," the next were "bad enough," all
were "particularly unlucky," and "always" they occurred while he
was with the "family." A permissible inference is that in Paris
approximately on April 15, 1862, while irked at having to guard
three dependent Adamses, Henry bought the favors of a prosti-
tute.[49]

As soon as Mary's teeth were in order, Henry led Mrs. Adams,
Mary, and Brooks to London. He then supervised the moving of
the Legation to Mrs. Sturgises' comparative palace. Auspiciously a
blazing sun came out in the English sky. Minister Adams, en-
sconced in a corner study, its large west windows aglow with sun,
its north windows overlooking Regent's Park, wrote to Charles, "I
eschew N° 5 Mansfield Street as gloomy, and hail 5 Upper Portland
Place as the abode of genial warmth and smiling content."[50]

Lest the official secretaries fail to grasp the significance of the
move, the Chief went down to their new quarters and told them
that the Legation "must have no more slut holes." When their
superior had left, Wilson asked Moran what such language could
have meant. The second secretary replied that the first secretary
was no longer free to make a pig sty of their room "by covering the
floor with newspapers."[51]

Anticipating dismissal, Mrs. Hollidge quit. A new cook was
hired. Henry called her "a good one" but a "vixen" and said she
"frightens our poor lady to death." The vixen was needed. London's "season" was in full swing. The elder Adamses were accepting
invitations and wished to reciprocate by giving dinners.

Henry too was caught in the social torrent. His mother and
Mary informed him that he must gain positive acceptance in
English society: it was his duty. Pure duty it would be, to his way of
thinking. He wrote to the lieutenant, ". . . [I] am steeling myself to
stand all the labor and disappointment of a struggle to acquire a
position in this great, dreary, scandal-mongering, censorious city."

Steeling could not prevent his sustaining the hurts commonly
inflicted by London on foreign guests. He went to a party given by
Margaret Seymour, the Duchess Dowager of Somerset. To enliven
the festivities, the aged duchess, "a terrible vision in castanets,"
accosted him in the ballroom and announced that he and the
Turkish minister's daughter were to dance a Highland Fling. He
felt "unutterable horror," yet achieved "a double-shuffle in the

shape of a Scotch reel, with the daughter of an unbelieving Turk for a partner."[52]

Horror awaited him also at Lady Palmerston's At Homes. There he usually found himself alone and stared at amidst civilized men and women not one of whom would greet him and ask his name. Moran suffered parallel inspections and thought them puzzling. He once recorded: "Henry Adams and I got together, and for a time amused ourselves like little Jack Horner in a corner[,] philosophising over the company. . . . Introductions rarely if ever occur, but why I don't exactly know."[53]

Since the outbreak of the American war, the Union cause had been championed in Parliament by a band of Liberals and Radicals led by Richard Cobden, John Bright, William E. Forster, and Richard Monckton Milnes. The leaders had paid the Adamses friendly visits.

Like other Englishmen, Cobden, Bright, Forster, and Milnes believed that the secession of the South in America was irreversible. As a corollary, they supposed it natural and right that C. F. Adams should have to vie for favor in England with a Confederate special commissioner, the once-captured but now-present James M. Mason, although admittedly the Confederacy remained unrecognized, and Mason was yet to be received by Queen Victoria at court.

In the circumstances, an urgent duty of the Union's envoys in London was counteraction of English wrongheadedness. A duty still more urgent was successful resistance to the supplying of English arms, especially warships, to the rebels. Despite strong protests by C. F. Adams, the *Florida*, a cruiser fitted out in British yards for the Confederate Navy, had recently gone to sea as a raider against Union merchant ships. In the Legation's view, the rebel cruiser had been downright emboldened to sail by the non-enforcement of British law. And there was serious danger that the outrage would be repeated. Warnings had come that a second cruiser, not yet named but designated the "No. 290," would be ready for sea at Liverpool very soon.

The menace posed by the cruisers gave the Legation much to do. Yet oddly the surge of business confirmed the Chief in his delusion of retirement. He wrote to Charles, ". . . it cannot be long before I bid my friends here farewell, and devolve all cares as well as honors upon a successor."[54]

Henry also wandered in dreams. A few days earlier, he had written to the lieutenant, ". . . if you're wounded, you can come out here and we'll exchange places. . . ." The proposal had the defect that Charles might be wounded badly or even killed. Ignoring all such chances, the third son imagined returning to America, possibly to be a soldier.

On May 11, the Chief and Henry went for separate afternoon walks. While they were gone, Mrs. Adams greeted a visitor, Sir Charles Lyell, the world-famous geologist, a good friend of the United States. A tall man, adorned with a monocle, Sir Charles got to talking with his hostess about the predictions that British editors liked to make concerning the rebellion across the sea—predictions, he said, which, printed one day, were commonly shown to be wrong by trustworthy news brought by arriving steamers the very next day.[55]

To the American Unionists in London, the Union's victory seemed imminent. In Virginia, General McClellan had been moving the great Army of the Potomac southward by water to the peninsula between the York and James Rivers, not far from Richmond. In Tennessee, at a place called Pittsburgh Landing, the large army headed by General Grant had repelled a heavy Confederate surprise attack in a pitched battle frightful for bloodshed on both sides. On the Mississippi, bursting past a rebel stronghold, "Island No. 10," a Union force had advanced a long stride down the river. Most astonishingly, where the Mississippi entered the Gulf of Mexico, a fleet under Admiral Farragut was ascending the river, intent on the seizure of New Orleans.

Unhappily, news had stopped. McClellan's operation was slow and cautious. Farragut's progress was swathed in silence. Henry, often prescient, felt on the edge of something but could not tell what.

Prescience was made the harder for him by the clamors of the London press, which he constantly was reading, and which seldom showed understanding of Union aspirations or prospects. He explained to Charles that the English were "a people who read everything backwards that regards us, and surround us with a chaos of croaking."

Thurlow Weed, gone for a time on the Continent, returned to London. His reappearance coincided with worsening friction between Minister Adams and the British foreign secretary, Earl Russell. The Legation was straining to prevent the delivery of the "No. 290" to the Confederate Navy. Henry told Charles, "About once a week the wary Chieftain sharpens a stick down to a very sharp point, and then digs it into the excellent Russell's ribs. The first two or three times the joke was born[e] with well-bred politeness and calm indifference, but . . . the sticks became so devilish sharp that now things are being thrown round with considerable energy. . . ."

Affairs had reached this condition when the minister and Henry went for walks. The Chief was first to return. Entering the room where his wife and Lyell were talking, he held out a telegram he had found downstairs on the table. From Seward, it reported, "New Orleans is in our possession."

The telegram asked that the news be relayed to the Union minister to France, William F. Dayton.[56] Happy to go to the telegraph office, the Chief and Lyell descended the stairs and crossed the threshhold. Seeing that Henry was approaching, the minister waved the telegram and cried, "We've got New Orleans." The son ran forward, snatched the missive, and sped away. ". . . leaving Sir Charles Lyell regarding my abrupt departure through one eyeglass with some apparent astonishment, I took a cab and drove down to Mr[.] Weed. Meeting him in the street near his hotel, I leaped out of the cab, and each of us simultaneously drew out a telegram. . . . His was Mr[.] Peabody's . . . . We proceeded then together to the telegraph office and sent a despatch to Mr[.] Dayton at Paris; and . . . I went round to the Diplomatic Club and had the pleasure of enunciating my sentiments. Here my agency ended; but Mr[.] Weed drank his cup of victory to the dregs. He spread the news in every direction, and finally sat down to dinner at the Reform Club with two sceptical old English friends of our side, and had the pleasure of hearing the news-boys outside shout 'Rumored capture of New Orleans' in an evening Extra, while the news was posted at Brookes's, and the whole town was in immense excitement as though it were an English defeat."

American politicians sometimes made unscrupulous trades. At the Republican Party's nominating convention in Chicago in 1860, Lincoln's managers had secured the deciding votes in favor of their candidate by promising a Cabinet place to Senator Simon Cameron, the Republican boss of Pennsylvania. Once in office, Lincoln made good on his managers' promise, naming Cameron to be secretary of war.

The president found the Pennsylvanian to be incompetent, yet not unwilling to leave the Cabinet. In 1862, another problematical Unionist, Cassius Clay of Kentucky, vacated the Russian mission. Lincoln seized his chance, made Cameron minister to Russia, and named Edwin L. Stanton as replacement head of the War Department.

En route to St. Petersburg, the new minister stopped in London and visited the Legation. Before joining the Adamses, Cameron spoke with Moran, who thought him "insincere" and "brusque" but credited him with "a much better face than I expected."[57]

It fell to Henry to introduce Minister Cameron to a Union champion in Parliament. He turned to Monckton Milnes, who agreed to see them. ". . . [Cameron] was the object of considerable interest . . . ," Henry wrote to Charles. "I can't say that I was proud of my charge, nor that I like his style. Thurlow Weed is quite as American, and un-English, but is very popular and altogether infinitely preferable. We all like Mr[.] Weed very much, and are sorry that he is going home this week. As for Cameron[,] I hope he will vanish into the steppes of Russia and wander there for eternity."

Weed had courted notice in London only to the extent of writing sensibly pacific letters to *The Times* and the *Telegraph*. For the most part, he had promoted Union interests by arranging unpublicized private meetings. The end of his mission was viewed as important by those who had met him and knew he was gone.[58] Such persons included Prime Minister Palmerston and Foreign Secretary Russell.

The departure of Weed was simultaneous with uneasy adjustments in English opinion about the war in America. New Orleans was the largest city in the South. To the English, its capture by Union forces had seemed an impossible and wrong occurrence. The Chief said about his hosts: "It took them three days to make up their minds to believe it. The division of the United States had become an idea so fixed in their heads that they had shut out all the avenues to the reception of any other."[59] But after a time, more than conceding that New Orleans had fallen, a few of the Union's warmer friends in Parliament veered to a new supposition that the Federal side in America had practically subdued the Confederate.

Henry learned that Speaker Denison of the House of Commons, encountering C. F. Adams, had dubbed him "The Conqueror." Thrilled by the speaker's phrase, Henry himself used heady language. He boasted to the lieutenant, ". . . the position we have here is one of a great deal of weight, and of course so long as our armies march forward, so long our heads are elevated higher and higher until we bump the stars."

On June 11, 1862, two weeks after Weed had gone, the Chief and Henry came back from an afternoon engagement and entered the corner study. An envelope awaited the minister's attention. He opened it, took out two documents, read them, and said curtly to Henry, "Palmerston wants a quarrel!"[60]

One of the documents was a short note from the prime minister to the Union envoy marked "Confidential." The other was a news report clipped from *The Times*.

Both documents concerned a disturbance in New Orleans. After its capture, a number of usually temperate but momentarily impassioned women, all intensely Confederate, subjected Union troops to derisive gestures and verbal barbs likely to breed retaliation. With the object of precluding worse disturbance, the Union commander, General Butler, ordered that henceforward women displaying such conduct be arrested and jailed as prostitutes. The extract from *The Times* sent by Palmerston quoted Butler's order verbatim.

Note and clipping passed from the Chief to Henry. He read them. What he concluded was not recorded, but any intelligent person who read what C. F. Adams had received would have gravitated towards three conclusions: that, knowing Weed had left, Palmerston thought the time had come for a definitive test of Minister Adams and supposed him weak and readily demolished; that the English leader had suffered a perturbation not easy to analyze; and that his lordship, anticipating questions that might be asked him in the House of Commons about the Ministry's view of Butler's order, had armed himself with a strong reply by sending an insulting note to the Federal government's official envoy.

Being confidential, the prime minister's note could be disclosed by its author but not by its Federal recipient. Oddly, Palmerston assumed that General Butler had wanted the women of New Orleans raped, meaning *all* the women, not just those who might renew the taunting of Federal troops. His lordship's note accordingly said, in full:

> I cannot refrain from taking the Liberty of saying to you that it is difficult, if not impossible to express adequately the Disgust which must be excited in the mind of every honorable man by the general order of General Butler given in the inclosed extract from yesterday's Times. Even when a Town is taken by assault[,] it is the Practice of the Commander of the conquering army to protect to the utmost the Inhabitants and especially the Female Part of Them; and I will venture to say that no example can be found in the History of Civilized nations, till the Publication of this order, of a general guilty in cold Blood of so infamous an act, as deliberately to hand over the Female Inhabitants of a conquered city to the unbridled license of an unrestrained soldiery.
> If the Federal Government chooses to be served by men capable of

such revolting outrages[,] they must submit to abide by the deserved opinion which mankind will form of their conduct.[61]

To sense the message as it was sensed by the two Adamses, one must recall that England in 1862 was the greatest of powers. The Chief and Henry had no one to help them, other than Wilson and Moran, whose assistance they did not seek. The father believed that Palmerston meant to place the insulting note before the public, and very soon. Were the English leader permitted to do so, the U. S. minister would have to resent the action; Palmerston would get his quarrel: the Adamses might probably leave the British Isles; and C. F. Adams's career as a politician might end, not precisely in failure, but in sudden ejection from diplomacy.

Quickly a reply went to Palmerston. It drew the prime minister into a correspondence which continued till six notes, three on each side, had been delivered. The first American note demanded explanations and elicited an evasive answer. The second re-demanded explanations and won a fresh evasion. The last ended with a sentence which Henry would later describe as "excessively strong."[62] Saying that Minister Adams would not again accept any communication from the English leader, the sentence required that Palmerston reach him thereafter only through Foreign Secretary Russell, with whom Minister Adams proposed to continue his usual dealings. The sentence read, ". . . [it is] my painful duty to say to your Lordship that I must hereafter, so long as I remain here in a public capacity, decline to entertain any similar correspondence."[63] And the sentence seemed effective. The prime minister said nothing in Parliament about his combat with the Legation.[64]

In the struggle with Palmerston as Henry saw it, war was never the issue. England's chance to war against the Union had been the *Trent* affair, and the Ministry had been prevented from taking it. The issue in the present case was the survival of C. F. Adams as minister, and Palmerston's note and clipping were a *second* insult. During the *Trent* affair, the Chief had been barred from taking a role. The British government had shut him out—had exclusively conducted its dealings with the Union government through Lord Lyons, its minister in Washington. Oppositely, in the present case, the Chief had been treated as a vulnerable target. Whatever Palmerston may have felt about events in remote New Orleans, his note of June 11 was a cannon shot meant to sink a supposed Yankee cockboat near at hand, the little-respected official envoy of the Federal government in London.

The situation being clearly defined, Henry knew what to do.

With respect to the three American notes, he acted almost exclusively as listener and copyist, seldom or never as a maker of suggestions, and never as reviser or writer.[65] The precautions were indispensable. Palmerston had to be beaten by the man he had taken for weak.

To that point, Henry's share in the matter could seem recessive. His share none the less was wholly or almost wholly assertive. Two reports of the Palmerston correspondence were prepared and sent to Washington for Seward's perusal. Signed by the Chief, the reports were penned by Henry in his astonishing script, which recently had simplified and expanded, and which in the present instance again expanded, acquiring an impressiveness one might associate with the Declaration of Independence. Preserved by the State Department, the second report is now in the National Archives. (The first is missing.) Seen at first- hand, it leaves no doubt that its meanings included a meaning important to the penman.[66]

That meaning was a silent change in Henry's rank at the Legation. Beginning on June 11, 1862, *two* Adamses held the English mission. The father was minister. The son was minister. The elder's rank was official and incessantly stated. The younger's was unofficial, unspoken, and as much as possible unthought. The son remained an all-purpose servant. In title, he still was "private Secretary." But in fact he was other minister, and his being also private secretary had become a mere usefully protective aspect of his being a principal diplomat, in place, irremovable, and hard at work.[67]

Henry had not sought or wanted the changed status he calmly took. The change was occasioned by an attack. Following the departure of one unofficial Union emissary, old Weed, another unofficial emissary, the younger Adams, was suddenly brought forward by the arrival of an intendedly ruinous English note.

With equal suddenness, C. F. Adams and H. B. Adams were made a team. An iron bond linking son and father was so welded it could not break. Henry would later try not to know it, would even act as if he did not know it, but his freedom to go home was extinguished. He and the Chief would leave the English mission when its two ministers left together—not otherwise, and not sooner.

3

Hopes for Us All

Correctly, the modern Adamses believed that the founder of their family in America was Henry Adams, an Englishman who emigrated to Massachusetts in the 1630s and farmed, died, and was buried in the area later named Quincy. Incorrectly, they thought he came from Devon. On the basis of family belief, John Quincy Adams had placed an impressive commemorative plaque on the founder's grave.[1]

In the 1840s, a small grandson learned about the old Henry Adams and the plaque. Also he learned that he was named Henry Brooks Adams by his mother in memory of her deceased brother Henry Brooks.[2] He combined these disparate items of data and, without intending it, put himself in the way of a strong temptation. He saw he might change his name, drop the Brooks, and become a new Henry Adams.

That he was tempted is clear. During his first life, he signed his writings Henry Brooks Adams, H. B. A., Henry B. Adams, and H. B. Adams, somewhat favoring the last. Forms he could just as easily have used were Henry Adams and H. A. He did not use them. Temptation could be seen in his being careful not to write them.[3]

While starting his second life, he showed restlessness concerning his name. Eleven of his letters survive from the three months following his vacation in Paris. One he initialed H. B. A. Three he signed H. B. Adams. Four he left unsigned. The rest he signed Jones, Brown, and W. E.—the initials of William Everett, a cousin on his mother's side who was a student in England, an undergraduate at Cambridge. The pattern tended towards outright erasure of Henry Brooks Adams. It possibly indicated a two-part plan: he meant to drop the Brooks, and he meant to wait for what might seem a perfect moment.[4]

He had nothing against the Brookses; indeed he was obliged

to them to the tune of an inheritance. Yet he felt he was not *of* them. He felt he was strictly an Adams and a Johnson. When he named himself Henry Adams, his new name would say who he was. It would say he was an important Adams; either that or *the* important Adams.

Louisa Catherine Johnson's name was changed in a usual way, by marriage. Henry may have hit on the idea of changing his name by musing when a child about what happened to her. *His* new name, when he got it, would be his own free choice. That would be apt; for the shared life of Louisa Catherine Adams and Henry Adams, beginning with her birth in 1775 and going forward till his eventual death, was itself a free choice—an imaginative invention based on love and resemblance.

For a person who thought historically, dates were sometimes fraught with meaning. The shared life of Henry and his Adams grandmother began in 1775, the year that was also the birth year of the American Union. It followed that in some degree she and he *were* the Union. By the same logic, the person later to be known as Henry Adams could feel *he* was the Union. This was no joking matter. His actions in later years would be the actions of a man who believed that, as nearly as such a thing was possible, he was the United States.[5]

While a student at Harvard, Henry was friends with "Rooney" Lee, a son of Robert E. Lee, a respected colonel in the U. S. Army. Rooney left college when a junior to take a lieutenancy in the army.

In February 1861, during his winter in Washington, Henry dined with several of the Lees (the colonel was absent) at their house in Arlington, overlooking the half-built Washington Monument and still domeless Capitol. A few weeks later, Colonel Lee deserted his country. He left the U. S. Army to take command of seceded Virginia's forces. (Rooney too left the army and became a rebel officer.) As felt by Henry, the action of the father was treason deserving of death by hanging.[6]

In June 1862, word reached London that General Lee had been given command of the rebel Army of Northern Virginia, defending Richmond. Henry was twice-sensitive to the news because distrustful of Lee's Union opposite, George B. McClellan. He believed that poor leadership by McClellan had taught the Army of the Potomac "a strange want of life." The Union force, inching closer to the rebel capital, was being kept "on the defensive even when attacking."

On June 25, battle came. The Army of the Potomac advanced

within sight of Richmond but, after seven days of clashes, retreats, recoveries, more clashes, and worse retreats, was hurled back to the James River, there to stanch its wounds and count its dead and missing.

Few Unionists had anticipated the news of the Seven Days. In London, the members of the Legation read reports of the long battle's uneven course and were shocked and dismayed. Henry wrote, "We suffered . . . very great anxiety, knowing that the current here was rising every hour . . . against us. . . ." Wanting to be helpful, he "avoided contact with everyone except friends" and assured all hearers who would listen that the rebels had been "as much crippled by their victory as we by our defeat."

Ironically, and from the Union point of view very luckily, Lee's success gave the English an opportunity to disappoint the Confederate States. A Conservative member of Parliament, William S. Lindsay, had said he would move for full recognition of the South. Before he could offer his motion, the news of the rebels' victory restored the English to complete agreement that the partition of America had been achieved. The House of Commons accordingly did nothing to aid the Confederate States. The season having ended, the members of Parliament, indeed the English educated and moneyed class in its entirety, left the metropolis as custom required and went to the country.

Soon after, the English disappointed the Union. The Adamses and Moran had hoped and expected that the law officers of the Crown would detain the "No. 290." The officers acted too late. On July 28, in Moran's expression, the cruiser sailed from Liverpool "without register or clearance, armed and manned to war against the U. S."[7] Once at sea, she unveiled herself as the Confederate warship *Alabama*.

In the resulting state of things, C. F. Adams scandalized Moran by saying openly at the Legation that, if the Union government would first free the slaves in the states and territories in its possession, he for one would accede to the Confederacy's independence.[8] In the same state of things, H. B. Adams did *not* say he would accede to the rebels' independence. He instead applied himself as a diplomat. Using terms unprecedented in his writings, he spoke of "the dignity of our calling."

Henry's principal worry was a looming diplomatic contest between the United States and five European powers: England, France, Spain, Austria, and Russia. The five powers threatened to intervene concertedly in the American war. If they did, their act, intentionally or not, would tend to secure the independence of the

Confederacy.[9] Yet Henry thought preventives were available, the best being a Union emancipation of the rebels' slaves. He wrote to Charles: ". . . it is the slavery question from which we can derive the greatest strength in this running battle. You see[,] we are stripping and squaring off, to say nothing of sponging, for the next round."

The mood of Henry's lines was sanguine, and he had much to be sanguine about. For an American man of affairs, London was a continuously helpful place. It helped particularly with respect to making political acquaintances. In July, he met an American, David A. Wells, of Connecticut, a dry statistical person, very well versed in economics and public finance. Henry wrote the visitor's English address in his engagement book: "24 Ovington Sq. Brompton."[10] Wells, it seemed, was a man with whom a rising Adams would want to have additional dealings.

Its British residents being absent, London's West End was forlorn and empty. Mrs. Adams wished the family would go to the country for a time by renting a house. They instead decided to travel for three weeks, return to Upper Portland Place, and move to the country later, thus escaping London's autumnal fogs. Henry made the arrangements; and the family toured in a pleasant circuit, by way of the Malvern Hills and Bath, as far as Cornwall and Devon.

While traveling, C. F. Adams received a plea for sick leave from unfunctional Wilson. The Chief granted leave, and the first secretary sped away towards Chicago. When the Adamses returned to London, secretarial burdens fell on two toilers only, Henry and Moran.

Henry meanwhile had undergone a secret change of heart. He assumed that the Union's failure to capture Richmond meant that still larger, deadlier battles were imminent. The prospect revived a sensation he had twice experienced in his first life, a wild need to share in the battles. He worked unflaggingly in the study, yet at the same time he silently imagined he should board a steamer, get to Boston, and through John—a member of Governor Andrew's staff—obtain a commission as a second lieutenant under Charles in the First Massachusetts Cavalry.

The family had gone to Devon partly out of interest in the English Henry Adams. In September, the new Henry initiated searches in London for records relating to the progenitor. They were unavailing.[11]

At Port Royal, a letter reached Charles from Henry saying that the Unionists and the rebels were fighting a running battle; the Europeans threatened to intervene; and the Union would do well to emancipate the rebels' slaves. The lieutenant replied, ". . . I see your conclusions are not very different from mine. . . ." Their conclusions were wholly different. In his letter, Charles set slavery aside. He merely wanted the North and South to negotiate boundaries, then join in declaring the South's independence. He said he was "ready to concede the question of separation, as best for us, for the South & for the world."[12]

The reply placed Henry in opposition to both the Chief and Charles concerning the Union's proper course. On September 5, he advised his soldier brother that he was in earnest about the Union, the war, and emancipation for the blacks. He conceded that a portion of the South might win transient independence as a passing accident, but he wanted victory for the Union and annihilation for the Americans who had turned against it. He explained, ". . . there can be no peace on our continent so long as the southern people exist. . . ." ". . . we must exterminate them in the end, be it long or be it short, for it is a battle between us and slavery."

Henry's new letter would find Charles at a new address. Unvictorious McClellan had been replaced by General Pope. Union soldiers had been pulled back by water from the James and redeployed in defense of Washington. Troops were withdrawn as well from Port Royal. Lieutenant Adams was among the soldiers repositioned. In his own words, he was shipped to "the dark and bloody ground in Virginia."[13]

In the 1840s in Boston, Charles and Henry had played with brothers whose ages matched theirs, Henry Lee Higginson and James Jackson Higginson. In mid-September 1862, Charles Adams and Henry Higginson were officers in the First Massachusetts Cavalry. Henry Adams and Jim Higginson were civilian shirkers, or so it could appear, in Europe. Ending a sojourn on the Continent, Jim was going home to get a commission in the First Cavalry. He stopped in London and found that Henry was the only Adams at the Legation. The elder Adamses and Mary were visiting Thomas Baring at his country seat, Norman Court. Brooks was visiting on the Isle of Wight.

Free to talk, Jim suggested that he and Henry act together and join their brothers. The suggestion had weight. If there was ever to be a time when every fit Union male should obey the call to arms, it could only be the present instant. Hideous news had come that General Pope had blundered the Army of the Potomac into a rout at Bull Run, the very spot in Virginia where the same army had panicked and fled the previous summer in the first large battle of the war.

Jim went home and Henry stayed, amazed to have stayed and scorched by doubts. His parents and Mary came back from Norman Court. They too were in torment. They had learned of Pope's debacle while guests at an English house, surrounded by English company. Retreat to the Legation scarcely helped. National disgrace was palpable within its walls.

A climactic misfortune seemed very near. Henry thought a "crash" would occur "within three months" and believed it would precipitate the "ship-wreck" of their mission. In that belief, he had made the bravest choice he could make and stayed on the sinking ship.

For lack of a better course, the family readied for a move to the country. Henry had found a rentable house, and the Chief was poised to sign the lease. But without warning on October 10, 1862, William Gladstone, the chancellor of the exchequer, said in a speech at Newcastle that President Davis and his fellow Confederates had "made a nation."[14] Fearing that the comment was authorized by the Ministry and signaled a final tempest, C. F. Adams did not sign the lease.[15]

Miserably the family held on in London. Mary's health had worsened, and exercise was recommended. Henry agreed to ride with her in the afternoons. Horses were cheaper to own than hire, so the Chief bought his daughter a handsome mount, known as Hodson.[16] Henry economized by buying a usable mare, name unrecorded.

The tempest signaled by Gladstone did not blow. The Adamses were freed from one alarm but shaken by another. Led by two generals of evident ability, Robert E. Lee and "Stonewall" Jackson, Confederate armies advanced west of Washington. Again commanded by McClellan, Union forces bunglingly attacked in battles at South Mountain and Antietam Creek, losing streams of soldiers. Reports of Union casualties were borne abroad. Always in dread of seeing his brother's name, Henry read the lists. The family learned at last that Charles was present on both battlefields but saw no action.[17]

Henry might have been less fearful, had he retained a shred of confidence in McClellan. Paradoxically, the Unionist he trusted was his fearful self. Moreover, there was something he could do. Loose on the oceans, the *Florida* and *Alabama* were sinking Union merchant ships as rapidly as found. For every loss, in Henry's opinion, the English were as much to blame as the rebels. He therefore was studying international, American, and English law as related to ships. He explained to Charles, ". . . I am tired of waiting for events; I have wholly drawn out of all society except American; I am occupied to my own satisfaction with other studies; and I am ready to go straight ahead until knocked down."

For two weeks, the family rented a house in Tunbridge Wells. Mrs. Adams and Mary stayed there continuously. The Chief and Henry left London only by turns. Helped by the alternations, Henry finished his article on Smith's non-rescue by Pocahontas. He wrote to Palfrey, "I have dished out our friend Capt. John to my satisfaction, and so he rests for the present."

The article was finished, but Henry showed no inclination to publish it. He had realized that, if printed in an English magazine and revealed to be the work of a meddling Yankee, an article exposing Smith's imposture would bolster English sympathy for the Virginians and deepen English frigidity towards the Federals.[18]

Henry tended to grow despondent in November. The reasons for the failing were evident enough. As a child, he had annually lost the company of his Adams grandmother. Her husband, ex-President J. Q. Adams, was pursuing a second career as a congressman and foe of slavery; and in consequence, every November, she left Quincy and traveled to Washington, where she had another home, a corner house on F Street.

For Henry, November abandonment went hand in hand with November affliction. In that month, he and the other children were moved to their parents' winter house in Boston, a city where he always felt a stranger, and where increasingly he was sent to school, an ordeal he tried to endure with profit, yet hated as equivalent to prison.[19]

In November 1862, he fell prey to his usual despondency and at the same time was depressed by news from Washington. President Lincoln, again removing General McClellan, had substituted another incompetent, General Burnside. "As I do not believe in Burnside's genius," Henry wrote, "I do not feel encouraged. . . ." He might better have said he was wholly *dis*couraged. Forgetting or disregarding the bad examples set by the Chief and Charles after the Seven Days, he lost all hope of victory, even hope of Union coherence. He discounted the Union's *politicians*. Lincoln and Seward he saw as voids. He confessed to Charles, ". . . as we can find no one to lead us and no one to hold us together, I don't see the use of our shedding more blood."

When cast down, Henry would sometimes mix saying things he believed with saying things he did not believe. In his present despondency, he claimed that since leaving college he had "steadily lost faith in myself"; also he swore he possessed a mind like Hamlet's, so balanced against itself as to preclude heroic action. The utterances were at odds with fact, yet true to momentary feeling.

The third son's condition had another, more hopeful face. Henry had developed faster and more securely than his brothers and sisters. Resistance to despondency had been the means by which he had achieved his accelerated, sturdy growth. In 1862, resistance was much in evidence. For a person in a poor frame of mind, he was strangely full of ideas. He unfolded for Charles a part-humorous plan for their American generation. "We want a national set of young men like ourselves or better, to start new influences not only in politics, but in literature, in law, in society, and throughout the whole social organism of the country. A national school of our own generation. . . . In England the Universities centralize ability and London gives a field. . . . But with us, we should need at least six perfect geniuses . . . spotted over the country and all working together. . . ." Charles was not a genius, nor ever would be. Henry all the same applied the plan to his brother. ". . . if you're an able man," he said, "there's your career."

As for his own situation, he made plain that, when meeting people in London, he was telling a useful lie. He said he was assuring all inquirers that he was a "visitor temporarily living with my father in England." "Under cover of this character I can move much more freely than in any other. . . ."[20] He went on to say he could make no plans while obliged to remain with the Chief.

The latter idea, true in one sense, was in another a completest lie. Henry *always* had a plan: the one he settled upon in his teens. Currently, also, he had a career, in fact two careers. During most hours, he was other minister and all-purpose servant. During the remaining hours, he was a separate Adams working hard at self-education or self re-education. Truthfully he told Charles that his work had two branches and that the second branch required his studying the "history and politics which seem to me most necessary to our country for the next century." The phrase revealed the unchanging inclination, the native tilt, of his mind. Though keenly alive to the present and actively interested in the past, he was most interested in the future. Literally, in 1862, he was living and studying for 1962.

Still writing to Charles, he dropped a colorless remark: "One man who has great ability may do a great deal. . . ." The line described his future. In ways adapted to him, he would develop "great ability" and "do a great deal." The plan he had offered for his American generation was emphatically not a plan for *him*. He of course would act as a member of his generation in America, but he was adapted as well to interacting cooperatively with persons of other generations and any country. His sympathies extended to persons in all times and places. He meant to impose no boundaries on inquiry, action, or aspiration.

Among the Englishmen he knew, Henry most liked John Bright.[21] He found a sponsor, however, in Richard Monckton Milnes. Notoriously a collector of pornography, Milnes was also and more constructively a collector of talented men. During the past season, he had once invited H. B. Adams to tea. In November 1862, he urged the American to "rail down & spend some days" at Fryston Hall, his house in Yorkshire.[22]

Adams arrived on December 3 and learned there were other guests. One, met previously at Lady Palmerston's At Homes, was young Laurence Oliphant, an English diplomat and journalist newly back from Japan—"a thorough anti-American."[23] Second was a Scottish gentleman, Stirling of Kier. Last was a boy, or what seemed a boy, named Algernon Swinburne. Milnes took Adams aside and warned him that Swinburne was a poet. Perhaps he also offered discreet assurances that Adams was an American but an exception, a traveler, linguist, diplomat, and potential writer.[24]

By December 8, when their "very jolly little bachelor party" broke up, Adams had cemented ties with Milnes.[25] He had formed cordial, even friendly relations with Oliphant. He had not adapted to Swinburne, and who could? The poet had talked torrentially, hilariously, for hours at a time. He had declaimed his and others' poetry in a profusion of languages, ancient, medieval, and modern. He unquestionably was a genius, out of control.[26] Fatally for close relations, he was mad.[27]

Henry no sooner returned to London than he was sent to Copenhagen. Princess Alexandra of Denmark would soon be married to the Prince of Wales, and an official gift of the United States waited conveyance to the Danish Court. The Chief believed that bearing the gift would give Henry "a chance to see a new portion of Europe, and one not commonly visited."[28] Henry disagreed. Concurring with Hamlet's jibe that Denmark was a prison, he assumed that Copenhagen's one attraction would be its picture gallery. He accordingly slept on a Channel steamer and trains, delivered the gift, inspected the pictures, and hurried to Berlin. There he enjoyed a two-day holiday and revived his German.

Again restored to London, he found the Legation overwhelmed with work. The list of Union merchant ships sunk by rebel cruisers was lengthening steadily, and notes to the Foreign Office were numerous in proportion. Having to make three correct copies of every note, and often a copy for the Union's most active ally in the House of Commons, William E. Forster, Henry and Moran were soon "worked to pieces."

There meanwhile was news of an impending measure by President Lincoln. The Union leader had announced that he would issue an Emancipation Proclamation. The act, constitutional under the war power, would free the slaves in the rebellious states.[29]

The mere promise of Lincoln's proclamation stirred a tumultuous response among the English lower classes. A great meeting was held in Manchester on December 31, 1862, in support of the Union president and his action. Soon in London, a still greater meeting, held in Exeter Hall in the Strand, drew crowds into the streets of a size, Henry said, "unheard of since the days of reform."

The war news improved. General Burnside had misdirected his army to a grim defeat at Fredericksburg in Virginia; but more recently a Union army under General Rosencrans had attacked a Confederate army at Stones River near Murfreesboro in Tennessee, brought on a battle, and won a much-needed victory.

Charles was promoted to captain. Feeling more confident week by week, Henry predicted, "The war can hardly last six months more of active campaigning." He imagined that Charles would then come abroad, not to serve at the Legation, but instead to travel with their elders. "You will . . . take my place. The Chief may ask leave of absence, and travel, and in such case you will be wanted to travel with them."

William Henry Seward was a lifelong admirer of J. Q. Adams. Since May 1860, the powerful New Yorker had enjoyed the adulation of C. F. Adams. In Washington in the winter of 1860–1861, when still a senator, he had repeatedly spoken with H. B. Adams, whom he liked and was eager to promote.[30]

Since coming to London, Henry had opened a channel of indirect communication between himself and Secretary Seward by writing to his son, Frederick W. Seward, who held the place of assistant secretary.[31] On January 23, 1863, Henry took a different course and wrote directly to the secretary. First stating, "My father requests me to say . . . ," he asked Secretary Seward to have his aides find and copy a series of old diplomatic papers and send the duplicates to the Legation.

The copies were wanted in London because Henry, no one else, was looking into old international frictions. In 1794, England was at war with France. The U. S. government—in claimed mere innocent sympathy with revolutionary France—permitted American privateers to sail from American ports, capture English merchant ships, and bring them to American ports as allegedly legal prizes. The English resented the American captures. The British minister to the United States, George Hammond, wrote letter after letter to Thomas Jefferson, the American secretary of state. Jefferson replied. Tapping sources in London, Henry had obtained the texts of Jefferson's replies but only the dates, or mere approximate dates, of Hammond's remonstrances.

In Washington, Seward welcomed H. B. Adams's request and ordered it met. Hammond's letters were found and copied; the duplicates were forwarded to London; and on arrival they passed to Henry. He read them and put them out of sight in a drawer. The episode seemed closed but was suspended and would later be resumed.

Like a ghost, clothes unbuttoned and hair uncut, Charley Wilson crossed the Legation's doorstep, reporting for work after a half-year's idleness with pay. The elder Adamses responded by barring *both* official secretaries of legation from their entertainments. Moran grew furious. By way of revenge, he excoriated two Adamses in his private journal. He seemed not to realize that his words described the Chief and Henry as equals. "The two sit up stairs there exchanging views on all subjects, and as each considers the other very wise, and both think all they do is right, they manage to think themselves Solomons and to do some very stupid things."[32]

Moran could scold, but past Adamses had been comparative Solomons, and Henry was on his way to becoming the greatest Solomon of the family. He was *helped* in his progress by studying all subjects. He was helped too by being in London. And immeasurably, in February 1863, he was helped by particular English books.

Everywhere in Christendom, believers were giving credence to verses in Genesis about the Creation. Simultaneously, many people, commonly the same people, were believing reports by scientists concerning fossils which allegedly indicated that human beings had walked the earth in years incomparably more ancient than the ecclesiastically dated lifetimes of Adam and Eve. Fossils were said to prove as well that humans had lived among saber-toothed tigers, hairy mammoths, and other animals no longer extant and nowhere mentioned in the Bible. Credence thus being doubled, if not confounded, Sir Charles Lyell had proposed to set forth the newest findings of science in an unprovoking manner. He had written a book called *The Geological Evidences of the Antiquity of Man, with remarks on theories of the Origin of Species.* Published in February 1863, it created a furor. Copies abounded. Typically, returning to London for the opening of Parliament, John Bright sent his wife a copy and urged her to read it.[33]

Henry read Lyell's book and two others of equal or greater interest, *The Voyage of the Beagle* and *The Origin of Species*, by an ally of Lyell's, Charles Darwin.[34] All three books were highly speculative and almost overfull of theories. For Henry, their principal value was not intellectual but personal. Lyell and Darwin were attempting to *explain* evolution. Without disrespect to their efforts, Henry with all possible energy was trying to *achieve* evolution. Emboldened by his reading, he wrote to Charles that he might leave law and politics to work in other fields. The notion so strayed from Adams precedent that the third son could hardly mean it. Yet he assuredly had conceived it. "My promised land of occupation," he exulted, ". . . my burial place of ambition and law, is geology and science."

For Henry, a practical benefit of reading *The Antiquity of Man* was friendlier and more serious relations with Lyell. Sir Charles often told him he should meet Darwin as soon as Darwin came to town. It gradually emerged that Darwin never came to town. The fact was regrettable; for Henry wanted first-hand dealings, the more the better, with the ablest persons of the age.[35]

He meanwhile was making rapid progress. Invited to dinner by the Duke of Argyll, he "took particular pains to be introduced" to John Stuart Mill, "as I think him about the ablest man in England."[36]

Monckton Milnes took a hand in Henry's advancement. He gave the American visiting privileges at a club for writers, the Cosmopolitan. Henry went there, looked across a room, and recognized Thackeray. It did not spoil the experience that the writer's club-house talk, spoken in a loud voice that an onlooker could not help but overhear, proved "stupid or vulgar or both."[37]

Persisting in kindness, Milnes nominated Henry for membership in a club for diplomats, the St. James's. The nomination was seconded by Laurence Oliphant, Frederick Cavendish, and Lord Hartington.[38] Soon elected, Henry could rightly have asked himself how many foreigners were similarly admitted to comparable English clubs when twenty-five. In later life he would suggest in print that, of the persons born when he was born, he possibly had advanced with the greatest speed.[39]

London taught Henry something so interesting he kept it to himself. On March 26, 1863, another great meeting assembled in St. James's Hall in support of Lincoln's proclamation. The gathering purportedly was organized by the leaders of certain English trades unions. John Bright presided and spoke.[40] Henry attended as observer for the U. S. government and listened while English workingmen gave cogent speeches linking the Federal cause in America with hoped-for democracy and socialism in Europe. He wrote an account of the meeting for Secretary Seward.[41] But he learned *and did not tell Seward* that the meeting in fact was organized by a "little Socialist group" under the guidance of a German socialist revolutionary self-exiled to London, Dr. Karl Marx.[42] It seems inescapable that he and the socialist were introduced, for Marx was there in the hall.[43]

When writing to Charles about the meeting, Henry again did not name Marx. Avoidance usually had a reason. In this instance, the probable reason had to do with leaders of revolutions.

To Henry's mind, there were revolutions and revolutions. If all went as he desired, no other revolution would compare with the one being worked by American democracy.[44] He believed that he himself was that revolution's leader-to-be. He merely would not say so.

In symmetry, Henry would not name the leader of the rival, lesser revolution being worked, sometimes violently, sometimes peaceably, by the socialists of Europe. Avoiding both names, he contented himself with telling Charles: "I went last night to . . . a democratic and socialist meeting . . . most threatening and dangerous to the established state of things. . . . I can assure you this sort of movement is as alarming here as a slave-insurrection would be in the South, and we [the Unionists in London] have our hands on the springs that can raise or pacify such agitators; at least as regards our own affairs."

The phenomenon Henry was watching was that of the American revolution impinging both on the European revolution and on European conservatism. The sight was reassuring. He told his brother, "I never quite appreciated the 'moral influence' of American democracy, nor the cause that the privileged classes in Europe have to fear us, until I saw how directly it works."

❖ ❖ ❖

As judged by the Legation, the right policy for the English and French governments with respect to the war in America would have been one of support for the Union and sharp repulse of the rebels. Experience had shown the Adamses and Moran that the actual policy of England and France was one of slight sympathy with the Confederates and masked antipathy to the Federals.[45] Henry reacted two ways. He permitted himself the satisfaction of private rage. In April 1863, he erupted to Charles, ". . . I hope to see the time when America alone will take France and England both together on her hands, and be strong enough to knock their two skulls against each other till they crack." But simultaneously he sought chances to cooperate with English politicians who might induce the Ministry to move to a policy supportive of the Union.

In his view, the ablest politician among the English was Richard Cobden. For several months, in despair of Union success on the battlefield, Cobden had been avoiding C. F. Adams. On April 15, 1863, changing his ways, the English leader visited the Legation. The occasion for his return was a not-yet-drafted speech. He intended to speak in Parliament in relation to the Foreign Enlistment Act. The speech would attack the Ministry for failing to prevent British subjects from supplying warships to the unrecognized Confederate States.

Cobden's reappearance gave rise to a political meeting at the Legation on April 21, a Tuesday. The hosts were C. F. Adams, H. B. Adams, John Bigelow, and Robert J. Walker, but not Wilson or Moran. The guests were Cobden, Bright, and Forster.[46]

Unexpectedly on Wednesday evening, while drafting his speech, Cobden was interrupted by a messenger bringing a letter from H. B. Adams. The letter concerned a matter the Englishman would think important: the history of America's neutrality laws. Adams asked Cobden to look back to the 1790s, when England and France were at war, Jefferson was secretary of state, and Citizen Genet was the minister of revolutionary France in America. (Adams digressed to mention some letters from Genet to Jefferson and the secretary's replies, which he said were the "best things" Jefferson ever wrote, "next to the Declaration of Independence.") His letter continued:

> . . . one side of the affair has remained a good deal in the dark. Geo. Hammond was then your Minister . . . of whom Jefferson complained privately that he overwhelmed him with letters and remonstrances; yet few or none of these have ever been published, nor do they exist in the archives of this Legation, nor anywhere else so far as I know, except in the State Paper Office, the Washington Archives, and a copy which I have in my drawer.

Hammond, to repeat, wrote to Jefferson because American privateers were seizing English ships in claimed excusable support of France and England strongly wished to obtain redress. It happened that, in seeking redress, Hammond voiced in 1794 the selfsame grievance that C. F. Adams was voicing in 1863 with regard to Union merchant ships destroyed by the *Florida* and *Alabama*. H. B. Adams said about the British remonstrances in his possession, ". . . the principle [supporting the] . . . claim of redress is laid down [in them] with great clearness; and certainly my father never stated it with more force."

Adams's object in sending the letter was to offer Cobden use of the set of Hammond's remonstrances. The Legation's messenger was waiting for a reply. Cobden sped the messenger back with word that the papers should be delivered at once. They were. Cobden scanned the papers and sent Henry a note asking whether pressure exerted by Hammond had caused the passage of America's early neutrality laws. Adams replied that Congress had passed such laws but that another consequence of Hammond's efforts had been agreement by the United States that it should pay damages to Great Britain in money. ". . . Mr[.] Jefferson accepted the principle of pecuniary compensation."

When finished, Cobden's speech would say nothing about pecuniary compensation. Yet its cornerstone, evident in its fifth paragraph, would be the Hammond-Jefferson correspondence.[47]

The English leader delivered his speech in the House of Commons on the evening of April 24. It prompted a debate lasting till midnight. Moran was present and recorded that the speech was "powerful." ". . . [Cobden] attacked the pretended neutrality of England in the war, condemned the shameless violations of the law . . . in building pirate ships and arming them for the rebels, pointed out in forcible language the bad effects of this course, and in a spirit of high statesmanship warned the House of the consequences of the bad precedent the nation seemed disposed to establish in this dishonorable proceeding. . . . Lord Palmerston staid the debate through. . . ."[48]

Without prompting from other persons, Cobden had ample motive for making a powerful speech. He was concerned about the effects on his countrymen of their flouting their own laws. He wanted the English no longer to sink to the level of profit-minded shipbuilders willing to perform any act that might win the Confederate Navy as a buyer. But Cobden had an open mind. After receiving a set of documents from H. B. Adams, he placed his speech on an international footing. As delivered, the speech led its hearers back to 1794, recounted American offenses against England, recalled England's strenuous protests, and said that the Americans, led by President Washington, granted the justice of England's case. ". . . they gave us all the protection which they now ask us to give them."[49]

With these and similar expressions, Cobden cleared a path towards Anglo-American cooperation. To his further credit, he returned to H. B. Adams the papers that Adams had lent him. Moreover, he preserved the two letters he had received from Adams on Wednesday evening. And it was not *his* fault that the American's letters, eventually acquired by the British Museum (later the British Library), would go unheeded by historians and biographers until the early 1960s.[50]

Even more than the enactment of his plans, Henry Adams wanted private happiness. He would be slow to say so, but most of all he wanted to marry for love. Almost equally, he wanted intimate friendships.

When a child, Henry had found a prospectively permanent friend, George Harrison Otis, a boy in Boston. George died suddenly of an illness. From that time forward, while making many acquaintanceships and not a few near-friendships, Henry had never met a contemporary whom he had sought as a true friend.[51]

To bridge the gulf, he had cultivated the more accessible of his brothers. The effort afforded him better knowledge of the virtues and faults of Charles and Brooks; but it was always a makeshift; and it raised the primordial question whether brothers, by dint of being brothers, had hurtful tendencies. The episode of "A Visit to Manchester" had shown that brothers in the Adams family could come close to repeating the tragedy of Cain and Abel. Henry had not forgotten the episode. His subsequent letters to Charles, though affectionate and often candid, had been risk-free and less than trustful.[52]

On April 27, 1863, Henry walked to Brook Street expecting to do no more than enjoy a talkative breakfast with Sir Henry Holland, one of the Chief's acquaintances, a retired physician, formerly physician to Queen Victoria. At the door he met an English youth "in the act of rapping the knocker." It developed that the stranger was Charles Milnes Gaskell. Known as Carlo, he was related on his father's side to Monckton Milnes. Four years younger than Henry, he had not yet completed his undergraduate studies at Cambridge. He chanced to be acquainted with "Piggy" Everett, Adams's cousin.[53]

The occasion was personally epochal. Adams saw with surprise and relief that his privation had ended. In adulthood in a foreign land, he had met a friend he would fully want. On his side, Gaskell had such perceptions and sympathies that he understood the person he was meeting. Practically at a glance, he knew what Henry Adams was.[54]

The knowledge made a basis for a never-to-be-altered wish. Gaskell was disposed to secure for Adams every benefit that he and his family could offer. The benefits would be great. Even by English standards, his parents were very rich. His mother, originally Mary Wynn, and his father, James Milnes Gaskell, belonged to families powerful in Wales and Yorkshire. A member of Parliament for thirty years, the elder Gaskell was an indolent politician but a voracious reader and capable critic. Earlier associated with Alfred Tennyson and Arthur Hallam, he had known most of the British writers of recent decades, including many who had been famous in the era of the first Napoleon.[55]

Carlo too had a literary connection. That first morning at breakfast, Henry learned that his friend-to-be had a sister Cecil who had married a man of unusual powers, Francis Turner Palgrave. He learned too that Palgrave had produced an attractive book titled *A Golden Treasury of the Best Songs and Lyrical Poems in the English Language*. He shortly bought two copies, kept one, and sent the other to Charles.

About two weeks later, Captain Adams unwrapped a gift Henry had sent him and threw it down as unwanted. Reconsidering, he took it up and started to read it. Eventually, he wrote to the Chief, ". . . it seemed such an odd book for a camp and the field; but strangely enough I find that I read it more than any book I have. . . ."[56]

Friendship with Gaskell released Henry from all necessity of making substitute friends of Charles and Brooks. Additionally it freed him to look for ways in which Charles and Brooks might safely join with him as political allies. Charles had expressed a wish to stay in the army as a career.[57] Henry thought the idea so bad as to require intervention. On May 1, 1863, he wrote to Charles on the subject dismissively. In the same letter, he reverted to the idea of their practicing law and dismissed that idea also. He explained: "We are both no longer able to protect ourselves with the convenient fiction of the law. Let us quit that now useless shelter, and steer if possible for whatever it may have been that once lay beyond it."

Henry's lines pictured himself and Charles as sailors. As

Charles would realize, the intended meaning of the metaphor was political. The Chief had decided that the occasion for his retirement would be the election of 1864. He was planning a journey to Italy in the spring of 1865, following his retirement as minister. John would then be free to assert himself unrestrictedly as a politician. Henry thought John a good fellow and liked him heartily. Yet, rather than yield ground excessively to John, Henry wanted to see a share kept for Charles, and he wanted Charles to begin suitable preparations.

Henry himself had long been seizing ground. To the limit of possibility, he had been politicking for fifteen years, since 1848, when John Quincy Adams died and he, a boy of ten, went to the funeral as a little-noticed lesser grandson. How much Charles had done since that fateful year was best not asked, but Henry wished his slower brother would use his mind and get to work.

According to reputation, the best lawyer in the United States was William Maxwell Evarts, born in Boston, but a confirmed New Yorker. In the spring of 1863, Secretary Seward sent Evarts to London to act as counsel for the Legation. He arrived at 5 Upper Portland Place on May 1, the very day that Henry wrote to Charles about their steering beyond the fiction of the law.

Evarts exchanged words with C. F. Adams but was abducted by H. B. Adams, who led him to a steamer on the Thames.[58] "We had a two hours' voyage up to Kew," Henry wrote, ". . . [and] had just time to run over the gardens. Then we took a cab and drove up to Richmond Hill, where we ordered dinner at the Star and Garter, and then sat in the open air and watched the view and the sunset until our meal was ready."

Forty-five and very thin, Evarts was friendly, active-minded, and astonishingly funny. His conversation abounded in original puns and laughable stories. After having chances to compare the arrival's mind and his own, Henry would say, part in earnest, "I am slowly but certainly becoming a dead-head."

In theory, the United States was governed by elected and appointed officials. In practice, the country had increasingly been governed both by officials and by persons who were not officials. Politicians in office and politicians not in office frequently worked in combinations. Since the summmer of 1860, a combination of New Yorkers led by Seward and Weed had asserted pervasive, even dominant control of the nation's business. Seward and Weed had several trusted associates. One was Raymond, currently both editor of the *New York Times* and a leading Republican Congressman. A second was Bigelow, formerly editor of the *New York Evening Post*, presently consul general in Paris. Evarts was a third associate. He was to serve as temporary counsel in London but could be presumed to be abroad on a secret errand. His hidden task would be to make a private survey of Union and Confederate activity in England and France. When ready, he could send his findings to Seward and Weed by private letter.[59]

Henry's taking Evarts to Richmond Hill was a political event. The abductor knew more about the New Yorkers and had more effectively taken part in their activities than they themselves could imagine. Raymond, Weed, Seward, and conceivably Bigelow had each been aware of some of Henry's involvements in their work; but none knew the full scope of his activities, still less the ultimate reach of his ambitions. The reason was partly Henry's requirements of secrecy, partly the fact that the New Yorkers' actions tended to be compartmentalized. Thus Henry could tell Evarts *as new information* important things about his past doings in Washington and in London. Yet one may doubt that the abductor said much to the lawyer about himself. Old secrets, for the present, were best allowed to sleep.

The only surviving record of what was said at Richmond Hill is two sentences written by Henry to Charles: "Much conversation had we, and that of a pretty confidential nature. We discussed affairs at home and philosophic statesmanship, the [Union] Government and the possibility of effectual reform." The sentences concerned the *spoken* aspect of their meeting. More essential was the unspoken. Henry was reaching for new access to the New York combination through the ablest of its younger members. He was never more successful. He and Evarts were not four hours together when they were close political friends.

Piggy Everett turned up in London. Apprised that Mr. Evarts and Henry would be pleased to visit Cambridge, he invited them to join him at the university during the Whitsuntide holidays. They accepted and went, but under difficult conditions. At home, fateful issues were hanging in the balance. In the west, Grant was attempting the capture of Vicksburg, the last rebel city on the Mississippi. Baffled at first by swamps, his army had contrived to slip down the river past the city, had attacked it from the south, cut its communications, and begun a siege. In the east, General Hooker—the latest replacement commander of the Army of the Potomac—had ordered his troops to cross the Rappahannock in search of a final clash with Lee's Army of Northern Virginia. The new Union commander was allegedly aggressive.

While at Cambridge, Adams again saw Gaskell.[60] Everett arranged that Mr. Evarts and Henry meet appropriate people and glimpse the university's inner workings. The experience gave Henry a new idea of the possible beauties of academic life. He said in a letter to Charles, ". . . it is astonishing what good fellows these gowned individuals may be, and how well they do live."

Back in London, Henry pondered the latest news. A peculiar battle had been fought in Virginia at Chancellorsville. General Hooker had shown remarkable incapacity; "Stonewall" Jackson was killed accidentally by his own men; and victorious General Lee lost a fifth of his army. Henry offered Charles a hopeful judgment. ". . . the Confederacy has got into damnably shallow water."

Charles sent conclusions still more hopeful. He all but claimed that the Army of the Potomac could dispense with a commander and win without one. His words portended better fortunes. He said the army was "large, brave[,] and experienced." "The men do not seem cast down or demoralised. . . ."[61]

A London season was in progress. ". . . I abhor it!" Henry reported, "but I go, in silence." Yet his hours in society were sometimes happy. He enjoyed relaxing at an English table while Sir Edward Bulwer-Lytton and Robert Browning exchanged opinions about immortality. It pleased him that Charles Dickens joined in one of the Legation's well-managed dinners. He was particularly delighted by a walk. "I had occasion to go last night to a reception over in Kensington . . . [and] walked part of the way. . . . I passed through Grosvenor Square and round Hyde Park to Apsley House, and the streets seemed alive with carriages in every direction. Gentlemen in white cravats were scuttling about, like myself; cabs were rushing furiously in all quarters; hundreds of carriages were waiting, or setting down or taking up their people before great houses. . . . There was a rush and roar all through the West End, that one can see only in London. Six weeks hence if I go through the same streets again at midnight, there will not be a soul there. . . . Acres and miles of houses will be as silent as a Virginia forest."

Acting against the *Alexandra*, a cruiser built for the Confederate Navy, the Liberal Ministry committed the warship's fate to the courts. Evarts helped prepare the Union case presented before Chief Baron Pollock. Henry, bitten during his first life by an English judge in the case of the rebel steamer *Nashville*, was

disappointed, not astonished, when Pollock so instructed the jury
that the *Alexandra* was freed.

Troubles seemed always to mount. Two powerful warships,
armored "rams," were nearing completion at the Laird yards in
Liverpool, purportedly for the Confederate Navy. In Parliament, a
fresh champion of the rebels, John Arthur Roebuck, said he would
formally propose assistance to the South.

Troubles equally subsided. Pollock's conduct made possible an
appeal, and the *Alexandra* was again detained. Roebuck entangled
himself in an intrigue with Napoleon III. Meanwhile England
basked in what Henry said was "wonderfully fine, clear, hot
weather." He thought the weather decisive. ". . . literally the sun
has carried us through."

Moran went to Paris on vacation. Evarts would soon return to
New York. Henry scanned French newspapers at the St. James's
Club and at night read heavy books. His advancing re-education
had brought him to J. S. Mill and Alexis de Tocqueville. He
humorously wrote to Charles, ". . . I have learned to think De
Tocqueville my model, and I study his life and works as the Gospel
of my private religion."

In Virginia, the armies were again in motion, but to what
purpose remained in doubt. The Union cavalry was much engaged.
On June 17, the First Massachusetts was drawn into a violent
skirmish by rebel cavalry at Aldie's Gap. Major Henry Higginson
suffered a sabre wound in his face and a bullet lodged in his spine
but was rescued and sent to Boston to begin a long, successful
convalescence. Lieutenant Jim Higginson was captured. Captain
Adams came away unhurt, but almost two-thirds of the troopers in
his squadron were captured, wounded, or killed. He sent an account to John.[62] Understandably, details of what happened were
only slowly forwarded to the Adamses at the Legation.

As they had been doing from the outset, Confederate propagandists were feeding the English enormous lies.[63] Recently, London newspapers had reported the surrender of Hooker's army at
Chancellorsville. They now reported the surrender of Grant's
army besieging Vicksburg.[64]

A steamer brought news more astounding than any lie. Lee's
Army of Northern Virginia, going over to the attack, had crossed
Maryland west of Washington, had entered Pennsylvania, and was
racing northward towards Harrisburg. The rebel commander had
never tried anything so daring or unaccountable. Out of excitement more than worry, Henry again craved involvement in a
battle.[65] "If it were not for the Chief," he exclaimed to Charles, "I

would not stay here a moment, but at least I hope my presence here is necessary for him, since I feel as though it were simple suicide for myself."

Frenzy changed to amazement at his own failure to appreciate where he was and what he was doing. "I want to go into the army! to become a second lieutenant in an infantry regiment somewhere in the deserts of the South! I who . . . have lived a life of intellectual excitement, in the midst of the most concentrated society of the world . . . . Why the thing's absurd! Even to retire to a provincial life in Boston would be an experiment that I dread to look forward to!"

He explained that London's "peculiar attraction" was its permitting him to do "every day and without a second thought, what at another time would be the event of a year; perhaps of a life." He gave an instance. He had just seen the English aristocrats behaving as they behaved when by themselves. ". . . we were asked out to a little garden party by the old Duchess of Sutherland at Chiswick. . . . Dukes and Duchesses, Lords and Ladies, Howards and Russells, Grosvenors and Gowers, Cavendish's [sic], Stuarts, Douglases, Campbells, Montagus, half the best blood in England was there, and were cutting through country-dances and turning somersets and playing leap-frog in a way that knocked into a heap all my preconceived ideas of their manners."

The English press announced that Lee's army, turning eastward, had "insulated Washington and taken possession of the Capitol." Mason, the Confederate commissioner, repeated the lie at a public dinner.[66]

Fresh reports by the steamers placed Lee's army where it had been before, but faced about and attempting to return to its old positions! General Hooker had been replaced by General Meade. Before Meade could fully take charge, the Army of the Potomac had sped to intercept and block the flying rebels; and at Gettysburg, Pennsylvania, a terrific battle had raged for three days ending in the evening on July 3.

Thousands of miles from the fighting, Unionists in London waited in hushed solemnity for more reports. "At this distance," Henry told the captain, ". . . it's very grand and inspiring. There's a magnificence about the pertinacity of the struggle . . . closing, so far as we know[,] on the eve of our . . . national anniversary . . . that makes even these English cubs silent. . . . Our generation has been stirred up from its lowest layers[,] and there is that in its history which will stamp every member of it until we are all in our graves. We cannot be commonplace. . . . I have hopes for us all. . . ."

Confirmation came that at Gettysburg the Army of the Potomac had withstood and much outfought the Army of Northern Virginia, which, cruelly thinned, had moved off towards Richmond. Simultaneously a telegram from Seward announced the capture of Vicksburg on July 4 and the full opening of the Mississippi to Union traffic.

Invited by Milnes to meet some English guests that evening, July 19, 1863, Henry was greeted in contrasting spirits. "Milnes . . . received me with a hug before the astonished company, crowing like a fighting cock. But the rest of the company was very cold. . . ." Coldness went hand in hand with open hostility. "I went with Mr[.] Milnes to the Cosmopolitan Club afterwards, where the people all looked at me as though I were objectionable. Of course I avoided the subject in conversation, but I saw very clearly how unpleasant the news was which I brought."

Ecstatic, and desperate for a rest, Henry ceased work in the study. Snatching up some books and inviting Mary and Brooks to come along, he hastened to Mount Felix. Mrs. Sturgis was glad to see them. He wrote: "It was as good as cool molasses-and-water to get back again among the greenth. I lay in a hammock under the trees, and smoked and read and dozed beside the silvery Thames. . . . Parliament has broken up; London is deserted; my friend Monckton Milnes has got a peerage and is now Lord Houghton; the [London] Times has acknowledged the capture of Vicksburg; and generally, the world keeps moving."

4

EXTREME RESTLESSNESS

The family again wished to travel. Henry sent parents, children, and servants to York, waited alone in London for a despatch bag, overtook the party, and guided its members to Edinburgh, Glasgow, Loch Katrine, Loch Lomond, and at 6:00 A.M. on August 12, 1863, to a dock in Banavie on the Caledonian Canal. After the others boarded a steamer (they would visit Edward Ellice, a member of Parliament), Henry and Brooks rented a light carriage or "dog-cart" and hastened westward over the mountains. They were starting their first ambitious joint project.[1] To justify the escape, they had declared a wish to imitate Johnson and Boswell's tour of the Hebrides. As preparation, Henry had read Sir Walter Scott's *Pirate* and studied Hebridean geology.

At Arisaig, they hired a boat and rowers. The three-hour crossing to the Isle of Skye afforded unforgettable views.[2] In Henry's words: "The long, mountainous coast of Scotland, lighted by the sunset and twilight, looked very grand in the distance, and on our left were the mountains of Skye covered with heavy folds of mist." He felt unaccustomed sensations. ". . . [I was] free on the Sound of Sleat." "I felt as peaceful and as quiet as a giant. . . ."

In inspiration, the brothers' journey was scientific. They wished to go where they would see no other humans, almost no traces of human effort, and small evidence of the evolution of organic forms, there to experience what they might feel as the very start of the world. Brooks was seasick during the crossing and repelled by the meals served at Skye's wretched inns, but Henry dragged him along stony roads, advancing always towards the Cuillin Hills. At last, on rented horses, they took a rising path over heaps of rock and earth called moraines, vestiges of the ice-age. "Along the whole seven miles there is no human habitation, no cultivation, not a tree or a shrub. . . . I walked much of the way, and climbed on foot the steep hill at its end."

From a high ridge, they saw a broad, empty expanse of air, earth, and ocean. At its center was a geological formation, Lake Coruiskin. ". . . [the sight] made an impression on me that few things can, and like all great master-pieces, the more I think of it, the more extraordinary it seems to be." The desolate lake had been created by the melting of an archaic glacier. "When the glacier yielded to some unexplained change of temperature, it left behind it nothing but this lake among the rocks close to the sea. . . . I might give you a good-sized volume of epithets without conveying the least idea of the really awful isolation and silence of this spot."

Starting at Edinburgh two weeks later, Henry and Brooks began another escape, a visit to the middle ages.[3] They hiked to Rosslyn and saw the keep and its "little jewel of a chapel." Next day, they inspected ruined Kelso Abbey and all-but-vanished Roxbury Castle, went to Jedburg, lounged in the ruins of its abbey, and walked two miles out of town to study a keep which Henry was determined not to miss. They slept at Hawick and in the morning took a southbound train. Near the English border, they got off at a lonely station. No road went their way, but Henry knew the direction they should take. After long hiking across brown hillsides through thick wet grass, they "saw from afar off the large and solitary castle that we sought." They found on arriving that Hermitage Castle was "still perfect," except for lacking its roof. The deserted structure was "a large, square granite pile, with a great Gothic arch at two ends, as though the builder had once seen a Cathedral, and had tried to make a castle with ecclesiastical reminiscences." They entered, mounted stairs, scaled walls, debated the probable uses of rooms, and, satisfied with their effort, stretched out on what Henry supposed was "the wall of the moat."

At Kiswick in the Lake Country, they rejoined their relations. The Chief had learned that the rams built at Liverpool would soon be delivered to the Confederate Navy. Concerned, he hurried to London. Henry shifted Mrs. Adams, Mary, and Brooks to the Lowood Hotel in Windermere. There he wrote a long letter to Charles—a "volume of travels"—recounting his and Brooks's adventures. He apparently permitted their mother to read the letter. It affected her feelings. She was reminded that in 1860 Henry had written Charles a series of travel letters from Italy which Charles let her read when received. The letters had ended with one from Sorrento. Remembering that particular letter and anticipating the journey to Italy which she and her husband were planning for 1865, she began to feel that she could not go home to retirement and old age in Massachusetts without visiting Sorrento in a party that included her Henry.

In London, C. F. Adams ascertained that the delivery of the rams was imminent, as reported. He accordingly sent Earl Russell a "solemn protest" against the failure of the British authorities to intercede.[4] While the Chief's protest was in transit, a note sent by Russell from Scotland reached the Legation. It seemed to blast every hope that the warships would be detained. Moran recorded, "Lord Russell . . . positively refuses to interfere with or stop Laird's Ironclads, and assumes his usual tone of insolence. . . ."[5]

Henry and his party returned to 5 Upper Portland Place on September 4, 1863, just after Russell's declaration was received. He read the latest communications and agreed that affairs were "in a very bad way." Looking back, he would shortly write, "We were . . . in the middle of the crisis . . . and . . . it was going against us." There *was* a crisis, but no cause for deep alarm. Since the *Trent* affair, each crisis had been less threatening than the one before.[6] He reported to Charles, ". . . disastrous as a rupture would be, we have seen times so much blacker that we were not disposed to bend any longer. . . ."

The Chief sent a note to Russell which Henry called "a counter-declaration, short but energetic, announcing what was likely to happen." The note would later stand as the most famous of C. F. Adams's papers.[7] Writing it, the father kept to his usual style. Saying no nation could tamely submit to such actions as the building by the British of warships for the Southern rebels, and saying he would have no further dealings with Russell until the Ministry detained the ironclads or new instructions reached him from his superiors in Washington, he offered the bristling comment, "It would be superfluous in me to point out to your Lordship that this is war."[8]

The counter-declaration was delivered to the Foreign Office at 3:00 P.M. on the 5th. Simultaneously a British message brought assurances to the Unionists that the matter of the rams was under "serious & anxious consideration."[9] Henry saw "confusion" in the British notes. He wryly observed that the English, "in their hatred of absolute Government," had "rendered all systematic Government impossible." The Liberal Ministry seemed capable neither of adhering to an established policy nor adopting a new one.

After a three-day wait, word came that orders to detain the rams had been in full operation for many days! A change of British policy had earlier occurred, but in secret. When no longer able to doubt it, Henry concluded, ". . . this is a second Vicksburg."

A week later, his mind still fixed on the vagaries of English politics, he was thunderstruck by news from another quarter. Rebel Commissioner Mason had terminated his dealings with Her Majesty's government and was going to France. "We have routed him," Henry exploded, "horse, foot[,] and creeters! We have pitched him into the Channel. . . ."

On September 23, the Legation's butler-messenger, Charles Light, was caught in a lie. The day after, he disappeared. Acting as "detective policeman," Henry opened Light's desk and found evidence of misdeeds ranging from the stealing of money and interception of mail to the consumption of 180 bottles of liquor. Shown the evidence, the Chief described the fugitive as "the most steady liar I ever knew, besides being a drunkard, a thief, a swindler and a forger."[10]

Astonishingly, Light returned. Henry wrote to Charles: "Now here is a case that has completely puzzled all my preconceived ideas . . . I knew that he was a liar . . . but believed that this was the result of education and that his disposition was good. When we discovered his true character, I at once supposed him to be a thorough villain, and took it for granted that he had fled the country. After an absence of three days, he came back, penitent, and wanting to be forgiven. . . ."

The butler-messenger was not forgiven, and his crimes lent impetus to a flurry of actions. Mrs. Adams demanded rescue from the horrors of London. Henry took her to a hotel in Hastings, with Mary for company. He then found a rentable house in nearby St. Leonard's, at 96 Marina, overlooking the Channel. The Chief rented it for two months.

On October 11, having settled mother and sister comfortably at the seaside, Henry reappeared at 5 Upper Portland Place. C. F. Adams told Moran that he and Henry would be trading places, each spending half his time at the Legation, half at St. Leonard's. He further said that during his absences the mail was to be opened and read by Henry before passing into others' hands. The father set out for the Channel, Henry made some effort to work, and Moran resisted. Asserting that he was a commissioned diplomat and H. B. Adams was not, the assistant secretary demanded that *he* control the mail.

Henry must have telegraphed, for Mrs. Adams invited Moran to St. Leonard's. On October 17, a Saturday, he went to the seaside for the weekend. Somewhat pacified, he enjoyed a walk on the coast and a visit to Battle Abbey in Hastings.

Henry too had come to 96 Marina. On Monday evening, he and Moran returned to London together. By then, the arrangement relating to the opening of mail was better understood. On Tuesday, however, bringing tea to H. B. Adams, the footman, Henry Hard, dropped the tray on the stairs. On Friday, the Chief dismissed him for drunkenness.[11]

Themselves offended by London's horrors, the Chief and Henry lengthened their stays at St. Leonard's and shortened their stints at the Legation. Their new schedule gave them intervals together by the water. As male Adamses had long tended to do, they went swimming and did not desist till mid-November. Henry rejoiced to Charles, " . . . your excellent father and myself . . . if possible indulge daily in a bath on the sea-shore—ye holy saints, how cool."

Large events seemed supplanted by small. Yet the family's part-withdrawal from London was encouraged by a fateful change. The British authorities were wholly interdicting the Confederacy's acquisition of warships. Henry wrote, ". . . you cannot conceive how differently we feel here. . . . There is no longer any perpetual bickering and sharp prodding necessary to exasperate this Government into doing its duty."

Time out of mind, Adams children had been raised to be Christians and church-goers. The children in Henry's generation were raised in the same way, yet were drifting away from religion. Henry may have drifted the least. On leaving college, he became a permanent avoider of church, yet remained a believer. In secret, he sometimes prayed.[12]

His remaining a believer may have rested as much on new experience as on old instruction. His stays at St. Leonard's gave him opportunities to gaze for long periods at the open ocean. He wrote to Charles, ". . . the more I look at it, the more I feel how far the ocean is superior in grandeur to every other object in nature." The words were palpably religious. They indicated that, for Henry, sight of the ocean was at times equivalent to sight of God.

John and Charles had nicknamed Henry "the philosopher." He had accepted the label and hoped to earn it. By striving constantly to find out what he thought, why he thought it, and whether he should modify his ideas, he had become the tentative holder of a philosophical position. Partial to both science and religion, partial also to commonsense views, he called himself "a sort of experimentalist." He held to four tenets especially. He acknowledged the reality and immensity of the universe; he as-

sumed its components were related and even alike; he believed the
occurrences experienced by humans were not yet well understood;
and he preferred to suppose that full explanation of all reality was
possible. He accordingly said in a current letter, ". . . my philosophy
teaches me . . . that the laws which govern animated beings will be
ultimately found to be at bottom the same with those which rule
inanimate nature, and, as I entertain a profound conviction of the
littleness of our kind, and of the curious enormity of creation, I
am quite ready to receive with pleasure any basis for a systematic
conception of it all."

His philosophical assertions could be deceiving. On October
30, 1863, speaking—so he said—as a "full-blown fatalist," he remarked to Charles: "The world grows . . . just like a cabbage. . . .
The result will come when the time is ripe, and the only thing that
disgusts me much is the consciousness that we are unable to govern
it. . . ." It disgusted him too—so he said—"that a man of sense can
only prove his possession of a soul by remaining in mind a serene
and indifferent spectator of the very events to which all his acts
most eagerly contribute." But the outbursts, it is clear, were
amusedly fatalistic. Both his philosophy and his conduct were *anti-*
fatalistic. His usual state of being was eager activity. He was consistently opposed to mere passivity and indifference. What he wanted
and was trying to get was improved control—better government—
of himself and events.

Increasingly the part of his work that mattered to him was his
attempt to re-educate himself. His letters permitted glimpses of a
two- and-a-half-year effort. "I labored at financial theories, and
branched out upon Political Economy and J. S. Mill. Mr[.] Mill's
works . . . led me to the examination of philosophy and the great
French thinkers of our own time; they . . . passed me over to . . .
the monarchist Hobbes; the atheist Spinoza and so on." "My can-
dles are seldom out before two o'clock in the morning, and my
table is piled with half-read books. . . ." "I am deep in international
law and political economy. . . ." ". . . I jump from International
Law to our foreign [i.e. diplomatic] history. . . ." "Other hours I
pass in sleepy struggle with philosophers and political econo-
mists . . . ."[13]

It could seem that his studies were highly theoretical. Yet they
always were practical. His object was to improve his chances to work
effectively as an independent writer and politician linked with the
executive branch of the U. S. government. His success was already
great. Incessant efforts since April 1861 had advanced him far
ahead of all other Americans his age in mastery of foreign affairs.

He thus could anticipate going forward without interruption in a career involving meaningful association with the State Department. But it needs stressing that his interest in domestic affairs was easily as strong as his interest in foreign. He had an unusually high opinion, possibly too high an opinion, of the centrality and influence of the U. S. Treasury.[14] Because his reading had moved him ahead of other Unionists his age in mastery of public finance, he could anticipate good relations with the Treasury's topmost officials. The prospect strengthened his resolve to become a first-rate all-round economist. Perhaps with that particular resolve in mind, he remarked in mid-October 1863, "I am ruining my constitution by studying far into the small hours. . . ."

Knowing that the risks to his health were real, he sought ways to exercise. He had selected a house on the Channel partly in hopes of buying a sailboat. Unfortunately the Chief agreed to rent at a great distance from London on condition that Henry pay his own rail fares. Since the money budgeted for the boat would be spent instead on fares, Henry moved the horses to St. Leonard's and he and Mary went for rides. Their outings were often medieval. On the same coast eight centuries earlier, William the Conqueror had landed with an army and fought the Battle of Hastings, defeating Harold the Saxon, who was killed by an arrow. "Mary and I," Henry remarked, "ride over the hills and among the valleys . . . and I have frequently had occasion to study the battle-field where the admirable Harold got so durable a thrashing."

His experiences had a way of reminding him of religion. Not as work but for enjoyment, perhaps mostly on trains, he read a bulky tome, Arthur Hallam's *Middle Ages*. The effort confirmed him in a fond idea that, had he lived a millennium earlier, in 863 A. D., he would have aspired to become an abbot in "one of those lovely little monasteries which I used to admire so much among the hills in Italy."

The previous May, before he was wounded at Aldie's Gap, Henry Higginson had written a letter to Henry Adams in London, asking him to order some uniforms. Major Higginson entrusted the letter to Charles for mailing. Captain Adams put the letter in one of his pockets and forgot it. In August, he found it and sent it to Henry, who, not knowing about the major's wounds, ordered the uniforms from Poole's and, lacking a better address, sent them to Massachusetts in care of John. Higginson during the same months formed a mistaken impression that Henry Adams did not like doing errands. All the same, he wrote to Adams again, this time directly, and in the process announced his engagement to Ida Agassiz.[15]

Higginson's new letter bore on Adams's strongest desires, his wanting to marry for love and his wanting continuous dealings with intimate friends. For the present, he had no hope whatever of marrying. He could however list Americans he would welcome as friends, opportunities permitting. One was John Hay, the younger of Lincoln's private secretaries. They had met in Washington in 1861 but had not tried to correspond. A second was H. H. Richardson. A third was Henry Higginson, and it seemed pure gain that Higginson was marrying Ida Agassiz. Not only did Adams owe his conversion to geology to Ida's father, but also at college he had somewhat known her brother Alexander. A potential fourth friend, Alex possibly was the ablest fellow on the list.[16]

In late autumn, the weather at St. Leonard's changed from good to bad to infernal. Their lease having expired, the Adamses resumed continuous residence in London. Thence on December 18, 1863, Henry wrote again to the major. He took positive interest in Higginson's marriage. "I have not the honor of knowing Miss Agassiz. . . . But I have heard a great deal about her. . . ." He asked a favor. "It is that you will give me photographs of you both." And he asked the groom to befriend him. ". . . my long residence in England has not increased the very small number of friends I ever had. . . . Do try and send me a little . . . news. . . ."

At year's end in 1863, Mrs. Sturgis gave parties at Mount Felix both at Christmas and on New Year's Eve. At her Christmas party, she kissed Henry under the mistletoe. At the New Year's party, he tried to join in the fun but ended feeling "devilish blue." Writing to Charles, he said that what distressed him was the flight of time. " . . . while the bells all over the country are ringing . . . we gather to the open windows and listen in silence till the last stroke. . . . Bright and gay; kind and affectionate; healthy and happy; by the eternal symbol of the prophet, I always suck my whiskey-and-water with a gulp after this ceremony, and curse me if I don't feel very like crying."

Henry was aware that his life was entering a difficult, possibly calamitous phase. His worries began with the Union's incomplete success on the battlefield. The war had gone well the previous summer, but its continuance created worries relating to politics. The new year would be an election year, and he was thinking alarming thoughts. On the Sound of Sleat the previous August, he had felt as calm as a giant. In the first hours of 1864, he felt anxious and afraid. He broadly admitted to Charles, ". . . it is . . . the vague dread and helplessness of the future, that makes me feel such a shiver. . . ."

Evarts, long in New York, recrossed the ocean. Finding his legal prowess unneeded in London, he escorted Mrs. Adams and Mary to Paris. On January 19, Henry too slipped away. Thinking that Henry had left "rather mysteriously," Moran made inquiries and was told that the younger Adams had gone to Paris and had taken his uniform.

The costume in question was official court dress. On arriving in London in 1861, Minister Adams had directed that an ornate costume be tailored for himself and that costumes less ornate be tailored for Henry, Wilson, and Moran. Thanks to the minister's out-of-date ideas, the costumes supplied were of antique design, involving a gold-braided coat, white breeches, a three-cornered hat, and a gilt sword.

For Moran in 1864, Henry's taking his uniform to Paris had an all-too-apparent meaning. An arrangement had been made for Evarts and Henry to be presented to Napoleon III at the imperial court.[17] The presenter would be John Bigelow, newly promoted to chargé d'affaires. The presumable maker of the arrangement was H. B. Adams.[18]

Four weeks later, in the early morning of February 16, 1864, his twenty-sixth birthday, H. B. Adams boarded an English mail boat at Liverpool and went to sea. He had obtained English permission to meet the Cunard steamer then arriving from New York, together with permission for a passenger, Captain C. F. Adams, Jr., to shift from steamer to mail boat and thus proceed to London with all possible convenience.

On furlough, Charles was making his first trip abroad. That afternoon, looking from the train as it hurtled across the Midlands, he saw with astonishment the "wonderful development" of England's cities, industries, and means of communication and transportation. He wrote in his diary, ". . . this country is actually finished!"[19]

Charles had never thought well of Henry's views, tastes, or inclinations. He found the third son "not improved" in his "philosophy of life." Yet he noticed that Henry was kindly attending to his wants. The boy, too, was "much older." Indeed, like no other Adams, Henry had become sophisticated. He even knew how to telegraph.[20]

For their parents and Mary, seeing Charles was one joy and seeing his cavalry uniform was a second.[21] Wanting to please him, the elder Adamses resolved on his being presented to Queen Victoria. An application was made for the levee on March 2. Also invitations were sought for everyone (Wilson and Moran excepted) to Lady Palmerston's reception on March 4. Mrs. Adams meanwhile gave a reception of her own at which Captain Adams was encouraged to play the social lion.[22]

On March 1, 1864, happening to enter the downstairs office, Henry incautiously said he would attend the queen's levee. Still more incautiously, he alluded to a rule at court which extended favors to near relations of principal diplomats. Moran knew or suspected that the rule would not permit Henry's doing what he evidently proposed to do: follow the Chief and Charles but precede the secretaries of legation when passing before the queen. The assistant secretary also knew that rules of protocol were not absolute, even at the Court of St. James, and might the more easily be relaxed for C. F. Adams, who, being an American, was a minister the queen had not invited to dinner and never would. But Moran had had enough of the Adamses and their uniforms. The Adams who most maddened and baffled him was Henry. In his opinion, the son was a diplomatic pirate showered with unheard-of prerogatives, one of which was a rank impossible to define. Being higher than Wilson's, what *was* Henry's rank in the English mission? And by what right had he acquired an official uniform, worn it when presented to Queen Victoria in 1861, and again when presented to Napoleon III in 1864? The questions were legitimate, yet forbidden; and it lacerated Moran that there were "two Legations," one upstairs in which an interloper could flourish, and one downstairs in which he, a diplomat by commission, experience, and hard work, was stalled with uncleanly Wilson.

Sir Edward Cust, the arbiter of fine points of protocol at court, stopped that morning at the Legation. Moran caught his ear and asked about the privileges that might be extended to two sons of a minister attending the levee next day with two secretaries of legation. Cust replied that, if the sons wanted permission to precede the secretaries, they would be seeking a privilege which could in strictness be granted only to the minister's daughter. Unsurprised, Moran went upstairs and imparted Cust's response to Minister Adams. Henry was in the study a few feet away. To the assistant secretary's complete surprise, Henry turned very red and said he would never again go to court.[23]

Henry's face was reddened by violent exasperation. The causes of the feeling reached back to 1861. When named minister, C. F. Adams had made no effort to secure the appointment of suitable aides. While the Chief did nothing, the place of secretary of legation had been given by Seward and Lincoln to Wilson merely because American habits relating to government permitted the awarding of federal posts to party underlings who had no intention of performing the relevant duties. Wilson having been given the place of first secretary, Henry had as good as forced the government to retain Moran as assistant secretary—a fact Moran thereafter had been shielded from learning. Henry at the same time had reserved for himself the non-place of "private Secretary." He had done so in the knowledge that his father's chance of succeeding in London with Moran alone for a functioning aide was far worse than unlikely; it could hardly be imagined.[24]

With respect to the levee, developments were negative. Captain Adams postponed his presentation till March 12. On March 2, the Chief went to Buckingham Palace with Wilson and Moran and discovered on leaving that the two footmen had drifted away from the carriage. In no good mood, he discharged one of the two as punishment.[25]

Mr. Evarts was again in London but was going to Rome. Charles and Henry asked to accompany him as far as Paris. The three men "started gaily"—to use the captain's expression—and soon arrived. Evarts went on towards Italy. Charles and Henry, in Paris, passed an interval in unknown but imaginable employments.[26]

The brothers returned to London. On March 12, rather grumbling at having to go, Charles went with the Chief and Moran to be presented to Her Majesty. Henry did not go. Not going, he gained the solace of keeping his word. Possibly, as added solace, he told himself that a true American would scarcely suffer if he never again saw the queen.

Charles had booked passage to New York on the *Persia*—the Cunard steamer on which Henry had first crossed to Europe. He and Henry took the night train, reached Liverpool at 4:00 A.M., and went to the ship on a tugboat. Their last interchange was silent. Charles wrote: ". . . on board the steamer & soon Henry nodded to me good-bye from the tug[;] & I, with a bitter taste . . . in my mouth, was off for home."[27]

In earlier times, three gentlemen in Boston, C. F. Adams, John Gorham Palfrey, and Charles Sumner, had shared prominently in the creation of the Free Soil Party, later merged into the Republican Party. In 1851, as a Free-Soiler, Sumner was elected senator from Massachusetts. He clung possessively to his role as senator, but his true interest was foreign relations, and he aspired to either of two positions: minister to England or secretary of state. The victory of the Republicans in the election of 1860 brought him successive disappointments. In December 1860, Lincoln chose Seward to be secretary of state; and in March 1861, Seward arranged the choice of C. F. Adams as minister to England. Envious and angered, Sumner ceased relations with Adams.[28] Yet the senator became a power in Union politics (but not in diplomacy) by being chosen new chairman of the committee on foreign relations.

When a child, Henry had become acquainted with his father's political allies. In the early 1850s, he formed a friendship of his own with Sumner. Their friendship was made practicable in part by Sumner's being a bachelor. Sumner and Henry's separate friendship did not end in March 1861. It fell into abeyance. Also Henry continued it at one remove. The device he used was letters to Palfrey. He wrote continuously to Palfrey in part because the historian—currently postmaster in Boston—was always in touch with Chairman Sumner.

On April 15, 1864, Henry wrote Palfrey a letter expressing, among other things, his objections to London. He complained: ". . . London never seems to me to allow any homelike feelings. I never quit it even for an afternoon at Richmond or a Sunday at Walton, without feeling a sort of shudder at returning, to be struck as freshly as ever with the solemnity, the gloom, the squalor and the horrible misery and degradation that seem to me to brood over the place. The magnificence I know and can appreciate. It has done its best to make me a socialist and has nearly succeeded."

The passage could give wrong impressions. Henry saw America and Europe as opposites. England he mostly hated but partly liked. English magnificence had made him *almost* a socialist, but Europe generally would make him *never* a socialist. He was growing more and more certain that socialism as developed by Europeans and democracy as developed by Americans were fundamentally unalike and even inimical.[29]

In the same letter to Palfrey, Henry showed positive interest only in *American* possibilities. He took the position that the victories needed to end the rebellion were close at hand. Without giving reasons, he also took the position that the five Adamses currently abroad simply *had* to go home at the earliest possible moment. It followed that a new minister would have to be named. "After this season is over, we shall become very restless[,] and if the war is over, as we strongly hope, we must leave here. I wonder whether Sumner wouldn't take the place. I suppose he might get it if he wanted it. . . ."

Concerning his own future, Henry seemed both decided and undecided. On the one hand, he had revived the dead idea of becoming a lawyer and supposed he might enroll at the Harvard Law School. On the other, he supposed he might momentarily relax and do very little. As if the two sorts of behavior could be easily harmonized, he explained, ". . . [I] am ready to leave the society of Courts to those that are courtiers, and rest awhile at the law-school in Cambridge or elsewhere."

A notable feature of Henry's letter was its saying not a word about his living in Washington. Silence was indispensable. He knew that the Chief was thought eligible for promotion to the Cabinet. Following the election of 1860, Seward and Weed had tried to persuade future President Lincoln to give Congressman C. F. Adams the appointment as secretary of the treasury. Henry at the time had passionately hungered for his father's promotion. Subsequent experience had taught him to view his father's political fortunes in a wholly different spirit.

The prospective risk for Henry in 1864–1865 was only too obvious. For whatever reason, Seward might cease to be secretary of state, and C. F. Adams might replace him. In that event, Henry would be ordered to Washington. It was bad enough that he would again be dragooned as all-purpose servant. It was worse that he might be pressed to accept an official position as assistant secretary of state. The worst would be that his real duty, expressed or tacit, would be to help bring about his father's ultimate promotion: a term or two as president.[30]

Lincoln had given overall command of the Union armies to General Grant. The supreme commander had come east and was directing operations from a cabin on Chesapeake Bay at City Point. It had grown apparent that Grant meant to attack with two main forces, his own former army in the west, headed by General Sherman, and the Army of the Potomac, headed by himself, assisted by Meade.

The objectives Grant assigned the two forces were plain to see. Sherman would attempt the capture of Atlanta, the railroad nexus of the South. Grant meanwhile directed the Army of the Potomac straight at Lee's Army of Northern Virginia, intending to destroy it. His orders thrust the Army of the Potomac into a terrible region of Virginia, a waste of pines known as the Wilderness.

The British press had discovered anew that the federals were losing the American War. Henry again grew afraid for Charles, whose unit was poised for battle. On May 20, 1864, he wrote to his brother: ". . . I hear this morning that you have crossed the Rapidan. . . . The violence of the excitement will I suppose come next week. . . ."

The week did not bring the violence. Almost as alarmed by delay as he would have been by a Union defeat, Henry "invested in French novels, to amuse my mind." The next steamers brought word that the Army of the Potomac had fought through the Wilderness at great cost and was positioned on better ground.

At Spotsylvania, Grant attempted to shatter Lee's army, failed, and readied to strike again. Henry studied detailed maps and all arriving reports. As usual looking ahead, he was trying to foresee the moves of the armies. He told the captain, "Grant is such an awful fighter that I fear another battle[,] which, so away from our base, must be a more than usually severe one for the wounded. . . ."

On June 10, more or less parenthetically, Henry wrote Charles some lines that Charles might dismiss as more of Henry's nonsense. The lines involved a future book. ". . . I've long seen what so many Americans will not see, that our system and the English system are mortal enemies. I mean to write a book about it one day—not for publication however; as I consider stupidity a necessary condition of a good book, and the public read only amusing works. It shall be written for you, my dear boy; for you! to read—if you can!"[31]

Henry's talk of a book was part-provoked by the London season. No longer a stranger, he if anything was too much the wanted guest, invited specifically because English-speaking and thus not "foreign." His busiest night was June 14, 1864.[32] He went first to a musical party at Countess Berstorff's, stopped next at Lady Colchester's, proceeded to Devonshire House for a word with the duke, put in an appearance at Mrs. Schenley's ball, and after midnight joined his parents and Mary at a ball at Miss Burdett Coutts's, "a regular chaos," at which he "sweltered in a beefy and suety crowd till near two o'clock."

While returning to Upper Portland Place in the family carriage, he was informed by his relations that some of Miss Coutts's English guests had laughed delightedly when told of reports, just received, that Lee had defeated Grant and that Sherman was repulsed "with severe loss." In his worried state, Henry believed the alleged reports. Once in his room, he did not undress. He did "what I have done many times." ". . . I sat at my window and watched the cold gray light spread over the Park and Hampstead . . . and contemplated the failure of our campaign." At sunup, he went out for the newspapers and found that there had been no defeats, only another burst of Confederate lies. The anticlimax helped him control his fears. Two added days permitted his writing, ". . . Grant appears to me now to have the game in his hands. . . ." The commander's strategy seemed to turn on Sherman's success in Georgia, even more than his own against Lee's Army of Northern Virginia. Henry judged the strategy excellent and expected that it might work. "I consider everything to depend on the fall of Atlanta . . . and believe it would make the fall of Richmond inevitable."

On June 24, 1864, Lady Waldegrave gave a party at Strawberry Hill, her Gothic residence near London, once the plaything of Horace Walpole. Those present included Lady Fife and Lady Constance. Walking in the garden, they noticed two gentlemen smoking cigarettes in the shadow of a summer house. Lady Fife glared in at the entrance. Lady Constance tried to make out their faces.

The skulkers were Henry Adams and Laurence Oliphant, and Henry was doing things far worse than smoke in an English garden. He and Mary had hatched a plot, with Brooks as junior accomplice. The purpose was to assure the early return of several Adamses to America, possibly *not* including the minister. Telling Charles what had happened, Henry said he expected to be home "next winter." He spoke as if he and the Chief could separate. "Mary and I are plotting to make sure that this be our last season. . . . I am getting old, and must be at work. The Chef can do without me, if he only tries, and Brooks had better go home with me. We will both settle in Cambridge. All this however is as yet unknown to the heads of the family. . . ."

Henry's reaching out to the children was evidence of a fresh return of fright and anxiety, this one more severe. In part, the drop in his spirits was brought on by a possibility so harsh that he previously had not faced it. Like other Unionists, he had assumed that Union victories would induce the rebels to sue for peace. But the rebels might not sue for peace. They might fight till no soldiers were left to continue the fighting. Indeed the killing was well advanced. The annihilation which he had once said would have to be wrought on the traitors was in process of infliction. It was wanted by the victims![33]

News reached London of actual setbacks for Grant and Sherman. They were momentary, yet sufficed to tell Henry that the killing of the rebel armies might consume many months, even a year. This new calendar of death brought last gorgons into sight. The gorgons were political.

In 1860, the Republicans had polled less than half of the

popular vote. During Lincoln's presidency, they dismally failed to increase their numbers. Democrats continued to swarm. They were expected to nominate ousted McClellan for president and openly were recommending peace with the South. Realities being what they were, the re-election of Lincoln was impossible apart from saving great victories won in good time, before November 8, when the voters would go again to the polls.

Henry had been saying that the war news was "exactly like a fever; now a chill, and now a boil." The simile suited the news, yet also reflected his swings of mood. Writing to the captain on July 8, he said: ". . . the struggle to die is painful. The next nine months will be slow to pass. . . . I would like much to go to bed, and sleep peacefully till next March. I want to escape the alternations of hope and dread; the hectic phenomena of our decline; and bid farewell to my strangely disastrous experience as a politician."

The lines raised questions that had no answers. Which Adamses were dying? Which declining? For that matter, how had *his* experience as a politician been disastrous? Yet some things were clear. Henry knew that the anti-slavery movement lacked decisive backing by the voters. He knew Lincoln could not win re-election in November—not if running as a Republican. He foresaw that McClellan, if elected, would no sooner take office in March 1865 than he would reach a settlement with the traitors; the Confederate States, recognized and protected by Old World powers, would be securely independent; and the United States would be reduced in size, shrunk in aspiration, and, almost as much as in the past, disfigured by slavery.

Marrying an heiress, C. F. Adams had set an example to his children. Louisa married Charles Kuhn, a rich Philadelphian; John married Fanny Crowninshield, a rich Bostonian; and their lives since they married had reflected their ample means.

John stayed in Quincy, where he and Fanny were raising a family. He was becoming a gentleman-politician, popular and likable, but showed more interest in fishing than in winning elections.[34]

For a time, Loo and her husband tried living in New York. She had a baby, a girl, who unhappily did not survive. The Kuhns next tried a stay in Europe. In 1860, they returned to America. They had since spent their time mostly in Rhode Island at fashionable Newport.

Loo recently had been ill. Fashionable in medical treatments as well as places to live, she was treated by her doctors with mercury, a deathly poison. When recovered sufficiently to make the voyage, she came abroad with her husband and joined her relations in London.

Henry tried to judge her condition and thought her health had been radically undermined. He reported to Charles, "Loo has been ailing, and I am very much afraid she always will be ailing."

The situation Henry occupied had an aspect too disturbing to be talked about. As he knew to his sorrow, few politicians were leaders. The rest were followers. John Adams and John Quincy Adams unquestionably had been leaders. In the 1840s and 1850s, Charles Francis Adams had seemed a leader, but by temperament he was a follower. When a congressman, in Washington in May 1860, he had suddenly and inalterably become another of the myriad followers of Senator Seward. Henry had been in Europe when his father became subordinated to the bold New Yorker. He later watched his father and Seward in Washington. Since coming to London, he had studied and copied their many communications. The lesson of the experiences was always the same. In large matters, when Seward commanded, C. F. Adams would obey.[35]

Onlookers might be slow to sense it, but Henry was a leader. During the early summer of 1864, the other Union leaders who most concerned him were Seward in Washington and Evarts, again a prosperous lawyer in New York. On July 20, Henry wrote Evarts a letter in which, in effect, though not in so many words, he asked the lawyer to learn for a fact from Seward whether the Chief could leave the English mission, effective January 1, 1865. He told his relations that he was writing to Mr. Evarts and would send him and his daughter their good wishes. He however did not show them the letter. He could not. It was necessary that its existence be *his* responsibility.

The letter has not been published.[36] It will be given here complete—with Henry's spellings. Better than any letter of his so early in date, it shows him writing with little or no self-restraint. It can be taken as equivalent to a few minutes of his freest conversation. It touches trivial subjects. Yet also it concerns American matters of the first importance.

As was usual, Henry put the letter into the despatch bag for rapid conveyance to the State Department. The envelope bore the legend "Hon. William M. Evarts./ New York City./ N. Y." The department would place the letter in another envelope and forward it. If he was keeping to his usual habits, Evarts would be at his summer house near the Connecticut River in Windsor, Vermont. The letter would reach him there.

London. 20 July. 1864.
My dear Mr[.] Evarts:

You are, or should be, by this time, studying agriculture and practice at your Vermont bar, which may allow you time to meditate and read letters. I had intended to write sooner, rather in the hope of getting something from you in return, telling us what to think and expect, than with any idea of enriching you with another autograph. But I have postponed doing so from week to week, believing that each steamer would bring decisive news either of victory or defeat, until now the season is over and we are on the verge of a flight to the mountains, and there is no choice but to write or give up the idea.

Extreme restlessness is the order of our existence just now. We have never had a season nearly so quiet as this has been in a political point of view. American affairs have attracted little attention in London. There has been scarcely any correspondence with this Government, and at present there is no question under discussion. In a diplomatic point of view, our success here over the rebels has been complete and final, for I see no reason to suppose that the question of recognition or rebel armaments will be raised again, except in case of some conclusive military disaster. The only point that offers a chance of trouble seems to be in the case of the yacht Deerhound, and I confess I don't see how we can make an international grievance out of that.

Our affairs then seem to be in a very good way, so far as I can see, and likely to continue so. But we are becoming more and more restless as the year passes away, and all of us are now eager to be off. It seems to be in the interest of the administration to make such changes as it has to make, as early as possible. If we are beaten in the [military] campaign, I take it that the Democrats will come in, and perhaps it's best they should. But if we have success and Lincoln is re-elected, it seems to me best for everyone that his changes should be made before the first of January. The new Minister ought to be in London at least a month before Parliament meets, so that five months more ought to see us free. The truth is, I think I shall have to return home then at any rate, and probably should take my brother and sister with me, but it would be very much against my will to leave my father and mother here alone.

As to our successor, why not Mr[. Salmon P.] Chase? You know what objections there may be to him better than I do, but if he would take it he would do well here and make an extremely creditable representative.

Apart from the natural stupidity and formality of London, which, as you know, fatigues a person in two seasons, to say nothing of four, we have now the consciousness of feeling that any other person might have done just as well here as the present Minister, since there has been for months past nothing at all to be done. But besides this, it has always been doubtful to me whether it is good policy to keep a foreign

Minister long at one post. He needs continual contact with his own country to keep thoroughly up to it's [*sic*] time.

At the same time, though there seems to be no reason to suppose that there will be anything to do here, if the campaign goes well, I suppose you are prepared for having the rebels recognised if we are beaten again. In fact there are very general rumors about which credit Napoleon [III] with an intention to act soon. I don't believe there is any danger unless Grant fails, but it's not diplomacy that will save us in that case.

I don't know that I have anything very new to tell you of your friends here. Poor [Nassau] Senior died, as you know, and his friends lamented him with a good deal more sincere grief than is common in this world. In fact his decease was a matter of acute feeling, more especially in France, where Thiers and others were thrown into quite a panic by it, and sent over here more than one agent to implore Miss Senior to preserve her father's secrets in their proper seclusion. As Mme[. Jules] Mohl was one of these messengers, and told me of the negotiation, there is no doubt in the fact. Some people say that Miss S. is levying black-mail on her miserable victims, but I don't suppose this is true. As you have an interest in the matter, you may like to know about it.

Whether the famous journals are to be published or not, I cannot say. It is certain that Miss Senior was unwilling to promise not to publish them, and I rather fancy she intends to make some use of them, either in the form of extracts, or mixed with other matter as in the case of de Tocqueville. You may then hope to see yourself in the same box with Thiers, Guizot, and three-fourths of the other distinguished persons on the continent. When your part comes out I will send you a copy early.

I breakfasted with the Hollands one morning last week, taking my brother-in-law [Charles Kuhn] there to share the noble hospitality of the baronet. Since the famous occasion when I was asked to come and bring my breakfast, I had not been at 25 Lower Brook Street; but the style seemed in the interval to have suffered no change. These ancient parties will die but they will not grow older. Sir Henry and his lady are precisely what they were three years ago. So is Lord Wensleydale, who has to its full extent still that strange rage for this laborious nonsense which they call society, which drags him and his lady to every entertainment, dance, dinner or rout, which anyone will ask them to. I know a number of elderly people who seem to have this London fever, and I regard with horror the idea that I too might in time catch the infection, and learn to think it pleasure. You knew, I think, young George Howard, Lord W.'s grandson, and you have heard of his engagement to Miss Stanley, the younger sister of Lyulph who is in America. Lady Stanley, who is detested throughout London, has at once received all the credit of the match, and the Wensleydale's [*sic*] have seemed rather to countenance the idea that George might have done better. You know how ill-natured this city is, and how they always attribute in society the lowest motives and the meanest capacities to everyone from Queen to footman. Poor George Howard and his fiancée have shared the common fate, aggravated by the hatred everywhere felt for the mamma-in-law. I have occasionally ventured to hint that I believed Miss Stanley was pretty, amiable and the most accomplished and cultivated girl in London; but "poor George" has become a sort of proverb, beyond redemption.

I was at the Argyle's [sic] yesterday, on a visit with some of my family. We saw the Duchess who was as bland and placid as usual; since the first time I ever saw her, I have never seen her change a hair's-breadth, or develope the least symptom of expansion, except perhaps physically. Some people like this perpetual calm and reserved dignity. I believe Mr[.] Dana considers it a mark of society such as the Gods patronize, and values above almost any other experience his visit here. I am almost afraid to say that I believe it nine times out of ten to be merely the indication of mental sluggishness, and after watching the Sutherlands pretty carefully in different generations, I have not been able to get up any great amount of enthusiasm for any of them. The ducal coronet seems to be a precious heavy thing to carry. Where it does not utterly swamp people, it turns them into a sort of show-humanity, as Chatsworth and Blenheim are show houses.

We are meditating a change in our department below. Wilson has resigned his place. This is still a secret and I hope you will not mention it until it is announced from his own authority, as Mr[.] Seward's appointment would perhaps be embarrassed by publishing the vacancy. Moran has applied for it. I suppose most people would consider it a matter of course that I should push for a piece of the convenient patronage too, but I hope you know me well enough to give me more credit. It is curious that one hears much of nepotism as a discredit to the parent, but I do not recollect ever to have heard it cast as a reproach upon the nepos. To my mind the blame is at least as much due to the latter as to the former, and if the country stands in need of my services here, it will have first to remove my father. To be sure, I would not take the place even then; but that is beside the question.

I have written you a long letter; longer than I intended. I hope you may in return find time to tell me something about our affairs. By that time something *must* be visible. I am suffering infernal torments with a growing suspicion that we have failed. My family send their best regards both to you and Miss Ellen.

Very truly Yrs   *Henry B. Adams.*

August neared. Five Adamses and two Kuhns expected to travel in Wales. Henry perforce made the arrangements. Prior to the others' departure, Wilson left for America, hoping for a federal appointment wholly suited to his wants.

The Chief and Henry had already recommended promotion for Moran. The authorities in Washington complied. Soon in Wales a message was delivered to the Chief. From Seward, it offered Henry an interim appointment as assistant secretary, till March 1865.

Twice in 1861, without success, Seward had offered the

younger Adams the place of second secretary in London. From Rhyl on August 24, 1864, Henry wrote to the secretary about the newest offer. He thanked him but said he had to decline it "without delay." He explained that all he had seen in the past three years in England had "only strengthened my earlier belief that I should not be acting in the best interests either of the service or of the Minister, or of myself, in accepting any official position in the Legation."

The travelers returned to London. There Henry received an answer from Evarts, sent August 22. The lawyer strongly implied that he had not communicated with Seward. There however had been time for him to send Henry's letter to the secretary and get it back with suggestions. Evarts can be assumed to have followed that course. In a tone of decision and finality, speaking of the Chief and Henry as a unit, and almost as a single person, he said, ". . . there is no foundation for your hope that you will be allowed to come home. . . ."[37]

What Henry did with the reply is evident enough. He showed it to no one and said nothing about it. As he knew, the Chief was hoping that Seward would consent to his retirement. From every point of view, it was better that C. F. Adams should continue hoping, undisturbed.

This is not to say that Henry's appeal to Evarts and the Evarts-and-Seward reply were simple documents. They instead were forceful, yet subtle messages bearing on an unspoken matter. Grand in some respects, American government was petty and small in others. As was known to numberless people, Henry B. Adams included, no love was lost between Secretary Seward and Chairman Sumner. Thus, for Seward, keeping C. F. Adams *in* the English mission had the valued advantage of keeping Charles Sumner *out* of the English mission. If only to serve Seward that private purpose, the elder Adams would be tied to London as long as Seward could manage to tie him.

With the help of detailed maps and every available report, Henry had been studying what he believed was a great event of the time: Sherman's closing in on Atlanta. The Union general was resisted by Confederate generals seemingly as capable as himself. The opposed armies were engaged in a protracted struggle involving surprises and counter-surprises. Scrutinizing his maps and the latest newspapers, Henry mis-anticipated the outcome. Word came that Atlanta was captured, and he was "almost incredulous."

More than most people, Henry wished not to form mistaken

anticipations. His error troubled him. After more study, he wrote
to Charles, ". . . I shudder to think what a close thing it was, and
how nearly desperate that superb final march was, in the sense of
its being a last expedient." The deciding factor, it was evident, had
been sheer ability on the part of Sherman. As if individual ability
were something he had never given serious thought to, Henry
asked the captain, and also himself, "How could I reckon on the
mere personal genius of one man?"

Together, the Evarts-and-Seward reply and the capture of
Atlanta placed Henry in a situation he did not like and meant to
counteract. He however could not immediately attempt a corrective
effort. For the present, he was caught in a swirl of activities
involving several families and several houses.

The year before, on June 20, 1863, he had been a guest at a
dinner given by the parents of Charles Milnes Gaskell at their
London house on Stratford Place.[38] After meeting him, Mrs.
Gaskell actively favored Henry as *the* friend for her son Charles.[39]
The mother's campaign was assisted by the progress of her son's
studies. In the autumn of 1863, having finished his undergraduate
course at Cambridge, Carlo moved to London to study law at
Gray's Inn. The move permitted Henry and Carlo to see each other
more or less continuously.

The senior Gaskells owned two country houses. James Milnes
Gaskell had inherited Thornes House in Yorkshire, notable for its
excellent library. Had his political ambitions been strong, he might
have tried to enter Parliament as a Yorkshire member. Instead he
did something that was acceptable by English standards at the
time: he bought a permanent seat in the House of Commons as a
member from Wenlock, a rotten borough in Shropshire. In 1857,
partly to be near his constituents, and partly to accommodate his
wife, whose relatives lived in the area, he in addition bought a
remarkable property in the Shropshire village of Much Wenlock.[40]
The property was the site of a ruined Cluniac abbey. A single
structure survived intact: a fifteenth century house, once the residence of the abbot. Adjoining the house were some fragmentary
walls and arches, the slight remains of what had once been a
chapter house and a great church in the Gothic style.[41]

In September 1864, the Adamses had no choice but to rent
again away from London, for Mary was suffering attacks of "congestive asthma."[42] They sought a house in suburban Ealing. The
Chief had lived there as a boy, when J. Q. Adams was minister. The
house they rented in Ealing, Hanger Hill House, bore no resemblance to their previous houses out of town. They moved on

September 29, accompanied by the Kuhns. Moran was shortly asked to visit. He recorded that the house was on high ground and was surrounded by 1400 acres of park. "It is a very fine place and is perfectly secluded—indeed it is in an eddy between two great roads to London. . . ." Views of the surroundings were blocked by stands of trees. "Some of these are very massive and grand— particularly the Cedars of Lebanon."[43]

Henry moved to Ealing with the others but two days later went to Shropshire. He had been asked by the Gaskells to Wenlock Abbey. He arrived and stepped into heaven. The house and ruins affected him as no place ever had. He slept that night in a room whose walls were "stone, three feet thick, with barred, square Gothic windows and diamond panes; and at my head a small door opened upon a winding staircase, long since closed up at the bottom, and whose purpose is lost." Daws woke him early with their "infernal chattering around the ruins." He felt freed and entirely at ease. ". . . in the evening we sat in the dusk in the Abbot's own room of state, and there I held forth in grand after-dinner eloquence, all my social, religious and philosophical theories, even in the very holy-of-holies of what was once the heart of a religious community."

Carlo and Henry turned archaeologists, found tools, and started to dig. "We excavated tiles bearing coats of arms five hundred years old, and we laid bare the passages and floors that had been three centuries under ground." Sometimes walking, sometimes riding, they explored Wenlock Edge, a formation rich in fossils. Wandering the countryside, they seemed to enter and leave past epochs in jumbled sequence. ". . . we rambled over the Shropshire hills, looking in on farmers in their old kitchens, with flitches of bacon hanging from the roof, and seats in the chimney corners. . . . And we picknicked at the old Roman city of Uriconium, in the ruins of what was once the baths; and . . . [ate] partridge and drank Chateau Léoville, where once a great city flourished, of which not one line of record remains . . . ."

Henry went back to Hanger Hill House and his duties. Now there *were* two Legations: one in London, left to Secretary Moran, the other at Ealing, monopolized by the Chief and the pirate. The monopolists came as necessary to London, mainly to open the despatch bag, divide its contents between themselves and Moran, and prepare the return bag for conveyance to Washington. The monopolists, however, had almost nothing to do. The Chief seemed already retired. He evidently was waiting in seclusion for his term of office to end.[44]

Soon Henry would picture the Kuhns as "two sparrows kicking up an eternal little row around their busy selves."[45] He loved his elder sister and got on well with Charles Kuhn but was far from sharing their mode of life. Loo's marriage had possibly been an error, but for her no other marriage might have been better. Her principal tragedies were her sex and her talents. In a world agreed that women should be recessive, she was cursed with exceptional powers of mind and will. Knowing she could not be a politician, soldier, diplomat, explorer, or anything comparably dominant, she had chosen a negative career and become an idler. Persistence in idleness had made her changeable, tempestuous, vituperative, and bored. Her mental condition seemed harmful to her physical. Henry wrote to Charles, "I am more and more astonished that any frame is capable of enduring the tortures of so restless a spirit."

News was awaited concerning the election. Henry's alarm about the Republicans' prospects had been shared in America by the inmost counsels of the party. It had been realized that Lincoln simply could not win on a Republican ticket. In haste, the Republicans and some renegade Democrats had joined to form a National Union Party. Andrew Johnson, a Tennessee Democrat, agreed to serve as Lincoln's running mate. Promotion of the new party became the responsibility of Henry J. Raymond, currently speaker of the House and a vigorous organizer.[46]

At Ealing, word came at last that the improvised National Union Party had won by a slight margin and Lincoln was reelected. For Henry Adams, the victory was good and bad. He rejoiced that Lincoln and Seward would continue as president and secretary of state. He regretted that Seward would keep the Chief in the English mission.

Since that would be Seward's design, Henry planned to fight it. The means at his disposal were Mary's illness, their mother's wish to make a journey to Sorrento, and his own abilities as a deviser of travels. The means were slight, but he would use them. He would try a "last expedient." He would lead a "final march."[47]

Loo and her husband would soon be going to the Continent. Well before Christmas, the Adamses would leave Ealing and begin a visit at Mount Felix with the Sturgises. Henry's plan would take effect in early January. Mrs. Adams, Henry, Mary, and Brooks would cross the Channel and keep moving till settled comfortably by the Bay of Naples in a hotel at Sorrento.

The Chief would know about the march and would have three choices. If he preferred, he could arrange to travel with his wife, Henry, and the children. Equally he could arrange to follow them to Italy after they left. His third alternative would be to stay indefinitely at 5 Upper Portland Place, assisted by Moran. To choose either the first or second courses, he might have to resign as minister. If he chose the third, his choice would involve his remaining passively in office.

5

THE CHARGE OF A FAMILY

From Ealing on November 25, 1864, C. F. Adams wrote a private letter to Seward asking release from his mission. The plea fell afoul of impinging events. Lord Lyons absented himself from Washington, on sick leave to England. In Paris, Minister Dayton died. Either occurrence gave Seward ample pretext to ignore or evade the Chief's request.

Secretly by the same mail, Henry asked Charles to visit Seward and say that, whatever the administration might do or not do, Mrs. Adams, Henry, Mary, and Brooks were going to Italy and then to Massachusetts. Henry's plea likewise came to nothing. Charles had accepted a lieutenant colonelcy in a Massachusetts regiment of black cavalry. Earlier overtaken by malaria, he was at home on sick leave. He soon returned to Washington and made some effort to call on Seward, but he reported to Henry that he "did not succeed." Far from regretting his unsuccess, he ventured that the five Adamses in Ealing should "submit with a good grace to an indefinite further enjoyment of English life."[1]

The interim appointment as assistant secretary declined by Henry in August had been awarded to a likable young Pennsylvanian, red-haired Dennis Alward. The appointee arrived at 5 Upper Portland Place on November 27 and started work in the downstairs office.[2] His arrival could be viewed as Seward's reply-in-advance to the Chief's plea for release. Expressed in persons, not words, the reply was clear and firm. Its three official positions being filled, the Legation was wished to proceed with its work as usual.

Riding near Hanger Hill House, Mary fell from her horse and suffered a head wound which twice opened and was slow to heal. The Kuhns left for the Continent. The Adamses quitted Ealing, as planned, and began their visit at Walton-on-Thames. Henry described Mount Felix as an "oasis in the English desert." Always glad to be with Mrs. Sturgis, he said his friend was "a woman who has been kind to me . . . and shows an interest in what I am doing—who has put her house and her household at my service as much as if I were her son."

Electrifying news arrived by the steamers. Sherman had launched an unimaginable campaign. His 60,000 soldiers, burning Atlanta as they left, living off the land, and destroying as they moved, were marching towards Savannah, the rebels' best deepwater port. Because it showed that the Confederacy's defenses were near collapse, the march caused ever-mounting concern in Europe. On December 28, 1864, returning from the bank to Walton, Russell Sturgis brought word that Sherman's army had reached the sea. Henry wrote to Charles: "You may judge of our exultation. . . . The combinations of this war are getting so tremendous that there will be nothing left for us in a foreign war except to make the moon a basis, and to march our armies overland to conquer Europe."

The elder Adamses and Brooks resumed residence at 5 Upper Portland Place; Mary stayed at Mount Felix; and Henry shuttled between the two. Also, unexpectedly, he received—and accepted—an invitation to visit Thomas Baring at Norman Court.[3]

The Chief seemed eager to travel, yet feared his departure might be delayed. Seward was silent and had not replied. Henry, as silent as Seward, knew there would never be a reply. The fox in Washington would act by failing to act.

Mrs. Adams caught cold and took to bed. On February 1, 1865, a week or more late, a party of six boarded the 10:00 A.M. express to Paris. The party included an Italian courier, Giorge, engaged to help with arrangements. The Chief accompanied the travelers to Folkestone, where they would take the Channel steamer.[4] Thinking a reply from Seward would have to come, he meant to wait in London for its arrival.

On setting out, Henry ceased to shave, intending to grow a beard. The march he planned permitted his troops two nights in Paris. He fed them at the Palais Royal and the Trois Frères Provençaux and otherwise prepared them for easy, one-day advances to Dijon, Lyon, and Avignon, where they would pause. By good fortune in Paris, he encountered a Harvard acquaintance, Francis Barlow, who had risen to brigadier general and corps commander in the Army of the Potomac. Frank had lost a leg and an arm at Gettysburg.[5] Wonderfully recovered, he was traveling in Europe and would shortly go to London. Henry gave him letters of introduction in which he said that Barlow was "a very live Yankee."

Avignon surpassed anticipation. Its Roman and medieval buildings interested Henry extremely, and he wished his father might

see them. Later, from Nice, as if the advice were practicable, yet
knowing very well it was not, he would coolly write to the Chief:
". . . [Avignon is] beyond all comparison the most attractive specimen of antiquity I have seen in France. When you come through,
by all means break your journey . . . and see it."

As he traveled, Henry could reasonably have expected to rejoice. Among his numerous objects in life, few mattered more to
him than acquisition of languages. In 1858, when finishing his
course at Harvard, he had sketched a plan to live *three* years in
Europe, to gain fluency as a speaker of German, French, and
Italian.[6] He had pushed his father to the limit by asking and getting
two years. Once abroad, he achieved fluency in German and French,
improved his Latin and Greek, and, as if two years could serve as
three, went twice to Italy and attempted a start in spoken Italian.
Now, in 1865, he was on the point of gaining more weeks in Italy,
weeks belonging to the third year abroad that he had wanted in
1858 but had not felt free to request. All the same, he did not
rejoice. On the contrary, he experienced an intuition that he was
moving towards imminent death—death for himself.

Understandably, he wanted to pray. He as usual had brought
books. Assisted by an Italian-English dictionary, he was reading
Petrarch's sonnets in Italian. He noticed that the sonnet beginning
"*I 'vo piagendo i mei passati tempi*" came close to expressing his sense
of impending death and his impulse to pray.

During two days, the party advanced to Marseilles and Nice.
On the trains, Henry attempted so to translate Petrarch's sonnet as
to produce a sonnet in English which would be a passable poem
and also his prayer. He valued the result and later published it in
his pseudonymous novel *Esther*, together with a remark that it cost
its maker two days' labor on trains to Marseilles and Nice.[7] The
translation read:

> For my lost life lamenting now I go,
>> Which I have placed in loving mortal thing,
>> Soaring to no high flight, although the wing
> Had strength to rise and loftier sweep to show.
> Oh! Thou that seest my mean life and low!
>> Invisible! Immortal! Heaven's king!
>> To this weak, pathless spirit, succor bring,
> And on its earthly faults thy grace bestow!
> That I, who lived in tempest and in fear,
>> May die in port and peace; and if it be

That life was vain, at least let death be dear!
In these few days that yet remain to me,
And in death's terrors, may thy hand be near!
Thou knowest that I have no hope but thee!

The railroad went no further than Nice. To proceed, Henry could choose either of two conveyances. The party could speed to Naples by steamer, at the cost of seasickness for himself and probably for the others. It could plod by old-fashioned carriage or *vettura* along the famous road above the cliffs and slopes of the Riviera. He chose the road, a route he had not previously traveled.

Giorge found a driver with a suitable *vettura*. For twenty Napoleons, in glorious weather, the party rolled to Mentone, San Remo, and Genoa. Paying fourteen more, they proceeded to Spezia. Along the way, Henry reported to the Chief that the scenery through which they were passing was "equal to everything I ever have heard of it." He said the best days of their journey were "summer idealised."

A railroad permitted easy progress from Spezia to Pisa. There, on the board of the hotel, Henry spied the name of a young English baronet he had heard much of, Gaskell's cousin and closest friend, Sir Robert Cunliffe. Wanting to meet the baronet, Henry wrote a letter to Gaskell in care of Cunliffe and had it delivered by the hotel staff. Sir Robert paid the Adamses an immediate visit; he and Henry liked each other; and an unusual friendship sprang into being—unusual because it linked two Englishmen and an American.

By train to Livorno, steamer to Naples, and local vehicles around or across the bay, the party arrived at Sorrento. Their hotel was the Tasso, possibly the one at which Henry had stayed in 1860. There he wrote Charles a letter which dramatized the typical conduct of their mother. It represented her as saying at night before retiring:

"... I confess I do not understand at my time of life the pleasures of traveling. I have seen nothing yet on this journey that any one could call pleasure, and if it weren't for Mary's sake, I never would have left home. Mary's health was our single reason for taking this journey and I do think that Mary is the most perverse and obstinate girl I ever saw in my life. . . . She will sit with draughts blowing right on her, and there! she's sneezing! yes! she's caught cold! I told her she would in that carriage today."

"And you knew I wanted so much to get to Sorrento. . . . Oh Henry, how you do look with that beard! I really think it is wicked in you to go so, when you know how it pains me and disgusts me to have you seen so!"[8]

In the same letter, Henry asked God's forgiveness for ridiculing his mother. Yet he seemed not entirely respectful of his father. As if bringing the party to Sorrento had been wholly a task imposed on him by the Chief and in no way an outgrowth of his own secret planning and skillful management, he told Charles: ". . . I have performed my duty. I have brought the party safely here. And I wait new orders from London, whether to return or to stay. You know I am but a subordinate, and obey orders with military precision and silence."

A description Henry gave of himself at Sorrento was "sheepdog." On steep hills above the bay and the sea, ostensibly happy, he was walking with Mary and Brooks in the shade of citrus groves—"beneath thousands of oranges and lemons which look as poetic as the heart of man could ask." But, if happy, he was also unhappy. His sense of impending death had not lifted. What seemed to change was the likely victim. No longer in fear of *his* death, he instead was imagining the demise of his elder sister. He warned Charles that future dealings with the Kuhns would be cautious and infrequent. "Loo is near insane, and will kill herself ultimately, I think."

Mrs. Adams was suffering a journey almost opposite to the one she had anticipated. Her Henry was with her, but she had thought all the family would travel southward, see Sorrento, and be done with Italy in six weeks. As things stood, weeks and weeks were swiftly passing; her husband was detained in London; and what was to happen?

The sheepdog had an answer. By letter, he asked the Chief for new orders and simultaneously made a two-part suggestion. The first part could seem agreeable. ". . . you are quite free to dispose of me as you can make me most effective. I am contented enough, and am working hard on Italian. . . . My time therefore is not lost to myself." The second part was full of menace. ". . . if you really decide to stick to your post another year, I suppose the least expensive and troublesome way would be for me to settle the family somehow quietly on the continent, at Florence, or in Switzerland, until you could join them. I could probably manage to return to you in that case."

To help his meaning sink in, Henry let three weeks pass without writing the Chief another letter. But silence would not avail, any more than words or travels by a wife and three offspring. Really nothing Henry could do would alter the disposition of his father to sit in London, tacitly instructed by Seward not to move.

As an engine for tugging C. F. Adams from the English mission, the march to Sorrento had failed. The issues, however, were not simple; and changes had occurred concealedly at high speed. That the march would fail with respect to its original purpose had probably grown evident to Henry while he was still in England.[9] He none the less had energetically pushed the march; for the maneuver, while doomed for one purpose, offered cover and camouflage for a more important purpose.

Beginning with Wilson's resignation and Moran's promotion, a contest had been in progress between Secretary Seward and private citizen Henry Adams concerning the latter's future. To his credit, Seward cared about the United States government and intended to bring forward young men he thought capable of being national leaders. Rather obviously, in August 1864, he had wanted Henry to accept the short-term appointment as second secretary of legation in London so that in March 1865, at the start of Lincoln's hoped-for second term, he, Seward, could the more easily sack Moran and make Henry first secretary; hence possessor of a $2,500 salary and a commission lasting four years, till March 1869. A term as first secretary, needless to say, would provide a basis for rapid, future advancement.[10]

Seward's object had not been lost on the intended beneficiary, but Henry wished not to rise in the nation's service as anyone's protégé, and not to rise as an official. All along, he had acted strongly in his own defense. He had explained his position to Evarts—and thus to Seward; he had refused the short-term appointment as second secretary; and he had sent Seward a message via Charles that he would shortly be going home to Massachusetts. Now it was March 1865. Henry was not *second* secretary. He was not at the Legation. He had gone to irrelevant Italy. It was appointment time for the new Lincoln administration. Seward may still have had ideas that Henry B. Adams should be *first* secretary, displacing Moran, but also Seward knew for a virtual fact that Henry would refuse an offer and disdain it as nepotistic. On that account, the English mission would be re-manned as *Henry* wanted it re-manned. At a distance of 4,000 miles, without anyone's having to tell him, he knew the future. The Chief, Moran, and Alward would all be given new, four-year commissions.

He knew as well that the places in London were in reality four in number and were both official and unofficial. One place was reserved for him, and the place would have great advantages. He would remain a private citizen and thus would not be subordinate, still less beholden, to the secretary of state. As before, he would be a principal diplomat. His rank as other minister—without commission—was happily not impaired. Better yet, it had been kept from notice.

During his visit to Europe, Charles had learned that Henry had become an economist just by reading. Wishing to do the same, the elder brother had since written to Henry for assistance in getting books.

Henry was glad to comply. Before starting for Italy, he had sent Charles a volume on taxation by Hugh McCulloch, an official at the Treasury, earlier an Indiana banker. As for other works, he had said: "[John Stuart] Mill is best on Currency, and indeed on all other subjects, but large and expensive. You had best get him from Washington."

In Henry's view, a strong point of the first Lincoln administration was the president's "character," presumably meaning the whole range of Lincoln's better qualities. The administration had been strong too in having Seward to head the Cabinet and the State Department. It unfortunately had been abysmal in giving Cameron the War Department; and it had been misguided in trusting the Treasury to Salmon P. Chase. The Ohioan was a blunderer in public finance, and not an economist.

News reached Sorrento that the second Lincoln administration had been safely inaugurated. McCulloch supplanted Chase as head of the Treasury. Henry wrote to the Chief: "The President's character is now a greater source of strength . . . than ever. From M'Cullogh's [sic] beginning I infer that he at least has a policy, which is consoling. Meanwhile the rebels seem scarcely to preserve an appearance of hope."

Near Richmond, Lee's Army of Northern Virginia was fighting still, but faced three enemies. Grant's Army of the Potomac had thrust south of the city and around it, cut its communications, and drawn Lee's defenders away from the place they were expected to defend. Sherman's army, after taking Savannah at Christmas, had begun a march through Georgia and the Carolinas to Virginia. It would shortly close in on Lee's defenders from the southwest. A third Union army, commanded by General Sheridan, was bearing down from the northwest. Thus entrapment was complete and Confederate ruin a matter of days.

By letter from London, C. F. Adams rearranged the affairs of his wife and children. He directed that they return to England, but by stages, making leisurely stops.[11] News simultaneously reached Sorrento that Charles was engaged to Mary Ogden, a member of a well-to-do family prominent in New York and Newport. The engagement was cheering for Mrs. Adams and would have been cheering for Henry, were it not that Charles had been raised to command of his regiment with the rank of colonel, was racked by dysentery, jaundice, and malaria, was staying constantly with his unit, and was exposed to every risk of battle. His chances of survival had never seemed so poor.[12]

John Hay had never suffered lack of opportunity or lack of consideration. As payment for his work as the younger of Lincoln's private secretaries, he had been made a major in the army. But all was not well with him. He felt "restless in the White House." He had found that Lincoln, careworn and often prey to melancholy, was not good company in the evenings, as compared with ebullient Seward. He often visited the secretary of state at his rented house, a few steps distant from the executive mansion on Lafayette Square. Early in 1865, speaking with Seward, he "asked and obtained the promise of an appointment abroad." In March, Seward offered him the place of first secretary in Paris. He accepted on March 22, but Lincoln stipulated that he stay a month at the White House to train the man who would replace him.[13] Word that Major Hay would go to Paris was meanwhile carried abroad by news services and the Union press.

It should be noticed that Henry Adams, by averting his own appointment as first secretary in London, and by deflecting that appointment towards a capable incumbent, Moran, had left Seward only the first secretaryship in Paris as a tempting gift to offer a protégé. The gift sufficed, and Adams learned that none other than John Hay was started along a path that he might himself have walked but had successfully avoided. The path was official service in the State Department with the prospect of moving from one appointment to another, rising eventually to the Cabinet and conceivably to the White House.[14]

The problem most bothersome to Henry Adams was being wanted by others to be a person he was not. There was the case of his mother's wanting him to be a Brooks and naming him Henry Brooks Adams, when, as it happened, he was indefeasibly an Adams and eventually would name himself Henry Adams. Similarly, the Chief, John, and Charles were always wanting him to be third son. In words, he would oblige. Ending the letters he had been writing to the Chief since leaving England, he was using the phrase "Ever your son." Yet it is evident that, in his feelings, Henry was not a son—never had been; and it is all-important to know very precisely who and what he was.

The best statement appears to be one that says he had taken two identities. It has already been noticed that the Adamses could be imagined to need a new Henry Adams to match the old Henry Adams who came to America in the 1630s. The Adams born in 1838 *was* the needed person. Matching the first of the Adamses, the new Henry would be the last; that is, he would figure as the ablest and most accomplished.

With equal reason, *the Adamses could be thought to need a George.* Charles Francis Adams had two elder brothers, George Washington Adams and John Adams II. It was Henry's understanding that his Uncle George committed suicide—drowned himself in Long Island Sound in 1829. He learned too that his Uncle John, in 1834 in Washington, strangely declined and died without evident cause.[15] Sorrow at their deaths had become a central fact in the life of their mother, Louisa Catherine Adams. When a child, Henry had felt her sorrow, and its transmission from her to him had given him an added role and had put him in the way of assuming, in secret, a second new name as an added George. In his added role, the Adams born in 1838 became the protector and guardian of his grandmother's surviving son Charles Francis; also the protector and guardian of the surviving son's wife and younger children.[16]

At Sorrento in 1865, Henry could try to assume he was merely Henry B. Adams. He could want *not* to be the last of the Adamses. He could propose escaping from the arduous role of protector and guardian of his father, mother, Mary, and Brooks. But Henry's conduct was more than ever that of the new Henry Adams and that of a second George. What, after all, was a sheepdog? And how long had the grandson born in 1838 been working as a sheepdog? Had not the counterpart of Louisa Catherine Adams been a protector and guardian from the very outset?

Meeting him at Sorrento, a stranger would not have guessed that the sheepdog was twenty-seven. Admittedly, his health and fitness were in keeping with his years. Shortly, however, he would write to Gaskell that he was "prematurely grey and bald." He would add that his worn appearance was caused by "the charge of a family." He possibly meant, half as a joke, that he had been quickly aged by the new responsibility of leading a "small regiment" of relations here and there in France and Italy. But it was habitual with him to make statements that had double or multiple meanings. His deeper meaning in this instance was that the charge of a family had weighed on his shoulders from a very early time. The weight would not be lifted. The charge would continue being his as long as his bearing it might be necessary.[17]

On March 28, 1865, as directed, Henry moved Mrs. Adams, Mary, and Brooks from Sorrento to Salerno, Paestum, and Amalfi. He held them for a time in Naples. Finally he advanced them to Rome. There they would stay through April, occupying rooms at 95 Piazza Barberini. [18]

In 1860, a month's stay in Rome had taught Henry to associate the city with working sculptors. The sculptor he knew best in the city was William Wetmore Story, an American expatriate, originally a Bostonian. On seeing Story's work, he had thought him an important artist. He had been fascinated by a marble representation of Cleopatra newly unveiled in Story's studio. A seated figure, the statue showed the queen on the verge of suicide. Later displayed at the London Exhibition, it won its signer a world reputation.[19]

Story and his wife were rich and were settled permanently in the Palazzo Barberini. To speed his work, the artist hired skilled assistants. On April 13, 1865, without advance notice, Henry returned to Story's studio with two American acquaintances. The arrivals "interrupted the great sculptor in the act of giving a sitting to no less a person than General McClellan, who is now his guest."

The defeated Democratic candidate for president made a poor impression. Henry reported to Charles, ". . . a more common, carrotty, vulgar-looking hero than he of Antietam, I have not frequently seen." Yet the visit to the studio was rewarding. Two newly completed statues were on display. One represented Saul. The other evoked "Medea meditating the death of her children." Henry believed that the Medea was the "best thing" Story had done. "It is a standing figure . . . draped simply. . . . The left arm is folded across her, and on the left hand she is resting her right elbow, so that her right hand comes up to her chin. . . . But the face is something to remember in one's dreams."

Dwelling on the Medea, Henry mentioned to Charles that Story had given an attitude to the statue's head, body, and limbs that suited a person at "the instant of determination, or just before the completion of a decisive plan." He neglected to add that the stone Medea was holding a knife—presumably the weapon with which she would kill her children. He likewise chose not to mention that he had newly experienced an instant of determination and that he already was enacting what he meant as his decisive plan.

Though nowhere set forth in records, Henry's plan would be revealed very clearly in his conduct. His plan was his old one—to be a politician, a writer, a Washingtonian, and a traveler—but modified with an addition. The addition was an extreme devotedness to work. In the interest of work, he would not have children. There could be no question of his starting a family. To his joy and sorrow, he *had* a family. If he married, it would be for love and in the interest of work.[20]

He had formed his modified plan principally by reversing mistaken wishes. Where earlier he had wished to insure the Chief's departure from the English mission and return to America, he wished to keep his parents and Mary away from America in the safety of the English mission. Where before he had supposed he had to get back to America himself, he meant to stay a while in Europe. Where earlier his foresight had been muddied, he had cleared it, plotted his nearer future, and possibly his entire route to a cheerful grave.

For an unknown period, he had been an attentive reader of the *Revue des Deux Mondes*, a journal of ideas published quarterly in Paris.[21] It seemed to him that the journal's editors and contributors were setting high standards for themselves as political analysts and litterateurs. While profiting from the magazine's contents, he possibly had gained still more from its title. Casting away every thought of a small life clerking in a Boston office or cramming at the Harvard Law School, he was going on in a great life conducted for the present in *two worlds*. Eventually, when he had better resources, he would want all the earth as his province. For nearer purposes, his chosen space would be the easily accessible portions of North America and Europe. Within that limited region, he would travel as widely and often as he could. At a propitious moment, ideally the fall of 1868, concurrently with the next presidential election, he would settle in Washington. There, without taking office, he would act as a writer and politician. When not at home and not traveling, he would live by preference in one or another of the great cities of Europe. Since his momentary business was delivery of three Adamses to London after stops at Florence, perhaps Venice, and certainly Paris, his modified plan was already in full effect.

On April 16, 1865, the American Unionists in Rome learned of a report that Richmond had fallen. That evening, invited to the Storys to dinner, Henry turned the conversation to the report. General McClellan scouted it as false; but it was true; and it was followed by the great good news that Lee had surrendered, the surviving rebel soldiers were at the mercy of Grant, and the Confederacy had expired.

Seeing Story again directed Henry's thoughts back to art. Story's best works, reconsidered, affected him as puzzles. He ruminated to Charles: "How Storey [*sic*] can make such statues I cannot understand. He is not a great man. He is vain, flippant, and trifling, and what is worse he has a wife who is a snob! Tudieu, what a snob! And he is under her influence habitually."

News continued to come. In England, Cobden had died. In Washington, Seward was injured. Out for a drive in his carriage, the aging secretary had suddenly noticed that the reins had fallen to the ground. Thinking he might retrieve them, he leapt from the carriage but in so doing caught his heel on its edge. His crash to the ground dislocated a shoulder and broke his jaw.

On April 26 at midnight, a telegram from the Chief reached Henry at 95 Piazza Barberini. It said that Lincoln and Seward were felled by assassins. Lincoln was wounded mortally. Seward was dealt new injuries so severe that his survival was doubted. In the circumstances, the Chief was expecting a summons to the State Department.[22]

The cataclysm found Henry ready. Correctly he guessed that Seward would mend and return to work. Responding by letter, he advised the Chief, ". . . your remaining at London seems now necessary." The quiet tone of the message reflected the quietness of its sender. In the situation created by the assassins, the other minister to England was the minister more in charge.

A week later, on May 3, the absentee Adamses left Rome in a *vettura* by a route leading into the Apennines. Again Henry chose a path he had not traveled. He soon reported to Gaskell: "It was full summer, hot, green[,] and fascinating. . . . I dragged my party round by Terni and Perugia, and came down to Siena, before reaching Florence . . . ."

Letters from Charles waited in Florence. On March 13, the family's soldier had been made a brigadier general of volunteers by brevet; on April 3, the Confederate government had abandoned Richmond; and the day following, at the head of a column of blue-uniformed, veteran black troopers, Charles had ridden into its streets—one of the first Union soldiers, possibly *the* first, to enter the burning city.

For General or Colonel Adams (both were applicable), the march into Richmond was a "culmination." Had he been more

COSUMNES RIVER COLLEGE
LEARNING RESOURCE CENTER

than a mere skeleton of his usual self, he might have stayed in the army. Diseases required his devising a short-range plan. First he would leave the army and try to regain his health. If he recovered, he would marry. He and Minnie would take a wedding journey, for the most part to Italy. Meanwhile he divulged the plan to his relations in Europe.[23]

For Henry too, the news of his brother's entry into Richmond was a culmination. Answering from Florence on May 10, 1865, he urged Charles and Minnie to come abroad as soon as possible. ". . . in another year," he explained, "railways will run in every direction about Italy, and . . . the antidiluvian [sic] character of the place will be lost."

In the same reply, Henry made some remarks which Charles might assume were attempts at whimsy. The younger brother said, "I have already buried Mr[.] Lincoln under the ruins of the Capitol, along with Caesar. . . ." He claimed also to have amused himself in Rome by conducting "my private funeral service over the victims."

The lines were serious in meaning, if not in manner. Henry had said who—politically—he believed himself to be. His remarks echoed Shakespeare's *Julius Caesar* and drew obvious parallels. Ancient Rome had its equivalent in modern Washington. Murdered Caesar was matched by murdered Lincoln. Mark Antony lived afresh in Henry Adams. Antony and Henry were survivors. Both knew what to do.

Again adverting to Lincoln's murder, Henry told Charles that "this great change" seemed to him "a step downward to our generation."[24] In one sense, the comment was knowingly false. In America, as before, older persons were shaping the Union's public affairs. The most visible such person was the replacement president, Andrew Johnson.

Less visible was still-powerful Thurlow Weed, and news concerning Weed had come from London. Aware that Seward might die and that Johnson might have to name a new secretary of state, Weed had broken a silence of several years and written to C. F. Adams. The Chief, in turn, had mentioned Weed's letter when writing to Italy.

Following Weed's departure from London in May 1862, Henry had avoided writing him letters but had repeatedly sent him best wishes by way of letters to Fred Seward.[25] One reason for Henry's not writing to Weed was a discovery that may have dated from the first hours of the unofficial envoy's times in London. Though to all appearances he had liked C. F. Adams, the Albany magician had formed a qualified, even negative opinion of the Chief's abilities.

Watching them together, Henry had detected Weed's well-concealed disapprobation.[26]

Mindful of Weed's estimate, Henry confided to Charles, ". . . I cannot believe that he has any real taste for our advancement." But for Weed the problems of April and May 1865 were very difficult. A dearth of well-prepared politicians plagued the government. The dearth was so severe that, in Henry's words, there were "but two men with the proper knowledge for the State Department; Sumner and our Minister at London." Hence, if Seward died, Weed would have no choice. He would plump vigorously for an unwanted Minister Adams as the only viable means of fending decisively against a still-more-unwanted Senator Sumner.

Henry further told his brother Charles that their father was not a candidate for the place of secretary of state. ". . . the Minister does not mix in the fight." Far from being a statement of fact, the remark was a proof of disagreement within the family. On one side were the Chief and John. Both could be classed as *expectant* Adamses. Each was an expecter of office who, on getting office, would expect in time to get higher office.[27] The Chief did expect to be secretary of state. He would later expect to be president.[28]

On the other side was Henry, best classed as an *experimental* Adams. He had developed a political credo more ambitious than any held before in the family. He believed he could renew and increase the family's political ascendancy. The means would be the not-holding of public office. The means would permit his being a leader of persons American or foreign; male or female; older or younger, in or out of his family; in office, out of office, or never in office.[29]

Given favorable opportunities, Henry might try to convey elements of his heresy to Charles, Mary, and Brooks; but he knew he would impart none of it to the Chief or John. With that foreknowledge at heart, and speaking as if the Adams males would share a single fortune (although he knew they would not), he told Charles that the family's political horoscope was as black as clouded night. "I do not know where to discover . . . a single star whose influence would be favorable to us. Except Seward we have not one friend."

The underlying issue was hardly friends. It was the unmentionable division between leaders and led. For Henry, politics in the United States was a neverending game of cards played by—and with—living people. The rule of the game was that only a very few politicians could be players. The rest were cards. Applying the rule, he said to Charles, ". . . we stand merely as cards for other men to play."[30]

As his confiding itself made evident, Henry knew himself to be *not* a card. Among the living Adams, he alone was a player. He had advantages no other American his age could claim. Indeed he had advantages no other Americans at all could claim. Like Weed, he was acting on the premise: to be always in office, be never in office. Yet unlike Weed, who was always partnering with Seward, he expected to work alone. It made no difference that the Chief and he shared the English mission. He still was alone. Apart from remembered Louisa Catherine Adams, he had no counterparts. In or out of the family, his abilities were placing him by himself. He knew it and was also acting on a deep premise even better than Weed's. The premise was loser take all.[31]

Year by year, he was proving that his ideas were right and that he was going to win in American politics. He unquestionably had superior vision. Thanks to residence in Europe, he could see the United States from without as well as within. By dint of incessant study, he could see his country in three *times*. Always studying its history, he knew well what the United States had been in 1788 when General Washington was elected president. Always a devourer of newpapers and journals of opinion, he recognized the Union's condition for the jumble it suddenly was, now that ex-Democrat Johnson held the presidency intended for ex-Republican Lincoln. Always most concerned about the future, he foresaw what the United States might be if Americans did no better than indulge their more destructive tendencies. Yet, always hopeful, he was trying to imagine what the Union could be if he and others designed and effected an improvement.

Going on about his business, Henry tended to say things which other Adamses might think conceited, affected, or not worth trying to follow. He wrote to Charles from Florence: "I have become much more radical in my convictions than is usual in America, where you exist in amusing ignorance of the fact that you are rapidly being caught up with and will soon be left behind by Europe. Of course you may answer this by the usual platitudes about the great republic. It's true enough that you and I never shall see the day when America will stand second, but the fact remains that since 1788 we have with difficulty sustained our position, while Europe has made enormous strides forward."

The passage disclosed that Henry wished to lead the United States in a race with Europe.[32] It did not much disturb him that the Europeans might move forward in a way he would view as *pretend-*

edly democratic. But it greatly disturbed him that, in a race that he believed was far-advanced, his fellow Americans might ignorantly yield their leading position. He thus arrived at the question which stood at the center of his radical democratic experimentalism. What, he wondered, could Americans do to renovate their country? Or in his words, sent from Florence: ". . . when all the world stands on the American principle, where will be our old boasts unless we do something more[?]"

At a pace the Chief thought "rather procrastinating," Henry brought his party to Bologna, Venice, and Milan, through Switzerland, down the Rhine, and at last to Paris.[33] Edward Brooks, one of Mrs. Adams's brothers, was there with his wife. Mrs. Brooks was in the last throes of illness. She shortly died. Henry witnessed her death and joined in talks with his mother and uncle. All agreed that Brooks Adams should accompany Edward Brooks to Boston. Their ship would leave two weeks later from Liverpool.[34]

Because he and his wards were again in Paris and again detained, it might be supposed that Henry repeated an old experience and resorted to prostitutes. Available evidence suggests he did the opposite and abstained. During the three year interval from the spring of 1862 to the spring of 1865, he had called himself a "placid hermit" and said he was loath to marry.[35] Not a hermit, not always placid, and secretly disposed to marry for love, he was sexually a normal male. His amended plan, however, called for work, always work; and he in consequence had reformed. Regardless of risk, he was courting the torments of a second virginity. In Paris, one may be sure, he closed his eyes to *all* women, the good with the bad.

On June 25, he moved his flock to the Channel.[36] The return was anything but pleasant. "I cursed my fate," he wrote, "when I once more stood on the beach at Folkestone and saw the watery, grimy, despondent sky and coast of England."

The Chief had come to meet the Channel steamer.[37] Rejoined, five Adamses proceeded to 5 Upper Portland Place. Henry found that "an enormous mass of copying" had accumulated in the study, for him to do. "Luckily for me," he wrote, "I had no time to think, and had to go to work again so hard that my low spirits passed away in state papers."

While laboring in the study, he carefully observed his father. He reported to Charles: "I find the Chief rather harder, less a creature of our time, than ever. It pains me absolutely . . . to see him so separate from the human race. I crave for what is new. I hanker after a new idea, in hopes that it may solve some old difficulty. He cares nothing for it, and a new discovery in physics or chemistry, or a new development in geology never seems to touch any chord in him . . . . I am continually puzzled to know how we get along together."

Edward Brooks and Brooks Adams left for Liverpool on July 7. A balanced array of Adamses was left at the Legation. The Chief and Mrs. Adams were the elder pair, Henry and Mary the younger. To all appearances, they shared one idea, an urgent wish to return to America.

The immediate departure of Brooks was prompted by doubts that he could win admission to Harvard. His performance at school had been patchy.[38] He reached Quincy and hastened to Cambridge. As if such a thing were easy, he arranged to be primed for the Harvard entrance examinations by a man who could virtually guarantee his admission. The wonder-worker was an assistant professor of Latin and Greek at the College, Ephraim Whitman Gurney, known as Whitman.

Gurney had joined the Harvard faculty as a tutor in September 1857, when Henry was starting his senior year. The information would matter to Brooks; for he had become an adorer of Henry, talked about him incessantly, wished to imitate him, and would want to hear whatever Gurney could recall about the paragon's achievements when an undergraduate in the 1850s.[39] Admittedly, Brooks did not fully understand his heroic brother. Indeed he misjudged him in numerous particulars. Yet, in the gross, Brooks was right. Like Gaskell, he knew Henry's worth. Carrying news of it to America, he brought first sparks of Henry's fame.[40]

The Chief understood his renewed commission as minister to be a makeshift necessitated by Dayton's death, Lord Lyons's illness, Seward's redoubled wounds, and Lincoln's murder. As nearly as he could comprehend his own feelings, Minister Adams had no desire to remain in diplomacy. Several weeks earlier, on May 20, he had sent Earl Russell a note reciting the grievances of the United States against England and asking reparations; that is, he presented what were coming to be known as the "Alabama Claims." Because his note stood at the end of many notes concerning the grievances, he thought the topic "pretty much exhausted." Further efforts seemed best left to his successor.[41]

The elder Adamses and Mary may or may not have remembered that, in July 1864, Henry had written to William Evarts. In July 1865, they learned that he was writing a strongly-worded letter to Mr. Evarts asking for news concerning their release from the English mission.

Henry's old letter to Evarts had been mostly secret. The Chief, Mrs. Adams, Mary, and Brooks had known it was sent but did not read it. Also the old letter was straightforward. It asked Evarts a plain question with a view to provoking a plain answer.

Henry's new letter to Evarts was open, even more straightforward, and calculated to deceive its earliest recipients. It was read by the elder Adamses and Mary prior to being sent (either that or Henry told them fully what it said). It thoroughly deceived them. It might not similarly deceive Evarts or Seward (it did not need to); but it gave the Chief, Mrs. Adams, and Mary the very necessary wrong impression that Henry wished to go home to America, as they did.

Deception was needful, yet comparatively unimportant. The main purpose of the new letter was to decide the family's future. Past experience considered, Henry could assume that an appeal to Evarts would be passed to Seward. He could assume as well that Seward would welcome a fresh opportunity to answer through an intermediary without himself seeming to speak. Last, Henry could assume that the Evarts-and-Seward answer would definitively forbid the Chief's retirement.

The second letter to Evarts—till now unpublished—will be given here complete.[42] Better than any other of Henry's letters, it shows how prepared he was to deal with America's ranking politicians on a basis of equality. It even shows him asserting his emergent superiority.

London. 14 July. 1865.
My dear Mr Evarts:

I am going to make another attempt to get some information from you, though my last effort a year ago was rather a failure. As you know, true American news is rare in London, and yet we need it here and in fact are rather out of temper, at being always in the dark. You can't imagine what a chaos America offers to our eyes at this distance. New questions, new parties, and new men at every turn; the President [Andrew Johnson] hobnobbing with rebels from Charleston; Dana and Sumner performing a pas gymnastique in the opposite direction, each telling the other he's utterly wrongheaded; old friends separating, and no one knowing to all appearance where under the sun he is, what he wants, or how he is to act. Sumner writes, I hear, that he and his friends will make a struggle for negro suffrage, and expects to carry it by a close contest. I suppose Massachusetts follows him. But what do you say to it, and what does Mr[.] Seward say to it, and how is Mr[.] Seward, whose troubles are enough to break the heart of a stone? If it weren't for them I think we might give him some trouble here by coming home in spite of him, like Burlingame [the U. S. minister to China] who is now in Paris. Six months ago I took all our family off to Italy in the full conviction that my father's successor was appointed, and would be out here in time to allow my father to join us in Italy. Why didn't he come? If the mission could be offered to one man, why not to another? If this sort of practical joking is to go on indefinitely, it is well to know it beforehand, because we want to enjoy it as well as the rest of the world. There is no use in talking now any more stuff about the necessity of our remaining here on state grounds, for there are no such state grounds. The truth is we are kept here for somebody's convenience, and I, individually, am curious to know who that somebody is. I don't think Mr[.] Seward would do it if he could help it, but why can't he help it?

If you can really tell me anything worth knowing on these matters, you may do some real good. As I've intimated before[,] we are not in the best of humors.

On returning to England after a five month's absence, we found a change. Respect is the order of the day. "What are you going to do with Mr[. Jefferson] Davis?" is now the only American question asked. Curiously enough our own friends, Bright, Forster, Lyulph Stanley &c. are maddest on this point. In fact one of the few reasons I know for sparing Davis, is that the liberals in Europe think it would damage them to have him executed. They are really very nervous about it, and press us very hard to change our minds. Can you tell me anything to console them?

Speaking of them, we are now in the very middle of the general election, which is a species of legally appointed riot. On the whole, parties will stand about as they were, and we expect a new Parliament not unlike the old one. The only change is, as a Tory said to me last night, that the radicals have put in a new set of men, too strong to be kept quiet. Bright and Forster come in uncontested; Goschen at the head of the poll; while John Stuart Mill beats the most bitter and factious opposition at Westminster; Tom Hughes and our friend M'Cullagh Torrens are chosen by tremendous popular demonstrations at Lambeth and Finsbury; Fawcett, the blind Professor we met at Cambridge, gets his seat at last at Brighton; all radicals, and all men who must be listened to. Bright has announced his reform policy in a superb hustings speech at Birmingham. It has made the Tories very bitter. I have always looked myself to the end of our war as the time for Europe to begin another forward movement. How long it will take, no one can guess, but now I believe that the struggle will begin in earnest.

Amberley is beaten at Leeds, to the great regret and mortification of his family and of the Stanleys, but of no one else that I can hear of. Lyulph Stanley dined here last night, to meet the Hales. He has been very active in J. S. Mill's election and exults largely about the result, but seemed to think poor Amberley had suffered a pretty serious disaster to his future prospects. Lord Russell however, and Lord Palmerston, are as imperturbable as ever, and the latter is not going to retire at all. I shouldn't wonder if Reform split his Cabinet, after all, before he retires.

We enjoyed Italy very much, and find London as attractive as you can imagine after such a journey. Lord Wensleydale is still well, but troubled about Alabama claims. Pray write me, if you have leisure, and tell me good news of our release.

Very truly Yrs
H. B. Adams.

6

MY REIGN

At the Legation on July 29, 1865, Secretary Moran was told by the Chief that in his absence the despatches were to be opened by Henry. Moran recorded on the 31st: "Henry B. Adams yesterday opened the Despatches. The insult rankled deep but I have said nothing about it. Probably no Minister ever so insulted a Secretary of Legation."[1]

In August, Henry led his parents and Mary on a tour of Ireland. On their return, Mary caught a bad cold. The Chief wrote: "Her situation here does not satisfy me any more than Henry's. Both of them properly ought to be in America. As indeed I ought to be myself."[2]

With Mary's health as a justification, Henry visited lively, amusing Brighton and found a house facing the Channel to which the family could retire for the autumn, beginning in late October.[3] Evarts meanwhile went to Washington, elicited a response from Seward, and wrote to Henry: "The difficulty about your father's being allowed to come home is that he is the best man for his place, both originally and by his service in it." Better yet, Evarts described the Chief's future service in terms of *years*. ". . . there are always some places where there must be strength as there is stress. The English mission has been for four years such a place & will be for some years longer."[4]

Shown the reply, the elder Adamses and Mary would be dismayed. Yet the Chief was predisposed to yield. While alone the previous spring, he had realized that he was one of the "few grounds of confidence" that the Union had established in England during the war. He had said so by letter to Henry in May. He had said too that resigning as minister was a "responsibility" he could not assume; also that a postponement of his retirement till early 1866 was "inevitable."[5] Thus the undecided question was the *term* of the postponement. With the arrival of Evarts's reply, the term was set at "some years." From Henry's point of view, this vague but large expression was very welcome and satisfactory.

Because they were staying in the English mission, the Chief and Henry were mindful of an American wonder, Cyrus Field's attempts to lay an Atlantic cable. The first attempt had failed but a second was in progress. If it succeeded, the cable would change the mission, greatly diminishing both its freedom and its importance.[6]

The two Adamses meanwhile were burdened with the Alabama Claims. With British aid, the Confederate government had launched attacks by nine cruisers, the *Alabama, Florida, Chickamauga, Georgia, Nashville, Retribution, Shenandoah, Sumter,* and *Tallahassee,* against the Union's merchant ships and whaling fleets. In response, the United States government had made claims against England relating to all nine but centering in the Ministry's failure to prevent the escape of the *Alabama* from Liverpool in July 1862.[7]

As much as anyone, Henry had shared in assembling the evidence and framing the arguments at work in the Union grievance. On January 9, 1863, he had written to Assistant Secretary Fred Seward: "I have set my heart on our gaining this case, as a matter of international law. I certainly trust your father won't abandon it, and I shall do all I can to urge my father to keep it well before the public here. . . . Of course there is no chance for the damages now; but a steady and firm pressure will do more with England than a thousand shocks."[8]

Writing in this vein, Henry had seemed interested principally in the improvement of international law. Yet he also was interested in pretexts the United States might have for starting a war with England and giving the English a vengeful thrashing. On March 20, 1863, again to Fred Seward, he had offered the suggestion: "If we were in better days[,] we might go to war with England. . . . Luckily we shall have the war cards to play at any time. The Alabama has furnished casus belli enough for twenty years to come."[9]

Speaking in this different vein, Henry could seem eager for war and only waiting for the best time to attack. But from an early stage he had noted a complication. The English had *not* broken their own laws. The reason had been that the oddities of English law were extremely odd. In this third vein, on June 25, 1863, he had written to Charles: "There is no law in England which forbids hostile enterprises against friendly nations. . . . Any number of Alabama's [*sic*] may now be built, equipped, manned and despatched from British ports, openly for belligerent purposes, and provided they take their guns on board after they leave the harbor, and not while in dock, they are pursuing a legitimate errand."[10]

To complicate matters further, Henry had favored peace on warlike grounds. He had argued that the Union could ruin England completely by remaining at peace and contriving to prosper in industry and commerce. In this fourth vein, on July 23, 1863, he had told Charles: "As for war, it would be folly in us to go to war with this country. We have the means of destroying her without hurting ourselves."[11]

Such had been four of Henry's outbursts in 1863. They showed that he was capable of volunteering highly energized assertions. Yet the assertions were secondary and misleading. All were fragmentary offshoots of a pattern of ideas the leading parts of which he would usually *not* express. The pattern, seen as a whole, favored permanent peace and friendship between the United States and England, to benefit both countries and to benefit mankind. That had been his position when most severely tested, in the *Trent* affair. Nothing since then had shown him to have modified his position, and he never would.[12]

Early in 1865, when the Rebellion was near its end, Seward had sent instructions to C. F. Adams which, if followed, would have lent an exceedingly aggressive tone to the latter's dealings with Earl Russell.[13] Shortly thereafter, the adventurous secretary of state was silenced by wounds. Somewhat independently, in his note of May 20, 1865, the Chief had reviewed for Russell's consideration the whole matter of the Alabama Claims. Russell weighed the note for three months and replied in a negative fashion. Persistingly, the Chief sent the foreign secretary a second communication asserting the claims.[14]

In September, Henry wrote "two pugnacious epistles"—as he later called them—to Charles. Both unfortunately are missing. By then, Henry had studied the correspondence between the Chief and Russell. The pugnacity of the "epistles" perhaps reflected the correspondence.

On October 10, to Henry's astonishment, or professed astonishment, the Adams-Russell correspondence was published in the *London Gazette*—a most unusual occurrence. Conveniently, five days later, Lord Palmerston died. Henry celebrated by assuring Charles: ". . . [the prime minister] had one really active antipathy, and that antipathy was America. He would have worked with her, or flattered or conciliated her, if necessary, for he was as callous as a rhinocerous. . . . But he would have much preferred to do her a harm, and he did what he could for that purpose. We not only

survived his attempts, but we have survived him, though he lived
long enough to see us resume our offensive, and throw England
on her back."

New tones were audible in Henry's lines. He seemed to think
the Legation was an autonomous, powerful agency, capable of
shaping world events. He boasted expansively to Charles: "We hold
at this moment the whole foreign policy of England in our hands.
. . . We wield a prodigious influence on European politics. . . . Lord
Russell is no match for us. . . . A new Ministry must inevitably
devote itself to internal affairs and face serious questions at home.
Our attitude therefore will become more than ever embarrassing
to them. . . ."

Large words within the family were a fresh instance of Henry's
acting to decide the family's future. Such words would help fix the
elder Adamses contentedly in Europe. Also they would mask an
effort by Henry to *reduce* the diplomatic initiatives of the Legation,
so that the Chief would effectually retire while in office, yet appear
not to do so. In addition, large words would camouflage a shift of
emphasis at the Legation from the diplomatic to the social.[15]
Finally, they would serve a new, most-hidden, special object.

Henry intended to create a myth. He meant to establish his
father before the eyes of present and future generations as a great
American, not inferior to the Adams presidents. This did not seem
a hopeless task. Current experience spoke strongly in its favor.
Many people in Europe and later many in America *read* part or all
of the Adams-Russell correspondence newly published in the *London
Gazette*. The result was dramatic. The stock of C. F. Adams rose
as the stocks of J. Q. Adams and John Adams had never risen when
they were ministers to England in earlier epochs. The Chief was
hailed as a diplomatic nonpareil. As if by legerdemain, a basis was
laid for Henry's intended myth.[16]

As planned, the elder Adamses, Henry, and Mary moved to
Brighton. Attention shifted to a private matter. Major Higginson
had mended and married; Colonel Adams was doing the same;
and the subject of a wife for Henry Adams was one he could no
longer hope to dodge.

In a final letter to Charles prior to his and Minnie's sailing for
Europe, Henry said there would be no wife. He gave a reason.
"Only a great passion could finish me now, and though I can
imagine a great passion, I do not think I could ever feel it." In the
next breath, contradictorily, he pictured the wife he imagined
would be best for him. "When I marry, too, I want a woman who

will take care of me, and keep me out of mischief, a good, masculine female, to make me work, and be blind to Burgundy and French cooking."

Charles and Minnie arrived at Liverpool on December 2. There to help, Henry led them to Chester, where he had reserved rooms at a Tudor inn. Face to face, Minnie was a pleasant surprise. Charles had married a New York woman, not rich, but self-confident and attractive.[17]

Henry went with the newlyweds to Brighton. At Christmas, several Adamses attended an especially festive party at Mount Felix. Henry missed it. Invited to Thornes House in Yorkshire, he spent the holidays with the Gaskells.

Privately, Henry was busy. Beginning on an unknown date, he had been collecting evidence—old books, pamphlets, financial reports, and the like—relating to the strain imposed on England's economy during the twenty years of the Napoleonic Wars, from 1795 to 1815. The strain that interested him had been much heavier than that imposed on the economy of the United States during the four years of the Rebellion, from 1861 to 1865. In the course of their trial, the English had suspended specie payments; that is, they interrupted the free exchange of English bank notes for English gold coins in the same amount. They later resumed such exchanges. What Henry was doing in late 1865 and the first days of 1866 was studying the evidence and perhaps collecting added items.[18]

On February 8, 1866, he accompanied Charles and Minnie as far as Paris. It appears that this visit to Paris was his first chance to renew his acquaintance with John Hay. Many meetings would be needed before he and Hay could be close friends. Though agreeable and easy to meet, Hay was reserved and hard to know. It would later be said that Adams was "the only person, outside of his intimate family, whom John Hay was ever able easily to call by his first name."[19]

In London on February 27, in uniform, Henry again was presented by the Chief to Queen Victoria at Buckingham Palace. Moran was to go. He stayed away, on account of a sore throat, feigned or real.[20]

The Adamses just then were moving from 5 Upper Portland Place to a smaller house at 54 Portland Place which had no room that could be used as a downstairs office. Moran and Alward were shunted to a separate building at 147 Great Portland Place. The new arrangement was one that C. F. Adams might have liked in

1861, if he had had it. There were no strangers downstairs. In appearance, he and Henry *were* the mission.[21]

The banishment of the secretaries to another street very sharply curtailed their chances to observe the doings of the Chief and Henry. It possibly was caused in part by suspicion that Moran was keeping a journal. The secretary was doing just that, and his pages sometimes showed hurt, disappointment, and fury. On seeing the quarters to which he and Alward had been shunted, he said he had been reduced to toiling within sight of Bolsoner Street—"until lately one of the most notorious brothel resorts in London."[22]

About ten weeks later, a Bostonian, Dr. Robert Hooper, appeared in London accompanied by the younger of his unmarried daughters. Word that the Hoopers were in town reached the Adamses, who were preparing to give a large dinner party on Derby Day, May 16. Henry sent them an invitation and received their acceptance. In his engagement book, he found room at the bottom of a page to list the thirtieth and thirty-first guests: "D^r. & Miss Hooper."[23]

It should be said at once that Miss Hooper and Henry Adams would later marry. The story of their marriage is an open secret, easy to read; but the story of their relations from the day she went to the Legation dinner in 1866 to the eve of their engagement in 1872 was later suppressed. Except for the words "Miss Hooper," quoted above, all the records needed to tell the story of their meetings were destroyed, presumably by Adams when a widower. This need not mean that Adams saw their courtship as discreditable, hence best concealed. It may simply mean that he wished to protect their privacy against potential intruders, of course including imaginable biographers.[24]

Miss Hooper had two names. Legally she was Marian Hooper. In everyday practice, she was Clover Hooper. Born in Boston on September 13, 1843, she was five years and seven months younger than Henry Adams. When she arrived in London, she was twenty-two.

Marian and Henry may have glimpsed each other previously in Boston. Every winter in the 1840s and 1850s, she had lived with her father at 44 Summer Street, south of the Common. There possibly were encounters; for Henry had lived with his parents at 57 Mount Vernon Street, north of the Common, about six blocks distant.

When they met in London, they already knew each other by

reputation. It was part of the business of the Adamses to know about the Hoopers and part of the business of the Hoopers to know about the Adamses. Both were leading Massachusetts families. By Boston standards, the Adamses were rich and the Hoopers very rich. The Adamses were famous, but things had happened which made the Hoopers objects of curiosity. To force comparison, the Hoopers were newly *political.*

Samuel and Robert Hooper, brothers raised in Marblehead, were heirs of a fortune made in seafaring and banking. They married sisters: Anne and Ellen Sturgis. Anne and Ellen inherited fortunes from their father, William Sturgis, of Barnstable on Cape Cod, who profited greatly in the China trade and became one of Boston's merchant princes.

Samuel Hooper, sometimes called "wicked Sam," was presently a member of Congress.[25] Robert Hooper had trained in Paris to be a physician but with some exceptions never practiced. Ellen, his wife, died of tuberculosis in 1848. Their children were a new Ellen, Edward, and Marian—or Clover. In place of a career, Dr. Hooper brought up the children. His course seemed harmless but was too extreme. In demeanor a calm, obliging person, the doctor concealed a streak of fierce impulsiveness and undeflectable will. To his mind, it was not enough to give the children their due. He gave them his life.[26]

At twenty-two, Marian was prepossessing. Her advantages began with vitality. Small, she had an enviable figure, shapely limbs, tapering fingers, and very small feet.[27] Her greatest charms were of mind and spirit. In keeping with her two names, she had two quite different and discernibly separate natures. On the one hand, she was unchangeably innocent and exceedingly kind. On the other, she was seriously political, intelligently domestic, and very funny.[28] Fittingly, her two natures had interested two Americans of promise, Oliver Wendell Holmes, Jr., and Henry James, Jr. Holmes—possibly—somewhat loved her. He currently was in London and was accepting invitations from the Adamses.

Counting Mary, seven unmarried young women attended the Derby Day gathering at the Legation. Miss Hooper perhaps was the best educated. Yet on two scores she was disadvantaged. Except for visiting Washington to see the victory parade of the Union armies, she had not traveled. Worse, she disliked her face. Not ill-looking, indeed striking, she had dark hair and light eyes. She however lacked what were called "good features." Sometimes, if moved, she would cover her face with her hands.[29] The gesture presumably was native with her. Yet it could lead a witness to surmise that she had read and taken too much to heart a story by Hawthorne, "The Minister's Black Veil," in which a Massachusetts minister named Hooper permanently and without explanation covered his face with black cloth, whereupon his protesting fiancée, at last divining the motive behind his dark metamorphosis, sympathetically covered *her* face for a moment, not with cloth, but with her hands.

Meeting in 1866, Henry Adams and Marian Hooper could feel pressed towards one another by chance associations. His father had left a seat in the House of Representatives to be minister to England. Her uncle had been named to a vacant seat in the same body. Her brother Edward had been sent to Port Royal. So had his brother Charles. She was friendly with Henry's friend George Sohier, and her best friend was Ida Agassiz, now Mrs. Henry Higginson.[30] Finally, her deceased mother was a second cousin of the Adamses' benefactor Russell Sturgis.

Records would vanish, but the Hoopers had long memories. A century later, repeating what they called "a tradition in the family," two of Edward Hooper's daughters would certify that at the Legation on May 16, 1866, Dr. Hooper mentioned to Minister Adams that his daughter Ellen, then living with her brother Edward in Cambridge, wished to learn Greek but could not find a tutor. Helpfully C. F. Adams replied that his son Brooks had found a tutor in Cambridge, Professor Gurney, who could be recommended unreservedly.

Dr. Hooper soon forwarded Gurney's name to Ellen. She enrolled as another of Gurney's private pupils and, while taking lessons, became acquainted with Brooks Adams. Clover, on returning from Europe, also met Brooks repeatedly. A few glances were enough to tell Brooks that Clover was the woman his brother Henry ought to marry. Never a person to conceal an idea once he had it, Brooks began to say so.[31]

A notable achievement of the U. S. government since its inauguration in 1789 had been the minting of a superb coinage. Before the Rebellion, a holder could exchange U. S. bank notes for U. S. gold coins in the same amount. As the phrase went, the dollar was "sound money." The Chief believed in sound money. It has been mentioned that in 1861, when Lincoln was choosing his Cabinet, Seward and Weed suggested him as the man to head the Treasury. Denied the Treasury but given the English mission, C. F. Adams had became a distant, unhappy watcher of Salmon P. Chase as overseer of the Union's finances.

The Union government could have financed its suppression of the Confederacy by a variety of means. In December 1861, the U. S. Treasury started issuing floods of "legal tender"—inconvertible paper "greenbacks." Not long after, the Treasury suspended specie payments. As compared with gold, the greenbacks lost much of their purchasing power. Hence, in 1865, when Secretary McCulloch announced that the Treasury meant eventually to buy up the inconvertible paper money and resume specie payments, C. F. Adams's enthusiasm knew no bounds.

Henry believed in sound money but thought it had limitations as well as advantages.[32] Also, for him, sound money, though important, was subsidiary to other concerns. Without question, his most pressing public concern was the *future* of United States. A public concern that would not let him rest was the *history* of the United States. The two were connected. It is helpful to turn first to the history.

The *era* in American history that most interested Henry was that of the first presidents, from General Washington through J. Q. Adams. The *event* in the American past that he most cared about was the forming of the American nation. He especially noticed that the nation was formed when—and conceivably because—Americans were in conflict with other nations, principally Great Britain. To his way of thinking, the history of England and the history of the United States were intertwined.

To repeat, Henry had been collecting data relating to past British financial woes during the Napoleonic wars at the start of the century. This was not a simple action. One of its purposes concerned his future *History of the United States*. Collecting old British data, he by the same act was collecting data he might need when writing a great history that would recount, and if possible explain, the forming of the American nation.[33]

His action also had near-term purposes. For some time, he had been trying to complete an article, "British Finance in 1816," for publication in the United States. He presumably wished the article to appear in 1866, the fiftieth anniversary of the date in its title. By limiting the article to the financial woes of a foreign country in a past era, he in pretence was keeping his promise not to publish on political subjects while he and the Chief remained at the Legation. The pretence was thin. The article in fact was political, even topical. It presupposed that past financial woes in Great Britain deserved the attention of modern Americans for whatever instruction past British woes might offer with regard to America's present and pending federal programs.

In July 1866, he had his sights on two magazines: the *Edinburgh Review*, published in London, and the *North American Review*, published in Boston. Both were old quarterlies. Though very limited in circulation, they were unrivaled in influence. Henry Reeve, the editor of the *Edinburgh Review*, had translated de Tocqueville's *Democracy in America*. He bore himself as a friend of the Great Republic and was one of the Legation's English contacts.[34] Had he been so inclined, Henry Adams could have approached editor Reeve about becoming a contributor. As it happened, Adams had no wish to make an early debut in Reeve's magazine. What he wanted was free access to the *North American Review*.

Unfortunately for him, his efforts to finish "British Finance in 1816" were succeeding only slowly. One reason was the topic. Past financial woes could not easily be transmuted into readable paragraphs. The main reason was ambition. His article was not merely an article. A politician as much as a writer, he meant to re-direct readers' minds and thus originate events. To have this effect, his utterances would have to be masterful. So he was writing the article over and over.

While rewriting, he revised his tactics. He decided *not* to offer the editor of the *North American Review* an article titled "British Finance in 1816." It might be *accepted*—thus spoiling a chance for large gains.

In pursuit of the largest gains possible, he reverted to his never-published article on Smith. After letting it sleep in London, he had sent it to Palfrey in Boston. It then had passed into storage in care of John at Quincy. Four years of sleep and storage had transformed it from an article to a key, with power to open a massive door.

He wrote to John asking for the article. He wrote also to Palfrey. Pretending he needed counsel, he explained: "My mind has run back to my old friend Smith of Virginia, whose reputation needs smashing. I have sent to John for the M.S. which I propose to re-examine and perhaps re-write. . . . But what do you think a proper form of print? The thing is too long for a review [meaning a quarterly magazine]. I've a mind to print it separately and call it a Monograph."

John sent the manuscript. Palfrey wrote to say that Charles Deane had privately printed an annotated edition of Smith's first book about America, *A True Relation of Virginia*, published in 1608. Also Palfrey announced that Deane was coming to London.

Deane arrived and gave Henry a copy of the annotated reprint.[35] Henry studied its notes and concluded that Deane had "left nothing for me to do." There was everything to do. The matter Deane and Adams had investigated, whether Smith lied in 1623 when he asserted in his *Generall Historie of Virginia, New-England, and the Summer Isles* that he had been rescued by Pocahontas, posed a problem of evidence and logic which even the most tireless, perspicacious historians could have been forgiven for avoiding. The problem could not be solved in short order. Deane and Adams doubtless were momentarily pleased with their first solutions; but year after year the problem would lead them towards improved, simpler, more convincing solutions.[36]

On second thought, in 1866, Henry realized he could not afford to be stopped by Deane. Writing again to Palfrey, he said he could "do nothing in the way of original speculation or statement," yet proposed to recast his article as a seeming response to Deane's important discoveries. By computing the word-length of articles in issues of the *North American* handy in London, he had found that his manuscript, if pruned, would be appropriate in length for the Boston magazine. Thus armed, he told Palfrey: "I am absolutely ignorant who edits. . . . If, however, you know any of those wonderful beings who read M.S.S. and can get him to promise me room for any particular number of his honored but heavy publication, I will be sure to be ready. The thing would want about thirty five pages of the North American."

As wished, Palfrey wrote to Charles Eliot Norton, editor of the *North American*, asking whether space could be reserved for an article about Captain John Smith by a son of C. F. Adams, residing in London. Replying on August 2, Norton warned that he could not "accept any paper absolutely before reading it," yet said he would be "much pleased" to read the manuscript. He only stipulated that the package be mailed to him directly.[37] In turn, Palfrey forwarded Norton's reply to Henry. To all appearances, Palfrey's role in the affair had ended.

Judged by popularity and sales, the leading historian in the United States was George Bancroft. Born in Boston in 1800, but likely to be found in other places, he was both a politician and a historian. Long a prominent Democrat, he had served in the 1840s as secretary of the navy and minister to England. Presently residing in New York in winter and Newport in summer, he was still politically active. Secretly, in 1865, he had written President Johnson's Annual Message.[38] His great work as a historian was a many-volumed, slowly-appearing *History of the United States*. It could be thought mistitled. An account of Europe's colonial settlements on the Atlantic seaboard, it was moving chronologically *towards* the formation of the United States but had not arrived.[39]

Born in Boston in 1838, and a would-be author of a history of the United States, Henry Adams could not avoid considering the problem of his relation with Bancroft. While reworking his article on Smith, he grew curious about Bancroft's response to Smith's story of rescue by Pocahontas. He looked into the first volume of Bancroft's *History* both as originally issued and in corrected editions. He saw that the historian accepted Smith's story as true and retold it in heightened, romantic language. He saw too that Bancroft reported having read the story in Smith's *True Relation of Virginia*, where it was not to be found, rather than in Smith's *Generall Historie*, where—and where only—it appeared. The departure from fact was extraordinary.

Extraordinary also was Adams's knowledge of doorways to acquaintance. In the course of revising "Captain John Smith," he inserted a passage convicting Bancroft of credulity, rhapsody, and illusion. He told Palfrey about the insertion, saying it would "point a sharp moral, and adorn Mr[.] Bancroft's tale." The moral Adams wished to point was that historians ought not to be donkeys. One purpose of the moral was to *improve* Henry's chance of good relations with Bancroft. Henry's manners were surpassingly excellent. He even knew how to sting but not hurt—as a start towards intended friendship.[40]

In September 1866, Palfrey received a package. Sent from London by Henry Adams, it contained a letter and a portfolio. The letter asked Palfrey to open the portfolio and read one thing it contained. Opened, it contained three items: an unsealed letter from Adams to Norton and two articles. One was the article on Smith that Norton had said should be mailed directly to him. The other was titled "British Finance in 1816." Without preliminaries, it hurled the reader into an account of old British financial agonies, their causes and cures. It began: "Lord Liverpool's administration, at the close of the great French war, contained perhaps not a single member endowed with less originating power than Mr. Vansittart, the Chancellor of the Exchequer."

Adams's conduct was somewhat excused by the letter to Palfrey, *outside* the portfolio. Henry said, "I hope you will not entirely renounce my acquaintance when you find that instead of one article for Norton, I herewith send him two." He asked a favor. "I would be greatly obliged by your reading the second Essay, (I care little about the Smith) and if you really conclude that its publication would on the whole not do me credit, I beg that you will at once suppress it (as well as my letter to Mr[.] Norton which I leave open for you to read). . . ."

There were other surprises. In the letter to Norton, *inside* the portfolio, Adams apologized for sending two articles but mentioned a third! He said he could write an article answering approximately to the title "The Suspension of Specie Payments in England from 1797 to 1818." He further declared that he would neither write nor send the third article unless one of the two already supplied was accepted and published in the editor's magazine.

Sifting the evidence put before them, Palfrey and Norton would conclude that the *North American* had been offered, not an article, but a contributor, except that Adams was a contributor who at the start had wanted an article accepted in advance of being read and now seemed to ask that further articles of his be accepted before being written.

To cap the climax, the contributor was welcome. Palfrey and Norton liked the two articles already supplied. Norton slotted "Captain John Smith" for the January 1867 issue and "British Finance in 1816" for the April issue to follow. The contributor's not-yet-written third article was accepted also. Victorious Adams could write it fully confident that it would be published when received, in the form he gave it.[41]

Palfrey and Norton had learned a mere fraction of Adams's strategy. He did not mention the *Edinburgh Review*. He did not say he wished to publish at his convenience both in the leading quarterly in America and in the foremost English-language magazine in the world. He did not explain that he hoped to serve the *North American Review* as editor for politics and the *Edinburgh Review* as editor for articles relating to America. He gave no sign that he would live in Washington.[42]

Colonel Adams wished to try a second time to succeed as a lawyer in Boston. En route from Italy to Massachusetts, he and Minnie paused in London. There he was told that articles by Henry would be appearing in the *North American Review*. Once in America, Charles lingered in Newport. He too wished to write for the Boston quarterly. He planned an article titled "Railroads." His knowledge of railroads was slight, but the projected article would be less informative than philosophical, somewhat in the manner of Emerson's essays.[43]

Incorrectly, Charles understood that Henry had sent *three* articles to Norton, including one on England's suspension of specie payments in the period 1797–1819. The matter had attractions for Charles, and he proposed to write an article about it. Needing advice concerning the subject's difficulties, he twice wrote to Henry for assistance.

At the moment, the diplomatic Adamses were making a tour of Germany, as far as Potsdam. From Berlin on November 10, 1866, Henry sent advice concerning the difficulties but added: ". . . you are treading on my toes. You are mistaken in supposing that the North American has an article of mine on the return to specie payments. I am going to go to work on that article immediately on my return to London. . . ."

About the time this answer reached him, Charles submitted "Railroads" to Norton. The editor accepted it, but someone told Charles disturbing news.[44] Issues of the *North American Review* began with long articles, sometimes signed, and ended with book notices, never signed but sometimes initialed. In the January 1867 issue when published, an unsigned article by Henry, "Captain John Smith," would be Article I. In the April 1867 issue, Henry's unsigned "British Finance in 1816," Article II, would much precede Article V, "Railroads," signed "C. F. Adams, Jr."

Success in soldiering had made Charles imperious. Though at a loss for a career, he knew he wanted to advertise himself and be important very soon. He would *not* say that the rights of an elder brother were about to be flouted in Norton's magazine; but, wanting Henry to advertise himself and be important too, he *would* make an issue of Henry's insistence on publishing anonymously. He accordingly wrote two letters to Henry assailing him for cowardice and for changing his course in life. In the first letter, he dwelt also on his own predicament. His revived hope of being a lawyer was already dashed. Desperate, he ended the letter with "thoughts of suicide."[45]

On returning to London, Henry found two letters from Charles. He read and destroyed them. On December 21, 1866, he replied with a letter as valuable as any he would ever write. In earnest, he described himself. The description ran to three words: "unique," "positive," and "complete." He denied having changed his course. "I have never varied my course at all. From my birth to this moment it has been straight as an arrow." "As for the suicide, I quite agree with you, having long ago made up my mind that when life becomes a burden to me I shall end it, and I have even decided the process."

Henry noted that Goethe, a "great practical genius," had offered a principle: " 'There must always be a sequence in life.' "

For Charles, sequence had vanished. In Henry's words, the elder brother would have to "recommence . . . operations from a wholly new point."

The suggestion was apt, except that operations had already started. In Newport, perhaps helped by sending violent letters, Charles independently had found the "point" from which to "recommence." His career would relate to railroads.[46]

The worst rub, Charles had said, was Henry's insistence that his writings be published without his name. Henry replied by insisting on the insistence. In terms Charles might find obscure, he disclosed the logic of anonymity. ". . . by the time this reaches you . . . I shall be out in the North American. . . . I would rather my name were wholly unmentioned. . . . The estimate the world has of a man, filters ultimately through the masses better in darkness than in the heat of the sun."

James T. Fields, publisher of the *North American Review*, knew that the lead article in the January 1867 issue was written by Henry Adams. Fields read it the moment the issue appeared. Accidentally encountering Charles Deane, he recommended it to him as "most gracefully done." Deane read the article and wrote to Henry, "Your notice of Bancroft is most excellent, nothing could be better."[47]

By dint of his own and the Legation's social efforts, Henry had formed a near-friendship with an expert on the period in which Smith lived, the Irish historian James Anthony Froude. When copies of the January *North American* reached London, Henry sent one to Froude, asking an opinion. On February 1, Froude answered that there could be "no doubt at all of the legitimacy of your conclusions." Froude said too that Smith's fabrication seemed very nearly unconscious. "You have succeeded admirably in tracing the way in which Smith's story grew & how he lied almost without knowing that he was lying."[48]

Through an arrangement with Trubner and Company in England, the *North American* enjoyed some circulation abroad. A copy of the January issue fell into the hands of the editors of London's *Pall Mall Gazette*. They read "Captain John Smith" and thought it defamatory. Word came their way that the author was Henry Adams, a son of the American minister to England; also that the article was his first published work. To the editors' way of thinking, it would have been bad enough if Adams had simply undercut Smith, whom they considered "as much an English as an American hero." But he had joined the lamentably numerous persons who were writing history in a new, merely truth-seeking spirit, as if life were never romantic and heroes never existed. The editors accordingly published a two-column outcry against the new spirit in history. Ruefully they announced: "Mr. Henry Adams, a son of the American Minister in England, has fleshed his maiden sword in no less a personage than Captain John Smith, the founder of the colony of Virginia, and we regret to say that he has done so with considerable effect."[49]

American political parties commonly experienced division. The Republicans had long been divided between those who claimed to be "strong Republicans" and those they criticized as "ultra men." In recent years, the ultra men had basked as "radicals" and scorned the strong Republicans as mere "conservatives."

Following the murder of Lincoln and the re-injury of Seward (both were classed as conservatives), two radicals in Congress, Charles Sumner in the Senate and Thaddeus Stevens in the House, seized the reins of government. Lurid quarrels broke out between the radical Republicans in Congress and ex-Democrat Andrew Johnson in the White House. Dangerous to all involved, the quarrels had the effect of dislodging un-radical Republicans from office. Governor John Andrew of Massachusetts, a conservative, visited Washington, witnessed the quarrels, and abandoned politics. Congressman Henry J. Raymond, likewise a conservative, attempted to lead a new National Unionist movement. He and other would-be Unionists held a convention in Philadelphia in August 1866. Realizing that by attending the convention he had destroyed his standing as an officeholder in Washington, he refused to seek reelection to Congress and went back to full-time labor as editor-owner of the *New York Times*.[50]

John Quincy Adams II had served in the Massachusetts legislature and on Governor Andrew's staff. He attended the National Union convention. Finding himself at the edge of a political chasm, he leapt sidewards and became a Democrat! Politically, the leap was fatal. In the nation at large, the Democrats were disgraced. The authors of the Confederacy had been Democrats, and the party could always be blamed for the Rebellion, with all its costs. The addition of an Adams would not improve the party's national prospects. Neither would it mend the party's fortunes in Massachusetts. Were John's new political fellows to nominate him for elective office, they would do so to flaunt his name. He would lose. A few voters would perhaps support him as a new face. More would oppose him as a mere political ornament.[51]

For five years, John had overseen Henry's investments. Late in

1866, when Charles was hoping afresh to succeed as a lawyer, Henry had shifted control of his investments from John back to Charles. Thus, in February 1867, while not fully a lawyer, Charles again had a client. Moreover, he had a workable idea. It seemed to him that Massachusetts was in need of a railroad commission. He was lobbying at the State House to push through the requisite legislation. If he succeeded, he could expect to be named as one of the commission's initial members.[52]

As an investor, Henry was an active gain-seeker but not a gambler. He was disposed to seek profits either as a bull or a bear. At the moment, he was poised to make a killing by mail on the Boston Stock Exchange. He thought the quarrels in Washington had so intensified that Senator Sumner and Congressman Stevens would have to attempt the removal of Johnson from the presidency on false charges, no true ones being at hand; and he foresaw that the attempt would cause a sharp drop in the value of securities, followed by a recovery.

Charles was a gambler who assumed that the way to make money was to borrow heavily and invest in volatile stocks.[53] In mid-February 1867, he received a perplexing letter from his client. Henry said: "The President will be impeached. You must see that the radicals have no other course; to stop is ruin to them, if to go on is ruin to the country. They will go on, and our credit will go down as they go on." The client ordered the sale of his American bonds. ". . . I see troubled waters ahead, and hope to fish in them. . . . Hell is about to break loose."

Thinking his client's order a mistake, Charles would not carry it out. In new letters, Henry was obliged to say, ". . . I see nothing to change my opinion that the President must be impeached. . . ." At the Capitol, the radicals were enacting whatever bills they pleased. Henry did not like the bills. ". . . I hope not only that you have sold all my U. S. securities, but that you have not invested. . . ." He said, ". . . the high-water mark of radicalism is at impeachment . . ." "I think that the month of March or April ought to settle the question, and I look for a struggle for gold combined with a panic and struggle for credit, a crash in prices, a crash in banks, a Congressional attempt to expand the currency, and a howl of agony from the whole country. . . ."

Many Republicans, Charles among them, shared a fear that the Southern Democrats might regain ascendancy in the federal government. Henry did not share the fear. ". . . I care not a damn whether the South rules us or not. In the worst of times they never ruled us so badly as Congress rules us now."

Stranger yet, Henry seemed indifferent to parties and even to government. Quoting Shakespeare, he called Seward an "old mole." "The world is out of joint, and Hamlet was a damned fool for trying to set it right instead of trying to make money on it."

Charles sold a few of his client's securities and wrote that the events the client foresaw would not occur. Henry modified his ideas but would not give them up. He seemed to think himself an accurate prophet. As if *his* experience was predictive of the general public's experience, he wrote on April 3, "Depend upon it that what affects me so violently will affect the average man at last."

Dropping everything else, Henry Adams and Carlo Gaskell undertook a "military and strategic excursion" to the French-German border. Till then a Germanophile, Henry learned things during the excursion that tilted him the other way. From London, he wrote to Charles, "I come back inclining to France." ". . . I detest the German rot about nationality. . . . Luckily both nations are now so equal in strength that they hesitate before fighting. . . . But sooner or later they *will* fight, and it is just as well to remember that fact."

Payment reached Henry for "Captain John Smith." The check gave him $80 in depreciated American greenbacks. Considering that the article had cost him large amounts of labor, his prospective income from writing articles was ruinous. Yet the amount paid was perfectly usual.

Minor events, or seeming minor events, unfolded one after another. Norton's April 1867 issue arrived, containing "British Finance in 1816" and "Railroads." Henry learned that a weekly magazine, *The Nation*, had been started in New York. He asked Charles to get him a subscription. "There seems to be merit about it."

Without orders, Charles had invested $1,700 of his client's money in securities issued by the Boston, Hartford & Erie railroad. Told of the purchase, Henry agreed that the case was "exceptional" and the sum "not large." ". . . I readily approve the investment." Yet explicitly he *disapproved*. ". . . I consider the money . . . a stake on a roulette table. It is a pure gambling operation. I have carefully read the statements you sent to me. . . . But there is one fact which to me seems the most important, and which I have not got at. Who manages the undertaking?"

By reading newspapers, Henry had been tracking manipulations on the New York Stock Exchange. The securities manipulated were those of the Erie Railroad Company, managed by Daniel

Drew. Their prices had risen. Likewise the securities Charles bought with the $1700 might rise. Time would tell.

The more serious problem was Charles's innocence. In his letter, Henry did not advise his brother in so many words that Drew, while openly managing the Erie, might in secret be managing the Boston, Hartford & Erie also; but he did warn that the latter corporation was "sure to become the 'Erie' of the Boston Stock Exchange."

If Charles had only done as asked, Henry would have made his killing. The client had meant to sell, bank the cash, wait till prices dropped, buy near the bottom, and profit on a subsequent rise. The opportunity was real and unusual. While Charles defied the orders to sell, some of Henry's unsold securities lost 23% of their value. Drawing attention to the fact, the client told Charles a few weeks later, ". . . there has been this spring a more severe and a more general fall in prices and destruction of credit than has happened since 1861. . . ."

While growing up in Boston, Henry had been a close neighbor of a girl his age, beautiful Alice Mason, daughter of an impecunious artist.[54] In 1857, Alice married her Sturgis cousin, William Sturgis Hooper (known as Sturgis), son of Samuel and Anne Hooper. During the war, in 1863, on army duty in Louisiana, Sturgis died. Widowed Alice, left sole parent of their daughter Bel, inherited her husband's money and became a favorite companion of his Hooper cousins, Ellen, Edward, and Clover.[55]

Samuel Hooper had meanwhile become a congressman. When in Washington, he and Anne lived in a commodious house at 1501 H Street, just east of Lafayette Square. They invited Alice and Bel to stay with them through Washington's 1865–1866 social season. It soon was noised about that the country's most powerful politician, Senator Sumner, although more than thirty years her senior, was showering attentions on Alice in what could only be a hopeful spirit.

The following August in Massachusetts, widowed Alice and Senator Sumner became engaged.[56] The disclosure of the match was a national event. Sumner unintentionally added to the sensation. He sent news of his engagement to Mrs. Charles Francis Adams in London without thinking to name the person he expected to marry.[57]

The wedding was held in Boston on October 17, 1866. The newlyweds went to Newport for a honeymoon. With Bel, they proceeded to Washington and moved into a furnished house they had rented on I Street. It happened that two of Henry Adams's relations were owner-residents at a nearby house at I Street and Sixteenth Street. The elder was his Aunt Smith, a sister of Louisa Catherine Adams. The younger was his Aunt Mary, known as "Mrs. John," the widow of his father's brother John. Mrs. John and Henry were always on good terms. It seems next to certain that they corresponded, but the letters have not been found.[58]

The Sumners disliked their rented house and wished to move. It meant straining his means to the breaking point, but the senator bought for $30,000 a house then being built at the corner of Vermont Avenue and Fifteenth Street. One reason for the purchase was location. While not on Lafayette Square, the house diagonally looked into it and glowered, so to speak, at the White House and President Johnson. Also the house was only a few steps distant from the Samuel Hooper house in which the Sumners' romantic attachment had had its origin.

By mid-February 1867, it became known to the well-informed in Washington that Alice and the senator were quarreling about her arriving alone and staying alone at dances and parties, and that flagrantly she was enjoying the company of a diplomat her age, Baron Friedrich von Holstein, the Prussian secretary of legation.[59] (The baron had previously been stationed in London and had visited the Adamses at 5 Upper Portland Place.[60])

On April 16, 1867, the Prussian government sent a cable to Washington recalling Holstein to Berlin. He decamped as instructed. In June, ostensibly still man and wife, the Sumners traveled together to Boston. In secret on arriving, Alice slept separately by her own choice.[61]

Midway in the same interval, on May 8 in London, Henry Adams wrote a letter in which he mentioned two of his father's former political allies: Senator Sumner, owner of a not-yet-lived-in house looking into Lafayette Square, and Richard Henry Dana, famous as the author of *Two Years before the Mast*. Adams said of Dana, "His fear of Democracy is very like an English Bishop's hatred of dissent." The noteworthy part of the letter was Adams's capitalizing the "d" in "Democracy." The word, so written, may have recorded cryptically that Adams had chosen *Democracy* as the title of his novel; moreover that he was developing the novel's plot. At all events, when drafted, his novel would have at its center a young widow's involvement with a powerful senator.

The economist Adams had met in London in 1862, David A. Wells, of western Massachusetts, had received a four-year appointment at the Treasury as Special Commissioner of the Revenue. His duties required his personally examining the revenue systems and industrial conditions of Great Britain and other countries in Europe. In 1867, he returned to London, especially hoping to confer with John Bright. Normally such a hope could take him to 54 Portland Place and thence to a meeting with Bright arranged by Henry Adams. Something of the kind occurred. On June 26, Bright wrote to his wife, "Mr. Wells the American has been with me for a couple of hours this morning talking taxes & tariffs & finance—he is very intelligent on these questions. . . ." Four days later, Wells dined with all the Adamses at their house.[62]

Grapevines being what they were, Wells may have learned while still in Washington that the anonymous financial article in the April *North American*, "British Finance in 1816," was Henry's work. But the commissioner would not know that his return to London was simultaneous with Henry's completion of another financial article—now titled "The Bank of England Restriction. 1797–1820."

Henry's articles showed improvement. "Captain John Smith" could be described as a discussion, loosely organized. "British Finance in 1816" was a discussion too, but tightly organized, terse, lucid, in places hilarious, and filled to its margins with energy and vitality. "The Bank of England Restriction," as described by Henry, was "unexpectedly difficult." It took the form of an organized *narrative*— a short "history."[63] Creating the history was no easy feat and consumed six months.

Public financiers wrote, not articles, but reports. Independently, Henry had completed a detailed, highly-readable report on the English currency. The report was in two parts. The first was a discussion, already published. The second was a narrative, still in manuscript. The parts embraced seventy years of British financial experience, from 1797 to 1867, but mainly fixed on the interval when the Bank of England suspended specie payments.

There could be no question about the usefulness of the report to the U. S. Treasury, and there was no possibility that the Treasury's chiefs would fail to read it. In the past, Secretary McCulloch had attempted to explain England's financial vicissitudes in the Napoleonic era, had developed a theory, and had published it. The narrative part of Adams's report took up McCulloch's theory and showed, or tried to show, that it did *not* explain the vicissitudes.

In view of Adams's report, also in view of his later dealings with the special commissioner, certain conjectures about Wells and Henry Adams assuredly are true. In June 1867 in London, they arranged to speak by themselves. Adams affirmed his authorship of "British Finance in 1816" and lent Wells the manuscript of "The Bank of England Restriction," asking an opinion. Wells read it. Pleased immeasurably by what it said, he accepted Adams on the spot as an ally in politics and a partner in public finance. In this way, the association with the heads of the Treasury which Henry had wished to initiate later in Washington was started at once in London. The gain was a year and a half.

Henry's success was so complete that he went to unusual lengths to conceal it. He wrote to Palfrey on June 28 that "The Bank of England Restriction" was "very long, very dull, and worse written than either of its predecessors." Rather than send the manuscript to Norton, he sent it to Charles, preceded by assurances that it was "dull." ". . . you might run your eye over it, and when you come to the law of Lord Stanhope's Gold Bill, see if I've made any mistakes. The study has taught me a great deal, but my article is ghastly to be sure." If willing, Charles was to pass the manuscript to Norton.

Taking no chances, Henry wrote to Norton on June 28, saying the third article had been sent in care of Charles. He asked again that his name not appear. Admitting that the new article was overlong, he said the fault could not be mended. ". . . I have crowded books into sentences and years into lines. How to compress further, with any regard to the unity of the argument and story, I confess I do not know."

Henry said in the same letter that his contributions had ended! "This will in all probability be the last time I shall trouble you with my manuscripts." A needful ruse, the announcement was his first step towards later re-attachment to the magazine. He would eventually return, or so he believed, as both contributor and editor for politics, living in Washington.[64]

The *North American Review* was kept in existence only through hard labor by unpaid editors. Norton for the present was dividing the labor with James Russell Lowell. As a Harvard teacher, in 1857 or 1858, Lowell had helped Henry Adams by urging him to go to Europe. In 1867, aware that events had come half-circle, a more experienced Henry Adams found himself dreaming that, if his old teacher could magically come to London, he would introduce him to the English.

The dream was ill-timed. At long last, the diplomatic Adamses were starting their withdrawal from the English mission. Yet Henry could not resist telling Norton: "Nothing would have given me greater pleasure than to have danced attendance on Mr[.] Lowell through every drawing-room in London, and smoked indefinite cigars with him in all the out-of-the-way holes where men of genius stuff themselves. But I'm afraid that it's now too late; my reign here draws to a close."

Charles found nothing amiss in "The Bank of England Restriction," and the article passed to Norton. It would be published, unsigned, in the October 1867 issue, and Norton would regret its author's abrupt disappearance.

"Captain John Smith" had shown that Henry was a shrewd analyst of historical evidence, all but impossible to deceive. "British Finance in 1816" established that he was also a proficient economist, at home in public finance. "The Bank of England Restriction" was more impressive. With sustained force and clarity, its narrative conveyed the simple message that the English had suffered cruelly in an earlier age because of financial incompetence on the part of their government. Valuable for what it said, the narrative was valuable too for what it indicated about its author. It was Adams's first outright success as the writer of a historical narrative fairly large in scale, and it showed him to have the makings of a great historian, a counterpart of Gibbon or Thucydides.

The best judges of "The Bank of England Restriction" would be readers not privy to its authorship. Such readers would encounter the article in an American magazine. They would infer from the text that the writer was male, but they would scarcely think him American. The article told an English story and told it in felt, even passionate terms. The teller's knowledge of English history and affairs, financial, industrial, legal, political, and diplomatic, was thorough and secure. Thus he certainly was English. Yet, for all his passion, the teller was impartial, clear-headed, and balanced. He thus might seem un-English. Informed that the author was an American not yet thirty, capable readers might repel the information. They might insist that the narrative could only have come from the pen of a cosmopolite, English by birth and long in Parliament, but frequently absent from England and familiar with everything. The article demanded some such origin. For eighty-five paragraphs, it transcended nationality without a waver.

7

THE ASCENT OF OLYMPUS

Adams had found an added friend in Gaskell's brother-in-law, Francis Palgrave. Very knowledgeable in the arts, Frank liked to teach. Henry obliged by becoming a pupil. In March 1867, "instigated" by Frank, he attended an art sale at Colnaghi's and bought an ink-and-wash drawing by Aelbert Cuyp, "A View of Rhenen," for £12.0, a price his mentor thought "dirt cheap." Frank did the bidding. Henry explained to Carlo, ". . . drawings are my mortal point and I can't resist."[1]

In truth, Adams's mortal point was not drawings. His mortal points were houses, statues, and his own books. Most mortal was the house he wished to occupy, or even own, on Lafayette Square in Washington. His means considered, he had no prospect in 1867 of renting or owning his wished-for house. None the less, he commenced its ownership while in London. The logic of his behavior was comic, yet also serious. A house in London often *was* its pictures.[2] It followed that a picture could be the beginning of a house. Thus, while far from owning his Washington house complete, he had bought part of it in the form of his bargain Cuyp. On the same principle, he bought pictures from other suppliers, notably an English sculptor and dealer, Thomas Woolner.

In early July 1867, while considering some works readied for auction at Sotheby's, Palgrave noticed an unsigned drawing purportedly by Raphael. He wanted Adams to own it. Knowing he would not be free to attend the sale himself, he sent his pupil instructions. "Verify the fact that the red chalk Raphael is in that lot & then tell the auctioneer to buy it for you. . . . If you bid, attention will be roused . . . . The more I think of it the more I incline to think it either genuine, or a firstrate [*sic*] piece of work of the time."

Prices at London auctions were sometimes amazingly low. Adams attended the sale, made sure the "Raphael" was in lot 146, but, possibly out of shyness, said nothing to the auctioneer. He compounded the omission by going to lunch. On returning, he learned that lot 146 was sold. When all was lost, he rallied, found the buyer of the lot, and said he had missed the opportunity to bid for it. Removing one drawing only, the buyer sold him the others, the "Raphael" among them, for the lot's auction price: 12 shillings.[3]

Adams was continually on the lookout for writers with whom he could feel he had affinities. In 1867, he bought and read a newly-published, first correct edition of Blake's *Songs of Innocence and Experience*.[4] Also in 1867, he became so taken with Rousseau's *La Nouvelle Héloïse* that he was quoting it aloud in French.[5] As much as any other writers, even Shakespeare and Milton, Blake and Rousseau would continue to appeal to him and influence his thinking.

In a friendly spirit, Adams and Gaskell began to vie as writers. Gaskell had a gift for sophisticated parody. While Henry was laboring to finish "The Bank of England Restriction," Carlo confected "The Easter Trip of Two Ochlophobists," a spoof of travel books. The spoof was dated May 14, 1867. Written in a mixture of English and French, it recounted in the first person the travels of a fictitious overeducated Englishman, Henry Stuart, not unlike Gaskell. To escape crowded London, Stuart wanders to Luxemburg and the French-German border in the company of a fictitious English friend, Granville, very like Adams. Granville is described as "eminently pleasant to travel with; *insouciant*, well-informed, and very good-humoured." Regrettably, he is a proponent of "odious realism" and an inflexible disapprover of literary egocentricity.[7]

The spoof was accepted by *Blackwood's Magazine* and would appear, unsigned, in the July and August 1867 issues. For Adams, its acceptance was a challenge. Since he too had a vein of humor (much echoed in "The Easter Trip"), he was defied to write a successful parody or satire himself.[8] He simultaneously was paid the compliment of being incorporated into English literature as an *English* character.[9]

Several months earlier, John Hay had gone back to America. Service in Paris had helped him learn French and write attempted poetry, but it had not disposed him to stay in the government service as a diplomat. Late in 1866, Minister Bigelow had resigned. Hay quit also. Sooner than the minister, he took ship for America, but not via London.[10]

Bigelow had been trying to recover the long-lost manuscript of

Benjamin Franklin's *Memoirs*. It was assumed to be somewhere in France. In January 1867, while in London poised to take a steamer, he received word from France that he could buy the manuscript, some letters, and a portrait of Franklin for 25,000 francs. He at once affirmed his willingness to meet the price. Simultaneously he was visited at his hotel by Minister Adams.

The Franklin materials were shipped to London. Bigelow took them to America and, at his home near West Point, discovered that the manuscript of the *Memoirs*, in addition to including eight pages never previously published in English, differed from the best existing English edition at more than 1200 points.[11] He began at once to prepare a new edition—issued in 1868 by J. B. Lippincott in Philadelphia under the title *Autobiography of Benjamin Franklin*.[12]

Hay meanwhile had gone to Washington. While there, he refused a staff position Seward offered him in the State Department. He dined with Senator and Mrs. Sumner at their rented house on I Street and, so doing, met Clover Hooper, who had come to the capital to see her relations. He next went to New York to speak with publishers about a large-scale biography of Lincoln, to be written by John Nicolay and himself. The project kindled no enthusiasm in the publishers. They also spurned an outline he showed them for a novel. Determined to become a writer, yet sadly lacking in encouragement, he drifted to Illinois. There he read in a newspaper that he had been commissioned by Seward to serve in Vienna as chargé d'affaires.[13]

This unexpected change, important to Hay, was important also to Henry Adams. Till recently, the U. S. minister to Austria had been John Lothrop Motley of Boston, a long-time friend of the Adamses. A politician and historian, Motley was the author of *The Rise of the Dutch Republic* and a *History of the United Netherlands*. To a degree unusual even among Bostonians, he was a believer in aristocracy. In 1861 in London, he had remarked in Henry's hearing that "the London dinner and the English country-house" were "the perfection of human society."[14] In 1866, in the hearing of an unforgiving American taxpayer, George W. McCrackin of New York, he similarly averred, "An English nobleman is the model of human perfection." McCrackin protested by letter to President Johnson. The president ordered Seward to investigate. Riled by the inquiry, Motley tendered his resignation; Johnson accepted it; and Seward named Hay as first secretary and chargé d'affaires, with a salary of $6,000, few duties, and chances of learning German.[15]

En route to Vienna, Hay made his first trip to England. On

July 10, 1867, he visited his counterparts, Moran and Alward, in their den on Great Portland Street. Moran took him to call on C. F. Adams—presumably also on H. B. Adams—at 54 Portland Place. Next day, he had lunch with Mrs. Adams, Mary, Charles Kuhn, and "piquante" Louisa Kuhn. Henry was not at the table. He had been invited to Norman Court by Thomas Baring, was catching a train at 5:10, and perhaps had to work. Talk at lunch partly concerned the Sumner marriage. C. F. Adams had been told it had been a "mistake." Hay recorded: "We tore our friends to pieces a little while. Motley got one or two slaps. . . . Sumner and his new wife were brushed up a little."[16]

Henry returned on July 16. One may assume that he and Hay had a conversation and he was told that Hay and Nicolay wished to write a biography of Lincoln, in effect a history of the United States during the Rebellion; also that Hay had hopes of writing a novel. Assuming Hay made these disclosures, Henry, at a guess, *postponed* replying that he at a future date would write a history of the United States during the time of the early presidents. What is certain is that Henry did not tell Hay that he would soon be starting *Democracy*, a dangerous novel. He would eventually share with Hay the secret of his authorship of the novel, but never the secret of its genesis. Permanently, in that regard, Hay would be kept uninformed.[17]

On August 9, 1867, three traveling congressmen, Justin S. Morrill of Vermont, James G. Blaine of Maine, and James A. Garfield of Ohio, dined at the Legation. All were interested in public finance. Garfield and Blaine were rising politicians under forty. For Henry, acquaintance with each of the three was welcome and important.[18]

Having finished a year at Harvard, Brooks came abroad and rejoined his relatives. The Adamses and Kuhns went together to Paris to visit the great Exhibition. The Chief stayed in Paris to sit for his portrait; Charles Kuhn took a separate path; and Henry led Mrs. Adams, Loo, Mary, and Brooks to a hotel in Baden.

Mrs. Adams, not in good health, began to take the water cure.[19] Brooks went home to resume his studies. Henry stayed with the ladies. Secretly he was writing. Gaskell was writing also. Henry reported to him on August 25: "I hope you keep on writing but . . . writing is only half the art; the other being erasure. . . . I . . . have expunged all my last thing." The thing expunged was presumably an article relating to sculpture and William Wetmore Story.[20]

His table being clear, Henry began to draft *Democracy*.[21] He had long possessed its essential settings: the city of Washington; the White House; a rented house on Lafayette Square; the Lees' house in Arlington; and, a few miles down the Potomac, the house and grounds of Mount Vernon.[22] He recently had acquired the nexus of its plot: the marriage—or, better, the narrowly-averted marriage—of a young widow interested in politics and an aging politician destined not to be president.[23] Lesser characters waited for cues. One, a young lawyer named Carrington, might conveniently be a Virginian, a rebel veteran, and a relative of the Lees.[24] A second, much older, a foreign diplomat assigned to Washington, might usefully be a baron.[25]

What was much more important, Adams felt the extraordinary stimulus, one may even say the terror, of a literary miracle. He and all the world had learned of a new English book titled *Alice's Adventures in Wonderland*. The author was not identified. The book was published as the work of Lewis Carroll—a pseudonym. It told of a child's having to grow up in trying situations during an interval underground.[26]

For Carlo Gaskell, the story served as a commentary on his courting a young Englishwoman.[27] For Henry Adams, it served as a standard for great writing while he was attempting to write *Democracy*. For Adams, too, the book had the surpassingly valuable property, not of casting lights on the misadventure of Alice Mason Hooper, who had gone to Washington at her peril, but instead of describing Henry Adams, who, though not a child, and not a girl, felt himself as growing and as perpetually having to deal with trying situations.[28] By describing *him*, the book moved Adams to look beyond his incipient novel and projected history of the United States to their intended sequel. As conceived in 1860, the sequel would be a book about himself. Or would it?[29]

Under numerous pressures, principally Carroll's *Alice* and Franklin's *Memoirs*, Adams reconceived his third book as innovative, very ambitious, and anti-egocentric.[30] As redesigned, it was asked to meet severe tests. The main tests would be four in number. It would attain its wanted value if it resembled no other book; if it was mostly *not* about its author's actual self; if it none the less made the utmost use of his experience; and if it succeeded in affording its readers new eagerness and ability to create a better world.[31]

Alice Sumner had long since left her husband. The Adamses returned to London, and Henry secretly continued writing. Alice hurriedly came abroad and joined her sister in Paris. There by chance she encountered Baron Holstein. In her sister's company, she turned back towards America, traveling via London. On October 23, 1867, the Chief recorded being told that Mrs. Sumner would sue the senator for divorce "on the ground of impotence." Three days later, she sailed from Liverpool.[32]

As usual, ships on the Atlantic were bringing newspapers from New York. On October 21 and 22, a Democratic organ, the *New York Evening Express*, under the heading "FROM BOSTON," had published an anonymous letter which claimed to set forth the "substance" of the Sumner scandal. A masterstroke of villainy, the letter declaredly was written to "stop the tongues of the thousands" who were making more of the Sumners' troubles than the "few facts" would justify. The letter's true purpose was the *loosing* of tongues. It succeeded. A larger Democratic newspaper in New York, *The World*, instantly reprinted the letter.[33]

In London, Henry Adams read the letter in the *Express*, *World*, or both. He made use of one of its lines to help shape *Democracy*.[34] He at the same time was disturbed by news concerning a Democrat, his eldest brother. In Massachusetts, elections for governor were annual. The Bay State Democrats had nominated John for governor, without hope of victory. At the polls in November, he received 65,000 votes, enough to be defeated badly.[35]

The disturbance for Henry was not the defeat. It was the willingness of his fellow Adamses to stand for office. On November 16, after learning that John had lost, he wrote to Charles: "Supposing we run *you* for Gov. and John for Congress. Then I think we should try for as many offices as we can conveniently hold."

The lines had a meaning which Henry would not spell out. The Chief was expecting to be elected president—not in 1868, but in 1872.[36] The situation called for comment. Henry produced a comment remarkably vocal about the three eldest sons but silent about their father. He told Charles:

> John is a political genius; let him follow the family bent. You are a lawyer, and with a few years patience will be the richest and the most respectable of us all. I claim my right to part company with you both. I never will make a speech, never run for an office, never belong to a party. I am going to plunge under the stream. For years you will hear nothing of any publication of mine—perhaps never, who knows. . . . If you see me come up, it will be with an oyster and a pearl inside.[37]

The comment was carefully worded. In making John a political genius and Charles a successful lawyer, it gave them distinctions they would never have. Picturing Henry as a pearl diver, it indicated that he would be neither a politician nor a lawyer and thus would have nothing left to be but a harmless writer. Indeed the image seemed to indicate that he was already reduced to being a writer, moreover a perfectionist or dabbler whose works would not incur the disgrace of being published.

The truth was not so simple. As he knew, Henry was no longer a Republican, would never be a Democrat, would never make a political speech, and never stand for election. Yet he would remain a politician—*more* than his father or brothers. In addition, he would try to outpace his American contemporaries as a writer. His books, at least the three that he knew about, would be meant to outlast the ages.

His most pressing current difficulty related, not to politics, but to writing. He found *Democracy* hard to draft. He wrote to Carlo on November 26, 1867: "Work comes forward very slowly. My progress is not only far from rapid but very unsatisfactory. I pass most of my time every day in erasing what I had written the day before. . . . Of course all this is for your eye exclusively."

Since the publication of *The Antiquity of Man* in 1863, Sir Charles Lyell and Charles Darwin had achieved almost universal notoriety. As a direct result of their writings, quarrels between religionists and scientists raged on every hand. Unrepentant, Lyell meant to stoke the quarrels. He had prepared a revised, tenth edition of his standard treatise, *The Principles of Geology*, in two volumes, and had received advance copies from the publisher. Wanting the new edition properly noticed in America, he talked with Henry Adams at the Legation.

Adams had read a good many works of science, but he had never tried to read the writings of scientists well enough to distinguish their better ideas from their worse, much less offer criticisms that the scientists would value. Merely as an experiment, he volunteered that *he* could write the American notice. To his astonishment, Lyell agreed and gave him the volumes. They further decided that, for a time, Henry's effort would be a secret.[38]

This revolution occurred at a critical moment. Henry had been trying to schedule the return of his parents, Mary, and himself to America for August 1868. The intended date was political. He wanted the Chief to arrive in New York *after* the Republican and Democratic conventions, especially the latter, which would begin in New York on July 4.[39] His effort seemed likely to fail. The Chief had asked Seward to name a replacement minister, and there was every prospect that the family would disembark at New York in June, *before* the Democrats were to meet.

While plans were still in flux, Henry announced that in January 1868 he would be leaving for Italy. He would be away two months, with Gaskell and Cunliffe. The excuse he offered was "delicate" health.[40]

How Henry's latest device might affect future scheduling was quite uncertain.[41] Meanwhile in London he shifted from one secret project to another. He put aside his attempted draft of *Democracy* and faced the hazards of reviewing Lyell's *Principles*. As preliminaries, he would have to study the new tenth edition, compare it with earlier editions, study relevant publications by Darwin and other writers, and think to a purpose about what might prove a mass of conflictive testimony. The task was enormous. He began it immediately.[42]

At some point, too, he mailed a package to Washington. He had read in the press about a new agency, the U. S. Geological Exploration of the Fortieth Parallel. The Survey had been created the previous March and was administered by the army chief of engineers, General Humphreys. The geologist-in-charge, Clarence King, had trained at Yale and worked in the field in California. King had political talents and had lobbied through Congress the bill creating the Survey. To help direct and perform the agency's work, he had recruited three aides: Arnold and James Hague, brothers from Boston, and Samuel Franklin Emmons, Adams's neighbor in Quincy and one-time host in Paris.

These details mattered because Lyell had decided to send two copies of his tenth edition to General Humphreys and had written to Adams requesting him to do the mailing. Henry complied, thought the errand significant, and preserved Lyell's note. In the same spirit, he possibly enclosed with the books a suggestion to General Humphreys that one set of Lyell's *Principles* be forwarded to Clarence King.[43]

On January 5, 1868, Adams started for Italy with Gaskell and Cunliffe. At Cannes they entertained two young English women of their acquaintance. Their next stop was Florence, where they glimpsed the Kuhns. Robert had to turn back; but Henry and Carlo hurried to Venice, saw Bologna heaped in snow, visited Perugia, and stayed briefly at Sorrento and Amalfi. During a month in Rome, Henry passed his thirtieth birthday. Obliged to leave, he returned to Florence, was detained by Loo to attend a dance, hastened north, and on March 9, in excellent health, was again in London.

That evening it was decided that the Chief, Mrs. Adams, and

Mary would go to Italy in May and June. Next day, accompanied by Henry, the Chief went to the Cunard office and tentatively reserved passage on a steamer scheduled to reach New York on July 8, some days *after* the start of the Democratic convention. C. F. Adams understood the delay to be a means of avoiding involvement in that party's affairs. He wrote in his diary: ". . . I am clear of complications consequent upon the Fourth of July in New York. This is a great relief to my mind."[44]

Two weeks later, on March 23, a letter reached the Legation. From John, it asked whether the Chief would accept the Democratic nomination for president. John apparently was acting on behalf of the head of the Democratic national committee, August Belmont. C. F. Adams recorded: "To me, this is alarming, for it dissipates all my plans of comfort, if I entertain the proposition, and it thrusts a great responsibility on me as a patriot if out of sheer cowardice or selfish indulgence I refuse to do what I can to aid the country in its difficulties."

On March 26, C. F. Adams sent an answer which mixed the positive with the conditional. In his words, ". . . my answer is a thoroughly independent one, and will not commit me to accept any platform excepting such as I can fully approve." The case, however, was one in which physical movements were going to be decisive. The Chief's reservation of cabin space was already confirmed by the Cunard Line. It would not be changed. The Adamses would sail a month earlier than Henry originally had wanted, but at an even better time. When the Democrats met in New York, C. F. Adams would be on the ocean and out of reach.[45]

On an unknown date, Henry advised the Chief that, after staying at Quincy through the late summer, he would try the "experiment" of living for a winter or two in Washington, to write more articles.[46] The disclosure came as a fearful blow. Had he been asked what destroyed his brothers, C. F. Adams could have answered, "Washington."

During John Quincy Adams's years in the capital as secretary of state and president, his sons successively had fallen victims to the amorous advances of an adopted member of the family, their mother's orphaned niece, Mary Catherine Hellen. Charles broke free, but George became engaged to Mary and stayed so for two years. She then changed favorites and welcomed a courtship by John. They married in Washington in 1828, but their chances for happiness had already vanished. John and George were both in irreversible decline.

Following George and John's deaths in 1829 and 1834, Mrs. John took charge of household details for John Quincy and Louisa Catherine Adams. The arrangement brought her every summer to Quincy. The change eventually resulted in her becoming a special friend of Louisa's grandson Henry. But oppositely, after the death of Louisa in 1852, Mrs. John ceased summering in Quincy. As a result, she and Henry saw each other only during short visits she made to his parents.

In 1868, when Henry disclosed his plan to the Chief, Mrs. John as usual was at her house in the capital. Old Aunt Smith was with her. Henry's plan thus had the advantage that the aunts could provide a welcome.[47] The Chief made no objection. Yet from the start he thought the plan an error. In his view, the aunts were exceptions. They were not New Englanders; and, in the opinion of New Englanders, Washington was not a possible place of residence. It was a mere center for the transaction of public business. No one went there to live.[48]

Henry's talk of an "experiment" was a fiction intended to conceal his actual purpose. He would not say so; but he was moving to Washington for life, happily could afford it, and knew what he would do when he arrived. His income, supplemented by an allowance from the Chief, would more than meet his expenses. His time would be wholly free. He would use it to act as an office-avoiding politician. He also would write. When possible, he would travel.

Charles in January 1867 had received a warning from Henry that he would not pursue a career in Boston. The warning made no impression. In March, in his capacity as caretaker of his brother's money, Charles wrote to Henry asking whether, for tax purposes, he wished to remain a resident of Quincy or change to Boston. Henry replied on March 28: "I've no property in Quincy, nor do I reside there, nor do I mean to reside there. I did once cast a vote there, the only vote I ever did cast, and possibly the only vote I ever shall cast. . . . I doubt the propriety of changing to Boston. . . ."

Had he read the answer with an ear to its implication, Charles might have recalled that citizens residing in the District of Columbia were deprived by law of the right to vote. He might then have realized that Henry was moving and would settle in Washington.

Charles missed the implication—and no wonder. The news from the capital was inconceivably bad. In February, the radical Republicans had driven a measure through the House impeaching

President Johnson. The measure accused the chief executive of eleven "high crimes and misdemeanors." The trial before the Senate was under way. The charges against the president were flimsy, where not false. Johnson had chosen not to appear and was depending for his acquittal on a battery of lawyers led by William M. Evarts and Benjamin R. Curtis. The speeches of his main attackers—Thaddeus Stevens, George S. Boutwell, and General Butler—could be expected to resound at enormous lengths. An early verdict would not be forthcoming. The outcome was wholly doubtful.

Henry had formed his principal ideas of government, not in manhood by studying the writings of Alexis de Tocqueville, J. S. Mill, Hobbes, Rousseau, and comparable writers, although he read them, but instead in boyhood by talking with J. Q. Adams. Every summer in the 1840s, the ex-president, freed from his wars at the Capitol as an anti-slavery congressman, had returned from Washington to Quincy. Learning politics directly from his grandfather was one of the causes of Henry's comporting himself in maturity as the leading member of his family, and it gave his perspective the curious property of being annual.[49]

Later Henry conferred in the summers with Senator Sumner, when *he* came back from wars at the Capitol against the Slavepower. Again the hearer's perspective was annual.

At twenty-three, Henry wrote the article called "The Great Secession Winter of 1860–61"—the one he suppressed and gave to Charles. The article was annual. It reviewed the nation's politics during the year preceding the outbreak of the Rebellion.

Since coming to the Legation, Henry had learned he was not alone in his idiosyncrasy. He had watched Lord Robert Cecil invent for the *London Quarterly* "an annual review of politics called 'The Session.' "[50]

For Henry in 1868, the upshot of these accumulated experiences was a plan for five articles. As perhaps was inevitable, the articles arrayed themselves as an ascending series.[51] First he wanted to place his review of Lyell's *Principles* in the October 1868 issue of the *North American*, signed with his baptismal name. So signed, the article would announce to New Englanders that "Henry Brooks Adams" was a promising Adams, a writer of articles.

Next he would write a pair of articles for simultaneous publication on both sides of the ocean. One would be shaped for English acceptance. Reversing his former tactic of writing about English financial woes for American publication, he would offer Henry

Reeve an article titled "American Finance, 1865–1869," timed to appear in the April 1869 issue of the *Edinburgh Review*. In keeping with the rule of the quarterly, the article would be anonymous.

The other article of the pair would be written for inclusion in the April 1869 *North American*. It would be signed and would review the past year of American politics. Its title—stolen from Lord Robert Cecil—would be "The Session." Unavoidably, it would show ambition. Reading it, the public would be apprised that Henry Brooks Adams was concerning himself with national politics.

The fourth article would be another "Session," written to appear in the *North American* sometime in 1870. Likewise signed, it would indicate that Henry Brooks Adams intended to review the nation's politics annually for an extended interval.

The fifth article rose in prospect as the best but was highly conditional. Assuming Reeve accepted "American Finance" and thought it a success when published, Adams would try to furnish the *Edinburgh Review* an anonymous article of great value. It would need an extraordinary subject. Its preparation and authorship might best be kept secret as long as possible. Although its contents could not be predicted, it loomed as the point and purpose of the five-part series.

The English often liked Americans but were seldom unhappy to see them leave. The Gaskells and Palgrave so loved Henry Adams they voiced a criticism: he did not appreciate the poetry of Wordsworth. The Chief agreed and offered Henry his set of Wordsworth, provided he read it through. Henry declined the gift but borrowed the books.[52]

The Adamses' tenure at 54 Portland Place would end on April 27, 1868. Henry wrote to Norton on April 10 reserving space in the October 1868 *North American* for a "review of Sir Charles Lyell's 'Principles of Geology. Tenth Edition.' " The returned contributor advised the editor that his "leaning," while "not strong," was "towards" Lyell and Darwin. Warning was apropos. Cultured Bostonians, upset by reports concerning Darwin and Lyell's theories, had sought reassurance from Professor Louis Agassiz at Harvard. To their relief, the Swiss geologist had thrown cold water on the writings of his English rivals in science. Henry accordingly offered *not* to write. ". . . if you are afraid of Sir Charles and Darwin, and prefer to adhere frankly to Mr[.] Agassiz, you have but to say so, and I am dumb." His offer was *pro forma*. Norton and Lowell would not turn away such a contributor as Adams—who knew it. He was sure in advance that space for the article was his.

For writing purposes, he sheared his review of Lyell into halves: a safer half on geology, to be finished in Europe, and a riskier half on evolution, to be finished in Quincy. Required to escort Mrs. Adams and Mary to Paris for new arrays of clothes, he went to Paris but asked them to do their errands without him. Thus freed, he "passed my days and nights in my room geologising." He was writing the safer half.

On May 14, the Chief came to Paris. Next day, Henry ushered parents and Mary to the Gare de Lyon and a train bound towards Italy. He himself caught a northbound train at another station, returned to London, and moved into Cunliffe's quarters at 9 Holles Street, Cavendish Square. Robert had lent him "charming rooms." Hosts and hostesses fed him "excellent dinners." He wrote to Cunliffe that he had turned into a "magnificent pauper." "Nothing that I have is my own. . . ."

Lyell asked Adams to dinner. Adams had to decline. The Gaskells wished him to spend his last days in England as much as possible at Wenlock Abbey. Leaving the completed half of his article with Lyell, he went to Shropshire. Sir Charles studied the pages and responded: "I read your M.S. with much pleasure. It seems to me geologically correct in the main & much better calculated to set people thinking than if you had attempted to embrace a greater number of themes. . . ." He made some slight objections and seemed fearful that his reviewer in the second half of the article might misrepresent how Darwin accounted for the evolution of species.[53]

Adams returned to London, recovered his pages, and went back to Shropshire. When not riding or walking with Carlo, he wrote to Lyell. The letters are lost, but they elicited notable replies. Sir Charles averred that human beings originated in one place only, evolved for a long time in a single way, but later, while migrating dispersedly, acquired the differentiations which set them apart as several "races." He as much as said that evolution is creative. "It is very difficult if one adopt[s] the doctrine of progressive development & an ascensive scheme[,] to exclude the term creation from that force or causation which is capable in the course of ages of turning a fish into an ape or an ape into a man. . . ."[54]

Carlo wanted a portrait of Henry and preferred that it be a drawing. He had summoned an artist, Samuel Lawrence. With pencillings beautifully clear, Lawrence drew a seated Adams, neither young nor old, balding but not bald, clean-shaven except for a moustache, eyes attentive, but otherwise non-committal and passive. Without faulting the drawing as art, a critic could hold that the artist drew the opposite of a likeness. As pictured, Adams was an English aesthete, a variant Gaskell, lacking vivacity. Will and energy disappeared.[55]

The elder Adamses and Mary came back from Italy. The parents would set out for the steamer *China* without a word to Moran. It was left for Henry to pay the secretary a parting visit at Great Portland Place. To the last, Moran was kept from knowing that it was Henry who had secured for him his long continuance as a diplomat.[56]

Two diplomatic families, the Adamses and Motleys, crossed together on the *China*. Henry improved his time on the voyage by reading Wordsworth.[57] The ship arrived in New York harbor during a heat wave late on July 7, 1868. The families appeared at the Brevoort House on Fifth Avenue towards midnight. John and Charles greeted them with news that the Democrats were still meeting and had not yet chosen a candidate. The Chief was *not* in the running.[58]

The elder Adamses, Henry, and Mary had been absent from America for seven years and two months. They proceeded to Quincy and returned to their usual rooms in the Old House. Expecting not to see Europe again, C. F. Adams would write to none of the English leaders who befriended him during his mission.[59] Henry wrote immediately to his closer friends. His first letters were lost, but answers survive from Palgrave and Gaskell. "I am glad you take more pleasure in Wordsworth," Palgrave replied. ". . . he has done more for us in poetry than anyone since Milton. . . . Your departure has made a blank which every day's walk through Portland Place brings very closely before me."[60]

Weary of carrying the *North American Review*, Norton and Lowell had passed it to Whitman Gurney. His responsibility as editor began with the October 1868 issue. Sight unseen, his predecessors had accepted for the issue a review of Lyell by Henry Adams.

To meet editor Gurney, contributor Adams merely needed to take the familiar road from Quincy to Cambridge. Brooks was staying at the Old House, knew Gurney, and would have been pleased to arrange a meeting. As it happened, Henry would stir not an inch in the editor's direction. A holder of power, he would show it by interposing Charles and Brooks between himself and other people as emissaries, shields, spies, partners, even superiors. Presumably, in August, having completed both halves of his article on Lyell, he asked Brooks to read it, suggest revisions if inclined, and convey it to Gurney.[61]

Charles and Minnie were in Newport. Henry paid them a visit. By then, he and Charles had produced seven articles for the *North American*. In 1867, Charles had drafted an article about two cities, Boston and Chicago, and sent it to Henry in Europe for criticism. Henry in effect had been asked to do the work of an editor. Editing was needed. Confronted with the affectedness, nervousness, and verbosity of his brother's style, Henry had tried to curb at least the verbosity. ". . . my great objection," he had said, "is to your profuse expenditure of words."[62]

Charles had since returned to railroads as a subject for articles. He had studied a titanic struggle in New York for control of the Erie Railroad Company. Initially the clashing titans were Daniel Drew, trying to keep control, and Cornelius Vanderbilt, gambling fortunes to obtain control. Others leapt into the fray. In the end, two dissimilar opportunists ruled the corporation as absolute suzerains: saturnine Jay Gould and flamboyant James Fisk, Jr.

Charles was not afraid of Drew, Vanderbilt, Gould, Fisk, or the nation's plutocrats in a body. Working rapidly, he had written an article on the Erie struggle good enough to be offered to Norton and Lowell. They had accepted it but showed it to Gurney, who thought it too strong in its personalities and sent it to Charles for revision. Henry saw the manuscript at Newport and gave his brother advice. He said that Charles—obeying impulses he himself was feeling—should intensify his studies of the Erie war, try to improve as a writer, and re-submit the article when much expanded. The advice had a practical meaning that perhaps was not apparent. Since the article would eventually appear in the *North American* and since Henry was taking a hand in its development, Henry was already beginning to serve, albeit unasked, as Gurney's editorial associate.[63]

At Quincy, the Chief was contemplating two projects: renovation of the Old House and publication of the diaries of John Quincy Adams. On returning from Newport, Henry copied extracts from the diaries, partly for his own uses, partly to help his father start his project.[64]

Copying was drudgery, but Henry used it as a gate to opportunity. He knew that his Adams grandmother had tried to write. Without making a show of the search, he took stock of the papers of Louisa Catherine Adams. He learned that some of her papers could be combined to form a short, coherent book.

Edward Atkinson, a Boston economist, had read and liked "British Finance in 1816" and "The Bank of England Restriction."

Sometime late in the summer, perhaps at the suggestion of their common friend, David A. Wells, Atkinson and Henry Adams talked. On October 5, 1868, Henry wrote to Atkinson requesting a letter of introduction to Edwin L. Godkin, editor of the *Nation*, whom he wished to visit in New York, while on his way to Washington. Atkinson obliged.[65]

Simultaneously two Adams sons reached critical moments in their careers. On October 9, 1868, John Quincy Adams II was to give a speech in Columbia, South Carolina, as part of a scheme the Democrats had conceived to make him a national figure. Nervous drinking and over-eating prohibited his appearing. New arrangements were made for October 10 and then for October 12. At a banquet on the latter date, the speech "may finally have been delivered, probably in part." John's failings were as much as possible concealed, and the family later published the speech as if he had delivered it in full, without delays.[66]

That same day, October 12, 1868, Henry left Quincy for New York and Washington. His parents were heartsick to see him go. The Chief wrote in his diary an entry unparalleled by any other in its many volumes: "I shall miss him every day and every hour of the rest of my life, as a companion and friend. Nobody has known so much of me, as he."[67]

In New York, Henry talked with Godkin. Originally an Englishman, the editor ranked high among America's reformers. He would naturally suppose his visitor to be a reformer also. Henry apparently told him he would be trying the experiment of living in Washington and would be writing articles. If an offer was made, Godkin presumably had to make it, giving the visitor to feel that any contributions he might send to the *Nation* would be accorded immediate reading.[68]

By accident in New York, Henry ran into Evarts. The previous May, after a two-month trial, the legal team headed by Evarts and Curtis had won the acquittal of President Johnson by a margin of one Senate vote; and on June 22 Johnson had nominated Evarts to serve as attorney general. In view of his new responsibilities, Evarts had moved to a rented Washington house. When he and Henry met, he was on the point of taking a train to the capital. Told Henry's itinerary, he required that they travel together and that Henry accept a bed in his house.

Occurrences had started that Henry could not control. Arriving in Washington with a member of the Cabinet had not been part of his plan. Neither had he counted on the train Evarts chose. It was equipped with sleeping cars, an innovation that Henry, usually quick to adapt, failed to like. In the morning, Evarts led him directly to the White House and introduced him to President Johnson. Henry was unprepared for the impression made on him by the Tennessean. Seen face to face, Johnson was "a true president" and a powerful figure.[69]

Perhaps on the same day, Henry went alone to the State Department and paid his respects to Seward. The news that an Adams would be wintering in the capital affected the scarred but lively secretary as a jovial surprise. He invited Henry to join him at his house whenever convenient. In addition, rooms being scarce in the capital, he ordered his major domo to go in search of a suite adapted to Henry's needs.

The major domo found excellent quarters. On G Street west of 20th Street, they included a spare bedroom and facilities for giving dinner parties. Henry ordered numerous improvements costing $200—equal to a workman's pay for three months. When the work was done and he moved in, he would enjoy a special benefit. His windows would give him a broad view of the Potomac, downstream towards Mount Vernon.[70]

In the United States, as elsewhere, possession of money went a long way towards assuring prominence and social standing. On October 13, 1868, Professor E. W. Gurney married his former pupil, Ellen Hooper. Two years before, when they met, Gurney's salary as an assistant professor had been $1,500 a year. When they married, Ellen had a fortune a hundred times that sum. In proportion, their marriage transformed Gurney's standing in the community and his standing at the College.[71]

Gurney had published Henry Adams's review of Lyell as Article IV in the October *North American*. It seems probable that he formed a judgment of its author only different from Norton and Lowell's in being still more approving. The review—titled "The Principles of Geology" and signed "Henry Brooks Adams"—was unforeseeable in what it said. Its opening pages revealed that Adams's knowledge of geology was wide, discriminating, and precise. Its later pages disclosed that he was neither a Darwinist nor an anti-Darwinist. He said humans had evolved. That, he said, was a palaeontological fact. But whether human beings originated in one place, as seemed probable, or in several places, as seemed possible, no one in England or elsewhere had shown; and *how* humans evolved—or how all pigeons evolved from the rock pigeon—was, he suggested, almost as mysterious in 1868 as it had been before

Darwin purported to explain the process in 1859 in *The Origin of Species.*

Without yielding even slightly to the conservatism then the fashion in Boston-Cambridge, Adams had written an American declaration of independence from British science. His review was also a declaration of independence by a younger writer after hard study of vaunted works by older writers. He showed particular reluctance to credit theories advanced by persons who published their ideas before they exerted themselves to consider the available data. He left no doubt that Lyell's geological theories were partly at odds with well-known evidence.

His main response was one of caution. He said the stumbling block for the present in geology and biology was a crippling insufficiency of facts. ". . . the more geology is studied," he reported, "the more its incompleteness becomes obvious; it cannot make progress without theorizing, yet very few of its theories have the proper number of legs to run upon; the facts, if not contradictory, are wanting."[72]

From the time he first went there, in May 1850, Adams had loved Washington. On returning in 1868, he loved it still. Past visits had shown him the capital in winter, spring, and early summer, but not in autumn. Having been so long abroad, he had lost remembrance of what American autumns were really like. Shortly after arriving, he began to take long walks in the woods on hilly slopes along Rock Creek. To his surprise, the result was "a fit of low spirits."

As he continued his walks, his melancholy deepened. As nearly as he could tell, the cause was the brilliant colors of Washington's trees. The sight of their ever-changing tints passed endurance. His condition approached being perilous. Thinking back many years later, he would write about his extremity, "Life could not go on so beautiful and so sad."[73]

Always his own best physician, he treated his melancholy with work, careful diet, contact with other people, and continued walking. After a brief stay with Evarts at the corner of H and 14th Streets, he lived with his aunts at the corner of I and 16th Steets. Possibly at their urging, he called on Mrs. Zachary Taylor, the aged widow of President Taylor. Without intending it, he made friends with her son. A former rich Louisiana planter and Confederate lieutenant general, Richard Taylor had been left penniless at war's end and was struggling to make a living. Cultivated, humorous, and extraordinarily intelligent, he was able to deal with Adams on a basis of easy give and take.[74]

The work Henry started soonest was letters to the Chief. Wishing to write every Sunday, he suggested mid-week replies. The plan was followed; but, of the fifty-odd letters they exchanged between late October 1868 and June 1869, those by the Chief were kept and those by Henry, the last excepted, were at an unknown time destroyed, presumably by Henry.

The father's answers were evidence that the son said or implied that he would winter in the capital indefinitely. C. F. Adams wrote back, "I confess myself a sceptic in regard to the possibility of permanent residence at Washington." Equally forthright on other topics, he said that Seward was a "great man" and the only great man in "the school of my father." He attested that John, again running hopelessly for governor of Massachusetts, stood alone among younger Americans as a "philosophical statesman." "I do not overrate John if I say that he has not his equal in his own generation. . . ."[75]

As he had long anticipated, Henry's work led him to the Treasury. "American Finance," planned for the *Edinburgh Review*, would take the form of a response to Secretary McCulloch's Annual Reports. A new Annual Report was in preparation; also a separate report by Commissioner Wells. Needing advance copies, Henry visited the commissioner. Wells seized the chance to introduce his friend to McCulloch. The secretary greeted Adams in part by patting him on the back.[76]

Confident he could make his article a success, Adams wrote on November 8 to Henry Reeve, offering him the article for his April 1869 issue. Reeve promptly and encouragingly replied.[77]

Lyell had been sent the October *North American*. He wrote to Adams: "I have lost no time in reading your very interesting article[,] the most original that I have yet seen on my new edition & the only one which has called due attention to what is new in this my last version of the 'Principles'. I am very glad that you maintained your own opinion on climatal & other subjects . . . & when I have next an opportunity of again going fully into that difficult question [changes of average temperature in the atmosphere] I shall carefully consider how far the objections you have started or [ought?] to modify my views." He ventured to add, ". . . your friends . . . will be not a little surprised when they see how good a grasp you have taken of some of the most difficult points of controversy which have been agitating the scientific world." To affirm his good opinion, he sent Henry his field compass.[78]

The members of the Fortieth Parallel Survey, after spending each summer in the Rockies to survey and map large areas of wilderness, came to the capital each winter and labored to prepare what eventually would be a massive Report. Perhaps at the Survey's rooms, but without meeting Clarence King, Adams talked with Emmons. Because his mind was focused on the nation's disturbed economy, he asked Frank about the pay of the Survey's members and learned what he could have predicted: the agency's scientists, apart from King, who drew a salary of $3600, were remunerated at half the rate of its cooks and mule-drivers. For his part, Emmons read "The Principles of Geology" and discovered that Adams had become the country's ablest geological critic.[79]

On November 10, Gurney sent Charles Adams a note requesting his brother Henry's address. The editor wished to initiate a direct, important correspondence with Henry in Washington. Such a correspondence later started. Evidence that it became important may be seen in the telling fact that all the letters ever exchanged between Whitman Gurney and Henry Adams later vanished, apparently because Adams after Gurney's death had chances to recover his own letters, did so, and burned everything.[80]

Fortunately, letters were not the only documents. Starting on November 1, Adams had begun a calendar of "Letters sent." It showed he did not write directly to Gurney till January 3, 1869. The one American editor he earlier wrote to was E. L. Godkin in New York, on November 28.[81] Thus the evidence was strong that Adams was trying to keep himself at a remove from Gurney. The policy would have as one of its effects his avoiding or at least postponing possible meetings with Ellen Gurney, her sister Clover, and their cousin-by-marriage, Alice Sumner, who again was living in Boston.[82]

Of the many concerns Adams had to deal with in Washington, the most pressing was the state of his private feelings. Rising politically, he was sinking emotionally. He confided to Gaskell, "The sad truth is that I want nothing and life seems to have no purpose."

His correspondents included an English lawyer, Ralph Palmer, a friend of Carlo's. Writing to Palmer, he said his problem was failure to marry. "I wish some-one would take the trouble to marry me out-of-hand. I've asked my mother and all my aunts to undertake the negociation[, *sic*] promising to accept anyone they selected. Damn *me* if, one and all, they didn't think I was joking. . . . That is what society has come to, in this country."[83]

❖ ❖ ❖

The quality most sought in nominees for president was likeliness to get elected. From the time when units under his command first won a battle, Ulysses S. Grant had been thought to have it. In the present year, both the Democrats and Republicans had wanted him as their candidate. He had acceded to nomination by the Republicans and on November 3 had defeated Horatio Seymour. Barring an untoward event, he would be inaugurated on March 4, 1869. He was expected to announce some or all of his Cabinet choices before that date.

To an unusual degree, the president-to-be was set apart from the citizenry. Like no previous American, even George Washington, Grant had been made a full general, wearing four stars.

His margin of victory at the polls had been narrow, and a possible cause was silence. What he stood for, other than national unity, was yet to be divulged. Inscrutable as a cannon that might or might not be loaded, he awakened awe and fear as often as hope or trust.

Rumors spread concerning the Cabinet appointments. One of the most plausible said that the State Department would go to C. F. Adams. It was known that Mr. Adams had been assisted when minister to England by one of his younger sons. Since Seward for eight years had had the help of his son Frederick as assistant secretary of state, no wild fancy was needed to paint Henry Brooks Adams as Fred Seward's assured successor. Significantly, or so it could seem, H. B. Adams had arrived in Washington—was already on the ground.[84]

Henry wished to view his future realistically. He wrote to Carlo, "In about five years I expect to have conquered a reputation." The estimate took no account of recent experience. Henry's meeting Evarts in New York and their coming to the capital together, the introduction to President Johnson, Seward's ordering the major domo to look for rooms, McCulloch's patting Henry on the back—all were occurrences with a meaning that far outran expectation and any imaginable rumor.

The meaning was first impressed on Henry by a use Evarts made of him. From the hour of their meeting in New York, the attorney general recited to him possible arguments the administration might depend upon in two cases soon to be decided by the Supreme Court: *Hepburn v. Griswold* and *Bronson v. Rhodes*. The government's opponents in the cases alleged that the Legal Tender Act of 1862 was unconstitutional. Being attorney general, Evarts had no choice but to argue that the act was constitutional. What he wanted was disputations between Henry and himself during which

Henry would argue that the act was *not* constitutional. Evarts said he needed an "anvil" to hammer ideas on and the anvil should hammer back. It did not matter that Henry was not a lawyer—that his formal training in law consisted of three days as a clerk in a Boston office before the war. Evarts knew Henry well and considered him a first-rate lawyer.[85]

Surprise followed surprise. Henry was welcomed by *five* of the seven members of Johnson's Cabinet. Fourth was General Schofield, the secretary of war, whom he had met in London. Fifth was A. W. Randall, the postmaster general, whom he shortly began to visit.[86]

Welcome led straight to an unheard-of accommodation. As if by instinct, numerous officers in the government recognized Henry's discretion, abilities, and willingness to work. They could not give him an office. He so conducted himself that his holding office was obviously beside the way. Yet tacitly they accorded him something practically equal to Cabinet rank. Had a joke been in order, someone could have said he was brought into the government as a private secretary.

His elevated status might seem an aberration, doomed to expire when President Johnson passed from office. Not an aberration, it was part and parcel with a permanent reality. So long as he passed his winters in Washington, this particular Adams would have, or could speedily re-acquire, high *de facto* rank in the national government. This unexampled prerogative rested on two bases, each sufficient: the Adamses' collective history and his very individual and capable self.

Still not recovered from his melancholy, Adams moved to his rooms, hung his pictures, hired a cook, and began asking friends to share his meals. When so inclined, he visited Seward.[87] He called also at the house of Chief Justice Chase—with astonishing results.[88]

In 1862, when secretary of the treasury, Chase was a proponent of the Legal Tender Act. He subsequently watched the value of the dollar drop to 32 cents, compared with gold. Regretting the passage of the act, he became an enemy of "legal tender" and wished the country could return to sound money. He left the Treasury but was named by Lincoln to be chief justice of the Supreme Court. In November 1868, to his great discomfort, the court was preparing to decide whether the act he had favored in 1862 should be upheld as constitutional, or struck down. It was irregular, indeed worse than irregular, but Chief Justice Chase told Henry Adams in confidence that arguments against the constitutionality of the act were in short supply. He hoped they existed, seemed not to know what they were, and asked Adams to go and find them.[89]

At the Capitol during three days ending on Thursday, December 10, 1868, the Supreme Court heard the opposing lawyers present final arguments in the legal-tender cases. Adams attended. The government's position was summarized by Attorney General Evarts, assisted by Benjamin Curtis. The latter spoke first and presented his argument in simple terms in an hour. Evarts spoke longer and used forensic devices of all kinds. The lawyers opposing the administration were men of small standing in the legal fraternity. One wholly avoided the question of constitutionality. The other, a New Yorker named Potter, tried to attack the position taken by Curtis and Evarts but seemed a lamb in conflict with lions.

On Friday, Adams mailed an article to the *Nation*. Titled "The Argument in the Legal Tender Cases" and signed "H. B. A.," the article was brief—ten paragraphs—but attempted several things. It reminded the reader that the Supreme Court had asked to hear final statements by the lawyers in the cases. It repeated a three-way joke that Evarts had made about paper money: that "people will make too much of it." It said it was "no reflection" on Potter that he did not have "the force necessary for supporting alone . . . so burdensome a cause" as the one he tried to win. And succinctly it counteracted the administration's claim that the Legal Tender Act was constitutional.

Godkin published Adams's short article in the *Nation* on December 17, 1868. Its appearance marked an epoch for writer and editor, who thereafter were friends, so much so that Adams would tell Godkin some of his most guarded secrets. But Adams, much though he might seem one, was *not* a reformer. He was a writer of incalculable powers, a practical politician, and on occasion both at once. Also, in his special way, he was consistently a *radical*. An instance was his article.

Evarts and Curtis had claimed before the court that their arguments formed a unified position. H. B. A. replied in the *Nation* that their arguments only "met without connecting."

Curtis had held that the government's power to issue irredeemable legal tender could be inferred from a power explicitly stated in the Constitution: the power to borrow money. He said that the inferred power was "subordinate, appropriate, and necessary" to the stated power. But H. B. A. rejected the argument on the ground that it claimed for the government a right to declare the dollar worth more than it was and a right to force the citizens to accept a declared value as if it were a real. In other words, Curtis had mistakenly said that the government was empowered by the Constitution to be dishonest and tyrannical.

Evarts had held that the government had a right to issue irredeemable paper money *in an emergency* because it could be inferred from the Constitution that the government had the right to protect itself. He held in addition that the right to decide what was or was not an emergency had been vested by the Constitution in Congress. Finally he held that the Legal Tender Act was constitutional because a famous clause in the Constitution, at least as *he* construed it, gave Congress "authority for *all* legislation that is necessary and proper" for the government to perform its listed powers. But H. B. A. rejected Evarts's arguments on the ground that the attorney general had claimed unlimited powers for a limited government.

Adams's reply would be read in Washington. Evarts would read it, perhaps with a sense that the anvil was hammering hard. Chase would read it and wish the other justices of the court would read it also. McCulloch and Wells would read it, possibly with rising hopes of the country's regaining the lost paradise of a redeemable currency. But Adams had not contributed his short article to the *Nation* with a view to earning the good opinion of high officials in Washington. The language he had used was that of an American speaking openly and seriously to all other Americans.

The key sentence of his article said, "Our Constitution, with its doctrine of limited powers, was supposed to have settled the principle that our Government, unlike most other governments, could legally do only those acts which of right might be done; that there was in it, speaking in general terms, no supreme power, even in the last resort, to make wrong right or false true." The sentence could seem a stumper, hard to read. It however could be read, and readers who read it would know that H. B. A. was a defender of the Constitution, of freedom, and of honesty in government who would not easily be induced to sacrifice the people's inalienable rights. What perhaps was still more important, he could capably resist the government's overstepping its rightful powers.

8

A TIME IN THE CLOUDS

The Chief met Senator Sumner at a dinner in Massachusetts and took pains to be courteous. He knew Sumner was starting south for the convening of Congress, and he thought courtesy on his part would be helpful to Henry. He advised his son, "This will smooth your path. . . ."[1]

Soon in the capital, Henry spied the senator at a distance. He ran to greet him. Sumner was taken aback, had no idea an Adams might be in Washington, yet responded politely, grew indulgent, affable, even warm. Their old friendship seemed to stir and come back to life.

Henry reported the encounter to his father. C. F. Adams took a dark view of Sumner and feared he would overshadow Grant, either by forcing Grant to make him secretary of state or by continuing to domineer in the Senate. ". . . he means to be Dictator," the Chief replied, "whether in or out of the Cabinet."[2]

Moorfield Storey, a Harvard graduate and law student, had come to Washington as Sumner's amanuensis. One evening, Storey visited Attorney General Evarts and was thrown into the company of a "strange young man . . . who was monopolizing the conversation, as it seemed to me, and laying down the law with a certain assumption." "I took quite a prejudice against him . . . but the next day I met him in the street and he was so charming and his voice was so pleasant that my prejudice vanished. This was Henry Adams . . . ."[3]

Acquaintance with Storey improved Adams's chance of renewed, complete acceptance by Sumner. When last seen by Henry in the capital, in March 1861, the senator had lived in rented bachelor's lodgings. In December 1868, he lived grandly as owner of a new house looking into Lafayette Square—a relic of his abortive marriage. Not a rich man, he could hardly afford so large a dwelling. Yet he seemed to prize it and was bounteously hospitable. Henry became a frequent guest at his table and found the meals excellent and the conversation instructive.

At another function in Massachusetts, the Chief met Grant, chancing upon him when the president-to-be was putting on white gloves. He and Grant dined in close proximity, and the Chief sent Henry word that the general was obstinate, silent, and cold.[4]

Henry meanwhile had become acquainted with Brigadier General Adam Badeau, a neighbor on G Street who had served on Grant's staff. Badeau was writing Grant's biography and waiting for a federal appointment. Henry read the published portion of the biography and thought it "no ordinary book." He and the biographer discovered they could trust each other. Responding to Henry's inquiries, Badeau said that Grant was not intelligent; not, that is, in the usual sense. At army headquarters during the war, the supreme commander had listened to ideas developed by others and had shown exceptional ability to choose a course and pursue it with energy. Henry took the information to mean that Grant *was* intelligent and when president would act.[5]

"American Finance, 1865–1869," Adams's article for the *Edinburgh Review*, was outlined in his mind before he started to write it. In the privacy of his rooms, he wrote and rewrote the article for six weeks, making every improvement he could devise.

When far along in his task, on Tuesday, January 12, 1869, he wrote to Commissioner Wells, "I hope I shall have the chance of a talk with you before long." On Saturday, Wells replied by messenger. He said that Atkinson was staying with him and he wished Adams would join them on Sunday evening. Congressman Garfield would be there, and "possibly one or two others." In fact, one other person was invited, Deputy Commissioner of the Revenue Francis A. Walker, of western Massachusetts. Like Garfield, Walker was a former Union general.

Held at Wells's residence, the Sunday gathering was secret. Present were men in office—Wells, Walker, and Garfield—and men not in office—Adams and Atkinson. All were aware that Grant had failed to outline a national program. Their purpose in meeting was to sketch the domestic portion of such a program. When fully sketched, it would be given to Grant, if he were willing to take it.

An excellent judge of his own writings, Adams knew in advance that Reeve would accept "American Finance, 1865–1869" and publish it when desired, in the April *Edinburgh Review*. The article was designed to perform six main functions. It provided a history of the way the U. S. government financed the War of the Rebellion.

It told English readers to beware of American prosperity and not expect impossible returns from American investments. It supported Commissioner Wells, whose appointment had months to run and could be renewed by Grant. It invited the attention of the incoming secretary of the treasury by summarizing the work of his three immediate predecessors. It outlined the domestic part of a suggested national program. And it said that Grant's inaugural address would be "energetic."[6]

The article was far better than Adams would ever admit.[7] That he knew its value showed in his asking Reeve to supply him copies printed as pamphlets. The pamphlet copies were needed. It was urgent that Wells, Walker, Garfield, Adams, and Atkinson have the article in their hands in convenient form. Published anonymously in London, the article would set forth the domestic program they wanted Grant to adopt.[8]

While completing the second article of his projected series, Henry looked ahead to the climactic fifth, to be written in 1870. He supposed its subject might be "rings," meaning combinations of persons in the United States, in and out of office, who were using office for personal gain, sometimes on a large scale. He wrote to Charles on January 22, 1869: "I want to be advertised and the easiest way is to do something obnoxious and do it well. I can work up an article on 'rings' which, if *published in England*, would I think create excitement . . . and cover me with odium. . . . No home publication will act on America like foreign opinion. I am not afraid of unpopularity and I will do it."

On January 27, Henry wrote again about his possible article. He said his "Rings" could not be written rapidly. "I am going to make it monumental, a piece of history and a blow at democracy. I mean to put into it all I've got in matter, thought and style. . . ."[9]

He seemed excited, even inspired. He told Charles he also had an idea for a popular article about the expedients of traders who made profits out of the currency. ". . . these fields are gloriously rich and stink like hell if only we were of the force to distil their flowers."

Telling Charles he might work up an article that would be "a blow at democracy," Henry could seem to say he disliked democracy. He in fact loved democracy and for that reason hated its all-too-numerous disfigurements.[10]

Among the causes of his excitement, none was more present in his thoughts than the unfinished draft of *Democracy*. The draft had taken for its starting point the meeting of Mrs. Sturgis Hooper and Charles Sumner in Washington. Its pages inescapably were redolent of Alice and the senator. That the public would relish a *roman à clef* was a foregone conclusion, and the public's weakness could certainly be played upon to advantage, if that were an object; but Henry had himself to please; and he had no wish whatever to write a novel in which the characters could be "identified." On the contrary, he was bent on writing an actual novel with independently realized, original characters.[11]

As things were, he was still unready to write it. The inevitable followed. Unprepared to go forward in the one and only novel he cared to write, he continued thinking about it. Daily in Washington, he entered houses such as its characters might rent or own. Week by week, a possible plot grew clearer. As before, an aging ambitious senator, lonely and displeased by his rented lodgings, could crave a better life as the married resident-owner of a fine house, and, beyond that, a term or two as president. But on second thought the ambitious senator could be leaving the Senate to enter the Cabinet in a new administration. He could become, not the new secretary of state, but the new secretary of the treasury. The widow he meets could be a New Yorker, mother of an infant who died. (Loo had lived in New York when first married, and had lost a child.) It would suffice if the widow and the senator did not marry; if instead they merely came close to being engaged—only to see their near-engagement unravel.

Ideas for *Democracy* were a gain but not the gain that Henry needed most. Of his problems, the hard-to-develop novel and the fifth article for English publication, the knottier was the article. He was yet to learn what the article would be about. He was having ideas, none convincing. What he lacked was a great or overwhelming subject.

Before the war, Senator Sumner had been much in Europe. He was introduced to Richard Cobden and John Bright and began correspondences with both. The correspondences were semi-public and worked strongly to Sumner's advantage. In January 1869, his still-continuing exchanges with Bright were understood in America and England to be important.

Henry Adams had known Cobden; he knew Bright far better than Sumner did; and he was on excellent terms with another English leader much interested in the United States, William E. Forster. If he wished to correspond with an English politician, he could reasonably try writing to either Bright or Forster. When less than a month in Washington, on November 13, 1868, he had written to Forster.[12]

Simultaneously with Adams's sending his letter, a new British government had been formed. Gladstone became prime minister and Forster minister of education. Bright, the first nonconformist ever admitted to a British Cabinet, was named president of the Board of Trade.

The interim U. S. minister to England, replacing C. F. Adams, was Reverdy Johnson, formerly senator from Maryland. Johnson and a new foreign secretary, Lord Clarendon, speedily negotiated a treaty creating machinery for a settlement of the Alabama Claims. The treaty was signed in London on January 14, 1869. To take effect, it would have to be ratified by a two-thirds vote of the U. S. Senate.

Sumner remained chairman of the Senate foreign relations committee. If he entered the Cabinet as Grant's secretary of state, he would have a voice concerning the treaty. If he stayed in the Senate, he could keep his chairmanship and work effectively to ratify or defeat the treaty. In either event, his hatreds and frustrations would come into play. From his point of view, Minister Reverdy Johnson was a Southern Democrat who had been appointed minister to England by another Southern Democrat, President Andrew Johnson. The Senate had confirmed Reverdy Johnson's appointment unanimously; and later the Senate had failed to convict Andrew Johnson, remove him from the presidency, and create an opening for a radical Republican. For all these reasons, in late January 1869, it was expected that Sumner would try to nullify Minister Johnson's "Alabama treaty."

Since mid-December, in secret, Henry Adams had waited for an answer from William Forster. None had come, and he had to wonder why. On February 3, 1869, he tried again by writing to John Bright. He told Bright he had moved to Washington and become a writer. Yet his letter was political. Bright would at once understand that Adams was in Washington as both writer and politician. Such double activity was familiar in England. Recently-ejected Prime Minister Disraeli had enlivened the world with several novels.

Adams's letter to Bright differed from Sumner's letters to Bright in being secret. Moreover, Adams's letter was not really a letter to Bright, nor even a letter that Bright alone could be expected to answer. Its contents were such that, on receiving it, Bright would have to show it to Lord Clarendon. Both men would have a say in the answer, should there be one. And there might not be one.

Once they studied Adams's letter, Bright and Clarendon would see that Bright's new correspondent was presenting them a choice. They could trust Sumner, from whom Bright had received streams of letters, or they could trust Henry Adams, whom Bright knew well and had talked with many times. Trust was the issue, for Adams asked Bright to join him in a secret effort to improve relations between their countries. He explained, "Long before returning to America I had made up my mind to live in Washington, and, since the field of public position was by our arrangements practically shut to me, to devote myself to a literary career." He said he was writing, not for newspapers, but for "more elaborate periodicals." He further said: ". . . I hold opinions on two points, for which my English education and especially your own influence and that of Mr[.] Cobden are principally responsible. On one side I have warm feeling of good-will to England, in spite of all she made me suffer. On the other hand, I am a firm free-trader. . . ."

Adams explained that the occasion for his letter was the necessity of his publicly declaring the opinions of a new school in American politics. He was ready to state opinions about free trade and about America's political corruption, which he said was worse than England's. He needed help only in relation to American foreign policy—a "delicate" subject. The general consensus was that the Alabama treaty would not be ratified by the Senate. He had learned from Sumner that Bright had written anxiously to him about the treaty. Adams feared that Sumner would oppose it. He knew that Grant was against it. Assistance being needed, he said to Bright: "I want you to write me precisely how you feel about it, and I shall make use of your letter in the most effective way I can, without absolute publication. If you would do this so that I could have your opinions within a month I think I could help [in?] the struggle."

Adams requested a reply within a month because he wanted to receive and use the reply prior to Grant's inauguration. Clearly he intended to influence the new president and secretary of state even before they took office. But just as clearly Bright could not gratify Adams's wish without serious risk. In relation to a matter of the utmost weight, Adams was urging the use of informal, indeed irregular, methods.

As seen by onlookers in Washington, H. B. Adams had been in the capital for three months with no occupation other than recently beginning to grow a full beard. He obviously was killing time, often in the company of two Bostonians younger than himself, Moorfield Storey and Samuel Hoar, Jr., the pardon clerk in the Justice Department.[13] By Washington standards, Adams's behavior was normal and easy to account for. He was either the already-chosen but unannounced future assistant secretary of state or something comparable in the Treasury.

Henry got wind of the gossip about him. He was angered enough to tell Charles he wished he *were* tendered a political plum. If he were offered a desirable place, he could refuse it and forever be "secure from such suspicions." "If Evarts gets the State or the Treasury, I shall be supposed to have my choice of positions, which will answer the purpose just as well."

The third son seemed irritated, yet self-assured. His letters to Charles contained very strong statements. He claimed he could prosper in any political circumstances. He said he cared "very little" about the incoming administration—could easily "get on without it."[14]

Charles alerted their father that Henry was deluding himself with dreams of prosperity. In kindness, the Chief wrote to Henry, "I warn you not to be too sanguine of early success from any efforts you may be able to make."[15]

With positive concern, C. F. Adams learned that Henry was squandering time on "private theatricals" and "silly young women." He did not want to criticize. Indeed he did not. He assured the prodigal, ". . . you know best."[16] But there was no doubting that Henry had unusual tendencies. He said in his letters that the people he liked best were ordinary people who were enjoying themselves; also that what he wanted most was a sense that he could experience *feelings*. In a letter to Charles sent on February 3—the day he wrote secretly to Bright—he mentioned that he was leaving Washington to pass an evening in Baltimore. "I am going to a masked ball. My jaded appetite needs the stimulant of mask and domino, under which I can invent sentiment."

Eight years earlier, in February 1861, the Chief and Henry had watched an unprecedented horde of office seekers appear in Washington, mostly fellow Republicans. In 1869, Henry watched the onrush of another Republican horde. The sight was expected but upsetting. He wrote to David Wells that his "disgust" was "too strong for comfort."

One cause of disgust was a contrast. Many of the office seekers in the capital were persons who hoped to be paid but not work.

They were variant Charley Wilsons. Henry meanwhile was performing hard work for which he was not being paid. He and
industrious Charles had been writing articles for two years with
very slight reward in dollars. Henry wrote to Charles, "Our labored
work does not gain us all it ought." He said his own articles were
"work absolutely thrown away."

A greater cause of disgust was knowledge of the country's
political history. During the first ten administrations of the U. S.
government, from the inauguration of Washington through the
retirement of J. Q. Adams, lesser employees in the executive branch
had mostly been kept in their posts if doing good work and not ill-
behaved. Beginning with the inauguration of Andrew Jackson in
1829, a new system was introduced on a large scale. Incumbents
were removed and their places given to supporters of victorious
Jackson. Once tried, the "spoils system" was retained. Like the
system it supplanted, it was a mere custom, subject to change. Its
disadvantages were many. It made membership in a political party
the basis for the awarding of office. It placed no value on willingness or ability to work. It diminished the power of the executive
branch to choose its employees and in like amount transferred that
power to party managers, the members of Congress, and more
recently to an organization of Union veterans, the Grand Army of
the Republic. Moreover, it resulted in forced taxation. Under the
threat of losing their jobs, employees in the executive branch were
often required to divert a fraction of their pay to party coffers.

Adams had a name for these and similar disadvantages. They
were what he meant when he spoke of "political corruption." As
part of the suggested national program that he and others were
developing, he wanted a government that could capably govern.
He had no revolution more at heart than the awarding of public
office only to public servants who would serve. With this object, he
hoped to restore the old power of the government's executive
branch to choose, keep, reward, and promote its lesser officials.[17]
Indeed he believed such a change would *have* to be effected. He
wrote to Atkinson: "The whole root of the evil is in *political*
corruption. . . . The more I study its working, the more dread I
feel at the future."

John Lothrop Motley wanted to be minister to England, was
rich, and had Sumner's backing. He conferred in Boston with C. F.
Adams. The Chief wrote to Henry, advising him that Motley would
soon be in Washington and would be staying with Congressman
Hooper. The implication was that Motley might want to confer

with Henry also, most easily during opportunities at Sumner's house or at Hooper's.

For lack of evidence, no account can be given of Henry Adams's dealings with Hooper, except that the Boston congressman chaired the House committee on ways and means and Henry had seen fit to quote and commend him in "American Finance, 1865–1869." The article put Wicked Sam in a favorable light. Believing an action by the House had been "hostile to the public interest, and injurious to the national character," Hooper had reacted, Adams said, with "extraordinary defiance."[18]

Disappointing many persons, Grant had said his Cabinet appointments would not be disclosed prior to his taking office. Adams tried to view the news as good. Looking in one direction towards Grant's "silent despotism" and in the other towards Congress, "the many-headed monster," he applauded the despotism.

So aided, he entered a twenty-day phase of expiring hope. In the absence of further news, the country invented lists of possible future Cabinet members. The lists tended to converge towards a single list, very dismal to read. Henry wrote to Charles on February 23: "We here look for a reign of western mediocrity, but perhaps one appreciates least the success of the steamer, when one lives in the engine-room." He drew a conclusion: "Life is not worth living— of that I am satisfied. My pleasantest and most satisfactory hours are those I waste in innocent but frivolous society."

No answer came from Bright. On Thursday, March 4, 1869, Grant was sworn in as president and gave an inaugural address that was not energetic. It emphasized a line, "Let us have peace." The line was memorable but in Henry's view unclear. It was left in the air and related to nothing.[19]

Like everyone else, Henry was anxious to learn who would serve in the Cabinet. On Friday, March 5, he went to the Capitol and stood near the doors of the Senate. The Senate closed the doors, went into secret session, obtained Grant's list of names, and, in deference to his four-star rank, confirmed the choices without ado.

The doors opened, and the names were announced. Some were welcome, but two were grotesque. The State Department was given to aged Congressman Elihu Washburne of Illinois, a stranger to foreign affairs. The Treasury was given to a New York businessman, the inventor of the department store, aged Alexander T. Stewart, a stranger to public finance. *Not* chosen to head the State Department, Senator Sumner was dealt an injury too grievous to be measured.[20]

Reviewed, the Washburne appointment related personally to Grant. The new secretary of state was one of the general's long-time backers for the presidency. The Stewart appointment seemed to relate personally to the president and his wife. Ulysses and Julia Grant had recently sought the company of New Yorkers and evidently were impressed by money. They had met Mr. Stewart, and he possibly had impressed them most. Still active in business, he reputedly was worth $40,000,000.

Sometime earlier, Gurney had learned that Henry Adams would contribute an article titled "The Session" for the April *North American*. He notified Adams that the manuscript would have to be mailed from Washington by March 11, a Thursday.

When he left the Capitol on March 5, Adams had not yet begun the article. The moment was exceedingly worrying for him. He was shaken by the Washburne and Stewart appointments. He had received not a word from Reeve about "American Finance, 1865–1869." He continued not to have answers from Forster and Bright. And he saw decided possibilities of war between the United States and England.[21]

Several times in recent weeks, Adams had been admitted to Chairman Sumner's study on the second floor of his house. There the senator had freely expressed his "views, policy and purposes," which, as Adams later wrote, "were sometimes even more astounding than his curious gaps or lapses of omniscience."[22] The dates of these private meetings are nowhere stated in surviving evidence; but the views, policy, and purposes that most astonished Adams could only have been imparted at the first workable hour after Sumner was apprised that Grant had not chosen him to be secretary of state. That hour must have been late on Friday, March 5, or sometime on Saturday, March 6.

To share Adams's astonishment requires knowledge of recent American foreign policies. Since 1861, control of the foreign affairs of the United States had been wielded in large measure by Seward. His work could be thought superb. During the Rebellion, he successfully avoided war with England and France without making concessions to either power. In the circumstances, his performance was stunning, and the performance was tantamount to a policy.[23]

Adams himself had a policy, in four parts. He favored peace at all times with all countries. He favored permanent peace and close friendship with England as a step toward general peace in the world. He opposed acquisitions of territory, believing the United

States had sufficiently enlarged its borders and should set the world an example by minding its business. And he favored free trade.[24]

Ironically, the policy that Seward had pursued during the war was not the policy that Seward would have preferred. As viewed by Adams, Seward's *preferred* policy was egoistic—framed, that is, to enhance its author's reputation for statesmanship; also the policy was partly secret; and it was harmless in practice only because Seward's efforts to put it into effect were delayed by the creation of the Confederacy. After the war, Seward purchased Alaska from Russia. He also attempted to purchase the Isthmus of Panama and the Danish islands in the West Indies. Trouble entered when one realized that Seward's achieved and attempted purchases were mere beginnings of a series of wished-for acquisitions which would transform the United States into an American Empire. The imagined acquisitions would bring under one government all of North America, including British Columbia, Canada, perhaps Bermuda and the Bahamas; all of Central America; Cuba and the lesser islands of the West Indies; also the Sandwich Islands and other archipelagoes in the Pacific. Persons who knew the scope of Seward's dream sometimes tended to discount it as braggadocio or insincere grandiosity. Adams thought the dream an actual danger, if only because the territories Seward had been part-secretly meaning to buy belonged almost entirely to owners unwilling to sell them.[25]

Sumner too had a policy. In his study on March 5 or 6, he fully revealed it to Adams. The senator's dream resembled Seward's in being vast. Sumner explained that, although he had been denied the appointment as secretary of state, he alone would conduct the country's foreign affairs. He affirmed that he would annul the Alabama treaty by opposing it in the Senate. He said he immediately would require Great Britain to make amends, not only for the destruction of Union merchant ships by rebel cruisers during the war, but also for all British additions to the fighting power of the South—for every British act which had prolonged the Slavepower's hated life. He said the British government in response might cede Canada and British Columbia to the United States, but he did not anticipate such a response. He instead expected that the British would balk and that the United States would initiate a universal war. Naval and military engagements would be fought on the planet's oceans and continents. The British Empire would shrink. The roles played in the world by Russia and the United States would expand. Russia would emerge possessor of India. The United States would emerge possessor of Canada.[26]

Adams liked Sumner, even admired him.[27] After their hour together that Friday or Saturday, he seemed as friendly to Sumner as before. As if nothing had happened, he went to his rooms and started drafting "The Session."

On Sunday, Sumner spoke with Grant at the White House. Later in the day, he visited the British minister, Edward Thornton, and harangued him in cryptic terms. In consequence, on Monday, the minister reported to Lord Clarendon at the Foreign Office. Thornton's letter was detailed, interesting, and important.

> . . . [Sumner] told me that he had seen General Grant . . . and had had a long conversation with him about the questions with England. He found that Grant's whole foreign policy referred to that country and particularly to the "Alabama" question; that he [Grant] had said that a Minister must be sent to England with peremptory instructions upon that subject; that England must meet the case at once and acknowledge her liability; that there was to be no mention of money; . . . that there was no amount of money which would ever pay [for] the damage and injuries she had done to the United States. I replied [to Sumner] that we had yielded [in the Johnson-Clarendon treaty] all that had been asked of us, and had perhaps done more than we ought to have done in order to show our good will towards the United States; but in spite of all my efforts, Mr[.] Sumner would not be induced to say what it was that General Grant expected us to do, or would instruct his Minister to ask; as however he [Sumner] repeated two or three times with great emphasis that there could be no question of *money*, I have no doubt in my own mind that the United States mean to demand, as the only acceptable compensation for the wrongs done them, the cession of Canada and British Columbia; and that if this be not granted, they will leave the question open until they shall have an opportunity of taking our possessions in spite of us. . . .
>
> Mr[.] Sumner added that he had recommended General Grant to send Mr[.] Motley as Minister to England. I believe you already know this gentleman; I am only just acquainted with him; but I understand that he is extremely bitter against us for the course we pursued during the late war in this country.
>
> It is possible that all Sumner told me as having been said by Grant, may have been said by himself to Grant, but I much fear that the latter has strong feelings . . . against England.[28]

By writing "ten hours a day for four days" while giving other hours to "politics," Adams finished "The Session" and mailed it on March 11, meeting his deadline. In the interval, several developments crushed him with work and greatly altered his prospects.

The developments were concurrent. Evidently on Monday, March 8, he received a tardy letter from Reeve saying "American Finance, 1865–1869" would appear in the April *Edinburgh Review*.

The editor deemed it a work of the "greatest importance"—"the best article on American affairs ever printed in an English periodical." Proofs accompanied the letter. Adams corrected the proofs and mailed them on March 9, but they had been so late in coming that they could not reach London before the issue went to press.[29]

At an early but unrecorded moment, an unidentified person—conceivably but not probably Henry Adams—mentioned to Chairman Sumner that Alexander Stewart could not lawfully serve as secretary of the treasury. To serve under existing law, Stewart would first have to divest himself of his businesses.[30] Sumner acted on the tip; Grant acceded to Stewart's departure from the Cabinet; and, as his replacement, the president chose George S. Boutwell, a radical Republican Congressman from Massachusetts whom Adams in confidence had once lumped with Sumner as "permanently insane."[31] Other than his political ties with Sumner, Boutwell had no qualifications for the office.[32]

Washburne too was removed. Julia Grant had been kindly treated by a new-made friend, Julia Fish, of New York. Mrs. Grant wanted Mrs. Fish's company in the capital. A possible means of securing the first lady's object was the appointment of Mr. Fish as secretary of state. Washburne therefore was prevailed upon to yield the State Department and take the French mission and Hamilton Fish was named to succeed him. An inoffensive gentleman-politician, Mr. Fish was remembered for mute inaction when governor of New York and senator before the war. He was greatly surprised at being required to head the State Department, but he hoped not to disgrace the office.[33]

From Adams's point of view, Fish, though perhaps better than Washburne, was a national setback. Boutwell was a national disaster. On March 11, Henry wrote to Charles: "Boutwell is not a Wells man." The appointments, he said, were not the ones that were needed. "But we are in the boat and have got to stay there."

The phrase "in the boat" meant in the government. Despite the Fish and Boutwell appointments, Henry Adams meant to come and go as an uninvited guest in the palace of Grant's administration. The "we" he spoke of included himself, Wells, Walker, Garfield, and Atkinson. In his view, a new school in American politics had existed, albeit secretly, for many weeks. Wells had been the initial director. The present director was Adams. The school's purpose was the enactment of a domestic program with Grant's consent, mainly by deciding the policies and procedures of the Treasury. By appointing Boutwell, Grant had gone a long way to defeat the purpose. Thus the success of the school could well depend on Boutwell's being dislodged. Meanwhile the school would gain if it added members. The best candidate appeared to be another Ohioan and former general, the new secretary of the interior, Jacob Dolson Cox. A second recruit would be Charles.

Motley, Norton, and Lowell were all in Washington seeking missions. Back from Austria, Hay was angling for the mission to Portugal. In appearance, Henry Adams was wholly at leisure. On March 30, he wrote to Gaskell that he was "quietly waiting for the explosion of my two fire-crackers on the 1st April. . . ."

Waiting meant reading. ". . . journeys always do interest me; I have done nothing this fortnight but read books of travel." Waiting also meant walks. Spring had come, bringing alternations of rain and sun. ". . . I devote four hours every day . . . to rambling over the country here and picking up a sort of familiarity with nature. . . . I live comfortably and rather cheaply on the whole; at least, well within my means, and as there are few men here who have any means, and the members of Congress and the Cabinet have only about twice my income or less, I . . . am thought a Croesus. . . . My despondent fit has . . . been succeeded by cheerfulness and contentment, thanks, I believe, to my long walks and careful life, without medical interference, but I am thin and bearded and very—very bald."

Judge E. Rockwood Hoar, a Massachusetts radical Republican, but friendly to the Adamses, had been named by Grant as attorney general. An early result of Hoar's appointment was a letter to Henry Adams from Francis Barlow. Currently a successful New York lawyer, the much-wounded former general had learned that Adams was in Washington and was not there for nothing. He asked Henry to help him get the appointment as federal attorney in the southern district of New York.[34]

Henry's reply was lost, but a second letter shortly came, likewise asking for help in getting an office. The writer was Charles. Henry was forced to say, and may previously have said to Barlow: "I can't get you an office. The only members of this Government that I have met are mere acquaintances. . . . Wells has just about as much influence as I have. . . . Judge Hoar has his hands full. . . ."

Meanwhile, Henry had *not* been waiting. In secret, he had moved from a strong political position to a still stronger political position. Oddly, the move had academic beginnings. Many weeks before, the presidency of Harvard had fallen vacant. C. F. Adams had been offered the place and had refused it. The candidate preferred by the faculty was Professor Gurney. Obliged to work simultaneously as teacher, editor, and candidate for the country's most prestigious academic appointment, Gurney was overwhelmed with duties. In part to lighten them, he arranged that Henry Adams should serve the *North American Review* as editor for politics, with a free hand concerning political articles and freedom to publish his own articles as signed editorials. The change possibly followed talks in Washington between Adams, Lowell, and Norton. It became effective with the April issue and at first was known only within a very limited circle of persons. One was Charles. Another was Godkin, with whom Gurney was newly close.[35]

The April *North American* did not immediately go to press. Adams wanted the issue to be more political. He asked that the manuscript of "The Session" be returned to him for revision. He would not make the revision till Sumner spoke in the Senate concerning the Alabama treaty. As revised, the article would principally relate to foreign affairs and would be balanced by an article on domestic affairs titled "The Financial Condition of the United States." The balancing article would be written by a frequent contributor to Godkin's *Nation*, a Wall Street stockbroker and economist, James B. Hodgskin.[36]

Bright had received Adams's letter and evidently showed it to Lord Clarendon. An answer was ruled out; either that or much postponed.

On March 21, 1869, a disturbing letter reached the foreign secretary from Edward Thornton. Clarendon instructed an aide to copy a portion of the letter. Next day, marking it "Private," he sent the copied portion to Bright with a covering note:

> I enclose an extract from Thornton's letter recd yesterday. Sumner is now our worst enemy in the U. S.[,] & it will remain to be seen how far he can influence the President[,] who is not I fear overfriendly to us.[37]

Bright apparently studied the note and extract, talked with Clarendon about possible courses of action, and was encouraged to write privately to Henry Adams. On March 24, he sent Adams a skillfully-worded, very legible, eight-page letter.[38]

Henry meanwhile seemed more idle than before. He wrote to Charles: ". . . I dawdle here. The life is pleasant. . . . Besides, I want to see what the devil is going to happen." He mentioned that he could not fathom Grant. "I am astonished by his behavior, but I am even more puzzled than astonished. . . ."

With the help of pretended idleness, Henry was improving his contacts. Old Sam Ward came to Washington on one of his famous visits. A New Yorker, international celebrity, and occasional lobby-ist, Ward knew everyone and was welcome everywhere. He and Henry Adams possibly had earlier crossed paths in Europe. They somehow met in Washington. Instantly, they assumed the attributes of boon companions.

The new assistant secretary of state was J. C. Bancroft Davis, of Massachusetts, a nephew of George Bancroft. In June 1862, Davis had dined with the Adamses, Bright, and others at the Legation.[39] Similarly, in London in July 1863, he had attended a breakfast given by Evarts for Cobden, Cyrus Field, Henry Adams, and others.[40] Davis and Adams may not have met since; but in April 1869, if so inclined, Adams could call on him as an acquaintance; and Davis was not so high-ranking that he could not go to Adams's rooms and share his meals.

Bright's letter reached Adams on April 8. What he did with the letter is not known, but it was Bright's intention that his letter be put to use. Possibly Adams lent it to William Evarts, who was still in the capital. He may have lent it to Sam Ward. Either man could freely visit the State Department for a word with Hamilton Fish or Bancroft Davis. Neither would be thought to have in his pocket a letter from the English Cabinet addressed to Adams. Once closeted with Fish or Davis, the bearer could produce the letter and make explanations.

Marked "private," Bright's letter was measured and clear. It was partly given to a defense of U. S. Minister Reverdy Johnson. Its main idea was that Americans would find they had warm friends among the English, if they only would seek them. But the contents of the letter were as nothing compared to its sheer existence. Its having been written and mailed were proofs that Chairman Sumner, the much-publicized American contact of the English radicals, was discredited in their eyes and superseded by private citizen Henry Adams. Any careful reader of the letter would see that it was written with Lord Clarendon's consent. No other assumption was possible.

A last consideration was still more important. The British letter was a reminder that, of the persons then in Washington, precisely one had known at first hand in London the frictions and animosi-ties felt between the United States and Great Britain subsequent to the outbreak of America's civil war. It followed that, in the vacuum that Sumner would create if he induced the Senate to reject the Alabama treaty, Henry Adams might best be asked to design a more acceptable treaty. That of course could be done without noise or the making of records.

On April 12, 1869, the Senate confirmed the appointment of J. L. Motley as minister to England. On April 13, Chairman Sumner denounced the Alabama treaty before the Senate with such effect that the members would later reject it with only one dissenting vote. On the 15th, the chairman's speech was published.

When he spoke, Sumner seemed heroically strong, both in force as a speaker and in ability to decide the course of the federal government. Almost alone, Henry Adams saw him as weak. Six weeks before in the senator's study, he had heard Sumner declare that, though barred from the highest place in the Cabinet, he would rule none the less as king of the Senate. The declaration was itself sufficient notice that the declarer was too disturbed to prevail. Sumner's speech against the Alabama Treaty again revealed weakness. It was a bid for general power made at the predictable cost of the bidder's influence in the government and the nation. Not without sadness, Adams would later recall, "Of all the crazy acts . . . Sumner ever did, and they are many, I think his speech on that occasion the maddest."[41]

There were unresolved problems relating to Minister Motley. One was the problem of securing him capable aides; the other the problem of his instructions. Prior to Motley's confirmation as minister, Adams had written to Gaskell: ". . . no doubt I might go with him if he goes, but you can imagine that I don't care for such a position. I shall however try to put a good fellow into it. . . ." Better than his word, Henry put *two* good fellows into office as aides in the English mission. One was Benjamin Moran, again retained as first secretary. The other was General Badeau as assistant secretary. The general had asked for a well-paid consulship in England and was showering attentions on Mrs. Grant to get it. His procedure would eventually lead to the desired result but for the present was ineffective. He accepted the second secretaryship in London as a stopgap.[42]

Norton and Lowell did not get missions. Hay was limited to being first secretary at Madrid, to learn Spanish. Luckless Motley had won the best mission but might better have lost it. A fierce contest began in Washington about his instructions. The contest was less about what he should be told than who should tell him. Sumner presupposed he could override the combined forces of Grant at the White House and Fish and Davis at the State Department. His error was egregious, yet would show itself for an error only slowly.

Adams wrote to Gaskell on April 19 and spoke as a man who had come to conclusions. "My hopes of the new Administration have all been disappointed; it is far inferior to the last. My friends have almost all lost ground. . . . My family is buried politically. . . . But I rather like all this, for no one can touch me and I have asked nothing of any living person. I express pretty energetic opinions all round, and I wait till the cards are played out. I can afford to wait."

By April 29, the flood of office seekers had practically vanished. Henry wrote to Charles: ". . . Washington is almost empty, and the country perfectly lovely. All the trees are in leaf, even the oaks. Such a place for wild-flowers I never saw."

A month late, the April *North American* appeared at subscribers' doorsteps. It contained an article, "The Session," signed by Henry Brooks Adams. The article spoke not only for its signer but also for the magazine—"this Review."[43] It had the marks of an editorial and served in part as an announcement of Adams's editorial status.

A copy of the issue was delivered to Sumner. He certainly noticed "The Session," scanned its pages, and saw that it was written by Henry Adams. He presumably saw as well that Henry sometimes referred to him by name, always in complimentary terms; also that the paper's treatment of Seward's foreign policy was openly critical. After such enjoyments, Sumner may well have closed his copy of the issue.

Adams had originally meant "The Session" to be an orderly review of a year of the nation's politics. Under the pressure of events, he had had to turn it into something wholly different, an undisguised political act. As published, the editorial ran to fifty paragraphs. Thirty concerned foreign affairs. In the thirty, Adams revealed the scope of Seward's visionary American empire. He outlined the history of the Alabama Claims since the demise of the Confederacy. He turned to the most dangerous aspects of the case, the hatred felt by Americans towards England and the opportunities their hatred might offer to politicians in Washington. He pointedly said: ". . . if there comes an appeal to arms, no great effort of the imagination is needed to foresee a political conspiracy, which will have for its object to throw British America into the arms of the United States and British India upon the bayonets of the Russian army."[44]

Without naming any particular member or members, the editorial attacked the Senate for voiding treaties already signed by the country with whom the United States wished to improve relations. Going further, it attacked the Senate for trying to take exclusive control of foreign affairs, at the expense of the White House, the State Department, and the nation's diplomats abroad. In both attacks, the word "Senate" was used in place of "Sumner." Yet Adams's editorial was really an assault on one politician, Sumner, and one foreign policy, his. If Sumner would never know it, a presumable reason would be that his unchecked egoism had rendered him fully able *not* to read.

Franklin Benjamin Sanborn, editor of a leading newspaper in Massachusetts, the *Springfield Republican*, received the April *North American*, read an editorial it contained, and rushed into print. On May 1, he published an editorial of his own. Titled "Another Adams," it concerned Henry Adams, third son of Charles Francis Adams. Mistakenly, it assumed that young Adams was presently in Massachusetts. Though meant as a compliment, it was marred by errors concerning Henry's history. Among other things, it said: "During his father's residence in England, Henry Adams lived abroad, and amused his leisure with writing articles for a Boston newspaper. Of late he has been a contributor to the Nation, and during the past winter, while living in Washington, he divided his time between 'society' and journalism. He had the reputation of being one of the three best dancers in the capital. . . ."

When he saw the editorial, Henry would be amused by the praise of his dancing. Yet what Sanborn principally tried to do was commend a new Adams for mastery in politics. The editor directed attention to the April *North American*, to which Henry Brooks Adams had contributed a "long and brilliant paper on 'The Session.'" Sanborn explained, ". . . with some conceit and some pedantry, but with more ability than either, he [Adams] reviews the doings and omissions . . . of the fortieth Congress; including . . . the rejection of the Alabama treaty."[45]

The *Springfield Republican* was read in Boston. Charles learned that Henry had been described in the *Republican* as conceited. He wrote to him and repeated the accusation. Henry fired back: "High appreciation of ourselves was always a strong point in our family, though I protest by Heaven that my conceit is not due to admiration of myself but to contempt for everyone else." Changing the subject, he turned to an actual problem. "Wells has gone." ". . . Sam Ward and I are monarchs of all we survey." "Boutwell however is too much for us. Grant's Cabinet[,] except Cox and Hoar, is all pretty rough, but this particular damn fool is the damnedest of all."

Henry's punishment had not ended. The Chief too thought him conceited. He mailed him a copy of Sanborn's editorial and subjected him to a vigorous lecture. Conceit, the father explained, was "a weakness even many strong minds fall into at first quite unawares." ". . . as you clearly expect to mix much with men, I advise you to remove this obstacle to your influence with them altogether."[46]

A package came to Henry's rooms. From London, it contained six copies of "American Finance, 1868–1869" in pamphlet form. When distributed to the members of his school, the copies would consolidate his leadership with regard to domestic affairs.

A check followed from editor Reeve. It gave Adams £30 in English gold, equivalent to $200 in depreciated American money. Although not large, the amount compared favorably with the $75 in greenbacks which Whitman Gurney could spare his associate editor for "The Session."

Comments multiplied about the country's new Adams. Persons who neglected to observe the rising star were instructed by Godkin to do so. On May 6, the *Nation* reviewed the *North American* and advised: ". . . ["The Session"] is a thoughtful, forcible, and highly suggestive article, which, let us hope, will get a great deal of attention. What it says of the Alabama treaty, the treaty for the purchase of St. Thomas, Mr. Seward's diplomacy, the economic measures of the present Administration, the 'rings' that control the Senate and the House, the Tenure-of-Office Bill—is all talk upon subjects upon which everybody has talked; but these subjects have seldom been treated of [with?] anything like the independence of thought and plainness of sensible speech that Mr. Adams brings to the discussion of them."

Henry's gains were impressive even to him. He wrote to Gaskell: "My article on 'The Session' . . . has been read. For once I have smashed things generally and really exercised a distinct influence on public opinion by acting on the limited number of cultivated minds."

Motley received his instructions on May 10. He returned to Boston and, before sailing, conferred a second time with C. F. Adams. The Chief reported to Henry: "We talked freely and kindly together and I told him in confidence of much which he did not know in my time of service and especially of the Palmerston correspondence." He seemed to think that Sumner had ruined

Motley's mission before it could start. "Never was a man placed in a situation more awkward and disturbing."[47]

Henry's case was the obverse of Motley's. Charles could disparage and the Chief could instruct, but Henry was his own master. No one could give him orders. He had means at his disposal to affect domestic and foreign affairs. He had long since learned how to use them.

Of his means relating to foreign affairs, it could seem that the most important would be a continuous exchanging of letters with Bright. Henry judged differently. He had found to his satisfaction that his decisive contacts for the purpose of establishing permanent peace and close friendship with England were his contacts with *Americans*—with the Chief, William Evarts, and Bancroft Davis. He saw the advantage of getting many letters from John Bright, but he was keen enough to see that he might better write just two more letters to English Cabinet members and then keep silent.

It had occurred to him that Forster had been silent because excessively busy. Sometime in May, he wrote the minister of education a new letter accompanied by a copy of the April *North American*. The letter requested both that Forster read "The Session" and that he read as Henry's the unsigned article in the current *Edinburgh Review* titled "American Finance, 1865–1869." The request was not small. Forster was asked to read sixty pages of print.[48]

Bright was older than Forster and no longer in good health. Adams wished not to impose on his strength or his time. He waited till May 30 and then sent Bright a letter confined to topics concerning which Bright and Lord Clarendon would most need advice.

A pressing topic was Sumner. Adams told Bright that for a long while he had known that Bright "did not understand Sumner." ". . . I suspect that since his speech you understand him still less. . . ." The reason for lack of understanding, Adams explained, was an erroneous idea of the senator's mental powers. "He passes everywhere either for worse or better than he is, merely because people over-rate his mind."

Adams said that Sumner's speech had been "applauded universally." When it was given, Seward was no longer in Washington. Except that two other men spoke against it, Evarts and George T. Curtis, Adams had been "alone" in his opposition, "both in the press and in society."

The administration had quickly realized that the speech would have to be counteracted. Grant and Fish saw that "Sumner and the Senate must not be permitted to seize control of our foreign policy." Adams spelled out the consequence. "Mr[.] Fish therefore would have nothing to do with the speech, and Motley's instructions were not based upon it, as Mr[.] Sumner had intended."

Sumner had then joined with Fish in an effort to renew negotiations with England. At the critical instant, President Grant intervened. He "obstinately declared that he did not want a settlement with England, as he preferred what he calls the 'precedent'; that is, to do ourselves at some future time precisely those dishonorable acts of which we have so steadily complained when done by England."

Washington was deadlocked. Grant was hostile to England. Sumner was uneasy and worried. Fish leaned towards Seward's ideas but could not stir. There remained the people; and, if Henry Adams was well-informed, popular feeling could very easily turn towards war.

> . . . a war-fever once started would sweep all resistance before it, especially in the north-western States, where the temptation of seizing Canada is greatest. I do not want to be an alarmist, but I cannot see any likelihood that either the Republican or the Democratic party would dare to advocate peace if once war were proposed, and whatever individuals may say, these party organisations have little honesty in them and are ruled by ignorant and ambitious men.

In such a case, the U. S. government could not begin new talks with England without making demands that would sooner or later transform to an ultimatum, which if rejected would bring the nations to the point of war. Grant however had opposed all talks, and Adams was glad of it. "To wait is dangerous[,] but it is still more dangerous to act."

Adams suggested that after a year or two the Americans might have different and better ideas with respect to foreign policy. Meanwhile England could reduce—perhaps even remove—the risk of war. The needed measure was immediate independence for Canada. ". . . the essential point is that [England] . . . should without delay sever her political connection with Canada and all her territory on our continent. . . . If after that concession to us, we still make war, we shall hurt ourselves more than you."[49]

The letter to Bright did not seek, and did not get, a reply. And Adams was right in thinking that Forster had been silenced by excessive work. The minister of education had been so delighted to hear from Henry the previous November that he had carried his letter with him as a reminder to write. But elevation to the Cabinet made Forster too busy to write; a first delay had shortly made him too ashamed to write; and the labor of getting a bill through Parliament reforming the endowed British schools had made writing seem impossible.

The arrival of a new letter from Adams broke the spell of Forster's preoccupation. He read Henry's two articles. Simultaneously Motley reached London and tried to function as minister. Glancingly Forster and Motley met, without result.

Forster at last wrote to Adams. He said, "You are the most forgiving of men." He reported: "I have . . . managed to read both your articles . . . my sole reading barring blue books & newspapers for months, & have really enjoyed both. I admire your courage[,] candour & clearness, & much like the style." He invited Henry to write again. ". . . you would very much oblige me if you would tell me from time to time what you hear & think." Also he promised he would have nothing to do with Sumner's minister to England. "I have had but little talk with Motley. In fact[,] unless he himself seeks it[,] I fear I might do harm rather than good by venturing in the business of his mission."

Neither of Adams's letters to Forster has been found. According to Forster's one reply, Adams's second letter contained some "very interesting comments on our international relations." Again according to Forster, they were "strictly confidential."[50]

The drift of Adams's lost "comments" can perhaps be reconstructed. Henry had induced Forster to read two letters and two articles. In "The Session," Forster read a statement by Adams that the history of the Alabama Claims was pointing towards *a settlement in money, to be awarded by an international court of arbitrators.* Moreover, "The Session" mentioned a correspondence in the 1790s between British Minister Hammond and Secretary of State Jefferson. The article referred to a treaty devised at that time. Never ratified, the treaty had involved "a commission of five persons."[51]

The *wording* of Adams's lost comments did not matter. What mattered was their gist. Adams can be thought to have sketched an expectation: that Canada would become independent; that there would be a new treaty replacing the one rejected by the U. S. Senate; that the treaty would create a five-person international tribunal empowered to arbitrate the Alabama Claims; that the tribunal would impose a settlement in money; and that the settlement would lead to permanent peace and friendship between England and the United States.[52]

So envisioned, the near future would be unpleasant for England. She would have to prepare to hear an international decision, and then she would have to pay the United States. When payment was imposed, however, American hatred would end. Peace and friendship would begin to show their value.

9

SEASONS OF DEATH

I n one of his Sunday letters, Henry told his father he wanted to assemble some writings by his Adams grandmother and create a book. The Chief replied, ". . . I should like nothing better." He had sifted his mother's papers and "reduced their volume." Apprised that Henry wished to start at once, he expressed the papers to Washington.[1]

One was a narrative Louisa Catherine Adams had written of her life to her thirty-sixth year, another a narrative of a journey she had made from St. Petersburg to Paris in 1815. Henry so combined the narratives and a selection of letters as to form a continuous chronicle. The work agreed with him. He wrote to Gaskell: "I am . . . preparing a volume of Memoirs. . . . It is not an autobiography—n'ayez pas peur! An ancient lady of our house has left material for a pleasant story." Copied, the selected papers formed a unified 180–page manuscript. It ended with a letter to Louisa from a friend, Pauline Neal, saying, "Do not then quite forget her who loves you so well."[2]

Carlo sent news that his mother and her sister had died within days of each other. Henry had grown much attached to Mrs. Gaskell and was hurt by her death. In response, he urged his friend to marry soon and become a father. ". . . you can't, like me, become a Bohemian. You must look ahead and build up a new family in place of the one destroyed. . . ."

When about to return to Quincy, Henry faced a death. On June 30, 1869, he advised the Chief: "Poor old aunt Smith, after a short illness of only about three days, died an hour ago. . . . Of course this will delay my journey . . . as I must stay [for] . . . the funeral and try to quiet Mrs[.] John[,] who has been made rather nervous by the responsibility." Henry and Mrs. John arranged the funeral jointly. Aunt Smith was interred in the oldest burying ground in the District, the yard of St. Paul's Episcopal Church, known as Rock Creek Cemetery. At an unknown moment, possibly when he went there for the burial, Henry realized that he would want to be buried in the same ground.

Likewise at an unknown moment, perhaps the same moment, he decided that the *Memoirs* he had prepared would not be published, nor even privately printed.[3] Louisa Catherine Adams had written autobiographically, but with misgivings about the consequent appearance of egoism. When he began to assemble and copy her writings, Henry thought autobiography a literary mistake; hence his hastening to say that the volume he was creating was "not an autobiography." Because his relationship with his grandmother was one of shared identity, he could have added that *her* writings were *his*. As he continued it, his work as arranger-copier of her papers affected him as work towards the writing of his own third book. The labor confirmed him in opposition to autobiography and assisted his completing an important discovery.

It has been mentioned that, in Europe in 1859, he had written but not published an article on education.[4] In his letters, he had adverted to education fairly often.[5] In an especially striking letter, he had said he would plunge under the stream, remain under water a long time, and possibly bring to the surface an oyster containing a pearl. Moreover, the Chief, in his letter approving the assembly of his mother's *Memoirs*, had chanced to say that he was required for many years to live "under the shadow of my father's name."[6]

These seemingly diverse matters were convergent. In 1907, a much older Henry Adams would astonish friends and relatives by giving them copies of a book he had secretly written and privately printed. Its title would be *The Education of Henry Adams*. The title page would name no author. A passage in the first chapter would evoke Louisa Catherine Adams. The opening words would be "Under the shadow. . . ."[7]

The pearl Adams offered for inspection in 1907 was a new literary form, discovered by himself. Not memoirs, and antithetical to autobiography, the form was *the education*—a sort of story recounting a person's attempt to learn, or the person's undergoing the imposition of learning, or both. Since he did not produce a full-length model of the form till 1907, emulation had to wait till that year; but he began the discovery of the form in 1867 in London and completed its discovery in June 1869 in Washington.[8]

The *New York Times* was reporting the comings and goings of President Grant, especially as they related to New York. In mid-

June 1869, the president and his family stopped in the city. They stayed at the home of his sister Virginia—known as Jennie—and Abel Corbin, her new-found husband. Without Mrs. Grant and the children, the general proceeded by boat and train to Boston, where he was scheduled to make an appearance at the Peace Jubilee, a week-long civic celebration.

The large, handsome steamboats carrying passengers between New York and Fall River, Massachusetts, a short train ride from Boston, were owned by James Fisk, Jr., best known for sharing with Jay Gould the capture of the Erie Railroad Company. When Grant went to Fall River, Messrs. Gould and Fisk also traveled on the boat and treated him to dinner. Fisk accompanied Grant to Boston and contrived to appear at the Peace Jubilee as his continuous companion—a feat of ostentation that earned him the nickname "Jubilee Jim."

The president returned at once to New York and rejoined his wife and children. During the evening of June 18, he and his family went with the Corbins to a performance at a theatre. Jim Fisk owned the theatre. They sat in his private box. On June 19, without mentioning Fisk, the *New York Times* reported: "President GRANT is stopping in the City on a private visit of a few days to his brother in law, in West twenty seventh Street. . . . Yesterday a large number of his personal friends and admirers called upon him. . . . Mrs. GRANT went shopping in the afternoon. . . . The President and family accompanied his brother in law and wife to the Fifth avenue Theatre in the evening, witnessing a performance of opera bouffe. . . . The party appeared to enjoy the performance."9

In the same issue, the *Times* announced the death of its owner editor, Henry J. Raymond. The newspaper offered a minimum of particulars. It said that, between 9:00 and 10:00 P.M. on the 17th, he left his house to attend a political consultation; that at 2:30 A.M. he was found unconscious in the hall of his house, near the entry; and that he had locked the outer door from the inside. "The most eminent medical aid was at once summoned, and the utmost that science and skill could do were done, but in vain. He remained unconscious, and died tranquilly about 5 o'clock in the morning." Perhaps as an offset to its avoidance of particulars, the newspaper merged its news account into an immense editorial eulogizing its departed chief. The first sentence of the editorial attributed his death to "an attack of apoplexy."

Sceptical readers, comparing the paucity of details and the size of the editorial, could easily form an impression that the true story had not been told. The episode had about it an odor of midnight violence. Henry Adams would later act as if sure that Raymond was fatally injured at the direction of Abel Corbin.[10]

C. F. Adams, Jr., took office in July 1869 as a founding member of a Massachusetts Railroad Commission. In the same month, under Henry's aegis as Gurney's associate, Charles published in the *North American* his massive article, "A Chapter of Erie," subjecting four titans of New York finance, Drew, Vanderbilt, Gould, and Fisk, to a 77–page thrashing, much-documented and always dramatic.[11]

July for Henry meant a secret conclave. He alerted Charles from Washington: "Wells and Garfield are coming to Boston. I have invited them to Quincy. We will have Atkinson too . . . and cut out our work." The meeting at the Old House would mainly differ from the one Wells organized the previous January in that Henry would act as acknowledged director. In that capacity, he gave Charles necessary instructions. "Garfield will talk about a railway-schedule with you. . . . So get ready to help him, for he may help you some day. We may never come up, but he probably will swim pretty strong."

Henry arrived in Quincy and ran the meeting. He at the same time was dogged by a sense that life had no purpose. He confessed to Carlo: "I should be better pleased if I could only find out what I myself want. Certainly not office, for except very high office I would take none. What then? I wish some one would tell me."

The offices Henry *would* take were already held, unfortunately without being filled. Secretary of State Fish was a diplomatic beginner. Secretary of the Treasury Boutwell could not be mistaken for a financier. Neither was likely to resign; and, if either did, there was no chance whatever that his post would be given to the Adams newly at Quincy. It none the less made a practical difference for Henry that Fish and Boutwell were what they were, and not more. Henry had advantages and was going to use them. The advantages were freedom from office and freedom to rise. He ventured to Carlo that his coming winter in Washington would be given to "prodigious efforts." The tone was mocking, but the threat was meant.

Though different in character, John Quincy Adams and Henry Adams were alike in being unconditional democrats and whole-hearted republicans who held that the federal government should originate and conduct major programs. During the past winter, seeing that Grant suggested no program and permitted no one of ability to head the government's most important departments, Henry Adams had defined a national program, both domestic and foreign. His program had not included all the things he personally favored. It instead was narrowed to four that might be workable. Two were friendship with England and avoidance of acquisitions of territory. The others were civil-service reform and revenue reform. The four together were inherently *presidential*.

Civil-service reform was a live issue. Decisions concerning the holding of office were being made in numerous ways that were open to serious challenge. Within the Cabinet, views differed about appointments to and removals from office. The way was clear to a battle.

Revenue reform, as understood by Adams, meant amelioration of economic inequity. It was needed because the rich were rapidly getting richer, to the ruin of the poor, who were getting poorer. This brutal injustice, inimical to democracy, could be corrected, Adams believed, but on one condition. The Treasury would have to be headed by financiers disposed to promote fairer distribution of wealth and capable of devising means to secure the object.[12]

A radical in ideas but a centrist in tactics, Adams was placing himself and his allies between the country's liberals and conservatives in order to deal with both. The program advanced by his school would appeal to many diverse groups and interests. The only persons likely to oppose it strongly were the unfairly rich and the criminal.

The program was not a citizens' program, for citizens to carry out. Emphatically it was a leaders' program designed for enactment by the executive branch of the federal government. Its designers realized that no part of the program was likely to be enacted unless an incumbent president pressed hard to enact it. They had begun with hopes that General Grant when president could be told what to do and would do it. The general's drift was no longer in doubt. The white gloves had been a portent. Attired in Brooks Brothers coats and trousers more formal than those usually worn by American politicians, the supreme commander had attached himself to the rich. That explained the choice of Alexander T. Stewart to head the Treasury. It also explained the accommodation made by the president for his wife and Julia Fish.

The situation swarmed with difficulties. General Grant was president, officially. No one aged thirty-one could be president in his stead, officially. The Constitution closed the office to persons under thirty-five. And really *two* questions were at issue. The lesser was the enactment or non-enactment of an intelligent national program. The greater was the bent that America should take in the post-Lincoln age. Henry Adams saw clearly that the events of 1869 and 1870 could decide the character of American life and government for a century or longer. The future was forming in the instant.[13]

The work cut out for Henry at the Quincy conclave included an additional article, "Civil-Service Reform," to appear in the October 1869 *North American*. The article would be strengthened with little-known facts. In Washington, perhaps assisted by Badeau, he had obtained a large fund of data concerning the State Department's consular service. Meaning to fit the data into the article, he went back to his pen.

When not writing, he swam in the Atlantic surf. Often he played with John's children at a house the eldest son had built in Quincy at a remove from the family property. Ever delighted to be with children, Henry treated them as equals and talked with them in ways attuned to their knowledge of words. Six-year-old George Caspar Adams responded warmly. Uncle Henry and nephew George were soon fast friends.

When himself a child, Henry had known the family's Quincy property, with its garden and orchard, as a summer paradise. During the past year, the Chief had renovated the Old House. He was adding a library, a separate building with two floors of shelves, large windows, and every facility for writing and study. The Stone Library could seem ideal for a writer, and Henry among other things was a writer. Yet he was far from happy in Quincy. He confided to Carlo: ". . . nothing but sheer poverty shall ever reduce me to passing a whole summer here again. It is pleasant enough, but it is dead."

"Civil-Service Reform," like "American Finance, 1865–1869," was much rewritten. After six weeks of "hard labor," on August 27, Henry reported to Carlo: ". . . I am just accouché of another ponderous article. . . . You can form an estimate of my impudence when I tell you that I mean to circulate this as a pamphlet and send copies to all members of the Government and of the [national] legislature. . . . I expect to get into hot water, but have nothing to lose."[14]

Henry's poverty, as he called it, was mere strict economizing to make possible a return to Europe in the summer of 1870 and a journey "to the Pacific" in the summer of 1871. Saving money, he cancelled a trip to Canada he had wanted to take in September. In place of traveling, he read. Buying or borrowing a set of Gibbon's

Decline and Fall of the Roman Empire, he ploughed through all ten volumes.[15]

His summer acquired an added dimension. His letters—those that survive—said nothing about his meetings with Gurney, whether in Cambridge or elsewhere. They said nothing about his introduction to Ellen Gurney, assuming it occurred. They nowhere indicated that he again saw Clover Hooper, supposing it happened. They instead were so worded as to create an impression that he never left Quincy. While largely true, the impression was also significantly false. He and Gurney formed an extremely close relation. They must have met, and their meetings presumably involved Henry with one or more of the Hoopers.[16]

By summer's end, his discontent amounted to illness. The nearest causes were Quincy and a surfeit of Adamses. A greater cause was the United States. He wrote to Cunliffe: "There is a lull in everything. Life seems to stand still, and one grows older without hope."

Adams and Commissioner Wells had been attempting to trace all the many consequences of England's paper money being redeemable in gold and America's not. From Connecticut on September 10, 1869, the commissioner wrote to Adams asking his opinion on a complex question: how America's paper currency injuriously affected the American farmer, whose wheat sold for the gold price of London. Wells explained, "I have my own ideas on the matter but should value yours."[17]

The question was apropos. Since 1862, when Congress passed the Legal-Tender Act, the United States had had two competing currencies: U. S. gold coins, which were mostly being hoarded, and $400,000,000 in Treasury "greenbacks," which were in use and sufficed for the payment of domestic debts. Foreign debts, however, were payable only in gold. The result had been the emergence of a Gold Room, a Gold Exchange Bank, and other facilities in New York to make possible the ready exchange of greenbacks and gold. Rightly or wrongly, the new facilities also permitted speculation in "phantom gold"—contracts "on margin" to buy or sell an amount of gold at a stated price and pay the broker the difference in greenbacks, should the market price change adversely.

Since Grant's inauguration, the price of $100 in U. S. gold coins had fluctuated between $131 and $144 in greenbacks and had shown evidence of manipulation. In early September, the "premium" rose almost to 138, then fell below 135. On September 14 and 15, 1869, the premium rose so sharply as to make a prima

facie case that something was disturbing the market. Wall Street
grew instantly nervous. Gold stayed high through the following
Tuesday, September 21. Nervousness gave way to fear. On Wednesday, the premium approached 142. It was alleged that Jay Gould
had effected the most spectacular of manipulations, a corner in
gold. Jim Fisk was said to be helping him sustain the corner. On
Thursday, the Erie barons appeared in the financial district together. Gould stayed in the office of a Fisk associate, William
Belden, a Broad Street broker. Fisk visited the Gold Room and
loudly bet that the premium would reach 200. It edged past 144,
creating ever-mounting terror and rage. Dozens of firms and
thousands of speculators were poised at the edge of ruin.

On "Black Friday," September 24, the *New York Times* raised a
cry that the administration might have a role in the corner. Gould
and Fisk commandeered the back room of a different brokerage.
Bank examiners arrived from Washington. By constant sending of
messengers to brokers, Fisk bought outrageously at the Gold
Room. The premium soared to 162 or higher; something or
someone broke the market; the price crashed to 133; news spread
that the Treasury would be selling gold; Fisk and Gould fled for
their lives through an alley; firms and individuals were ruined en
masse; records were in inextricable confusion; accounts could not
be settled; and business came to a halt.[18]

There had been a September hurricane. It seemed not to have
ruined Gould. At a distance of 200 miles, it saved Henry Adams,
giving him the subject of a climactic article, to be published in
London. He told no one that he would be writing an article on the
gold panic. In outward appearance, his conduct did not change.

As sent to the printer in August, Adams's added article, "Civil-
Service Reform," was harsh—"very bitter and abusive of the Administration." Being political editor of the *North American*, Adams
was free to alter political articles even in page proof. In this case,
he manifestly did so. As published in the October issue—also when
reprinted as a pamphlet—"Civil-Service Reform" would be signed
Henry Brooks Adams. It would mention several Cabinet members
by name. But it would nowhere be bitter and nowhere abusive of
the administration.

With Gurney's consent, Henry was reshaping the *North American* as a quasi-political organ. He solicited three political articles for
the January 1870 issue in support of his national program. The
articles would be written by Charles, Simon Newcomb, and Gamaliel Bradford.

Meanwhile, in October 1869, Henry and Charles went together to New York. They visited Fisk at the Erie headquarters on West 23rd Street, an establishment that had cost the stockholders $1,000,000 and included an opera house. They did not see Gould. Charles returned to Boston. What Henry wanted was secret use of a daily newspaper. During the next few days, he talked with Evarts and "saw many editors; some thieves; and many more fools."[19] He could not consider the *New York Times*. He had reason to believe that Raymond had been murdered; Bigelow had replaced Raymond but resigned, effective Black Friday; and the *Times* was uncaptained and adrift.[20] After surveying alternatives, none encouraging, he turned away from newspapers and reverted to the *Nation*. He made an agreement with Godkin to supply newsletters from Washington at three-week intervals, beginning soon.

A sensitive aspect of his stop in New York was his communing with James B. Hodgskin. The broker-economist was a principal figure in both the Stock Exchange and Gold Exchange. His office at 14 Broad Street was only a few steps from the Gold Room. He was studying the September panic virtually as an occupation. So was Adams.

The press all along had been clamoring for a congressional investigation. Adams and Hodgskin knew that any thoroughgoing investigation would automatically transform from an investigation of Jay Gould and James Fisk, Jr., into an investigation of Gould, Fisk, Secretary Boutwell, and President Grant. Their own inquiries had already undergone that far-reaching metamorphosis. Evidence was accumulating that Gould had bribed a federal officer in New York, the assistant treasurer, General Butterfield. It was established too that Gould's associates in the corner, up to a critical moment, had included Abel Corbin. (A man of sixty, formerly a Washington lobbyist, Corbin had long known Mrs. Grant. Surprisingly, he and Jennie Grant had married in May.) The *New York Sun* accused the president himself of wrongdoing. Grant answered by issuing a letter denying knowledge of "the 'disreputable proceedings' of the Gold Ring."[21] Suspicion was mounting that he had lied.

A developing worry related to Henry Reeve and the *Edinburgh Review*. Adams's dealings with the English editor had been successful but not comfortable. At an unknown moment, presumably from New York, Adams wrote to Reeve offering him an extraordinary article about the activities of the Gold Ring in Wall Street. Yet Adams half-believed the article would be better given to another magazine. The one that most attracted him was Lord Robert Cecil's vehicle, the *London Quarterly*.

Adams proceeded to Washington. On November 1, he mailed copies of "Civil-Service Reform" to the Cabinet secretaries and the members of the Senate and House. The latter persons had not yet arrived. He reported to Carlo, "Except for Cabinet officers I am alone in the city, and have nothing to do but to set my springes for future woodcock."

On November 8, Adams wrote to Secretary of Interior Cox suggesting he organize "a majority of the Cabinet" to join in "declaring the solid principles of reform." He exhorted: "Give the country a lead! We are wallowing in the mire for want of a leader."

Before Cox could begin to act, on November 11, the *Nation* hailed Adams as a national leader. Under the caption "The North American Review for October," Godkin's journal announced:

> By far the most striking and readable of the long articles in the last *North American* is that of Mr. Henry Brooks Adams, who has by this and one or two similar essays made for himself an enviable reputation as a courageous politician in the best sense of the term, and as an excellently clear and forcible writer.

A passage in Adams's "Civil-Service Reform" contrasted Secretary of the Treasury Boutwell, ousting Democrats from the Treasury to make room for Republicans, with Attorney General Hoar, who would not discharge his messenger for being a Democrat even though the messenger, ill and bed-ridden, was long absent from duty and Hoar was running his messages himself. The *Nation* said the contrast was "restrained and dignified," yet also said it was "very telling." The Chief similarly approved. He assured Henry that "Civil-Service Reform" was "the best, both in what it does and what it avoids, that I have read of yours. There is no trace in it of the defects that I pointed out last spring."[22]

Henry's motive for restraint and dignity had not been fear of seeming conceited or self-important. He was governed by the recent history of presidents. Lincoln had been murdered. Johnson had come within one vote of unjust dismissal. In view of past calamities, Adams wanted no injury done to President Grant if injury could be avoided. Even more, he intended to bring assistance. "Civil-Service Reform" betrayed extremest concern to secure for Grant a second chance to be what many Americans had hoped he had meant to be, a help to the country, a new George Washington, superior to faction, above corruption.

Adams especially was trying to free Grant to assert the rightful powers of the executive branch in the face of an encroaching

Congress, imperious party bosses, and importunate Union veterans. To this end, "Civil-Service Reform" provided an account of the State Department's largely frustrated, sixteen-year attempt to wring appropriations from Congress for the training of consuls. The account took the reader inside the executive branch and revealed its difficulties. It showed that the State Department's besetting problem had been the ignorance, stupidity, and greed of particular congressmen and particular senators.

Unfortunately, "Civil-Service Reform" *existed* because of developments still more ominous. Grant had yielded to whomever it was that wanted the appointment of Boutwell. The president and the Cabinet had yielded to innumerable pleas concerning subordinate appointments. Equally bad, the Cabinet lacked coherence and could not function as a body. Henry recognized the evils and saw where they led. His article warned that restoration of good government in Washington would require efforts and appeals to the public sustained for a very long time.

The best potential recruit for the new school of politics remained the secretary of the interior. Cox answered on November 18: ". . . [I] assure you that I fully understood your article in the North American, which I read with real satisfaction. . . . I propose (*entre nous*) to speak plainly on the civil service in my report." The Ohioan was wary but did not close the door to collaboration.

Congress would soon convene, and Henry was greeting throngs of arrivals. He shook hands continuously but felt isolated and friendless. "I am as lonely as a cat here," he told Carlo. "Acquaintances without number I have, but no companion. And what avails it to be intimate with all men if one comes home at five o'clock and abhors life!"

Autumnal rains drenched the city. The risk of self-harm increased with nightfall. He confessed: ". . . it is one of the dankest, foggiest, and dismalest of November nights, and . . . I am as out of sorts as a man may haply be, and yet live through it. . . . Well! one can't have life as one would, but if ever I take too much laudanum, the coroner's jury may bring in a verdict of wilful murder against the month of November."

The previous July, after going there on an errand, Evarts had written to Adams, ". . . Washington . . . without you, was intolerable."[23] The five words told two truths. People greatly liked Adams. But the city he loved they hated.

He could sympathize with the haters. In the first of his anonymous newsletters in the *Nation*, dated November 20, he said of the capital: "Americans commonly regard it as a centre of corruption and intrigue; foreigners only know that it is dull. This is its unpardonable sin. There is not a theatre, except by courtesy; there is no art, no music, no park, no drive, no club. . . . The worst annoyance of all is that society itself exists only in disjointed fragments. . . ."

The pace of events had quickened. He told Carlo: "I am writing —writing—writing. You must take the New York Nation if you want to read me. I have written that animal Reeve a letter, offering him an article—such an article!—and he does not even answer it!" "I have written to Palgrave to make advances to the [London] Quarterly, and I will make my article *SUPERB* to disgust Reeve."

Scenting possible appointment as consul-general in England, Badeau had resigned his assistant secretaryship, returned to Washington, and resumed his attentions to Mrs. Grant.[24] He brought Adams confirmation that Lord Clarendon, ignoring Motley and thus also Sumner, would be transacting business with the United States solely through Minister Thornton. The news was glorious— except that Adams was hesitant to deal directly with Thornton and still more hesitant to deal with his aides. He informed Gaskell that the United Kingdom was represented in Washington by "the queerest lot of Britishers it was ever my bad luck to meet." "You have six or seven men, and four or five women here, who are too much for this vile world, and should be translated to a better. . . . All the women are a little mad. All the men (those that dont [*sic*] drink) are apparently fools. A state of things I regret."

A letter came from George in Quincy. New to pens and paper, he had written in capital letters. Uncle Henry replied:

> . . . when you are twelve or fourteen years old . . . you will come on here to Washington and pay me a visit. Then I will take you up to the Capitol where all the Senators and Judges are sitting in great rooms; and you shall call on the President and ask him how he likes it, and you shall go down to Mount Vernon and see where the great General Washington lived. . . . I have become a member of a boat-club and next spring I mean to keep a little wherry or row-boat on the river. Perhaps one of these days I shall have money enough to keep a sailboat. . . .

The answer promised that the political careers of the Adamses would be unendingly successful and that Henry would wait for George in Washington as long as necessary, or forever. Yet all signs pointed to an opposite future. Alone at her house, Mrs. John was failing in health. The Chief's mid-week letters were uniformly pessimistic.[25] John had again run for governor, as if defeat were a positive object. And in design and intention, Henry's efforts were the *last* great efforts of a great family and were succeeding on just that basis.

What Henry had and other Adamses lacked was resilience assisted by humor. In early December, dressed as usual in London clothes, he was walking near the capital's limits when he heard a "rushing noise." Too soon to permit his reacting, he was hit on the back of his head so forcibly he was knocked to the ground. He sent Carlo an account of his mishap. ". . . I did not even make an effort to save myself." Hurt in a knee and three fingers, he "jumped up mechanically" and reached for his hat. He saw his attacker. ". . . flapping painfully, and gazing at me with eyes to the full as amazed and bewildered as my own, was a huge, white, tame goose." The collision belonged less to modern life than to ancient myth. "Dædalus was nothing in comparison. He melted at the rays of the sun. But I was floored by the stupidest, dirtiest and coarsest of domestic dung-hill fowl."

Badeau's return made possible an improved arrangement. The suite of rooms below Henry's chanced to fall vacant. Badeau rented it and agreed to "combine for society" at Henry's table. Their meals would be intended as occasions. "We dine every day in state, and full dress, including white cravats, and we entertain freely, or mean to. Between us we know everybody, and those we don't know, know us."[26]

The officials Henry most needed to confer with were Fish, Davis, Hoar, Cox, Wells, Walker, and Garfield. He did not see them often but saw them often enough. ". . . I am . . . winding myself up in a coil of political intrigue. . . . My progress in a year has alarmed me, for it is too rapid to be sound. I am already deeper in the confidence of the present Government than I was with the last, although that was friendly and this a little hostile."

The first persons to occupy the White House had been Henry's great-grandparents, John and Abigail Adams. His grandparents, John Quincy and Louisa, had lived in the executive mansion for a full term. The Chief had lived there intermittently, Mrs. John continuously. Belated Henry had entered its doors a mere three times: in 1850, to exchange a few words with Zachary Taylor; in 1861, to shake hands with Abraham Lincoln; and in 1868, to pay respects to Andrew Johnson. After each encounter, he never again saw the president he had met.[27] Viewed "subjectively," the phenomenon could seem magical. When seen once by a certain Adams, three presidents had disappeared.

On Sunday evening, December 12, 1869, Badeau and Adams went to the White House. They found the president smoking with some of his intimates. Dull talk was in progress. Adams was introduced. Supposing the place was one where people could be natural, he expected to relax. ". . . Mrs[.] Grant strolled in. She . . . is not much more vulgar than some Duchesses. Her sense of dignity did not allow her to talk to me, but occasionally she condescended to throw me a constrained remark. . . . One feels such an irresistible desire . . . to tell this kind of individual to put themselves at their ease and talk just as though they were at home. I restrained it, however, and quite performed the part of guest, though you can imagine with what an effort."

If the citizens of the new America of 1869 and 1870 wanted a ceremonial president who would reign but not govern, they had found the man they desired. Grant resembled a statue. He had the ability to sit motionless at dinners saying nothing and inviting silence from persons near him. Julia Grant was more alive. The first lady was trying to govern. Slave-holding by birth, she had a program: the nurture of aristocracy.[28] Despite an ungainly frame and a misalignment of the eyes, which, in Adams's unforgivable phrase, made her squint "like an isosceles triangle," she seemed in a fair way to advance her program.

For the moment, in Henry's observation, events in Washington had the qualities of "a play." Citizens and officials were actors performing roles. An actor himself, Adams had a flair for playing the unassuming companion of whatever person he chanced to be with. He and Badeau were short—one thin, one stout. Badeau could seem European and noble. Telling Carlo about the visit to the White House, Henry spoke of Badeau and himself as "an old-fashioned nobleman and his wife." The wife had a full beard. Her name was "H. Pocahontas Adams."

Adams could joke, but better than others he knew that politics in America was an activity in which the more ambitious participants were likely to be injured or even killed. His Sunday call at the executive mansion brought face to face two very different male Americans, one of whom at least would be harmed by the other. Adams was the more assertive. He was attempting to mobilize the executive branch of the government, restore its powers, and put it to work. In Lincoln's phrase, he wanted government "for the people," and he intended to get it.

Grant was an entirely opposite sort of being. He had said when inaugurated, "Let us have peace." Originally puzzling, the words were clear. The general-turned-president assumed that the government in peacetime should mirror the army in peacetime: it should not act, only be. Fitfully his administration might attempt initiatives. Grant himself might occasionally stir. Yet in the main, while peace continued, the clock of government would not be wound. The president would have the key in his pocket. The hands would not move.[29]

The House of Representatives resolved on December 13, 1869, that its committee on banking and currency should "investigate the causes that led to the unusual and extraordinary fluctuation of gold in the city of New York, from the 21st to 27th of September."[30] The committee's chairman was James Garfield. He asked Adams to go with him to New York to make a preliminary inquiry. Adams pled other engagements.

Even if free, Adams would not have gone. He saw Garfield, not as a person suited to investigate the Gold Ring, but rather as a patriot, conscientious legislator, and loyal Republican predisposed to believe that the "wicked and cunningly devised attempts of the conspirators to compromise the President of the United States . . . utterly failed."[31] The words, eventually found in the printed report of the House committee, were also written in advance in the forefront of the chairman's mind. Garfield knew no higher duty than that of honoring presidents, and for him all *Republican* presidents were blameless by definition.

Conscientious as always, Garfield tried a second time. On December 30, the chairman sent Adams a message that he was leaving at 9:00 that night for New York and wanted Henry to accompany him. If that was impossible, he wished Henry would give him "memoranda" that would aid him in finding "the men who know about the inner history of the panic." He would send for the memoranda at 6:30.

Adams supplied Garfield a letter of introduction which would secure for the chairman the guidance of a New York broker-economist, James Hodgskin. In addition, he wrote a letter of advice in which he said about Hodgskin: "His position on the Stock Exchange has put him in the way of studying the whole matter. He is very intelligent and shrewd. As you will no doubt be surrounded by false lights, I recommend you to use [him] . . . as a sort of preliminary text-book, to be consulted privately when difficulties turn up."

Garfield went to New York and consulted Hodgskin. Adams stayed in Washington, where his doings were never so secret. The new year, 1870, felt momentous to him, and in part for a personal reason. 1870 was the starting year of a new plan for himself, just completed, which targeted a date for the publication of his *Democracy* and possibly dates affecting his *History of the United States.*

That he had such a plan appeared in a letter alluding to a wedding in Washington. On January 13, he wrote to Carlo: "Eight bridesmaids were selected from the prettiest and most fashionable girls here. . . . Your humble servant is supposed to be attentive to one of these young women, just on the thresh-hold [sic] of twenty. . . ."[32] Henry was not in love with the young woman, nor even near it, yet he was quoting poetry to her and simulating attachment. "Perhaps in your vulgar mercenary eyes her chief attraction would be £200,000. In mine her only attraction is that I can flirt with the poor girl in safety as I firmly believe she is in a deep consumption and will die of it. . . . You may disbelieve it if you like, but . . . every sentimental speech or touching quotation I make to her, derives its amusement from the belief that her eyes and ears will soon be inappreciative. . . . I have marked it for a point in my novel, which is to appear in 1880."[33]

Behind closed doors at the Capitol on January 15, 1870, the House committee on currency and banking began to take sworn testimony from a carefully ordered sequence of witnesses who might be able to provide information concerning the gold panic. The first to be called was James Hodgskin. He had readied a statement, a sort of financial map, which might help the committee choose its road. The statement was purely his work and in no way Adams's. Their labors relating to the panic had overlapped but were not alike.[34]

The committee had ten members, eight Republicans and two Democrats. Their investigation of the panic became arduous and, for some members, too alarming to continue. Gould and Fisk testified on January 22—the fourteenth and fifteenth witnesses.[35] The twenty-ninth, Abel Corbin, appeared on January 27 and 28.[36] The testimony was secret, but some of its substance daily transpired after the witnesses had appeared and spoken. Increasingly the testimony raised questions of such kinds that the committee would *have* to subpoena Julia Grant and Jennie Corbin.[37]

President Grant accordingly asked Secretary Cox to write to Chairman Garfield and secure those ladies against disturbance. On February 1, Cox wrote the requested letter to Garfield. President, secretary, and chairman were all former Union generals, and Grant's plea had the force of a military order. Garfield willingly complied, and the president's wife and sister were exempted from participation.[38]

The committee Democrats were Thomas L. Jones of Kentucky and S. S. ("Sunset") Cox of New York. Partly at their insistence, Chairman Garfield visited the president and asked him to read and respond to those parts of the testimony which alleged wrongdoing by him and members of his family. Grant refused to see the parts. On February 4, a motion to subpoena the president was defeated by a Republican majority in the committee on the ground that the committee's "only mode of reaching him for official acts was by impeachment." A Republican majority in the committee likewise voted down a motion merely "requesting" the president to appear and testify.[39] Yet when the last witness—the fifty- seventh— was being questioned on February 15, the matter most at issue was a possible shifting of money to Mrs. Grant.[40]

Changes meanwhile had continued at Harvard. In October 1869, its presidency had been given to Charles W. Eliot; and, in January 1870, Gurney had been made the institution's first dean of the faculty and its second-ranking executive officer. Gurney none the less was obliged to teach. He still was editor of the *North American*. His roster of tasks was no longer possible to perform.[41]

Adams had become more an editor. By mid-January 1870, three of his Washington newsletters had appeared in the *Nation*, unsigned. For reasons that can only be guessed, a new arrangement was devised. Rather than newsletters, he was to supply fortnightly anonymous *editorials*.

The opportunity was not small. Between January 27 and May 5, eight unsigned editorials by Adams would appear in the *Nation*, so positioned in the issues as to have the journal's full backing and to create impressions that Godkin might be the author.[42] Between January and May, Adams would also supply unsigned editorials to a sister publication, the *New York Evening Post*, a daily newspaper edited by William Cullen Bryant.[43] In addition, Adams would offer his rooms as a meeting place for reformers, editors, and politicians, whether Republicans or Democrats. By these and other devices, without trenching on the interests of other editors, indeed by lending desired assistance, he would begin to assume the function of a national editor-at-large.

For Adams, however, events had an outside and an inside. The only correct gauge of his progress was not the people he knew nor the meetings he organized, nor even what he published, but what he succeeded in finding out. In late January or early February, his situation was altered by a disclosure. He was convincingly informed that Julia Grant had received and possibly solicited from Jay Gould, through Abel Corbin as active intermediary or broker, $100,000 in

U. S. bonds, equivalent to her husband's salary as president for four years.[44]

From whom Adams got the information is unknown and is a question of lesser importance. (One of his informants may have been Badeau.[45]) What principally mattered was, first, the magnitude of the information and, second, the information's coming to *him*. It was a commonplace of the stage that the hero or heroine of any serious drama was likely to know something that could not be said, yet *had* to be said. After February 1, 1870, or thereabouts, Adams shared the situation of Hippolytus or Hamlet. He knew. But what should he do?

In Washington the year before, Adams had read *The Ring and the Book*, a long new poem by Robert Browning. The poem's main claim to a reader's interest was its telling a shocking story as viewed from the standpoints of many participants and commentators. By coincidence, subsequent to Black Friday, Adams was preoccupied by *his* ring and *his* book. The ring was his climactic article, to be titled "The New York Gold Conspiracy." The book was *Democracy*. They were twins.

The ring and the book had to be fitted into a four-part writing schedule. One part was Adams's series of editorials in the *Nation*, already started. The second part was "The New York Gold Conspiracy," which would have to be written with all possible suggestiveness. The third part was his annual review of politics for the *North American*, to be written for the July issue under the unchanging title "The Session." Fourth was *Democracy*, and it might at times have seemed to him that the novel could wait. Really nothing could wait. Materials had to be apportioned instantly between the editorials for the *Nation*, "The New York Gold Conspiracy," the new "Session," and *Democracy*.[46] There might otherwise be regrets.

An emergency supervened. Attorney General Hoar had inherited from Evarts the duty of upholding the constitutionality of the Legal-Tender Act. Grant had joined with Hoar in the act's support. On February 7, the Supreme Court declared the act unconstitutional in one of its bearings—a victory for Henry Adams. But on the same day, at the suggestion of Secretary Cox, Frank Walker was named to head the 1870 census. It happened that, secretly, Adams had wrung from Walker the promise of an article for the April *North American* on the history and demerits of the Legal-Tender Act. Having accepted the assignment as chief of the census, Walker could not continue work on the article. In haste, Adams himself wrote the article, partly on the basis of Walker's notes.

The article was published under the title "The Legal-Tender Act" and signed Henry Brooks Adams.[47] Blame for the article would thus be directed at Adams only. Blame was likely. Forsaking dignity and restraint, Adams shaped the article as "a piece of intolerably impudent political abuse."

"The Legal-Tender Act" served a single purpose: to show that the Unionists who bore responsibility for financing the Civil War had knowingly rejected the simple, effectual method used by Albert Gallatin to pay for the War of 1812 and had substituted in 1862 a financial idiocy, a Legal-Tender Act which vastly increased the cost of the Civil War and turned the Unionists into a nation of speculators, gamblers, and worse. While telling the story, Adams shrank from nothing. A few politicians had tried to prevent the disaster. He praised one without limit. ". . . the speech of Owen Lovejoy of Illinois was in its short space as clear, as vigorous, and, from a rhetorical point of view, as perfect, as the oldest statesman or the most exacting critic or the deepest student of finance could have hoped or wished to make." Equally he blamed and scorned. The politicians he attacked by name included Salmon P. Chase, Charles Sumner, and Samuel Hooper. He insulted the American people—his readers—with similar freedom. "In the popular humor of the moment, it is more than ever doubtful whether any advice that is wise would be listened to, or whether any advice that has a chance to be listened to could possibly be wise."

The psychology of Adams's conduct was that of a man who thought his associates the best then living, yet also that of a man who outclassed his contemporaries and stood alone. A fair test of his contemporaries was the challenge presented by the gold panic. The report of the House committee, completed in the last week of February and signed by the eight Republicans, shrilly assailed three men in New York, Jay Gould, James Fisk, Jr., and Abel Corbin; but it obeisantly lauded two men in Washington, Ulysses S. Grant and George Boutwell. The Democrats, S. S. Cox and Thomas Jones, complained in their dissenting opinions that the investigation had been aborted; that the majority had refused "to take such testimony as would unravel this mystery." Cox and Jones declared, "No explanations are permitted." But, taking shelter behind the statement, they held, or rather pretended, that no opinion was possible![48]

Printing of the report was ordered on March 1 but would take time to complete. The *Nation* did not wait to see the testimony. If Godkin was representative, the gold panic was simply too horrifying for America's reformers to confront. His weekly said on March

3, 1870: ". . . nothing could have been more sensible or upright than the President's course throughout the whole affair. He committed in it only one error, and that was accepting the hospitality of, and entering into conversation with, such people as Gould, Fisk, & Co. were then known to be."[49]

By March 7, Adams's situation was critical. In London, Reeve had been unable to grasp what an article concerning a Gold Ring in New York might be about. After a three-month silence, he had written to say he could not use an article on American currency. Adams had no wish to continue with the *Edinburgh Review* and preferred the *London Quarterly*. But, amazingly, Palgrave had not responded.

The hour being late, Adams confided a part of his predicament to Gaskell. "I am about to write an article on a very curious and melodramatic gold speculation that took place in New York last September. It involves a good deal of libelous language which I can't well publish here."[50] He added a statement which seemed to have a large meaning—either that or a *very* large. "As I have been pulling wires behind the Congressional Committee of Investigation, and have been up to my neck in the whole thing, I know all that is known."[51]

The Chief wrote to Henry to relay a message. Gurney could not go on as editor of the *North American Review*; the magazine's continuance was in jeopardy; and Eliot and Gurney wished that Henry would drop everything else and start work as sole editor.[52]

The proposal rested on a misunderstanding. Like Faneuil Hall or King's Chapel, the *North American* was an integral part of Boston. Its editorship could be awarded only to a year-round resident of the Boston area. The Chief, Gurney, and Eliot could not absorb the strange fact that Henry by preference, and virtually from birth, was a Washingtonian. Out of friendship to Gurney, Henry offered to be editor-for-politics in a publicly formalized manner. His offer was beside the point, and the magazine's problem remained unsolved.

Meanwhile in the capital, politics became a melee. Furious combats broke out between officers of all three branches of the federal government. Grant, Fish, Boutwell, Hoar, Sumner, Chase, and a long list of others dueled and fought in bewildering combinations. Henry entered the melee and enjoyed it. The mood of his activities greatly changed. There was no longer any telling how many articles he was going to write. His detailed plans were hidden, but his general plan was not. He meant to persist in Washington until a constructive national program was in full effect. His hopes for the country were unlimited. His hopes for himself were rising. In one of his editorials in the *Nation*, he wrote, ". . . we believe God intends the human race to be governed finally by what is best in intellect, and not what is most voluminous in sound or most intense in feeling."[53] Which American did he suppose best in intellect? The answer was clear: the Adams in Washington.

As Adams knew in advance, "The New York Gold Conspiracy" would be the most dangerous American political article of the epoch.[54] With three exceptions, Gaskell, Palgrave, and the editor of the *London Quarterly*, the secret that he was writing it had been imparted to nobody. He finished the manuscript in eight weeks and mailed it on April 28. Palgrave by then had wrested a promise from the *Quarterly* to consider it, when sent.

In pretence, the article was a review of two works: the 483-page report by the House committee on currency and banking, titled *Gold Panic Investigation*, and a best-selling pamphlet, *A Chapter of Erie*, by C. F. Adams, Jr. In fact, the article was a historical narrative about the United States and especially about the threats posed to the nation by "an empire within a republic"—the Erie Railroad Company. The narrative was in one sense impossible to write. Adams had learned too much for an article to hold, too much for a magazine to print, and too much for an author to say. He knew the inner history of the gold panic but could tell the history only with the help of omissions.[55] That being the case, he took three of its principal elements—Julia Grant's $100,000 in U. S. bonds, a new president who had not the beginning of an idea what his office might be or what he should do, and a Washington specialist in bribes—and allotted all three to *Democracy*, where they eventually would do good work.[56] "The New York Gold Conspiracy" was thinned in proportion, yet not so thinned as to lose its meaning.

The article could seem contradictory. It began by explaining that mismanagement of the Union's finances during the Civil War turned all the Unionists into speculators at best. It ended by saying that the Union's affairs were returning gradually to normal. It then added that entities like the Erie corporation might corrupt and govern the Union altogether—which would be a far cry from return to normal.

The middle pages of the article could seem fairly simple. They presented an ancient drama in modern dress, a plot recoiling upon its author. The originator of the drama was Jay Gould, a designer of swindles. Gould had become enamored of a three-part idea suggested to him by an English associate, James McHenry: (a) that a rise in the price of gold—that is, the price in U. S. greenbacks—would increase the flow of American wheat from farms in the midwest to New York and thence to the ports of Europe; (b) that more trains loaded with wheat would ride the Erie tracks; and (c) that Erie profits would rise. Believing the idea true, Gould maneuvered to force up the price of gold with the help of associate buyers. He hoped to keep the price at 140 or 145 through the harvest season. The raised price would benefit the farmers, the railroads, the exporters. It would even be patriotic.

Such was the start of the drama. But what Adams had to do was disclose an operation involving *three rings*. The members of the first ring were Jay Gould and two associate buyers, Arthur Kimber and William Woodward. Gould, Kimber, and Woodward, as they knew, could not corner gold unless dead certain the Treasury would not sell gold at all or would sell it only, and dependably, at a uniform, slow rate. Unluckily for them, Boutwell was selling gold in irregular amounts and fast. To make matters worse, the secretary thought himself exclusive lord of the Treasury. He could be influenced only by Grant. Gould's problem accordingly was plain. In Adams's words: ". . . it was therefore essential that Mr. Gould should control the government itself, whether by fair means or foul, by persuasion or by purchase."[57]

The organizer of the second ring was Abel Corbin, the aging husband of the president's sister. As Adams told the story, Corbin provided Gould "a channel of direct communication with the President."[58]

Jim Fisk—later head of the third ring—was averse to buying gold but liked to cooperate with Gould and chanced to own the steamship line that provided service from New York to Fall River, not far from Boston.[59] On June 15, 1869, Corbin, Gould, and Fisk so arranged things that Grant left for Boston on one of Fisk's steamers. That night on the steamer, after dining with Fisk, Gould, and others, the president heard all that Gould wished to tell him about gold, wheat, and patriotism. Talk continued for hours. Persuasion failed.[60]

Had he been free to write what he knew, Adams would have told how Gould went at once to New York, visited Corbin and, through his mediation, purchased *Mrs. Grant* for $100,000 in U. S. bonds.[61] Julia Grant led the president on vacation to Mount Washington in New Hampshire and to her cousins's house in Washington, Pennsylvania.[62] Along the way, she so persuaded the "unsuspicious President" that he sent an order from Corbin's house directing Secretary Boutwell to sell regular small amounts of gold and make no change without getting new instructions.[63]

Adams was far from free. He could say only as much in his article as could be accepted for publication in a British quarterly. Thus, at the crucial point in his narrative, he eased the reader into a passage which, without mentioning *bonds*, left no doubt that the workability of the plot hinged on the presence of *wives*; that persuasion of the president was purchased; that Grant sent Boutwell the necessary order; and even that Fisk and Gould in New York received a message from Grant in Pennsylvania which—as Gould and Fisk understood it—confirmed that the president knew he was bought and was acting as they wished.[64]

Grant's order to Boutwell from New York made the corner possible. Gould bought until sellers had contracted to supply him $50,000,000 in phantom gold. Inopportunely, a member of the first ring, Kimber, got into financial difficulties. He sold his gold and withdrew from the market.[65] Gould, his own resources strained to the uttermost, intimated to Fisk that assistance was in order. Fisk plunged into the market as a separate buyer and head of a separate ring.

Along the way, out of nervousness or inexperience, Gould had made gross errors of excessive effort. One was an attempt to bribe Grant's secretary, General Porter. The worst was a letter Gould induced Corbin to write and send by messenger to Grant at the home of Julia's cousin in Washington, Pennsylvania. The letter asked and elicited a reply. After the messenger left, the Grants reconsidered and panicked.[66] Mrs. Grant wrote to Jennie Corbin saying her husband must dissociate himself from gold speculations immediately.[67] Jennie gave Abel the letter. Earlier Corbin had extracted from Gould a check for $25,000. On September 22, he showed Gould the letter from Mrs. Grant to the president's sister and on the spot tried to extort from Gould a check for $100,000.[68] Gould asked for time. He knew that Fisk's ring was buying gold. He knew also that Fisk, by buying in an insanely public manner, would have the financial community, the press, and the Treasury down upon them within two days or less. Without Fisk's knowledge, Gould rapidly sold his $50,000,000 hoard of gold, mostly to Fisk. It was Gould's untraceable sales that undermined the price on Black Friday and caused the crash to 133. Fisk was equal to the occasion. By disclaiming his orders, he ruined the others in his ring and saved himself.

❖ ❖ ❖

Until he entered the labyrinth of "The New York Gold Conspiracy," Adams was not a major writer. The short narrative he produced allowed no morsel of comedy to escape its notice, yet was tragic and somber. Readers might think the article strangely elevated. It could seem conceived in distant retrospect, from the vantage point of a later age. Yet it was written by a Washingtonian caught up in scores of current matters, all clamoring for his attention.

There was geology. Without any urging by Clarence King, Congress had awarded the Fortieth Parallel Survey a new three-year appropriation. Emmons, meeting Adams in Washington, invited him to join the Survey in the Rockies as a guest geologist. Adams could not accept for the present summer, yet wished to go. They agreed that he should join King's surveyors in the summer of 1871.[69]

There was a conclave. On April 28, 1870, an unsigned report in the *Nation* advised: "A meeting of revenue reformers, in which the wicked Wells, General Hawley of Connecticut, Mr. White of the *Chicago Tribune*, Mr. [Francis] Amasa Walker, Mr. Grosvenor of the St. Louis *Democrat*, Mr. Nordhoff of the [*New York*] *Evening Post*, and Mr. McCulloch, the ex-Secretary of the Treasury, bore a prominent part, was held in Washington, last week. . . ." The presumable reporter was Godkin; he did not mention that the revenue reformers met in Adams's rooms; but he plainly stated their purposes. ". . . it was . . . resolved that these things should be pushed at all hazards, in the Republican party if possible, but out of it if necessary. After the usual distribution of 'British gold' by the butler from the [British] Legation, the meeting separated, with the intention of having a more formal gathering somewhere in the West early in the fall."[70]

Starting the following day, April 29, Adams had to write his new "Session." Uncertain what it should say, he had begun by thinking of the Senate. During that body's debates, one senator, perhaps more, had abused him by name. More as an ebullition of vigor than an actual purpose, he considered hurting some senators. He wrote to Carlo, "In my review of the Session . . . I am going to make an example or two *in terrorem* and go to England to escape retaliation." ". . . I am Aristophanes."

A new occurrence in the Senate opened the way to a better idea. Two senatorial peacocks, Roscoe Conkling of New York and Charles Sumner of Massachusetts, suffered the indignity of being named to the same committee. In the *Nation*, Adams said about them, "Two Jupiters may not exist together on any Olympus."[71]

Applied to senators, the metaphor was comic, but if used in another connection it would be mortally serious. Till that time, Adams had avoided signed conflict with Grant. He could wait no longer. The new "Session" would do two things: support revenue reform and injure the occupant of the White House. He began writing and quickly finished.

Adams had not gone into opposition. He was preparing for a third winter in Washington during which the melee of 1870 would give way to orderly progress. Two facts were uppermost. Grant was at the top of the mountain, officially president but a specious Jupiter. A different Jupiter, Henry Adams, was also at the top of the mountain. The purpose of the new "Session" would be to drive Grant a long way down from the summit. The contest would be one of stasis assaulted by action. Adams would use the method of "Civil-Service Reform" as revised. He would phrase the new "Session" in the most *moderate* terms he could find. By this insidious, two-edged means, he would maim Grant sufficiently to afford a useful beginning. Boutwell, in good time, might be expelled from the Treasury.[72] A man of ability, possibly Jacob Cox, might step forward as national leader.[73]

Thanks to Julia Grant, Badeau had received the consul-generalship in England.[74] He and Adams booked passage on a steamer leaving from Baltimore. They would reach London near the end of the season. Adams was anticipating a holiday with Gaskell, Palgrave, Cunliffe, Forster, Lord Houghton, and others, including Motley. He might dash to Italy to see the Kuhns. Sadly enough, Loo's brother-in-law, Hartman Kuhn, whom Henry had known and liked, had been killed near Rome, thrown while riding on the Campagna.[75] Loo in consequence was wearing black.

The first thing Adams learned in England was that the *Quarterly* had rejected "The New York Gold Conspiracy" out of fear of reprisals, legal or physical, by the Erie barons and their English squires.[76] Adams appealed to James Anthony Froude. Currently editor of *Frazer's Magazine*, the historian was away in Ireland. On June 30, responding to Adams's inquiry, Froude said he would be "delighted to publish what you have written . . . provided you do not object to signing your name."

Froude's answer was brought to Adams's London address but had to be forwarded to Italy. A telegram had come, and he had gone to the Continent. Previous messages had informed him that Loo had suffered an accident driving her carriage. They said her foot was crushed but was mending. Oppositely, the telegram specified that tetanus had set in; that she possibly was dying and he must come.

The Kuhns lived in Florence but, in search of cooler air, had gone to Bagni di Lucca, taking rooms at the Hôtel d'Amerique. Henry arrived and saw his sister. Her affliction had been correctly diagnosed, but tetanus was a disorder of unknown cause for which no effective treatment existed. Victims suffered convulsions of the entire body. The lucky survived. Many died.

Medicine was not yet a science. Professional nursing was a recent invention not in wide use. For help when sick or dying, Americans and Europeans depended on relatives and friends. Charles and Louisa Kuhn had many acquaintances of many nationalities. Several were faithfully acting as nurses. Outwardly different only in staying with his sister for very long intervals, Henry melted into the throng.

Letters came. One was Froude's offer to publish "The New York Gold Conspiracy," if signed. Adams met Froude's condition.[77] Others were communications from President Eliot. They offered Adams a place on the Harvard faculty as assistant professor of history, provided he edit the *North American Review*. The offer was not a surprise. Adams knew that Harvard had two permanent history teachers, Dean Gurney and Professor Torrey, and had decided to add a third. He knew also that his father, speaking as a University overseer, had "casually expressed an opinion" to President Eliot that his son Henry might serve creditably as the third teacher, provided he showed the requisite "industry." The Chief had not thought his opinion greatly mattered. He however had mentioned it to Henry in a letter sent on June 13, prior to Eliot's sending Henry the offer of the position as teacher-editor.[78]

Henry could not delay replying without creating hopes that he might accept the appointment. On July 3, 1870, he wrote to Eliot saying the offer was "not only flattering but brilliant," yet he could not accept it. He explained that two years earlier he had chosen a career and that he remained "determined to go on in it as far as it will lead me."

Good to that point, Henry's answer was incomplete. The presidency given to Eliot had been offered first to C. F. Adams and was refused. Were H. B. Adams curtly to refuse the brilliant offer made to himself, an impression might be created that the Adamses were unappreciative of honors, even those bestowed by their alma mater. He accordingly cushioned his refusal by assuring Eliot in a closing statement: ". . . I may have an opportunity to see you in the autumn, and at all events I shall make the attempt."

❖ ❖ ❖

As children, Loo and Henry had been much attached to one another. As adults, they had been separated by what seemed a basic difference of character. To use his word, Henry was "positive." He had said the previous November that he might do away with himself some rainy night by taking laudanum, but he never would. On the contrary, he would try to make something positive of his every waking and sleeping hour.

Loo had been exceedingly negative. Henry had said his sister was "near insane" and would "kill herself ultimately, I think." Really she had killed herself all along. Afloat on the tides of display, fashion, and expatriation, she had squandered a dozen years on the merest "society." Her great ambition was better jewels.[79]

Illness had a way of bringing relations together. On July 8, 1870, a Friday, when Loo had resisted tetanus for fifteen days and Henry had been attending her for eight, Henry wrote to Carlo about the eight: "They have been in many ways the most trying and terrible days I ever had. . . . We have swum in c[h]loroform, morphine, opium, and every kind of most violent counteragent and poison. . . . One night my sister, reduced to the last extremity, gasped farewell to us all, gave all her dying orders, and for two hours we thought every gasp was to be the end. Her breath stopped, her pulse ceased beating. . . ."

The Louisa at Bagni di Lucca differed from the one whom Henry had drifted away from. She had thrown off the garments of idleness and was fighting for her life. She revived, failed, and revived. The cycles created hope. Henry continued: "She never loses courage nor head. She knows perfectly what is the matter . . . but in the middle of her most awful convulsions, so long as she can articulate at all, she gives her own orders and comes out with sallies of fun and humorous comments which set us all laughing in spite of our terror. . . ."

Often and unfairly, Henry had described himself as a coward. In the sickroom, his terror was double. He feared the disease and feared the remedies. A disbeliever in doctors, he knew that his sister's physicians, in Italy as in America, used poisons as cures. He was present while poisons were advised and she took them. Being a layman, he was ineligible to interpose. Yet he watched, and while watching treatments he thought were hurtful, he found out that he was brave. In his letter to Carlo, he righted an injustice and gave himself credit for courage. "As for me, I was at first a wretched coward, but now I . . . face a convulsion, with death behind it, as coolly as my sister herself."

On July 13, Louisa died "in convulsions."[80] Persons interested in her favorite brother might give thought to the interval between Friday, when he wrote to Carlo, and Wednesday morning, when she died. What truly mattered may not have been that a woman died. It may have been, instead, that, for sister and brother, other persons lost significance.

In that event, Loo and Henry increasingly felt they were by themselves. Loo continued to struggle. Henry was with her. If striving and courage could keep her alive, she would live. In deepening unison, they lived for five days and nights. All were eternities.

PART TWO

10

BOTANY BAY

The day after Loo's death, a war began between Germany and France, the war that Henry three years earlier had said was a coming "fact."

Loo had asked to be buried in Italy. Immediately after the funeral and burial in Florence, Kuhn and Adams started towards London. They paused at Stresa on Lake Maggiore, then proceeded to Switzerland via the Simplon Pass. During a stop at Ouchy on Lake Geneva, Henry wrote to Carlo about the war: "My single hope is that France will get so thrashed as to make her mind her own business in future, and that Germany will have the same fate. How both can be beaten at once, I don't know, but I hope it may turn out so."[1]

Despite the mobilization, Kuhn and Adams easily crossed France and reached London. They put up at the Albemarle Hotel in Dover Street. Wanting to go at once to Quincy, Kuhn left for a steamer. Adams planned a month in England, to be followed by a visit to Quincy and winter as usual in Washington. As if 1870 were 1864 or 1862, he studied maps and reports of battles. The Germans could not be stopped. The Europe of Napoleon III was yielding rapidly to a Europe of Bismarck.

Adams had advised Gaskell that he wished to avoid "society and condolence," yet see friends and talk with "the political people." How much he talked with *English* politicians is unknown. Bright had suffered a breakdown and was not in London. Lord Clarendon had died, and Lord Granville was foreign secretary. Possibly Adams conferred with William Forster and even the foreign secretary, but evidence of such meetings is lacking. *American* politicians were accessible. He talked with Wells, who, no longer commissioner of the revenue, opportunely had come to Europe. Also he visited Motley.

Affairs at home remained a melee, and Motley was a victim.

The more prominent feudists in Washington were Grant, an expansionist to the South, and Sumner, an expansionist to the North. Grant hoped to annex part or all of San Domingo in the West Indies, and an emissary he sent there negotiated a treaty of annexation. Sumner induced the Senate to annul the treaty. In reprisal, Grant ordered the removal of Motley from the English mission. The letter asking Motley to quit had reached him in July. Outraged, he refused. When Adams visited him in August, he was in a mood to tell his caller all that was known in London about the feudists in Washington.[2]

In two respects, as seen by Adams, the news from America was excellent. Desistance from territorial acquisition had occurred. If only because Grant and Sumner were beating one another, the United States was staying within its borders. There was hope too of a settlement with England. Once Motley was removed (and Sumner punished), Grant might accede to a treaty committing the Alabama Claims to arbitration.

In a third respect, as seen by Henry, the news was as bad as possible. When they met in his rooms the previous April, the revenue reformers had had an unstated purpose, to begin the process of replacing Grant. Those present wished to meet again in the autumn. Inevitably, the necessities of the autumn meeting would be to devise a winning strategy and choose a winning presidential candidate for 1872. The reputation of Charles Francis Adams as a great diplomat was unimpaired, and he had no strong enemies other than Sumner. A movement favoring him as the reformers' choice was sure to start.

How well a C. F. Adams boom might prosper would mainly be decided, not later by the Chief, but sooner by persons attending private meetings. The meeting between Wells and Henry in England was crucial, but no record survives of what they said. Moreover, no assumption should be made that Henry was forthright with Wells on the subject uppermost in their minds.

As before, Henry wished to sustain and improve the Chief's reputation. He none the less would act to block a run for president by *any* Adams. It was later disclosed that the meeting of revenue reformers, originally planned for the west, would instead take the form of a "conference" in New York. The change possibly was agreed upon by Wells and Henry in England at Henry's urging. A reason suggests itself. A conference in New York would be more susceptible to his control.

❖ ❖ ❖

Frank Palgrave was scouting for pictures for Adams's rooms in Washington. When Adams returned from Italy, the Palgraves had just lost a newborn son and Cecil was ill. It happened too that Frank had come upon a soon-to-be-auctioned masterpiece, a purported Mantegna. Henry had promised to go to Shropshire to stay with Carlo. Frank kindly attended the auction, bought the Mantegna for 22 shillings, and reported to Henry, ". . . I think this the best bargain you ever made— even remembering the famous Raphael." He shortly wrote to add that the attribution had been confirmed. "It is on the whole the most beautiful piece of work I ever saw by that great man."[3]

While at Wenlock Abbey with Gaskell, Adams heard from Froude. The editor had fully meant to publish "The New York Gold Conspiracy." Perusal of the manuscript had made him fear a suit by the Erie lawyers. He explained to Adams that "in the face of a possible prosecution" he had consulted the magazine's owners. They were "unwilling to run the risk." Therefore, with "great regrets," he returned the manuscript.[4]

Written to appear in London simultaneously with his new "Session" in Boston, Adams's climactic article had been rejected unseen by the *Edinburgh Review* and rejected after reading by the *London Quarterly* and *Frazer's Magazine*. The article's existence was known only to Adams, Gaskell, Palgrave, and British editors. Adams wished the secret kept and again sought a publisher. He booked passage for New York on the *Cuba*, sailing from Liverpool on September 4, 1870. At the last opportunity, he sent the manuscript to Dr. John Chapman, editor of the *Westminster Review*, in London.

The *Westminster* was owned by Trubner and Company, the English distributor of the *North American*. Adams had no way of knowing whether Chapman would accept the article, but he knew that the *Westminster* was published not only in London but also in an "American Edition" issued separately in New York. A chance thus existed that Chapman might publish "The New York Gold Conspiracy" in October in both countries.

Henry reappeared at the Old House in Quincy on September 15. His parents had not seen him for almost a year. They were overjoyed at his return but wished to be spared the details of Loo's last hours. Their own news was quickly told. Mrs. John had died of apoplexy on August 31 in New Hampshire.[5] The linked appointments offered to Henry as editor of the *North American* and teacher of history at Harvard were unfilled and remained available to him.

The parents' explanations disclosed a story which Henry had

known only incompletely. President Eliot, Dean Gurney, and others had wanted to effect a revolution at Harvard. They had spearheaded the revolution with a lecture series. Some of the lecturers had been considered heterodox; and one, John Fiske, had lectured on the "positive philosophy" of Auguste Comte, a topic viewed with horror by many in the community. In February 1870, to relieve Gurney from teaching, Eliot and Gurney had given Fiske a temporary professorship and asked him to undertake the "interpretation of mediæval history to the senior class."

This near-approach to making Fiske a voting member of the faculty had caused a crisis. A special committee chaired by Overseer C. F. Adams upheld the fitness of the Fiske appointment, and Dean Gurney won agreement that a third professor of history should be appointed permanently to teach courses in "the political history of the Middle Ages and *mediæval institutions*"—in lay terms, medieval law.[6] Fiske wanted the place and was qualified in both fields; but Eliot and Gurney's adversaries succeeded so well in branding Fiske an atheist and positivist, though he was neither, that his candidacy could not be so much as entertained. Hence, in June, Harvard's first medievalist—in Henry Adams's expression—was "turned out because he was a Comtist!!!"

Thereafter, determination to appoint a permanent history teacher had become entangled with fear that the *North American* might expire. The quarterly was not a Harvard publication. All the same, Eliot and Gurney viewed its survival as a Harvard responsibility. They turned to Henry Adams. It was hoped that he would serve five purposes: save the magazine, free Gurney from editing, insulate Gurney against excessive burdens as a teacher, add a vote to the reform bloc in the faculty, and initiate the regular teaching of medieval history. As compensation, he was offered a five-year contract, an assistant professorship, a $2,000 salary, every chance of promotion, and a free hand, but no salary, as editor of the magazine.

When Adams's refusal reached them from Italy in late July, Eliot and Gurney turned to Godkin. Knowing he was married, had children, and could not easily be induced to abandon the *Nation*, they tempted him with a full professorship and a $4,000 salary. He hesitated at length but refused on August 25.[7] Rather than approach another candidate, Eliot and Gurney waited for Adams's return to Quincy. They disclosed their course to his relations, all of whom greatly wished that Henry would reconsider and accept the Harvard offer.

In July, Henry had been told what the Chief preferred. In a

letter about the revolution at Harvard, the Chief had explained to
Henry that the students had been freed to design the latter part of
their four-year programs. He had ventured to say that education
had become "the field of widest influence" in the country. He had
even predicted that the teacher who made "the greatest mark"
would become "all powerful" in the America of the future.[8] Truth
perhaps could be found in the father's words, and the distant vista
was grand, but the nearer prospect was familial and narrow. The
Chief's letter had implied that errant Henry should desist from
experiments in Washington, come home, teach respectably at Harvard, reside when possible at the Old House, freely use the Stone
Library, and, as necessary, assist his mother.

Following his arrival in Quincy, Henry for several days did
nothing that warranted the making of records. Attention was
mostly fixed on his elder brothers. John had bought a yacht on
which the sons could sail on weekends. Charles was planning a
large, expensive house on the family's Quincy property, at the top
of President's Hill.

In Cambridge, Gurney had built a new house, a mile or so
from the campus, on Fayerweather Street. On September 21, a
Wednesday, Charles and Henry went to Cambridge, dined with
Gurney, and saw the house. The brothers returned to the Old
House and talked awhile by themselves. Henry spoke separately
with their parents, but not at length.

That same night, Charles wrote in his diary: ". . . went out to
Cambridge & saw Gurney's house,—Henry & I dined with him,—
got home at 7 o.cl. & discussed Henry's professorship. . . ."[9]

Mrs. Adams too was keeping a diary. Before retiring, she
recorded an event that Charles did not mention. ". . . on his return
Henry told us he had agreed with Mr. Gurney to become the
Editor of the 'North American Review.' I am sorry[,] for it is hard
work & no pay."[10]

In 1870, three periodicals in the United States aspired to
superiority high above the squalid journals aligned with the Republican and Democratic parties. They were the *North American* in
Boston and the *Nation* and *Evening Post* in New York.

The July 1870 *North American* had contained three articles that
fell within Henry Adams's province as editor for politics: his new
"Session," Hodgskin's "Our Currency, Past and Future," and
Simon Newcomb's "The Labor Question." Henry had left for
Europe too soon to correct all the proofs. He evidently had depu-
tized Charles to do the work. The issue was very late in appearing.

It otherwise did not seem unusual, except that it received a most vigorous boost from Godkin. On August 11, the *Nation* printed a two-column reaction, mostly laudatory. Seven of its paragraphs concerned Henry's "Session."

In adverse situations, Henry tended to be agreeable, listen, and draw people out. The situation that awaited him in Quincy in September 1870 was adverse in a high degree. Its history dated from the meeting of revenue reformers in Washington the previous April. Charles had attended the meeting. All present had joined in an agreement that they would push their program "at all hazards, in the Republican party if possible, but out of it if necessary."[11] Nothing in their agreement encouraged trafficking with the Democrats.

Roughly on August 1, before the delayed July *North American* was mailed to subscribers, Henry's "Session" was given to the Democrats. It was sent to Illinois, apparently in the form of proofs, and on August 5 was published in the *Chicago Times*, a Democratic organ.[12]

The article was similarly printed in the foremost Democratic paper in New York. On August 8, perhaps on the basis of the article as published in the July *North American*, Manton Marble's *World* printed an incomplete version, shorn of almost a quarter of the text.

As incompletely printed in the *World*, the article passed to the National Democratic Executive Resident Committee in Washington. The committee understood it could reissue the article as a campaign pamphlet. Planning to circulate 250,000 copies, the committee reprinted Marble's version under a blaring cover:

A Radical Indictment!

The Administration—Its Corruptions & Shortcomings.
Its Weakness and Stolidity.

Thorough Analysis of Grant and Boutwell's Mental Calibre.
No Policy—No Ability.

A Graphic Review of Our Recent Political History.[13]

One might suppose that the seizure of one of its articles for partisan use was resisted or even stopped by the *North American Review*. No resistance was offered. Just the reverse, the article was given to the Democrats by persons who thought themselves possessed of authority. Their identities could not be mistaken. They were Henry's elder brothers, asserting the authority of Charles as Henry's deputy while Henry was abroad; also asserting the political rights of John and Charles as senior males in the Adams family.[14]

How much Henry knew about the reprinting of "The Session" when he went with Charles to dine with Gurney is uncertain. Possibly Henry's knowledge was a mere outline. Yet in two ways his knowledge can be assumed to have been complete. He knew that John and Charles had wrecked his carefully established position as a political independent, beholden to neither the Republicans nor the Democrats.[15] He also knew that the eldest sons were bent on the Chief's being elected president in 1872. In the minds of John and Charles in the summer and fall of 1870, damage to Grant had value because it might improve the likelihood that their father would be Grant's successor. Mentally they remained where they had been in 1868 when August Belmont had wanted to run their father for president and for some reason he had not arrived in America in time to be given the proffered place as Grant's Democratic opponent.[16]

While visiting Gurney, Henry had agreed to assume the editorship of the *North American* for one year and try to make it pay its costs.[17] He emphatically had *not* agreed to accept the place as Harvard's added teacher of history. As Mrs. Adams said, he consented only to perform—*unpaid*—the hard labor of editing the magazine.[18]

It went without saying that the decision was very odd and must have reflected a very strong motive. The last thing Henry had wished to do was accept responsibility for a revered institution in Boston. Only one motive could explain his consenting to take the headship of the *North American*. He wanted to recover control in American politics, control in the Adams family, and control of Charles; and he saw that a ready means to all three ends was calmly to become chief editor.

At Gurney's request, on Sunday, in the absence of Charles, Gurney and Henry talked again. They had already agreed that Henry would begin his editorship with the January 1871 issue. The reason for the new conversation was that Gurney more than ever wanted Henry to accept the place as third teacher of history. When they met, Gurney ought to have spoken only as dean of the faculty. He spoke mainly as an affectionate friend. He asked a great favor and openly expected its being granted. He at the same time guaranteed that Henry when a teacher would be autonomous, in effect would have his own department, and within his department could make whatever arrangements he thought best.

Henry would not agree to become either permanent editor or permanent teacher. He absolutely would not leave Washington as a permanency. In honor, he must have warned Gurney that, even if holding a five-year Harvard contract, he would move back to the capital as soon as his doing so might be possible. Yet he met Gurney's plea to this extent: he said he would visit President Eliot.[19]

On Monday, Adams saw Eliot in his office and protested that he knew nothing about medieval history and nothing about teaching. Eliot answered that Adams "knew just as much as anyone else in America knew on the subject, and . . . could teach better than anyone that could be had." It was assumed that the offered five-year contract had been accepted.[20] Adams left the room a member of the faculty, lacking only confirmation by the president and fellows at a meeting the following Saturday.[21]

Adams's earliest memory of Harvard was one of going there in the mid-1840s with his mother to visit her sister Charlotte, wife of Edward Everett, then president. He remembered that the president's house had a drawing room on the ground floor, off which there was a kitchen. On the strength of the memory, he walked to the bursar's office and asked about the "old President's house." Recently renamed Wadsworth Hall, the structure was located a few yards from Harvard Square. The bursar advised that rooms were available in the hall for faculty. Adams took ground floor rooms and a room above, connected by a private stairway.[22]

At Quincy later in the day, Henry informed his parents that he had accepted the professorship. His mother wrote in her diary: ". . . Mr. Gurney and Charles have persuaded him into it. We are very glad, we shall not only have him with us . . . but I think his life will be more useful and settled. . . ."[23]

News spread in Cambridge that Henry Adams had joined the faculty. In excited accents, Henry James, Jr., wrote to a friend, Grace Norton: "Do you know Henry Adams?—son of C. F. A. He has just been appointed professor of History . . . and is I believe a youth of genius and enthusiasm—or at least of talent and energy. . . . The Professorship of History was (I believe it's no secret) offered to Godkin, who declined."[24]

The person most excited was Brooks. About to start his first year at Harvard Law School, he had been hoping to live with Henry. It was settled that he should have the upstairs space in Wadsworth as a gift. Thus, after years of delay, their old dream of an interval together in Cambridge was becoming a reality.[25]

The semester would start at the end of the week. Because

history was an "elective" subject, seniors and juniors could take any history courses that were offered. Word got about that Henry Adams would be teaching courses on medieval history for seniors and juniors and a course on medieval institutions open to both. A flood of applicants enrolled. When Professor Adams met his classes, a third of the seniors and juniors would be in the class-rooms, waiting to examine him.

Adams meanwhile had gone to Washington to break up his G Street establishment. While in the capital, he "passed an hour" with Secretary Fish, whom he described as "very talkative." The Grant administration, never strong, was losing strength through resignations. Secretary Boutwell was immovable, but Attorney General Hoar had resigned early in the summer, and Secretary Cox would be resigning soon. Adams had settled on Cox as the candidate the revenue reformers would best support to carry the election of 1872. If one may judge from their later dealings, Adams visited Cox, explained that he had accepted the editorship of the *North American*, said he intended to support Cox for president, and asked whether Cox could write an article on civil-service reform for the January issue. Understandably, the secretary promised to supply the article.[26]

Writing to Gaskell from Washington on September 29, Adams confessed that he had become a Harvard history professor and "avowed editor" of the *North American*. He seemed cheery enough. "Do you imagine I am appalled at this prospect? Not a bit of it!"

Until that moment, Henry's letters to Carlo had been open and confiding. His new letter was misleading. He wrote as if his predicament had been a mere matter of being insistently urged to teach. ". . . I found the question of the professorship sprung upon me again in a very troublesome way. I hesitated a week, and then I yielded." He painted the professorship as advantageous, even welcome. He said he had been "brought in to strengthen the reforming party in the University." He would be "responsible only to the college Government" and was "sure of strong backing from above." He would be teaching *medieval* history, "of which . . . I am utterly and grossly ignorant," but he would be free to "teach what I please within the dates 800–1649." ". . . my great wish is to get hold of the students' imaginations for my peculiar ideas."

On some subjects, the letter to Gaskell was silent to the point of evasion. It said nothing about the problem of America's presidents, the standing of Henry's father, or the conduct of his elder brothers. It gave no sign that the critical question had been the *editorship*; that in a desperate situation Henry had opted to take charge of the *North American* for hidden reasons all his own.

Yet the letter could be forgiven. It reflected a great event of the time: a tragic flight of capable men from Washington and from the federal government. Its best lines were entirely frank and rather sad. ". . . there are few of my political friends left in power now, and these few will soon go out. This reconciles me to going away, though I hate Boston and am very fond of Washington."

Senator T. O. Howe of Wisconsin was a Republican intensely loyal to General Grant and Secretary Boutwell. He understood that Henry Brooks Adams, a young member of the Adams family, deeming himself a "Massachusetts politician," or even a "Massachusetts statesman," had contributed an article to the July *North American* titled "The Session" that purported to survey the actions of the federal government during the preceding year. To Howe's knowledge, the Boston quarterly as a rule was "indifferent to all parties in politics—to all sects in religion—to all sides in morals." Howe read the article and ascertained that young Adams was *not* indifferent. He was a "Democratic expositor." His article was a "Democratic broadside." It had been given to the Democratic *Chicago Times* in such haste that it appeared in that party organ on August 5, "two days before the [*North American*] *Review* could be bought in Chicago." Thus what might have passed for the work of an impartial critic was revealed to be the work of a malignant Democrat criticizing the Republicans out of "party spite."

Howe was well-posted on the Adamses, who in his opinion were the Republican Party's principal apostates. He thought them dangerous as well as despicable. Meaning to counteract young Adams's article, he wrote a point-by-point rejoinder and arranged its publication in the *Wisconsin State Journal* on October 7. He also arranged its issuance as a pamphlet. Printed on newspaper stock for free distribution, the pamphlet bore the headings:

Political History

The Republican Party Defended.
A Reviewer Reviewed.

"The Session," by Henry Brooks Adams, reviewed by Hon. T. O. Howe, U. S. Senator from Wisconsin.[27]

The rejoinder was meant to hurt. It can be assumed that Howe sent a copy to Fields, Osgood & Company in Boston, the publisher of

the *North American*; that the copy was forwarded to Adams as editor
of the magazine; and that, at the very latest, Adams received it in
the morning on Monday, October 24.

Meanwhile, in appearance, the Adams family was united.
Henry had shipped his possessions from Washington to Cambridge, moved into Wadsworth, and started to function as a
teacher. On weekends, he went to Quincy. On Sunday, October 16,
all four sons sailed on John's yacht. On October 23, John, Charles,
and Henry sailed again.[28]

When meeting his students, Professor Adams claimed only to
be a learner. He did not disguise how little he knew about medieval
politics and medieval institutions. Yet very quickly the students
witnessed his speed, directness, and energy when entering a subject.

Two of the seniors, Michael Simpson and Henry Cabot Lodge,
were inseparable friends. Lodge till then had not been serious
about his studies. While traveling in England four years earlier, he
had become acquainted with Mary Adams, and at Harvard he had
grown very friendly with Brooks, but he had only heard of Henry.
According to his own account, he "stumbled" into Professor
Adams's course on medieval politics and learned to his complete
surprise that he was "fascinated by the stormy careers of the great
German emperors, by the virtues, the abilities, the dark crimes of
the popes, and by the tremendous conflicts between church and
empire." In a matter of days, he found himself transformed. ". . . I
worked hard. . . ." ". . . I discovered that it was the keenest of
pleasures to use one's mind. . . ."[29]

Living together in a Harvard building was a new experience
for Henry and Brooks, and one that bore on Henry's name. Their
mother had named one son after her dead brother, Henry Brooks,
and another after her rich father, Peter Chardon Brooks. When
the older was small, she often called him Brooks; and, as Peter
grew, she called *him* Brooks continuously. For this reason, friends
of the Adamses had learned to speak of Henry Brooks Adams as
"Old Brooks." The name had pursued him even when a collegian.[30]

It had not been Henry's tendency to complain about his name.
While at the Legation, he had ordered a bookplate from an
engraver bearing the name Henry Brooks Adams and a matching
device in Latin, *Humani Bona Animi*.[31] He had pasted the plates into
many of his books. Each book seemed silently to testify how much
he *liked* his name.

In late October 1870, Henry Brooks Adams received a letter
from Henry Higginson saying he was delighted by Adams's return

to Harvard. Answering on Monday, October 24, Adams explained that he had returned to the college "not so much to teach as to learn." "I am writing this at a faculty meeting, and there is not a student here who could feel less at home in the company than I do." He admitted siding with the students. "Am I not one of them myself?" And he invited Higginson to visit him at "No. 1 Wadsworth Hall." "There I renew my youth."

Finishing his answer to Higginson, Adams signed it with the two words "Henry Adams." He had quietly changed his name. Next day, perhaps from habit, he signed a letter to Gaskell "H. B. A.," but he also signed more letters "Henry Adams." Thereafter he did not vary. His name was Henry Adams or H. A. The "Brooks" and the "B." were gone.

It can be assumed that Henry's relations were among the first to sense that he had changed his name. Being Adamses, they were likely to ask why he did it. Being Henry, he was likely to respond, not by giving the truest reasons, but by giving reasons that were true and likely to stop discussion. For a start, he could say he had changed his name because he and Brooks were living together and needed not to be confused. He could say he wanted never again to be called "Old Brooks." He could say in addition that Brooks might become a writer, in which case he and Brooks would need easily remembered names that would keep them separate, yet give them the appearance of a pair.

A factor that bore on Henry's changing his name was the pamphlet circulated by Senator Howe. The senator had begun his rejoinder to Henry Brooks Adams by saying that Adams's "Session" was the "first broadside against the Republican party in the campaign of 1870." He named four members of the Adams family: John Adams, John Quincy Adams (whom he called "the greatest"), Charles Francis Adams, and Henry Brooks Adams. He treated the four as the Adamses who mattered. He went on to say that all four had gained by belonging to political parties and had then deserted them. John Adams and Henry Brooks Adams had each completed such a betrayal once. John Quincy Adams and Charles Francis Adams had each completed a betrayal twice. All, however, were thorough infidels, truthless to their chosen parties.[32]

Of course, if betrayal was defined as moving from one party to another, the conspicuous apostate among the younger Adamses was John. Henry's sins, if they were sins, were his shifting from the Republican Party to no party and more recently his organizing a political movement of "revenue reformers." But Howe's pamphlet did not trouble itself with details. It lumped four living Adams sons into *one* son, Henry, and made him a quondam Republican who had turned into a Democrat.

Howe's pamphlet was easily the most important attack on an Adams in many years. The senator's reason for making the attack had nothing to do with the fall elections in 1870 and everything to do with the presidential election two years in the future. The meaning of the attack was clearest in an especially derisive passage. Howe said about Henry Brooks Adams:

> The author is proclaimed to be not only a Statesman himself, but to belong to a family in which Statesmanship seems to be preserved by propogation [*sic*]—something [somewhat?] as color is in the leaf of the Begonia, perpetuating resemblance through perpetual change. He may fairly be said to have been sired by at least two Presidents and a half.[33]

The last words were prophecy. Howe was saying that Charles Francis Adams would be nominated for president by the Democrats in 1872 and would be *half* a president in the sense that he and Ulysses S. Grant would divide the space on the ballots. Also, by saying "at least," Howe conceded that C. F. Adams might possibly be elected. It was precisely because the father's candidacy looked strong that Howe was answering the "broadside" by the malignant son—the heir apparent of the future candidate, and revealedly his accomplice.

No evidence exists that Henry showed his relations the attack by the Wisconsin senator, still less that he urged their reading it.[34] There is evidence, however, that he read it himself; and there is reason to believe that the precipitating factors that moved him to change his name were *printed statements*. A pertinent statement appeared in Howe's pamphlet. The senator ascribed the writing of "The Session" to "Brooks Adams" and the assassination of Lincoln to "Wilkes Booth." The wording was very strong. It suggested that "Brooks Adams" had tried to assassinate both Grant and Boutwell by means of lies.

Additional statements appeared in an anonymous critique of "The Session" that Henry clipped from an unidentified periodical, possibly a Boston newspaper, and preserved in his files. The critique spoke of "Mr[.] Harry Brooks Adams." It contained phrases even more misleading: "This article on the session by the great Brooks Adams"—"Mr[.] Brooks Adams's great dissertation"— and "B. A's views." Also it offered the sly comment: "Mr[.] Brooks Adams should have sent this part of his article to some New York newspaper, with sensational headings."[35]

The printed statements considered, it was time for Henry Adams to step forward as Henry Adams. The world needed to be informed that a living male Adams distinct from other living male Adamses possessed a distinctive simple name. Confusion had to stop.

In his first letter to Carlo after reaching America, Henry had mentioned the death of an aunt with whom he had been "very intimate." His next sentence said, "I found myself growing in consequence."[36] Also he revealed his income. ". . . what with one thing and another[,] my income is about doubled, and I have about £1200 a year."

Mrs. John was predeceased by her only child. No will in her name was recorded in the District of Columbia.[37] What happened to her assets when she died is unclear; but it seems likely that by a private means, perhaps through the agency of the Chief, she left Henry money. The income Henry revealed—$6,000—was a third more than President Eliot's annual salary. In income, the new professor was one of the richer inhabitants of Cambridge.

While getting richer, Henry grew younger. The idea that he was a student had more validity than might appear. He was eating meals on occasion with law students and seniors. He was living in what could just as well have been student rooms. In addition, he was looking for new friends. As would happen on a campus, he was seeing new faces by the hundred. He told Carlo, "I hope to pick up a few new acquaintances whom I like, for my old friends don't amuse me much . . . ."

Another change was more important. While Loo was dying, Henry had undergone a strain as great as he could withstand, consistent with his survival. The strain left him stronger and more perfectly defined in character. He however won these invaluable gains at the cost of transient tiredness and debility. It was during this interval of impairment that he was faced with complications created by his elder brothers and the Harvard authorities. He acted rightly and strongly; also he kept Gurney's friendship; but tragically he lost his home. It would take time and effort for him to return to Washington. He meanwhile had not entirely recovered; and there was no one in Cambridge or Boston, not even Gurney, in whom he felt perfect trust.[38]

On October 25, writing Carlo another letter (the last he signed H. B. A.), he moved back towards candor. His expressions showed pain and hardship. He said he had repitched his camp in a locality that had serious disadvantages. "I lose by the change. The winter climate is damnable. The country is to my mind hideous. And the society is three miles away in Boston."

His severest complaints related to Harvard. He was beginning to teach at a university he did not respect. ". . . I don't believe in the system in which I am made a part, and thoroughly dislike and despise the ruling theories of education in the university. So I have undertaken to carry on my department on my own bottom, without reference to the Faculty or anyone. . . . I shall quietly substitute my own notions for those of the College, and teach in my own way."

When taking over as editor, Henry insisted that Charles be secretly involved. After much discussion, Gurney, Henry, and Charles agreed on a program for the *North American* that might cut costs and increase circulation. They met with James Osgood, the publisher, and Henry unfolded the program. Osgood accepted it and helped put it into effect—did "everything I have asked."[39] Yet the quarterly's survival would be hanging by a thread, and in one respect the thread would be thinner than Osgood may have anticipated. Henry wished to keep the magazine partly political, but the magazine would contain no new political articles by Henry Adams.

This revolution did not mean that Adams was no longer a politician. He was more than ever a politician and was pursuing his political objects by new, less fathomable means. One of his means was to do what a politician could do when clothed as chief editor of the *North American*. He already had won the promise of an article from Secretary Cox. In a letter sent on October 21, he had placed the old quarterly at Minister Motley's service.[40] The politicians next on his list were David Wells and one of the senators from Missouri, Carl Schurz.

Wells had returned from Europe and was employed as tax commissioner by New York State. On October 25, Adams asked him for an article on revenue reform. "Don't try to get out of it. I have a fair claim on your assistance. . . . I shall expect the article to be in my hands on the 1st of March [1871] punctually."

Highly ambitious but foreign born, Senator Schurz was barred by the constitution from being president. The bar appeared to have made him an inveterate promoter of persons who might be president. He had risen to prominence in 1860 as a publicist appealing to German-Americans to vote for Lincoln. He was made minister to Spain, and briefly visited the Adamses in London, but left diplomacy to become a general.[41] When elected to the Senate, he was assigned to the committee on foreign relations. In the spring of 1870, Henry Adams had badgered him without success to write an article for the *North American.*

Currently Schurz was leading a reform movement of "Liberal Republicans" in St. Louis and other midwestern cities. The movement showed evidence of wanting to choose a president. Writing from Cambridge on October 27, Henry invited the senator to contribute an article on "the political condition of Missouri and the West." ". . . I would be glad to extend the range of your influence so far as is in my power."

There was little risk that either Motley or Schurz would contribute an article. Henry's true object in writing to them was the maintenance of good relations. Good relations were necessary because political movements were multiplying. The most threatening to Henry was a movement by distinguished New Yorkers to bring Charles Francis Adams before the public. The Chief had completed an arrangement with the New York Historical Society to address the members at the society's anniversary meeting in December. His address would concern the historical background of the Alabama Claims. Though historical, the address would be heard and reported as incipiently presidential.[42]

The news that C. F. Adams would soon be coming to the city inspired a leader of New York society, Mary Schuyler, to invite the Chief and Mrs. Adams to stay as guests at her and her husband's home. Closing her invitation, Mrs. Schuyler asked Mr. Adams to convey a message to his wife: ". . . tell her, I have not forgotten that she once told me, that Henry was her most clever son."[43]

The message from Mrs. Schuyler reflected two increasingly important facts. People were expecting that C. F. Adams would be the next tenant in the White House, and people could not think about the Chief without thinking about his cleverest son.[44] Menacingly for Henry, the two facts were really one. As if by a common instinct, many Americans were turning for leadership to a supposed team, a father generally known as the country's greatest living diplomat, and a son who was publishing incisive articles relating to the current administration.

Two winters before in Washington, Henry Adams had devised a political program attractive to diverse groups and even to groups not usually held together. In late 1870, his program was so firmly rooted that in numerous minds it was a given. What remained was its execution.

Also, for two years, Adams had been building a movement. It

had no name. Its members dubbed themselves "revenue reformers," but the tag reflected only one element in their program.

The New York conference of revenue reformers, scheduled to occur on November 22, 1870, would be *private*, meaning closed to reporters. The Free Trade League, a new organization with chapters in several cities, would serve as nominal sponsor. Those invited would be Republicans or persons without party attachments, but sympathetic Democrats would be waiting nearby, in case their inclusion was desired. A sizeable portion of the participants would be editors. Henry Adams would attend, explicitly "to press the interests of my Review." He would not seem to be in charge.

Approximately on November 1, Adams obtained the October issue of the *Westminster Review* as published in New York. It contained "The New York Gold Conspiracy," printed as Article IX, unsigned. Sight of the article in print was Henry's first knowledge that Chapman had ventured its publication.

The effect of Chapman's courage was final. Thereafter, Adams would *reprint* political articles he had published, and possibly he might revise or improve them, but he would never write a new one. In his view, those already published made a completed, extremely successful unit, best not disturbed with sequels.[45]

Word came that Motley's resistance to ejection had resulted in his outright dismissal by Grant and Fish. In the absence of a minister, Moran was serving as chargé d'affaires.

Henry had firmly sworn in 1867 that he would never in future belong to a political party. In 1870, he gave some appearance of deviation from that ideal. On November 19, three days prior to the New York conference, he explained to Carlo: "The retirement from Washington has by no means thrown me out of politics. On the contrary, as editor I am deeper in them than ever, and my party is growing so rapidly that I look forward to the day when we shall be in power again as not far distant. Two or three years ought to do it."

It was November, yet Henry's letter was cheerful—one could say unaccountably cheerful. He said he was sorry for Motley, "especially as he has now received his *coup de grace* in peremptory dismissal." He mentioned that "The New York Gold Conspiracy" had been published in the *Westminster Review*. "I sent it to the editor just as I was coming away . . . and heard no more of it till I saw it in print. The editor has not written to me on the subject, and I have not written to him."

November 21 was the Monday before Thanksgiving. Late in the day, Henry, Charles, and Wells converged at Fall River and caught the night boat to New York—one of Jim Fisk's luxurious steamers.[46] In different ways, the travelers were in the dark. Neither Charles nor Wells knew that Henry had just published an article which concerned, among other things, a dinner arranged for Grant on a Fisk steamer so that Gould could persuade the president to accept McHenry's "crop theory" and permit a rise in the price of gold.[47] For his part, Henry did not know that in New York someone connected with the *Nation* had just encountered a wondrous *British* article about American affairs. Always eager to advise subscribers concerning things they might wish to read, the *Nation* was preparing to commend the article as a reversal of the time-worn rule that British commentaries on America were ill-informed.

The conference on November 22 began with a day session attended by roughly twenty persons and climaxed in an evening session attended by roughly forty. During the evening session, measures were proposed and votes taken. Charles recorded: "A vile rainy day, wh. was occup^d w^h our conference,—it was very import^t & very satisfactory,—about 20 present & a great change since last Spring,—the tone now was confid^t & bold. Henry & I had clearer ideas of what we wanted than anyone else & finally shaped the course of events,—we didn't get through till midnight."

Godkin attended the evening session. In a diary he was keeping for later sending to his absent wife, he noted free-spokenly: "Went in the evening in torrents of rain to the meeting of revenue reformers. There were about forty present. It was very successful. . . . The two Adamses were there. C. F. is growing quite fat and chubby, and looks more comical than ever."

Somewhat as a postscript, Charles recorded on Wednesday, ". . . met Godkin & lunched with him;—saw Hodgskin for a few minutes & home by Fall River boat." He did not mention Henry.

Godkin made a parallel Wednesday record: ". . . [I] had lunch with the Adamses, and went about with Henry arranging with booksellers to push *N A Review*."[48]

The most evident result of the conference was open enthusiasm concerning a large *public* dinner for interested persons, to be held at Delmonico's the following Monday night. Reporters would be welcome. Henry so arranged things that Charles and John were *invited*. They would not *attend* but would respond with letters that would be read to the participants at the start of the proceedings.[49] Henry would neither attend nor send a letter. He effectively would vanish.

Disappearance was indispensable. Henry had exerted a controlling influence on the doings of the *private* meeting, especially during the evening session. Those present had included himself and Charles, Godkin of the *Nation*, William Cullen Bryant and Charles Nordhoff of the *New York Evening Post*, Samuel Bowles of the *Springfield Republican*, William Grosvenor of the *St. Louis Democrat*, and Horace White of the *Chicago Tribune*. At the start of the session, there were preliminaries relating to James G. Blaine, the Speaker of the House, with whom the revenue reformers had been attempting to have some dealings. The main discussion centered on civil-service reform and revenue reform. ". . . it was . . . decided that the two measures should be advocated together and that for the present our agitation should be restricted, so far as we acted as a body, to these two issues. . . ."

To that point, there were no dangers. But the participants went on to added matters. Many said they considered themselves a "new party." They wondered whether to effect "a permanent organisation." Next they voted to create a "central committee" with power to call a "convention" the following summer. And they came to the verge of naming Jacob Dolson Cox as first member of the central committee.

Henry interposed. Saying the participants were in "great danger" of acting "without sufficient preparation," he urged *against* naming Cox as a committeeman. He said it had not been learned whether Cox was willing to serve. His objection was supported by Charles and Nordhoff of the *Evening Post*. All present at last agreed to adjourn "without naming the committee."

The committee had been created to call a party convention in the summer of 1871. No committeemen having being named, it was decided that the party would simply "wait the doings of Congress, holding our Convention as a threat over the [Republican] party." It was felt that waiting would do no harm. If the Republicans in Congress misbehaved, a call for a convention could go out as early as the spring.

The reformers present, Charles and Nordhoff among the rest, had not grasped what the struggle about the committee was all about. The issue was presidential. Henry—in secrecy so secret that no one guessed his motive—had wanted the revenue reformers to promote for president a man *not of their number and not an Adams*. If the evening participants had done what they almost did, if they had made ex-Secretary Cox the first member of the central committee, Henry's hopes that the Ohioan might be a candidate for president would have been defeated. Cox would have fallen instantly to the status of a mere committeeman. But since Henry interposed successfully, the possibility that Cox might become a presidential candidate was still alive, and ironically Henry succeeded in part through timely support by Charles.

This is not to say that Cox had good prospects of becoming president. The Ohioan was a fine man. Perhaps no better candidate could be found in the country. But he was very unlikely to be nominated in the election of 1872, either to replace Grant as the Republican candidate or to run against him as the candidate of another party, old or new. The great barrier in his way was another man's supposed ability to get elected. The country boasted editors and politicians who claimed to know who could be elected and who not. Such editors and politicians were seated in the room, and the man whom almost all of them would want to nominate for president in 1872 was C. F. Adams.

When the participants rushed to have a committee and rushed toward naming Cox as its first member, they also were rushing towards an unspoken object: the choice of the elder Adams as their future candidate. Henry stopped the rush and achieved three objects at a blow. He held back some of the country's strongest supporters of a potential president, the Chief. He preserved the slender prospects of another potential president, Jacob Cox. And he took a step towards transforming the revenue reformers from a self-styled new party into something more effective. That something would be a political junto; that is, a *terrifier* of existing parties—a small unanimous body capable of reshaping the existing parties' intended acts.[50]

The effectiveness of Henry's management was not sensed, which made it the more effective. When the conference adjourned, the participants, Henry excepted, understood themselves to be a new party preparing to hold a convention in 1871, a year in the advance of the next election. Henry would not object to the reformers' saying they were a party. He at times might say so himself. But the reformers would operate at one level of political acumen and sophistication, and he would operate at a higher but secret level. He needed to prevent the nomination of the Chief for president, by any or all parties. He needed to implement his own national program. He was managing rather well, but to continue in his success he would resort to added means.

Presumably by the night boat on Wednesday, he returned to Fall River and thence to Boston. Soon in Cambridge, he received the issue of the *Nation* for November 24. In the section headed "Notes," he read an unwitting commentary on himself. The magazine alerted its readers to a remarkable British analysis of the gold panic.

> One of the essays in the last *Westminster* shows quite sufficient knowledge of American affairs. It tells the story of the famous "corner" in the Wall Street Gold Market, which was effected by Mr. Jay Gould and Mr. James Fisk, jun., in September last. It is no more than fair to say that one might look far in our native newspapers and magazines before coming on any writer who has brought more local knowledge to the handling of this particular American topic. . . . To one aspect of American life . . . our English brethren have at last done something like justice.

Warning came from Cox that his article on civil-service reform for the January 1871 *North American* would be a few days late. Since becoming acquainted in Washington, Henry and the Ohioan had exchanged some seven letters, all secret. Henry replied on November 28 and gave an account of the conference. As far as it went, his account was doubtless true. It none the less was most notable for omissions; also for subtlety of expression. He did not tell Cox that his elder brothers, unlike himself, wanted C. F. Adams to be the country's next president. He did not explain that his own *opposition* to an Adams candidacy was a total secret, unknown to his brothers and unknown to his father. Still more to the point, he left it to Cox to discern what the struggle concerning a central committee had involved.

Cox's article arrived. Once it was set in type, Henry ordered the publication of his first issue of the *North American*.

A few days later, on December 13, potential-president Charles Francis Adams addressed the New York Historical Society on "The Struggle for Neutrality in America." His address reviewed the history of the United States in its relations with other countries. The subject appeared to engage the speaker's deeper feelings. Certain details stood out. He lauded Albert Gallatin as a diplomat. He noted that the Treaty of Ghent with Great Britain was signed the day before Christmas. Moving forward to the Rebellion, he described the *Trent* affair as "the most perilous hazard of the war."[51] He seemed to think the affair had been more perilous than a great battle, even the Seven Days, Antietam, Vicksburg, or Gettysburg. The suggestion was new.

The departure of J. L. Motley from office encouraged the British to attempt new dealings with the touchy Americans. An English politician, Lord Tenterton, submitted a memorandum to the Foreign Office on November 21, 1870, recommending an initiative avoiding direct reference to the Alabama Claims. England instead was to raise with the Americans a list of disputed issues relating to Canada. The two countries might then agree to submit the Canadian issues to "a Joint International Commission, such as that which preceded the Treaty of Ghent." That done, the Americans might be led to insist that the British *as a concession* permit the Alabama Claims also to be submitted to the commission. By this ingenious means, the British would appear to yield and the Americans would gain an appearance of force and dignity such as they seemed to want. Progress towards a general settlement might follow.

Five days later, Sir John Rose, a London banker trusted by Lord Granville, submitted a memorandum to the Foreign Office which suggested that an unofficial emissary be sent to Canada and thence to Washington with a view to speaking with Secretary Fish concerning matters of mutual interest. Born in Scotland but raised in Canada, Rose was married to an American, knew Fish and other Americans prepared to discuss the Alabama Claims, and had a gift for avoiding conflict. As perhaps had been intended all along, Rose was asked to serve as emissary. His instructions, dated December 19, empowered him go to America and find out "if some agreement acceptable to both parties may not be reached."

Moran was told about Rose's mission. He understood that the visit would be "without official character" and of a "purely private nature." He cabled news of it to Fish.[52]

At Harvard, the only considerable breaks in the academic year were summer vacation and Christmas recess. On December 19, Henry Adams sent Gaskell another letter. He said a senator had called him a begonia. He mentioned a meeting. "I went to New York a month ago to a political meeting, and we laid vast and ambitious projects for the future." He revealed that James Mc-Henry wished to sue the author of "The New York Gold Conspiracy"; that editor Chapman had informed the author that McHenry might sue for libel; and that the author was delighted. "I have written over that this is precisely what would suit me, and that he may try it if he likes."

Henry added cheerfully that he had *worked*. "My happy carelessness of life for the last ten years has departed. . . . As for society, I have not seen the hem of a female garment since I came out here. Life has resolved itself into editing and professing."

A metaphor Henry had used for his altered life in Cambridge was "banishment."[53] In his letter, he gave the metaphor a part-biting, part-comic form. He said to Carlo, "What a droll idea it is that you should be running about England, visiting people, and I shut up in this Botany Bay, working like a scavenger."

The image made Henry a *British* felon, transported to forced labor in Australia. Yet the felon was in high spirits. ". . . I shall go on to Washington for the holidays. . . . What do I do after getting there? I go to my dentist's, oh my friend! Yes! I pass a fortnight with my dentist."

As tended to happen, the letter was interrupted. Henry was unable to complete it till the day before Christmas. Yet his mood remained the same. ". . . I start for Washington in an hour. . . . I am just *done*! Run to death by printers and students. But my work is finished and time is up. I am going to have some fun."

11

ENGAGED AND DISENGAGED

When traveling either way between Massachusetts and Washington, Adams liked to pause in New York. During his absence from Cambridge in December 1870 and January 1871, he possibly had friendly meetings in New York with Hay. After an interval of service as first secretary in Madrid, Hay had retreated to Illinois and written a book, *Castilian Days*. He then moved to New York to become an editor of the *New York Tribune*, working with owner Horace Greeley and chief editor Whitelaw Reid. Simultaneously, his book was accepted for publication by William Dean Howells, a new editor at the *Atlantic Monthly*. The first instalment appeared in the December 1870 *Atlantic*.

Where or with whom Adams stayed while in Washington is unknown.[1] It is known that he called on Hamilton Fish and that the secretary of state, without asking that the story not be repeated, mentioned to him "that Grant took a dislike to Motley because he parted his hair in the middle."[2] What else Fish may have said to Adams can only be guessed, and what Adams said to Fish is a perfect mystery.[3]

Adams presumably left the capital on Friday or Saturday, January 6 or 7, 1871. Sir John Rose, the English emissary, arrived on Monday and immediately dined with Fish and Davis. Also on Monday, as a means of offending Sumner, the administration gave the Senate and the press a mass of documents relating to Motley's ouster.[4]

On January 13 from Cambridge, Adams wrote to Charles Eliot Norton: "I was at Washington last week and found anarchy ruling our nation. I don't know who has power or is responsible, but whoever it is, I cannot find him. . . . The official figure-heads at all events are not the ones in power. . . ."

Four days later, Adams wrote in confidence to Wells: "I was sorry not to see you in Washington. . . . I found things badly changed. . . . The President has succeeded in breaking down everybody of any value, including himself. . . . Unless we are lugged into foreign difficulties we shall come out right in the end, but meanwhile, it is all chaos."

Wells had chaired the revenue reformers' conference in New York. At the time, the participants had acted as if their power to dismiss Grant in 1872 was assured. In view of their hopes, Adams's communication to Wells contained a harsh surprise. He said about Grant, ". . . the prospect of getting rid of him is distant." The implication was that Grant would be reelected.

The outlook for the reformers, recently so bright, had blackened horribly. Possibly Grant's ability to stay in office had been underestimated. Possibly the ability of the reformers to dislodge him had been wildly exaggerated. In either case, if Henry Adams was right, the reformers faced a huge gap of time, more than six years, during which they could expect to be powerless in Washington. Meanwhile the main spring of the revenue reformers' movement, Adams himself, seemed disengaged from the mechanism. Perhaps some change he knew about but would not disclose had transformed his necessities.

For winter purposes, Dr. Robert Hooper had moved to a new house in Boston, at 114 Beacon Street, in an area called the new Back Bay. Of his three children, only Marian, or Clover, was unmarried. Clover as usual was living at home. Socially active, she was watchful—to use her words—for "chances for flirtations." She however was not taken with certain men she was seeing. One of her enjoyments was sending bulletins to Mrs. Alexander Whiteside, formerly Eleanor Shattuck, who had moved to Champlain, New York. On January 10, 1871, she wrote to Elly (her punctuation is kept): "Do let me think of all the most unimportant things I can tell you. A pleasant dinner at Brooks' with soup, fish Sayles and Gray—ditto at James on New Years, with the variation which Boston affords of raw oysters, then soup Gray and Holmes."

Clover read newspapers. She sometimes found hilarities in national politics that were lacking at Boston dinners and dances. She continued to Elly (her spelling is kept): "Such larks today to get the Motley and Fish correspondance. . . . I should think Mr. Fish's letter to Moran would sting Mr. Motley dreadfully. . . . What a nice piece of gossip the whole thing is! And no one thinks that they are gossipy in discussing *men's* affairs, but only 'showing a proper interest in public questions of the day!' "[5]

A man had come into Clover's life whom her bulletins did not name. Henry Adams had replaced her brother-in-law, Whitman Gurney, as editor of the *North American*. Professor Adams was visiting frequently at the Gurneys' house in Cambridge, and his arrivals had placed him in continuous touch with several Hoopers. He had shown likings for Ellen and Edward. He had had encounters with Clover, with no visible effect.[6]

In November and December 1870, Adams had sometimes gone to Boston to dine with his parents and Mary at 57 Mount Vernon Street. Following his return from Washington, he regularly did the same. Possibly beginning in November, his dinners in Boston had served as cover for another activity. After each dinner, without its being noticed, he walked to 114 Beacon Street to see Clover Hooper, then went back to Cambridge. His not mentioning his meetings with Clover was matched by her not mentioning them either. Both were keeping secrets.

In addition to concealing their meetings, they were concealing truths from one another. The reasons for silence were strong. The question between them was not everyday love leading to ordinary marriage. It was love of different kinds, each raging and undeclared.[7]

Henry's feeling was what writers of novels and romances called true love. He had fallen in love with Clover in every atom of his being. A radical in love as in everything else, he wanted, not a marriage, but a perfect marriage. As he saw her in late 1870, Clover was perfect in two ways, at some moments sweet and peaceable, at other moments funny, practical, political, and in every act and word original.[8]

Daughter of a non-practicing physician, Clover felt the passion of a woman capable of benefits and cures. She knew Henry as strong but in need of care.[9] His most singular attributes were a steadiness not easy to account for and an often-visible trace of defiance. He had the air of a fighter engaged in a battle or combination of battles that he intended not to lose; yet, in the instant, he was homeless, friendless, and mateless. He had been torn from Washington, a place he said he greatly liked, and chained to Cambridge, where his rooms, though useful for meeting people, working, and keeping books, were not a desirable place to live. He was friendly, yet discernibly had no intimates. In any usual sense, he seemed not to want a wife. In addition, he had an ailment, invisible to most, that Clover possibly could see. He was absenthearted. He had loved, but only within a segment of the Adams family. Attached to a grandmother and other Adams women no longer living, he was too continuously with the dead.[10]

It needs repeating that Henry was a writer. He believed that the controlling fact in Clover's life was that at five she had lost her mother. He knew that her mother, Ellen Sturgis Hooper, was a poet and left a sheaf of poems much valued by her children.[11]

Instead of telling Clover his thoughts and feelings, Henry wrote them. He knew a sonnet by Petrarch that he wished to translate.[12] Possibly a few days prior to February 16, 1871, his thirty-third birthday, he finished a corresponding sonnet in English:

> Oh, little bird! singing upon your way,
>   Or mourning for your pleasant summer-tide,
>   Seeing the night and winter at your side,
> The joyous months behind, and sunny day!
> If, as you know your own pathetic lay,
>   You knew as well the sorrow that I hide,
>   Nestling upon my breast, you would divide
> Its weary woes, and lift their load away.
> I know not that our shares would then be even,
>   For she you mourn may yet make glad your sight,
> While against me are banded death and heaven;
>   But now the gloom of winter and of night
> With thoughts of sweet and bitter years for leaven,
>   Lends to my talk with you a sad delight.[13]

Henry's sonnet was important in several ways. It commemorated his secret meetings with Clover at her father's house. The meetings were secret in that their Adams and Hooper relatives, Dr. Hooper excepted, knew nothing about them. They were secret also in the sense that Dr. Hooper would have to wait if he wished to be told their meaning.

Also the sonnet named a battle. It revealed Henry's belief that "death and heaven" were leagued against him, even to the extent of barring him in another life from persons he had loved.

Interestingly, the sonnet showed that Henry did not know Clover. His lines assumed she was a Christian with usual beliefs and hopes. They left no room for her being what, by then, she must already have become: a convinced but unquarrelsome agnostic.

At a future time, Henry might tell Clover that he had translated a sonnet of Petrarch's. He might mention the date he finished the translation. He might place it in her hands. If he did, she would quickly see that his lines were a marriage proposal. She would see as well that it was meaningful to him that her mother was dead but left some poems. She would learn, too, that he supposed her happier than he was, with every prospect of seeing her departed mother.[14]

Henry would not immediately let her see his translation. The brake was awareness that he meant to separate a father from his last unmarried child. Knowing they were close, he wished to give father and daughter sufficient time to prepare for parting. Preparing might take a year.[15]

David Dudley Field—brother of famed Cyrus Field, the promoter of the Atlantic cable—was an eminent luminary of the New York bar, yet also was chief counsel for the Erie Railroad Company. In December 1870, the *Springfield Republican* printed a charge that the Erie counsel had been paid more than $200,000 by the corporation in a single year.

On December 27, Field wrote a private letter of protest to Samuel Bowles, owner-editor of the *Springfield Republican*. As has been noticed, Bowles was one of the revenue reformers. He so cuttingly replied that a secret war of letters broke out between Bowles as attacker and Field and his son, Dudley Field, as defenders. In the twelfth letter of the exchange, on January 12, 1871, David Dudley Field said he had printed the correspondence as a pamphlet and was giving copies to friends. He enclosed a copy.

Bowles saw that Field's pamphlet did not reprint the charge in the *Springfield Republican* that had moved the Erie counsel to write his initial letter. New letters were exchanged. In the twentieth letter, Bowles warned that *he* would publish the correspondence.

On January 28 in New York, the *World* published Field's pamphlet—not, Field said, with his permission. In reply, the *Springfield Republican* issued a 21-page pamphlet titled *David Dudley Field and His Clients*. The latter pamphlet gave the complete correspondence to the public, with supporting explanations.[16]

As published by Bowles, the correspondence was accompanied with a quotation from an editorial paragraph that had appeared in the *Springfield Republican* on December 8, 1870. The quotation included a pithy statement:

> . . . a first-class British review, the Westminster, has broken ground in vigorous rebuke of that eminent lawyer, Mr[.] David Dudley Field, for . . . prostituting the law . . . to the gross schemes of speculation, corruption and robbery, in which his distinguished client, James Fisk, Jr., has been engaged. . . . [17]

Though not so intended by Bowles, the reprinted statement would incite counsel Field to initiate an added protest.[18] As Field knew, the statement was in a measure correct. An unsigned article in the October *Westminster Review* had impugned him in his capacity as Erie counsel. Believing he must strike back, Field wrote a six-part objection. He sent it to editor Chapman on February 13, 1871.

Field's objection was meant for and demanded immediate publication in Chapman's magazine. Field understood that the author of the offending article was English. He had no idea—nor had Bowles—that the author was Henry Adams.[19]

On his side, Adams did not know that Field had sent Chapman an objection to his article. Adams, however, was ahead of things. He already had set a train of events in motion. Having learned from Chapman that James McHenry meant to sue, he had shifted the burden of "The New York Gold Conspiracy" from Chapman to himself.[20]

His means were simple. He asked Chapman to disclose the article's authorship to McHenry on a given date in February. (The letter is missing, but its contents can be inferred.) When told the authorship, McHenry necessarily would cable it to Cyrus Field in New York, both for his own use and for the attention of his brother David.

Aware that he and the Field brothers would soon be legal antagonists, Adams had begun to arm. He had contacted two lawyers in New York, Frank Barlow and Albert Stickney. Younger than David Dudley Field, they were decidedly his superiors in ability, not to mention courage. For reasons of their own, they were spoiling for a contest with the Erie counsel. As they saw it, the contest would open a path to the overthrow of Gould, Fisk, and their innumerable satraps in New York State, New York City, and the New York bar.

At Adams's instigation, three writers took up their pens. Barlow developed a long bill of particulars attesting professional misconduct by the Erie counsel, to be published by Reid and Hay in the *New York Tribune*. Soon completed, the bill took the form of letters to the editor that filled eight columns. Barlow signed the letters.[21] Simultaneously, C. F. Adams, Jr., prepared a long article, "An Erie Raid," that would exhibit Gould and Fisk as sponsors of physical violence, including the use of firearms. One of the persons named in the article would be David Dudley Field. The article would be finished in time for inclusion in Henry's April 1871 *North American*. Charles would sign it. Concurrently, Stickney wrote an article titled "Lawyer and Client" that likewise would appear in the April *North American*, signed. Stickney's article would present itself as a response to the Field-Bowles correspondence. In legal language, it would reiterate against the Erie counsel the charge of professional misconduct. Prior to publication, it would be sharpened and honed by additional lawyers.

One purpose of the three devices, all engineered by Henry Adams, was the extinction of David Dudley Field as a lawyer.[22] Another purpose, less evident, was the silencing of James McHenry. The chief purpose was incitement of a non-partisan revolt in New York against the Erie lords and the corruptest Democrats in the state and city, most notably Boss Tweed.

Adams's life had entered its most complicated phase. For a time, he would be doing a large variety of essential things all at once.

Apparently in the afternoon on Monday, February 20, 1871, he left for New York, declaredly to attend a Harvard alumni dinner on Wednesday evening. There also would be a Brown alumni dinner on Tuesday evening. Hay would speak at the Brown dinner on Tuesday. Evarts would speak at the Harvard dinner on Wednesday.[23]

Adams's reappearance in New York coincided with an explosion. Word came from London that the author of "The New York Gold Conspiracy" was an American, Henry Adams, a younger member of the Adams family. Once learned by a few, the news was repeated in all directions. Copies of the October *Westminster* were hastily found and passed about. Knowledge that a seemingly English article was an article by *him* lent previously unnoticed meanings to every page.

Reactions were extreme. The city reverberated with rumors that hearers passed along and no one dared to print. On Tuesday, February 21, a New York correspondent of the *Springfield Republican* sent the paper some paragraphs of news prefaced by three smoky sentences:

> The air is thick with rumors of all kinds, some of them of dire import and of the most scandalous nature, assailing the character of one of the most prominent men in the country. These I have no right nor wish to mention. If they are well-founded, the truth must in time come out, and it will cause an unprecedented sensation. . . .[24]

The dire rumors evidently concerned a man more centrally placed than counsel Field. The scandal allegedly involved was of such a kind or such a size as to have no precedent. In fear of it, the reporter made use of slippery terms and was hesitant to speak at all.

In "The New York Gold Conspiracy," Henry Adams had described a dinner on a steamboat between New York and Fall River, Massachusetts. The guest of honor was President Grant. During and after the dinner, Jay Gould tried to persuade the president that an increase in the price of gold sustained through help by the U. S. Treasury would be a patriotic measure. Two other patriots were at hand to assist in the persuasion: Jim Fisk and Cyrus Field. The article went on to say that persuasion failed and Gould had no choice but to look towards other means.

Cyrus Field had the advantage of knowing Adams if he saw him. He had met the author in London in the 1860s.[25] He studied the offending article in the October *Westminster,* especially studied the passage about the dinner, and resolved to threaten Adams with a suit for libel.

Adams attended the Harvard dinner on Wednesday evening. One morning, presumably Thursday morning, Cyrus Field called at Adams's hotel. Adams was still in bed, and the promoter had to wait. After a few minutes, he thought better of his errand and went away.[26] Adams shortly learned that Cyrus Field had called and left. Guided in part by that information, Adams returned to Massachusetts and negotiated a contract with James Osgood and Company for a book of essays.[27]

The planner of the book was Henry, but he gave it a shape that Charles would heartily approve. The book's first effect would be to establish C. F. Adams, Jr., as America's leading authority on railroads. At first glance, the book would seem to have one author. The backstrip would display a title and a surname:

Chapters

of

Erie

and

Other Essays

———

Adams

The impression given by the backstrip would be confirmed to some extent by the contents. No preface or introduction would appear. The title page would name *two* authors: "Charles F. Adams, Jr., and Henry Adams." The table of contents would list eleven essays written by Charles Adams, Henry Adams, and Francis A.

Walker, with emphasis on those by Charles. The essays would include his longest railroad articles, "A Chapter of Erie" and "An Erie Raid." Under a new title, "The Railroad System," four more of his railroad articles would be grouped as a single effort. There would be five essays listed as by, or partly by, Henry. One of the five, "The Legal-Tender Act," would be listed as by "Francis A. Walker and Henry Adams"—a misleading, indeed a wrong, attribution. Thus roughly three-fifths of the pages would be ceded to Charles and two fifths would remain for Henry and Walker. Readers would be led to assume that Charles was the leading figure and that Henry and Walker were mere coadjutors or make-weights.

Chapters of Erie was the earliest of Henry Adams's important published anti-autobiographical fictions. On the basis of the essays listed by the book as his or partly his, an impression would be put about that he was a writer of scattered tendencies. Three essays— "The Bank of England Restriction," "British Finance in 1816," and "The Legal-Tender Act"—would present him as a devotee of economics, the dismal science. A fourth—"The New York Gold Conspiracy" (the only essay not reprinted from the *North American*)— would be printed towards the front, positioned modestly between the long essays by Charles, "A Chapter of Erie" and "An Erie Raid." Because bracketed by works relating squarely to the Erie corporation, the essay on the Gold Panic would be given an appearance of relating mainly, not to Washington and Grant, but to New York, Gould, and Fisk. The remaining essay—"Captaine John Smith" (considerably revised)—would concern *colonial* history, a worn-out subject. Thus Henry would be falsely advertised as subordinate to his brother, rather dry, and, even when engrossed in economics, given to antiquarian topics.[28]

An un-subordinate, un-dry, and un-antiquarian motive underlay the plan for *Chapters of Erie*. Henry needed a vehicle for making "The New York Gold Conspiracy" permanently available to buyers. The book of essays was the vehicle. In the book, the explosive article would be swathed in harmless works by Charles and lesser pieces of Henry's own making. Yet predictably, despite the barriers in the way of its being noticed, or perhaps in part *because* of the barriers, the article would be sought for, read, and read again.

The greatest attraction of "The New York Gold Conspiracy" would be its exerting a kind of power usually associated with institutions of government. The article was an act of gradual execution. Following the disclosure of its authorship, Gould would live with a streak across his name which no effort could lift off. Though protected by deference to the high stations they had come to occupy, the Grants would recede steadily towards oblivion as misplaced residents of the White House. In the months following the panic, aging Corbin had been crushed by notoriety; but, following the publication of Henry's ingenious book of essays, he might sink to greater fame. In a later time, he might even be recognized as the nerviest, most enterprising criminal ever schooled on Capitol Hill.[29]

A nearer measure of the article's power was the protection it afforded Henry Adams. Cyrus Field was not the only person who read "The New York Gold Conspiracy" and on second thought decided not to seek a contest with the author. There were many. Voluntarily, Adams revealed his responsibility, walked among them, and was not touched.

Great Britain and the United States had advanced towards a settlement as if guided by metal rails. Informal talks between Sir John Rose and selected Americans had produced an agreement creating a Joint High Commission modeled on the one that negotiated the Treaty of Ghent.

The Commission would convene in Washington. On February 1, 1871, Minister Thornton notified Secretary Fish that Great Britain was ready to send five commissioners, as required by the agreement; and, on February 9, President Grant proposed to the Senate for confirmation the names of five American opposites. It angered C. F. Adams that Grant did not select him as one of the nominees. On February 29, when the Commission started work in Washington, a person far angrier was Sumner.

The chairman of the Senate committee on foreign relations wanted the British flag removed from the western hemisphere. In common with hosts of other Americans, Grant and C. F. Adams among them, Sumner had believed that Canada would shortly be absorbed in the United States. Earlier a colonial patchwork, Canada had been confederated in 1867. The inhabitants had become the citizens of a new entity, the Dominion of Canada. They had not wanted and had not received complete independence, and it seemed still possible that they might find themselves absorbed as new citizens of the United States. Grant, however, was prepared to let Canada go if Sumner could be demoted.

Sumner hastened his undoing. He wrote a demand for British hemispheric withdrawal and presented it to Fish, as if the British would care to see it. He snubbed Fish at a social gathering, as if Fish would be the loser. He tried to continue chairing the Senate committee on foreign affairs when no longer on speaking terms with the secretary of state. For these and other reasons, when the Senate reorganized in March, he simply was dropped from the committee. His removal on March 9 assured the success of the Joint High Commission. It was a foregone conclusion that there would be a Treaty of Washington and that the treaty would submit the Alabama Claims to arbitration by an international tribunal.[30]

For Henry Adams, the Senate's action became a means to a private end. Schurz had succeeded Sumner as chairman of the foreign relations committee. By an unknown means, perhaps a letter, Adams assured the Missourian that he—Schurz—was uniquely qualified to contribute the annual review of politics titled "The Session" for the July 1871 North American. Whether a senator could with propriety write such a review was doubtful, and whether Adams suggested Schurz sign his article is unclear, but an actual article was not the issue. The presumable objects of Adams's tactic were, first, that Schurz be pleased by the invitation and, second, that he slowly be encouraged to admit that the article would not get written. In this way, Adams would acquire a means of explaining why the annual review of politics could not appear. The explanation would be simple. The only qualified contributor for 1871 was just too busy.[31]

The previous May in Washington, Adams had attended a lecture with geologists belonging to the Fortieth Parallel Survey and was introduced to Clarence King. Meeting King had not seemed probable. Reportedly the geologist-in-charge always was traveling, or had just left, or had not arrived.[32]

A several-sided genius, King by reputation was an unrivaled talker and spinner of tales.[33] Not married, he had the problem of a dependent mother and other relatives in need of money. Partly to increase his income, he contracted in February 1871 to write some humorous sketches for the Atlantic Monthly under the general title Mountaineering in the Sierra Nevada.[34]

Being a Boston editor, Adams was one of the first to know that he, Hay, and King would soon be placed in accidental collocation. During the autumn of 1871, James Osgood and Company would publish not only Chapters of Erie but also, in book form, King's Mountaineering in the Sierra Nevada and Hay's Castilian Days.

In March 1871, prior to publishing his tales of mountaineering, the Atlantic Monthly published an article by King, "Active Glaciers within the United States." The article concerned discoveries by his Survey. In passing, it named Arnold Hague and S. F.

Emmons as his principal associates. Not humorous, the article was scientific.

That same March, declaredly because his mother had sprained her ankle, was housebound, and wanted company, Henry Adams changed his habits and walked to Boston "nearly every evening to dine with my family." His returns to the company of his parents and Mary tended to dash his spirits. He was dismayed to participate in their self-imposed repetitions of Boston's preferred routines. He keenly regretted "the quiet disappearance of our lives." "I lose all patience when I think how little we do that is worth remembering."

The true reason for his walks to Boston was continued meetings with Clover Hooper. The secret meetings could not be extended indefinitely. Dr. Hooper had finished building a summer house at Beverly Farms on the North Shore, about twenty miles from Boston. In mid-May, he and Clover would move there to enjoy a first season of residence. Till then, Clover and Henry would meet as often as possible at 114 Beacon Street, but thereafter Henry would be able to see her only by taking trains—a very different matter.[35]

With the coming of spring, Henry and Brooks went for walks. As if Henry were incapable of the idea, Brooks told Henry he ought to marry Clover Hooper. Henry so replied that Brooks gained not the beginning of a hint that Henry was courting the suggested person.[36]

While successfully evasive about one subject, Henry kept silent about two others. He was wondering whether Palgrave might find a picture that would make a suitable gift for a young woman in America, and he was thinking that during the next academic year he might live in a civilized manner and rent a house.[37]

The May *Atlantic* contained an instalment of Hay's *Castilian Days* immediately followed by the first of King's tales of mountaineering. Titled "The Range," King's sketch was adapted to a popular audience. It combined geology with an amusing story of a long ride he and a friend had taken in the California wilderness in 1866 on mules.[38]

Adams was undecided about his summer vacation. Emmons's invitation to him to join the Fortieth Parallel Survey was still standing and could be accepted. King's pieces in the *Atlantic* acted as reminders. After some hesitation, Adams wrote to Emmons— the letter is missing—confirming his arrival in Wyoming sometime in mid-July.[39]

Since he would be in the West during almost all the Harvard

recess, Adams would have to prepare both the July and the October issues of the *North American*. (He simultaneously would read the proofs of *Chapters of Erie*.) For the July issue, he obtained from Josiah Whitney, King's one-time mentor and employer in California, a book notice titled "King's Fortieth Parallel Survey." The notice would review a newly-published volume of the Survey's immense Report. When he started for the Rockies, Adams would take with him copies of Whitney's notice for King and Emmons.[40]

King had wished his Survey to make full use of the tools afforded by modern technology. In this spirit, he had engaged several gifted, well-equipped photographers. Evidence is lacking, but it appears that Adams had seen in Washington remarkable pictures made by the Survey's photographers, especially attempts to take an ideal view of a wall of rock, El Capitan, in the Yosemite Valley.[41] Adams himself was drifting towards photography. He was thinking he should buy a camera and related equipment and teach himself to take good pictures. He showed little interest in taking photographs of people. His concern was great buildings. It vexed him that he was trying to teach medieval history without the help of good photographs of Europe's cathedrals.[42]

The Joint Commission had meanwhile negotiated a Treaty of Washington. The Senate had ratified it. The treaty called for the creation of a five-person Court of Arbitration, to meet at Geneva. Great Britain and the United States would each choose one arbitrator. The other three would be citizens of other countries. Fish urged Grant to give C. F. Adams the place as American arbitrator, but Grant was disinclined to choose him, as too much a Democrat.[43]

The Chief, Mrs. Adams, and Mary made their annual spring migration from Boston to Quincy. Dr. Hooper and Clover moved to Beverly Farms. In place of meetings, Clover and Henry exchanged secret letters.[44] On May 22, 1871, after Clover left for the summer, Henry wrote to Carlo about his life in Boston-Cambridge. He said, among other things:

> . . . there is but one house at which I am intimate; that of Prof. Gurney, Dean of the Faculty, and my predecessor as editor of the *North American*; he married a clever Bostonian of about my own age, and his house is an oasis in this wilderness.

The wording showed how completely Henry was in love. Ellen Gurney was studious more than "clever," but Henry could not avoid reaching for a word so similar to Clover.[45]

Seven weeks later, Henry would himself be traveling to Wyoming and points beyond. That he should plan to go a long distance away from the woman he wished to marry could seem unnatural and could even suggest he was not in love. But his plan, so far as it related to love (it had several motives), was natural. That *he* loved he knew. Indications that *Clover* loved had been given to him at Beacon Street, and others were coming in the mail; but for some reason, possibly shyness, he did not fully comprehend them. So, thinking separation the test of love, he would go away and wait to learn what his going might reveal.[46]

Among his undated works, one that might seem impossible to date is a sonnet named "Eagle Head." Read with attention to all its features, the sonnet can be taken to be self-dating and highly communicative.[47] It appears to have had the following history.

In June 1871, Henry made a visit to Beverly Farms and went with Clover on horseback or by carriage to Eagle Head, a rocky promontory on the Atlantic coast where eagles formerly had lived. During his hours with Clover among the rocks above the sea, he silently asked himself about the houses he and she might live in when they were married. He realized that, of the houses *he* could want, one would be a summer house they could build on the North Shore, close to her father's.[48] At the same time, watching the breaking surf, he was reminded of his dying sister. When she had her accident, Loo was not a passenger in her carriage. Perhaps crazily, she was *driving*. She fell to the ground, and her foot was smashed by her carriage's passing wheel. Once ill with tetanus, she was sane. Self-exhaustingly, she tried to live.[49]

The visit to Eagle Head gave Henry the requisites for a poem in two parts, the first involving one person and that person's reflections, the other concerning two persons and what they might do.

Eagle Head

Here was the eagles' nest. The flashing sea,
  Sunny and blue, fades in the distant gray,
  Or flickers green on reefs, or throws white spray
On granite cliffs, as a heart restlessly
Beats against fate, and sobs unceasingly,
  Most beautiful flinging itself away,
  Clasping the rock by which it must not stay,
Sublimest in revolt at destiny.
Here where of old the eagles soared and screamed,
  Answering the ocean's restless, longing roar,
While in their nest the hungry eaglets dreamed,

—Here let us lie and watch the wave-vexed shore,
    Repeating, heart to heart, the eagles' strain,
    The ocean's cry of passion and of pain.

The poem was sexual. It began with the solitary and continued with the mated. It suggested that two persons would be sexually active to a degree that would call for strong descriptions. It did not differentiate male and female with respect to strength of passion. It left open the possibility that the *woman* had led the way to Eagle Head and that, in daylight, in a manner she desired, a coupling had occurred.[50]

Adams later wrote that the "critical point" for his generation in America was the summer of 1871.[51] With the July *North American* in his bags, he left Cambridge on July 8. He rode trains as far as Cheyenne, in Wyoming Territory, expecting to join Emmons's party at Fort Bridger and accompany it on "an expedition down the cañon of the Green River, an upper branch of the Colorado." At Cheyenne in the station restaurant, he "happened to tumble over the leader of the very party I was on my way to join"—a phrase which could seem to mean Frank Emmons but in fact meant Clarence King.[52]

King and Adams exchanged information about their plans. King was traveling eastward. One of his errands would be to read the proofs of *Mountaineering in the Sierra Nevada* at the office of Osgood's printer in Cambridge.[53] Apprised that Adams would be meeting Emmons at Fort Bridger, he directed a change. He told Henry to join Hague's party, which had come into nearby Laramie for supplies. One purpose of the change was to give Henry the opportunity to travel successively with both the Survey's exploring parties.

As directed, Adams attached himself to Hague's party and was led on an expedition of several hundred miles through the Rockies, ending at Estes Park near Denver. King meanwhile went to Cambridge, read his proofs, and journeyed west to Colorado. In the evening of August 5 or thereabouts, he arrived by buggy at a cabin at the entrance of Estes Park. Its owner was Griff Evans, a Welshman.

That night there was a sound of hoofs. Going out to investigate, King and Evans saw a man approach on a mule. It was Adams.[54] Far up the mountain trail, fishing in a brook for trout, he had lost track of time. Overtaken by darkness and afraid he could not retrace the way to Hague's camp, he remembered a cabin at the entrance of the park. He mounted his mule, reined it downhill, and assumed the mule might find the cabin. In result, though not intention, he had come down from the camp to welcome King. The occurrence seemed uncanny.

Next day together, King and Adams ascended the trail. After a day or two with Hague, they started towards Utah.[55] Soon after, at Fort Bridger, waiting to connect with Emmons, Adams read in a newspaper that Grant had appointed the Chief to serve on the Court of Arbitration.

The president's change-of-mind was an important event in Henry's life. The change-of-mind perhaps could be part-explained by Grant's good relations with Secretary Fish, made better by the secretary's dismissal of Motley and the Senate's removal of Sumner. Yet it could also be explained in another way. Mrs. Grant must have heard about and must even have read a damning article, "The New York Gold Conspiracy." She must have heard in addition that the article was written by the Adams son who worked with C. F. Adams when he was minister to England. The article and its authorship considered, it could be guessed that Julia and Ulysses Grant privately joined in deciding that the Adamses should be conciliated, grandly flattered, and sent abroad.

In late August, Henry accompanied Emmons's party on its expedition along the Green River, an excursion he thought a "stunner." He came away with new ideas. Thanks to travels with Hague and Emmons, he had learned that, if discoveries were the criterion, King had no superior among geologists, perhaps no equal, and, though only twenty-nine, was unquestionably a leader among the scientists of the world. He learned too that King's opinions were in contrast with those of Lyell and Darwin. To some of their tenets, his Survey's discoveries were a convincing refutation.[56]

King meanwhile had resumed his peregrinations. They so wearied and injured him that, not long after, sick and forced to pause, he would cross to the Sandwich Islands for an extended rest. While visiting Hawaii, the largest island, if his tale could be believed, he would become acquainted with Princess Keelikolani and would visit her at her royal house, "shaded by a massive umbrella tree and brakes of bamboo, seventy feet tall." It would not be lost on hearers that the tale involved a pun. It was apt that a princess was visited by a King.[57]

❖ ❖ ❖

Adams had just time to return to Massachusetts. On his arrival, he needed to be at three places, Quincy, Cambridge, and Beverly Farms. He went to all, but his base was Quincy. The Chief's appointment had reconstituted the five-person family that had lived at the Legation.

The five Adamses were reassembled but would soon be divided. In November, the Chief would leave for Geneva. Brooks would accompany him as secretary. Mrs. Adams would not risk an autumn voyage. Mary too would stay home. Henry, after helping the Chief and Brooks get ready for their mission, would move to Boston and live with his mother and sister. His Cambridge rooms would serve him only as an office and a place for keeping books. He meanwhile—in "a hopeful state of mind"—was well-started in a second year of editing and teaching. ". . . I am not unwilling," he said. "The work is not so nasty as some. . . ."

Had he been free to teach quite literally as he wished, he might have shifted his students' attention to cathedrals. He had seen them and studied theories of their development.[58] He was free, however, only within a fixed pattern of expectation. As before, he was required to acquaint the students with medieval politics and medieval institutions. Perhaps as a concession, he was allowed to offer three courses: Medieval Institutions; History of Germany, France, and the Church from the eighth to the fifteenth century; and History of England to the seventeenth century. The difference was his being permitted to give separate attention to *English* history.[59]

By October 1, 1871, *Chapters of Erie* was available at bookstores. The tide of battle turned in New York City later in the month, when Mayor Tweed was arrested. Outright victory was achieved by the opponents of Erie in city elections in November.

Chapters of Erie changed the relation between the public and Henry Adams. Since the book exhibited his corrected name and reprinted "The New York Gold Conspiracy," it connected two essentials: who he was and what he had written that was most important.

On November 9, Adams wrote to Samuel Jones Tilden, the leader of the reform Democrats in New York, requesting an article for the *North American* on the "Tammany frauds." The frauds referred to were those that had permitted a united phalanx of New York reform Democrats and reform Republicans to defeat, disgrace, impeach, and imprison a series of the city's oppressors. Wanting the story told from within, Adams explained: "I know of no one except yourself who is capable of doing this properly. You alone know the private history of the affair. . . ." It was not a tragedy that Tilden could not oblige. Henry had placed himself in communication with the ablest Democrat of the age.[60]

C. F. Adams's return to public life increased the ardor of enthusiasts who thought the country needed him to be president. Foremost in zeal was Carl Schurz. The Missouri senator had an advantage over most of the Adams boosters. Schurz at least had met the famous diplomat.[61] With few exceptions, the other enthusiasts had never seen him.

If he wished to run for president in 1872, the Chief could perhaps announce his availability at a later date. Till he and Brooks departed, he mostly remained secluded at the Old House. His work at Geneva would possibly add lustre to his already lustrous reputation, but his absence from the country would work strongly *against* a successful candidacy. As a counterbalance, he could name one or another of his sons as his spokesman while he was gone, so that the son could pull together the makings of an organization and reach out for wider support. John, Charles, and Henry were all in Quincy. Yet it grew evident that no son was named and no organization would be built.

The Chief and Brooks sailed on November 14. Mrs. Adams, Henry, and Mary moved to 57 Mount Vernon Street. In appearance, Henry was more than ever the uncomplaining teacher, the tireless editor, the restored general family servant, the accommodating brother and perfect son. He seemed to have no private history.

Silence and the performance of duties concealed already-completed revolutions. For one thing, Henry had changed his family ties. In his feelings, while remaining an Adams, he had joined another family and become an addition to the Hoopers. When the time was right, he would ask Clover to marry him, but he would not want her to leave her family. To the extent that leaving was necessary, he would be the person to do the leaving.

In its way, the impending union would seem an ordinary American marriage. Clover in name would be Marian Adams or Mrs. Henry Adams.[62] Yet her rights if anything would increase. Because of the attitudes of her husband, she would be freer to be the double person she was: compassionate Marian, original Clover. In her amorous drama, she would be the leading figure, a Puritan Cleopatra, freed to rule. Her husband would be an American Antony unalarmed by his queen, though increasingly aware of her attractions and varied powers.

Henry's allegiance to Clover and the Hoopers was concurrent

with allegiance to Clarence King. In August in the West, he and King had become close friends and associates. Talking at Evans's cabin, again at Hague's camp, then while traveling to Fort Bridger and camping in Utah on the Uintah range, they had formed a partnership in learning. Partnership was possible because both were historians. King's work in geology was through and through historical. When published seven years later, his portion of the Survey's Report, *Systematic Geology*, a massive treatise, would outline the *history* of the earth's surface in the large western area his Survey had explored.[63]

Until he and King became associates, Adams had subordinated writing to politics. He allied himself with King at the instant when a shift was possible and the emphasis could be reversed. He came back from the West already changed, predominantly a historian. The shift required that he set limits on his involvement in politics. The limits he set were strict. While working as a historian, he would engage in politics only in relation to the country's choices of presidents and its choices of secretaries of state.

The Chief and Brooks having gone, Henry turned to history. The spirit of his enterprise was as ambitious as possible. During the next twenty years, he intended to make an effort that would place him in rivalry with the greatest historians of whatever times and countries. The effort would center in two difficult projects, a new and an old. The new would be a history of early England as it related to democracy and thus to democracy in America. The old would be his *History of the United States*.

Characteristically, he sought a means of memorializing the beginning of his effort. The foremost British historians were J. A. Froude and Edward A. Freeman. Froude had recently published a book of *Short Studies on Great Subjects*, and Freeman had recently published a book of *Historical Essays*. In secret, Adams wrote a two-part review of their books titled "Two Historical Essayists." He sent it to Godkin for the *Nation* with a request that his authorship be permanently concealed.[64] Under the sub-titles "Mr. Froude" and "Mr. Freeman," the *Nation* published the parts on December 14 and 21, 1871.

Adams's review of Froude and Freeman was important in two respects. He declared an American's right to mine for evidence and adduce conclusions in *English* history, and he undertook to explain what history was all about. The explanation was the more worth reading because it was the only one he would ever publish. He said:

. . . he [Edward Freeman] has seized more clearly than any other historical writer of the day the all-important truth that the investigation of history is, call it by whatever names you will, merely the investigation into evidence, and that the duty of a historian is not to say fine things about the philosophy of history, but to investigate into the evidence of the facts on which such philosophy, if worth the paper on which it is expounded, must rest. This truth lies at the very foundation of historical research. Its importance vindicates the stress which Mr. Freeman lays upon minute accuracy, and to have seized this truth and held fast to it in the midst of an unbelieving world, is Mr. Freeman's great claim to the reputation which he already possesses, and which will, we conceive, ultimately increase on both sides [of?] the Atlantic.

On December 15, while Henry was secretly publishing his principles of history, the many officials concerned in the arbitration of the Alabama Claims met at Geneva. The government of Great Britain and the government of the United States each delivered its printed case to the other government and to the Court of Arbitration. An Italian arbitrator, Count de Sclopis, was chosen to act as presiding officer of the tribunal. Without delay, a majority of the arbitrators voted to recess *for six months*, so that the two governments could study each other's cases and prepare counter-cases.

The long recess took arbitrator C. F. Adams by surprise and found him at a loss. He could not think of a good means of filling the six-month vacuum. Winter being at hand, he took Brooks as far as Naples. There he considered a voyage to Alexandria.[65]

Henry simultaneously faced a crisis as editor of the *North American*. Some of the contributors for his January 1872 issue did not supply their contributions or would be sending them too late. The shortage was two full-length articles and several short critical notices.

Unexpectedly, an article arrived from Palgrave about a little-known Elizabethan poet, Thomas Watson. Received just in time, it filled one of the larger gaps. To fill more gaps, Henry wrote a notice of an English book he could heartily admire, Sir Henry Maine's *Village Communities*, and wrote a second review of Freeman's *Historical Essays*, this one from a different, much more critical perspective. When published, both notices would be unsigned.

To fill the remaining gap, Henry produced as if from nowhere a long article, "Harvard College. 1786–87," mostly made up of quotations from a diary kept at Harvard by an unnamed student. The student was John Quincy Adams, and the quotations were invaluable evidence of the conditions under which American students had once had to try to learn. The article would be signed "Henry Adams." In part, it would be a forthright expression of Professor Adams's principles as a teacher.[66]

During the Christmas and New Year season, well-placed reformers of several kinds would be meeting in Washington. Schurz, Wells, and Atkinson would be there. Henry was urged to come. The reform that the reformers most wanted was the election of C. F. Adams as president in 1872 by Liberal Republicans and reform Democrats acting in concert.

Henry did not attend. He claimed a change of dentists, spent most of his holiday in New York, and went to Albany in connection with "future literary and political experiments."[67]

Adams's personal history showed progress, but events in general were still chaotic. On January 6, 1872, on the stairway of the Grand Central Hotel, a gentleman in New York, Edward S. Stokes, fatally shot another gentleman, James Fisk, Jr., in a contest for ownership of a high-priced lady, Josie Mansfield. News of the murder reached London just when the *Pall Mall Gazette* was attempting to review an American book. Not untypically, the English editors confused *Chapters of Erie* with a previously published pamphlet named *A Chapter of Erie*, and the English reviewer ascribed the pamphlet to "James F. Adams, jun." The mistaken name carried confusion and chaos very far. Depending on how one read it, it could include as little as one part Charles and as much as three parts Fisk.[68]

Henry meanwhile returned from Albany and found his mother in nervous collapse. The evident cause was separation from her husband. Seizing her collapse as an opportunity, Henry took charge of his parents. In weekly letters to Europe, he instructed the Chief to come home as if on business, wait quietly in Boston till spring, and return to Europe accompanied by his wife and Mary. All this was to be accomplished in such a way as not to worsen Mrs. Adams's nervous illness and possibly even to cure it.

For no reason that onlookers could guess, Henry interested himself in Boston society and went to balls but no longer danced. Surprisingly, he invited some "young birds" of the "ultra-fashionable set" to a luncheon at his Cambridge rooms. During the repast, the birds drank champagne cocktails. News of the offered drinks circulated in Boston-Cambridge and ruffled conservative feathers.

As wished, the Chief went to Paris, left Brooks there to fend for himself (a dangerous expedient), and returned alone to New York. At the request of Secretary Fish, he proceeded straight from the steamer to Washington to confer with the secretary and President Grant. He at last reached 57 Mount Vernon Street in Boston on Sunday, February 25.

Beginning with the Chief's arrival, Henry took a course which can be reconstructed in essential outline and possibly guessed in certain details. His problem had been to arrange his marriage to Clover on a basis of minimized hurt to Robert Hooper. Presumably late on Sunday, without Clover's knowledge, he walked to 114 Beacon Street and spoke to Dr. Hooper. He asked permission to marry Clover, assuming she would consent. Dr. Hooper did not rejoice. He felt "resigned." Yet he immediately gave permission.

Before leaving, it appears, Henry asked Dr. Hooper for a letter he might show to Clover on Tuesday. Robert Hooper kindly supplied the letter, either at once or through the mail.[69]

As usual, on Monday, Henry taught at Harvard. On Monday evening, he attended the weekly faculty meeting.[70]

Clover had two gentleman visitors at tea-time on Tuesday, February 27, 1872: Henry Adams and Fred Shattuck, the brother of Eleanor Whiteside. Fred stayed and stayed but finally left. Moments later, Clover passed through an experience of terror and moved safely beyond it. She learned that she and Henry could marry.

Explanations that Clover and Henry later gave to others concerning their engagement were fictional with respect to how long she and he had been seriously involved with each other.[71] Writing to her sister, Clover said she would do something that was frowned upon in the Hooper family: she would tell "a horrid dream." She said she dreamt that she and Ellen for a long time were caught in ice, also were separated by a wall of ice. More recently, because the sun had warmed things on her sister's side of the wall, Clover for four years had been enjoying "a nice time" with Ellen and her husband Whitman. And *very recently*—so said her fiction—the sunshine on Clover's side of the ice wall had become "so warm, that I tried to move and I couldn't." ". . . then, last Tuesday at about sunset, the sun blinded me so that in real terror I put my hands up to my face to keep it away. And, when I took them away, there sat Henry Adams holding them. And the ice is all melted away and I am going to sit in the sun as long as it shines. . . ."

The cause of terror could not be doubted. It was the assumed likelihood of deep injury to the feelings of a father who for twenty-odd years had been over-attentive to his motherless offspring. What is unclear is what suddenly brought the terror into play. Possibly Henry began by telling Clover that he had spoken to her father. Or possibly he began by holding before her a letter to himself from Dr. Hooper, saying she and Henry had her father's permission and could marry. Henry apparently did *not* show her a translation he had made from Petrarch. That could wait.

In any event, terror took hold of Clover; she covered her face; the terror passed. She saw she had dropped her hands and Henry was holding them. From that instant, it was easy to decide the things they were going to do. They would start by telling others they were engaged, but at first they would limit their disclosure to a very strict minimum of hearers, the relatives and friends they thought most concerned.[72]

12

ABU SIMBEL

Not knowing Henry would act as he did, Clover had promised to visit Mrs. Charles Russell Lowell and Mrs. Francis G. Shaw on Staten Island. It meant seeing "my good man" for only "10 hours," but she and Henry devised a plan to permit the visit and bring six people together in New York. Before departing, she wrote to her brother and the Gurneys about her and Henry's liberation. She at the same time asked the Gurneys to go to New York as guests of the Godkins. Ellen and Whitman responded by writing to Clover at Staten Island and going to New York as asked.

Henry meanwhile spoke in confidence to his parents and Mary. He wrote to Brooks in Paris. He did not speak to John or Charles.[1]

On March 8, 1872, her last day on Staten Island, Clover confided to Eleanor Whiteside, "Henry . . . vows he will never go away." The vow was serious and important. It went beyond usual vows to love, honor, and obey. It meant that Henry and Clover would continuously be found together and would live and act as one.

On March 9, Clover crossed to Manhattan and went to the Godkins' at 10 West 48th Street. Henry simultaneously arrived from Boston. Already a couple secretly, Clover and Henry became a couple privately by joining the Godkins and Gurneys at midday dinner. That afternoon and evening, they became a couple openly by traveling with the Gurneys to Boston. On arriving, they publicly announced their engagement.[2]

This shuttling to New York and back had a meaning that Henry's relations would apprehend only slowly. It was a first notification that the third son, long mistaken for a usable appendage to his parents and siblings, but in fact an independent Adams on whom certain of his relations could depend for valuable aids and services, had become far less usable, had joined with someone not an Adams, was half of a tight-knit couple, and, if mistakes were an object, could soon be mistakable in an opposite way, as a distant and shielded stranger.

The relative to whom Henry spoke most openly was his father. C. F. Adams had a rule of giving his sons augmented incomes from the family's capital when they married. Considering the money that would be coming his way, Henry was under constraints to speak very frankly. Writing to Brooks on March 13, the Chief remarked that Henry and his fiancée had "startling" plans of future residence.[3] He gave no details; but, to qualify as startling, the plans that Henry revealed must have been plans to live in places far removed from the other Adamses. He evidently said that he and Clover expected to live in summer on the North Shore at Beverly Farms, a long way from Quincy, and that they hoped to live in winter in Washington, which was to say in another world.

The Adams to whom Henry and Clover wished to extend their warmest welcome was Brooks. In his letter to Brooks, Henry gave instructions. ". . . you must stand by me. . . ." "I shall expect you to be very kind to Clover, and not rough, for that is not her style."

Eventually Brooks would adjust to the pairing he had urged. In the instant, he took the news of the marriage as catastrophic for himself. He confided to the Chief: "What I am to do when I get home I don't know. . . . Henry's engagement has utterly smashed all my plans."[4]

Of Henry's brothers, the one whose conduct most often was overbearing and insulting was Charles. The second son was as surprised by the engagement as the rest of the family. When first told, he viewed the impending marriage with tolerant indifference. In his writings, he referred to Henry's wife-to-be as "his young woman," "his Clover," and "Miss Hooper."[5] The expressions indicated lack of acquaintance and perhaps incipient dislike but nothing approaching disapproval, jealousy, or hatred.[6] The latter feelings would develop only with the help of time and rumination.[7]

Being members of leading Massachusetts families, Henry and Clover were accorded the fullest rights within the gift of Boston society. On returning to Harvard in 1870, Henry had been included automatically in the Friday Club, an association of young Harvard teachers and supposed young savants who met for dinner. He had attended some of the dinners and resumed old acquaintanceships, notably with Oliver Wendell Holmes, Jr. He also formed new acquaintanceships, notably with Raphael Pumpelly, John La Farge, William James, and Henry James, Jr.[8]

Clover and Henry viewed Boston differently. Clover saw Boston society in two ways, as an accepted member and as a highly percipient observer. This mixture of involvement and detachment was not likely to be tolerated very long. She was sure to be criticized because assumed or alleged to be critical. Henry had felt actually alien from Boston as long as he could remember and recently had been studying its more privileged citizens with the eyes of a traveler or ethnologist. He had written to Carlo: "In this Arcadian society sexual passions seem to be abolished. Whether it is so or not I can't say, but I suspect both men and women are cold, and love only with great refinement. How they ever reconcile themselves to the brutalities of marriage, I don't know."

As if to counterbalance deficiency of passion, Bostonians attached great importance to wedding ceremonies and wedding journeys. In 1861, in a time of national crisis, the Chief had voyaged to his post as minister to England only after a month-long delay. He waited because John was about to marry Fanny Crowninshield and the failure of a father to attend a wedding was unimaginable. On parallel grounds in 1872, Henry and Clover could require that other interests give way if in conflict with their nuptial preferences. Henry so required. He announced that he would shortly cease being editor of the *North American Review* and that he would be absent from Harvard during the coming academic year.

William Dean Howells was a salaried magazine editor and an aspiring writer. He had just published a novel, *Their Wedding Journey*, his first. It recounted the nuptial travels of a Boston couple to Niagara Falls and other scenic places. A copy survives that Clover inscribed "Henry Adams/ &/ Clover Hooper/ February 27th/ 1872"—that is, the Tuesday of Henry's tea-time visit and her terror. The copy is part of a cluster of evidence relating to her and Henry's plans.[9] Clover had scarcely weathered her terror than they settled upon a plan for a wedding ceremony and a wedding journey that partly kept within the bounds of custom and partly broke them. Except in two respects, the plan is best considered, not as projected, but as realized.

The exceptions have to do with travel and work. From an early age, Henry had wished to travel on a global basis. The places most attractive to him tended to be places as far as possible from Boston. When in college, he had written about a phenomenon that interested him, the great temple of Abu Simbel in Nubia on the Upper Nile. Since that time, wintering in Egypt had grown fashionable. Innumerable Europeans and Americans were hastening to Cairo and thence to the Pyramids and the Sphynx. Many ascended the

Nile as far as Thebes and Luxor, principally to see the temple of Karnak and the Memnonium. Doctors recommended such travels for health and pleasure, and the Egyptian winter climate was praised as unapproachably ideal.

For many reasons, beginning with Clover's physical well-being (she was underweight), Henry wanted to spend the coming winter on the Nile. If he and Clover could travel upstream to Abu Simbel—a long journey—he would be the happier. His anxiety to see the temple was an index, possibly the best index, of his sense of himself as a general historian. He would concentrate in English and United States history, but his field was universal history—the history of humankind. The temple was an important signpost within the field. Should he reach it, he would be attending to business, and Clover would approve. Her idea of married happiness, or part of it, was keeping her husband at his work.

On March 12, 1872, Erie stockholders forced Jay Gould to step down as president and yield control of the corporation. The act was hostile. The *New York Tribune* reported, ". . . [Gould] leaves the Presidency knowing he will at once be expelled from the Directory, and without any assurance whatever that he will not be prosecuted . . ."[10]

Shakily, in March, the United States and England advanced towards a settlement of the Alabama Claims. Bancroft Davis had prepared the case for the United States. Although Sumner had been thrust aside, Davis had included in the case complaints of "indirect" injuries of the kind that Sumner had liked to voice. The English, in reply, all but withdrew from the arbitration. Various persons rushed into action and repaved the road to peace. At a meeting in Washington, Secretary Fish gave C. F. Adams his firm assurance that an arbitration *could* occur.[11] So assured, the Chief arranged to sail from New York for Liverpool on the Cunarder *Russia* on April 24, 1872, accompanied by Mrs. Adams and Mary.[12] It can be assumed that Henry suggested both ship and date.

Henry meanwhile rowed invisibly through a squall at the *North American*. He had prevailed on a contributor to write for the April 1872 issue a long notice of Bayard Taylor's translation of Goethe's *Faust*. Taylor saw the notice and objected. Henry wrote a replacement notice himself but then decided to suppress it.[13] To fill the last-minute gap, he quickly wrote unsigned notices of Howell's *Their Wedding Journey*, King's *Mountaineering in the Sierra Nevada*, and a bad book by Sir Henry Holland, *Recollections of Past Life*. These productions were slight, and it was Henry's settled wish that he cease editing the magazine when he married. Yet his situation had become suggestive. If he later resumed the editorship, he would come back to a magazine for which he had written seven new contributions: six unsigned notices and his signed article, "Harvard College. 1786–87." All seven were personal. Each concerned a subject he cared about. And all were what he called *sketches*, meaning things lighter than essays.

The existence of his seven sketches pointed towards an obvious conclusion. Were he to resume editing and publish more sketches, the series might grow into a book, printed piecemeal in the magazine, and for the most part unsigned. Such a book, hidden but complete, was a project he might view as worth the effort.

When practicable, Henry had sent Gaskell and Cunliffe word of his engagement. (Cunliffe had married; Gaskell had not.) In his letter to Carlo, he described his fiancée. "She is certainly not handsome; nor would she be called quite plain. . . . She is 28 years old. She knows her own mind uncommon well. She does not talk *very* American. Her manners are quiet. She reads German—also Latin—also, I fear, a little Greek, but very little. She talks garrulously, but on the whole pretty sensibly. She is very open to instruction. *We* shall improve her. She dresses badly. . . . She has enough money to be quite independent. She rules me as only American women rule men, and I cower before her. Lord! how she would lash me if she read the above description. . . ."

In one respect, and temporarily, Henry did *not* confide in Clover. He did not give her a full idea of his situation as a politician.

As before, he was living with his parents and Mary at 57 Mount Vernon Street. The arrangement assured him continuous proximity to the Chief. The elder man's standing was at its apogee. He was an international figure, serving on an innovative court created to settle a dispute between great powers; and he was a national figure, thought by many to be the safest, most trustworthy replacement for less-than-sufficient Grant.

Henry was in a position to affect what happened to the Chief in both international and national spheres. His conduct would have two sides. He would help his father as an international figure provided help was wanted. He would leave him alone as a national figure even if help was asked. This split in the son's behavior was based in part on the father's states of mind. With regard to his work at Geneva, C. F. Adams was clear-headed and capable of saving action. With regard to becoming president, he was expectant, irritable, and daft.

Senator Schurz believed himself a highly capable political manager. When C. F. Adams was first in Europe as arbitrator, the
Missourian and several allies had issued a call for a Liberal Republican convention, to meet in Cincinnati on May 1, 1872. Because
Schurz would chair the convention, the task of organizing support
for Mr. Adams's candidacy was devolved on David Wells. He wrote
a letter to Atkinson that could be shown to the candidate. The
letter suggested that Mr. Adams's sons—meaning John, Charles,
and Henry—could be sent to Cincinnati and there act as a "council"
on his behalf. But C. F. Adams repelled the suggestion.[14] Wells then
wrote directly to Mr. Adams suggesting that one person—*any*
person—be given authority to speak for him at the convention.[15]
The Chief replied. On April 18, he sent Wells a letter which could
be taken to say that he resented being thought a candidate; that he
did not want the nomination; that he would not accept the nomination; that he would consider accepting the nomination only if it
was given to him in the complete absence of encouragement by
him; and that he would of course accept the nomination, if it was
given. A letter more aspersive and confusing could not have been
invented.[16]

The Cincinnati convention was two weeks distant. Schurz,
Wells, Atkinson, Godkin, Bowles, and similar enthusiasts had talked
themselves into a condition of extraordinary over-confidence.
Though not blind to the oddity of their candidate's reply, they
searched it carefully for merits. It had no merits, not even brevity.
All the same, Wells gave it to Bowles for eventual publication.

In the next few days, several Adamses grew very excited about
the three-part possibility that the Chief would be nominated for
president by the Liberal Republicans at Cincinnati; that he would
also be nominated by the Democrats at their convention in Baltimore; and that he would easily win election as president in November. Earlier a sceptic, Charles became a near-believer. He wanted
"the Governor" in the White House, believed it possible, and was
consumed with excitement.

Henry gave no sign, even to Clover, that he did not share the
excitement. In secret, he thought the Cincinnati convention a
"trap."[17] He strongly wished his father would *lose* the Liberal
Republican nomination. He believed, moreover, that a campaign
for the presidency would cost the Chief his life.

On April 23, 1872, the Chief, Mrs. Adams, Charles, Henry,
and Mary took the 8:00 A.M. train for New York. To minimize
separation, Clover went part way to New York and would wait for
Henry to join her when returning. Charles recorded: ". . . we had

a very pleasant day & a good time, got to New York at 4 o'cl, and had a tip-top dinner at the Brevoort. The movement in support of the Gov' looks to-day as if it were assuming very big proportions."

Charles expected that next day, when boarding the *Russia*, the Chief would be visible to a crowd and receive a rousing send-off. His expectation was disappointed. He recorded the following evening that "the departure was bitched and we got on board by a sneaking process, quite disgusting." He later wrote to the Chief that he and Henry "sneaked on shore in the same humiliating manner in which we had previously sneaked on board." It went without saying that the Adams who had contrived the sneaking was Henry. He had arranged that the candidate's party would board the *Russia* using means invisible to any crowd that could gather, and the boarding procedure was well under way before Charles could urge a shift to anything different.[18]

Following the departure of the ship, Charles and Henry shared dinner at the Brevoort and attended a theatrical performance, "Black Friday," at Niblo's Garden on Broadway near Prince Street. Next morning, April 25, according to Charles, Henry returned to Boston by an early train, "picking up his Clover on the way." Charles lingered briefly in New York, breakfasted with Godkin, and "debated the Gov's letter[,] wh. astonished me by beᵍ out." The letter was published in the *Springfield Republican* and again, slightly altered, in the *New York Times*. ". . . it is good," Charles recorded, "but will it make or mar him!"

The letter marred the father very quickly. Charles reached Quincy that night and there recorded that he was "watching the effect of the Gov's letter." ". . . everyone is puzzled."[19]

The second son felt ever-mounting excitement. Very differently, the third son felt a needed measure of relief. Henry wrote to Carlo on April 27: "My family sailed three days ago for Liverpool. . . . It was quite time, for a new presidential canvass is beginning and all the elements of discontent with the present administration have agreed to meet at Cincinnati next week and strike hands. The gathering will be tremendous and my old political friends are deep in it. We do not know what will be done there, but as yet my father commands much the most powerful support for the nomination, and it is not improbable that all parties will combine on him. . . . Of course I keep out of it with great care. . . . But my father's absence is a perfect blessing and I groaned with pleasure when I saw him fairly on board the Russia."

Even to Henry, the future remained uncertain. Without quite telling Carlo that he was *against* his father's becoming president, and without saying that he had been shaping his conduct for many years to reduce the likelihood of that occurrence, he told his English friend that a point to consider was the saving of human life. Also he fibbed arrantly about Clover. "That one's father should be President is well enough, but it is as much as his life is worth, and I look with great equanimity upon the event of the choice falling on some other man . . . . My fiancée, like most women, is desperately ambitious and wants to be daughter-in-law to a President more than I want to be a President's son. So we are altogether in a chaotic condition."

The idea that C. F. Adams would win easily at Cincinnati was an idea without foundation. There were three contenders. Lyman Trumbull, an Illinoisan, was willing to be vice-presidential candidate on a ticket headed by C. F. Adams but wanted first to try for the leading place. Meanwhile Horace Greeley greatly hungered for the nomination and commanded the help of managers and delegates who were disposed to accept new support regardless of where it came from.

The mood at the convention was feverish from the start. Rapturously confident that their candidate was going to win, the promoters of Mr. Adams were slow to convert Trumbull votes into Adams votes and secure a majority.[20] Six ballots were taken without a decision. The Adams managers then obtained sufficient promises of Trumbull votes, but the votes could not be voiced. A frenzied Greeley stampede had already begun on the convention floor. It carried all before it.[21]

Charles was at Quincy while the ballots were cast at Cincinnati.[22] His diary showed confidence. ". . . for the first time I thought the Govr pretty sure of the nom^n and went to bed excited in that faith." He very soon was obliged to add: "Greeley nominated!!!—Words would fail to do justice to my disgust and surprise. . . ."[23]

The news was cabled to Europe at the moment when the Chief, Mrs. Adams, and Mary were en route from Liverpool to London. Though perhaps of several minds, the Chief expected that the Liberal Republicans and the more enlightened Democrats would unite to back him. At the railway station in London, he was informed by a stranger who had been a passenger on the *Russia* that the Liberal Republicans had nominated Horace Greeley. C. F. Adams wrote in his diary: "This was odd enough. The unexpected is what mostly turns up. . . . My first sense is one of great relief in being out of the melee. . . ."[24]

Gaskell visited the elder Adamses and Mary in London. Not

realizing that to do so meant walking on perilous ground, he read aloud from Henry's letter of April 27 about the impending Cincinnati convention and the chance that his father might be elected president. C. F. Adams fortunately did not gather from what he heard that Henry's hopes were *against* nomination and election. As much as before, the Chief assumed that all his sons ardently favored his advancement. He wrote to Henry consolingly, ". . . I could not help fearing that you might very naturally feel more of disappointment than is altogether pleasant." Falsely, he claimed he had not expected that the Liberal Republicans would nominate him. Perhaps more truthfully, he professed to *like* the result of the Greeley stampede. ". . . I was rescued from a very critical situation[,] with the preservation of my character."[25]

Among the persons who had decided the outcome at Cincinnati, the most influential very possibly was Henry. When he said that with great care he was keeping *out of* the operations relating to his father's candidacy, he with the same words had said he was keeping *in* them to the utmost limit. One of his expedients was glaring. As in 1868, so again in 1872, he had placed his father out of reach on the ocean.

A second expedient was total and silent non-support. It made a difference. The difference was proportional to Henry's earlier standing among the revenue reformers. The balance of forces at Cincinnati was almost even. Pounds not on the scales counted as hundredweights. The scales leaned towards C. F. Adams but leaned only uncertainly. One push and they tilted to an alternative, Horace Greeley.

Having won the honor of nomination, Greeley was saddled with the hopeless labor of waging a successful campaign. He required Reid and Hay to assist his effort. Hay suggested to Reid that Henry Adams might possibly furnish the *Tribune* a series of articles destructive to Grant. Reid went further and invited Adams to serve the paper as an associate editor, starting at once. Henry replied on May 15 that nothing would give him more "satisfaction and amusement" than to "obtain an education for the press under your head, on the *Tribune*." Yet he refused. He said he was "starting for Europe on a year's vacation."

To be precise, Henry was starting for Beverly Farms. His marriage would occur on June 27 at Dr. Hooper's "cottage." A month ahead of time, approximately on May 25, he moved to the cottage, was given a room, and unpacked his things. By means of trains to Boston and horse cars or walks between Boston and

Cambridge, he continued his work as editor-teacher, which soon would stop.

The third son's political worries had decreased but had not ended. Writing from the cottage on May 30, he reported to Carlo: ". . . there is not much to tell you. My father narrowly escaped being the next President, but has come out of the fight very sound and strong, while his successful rival is likely to be not only disgraced but beaten. . . . Otherwise all is dark as Erebus."

If Henry's lines appeared to say that his father could have beaten Grant at the polls, they did just that: they maintained appearances. Meanwhile the empire of darkness had departments that Gaskell would not imagine. 1872 differed from other election years in involving a split between "Stalwart" Republicans and Liberal Republicans; also a split between Democrats willing to drift with Greeley and "Straight-out" Democrats bent on going a separate way. Some days prior to the Cincinnati convention, a Stalwart manager, Senator Conkling of New York, had sent Frank Barlow to Boston to offer C. F. Adams the chance to be Grant's running mate, get elected, and return to Washington as the nation's vice president.[26] The Chief had declined the offer. But in the not-distant future, on September 3, the Straight-out Democrats would hold a convention at Louisville, nominate Charles O'Conor of New York for president, and nominate John Quincy Adams II of Massachusetts for vice president. John would accept the nomination.[27] Though separated by five months, the episodes would have a single cause and a sinister meaning. Stalwart Republicans and Straight-out Democrats wished to advertise themselves as not corrupt. They accordingly viewed the Chief and John as possibly usable figure-heads—deceptive labels.

As Henry saw things in mid-June 1872, President Grant's reelection was an already accomplished fact. For Clover and Henry, the event had serious effects. It made Washington a place to which they could not move as winter residents. They might visit the capital, but they could not live there—not for five years to come. The knowledge transformed Henry's professorship into something of value, a port in a storm; and it made Henry and Clover all the happier that they would soon begin a year-long wedding journey to Europe and the Nile.

In preparation for the journey, apparently in May or June, Henry and Clover took photography lessons at a Boston studio. (Lessons were indispensable. Wet-plate photography was intricate and required the use of poisonous chemicals.) They presumably bought and used a practice camera, and they sent an order to London for a complete apparatus, including a mid-sized camera and supplies for a winter's campaign of picture-taking. Henry's desire to photograph was the stronger at the beginning, but Clover's interest was started and would increase.

Their journey promised to help solve a problem related to Henry's professorship. His two years on the faculty had involved his depending very heavily on other writers' ideas. His dependence had been greatest in relation to medieval institutions. To keep ahead of his students, he had had to read shelves of books in several languages, mostly in German. He had cured his ignorance, but he had possessed neither time nor materials to attempt original research.

As a teacher, he had tried various methods but treated one as best. The method was to assign each student a subject which the student would investigate by finding such evidence as he could and by following whatever leads the evidence might provide. At an agreed time, the student would report before the class.

The method was a classroom adaptation of a method Adams had used since boyhood when looking into subjects that interested him. It was the natural procedure used everywhere by adepts at self-teaching and self-education. When he spirited it into the alien world of institutional instruction, he understood that his action was subversive. By and large, his students welcomed the subversion. They responded to his unheard-of attitude and especially his assigning individual subjects as little short of revelations. Instead of teaching them what they should know, he was freeing them to learn whatever their efforts might permit their finding out.[28]

Adams himself had used the method while exploring "medieval institutions." Early in his inquiry, he had been jolted by a writer younger than himself (a contemporary of Gaskell and King) who had written what he thought "a great work"—"apt to remain new for a great many years." The writer was Rudolph Sohm, a German historian. The book was *Die Frankische Reichs-und Gerichtsverfassung*. It concerned the Franks, barbarians of northern Europe in the time of the Roman Empire, and it expressed a new idea. As described by Sohm, the Franks were free men who practiced free government. They shared with other Germans a local court with judicial functions—in English parlance the assembly of the hundred. Sohm's idea was that the court was *long-lived*. It "existed in the epoch of Tacitus," " 'survived through all historical vicissitudes,' " and vanished in Germany only " 'in the sixteenth century.' "[29]

Adams was disposed to treat himself as he treated the students. Presumably after his father lost to Greeley at Cincinnati, he decided to undertake an investigation. He assigned himself as his subject the possible persistence of the German local court *among the Anglo-Saxons and their English descendants*. His inquiry would be original, yet also declaredly subsidiary to Sohm's. In addition, it would be expensive and very laborious.

While classes continued at Harvard, Adams searched for titles of books he might obtain in Germany, France, and England for use in his investigation. The books he most wanted were not histories or monographs but works containing *evidence* relating to English history in its earliest, least-known phase. If he succeeded in obtaining the evidence and if his investigation prospered, he would write a short history of England, chiefly adapted for American reading.

During the academic year then closing, one of Adams's students made a discovery concerning an American subject. The student was J. Laurence Laughlin. He had enrolled in Adams's course in medieval institutions. While studying institutions, he sometimes studied the teacher. In his recollections, written long afterwards, he said that Adams was intellectually "robust and virile." His conduct in the classroom was "original, unexpected, and even explosive." "His method of attack was direct, not subtle. . . ." He had "a genius for starting men to think." "He was so stimulating . . . that he conveyed to one unconsciously the true concept of education as the power to think in a subject. That was something of a miracle. . . ."

Laughlin's made his discovery while taking an examination in Lower Massachusetts Hall. The teacher was in the room. Looking up in the intervals of writing, Laughlin was "struck by the likeness of Henry Adams to the full-length portrait of John Quincy Adams on the eastern wall."[30] Comparing grandson and grandfather, he saw that the grandson was indeed an Adams: the physical resemblance was very marked. Also he saw that the president and the teacher shared a quality: they had "the same air of self-contained strength." But in addition he saw something very much worth noting. The two Adamses were not equals: the grandson was an improvement. "In the younger[,] the pugnacity was genial. His nature was positive, not negative. His smile had in it fellowship, welcome, and heartiness. . . ." ". . . his laugh was infectious. . . . It might often be ironical, of course, but always good-humored. . . . His manner was animated and brusque, but kindly."[31]

❖ ❖ ❖

On June 3, 1872, when he had been living with Clover and her father for a week or more at Beverly Farms, Henry went to Quincy and stayed the night at Charles's house at the top of President's Hill.[32] The reason for the visit was unrecorded but apparently related to the *North American Review*.

By then, Henry had readied seven issues of the quarterly for publication. The issues had been successful. James Osgood, the publisher, believed the old quarterly was attracting subscribers as a magazine of general interest. He attributed its viability to Henry and considered him *the* editor on whom a publisher could depend.

There was no denying that under Henry's management the *North American* had published articles and notices of importance. Two examples deserve attention. The issue for October 1871 contained a long book notice by Charles Peirce, a native of Cambridge, and, for Adams, a former schoolmate and college acquaintance. The notice, "Fraser's Works of Bishop Berkeley," reviewed the history of western philosophy from the middle ages to modern times. With justice, it could be called the preface to Peirce's scientific realism, a new philosophy intended to supersede the philosophies of Europe and ancient Greece. That Adams effected its publication might eventually stand as one of his principal achievements.

The other example was very recent. The latest issue, for April 1872, contained a 68-page article by Ernst Gryzanovski, a Prussian cosmopolite. Titled "On the International Workingmen's Association; Its Origins, Doctrines, and Ethics," the article concerned the socialists in Europe and the beginnings of an attempted world revolution. To say the least, the article was informative.

A weakness of Adams's issues had appeared at the point where he had most tried to lend them strength. He had published an article by J. D. Cox and another by Davis Wells. It had been thought that the articles might be rallying cries for the revenue reformers. They failed. The *Nation* said of Cox's article that it contained "not much that has not been in print before." Wells's article was greeted as chiefly interesting for its comments on personalities.[33]

The prospect that Adams would cease being editor created a hubbub in Boston-Cambridge that resulted in a new arrangement. Apparently Osgood insisted that Henry continue as editor but take a leave of absence; Henry refused; the magazine's survival was thought jeopardized; and a compromise was reached. Though both were shortly leaving for Europe, James Russell Lowell and Henry Adams consented to be permanent co-editors. It followed that several issues, beginning with the issue for October 1872, would have to be cobbled together by whichever persons could do the cobbling. Lowell and Adams hastily assembled materials for the October issue. William Dean Howells was prevailed upon to proof-read it.[34] Subsequent issues would have to be assembled by an interim editor, yet to be found.[35]

Henry's particular business, visiting Quincy, was to arrange that during the coming September Charles would write an article to complete the October issue. Its subject would be "The Political Campaign of 1872." It would concern a presidential election in which the second son had been denied an important role. By writing an authoritative commentary, Charles would assert himself significantly after all. The one condition Henry imposed was that Charles's authorship be forever secret. No one was to know that the commentator was a disgusted Adams.

In 1870, Charles had argued that Henry should leave Washington and edit the magazine. As events had developed, Henry was sole permanent editor. (Lowell's co-editorship was *pro forma*.) His secret arrangement requiring Charles to write a political article implied an additional secret. On that future date when Henry's leave of absence was over, Charles would begin service as co-editor with responsibility for *political* articles, and his service would be entirely concealed.[36]

Four days prior to his wedding, on June 23, 1872, Henry again wrote to Gaskell from Beverly Farms. He said people might think it "peculiar that I should calmly come down here and live with my fiancée for a month before our marriage. But my father-in-law . . . is a sensible man in such matters. . . ." "When you know my young woman, you will understand why the world thinks we must be allowed to do what we think best. From having had no mother to take responsibility off her shoulders, she has grown up to look after herself and has a certain vein of personality which approaches eccentricity. This is very attractive to me, but then I am absurdly in love, and I wont [sic] guarantee your liking it."

The wedding took place in the Hooper cottage as scheduled and was viewed by Charles as "no wedding at all." In addition to Dr. Hooper, Clover, Henry, and the minister, the persons present were Clover's sister and brother with their spouses, Henry's elder brothers with their wives, and Betsy Wilder, a Hooper servant. Henry thought the occasion "very jolly." Charles liked nothing about it. The ceremony was edited to an irreducible mimimum and in his words "lasted in the neighborhood of two minutes." Formality was dispensed with. ". . . we all bundled into luncheon and sat down anywhere and the bride, at the head of the table, proceeded to calm her agitation by carving a pair of cold roast chickens." ". . . the champagne wasn't cool and made its appearance only in very inadequate quantities. . . ."[37]

The newlyweds left early, made their way to Cotuit Port on Cape Cod, and took possession of a summer mansion lent to them by Clover's Uncle Sam. The congressman also lent them his sailboat, complete with skipper, George Child. During the next few days, in broiling heat, Mr. and Mrs. Henry Adams went fishing, caught fish, and came ashore with sunburned noses. Writing to Dr. Hooper, Henry described himself and Clover as "flourishing and very elderly married people."

Saying there had been no wedding, Charles was close to right. The officiating minister, Charles Grinnell, was a young friend of the bride and groom who would shortly leave divinity to become a lawyer. The abridged ceremony suited Clover, who, though not against religion, was exceptionally without it. The place chosen for the ceremony shielded the newlyweds from public observation, and the availability of Uncle Sam's cottage at Cotuit Port permitted them to continue living together in Hooper houses as if little or nothing had happened.

A consequence of the wedding was its bringing into the open the fact that Charles was becoming disgruntled about Henry and Clover. Writing to the Chief, he criticized them for cheating Boston society of one of its favorite pleasures. "Why it is necessary or desirable to thus hold the world at arm's length and to carefully remove what little of foam and sparkle comes in one's way in life, is 'not perfectly clear' to my mind, but everyone to his taste."[38]

As for giving the couple a present, Charles tried to become co-donor of a present given by Mary and co-donor of a present given by Brooks. Each loved Henry greatly, each insisted on being sole donor, and Charles was two times rebuffed.[39]

On July 9, after an overnight stop at the Old House, dinner with John and Fanny, and good-byes to Charles and Minnie, Henry and Clover sailed from Boston on an old Cunarder, the *Siberia*.[40] The passengers included Henry's editorial "confrère," James Russell Lowell, and the man Henry considered the country's "best" historian, Francis Parkman.

The *Siberia* was a slow, unsteady ship that rolled and pitched even in moderate weather. Soon most of the passengers were seasick. The sick included the Adamses and Parkman. Henry and Clover had taken a double cabin on deck which was large enough to accommodate an added person. Earlier acquainted with Parkman only well enough to know he was "very agreeable," they were disposed to assist him. They suggested he leave his less-ventilated cabin and sleep in their extra space. He accepted and became a friend.

Gaskell awaited them in Shropshire. Clover thought Wenlock Abbey "ideal." ". . . Henry's and my rooms . . . are in the old Norman wing,—eight hundred years old,—with long narrow lancet windows, old carved furniture, and modern luxury combined in a delightful way."

The couple proceeded to London, sent their photographic apparatus ahead to Egypt, and called on the Palgraves. Frank showed them a sheaf of excellent drawings by Rembrandt, Vandyke, Raphael, and others. As a wedding present, he gave them a drawing by Blake of the prophet Ezekiel mourning for his newly-lost wife. Moreover, he confronted them with a Blake color print of Nebuchadnezzar, naked and insane—"on his hands and knees, eating grass." The picture was terrifying, but Henry liked it and would later buy it.

By way of Antwerp, the Hague, and Amsterdam, the Adamses proceeded to Bonn. Henry spoke with a professor at the university, Heinrich von Sybel, and learned that the books he hoped to obtain were not easily come by. In Clover's words, "They had never heard of any book Henry asked for." The one place the books might be purchased was Berlin.

At Cologne, a letter from Brooks required a change of itinerary. Henry and Clover hastened south, paused at Berne, connected briefly with Henry and Alice James, and reached Geneva. Charles Kuhn met their train and escorted them to the Château la Boissière, where the Chief and his party were residing.

The arbitration had reached its final stage. Evarts and Davis had finished presenting the American counter-case. The court's deliberation came next and was speedily concluded. The arbitrators decided that Great Britain should pay the United States $15,000,000—by coincidence the exact amount the United States had paid Napoleon I in 1803 for the Louisiana Purchase.

It could be said that three beneficiaries of the settlement were Great Britain, the Grant administration, and arbitrator Adams. Compared with what Sumner and other vengeful Americans had demanded, the British were required to pay extremely little. The Grant administration took credit for a masterstroke of statecraft. C. F. Adams again retired, this time with much satisfaction, everyone's blessing, and, in relation to diplomacy, a splendid record.

A meeting of emperors made it inopportune for Henry and Clover to go directly to Berlin. They went to Nuremberg and paused in Dresden.[41] The U. S. minister to Germany, George Bancroft, also visited Dresden. The Adamses learned that he was there and invited him to dinner.

Clover was related to *Mrs.* Bancroft—both were Davises—but she knew the minister-historian only by sight. After dinner, Bancroft adjourned with Henry and Clover to their parlor and in her words "talked Alabama, English gossip, and so on." Reporting the experience to her father, she said that Bancroft was "wearing a long white beard and talking German with much enthusiasm."

The emperors disbanded. The Adamses and Bancroft traveled separately to Berlin. The city was drenched with incessant rain. On September 13, as a step toward getting books, Henry called on a librarian and historian, Georg Heinrich Pertz. Also he called at the U. S. Legation. Minister Bancroft was there alone. (Sickened by Berlin's trying climate, Mrs. Bancroft had fled to Baden.) He invited Henry to share a dinner he had arranged for that very evening. Henry demurred, said he was dining with his wife, and mentioned who Clover was. According to Clover's later account, Bancroft became "much excited and pretended I was his dearest friend and insisted I must come too."

Henry sped back to Clover. In an hour, she "scrambled into a gown, not knowing whether it was a big affair or not." The affair could not have been bigger in relation to history. The principal German guests were Theodor Mommsen, the historian of Rome, and Ernst Curtius, the historian of Greece. Clover thought the dinner "lively." ". . . there was much good talk, but unhappily for me it was chiefly in German and so rapid that most of it was lost on me."

Beginning at dinner, Bancroft made Clover *his* cousin and said she and Henry must call him George. Thereafter for two days, with success, he helped Henry find elusive books. Clover thought his behavior "very kind," but kindness was not the only motive.

Born in 1800, Bancroft was in his seventies. He had not retired as America's national historian. His *History of the United States* was unfinished; several volumes were waiting to be written; and he could not afford to view himself as enfeebled and prepared to quit. His new friend Henry was an ambitious historian. The evidence was his list of seldom-asked-for German books. Reacting to the list, Bancroft accepted him as both a friend and a companion in history.

What Bancroft did not know was that Adams was his *successor*.

Henry too was America's national historian. He himself had a *History of the United States* to finish. The difference was that none of his volumes was even started, and for several years none would be. By the time he was ready to start them, Bancroft might be eighty.

In quest of sunny skies, Henry and Clover traveled west to Frankfurt and south to Switzerland. At every opportunity in Europe, they had taken advantage of good days to have pleasant experiences. At Frankfurt they strolled through the historic ghetto "where the Rothschilds started in life." At Lucerne, they rowed "to a most enchanting island, where we landed and feasted on a view such as one can see only now and then in a lifetime. We found roses in bloom, though it is cool enough to frighten away all that belongs to summer."

Autumn was setting in. They crossed the St. Gotthard pass into Italy, stopped for a week at Lugano, and shifted to Cadenabbia on Lake Como. There they were "greeted by three days' deluge,— such pitiless hopeless rain." Henry had sent books to America but also had selected a "small library" to study while in Europe and on the Nile. Rain did not at first trouble him. He contentedly studied. Clover wrote to her brother, ". . . we jog along, row on the lake when the sun does come out, and try to be philosophical."

Downpours, the worst in decades, pursued the couple to Venice. Being experienced travelers, they drew every possible benefit from their visit. "We plunge into the dirtiest alleys and market places and lose our way and watch the busy, squalid, everyday life and forget that gondolas and palaces exist." The city however was thrice-flooded, by sea, rain, and savage mosquitoes. They soon regretted having come. In memory, their days in Venice would come to seem a "fatal mistake."[42]

In Florence, very differently, the skies were bright. Henry wrote to Dr. Hooper that, despite almost continuous adverse weather since leaving Boston, Clover had "gained flesh and strength" and was "in better condition . . . than I [have] . . . ever known her to be." "Not that she had or has forgotten you . . . or has in the least lost her attachment to America. I have no fear that she will ever do that . . . ."

On schedule, the Adamses returned to the Adriatic at Ancona and took the steamer *Malta*, bound for Egypt. On November 22, 1872, in Alexandria, they rented a houseboat on which they would live for three winter months on the Nile. Adapted to European aristocrats, the houseboats—called *dahabiehs*—were large and luxurious. Henry and Clover chose a small one, the *Isis*, which was "clean and cheaper than we expected." Also they met their crew and their dragoman, Giovanni.

While Giovanni and the crew warped the *Isis* upstream to join them, the Adamses went ahead by rail to Cairo. During a visit to the Pyramids, they ran into Samuel and Anna Ward, a Boston couple they had met in Italy and knew would precede them to the Nile. More conservative than the New Yorker of the same name with whom Henry had been friends in Washington, Samuel Gray Ward was the U. S. agent of Baring Brothers and in Henry's words a person of "bankerial and artistic tastes."

The Wards too would be wintering on the river. They had chosen a large, handsome boat, the *Lotus*, and would be sailing before the *Isis* was ready. The couples agreed that, as soon as possible, they would join forces and ascend the river together. One reason for the plan was fear that British travelers might be around them in quantity. The fear was justified. Henry and Clover later saw eighteen *dahabiehs* anchored in a single spot, all housing British inhabitants.

At Cairo, Adams received a letter from Henry Cabot Lodge. It was the second of two letters. Behind the two was an eventful story.

Lodge was familiarly known as Cabot. After graduating from Harvard in 1871, he had married his cousin Anna Cabot Mills, known as Nanny, a prepossessing person—later one of Adams's closest friends. Cabot and Nanny went to Europe on a wedding journey. Cabot's chum, Michael Simpson, also went to Europe and was much in their company. They separated at Rome. Soon after, Simpson died of typhoid.

Shocked and feeling at loose ends, Lodge wrote to Professor Adams at Cambridge requesting advice about careers. Replying on June 2, 1872, Adams suggested that Lodge consider becoming a historian. Lodge went back to Harvard, enrolled at the Law School and at the same time tried to read the writings of Rudolph Sohm. Finding the work discouraging, he wrote again to Adams, who was himself on a wedding journey. Adams received the letter but was not at once inclined to answer.[43]

The *Isis* was ready for its voyage. Henry and Clover boarded on December 5 and started a twenty-eight day ascent to Thebes and Luxor. In effect a yacht, the boat afforded excellent quarters for study. Day after day, Henry read German books related to his inquiry concerning the possible role of the German local court in English history. At first with poor results, he also started to photograph.

His great hope was seeing and photographing Abu Simbel. The distance from Cairo to the temple by river was five hundred miles. Moving against the current, the *Isis* was slow, yet advanced. Gradually the scenery changed, and the weather grew milder. Clover wrote: "Egypt is certainly a wonderful country and impresses one more and more. It is on such a grand scale that other places must seem commonplace after it, though infinitely better to live in. The scenery is much more beautiful than I expected and has more variety . . . . The number of towns and villages that we pass every day is astonishing. . . . Troops of young girls come down to the river's edge to fill the large earthen water jars which they balance most gracefully on their heads. They wear one garment only, a long dark blue cotton mantle which covers their head and falls to the ankles, but in spite of their dirt and squalor they all wear silver bracelets, and I quite envy some of them, they are so becoming."

From Luxor, on January 2, 1873, Henry wrote to Lodge. He offered fresh encouragement concerning opportunities in history. He defended medieval history as a training ground where historians could learn good methods. He seemed engrossed in legal and institutional history. Saying his professorship required that he learn Anglo-Saxon, he implied he had started the labor and half-suggested that Lodge do the same.

As if he were thinking aloud, he defined the purpose of universal history and, with the same words, defined his own ambition as a historian. "America or Europe, our own century or prehistoric time, are all alike to the historian if he can only find out what men are and have been driving at, consciously or unconsciously."

Next day, the *Isis* overtook the *Lotus*. Thirteen added days and the two American *dahabiehs* were safely hauled beyond the first cataract and anchored at the temple island of Philae. Because a quarantine barred all boats from advancing towards Abu Simbel, the Adamses and Wards contented themselves with a long stay at Philae. Henry took excellent pictures of temples, and one of himself, but none of Clover. She disliked being photographed.[44]

Remaining anchored was agreeable, and the Adamses felt no wish to move. Clover wrote to her father, "I doubt if we find any place as beautiful as this." Unexpectedly, however, the quarantine was lifted. The *Isis* and *Lotus* pulled anchor and together moved upstream.

Without incident, amid lovely scenery and delicious air, the

American boats advanced the last 170 miles. Each night the Southern Cross rose higher above the horizon. The days changed color. Clover wrote, "The desert is more golden in Nubia than in Egypt and the cliffs and mountains [are] very striking."

In the evening of February 2, the boats "pulled up by the great rock temple." Above loomed the four seated figures of Abu Simbel—"immense colossi . . . between sixty and seventy feet high." When at college, Henry had understood that the figures all were kings. At some early time, the second from the left had fallen in ruins. The other three were intact, seated on thrones, hands on knees, eyes open, looking immortally across the river. Clover studied their faces and said they were "quite perfect." ". . . the expression of power and sweetness is very striking."

In the morning, Adams and Ward tried to find the best vantage point for the Adamses' camera. What Henry wanted was to catch the "spirit" of the temple. Despite "much trouble," he could find no vantage point that appeared to serve. Ward however discovered one and Henry used it, confident that a picture from that direction would achieve his object. He developed the plate and liked the result. He later sent Carlo a print and accompanied it with the boast that his photograph was "worth half a dozen of any I have yet met."[45]

During the two nights and a day the Adamses stayed in their presence, the ancient figures kept their places and Henry had opportunity to think of *words* to express their spirit. If effectual words occurred to him, he did not put them down in any record that survives. He only said when writing to Carlo, "As a sight, there is nothing I have seen in the world equal to this temple. . . ."

Descending the river was easy and swift. On February 10, Clover wrote that they had said good-bye to the Southern Cross and were at Philae, having come from Abu Simbel in six days. "We all think Nubia much more attractive than Egypt, and for people in search of health the climate is perfect. We found a few temples to explore as we came down, some nearly buried by sand, but by creeping in through the choked-up entrance we came into chambers where the figures were beautifully colored and little injured considering the thousands of years which have passed over them."

If for Henry and Clover one place represented the early phase of their marriage more than any other, the place was the temple of Philae. At sunset on February 10, they went there for the last time. Before retiring, Clover wrote to her father: "We hope to go over the great cataract at 'El Bab' tomorrow morning early. It ought to

278 BETTER IN DARKNESS

be very exciting. . . . I will add a line at Assouan to tell you we are all right."

The cataract was safely passed, but there came a spell of bad weather. Below Luxor, in Henry's words, ". . . the weather was diabolic." The *Isis* and *Lotus* were slowed for a week by a cold, hard north wind. "The wind blew a tempest every day, making me quite seasick, and shutting us up in our cabins." Yet the storm "did us no harm."

The Adamses and Wards separated at Cairo. When first seen, Alexandria and Cairo had repelled Clover as dirty or worse. On returning to Cairo, she thought it fascinating. "The weather has been enchanting and we have trotted round on donkeys all day long to Syrian and Turkish and gold bazaars and bought many nice things. . . ." One of their purchases for Clover was a silk scarf large enough to wrap a human figure, yet so fine one might think to draw it through a wedding ring.[46]

The Wards were en route to Syria. At Alexandria, Clover seized a moment and wrote a letter to Mr. Ward. Her letter was happy. "We long to hear that you get comfortably to Syria & enjoy it as much as the Nile. From much we have lived through this winter[,] we feel as if we went home with a new lease of life and happiness to begin with . . . ." That same morning, March 10, 1873, she and Henry sailed on a French steamer bound for Naples. She wrote to her father from shipboard: "Our winter in Egypt has been a great success. We feel as if we had had a great bath of sunshine and warmth and rest, and are quite made over new."[47]

13

By an Atom

Sometime earlier, at the latest on the *Siberia* when they were
beginning their journey, Henry had told Clover about his part-
written *Democracy*.[1] He had no choice but to tell her. He had to
disclose that he had tried to write the novel in 1867 after the news
reached London that Senator Sumner, his long-time friend and
Clover's long-time acquaintance, had married Alice Mason Hooper,
his former acquaintance and Clover's cousin-by-marriage. Disclosure was the more necessary because Mrs. Sumner and her daughter Bel had settled in Europe and there was every chance that the
Adamses would meet them. As it happened, Henry and Clover
agreed to see them in Switzerland and again in Florence. Both
arrangements miscarried.

In England, soon after leaving the *Siberia*, Clover obtained and
started to read the first instalments of *Middlemarch*, a new novel by
"George Eliot" (Mary Ann Evans), currently appearing bi-monthly
as eight separate "books."[2] Her reading was interrupted while she
and Henry were on the Nile, but she bought the concluding books
when leaving Egypt and read them on shipboard en route to Italy.
Henry too read *Middlemarch*. Presumably he finished before their
arrival in Naples.

Henry was interested in Eliot's novel generally but was struck
particularly by two epigraphs. Beginning Chapter 74, Eliot quoted
a marriage prayer from the Book of Tobit: "Mercifully grant that
we may grow aged together." Beginning Chapter 85, she quoted
the passage in *Pilgrim's Progress* in which Faithful is wrongly condemned to death by a jury of twelve "persecuting passions."

Three years later, in March 1876, the Adamses would acquire
a copy of *Pilgrim's Progress*. Clover would sign it as hers; and Henry
would inscribe in it the Biblical marriage prayer, cite the Book of
Tobit as its source, and sign the inscription with his initials.[3] So
inscribed, the copy was part-deceiving. It concealed the fact that

for Henry and Clover the effective source of the prayer was not the apocryphal Book of Tobit, for which neither may have cared a button, but instead was the ambitious English novel they had read on their wedding journey.[4]

It appears that *Middlemarch* was mainly important to Henry and Clover because of its relation to Henry as a novelist. To see how Eliot's book acquired that importance, one should consider a salient fact. Dorothea Brooke, Eliot's heroine, commits in fiction an error comparable to the error that Alice Mason Hooper committed in life. Virginal Dorothea marries a self-involved clergyman of fast-dwindling vitality. Widowed Alice married an egotistical, aging politician of unusual or absent sexuality. For Henry and Marian Adams, the great difference between the unhappy cases was not the difference between fiction and life. Neither was it the difference between Dorothea's innocence and Alice's experience. Rather it was the difference between disastrous marriage in relation to an English clergyman and disastrous marriage in relation to an American politician.

Such evidence as survives indicates that Clover, on hearing about Henry's part-written novel, wanted *Democracy* finished and published. She approved its prospective plot, in which the American heroine, a young widow, would at the last minute *avoid* a disastrous marriage to a much older, very self-centered, high-ranking American politician. But an obvious possibility developed: a second novel by Henry.

Clover perhaps saw the possibility sooner than Henry. He had not intended two novels. He had intended one, of such strength and appeal that it might be read for an indefinite time. Moreover, because he had conceived it when a bachelor, *Democracy* was strictly his. But as early as the day they arrived in Naples, March 15, 1873, he and Clover were in a position to imagine his writing a novel truly *Clover's*. The plot for the possible second novel was ready-made. At the last minute, on grounds of her agnosticism, an American heroine would avoid a marriage to a self-centered, high-ranking American clergyman.

While still in Egypt, the Adamses received news that Gaskell's father had died and that Gaskell, already owner of Wenlock Abbey, had inherited a large fortune and two more residences: Thornes House in Yorkshire and a townhouse in London. Because he would not need his townhouse while in mourning, Carlo urged Henry and Clover to use it before going home. They declined the offer as excessively generous, yet felt it as "a great temptation."

The Adamses had come to Europe partly to buy furnishings for their future houses. In Henry's words, they meant to conduct "a very lively campaign among the shops." They were fully prepared for the campaign. Henry said they felt "a good healthy energy of enjoyment such as grows only under the sun of the East." Their needs included rugs, china, silver, linens, fabrics, drawings, watercolors, ancient Greek vases, Tanagra figures, even fourteenth century Japanese bronzes.

Illness somewhat interfered. Naples, new to Clover, was lively as always; but the threat of fever encouraged an early departure. At Sorrento, their spirits remained high, but they both came down with colds. Though not recovered, they advanced to Rome and connected at last with Alice Sumner and daughter Bel. Clover reported that Alice and Bel were "fat and flourishing." She and Henry, however, summoned a doctor and, to forestall malaria, stayed in their rooms. Henry James paid them a call and wrote that they were "the better for Egypt, but the worse for Naples, which has made them ail a little."[5]

When well enough, they left their hotel and visited William Wetmore Story. In Clover's words: "We went to Mr. Story's studio, and oh! how he does spoil nice blocks of white marble. Nothing but Sibyls on all sides. . . . Call him a genius! I don't see it. . . . He himself was handsome and pleasant; Mrs. Story is very stout and tells lies. . . ."

Fully recovered, they went to Florence. Charles Kuhn had built a tomb for Loo. Henry and Clover possibly were shown it. The Chief had earlier been given the opportunity—for him exceedingly unwelcome.[6]

Henry wanted Clover to travel by carriage, as he had, along the Corniche to Nice. At Spezia, they hired a carriage. Their first day's drive was spoiled by rain and hail, so they "made a sudden change of base" and returned to railroads. A train sped them under the Alps via a new tunnel at Mont Cenis. When the train paused at the tunnel's northern end, they got out and "ate snow and made and fired snowballs, which was a great excitement after a winter of golden sand."

Knowing Paris had been heavily damaged in 1871 while held by the *communards*, they doubted that good accommodations would be available. Luckily they found clean small rooms high up in a hotel at the corner of the Rue du Rivoli and the Place Palais-Royal. Thanks to a bomb, their parlor had been refurbished, but along the Rue du Rivoli what remained of the Tuileries was a "dreary ruin," unrepaired and vast.

Three veterans of the First Cavalry, Henry Higginson, Greely Curtis, and C. F. Adams, Jr., had been sent abroad as Massachusetts State Commissioners to the Vienna Exposition. The commissioners stopped in Paris, and Charles called on Henry and Clover. They again had bad colds, yet they offered him a bed in a cubbyhole adjoining their parlor. He stayed the night but proved an ungrateful lodger. He wrote to Minnie: "My brother has grown to be a damned, solemn, pompous little ass, and his wife is an infernal bore;—they are the most married couple I have yet seen;—and when I came into the room (& Lor, how I hate her!—she talks in a low voice . . . and she's always saying something to me—she's doing it now!)—well I found them sitting together & she holding his hand, and then she makes cups of Turkish coffee all day and makes everyone drink them, even me. . . ."[7]

First on the *Isis* and at intervals since, Henry had been teaching himself Anglo-Saxon and searching for evidence relating to the question of the hundred court in early England. While in Paris, he formed acquaintanceships with two young French historians, Gabriel Monod and Marcel Thévenin. The latter was a medievalist supportive of Sohm's discoveries, was adapted to writing critical notices for the *North American*, and eventually would do so.[8]

Clover knew many details concerning the Sumners' attempted union and at some point in America had been introduced to Baron von Holstein. Walking in Paris, she met the baron. Mutual recognition could not be avoided. She later informed her father from London: "Holstein is in Paris; I met him face to face on the Boulevard and cut him."

Gaskell was determined that the Adamses use his London house. By offering it for rent at a prohibitive figure, £800 a month, he kept it vacant. To force their taking it, he asked them to consider their occupancy a wedding present. He also required that they visit him at Thornes House in Yorkshire and a second time at Wenlock Abbey.

Henry, overwhelmed, consented by letter from Paris. Again recovered, he and Clover crossed to London on May 10, 1873. The season being in full swing, their hotel admitted them for one night only. Lacking a hotel for the following nights, they took annex rooms on Suffolk Street and Albemarle Street.

At his earliest chance, Carlo came to town, gave them keys, lent them two servants, and returned to Shropshire. Relieved and happy, his guests took possession of 28 Norfolk Street, Park Lane. Although borrowed, the townhouse counted as the first house the

Adamses could feel as theirs. It had advantages parallel to those of a Washington house on Lafayette Square. Four rooms overlooked Hyde Park. At ground level there was a "large sunny dining-room." Above was a "large and very handsome parlour with a piazza." Higher still were Clover's bedroom and Henry's dressing room. There were two spare bedrooms.

The Adamses' marriage did not stand alone but was paired with the Gurneys' marriage. The two unions, however, were opposite in spirit. Ellen had been much attached to a man who died in the war. She consented to marry Whitman only after he several times proposed. When she at last consented, she did so with augmentedly romantic feelings. Their marriage in consequence was "very lover-like."[9] Yet it also was reserved and very conventional.

The Adamses' marriage had both closed and opened doors. From the first, Henry and Clover had made their union not private or secret but secretly secret. From the first, too, they had made exceptional efforts to accommodate other people. They invited Brooks to go with them to Egypt and share their *dahabieh*. (He refused and went on in law school.) They asked Dr. Hooper to join them for the season in London, assuming they could rent a house. (He would not leave Beverly Farms.) On their roster of necessities, active hospitality stood fourth after love, work, and rest; and it stood a very high fourth.

Being hospitable themselves, Henry and Clover encouraged hospitality in those they met. The day they moved to Park Lane, they went to dinner at the Thomson Hankeys and met Sir Charles Clifford, a member of Parliament and fellow of All Souls, Oxford. It developed that Clifford was friendly with Cunliffe, then also a member of Parliament. In the course of conversation, the Adamses touched on their planning to visit Oxford. Henry wished to see Anglo-Saxon manuscripts and was anxious to meet Professor William Stubbs, the university's leading historian of early England. Clifford immediately invited the Adamses and Cunliffe to join him at Oxford during Parliament's Whitsuntide recess.

Next day, going about in a rented brougham, Henry and Clover left cards and paid calls. They hired an excellent cook who unfortunately was cross. Using their Dresden linens, Danish china, and other properties where possible, they began to offer meals. Cunliffe dropped in and chaffed them for "being such swells as to take a house in Park Lane." He told them they had "reached the summit now and after this must decline steadily in our fortunes."

Gaskell persisted in kindness. Clover absolutely declined to be first user of a brougham he had just bought and wished she would try. She said his gift house was sufficient "gorgeousness." As guests continued to arrive, she wrote to him in mock alarm: "The Lord Chancellor and Dean Stanley smoke in the *drawing room* and borrow your choicest books and dog's-ear them! *You* must do something about it."

At the end of May, she and Henry shed their irritable cook and went to Oxford for a four-day visit. To his great satisfaction, Henry saw "the early English M.S.S. in the Bodleian." Assisted by Clifford, he spoke with "all the men I expected to see," chiefly Professor Stubbs. He also met "a number I did not expect to see." The most notable was Sir Henry Maine, an authority on ancient law. Earlier, in the *North American*, Adams had anonymously reviewed and praised Maine's books.

On June 4, 1873, returning to the London maelstrom, the Adamses started afresh. Lady Rich sent them a cook who was good-tempered as well as excellent. Their first sleep-in visitor was Charles. His jealous hatred of Clover could not have been unapparent, but he stayed two nights.[10] Henry Higginson stayed a week. Lowell stayed before and after a trip to Oxford to receive an honorary degree.[11]

A letter to Adams from Lodge awaited an answer. Lodge did not have to earn an income, was far along in his course at the Law School, and wished to become a historian under Adams's tutelage. Henry replied that he had been "accumulating notes upon some points of early German law." "If you like, I will put these notes in your hands next term, and we will proceed to work the subject up together." The proposed joint venture would require Lodge's "best knowledge of German, French, Latin and Anglo-Saxon." It also would require their sharing space on the campus. ". . . polish up your languages and on the 1st October, if you are ready to begin, establish yourself in my rooms at Wadsworth."

Henry and Clover celebrated their first anniversary, June 27, by giving a "family dinner." Carlo, their "fairy godfather," came from Shropshire to attend, then swept them northward to York-shire. Clover thought Thornes House a "lovely quiet old place" but "immense." Most astonishing was the "library—huge—with five thousand books."

England was the setting which best showed Henry's quality of being America. Fully as much as Henry, *Clover* was America.[12] Their sharing the attribute went a long way to explain their marriage. Once united, they comported themselves as a quintessentially American couple. Their dealings with the English were designedly American and included American take-offs of English ways. Learning that Carlo stood to inherit a fourth house from a ninety-year-old uncle, they chaffed him for being an "insatiate heir" and told him his country's "social fabric" was wobbling and would crash. In the circumstances, they recommended he invest his riches outside of England, meaning in the U. S. A.

The disparities between England and America were partly amusing, partly not. At Thornes, a doubt arose concerning precedence. It was debatable which Englishman should take Mrs. Adams to the dinner table. Recounting the experience, Clover said, ". . . I told them they might fight it out among themselves, that their 'effete monarchical customs were a matter of no concern to me. . . .' " In the same letter, she stated her and Henry's strongest criticism of the United Kingdom. They could see no excuse for the cruel inequalities of British life. She said, "England is charming for a few families but hopeless for most. . . . Thank the Lord that the American eagle flaps and screams over us. . . ."

Carlo, Clover, and Henry went back to London and entertained for a week as a threesome. When the week had passed, the Adamses had seen nearly "all our imaginable friends." Carlo left, first making sure that Henry and Clover would rejoin him in Shropshire before going to Liverpool and their steamer.

Sir Henry Maine asked the Adamses to dine, and Clover was pleased to see that of sixteen guests she already knew eight. In several ways, she was prospering. She excelled as a hostess. "I like giving dinners in such a big society—one can get more variety of material than in Boston." Her dealings with servants were practical and democratic. She said of her new cook: "We shall weep on each other's necks when we part. . . . She asks how many guests, makes out the menu, submits it, and cooks it to perfection; we eat it and pay for it."

As a concluding pleasure, Clover caught a glimpse of the life Henry had known ten years before. John Bright came to dinner. Though in decline, he remained good company. Henry noted, "We had much gay talk."

The Adamses had spent a large amount—£2,000—on new possessions. A caravan of wooden cases was carried away by the shippers, labeled for conveyance by sailing ship to Boston. Not packed was the camera and attendant equipment. Believing they would not see Europe again for many years, Henry and Clover took the camera to Wenlock Abbey. Henry photographed the house and adjoining ruins. Carlo, Clover, the Cunliffes, and other guests submitted to being posed in informal groups. For one of the pictures, Clover was cajoled into taking center place.[13]

Intending his remark as helpful, the Chief had written to Henry suggesting that on his return he should at last apply himself "to the serious work of life."[14] Henry and Clover crossed to New York on the *Cuba* and went at once to Dr. Hooper's cottage at Beverly Farms. Henry shortly visited at Quincy. Perhaps to avoid seeing Charles, Clover did not go with him.

Since 1871, Henry had kept in touch with Clarence King. (Details are lacking. Their early letters are missing.) As soon as practicable, Henry and Clover journeyed to Newport to pass a weekend as King's guests. The meeting of wife and friend apparently was agreeable, and one reason was a house. The Kings had lived in New York and Newport. In former times, they had prospered as merchants in the China trade. Except that they suffered shipwrecks and calamitous deaths, they were counterparts of Captain William Sturgis in Boston and early seafaring Hoopers in Marblehead. In 1873, their old Newport house, at the corner of Church and High Streets, was still redolent of the past, its interiors "bright with the rich fabrics, grim with the weird carvings . . . and fragrant with the strange scents of the Far East."[15]

By mail from abroad, Henry and Clover had been trying to buy an apartment or house in Boston and to scout for land at Beverly Farms on which to build. Within a month of their return, they bought a house in Boston at 91 Marlborough Street, at the corner of Clarendon Street, a fashionable location in the new Back Bay, a short walk removed from Dr. Hooper's house at 114 Beacon Street. Henry described their house as "quite pretty" but "very small." It had many windows facing south and a "gem" of a library, shelved to accommodate "about 2,000 books." He estimated to Carlo that the cost of the house and furnishings would be about £10,000.

Immediately after the Adamses bought their house, on September 18, 1873, Jay Cooke and Company failed in New York. A panic followed. "The next day Fisk and Hatch . . . went down. Wall Street was in terror, and the New York Stock Exchange was closed for eight days."[16]

Henry and Clover saw bankruptcies all around them but were themselves uninjured. The principal change they made of a business sort was one of investment supervision. Henry shifted oversight of his capital from Charles to Edward Hooper, who in 1872 had been named to the Harvard corporation as treasurer.[17] Apart from the break with Charles, the transfer had two advantages. It placed Henry and Clover's assets in a single overseer's accounts, and it drew upon the talents of the man entrusted to manage Harvard's endowment.[18]

The person pressed into service as interim editor of the *North American Review* was Thomas Sergeant Perry, a young Harvard teacher.[19] Perry found an eager helper in Henry Cabot Lodge. Adams's permanent editorship remained in force (Lowell had been dropped), and his responsibilities would re-begin with the April 1874 issue.

One day in September 1873, Adams shuttled from Beverly Farms to nearby Nahant and visited the Lodges. After lunch, he and Cabot walked together on the road leading to "the wagon for Lynn." As they walked, Henry asked Cabot to join him as official assistant editor. The opportunity was not a small one. In Lodge's words, ". . . the whole world was changed."[20]

When classes started again at Harvard, Adams taught courses in medieval politics and medieval institutions; he began a new course in English constitutional history; and he instituted a graduate program of his own design. Its governing idea was joint research by teacher and students. He arranged to conduct a research project with Lodge and another former student, Ernest Young. Partly to speed the project, he continued to rent 3 Wadsworth House—Brooks's former upstairs room.

Word got about that graduates who studied with Assistant Professor Adams might eventually earn the degree of doctor of philosophy, then new at Harvard. The liberties extended to Adams quickly grew. He soon had several assistants. He wrote to Gaskell, ". . . as my old students are some of them still hanging about and wanting occupation, I have managed to harness a few of them to the wheels in such a way as to relieve me of a good deal of work." The students harnessed were Lodge, chiefly to deal with the printing of the *North American*; Young, to help teach medieval politics; and Ephraim Emerton and J. M. McVane, to work with Young as sub-assistants.[21]

Assistants were necessary. Henry was staying at Harvard for long stretches three days a week, was expected at Monday evening faculty meetings and sometimes went, was reading with a constancy that might endanger his sight, and again was busied by the *North American*.[22]

Clover meanwhile was organizing their household. They moved to 91 Marlborough Street on October 20, 1873. In the library, they hung only Blake's "Nebuchadnezzar." In other rooms, they hung numerous drawings and watercolors. By turning two of its corners under, they fitted into the dining room a large carpet the color of Nubian sand. Soon all their furnishings were given places. The general effect was that of a Hooper home, expensive and very tasteful.

Between semesters, in February 1874, the Adamses went to Washington for a fortnight. The reasons they gave were Henry's recess from teaching and their being invited by Congressman Hooper to join him at his house. The reasons evidently masked a third reason relating to a future move. Henry wrote to Carlo: ". . . I find myself again with my foot upon my native asphalt, rejoicing in delivery for a time from the ways of Boston. It is no end of fun to come back. . . . No one seems to have any idea of what is to happen here, but my own notion is that our next election will throw a crowd of new men into office. . . ."

Assuming that the Adamses meant to live in Washington beginning in 1877 after Grant completed his second term, and assuming too that they would want to rent a house on or near Lafayette Square, it behooved them to apprise the owners of houses or their agents three-and-a-half years ahead of time. Moreover, their problem was one that required both good management and good luck. The most desirable houses on the square were those on H Street facing south towards the White House. Because St. John's Church occupied the northeast corner of H Street and 16th Street, such houses were few and proportionally in demand. The prospect of getting one could not have looked bright.

While the Adamses were abroad, on September 4, 1872, the *New York Sun* had alleged that Congressman Garfield, Vice President Colfax, vice-presidential nominee Henry Wilson, and other leading Republicans had accepted stock in Credit Mobilier, a construction company created by the promoters of the Union Pacific railroad to divert the company's construction profits to themselves. In addition, the *New York Tribune* alleged that the speaker of the House, James G. Blaine, had accepted $2,000,000 of stock in the Union Pacific railroad while it was part of the Erie empire.

A Congressional investigation had followed. Garfield was exonerated. Blaine was cleared but seemed likely to escape one accusation only to incur another. Stories lingered about members of Congress who had not been investigated. Blaine's biographer "Gail Hamilton" (Mary Abigail Dodge) would eventually repeat in print an allegation that " 'Sam Hooper,' of Boston . . . walked daily back and forth before the Speaker's chair, with his pockets stuffed full of Credit Mobilier stock, a single dividend bringing $100,000, not only unharmed, but unassailed and undisturbed; and Bingham of Ohio, when asked if he had any, shouted 'Yes, and only wished he had ten times more. . . .' "[23]

When Henry and Clover joined Congressman Hooper in February 1874, the American statemen most in their minds were Senator Sumner, President Grant, and Speaker Blaine. At his house a few steps distant, aging Sumner was stricken with angina. It pleased him that Henry and Clover came to visit, but he clearly was failing.[24]

Though Henry had said to Carlo that he expected new men would take office in 1877, there was ample reason to doubt it. Hope that Grant would vanish after two terms was a hope, nothing more. The limiting of presidents to two terms was a matter of custom, not law, and Grant had supporters who would back him for any number of terms.

In Henry's opinion, a worse possibility than a third term for Grant was a first term for Blaine. On the basis of direct acquaintance, data obtained by word of mouth, and information in the public prints, Henry had come to think that Speaker Blaine was corruption incarnate and that *his* being president would make the peculations of Julia Grant seem a timid prologue. To make matters worse, the odds that Blaine could be elected were steadily improving. It was no deterrent that the Maine politician, originally poor, was leading the life of the rich. In the eyes of many, he was partly a *reformer*. He assuredly was a church-goer. He routinely taught classes in Sunday school.

The Adamses returned to Boston. Immediately thereafter, Sumner weakened. On March 11, 1874, he died. His death created a vacancy in the Senate, and an effort was made to obtain the place for the Chief. Though not strong, the effort was strong enough to elicit from Henry a sweeping comment about the condition of American politics. He wrote to Carlo, ". . . the badness of our government . . . is desperate; not so much corrupt as incompetent; enough to make one a howling dervish for life."

In the next breath, Henry said he would stay in Massachusetts well past the time of the next presidential inauguration. "The winter has now pretty well passed. . . . We are meditating on our summer cottage and new work for next year. Altogether, life is calm and very enjoyable, so that I look forward to at least five years of perfect quiet here, only varied by Boston, Cambridge and Beverly in regular succession."

Being written to Carlo, Henry's forecast could seem deserving of credence. In coming months, he would make other statements indicating that he would not move to Washington soon. But his various prophecies were evidence, not of willingness to stay in Boston, but instead of secret plans. At bottom, the Adamses' situation was simple. Henry was hardened in his determination to move to Washington in 1877. With respect to the move, he trusted no one but Clover. He feared he would get back to the capital only with the help of new efforts as a politician; and till ready to move— or forced *not* to move—he wanted the cover of claimed intentions to remain contentedly at Harvard.

Meanwhile it was true that the Adamses were meditating their summer cottage. Perhaps because of the crash, tracts of land close to Dr. Hooper's were becoming available. Henry and Clover wished to buy them and build a convenient house that they themselves would design.

For the present, Henry was happier than he had ever dreamed to be. Yet he also was exceedingly, even painfully, unhappy. Residence in New England was cutting him off from the United States. He told Carlo, "Boston is very well up in all things European, but it is no place for American news." Persons from other states seldom came to Massachusetts. He wrote to Garfield, "One might as well live in Walrussia as here for anything one can see of the world."

His particular horror in Boston-Cambridge was institutionalized group complacency, saffroned with culture. In 1871, apropos of the Friday Club, he had reported to Carlo: "I go every month to a club dinner at which we are all young editors, or writers for the press, or lawyers. . . . We talk culture. . . ." Wanting *not* to talk culture, and judging himself "too bad for such excellent surroundings," he had attended at the cost of silence and restive listening.[25]

In 1874, he again was a member of clubs (it is uncertain which), but his preferred course was avoidance. A club he kept very far away from was the most publicized in the country. Created in Boston in 1867 and open to both men and women, the Radical Club at its monthly winter meetings heard and discussed papers on religious and cultural topics prepared by distinguished speakers.[26] The papers were much in the tradition of Ralph Waldo Emerson, Margaret Fuller, the *Dial*, and transcendentalism. The proceedings were reported in the *New York Tribune* by Mrs. Louise Chandler Moulton, a well-known poet who was also the newspaper's

Boston literary correspondent. Her reports were widely read. In the words of her biographer, Lilian Whiting: "Extracts from them were copied all over the United States, and they came to be looked upon as a sort of authorized report of what was doing in the intellectual capital of the country."[27]

Adams had recently exhibited irritation, even temper. The January 1874 issue of the *North American*—Perry's last issue—contained a notice signed "H. A." The notice jousted belligerently with Edward A. Freeman with reference to a revised American edition of his *History of the Norman Conquest of England, its Causes and its Results*. Teachers and students at Harvard instantly knew that the attack on Freeman was written by Professor Adams. Freeman reached the same conclusion, resented the notice, and later answered it in print and in person.[28]

The idea at work in Adams's attack was that English historians were the historians *least* likely to understand English history. He believed that the thread of English history was best followed through the labyrinths of evidence by inquirers not purely English. How he himself understood English history was as yet only slightly apparent, but he made the attack on Freeman partly because, assisted by Rudolph Sohm, he was following a thread.[29]

Beginning with his and Lodge's first issue of the *North American*, that for April 1874, the magazine became much more historical. Adams contributed three unsigned notices at the back of the issue. Two of the three related directly to his courses at Harvard; and one of the two, a notice of Marcel Thévenin's French translation of a book published by Sohm in 1867, was astonishingly recondite. Its publication seemed to promise that the magazine in its back pages would try to serve as a newsletter for America's most serious historians.

Henry's practices as the magazine's chief editor were hard-headed and secretive. He sometimes would not tell Lodge the names of anonymous contributors. In such cases, he might list himself as the writer-of-record of an article or notice actually written by somebody else.[30] Other secrets related to money. Because he wanted to pay outside contributors substantial amounts for their articles and notices, he meant to fill the issues when possible with contributions he could get for nothing. Unpaid contributors would include Lowell, the Chief, Brooks, Lodge, himself, and secret political co-editor Charles.[31]

A prodigious worker, Lodge assumed as many duties as assistant editor as Henry would provide him. Busy as he was, Lodge may not have realized that, by writing anonymous notices for the back pages, Adams was continuing a process of publishing "sketches" on subjects important to him. His sketches were becoming a sort of journal of his intellectual development. If doubled in number, they would bulk large enough to make a book.[32]

In May, the Adamses moved to "a small box" they had rented for five months at Beverly Farms. While commuting to Cambridge to meet classes, Henry prodded Charles and Brooks to finish political articles for the July issue. He wanted his brothers to speak their minds, and he possibly seemed to share their ideas, but in reality he occupied a unique position. The drift of their articles was plain in the title Brooks gave to his: "The Platform of the New Party."

Cunliffe and Gaskell had been beaten in recent elections and faced doubtful futures as politicians. Henry wrote to Cunliffe: ". . . I am heartily sick of the condition of politics in my own country. . . . We are growing rapidly in wealth, education and even in the higher refinements of taste, but politically we were never so low as now." The lines stated Henry's political problem. He wished to prevent politics in the United States from sinking lower. To that end, he needed a means of stopping the Republicans from nominating Grant or Blaine in 1876. In name and appearance, such an implement might well be Brooks's "New Party," but Henry would want to wield the implement and give it an uncommon but effectual character.

For Clover, Beverly Farms had many advantages, including easy visits to her father. For Henry, its advantages were the ocean, exercise in the open air, and escape from heat. He liked to swim and take long walks. Since summer for him partly meant heavy reading to prepare new courses, it greatly helped that the North Shore was "the coolest place between here and Patagonia." He wrote to Carlo that the present summer was "the loveliest season I ever saw in this climate; deluges of rain; cool days, and foliage fresh and almost as thick as in England."

Unhappily, for Henry, the advantages were offset by deprivations. Even more than Boston, Beverly Farms was isolating. "As for news," he continued, "you can expect none from a fellow who lives in a corner of creation like this. I am fond of the place, but it is more out of the world than any Scotch moor. I wander in pine woods which have no end, or along the sea-side. . . . The newspapers are deadly dull. . . . Politics are contemptible to the last degree, and growing more and more sordid and aimless. There is nothing but my profession to interest me, and even there solitude mostly prevails. . . ."

From an unknown owner or owners, Henry and Clover bought a tract of land nearly bordering on Dr. Hooper's property. A house site at the end of a 1500 foot drive afforded a view of the ocean. A quarter-mile path through the pines connected the house site and Dr. Hooper's cottage. Also the tract could be expanded. Neighbors were willing to sell. The Adamses might eventually own twenty acres.[33]

In late August, Henry and Clover went to the Adirondacks, returning by way of Montreal and Quebec. The excursion did not raise Henry's estimate of Canada, which he thought a country "without a vestige of literary or artistic aspiration." ". . . on the other hand," he said, "Quebec is the most superbly situated place I ever saw in any country."

In September, while "cutting trees" on the newly-purchased tract, Henry hurt his foot. (He perhaps was trying to improve the ocean view and wielded the ax with too-impetuous energy.) The wound would heal, but for a time he was hobbled by dressings. He seized the interval to draw complete plans for their cottage: a three-story wood house with breezy porches. His plans were sufficiently detailed to be translated by a builder into blueprints. Construction would start early in 1875. He and Clover would occupy the house in the late spring of 1876.

On September 22, 1874, a never-identified writer made a brilliant attack on Boston's Radical Club. It took the form of a letter to the editor of the *New York Tribune*. The letter was long— eighteen paragraphs of data and analysis. It was sent from "Boston" and signed "R. W. L." Teasingly the initials suggested both Ralph Waldo Emerson and Henry Wadsworth Longfellow. The attacker had certainly attended meetings of the club and conceivably was a member in good standing. There was no guarantee that the attacker was not a woman. Because the letter began by saying "The Boston Radical Club is dead"—a very Swiftian touch—the letter would come to be known as an "obituary."[34]

After a half-month delay, on October 7, the *Tribune* published the obituary under the headings:

The Boston Radical Club.

———

Its Death, and How it Came to Die.
The Interest Surrounding Its Early History—

the Time of Its Formation an Auspicious One
—the Character of the Discussions—Literary
Pyrotechnics—a Lofty Contempt for Facts—
Bright Talk Varied with Sublime Rubbish.

According to "R. W. L.," nine persons had given the club its
"guiding impulse" and "habitual tone." The six persons first mentioned were

Dr. Bartol	—"a very venerable and very clerical looking man"
John T. Sargent	—"a somewhat superannuated ex-minister"
A. Bronson Alcott	—"over 70 years of age"
D. A. Wasson	—"an ex-minister, of middle age, a man of vigorous intellect"
T. W. Higginson	—"who needs no description"
John Weiss	—"a man of marked characteristics, the most prominent being vividness of imagination."

Three others mentioned were "Samuel Longfellow, a minister
and poet, brother of the more famous poet of the same name;
Mrs. Julia Ward Howe; and Mrs. E. D. Cheney, widow of the artist
Cheney."[35]

"R. W. L." thought the list of persons revealing. ". . . note the
curious fact that the men are, or were, all ministers (with one
exception), and even the women are sometimes preachers." More
to the point was the fact that the leaders' preachments were
outmoded. The club could be considered dead because it had tried
to resuscitate the past. "It was narrow in its theological sympathies,
narrow in its philosophy, and in its method of thinking . . . almost
the reverse of radical. . . . It was an attempt to bring back a kind of
culture for which Boston gained some reputation 30 years ago, but
which the real intellectual progress of the world has already left
far behind."

Henry and Clover read the obituary but at first did no more
than remember what it said.[36] Henry had started his fourth year
of teaching and had made several changes. In his place, Ernest
Young was teaching "The Political History of Europe from the 10th
to the 15th Century." Henry was continuing to teach "Medieval
Institutions" and "History of England to the 17th Century." He
was introducing a wholly new course in the "Colonial History of
America to 1789," meaning to the first inauguration of President
Washington.[37] Also his research project had been formally recognized by the Harvard authorities and turned into a graduate

seminar. Young and Lodge were officially enrolled as doctoral candidates. J. Laurence Laughlin had joined them as a welcome third. Teacher and students hoped to ascertain "the share that Germanic law had in forming the Common Law." In time, both teacher and students would be writing learned essays.

The death of the Radical Club had come as news to its members. As if nothing had happened, the club looked forward to a new winter of monthly meetings. The first meeting was held as usual during the morning of the third Monday of October. The place as usual was the large house of John T. Sargent and his wife at 13 Chestnut Street. Professor Charles C. Everett read a paper on "The Tragic Element in Life and Literature." Outwardly there was no change.[38]

The club's seeming vitality was due in a measure to the vitality of a weekly religious newspaper, *The Index*. The editor was a capable man of forty, Francis Ellingwood Abbot, a religious reformer.[39] Thinking the Boston Radicals had nothing to fear from critics and might even thrive on criticism, Abbot reprinted the *Tribune's* obituary on November 12. In his next issue, he published a reply to "R. W. L." by one of the club's leaders, Colonel Thomas Wentworth Higginson. These tactics were not without risk. Colonel Higginson did not squarely meet the mysterious critic's charges. Rather lamely, he tried to defend the club as a mere private body, without a mission and averse to fame.[40]

In the same month, William E. Forster visited Boston. The Adamses asked him to come for dinner on November 26. Henry wished to make the dinner a notable occasion. Believing Forster might think them interesting, he invited William Lloyd Garrison and "some other venerable war-horses" as fellow guests. Garrison was both America's most famous abolitionist and a leading proponent of women's rights. Of the topics likely to be raised at the Adamses' table, the rights of women was for Henry the most unsettled. His own position was clear. He favored equality for men and women; also for children, persons of student age, the elderly, the dead, and the not-yet-born; but he currently was antagonized and sickened by the country's noisiest advocates of a revolution for women, Theodore Tilton and Victoria Woodhull.[41]

The guests arrived, and Henry enjoyed "the drollest dinner I ever saw." "Forster . . . poked fun at Garrison about woman's rights. . . . We had a most fundamental discussion of the topic. . . ." To that point, the behavior of all present was reasonable, though lively. But Boston war-horses did not limit themselves to one or two philanthropies or enthusiasms. Henry continued: "After dinner,

Garrison rose to his feet in my library and[,] producing about a dozen spiritual photographs from his pocket, proceeded to give us a lecture on them." Forster was unprepared for the visitation. ". . . he could stand woman's rights, but spiritualism was a new and grizly horror."

The spiritual photographs and unscheduled lecture were a turning point. Possibly at Clover's instigation, Henry agreed to attend a meeting of the Boston Radical Club.[42] A meeting would be held at the Sargents' house on January 18, 1875. John Weiss would be speaking on "The Bible and Science." Guest invitations could be applied for.

On the appointed morning, more than two hundred persons crowded together for the meeting. Weiss read his paper. Three listeners were Ellen Gurney, Clover, and Henry.[43] Dressed in his usual English clothes and holding his London "tile," or top hat, Henry was seated "near the door." Possibly he had entered late.

Louise Chandler Moulton was present, joined in the discussion, and reported to the *New York Tribune*. Published three days later, her report showed loss of patience. She alluded to the obituary and half-humorously said the Radical Club "has had a resurrection." Her summary of the proceedings was disrespectful. Indeed she interrupted it and turned it into a reminder that Boston looked unforgivingly on mockery of its institutions. "John Weiss read a paper, and of course it was about the conflict between science and supernatural religion; and then they discussed it, and we all looked wise, and pretended to one another that we understood every word. Did I ever give you the Rev. Petroleum V. Nasby's definition of the Radical Club? He said it was the 'Den of the Unintelligible where they talked about the Unknowable.' Boston hasn't been a safe place for the reverend gentleman since then."[44]

The "new party" that Brooks had written about had acquired a name. Its members were self-styled "Independents." In Boston in November and December 1874, several Independents—notably C. F. Adams, Jr., Brooks Adams, Henry Cabot Lodge, and Moorfield Storey—had sponsored meetings critical of the Grant administration. Henry Adams had taken part in the meetings, increasingly as manager, seldom or never as a talker. The inevitable question had been raised: who should be president?

The Independents were in touch with Senator Schurz. The Missourian had severely injured his political credit in 1872 by failing to secure the Liberal Republican nomination for C. F.

Adams. He had somewhat recovered credit in recent months by taking the place of Senator Sumner as President Grant's most visible antagonist in the government.[45] His immediate plans were definite. He was retiring from the Senate and for an interval would be in Europe. Later possibilities could be imagined. Always looking towards higher roles, Schurz might be pleased to figure once again as the nation's king-maker.

In February 1875, Henry and Clover again traveled to Washington to stay with Uncle Sam. The congressman's family was abroad, and he was anxious for company. On arriving, the guests found their host "dangerously ill of pneumonia." From Hooper's house on February 15, Henry sent Carlo a rush of news. He and Clover had had to take charge; Uncle Sam grew steadily worse; he died early on the 14th; there would be a funeral on the 16th at the Capitol; and Henry, although reluctant, would have to serve as one of "three chief-mourners."

The funeral for Congressman Hooper fell by chance on Henry's birthday, February 16, 1875, his thirty-seventh. Another chief mourner was Bancroft. At the start of Grant's second term, Bancroft had been displaced as minister to Germany. Instead of returning to New York, he and his wife had moved to Washington. They were living in a house just west of Lafayette Square at 1623 H Street.

For all these reasons, the Adamses's intended stay with Wicked Sam turned into an opportunity to renew their friendship with the national historian and begin a friendship with his wife. It chanced too that, during their residence in Hooper's house, Henry and Clover were introduced to a man they greatly liked, a senator from Mississippi, Lucius Q. C. Lamar, formerly the Confederate minister to Russia.[46]

Henry's most urgent motive for visiting Washington related to the Independent Party. He had assumed the function of uncontested behind-the-scenes manager. He would not say so, but he meant to use the so-called party as a short-lived junto, meaning a political bludgeon held over the heads of the major parties, particularly the Republicans. His first necessity was renewal of acquaintance with Senator Schurz.

Brooks Adams and Cabot Lodge also came to the capital, to work under Henry's supervision as Independent Party operatives. They were shown a most cordial welcome by Speaker Blaine, who may or may not have guessed the reason for their arrival.[47]

Privately, Henry talked with Schurz. Dates and places are lacking, but the substance of what was said can be gathered from later evidence. Adams proposed that he and Schurz be co-leaders of the Independents. Adams would set things in motion. He would then withdraw "from all share in the movement," permitting Schurz to be sole chief.

In his letter to Gaskell from Washington, Adams candidly sketched the outlines of his project. "Here I have been cooking and cooking a plot which is expected to explode and blow us all up. . . . I am losing my own self-respect in this underhand work of pulling wires, but somebody must do it and I am amused by it. Just now I am engaged single-handed in the slight task of organising a new party to contest the next Presidential election in '76. As yet I have only three allies; a broken down German politician [Carl Schurz]; a newspaper correspondent [possibly Horace White], and a youth of twenty who is to do all the work [Henry Cabot Lodge]. With these instruments I propose to do no less than decide the election. . . . You will see."

The plan Adams divulged to Schurz proved insufficient. By April 1, 1875, it became evident—in Henry's words—that "something must be done immediately or the whole thing would fall through."

Assisted by Lodge, Charles, and Samuel Bowles, Henry contrived to schedule a dinner in New York on April 27 in Schurz's honor. While arranging the dinner, Henry taught his associates his own ideas relating to political tactics. The organization he was constructing would be situated *between* the Republicans and the Democrats. "My scheme," he reported to Gaskell, "is to organise a party of the centre and to support the [major] party which accepts our influence most completely." In truth, his "party of the centre" was not a party at all. It was a junto organized to decide just one election.

On April 27, two hundred Independents dined at Delmonico's in New York. Henry Adams was present. Evarts presided. Schurz was adulated. C. F. Adams, Jr., gave a speech saying that in 1876—the Centennial Year—nominees "more unselfish" than usual should be put forward to lead the country.[48] The newspapers concluded that the purpose of the gathering was, in Henry's phrase, "to make my father President next year." Henry added, ". . . I believe this is to be Schurz's most earnest wish and hope, but emphatically it was no part of my plan. . . ."

A "movement" existed. That at least was achieved, and Henry took credit for its existence. Telling Carlo about his "devious and underground ways," he shortly said, ". . . we had a *demonstration* . . .

which, as it was originated, hatched and generally brought into life by me as a result of six months incubation, I may call mine."

Meanwhile, with good reason, Henry shifted to a new plan, opposite to his old. Schurz was to stay awhile in Europe and come back to take control, but Henry would not withdraw. The reason was a difference of motives. Henry's motive was denial of the Republican nomination to both Grant and Blaine. It was wholly serious and possibly workable. Schurz's *seeming* motive, the elevation of C. F. Adams to the White House, was impracticable and mostly pretended. His controlling motive was personal. He wished to regain his former prominence and trade on it to get a place in a future Cabinet.[49]

Repeating their action of the previous summer, Henry and Clover moved to the rented box at Beverly Farms, probably on May 1, 1875, a Saturday. Henry's state of mind was one he had previously experienced. It perhaps had been best expresssed in a letter he had written in January 1872, when he and Clover were not yet engaged and his father was still in Europe. He had told the Chief: "Boston is so quiet that one feels oneself a little of a blackguard in it, for wishing to vary the life. . . . But I sometimes groan in spirit for the larger interests and more serious dangers of Washington or London. To have a real risk to meet or a thoroughly alarming battle to fight, would occasionally seem an agreeable variation."[50]

Boston had seven leading newspapers: the *Advertiser*, *Globe*, *Journal*, *News*, *Post*, *Transcript*, and *Traveller*.[51] A self-respecting but lesser newspaper was the weekly *Boston Times*, published on Saturday evening for Sunday delivery. During the first week of May, the editor of the *Times* received an unsolicited contribution from an unidentified writer. The contribution was a satirical poem in twenty-four stanzas. It was titled *The Radical Club*. It purported to be "by an Atom." Its stanzas were followed by a mock-signature, "D. Scribe."[52] The stanzas mimicked the form and language of Poe's "Raven."[53]

The contributed poem greatly excited the editor, and he intended to publish it in his next issue. Wishing also to comment about it, he wrote an editorial and had it set in type but changed his mind and used part of the editorial as a preamble to the poem.[54] In consequence, his issue for May 8, 1875, offered on its second page a package of materials. The package was composed of some startling headlines, an editor's preamble, twenty-four rhymed stanzas, and the foolish mock-signature "D. Scribe." The headlines and the essential portions of the preamble read as follows:

The Radical Club.

———

A Poem,

respectfully dedicated to

"The Infinite."

By an Atom.

———

[Contributed to the Boston Times.]

This Club was once quite famous and promised to rival the renowned salons of Paris. But its glory has departed. . . .

If the Radical Club is remembered at all, it will be quite as likely to live in the brilliant sarcasm that we print . . . as in the reports of its own debates. Those who have been in the habit of attending its æsthetic seances will instantly recognize the members as one after another they appear. . . .

We do not know the author. We found the manuscript on our desk one morning without note or comment, or any clue whatever to its authorship. If it is the production of a new writer, we can only say of him as Pope said of Johnson, "he will soon be deterred"— although nothing seems to *deter* him. [P. S.—This is a pun.]

All things considered, the Bostonians who opened the newspaper at page 2, read the headlines, and read the poem and signature found themselves face to face—and in at least three ways—with a puzzle that was not a puzzle. One may imagine a hypothetical Bostonian who saw that the poem was "BY AN ATOM" and saw also that it was by "D. Scribe." The hypothetical Bostonian could sense at once that "AN ATOM" was *an Adams*. Being also a "Scribe," the Atom was *Henry Adams*. That particular Adams was known to have served in Washington and London from 1860 to 1868 as his father's secretary. Thus the poem was not anonymous. It was signed.[55]

The poem was read by actual, not hypothetical, Bostonians. Moreover, the case was a case both of mere inky words and of unexampled nerve. How nerve entered could be seen with the help of a question. Were the meanings of the adult pun "Atom" and the puerile pun "D. Scribe" intentionally so obvious and hard-hitting that they would *silence* the Bostonians who saw them? If so, the poem as published on May 8, 1875, was an act of frightening literary aggression and successful violence.

For many readers who were not Bostonians, and some who were, the Atom's poem could almost pass for entertaining comic verse. The opening and third stanzas were explanatory.[56]

> Dear friends, I crave attention to some facts that I shall
>   mention,
> About a Club called "Radical," you haven't heard before;
> Got up to teach the nation, was this new-light federation,
> To teach the nation how to think, to live, and to adore,
> To teach it of the heights and depths that all men should
>   explore;
>   Only this, and nothing more.
>
> And first, dear friends, the fact is, I'm sadly out of practice,
> And may fail in doing justice to this literary bore.
> But when I do begin it, I don't think 'twill take a minute
> To prove there's nothing in it (as you've doubtless heard
>   before),
> But a free religious wrangling club—of this I'm very sure;
>   Only this, and nothing more.[57]

The next nineteen stanzas recounted the meeting of the club on January 18, 1875 (with one fictional addition). The poem functioned somewhat as a play. One after another, without their names but identified by varied means, leading members of the club were caused to perform.[58] John T. Sargent played the host as Mr. Pompous; John Weiss, the speaker for the day, made himself sufficiently ridiculous as Wiseman; Charles Bradlaugh, an English visitor, roared as British Lion; and Francis Ellingwood Abbot interposed as Mr. Fairman. Additional worthies—Mrs. Sargent, Colonel Higginson, Dr. Cyrus A. Bartol, and the Rev. C. P. Cranch—identifiably advanced the action. The effect was intimidating as well as funny, for humor was put in place in precisely calibrated measures. The thirteenth and fifteenth stanzas concerned A. Bronson Alcott and Louise Chandler Moulton. The treatment of Alcott was cutting. That of the poet and literary reporter could be read two ways, either as kind or as inexcusable.

> But the interest now grew lukewarm; for an ancient Concord
>   bookworm,
> With authoritative tramping, forward came and took the
>   floor;

And in Orphic mysticisms talked of light and life and prisms,
And the Infinite baptisms on a transcendental shore,
And the concrete metaphysic, till we yawned in anguish sore;
    But still he kept the floor.

Then a matron made for kisses, in the loveliest of dresses,
And with eyes that shone more brightly than the diamonds
    that she wore,
Spoke in tones of lute-like sweetness words of such exceeding
    fitness,
Phrases of such happy neatness, that we clapped our hands
    for more. . . .

One personage in the satire was uniquely hypnotizing. Disputes might arise about the identity of the young lady introduced—and whether she existed. (She is the poem's only fiction.)

Then a lively little charmer, noted as a dress-reformer,
Because that mystic garment called a chemiloon she wore,
Said she had no "views" of Jesus, and therefore would not
    tease us,
But that she thought t'would please us to look her figure o'er,
For she wore no bustles *anywhere*; and corsets she felt sure
    Should squeeze her *nevermore*.[59]

Signs that the Atom meant to kill appeared as early as the twelfth stanza. It evoked Julia Ward Howe and, closely read, would be seen as aiming at an object larger than injury to *her*.

Then a lady fair and faded, with a careworn look and jaded,
As though she saw the glory of the coming Lord no more,
Crushed the British Lion's roaring with a reverent outpouring
Of a faith forever soaring unto heaven's golden door;
She was listened to intently by each member on the floor,
    For her genius they adore.

Later stanzas confirmed that, to survive, the club would have to defend its women.[60] The lady members most savaged were Boston's most sacred celebrity, Miss Elizabeth ("Biddy") Peabody, sister-in-law of Nathaniel Hawthorne, and Mrs. Edna D. Cheney, the club's most formidable lady preacher. The ladies were preceded by a "tall and red-faced" bishop, identifiable by Bostonians as Julius Ferrette. He appeared in the twentieth stanza. Miss Peabody and Mrs.

Cheney filled the twenty-first and were identified by assorted clues, mainly their being overweight.

> The Kindergarten mother clucked an answer to this brother,
> And her curls kept bobbing quaintly from the queer head-
>   dress she wore;
> And another *magnum corpus*, with a figure like a porpus [*sic*],
> In wonder did absorb us, as she viewed our numbers o'er,
> And talked about the "Oversoul" and other mystic lore,
>   Nameless here, forevermore.[61]

The abominations concerning Miss Peabody and Mrs. Cheney formed a climax, and little attention would be given to the poem's concluding stanzas. Yet the twenty-third was all-important. It introduced three last persons: Look-sharp, Wriggle, and Ziegel.[62] By treating Looksharp and Wriggle with loving amusement, it raised the possibility that these persons were friends or relatives of the author, and by stating where Ziegel was seated in the room, it practically shouted that Ziegel was the author and that murder could be fun.[63]

> There are others I could mention that took part in this
>   contention,
> And at first 'twas my intention, but at present I forebear;
> There's young Look-sharp, and Wriggle who would make an
>   angel giggle,
> And a young conceited Ziegel who was seated near the door;
> If you could only see them, you'd laugh till you were sore,
>   And then you'd laugh some more.[64]

14

DOCTOR BARBARICUS

Adams bore full responsibility for *The Radical Club*, being its author, but his marriage was such that he and Clover felt an action by either was an action of both. Knowing that the poem was hers as well as his, Clover would take an active interest in its fate.[1]

When the poem was published, the Radical Club seemed proof against attack. The unexpected onset of the Atom evoked two responses, one public, one secret. The public response was attempted by Francis Ellingwood Abbot. He tried to meet the emergency with a new display of fairness. The *Index* announced on May 20 that John Weiss's "scintillating" lecture on "The Bible and Science" would appear in its next issue. The lecture appeared on May 27, as promised; and on June 3, by way of balance, the *Index* pirated *The Radical Club* from the *Boston Times*. In an editorial note, Abbot recommended that the Atom's poem be welcomed as humorous. He said a "satirical wag" had attended meetings of the club "to make fun of it." ". . . his parody of 'The Raven' is extravagant caricature all through; and surely no radical will be so weak as to be seriously offended by a mere *jeu d'esprit* of this sort. Let us all join good-humoredly in the little laugh at our own expense."[2]

The secret response of the Club was literary; that is, in form. A member "*immediately*" wrote a poem. The work was titled:

The Radical Club.

A Poem

Respectfully dedicated to

An Atom.

By a Chip.

The counter-poem—twenty-one stanzas—was hand-copied, not printed. Its authorship was successfully concealed, and readings were "reserved for the private ear of the Radical Club alone."[3]

The Chip stated a reason for the counter-poem's existence: harm had been done by youth to age. By way of comfort, the counter-poem paid versified compliments to lacerated elders. Commendatory stanzas were devoted to "gracious" Mrs. Sargent, "self-sacrificing" Colonel T. W. Higginson, "honored" Bronson Alcott, "thoughtful" Julia Ward Howe, and "sacred" Elizabeth Peabody.

All the same, the counter-poem's business was to point an accusing finger. Within narrow limits, the Club's leaders knew the identity of the Atom. The knowledge appeared in the last stanza in a passage that could seem to say no more than that the Club had erred by meeting too infrequently to achieve its best possible wisdom. The passage read:

> Could the great minds oftener meet,
> And by interchange grow wiser . . .
> Even "*Atoms*" might learn wisdom,
> And respect the aged more. . . .

The meaning was clear. "*Atoms*" were the young. The "*s*" conveyed particular implications. The attack in the *Boston Times* had been the work of a young *Adams*.[4] Alternatively it was written by an Adams *couple*.[5] Conceivably it was written by *the wife*.[6] Which attribution was correct was a comparative detail. The chief concerns were that the offense had been heinous, that deep wounds had been inflicted, and that blame was fixed sufficiently to permit discussion of what to do.

At Beverly Farms, builders had started the Adamses' cottage, to be known as Pitch Pine Hill. Henry spoke as if its construction were his and Clover's one excitement. On May 19, he wrote to Lodge: "The country is glorious. . . . *The house is BEGINNING, and SUCH a house.*" (The line was Biblical. It echoed the opening words of Genesis and John.)

A matter always in Henry's mind was his progress as a historian. From the moment in September 1871 when he returned from the West and his meetings with Clarence King, he had considered and reconsidered the question, How best could a historian conduct his inquiries? Looking for answers, he had studied the supposed best German, French, English, and American historians and had written and published sketches about their writings.[7] During the same interval, he had considered the very different question, What in outline was the history of humanity? By reading many books in several languages and by traveling to Egypt, he had reviewed the advance of human beings from prehistoric brutality to their current, most-developed state of being. He also had studied masses of evidence relating to the Germans and the Anglo-Saxons. His efforts had yielded conclusions, with the result that a changed idea of history was appearing, albeit scatteredly, in his unsigned sketches in the *North American*.[8]

While pressing his inquiries, he had recognized that the task he had set himself—to inquire concerning the survival of the hundred court among the Anglo-Saxons and the English—could not be quickly performed by a single historian. He brought Lodge, Young, and Laughlin into the inquiry principally because he wished it finished swiftly.[9]

He and his helpers were to labor as historians of law.[10] Their subject was Anglo-Saxon law—or, in Laughlin's words, "the institutions which through the Normans and Anglo-Saxons formed the basis of English and . . . American legal development." To speed the work, Adams divided the subject four ways and made four assignments:

Adams	—the Anglo-Saxon courts of law
Young	—Anglo-Saxon family law
Lodge	—Anglo-Saxon land law
Laughlin	—Anglo-Saxon legal procedure

The team was to investigate "exhaustively." Adams insured access to necessary books mainly by purchasing them himself. The result, in Laughlin's phrase, was an "amazing excursion." Part-cooperatively, part-independently, teacher and students "searched the early German codes of the Visigoths, Burgundians, and Salian Franks," then studied evidence relating to their individual assignments. Laughlin summarized: "Besides the early codes and the writings of Waitz, von Maurer, Sohm, and other Germans, we read and searched many times the whole collection of Anglo-Saxon laws, and ploughed through twenty-five thousand pages of charters and capitularies in mediæval Latin."[11]

The requirement always before the team was learning whatever the evidence imparted. The work was appallingly arduous, yet was done. Meeting at intervals in Adams's library at Marlborough Street, the members reported what they found. Discoveries were pooled, but each researcher outran the others in knowledge of his specialty. Teacher and students would write their essays separately. Those written by Lodge, Young, and Laughlin would be presented to the faculty as bases for their receiving doctorates, and Adams would arrange the publication of all four essays as a book, to be sold through usual channels.

What Adams valued most in students was highly energetic intellectual initiative. He had found it in only two students, Michael Simpson, already dead, and Ernest Young.[12] The respect he felt for Young showed in his asking him to investigate Anglo-Saxon family law while he himself looked into the Anglo-Saxon courts. The subjects were matched in breadth. An essay on either would have to concern itself with the individual, the family, the nation, and the state.

To an onlooker, it could appear that the inquiry Adams was leading bore no relation to contemporary life in the United States. Certainly to Adams and Young, the inquiry bore directly on both past and present life. The nearest example was its bearing on the marriage of Henry Adams and Clover Hooper. Doubtless their marriage accorded with their personal wants; but it remained a fact that, when he married, Henry had been investigating barbarian marriage in pre-feudal Germany. He knew that barbarian marriage harmonized with his and Clover's wish that she not become subordinate to him when consenting to be his wife; that she stay fully a Hooper while becoming an Adams; and that she not become subordinate to the near-patriarch he had called the Chief.[13]

Again, to an onlooker, it could seem that the discoveries possible for the team would be small. But Sohm had made large-scale discoveries concerning the institutions of barbarian Germany. Following his lead, but possessing will and ability to disagree with his findings should evidence warrant, Adams and his students read evidence relating to the Anglo-Saxons, a cluster of Germans who moved from Denmark to southeastern Britain in the fifth century and came to dominate what would later be known as England. He and the students made discoveries beyond the ones that Sohm had published. In addition, another American, Lewis Henry Morgan, was making discoveries relating to the North American Indians that accorded both with Sohm's discoveries and with theirs.[14]

An instance of discovery by the American team related to the question whether the barbarians of northern Europe in the time of the Roman empire were tribes or nations. When he began his review of history in 1871, Adams had supposed the barbarians were nomadic tribes. That was the usual opinion. As he and his helpers pursued their study of German and Anglo-Saxon records, they found that the Germans—with some exceptions—*did not move*.[15] They found too that the Salian Franks "had no tribal ideas" and were not a tribe. Neither were their neighbors. In a sketch in the *North American*, Adams had said in April 1875:

> ... German society, when it first emerged into the view of the civilized world, was not founded on a tribal system. ... The state ... was ... supreme. The political, the judicial, the military, and the religious systems were none of them tribal. In all, the individual full-grown man, associated with other men in artificial groups, constituted the state. If often the individuals whose union made the village community were united by ties of [blood] relationship, this may have been the result of propinquity quite as well as of the fiction or reality of a common origin.

Male adult barbarians—those not slaves—met in assembly as equals and practiced free government.

> ... the entire free [adult] male population met in assembly in each geographical district, and this assembly was, as occasion required, parliament, law-court, or army. To the obligations thus imposed all persons were equally subject. The tribe was unknown, and the family, however powerful it might be, was in law wholly subordinate to the state.

The family was not patriarchal. Grown sons were their own masters.

> The German *magenschaft*, or kindred, was a loose organization, without a patriarchal head and without a common property. It included the mother's as well as the father's relations. In it, the duties and privileges of its members were confined to a sphere of reciprocal assistance in case of trouble. ... The son came of age at a fixed time of life, and became at once *sui juris*, with all the rights of our own [American; *not* English] law.[16]

These findings were published by Adams in contradiction of a new work by Sir Henry Maine, *Lectures on the Early History of Institutions*. All along, Adams had wished to lead the *North American's* subscribers and his Harvard classes away from veneration of English authorities as models. He had spiced the magazine and his Harvard courses with sharp criticisms of Edward Freeman.[17] With surprise and regret, he had found that his disagreements with English historians extended to the newest opinions of Maine, a man of superior powers.

The advantage enjoyed by Adams and his team was their studying evidence exhaustively. Maine had not. Though ragged, the evidence relating to the Anglo-Saxons suggested meanings which were unmistakable, if unexpected. Simply because he and his helpers were attuned to the full evidence then available, Adams supposed that *Americans*—especially he and Ernest Young; also

Lewis Henry Morgan—had seized the lead among the historians in the English-speaking countries.[18]

In May 1875 at Beverly Farms, Adams finished a sketch concerning a comprehensive new history of England by an Englishman his age: *A Short History of the English People*, by John Richard Green, an examiner at Oxford.[19] Also he finished his research and made ready to draft his essay. "I began my summer furiously in violent desk-work, intent upon my magnum opus. . . ."

The opus, titled "The Anglo-Saxon Courts of Law," took the form of a compact, closely reasoned argument supported within the text by evidence in Anglo-Saxon and Latin. Although in name and appearance an essay, the work was a skeleton book. Its purpose was very broad. It suggested a changed outline of England's history from the arrival of the Anglo-Saxons late in the fifth century A.D. to the Norman conquest six centuries later. Because put forward by an American, the changed outline, if read in England, might seem an astonishing intrusion.[20]

While writing the skeleton book, Adams showed indications of extreme impatience. On May 26, he wrote to Lodge, ". . . I care a great deal to prevent myself from becoming what of all things I despise, a Boston prig (the intellectual prig is the most odious of all) and so I yearn, at every instant, to get out of Massachusetts and come in contact with the wider life I always have found so much more to my taste."

In June, Adams tried to effect a change in his arrangements as a teacher. He proposed to President Eliot that without pay Lodge replace him in the autumn as teacher of American colonial history so that he could himself initiate a course in the history of the United States. Eliot could not approve the plan. The autumn schedules were fixed. But he promised to support the plan for the academic year to follow, 1876–1877, which possibly was a help.

Adams completed "The Anglo-Saxon Courts of Law" very rapidly. Its argument was clear and brief—brief enough to be printed in fifty-four pages. Unfortunately, rapid writing cost a price. He suffered eye trouble. ". . . for the first time in my life, my eyes put an end to all my ambitious schemes and left me to lounge among my workmen."

Through July and August, he did only as much reading and writing as was absolutely necessary. For occupation, he and Clover haunted the site of their growing cottage. They took an enjoyment in its construction far exceeding the ordinary. Being the designers of every detail, they felt the structure as fully theirs.

❖ ❖ ❖

In later years, Louisa Chapin Hooper, second daughter of Edward Hooper, noticed that her Aunt Ellen and Aunt Clover had no children and decided to learn the reason. She pursued the inquiry among her older relations until she obtained an answer she believed had a basis in actual knowledge. The answer was not one she could easily communicate. The gist of what she learned was that her aunts were sexually active with their husbands but prevented conception. The aunts acted in concert; their childlessness was voluntary; and the explanation of their success was "something from the East"—probably meaning from China or Japan. Louisa knew what the something was, whether a practice, substance, or device; but she was too reserved to describe it.[21]

The marriages of Henry's elder brothers were steadily producing children. The summer of 1875 brought news of the births of Charles and Minnie's fourth and fifth children, twin boys, the elder of whom was named Henry Adams II. News came as well that Sir Robert Cunliffe had a son. Writing to Cunliffe on August 31, Henry said, "I am . . . so firm a believer in the necessity of propagating our kind that nothing gives me more pleasure than, like Artemus Ward, to see all my able-bodied friends and relations devoting themselves to this end." Though worded as a joke, the statement told the truth. Henry wanted humanity perpetuated but did not himself want children. He instead wanted marriage, friendships, and the steady completion of his work. Clover knew what he wanted and was determined that they have it.[22]

In September, Henry wrote three concluding sketches, to appear in the October *North American*, unsigned. His series had grown to twenty-three sketches. They concerned education, literature, and history, especially history. Were they ever pulled together and published as the loosely-organized book they were, his *Sketches* would stand next to "The Anglo-Saxon Courts of Law" as one of a pair of hidden books. Each could be read satisfactorily apart from the other, yet each justified the other, and they would best be read together.

When classes resumed in October 1875, Adams repeated his courses of the year before. His time seemed wholly taken up by teaching and perpetual editing. He had decided to bring out a Centennial Issue of the *North American*, consisting solely of articles summarizing the achievements of the United States since 1776 in six fields. The issue would be a national history written by six authors, not including himself. He would not declare it, but the looming Centennial Issue was a step towards ending his editor-

ship.[23] Heavy quarterlies, no matter how well edited, were unwanted in the new age that had begun in 1870. He had written the
year before to one of his contributors: ". . . the numbers [of the
North American] always seem to fall dead as the Pharoahs. No one
ever takes the trouble to think whether they are good or bad."[24] He
accordingly could want only two fates for the magazine, either to
expire or be reconstituted as a monthly, and he was anxious that
his departure as editor precede the one or the other.

A year in advance, he meanwhile was preparing the last new
course he would teach at Harvard—"History of the United States
from 1789 to 1840." This meant he at last was continuously
working as author of his future *History of the United States*. For the
present, the work for the most part took the form of acquiring and
reading evidence—old books and pamphlets, diaries, journals,
letters, maps—an immense profusion of material. He could not
hope to acquire *all* the evidence most useful for a writer of United
States history. But he had begun to try.

On the third Monday morning of October 1875, what formerly
had been Boston's Radical Club met under an altered name as the
Chestnut Street Club. The members seemed intent on averting a
new attack. The change of name was a retreat, indeed a rout.[25]

It further developed that Louise Chandler Moulton would no
longer be writing about the Boston Radicals. She had dropped the
subject. She was going to Europe for an extended stay and would
be writing for the *New York Tribune* as a traveling correspondent.[26]

A stranger development involved a young writer from Mississippi. Wife of an improvident husband and mother of a small
daughter left in the South, "Sherwood Bonner"—Mrs. Katherine
Sherwood Bonner McDowell—had migrated to Boston-Cambridge
and was desperate for money. Sometime in the autumn of 1875, a
never-to-be-identified donor gave her a trip to Europe and a
sufficient purse to permit her staying for many months. During
her trip, she would earn added money by writing travel letters for
the *Boston Times*.[27]

Mrs. Moulton and Sherwood Bonner agreed to go to Europe
together. They were to sail from New York on January 22, 1876.[28]
Three weeks prior to their departure, the *Boston Times* reprinted
The Radical Club, by an Atom. As before, the poem was signed "D.
Scribe." In a prefatory paragraph, the editor mentioned that the
Atom's poem had been partially or fully reprinted by several other
newspapers. He went on to say: "Notwithstanding that it has been
so widely circulated, we are constantly receiving applications for a

copy of the poem as it first appeared, and in deference to these frequent solicitations we . . . reproduce it. Since the poem was first published[,] the famous Radical Club has expired, or, at any rate, undergone a metamorphosis, what is left of it being now known as 'The Chestnut Street Club,' so that . . . the defunct club will be quite as likely to live in this pungent sarcasm as in the reports of its debates."[29]

The two correspondents sailed; and on February 27, 1876, the *Boston Times* published a letter sent from Liverpool. The letter was bland and pleasant. The headlines preceding it conveyed a sensational surprise.

Sherwood Bonner's Letter

"D. Scribe" Renews Acquaintance with Times Readers
Pencillings En Route for England

by the
Author of "The Radical Club."

The announcement in the *Times* that "D. Scribe" was Sherwood Bonner had two immediate effects. First, it opened a chasm between the innocents and fools who might believe the announcement and the non-fools and the injured parties who would see that it was false.[30] Second, it made possible the marketing of the poem as a separate publication.

A week later, the *Times* advertised that it had printed *THE RADICAL CLUB, a Satirical Poem*, by Sherwood Bonner, in a form that was "very attractive" and "suitable for preservation." As reissued, the poem was a small, ornately printed pamphlet. "Copies can be obtained at Loring's, and at the Times Counting Room. . . . Single Copies 5 Cents."[31]

Four things were indisputable. The poem was in great demand. The *Times* was promoting its sale with gleeful energy. What was left of the Boston Radical Club was under new attack by a lurking adversary who was preternaturally adroit. And fact and fiction had been confounded and interchanged.[32]

The false idea that Sherwood Bonner had written the poem had been impressed on the public's mind and could never be erased. In that limited sense, the false idea would remain forever true. But the idea was not just false; it was comically *impossible*. Of the knowledge required to write the Atom's poem—knowledge of Boston, of Bostonians, and of particular Bostonians who had either sustained or shunned the Radical Club—newly-resident Sherwood

Bonner had not a tenth. Of the disposition required to write the poem, she had not a millionth. At the time the poem first appeared, her attitude toward the Boston Radicals was one of anxiety to please. She had just published an adulatory article about Mrs. Julia Ward Howe.[33] Since its appearance, she had become the secretary of Henry Wadsworth Longfellow.[34]

Only one explanation could account for the poem's mis-attribution. Twenty-six-year-old Sherwood Bonner had been offered a paid trip to Europe and an opportunity to be a correspondent of the *Boston Times* on the express condition that she permit the newspaper to say in print that she was "D. Scribe" and that the poem was her invention. She took the offer. The best extenuation that could be made of what she did was her being a "Bohemian." She could not entirely disavow the failing. Before she left, her deserted employer, Henry Wadsworth Longfellow, had gently regretted that she had it.[35]

In the new state of affairs, the leaders of the no-longer-extant Radical Club were moved to act. They gave their secret poem of the previous May to a Boston publisher, William F. Gill & Company, for issuance and sale as a counter-pamphlet: *THE RADICAL CLUB, A Poem Respectfully Dedicated to An Atom,* by a Chip. In an introductory Note, the counter-pamphlet explained that the "reply" by a Chip had been written the year before. It further explained, "The recent republication in a *permanent* form of the verses by 'An Atom' has induced a demand for the publication of the reply. . . ."

Beyond a doubt, the public sale of the counter-pamphlet was authorized by the murdered club. To meet the needs of the occasion, the Chip's poem was amended in one place. The amended passage read:

Those strange rhymes, so *"very* free."

By "S. B."

The passage did not accept the identification of "D. Scribe" that had appeared in the *Boston Times.* It only took note of it.

The true motive for publishing the counter-pamphlet related to blame. As much as it dared, the club wished to name the actual author of its demise. The counter-pamphlet, if read with close attention to its title page, its Note, the Chip's assertions about the "Atom," and especially the Chip's finger-pointing passage concerning *"Atoms,"* returned the strange rhymes of May 8, 1875, to their original claimant, the Atom, and it denounced the rhymes as monstrous.[36]

❖ ❖ ❖

Ohio was one of the states in which Liberal Republicans and Independents, though not preponderant, were strong. It was also a state in which the Republicans were accustomed to defeating the Democrats. During the summer of 1875, the Ohio Republicans feared defeat by the Democrats in state elections, to be held in mid-October. The result was an emergency measure.

On October 4, 1875, Adams wrote Gaskell an account of the Independents' prospects. "As yet we independent liberals hold the balance of power and gain strength. . . . We called Schurz back from Germany to fight the democrats in Ohio. If he succeeds in beating them there, my friends will pretty surely control the next presidential election. Tilden may be our man, or some other."[37]

The lines were elliptical and over-sanguine. Especially they concealed a serious setback for Adams as the Independents' manager. Adams was an authentic Independent, wholly estranged from the major parties. He was assuming that, in 1876, the Democrats would nominate Governor Tilden of New York and the Republicans would nominate Speaker Blaine. His hatred of Blaine had grown—was so intense he would not name him in his letters. He saw the Independents as increasing in numbers but still limited in strength. He believed that, to decide the election, they would need to wield their strength with skill and act unitedly. He was hoping that the Independents, if all went right, would swing the election to Tilden, the Democrat, by supporting him as a body.

Things could hardly go right. Schurz was not a true Independent. He remained what he had been in 1872, a Liberal Republican, meaning in his case someone likely to return to the Republicans and submit himself afresh to party discipline. In addition, the ex-senator was more than ever imbued with Adams insanities. His latest idea was that both major parties should nominate C. F. Adams as a national unity candidate for the Centennial Year.

Henry had not opposed the recall of Schurz from Germany to save the Ohio Republicans. He could not. The Ohio problem needed a solution. Unfortunately, Schurz's recall meant instant empowerment of the Missourian as head of the Independent Party. The loser was Henry. He had begun as the movement's invisible but highly effectual creator. Events reduced him to a mere adviser whose advice might not be asked.

The situation being what it was, Henry looked forward to the time when Schurz, getting nowhere with his C. F. Adams scheme, might agree to a better. Rather than complete his letter to Gaskell, he waited. The Republicans won the state elections in Ohio; and, on October 15, Henry finished his letter. He said nothing about

Tilden. Indeed he seemed to swing about and anticipate a *Republican* victory in 1876. " . . . after an awful strain on the nerves we feel at last sure of having effected our object. The democrats are beaten. . . . You will hear more of us next year. We will play for high stakes. . . ."

Like its predecessor, the new account left essential things unsaid. Schurz had begun to learn that C. F. Adams could not be thrust on the Republicans and Democrats as a national unity candidate. Moreover, a new presidential hopeful had appeared. Simply by winning a third term as governor of Ohio, Rutherford B. Hayes had emerged as an alternative to Blaine or Grant for the Republican nomination.

As before, Adams was leading Young, Lodge, and Laughlin towards a speedy finish of their work. He contacted a Boston publisher, Little, Brown, and Company, and arranged the publication of their book. It would be titled *Essays in Anglo-Saxon Law*. In place of a preface, it would begin with a list of sources. The stress would be on substance, not authorship. The authors' names would appear in the table of contents but not on the cover or title page. The essays would be placed on an equal footing, except that the essay by the teacher would precede the essays by the students. A dedication to President Eliot would describe the work as a "fruit of his administration."[38]

Ernest Young had permanently succeeded Adams as teacher of medieval politics. Cabot Lodge was preparing to succeed him as teacher of colonial history. On his own initiative, Lodge also was starting two historical projects well-suited to his individual tastes: a series of publications relating to Alexander Hamilton, whom he all but worshiped; and a biography of his grandfather, George Cabot, a leading New England Federalist of Thomas Jefferson's time.

That Lodge had the faculty of doing many things at once made him invaluable to Adams, but Adams thought Lodge by nature not a historian and not a teacher. Silently, for a considerable interval, Henry had been guided by the thought that Lodge was a future senator from Massachusetts—another Sumner.[39] With that eventuality in mind, he wished to give his helper political advantage and experience.[40]

The Centennial Number of the *North American* appeared, as planned, in January 1876. While perhaps a fair success, it did not conform to Adams's original design.[41] To obtain the necessary six articles, he had had to appeal to eleven prospective contributors.

Finding no one who would write an article on Literature, he substituted an article on Education. The writer was Daniel Coit Gilman, the president of newly-founded Johns Hopkins University in Baltimore. The last-minute arrival of the article placed Adams and Gilman on very cordial terms.

A letter from Schurz, received on February 5, 1876, afforded Adams a slight new chance to reassert control of the Independents' strategy. Adams spoke with Lodge. Under his direction, Lodge took the night train to New York and met with Schurz.

The ex-senator asked Lodge to go at once to Washington and visit Grant's current secretary of the treasury, Benjamin H. Bristow. The reason for Schurz's request was a change of imagined presidents. C. F. Adams had receded. Bristow had been taken up. A Kentucky Republican, Bristow had won the nation's approval by prosecuting a Whiskey Ring. He and his aides had brought about the indictment of Grant's private secretary, General Babcock, and 238 other persons for defrauding the government of taxes owed by distilleries. What Schurz wished Lodge to learn was whether Bristow would "give us any sort of assurance that he will if necessary accept an independent nomination."[42]

Lodge undertook the mission but first returned to Boston and spoke with Henry Adams. Opposed ideas of politics were in play. Schurz was acting as if the presidential election of 1876 would be open to easy management. Adams thought the opposite. Yet he wanted to win Schurz's agreement to a strategy that at least *might* succeed and that deserved to be tried. He wrote to Gaskell on February 9:

> . . . although we have unquestionably the power to say that any given man shall not be President, we are not able to say that any given man shall be President. Our first scheme was to force my father on the parties. This is now abandoned, and we have descended to the more modest plan of pushing one of the regular candidates or splitting the parties by taking one of their leaders. I am no longer confident of doing good and am looking with anxiety to the future. But things are getting beyond my capacity to influence or even to measure.

Lodge reached Washington on February 12, stayed two weeks, and did his best to explore the ground. Even before Lodge departed, Adams silently foresaw that Lodge would not get the assurance that Schurz had said should be obtained. Adams's foreknowledge was borne out. Lodge talked repeatedly with Bristow and his aides, realized it would be too risky to ask the secretary's assurance, and never asked it.[43]

Immediately after Lodge set out, on February 14, Adams wrote

Schurz a letter of advice. Rather than send it directly to Schurz, he sent it to Lodge in Washington for him to read and forward. Very carefully worded, the letter suggested a plan that Adams, one may assume, had secretly favored from the time the Independents first were organized. He said:

> The essential point of any policy must be to hold our friends together. Whatever support is given to Mr[.] Bristow or to anyone else, it is all important that we should act . . . as a unit. . . .

> . . . it will be necessary to make a [new] demonstration. . . . My recommendation is that you and half a dozen other gentlemen should write a circular letter addressed to about two hundred of the most weighty and reliable of our friends, inviting them to meet you, say at Cleveland or Pittsburg, one week after the republican Convention meets, there to decide whether we will support the republican candidate or nominate a candidate of our own. I enclose my notion of the draft of the letter.

Adams nowhere mentioned Blaine. He presented himself as concerned about one thing only: corruption in the nation's politics. He attributed corruption, not to persons, but to the established parties, to party discipline, to quadrennial nominating conventions, and to "caucus dictation." He assumed that parties were inescapable and said the Independents might become a major party; but he insisted that they should act for the present as something much more integrated than a party: a short-lived junto. ". . . I know no other way of fighting the caucus than with the junto."

The June meeting of Independents that Adams suggested was timed to *follow* the Republican convention (without regard to the Democratic convention, scheduled two weeks later). The circular letter Adams suggested would be mailed *prior to* the Republican convention and would be highly publicized. In appearance a mere invitation to Independents to participate in a meeting, *the proposed circular letter would itself be the principal demonstration.* It could be expected to have two powerful effects. It would "unite our friends." It would "alarm the [Republican] Convention at Cincinnati."

If used, the engine Adams had designed would work against the nomination of Grant for a third term. Still more, it would work against the nomination of Blaine. Although in these respects preventive, the engine was also positive. It looked towards a possible swift expansion of the Independents' ranks, the full emergence of a new party, a shake-up of old parties, and an era of better government.

The problem was Carl Schurz. The ex-senator had traded one chimera for another. To tell him that Bristow could not be nominated for president by the Republicans was risky, but Adams told him.

> . . . nothing is more certain than that Mr[.] Bristow cannot be nominated. We must not let our hands be tied by any delusion as to his strength. . . .

Adams further explained that the Kentuckian was a "firm believer in party loyalty" and thus could not accept nomination by a nascent third party, the Independents. On that precise understanding—that Bristow would not join them—Adams urged that the Independents immediately favor Bristow for president. This canny idea pointed towards a future building of Independent strength. ". . . let us . . . work earnestly for Bristow. By establishing close relations with Bristow's friends, we shall probably carry a portion of them with us. If the [Republican] Convention makes a very bad nomination we may carry nearly all."

Schurz might not agree that a Bristow victory at the Republican convention was impossible. So Adams allowed he might be wrong.

> If the [Republican] Convention nominates . . . Bristow, well and good! Our meeting [one week later] will merely confirm their action. If not, the serious responsibility will fall upon us of placing a candidate before the people. Our meeting must consist of men who will not shirk that responsibility. . . .

The passage made plain what "junto" meant. Henry Adams had invented an engine for displacing the major parties and taking control of the federal government. The Independents' circular letter was to subject the Republican convention to a most serious threat: nominate a person acceptable to us or lose in November to the Democrats and thereafter see the Independents emerge as the dominant political power.[44]

The other Adamses had no knowledge of Henry's letter to Schurz till after he had mailed it. While waiting for a reply, Henry brought the Chief abreast of the Independents' newest activities. He confided next in Brooks. Charles was too ill with erysipelas to think of politics, but when recovered would be informed. John was near at hand but, being a Straight-out Democrat, had his own problems to consider.[45]

The receipt of Henry Adams's letter presented Schurz with a choice. If he acceded to Adams's proposal, he would do so at the cost of becoming a genuine Independent and possibly at the cost of not being invited by the next administration to accept a place in the Cabinet. Thus the choice was very simple. It was country versus self.

Schurz replied to Adams on February 24 from New York. As manager, he insisted on an opposite strategy. ". . . I must adhere to my first opinion: we shall be utterly powerless if we put off our demonstration until after the Republican convention. . . . My present intention is to issue invitations for a meeting to be held about the middle of April, two months before the Republican Convention. That meeting is to be a free conference, to be governed in its action by the circumstances of the times, so that, if such a course be thought best, it may adjourn to some day after the Republican convention."[46]

Aware that his letter reversed the plan Adams suggested, Schurz added verbiage. The verbiage made clear that he wished not to acknowledge and in fact would misrepresent the suggestion Adams had made. It also made clear that Schurz, having acquired the power to make the Independents' decisions, would continue to assert it. Adams had sent him a draft of a circular letter. Schurz welcomed the draft and simultaneously repelled it. He said it was "excellent" but would "have to be amended somewhat to serve a different purpose."[47]

Schurz's rulings were destructive. Agreeing to send out a circular letter, yet requiring that both the letter and the Independents' meeting precede the Republican convention, the ex-senator had converted what could have been a united junto and potential new major party into what predictably would be a collocation of talkers—in Adams's phrase, a "rope of sand."[48]

Adams was not surprised. On February 27, in place of writing again to Schurz, he sent Lodge a list of reasons why Schurz's convention in April would harm the Independents. Also he asked his helper to take a needful precaution. "Lose no opportunity of putting your foot on any revival of the [C. F.] Adams scheme. We are well rid of it."

The precaution was needed. On March 7, Schurz wrote to Lodge advising that the Independents would have to return to their "first love"—C. F. Adams. He said that Bristow seemed unequal to the "exigencies of the situation." ". . . nothing is left us but to raise the Adams flag. . . ." "Has not Henry Adams changed his mind also. . . . [?]"[49]

Anticipating that Schurz would revert to C. F. Adams, Henry already was seeking a means to raise a cry for Bristow. He learned that a Democratic organ, the *Boston Post*, was on the market. By approaching some well-to-do Bostonians, he got ready to buy the paper. He notified White, Nordhoff, Walker, and Schurz that the *Post* might soon be hiring a well-paid chief editor.

The purchase of the *Post* fell through, but Henry was practicing the maxim that quarrels were best avoided and friends were best assisted. He seemed to sense opportunity. He wrote to Walker: ". . . I want all the strings to my bow that are anywhere loose. . . . I have reduced my pedagogic work to the narrowest dimensions and am working more and more back into active life."

Schurz slightly changed his plan. Aided by Lodge as secretary, he issued invitations to a "free conference" of Independents, to meet in New York in May, a month before the Republican convention. Henry took no part in the call.[50] His optimism—to the extent that he had some—no longer related to the Independent movement. He considered Schurz the inverse of a leader and thought the Independents in process of dissolution. On March 20, writing to Wells, he said, "We have . . . no leader nor organisation." ". . . the Lord only knows what is to be our fate. I give it up. Perhaps we shall see light when we least expect it."[51]

In April, Henry was summoned urgently to Quincy. Three of John's five children were down with diphtheria. George survived, but Fanny died on April 10 and Johnny on April 12. Henry sat with the parents through the night while Johnny failed.[52]

If the assumption was still being made that Adams males could be elected to political office, the assumption died completely when the girl and boy were carried off. Writing to Carlo, Henry said: "The death of my brother's two children was a very serious blow to us, not merely because the boy was the oldest and brightest in that generation, and his loss takes away the natural head of the family in the future, but because the blow upsets my elder brother's career and changes all his life. He was desperately attached to his children. He is too rich to care for his profession as a lawyer, or to enjoy his scuffles in politics."

A week prior to Schurz's conference in New York, Henry and Clover moved to Beverly Farms as owners and occupants of Pitch Pine Hill. Henry told Carlo he was "only too glad" to "bury myself in our woods." "Our new house is more than all we ever hoped. . . . I am perfectly happy here. . . . We have a dog, too, a little Scotch-terrier pup, which we call Boojum. . . . He affords us incessant and unmitigated joy. I only trust that I may be left undisturbed here all summer."

The conference met on May 15 and 16 at the Fifth Avenue Hotel. Recovered from erysipelas, Charles attended. Henry did not. Schurz had foreordained the meeting's business in all possible detail. Lodge called the first day's session to order and hastened formalities to completion.[53] The *New York Tribune* said of the second day:

> Resolutions taking a strong position for civil service reform were unanimously adopted. Carl Schurz and Colonel T. W. Higginson discussed the best way of giving the movement weight with the country. Charles Francis Adams, Jr., made a stirring speech, and declared that Secretary Bristow should be the Republican candidate for President; if the action of the Cincinnati Convention should be unsatisfactory he said he would gladly support Gov. Tilden if nominated by the Democrats . . . . Sidney Thomas [of Chicago] offered a resolution putting forward Charles Francis Adams[, Sr.,] as a candidate, but it was rejected, the sentiment of the Conference being in favor of naming no man, but of looking first to the Republican Convention for a candidate; second, to the Democratic Convention; and if both failed to give the country a reform candidate, then to nominate an Independent Reform ticket.[54]

The meeting lived up to the reasons Henry had listed privately for Lodge *against* its being held when Schurz directed. Far from having good effects, the meeting advertised the Independents as a small chorus of political incompetents who came together, named an executive committee, made speeches, and went home.[55]

Awareness of failure must have grown painful while the meeting was going on. When the proceedings ended, Schurz thought he might say a word to Lodge. He was too late. Lodge had vanished.[56]

Adams's doctoral candidates completed their essays, submitted them for reading, and qualified for degrees. Young was asked to speak at Commencement and for the purpose wrote an added essay on "The Patriarchal Theory." It occurred to Adams that Schurz should be brought to Harvard and made an honorary doctor of laws. He suggested the idea to President Eliot. The president demurred; but Adams, helped by Lodge, persuaded Francis Parkman, Edward Hooper, and the Chief to apply "a little pressure." Eliot decided that the ex-senator should be awarded the degree, after all.

If it appeared at times that Henry Adams was too anxious to help those who rejected him, or too willing to forgive those who injured him, the oddness of his behavior could be explained without reference to Christian precepts. Henry cheerfully helped others in part because he also cheerfully took pains to help himself. True, his Alma Mater would shortly give doctoral degrees to Carl

Schurz, Henry Cabot Lodge, J. Laurence Laughlin, and Ernest Young, and when the ceremonies ended Assistant Professor Henry Adams would be, as before, a lowly bachelor of arts, Class of 1858. But the Henry was not the loser. He had provided for himself.

One of his rewards was the satisfaction of work well done. His and his students' *Essays on Anglo-Saxon Law* were a superbly researched historical comeuppance for the English historians of England. The *Essays* served to demonstrate that early England through five centuries was healthily democratic. They showed as well that the consolidation of England into a single nation under a single state (in itself a healthy innovation) was simultaneous with the introduction of feudalism, the differentiation of lord and man, and the establishment of primogeniture; that is, with "depravations"—forms of social breakdown and disorganization. Last, they showed that English historians had been too imbued with feudal ideas and too casual as researchers to effect an accurate reconstruction of their country's early history.

Adams's essay "The Anglo-Saxon Courts of Law" was a juggernaut of persuasion. One of its points was that the German system of government by assembly (annual national assembly and bimonthly district assembly) was brought from Denmark by the Anglo-Saxons and—thanks to English conservatism—long persisted. Another point was that the consolidation of England involved a reordering of names. What had been self-governing Anglo-Saxon *nations* turned into *shires*. What had been self-governing Anglo-Saxon *districts* (first named "hundreds" by King Alfred) turned into *parts of shires*. Both points were hard to establish because of confusions of terms and incompletenesses and corruptions of evidence. Especially by recovering the meaning of the Anglo-Saxon word "socn" or "soc" (*socnam* in Latin), Adams showed that the Anglo-Saxon courts of law of the tenth century were district courts inherited from fifth century German district courts, which possibly were themselves survivals from archaic courts that had existed time out of mind.[57]

Adams was proud of his "Anglo-Saxon Courts of Law," as indicating that English history was comprehensible; as indicating that self-government and democracy had originally been dominant in England; and as indicating that self-government and democracy were inheritances extremely old, possibly known among the barbarians from their beginnings. But he also thought his skeleton book ridiculous—too expensive in effort, time, and money. He thought its author should be given, not a diploma, but an epitaph. He accordingly readied one and gave it to himself. Worded in twelfth century Latin, it was suitable to a graveyard in medieval Rome.[58]

[Adams's Latin]	[an American translation]
HIC JACET HOMUNCULUS SCRIPTOR DOCTOR BARBARICUS HENRICUS ADAMS ADAE FILIUS ET EVAE PRIMO EXPLICUIT SOCNAM	Here lies an atom-sized scribe, a German teacher, Henry Adams, a son of Adam and Eve, who was the first to recover the meaning of the Anglo-Saxon word *socn* (meaning profits of justice; whatever a court of law is able to collect)

The date when Adams gave himself the epitaph may have preceded Commencement. It was fitting if it did. May 1876 was for him a deathly month. He had wanted to insure that the new administration *not* be headed by Blaine or Grant. There instead was every prospect that Blaine would be nominated and elected. It had been his intention to move to Washington in the fall of 1877, when the next administration was a half year old. The prospect was blighted. His future generally seemed a ruin.

On May 27, 1876, writing to Lodge, Adams admitted, ". . . I do fear Blaine. . . ." One ground for fear was the speaker's unfailing air of presentability. The Republican contender was a most plausible Christian, family man, and statesman. Normally perspicacious Americans, Whitelaw Reid and John Hay among them, were wholly unable to penetrate Blaine's manner and understand his history. The *New York Tribune* was backing him enthusiastically. Troops of Independents considered him a near-reformer, more than acceptable as chief executive.

Help came when not expected. The House of Representatives was again looking into a charge that its speaker had once corruptly profited in a transaction relating to the Union Pacific railroad. On May 31, a Boston bookkeeper, James Mulligan, testified before the House committee that he had with him some letters from Speaker Blaine that proved the allegation true.

Blaine was permitted to get near the letters. While others were looking, he *stole* them and falsely said they were his property under law.[59] On June 5, in the course of a long speech to the House, he claimed to read the letters verbatim and glossed them with all sorts of explanations. The speech was greeted with wild applause but did not account for the gulf between his imputable legitimate income through life and his evident affluence, exemplified by his Fifteenth Street house and his munificent use of it as a place of entertainment.[60]

Adams thought Blaine's speech matchless in "insolence." Yet he thought the country again was safe. Mulligan's evidence had not ruined Blaine, far from it, but it had somewhat reduced him for 1876.[61] Much though they might want to nominate him for president, the Republicans would have to reconsider. Prophetically, Adams wrote to Lodge, ". . . I am . . . contemplating the figures of Hayes and Washburn."

At the Republican Convention in Cincinnati, Bristow fared poorly. During a critical seventh ballot, Blaine's supporters failed to win a majority of the delegates. In consequence, Hayes was nominated.

Schurz convened the Independents' executive committee. Its members decided that a meeting of the party could be dispensed with and that each Independent should vote in the election as his conscience might direct. So encouraged, Schurz went back to Republican regularity.[62]

Adams did not attend the Commencement exercises. Lodge wrote to him about them. Young's essay on "The Patriarchal Theory" was well received.[63] Schurz became a doctor of laws. Lodge, Young, and Laughlin were given their diplomas.

The Democrats nominated Tilden. The news reached Adams simultaneously with Lodge's letter. Being a Massachusetts resident, Adams was eligible to vote. And being the author of "The New York Gold Conspiracy," he was entitled to remember that his article gave Bowles, Barlow, Stickney, Tilden, and many others an opening for effective resistance to corruption in New York, though not in Washington. He answered:

> I am not only as pleased as Punch about my Ph. D's; but highly delighted to have carried our point about Schurz. And to crown all comes Tilden. . . . I have no ill-will to Hayes. If he is elected, I shall support him loyally. But I can no more resist the pleasure of voting for Tilden than I could turn my back on a friend. I too fought with Erie!

15

BIOGRAPHER OF GALLATIN

Of all titles ever assumed by prince or potentate, the proudest is that of the Roman pontiffs: "Servus servorum Dei"—"Servant of the servants of God." In former days it was not admitted that the devil's servants could by right have any share in government. They were to be shut out, punished, exiled, maimed, and burned. The devil has no servants now; only the people have servants. There may be some mistake about a doctrine which makes the wicked, when a majority, the mouthpiece of God against the virtuous, but the hopes of mankind are staked on it; and if the weak in faith sometimes quail when they see humanity floating in a shoreless ocean, on this plank, which experience and religion long since condemned as rotten, mistake or not, men have thus far floated better by its aid, than the popes ever did with their prettier principle; so that it will be a long time yet before society repents.

The passage is the opening paragraph in Chapter VIII of *Democracy/An American Novel*. The novel was published anonymously in 1880, and for thirty-five years the authorship remained a mystery. Very few persons knew Adams wrote it. None revealed the secret. *He* revealed it, but by proxy. In 1915, with his silent passive consent, a person known to be a friend of his, William Roscoe Thayer, declared in print that the author was Henry Adams.[2]

As it happened, the authorship of the novel was only one of a web of interrelated secrets. A deeper secret was the *date* when Adams wrote it in its form as published. A still deeper secret was his motive for completing it at that time. There was also the problem of the links, if any, between his novel and his *History of the United States*.

An item of evidence that bears on these matters is the paragraph just quoted. It may at first seem difficult and perhaps not worth the effort required to grasp its meaning. Comprehension gets easier when one realizes that the paragraph is a speech. Often in novels, the person telling the story is a fictional narrator separate from the author. In *Democracy*, there is no such split. Author and narrator are one. The point needs making, for the paragraph is the only passage in the novel in which Adams stops his story and gives a speech.

The speech is serious, yet humorous. Adams says that human beings have gone over to the heretical doctrine that majority rule is godly; they believe they have profited by adopting their new faith; and they will not soon give it up. He pictures humanity afloat on a plank on a shoreless ocean. Somewhat in defiance of the church, confidently and ironically, he sides with humanity, the ocean, and the plank.

On July 4, 1876, Henry's plan to finish and publish *Democracy* was a secret shared only with Clover. (Gaskell only knew that Adams had attempted to write it.) His plan to write a history of the United States similarly was a secret. Clover knew about it, but no one else.

At the time, Americans subscribed to a view of the history of the United States that could fairly be called part fact but mostly wishful thinking. This view centered in the idea that the nation existed from the moment on July 4, 1776, when representatives at Philadelphia signed a Declaration of Independence. Throughout the hundred years between 1776 and 1876, this idea had been affirmed during holiday celebrations on the Fourth of July. Customarily the celebrations included speeches. George Washington Adams gave such a speech at Quincy on Monday, July 5, 1824. It was later printed.[3]

The idea that the United States had been created by the Declaration of Independence gained credence partly as a result of a coincidence involving Thomas Jefferson and John Adams. As all Americans knew, Jefferson and Adams took leading roles relating to the Declaration. Jefferson was chief author of the text, and Adams rounded up needed signatures. Astonishingly, precisely fifty years later, Adams and Jefferson died on the same day, July 4, 1826.

The Centennial Year was marked by many observances linked to the Declaration. One was a celebration in Philadelphia on July 4, 1876, opposite Independence Hall. William Evarts gave the oration. Evarts was chosen partly because he was the grandson of one of the writers of the final draft of the Declaration, Roger Sherman. A supplementary speaker was C. F. Adams.[4]

For Henry and Clover Adams, the summer of 1876 was one long celebration. It was their first season of residence at Pitch Pine

Hill. Henry had special cause to rejoice. For the first time, he had the use of a study designed and constructed to suit his needs.

During the summer, he gave the appearance of being occupied by many tasks. For one thing, he purported to be revising *Essays in Anglo-Saxon Law*, reading its proofs, and compiling its index. But his share of the proofreading may easily have been completed earlier, and during the summer he could call on Young, Lodge, and Laughlin to do some work. *They* could revise, proofread, and index. He did very little.

Adams put it about that, in preparation to teach United States history during the coming academic year, he would pass the summer reading historical documents. Writing to Lodge on August 31, he said he was "still buried in avalanches of State Papers." But Adams could be said to have been preparing to teach United States history since early boyhood; he had accelerated his preparations the summer before; and burial in state papers could give *pretended* occupation to any summer.

As usual, Adams and Lodge were editing the *North American*. On August 5, Adams suggested to Lodge that they each draft a book notice reviewing the American translation of *The Constitutional and Political History of the United States* by the German historian Hermann von Holst, then compare their notices, publish the better notice in October, or publish a notice written jointly. As Adams presumably foresaw, his suggestion incited Lodge to write, not a mere short notice, but a full-length article. Adams approved the article, and it was published in the October issue, signed by both Adams and Lodge. Readers assumed that Adams was the principal author, but the article is itself sufficient evidence that Lodge wrote all of it and Adams none of it.[5]

Two book notices for the October issue would be titled "Lathrop's Study of Hawthorne" and "Frothingham's Transcendentalism." The magazine's records would say that Adams wrote both, and assistant editor Lodge may have believed that Adams wrote the latter of the two; but in each instance Adams was the writer-of-record because he had agreed to conceal the identity of the actual writer. Thus his share in the two notices was largely a mere matter of reading proofs.[6]

At an early moment, Henry notified Lodge that he and his brother Charles would write a political article for the October issue. The article, also referred to as a manifesto, would be titled "The 'Independents' in the Canvass." During the summer, in his dealings with Lodge and others, Henry continued successfully to pretend that he was co-author, even sole author, of the promised manifesto; but secretly Charles alone would write it. Also Charles would perform the chores relating to another political article for the October issue.[7]

The lesson that could be drawn from these details was important. In the summer of 1876, Henry Adams pretended doing things he did not do. The two persons he was most careful to deceive were the two men who most believed they knew what he was doing: Charles and Lodge.

The reason for the deceptions was Henry's wanting perfect cover for a project that Charles and Lodge could hardly have imagined.[8] In July, possibly on the 4th, Henry went back to work on *Democracy*. While valuing his attempted draft of 1867, he started over.[9] At high speed, he finished the novel in an altered, expanded form, rich in memorable scenes. Perhaps for lack of time, he overlooked some minor errors.[10]

As completed, the novel was full of references to matters in American history dating back from the time of composition to earlier years, even to the boyhood of George Washington. Yet in two respects *Democracy* was anchored to July 4, 1876. Considered as a whole, the book was Henry Adams's centennial oration. A single part of it, the paragraph already quoted, was the oration over again, humorously reduced to five pithy sentences.[11]

Adams's persistent returns to Washington, his "native asphalt," had had many aspects, personal, political, literary, even mythical. One aspect related to history. There was no possibility of his writing his *History of the United States* without drawing heavily on records controlled by the federal government. A great many of the documents he would need to see and quote were unpublished papers in the library and archives of the State Department.

Historians routinely gained access to papers owned by the government, and Adams could anticipate admittance. His needs, however, would be unusual in scale. He would want virtually unlimited freedom to consult materials.

Worse, his visiting the State Department might be impossible. He had to weigh the chance that Hayes, if elected president, might be prevailed upon to install hated Blaine as secretary of state.[12] If the leading corruptionist in the country took charge of the State Department, Adams could not go near the department. Just the opposite, he would have to stay away till Blaine left.

When finished, *Democracy* was three things in one: a novel, a satire, and a political instrument. Adams kept his authorship secret for a reason relating to the novel's power. Once the novel was published, its anonymous author all by himself would have the influence of a revived—even improved—Independent Party; and the author would continue to have that influence as long as the public remained unsure about the authorship. Really two factors would be at work. One was the novel's power, the other the power of mystery.

His novel as finished bore the marks of three occurrences: his learning about the Charles Sumner-Alice Hooper marriage in 1866; his learning in late 1869 or early 1870 that a bribe of $100,000 in U. S. bonds had passed from Jay Gould to Mrs. Grant; and the country's learning at intervals that Speaker Blaine had corruptly enriched himself.

Of the occurrences, the one relating to Julia Grant was echoed in the novel with the help of a little German. For no apparent reason, the author introduced a minor character, a likeable young woman named Julia Schneidekoupon. Simultaneously the author centered the story around a bribe of $100,000 paid in the form of "United States Coupon Bonds."[13] Practically all readers would know that President Grant was married to Julia Dent. Some would know that *schneid* in German was the equivalent of "cut" or "clip" in English. A few would sense an implication, yet fear it. As the saying went, a Julia was "clipping coupons"—that is, collecting cash returns on a hoard of U. S. bonds.[14]

The Blaine horror had acquired an urgency for Adams that would be hard to exaggerate. With Blaine in mind, Adams reshaped *Democracy* to meet three requirements. The novel had to be so baited as to attract large crowds of readers. It had to be so barbed that if published in November-December 1876 immediately after a Hayes victory, it would stop Hayes from choosing Blaine to be secretary of state. And it had to be so barbed that if it was withheld while *Tilden* served as president but was published in the spring of 1880, it would destroy Blaine's chance of winning the Republican nomination for president in that year.

Although not long, *Democracy* afforded active roles to twenty-four characters, fifteen male, nine female. The presence of so many actors did not veil the centrality of three: a corrupt United States senator, a marriageable young widow, and a baron from the Continent.[15] Their prominence would alert many readers to the likelihood that the book owed its existence in a measure to the marriage of Charles Sumner and Alice Mason Hooper in 1866 and its dramatic sequel, the forced flight of Baron Holstein from Washington. Thus the novel was baited with an old but sensational mixture of the political, the intriguingly social, and the scandalously sexual.

The barbs were fashioned from the standard materials of corruption. If published in December 1876 to preclude the appointment of Blaine as secretary of state in March 1877, the novel would depend for its effect on an analogy between fiction and fact. In the novel, a fictitious politician, Senator Silas P. Ratcliffe of Illinois is chosen by President Jacob ———— (the last name is withheld) to be secretary of the treasury.[16] After taking office as secretary, Ratcliffe is revealed to the heroine, Mrs. Lightfoot Lee, to have been a willing party in the past to a bribe of $100,000. These fictional occurrences would bring to mind two moments in the history of the Republican Party: Lincoln's near-choice of corrupt Senator Simon Cameron of Pennsylvania to head the Treasury Department (January 1861) and his actual choice of Simon Cameron to head the War Department (March 1861). The novel would insure remembrance by mentioning Lincoln and making a display of Biblical names: Abraham, Daniel, Eli, Jacob, Jared, John, Jonathan, Nathan, Samson, Samuel, Silas, and Thomas.[17]

It can be assumed that Adams finished *Democracy* in September. It can be assumed as well that he strongly hoped the voters would vote for Tilden and he himself would not have to rush at once to a publisher with the manuscript of a novel. The reasons for his strong hope were many. One concerned a rentable house.

Because they were guests of Sam Hooper in the capital when he died, Henry and Clover had been afforded an opportunity to try to rent the house he occupied: 1501 H Street, just east of Lafayette Square.[18] Clover liked the house. She thought it a "charming old ranch." At the front, it had wisteria vines and "superb rose trees."[19]

In July 1876, the owner of 1501 H Street was William Corcoran, a Confederate sympathizer who stayed in France through the war. Corcoran owned several Washington houses, including houses on Lafayette Square looking south towards the White House.

At the latest in September 1876, Henry obtained a near-promise from Corcoran that he could rent 1501 H Street in the autumn of 1877. This development placed the Adamses in an intricate situation. Henry might soon be under great pressure to publish *Democracy*. Yet he and Clover were hoping to live in the one house in Washington which they could occupy only at great risk to themselves.[20] 1501 H Street was the house in which Charles Sumner had fallen in love, or whatever, with Alice Mason Hooper. If the Adamses moved into it in 1877, and if, before and after they arrived, *Democracy* was being read on every hand, the prospect would arise that readers of the anonymous novel would identify *their* drawing room as the drawing room in which Senator Sumner grew fatally attracted to beautiful Alice. The same readers would then assume it to be the drawing room in which fictional Senator Ratcliffe formed designs on fictional Madeleine Lee. It would not be a long jump from those ideas to excited allegations that Henry Adams or Marian Adams—if not both—was the author of the novel.

The case as yet was only potentially dangerous. But Mr. and Mrs. Adams were the architects of their danger. Already the case was comic, knotty, and bizarre.

In the last week of September 1876, the October issue of the *North American Review* was nearly ready for distribution. James Osgood, the publisher, looked into the issue and disliked it. Setting aside the notices at the back, the issue was heavily political. Article I, "The Southern Question," was contributed by William Henry Trescot of South Carolina, a leading Confederate. There were articles relating to corruption in the federal government and in New York City. Others were written by professed Independents who might actually be Democrats.

The trouble partly related to the Adams family. Election day was less than six weeks distant. Boston's better citizens were aligned fairly solidly in support of Governor Hayes. Notoriously the Adamses were supporting Governor Tilden. The father, C. F. Adams, had himself accepted the nomination for governor of Massachusetts on the Democratic ticket. No one imagined the great diplomat would be elected, but his candidacy was galling. At least in appearance, he and his sons had gone over to the Democrats in a body.

Article V was titled "The 'Independents' in the Canvass" and was unsigned. In style and substance, the article was a political editorial. After much flourishing, it plumped emphatically for Tilden. Osgood possibly knew that the manuscript of the editorial, as given to the printer, was in the handwriting of C. F. Adams, Jr. Charles currently was in the west on a business trip. The person responsible for the issue was the chief editor, Henry Adams. And there was room for belief that the actual writer of the editorial was Henry.

The issue being far advanced, it was too late for sweeping changes. So someone in the publisher's office remarked to Henry Adams, perhaps in mild, unquarrelsome terms, that the issue was over-political and that its political tendencies left something to be desired.

Classes at Harvard were on the point of resuming. Young would be teaching medieval politics. Lodge had joined the faculty on an unpaid basis and would replace Adams as teacher of colonial history. Adams would again teach English history and medieval institutions. The great novelty of the year would be History VI, Adams's course in the history of the United States from 1789 to 1840. Students were flocking to take it. They almost seemed to think the chance might never be repeated.[21]

At Beverly Farms on September 30, Adams finished and sent a letter to Gaskell that had been interrupted three weeks earlier. In its early portion, he had said that "for two blessed months" without interruption he had "sat still all day and read or written"; also that Carlo's personal affairs, as told in his letters, sounded "like a modern novel."

The new portion of Henry's letter was crammed with news. He mentioned that his Independent Party had "dissolved like a summer cloud." He said that he and Clover had just gone to Philadelphia to visit the Centennial Exhibition. He explained that his father was running for governor of Massachusetts, and he stated that the Republican and Democratic parties were both "impossibly corrupt."

> . . . I have devoted the whole October number of the North American to a review of the field. The result is sickening. But I consider my October number a historical monument, and am going to avail myself of a trifling disagreement with the publishers to . . . get rid of my editorial duties, leaving my monument behind me.[22]

Looking ahead a full thirteen months, Henry told Carlo in casual tones, "If the new Secretary of State is a friend of mine, I shall try the experiment of passing a winter in Washington, searching archives." As in 1868, he used the word "experiment." He gave no indication that he and Clover would be moving permanently. He did not say that the new secretary of state could very possibly be Blaine—the extremest opposite of a friend. Yet he spoke plainly about retiring as a teacher. "I regard my university work as essentially done. All the influence I can exercise has been exercised."[23]

During the first week of October, *Essays in Anglo-Saxon Law* was published by Little, Brown and Company in Boston. Fifty copies were shipped to London to be offered for sale by the Macmillan Company.[24] Copies were mailed to Gaskell, Palgrave, Sir Henry Maine, and K. E. Digby in England; to Lewis Henry Morgan in upstate New York; to Daniel Gilman in Baltimore.[25] Oliver Wendell Holmes, Jr., currently a teacher at the Harvard Law School, was reading the book in proof and readying a notice for the *American Law Review*.[26] William Francis Allen, a professor at the University of Wisconsin, would soon be writing a review for the *North American*.[27]

Suddenly during the same interval, in the first week of October, Adams quit as editor of the *North American*. Lodge quit also. Osgood, having no choice but to distribute the October issue as Adams shaped it, changed it only by adding a Publishers' Notice to the table of contents. The notice said the editors had "retired . . . on account of a difference of opinion with the proprietors as to the political character of the number."[28]

Nothing in the issue betrayed the part that Charles had had in it as secret editor for politics. It seems unlikely that Osgood knew for a fact that Charles had written the manifesto—Article V, "The 'Independents' in the Canvass." And Lodge may not immediately have learned that Charles alone had written it.[29]

At Bryn Mawr, Pennsylvania, on October 13, en route from the west to Quincy, Charles recorded with typical self-centeredness that his "political manifesto" had "made a row and burst the N. American." Ten days later at his Boston office, he was visited by Henry and Lodge. They presumably told him in some detail about their resignations.[30]

To outsiders, especially if Democrats, it would seem that the proprietors of the magazine were guilty of most exceptional interference with the editors; that Henry Adams and H. C. Lodge had written Article V; and that they had a right to sympathy as injured parties.[31] In their own view, Adams and Lodge walked away from their duties uninjured and in need of no special sympathy. Their names appeared at the end of Article III, "Von Holst's History of the United States." The names were their farewell.[32]

During the six months following his resignation from his editorship, Adams wrote few letters to Americans, said little in the few concerning politics, and less about his plans. He probably was more confiding in letters to Gaskell, Cunliffe, and Palgrave, but the letters are missing and their contents can be gathered only from replies.[33]

On November 3, 1876, four days before the voters went to the polls, Charles recorded: "I doubt if I have ever seen election excitement so intense as at present. The result,—so great, is near and is wholly uncertain." On election day, November 7, Tilden carried sufficient states and was elected president; but his victory was disputed. The Republican managers refused to concede that he had won. They challenged the election returns in Florida, Louisiana, Oregon, and South Carolina. Their course raised questions concerning the Constitution and possible means of deciding the outcome.

As seen by Charles, the Republican action was thievery on a grand scale, and he grew angry and excited.[34] Henry's response is not documented but probably can be inferred from things he had said before the election. He had written to Wells on July 15, "The main point is not to have any quarrels among our friends, so after [the?] election we may all unite again to support the new administration." He had urged Lodge on August 25, "Let us stay blandly on the fence." He had confided to Moorfield Storey on September 21, ". . . I very much hope that our friends will see the wisdom of remaining good-natured, ready to unite when the hurricane is over." And he remarked to Bowles on October 10 that, when the election was past and they were "all sane again," he hoped to see him "in Marlboro Street."[35]

Though he had braced for a hurricane, Henry could not have anticipated the form it would take, still less the consequences for himself. Rather terrifying to the country, the electoral crisis of 1876–1877 was amazingly favorable to Henry Adams. From its beginning on election day, the crisis opened a path for his return to Washington. It put to rest the fear that he would need to make immediate use of *Democracy*. And it permitted him to start an all-out effort to prepare for and write his *History of the United States*.

For an analyst as capable as Adams, the outcome of the electoral crisis was visible in advance. Tilden's victory was lost. It was a foregone conclusion that Hayes would be elected president by force, fraud, or both. The Ohioan would thus be placed on his best behavior and could not choose Blaine as secretary of state.

The mechanism invented to end the dispute was an Electoral Commission so chosen as to assure the Republicans their wanted victory. The claims of the Democrats and Republicans would be presented before the Commission by lawyers. The chief counsel for the Republicans would be Evarts. Since the outcome was predecided, Evarts's performance would be a mummery. In form, however, Evarts would *save* Rutherford B. Hayes, as earlier in fact he had saved Andrew Johnson. In the earlier instance, Johnson responded by making Evarts attorney general. In the new instance, Hayes could be expected to do something better.

The heavy losers in the electoral crisis were the Democrats, candidate Tilden, and New York. Because it was being robbed of a fairly-elected president, the Empire State would demand as solace the highest post in the Cabinet. A New Yorker suited to head the State Department was William Evarts. It actually helped that Evarts of late had forsaken the Republicans and become an Independent.

While the crisis was in process of resolution, Adams continued to meet his classes. In Boston on December 7, in Marlboro Chapel, he gave a public talk—a Lowell Lecture—on "Women's Rights in History." The text of his talk was not preserved.[36]

The Harvard calendar permitted Henry and Clover to go to New York and Washington either during the Christmas season of 1876 or in February 1877 after the fall semester ended. All that is known for certain is that Henry at some point was in New York.[37]

Though records are lacking, a firm inference can be made that, in the period November 1876–March 1877, Adams settled upon the general plan for his *History of the United States*. He also decided the spirit that would govern his effort to write it. Because the work would be the longest of his writings, and possibly the best, there is point in knowing both the choices he made and the alternatives he rejected.

Adams was born into a family that understood the history of the United States as much as possible in terms of its Constitution. John Adams wrote a three-volume *Defence of the Constitutions of the United States of America*, published in 1787–1788 and 1794. He renewed the "defence" in a fourth volume, *Discourses on Davila*, published in 1805. As viewed by him and his sons, the four volumes amounted to a single work, and the work was a history. John Quincy Adams caused a set of the volumes to be bound in calf and lettered *Adams's History of the Republic*. When a boy, Henry Adams very possibly saw his grandfather's set, handled it, and read about in it.[38]

In his early teens, Henry was asked by his father to help proofread an edition of John Adams's *Writings*. Obediently he joined his father in the labor.[39] In this way, line by line, he was taught indelibly that a history of the Union, if written by an Adams, might better take the form of a constitutional history.

Henry was brought to Harvard in 1870 partly to teach "medieval institutions." Rather than respond in a merely acceptable fashion, he undertook to inform himself completely about the constitutions inherited by, and modified by, the peoples of Europe following the decline of the Roman empire. He not only continued teaching medieval institutions; he taught English history with em-

phasis on the English constitution. He led a research team through
forests of evidence relating to the Anglo-Saxon constitution. As
leader of the team, he wrote "The Anglo-Saxon Courts of Law"—
a skeleton history of England.

The argument of the skeleton history was complicated and
turned on evidence in several languages. To accommodate readers
who would not wish to read the argument, Adams set forth his
thesis in the opening paragraphs. His thesis was that the state and
the law of modern England and the United States demonstrably
are inheritances from the democratic state and law of the ancient
Germans. He asserted that without error a historian can follow the
thread of inheritance through two thousand years, beginning in
the German "primitive popular assembly, parliament, law-court,
and army in one; which embraced every free man, rich or poor,
and in theory at least allowed equal rights to all." The later
paragraphs of his argument retold the story in detail. It showed
with evidence that, by a route through England, ancient German
democratic precedents survived—indeed survived in America in
1876.[40]

In the October 1876 issue of the *North American*, Adams and
Lodge signed an article on Von Holst's *Constitutional and Political
History of the United States*. As has been mentioned, the entire article
was written by Lodge. The article assumed that what happens in
history is determined by constitutions and by laws; in short, that
law makes history. The concluding paragraph affirmed that a legal
document performed a prodigy: the U. S. Constitution of 1787
"made a nation."[41] In what could seem a spirit of complete agreement, Adams wrote flatteringly to Lodge that the paragraph was
"*my*"—that is, Adams's—"centennial Oration."[42]

Adams did not immediately desist from speaking along these
lines. During the winter of 1876–1877, Lewis Henry Morgan
completed and published a book titled *Ancient Society*. On July 14,
1877, writing to Morgan in response to the book, Adams would
seem to say that the pinnacle of human activity was law. He roundly
declared: ". . . the history of law is the best that man has to show."

Adams's praises of law were less than half the story. Starting in
early youth and advancing by painful steps, he had moved towards
a very individual opinion of constitutions, laws, and lawyers. On
February 22, 1875, he had written to Sir Henry Maine about early
institutions and early law, ". . . the more I study this subject, the
less practical and positive are the results."[43] Sixteen months later,
on June 25, 1876, he burst out to Lodge, "I can *not* understand

things that to other men are plain as a poker, and above all I cannot understand law."

These seemingly exceptional remarks were warning signs of a change in Adams's thinking. The change was concurrent with the completion of *Democracy*, the election of Tilden, and the pseudo-legal election of Hayes by the Republican managers and their lawyers, headed by Evarts. Adams may never have quite believed that law made history. After the change, he fully believed the wholly different idea that, insofar as history was made, it was *human beings* that made it.

Since his marriage, Adams had been treating two men with particular consideration. They were Clover's friends in earlier years: Henry James, Jr., and Oliver Wendell Holmes, Jr. Though not of the marrying sort, James was sociable and had often visited at Marlborough Street. Adams liked him.[44] The relation between Adams and Holmes was entirely different. They were one-time schoolmates and showed tendencies to be competitive. In 1872, ten days prior to Adams's marriage to Clover Hooper, Holmes married Fanny Dixwell, daughter of the headmaster of the Boston private school he and Adams attended in the 1850s. The Holmeses traveled in Europe in 1874, starting in England, and Adams tried to assist them with letters of introduction.[45]

Late in 1876, Adams received from Holmes an inquiry about aspects of "The Anglo-Saxon Courts of Law" that struck him, Holmes, as unclear. Holmes was at work on his notice of *Essays in Anglo-Saxon Law*. Adams replied obligingly on December 5, but in the course of answering he wrote two remarkable sentences:

> I am not a lawyer. If I were, I should not be a historian.

Whatever their other meanings—there possibly were four or five—the sentences meant that Adams would *not* write a constitutional history of the United States. He instead would write a history in which the constitution and the laws would have only subsidiary importance.[46]

Interest in the history of the United States was very strong among descendants of the signers of the Declaration of Independence, descendants of framers of the Constitution, descendants of members of early administrations, of early members of Congress, and early generals and naval heroes. Knowing he was the most conspicuous descendant in the country, C. F. Adams had distinguished himself since retiring from the English mission by preparing a revised version of his biography of John Adams and by editing and publishing volume after volume of the *Memoirs of John Quincy Adams,* meaning his extraordinary diary, which was itself a history of the Republic. In 1876, C. F. Adams's historical productions were nearly finished. Sometime in 1877, the *Works* and *Life of John Adams* and the *Memoirs of John Quincy Adams* would all be in print. They would fill twenty-four volumes.

Thus, in 1876, Henry Adams was under no compulsion to memorialize his great-grandfather or his grandfather. He instead was free to obey whatever feeling *he* felt as a historian. Any appearances to the contrary notwithstanding, his feeling was *not* a descendant's feeling.

Henry differed from other living Americans, his father and brothers included, in the psychology of his relation to the founders and makers of the United States. Accidents of aptitude and experience had made him feel himself entirely at one with—wholly corporate and cooperative with—the founders and makers. He belonged with Franklin, Washington, John Adams, Jefferson, Madison, Gallatin, J. Q. Adams, and the rest except in one slight particular: he had not died.

In one sense, for Henry, the history of the United States was not history at all. When he wrote of Franklin or Washington or Jefferson, he perforce would be writing *for* them—also *with* them— as their last surviving coeval. Thus his *History of the United States* would have a double meaning. It would be a history. Yet it would also be the nearest that he meant to come to writing an autobiography.

Starting as early as 1846, when he was eight, Henry had been paid to make copies of letters by Elbridge Gerry to John Adams and letters by William Vans Murray to John Quincy Adams. The copies filled many hundreds of pages. Making the copies may have given him occasion to form the elements of his handwriting, which is one of the clearest and most distinctive ever developed by a famous American. What mattered more, making copies taught him to learn history in one way: by gathering, copying, reading, and understanding *evidence.*[47]

In 1846, George Gibbs, a Rhode Islander of thirty-one, published a stout two-volume work, *Memoirs of the administrations of Washington and John Adams, edited from the papers of Oliver Wolcott, secretary of the Treasury.* One may assume that the Adamses acquired a copy and that Henry in 1846 or soon after seized and studied the copy.[48] From his point of view, no book could be more interesting. Oliver Wolcott was appointed secretary of the treasury during the second administration of President Washington, to replace the first occupant of the post, Alexander Hamilton. The memoirist, George Gibbs, was related to Wolcott, had access to his papers, and had access to papers belonging to other families. A passionate fighter and an adherent of old-style Federalism, Gibbs wrote history on the premise that history was political warfare continued by other means.

In the *Memoirs*, Gibbs warred against the Adamses. That single fact might have sufficed to interest Henry Adams deeply, but the book had added values. Gibbs had the idea that writers of United States history should key their works to the federal government's successive administrations. He assumed as well that memoirs should bristle with evidence, including letters quoted complete. Still better, he was honest, and he could write.

Henry Adams did not fully know that he would write a great history of the United States till 1860, when he was twenty-two. At that time, the subject seemed preempted by other writers, most notably George Gibbs and George Bancroft. As things developed, however, the subject was not preempted. Instead, as Adams understood the matter, the entire subject was left open for him to pioneer.

Bancroft earned a doctorate in history at the University of Gottingen in Germany. He taught briefly at Harvard. When still young, he projected a *History of the United States from the Discovery of the American Continent*. In the first volume, published in 1834, he projected a grand narrative recounting American history from Columbus to the present. During succeeding decades, he carried his narrative forward as far as the provisional treaty ending the Americans' War of Independence against Great Britain. Adams reviewed the tenth volume in the April 1875 *North American*.[49] By then, it was evident that Bancroft could not possibly complete the grand narrative he had started.

After writing his tenth volume, Bancroft decided not to add more volumes under his existing title. He instead began a separate *History of the Formation of the Constitution of the United States of America*. Accordingly, in the academic year 1876–1877, it was anticipated that Bancroft would complete a particular portion of his intended story, the portion ending in 1787, when the U. S. Constitution was written.

At the same moment, Professor Adams at Harvard introduced History VI, History of the United States from 1789–1840. It could seem that Adams was staking a claim to the portion of United States history that Bancroft would not write. But Adams had no intention of writing a history of the United States beginning in 1787 or 1789 and ending in 1840. The dates he gave his Harvard course and the dates that would govern his future *History* were widely different. Moreover, the dates governing his *History* were then a secret.

Late in 1876, Adams knew the plan his *History* was going to follow. The plan would be reflected in its titles. Here the titles should be given, to speed explanation of the ideas that lay behind them. There would be no overall title. Instead four volumes would bear four different titles starting with seven repeating words.[50]

History of the United States of America
during the First Administration of Thomas Jefferson
1801–1805

History of the United States of America
during the Second Administration of Thomas Jefferson
1805–1809

History of the United States of America
during the First Administration of James Madison
1809–1813

History of the United States of America
during the Second Administration of James Madison
1813–1817

The first truth to be found in the titles is that Adams felt no need to intrude upon the epochs in American history attended to by Bancroft or Gibbs. He meant to start at the point where *Gibbs* had stopped. Nothing is more important than knowing his reason for starting there.

The principal reason turned on what Adams meant by "the United States of America." For him, a state was the people in a geographical area acting together to govern themselves and deal with other states.[51] To his mind, the United States, or the American Union, or the Union, was the people united and in action. In a word, his subject was the *nation*. He intended a national history.

The spirit governing Adams's historical investigations was solely attentive to evidence. At an unknown moment, conceivably as late as 1875, he had learned from evidence that *the American people—the nation—did not exist in 1800 and did exist in 1815.* As well as anyone, he knew that the nation was projectedly real in 1789 when Washington took office as first president. He knew that the

United States had some pretentions to reality in 1776 when Jefferson penned the Declaration. He knew also that a Union of sorts existed still earlier in acts of colonial cooperation. But he did not share the part-mythical idea of American history then operative in the minds of Americans at large. He moreover was the reverse of self-deceiving. In 1876, there was much he did not know about American history; but he did know that Americans abounded in 1800 for whom the United States was a nation only in unrealized dreams, or only in governmental arrangements *not* expected to endure, or a nation only on paper, or a nation in words to which no attachment at all was felt.

The occurrence that interested Adams was the historical action at the start of which Americans were more un-united than united and at the end of which they were a people, a race, a nation. He believed that the action was sudden; that it began in 1800 or 1801 and was completed prior to 1817. He was willing to make strenuous inquiries and write four volumes to find out if he was right. And he wished to get within the action well enough to see what it was and say how it worked.[52]

Adams's explanation of the American people's coming into existence would be an explanation involving both the people and their government. As the titles of his volumes showed, he accepted the Gibbsian principle that histories of the United States could properly be written administration by administration. Yet he and Gibbs diverged. Gibbs wrote memoirs *of* administrations. Adams would write a history of the United States *during* administrations. The difference was every difference. Like Gibbs, Adams would write an account of the United States government, but he would write it as integral with the history of the people.

Adams's explanation, too, would be an explanation involving both the Americans and other peoples. His narrative would have a center, the city of Washington. Very soon the narrative would move outwards from its center to other peoples and governments with whom the Americans at the time were in contact or conflict. The narrative's extension would become extremely large. The reader would go to London, Paris, and St. Petersburg; to Madrid and North Africa; to the West Indies and still-foreign Louisiana; to Indian territories in the Mississippi basin; to Oregon; to portions of Canada.

The places did not matter most. Peoples mattered most. In some instances, individuals would matter too. The diverse peoples and individuals active in the narrative, though living in the same years and in many countries, would be distributed historically in gradations between the primitive and the advanced. The peoples and individuals would be in contact at one time, yet representative of all human experience, late and early. The story of their interactions would be a story not simply of the Americans but instead of all humanity, the Americans being merely the newest of the races and the most advanced. In a word, Adams's *History* would end in showing direction. It would show where humanity was going.[53]

In part, Adams's plan for his *History* reflected a lesson taught to him by a British history. John Richard Green's *Short History of the English People* had been published in London in 1875. Of the anonymous sketches Adams had written for the *North American* while editor, the best was his response to Green's *Short History*.[54] The response culminated in a regretful passage concerning historical method. In Adams's opinion, Green had made the mistake of attempting a comprehensive history of the English people from the Anglo-Saxon landings in the fifth century to the reign of Queen Victoria. The attempt was a mistake because the historian could not at every point consult the evidence; and, even if able to obtain and read the evidence, the historian could not take time to understand it. In Adams's words:

> Any single mind has its limits, and even in the greatest human intelligence those limits are really not hard to reach. . . . A [comprehensive] history of England must inevitably overstrain the powers of any mind. . . . The field is too large. Great as is Mr. Green's ability and wide as is his learning, he cannot carry his own individuality thoroughly into every part of it. He cannot be equally sure of his judgment in every portion of the work. His mind must yield to human weariness. . . . It is true that, in the broad sense of absolute accuracy, there never was, and there never will be, a history written, so long as man is neither omniscient nor omnipresent, which can be more than approximately exact. . . . But the more the historian's task is limited, the better is his chance of mastering every detail. . . .

An American investigator who had solved the problem of limiting his task was Clarence King. Adams's plan to study the history of human beings was patterned after King's Fortieth Parallel Survey. Adams understood the logic of his friend-and-partner's investigation. King's exploring parties did not rush here and there in the Rocky Mountains for evidence. To use King's term, they practiced systematic geology. They surveyed and analyzed a limited area—a sample—across the mountain ranges of the West. The area chosen was a thousand miles by a hundred. It was large, yet not so large that a small team of geologists could not explore it to its furthest corners.[55]

The tendency of King's method, which became Adams's method, was to offer hope of learning an overall direction of occurrence within the data considered. King wanted to open the door to understanding of the planet Earth; hence of the universe; hence of all things; and he began by analyzing a large sample of rock. Adams wanted to understand all things but turned to human beings, usually as aggregates, sometimes as individuals. The sample that Adams meant to explore was the Americans and their neighbors in the time when the Americans became a nation.

In practical terms, Adams's problem in 1876–1877 was one of getting evidence. Because letters are missing and, too, because records were never made, it is impossible to trace in detail how he proceeded; but the outlines of his progress can be stated without a doubt. The place where evidence was easiest for him to get was Boston and elsewhere in New England. From the moment he and Lodge retired as editors of the *North American*, he redoubled his efforts to see, and where necessary copy, historical records held by New England families and institutions.

Washington was different. Adams could get evidence in Washington on the terms and in the amounts he wanted only if he had the fullest cooperation of the incoming administration. For him, success in Washington had long gone hand in hand with friendly acquaintance with politicians in New York. Raymond and Seward had died; but, in January and February 1877, there were two politicians in New York in whom Adams could confide about his need for evidence. William Evarts was living at a corner of 14th Street and Second Avenue. Thurlow Weed was living at 12 West 12th Street. Probably in January, Adams spoke privately and informally with Evarts. On the assumption that Evarts would be secretary of state in a Hayes administration, he said he would be needing access to the State Department archives and especially access to all the papers of Thomas Jefferson and James Madison. He presumably disclosed his plan to write the nation's history during the Jefferson and Madison administrations. Presumably, too, he asked Evarts to mention the plan confidentially to Weed or others who might be helpful.[56]

Evidence survives that Adams early in 1877 grew confident that he could move to Washington, rent 1501 H Street, gain full access to materials held by the government, and gain access to materials abroad. Part of the evidence was requests to Francis Palgrave and Thomas Woolner for pictures the Adamses would need if living in a larger house.

Some months earlier, Henry James, Jr., had moved to London permanently to pursue his career as a professional writer. Adams wanted to insure James's perfect welcome in England. In January 1877, he wrote him a friendly letter and enclosed a sheaf of introductions far from ordinary in tone. The letter is missing, but some of its details can be adduced from James's reply. Adams mentioned the building of Boston's Trinity Church, designed by H. H. Richardson, and the decoration of its interior with frescoes designed by John La Farge and painted in haste by a drove of artists, including Augustus St. Gaudens. Also Adams mentioned a painting by Turner that had found its way to Boston.

James did not know Adams well. He liked to think that Adams should stay in Massachusetts and try to become a counselor of Boston's politicians. He answered, "Your picture of Boston with its gorgeous Turner & its frescoed churches is really glowing, & I feel like hurrying home, to become the Vasari of such a Florence, where didn't I advise you to remain & become the Machiavelli[?]"[57]

Thanks to Adams's introductions, James formed friendly relations with Cunliffe, Palgrave, and Woolner. He cooperated with Woolner in choosing pictures for the Adamses and took pleasure in seeing that the pictures were safely shipped to Boston.[58]

Palgrave may also have sent pictures, but a matter more interesting to him was the possibility that Henry and Clover might return to London. Writing to Henry on February 9, 1877, Frank inquired, "When will you come over for a year or two?"

The basis for Palgrave's question possibly was news sent by Adams to Gaskell that he might have to come to Europe to search the archives of several governments. Some weeks later, perhaps to Palgrave, Adams sent news that he and Clover would return in 1879. The news reached Woolner and his wife. Woolner burst out in his next letter, "We are greatly rejoiced at the prospect of your being in England. . . ."[59]

The vicissitudes of politics had placed C. F. Adams on excellent terms with Governor Tilden of New York. In April 1877, the Chief had to deal with an emergency. Mrs. Adams "got into one of her conditions of nerves." In search of treatment, she went to New York, accompanied by Mary and Brooks. The party stayed at the Windsor Hotel.[60]

For a separate reason, apparently on Thursday, April 12, Henry and Clover traveled to New York. They stayed at a different hotel.

On April 14, the Chief arrived from Boston and relieved Mary

and Brooks, who went home.[61] That evening, Henry wrote a letter
to Gaskell outlining a sudden change.

> I am again in New York, devoting all my energies to the arrangement
> of a great mass of papers which have accidentally come under my
> hands, and which may give me some years' work. . . . My wife is with
> me. My father is at another hotel here with my mother who is again
> under medical treatment. . . . My political friends, or one wing of
> them, have come into power, but under circumstances which prevent
> me from giving them more than a silent and temporary sympathy .
> . . . Meanwhile I hob-nob with the leaders of both parties, and am
> very contented under my cloak of historian.

The explanation of Henry's conduct was possibly as follows.
Evarts put word about that Henry Adams would be setting up shop
as a historian of the United States and needed access to the papers
of Jefferson and Madison. Those informed included Weed or
Tilden. The persons involved all knew that the papers of Jefferson
and Madison were interrelated with those of Albert Gallatin. Evarts
moved to Washington and on March 12 took office under Hayes as
secretary of state. In April, Weed or Tilden ascertained that
Gallatin's papers were held by his son Albert R. Gallatin. One or
the other, presumably Tilden, learned that the younger Gallatin
was in quest of a person who could be trusted with his father's
papers and would be competent to write a biography. The result
was a message to Henry Adams in Boston, urging his arrival.[62]

What is definitely known is that Adams on arriving visited a
connection of the Gallatins, John Austin Stevens, librarian of the
New York Historical Society.[63] Adams spoke next with Albert R.
Gallatin. Mr. Gallatin gave him immediate possession of his father's
papers, in order to write the desired biography—also to prepare
an edition of his father's less-available important writings. The
arrangement being settled, Adams ordered the making of a large
wooden strong box. As soon as possible, he would load the papers
into the box and have it shipped to Boston.[64]

On Monday, April 16, Henry and Clover were still in New York.
The Chief recorded that John Bigelow had visited him at his hotel.
"After he left I walked to . . . the Governor's [meaning Tilden's
house on East 20th Street,] but he had gone to the Park. From
thence I walked to Mr. Thurlow Weed's and sat with him half an
hour." Later, at the Windsor, he was visited by Henry.[65]

When he wrote to Carlo on Saturday that he was very contented under his "cloak of historian," Henry had failed to say what
had happened. True, he wanted a cloak; but at the moment he was
taking off the cloak of historian and putting on the still better

cloak—more modest, less assuming—of mere biographer of Gallatin and editor of his writings. A modest cloak was wanted, for
Henry had much to hide. In the history of the United States,
certain persons counted for more, others for less. Albert Gallatin
was barred by foreign birth from becoming president. He was
restricted officially to being secretary of the treasury under Jefferson and Madison, peace commissioner at St. Petersburg and Ghent,
and later minister to France and minister to England. He however
was *the* American who continuously was at the right places at the
right times during the development of nationhood that Adams
wished to investigate. On that ground, it could be held that Gallatin
exceeded Presidents Jefferson and Madison in importance both
practically and officially. By capturing Gallatin's papers when just
beginning his investigation, Adams secured a gain almost too large
to measure. Admittedly the gain would not seem huge to others.
But Adams knew the dimensions of his gain, and for the next two
years he would want to wrap his extreme prosperity in modest
coverings.[66]

Presumably Henry and Clover returned to Boston on April 17.
Henry would not be free from teaching till the end of June. By
agreeing to write a biography and by promising to edit volumes of
writings, he had added a large labor to the extremely large labor
of preparing for and writing his *History of the United States*. Rather
than wait, he planned an instant start. Beginning in Boston and
continuing at Beverly Farms, he would advance with all possible
speed towards publication of *The Writings of Albert Gallatin*, including letters by and to him. He simultaneously would gather additional materials and ready his mind for the composition of *The Life
of Albert Gallatin*.[67]

His more visible activity was editing. He bought suitable paper,
employed a copyist, and set in motion the process of creating a
manuscript of the parts of the *Writings* that would be drawn from
handwritten originals. The copyist started work on April 29.[68]

Two developments, one definite, one indefinite, brought Adams
to a turning point. The definite development was the restoration
of Frederick Seward to his old position as assistant secretary of
state. The indefinite concerned 1501 H Street. William Corcoran
wrote to say that the house *might* be available; he was not entirely
sure.

Corcoran's letter arrived at the latest on May 4.[69] On that day,
Adams wrote a request to Assistant Secretary Seward. In his request, he gave the impression that he was a university teacher who,

to obtain materials for a biography and an edition of documents, also to improve his teaching, wished to take a leave of absence from Harvard and spend a winter in Washington searching collections at the State Department.

> Mr[.] Albert R. Gallatin of New York has put into my hands all his father's papers to be prepared for publication, and has requested me further to collect the materials necessary to a biography. Owing to the fact that Mr[.] Gallatin rarely took copies of his letters, I shall be obliged to obtain copies of all such as are recoverable. The largest single mass of these is in the State Department, among the Jefferson, Madison and Monroe Papers and in the official archives. To have all these copied would be an expensive and interminable labor. In order to perform the work properly I must examine the material myself and select what is important.
>
> I write therefore to ask whether permission can be obtained to examine the archives and the collections of the Department down to 1827.[70] Without this permission I am at a loss to see how there can be any thorough knowledge of our history. Certainly, as an instructor in that subject in our Universities, I cannot hope to teach or write with any accuracy without the knowledge which the State Department can alone supply.
>
> If permission can be obtained, I shall try to pass next winter in Washington for the purpose of collecting Mr[.] Gallatin's papers.
>
> I have already spoken to Mr[.] Evarts on the subject. Since then, however, Mr[.] Gallatin has given me the task which obliges me to ask for a more immediate decision.
>
> Believe me, it is with great satisfaction that I have seen you reestablished at the Department.

Fred Seward's permission reached Adams late in May. The terms were so encouraging that, on May 30, though he lacked a decision from Corcoran, Adams resigned from the Harvard faculty.[71]

The din in Cambridge was loud. John Fiske wrote excitedly to his mother: "Today HENRY ADAMS'S resignation. I went to Jamaica Plain to noonday dinner with Francis Parkman. . . . Talked of Adams's resignation." Fiske hoped to be appointed in Adams's place and at once made inquiries. Eliot or Gurney fobbed him off with the assurance that he might be appointed the following year.[72] They evidently were thinking that Adams might return. They almost acted as if he would.[73]

A short time later, three events occurred, each important to Adams. On June 25, 1877, Lodge obtained from Little, Brown and Company a copy of his first book, *The Life and Letters of George Cabot*.[74] On June 26, Clarence King gave a public address at Yale on "Catastrophism and Evolution." The address was the first announcement of his views concerning the evolution of species, which differed from those of Darwin and Lyell in significant respects.[75] And early in July, Adams wrote to his father in Quincy saying that he urgently wished to publish a book of documents and wanted access to the family papers.

By any standard, Lodge's biography of George Cabot was a creditable performance. Bancroft read it and wrote to Lodge's mother that her son's biography of his grandfather was "the most important contribution which has been made to our history for many a day."[76]

Adams had read his former assistant's *George Cabot* in proof and arranged with Godkin that he would review it in the *Nation* anonymously. He sent the review to New York in time to appear in the issue for July 5. In advance, he explained to Lodge about the review, ". . . I think it will excite interest in the book and sell the edition."

As it happened, Adams's review was both a preface to Lodge's book and a preface to the book of documents that he himself would be hastening into print. Two passages were especially relevant.

This book [Lodge's *Cabot*] is a considerable addition to the historical literature of the United States; in fact, it is a direct continuation of Mr. George Gibbs's 'Memoir of Oliver Wolcott,' which is better known as the 'History of the Administrations of Washington and Adams." Both are histories of New England Federalism, but Mr. Gibbs stopped short at the year 1801. . . . The 'Life of George Cabot' carries the story down to the extinction of Federalism in the peace of Ghent.

Mr. Lodge aims . . . at presenting his side of the picture, and, naturally, the view of his ancestor, in the most favorable light; but he writes with good temper, and, as a rule, is disposed to let his characters speak for themselves, which is a great virtue in a biographer. But, what is of more consequence, Mr. Lodge, like Mr. Gibbs, has had the courage and the honesty to conceal nothing and to print all his documents without omission or amendment.

Part of the meaning of the passages harkened back to the previous March, prior to Adams's becoming the biographer of Gallatin. At the time, Adams and Lodge had agreed to disagree about American history. As described by Adams, Lodge's views were "federalist and conservative" and Adams's views tended to "democracy and radicalism."[77]

A particular matter concerning which Lodge and Adams disagreed was the conduct of the New England Federalists after 1801. In that connection, they had collected many unpublished papers. Lodge published a selection of the papers in *The Life and Letters of*

George Cabot and did so in such a way as to maintain that the New England Federalists were blameless. What Adams wished to do was publish a volume of papers which would show that in the period 1800–1815 the same Federalists tried to divide the United States and unquestionably committed treason.

In his first letter to the Chief about the intended volume, Henry gave the impression that he might want to remove some papers from the Adams family's holdings. The Chief was happy that Henry should want to see the papers but he required that they stay within the Stone Library. He wanted the family papers "permanently fixed within these walls at least so long as I live." He added that the family papers were immense in scope and value; that he did not "know a hundredth part of what they contain."[78]

In a new letter to the Chief, Henry said he wished to publish a long-suppressed paper by John Quincy Adams relating to certain Federalists who, during the administrations of Jefferson and Madison, plotted to remove New England and New York from the Union. The Chief's impression was that the paper should stay suppressed. Yet he did not forbid Henry to publish it. He merely said, "I should like to look it over before you do."

Having mailed his letter, the Chief searched for the wanted paper, only to discover that it was lost in the vastness of the family's holdings. He could not find it.

By then the summer was well advanced and many things were happening at once. For two days in August, Henry and Clover visited at Quincy and found the wanted paper and other wanted documents.[79]

In England, Palgrave received a letter from Henry saying he planned a history of the United States when uniting, in 1800–1815. The plan struck Frank as surprising and possibly mistaken. He replied: "I don't see why you choose 1800–15 for your epoch. Surely the initial formative stage of the U. S. A. (which I suppose to be your subject) was hardly over before 1825. But I speak with diffidence."[80]

Because Gaskell at last was married, and to a very young wife, with every prospect of having children, Henry wrote to him about his own childlessness. He mainly said, ". . . if it were not that half the world will never leave the other half at peace, I should never think about the subject."

Word came from Corcoran that 1501 H Street was definitely available.[81] The Adamses began preparing for their move to Washington. They at the same time offered their Marlborough Street house for rent.

The *Nation* for August 30, 1877, contained an unsigned paragraph about Clarence King's "Catastrophism and Evolution" as printed in the August issue of the *American Naturalist*. The paragraph was written by Adams and was long and instructive. It apparently was supplied to Godkin after revisions by Emmons or perhaps by King.[82]

The paragraph was protective of King, who, Adams explained, had "hardly taken care enough to guard against misconstruction." The work of the Fortieth Parallel Survey had led its chief geologist to shift to a halfway position between Darwin and the old-style catastrophists. King had found evidence that sudden changes in environments were the great engines of evolution; that, following geological catastrophes recurring at intervals, some species died, some stayed the same, and others took new forms. This new theory, Adams said, was well-supported by the American geological record.

On September 17, the Chief sent Henry permission to publish John Quincy Adams's accusing paper. "I have just done reading over the reply to the [New England] Confederates. It is a masterly historical paper and I see no objection to its publication as such in toto. . . ."[83]

Henry arranged with Little, Brown and Company to publish his volume of documents and instantly began supplying copy to the printer. He simultaneously started to draft *The Life of Albert Gallatin*.

Four weeks later from Beverly Farms, he sent a report of progress and an account of expenses to Albert R. Gallatin. The report was businesslike. ". . . I have got so far in the preparation of your father's papers for the press that I can do no more here, and intend in three weeks to move to Washington[,] where I shall pass the winter. By the time I go from here, I hope to have all the important papers in my possession ready for the press. This leaves only the State Department, and the letters to Dallas, Crawford, Joseph H. Nicholson, Lafayette, and some few others, to be sought for." In further passages, he asked Mr. Gallatin questions about his father and missing materials. He said he would call on him in New York on November 7 in hopes of replies.

The expense account revealed that the Boston copyist had needed 1,625 sheets of paper. Adams said: "I hope this will be all I shall have to spend, but I may need a little more copying at Washington. We will try to make the publisher refund it all, but as yet I have not sounded publishers."

16

AN ENTIRELY NEW CAREER

Henry and Clover Adams arrived in Washington on November 9, 1877, and moved into 1501 H Street, a finer, larger house than the one they owned in Boston. Helped by three live-in servants, they struggled to make themselves at home. They called on the Bancrofts on November 11, the Evartses on the 14th, and Secretary of the Interior Carl Schurz on the 15th. Clover instituted five o'clock tea every day; also Sunday letters to her father. In the earliest that survives, she remarked: "We strut round as if we were millionaires. Henry says for the first time in his life he feels like a gentleman."

Henry's words reflected his being settled at last in a Washington house. Clover did not warn her father not to quote them. She instead encouraged him to show her bulletins to Henry's mother. But Boston was full of people waiting for news of the vagrant couple who had moved to Washington. When Clover's letter had been shared, talked about, construed, and reconstrued, a story would take hold in Boston that Henry was speaking disparagingly of Massachusetts and Bostonians.

Soon Henry walked to the State Department, recently moved to a new building adjacent to the White House. He came as biographer-editor of Gallatin, and his requests for documents accorded with the role. He wrote to Lodge, "I find a mass of new Gallatin matter in the Jefferson papers and am burrowing in rich soil."

Secretary Evarts knew that Adams's needs, though initially limited to Gallatin matter, extended to all matter in possession of the government that might assist completion of a history of the United States in the era of Presidents Jefferson and Madison. Evarts must have relayed his knowledge to his aides, for Adams found the department "magnificently hospitable." He was given space and a desk. He gained access to all the records of the executive branch that might help to underpin his work.[1] He similarly was afforded lifelong delivery and return of desired materials via regular wagon by the Library of Congress.[2]

It bears repeating that Adams had strong motives to return to Washington. On November 25, he wrote to Gaskell that he had started "an entirely new career." ". . . we have made a great leap in the world; cut loose at once from all that has occupied us . . . and caught new ties and occupations. . . . Our water-colors and drawings go with us wherever we go, and here are our great evidence of individuality, and our title to authority."

In terms that might seem extravagant, Henry claimed for himself and Clover the distinction of being the first twentieth-century Americans. Onlookers, he said, were watching them with puzzlement, like Alice in Wonderland.[3] "As I belong to the class of people who . . . believe that in another century [the United States] . . . will be saying . . . the last word of civilisation, I enjoy the expectation of the coming day, and try to imagine that I am myself, with my fellow *gelehrte* here, the first faint rays of that great light which is to dazzle and set the world on fire hereafter. Our duties are perhaps only those of twinkling, and many people here, like little Alice, wonder what we're at. But twinkle for twinkle, I prefer our kind to that of the small politician."

Small politicians included President Hayes and Secretaries Evarts and Schurz. But Henry and Clover showed no intention to criticize the country's official leaders. They proposed to be good citizens. In that spirit, they attended a White House reception on November 30.

To all appearances, Henry was no longer a politician. He told Gaskell, ". . . I am avowedly out of politics. . . ." He remarked to Lodge, "Of politics I keep quite clear, but hear a good deal of it." He and Clover especially heard politics from Secretary Schurz. "We met him again on Friday evening at the White House, and he insisted on our going home with him to smoke a cigar. . . ."

A particular action seemed to prove that Henry had become a mere biographer and historian. In the third week of December, Clover accompanied him to the State Department and helped him manage bales of letters by Gallatin, mostly to Jefferson and Madison.

Simultaneously the public learned from the December 13 *Nation* that "Little, Brown & Company have in press a collection of original papers relating to early New England Federalism and Secession, with notes by Prof. Henry Adams." The volume was appearing at Adams's expense.[4] He had asked that his name not appear on the cover. He thought it sufficient that the title page should bear the words "*Documents Relating to New-England Federalism./ 1800–1815./* Edited by Henry Adams."

Copies reached him on December 20 and showed that Little, Brown & Company had disregarded his request. Wanting the book to seem a near match of Lodge's *Life and Letters of George Cabot*, the firm had lettered the backstrip "*New-England Federalism/ 1800–1815/* Henry Adams."[5] Furious, Adams asked the firm to bind the remaining copies in covers omitting his name. Yet he used the specimens already bound. While Little, Brown sent the book to a list of persons he had provided, he gave Bancroft a copy and distributed copies to other persons.[6]

New England Federalism (the title as spelled in the page headings) was the first book published solely under Henry Adams's name. Judged by cover, title page, and table of contents, the book was uninviting. The text and appendix contained nothing but documents very slightly annotated. A four-page Preface began, "This volume has no controversial purpose."[7] It mainly said: "So far as the editor is concerned, his object has been, not to join in an argument, but to stimulate, if possible, a new generation in our universities and elsewhere, by giving them a new interest in their work and new material to digest."[8]

The thrice-repeated word was "new." The Preface closed with place and date, "Washington, November 29, 1877." Place and date had meaning. Affixed to Washington three weeks after Adams's return, *New England Federalism* was the starting point of his entirely new career.

Just as Adams had supplied the *Nation* an unsigned notice of Lodge's *Life and Letters of George Cabot*, Lodge supplied the *Nation* an unsigned notice of Adams's book of documents. The notice said that the book, although of course historical, was also literary and succeeded admirably as drama. "A collection of historical documents can rarely be called dramatic, but this term may be very fitly applied to [*New England Federalism*]. . . . In the political drama that is here unfolded[,] the various personages tell severally their own stories in their own language, state their own opinions, and reveal their own characters, while the editor preserves as scrupulous an impersonality as the most finished playwright."[9]

The comment was insufficient. *New England Federalism* is not a mere edited compilation. It is an organized book written by collecting and intelligently arranging related writings by various persons. The *montage* is very large. The text and an appendix fill 426 pages.

The text presents ten documents (some containing sub-documents) involving thirty-odd persons as writers and recipients. The appendix presents fifty-three letters involving nineteen additional persons as writers and recipients. The actors in the drama thus total more than fifty.

Adams's disclaimers notwithstanding, the book is the work of a still-active politician. Its contents turn on an error made by Thomas Jefferson six months before he died. In 1825, John Quincy Adams was president and Henry Clay was secretary of state. Virginia's politicians were sharply divided. Those supporting President Adams could be described as belonging to the school of George Washington and Chief Justice John Marshall of the Supreme Court, then still on the bench. Those opposing President Adams stood to gain if they could present themselves to the public as the political heirs of Jefferson. One of the latter was William B. Giles. In the early years of the century, when Jefferson was president, Giles had been a senator from Virginia much in contact with Senator J. Q. Adams of Massachusetts. On December 15, 1825, Giles wrote to Jefferson requesting information concerning what he called Adams's "pretended conversion" in 1808 from Federalism to Democratic-Republicanism. In the same letter, he asked Jefferson's opinion of the national program of "internal improvements"—mainly great roads and canals—newly proposed by President Adams.[10]

Jefferson's error was a two-faced response. On December 25, he sent Giles a letter in which he tried to recall a visit by Senator Adams to the White House in 1808. Complimentary to Adams but confused in its facts, the letter was written for publication. And on December 26, Jefferson sent Giles a letter highly critical of Adams's national scheme of internal improvements. The second letter was confidential.[11]

Giles perfidiously withheld the December 25 letter, written for publication and complimentary to J. Q. Adams. He waited till well after Jefferson died and in September 1827 published in the *Richmond Enquirer* the portion of the confidential December 26 letter that would injure Adams as president and undercut his planned improvements.

The perfidy was detected. Thirteen months later, Archibald Stuart, a Virginian supportive of President Adams, wrote to Jefferson's grandson, Thomas Jefferson Randolph, asking for the text of the letter complimentary to Adams. Thomas Randolph obliged, and Stuart published the letter in the *Staunton Spectator*.

Currently Giles was governor of Virginia. On October 21,

1828, he wrote a defense of his conduct to the editors of the *Richmond Enquirer* and appended the text of his original letter to Jefferson. The editors published the communications. President Adams meanwhile had seen Jefferson's complimentary December 25 letter about him in the *Staunton Spectator*. Because in the letter Jefferson described as simultaneous events separated by as much as five years, Adams wrote a clarification, worded as written *for* the president, not *by* him.

The clarification appeared in the *National Intelligencer* on October 21, 1828. It gave details about the only meeting that Adams had ever had with Jefferson when president. It itemized the confusions into which Jefferson had fallen in his December 25 letter. And incidentally it spoke of designs by several New England Federalists to separate the New England states and others from the Union in the period 1804–1815. It said that President Adams possessed documentary evidence of these designs, but not evidence sufficient to prevail in a court of law.[12]

The clarification drew fire from both Virginia and Massachusetts. On October 24, 1828, Governor Giles supplied the *Richmond Enquirer* a fulminating missive attacking President Adams's "Washington Exposé." Soon after, thirteen Massachusetts Federalists and sons of deceased Federalists sent a letter to the president demanding, first, that he *name* the leaders said in the White House statement to have intended disunion and the creation of a Northern confederacy, and, second, that he produce his evidence.

Replying on December 30, Adams refused to give the names or produce the evidence. Thereupon twelve of the thirteen signers—or "confederates," as Adams came to term them—published an *Appeal to the Citizens of the United States*. Dated January 28, 1829, the *Appeal* branded the president a false accuser.

So things stood five weeks later when Adams left the presidency, making way for Andrew Jackson. Rather than return to Massachusetts, Adams stayed in Washington, assembled materials, and started a paper addressed "To the Citizens of the United States." As he wrote, the ex-president learned that his eldest son, George Washington Adams, had disappeared from the steamboat *Benjamin Franklin* while traveling from Boston to the capital. George's suicide reduced his parents to extremities of shock and grief.[13] Yet the father persisted in writing his "reply to the appeal of the confederates."[14] Finished in Washington, the reply was a documented argument which, if printed, would require as many as 250 book-sized pages. Two causes prevented its publication. Advisers read the manuscript and urged the ex-president to suppress it. Simultaneously his neighbors elected him to Congress, with the effect that he began an entirely new career.

When J. Q. Adams died, in 1848, his suppressed reply was stored among the family papers. In 1850, William Plumer, an acquaintance of the Adamses in New Hampshire, began a biography of his father, also named William Plumer, who in the time of President Jefferson had been a senator from New Hampshire on close terms with Senator Adams. To help him write the biography, C. F. Adams gave the younger Plumer "free use" of the reply "in manuscript."

Plumer apparently was lent a duplicate. At the time, twelve-year-old Henry Adams was an experienced copyist of documents. One may assume he made the copy for Mr. Plumer and then recovered it as his personal property, for the assumption would account for three controlling facts. Henry at some early date became possessor of a copy; he was the only Adams deeply interested in getting the reply into print; and he rather assumed he had a right to publish it.[15]

The Life of William Plumer was published in Boston in 1857, while Henry was an undergraduate at Harvard. Nothing further was done with J. Q. Adams's reply till the 1870s. When engaged on *The Life and Letters of George Cabot*, Henry Cabot Lodge was given free use of the paper in manuscript. It is impossible to escape the inference that he studied it, not in the handwriting of John Quincy Adams, but as copied by Henry Adams in 1850 or soon after.[16]

Henry Adams planned *New England Federalism* almost as a trap. The book starts with documents tending to create a strong impression that John Quincy Adams when president was indeed a false accuser. It continues with the ex-president's long reply. It ends with an appendix of letters substantiating everything in the reply that a reader might have doubted could be substantiated.

J. Q. Adams was a first-class thinker who had detailed knowledge of the "political drama" (his term) that he intended to disclose.[17] Also Adams was a matchless speaker, inspiring in knowledge, frankness, and love of country, terrifying in his dismemberment of opponents' assertions and characters. In 1829, meaning to controvert beyond answer both Giles in Virginia and the confederates in Massachusetts, he wrote a concise history of the United States from 1799 to 1829 and detailed within it a history of the New England Federalists from 1800 to 1815.[18] He so fashioned these histories that each matter he thought relevant was attended to in full.[19] His pages drew heavily on literary works. He quoted a couplet from Pope's *Essay on Man*:

> Truths would you teach, or save a sinking land,
> All fear, none aid you, and few understand.

He linked his histories to *Paradise Lost*, pointing to the safe escape of lone Abdiel from Satan's legions; also to the paradise of fools. He included five borrowings from *Hamlet*, four from *Othello*, others from *Macbeth*, *Measure for Measure*, *As You Like It*, and *A Midsummer Night's Dream*.[20] These inclusions did not enter his text as grace notes or filigrees. They reflected what the orator was doing. Single-handedly, against both Southern detractors and Northern secessionists and their heirs, Adams was fighting for the Union.

In one respect, as finished in 1829, the reply was ill-adapted to publication in 1877. Writing as a speaker, J. Q. Adams used words to make ideas *hearable*. His address, if delivered in parts on three successive days, might have fallen on the ear as clear, convincing, and not too long. Yet if printed for absorption through the eye, the same address would overstrain the patience even of readers for whom the pages had gripping interest. In this unusual and limited sense, the grandfather—in Henry's words—was "a bad writer."[21]

When completing *New England Federalism*, Henry took some liberties. Since his grandfather's paper lacked a title, he supplied one: *Reply to the Appeal of the Massachusetts Federalists*. Also he abbreviated the argument. Using the excuse that J. Q. Adams attacked Harrison Gray Otis with a severity that became "merely personal," he made four considerable cuts—each duly indicated. The cuts reduced the *Reply* to readable length and if possible increased its force.[22]

What made *New England Federalism* a complete success was Henry's efforts as a researcher. He matched his grandfather in seriousness by obtaining a large array of relevant contemporary papers. Artfully coordinated in the same volume, the papers permitted the *Reply* to speak its message and be confirmed by the adversaries it denounced.[23]

Bancroft welcomed Adams's book of documents on its stated terms, as fresh material. He wrote to his neighbor on December 22, 1877:

> I began reading the volume before five this morning. . . . The "reply" to the "appeal" is written with masterly ability, self-possession, & forbearance. . . .
> To me your volume is intensely interesting, & no one can write the

history of the administrations of Jefferson & Madison without using
[it]. . . . [24]

For most readers, *New England Federalism* would have a different
value. It was not enough to say with Bancroft that it was interesting
and indispensable, nor to say with Lodge that it qualified as drama.
The book was a national event—mere print but none the less an
event.

In the Union of which Rutherford B. Hayes was president,
Henry and Marian Adams were politicians exerting strong influence by unusual, unofficial means. The couple's arrival in Washington added an informal governing power to the executive, legisla-
tive, and judicial powers already emplaced in the capital. The
Adamses would not rule, nor even impose. Clover would welcome
visitors at daily tea; she and Henry would give dinners for six or
eight; and endlessly they would listen to political talk. These
inoffensive proceedings would themselves affect the country's politics. Yet also the proceedings would be accompaniments to a series
of widely-spaced, important acts. *New England Federalism* was the
first act of the series. It struck hard, and it was signed.[25]

In its pages, a great politician long dead and a great politician
fully alive combined to change the balances in American life and
politics. The means employed was full disclosure of histories till
then concealed and brazenly denied. J. Q. Adams and Henry
Adams unitedly showed the public that efforts to disintegrate the
Union were mounted early by American politicians, were mounted
in attempted concert with the British government, were overthrown at great cost and by narrow margins, and were overthrown
most effectually by Americans capable of rescuing the Union from
threatened or actual civil or foreign war by successes in diplomacy
and international accommodation. Henry showed especially that
the sin of the *South* against the Union had earlier been the sin of
New England against the Union. In 1877, this revelation was revelation. It annihilated received opinion established during eight decades by false apologists.

For almost all Americans in 1877, United States history was
misty. It was something that had happened and left impressions,
but the impressions were largely shaped by accidents of memory
and imagination.

Differently, Henry Adams began as a possessor of inside knowledge. Exploiting the advantage of being an Adams, he had learned
all the United States history he *could* learn with the help of that
advantage. The knowledge he thus acquired had value far exceed-

ing what an outsider might expect. His *New England Federalism* was evidence of the value. Page by page, the book was richer in data and ideas than any other book relating to United States history that had appeared until that time.

For Adams, inside knowledge became a matter of great concern. He early realized that United States history was a house containing many secret rooms. While learning secret history as known to the Adamses, he had learned to think he should gain access to other secret histories. His obtaining the papers of Albert Gallatin gave him *Gallatin's* inside knowledge—knowledge complementary to the Adamses'. But his gain did not stop there. By virtue of his sweeping arrangement with Gallatin's son, he became a surrogate Gallatin. This extraordinary status entitled him to the inside knowledge possessed by the leaders with whom Albert Gallatin had shared the reins of power, beginning with Thomas Jefferson, James Madison, and James Monroe, but extending to Aaron Burr, John Randolph, and lesser figures.

While still at Beverly Farms, Adams had written for help to Hugh Blair Grigsby, president of the Virginia Historical Society, and, at Grigsby's suggestion, to William Wirt Henry, the biographer of Patrick Henry, and Sarah N. Randolph, a great-granddaughter of Jefferson. He told William Wirt Henry, ". . . I shall be very grateful for any information you can furnish me . . . regarding . . . any portion of Mr[.] Gallatin's career. . . ." He added that Gallatin's career involved "all the secret history of the Administrations of Jefferson and Madison, much of which, if known anywhere, can be only known in Virginia."[26]

Once settled in Washington, Adams extended his inquiries in person. His intention was far-reaching. Whether through official or private doors, he hoped to enter every important secret room of United States history in the period 1800–1815.[27]

While wanting access to evidence, Adams also wanted to shape his readership. Each of his books was designed to reach an audience of predetermined character. *New England Federalism* was so devised as to be available to concerned readers, closed to casual readers. He separated the concerned from the casual by means of a documentary barrier. He placed at the start of the volume some noxious, brambly letters by Giles which even at their clearest were deucedly hard to read.

A month's work at the State Department sufficed for Adams to plan and start a three-part project. He meant to round out his Gallatin inquiries and complete the promised Gallatin publications.

He meant to acquire and organize a powerful array of Jefferson's papers, till then largely secret. And he meant to do the same in relation to Madison's papers. The three tasks were best advanced concurrently.

On December 24, 1877, he sent a first instalment of *The Life of Albert Gallatin* to Albert R. Gallatin in New York. Later published as "Book I.—Youth. 1761–1790," the instalment was a twelfth of the *Life* as finished. It contained many letters in French, including some written by Gallatin to persons in his native Geneva. Several of the letters were by Voltaire. Adams did not translate the French letters. He offered four reasons: ". . . that it is always a little impertinent to suggest that one's readers are ignorant of French . . . ; that . . . most of this class of readers do understand it; that a translation requires a great deal of labor and will occupy much space; and finally that I have my doubts whether the man who thinks he can translate [Voltaire] . . . is not a little of a fool." Of course, the French letters were akin to the brambly letters by Giles that Adams had placed at the start of *New England Federalism*. In the new case as in the old, he intruded a barrier to casual reading.

What mattered was the motive that led Adams to intrude both barriers. The principal motive was a desire not to spoil his work. He was reasoning backwards from an anticipated occurrence he considered all-important. He assumed that his *History of the United States* would disclose the story most deserving of the nation's notice. In intention, the book would be the basis for a new American confidence in America, grounded in what Americans in fact accomplished in the past. To assure the story's being noticed by the nation generally, he wanted the volumes of his *History* to achieve the widest possible circulation. Wide circulation would be likelier if no other book preempted the field by disclosing a similar story or a story that *mistakenly* could be assumed to be the same.

In his *Reply to the Appeal of the Massachusetts Federalists*, John Quincy Adams disclosed a story Henry Adams thought invaluable. Henry agreed with it. Yet the grandfather's disclosure was based on minimum information. Its reach was relatively narrow. And it was simply not the story that the grandson would disclose in his intended *History*. All interests would thus be served if J. Q. Adams's eruptive *Reply* was assured a heedful and influential audience, but not a large one.

The Life of Albert Gallatin could not escape being also a history of the United States from 1789 to 1849 and more especially a history of the United States from 1800 to 1815. But Henry Adams in 1877 was not ready to write that history. He was still in the stage of gathering and organizing data. Whole areas of the subject were new to him.[28] Also his ideas in some respects were unsettled and changing. This was especially the case with regard to the history of American political parties and the question whether they were matters of serious importance to the nation's historians. These uncertainties were sure to show themselves in the *Life* and would injure it as history.[29]

It none the less was likely that, if read narrowly for what it said concerning Gallatin, the *Life* would be a truthful and moving book.[30] It occurred to Adams, too, that the *Life* could be a vehicle for the publication of documents. If very heavily freighted with letters not included in *The Writings of Albert Gallatin*, the biography would have the function of a documentary supplement.[31]

The moral of these considerations was that Adams knew what he was doing. He mainly was looking forward to writing and publishing a great book, his *History of the United States*, in which barriers would have no part. Through the sale and reading of that one book, he meant to bring about a new understanding of how the nation came into being. This new understanding would rest on fact and would replace an old understanding largely floated on hopeful fiction. The new understanding would give the nation its rightful past.

He meanwhile confidently expected that the younger Gallatin would approve the first instalment of the *Life*. In his letter to the son, he looked forward to an interval of hard labor. The second instalment, "Book II.—The Legislature. 1789–1801," would concern Gallatin's rise from obscurity in Western Pennsylvania to leadership of the Democratic-Republicans in the House of Representatives. It would disclose his securing the presidency for Jefferson (deflecting Burr) in the electoral crisis of 1801. It would end when Gallatin's becoming secretary of the treasury was imminent. Though easy to outline, Book II would be hard to write. It necessarily would be long. (As published it would fill 188 large pages.) Accordingly Adams warned Albert R. Gallatin that his progress would be slow and difficult.

The life that Henry and Clover led in Washington was agreeable but set them a serious problem. When they were only two Sundays in the capital, Clover received an unwelcome visitor. She told her father: "Mrs. Berry[,] a most intimate friend of the great Conkling[,] popped in offering to take me to church. I gravely said I was tired & thought *today* I would not go."

Clover's answer was a fib. She meant to go to church on no Sundays whatever. And meanwhile there was a question, How might she best break the news to other Washingtonians? Half-humorously, she continued to her father: "I must get a platform to stand on. . . . I think I'd best announce that I'm a Buddist (*sic*) or a Mormon[,] the Washington females are such church goers."

Neither she nor Henry wished to say so publicly, but Clover already had a platform, that of being an agnostic. Her intending not to go to church was an honest consequence of disbelief. She knew her own mind and knew very well what she wanted not to do. It was easily foreseen, however, that in Washington her not attending church would make her a sinner against the norm, a Hester Prynne, or worse. If her situation became precarious, Henry would want to lend support. Understanding the seriousness of the issue, he would seek effectual means of suggesting she go ahead and disbelieve.

In early January 1878, Henry, Clover, or both received from Boston an accusatory letter. Because a great many letters are missing, the episode can be reconstructed in most respects but not in all.[32]

The importance of the accusation centered in its indicating that the Adamses who had newly moved to Washington were being watched from afar by persons who were angry and disposed to criticize. On January 6, Clover told her father: "I want you to be very careful in quoting anything I say in my letters. I try my best not to commit myself, but this week a most annoying *pin* 500 miles long[,] twisted & sharpened[,] has come in a letter from Boston. I may have said to you that we found this house charming but as we are not used to such fine quarters Henry 'never felt like a gentleman before.' That as I say returns as a long sharp *pin*[,] & one would suppose Henry was a fool from the new interpretation put on it."

Clover's anxiety was intensified by fear of her cousin by marriage, the one-time wife of Senator Sumner. It did not help that Alice earlier had won a divorce. She had returned to Boston and was seeing Dr. Hooper. Clover advised: "Above all things please never quote a word or syllable to Alice Mason. Her tongue is a weapon which cuts right & left[,] & I am cowardly enough to stand even at this distance in terror of it!"

Dr. Hooper assumed that Brooks Adams was the person who had shot the twisted pin. On Sunday, January 13, Clover corrected him, ruling out that particular Adams. "Your answer to my pin complaint came in due course. You do *Brooks* injustice. He is far too busy & loyal to *nag* his absent relatives. I doubt if he even knows where we are. Tell him if you meet him that we are hoping for a visit from him some day."

That same Sunday, writing to the Chief, Henry alluded to the accusatory letter. (His letter is missing, but its drift can be inferred.) C. F. Adams knew what the accusation was. He thought it true. In the harshest Adams style, he replied, "If you do not like Massachusetts and its population, you are under no obligation whatever to stay there."

Henry shortly countered that there had been a misunderstanding. In his next letter, the Chief retreated enough to say: "With regard to the little matter touching accidental reports of words ascribed to you, which you disavow, I was very glad to find that they had no foundation in fact. As such I dismiss it."[33]

The trouble appeared to end. It in fact would grow worse. Evidently Charles was the accuser and, though Henry was the accused, the person wished more to suffer was his possibly more vulnerable wife.

All of Henry and Clover's new activities were undertaken within the framework of a plan. They were allowing two winters at 1501 H Street and two summers at Beverly Farms for Henry to speed his three-part project centering in Gallatin, Jefferson, and Madison. In September 1879, they would go to Europe and Henry would attempt a more difficult project: gaining access to the records of the English, French, and Spanish governments. There seemed no necessity to change the plan, but Henry was amazingly efficient and might get ahead of schedule.

It helped that the State Department was nearby and he could walk there in minutes. Arrangements at home encouraged work. Clover's teas ended promptly at six. Henry either joined the assemblies towards the end of the hour or did not appear.

Clarence King came for dinner in December and thereafter returned whenever possible, sometimes taking a room. His *Systematic Geology* was nearing publication, and he was saying that his next project would be "the great American novel."[34] The announcement was a joke, yet not a joke. In prospect, his boasted novel could seem very real.

Relatives who visited, one excepted, were not disturbing. Edward Hooper came soonest. Alice Hooper, a cousin not to be confused with Alice Mason, arrived in February. Dr. Hooper came in April. Charles eventually appeared for meals and briefly was a sleep-in guest.

Clover's visitors at tea were sometimes as many as twenty. She invited them on a basis of affection. They might be female or male, old or young, American or foreign, but the feeling they met on entering was a feeling they also brought. Her house was an affectionate house the affectionate greatly liked.

To conduct affectionate teas and friendly dinners in the national capital meant taking risks. ". . . in this social vortex," Clover wrote, "one has to steer gingerly—tack[,] reef & at times scuttle one's ship." Being perpetually at the center of things exercised her keenest as well as her kindest qualities. Often keenness and kindness were simultaneous in her expressions. John Hay had married Clara Stone, a Cleveland heiress. He brought her to Washington and introduced her to the Adamses. Clover reported to her father about the Hays: "Mrs. Hay is a handsome woman—very—but never speaks. He chats for two."

It was evident that Henry and Clover were Unionists of the deepest dye, enemies of aristocracy, and political and moral democrats. Yet no guests were happier to see them than well-placed Virginians. Sarah Randolph came to dinner. Clover judged her to be about forty—"nice-looking[,] bright & chatty." It came out that Sarah and her sisters kept a boarding school for girls. Clover continued: "She lives in a fox hunting country & herself follows the hounds. Think of a pretty foxhunting schoolmistress!"

A favorite friend was Senator Lamar of Mississippi. At dinner on February 13, 1878, he and Henry discovered they had both been in the House of Commons fifteen years earlier when John Bright vanquished Arthur Roebuck in debate. The discovery made them faster friends.

Spring came very early. Accompanied by Boojum, the Adamses reveled in long walks. On February 21, seeking flowers in the woods, Henry found opening hepaticas and budding arbutus.

A surprise visitor, Wayne MacVeagh, "dropped in for tea & talk" on February 27. Clover reported: "He is Simon Cameron's son in law but rejects the family principles or want of principles & stands as an out & out independent. . . ." Like no one else in American politics, MacVeagh had a gift for making other politicians absorb unwanted news. Skeptical at first, Clover said, ". . . [he] is believed to have much influence with Hayes & if he really says to him *half* the things he 'says he says' the White House must[,] when he is in it at least[,] be a palace of truth."

❖ ❖ ❖

It has been mentioned that in Washington in 1868 Henry had found a friend in Richard Taylor, son of President Zachary Taylor—also brother-in-law of President Jefferson Davis and a Confederate lieutenant general. Early in 1878, General Taylor paid the Adamses a visit. Perhaps because of his easy manner, Clover began by underestimating him. She wrote on March 3, "He is pleasant in his way but a light weight for a man who has commanded armies & led national councils." Acquaintance changed her estimate. Soon the general was one of her tea-time regulars.

A generation older than Henry and Clover, Taylor was the representative of the Confederacy most remarkable for education, wit, and powers of mind. His record in the Rebellion had been exemplary. Originally a sharer of the campaigns of Stonewall Jackson, he later directed winning battles against superior Union forces in the trans-Mississippi theater. At war's end, he commanded all the Confederate forces in the Department of Alabama, Mississippi, and East Louisiana. When he began his visits to the Adamses, he was finishing a personal narrative, *Destruction and Reconstruction*, later considered the best of all Confederate memoirs. While continuing to write his book, he learned of Henry's *New England Federalism*, read it with concern, and changed his views.[35]

That the general constantly reappeared at Clover's teas and profited by reading Henry's book had more-than-private meanings. Taylor's actions showed recognition of two realities. He understood that Henry was such an Adams as there had never previously been, simply the greatest of the breed, and that Clover was Henry's match.[36]

Possibly, of the two, Clover was the better. Marrying the greatest Adams and moving with him to Washington were very dangerous things to do. She had been brave enough to do them. How she conducted herself in Washington was a public matter. As Marian Adams, the name she used to sign her notes and letters, she was someone to be noticed. Taylor said to her that her teas were her "salon." Men attended as often as women. Her parlor was the country's active center. In all the Union, there was no comparable place for company and introductions, or even for the news.

On April Fool's Day, 1878, Henry and Clover led a party of seven to a 10:00 A.M. boat, steamed down the Potomac to Mount Vernon, were shown many rooms of Washington's house, and picnicked on the grass.[37] For the Adamses, the excursion was the first of three.

On May 9–11, they went to Edgehill, Virginia, near Charlottesville, and passed two days with Sarah Randolph. The purpose of the trip was to permit a great-granddaughter of Thomas Jefferson to escort a great-grandson of John Adams through Monticello. A notable occasion, it was Henry's only visit to Jefferson's residence.[38]

Gallatin too had a house. When nineteen, he exchanged the safety of Geneva, Switzerland, for the opportunities and dangers of the American wilderness. At the first chance, he built Friendship Hill on the banks of the Monongahela. Leaving Washington on May 13, Henry and Clover journeyed to Western Pennsylvania, saw the house, doubled back to New York, and proceeded to Beverly Farms to pass the summer.

Writing in his study at Pitch Pine Hill on May 30, Henry reviewed for Gaskell his and Clover's first season in Washington. "We have had a very cheerful winter. . . . I have worked hard and with good effect. My wife has helped me and has had a house always amusing and interesting. . . . Our little dinners of six and eight were as pleasant as any I ever was at even in London. And Washington has one advantage over other capitals, that a single house counts for more than half a dozen elsewhere; there are so few of them."

Boxes of Gallatin, Jefferson, and Madison papers arrived. Henry wrote to Bancroft on June 7, ". . . I am at work again, to my great joy." He was assembling Jefferson documents chronologically in volumes.[39] He simultaneously was hastening towards the completion of his Gallatin volumes, three of the *Writings*, one for the *Life*. The pace he set was fast. He reported to Gaskell on June 18 that he was writing "ten hours a day, till my mind is scoured like a kitchen copper."

Because President Hayes had pledged in 1876 that he would not seek a second term, the question before the country in 1878 was the election of his successor in 1880. Swarms of Republicans were poised to secure the presidency for Blaine. Other swarms were boosting Grant.

Adams had been saying to Lodge that the best course for the Independents for the time being was not to make an effort. On August 7, 1878, he assured his one-time assistant that the voters were tired of elections and "glad to repose under Mr[.] Hayes's respectable nullity." Perhaps on an impulse, he added several remarks. He said he was "a Grant man," but not "publicly." He said his one concern was the "democratic nomination" and he would be abroad when the Democratic candidate was chosen. He ended, "Presidential elections make me sick."

The remarks required translation. Henry was a Grant man to the extent of thinking Grant not as bad as Blaine, but he would say nothing publicly *as Henry Adams*. He did care about a nomination—the *Republican* nomination; and he intended to leave for Europe in 1879 and still be there in 1880 when the *Republicans* nominated their candidate. And presidential elections were making him sick because of the continued possibility that Blaine would be elected.

Henry and Clover had an elderly friend at Beverly Farms, a widow, Mary Dwight Parkman, who could be trusted with a secret and possibly give advice. They told her about Henry's *Democracy* and its chances of harming Blaine. Evidently, too, they asked her whether they could risk its anonymous publication after having lived in a Washington house with which the novel had connections. There is no evidence that Mrs. Parkman read the manuscript, only that she was told about it. She apparently urged publication.

That same day, August 7, 1878, Henry wrote informatively to Cunliffe: ". . . I am . . . straining my weary muscles to put four bulky volumes onto the tired world next year, and then we mean to cross the Atlantic again. I must grub in Foreign Office papers in London, Paris, Madrid, perhaps even St[.] Petersburg. We shall probably take a house in London during the spring of 1880, while I burrow for papers."

The obvious best strategy when seeking permission to read and copy old diplomatic papers in European archives with a view to their publication would be to begin by seeking British permission and, if successful, make that gain a basis for asking French and Spanish permissions. The strategy was easy to choose but hard to carry out. The British government—in Henry's words—was "very close about its papers." It was closer still about papers dating since 1799, meaning precisely the sort of papers that Henry wished to get.

Sir Edward Thornton was still the British minister in Washington. The Adamses knew him, but very slightly, having been kept at a remove by a bad impression of his wife.

The British official empowered to grant the permission Adams wanted was the foreign secretary, Lord Salisbury. On August 21, Henry asked Gaskell to assist him. ". . . the whole object of my journey is to study the diplomatic correspondence of the three governments, in regard to America, during the time of Napoleon, from 1800 to 1812. Unless I can get this object, I shall throw away my trouble, and so I am straining every nerve to open in advance the doors of three Foreign Offices. I shall come with an official letter from this Department of State, and shall ask Sir Edward

Thornton to give me another. But if you ever see the Salisburys, you might facilitate my movements by sounding for me there. I am afraid that Salisbury has such a suspicious temperament that he will hardly grant such a favor. . . ."

By mail in August, Henry negotiated with J. B. Lippincott in Philadelphia to publish *The Writings* and *The Life of Albert Gallatin.* The four volumes would run to 3,000 pages. He foresaw a winter mostly given to correcting proofs.

Whether by accident or design, the choice of Lippincott as the publisher of the Gallatin volumes placed Henry in juxtaposition with his father. The same house had published the Chief's twenty-four volumes relating to John Adams and John Quincy Adams.

Perhaps by accident, two invitations placed Henry and his father side by side within a book. A Boston institution, the New England Historic Genealogical Society, had been given a fund to support the publication of short biographies of its deceased members. The biographies would appear in annual volumes. Of the deceased members, the most distinguished were John Quincy Adams and Albert Gallatin, and the persons invited to write their biographies were Charles Francis Adams and Henry Adams. When published in the inaugural volume of *Memorial Biographies,* the father and son's contributions would appear on an equal footing.

For their second winter in Washington, Henry and Clover planned a change from walks to rides. In addition, Henry would begin to teach himself proficiency in reading Spanish.

In Massachusetts, they bought a fine horse, Prince, for Clover. They started south on October 28, saw much of Clarence King in New York, and proceeded on November 2 to Washington. There Henry received—in Clover's words—"a charming little bay mare sent up by Miss Randolph." They named her Daisy, possibly in honor of Henry James's recent success, *Daisy Miller,* a short novel. Both Adamses had read the story. Henry thought it "very clever."

Clover was glad to be back in Washington. She mentioned that she and Henry were living "à la Noah's Ark"— two Adamses, two men servants, two women servants, two horses, and a limit of two dogs. Their plan was to ride in the morning. ". . . Henry can get six solid hours of work between noon & dinner." Clover as usual would have daily teas at 5:00. Dinners would be at 8:00.

With regard to his novel, King had asked James Osgood, "Are you going to publish it?"[40] But the novel was postponed. A plan was devised to merge several geological surveys into a U. S. Geological Survey within the Department of the Interior. King wanted the appointment as the agency's first director. Adams would lobby in favor of the agency and King's appointment, and King would be much in Washington. Clover was delighted. "No one," she said, "is so good company."

Prince was too powerful and spirited for Clover, so she and Henry traded mounts. It happened that on November 30 Henry was required to attend a burial. The deceased, General Buchanan, a relative of Louisa Catherine Adams, had resided in the capital. Like Aunt Smith, he would be buried in Rock Creek Cemetery. Clover went with Henry to the burial by carriage and thought the cemetery "a beautiful place." Next day on horseback, she and Henry went again to the cemetery and by chance had "a curious chat with a handsome gay old gravedigger who came to this country as page to Fanny Elssler & lived before that with the Grotes in London." The experience was curious because Shakespearean. It ran parallel to *Hamlet*.

Taylor's *Destruction and Reconstruction* would be published in New York by D. Appleton and Company and would appear in the spring of 1879. It would not mention Adams. Clues in the opening paragraphs, however, would coordinate the book with Adams's *New England Federalism*, his *Life of Albert Gallatin*, and even his future *History*.[41]

Early in 1879, Adams wrote a Preface for *The Writings of Albert Gallatin* explaining the plan of the work. Volumes I and II contained otherwise inaccessible letters by and to Gallatin. (Counting enclosures, they totaled about 700 documents.) Volume III contained "such essays and publications of Mr. Gallatin as are believed to have historical value and are not easily to be found even in public libraries."

The plan showed determination to give inquirers large quantities of Gallatin resources while giving was possible. The plan was prescient; for Gallatin's papers, when Adams was done with them, would be held indefinitely in locked storage.[42]

The Report of the Fortieth Parallel Survey was issued by the Government Printing Office in tomes even bulkier than Adams's Gallatin volumes. The tomes were printed, not in numerical order, but as soon as finished. King's *Systematic Geology*—Volume I—had appeared late in 1878, was three inches thick and a foot tall, weighed eight pounds, and was richly illustrated, partly in color. A review was wanted by the *Nation*. Adams offered Godkin an anonymous review, was urged to send it, and wrote it with King's advice and in his presence.[43]

The King review was clear, full, and informative. Adams took pains to suggest the great range of evidence the Fortieth Parallel Survey had mapped and analyzed. "Here . . . is a systematic section, covering . . . some eight hundred miles of contiguous mountain ranges, and disclosing all the broader divisions of geological time through not less than 125,000 feet, or more than twenty-two miles thickness, of visible sedimentary deposits." He named the qualities most to be valued in a geologist. "Hitherto every geological report has been a geological itinerary without generalization or arrangement." "The most satisfactory part of Mr. King's work, next to its scientific thoroughness, is the breadth of view which embraces in one field the correlation of . . . extended forces, and the vigor of grasp with which the author handles so large a subject without allowing himself to be crushed by details."

To their surprise, the Adamses were invited by Sir Edward Thornton to make a wintry trip to Niagara Falls, beginning on January 13. Clover would have refused. Henry accepted. A considerable party was assembled. One of the guests was a young Miss Anne Palmer of New York whom Clover had met the previous winter and thought "very charming." Another was Charles Trevelyan, an English visitor the Adamses had known earlier and greatly liked.[44] King was invited but could not go. He moved into 1501 H Street during Henry and Clover's absence.

At one point while at Niagara, the Adamses, Anne Palmer, and Trevelyan formed a separate party and crossed an ice bridge from Canada to the American falls. Apropos of the falls, Clover wrote that Henry "brooded over it . . . and said he could not resist it." She took greater pleasure in a sleigh ride and a sunset walk. Although she enjoyed the holiday, she could not like her hostess. She confided to her father that Mrs. Thornton was "a singular & most unpleasant freak of nature"—"not a fine lady but a Birmingham imitation—a divorcée."

On January 20, a Monday, the Adamses reappeared at 1501 H Street. King greeted them with a fire and tea. General Taylor, Congressman Hewitt of New York, and Aristarchi Bey, a Turkish diplomat, came in at once, wanting news.

The following Thursday, the *Nation* published the King review. In Washington, it was not a secret that Henry was the author. At the Adamses' that evening, twenty celebrants joined in festivities in honor of King that continued past midnight.

Six evenings later, on January 29, Adams and Godkin visited Secretary Schurz and were talking with him and Senator Lamar when President Hayes stepped in. Hayes kept silent. Lamar was talking. Adams and Godkin listened. Before either thought to interrupt Lamar, Hayes left, walked back to the White House, and, meeting Charles Nordhoff, said to him that he had just met two "*reform* Democrats," E. L. Godkin and Henry Adams, both of whom were "dull owls."

Nordhoff relayed the president's opinion to the Adamses. Henry was delighted. Clover happily recounted the episode to Dr. Hooper and urged him to repeat the story to Henry's relatives.

For the present, a reputation for owlish dullness would possibly serve Henry better than any other. No such reputation was possible for Clover. At her teas and dinners, she was always herself and could not be silent. Her remarks frequently concerned particular people, were often kind, but tended also to be discerning. Sad to say, her remarks would *always* be misreported. Her conversation was inimitable and indescribable. When efforts were made to repeat it, some of her perspicacity might be saved. All her charity would be lost.

The month past, January 1879, had been a time of secret changes which, from scattered evidence, can possibly be reconstructed. Adams had been uncertain whether to publish *Democracy* and feared the risks might be prohibitive. He took advantage of the visits of King and Godkin to tell them that he had written a novel, *Democracy*, which, if published anonymously, might have political repercussions. He appears to have told them separately and asked them in the strongest terms never to divulge his authorship. His reason for telling King was the closeness of their friendship. Among the reasons for telling Godkin, not the least was the necessity of preventing harmful conjectures by the *Nation*, were the novel to appear and create a noise.[45]

As nearly as can be guessed, Adams sometime in January read the manuscript of Taylor's *Destruction and Reconstruction* and was so favorably affected by it that he lent Taylor the manuscript of *Democracy* in exchange. Taylor not only read the novel; he paid it the homage of writing a companion work for immediate anonymous publication. The companion work was a lampoon. There seems more than a possibility that Adams saw it as soon as it was finished.[46] Its relation to Adams's novel was that of a pistol beside a cannon, but it had superiorities as humor and as politics that would operate as challenges to Adams to cease his shilly-shallying and publish *Democracy*.

On February 2, 1879, Clover sent her father an anonymous article printed the day before in the New York *World*.[47] She asked him to read it and show it to Mrs. Parkman. "I fancy she will 'spot' the author." Dr. Hooper did as Clover wished, and Mrs. Parkman was moved to respond. In a letter that is missing, she asked the Adamses for news of *Democracy*. Henry replied: "The great work you are kind enough to remember, is still trembling on the edge of the fire and may at any moment become ashes. That way lies safety, if not immortality."

Henry's reply was quite untrue. Both he and General Taylor were steering for immortality. No longer mere cordial friends, they had been confiding with one another very freely.[48] The article Clover sent her father and Mrs. Parkman bore a suggestive title:

Political Aspirants

A Wise Man, Whose Ancestors Knew How It Was Themselves, Discourses on His Rivals for 1880

That Taylor wrote the article was manifest on evidence of style. His authorship was confirmed by the article's comic drift. The fictional "wise man"—the article's pretended author—purports himself to be an aspirant to the presidency whose father and grandfather had been aspirants to the office. He is writing confidentially to his sons, and he asks that they preserve his lines "sacredly and secretly among the archives of the family." He mentions, too, that his grand-father served as a minuteman in the battles of "Lexington and Bunker Hill, Bennington and Saratoga." The reader can thus assume that the wise man's family is a political family in Massachusetts. Hence the article, among other things, is a friendly spoof of Henry Adams.[49]

Taylor's "Presidential Aspirants" bears resemblances to *Democracy*. The lampoon runs to thirty paragraphs. It exposes the weaknesses of seven aspirants for election to the presidency in 1880: Grant, Blaine, Tilden, Conkling, Thurman, Hendricks, and Bayard (three Republicans, four Democrats). It does its work so effectively that the reader has little choice but to hope an eighth candidate will prevail. The *author* is the eighth. He is independent enough to lack a party, Adamsish enough to be Henry Adams, and old enough to be Dick Taylor.

Of the seven aspirants exposed as unfit, the most hurtfully treated is Senator Blaine. On the one hand, the wise man concedes that Blaine, before becoming a senator, "used the position of Speaker of the House of Representatives with commendable moderation." ". . . I readily believe he could have made more money out of the place . . . ." On the other, the wise man concedes that Blaine is not too poor to be president; that his thefts, though moderate, have sufficed to prepare him for candidacy. ". . . this is a recommendation not to be overlooked."[50]

On March 3, Congress passed the bill creating the U. S. Geological Survey. King won the directorship, at a salary of $6,000. It seemed for a time that he would rent a Washington house, in which the Adamses could store their possessions while abroad. (The house would not materialize.) His affairs and theirs were never so interlocked. Yet Henry and Clover had a secret they meant to keep from Godkin, from General Taylor, and even from King.

The moment had come when Adams would write his second novel. Suggested six years earlier by George Eliot's *Middlemarch*, the novel had been re-suggested by Clover's not becoming a Washington church-goer and suggested most of all by Henry's reconsideration of Hawthorne's *Scarlet Letter*. Henry apparently wrote the novel at top speed in March and April 1879. Partly to screen its relation to Hawthorne's masterpiece and partly to introduce an added theme, he borrowed the name of its heroine from one of Hawthorne's lesser tales, "Old Esther Dudley."[51] The leading idea of the tale is that the colonists who freed themselves from England and designed an American Union were an advance over previous nations—a "new race of men."

Adams's *Esther* is simply a novel. It represents a smaller effort than *Democracy*. The heroine, Esther Dudley, twenty-five and unmarried, is an only child, the motherless daughter of a well-to-do New Yorker. She has been accustomed for fifteen years to being "absolute mistress of her father's house."[52] She is a painter of no great ability, as she knows, and she emphatically is not a church-goer.

By use of rather creaky novelistic machinery, Esther is brought into such proximity with a young clergyman, Stephen Hazard, that she can correctly judge his qualities when away from his church, yet also watch him give sermons. By use of more machinery—six other characters, the death of her father, and other impingements—she and Hazard are maneuvered into love. At his insistence, she promises to marry him; then, without success, she tries to break the engagement. Her aunt devises a wintry escape for her to Niagara with several companions. Informed of Esther's whereabouts, Hazard pursues her. In a well-written scene, she tells him: " 'Some people are made with faith. I am made without it.' " He pleads and argues. She is moved to answer, " 'It must be that we are in a new world now, for I can see nothing spiritual about the church.' "[53] He is bested and retreats. Their engagement is dissolved. She is lovelorn, but she is free.

The place of *Esther* in Adams's life is sufficiently apparent. Novel-writing was an ability Clover believed she lacked. Henry wanted her to have a novel to her credit and wrote her novel for her. It was written with her knowledge, was designed to express her thoughts and feelings, and sufficiently succeeded.[54]

Read for its plain meaning, *Esther* is a hopeful book. Its heroine is a much weaker person than Mrs. Henry Adams. Yet, when confronting Hazard at the critical instant of the story, Esther capably and bravely fights her battle. Her platform is inborn lack of faith. She realizes she has no business becoming the wife of a clergyman. She claims no special merit, but she stands firm and holds her ground.

Taylor in early March suffered a severe attack of illness. King helped him move to New York, to stay with Samuel Barlow. On March 17, the invalid wrote to Clover: "For many weeks the event of each day was my visit to you. . . . Please say 'bien de choses' to Mr. Adams, who is one of the few men I can tolerate."

Henry was completing his Gallatin-Jefferson-Madison project ahead of time. Rather than leave for Europe on September 1, he and Clover could start in May. He wrote to the Cunard Line on April 2 asking for space on the *Gallia*, a new ship, scheduled to sail on May 28. Through the help of Samuel Barlow, he obtained the ship's best stateroom.

Taylor died on April 12, and Adams was invited to be a pallbearer. The others would be Congressman Clymer of Pennsylvania, Senator Bayard of Delaware, and Secretary Evarts. Adams declined. The explanation he gave to Barlow was rich in ironies. "The poor old General would have lifted his coffin lid and smiled his most sardonic smile at me, if I had seen him escorted to the grave by politicians."[55]

Last proofs of *The Life of Albert Gallatin* came from the printer on May 11. To use Adams's term, the work was a heavy biography. Prefaced and indexed, it would fill 700 pages, set in smallish type.

Presumably in May, Adams completed the miniature biography of Gallatin requested by the New England Historic Genealogical Society. When set in largish type, it would fill about nine pages.

Both of Adams's biographies of Gallatin were attempts to achieve perfection in the form. They are best read together, the long first, the short second. Because the short firmly outlines the story that the long had been hastily contrived to tell, the two together can have the effect of a single work better than either.[56]

The estimate Adams formed of Gallatin was so high that he stated it only where it would be less seen, in the short biography. The estimate had two sides. "As a practical statesman [Gallatin] . . . had no equal in his day, and his scattered writings show him to have had no superior as a man of science and study."[57]

In both biographies, Adams explained that Gallatin, late in life, founded in the United States the scientific study of *peoples*. "His ethnological papers on the American Indians and their languages, published in 1836, 1845, and 1848, may be said to have created that branch of science."[58] The branch in question, usually referred to as ethnology, was known to Adams also as history. Thus, among American scientists, Gallatin and Adams were related as precursor and successor.

Before sailing for Europe, Henry and Clover made necessary arrangements. Their plan was to sell the Boston house, place their Washington possessions in storage, and rent a different Washington house on their return. A Miss Lee in Virginia would shelter the horses. Boojum would stay with Alice Hooper.

On May 19, 1879, when they reached New York, Henry had with him the manuscript of *Democracy*. He sent it to a New York publisher, Henry Holt, under injunctions of absolute secrecy.[59] He asked that it be printed as written and that it be published anonymously on April 1, 1880.[60] Holt was delighted to be trusted with the book and agreed to Henry's terms.[61]

Once in Boston, Clover went to her father's house at Beverly Farms. Henry spoke with the Chief at his Boston office, hurried to Quincy, did not find his mother, and, when the Chief arrived, took up a grievance. In the father's words: ". . . [Henry] entered into an unpleasant business caused by the indiscreet conversations of his wife which have been reported and have more or less nettled all the family. I talked with him moderately but firmly. He bore it very well—but his mother did not get home in season, for which I was not sorry . . . . I am afraid that this commotion is driving Henry to exile in Europe . . . . But I am very sure that even that separation is far more safe for all the family than the thoughtless malice springing from jealousy . . . . Henry has always been one of my trusted supports. I have no feelings but those of affection and love for him. I pity rather than dislike his wife. But henceforth I must regard her as a marplot . . . ."[62]

Henry went twice again to Quincy alone. Clover went once alone. Simultaneously C. F. Adams visited Dr. Hooper. These shufflings may have done some good, but at Quincy after Henry said his goodbyes the Chief felt compelled to write, "There is a feeling of sadness when I reflect upon the departure of Henry that I cannot control."[63]

Reportedly the case had two aspects. One was Clover's alleged "indiscreet conversations" in Washington. The Massachusetts Adamses believed they knew what she had been saying. Several of their number, the Chief included, had mulled her supposed remarks. The experience was final. They had set their minds against her.

The other reported aspect was "malice springing from jealousy." There were only two things to be jealous of: Henry's having been carried off—as it may have seemed—by a Hooper, and his being an Adams who had lived for two additional winters in Washington. Perhaps several of his relations were jealous on both scores but in different degrees. Whatever their shades of feeling, the most jealous among the several was Charles.

Henry Adams, presumably in his campus rooms at 1 Wadsworth Hall, shortly after joining the Harvard faculty in September 1870. "My great wish is to get ahold of the students' imaginations for my peculiar ideas," young Professor Adams said. Fully a third of Harvard's juniors and seniors enrolled in his medieval history classes, since the instructor claimed to be "utterly and grossly ignorant," and proposed learning along with the undergraduates. *Courtesy Faith Thoron Knapp. Author's collection.*

John Quincy Adams in full diplomatic uniform, an oil portrait by Pieter van Huffel on the occasion of the Treaty of Ghent (1815), which the future president helped negotiate on behalf of the United States. His grandson Henry wore a similar uniform on formal occasions when serving in the U.S. Legation in London, 1861–68, during which time he was instrumental in preventing war between Great Britain and the United States. The physical resemblance between grandfather and grandson was noted in 1872 by one of Henry's students as he took an examination on medieval institutions in the presence of his instructor, and under the gaze of the sixth president's portrait. The often-irascible JQA looks almost puckish when compared to his momentarily menacing grandson. *Courtesy National Portrait Gallery, Smithsonian Institution.*

Henry Adams's "official" Harvard portrait, 1872. The full beard was grown the previous summer, which Adams spent trekking with Clarence King and the 40th Parallel Geological Survey. His imposing, stern physical presence intentionally conceals a curious and playful but determined intellect. "I shall quietly substitute my own notions for those of the College, and teach in my own way," he wrote to his intimate friend Carlo Gaskell. *Courtesy Harvard University and Massachusetts Historical Society. Author's collection.*

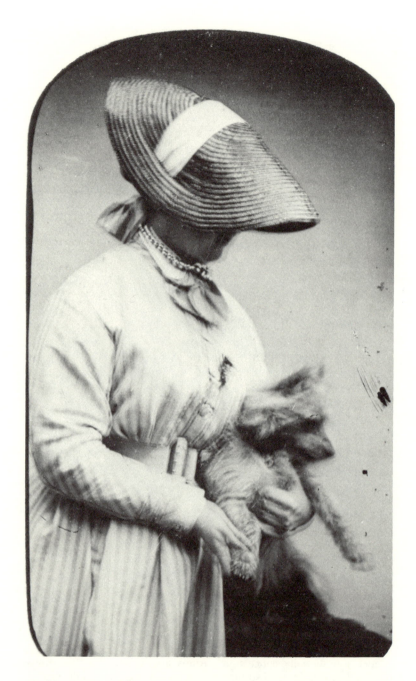

Marian Hooper (Clover) Adams with a young dog, possibly Possum, winter of 1881–82, presumably photographed by Henry Adams. Clover Adams strongly wished that she—and especially her face—be spared from exposure to cameras, a wish her husband respected. This is the only known photograph of her to have been taken in the United States subsequent to her marriage. *Courtesy Louisa Hooper Thoron and Massachusetts Historical Society. Author's collection.*

Henry Adams with a Skye terrier puppy, perhaps Possum, winter of 1881–82, presumably photographed by Clover Adams. This is the earliest known photograph of Adams taken by his wife, and was apparently made on the same occasion as Henry's portrait of her. The technical deficiencies of the two images may have encouraged Mrs. Adams to take a serious interest in photography, in order to memorialize their marriage, life together, and their friends by creating an array of suitably excellent photographs. *Courtesy Massachusetts Historical Society.*

Abu Simbel, photographed by Henry Adams on February 3, 1873. His efforts to capture the "spirit" of the temple literally left Adams speechless, but he later told Carlo Gaskell his photograph was "worth half a dozen of any I have yet met." *Courtesy Massachusetts Historical Society.*

Henry Adams on board the *Isis*, on the Nile, during his and Clover's wedding journey. Adams is looking at, and actuating with his thumbs, a mechanism that permits the photographer to trip the camera shutter from a distance. His self-portrait, taken in December 1872 or January 1873, is more an act of curiosity than of egotism, and shows a remarkable lack of vanity. The photograph is commonly—and mistakenly—credited to Marian Hooper (Clover) Adams. *Courtesy Massachusetts Historical Society.*

Henry Adams with Marquis, May 1883, on the back steps of the Adamses' rented Washington house at 1607 H Street. The portrait was taken by Clover Adams at the beginning of her serious work as a photographer. *Courtesy Massachusetts Historical Society.*

Henry Adams in his study at Beverly Farms, Massachusetts, August–September 1883. This is one of several photographs Mrs. Adams took of her husband at their summer home, Pitch Pine Hill. He is presumably writing a portion of his *History of the United States. Courtesy Massachusetts Historical Society.*

17

A CHECKERED OCEAN

After a gentle voyage on the *Gallia* and a brief glimpse of the Cunliffes in Wales, the Adamses went to London, joined the Gaskells for five days at 33 Grosvenor Street, moved for an interval to Claridge's, and settled at last in attractive lodgings at 17 Half Moon Street. They resumed their English associations and, partly with the help of Henry James, who lived in the next street, started adding new ones. Meanwhile, chaperoned by her mother, Anne Palmer arrived from New York. Rooms were found for the Palmers on Half Moon Street four doors away. Clover said of Anne, ". . . it is pleasant to have her to loaf with."

While still in America, Henry had been furnished one copy of *The Writings of Albert Gallatin* and an imperfect copy of the *Life*.[1] In London, he would be receiving copies of the *Life* in good order. The shipment mattered. He wanted access not only to papers owned by three governments but also to papers in private English collections. When appropriate, he could offer the *Life* as evidence of his competence and deservingness.

The U. S. minister to England was a Philadelphia merchant, John Welsh. Henry evidently called on him and elicited his help, and later the minister paid Clover a cordial visit. She thought him "a quiet Baptist deacon style of man, with no nonsense and no charm." It seemed to her that the place of minister had wholly lost its diplomatic importance and utility. "Why the two secretaries of legation and the Atlantic cable cannot do the work, I cannot see."

At a Foreign Office reception on July 2, 1879, Henry mentioned to Lord Salisbury that he needed access to the correspondence between the Foreign Office and the British ministers to the United States during the early years of the century. The foreign secretary encouragingly replied that Mr. Adams should submit a written application.

In his application, Adams explained that, for "purely historical purposes and in connection with the history of the United States, I am anxious to examine . . . unpublished [Foreign Office] correspondence." Because the existing rules permitted no papers to be shown of later date than 1802, he requested "an extension of time . . . to the year 1810, or, if it is not thought improper, even to the year 1815."

He soon received notice that his request was fully granted. On July 11, he sent thanks to Philip Currie, an aide of Salisbury's, and mentioned that, as compared with "the ordinary practice of other governments," the response was one of "exceptional liberality." He said nothing to Currie about copying or partly publishing the papers he would read; but tacitly, it seems, he had been given those liberties.

Papers of the sort Adams needed had been moved to the Record Office and were organized in volumes. Knowing the Record Office would close for the summer on August 10, he began his visits at once. He started by reading the despatches in Volume 46 from Minister Liston in 1800. As he read each despatch, he wrote its number, date, and a description in a ruled book. At the head of his list, he wrote instructions to the copyist: "Copy all the despatches marked *copy* but no printed matter nor any enclosures except when expressly directed." Since the papers he had wished to read extended to those in Volume 113 from Minister Foster in 1812, a long task awaited him. Yet his expedition was already a part-success. He was assured the capture of a trove of evidence no foreigner had ever seen.[2]

On June 23, 1879, J. B. Lippincott and Company had sent copies of *The Life of Albert Gallatin* to twenty-seven editors in the United States and England and copies of the *Writings* to twenty-three.[3] The *New York Tribune* reviewed the *Life* anonymously on July 4. In part complimentary but always desultory, the review warned that "extracts from letters in the French language . . . give a foreign aspect to the commencement of the volume that is not a little discouraging."

The Chief received the Gallatin volumes on June 28. He began by looking into the *Writings*. In July, he and Mrs. Adams went to Saratoga Springs to permit her taking a cure. By then he was reading the *Life*. He wrote in his diary on July 12: ". . . Henry's book . . . seems to me very well prepared. His sketch of the state of things and Gallatin's share in them is very lucid and masterly. And the agency is not overdrawn[,] as so often happens when the labor is to make an idol."

The father added on July 22 that the *Life* "is a masterpiece of political history." Next day, he continued: ". . . Gallatin's life thus far runs like a novel. I am clear that the narrative contains the whole history of the war of 1812." He completed his reading at Quincy, writing on August 9: ". . . [the biography] is long and it might fatigue the occasional reader, but it is not prosy and it throws a great deal of light on matters which have remained in obscurity. This is especially true as to the negotiation of the Treaty of Ghent and some of the later transactions of the Cabinet of Mr[.] Monroe. I feel gratified that my son has done it so well."

Charles received the *Life* and started to read it on July 19 while traveling to Saratoga to join his parents. He finished it three days later while returning to Quincy.[4] His hasty survey, and possibly glances at reviews in the *New York Tribune* and *Boston Advertiser*, sufficed to tell him that correctives were in order.[5] *He* would be the corrector, and his means would be an anonymous article in the *Nation*. He apparently alerted Godkin that an article reviewing Henry's book would soon arrive.

Like most other readers, Charles knew little about Gallatin until he read the *Life*. After reading it, he began to write on the subject as if it had always been known to him. In this respect, he was not exceptional. The Chief attempted a sketch on Gallatin.[6] Lodge published a long article on Gallatin; and John Torrey Morse, Jr., a cousin of Lodge's, published a slapdash review of the *Life*.[7] Charles only diverged in concealing what he did and in wanting to force an issue.

He completed his article on August 3.[8] It took the form of two instalments. He said in the second that the animus that moved him was "a positive sense of aggravation."[9] In his judgment, the great necessities were to awaken Gallatin's biographer to the gross errors which had spoiled the *Life* and to give the biographer an idea of the book he should have written. For Charles, the perfect biography of Gallatin was easy to imagine. It would have been a book adapted to the general reader, sprightly in style, printed in varied types, and light in the hand.[10] So he started his article by saying:

> About the year 1802 Albert Gallatin's tailor spoiled a coat for him in the making, whereat the then Secretary of the Treasury expressed the energetic opinion to his wife that "Every man, from John Adams to John Hewitt, who undertakes to do what he does not understand, deserves a whipping." Upon first handling the ponderous volume in which Mr. Henry Adams undertakes to tell the story of a very remarkable life, one is irresistibly tempted to substitute for the name of John Adams in the foregoing sentiment that of his great-grandson. In its superficial make-up this volume falls little short of being an

outrage both on Albert Gallatin and on every one who wishes to know anything about him. . . . He [Henry Adams] . . . seems . . . to have . . . set to work in a spirit of defiance, and made every detail of publication as repelling to the general reader as he knew how. The book resembles in appearance a volume of a cyclopædia,—it measures ten inches by six, and weighs nearly four pounds. It is printed—narrative, extracts, and correspondence—all in one monotonous type . . . and it bristles with letters in French which seem to say, as clearly as if in words, that the book is not for general readers.[11]

Godkin apparently felt the arrival of Charles's anonymous article as a commendation of himself. Since the first of the year, *two* Adamses had trusted him with secrets! Surprisingly, Henry had told him about *Democracy*, its possible publication, and the necessity that his authorship be successfully concealed. Still more surprisingly, Charles had supplied an article about Henry's *Gallatin* and wanted the authorship withheld, pending later instructions.

Had he been a better editor or a better judge of persons, Godkin might have declined to publish the elder brother's article, which on its face was trouble-making. There was a ready alternative. The *Nation* had obtained a review of Henry's *Gallatin* from an occasional contributor in New York, Arthur Rodney Macdonough.[12] But Godkin set Macdonough's review aside and published Charles's article. The instalments appeared on August 21 and 28, 1879.[13]

Henry's new stay in Europe was his fifth, Clover's her third. For several reasons, their new adventure had a special character. One reason was extra money.

In 1867, in his capacity as a stock broker, Henry Higginson had concluded that two copper mines in Michigan, the Calumet and Hecla, were good investments. The mines were controlled by his brothers-in-law, Alexander Agassiz and Quincy Shaw. Originally offered at $12.50, shares in the companies sometimes traded for as little as $5.00. The companies first paid dividends in 1869–1870 and were merged in 1871. Apparently through Higginson, at unknown dates but in rather large amounts, Clover Hooper and Henry Adams bought Calumet and Hecla shares. During the 1870s, appreciation and dividends were astronomical.[14] By 1879, the Adamses were spending money as if they had extra money to spend. At least part of the money was dividends in "Calumet."

A principal peculiarity of their new experience rested on Henry's having become a historian of peoples. The peoples he had to form opinions of, to be expressed in his *History*, were the Americans, the English, the French, the Spanish, the Indians, the whites of Louisiana and Canada, and the blacks of San Domingo. His great objects were to learn when and how the Americans became a nation, to learn how they compared with other peoples, and generally to achieve an overview of the history of humanity. These objects were much in his and Clover's minds. He and she accordingly were hyper-conscious of national traits, both their own and those of everyone they met.

Needless to say, national and racial peculiarities and differences were dangerous matters to investigate, think about, and especially talk or write about. The Adamses sensed the dangers but were going ahead as if the dangers were better risked.

In their letters to trusted recipients, Henry and Clover freely voiced impressions involving nationality, ethnicity, or race. On June 29, writing to her father, Clover remarked in passing that Lady Goldsmid was "a Jewess, and very nice."[15] On July 6, apropos of a dinner at the Charles Roundells', she mentioned that Henry and she had met John Richard Green and his wife. As author of the *Short History of the English People*, Green occupied a position in English life somewhat parallel to the position Henry was seeking to achieve in American life. Clover went on to say that after dinner Henry and she had "a nice talk" with the Greens. Appreciatively she added, "His wife [is] a pleasant little Irish woman, who is free-spoken as to the peculiarities of English females."[16]

After becoming acquainted, the Adamses and Greens met repeatedly. The husbands felt a double bond. They not only were historians of peoples; they had harmonious opinions. Henry reported to Gaskell that Green "bids fair to become my most intimate guardian and teacher . . . but is so awfully fragile that I always fancy I shall never see him again." He would later say that Green was "the only English writer of history whom I loved personally and historically."[17]

Adams and Green could be friends, but it remained a fact that the gulf between the Americans and the English was wide. An instance was an English review of Adams's Gallatin volumes. In an article in the *Saturday Review* surveying fifteen American publications, an anonymous English critic placed the *Writings* and the *Life* at the head of the list and denounced them. The critic said that Alexander Hamilton was the "greatest mind, if not the greatest character, of the Revolution and of the critical epoch that immediately followed"; moreover that, in contrast, Albert Gallatin was "a clever, pliant, ingenious, pushing French speculator." But Americans, the critic held, lacked all sense of proportion. Typically, an American biographer had placed Gallatin on a level with Hamilton, had ascribed to Gallatin "the first place in the negotiation of the treaty of peace with Great Britain," and had made him the subject of "four enormous volumes of the largest size now employed in any but scientific literature." The critic ventured that the volumes were "perhaps the most extravagant instance of disproportion between subject and treatment, the gravest offense against literary common-sense, which the *luce Boswelliana* has yet perpetrated in the United States."[18]

Henry heard about the denunciation and supposed he might enjoy it. He wrote to Gaskell on August 2: ". . . I understand that the Saturday has been launching thunderbolts at my head. . . . I have not seen the reproof, but if there be one subject on which the Saturday has always been more idiotic than another, it is America and everything American, so I can conceive that it may be amusing."

In Washington, the Adamses had often exchanged visits with the French minister, Maxime Outrey, his wife, and their small daughter Adeline. Clover had told her father in December 1878 that Adeline and Henry were carrying on a flirtation. "He rides on rocking horses in their nursery & has a special private invitation to her tree. . . ."[19]

Early in 1879, a kinsman of the Outreys, William Henry Waddington, took office as premier of France.[20] Waddington was a naturalized French citizen, married to an American. Evidence is lacking, but the Adamses appear to have secured from Minister Outrey a letter permitting them to initiate a visit to the premier and give him notice of Henry's wanting access to papers. Presumably from London, Adams wrote to Waddington. Also, by watching the French press, he and Clover kept track of his movements.

Roughly on August 7, Henry stopped work at the Record Office. His historical winnings were greater than anticipated. He told Gaskell he was leaving "three months labor for a copyist." Looking forward, Clover soon remarked: "Henry found so much stuff of value to him in the Record Office . . . that if Paris and Madrid are opened to him, and have as much, it will be tight work to get through by October 1880."

On an impulse, because they had not had a thorough rest since the previous October, the Adamses began a vacation by going to Furness Abbey on the Irish Sea in Lancashire. Clover wrote to her father from the abbey: "This is one of the most beautiful ruins in England; far more so than even Wenlock. The hotel is the Abbot's house restored to modern comfort."

Hoping for good weather and acceptable hotel space, both of which materialized, she and Henry proceeded to the Lake Country and relaxed at Windermere and thereabouts. While returning to London, they revisited the Cunliffes in Wales and tried to arrange joint travels in Spain. Unhappily the Cunliffes could not afford so expensive a holiday. The British upper classes were evidently short of money.

In London, Henry and Clover crossed paths with Alice Mason.[21] The meeting was friendly enough and turned the Adamses to thoughts of not-yet-published *Democracy*. For them, the novel was gradually ceasing to be a source of fear and becoming a source of high amusement. Apparently while still in London, Henry conceived the idea that Clover, when they got to Paris, should imitate a character in the novel and order a gown from Worth. The idea was in keeping with one aspect of the book. Though meant as a reflection on life, *Democracy* was also meant to be so written that life would conform to it. The purchase of a gown would figure in advance as a small-scale parody and burlesque of the novel's hoped-for power to shape events.

In appearance, the Adamses left London with no more pressing immediate purpose than a pleasure trip in Normandy and Brittany. En route to the Channel, they stopped at Canterbury and inspected the cathedral, new to both. Clover said it was "most impressive." Henry declared it "an uncommon good one."

Once in France, they visited another church. Henry wrote to Gaskell: "We slept at Amiens and strolled about the cathedral there, which is a whacker. Some points in it beat anything I know."

For several days, they haunted the Norman coast at Dieppe and Etratat. Their true object was a meeting with the Waddingtons. Without forgetting their object, they detoured to Rouen and visited three more great churches.[22]

At Dieppe on September 1, Henry had answered a letter just received from Hugh Grigsby, the Virginia historian, praising *The Life of Albert Gallatin*. As a rule, when speaking or writing to friends or officials about his intended works, Henry remained extremely wary. His explanations were always incomplete and in harmless ways might also be misleading. His letter to Grigsby was valuable for saying more about his future *History* than he usually would divulge. He told the Virginian that he intended a history of the United States from 1801 to 1815. ". . . [it] will be an affair of at least ten years work, and will exhaust all that I have to say. . . . To

compress this into three volumes and to expunge every unnecessary syllable, will be my great labor. . . ."

In one respect, the lines were inexact. There was no reason to
believe that Adams was seriously planning to write *three* volumes.
Yet, in another respect, the lines were helpfully suggestive. Compression and expunction were the usual hallmarks, not of history,
but of poetry. A narrative history compressed into minimum
volumes and shorn of every unneeded syllable would be a literary
wonder. And that was what Adams wanted: a prose history so
written that it would be poetry and would qualify as an epic.

Having told Grigsby a great deal, Adams was tempted not to
stop. He added a passage linking his *History* to the coming century.
"America is increasing so rapidly, and her future is so vast, that
one man may reasonably devote his life to the effort at impressing
a moral on the national mind, which is now almost a void. The old
days of Virginian and New England supremacy in power, are gone.
The America of the next century will be one of the greatest
problems of all history. To reach one's arm over into it, and give it
a shove, is at least an amusement."

At Deauville on September 9, the Adamses called on the
Waddingtons. They may have seen the premier. They assuredly
saw his wife. Clover told Dr. Hooper: "She was cordial and pleasant,
and suggested our dining with her, but we told her we were going
the next day."

The visit gave the Adamses encouraging information. Clover
continued: "Mr. Waddington . . . thinks Henry will be able to see
such papers as he wants, but here, as in London, vacation puts a
stopper to work until October 1st, which is aggravating when every
day is an object." She did not say so, but Henry must have inquired
about the possibility of *exceptional* access to the archives. He was led
to think that such access might be granted, beginning at any
moment.

Before calling on the Waddingtons, the Adamses had planned
further travels. Clover wrote: ". . . if the weather had promised
well, we should have headed for Brittany for a week's tour,—Mont
St. Michel, etc., but it blew a gale and the rain came in gusts, and it
seemed hopeless for a journey. . . . So we suddenly changed our
line and took the train to Paris."

In Paris, the Adamses stayed at the Hôtel du Parlement on the
Boulevard de la Madeleine. They found companions in Henry
James and Isabella Stewart Gardner, usually known as "Mrs. Jack,"
whom they had earlier known in Boston and Washington. At Henry

or Clover's request, Mrs. Jack introduced Clover to Worth, and she promptly bought a gown. Telling the story to her father, Clover reported, ". . . I so far yielded to Henry's wishes as to order a duplicate gown to one making for the 'Grand Duchess of Würtemberg,' which Mr. Worth ordered one of his young women to parade in." Her sentence did not divulge that she was very closely following Chapter XI of *Democracy*, in which Sybil Ross orders for a ball in Washington a Worth copy of a gown made earlier for "the reigning favourite of the King of Dahomey."

While silent about *Democracy*, Clover and Henry were silent about an article. Presumably soon after reaching Paris, they saw in recent issues of the *Nation* an unsigned article about *The Life of Albert Gallatin*. In their eyes, the article was annoying but self-explanatory. They thought it best treated as if Charles had never written it and Godkin had had enough intelligence not to print it.

At the start of President Hayes's administration, James Russell Lowell had accepted the Spanish mission. The appointment involved a risk. Spain in summer presented dangers to health.

While in London, Adams had wanted to write to Lowell about his need for Spanish papers, but he had learned that Mrs. Lowell was very ill. Rather than write, Henry postponed the letter.

The Adamses were held in Paris by continued assurances relating to papers. If he could gain immediate access, Henry might progress a long way before he and Clover left for Spain. There was time. Indeed there was a month. For fear of summer heat and bad drains, they would not risk Madrid till mid-October.

They learned in Paris that there had been no news of the Lowells for six weeks. On September 13, suspecting serious trouble, Henry wrote to Lowell offering his and Clover's help in any form that help was possible. Very briefly, he alluded to needing papers. "I am in search of documents in the [Spanish] government archives. . . . I am only waiting for cool weather to cross the Pyrenees."

Caution was justified. Not long before, the queen of Spain had died of typhus. Mrs. Lowell too had contracted typhus. She had gone mad, repeatedly almost died, recovered sanity imperfectly, and remained physically ill in ways that set endless problems for her nurses, beginning with her husband.[23]

On hearing from Adams, Lowell replied, "I am glad you are coming to Madrid, though I wish I were not going to be here when you come." He disclosed the severity of Fanny's case and said, ". . . my only longing is to get her away. . . ." Yet he had taken a step on Adams's behalf. "I will do all I can to help you in your researches. The Spaniards are very good about such things. . . . I spoke to the Minister of State . . . & he promised every assistance."[24]

In happier circumstances, Adams might have given Lowell a detailed picture of the future *History*. Instead he told Lowell only enough to identify the papers he wished to see. Writing again from Paris on September 24, he said he expected to write a history both national and multi-national. "I want to tell the whole truth, in regard to England, France, and Spain, in a 'History of the United States from 1801 to 1815'. . . . The British government has allowed me to see its most secret documents. . . . Mr[.] Waddington encourages me to believe that the same privilege will be granted me here. At Madrid I shall ask permission to read (and take copies wherever I think necessary) all the correspondence of the Spanish minister at Washington for that period. . . ." He wished also to see "the correspondence between France and Spain relative to Louisiana from 1800 to 1806."

To help the Lowells, the Adamses planned an early start for Madrid. They no sooner made the plan than they had to reconsider. On October 3, while visiting a certain Mme. Perraud, they met a celebrated French astronomer. The astronomer gave Henry a note of introduction to the minister of the navy. Next day, Henry learned of papers at the naval ministry that would greatly strengthen the *History*, if released. On the chance of his getting them, the Adamses put off their departure.

That same night, October 4, Clover received a first issue of the Sunday *Boston Herald* from her brother. Amid of welter of other news, the issue reported that Calumet and Hecla had topped $200 a share. In her next letter to her father, she remarked, "The *Figaro* and the *Rappel* have no such thrilling facts and fancies."

A further letter from Lowell brought bad news concerning the Spanish papers. "Did I tell you," he asked, "that the Minister for foreign affairs told me that the papers in his department are in great confusion? I believe it is true & not an excuse."[25]

There meanwhile was no decision about the French papers that Henry needed most, those at the ministry of foreign affairs. From Paris on October 12, Clover advised her father: ". . . we are still dangling on the Boulevards, the knots in French red tape being so hard and numerous that Henry's fingers are blistered with trying to pick them. You get a polite answer that when so and so returns you may, by applying to this one or that, get what you want. . . . So on Wednesday next we shall turn to pastures new and try our luck in Spain."[26]

❖ ❖ ❖

Henry James had formed his idea of Clover when she was single. He was prejudiced about Henry Adams, supposing him cast in an Adams mold that would make him quite unsocial. In London, he wrote to his brother William: "Henry A. can never be in the nature of things a very gracious or sympathetic companion, and Mrs. A. strikes me as toned down and bedimmed from her ancient brilliance. . . ." James reported soon after to Elizabeth Boott: "The Henry Adamses are here—very pleasant, friendly, conversational, critical, ironical. . . . Clover chatters rather less, and has more repose, but she is very nice, and I sat up with them till one o'clock this morning abusing the Britons. The dear Britons are invaluable for that."

With experience, James moved slightly towards improved opinions. From Paris in October, he wrote to his father: "The Henry Adamses, who are very good company, I frequently—almost daily—see; and we usually dine together at a restaurant. Henry is very sensible, though a trifle dry, and Clover has a touch of genius, (I mean as compared with the usual British females)."[27]

Though valuable to a point, James's comments were narrowed by his limitations. Himself the epitome of the solitary, he had before him a man and woman who were epitomes of the united. Clover in love was not a Clover he could easily understand, and Clover's husband was an Adams whom his abilities prepared him to like but never to comprehend. He seemed not to realize that Adams had the faculty of controlling the impressions he made on others and that, when dealing with Henry James, he chose to be ironical, critical, and a trifle dry, yet also pleasant, friendly, conversational, and very sensible—in short, good company; and Clover approved the choices.

There was the additional fact that Adams had accustomed himself to extremes of thought and feeling, had mentally reached out to an immense variety of concerns, and was not afraid of having ideas that departed from the norm. He *had* to be guarded about expressing his opinions, for commonly they were opinions his hearers might not be glad to hear.

Early in the summer, writing to Cunliffe, he had voiced ideas about England's politics of 1879 as compared with English politics he had previously witnessed. He said: "You will properly resent the remark that your politics are a shocking bore, but it is true, all the same; they are frankly imbecile; there is not a question now up, from Zululand to Dublin[,] which is worth ten minutes talk. A contemptible war with a horde of savages in a remote corner of a desolate wilderness; the establishment of a one-horse university in a provincial town; the futile reiteration of tedious truisms about Turkey. . . ."

Either Cunliffe had grown unused to Adams, or Adams had failed to gauge the amount of criticism that Cunliffe would gladly hear. Sir Robert's answer, which came late, showed both resentment and hurt. Henry responded at once: "You poor old Britishers are becoming sensitive. I can't make an innocent remark about England that I'm not met with the inquiry how it is in America. I can't persuade people that I am English enough to compare England with herself."

The underlying issue was powers of tolerance. Clover, Clarence King, and departed General Taylor could tolerate the hot and freezing temperatures of Adams's more unusual opinions and the extremes of language he sometimes used while saying what they were. Cunliffe was so jarred that Adams offered explanations. "All this . . . is for your private ear. I don't talk this way to other people. . . ." ". . . you must take it as quite private and evidence of my attachment."

"Tired as two dogs," Henry and Clover were greeted at the station in Madrid by Minister Lowell and Secretary Reed, who had arranged accommodations for them at the Hôtel de la Paz—"the best." The trials of the Lowells remained desperate. The minister told Reed that the Adamses' arrival was a godsend. Clover talked with Mrs. Lowell and studied her husband, who at times seemed reduced to a helpless child.

The first blow for Adams was word that the papers he wanted were lost but possibly could be found at Seville or elsewhere. The next blow was that most of the papers he wanted had been found in Madrid but were decreed by the foreign secretary, the Duke of Tetuan, to be of " 'too reserved a character to be shown' " to the American visitor.

While feeling the blows, Henry wrote to Carlo. His expressions were unguarded and rather strong. ". . . Madrid . . . is without exception the ugliest and most unredeemable capital I ever saw. . . . The hotels are bad; the streets vulgar, and the people simply faded Jews. . . . In short . . . I think Spain a hole. . . . This is the logical result of my statement of facts, and I am mortified to find how little even *my* remarkable wisdom has of logic, for I must own that . . . Spain does amuse me. Every day, with perfect regularity, a sky so blue you can scoop it out with a spoon; a sun so glorious that the shadows are palpably black; a dry, crisp air that tightens all one's muscles and makes life easy; and a good natured, dirty people who are always apologetic if one does not insult them."[28]

Sun yielded to incessant rain. On November 3, 1879, at an hour's notice, the Adamses packed, said good-bye to Lowell, and took the 6:30 P.M. southbound express. During a sunny morning stop at Cordova, they visited the great mosque and its court. In Clover's words: "We poked about . . . in the winding little streets, peeking into house after house, with their marble vestibule as clean as a Shaker could wish; a door of iron lacework in quaint Moorish patterns, and behind a cool patio or open court . . . with orange trees, roses, blue jasmine, heliotrope, and other gay flowers in masses of color. . . ."

At 2:30 P.M. on a train that would take them towards Granada, they shared a compartment with some Spanish travelers, "a family of four who seemed to have endless bandboxes and bags." The señora and señoritas showed Clover jewelry they had bought at Castellani's in Italy.

Clover had an idea. "I muttered to Henry that perhaps the Señor might know the Chief of Archives in Seville. . . . Henry, true to the characteristics of his first ancestor, wished me to 'bite first.' "[29] In Spanish, Clover put the question to the father. The señor said no, but "he could give us a card of introduction to a gentleman in Granada who would pass us on to the Chief of Archives."

All along, Granada had been part of the Adamses' plan for their time abroad. For beauty, Henry found the city second only to Naples. Thanks to the señor's card of introduction, their stay was providential. Don Leopoldo Equilaz, a fifty-year-old lawyer, antiquarian, and professor of Arabic, welcomed Henry warmly on November 6, guided the Adamses through the Alhambra on November 8, and showed them his house, a renaissance palace, on November 10.

At the palace on November 12, Don Leopoldo introduced the Adamses to two Moorish brothers "in full costume"—"lineal descendants of the Moorish king who began the Alhambra." All present agreed that Henry and Clover should hurry to Gibraltar, cross to Africa, stay a night at Ceuta, and proceed next day to Tetuan, the Moorish capital.

The Adamses' had several reasons for traveling to Tetuan. One was sheer desire to see the world. Another was the thought of softening the decree of the Duke of Tetuan by visiting his hereditary domain.[30] Before they set out, Don Leopoldo gave Henry a letter to a young professor in Seville, a Don Prudencio. The plan was that the Adamses, on leaving Africa, should go to Seville and, through Don Prudencio, get access to the archives.

They reached Ceuta on November 15, survived the hotel, and started for Tetuan next morning. Clover recorded: "Left at 7 A.M. on donkeys, a caravan of six or seven—Hebrew rabbi with long white beard, Henry, guides, postman and I. . . . The most enchanting road all the way for nine hours, close to the sea, sometimes over a long sand beach, then plains of heather in bloom and low palmetto; halt of ten minutes only."

Though situated at the west end of the Mediterranean, Tetuan seemed to Henry the most eastern place he had ever been to. Clover described it in strong language. "In the distance it lies white and beautiful in its frame of violet mountains; within, a howling mob of Moors, Jews, and Spaniards, half smothered in garbage. The streets are alleys reeking with filth, and yet they say it is free from typhus, which sweeps the neighboring cities. For two days and three nights we were comfortable and amused in a clean Moorish house kept by a Jew who also figures as British consular agent. I was amused to find that I was the first American woman who has ever visited Tetuan. Monday we wandered the streets; went to the Union Club, which consists of about ten members, Moors and Jews mixed—is fitted up like a miniature poor house; took coffee and played chequers with our fat Hebrew host [Isaac Nahon]."

There was no way of returning to Gibraltar without stopping a second time at Ceuta. Apparently during their second stay, Clover had a memorable experience. She later wrote to her father:

> Did I tell you that I had a nightmare in the inn at Ceuta, and saw the black man who waited on the table come into our room and felt him clutch my throat? When I told the landlady in answer to her friendly inquiry how I slept, she laughed consumedly, and then I found he was a pardoned galley slave sent to the galleys for cutting his wife's throat. Ceuta is an immense galley station, and as they [the unpardoned convicts] file through the town at sunset you can study villainy in every variety from their horrible faces.

On November 21, from Gibraltar, Henry summarized for Carlo his and Clover's travels since leaving Madrid. "Nearly a month has passed, and I feel as though I were a pure Spaniard— or perhaps a Jew, for of late I have been a bit more Jewish than anything else. Checquered is the ocean of life, my dear friend, and I think the part of that ocean in which Spain lies is decidedly more checquered than most."[31]

That life should be a checkered ocean was for Adams a datum very relevant to him. He felt he could not be a historian of nations without visiting people unlike himself, Spaniards, Moors, and Jews being examples; and he felt he could not visit other peoples without merging into them and wondering who he was. ". . . I enjoyed the trip, or parts of it, immensely. . . . But whether my name is now Abd-el-adem, or Ben-shadams, or Don Enrique Adamo, I couldn't take oath, for I have been utterly bewildered to know what has become of my identity, and the Spaniards have been so kind to us that I feel as though I owed them a name."[32]

With respect to the Spanish, Adams was moving from one impression to another. Like most Americans, he had more or less disapproved of certain famous acts of the Spanish: the expulsions of the Moors and Jews. He wrote a letter to Sir Robert on November 22 of which only part survives.[33] In the fragment, he told again the story of his and Clover's dash to Morocco. ". . . the ride [to Tetuan] was almost the most beautiful thing I ever saw, along the Mediterranean all day, with a view that justified self-destruction. . . ." To balance the *paradiso* of shore, sea, and air, there had been an *inferno*, Ceuta, an unspeakable seaport. On the way to Tetuan and returning therefrom, he and Clover had twice experienced "Ceuta and the hotel with its Jew Benshimol."[34] Moved by alternations of horror and beauty, he put into his letter a savagely ironic yet comic line: "I have now seen enough of Jews and Moors to entertain more liberal views in regard to the Inquisition, and to feel that, though the ignorant may murmur, the Spaniards saw and pursued a noble aim."

The line might easily be misread.[35] In Spain and Africa, Henry had been learning to be more fair-minded. He had been fair-minded enough in the past to be fair-minded on occasion about Jews and Moors of previous or recent centuries, but not fair-minded enough to be fair-minded about the Spanish of the present time or any time. The opinion he was mending was an unfair opinion of the Spanish. Mending was indispensable. The Spanish were a nation he would write about in his *History*.

The Adamses were kept three days at Gibraltar by lack of a steamer. At last they proceeded to Seville. There Henry had digestive troubles. Clover got a doctor and found better rooms. By the time Henry was well, the archives were closed, to honor a royal wedding in Madrid.

Henry called on Don Prudencio, who was not at home. When Don Prudencio returned the call, Henry was out. Clover prevailed on the young visitor to make special exertions, and through his help the archives were opened on Sunday for three hours, exclusively for the Americans.

The old archivist had served for sixty-five years and remembered the visits of William Prescott and Washington Irving, but not of George Ticknor. The archivist and Clover talked. Henry searched. "Among millions of bundles[,] Henry found what he was in search of, and while I talked to the old man he went through them, and found that negatively they were all we wanted. No other fellow can come here and trip him up by later information and spoil his work."

Don Leopoldo knew the Adamses' itinerary and meant to join them in Madrid. He was waiting on December 3 when they returned and instantly put them in the hands of another Spaniard, an aristocratic politician. Clover wrote: "Henry has got an ally here who is going to work for him, a young Marquess [*sic*] de Casa Yrugo, whose grandfather was minister to the United States during Jefferson's administration. . . . He is a member of the Cortes, a grandee, and can work to advantage. . . . He came for a long call Saturday P.M. and was most kind and civil, promising to get at the papers Tetuan refuses to show and tell Henry anything he can get from them. He has been diplomate [*sic*] in London and speaks English perfectly."[36]

The Adamses' adventures in Spain seemed half victory, half defeat. They had a prospect of Henry's being told by the Marqués de Casa Yrugo what the papers in Madrid contained. They had no prospect of Henry's getting to see the papers, still less have copies made.

In this new situation, the Adamses no longer needed their arch-benefactor, Don Leopoldo Equilaz. He none the less attended to their welfare continually. On December 8, when they left for Paris, he helped them onto the train and said a last good-bye.

On November 3, 1879, at his house in Quincy, Charles had written Henry "a long letter" of an "admonitory character." The letter is missing. What it concerned is unknown, except that it did not concern the Gallatin review.[37]

In Paris, Henry and Clover avoided the Hôtel du Parlement, which they had found was ill-managed and dirty. At the Hôtel du Jardin on the Rue de Rivoli, they took "a charming apartment looking over the Tuileries . . . large parlour, nice bedrooms on front, dining room, hall, and great closets behind, big wood fires and excellent cuisine."

They had hardly unpacked when news came from Madrid. Clover wrote: "Crisis in Spain. Duke of Tetuan kicked out!"

The news offered hope that the young Marqués de Casa Yrugo might not only read the papers in Madrid but also might have copies made, as necessary, and forward them, in care of Lowell or Reed. On that assumption, by mail, Henry commenced a new attempt to obtain every paper he might want.

On December 12, a Friday, at the palace on the Quai d'Orsay, Mme. Waddington gave the Adamses tea. Events were speeding forward. During Henry's absence, the U. S. Legation in Paris had won permission from the French authorities for Mr. Adams to see the naval papers.[38] On Sunday, Clover told Dr. Hooper, "Henry got his permission on Thursday to work on papers in the Marine and this week probably will get at his other archives; is up to his eyes all day in fascinating work and is very happy." On December 20, still prospering, Henry reported to Carlo: "As for Paris, I hardly know what it is. Except for a short walk after dark, I see nothing of it except manuscripts and books."

Presumably after insistent urging by Charles, Godkin wrote a letter to Clover in which he asked her to ask her husband what he thought of the *Nation's* review of *The Life of Albert Gallatin*. Delivered in Paris just before Christmas, the letter to Clover permitted Henry to break his silence about the Gallatin review. In answer, he told the editor: "You are the fourth person who has asked me *'for particular reasons'* to tell what I thought about the Nation's review of Gallatin. Apparently there is some mystery about that document. If there is, I don't want to know it and do want not to know it. . . . I don't propose to dance to other people's music. So if anyone else asks you what I think about the notice, you just tell them that I'm not yet quite a fool, and that I don't think anything about it."

Though promised, permission relating to the papers at the French ministry of foreign affairs did not come. To get around the impediment, Adams sought the help of Gabriel Monod, one of the historians he had contacted in Paris in 1873. Clover wrote that Professor Monod "turned up last week; is very angry at the discourteous delay and is trying to do something through his cousin in the department."

Clover meanwhile had consulted Mr. Worth about a second gown and ordered it. She described the *couturier* as "standing pensively by the window in a long puce-colored dressing gown with two exquisite black spaniels—twins—sitting on two green velvet chairs." There was even a question of Clover's getting many gowns. "I have become bored with the idea of getting any new gowns, but Henry says, 'People who study Greek must take pains with their dress.'"

Like the Duke of Tetuan, but with an even better result, William Waddington fell from office. On his last day as premier, December 28, 1879, he signed the document granting Adams access to the papers at the ministry of foreign affairs.[39] Apprised of the permission, Henry presented himself to Monsieur Faugère, the chief archivist, and set to work among unpublished correspondence of the first importance.

The Adamses could stay only six weeks in Paris before returning to London. Their problem was lack of a London house for the season. They planned to start on Sunday, January 24, 1880. Unexpectedly on the 20th, they saw in *Galignani's Messenger* that in place of Welsh, who had resigned, Lowell had been appointed minister to England.

This new stroke of luck created a problem for Henry that he was very anxious to solve. The services of C. F. Adams and Henry Adams in the English mission had commenced after a long delay and were further hindered by lack of appropriate rented space. Henry accordingly wished Lowell would begin his service with all possible promptness, in good quarters. He immediately sent Lowell congratulations and urged his hurrying to London. "To judge from my experience . . . I should say that every day you lose after the meeting of Parliament, will be unfortunate. We arrived [in 1861] . . . at least two months too late."

With both themselves and Lowell in mind, the Adamses left Paris in a rush, reached London on January 22, and heard next day from their house agent that he had a house to show them in Queen Anne's gate. They saw the house on the 24th, thought it "a perfect gem from top to bottom," and by making an instant offer secured a lease till August 1.

Lowell wanted Adams to know his plans. That same day, January 24, he wrote to say, "I shall come to London to present my credentials & then [come] back to Madrid on leave to fetch Mrs[.] Lowell." Thanks in part to the help of a British nurse, Fanny Lowell had improved, but was far from well. The minister added a postscript: "My greatest anxiety is that I am to be the successor of your father[,] who did more service than a dozen generals."

The U. S. chargé d'affaires in London, William Jones Hoppin, was an older man in his late sixties whom Adams considered sensitive. It was natural to suppose that Hoppin would want to be Lowell's host when he arrived. In his letter from Paris, Henry had urged the new minister to show Hoppin particular consideration. Yet he let Lowell know that he and Clover might shortly have a house at which the minister might find temporary shelter, should he need it.

After renting 22 Queen Anne's Gate, Adams ascertained that Hoppin's residence did not afford a space in which the arriving minister could sleep. In a new letter sent from London on January 28, Henry positively invited Lowell to stay with him and Clover. "We have plenty of room . . . and a large house near the Legation."[40]

In Madrid, Lowell had secured permission to read the papers Adams wanted but had no time to read them. He suggested that a new archivist might do the work in his place, for appropriate pay.[41]

Adams had meanwhile corresponded with the Marqués de Casa Yrugo. In his next letter to Lowell, dated February 10, he said he had sent instructions about the papers to the Spanish grandson and to Secretary Reed; also that permission to make copies could be assumed. ". . . I will leave the examination and selection of the papers to Casa Yrugo himself. I can trust him to send me the ones I want."

Received opinion held that no American minister of any importance had served in London since C. F. Adams. There was every chance that Lowell could at least make a good impression. Though scarcely known as a diplomat, he was very much in vogue as a poet, essayist, and arbiter of literary taste.

No. 22 Queen Anne's Gate was a four-story brick house in the best style, three windows wide at the front. Its rear windows faced west over Bird Cage Walk into St. James's Park. Its interiors had their original brasses and moldings, and the furnishings were the finest possible, consistent with being used. The Adamses brought with them still finer linens. They inherited a housemaid from the owner. Henry James sent them a man. Mrs. Henry Sturgis recommended a cook who not only prepared excellent meals but provisioned and planned them; also Mrs. Sturgis lent them silver; and Clover rented a coupé, interchangeable at need with a victoria.

Hoppin was keeping a private journal. He recorded dining with the Adamses on February 8. The other guest was Ralph Palmer. The chargé d'affaires disliked his host, whom he viewed as civil but professorial. ". . . he has been a professor at Harvard & retains a little of the pedagogic air which few people who have ever taught can shake off. He is always willing to illuminate with the rays of his wisdom those poor people like myself who sit in darkness."

General Badeau appeared in London and lingered, waiting for Lowell to appear. Hoppin dined again with the Adamses on March 4. He wrote no new criticisms of Adams. The guests included Mr. and Mrs. Matthew Arnold. "Arnold," Hoppin said, "was particularly genial & loquacious."

Lowell had a nephew in London and planned to stay with him. The minister was due at Victoria Station on Saturday, March 6, at 5:45 P.M. Hoppin, General Badeau, and the Adamses were there to greet him.[42]

As Hoppin was in process of finding out, Adams held a rank among American diplomats that showed itself in private arrangements. It was understood in Madrid that emergency messages to Lowell were to be addressed to Adams at 22 Queen Anne's Gate. Hoppin wrote: "At 5 on Monday Adams came to my house to say that a telegram had been sent to him from Madrid with such bad news about Mrs[.] Lowell that he was afraid to deliver it. It said that she was worse & that it was 'too late' & 'useless' for him to return. We concluded that she was no longer living." Adams and Hoppin delivered the message, which happened to be overdark. Mrs. Lowell rallied. Hoppin noted, "The next morning a more encouraging telegram came & each succeeding one has been better so that Lowell has recovered his spirits & is going through his duties."[43]

During his second stay in Paris, Adams had seen all the papers he wished to see and completed his orders to the copyist. Looking back at the experience from London on February 22, he had written to Lodge, "At the best of times Paris is to me a fraud and a snare; I dislike it, protest against it, despise its stage, contemn its literature, and have only a temperate respect for its cooking; but in December and January Paris is frankly impossible. It has all the discomforts of London without its mildness; all the harshness of New York without its gaiety. Yet I got my papers, which proved to be most interesting. I did a heap of reading which was indispensable and almost as interesting as the papers. I never have had a better-employed six weeks, and have seldom been gladder to finish them."

Adams spoke too soon. He did not get the copies he ordered at the French foreign office. French authorities wanted Mr. Adams not to receive the copies unless reciprocal advantages were granted to French inquirers seeking papers in Washington. The problem was one of international scope, requiring a concession by Secretary Evarts. It developed, too, that M. Faugère lost Adams's instructions to the copyist.

In London, Adams planned a month's reading of old newspapers at the British Museum—"Pure loss of time, but inevitable"—and another month at the Record Office. He also wished to complete an article he said he had started but "not touched since finishing Gallatin."[44]

For Henry and Clover, events were crowding together in bewildering confusion. On March 8, the day it was thought Mrs. Lowell had died, the Gaskells and Henry James were the Adamses' dinner guests. Carlo brought news of a sudden dissolution of Parliament and an impending election. British politicians, Cunliffe and Gaskell for two, would perforce spend several weeks among their constituents. Political excitement was expected to rise quickly to feverish heights.

On March 15, pending assurance from Evarts of rights for French inquirers, Adams sent instructions that the copyist at the French foreign office should "copy every document in full." Adams made the arrangement through Henry Vignaud, the U. S. assistant secretary in Paris. He told Vignaud: "I expect to pay a very heavy bill, but if I am the worse for it some poor clerk will be the better and doubtless needs the money more than I do. History is a stern mistress and more costly than an actress of the Variétés."[45]

Lowell departed for Madrid on March 18, on leave. He took with him a copy of *The Life of Albert Gallatin*. In a week's time, he succeeded in moving Mrs. Lowell as far as Biarritz. He wrote thence to Adams: "I read the Gallatin nearly through on the journey. It was a great distraction & I found it very interesting."[46]

In a note sent on March 29, Lowell added: "I haven't yet finished Gallatin which . . . grows more interesting as it goes on." Certain facts in the biography would have special interest for him. Gallatin's last post as a United States official was minister to England. The president under whom he served was John Quincy Adams.

For all intents and purposes on April Fool's Day, 1880, Henry Holt and Company in New York published an anonymous work titled *Democracy/ An American Novel*. The Republican convention would begin in Chicago two months later, on June 2. Whether *Democracy* would affect Blaine's chances at the convention would greatly depend on sales.

The persons given review copies included Wendell Phillips Garrison (son of William Lloyd Garrison), who, among other duties, served the *Nation* as book review editor. Apparently without interference by Godkin, Garrison secured a notice of *Democracy* for publication, unsigned, in the weekly's issue for April 22.[47]

American and British reviewers of the time thought of themselves as expert readers who fully understood the art of reading books. Rather than read *Democracy* for its story, the reviewer for the *Nation* tried to discover the nationality of the anonymous novelist. The effort led to complex results. The review began:

> *Democracy* is called "an American novel," but there are traces in it of other than American handiwork. The attentive reader will be in several minds about it; in parts it displays a thorough familiarity with "American institutions," while in others [it] seems so dissociated from any native sympathy as to spring wholly from intimate and long observation from without. In saying that . . . it leaves a general impression such as the work of some clever Englishwoman long resident in Washington and a practised writer, carefully revised and edited by an American, might leave, it is not meant to hazard a guess as to its author, but to give a description of the book.

More or less unthinkingly, the *Nation's* reviewer supposed the novel was written in recent months. On that basis, the reviewer asked the assumedly urgent question whether the novel obeyed the rules of good taste. The answer was negative. The novel sinned when attempting to picture a senator eager to be president and sinned grievously when picturing a president's wife. In the book, Senator Ratcliffe was endued "with the least admirable traits of several well-known public men who are easily recognizable" (the reviewer was pointing at Senator Blaine). The wife was "readily identifiable" (the reviewer mistakenly believed she was Mrs. Hayes). And precisely because its offenses against good taste were "grave," indeed "as sensational in some regards as if it had a blackmailing intention," the novel, so said the reviewer, was self-defeating. ". . . the effect of *Democracy* will probably be slight. . . ."

The reviewer's opinions were representative—except in one way. Readers generally agreed that nothing mattered more about *Democracy* than its authorship. They agreed, too, that the names of its characters in real life could be determined beyond a doubt. But they particularly agreed that the book's offensiveness was of a sort that needed to be experienced at first hand. They wanted to feel it.

Apparently in late April, C. F. Adams, Jr., caught wind of *Democracy*, ascertained that the book indeed was coarse, and mailed a copy to Henry in London. He alerted Henry that a book was coming but did not specify the title. Henry advised on May 19 that the promised book had not arrived.[48]

Henry Holt and Company had meanwhile discovered that *Democracy* was a publisher's bonanza. Most American novels sold in mere hundreds of copies. This one was selling in thousands. Copies could be sold as fast as they could be manufactured and hurried to the stores.[49]

Charles tried again. He wrote on June 4: "The book I sent you was the very 'coarse' novel—Democracy. I send you another copy. Not that I admire it, but I was rather pleased with the leading character—Randolph [actually Ratcliffe]—in which the author seems to me to show some insight into the mixed ability, cant, integrity and shrewdness of our Western statesmen."

While Charles was writing, the Republican delegates at Chicago were balloting. Grant was leading but seemed unlikely to get the nomination. The supporters of Senator Blaine and Secretary of the Treasury Sherman were so numerous that the convention was balloting repeatedly without result. Charles seemed half to regret the deadlock. In his letter to Henry, he continued: "Poor Grant!— Think of finishing at Galena at 55 after his career!"

Henry meanwhile was working with his usual success and speed. He wrote to Lodge on May 13: "I have finished with the Record Office, completed my search through the newspapers, collected the greater part of my pamphlets, and sounded all the wells of private collections I could find. In Madrid and Paris copyists are at work for me and ought soon to send their copy. I foresee a good history if I have health and leisure [in?] the next five years, and if nothing happens to my collections of materials. My belief is that I can make something permanent of it, but, as time passes, I get into a habit of working only for the work's sake and disliking the idea of completing and publishing."

Henry James had gone for a time to Florence. The Adamses' most congenial English visitors were John Bright and J. R. Green, and Green was reading *Essays in Anglo-Saxon Law*.

In connection with the *Essays*, Adams added to Lodge: "John Green is one of my intimate friends here, but how he objurgates you fellows for your German style. He says my Essay is bad enough, but you others are clean mad. We chaff each other thereupon." Nothing in Henry or Clover's letters showed that Green took issue with the ideas in Henry's essay. Possibly Green accepted Adams's opinion that the English, however much they were corrupted by French feudalism and imported ideas of hereditary royalty and aristocracy, were originally, and might remain, a democratic and republican people, little though they knew it.

Gladstone succeeded Disraeli as prime minister. Lowell returned to duty in London. Henry and Clover were hoping both Grant and Blaine would lose the Republican nomination. They worried, yet also looked forward with confidence. Clover wrote on June 6: "Our little minds turn anxiously to Chicago & we watch the Grant boom wane & look to see Blaine laid out afterwards. We want Hayes or Sherman, or even Harrison as a dark horse but this week must end the battle. . . ."

News was cabled on June 8 that the Blaine and Sherman forces, as a means of denying the nomination to Grant, threw their support to Congressman Garfield on the thirty-sixth ballot. The choice came as a surprise. Clover wrote: "The one interest of the past week to us . . . has been Garfield's nomination. It is most satisfactory & he will continue the regime of clean government which mild brother Hayes has so well begun. Garfield dined with us a few weeks before we left Washington last year . . . & was very outspoken as to Hayes['s] shortcomings."

To his extreme satisfaction, Adams was granted temporary possession of bundles of papers written by Spencer Perceval, chancellor of the exchequer and prime minister till assassinated in 1812.[50] Adams had long been trying to get the papers, which remained in private hands. Many had to be copied. He copied them himself.[51]

By applying well in advance, Henry and Clover had reserved the same cabin on the *Gallia* for their return voyage to New York on September 25. Their plan was to spend ten days in Beverly before house-hunting in Washington. They changed the plan, deciding to go first to Washington and then to Massachusetts to vote. Though long on the market, their house at 91 Marlborough Street had not found a buyer. Henry remained a legal resident of Boston and Beverly Farms. He could cast a ballot.

During their winters in Washington, Clover had said that Boston was home and had thought that her and Henry's returning to Boston was possible. On April 18, 1880, at Queen Anne's Gate, she had written to her father very differently: "I'm so glad to hear from you that we're missed in Washington—it was a wise move to go there to live. We've never flattered ourselves that the Hub missed us."

Through Edward Hooper, the Adamses had been seeking a still better Washington house. At the perfect moment, they were offered a house at 1607 H Street that Corcoran was renovating. They at once agreed to rent it. On June 27, Clover advised Dr. Hooper that their future residence had "many good points." Its location was "better than the house we left—more sun—& no overlooking neighbors."

She did not mention that 1607 H Street was on the north side of Lafayette Square. She apparently was familiar with its interior. She knew—but did not say—that the double window of Henry's study would look directly across the square to the west wing of the White House, where successive presidents had their office.[52] Evidently, from her and Henry's perspective, the news was too good for expression.

18

Some Good Influence

M ost of the Spanish papers arrived at 22 Queen Anne's Gate, transcribed in a stately hand.[1] The others were promised soon. Because uneasy about them, Adams arranged that the French papers already copied be kept at the U. S. legation in Paris, pending his return to that city. Meanwhile in London he obtained copies of added British papers relating to the New England Federalists.[2]

Adams was learning what his *History* was going to say, but he was making inconsistent comments about its form. He had told Grigsby that three volumes would embrace fifteen years. On July 9, 1880, writing to Lodge, he said that six volumes would embrace sixteen years. "My material is enormous, and I now fear that the task of compression will be painful. Burr alone is good for a volume, Canning and Perceval are figures that can't be put in a nut-shell, and Napoleon is vast. I have got to contemplate six volumes for the sixteen years as inevitable. If it proves a dull story, I will condense, but it's wildly interesting, at least to me. . . ."

The more trustworthy portions of Adams's comments related to dates. Although it would fix on the period 1800–1817, his *History* would most concern the interval from March 1801, when Jefferson took office as president, to December 1814, when Gallatin and others completed the negotiation with the English ending the War of 1812. Less credible were the portions concerning volumes. It seems likely that from the beginning he had planned a history in four volumes. In that event, his mentions of three or six volumes were mere screens and the four-volume plan was temporarily a secret.[3]

Clover had not seen Scotland. Intending to go there, the Adamses had accepted an invitation to visit Sir John and Lady Clark, residents of Aberdeenshire, whom they had recently met in

London. Also Henry and Clover planned a visit to the west coast, facing Skye.

In his letter to Lodge, Henry had sketched the Adamses' future. "I suppose we shall stay in Scotland till near September, and reach New York . . . on October 5th or thereabouts, whence we must go directly to Washington. . . . We have taken Corcoran's white house, next [to] his own. . . . When things are set going there, we shall come to Boston for a while. I rather hope to be there for the election, to vote. Then back to Washington for the winter, and I look forward placidly to recurring winters and summers in Washington and Beverly, until a cheery tomb shall provide us with a permanent abode for all seasons." In a separate passage, he said, ". . . I shall vote for Garfield."

The forecast reflected a happy truth. Henry and Clover were enjoying normal health and anticipated living to late ages. One truth was kept from sight. Their marriage had united persons who differed in relation to place. Henry was a Washingtonian and a cosmopolitan but not a New Englander. He *had* to live in Washington; he again would *have* to travel. Clover began as a New Englander but was governed by attachments to persons. She could enjoy long foreign journeys; she welcomed living in Washington in winter; but she needed hope of returning every summer to Beverly Farms. She remained strongly attached to her father.

As things stood, their difference was immaterial. Both were tired of travel and tired of Europe. Clover told her father: ". . . to a genuine New-England soul the '*discipline*' of a winter in Europe is no slight thing. Fortunately for me Henry is quite of my way of thinking & having passed more than eleven years out of the 22 since leaving college on this side of the water he doesn't want to pass any more."

Meanwhile the news from Massachusetts was unhappy. Henry's father was losing his powers of memory. Alice Hooper had died of illness; and Fanny Hooper—Edward's wife, mother of five small daughters—was very ill, her death a matter of months.

Hopes that the country would get a good president, at first sight improved, were dimmed and might soon be shattered. The *New York Herald* had greeted Garfield's nomination by reprinting Independent charges of 1876 that he had used his congressional office to extort and pocket money. Clover wrote: "I hope Garfield will come out & clear off the charges against him—if not disproved he is hardly fit to be Pres^t." That Garfield should clear himself seemed the more necessary because General Winfield Scott Hancock, the Democratic candidate, was not in the Adamses' judgment an acceptable alternative. Newspaper reports concerning Garfield continued to be less than reassuring.

Vacating 22 Queen Anne's Gate on July 31, 1880, the Adamses went to Edinburgh and thence to Tillypronie, the Clarks' house near Aberdeen. The house—"the perfection of good taste & luxury"—stood on a hilltop "looking far and wide over crimson moors and blue hills." Sir John and Lady Clark were a half-generation older than the Adamses. Clover wrote, ". . . [they] are profound liberals & radicals & speak their minds refreshingly." Everything about the visit was pleasing and enjoyable.

A few days later, on the west coast at Oban, the Adamses accidentally fell in with Bret Harte. The Californian and Henry had no difficulty getting acquainted. Clover wrote, "He and Henry are now chatting in the garden in front of my parlour window."

In London, Henry and Clover again saw Henry James. Writing to James soon after, Clover said something about *Democracy*. (Her letter is missing.) James replied, "I hear a good deal about the little book, *Democracy*, you mention. . . ." He said it was "much talked of" in Warwickshire, where he was visiting. He apparently had not read it.[4]

In Paris, the Adamses took a large suite at the Hôtel du Jardin. Their errands were collecting French state papers and buying Worth gowns. A "huge pile of material copied here since January" awaited Henry at the Legation. Clover increased her store of gowns to eight.

They did not need pictures. In England, assisted by Thomas Woolner, they had purchased many watercolors and three oils. The furthest thing from their minds was buying another painting. Walking one day on the Rue Lafayette, they saw a painting in a window that looked familiar. On the way from Tetuan to Ceuta the previous November, they had been joined by two Frenchmen, a photographer and an artist. During a stop on the road, the artist had sketched the Adamses' Moroccan guard on horseback. The painting in the window corresponded to the sketch. Henry wanted the painting, but the dealer had already sold it. A trip to the artist's studio outside of Paris did not result in discovery of the sketch. Moreover, the artist was away, in Spain.

Clover commented with amusement that their effort made "a tragic tale." The oddest part of the tale was a name. In North Africa, the artist had told the Adamses that his name was "G. Washington." They had not credited his word till they saw his signature on the painting in the Paris window. And most emphatically the tale had a point. Henry could not see or hear the name

George Washington without reacting strongly. On that score, his sensitivity, always great, was on the rise.[5]

The Adamses expected to spend their last days in Europe at Wenlock Abbey with the Gaskells and Cunliffes. The English couples were raising children. The Adamses were looking forward to Henry's working continuously till his *History* was finished. As they knew, their happiness was partly based on ceaseless, difficult work.

In a letter to Carlo sent from Paris on September 11, 1880, Henry so foretold the future that the *History* vanished and a different project was revealed: a design for a memorial at a gravesite. His tone mingled the solemn with the cheery. "I am heartily glad to feel that I shall have another holiday with you, for the shades of night are drawing down upon us and there is little to look forward to but the grave. I am going to order mine after my own design, as my last amusement."

The holiday at Wenlock was pleasant but brief. The Adamses boarded the *Gallia*. From Queenstown, where the ship paused for passengers and mail, Henry sent a note to Carlo that brimmed with finality. ". . . I have little doubt that we now are bidding good-bye to Europe forever. If we wander again, it will be when the doctors send us for health."

Happily, on the train from New York to Washington, the Adamses had the company of Schurz's daughters. They were joined as well by their potential best ally. Clover reported to Dr. Hooper, ". . . Wayne MacVeagh was on the train,—Cameron's brother-in-law. . . ."

A Philadelphia lawyer, MacVeagh seemed worthy of high office in the federal government. He was married to Virginia Cameron, daughter of Simon Cameron. He thus also was the brother-in-law of Senator James Donald Cameron, known as Don, the successor to Simon Cameron as boss of Pennsylvania. Clover continued: ". . . [MacVeagh was] full of politics and most interesting to our long-famished souls. He is an Independent, and the clan Cameron is not in sympathy with him."

In Washington, the Adamses rented 1607 H Street from Corcoran for six years, with hope of renewals. The house had thirteen foot ceilings, center halls, and large rooms.[6] Gaslight and modern plumbing were being installed. Henry and Clover wanted additional conveniences, beginning with sufficient bookshelves in Henry's study. (The room was to the right, as one entered from the street.) They would begin to make some use of the house as soon as the study was put in order.

Hardly pausing in New York, they went to Boston, arriving on October 14, 1880. Henry visited his parents. The Chief found him "well and active in mind"; also "amusing in the history of his experiences." Two mornings later, the Chief and Henry went to Boston together. The Chief recorded: "He has but one fault[,] the passion for roving—a difficulty incident to persons not favored with children."

The Massachusetts Adamses had not yet learned Henry was hard at work on a history of the United States. In the absence of that information, C. F. Adams was harboring the doubly wrong idea that Henry lacked a "permanent site" and lacked an "occupation." The best cure, the Chief believed, would be for Henry to accept a public office. "It is barely possible that in the changes that happen in public life he may catch some position that may give him the occupation that he needs. I trust it may be so and yet I fear."[7]

Henry and Clover meant to stay in Massachusetts only long enough to visit relatives, send properties to Washington, and attend to business details. Henry would *not* stay to vote. In his and Clover's opinion, the charges leveled at Garfield were unanswered and true. The Ohioan none the less was likely to be elected. That being the case, the best plan for Henry was an early return to Washington.

Possibly on October 16, Clover and Henry joined Dr. Hooper and the Gurneys, presumably for dinner. Astonishingly, in Clover's words, Dr. Hooper "opened fire" about *Democracy*. He said that Godkin "knew the author."[8] Whitman and Ellen's faces betrayed their knowing something. The Adamses could not guess how much and did not mean to ask.

Since leaving the *Gallia*, Henry and Clover had been twice in New York but had visited Godkin neither time. On October 24, Godkin wrote to Charles about his article concerning *The Life of Albert Gallatin*. The letter is missing, but its contents can be inferred. Godkin told Charles mistakenly that Henry and his wife were much offended by the article. What the editor wanted was permission to tell them who had written it.[9] As it happened, Charles was not in Boston. The letter had to wait his getting back.

Care of Boojum has been transferred from failing Alice Hooper to the Hoopers' servant, Betsy Wilder. Restored to the Adamses, Boojum accompanied them to New York on October 27, shopped for wall-papers, gas lamps, and other furnishings, and proceeded to Washington. Wormley's, the hotel at H and Fifteenth

Streets where they would stay, admitted him as a long-familiar guest.

Charles returned to Boston. He had represented his Gallatin article to Godkin as "medicine" that would do Henry needed good. On October 30, he opened Godkin's letter, gathered that Henry and Clover were much offended, and wrote to the editor, "I laughed consumedly as I read it, for it showed that my medicine was working."[10] Without refusing permission to reveal the authorship, he urged Godkin to take a different course. Indeed he gave instructions.

> . . . go to see them [in Washington] just as usual. . . . If it's on her mind[,] Mrs. Adams will not be able to help referring to that grievance. . . . Ask if she suspects who wrote it. Then bring on your mystery. Tell her that you wished you could tell her,—that it would astonish her,— that it was utterly impossible for you to decline the paper, coming from such a source &c &c, and generally convey the impression that it was Mr. Evarts, Henry Ward Beecher, Geo. Wm Curtis, or Gen. Grant,—that you are dying to tell, but can't. That fetches 'em—every time.

It had occurred to neither Godkin nor Charles that Henry and Clover had known at once that Charles had written the article. They had known too that humans varied greatly in intelligence; most were limited in mind; not a few were fools. In the present case, Godkin and Charles were equals in dimness but dissimilars in motive. Godkin thought the article was felt by Henry and Clover as an unexplained and grievous insult. He wanted to patch things up. He was bumbling, yet friendly.

There was nothing friendly nor even joking in the impulse felt by Charles. He wished it thought that his motive was correction of Henry, the more effectual if anonymous, but his conjurings to the editor revealed his controlling impulse. He hoped that criticism of Henry would torment Henry's wife. His newest hope was that her torment, which he believed considerable, might be doubled.[11]

During the Adamses' year in Europe, John Hay, on leave of absence from the *New York Tribune*, had returned to the government as assistant secretary of state, replacing Fred Seward, who had resigned. Clarence King remained director of the Geological Survey and was usually in Washington. In recent years, he had formed affectionate ties with the Hays. These developments brought five friends together in one place. On October 29, 1880, when the Adamses bivouacked at Wormley's, they, King, and the Hays were residents of Washington.

On election day, November 2, Garfield defeated Hancock handily in electoral votes but won the popular vote by the narrowest of margins. The future president seemed a weaker, less capable leader than had been anticipated. Rumors about his Cabinet proliferated quickly.

The most ambitious officeholder in Washington was Senator Blaine. His house was a political and social gathering place. That Henry and Clover had never called on the Blaines was known. Their avoidance of Blaine rested on three grounds. By their count, the senator's illicit pocketings of money hugely exceeded Garfield's. An artful adviser, he seemed capable of taking control of the new administration simply by sliding into it. Ominous too was his household, which included the senator, his wife, their children, and Mary Abigail Dodge, his secretary (also a journalist), known by her adoptive name, "Gail Hamilton." As seen by the Adamses, Gail Hamilton was the flag that most openly displayed the auspices under which Senator Blaine meant to continue and expand his depradations.[12]

Far from being Independents, King and Hay were confirmed Republicans. King was friendly with Blaine and his housemates. Hay was even friendlier. Both were aware that Republicans might sin, even did; but they would not forsake the party on that account; and, being officeholders themselves, they were more or less required to condone the offenses of the party's highest-ranking men as incidental crimes, the natural concomitants of government everywhere.

Adams returned to the State Department and resumed his mining of government documents. Charge of the department's library had devolved on a former clerk, Theodore Dwight. Friendly cooperativeness began between Adams and Dwight, who was an imposer on other people, yet had the merit of knowing where to find the department's papers.[13]

Work at 1607 Street proceeded. Henry's study was finished. Clover served tea to Secretary Schurz in the study on November 14 and thereafter offered daily tea at 5:00. She told her father, "The town is filling fast and we expect an interesting winter."

A letter from Godkin to Clover raised anew the question of the Gallatin article. His letter is missing but evidently said that any hurt the article had inflicted on Henry was chargeable, not to Godkin, but to the reviewer, whose name could not be revealed. Clover passed the letter to Henry.

On November 22, Adams advised the editor, ". . . we laughed consumedly over your wail. . . ."[14] He repeated that he had no interest in the article and was not offended. He pointed out that the person responsible for the article's appearing in the magazine was Godkin and if there had been offense (there had been none) the *editor* was the offender. In a last paragraph, he changed the subject. ". . . the real complaint against you is much more serious. It is that you have been talking about a matter concerning which you were pledged to absolute silence. Of this, I will not write."

The reply shook Godkin's plumes. He had assumed he was free to tell selected persons that *he* knew who wrote *Democracy* but could not divulge the name, being sworn to secrecy. A flurry of messages passed between Godkin, Henry, and Clover. It emerged that Godkin had not told the Gurneys that the author was Henry. Since Holt, King, and Godkin were the only persons who knew the authorship (Mrs. Parkman and General Taylor had died), and since King's silence remained complete, as had Holt's, Godkin's bragging had resulted in very little.[15]

On November 27, 1880, moving men completed the bringing of fifteen wagons of possessions into 1607 H Street, and the Adamses started full residence. In early December, painters transformed the exterior of the house from white to yellow. The changed was noticed. Perhaps beginning soon, people called the building the Yellow House.[16]

In America and England, persons of many sorts were talking about *Democracy*, buying it, and trying to read it. Interest was strong in Boston, where books were supposed to be taken seriously, and in Washington, where the book could be imagined to have particular application. In both cities, curiosity centered in the novel's authorship, but in Washington it also gravitated urgently towards the possible "real" identities of certain of the leading characters.

Beginning in December 1880, events occurred which cannot be accurately followed apart from accurate comprehension of *Democracy*. One point is fundamental. The only work by Adams containing living persons under invented names is *The Radical Club*. A second point is historical. *Democracy* overstrained the minds of its initial readers.[17] For the public in a later age, say the twenty-first century, it might be readable without disturbance. For the readers who saw it the 1880s, it was extremely agitating. It induced excitable souls to believe they were reading a *roman à clef*. They could only think they were reading about "real" people, which they were not.[18]

At worst a near-masterpiece, *Democracy* is less outrageous than

The Radical Club but more ingenious and incomparably more ambitious. It is a heavy comedy masquerading as a light.[19] Its characters are types. Some also are highly developed figments of the imagination. To that extent, the book sets out to be an authentic work of fiction and handsomely succeeds.[20]

The principal characters are numerous. There is a heroine who so slightly understands herself that it requires most of the cast to prevail upon her not to enter into a predictably horrendous second marriage.[21] There is a senator who turns into a secretary of the treasury and will never be president.[22] One may think him the villain; he is accused of having taken a large bribe; but one cannot be entirely certain that he has ever lied importantly; his history remains in doubt; and clearly, through life, he has spent no money but his salary.[23]

There is a female lobbyist who, while her lobbyist husband lived, practically ran the country and did it in her head, without keeping records.[24] There is an honest lawyer.[25] (The cast derives more from the evolution of the stage than the evolution of the novel.) There is a heroine's younger sister, a good judge of persons but a stranger to ideas. As is to be expected, the heroine is loved by the honest lawyer, on whom her sister has a crush. Add a foreign diplomat condemned by debts to exile in Washington.[26] Also add a Massachusetts historian who wants a diplomatic mission and cannot get one.[27]

Still other characters—other fictions—appear. All the fictions are built in part from shards of fact. Silas P. Ratcliffe cannot be any living senator or secretary of 1876 or 1880; he is too interesting; but, better than any other character, he shows what the author wished to put before the eyes of impressionable readers. Partly by sheer invention, partly by calling upon his exceptional knowledge of the breed, Adams created an archetypal American senator. He lent Ratcliffe fragmentary resemblances to real senators ranging from Blaine and Conkling to Sumner, Seward, and Douglas and, further back, to Webster. He then changed him into a member of the Cabinet and lent him fragmentary resemblances to such real secretaries as Seward and McCulloch—conceivably also J. Q. Adams and Albert Gallatin.

As Adams doubtless foresaw they would, the fragmentary resemblances sent readers on a goosechase after Ratcliffe's identity and gave the chase a direction. The direction was towards guessing, towards the past, and towards absurdity. If ever the goosechase was broken off, the panting chasers would be left with Silas Ratcliffe, a figure worth considering.

* * *

Senator Blaine and Gail Hamilton read *Democracy*. The latter had known Clarence King from youth. It seemed to her that he alone was capable of writing the novel. On the strength of her belief, in mid-December 1880, she and Blaine cut King's acquaintance.

Dr. Hooper read *Democracy* and supposed uneasily that Clover wrote it. He told her his suspicion. She replied on December 21: "I am much amused but not surprised at your suspecting me of having written *Democracy*, as I find I am on the 'black list' here with Miss [Harriet] Loring, Arthur Sedgwick, Manton Marble, Clarence King, and John Hay! We hear that King has been cut by Blaine and Gail Hamilton for his supposed authorship. John Hay says *he* has 'given up denying it'; that 'it will be known after the 4th of March.' Miss Loring has still the inside track, but Arthur Sedgwick is running her hard. All I *know* is that *I* did not write it. Deny it for me if anyone defames me absent, and say to them, as Pickering Dodge [said] of his parrot: 'If she could n't [*sic*] *write* better than that, I'd cut her ———— head off.' "

While giving her trusting father a list of six reputed authors of *Democracy*, Clover deceived him. Saying that all her knowledge of the book was that *she* did not write it, she flatly lied. If she seemed to carry things to extremes, she had the excuse that she and Henry were in a situation which might have been wildly funny had it not been dangerous, not to mention discouraging.[28]

One of the points of *Democracy* was that Americans were consumed by desire for place. To an extent that could be believed only if seen, males in the United States were prey to the impulse to try for office. Their overriding purpose in seeking and getting office was to preen the ego. The reigning question was what each egoist could get to *be*. Any idea that a government and its officers should *do* something of value was secondary, if not absent. In *Democracy*, the point is dramatized obtrusively by male officeholders and office seekers. Yet it also is dramatized by the heroine. Mrs. Lightfoot Lee has no idea that she wants to be a president's wife till near the end of the novel. She then realizes that that had become her controlling motive. She realizes too that an idea she had formed that she should sacrifice herself to help her sister Sybil was a self-deception, nothing else.

These considerations bear on the response of Blaine and Gail Hamilton when trying to read *Democracy*. They assumed the book concerned real persons. They concluded that its leading male character, Silas P. Ratcliffe, was a representation of Blaine.[29] They further concluded that the representation was a libel, an injurious diminution. Or, to put the matter differently, Blaine showed sufficient egoism to volunteer for the role of Senator-and-Secretary Ratcliffe, though injurious, and Gail Hamilton lent him womanly support.

It needs repeating that when he completed *Democracy* in 1876, Henry had before him the threat that Blaine might lead Hayes to make him secretary of state. In 1880, the threat was repeated. The danger arose that Blaine might lead *Garfield* to make him secretary of state. On December 21, when Clover said she knew nothing about *Democracy* except that she did not write it, she and Henry may have known or guessed that Blaine the day before had consented to serve in that capacity.

How Blaine and Gail Hamilton read *Democracy* was a matter of considerable importance. In late December, both were at a pitch of political and personal excitement. Blaine was reaching to control the choice of Garfield's secretary of the treasury. That achieved, Blaine would control the new administration.[30] And wondrously that exact success, if achieved, would make *Democracy* a prophetic novel. Blaine would repeat in life what Ratcliffe had already done within a portentous book.

When the news reached the Adamses that Blaine would head the State Department, it set them on their heels. There seemed little they could do. Yet they meant to do their little. Henry would continue working at the Department till Inauguration Day and would then stay home. He and Clover would continue not calling on Blaine. They would try by every means not to encounter the future secretary at other people's houses. Under cover of these avoidances (which would be noticed and might be ridiculed as Independent pique), they would secretly consider the means of removing Blaine from the State Department and, if possible, from Washington. They *had* to consider. The prospect was that assertive Blaine would direct the executive branch during two Garfield administrations, till March 4, 1889. He might be president thereafter.

Likewise, Blaine and Gail Hamilton had to consider. The author of *Democracy*, after all, might not be King. In that event, an unarrested novelist, male or female, was lurking somewhere in Washington's shadows. In the novelist's book, a senator-turned-secretary was effectively in charge of a new administration. *The book was clearly preceding Blaine and knew his intended moves!*[31] Possibly the author was a devil and the book was supernatural.[32]

❖ ❖ ❖

The Adamses' friends in the Hayes administration would not be staying in office under Garfield. Evarts was returning to private practice. Schurz had suffered in pocket by serving in the Cabinet and wished to find well-paid employment in the press. King was ill, in debt, and more than ever burdened by dependent relatives. He meant to give up his directorship and had already left on a six-week trip to the southwest and Mexico in search of health. Hay wished to free himself from both the State Department and the *New York Tribune*. He would settle in Cleveland, Clara's home city. There he would start writing his parts of the biography of Lincoln that he and Nicolay had long since projected.

When telling her father about Blaine's becoming secretary of state, Clover spoke almost as if the problem she and Henry faced was merely one of social awkwardness. She wrote on January 9: ". . . as we are on terms of great intimacy with several of the head officials in the State Department[,] the position is not easy. Henry will hurry up his work there so as to finish by March 4th, not wishing to be a protégé of a man that he does not recognise socially." In reality, the Adamses' problem was one of mortal enmity. One evidence of its being so was the guardedness of Clover's language. In her letters, she spoke of the future secretary of state in terms of mild disapprobation or near neutrality. Knives were hidden in soft garments.

King's absence reminded the Adamses how large a gap had been left by the death of General Taylor.[33] Yet new friends seemed always to appear. In the evening of January 13, 1881, the Adamses went to a reception given by Mrs. Hay. Clover found herself in conversation with a person she may sometimes have met but did not know. "Mrs. Don Cameron asked if she might come to tea and declined to wait till I called first. She is very young, pretty, and, I fear, bored. . . ."

Daughter of a Cleveland judge, Charles Sherman, Mrs. Cameron was also a niece of General William Tecumseh Sherman and a niece of the outgoing secretary of the treasury, John Sherman. Though honest about other subjects, she lied about her age. She said she was twenty-one but was twenty-three. What she was doing, married to a politician a generation older than herself, was a matter not discussed.[34]

At the moment, Senator Cameron was in Harrisburg, trying to recover control of Pennsylvania, which the "Stalwart" Republicans temporarily had lost. Mrs. Cameron's decision to visit Mrs. Adams could be viewed as a near-revolution. Her taking part in Clover's teas would lead her into company the senator had not usually approved. Clover said: ". . . [she] was quite frank in her remarks about men and things. Poor 'Don' will think she's fallen among thieves. . . ."

At 1607 H Street, the kitchen and servants' quarters were in a building set apart from the back of the house by a garden. Facing the garden, the house had a piazza. Clover advised her father on January 23: "Henry pegs away at his work and thinks his house charming. It is far more attractive than Uncle Sam's, and in spring will be most comfortable when the piazza and garden come into play. We have two spare rooms now ready. When will you come? The sooner the better. . . ."

Schurz favored the choice of Frank Walker as his replacement to head the Interior Department. On February 3, Adams made an unusual move. He wrote to George William Curtis, a New York Independent, the editor of *Harper's*, and asked him to lead a drive to get places in the Cabinet for two Independents, Frank Walker and Wayne MacVeagh. He said he had not consulted his brother Charles. ". . . he and I rarely disagree in these matters." What he wanted was pressure, and his tone was very urgent. "Publicity of course is to be avoided, but whatever is done should be done quickly."[35]

Office seekers were crowding Washington. The Adamses were barricading themselves against new visitors. To be certain of avoiding Blaine, they also were declining invitations to other people's dinners. On February 13, six weeks overdue, King—their "prop and stay"—returned from Mexico. Wormley's being full, he accepted one of their spare rooms till the Inauguration.

In Massachusetts, Fanny Hooper was nearing death. Clover rather wished she might go north and help her brother with the children. She wrote to her father: "I will be nurse or read story books all day long or play games or [do] anything to fill any gaps. Henry and Mr. King will do nicely together and I can leave at two hours' notice."

Fanny died. In keeping with a Sturgis family custom, the news was sent to Clover by letter, not telegraph.[36] The letter did not arrive till the day of the funeral. She again thought of hurrying north but told her father, "Henry flatly refuses to let me go alone and I am not willing to pull him up from his work."

As planned, Adams left the State Department when Garfield was inaugurated. The new president announced his Cabinet choices, other than Blaine, after taking office. Luckily, Blaine was rebuffed. The Cabinet was ill-adapted to his control, and the secretary of the treasury was a man he did not want. Unluckily, however, the Independents were half-rebuffed. Walker did not get the Interior Department.

One Independent was admitted. The new attorney general was Wayne MacVeagh. He started work on March 7. It did not seem so, but his role was double. Publicly he was managing the Justice Department and participating in Cabinet meetings at the White House. Secretly he was a member of a partnership. His partner was Henry Adams, across the square at the Yellow House. Their one idea was removing Blaine from his place as secretary of state and leading member of the Cabinet.

Garfield urged King to remain as director of the Geological Survey. King declined, resigning on March 13. Blaine urged Hay to continue as assistant secretary of state. Hay refused. Bancroft Davis refused the place as well, even when offered augmented pay.

On March 17, the Adamses, King, and the Hays shared a first dinner at the Adamses' table. The occasion reflected their impulse to band together. Indeed it seemed possible that if they made no effort to band together they would forever separate. Four days later, King would move to New York for good. As soon as possible, the Hays would move permanently to Cleveland.

In 1801, when Albert Gallatin left the House of Representatives to be secretary of the treasury, leadership of the Democratic-Republicans in the House was entrusted to a congressman from Virginia, John Randolph. He later became a senator and minister to Russia.

Since 1877, Henry Adams had been telling Henry Cabot Lodge that he was finding John Randolph papers, first among Gallatin's papers, later among those of Jefferson, Madison, and others. But Adams had *not* told Lodge that he was finding papers of great interest relating to Vice President Aaron Burr; also indirectly to Alexander Hamilton and Andrew Jackson. Some of the papers had turned up in *Spanish* archives.

Lodge and John Torrey Morse, Jr., were cousins. Morse was editing political biographies—the American Statesmen Series—for a Boston publisher, Houghton, Mifflin and Company, headed by Henry O. Houghton. Presumably from Lodge, Morse learned of Adams's special knowledge of Randolph. On April 1, 1881, or thereabouts, he wrote to Adams asking him to write a biography of Randolph for the series.

Adams did not at once respond. He hesitated partly because of the existence of a book. In earlier times, a gentleman in St. Louis, Hugh A. Garland, had exerted himself to collect John Randolph papers. He had produced a two-volume work, *The Life of John Randolph of Roanoke*, published in New York in 1850. The book was well-informed. Its narrative was interspersed with extensive quotations from the Virginian's better writings, including his choice comment that John Adams was succeeded by a "greater bear," John Quincy Adams.[37]

There is no evidence that Henry Adams had felt impelled to write a biography of Randolph. To his mind, the Virginian's life inverted what a Virginian's life might better have been in the generations following those of George Washington and John Marshall. But, for reasons connected with his *History*, Adams had intended a biography of Burr.

It has been stressed that Adams's *History* would fix most strongly on the period from March 1801 through December 1814. It must be added that Adams's frame of reference was the American people and their government during *seven* administrations, from 1789 to 1817. He designed an epic narrative which, like Homer's *Iliad*, would begin *in media res*. The histories of the American people during the first and second administrations of George Washington and the administration of John Adams would not be written. Contrariwise, the histories of the American people during the first and second administrations of Thomas Jefferson and the histories of the American people during the first and second administrations of James Madison would be written. The written histories would presuppose the unwritten, would be haunted by them, yet never mention them. Three sevenths of the total being kept from view, the four sevenths presented would receive all the attention that readers might care to give. Narrowed scrutiny would heighten awareness of meaning. Four volumes might have the weight of seven.[38]

Adams was a historian well-supplied with ideas. He was also a great-grandson and grandson of men who had battled to their satisfaction with Alexander Hamilton and Andrew Jackson. There was never a possibility that Henry Adams would write a biography of Hamilton or Jackson; but he possessed important new materials relating to Burr; and he realized that a short, readable biography of Burr, if published soon, would have advantages. It would advertise its author as the historian of the United States in the time of the nation's forming, and it would create a large readership for the four-volume *History* that Adams would start to write shortly after his *Aaron Burr* was finished.

More particularly, Adams's projected *Aaron Burr* would tell the story of the man who shot Alexander Hamilton. It would present a General Hamilton to whom the public was not accustomed. It would similarly present a General Jackson to whom the public was not accustomed. Both generals would be exhibited in comparative shadow. Strong light would fall only on melodramatic Burr, who, after killing Hamilton on the west shore of the Hudson, would travel to the Ohio and Mississippi, seek allies, a candidate being Jackson, and try to form a separate American empire.[39]

As it happened, Adams decided to write a biography of Burr *and* a biography of Randolph, beginning with the latter. On April 9, 1881, he wrote to Morse. As he had done with Lodge, he said he was burdened with a *six*-volume history. He claimed to have extended his time to complete the work from ten years to "fifteen." (He did not give a starting or ending date.) On that basis, having "five years to spare," he said he "might squeeze out of them a month or two for your book."[40] In a last paragraph, using language that Morse might not think agreeable, he also made an offer. "If I find Randolph easy, I don't know but what I will volunteer for Burr. Randolph is the type of a political charlatan who had something in him. Burr is the type of a political charlatan pure and simple, a very Jim Crow of melodramatic wind-bags. I have something to say of both varieties."[41]

Until he wrote to Morse, Adams had made no serious errors for many years. The exchange with Morse occurred at an unlucky moment. Ejected from the State Department, Adams was swept up in the problem of ejecting his ejector. He was too hard-pressed to give his full attention to any subject but Blaine. Because preoccupied, he did not consider that Morse was not an editor he would want. He similarly did not consider that Henry O. Houghton was a publisher with whom he had once come close to crossing swords.[42]

It was an outright error on Adams's part to offer Morse his projected *Aaron Burr*. The *Burr* was too important to be entrusted to Morse and Houghton. And Adams might better have refused to write a biography of John Randolph for Morse's series. Adams did not know that Morse and Houghton liked to think that statesmen were superior figures distinct from politicians, yet cared so little about their principle that Morse had promoted Randolph on a mere impulse and made *him* an "American Statesman." But Adams knew well enough that neither Houghton nor Morse was serious about books and authors. If only for that reason, he might better have declined to go along with Morse's wish.[43]

❖ ❖ ❖

With the coming of spring, Clover mostly discontinued giving teas, preferring when possible to be outdoors. She said she was "planting out my garden." "It's a patch about seventy-five by fifty feet and, the centre being grass with a red maple in [the] middle, I'm having [the] border filled with early spring and late autumn plants—lilies of [the] valley, daffodils, roses which in ordinary winters will bloom until Christmas, and lots of new chrysanthemums. I've engaged Bancroft's gardener to do it for me. . . . We've got so fond of this old house that we shall never leave until we are forcibly ejected."[44]

Dr. Hooper and Edward Hooper came for springtime visits. Brooks Adams came briefly. Charles Francis Adams III, a son of John's, stayed long enough for Henry to show him the capital's sights.

On April 16, 1881, Henry and Clover gave a dinner for eight. The guests included the MacVeaghs. Clover wrote to her father: "It was very lively. Mrs. MacVeagh I'd never seen before. . . ." The wife lent the Cameron family an altered meaning. ". . . Henry says she looks just like her father, old Simon Cameron. She is tall, spare, superb eyes, quick, good deal of humour, and very straightforward. I like her."

On April 23, the MacVeaghs gave a dinner for twelve at which the attorney general escorted Mrs. Adams to the table. It was Henry and Clover's first dinner away from home since February.

President Garfield had attempted to assert himself, but in answer Secretary Blaine had begun a more energetic, more artful effort to take control of the administration. The new conflict initiated by Blaine could seem, and partly was, a mere fight for place between two large Republican factions: the so-called Half-Breeds, including the Blainiacs; and the Stalwarts, mostly die-hard supporters of Grant, led by Senators Conkling, Cameron, and others.

Clover's persistent visitors included two who were well-connected with the Stalwarts. One was her new friend Elizabeth Cameron. The other was Miss Emily Beale, long known to the Adamses and much seen in Lizzie Cameron's company. Emily could be amusing but was not distinguished for power of mind. She recently had read two novels, anonymous *Democracy* and Frances Burnett's *Fair Barbarian*, and had suffered a double shock. Each contained a character modeled on herself! Clover reported the misadventure. ". . . she says she differs from the Biblical gentleman who said: 'Oh, that mine enemy would write a book.' She hopes hers won't write any more."[45] Emily's reaction was representative, though ludicrous. She assumed she knew how to read, and she was self-centered enough to think that she was a subject of the nation's current books.[46]

The opening months of 1881 were Clover's first opportunity to witness office seekers in Washington at the start of a new administration. The spectacle disturbed her. She told her father, ". . . the craving for the meanest kind of official existence is so intense as to form a division of lunacy by itself."

Paradoxically, some male Americans were happiest when *losing* the government positions they had angled long to get. King came back to Washington on a flying visit. Clover wrote on April 24: "He beams with joy at being out of office. He and Mr. Hay were as eager to get out as most fools to get in. . . ."

Under Blaine's renewed artful guidance, Garfield was attempting a series of seeming promotions and new appointments the result of which would be the shifting of Stalwarts to less-desired positions and the installation of Half-Breeds and Blainiacs in much-desired positions. The effort centered in a single office: collector of the revenue in New York. Garfield and Blaine meant to award the office to a Half-Breed, William H. Robertson. (It had earlier been held by Chester A. Arthur, the new vice-president, a Stalwart.) On May 13, 1881, Stalwart Senators Conkling and Platt of New York noisily resigned in protest. Their exit was viewed by onlookers as a victory for Secretary Blaine.

The applicants for office then in the capital included a native of Illinois, originally Julius Guiteau, renamed Charles at his own insistence. Guiteau was nearing forty and was new to politics. Unlike most office seekers, he preferred large designs. The office he requested was the consulship in Paris, or, failing that, the consulship in Vienna or in Liverpool. Since his arrival on March 5, he had made efforts to visit and correspond with President Garfield. He had simultaneously tried to impress his identity and his wishes on Secretary Blaine.[47]

According to later testimony, at the State Department on May 13, Blaine was approached anew by Guiteau, and the secretary shouted at the applicant, "Never bother me again about the Paris consulship as long as you live!" The encounter, if real, occurred at a moment when fact and fiction were growing more and more interactive.

The resignations of Conkling and Platt took the Adamses by surprise. On May 22, Clover wrote: "It's a good riddance, and now if we can get Blaine relegated to private life or a foreign mission we may clear things up a bit. Blaine does not carry much weight in the Cabinet and may resent it by and by. Mr. and Mrs. MacVeagh were here Friday evening and had much to say that interested us."

On May 23, Guiteau wrote to Garfield. He advised in strong terms: ". . . Mr. Blaine is a wicked man, and you ought to demand his *immediate* resignation; otherwise you and the Republican party will come to grief. I will see you in the morning, if I can, and talk with you."

Henry and Clover prepared to move Prince, Daisy, Boojum, and themselves from Washington to Beverly Farms. Henry readied for shipment the evidence he would need when writing two biographies fast.

The Adamses reached Pitch Pine Hill on June 1, after visits in New York, Cambridge, and Quincy. While getting settled, Henry wrote to Justin Winsor, librarian of Harvard, asking the loan of American newspapers from 1800 to 1809 and promising to be done with the volumes by October. Writing also to Frank Walker, he said he expected his work in life to be done in "ten years." "King and I then mean to go off to the South Seas and suck oranges till we die."

The two youngest of Edward Hooper's five daughters, Fanny and Molly, respectively four and two years old, would be staying for the summer with their Aunt Clover and Uncle Henry. While the aunt tended the nieces, the uncle began to write *John Randolph*. He started approximately on June 6.

Guiteau's intended meeting with the president on May 24 had not materialized. In late May, by a means or process not easy to reconstruct, he acquired a new idea. The person to be removed from office was not Secretary Blaine. It was President Garfield.

Knowing himself to be the president's remover, Guiteau borrowed $15.00. On June 8, he bought a revolver. Because unused to weapons, he briefly practiced with the revolver on the banks of the Potomac. He then stalked the president and had two opportunities to kill him. Each time he thought best to wait.

As head of a federal department, Attorney General MacVeagh was obliged to supervise political appointees who were unfit for their assignments. An especially unfit official was George B. Corkhill, the district attorney in the District of Columbia. In early June 1881, MacVeagh told Garfield his opinion of Corkhill. The MacVeaghs then left the capital and went to Boston. They visited the Adamses briefly at Pitch Pine Hill.

On July 1, Garfield decided to bring about the removal of

Corkhill but postponed the needed action. Next morning, he and
Blaine went together to the Baltimore and Potomac Railroad station to take a train. As male Americans often did at the time, the
president and the secretary walked arm in arm. As they walked,
they were followed by a slight person who suddenly produced a
pistol and fired two bullets at close range. The bullets struck
Garfield in the back. A scuffle ensued. The assailant was seized and
conveyed to jail. Every effort was made to help the president, who
was alive but badly wounded.[48]

At Beverly Farms, the Adamses learned only as much about the
attack as was given to the press. With a bullet unremovably lodged
in his spine, Garfield had chances neither of recovery nor survival.
His true condition, however, was successfully concealed.

On learning of the attack, MacVeagh returned to Washington.
Adams continued writing *John Randolph*. On July 9, he sent Mac-
Veagh a letter based on misleading reports of Garfield's condition.
He advised:

> As for the poor President, let us consider it as a fever . . . . Practically
> this is what has happened. He has been hit by one of the disregarded
> chances of life. What then?
>   Of course your business is to get him well. In that case he will have
> an eight-year, popular, irresistible administration. Today is a week
> since he was hit, and if he could live a week, I know not why he should
> not live a thousand.

Since the MacVeaghs' departure from Beverly Farms, Adams
had attended Harvard's Commencement. He mentioned the exercises in his letter and closed by writing an undergraduate cheer.

> John Randolph is finished. Rah, rah, rah.
> Now for Aaron Burr. Rah rah, '81.

There are dimly illumined areas in Adams's second life. One
has to do with letters he received from MacVeagh in mid-July 1881.
The letters are missing. They evidently said that the attorney
general wanted guidance. They gave no warnings that Garfield
could not survive.

The press was saying the president's recovery was assured. At
the same time, a drive was being launched to raise a large sum of
money as a gift to Mrs. Garfield. Corkhill remained in office. The
government's proceedings against Guiteau were in his hands, and
he was stating publicly that he meant to prove in court that Guiteau
was sane.

In this confused situation, on July 18, Adams replied to Mac-

Veagh. He suggested that a gift to the wife of a living president would dog the president and hurt his chances of reelection in 1884. On that ground, he urged that Garfield be asked whether the contributing of money should be stopped. He then turned to the proceedings against Guiteau. Like the rest of the country's citizens, he had been led to believe that the president would recover. On that basis, he assumed that the assassin could be confined permanently only if found to be criminally insane. The press was repeating and repeating that Guiteau shot the president because he wanted a consulship and did not get it. Adams was skeptical. He did not agree that the alleged reason was the full, sufficient reason. He accordingly asked MacVeagh:

> Why is the District Attorney so eager to prove Guiteau sane? You can't hang him. Your only chance of shutting him up for life is to prove him *not* sane. More than this, the assertion that Guiteau is sane is a gross insult to the whole American people. We are all of us ready to shoot the President or anyone else if we can find a good reason for it, but we don't go round banging away with horse-pistols at our neighbors without good cause. . . . The peculiarity of insanity is the lack of relation between cause and effect. No one has yet succeeded in establishing any *sane* cause for Guiteau's effect.

The pervasive idea in the passage was that the cause behind the assailant's act was a matter that MacVeagh himself should try to investigate. What Henry was most aware of was an unattended, far-from-solved, mystery.

Writing at blazing speed, Adams finished drafting his *Aaron Burr*. On August 6, in connection with a separate matter, the purchase of the *Nation* by the *New York Evening Post* and the editing of the *Post* by Carl Schurz, he wrote to Godkin: "Beverly is peaceful—Oh Lord, how long! I have written two whole volumes in exactly two months."

King visited at Beverly Farms, fell ill, recovered, and resumed his wanderings. Adams by then was reading American newspapers of Jefferson's time. He found them almost empty of information.

Gradually the truth was publicized that President Garfield could not live. He was moved for air to the New Jersey shore. There he died on September 19. King wrote to Adams from New York on the 22nd: "It was awfully comfortable and regulating to the mind to stay with you. . . . John Hay of course hurried back here after Garfield died and is doing his Tribune work well as you see."

In appearance, the president's death put Corkhill in the right. Guiteau had shot the president. The president died. If Guiteau could be shown to be sane, nothing further would be needed. Any jury would convict. The assassin would be hanged, and all inquiry could cease.

Chester A. Arthur, the new president, had the virtue of thinking his new office was above him. Garfield's Cabinet resigned, freeing Arthur to name another. Pending Arthur's decisions, the old Cabinet continued to serve *ad interim*.

The Adamses' attitude towards Godkin had softened but was less than trusting.[49] Henry wrote to the editor from Beverly Farms on September 23: "We shall probably be in New York about the 25th Oct. on our way to Washington to see the fun. I do not much care to get there before Blaine quits, for I would not seem to laugh at that national disaster; but I want to be there when McVeagh [*sic*] packs his trunk."

Henry gave an appearance of assuming that Arthur would reappoint neither Blaine nor MacVeagh. His actual idea was subtly different. He assumed that he and MacVeagh could more easily bring about the exclusion of Blaine from the new Cabinet if MacVeagh would *insist* on being permitted to retire.

It was generally supposed that Arthur's administration would be a Stalwart administration, dominated by a resurgent Conkling or resurgent Grant. Adams wrote to MacVeagh of September 25: "I assume . . . that the machine is to rule us henceforth. . . . The new President . . . will hardly deem it necessary to conciliate independents." The latter sentence had very particular implications: that Blaine might be reappointed and MacVeagh would not be. Adams went on to say: ". . . I keenly regret your retirement. I do not like to be left alone in Washington without a single individual to sympathise in my feelings. A single man in a hostile crowd is about equally ridiculous whether he cries out, or holds his tongue. You have rather a gift at crying out. I rather pride myself on the capacity to hold my tongue." The passage had an underlying meaning. Being well suited to work together, MacVeagh and Adams would not dissolve their partnership till either they or Blaine incurred a sharp defeat.

Adams was writing candidly to MacVeagh, only half-candidly to Godkin. On September 30, using the past tense, he assured the editor: "Between ourselves, *my* devil was Mr[.] Blaine. I shall be so well pleased to bid him good-bye that for a time I sha'n't mind any new devils. Garfield's administration, so far as it went, was [a] sort of *delirium tremens* vision with Blaine as the big and active snake."

In about a month, Adams and MacVeagh would be together again in Washington. They would make no blithe assumptions that the big and active snake was leaving the government. They instead would seek an effective means of preventing his reappointment.[50]

Relations between Henry and his brother Charles had dwindled almost to vanishing. On October 21, the eve of their departure for New York, Henry and Clover went to Quincy. They were invited to dinner at the house on Presidents' Hill. Clover wrote of the occasion, "Very smart dinner at Charles's baronial hall[,] which would not be out of place at Chatsworth." Her words were not reflective of good feeling.

In New York, King treated the Adamses and Hays to a dinner at Delmonico's so successful that the participants repeated the indulgence the following night. A motion was made and carried that they should form an association called the Five of Hearts.[51] Not original, and evidently proposed by the Adamses, the name was borrowed from the Five of Clubs, an association formed in an earlier time by Charles Sumner and four male friends in Massachusetts.[52] Hay shortly ordered official stationery for the members, bearing their playing card in red.[53]

The practical occasion for creating the Five of Hearts was the Adamses' telling the Hays that Henry wrote *Democracy*. The Adamses appear to have done so at the restaurant.[54] For them, the club was indispensable protection. The danger to be met was concerted charges by many accusers that *one* of the Hearts—most probably Clover—was guilty of *Democracy*. The best shield against concerted charges was preemptive unity. By openly associating, the Hearts could put onlookers in the way of imagining that the objectionable novel was written by the five associates jointly.[55]

The Hays and King treated Henry and Clover as the first and second Hearts. They lived in Washington, the scene of *Democracy*. Henry was first because he wrote the book.[56]

There was always something hollow about the suddenly-invented club. At the restaurant, the members possibly assured each other that, to match Henry's *Democracy*, Hay and King must each write a novel. Then and later, however, the Adamses withheld the fact that *Clover* already had the manuscript of a novel to her credit, written for her by Henry along lines she could approve. Clearly some secrets were much deeper than other secrets. The existence of *Esther* was not to be imparted.

In Washington on October 28, the Adamses resumed their former ways without apparent change. Clover wrote: ". . . Mrs. Senator Don Cameron and Emily Beale rapped on Henry's window with their umbrellas and of course got in; as Miss Beale explained, 'It's better than ringing because you can't say engaged.' "

On the first Sunday, Boojum sat on a window ledge, as he liked to do, and elicited greetings from passing friends as they went to church. In his study, Henry began to draft a volume which when completed would run to thirty-five chapters. It would be titled *History of the United of America during the First Administration of Thomas Jefferson—1801–1805*.[57] With regard to politics, Henry was far from sanguine. He wrote to Lodge on October 29, ". . . it will be hard for Arthur to begin worse than Garfield did, although he can but try."

Arthur urged MacVeagh not to break off his service as attorney general, as he proposed to do. MacVeagh affirmed his wish to quit and, with Mrs. MacVeagh, temporarily left the capital.

On November 6, in a letter to her father, Clover mentioned a rumor that Blaine had been offered the English mission but refused it. The idea implicit in the rumor was that Blaine would run for president in 1884 and get elected. Clover explained: "He is a crafty old bird and will now pose as Garfield's immediate successor. No one knows that better than Arthur."

On Sunday morning, November 13, the doorbell rang at the Yellow House. ". . . in walked the MacVeagh's [*sic,*] as cheery and jolly as you can imagine." The attorney general and Virginia had come from Philadelphia the night before with President Arthur, Secretary Blaine, and others in the president's private railroad car. "They stayed to lunch and we had a long intimate talk; they couldn't dine but are coming at nine o'clock for tea and more talk."

The visit of the MacVeaghs permitted Clover to send her father a correction. "Blaine has *not* been offered the English Mission. . . ." The source of the false rumor, she said, was Blaine himself.

Next day, November 14, 1881, two events occurred together. MacVeagh ended his service as attorney general.[58] The trial of Guiteau began at the Supreme Court of the District of Columbia.

At the trial, a plea of not guilty on grounds of insanity was made on Guiteau's behalf by his sister's husband, George Scoville. The case for the prosecution was completed on November 21, the case for the defense on December 2. Guiteau made a plea of his own, distinct from Scoville's. It had to do with his claimed insanity.

Guiteau was a would-be writer, as well as would-be evangelist, lawyer, and politician. On June 16, two weeks prior to shooting Garfield, he had written an "Address to the American People." It said in part: "I conceived the idea of removing the President four weeks ago. Not a soul knew of my purpose. I conceived the idea myself. I read the newspapers carefully, for and against the administration, and gradually the conviction settled on me that the President's removal was a political necessity. . . ."

Before going to the railroad station, Guiteau had also written two letters, one beginning "To the White House," the other addressed to General Sherman, head of the army. He had the letters in his pocket when he fired his shots. Both letters contained the sentence "I am a Stalwart of the Stalwarts." Read together, his "Address" of June 16 and his two letters of July 1 could be understood to say that, at the time of the assassination, Guiteau considered himself the highest ranking of the adherents of former-president Grant and the political sponsor of Chester A. Arthur, the president-to-be.[59]

The plea that Guiteau offered in court centered in a different account of his acquiring his idea; also a different conception of his rank. He testified: ". . . the Lord interjected the idea into my brain and then let me work it out my own way. That is the way the Lord does. He doesn't employ fools to do his work; I am sure of that; he gets the best brains he can find." He further explained that, being a selected instrument, he was not responsible. ". . . it was God's act and not mine. The Divine pressure on me was so enormous that it destroyed my free agency, and therefore I am not legally responsible for my act."[60]

The assassin's two accounts of his action were mutually exclusive. One might be true in some limited sense. Both might be false. If both were false, a third account would be needed, one that Guiteau had not chosen to volunteer.

Two Skye terrier puppies, Possum and Waggle, had joined the Adams household. Waggle died, but Possum lived and, while Guiteau's trial was in progress, achieved a social feat. "The great Don [Cameron] came to tea . . . and admired Possum. . . ."

At the Yellow House on December 6, a series of events began which could seem mere accidents of life, yet possibly were results of foresight and the making of arrangements. The Adamses shared "muncheon"—Clover's word—with Charles Grinnell, who had officiated at their wedding. In the interval since the wedding, Grinnell had become a lawyer and legal editor. He had a sister in Washington who was married to Dr. Charles F. Folsom of the National Board of Health. Next day, December 7, the prosecution at the trial would start its rebuttal by calling ten witnesses. One would be Dr. Folsom, speaking as a medical expert.[61]

Early on the 7th, Dr. Folsom sent the Adamses an invitation to the trial. At the court house in the afternoon, Henry sat among the medical experts in close proximity to Guiteau. Clover was given a seat near a window from which she could see the prisoner clearly, but only in profile.

After the court recessed, the Adamses looked on while Guiteau was put into a van to be returned to the jail. Folsom then suggested that the Adamses go with him to the jail, where, he said, he would have to examine the prisoner's eyes.

In the jail's lobby, Clover was introduced by Folsom to a courteous person. She suddenly realized that the person was Guiteau. The knowledge gave her a horrid turn. She had thought the assassin a "beast" and was unprepared for courtesy.

Folsom led Guiteau and the Adamses into the jailer's room, examined the prisoner's eyes, sat down for a talk, and, by way of starting a conversation, made a comment that harked back to the letters Guiteau put in his pocket on July 1, saying he was a Stalwart of the Stalwarts. Clover later reproduced from memory the entire colloquy.

FOLSOM. Well, Grant and Conkling seem to be running things now in the Republican Party.

GUITEAU. I think there is more harmony than there was on the first of July.

HENRY. What do you suppose Mr. Blaine thinks about that?

GUITEAU. We won't discuss that.

Henry's question took the prisoner by surprise. Guiteau gave him a "keen look," answered "drily," and made an immediate departure. "Put on his hat, took up his bundle of newspapers, and shambled out of the room without giving us another look."

One may assume that by the quickest possible means the Adamses told the MacVeaghs the news of the colloquy in the jail.

On Sunday, December 11, 1881, Clover wrote as usual to her father. She volunteered a one-sentence explanation of Guiteau's attack on Garfield. The explanation said nothing out of the ordinary. "He's a cunning, shrewd beast, deranged in a sense no doubt, but he miscalculated, believing he could murder Garfield and get off through the gratitude of the 'Stalwarts.' "[62]

Next day, December 12, Arthur nominated Frederick T. Frelinghuysen of New Jersey to serve as secretary of state, supplanting Blaine. The Senate instantly confirmed the nomination. On the 16th, at MacVeagh's suggestion, the president nominated Benjamin

H. Brewster of Pennsylvania to serve as attorney general. He too was speedily confirmed.

Meanwhile, on the 13th, Henry had walked to a government building. Later in the day, he wrote to Godkin: "I go in for Arthur. No harm he can ever do will equal the good of ejecting Blaine. Today has been a day of bubbling joy to me, and I have returned to my work in the State Department. I think MacVeagh and I were the only men who fully appreciated Mr[.] Blaine's many-sided virtue."[63]

The last words belonged to Clover. On December 18, she again wrote to her father. Three lines of her newest letter were possibly more meaningful than Dr. Hooper would realize.

> Poor Garfield paved his way to the grave with good intentions, and fell so body and soul under Blaine's influence that he lost his moral scent.[64]

> Arthur is astonishing all lovers of clean, strong government by the good quality of the timber he is putting in.

> Some good influence has been at work lately which does not appear.

PART THREE

19

THE AUTHORS OF *DEMOCRACY*

Nicholas Anderson of the Harvard Class of 1858 served as a Union officer during the Rebellion. Wounded at Shiloh and wounded badly at Stones River, he at war's end was a major general. His chief occupation thereafter was being rich. A native of Cincinnati, he disliked the city sufficiently to consider living in another. During a four-day visit to Washington in March 1881, he "to his own amazement bought a charming house"—No. 8, Lafayette Square. The remark about his action was written by Marian Adams, the wife of his Harvard classmate Henry Adams. One of Anderson's hopes was that he and his wife might enjoy the Adamses' company. He visited Henry and Clover on March 18, stayed for dinner, and told them about his purchase.[1]

H. H. Richardson when at Harvard had known Adams and Anderson. One of his architectural specialties was gentlemen's houses. Anderson was rich enough to afford a Richardson house, and a site was available in Washington on which a house would show to advantage. It soon was known in the capital that General Anderson, having bought a small old house on Lafayette Square, would be building a large new one on K Street.

On November 1, 1881, immediately following their return to Washington from Beverly Farms, the Adamses were visited by the Andersons at tea time. Clover wrote that their guests "were full of the new house which Richardson is planning for them here."[2] And on Friday, December 9, two days after the Adamses met Guiteau at the prison, Richardson paid Henry and Clover a brief visit. He had come from Boston to show the Andersons their plans. Next morning, he revisited 1607 H Street. Clover said of the occasion, ". . . we studied the new house plans, which are charming, and he dined quietly with us, the Andersons having a dinner engagement."

Varying a six-year residence in Europe, Henry James had returned to America. On November 6, 1881, he wrote to Clover from Cambridge that he was coming to the capital and would "stay as long as possible."[3] He reminded her that in London she had told him it would be " 'over there [in Washington] that we shall really meet *familiarly!* "[4]

In the letter, James recalled an interchange at a party in Paris. (It was possibly a fiction.) He said an American gentleman had asked him: "Did you read that charming little anonymous novel *Equality?* Have you any idea who it's by?"—to which he had replied: "Not the smallest. But there are plenty of people over there—at least there are two or three—clever enough to have written it." Thereupon, James said, the gentleman had pointed out to him that *"mock-lace,"* a term used in the novel, was English; hence the writer was surely English.[5]

James had come to America partly to be feted as author of his latest novel, *The Portrait of a Lady*, which, after appearing serially in the *Atlantic*, had been published in book form. At James's urging, Clover had waited and read the book version. Henry also began to read it but stopped—left it to others to appreciate and praise.

In December, James stayed with the Godkins in New York. The high point of his stay was a dinner given by Whitelaw Reid in honor of James G. Blaine. Reid believed that Blaine would be devoting his energies to being the next president and would succeed. The visiting novelist was pleased to meet the putative president-to-be.[6]

James had read *Democracy* and especially had hovered over Chapter VI and its presentation of an American girl, Victoria Dare, during an excursion from Washington to Mount Vernon.[7] In mid-December, he asked Godkin whether Mrs. Adams was the author. The editor replied that the rumor of her authorship was nonsense. Secretly he wrote to Adams about James's inquiry and his reply.[8]

From New York a week later, James wrote to Adams. His arrival had been postponed. He explained, "I am really waiting for Guiteau to be hanged. . . ."[9] After another week, he wrote from Cambridge asking Henry's help in getting Washington rooms. It perhaps was clearer to the Adamses than to James that their friend was about to reenact the venture of the heroine in *Democracy*. Like Mrs. Lee, James would try a new experiment, a winter's residence in Washington. Like her, he would visit the engine room of the United States. The outward difference was that he would live alone in furnished lodgings. He possibly would use his hours of solitude to write.[10]

Adams found rooms for James at 723 15th Street, near the Metropolitan Club. On January 5, 1882, James called at 1607 H

Street. He had already completed an inspection of the Capitol. Clover wrote to her father three days later: ". . . Henry James put in an appearance. . . . He is surprised to find that he can go to the Capitol and listen to debates without taking out a license, as in London. He may in time get into the 'swim' here, but I doubt it. I think the real, live, vulgar, quick-paced world in America will fret him. . . ."

James on the same day wrote to Sir John Clark, "I find here our good little friends the Adamses, whose extremely agreeable house may be said to be one of the features of Washington." He seemed a trifle irritated. His saying he had *found* his and the Clarks' "good little friends" combined whimsical falsity with mannerly denigration.

The Adamses invited him to midday dinner on Sunday, January 15, in company with the new British minister, Sir Lionel Sackville-West, and his illegitimate daughter Victoria. James wrote afterwards that Victoria was "a delightful little foreign daughter . . . the most perfect *ingenue* ever seen in America." Henry and Clover's kindness did not arrest his tendency to reduce and minimize. In letters, he mentioned that the Adamses had "a very pretty little life in Washington," that Mrs. Adams served afternoon tea "two or three times a day," and that she gave "frequent dinners at a little round table."[11]

James saw more of Clover than of Henry, who, except on Sundays, was fully occupied in writing United States history.[12] To James's way of thinking, Adams was indeed a historian and thus the opposite of a novelist. Yet James believed him capable of better. It was possibly during one of his calls that he urged Adams to seek a career as a writer more like himself.[13]

Met familiarly, Clover seemed to James a female politician even more political than her extremely political husband. James at the same time noticed an anomaly. Following the dinner with Sackville-West and young Victoria, he wrote with some astonishment that Guiteau was never mentioned in Washington. The subject had been dropped.[14]

Two days after the dinner, Clover had a scare. She heard from her father that he was ill. What was equally worrisome, his housekeeper, Betsy Wilder, was—in Clover's words—"a ghastly failure in illness." The scare passed, but while worried Clover asked her father, "Shall I take the train . . . ?" She knew that Henry would not object. "I will at two hours' notice[,] if it would amuse you or give you any pleasure. Boojum and Possum will take good care of Henry. . . ."[15]

James had assumed that the Adamses' usual practice was to keep open house and "receive a great deal."[16] He quickly learned that Clover's first concern was *not* to receive. It happened that another rising author, Oscar Wilde, was then in Washington. Wilde was famous partly because travestied by Gilbert and Sullivan in *Patience*. (The Adamses had seen the London and New York productions.) Clover had feelings about the "undecided" sexes—her expression—and wanted not to meet him. She accordingly asked James not to bring Wilde to tea. James complied and assured her that his rival in fame was "a fatuous fool, a tenth-rate cad."[17]

James learned too that the Adamses were extremely careful about the houses they visited. He possibly was not told that, during the four months that Chester A. Arthur had been president, Adams had not left his card at the White House.[18] He learned, however, that Henry and Clover would not set foot in the house of Congressman Robeson of New Jersey. He gathered that the avoidance was political.

Arthur had found the presidency a pleasure and, needing something to do, was renovating the White House.[19] Although deprived of office, Blaine remained a fixture in the capital. He was entertaining on an increasing scale and was building a large new house. He invited James to a banquet on January 19 at which the novelist sat next to Gail Hamilton. James most valued the occasion for permitting him an after-dinner chat with the president. Arthur had been acquainted with several Jameses in earlier times. He spoke pleasantly about them.[20]

It struck James that the Adamses were inquisitive. He told Godkin they were "eagerly anxious to hear what I have seen and heard at places which they decline to frequent. After I had been to Mrs. Robeson's they mobbed me for revelations, and after I had dined with Blaine, to meet the President, they fairly hung on my lips."

For particular reasons, James rather hated the capital. He added to Godkin: "Washington is too much of a village. . . . It is too niggerish. . . ."[21] Instead of servants in livery, persons in good society employed servants with dark complexions.[22] The Adamses were no different. Their Washington servants were blacks.[23]

Henry and Clover were aware how strongly James was reacting and may have guessed that he was busy. He was writing "The Point of View," an article in the form of letters, comparing aristocracy and democracy. He seems not to have told them about it. In one letter in the article, he tried to make some slight use of Clover's conversation.[24]

Blaine when secretary of state had been required to deal with complications incident to a war between Chile and Peru. In late January 1882, a scandal erupted concerning his response to the complications. James came to think that, with respect to Blaine, the Adamses were unbalanced. On Sunday, the 29th, he wrote to his mother, "The great news of the moment is the exposure of Blaine with regard to South America—over which the little Adamses, who are (especially Mrs. A.) tremendously political—are beside themselves with excitement."[25]

That Sunday, Adams wrote to Gaskell. He said his life was "as real and enjoyable as ever." ". . . if I felt a perfect confidence that my history would be what I would like to make it, this part of life—from forty to fifty—would be all I want." His forties, he continued, had "a summer-like repose"—"a self-contained, irresponsible, devil-may-care indifference to the future as it looks to younger eyes; a feeling that one's bed is made, and one can rest on it till it becomes necessary to go to bed for ever. . . ."

The description was too simple. Adams would not tell Gaskell, and would surely not tell James, but he and Clover were sustaining a devil-may-care indifference despite threatened occurrences that might destroy indifference at any time. Especially Adams would not tell why he and Clover wanted Blaine out of politics; why they hated his hanging on in Washington; and why they could seem beside themselves when a new Blaine scandal came to light. The most Adams said to Gaskell was that his Washington life was too exciting. "You know my life here, for I have described it to you many times. Poor Henry James thinks it revolting in respect to the politics and the intrigues that surround it. To me its only objection [in the sense of drawback] is its over-excitement."

A parent's illness brought James's visit to a close. That Sunday at 11:00 P.M., he came to 1607 H Street to apprise the Adamses that his mother was ill in Cambridge and he was starting north next day. Clover telegraphed on Monday to Mrs. Louis Agassiz and early on Tuesday got an answer. Mrs. James had died.[26]

Brooks Adams had had a setback. He was thirty-three. After running without success for the Massachusetts legislature and trying without success to win a young woman in marriage, he had suffered a mental and physical breakdown. One result of his illness was a change of temper. Earlier personable, he had become combative and saturnine.[27]

By letter, Henry and Clover had asked Lodge to join them in urging Brooks to come to Washington for a visit. Brooks had agreed to come at a later date, and Lodge invited himself for a week. On January 31, shortly prior to Lodge's arrival, Henry wrote to him: "History moves on apace. I am getting to Chase's impeachment and the close of my first four years, the easiest quarter of my time." Rather than stop to read his manuscript, he was drafting added chapters. ". . . I keep hammering ahead, day after day, without looking backwards."

By the end of January, it appears, Adams drafted twenty-six of the thirty-five chapters of his *History of the United States of America during the First Administration of Thomas Jefferson—1801–1805*. As he said, his progress was swift. Yet in a hidden way it was swifter than could be guessed. Writing the *First Jefferson*, as one may call it, he changed to a style unprecedented in his writings. Although written in prose, his narrative had the economy and scale of an epic poem.

While hammering ahead in the *First Jefferson*, Henry improved *Aaron Burr*. Other than Clover, no one knew he had written the *Burr*. He had told Morse that he *might* write it, but Morse had not understood that the idea was serious and had no inkling that the book was written.[28]

The only persons who were not only the Adamses' friends but also their political allies were Wayne and Virginia MacVeagh. The two couples were seeing each other whenever the MacVeaghs came to Washington. They communicated mostly in person. Letters were exceptions.[29]

King and the Hays were the Adamses' fellow Hearts but, being loyal Republicans, were political opponents. In New York, when not prevented by malaria, King was absorbed in mining ventures. The fact was not yet evident, but his epic work was already behind him, achieved at the cost of damaged health, physical and mental.[30]

The Hays were living in Cleveland. Hay was prone to illness; his best work was not yet started; and, were he to do it, he would have to do it in the intervals when feeling better. Meanwhile, in cooperation with Reid and others, he was warmly supporting Blaine.

There was no one in the administration or in the Congress whom the Adamses knew and liked. Henry mentioned to Gaskell, ". . . I am curiously without political friends, and know not a single man in public life who agrees with me." Yet he said he was hopeful concerning Blaine's Peruvian misconduct. ". . . I trust that Mr. Blaine is blown up forever. . . ." About Arthur's presidency, he admitted being depressed. ". . . I am more despondent about this new administration than about any other of late years. It is wretchedly feeble and characterless."

Two political friends stepped forward. Charles Nordhoff, the Washington correspondent of the *New York Herald*, had been an Independent but an approver of Blaine. Disclosures he himself was making converting him to an enemy of Blaine. A man who needed no converting was a newly-elected Democratic congressman from New York, Perry Belmont, son of August Belmont. Perry had been a student of Adams's at Harvard. Though a freshman in the House, he was a member of the committee on foreign relations. Early in 1882, he became Henry and Clover's secret representative on that committee, sharing their opinions.[31]

The Peruvian scandal was a far-ranging entanglement involving promoters, speculators, investors, bankers, and public officials in Paris, London, New York, Washington, and Latin America. In its connection, letters had vanished from the State Department's files. On January 31, Clover sent her father an account of the scandal. "We . . . hope the rat Blaine is in a corner at last. He is of course lying, and squirming, and bullying, but there is worse to come, and all the press is against him but the *Tribune*, whose editor, Whitelaw Reid, is a scheming tramp from Ohio, sold to Blaine, body and soul . . . . Nordhoff put a match to the fuse last Thursday, and now that the blast is in full force we remain at a safe distance and watch the splinters fly."

Dr. Hooper advised Clover to beware of party politics. She replied that Boston was not in Washington's latitude and did not sense the "feeling and interest" of events in the capital. Yet she promised to say less about politics in her weekly letters. As news, she said Emily Beale was "in bed with chills and fevers; looks like Blake's ghost of a flea." "Mrs. Don Cameron came home yesterday from a six weeks' illness in New York. I'm going to see the poor little woman now; she's drawn a blank in Don, I fear, for all his money and fine house, and she's not over twenty-three—a mere baby."

The Adamses were in good health, but Henry was hard worked by his *History*. The method he meant to use to build the *First Jefferson* was daily writing at high speed followed by rewriting and more rewriting. He had told Lodge on January 31 that the volume was moving swiftly. On February 20, he told Francis Parkman it was moving slowly. He said he was "struggling" with his "historical mud-pie" and doing his best "to give it shape and cohesion." He apparently had read the drafted chapters, seen the amount of rewriting they would require, and was not a little shocked. "The task is a slow one, and sadly discouraging to one who would like to do more than he knows how to do."

Slowness notwithstanding, he believed he could perfect and publish *John Randolph, Aaron Burr,* and half the *History*—the *First* and *Second Jefferson*—in orderly succession, beginning soon. On that assumption, he looked forward to preparing *John Randolph* for the press while still in Washington. He wrote to Morse on March 2, 1882: "You are a lucky editor, and I am a lucky contributor. By the time I start north, June 1, my MS. will be ready, if things go well, and then you can print it when you like, if you like, or not at all."[32]

Democracy had been published only in New York, and the trickling of copies to Europe had been slight. None the less, the English had taken it up and formed an opinion of its authorship. An English friend, Mrs. Anne Benson Proctor, would later write to Clover: "At first there were only three copies in England. . . . Mr[.] Smalley kindly lent me his. . . . Every one said it was written by *Mrs*[.] *Henry Adams.*"[33]

The earliest foreign reaction to *Democracy* known to have reached the Adamses came in a letter to Clover from Alice Green. Dated February 7, 1882, from Menton on the Riviera, the letter principally contained bad news. In the face of advancing tuberculosis that made him too weak to hold a pencil, John Green was writing books by dictating them to his wife. Mrs. Green sent the Adamses *The Making of England,* which he had completed the previous summer; and she inquired whether Henry, as one of the three people in the world her husband thought capable of seeing meaning in early English history, could write to him at Menton. She also said: "I hope you enjoyed *Democracy* as much as we did. Mr. James looked very grave and severe over it, but I am not sure whether it was on patriotic or artistic grounds. I don't understand the patriotic objection, for the author seemed to me profoundly convinced that America had made the only solution worth having of the problem of government."[34]

Simultaneously with news from Mrs. Green, Clover received news that her father was again unwell and that King had nearly died.[35] On February 19, she urged her father to voyage to Europe for his health and take King as his companion. ". . . ask him to go with you—his little sister is over there and he's never been. . . . He'll go anywhere on the spur of the moment."

Dr. Hooper did not follow the advice; but on March 9 King wrote to Adams disclosing that his recent illnesses had caused a recurrence of an old ailment and he hoped to sail for England in April to recuperate. Writing again on the 17th, he said: "I want awfully to go to you for a day and sit up half the night by the fire

& find out where you are by this time. Life is so fast that I am always afraid my swift minded friends will get clear beyond me. I am rather falling behind I know. Sickness is a singular, retarding drag to the mind."

The persons named in the Peruvian scandal included Jacob R. Shipherd, a New York promoter less than friendly to Blaine, and Levi P. Morton, a New York banker-diplomat, whom Clover described as the "Minister dis-credited by the Republic of the United States to the Republic of France." She wrote: "On the surface everything is quiet . . . but slowly and surely the Committee[s] on Foreign Relations in [the] Senate and House are ripping up the brilliant cloth of gold woven by Blaine and his pals since March 4th, 1881. Shipherd is to testify on Wednesday; Blaine is to be called up; Trescot to be sent for probably; [and] L. P. Morton was cabled to by [the] Secretary of State last week. . . ."

For no apparent reason, Secretary Frelinghuysen offered Adams the place of minister to Costa Rica, with responsibility also for U. S. relations with Guatamala, Honduras, Nicaragua, and El Salvador. Adams of course declined.[36] He later remarked to Gaskell: ". . . the world is ready enough to give one whatever one does not want and would not take. The only thing I want is that they should read my books, but against this there is a rooted opposition which amounts to conspiracy."

Adams's closing sentence was unwarranted, except that he had cause to mention conspiracy. The only possible purpose of making him minister to Costa Rica was to exile two Adamses from Washington, especially *Mrs.* Adams, the reputed author of a novel. The originator of the attempted appointment was evidently not Secretary Frelinghuysen but two persons behind him, Gail Hamilton and Blaine. Comically enough, their maneuver unsuccessfully imitated an appointment brought about in *Democracy* by Secretary Ratcliffe.[37]

H. H. Richardson returned to Washington to survey the progress of Anderson's house. It emerged that Anderson and his wife were angry. The point at issue was two Joshua Reynolds portraits offered for sale in Washington. The Andersons had wanted them. Clover did not know the Andersons were interested and, reacting swiftly, had bought the pair. To make matters worse, she had paid a bargain price.[38]

Hay had contracted diphtheria. Recovered, he came with Clara to Washington on April 5, and the Adamses saw them daily. In mid-April, after escorting Clara to New York, Hay returned alone, intending "a stay of two or three weeks." Henry and Clover wished to give him a room; but Brooks had taken one of the spares; nephews C. F. Adams III and George Adams were crowding the other spare; Alex Agassiz would need it when they left; and Anne Palmer would probably follow. Hay accordingly was driven to a lonely space at Wormley's.

To Hay's surprise, Adams asked him in confidence to read and criticize the manuscript of a biography—*Aaron Burr*. To Hay's redoubled surprise, Adams said he had written a somewhat parallel *John Randolph*. Adams did not let Hay see the *Randolph*, but he said he would shortly be readying it for publication and that it and the *Burr* would be published in successive years in Morse's American Statesmen Series.

Hay read the *Burr* and discussed it with Adams. He left Washington sooner than expected, very unwell and anxious to consult his New York doctors. He said before going that in July he would be sailing for Europe with Clara and their infants, to winter on the Mediterranean.

The *Burr* affected Hay as sensationally interesting. On April 26, writing to Adams from New York, he said that the book was sure to be "a great popular success." Also, in mild terms, he offered a suggestion. ". . . I can't help thinking you might give [Alexander] Hamilton a fairer show for his money. I know you do not rate him so highly as some of us do, but even with your judgment of him, he seems to me to deserve more considerate mention than you give him. . . ."

That same day, April 26, 1882, an attack on beleaguered Blaine by Belmont, the Adamses, and Nordhoff showed promise of succeeding. During a hearing at the Capitol, Belmont goaded Blaine beyond endurance. After other provocations, the congressman called the ex-secretary "a bully and a coward." In response, Blaine cried out: "Mr. Chairman, this man has disgraced his place. He is the organ of men who are behind him. He was put here to insult me. I beg to say that he cannot do it. I recognize that he is speaking for men behind him."[39]

On the 28th, Clover became so sick with a cold that Henry sent for Dr. Lincoln. She reported to her father on the 30th: "Boojum never leaves me and was unwilling to eat yesterday, owing to my staying in bed, except what I gave him. Possum has no sentiment in his nature and would cheerfully eat me if mixed with potato."

Adams had asked Hay to read the *Burr* in hopes that he would read it seriously. It did Adams's temper no good that Hay's one suggestion was mercy for Alexander Hamilton. He answered on the 30th: "To me the man is noxious, not because of the family quarrel, for he was punished sufficiently on that account, but because he combined all the elements of a Scotch prig in a nasty form. For that reason I prefer not to touch him if I can help it, and shall follow your advice by cutting out all I can cut, in regard to him, and emasculating the rest."

Adams had seen that *Democracy* agitated every American who came near it. He continued to hope the book might do Blaine a fatal injury. A possible means of causing new sales in the United States was to free an English publisher to sell unlimited copies in the British Isles. By an unknown process, a London publisher, Macmillan and Company, was induced to publish two editions of the novel during the current season. There would be a paper-backed edition at one shilling and a clothbound edition at usual prices in a choice of one-volume or two-volume forms. News of the book's availability in England would not be announced till May 27, 1882, but the decision to publish the editions must have been made at the latest in April.[40] Until evidence is found to the contrary, one may assume that Adams made arrangements with Macmillan with the help of an intermediary. A conceivable intermediary was MacVeagh.[41]

King had read *Democracy* but at a time when mentally so disturbed that he could not really follow what it said. On May 6, he sailed for England, chiefly to sell a mining company. He was acting both in his own interest and in the interest of two rich Boston investors, Alexander Agassiz and Quincy Shaw.[42]

James sailed for England four days later. Before leaving, he sent a message to Clover complimenting her as "the incarnation of my native land." She remembered that in his *Hawthorne*, a minor work he had published in 1879, James had described the United States as lacking in all the qualities a writer would want his country to have. She accordingly thought his compliment "most equivo-cal."[43] It might have revenged her to know that in England, while trying to write, he would be much interrupted by convivial Ameri-cans.[44]

Once in London, King entrusted his business errand to a deputy and went to Spain. Some weeks later in Paris, he wrote a story, "The Helmet of Mambrino." Restored to London, he took rooms opposite James's on Bolton Street and began to think about a novel.[45]

New rumors were echoing in London that the author of *Democracy* was Mrs. Henry Adams. Not content to speculate, an English acquaintance, Mrs. Stanley Clarke, simply wrote to Mr. Adams in

Washington and asked whether the author was his wife. On May 18, Cunliffe did the same; and on June 2, answering a letter from Adams, Woolner remarked: "You do not mention Mrs[.] Adams. . . . Did she write a book called 'Democracy'? Everyone tells me to read it, and some say it is by her. . . ."

The strengthened rumors about Clover's authorship had started, one may suppose, as shoptalk in the Macmillan office. To deflate them, Adams made use of Cunliffe, who, being in Parliament, could speak with statesmanlike authority. On May 29, he sent Sir Robert a disclaimer. "If you see Mrs[. Stanley] Clarke, please tell her that my wife has never yet written anything for publication. . . . Meanwhile I cannot enlighten you about the authorship of "Democracy[,]" which has been attributed to a score of people including Clarence King, John Hay and myself. It is an old and forgotten book here. Indeed I first saw it when we were living at Queen Anne's Gate."

Adams could assure Cunliffe that *Democracy* was forgotten in America, but Hay knew better. He learned in Cleveland that the Ohio press was treating the book as new. A newspaper had reported:

> An anonymous novel entitled "Democracy," which is an accurate and vivid picture of American politics, and scintillating with brilliant delineations and carricatures [*sic*] of public men, is just now puzzling the critics. It is thought that John Hay is the author.

Hay clipped the report and on June 6 sent it to Adams with the comment, ". . . if people get it into their heads that I wrote 'Democracy,' they will require of me a glitter of style and a lofty tone of philosophical satire as far beyond me as the sword of Goliath. . . ."

Adams recognized Hay's letter-and-clipping as an opportunity. He replied: "I am glad the secret is at last coming out. I was always confident that you wrote that book. . . ." Thereafter when writing to Hay, he reiterated in ingenious, ever-changing ways that Hay and Hay alone had authored *Democracy*. Hay joined in the game, and the game served a use. Their cordiality gave way to close friendship of a kind Hay had not previously experienced. He and Adams shifted to a footing of inseparable association. In their altered relation, Adams would be dominant but rather silent, Hay recessive and free-spoken.

On June 12, from Cleveland, Hay asked Adams a good question. He had noticed the order of Burr and Randolph's dates. Born in 1756, Burr had grown to manhood in time to serve in the

Revolution. Born in 1773, Randolph appeared so late on the scene that John Adams was president when he first ran for Congress. To Hay, it seemed an error to print the two men's biographies in anti-chronological order. He inquired: "Why do you print Randolph first? Aaron takes precedence in point of time, and if I were you I should be nervous at having such precious material lying for a year in my desk." The question-and-suggestion reflected both their closer tie and their complementary characters.

The Adamses delayed their annual return to Massachusetts. They gave reasons, including the chance that Clover for the first time might see the blossoming of laurels in Washington's woods.

More pressing reasons were politics and authorship. For all that the Adamses, Belmont, and Nordhoff could do, Blaine was sliding clear of the Peruvian scandal. Clover's letters were emphatic. "The Chile-Peru matter drags on; the general public cares little and knows less." "We don't believe anything is coming out of the Shipherd investigation, so-called. The [House] Committee—except Belmont—are in terror of any disclosures apparently and don't understand the drift of such testimony as they have got."

Henry meanwhile was heavily burdened by his writings. He did not leave the capital until he had readied *John Randolph* for the press, but the *First Jefferson* had prior claim on his energy, and it extorted such large shares that it hurt the lesser book. The last chapters of the *Randolph* showed evidence of fatigue and wavering concentration.[46]

On reaching Boston, Clover and Boojum joined Dr. Hooper at Beacon Street, and Henry and Possum went to Quincy. The visit was saddening. The Chief had lost almost all his memory. He seemed content enough, but Henry's mother had taken charge.

Dr. Hooper, Clover, and Henry proceeded to Beverly Farms. Morse lived nearby, and Henry gave him the manuscript of *John Randolph*. The editor pronounced it very clever and sent it to the printer.[47]

In Henry and Clover's opinion, the best number of dogs was three. Though unrivaled in sentiment, Boojum was yellow and not a model Skye. Heartless Possum showed good lineage. Wanting a still better representative of the breed, the Adamses bought a Skye puppy who reputedly was "the best and purest in the United States." The newcomer, Marquis, was the household's aristocrat.

Hay's good question about the publishing sequence of the *Burr* and *Randolph* did not receive an answer. When he at last wrote to

Hay, on June 25, 1882, Adams said nothing about the *Randolph* and mentioned that temporarily the *Burr* would be withheld.

> Thanks for your sympathetic interest in my ideal scamp. He was never a safe scoundrel to deal with, and may well run away and cheat the world again; but I tote about a hundred-weight of manuscript far more valuable than his, and he must bide his time. In truth I rather grudge the public my immortal writings. I neither want notoriety nor neglect, and one of the two must be imagined by every author to be his reward.

The hundred-pound manuscript was the *First Jefferson*. Adams was planning to print each volume of the *History* privately when in good order. Six copies would be made of each volume.[48] To insure against loss, he would keep copies in different places.

Also, being very concerned about possible errors of fact, he would be lending copies to competent readers. Writing to Justin Winsor on June 26, he said he hoped in about a year to send Winsor a volume for his "corrections and suggestions." Thereafter, perhaps "by 1885," he might "get a couple of volumes published." ". . . my great wish is to be accurate, and I shall keep them back until you and other sharp observers have struck out whatever you detect that is inexact."

Guiteau was hanged and silenced on June 30, 1882. During July and August, Adams worked forward in his *History*. He finished drafting the *First Jefferson* and may have started the *Second Jefferson*.[49]

During the same months, James Osgood planned a festive celebration in London, a dinner at the Hotel Continental, to be attended by his former authors. James, King, Hay, and Howells were among the many authors expected. Adams would not appear.

For twelve weeks prior to Osgood's dinner, Macmillan and Company flooded the British Isles with copies of *Democracy*. Many English magazines reviewed the book and treated it as important.[50] The July *Edinburgh Review* contained a thirty-page article in which seven American novels were paraded for inspection. First was *Democracy*. Second, third, and fourth were *The Europeans, Daisy Miller*, and *Confidence* by Henry James. Fifth was *A Chance Acquaintance* by William Dean Howells.

As perhaps was inevitable, the American writers who were gathering in England groused about *Democracy*. King and Hay placed themselves among the grousers. Their complaint was patriotic. Both said—mistakenly—that invariably English readers read the book as proof that English criticisms of the United States were fully warranted.[51]

On August 15, King confided to Hay from Paris: "I am glad and sorry for the success of Democracy. . . . I am moved to do a droll thing, namely to write a companion volume to be called 'Monarchy' . . . ." What King wanted was a counterpoise. He explained that, when writing *Democracy*, Adams had failed to understand his characters and especially had not realized that "Mrs. Lee"—the "woman from Boston"—made "pitiable social blunders" in Washington which were "infinitely more lamentable than anything the woman from Peoria . . . could possibly make." The remark was more than strange. *Democracy* contained no woman from Boston. It might appear that King was speaking loosely, but the truth was worse. In earnest about Boston, he was gripped by a slight insanity precipitated in part by stressful dealings through the mail with Agassiz and Shaw.[52]

King seemed unaware of his condition. In his letter, he treated his idea for *Monarchy* as sane though possibly extreme. As if his true concern was literary, he outlined his intended book. In subsequent letters to Hay, he reported that, under a changed title, *Aristocracy*, he had started to write it, or rather would shortly do so.[53]

Hay had meanwhile sent Adams a paper-covered copy of *Democracy* he had bought for sixpence at a railroad station en route to the Clarks at Tillypronie. Presumably the copy belonged to an edition published in London by Ward, Lock & Company.[54] It seems too that Adams's novel had scored an ultimate triumph. It was being pirated.[55]

Not to be outdone, Hay conceived a novel called *The Bread-Winners*, defending private property. He began it in August and advanced very rapidly. Without revealing that he was at work on the book, he warned Adams that, having sinned by writing *Democracy*, he, Hay, might write a sequel.[56] As it happened, his hint would be true in one respect. *The Bread-Winners* would follow *Democracy* in that the authorship would remain a secret. Hay would die before his authorship got out.[57]

One of the authors expected at Osgood's dinner was Charles Dudley Warner. He shared with Twain, Howells, James, and a few others the honor of being America's established novelists. He and Mark Twain had co-authored a novel in 1875, *The Gilded Age*, which in its Washington scenes could be said to have anticipated *Democracy*.

On September 13, the eve of Osgood's grand dinner, a small

gathering occurred. Those present were Howells, James, Hay, and King. A memorable aspect of the occasion was that Hay and King were obliged to listen to a new theory of the authorship of *Democracy*. Hay told the details on September 17 in a letter to Adams sent from Cunliffe's house in Wales. He said: "I have heard little except the authorship of D————— discussed since I arrived [in England]. The other day, to King, James and me, seated under the trees in Kensington Park, Howells suddenly broke silence and said 'Charles Warner and I last night both at once came to the conclusion that DeForest wrote Democracy; and we were both astonished that we had not thought of it before.' The next night at Dinner [i.e. Osgood's], Howells being in ear shot of me, somebody asked him who wrote Democracy. I heard him state without qualification that it was a gentleman in Hartford, named DeForest."

The Warner-Howells conclusion was adapted to soothe the egos of America's established novelists. Needing a supportive, reassuring way of accounting for the book that American and English readers were buying too eagerly and would not stop talking about, Warner and Howells awarded the authorship to a well-known writer, John William DeForest, author of *Miss Ravenel's Conversion from Secession to Loyalty* and other novels. The chosen author was male and a member of their fraternity. He was not present. He could not spoil their conclusion by saying it was not true.[58]

Several guests, King among them, had been expected at Pitch Pine Hill in the summer of 1882. King however had stayed in Europe. In part for business reasons, he cultivated the highest ranking Europeans he could reach, including the Prince of Wales and Baron Ferdinand James de Rothschild. He wrote to other people but not a word to the Adamses. He seemed mentally to have lumped them with Shaw and Agassiz.

Henry and Clover's other summer guests likewise failed to appear. Henry used the freed hours to press onward in his *History*; yet, loving King as he did, he worried about him.[59]

Publication of *John Randolph* was scheduled for October. As if Hay had never heard of it, Adams wrote to him on September 3: "I am bored to death by correcting the proofs of a very dull book about John Randolph, the fault of which is the enforced obligation to take that lunatic monkey *au serieux*. I want to print some of his letters and those of his friends, and, in order to do so, was obliged to treat him as though he were respectable. For that matter, however, I am under much the same difficulty with regard to T. Jefferson, who, between ourselves is a character of comedy. John

Adams is a droll figure, and good for Sheridan's school; but T. J. is a case for Beaumarchais . . . ."

John, Charles, and their families were spending the summers at a beach house on the Massachusetts coast south of Boston. On September 17, Charles sailed in his yacht *Winsome* from the beach house to Beverly Farms and slept at Pitch Pine Hill. Two days later, having occasion to be at the Old House in Quincy, he found Henry there. That night, Henry accepted a bed at Charles's house on President's Hill. The meetings evidently made for better relations. Charles took an improved attitude towards Henry's work, if not his life.[60]

From Beverly Farms on September 21, Adams wrote to Holt asking him to reprint *Democracy* by October 1 in "a twenty-five cent edition." He offered to compensate the publisher for any loss he might incur. Holt started work on the edition but not as rapidly as wished.

Adams's request was urgent. On the 29th, he sent Holt "a couple of sheets" he wished the publisher would add to the edition on a front fly leaf. The sheets bore extracts from reviews of *Democracy* in American newspapers. He later told Holt he wanted his novel not mistaken for British; hence the cheap edition. A better explanation was that Adams wanted the book reprinted in advance of the 1882 Congressional elections. At the same time, he wanted the reprinting to be very quiet. He insisted that the edition be announced but not advertised.[61]

On October 1, *John Randolph* was twenty days short of being published. Evidently by means of a note that was not preserved, Adams informed Morse that he had completed *Aaron Burr* for the American Statesman Series, lacking only preparation for printing. He seems not to have shown Morse the manuscript, only told him about it.

The news of the *Burr* created problems for Morse. Rather than ask to see the book, he consulted Houghton. The publisher wanted the American Statesmen Series to sustain a level of dignity consistent with its high-sounding title. He ruled against a biography of Burr on the ground that Burr was "not a statesman." Morse relayed the decision to Adams. Again the note was not preserved.

Replying from Beverly Farms on October 6, Adams told Morse, ". . . my offer to write Burr was an offer to *you*, not to Houghton, to help you out in your editing." ". . . if you will release me, I shall be glad of it; and you have only to tell Houghton that I have withdrawn my offer."

Adams wrote to Hay two days later and dressed his *Randolph* in repulsive rags. "My John Randolph is just coming into the world. Do you know, a book to me always seems a part of myself, a kind of intellectual brat or segment, and I never bring one into the world without a sense of shame. . . . This particular brat is the first I ever detested. He is the only one I never wish to see again; but I know he will live to dance, in the obituaries, over my cold grave."[62]

Ending his letter to Hay, Adams disclosed that Houghton had refused to publish *Aaron Burr* "because Aaron wasn't a 'Statesman.' " "Not bad, that, for a damned bookseller! He should live a while at Washington and know our *real* statesmen. I am glad to get out of Houghton's hands, for I want to try Harper or Appleton. Which recommendest thou? I incline towards Harper."

On the mistaken assumption that Houghton had seen the biography of Burr, Hay answered from Paris: "A publisher who would not jump at Aaron is an idiot. It is the best thing going: not only good, but very saleable. I should advise Harpers by all means."[63]

A key fact about the rejection of Adams's *Aaron Burr* was that he could feel it as a slight to himself. Unthinking Morse had been given a generous offer of an added biography, had paid it no attention, and, when told the book was done, had shuffled with the news to unthinking Houghton, who had lightly rejected it. Moreover, Houghton's verdict, fully reconsidered, pointed back to Adams's having been singled out by Morse to write a biography of unadmired John Randolph. In connection with the earlier matter too, Adams could feel he was slighted.

John Randolph and *Aaron Burr* had been drafted in one summer and could be imagined to be twins. It could seem a tragedy that they were separated—that only one would appear in Morse's series. The books, however, had been separate from their inceptions. Adams wrote the *Burr* of his own accord. The *Randolph* was an instance of what could happen when he was asked to write a book he had not thought to write.

There is testimony that *Aaron Burr* was the better book. Perhaps it was, as a biography. But Adams was always capable of surprises. In his hurried effort to write both books, he had turned *John Randolph* into something unexpected. It was a book that Morse could not refuse, yet a book with several aspects, including one that was highly original and that will later need explanation.

Clover was thirty-nine and felt no longer young. It seemed a comment on her age that she was troubled with nightly toothaches.

Rather than seek help in Boston, she waited for her and Henry's return to Washington, where they had confidence in their dentist, Dr. Maynard, and their physician, Dr. Lincoln.

They started south in mid-October. For them, King being abroad, New York would feel empty. They accordingly took precautions. In Henry's words: ". . . we carried Richardson and Ned Hooper with us; telegraphed to La Farge and St[.] Gaudens to dine with us; saw the worst play we ever yet saw . . . where Schurz and we cried with laughing at the pathos; lunched at Schurz's; dined with Godkin, and were refused permission by W. H. Vanderbilt to see his house, because 'Mrs. V.' said we mustn't." It was possibly at Godkin's house that Henry took a precaution of another sort. He arranged that the review of *John Randolph* in the *Nation* would be contributed anonymously by himself.

The MacVeaghs wished the Adamses would visit them at their dairy farm near Philadelphia, in Bryn Mawr. Clover's account of the visit said very little. "The house is a roomy one of gray stone just rebuilt after being burned a year ago. Tuesday was a fine day and we drove about the country both morning and afternoon, the rest of the time sat over the fire and talked politics mainly."

After twenty-two years of Republican rule, the nation was restive. The Democrats hoped to win many congressional seats in November and compete strongly for the presidency in 1884. Even Hay was ready for change. On October 22, 1882, he wrote to Henry from Paris: "I wish you would tell me what my politics ought to be next year. An humble seeker after truth, who would like to be on the winning side, has a path sown thick with difficulties in times like these. If all the Democrats I know would leave their party[,] I think I would join it."

Hay turned again to *Democracy*, this time not as a work by himself. He supposed it might be by Adams, and he assigned it a very high rank. " 'Democracy' still continues its devastating course on this side the great deep. It is as much talked about in Paris as in London. I have myself read it once more, with you in my mind, and I grieve to state that it fits you. . . . If you did it, you must take the fat with the lean. It is the best thing of the sort ever done. . . ."

For both Adamses, Washington meant home. Clover wrote: "Got here Wednesday P.M. [October 25], found everything in order, fires and nice dinner. Engaged two new women servants. . . . Am having a nerve killed with arsenic and so the last three days have been chequered, but after four months of nightly toothache . . . anything is a relief."

Washington was altered by new houses. In her next letter,

Clover noted that Blaine and Robeson had "put up huge piles of brick." Construction at K Street being slower than expected, the Andersons were still at 8 Lafayette Square. "Friday we dined there quietly with only Mr. Frederick L. Olmsted and Richardson. The Anderson house is a subject of much discussion and very opposite opinions are held about it; it is emphatically a gentleman's house and the lines are very fine; it is very stern and severe as a whole, but H. H. Richardson is satisfied and says windows and grading will give it all it now lacks."

Copies of *John Randolph* had preceded the Adamses to Washington and Richmond. For fifteen years, dating from the appearance of "Captain John Smith" in 1867, historians in Virginia had resisted Henry Adams and Charles Deane as historical despoilers.[64] They none the less were unprepared for Adams's *Randolph*.[65] Henry wrote to Lodge on October 31: "The Virginians are red-hot at my introductory chapter. . . . Luckily for me, the book is but a feeler for my history and I want the mud it stirs." Clover similarly told her father: "The Virginians are very angry with it—not that they defend Randolph, but the picture of his surroundings is not pleasing, though true. The Canadians liked Francis Parkman till he criticised Canada, then they foamed and swore."

When mentioning his *Randolph*, Henry seemed always to link it with his *History*. In this vein, he remarked to Cunliffe on November 12: ". . . I have just published a little biography . . . which is really, like my Life of Gallatin, only a preliminary essay. . . . I don't like it, and have taken very little interest in its reception. . . ."

In Boston, the biography was liked. Charles thought it "excellent reading!"[66] Morse admired it and, not realizing that his relations with its author had greatly worsened, sought Adams's help in finding someone to write a biography of Patrick Henry. A candidate he had in mind was a journalist, David Graham Adee. Adams contrived to obtain a scrapbook of Adee's newspaper writings and on November 19 sent Morse a positive recommendation. He at the same time chose to remark that Randolph's life could "now be read, thanks to Garland's indiscretions and to the papers we have printed." To end his letter, he reminded Morse that the qualities of a biography were sometimes determined by the subject. "If you like 'Randolph,' I am pleased, for you are the only person I was bound to satisfy. To me it is an unpleasant book. . . . The acidity is much too decided. The rule of a writer should be that of a salad-maker; let the vinegar be put in by a miser; the oil by a spendthrift. In this case however the tone was . . . decided by the subject, and the excess of acid was his."

* * *

E. Plon & Compagnie in Paris was preparing to publish *Democracy* in French.[67] As if he was not responsible for the project, Adams wrote to Hay: ". . . we are told that the work is being translated into French. For the love of fun, send me a copy. . . . You seem to think I am going to make myself ridiculous by denying its authorship, but, oh, my poet of the people, I have printed volume after volume which no one would read, and if now the public choose to advertise me by reading as mine Shakespeare, Milton, Junius, Don Quixote, and the Arabian Nights, shall I say them nay?"

Once again, *Democracy* was selling by editions. Holt's cheap editions were going fast; British editions the same. For travelers on the Continent, there was a Tauchnitz—a German edition in English.[68]

Dr. Hooper had been reading *John Randolph* and wrote to Clover about it. She replied on December 3: "I'm glad you like Henry's *Randolph*; the *Burr* is much better; he'll publish that next spring on his own hook." Her report seemed definite. Yet nothing was definite. Henry increasingly felt his *Aaron Burr* as a problem.

Clover found James's "The Point of View" in the December *Century* and read it carefully. The fictional letters that made up the article included one by the "Hon. Marcellus Cockerel" that was based in part on things James had heard her say. She assured her father, "Some of the remarks [in the Cockerel letter] . . . I plead guilty to, but that it should be spotted as 'one of mine' I can't imagine." Her chief sense was regret. She saw that James was reusing ideas and imitating his former works. "The whole article seems to me, with one or two exceptions, a dilution of his 'Bundle of Letters' of 1879."[69]

Clover was dogged by minor ailments. Her aching nerve was killed, but she was about to start treatment for a shrieking ear. To compound her discomfort, two Bostonians long resident in Italy were visiting Washington. "The S's are here and are being lunched and dined vigorously. I am sorry to find them both very antipathetic. . . ." The visitors were Mr. and Mrs. William Wetmore Story. She explained: ". . . there is a jaunty *ci devant* young-man-of-fashion air about him which riles my sweet temper. She is a silly, stout bore."

In England on December 12, hurried and in distress, James boarded a steamer. He had been called home by alarms about his father, who, as things turned out, died in Boston before he arrived.[70]

Next day from Paris, Hay wrote to Adams that he was waiting

to read the *Randolph*. "I have sent to Stevens [in London] for a copy and shall read it with love and reverence. But I pine for the advent of Aaron Burr. I want to read it once again before I die."

In New York the day after, December 14, 1882, the *Nation* published a notice of *John Randolph*, unsigned. Although it was worded with a sureness that could more suggest an author than a reviewer, the notice was received as an everyday appraisal and awakened no suspicions.[71]

King was alone in London. He wrote to Hay, "I am pretty full of ideas now for Aristoc. & think I shall get at it soon."[72]

Approximately at the same time, Lodge found out that Adams had written *Aaron Burr* and wrote to him about it. Adams replied on December 26: ". . . I have not yet decided what to do with Burr. . . . My hands are so full that I put things off."

Letters between Adams and Hay were constant and amusing. On January 7, 1883, Adams wrote Hay a letter that touched on several matters. Improbable though it seemed, a friendship had started between himself and Senator Cameron. Henry said: "WE were asked to a charming dinner there the other evening, and I am now tame cat round the house. Don and I stroll round with our arms round each other's necks. I should prefer to accompany Mrs[.] Don in that attitude, but he insists on my loving him for his own sake."

Adams reverted to Hay's favorite book. "Aaron Burr is not to be printed at present. . . . I hate publishing, and do not want reputation. There are not more than a score of people in America whose praise I want, and the number will grow with time. So Aaron will stay in his drawer and appear only as the outrider for my first two volumes of history, about a year before they appear, which may give Aaron three or four more years of privacy."

Hay could not know it, but Adams had shifted to a radically altered schedule of publication. He meant not to publish the *First* and *Second Jefferson* till 1887 or even 1888. The *Burr* would precede them by a year. Till that time, the *Randolph* would stand by itself.

In the same letter, Henry reported two notable developments. One was an alleged assertion by Blaine. Henry said: "I understand from my sister-in-law, Ellen Gurney, that Hon. J. G. Blaine at a dinner party in New York said that Mrs[.] H. A. 'acknowledges' to have written *Democracy*. You know how I have always admired Mr[.] Blaine's powers of invention." The other occurrence was a gibe repeated by a Washington newspaper. It was nothing less than that *Democracy* was written cooperatively by James G. Blaine and Gail

Hamilton. In Henry's words, "The '[National] Republican' in a list of reputed authors puts J. G. B's name first with Gail as collaborateur."[73]

Closing his letter, Adams asked the question which could no longer be put off. "Is King insane or not? Agassiz seems seriously to think he is, and I myself sometimes suspect it." The question reflected concern. Adams was next to certain that King was hurt irreparably. The damage being done, he was more than ever determined to show how much he loved and cared.[74]

The notice that Adams wrote of *John Randolph* was in every way characteristic, yet was not identified as his in his lifetime.[75] Its place among his writings will be clear if the biography and the notice are considered together.

In appearance and to some degree in substance, Adams's *Randolph* was what it was advertised to be: a short, well-informed biography. One merit of his notice was its just and candid estimate of the comparative values and complementary uses of his biography of Randolph and the earlier biography by Hugh A. Garland.

Though not advertised to be such, *John Randolph* was also Adams's book-length testament as a Unionist and a representative of the North in the Civil War. It offered a clear, unhesitating history of American doctrines relating to state sovereignty and of Randolph's role as a fomentor of rebellion by the Southern states. In his notice, Adams avoided explicit reference to the war, but he raised the question of state sovereignty and said that *John Randolph* is sectional and speaks for the Union and the North.[76]

The biography had a third aspect. As Adams said to Hay, the book was a "feeler" for his *History*. Most of the chapters of *John Randolph* concerned a short period in United States history, the interval immediately preceding the War of 1812. Similarly, Adams made that interval the main concern of his notice. So doing, he turned the *notice* into a feeler for the *History*. In fact, he permitted it to state one of the larger work's most salient conclusions, that the United States became a nation during Jefferson and Madison's presidencies.

A last aspect of the *Randolph* was one that Adams had not mentioned in his letters. It was this aspect that afforded the book its great distinction. Although printed as a biography and reviewed by him as biography, the book was something new. The novelty was evident, not somewhere in its text, but in the book throughout.

The leading idea of *John Randolph* is that the title character, by virtue of his inborn nature and early surroundings, received an education which barred him from affecting himself, his fellow Virginians, his fellow Southerners, his fellow Americans, or humanity at large in any but hurtful ways. The book showed Adams's command of the genre he had discovered: the education. Written truthfully about an actual American who received an eighteenth-century education and contributed to the miseries of the American Union in the nineteenth century, *John Randolph* stood opposite to a book of the future, *The Education of Henry Adams*, which when written would concern a fictitious "Henry Adams" who receives an eighteenth-century education and has the problem of shedding it and replacing it with a better. Admittedly the *Randolph* was complicated and served four uses; but Adams decided its prevailing character by giving it a first chapter, "Youth," which was a conscious anticipation of the first chapters of *The Education of Henry Adams*, rivaling those future chapters in strength, and written in a practically equivalent style.

It has been stated that Adams was a great writer who, while writing lesser works, meant to write three works of outstanding importance: a satirical novel, a large-scale scientific history, and the prototype of a new literary form, *The Education of Henry Adams*. The three works were interrelated. They tended to get written together. The tendency of the last to get onto the page was so strong that in late 1882 and early 1883, by proxy, it was being sold in the bookstores. The proxy was *John Randolph*—a foretaste of a new kind of book.[77]

That Adams was aware of the foregoing considerations can be seen in his unsigned notice of December 14, 1882. In the notice, without saying that his *Randolph* is not a biography, indeed while saying that it is, Adams shifts discussion from Randolph's life to his education and to the disaster Randolph incurred when his education unfitted him to a world abruptly changed.[78] The notice is brief. It reads as follows:

> We already have a larger and more complete life of Randolph, by Hugh A. Garland, but it has left full room for Mr. Adams's biography. The two sketch the Virginian from altogether different standpoints. His pride of ancestry, his arrogance and self-sufficiency, his contempt for all law except individual will and power, his greed for land, his thriftlessness, even his bad personal habits, are conscientiously detailed by both; but the ingenuous and unconscious sympathy of Garland, and the evident antipathy of Adams, make them almost biographers of their sections [the South and North] as well as their subjects, and will in conjunction give the reader a stereoscopic view of John Randolph in his round (or linear) entirety.
>
> The different attitude of Garland gives his work, viewed as biogra-

phy, the greater value, for Randolph was to him a man, with all the affections, purposes, and disappointments of a man. To Mr. Adams, Randolph is, if not quite a lay figure on which to hang historical drapery, at least a cadaver, to be curiously dissected for the instruction of an interested class. However this may detract from the interest of the book as a biography, it very much increases its value to the political student. From no other source can he get such clear light upon the nature and influence of the decade, beginning with the annexation of Louisiana in 1803, and ending with the declaration of war against Great Britain in 1812, which sealed the death-warrant of State sovereignty, and changed the whole current of the country's history. It found the United States theoretically a congeries of sovereign States, and when the wave had passed it left behind it a nation. It found Randolph at the head of the State Sovereignty Democrats; it left him stranded and helpless amid a new order of things, out of sympathy with his State, with his party, with the Administration, with the country, and with his whole political environment. It ruined his career, as it did that of every other leader who was not careful, while maintaining State sovereignty in words, to respect the national sovereignty in fact. Randolph, almost alone, endeavored to practise as well as preach the ancient theory, and he was as out of place in the Congresses of 1812–1830 as a survivor of the Tertiary period would have been in Barnum's "happy family." In presenting to view this change in the national life, Mr. Adams has done a distinct and excellent piece of work, and has given us in one small volume more of general, if less of special, interest than is contained in the two larger volumes of his predecessor.

20

A GREAT BOOK

Historians diverged in their ideas about their function. Adams's view was unconditionally scientific. His first purpose as a historian was to make "an attempt to ascertain what actually happened."[1] He had been successful in obtaining evidence and would collect and study evidence as long as necessary. Meanwhile he was feeling the necessity of a second purpose, relating to both science and art. As he said to Parkman, he was struggling to give his *History* "shape and cohesion."

In one respect, the form of his epic work was predetermined. He was predisposed to write a long, fully-organized narrative—an actual story, the hardest thing to write. To pull the story together, he was prepared to labor hard. As he advanced in the work, he would write and rewrite each part three times.[2] He would rewrite the parts both to insure cohesion and to make them readable. If successful, the result would be wholly self-attuned. Every assertion would anticipate or remember every other.

In a second respect, the form of the *History* had been settled very early. The work would be written and published as four volumes. Each volume would be slightly large. Each would bear a title beginning with the words "History of the United States of America." The publisher and the public would take these words to be a general title and might judge it a perfectly good one.[3]

In a third respect, the form of the *History* was evidently decided in 1882. Adams had to shape the work's smaller units. He found it easiest to draft the narrative in uniform chapters, neither long nor short. Many would be needed. (There would eventually be 153.) Also he found that the chapters took form as clusters or "books." Each book centered around a particular occurrence or consideration. And last he found that, throughout the work, *five* books would make a volume.[4]

To summarize, the *History* would be a fully organized, wholly consistent long story that would be the easier to read because developed in the form of twenty books.[5]

There would be nothing to add, were it not that the form involved some notable differences. The *volumes* were chiefly practical conveniences relating to the publication of the work in handy portions. The essential things were *the work in its entirety* and its most substantive divisions, the distinct, quite different *books*. Within the books, the *chapters* were mere incidental subdivisions.

It perhaps was important that, while Henry solved the problem of the form of the *History*, Clover was enjoying a long work in parts. Late in 1882 in Washington, she began to read George Sand's autobiography, as published by Cadot in 1854–1855. The book seemed not long because set forth as twenty "volumes." On December 3, she wrote to her father, "When you want a mild but readable book[,] try George Sand's *Histoire de Ma Vie*—lots of volumes but very quick reading." Dr. Hooper acted on the suggestion. Clover resumed on December 24: "I'm glad you're reading *Histoire de Ma Vie.* . . . I'm in the fifteenth volume and think the interest increases; the convent life is wonderfully described." On December 31, she asked: "How are you getting on with George Sand? To me it grows more and more interesting; volume eighteen is charming and I'm sorry it ends with volume twenty."[6]

During the same months, Henry was hard at work on the first half of the *History*—the ten books of the *First* and *Second Jefferson*. By January 1883, he was rewriting the *First Jefferson*. As nearly as can be determined, its five books were well-defined. The subject of each book was suggested by a brief title.[7] With the important exception that his book titles were later lost and that suggested possible titles have had to be inserted in their places, the books conformed to the following list:[8]

Book I	*1800: the Americans Not United*	6 chapters
Book II	*The Jeffersonian Revolution*	6 chapters
Book III	*Napoleon and Toussaint Louverture; the Sale of Louisiana*	8 chapters
Book IV	*Centralization*	7 chapters
Book V	*Quarrels with Spain and England*	8 chapters

How much Clover may have affected the effort that produced the *First Jefferson* in the form here listed is not known and seems difficult to guess; but if it was true that Henry owed some of his success in ordering the *History* to Clover's interest in his problem and to her simultaneously reading Sand's *Histoire de Ma Vie*, then for him the matter of his *History* was emotionally entwined with his and Clover's marriage and their private happiness. Moreover, if their happiness met with impairment, the *History* might suffer also.

The White House fronted on Lafayette Square, facing north. Across the square was the T-shaped intersection of H Street and 16th Street. Adjacent to the intersection were two private properties. The corner east of 16th Street was occupied by St. John's Episcopal Church. The corner to the west was held by Corcoran as a speculation. The lot, a large one, was emptied of buildings and inhabited by weeds and trees.

Having rented the house next to the emptied lot, Henry and Clover were the persons who lived most nearly across from the nation's president. In that sense, their winter residence was the most conspicuous possible. It also was very pleasant. Some of the trees in Corcoran's lot cast morning shade into their back yard and flower garden.

In the winter of 1882–1883, Corcoran sold his corner to a developer, Frederick Paine, who wished to build a thirty-family apartment house. Whether Paine could raise the money to finance the apartment house was unclear, but in prospect his structure greatly diminished the desirability of the Adamses' accustomed residence. If built, the apartment house would overlook their yard, garden, and back windows. Presumably the trees to the east of the garden would be cut down. An excellent place to live would be irreparably harmed.

For the Adamses, Paine's project was concurrent with a dearth of friends. The MacVeaghs were settled in Bryn Mawr; the Hays remained abroad; King lingered in Europe and never wrote; and Henry and Clover were reduced to three intimates: Mrs. Cameron and George and Elizabeth Bancroft. Of the three, they were closest to Mrs. Cameron. Said by all to be beautiful, she had an attribute that many observers overlooked. She had a much better than average mind.[9]

While lacking friends, the Adamses were depending for company on foreign diplomats, new-made acquaintances, and a constant traffic of live-in guests. They particularly liked an English surgeon and etcher then visiting the capital, Sir Francis Seymour Haden. In Henry's opinion, Haden understood the United States better than most Americans. Clover was especially pleased that on the steamer crossing to New York he had met and liked her friend Anne Palmer.

At Haden's urging, Clover advanced Anne's visit to Washington. She also invited Godkin, thinking he would like her. Anne arrived; but half way through her visit, on February 2, a cable about a sick brother required her rushing to New York, intending to sail for Europe.

Not important in itself, Anne's departure may have been a factor in Clover's writing an important letter. On Henry's forty-fifth birthday, February 16, 1883, she wrote to Clara Hay. The main idea of her letter was that the Hays should move to Washington and live in Paine's apartment house. Clover said that Secretary Frelinghuysen had three times asked her to suggest a replacement minister to Spain and she at last had recommended Mr. Hay. She continued: ". . . if by any chance the offer is made & declined, then please write or *k*able for the best flat in the new appartment [*sic*] building which is going up between us & St[.] John's Church. Corcoran has sold the land for 64,000 lately—it will be charming for you & so of course for us. Seriously now—they'll all be grabbed unless you engage one—& you could always underlet."[10]

Clover's suggestion was Henry's too and was inspired by both open and hidden motives. The Adamses wanted the company of the Hays and said so, but in addition they wanted a means of becoming less conspicuous. If the Hays would take the best apartment in Paine's building, *they*, not the Adamses, would be the president's most-noticed neighbors.

A month earlier, in January 1883, Adams had advanced in the *History* sufficiently to rethink its publication. He had written to Gaskell, "I hope to get out two volumes in 1885, and I mean them to be readable." To meet this schedule, he would start the private printing of the *First Jefferson* during the coming summer and the private printing of the *Second Jefferson* during the summer to follow. Once read, criticized, and improved with pen and ink, ten books— half the *History*—would go to a publisher for final printing and general sale.

The plan was simple, but the Adamses' situation was mixed and contradictory. Henry had two unpublished books in his desk: *Esther* and *Aaron Burr*. To serve as an outrider for the *History*, the *Burr* would have to appear in the fall of 1884. The biography could be expected to create a national sensation, especially if signed. But neither Henry nor Clover wanted immediate fame. They wanted the opposite.

Anonymous *Democracy* meanwhile was a European sensation. In mid-February, Hay bought the French version in Cannes and

sent it to Adams. In his next letter, he reported that the Prince of
Wales was commending the mysterious novel.[11] And, writing from
Boston, James mentioned to Clover that Prime Minister Gladstone
was said to have talked about the book for an hour at a dinner
party.[12]

On March 4, Adams acknowledged Hay's gift of *Democratie*. As
usual, he playfully supposed Hay wrote it. Yet also he counted it a
failure. ". . . your novel . . . is a failure because it undertook to
describe the workings of power in this city, and spoiled a great
tragic subject such as Aeschylus might have made what it should
be, but what it never in our time will be. The tragic element, if
accepted as real, is bigger here than ever on this earth before. I
hate to see it mangled à la Daudet in a tame-cat way. Men don't
know tragedy when they see it."[13]

As read by Hay, Adams's talk about unrealized tragedy might
seem to apply to current American novels generally. Or it might
appear related to Hay's secretly-completed *Bread-Winners* or King's
unwritten *Aristocracy*.[14] But in reality Adams's outburst had little to
do with novels and much to do with the first ten books of his
History.

When it came to history, Henry could fairly be counted as two
persons. He was a gifted scientist capable of assembling, understanding, and reporting on the meaning of large masses of evidence. He had begun the effort to write his *History* in a spirit
predominantly scientific. He had intended to do again in history
what King had done successfully in geology. He had meant to be
systematic—to inspect, study, analyze, and explain a large, well-
chosen sample of human action. By that means, he would attempt
to infer the general tendency of human action. The plan was
simple but ambitious.

Equally Adams was a gifted writer likely to wrest from his
materials a work even better than the work he himself had thought
was possible. As early as 1883, he grew aware that, while continuing
to work in a scientific spirit, he was writing a narrative that many
readers would experience less as history than as tragedy or epic.

It is not suggested that Adams the writer got the better of
Adams the scientist. The truth was simply that Adams was on his
mettle. He could not escape awareness that his *History* was acquiring
something of the character of Shakespeare's tragedies.[15] What was
more important, he started the third book of the *First Jefferson* by
explicitly linking his story to Milton's *Paradise Lost*.[16] The linkage
was definitive. He was writing the American epic, and he knew it.

What Henry was going through was mirrored by Clover. Ad-

mittedly there were limits to what Clover would read. She liked to
say self-deprecatingly that she was not a reader of poetry, though
she read poetry and would even quote it.[17] She had once launched
herself into Gibbon's *Decline and Fall*—with unknown results.[18] But
in the spring of 1883, she told her father she again was reading
Greek. On April 1, she continued by saying she had divided a
morning between trimming a bonnet and "reading a book of the
Iliad, which now runs as easily as French, and yet though I'm
reading it for the fourth or fifth time I could n't [*sic*] read a page
of *Paradise Lost* to save my head!"

The significance of Clover's remark did not stop with Homer
and herself. Every day she and Henry were married, they moved
into closer union. Her relation to his *History* was consultative,
cooperative, and even proprietary. Other than Henry, she was the
only person who read the books of the *First* and *Second Jefferson* in
handwritten form. She was so involved in their creation that she
never wrote about them to her father. Perhaps the closest she came
to a comment was her references to Homer. Apparently, in her
experience, Homer's *Iliad* and her husband's *History* were matched
great books, and she was treating herself to the benefit and joy of
reading both.[19]

In New York, Anne Palmer learned that her mother and sister
had already sailed for Europe and she was asked to care for her
father, who also was very sick. She took him to Florida and, when
able to get back to New York, wrote to Clover inviting her north
for a pleasant visit. Henry was a husband for whom separation,
even brief separation, was hard to bear. Since their marriage, he
and Clover had separated only when he had spent an occasional
night at Quincy. Yet, in the present case, he urged Clover to join
Anne for more than half a week.

The days intended were Monday through Thursday, April 9–
12, 1883. Anne and Clover's doings during the interval could seem
aimless and haphazard. They dined at the Godkins' with Carl
Schurz, his daughter Agatha, and Arnold Hague. They crossed
paths with Henry James, who would soon be coming to Washington
for a second visit, very fleeting. By postponing Clover's departure,
they attended Barnum's circus.

Viewed in another perspective, Anne and Clover's activities
showed consistency. They shared adventures involving art. The
first related to sculpture. The Bostonians wanted to raise a memorial to a relative of Clover's, Colonel Robert Shaw. During the
Rebellion, Shaw had been killed while leading a Massachusetts

negro regiment. The artist chosen to sculpt the memorial was
Augustus St. Gaudens. Clover wrote to her father: "Tuesday early,
[Anne and I] went to St. Gaudens's studio. He's a friend of Miss
Palmer; unhappily he was out and we had no time to get there
again. His great bas-relief monument to Bob Shaw is very fine,
they say—Anne Palmer has seen the cast or plan. It's to be inserted
in a wall by the sidewalk in front of the [Massachusetts] State
House. . . . Let us be grateful that William Story has not got this in
hand; I dislike the man and all his works."

A second adventure led to a portrait. Leaving St. Gaudens's
door, Anne and Clover walked to an exhibition of American
paintings. They thought it "very poor," with one exception. The
exception was a "very striking full-length portrait of a Miss Burck-
hardt by John Sargent, a promising Philadelphia artist whom we
fell in with at Seville in 1879. This picture made a sensation in last
year's [Paris] Salon—a youngish woman, not pretty, in a most
severely fascinating black satin gown; not one touch of colour
anywhere; only a white rose in her left hand." Clover did not say
so, but the portrait was interesting partly for resembling a black-
and-white photograph much enlarged.

The third adventure was simpler. On Wednesday, Anne and
Clover visited the painter F. D. Millet at his studio. Clover had met
him at Beverly in 1876. "He was cordial, and his wife pretty and
nice; and an exquisite young girl—infinitely prettier than [Lillie]
Langtry—who was sitting as model in Eden-like costume[,] stayed
after working hours to let him drape her in many charming
Eastern stuffs to amuse us."

The friends' wanderings had a meaning that Clover did not
recount. She had gone to New York on an errand relating to her
potentialities as an artist. It could seem that her talents extended
only to appreciation of works by other persons. Her interests in
Richardson's buildings, or Sargent's portraits, or James's novels, or
Story's figures showed discernment and were exceptionally strong.
But Clover preferred a different view of her abilities. She appar-
ently had decided to take up photography and be serious about it.
The evident secret object of her trip was to select and buy a camera.
She bought it and soon would call it "my new machine."

The photographs she meant to take would be memorials of
her and her husband's life. On reaching Washington, she took a
picture of Henry talking with Marquis on the back steps of 1607 H
Street.[20] Richardson was present when the picture was planned
and taken. With typical self-deprecation and generosity, Clover
attributed the success of the picture to Richardson. Later pictures

would be sufficient evidence that the success of the first could be attributed instead to her.

Alex Agassiz came for a visit and said he wanted to see the Andersons' nearly finished house. On April 16, Clover and Alex went through the house together. She told her father: "It does Richardson great credit. . . . Alex is anxious to buy a lot here and have Richardson build him a really simple cheap house, and I believe he can do it. Such clients as F. L. Higginson and Anderson are not educated as to what is ultimate . . . and being highly irritable, they take out their temper in railing at H. H. R., who sets out many temptations before them, as it's his business to; [but William] Dorsheimer and Ned [her brother] have found it possible to curb his extravagance. . . ."

The Hays were returning from Europe. Their steamer would dock in mid-May, a month before Henry and Clover would start for Beverly Farms. Clara had not responded to Clover's suggestion about taking a Washington apartment, but Hay urged the Adamses to meet the steamer and have some fun.[21] A meeting was possible for them but not convenient.

Henry meanwhile was writing letters to England about the Camerons. Having drunk too much bourbon whiskey at home, Senator Cameron planned a two-year stay abroad. Henry could not recommend the senator as someone to know, but he wanted kind attention shown to the senator's wife. He wrote to Hay about Mrs. Cameron: "I adore her, and respect the way she has kept herself out of scandal and mud, and done her duty by the lump of clay she promised to love and respect. Please say to Mr[.] Lowell that we expect him to take *her* under special charge." He added that Mrs. Cameron would be carrying many letters, but "none from us."

Wayne and Virginia MacVeagh also were going to Europe. On May 15, Adams wrote to Minister Lowell: "Don [Cameron] has good qualities, and some pretty poor ones [but] . . . is a good deal better than he seems. The Wayne McVeaghs (Mrs[.] McVeagh is Don's sister) are talking of going over. . . . McVeagh is a man of extraordinary ability and character; the only man in American politics who says what he thinks, and thinks honestly. His wife is a trump." Adams especially wished that Lowell would take Mrs. Cameron to a "big entertainment" and tell her which persons she should want to see and know. "You will fall in love with her, as I have."[22]

News came from Cleveland that Clara Hay's father, Amasa Stone, had committed suicide. By then the Hays were on the ocean.

They would learn the news in New York and predictably would rush to Cleveland. A reunion with the Adamses would have to wait.

Mrs. Cameron was happy to go abroad but knew she would miss Clover and Henry and knew they cared about her. She hated leaving them. On the night of May 16–17, the eve of her and the senator's departure, she stayed at 1607 H Street till 1:00 in the morning.

As foreseen, the Hays rushed to Cleveland. On May 20, Adams wrote to Hay: "Knowing the shock that waited you in New York[,] we have not tried to welcome you home or to meet you. We only hope that . . . your outing in Europe has given you . . . reserve strength to draw upon." In the same letter, Henry touched on the subject that Clover had previously raised. "My wife and I long to have you return here, but do not venture even to hope it."

The sentence was considerate but was silent about the under-lying realities. As the Adamses knew, it was a virtual certainty that the Hays would return to Washington. As much as practicable, Hay would want to live near Adams. In his own fashion, he would do things that Adams was already doing. *The Bread-Winners* was com-pleted and would soon appear because *Democracy* existed and was scoring an international success. The influence of Adams's *History* was even stronger. Hay and Nicolay's biography of Lincoln had been hanging fire. Nicolay held a government post in Washington and was collecting evidence.[23] To work easily as co-author of the book, Hay needed to live as near as possible to the collection. He luckily could do that and also live near Adams. Money was not a problem. Amasa Stone's will gave most of his fortune to his two daughters and the rest to Hay. In view of the change, Hay could afford a Washington residence. The only question was which.

In a new letter to Hay, on May 30, 1883, Adams reported progress in his *History*. "Washington is empty but we linger . . . waiting for the east winds at Beverly to abate. Huge masses of manuscript are piling themselves up in my drawers, but I am less and less willing to throw my mock-pearls before the swine who write criticisms. . . . The number of persons whose criticisms are worth having is amazingly small. . . ."

On June 10, writing to Gaskell, Henry sketched the work he planned for the summer. "In another ten days we shall be starting off to bore ourself for three or four months at the sea-side, chiefly to be near our families. . . . I have, too, a heavy load of MS. to put into type, and several volumes to be written, and idleness is not my industry."

The firm that would print the private copies of his *History* was the University Press in Cambridge, owned by John Wilson. Henry apparently had completed his arrangements with Wilson by mail from Washington.[24]

On June 18, accompanied by Richardson, the Adamses went north as far as New York. Secretly, on June 19 or 20, Henry offered *Esther* to Holt, but did not give him the manuscript. The offer was fenced by two unusual conditions. Henry required that the novel appear under a feminine pseudonym not suggestive of Clover. He required as well that it be listed as one of Holt's publications but not advertised. To excuse the conditions, he said that as an experiment he wished to test whether an unpublicized book could win a following. Holt wanted the book and accepted both conditions.[25]

Clover had become an enthusiastic admirer of Richardson's buildings. On June 20, rather than go directly to Boston, she and Henry took a Hudson River boat, enjoyed an evening cruise, and in the morning disembarked at Albany. There they saw the buildings Richardson had designed for the city of Albany and the New York state government.

On reaching the Boston area, Henry's first necessity was to give Wilson the opening book of the *First Jefferson*. By summer's end, if all went well, Books I-III would be delivered for printing.

When they had been a month at Beverly Farms, on July 26, Clover received a letter from Mrs. Cameron. She and Henry both replied. Henry told their friend, "I wish we could send you interesting details of our doings . . . but my wife does nothing except take photographs, while I do nothing except correct proof-sheets." In her letter, Clover recounted the detour to Albany to see Richardson's newest buildings. Her praises were decided. ". . . Governor Cleveland's private room is charming." "The Senate Chamber . . . seems to me by all odds the handsomest room I ever saw. Nothing in that played out old hemisphere in which you are wasting your young life can hold a candle to it. . . ."

Clover liked to include Mrs. Cameron as much as possible in her and Henry's life. In her freest style, she described their days at Beverly Farms. "My husband is working like a belated beaver—from 9 to 5 every day ungarbling the history of his native land as run by antedeluvian bosses—called Thomas Jefferson—Jimmy Madison—& James Monroe. At 12—we feed. We do not dine—today—as the Queen says in Alice in Wonderland[,] 'We have no gingerbread today[;] we have it yesterday & tomorrow'[;] then at 5—we ride."

In another passage, Clover said she had photographed Henry,

Marquis, and Possum. The picture showed them "sitting at the window of a small play house in the woods which I built two years ago for my small nieces." She then let slip some information. "H. has his type-writer there & works there a good deal."[26]

Until that moment, Henry's typewriter had scarcely mattered. He evidently had acquired it while still on the Harvard faculty. He had bought it for use by a typist engaged by him to copy Timothy Pickering letters and related documents at the Massachusetts Historical Society. He subsequently had moved it to Pitch Pine Hill and, perhaps as a game, had learned to use it.[27] Any idea that he would use it for *writing* would be an error. As a writer, he would remain exclusively a creator of penciled drafts, penned improved drafts, and penned reimproved copies. Just so, when photographed by Clover three weeks later in his study, he would be seated at his desk, pen in hand before a manuscript, most likely Book III of the *First Jefferson*.[28]

The presumable reason for Henry's working at a typewriter in the play house was secrecy carried to utmost lengths. He was making a copy of *Esther* to send to Holt. He and Clover viewed the novel as a *jeu d'esprit* and were happy to publish it, but they wanted it to enter the marketplace as unobtrusively as could be managed. Particularly they wished to preclude disclosure of the authorship to anyone in Holt's office or printery. Henry's handwriting was growing famous and—as Holt would later say—could be recognized as far as seen. The necessity was to eliminate handwriting, and the ready means was to type.

Perhaps by August 10, a copy text of *Esther* was spirited to Holt. Proofs were spirited back by early October. Henry or Clover— more probably Clover—corrected them while still at Beverly Farms.

The Bread-Winners began appearing serially in the August *Century*, unsigned. Hay's idea of anonymity bore no resemblance to Henry or Clover's. He had placed the action of his novel in and near a house which many readers would recognize as his and Clara's house in Cleveland. Concurrently with the novel's publication, he was identified as the author. He met the charge by denying it verbally and in print, sometimes angrily. Thereafter a truth too evident to be doubted was set aside merely because the author continued to contradict it.[29]

Writing to Adams on August 3, Hay raised the question of living in Washington. "Do you think I could buy S[t] John's Church? Or would M[r] Corcoran sell me his house and move to the Old

Ladies' Home? I would want not to be out of an invalid's walk from your door."

Adams knew that Anderson had quarreled with Richardson and was saying he wished to sell his new house without moving into it. The house was located at the corner of 16th and K Streets, three blocks from Lafayette Square. On August 10, Adams urged Hay to make Anderson an offer. He said it was "the handsomest and most ultimate house in America . . . and the only one I would like to own." At an irritated moment, Anderson had offered it to Adams for $90,000, but Adams thought it could bring $100,000. He told Hay, "If you meant business, write to Gen. N. L. Anderson, 8 Lafayette Square, Washington. D. C."

Henry said as well that he and Clover wished to pay the Hays a visit. "I have an idea of visiting Cleveland in October. I want to go down to Blennerhassett's island, and can easily go round your way." The island—in the Ohio River not far from Pittsburgh—had served as a focal point of Burr's conspiracy to divide the Union. Saying he wished to go there, Henry seemed almost to promise that he would soon be publishing his *Aaron Burr*.

Hay went to Colorado for a month of mountain air. On August 29, Adams wrote to him again. "I toil and moil, painfully and wearily, forward and back, over my little den of history. . . . I would I were on a mule in the Rockies . . . but at forty-five every hour is golden. . . ." As he tended to do, Henry was thinking in metaphor and had made himself a western miner and his *History* miner's gold. He continued, "I painfully coin it into printer's ink, and shall have a big volume of seven hundred pages to show *you* next winter."

In truth, the privately-printed *First Jefferson* would be shown to other readers sooner than to Hay. Clover and the Bancrofts would see it book by book as fast as Wilson sent copies of the books to Washington. Hay, MacVeagh, Charles, and presumably Winsor would later be sent the completed volume, handsomely bound. All copies would come back to Henry, with suggestions and criticisms.

It needs repeating that, other than Clover and Hay, no one had seen Henry's *Burr*. Two Boston publishers, however, had grown anxious to publish it. Recently, without success, Osgood had asked for the book; and in September, through Morse, Houghton proposed to publish it outside the American Statesmen Series.[30]

Adams continued to believe that he would publish the *Burr* but was far from being in a hurry. The reason was evident enough. He was finding that the *History* was highly susceptible of improvement;

improvement meant more rewriting; and rewriting devoured his time.

On September 26, 1883, he wrote to Morse about the *Burr*. His tone was part-friendly, part not. "If you want the volume for your series, with your name on it, I will not refuse it; but I don't propose to be dictated to by any damned publisher." He suggested that Morse simply tell Houghton he was not ready to publish. He added privately that he had "decided in any case to withhold the 'Burr' another year from publication." "If the 'History' [i.e. the *First* and *Second Jefferson*] cannot appear before 1886, the 'Burr' will not appear before 1885."

Autumn meant new beginnings. The Hays returned to Cleveland, and the Adamses left Beverly Farms. During a stopover in New York on October 18–21, Adams effected delivery of the corrected *Esther* proofs to Holt. It was understood that the book would be issued in the spring of 1884 as No. 3 in a new American Novel Series.[31]

Henry and Clover detoured from New York to Cleveland and were welcomed to the house described in *The Bread-Winners*. Hay was drafting chapters of *Abraham Lincoln/A History*. Nicolay and Hay's compendious biography and Adams's ambitious *History* could seem to have affinities, but they in fact were unrelated, if not opposed. The motive driving Adams's *History* was desire to know and tell. If Adams sinned, his sin was inquiring and writing on so great a scale that only vigorous and ambitious readers might wish to read him. Nicolay and Hay risked a different error: idolatry. In Hay's words, "every line" of the *Lincoln* was "written in a spirit of reverence and regard."[32]

Rail schedules being unpropitious, the Adamses decided not to go to Blennerhassett's Island. With a new idea in mind, they hastened to Pittsburgh and caught the Chicago express to Washington. The new idea was that Hay might be prevailed upon to buy the empty corner that Paine had bought from Corcoran. To their regret, Henry learned from Corcoran that Paine was determined to proceed with his apartment house.

As a next resort, Henry and Clover invited Anderson to Sunday dinner. (Mrs. Anderson was away.) It emerged that Anderson was vain about his Richardson house and would not sell it. Writing to Hay on October 31, Henry said of Anderson: "His house has cost him $86,000, and he is the most delighted house-owner you ever saw. . . . I don't think a hundred thousand would fetch him. He owned up that he had no idea of selling at present."

Defeated, Henry said as well that there was no nearby Washington house for sale that the Hays would want to live in. There seemed to be no way to move the Hays to Washington.

Mrs. Bancroft had read Books I and II of the *First Jefferson*. She sent Henry a note asking for news of Book III and in the note said disapproving things about President Jefferson. Adams wrote in answer that Book III had not arrived but he would be sending it just as soon as received. He also said it pained him that she did not "like my *dear* Jefferson." "I feared as much."[33]

Changeable Anderson swung about and said he would part with his new house at cost. Adams urged Hay on November 23: "I want you to try him with a hundred-thousand offer. It would agonise him, but I think he would refuse it, and then I could just jump on him."

Hay made the offer, but the Adamses already had started along another path.[34] On November 29, they invited Paine to "breakfast"—their noontime meal. Henry told the developer he was anxious to prevent the construction of the apartment house and wished that Paine would name the price he would accept for the entire corner. Henry guessed Paine would ask $77,000. He notified Hay to that effect.

Paine called next day and wanted $78,795. Adams sent Hay the news and explained that the property was so big that Hay could build on a large space and set aside two smaller spaces including one on H Street next to the Adamses' rented house. Referring to the smaller spaces, Henry said, "I wish I might be rich enough to build on the near one."

Hay sent a full answer on December 2. "I want the lot. I want to give more than it is worth—but I do not want to soar into the region of positive lunacy. . . . Perhaps I might . . . go to $72,000— but there is a line between great wit and madness, and I cannot help suspecting that 79,000 means Bedlam. If I were well and happy, I would do it, at all hazards. But as I am—to pay a price my judgment disapproves, then to build—against which my lethargy revolts—& to furnish a house;— all this daunts me more than I can tell you."

The reply being negative, Adams told Paine to go ahead and build. On December 4, Paine came down to $75,000. Adams telegraphed the price to Hay and said he would himself meet half of it. Approvingly, Hay wired back that they would "go halves."[35]

Next day, December 5, Henry sent Hay a letter and a hand-drawn map showing three lots of different shapes. He did not say so, but behind his letter-and-map was an impulse felt by Clover. Apparently on December 4, she had changed her mind. She wanted to buy the near lot shown on Henry's map and build an inexpensive Richardson house.[36]

What Henry *did* explain to Hay was that he wished to achieve two objects. ". . . one is to have you and Mrs[.] Hay next door; the other, to stop this infernal seven-story torture which is to be erected over my present house." Speaking for himself (and concealing Clover's change of mind), he said: "I don't want to buy land; I don't want to build; but the gratification of one's wishes costs money; and if . . . I must buy land and build, I can sacrifice the five or ten thousand dollars it will cost me to change my plans." He went on to say that if he paid $25,000 for the 44' × 131' lot outlined on his map, and if he built a house designed to cost $30,000, and allowed $5,000 for added features, his cost would be $60,000—a sum he could afford.

Writing next day to Clara, Clover said that she and Henry, knowing "exactly what we want *inside*," were "making plans." She said their new house would be "plain as a pike staff." She listed the rooms they wanted on the main floor.[37] Also, very pointedly, she mentioned that King might wish to build on the third space indicated on Henry's map. The space for King—50' × 55'— fronted on 16th Street. It would be just large enough to accommodate a smallish house.[38]

Hay telegraphed that he would pay $50,000 for the lots not wanted by the Adamses. His reply silently vetoed King's getting space. The Adamses would buy their lot for $25,000. Paine would get the $75,000 he had asked.[39]

Adams interpolated a frugal letter to Paine "saying that I must stop at 72; that I had wicked partners who declared it lunacy to offer more; that 72 gave [Paine] . . . a clear profit of $6,000, and that . . . I should stop there." Hay too thought $72,000 the right price. He followed his telegram with a letter to that effect.[40] Paine resisted Adams's offer of $72,000. To break the resistance, Adams offered to pay also some interest Paine owed to Corcoran, who had retained a mortgage on the property. Unsummoned, at 11:00 A.M. on Tuesday, December 11, 1883, Paine came to 1607 H Street. In the words Adams wrote to Hay a few minutes later: " 'Well!' said Paine; 'I will take it.' " The deal being agreed upon, the seller had only to wait for Hay's coming for a Thursday meeting.

The purchase of the valuable corner had resulted from moves initiated by the Adamses at every step. Yet Henry wished to create impressions that the principal negotiator had been Hay, and he wanted Hay himself to accept the fiction. Putting the fiction into immediate use, Henry said in his letter: "If you want me to do anything more, let me know. I shall not be quite easy about it until you have got here, and assumed charge of the whole affair. . . ."

On Thursday at the Adamses', Hay saw a photograph Clover had taken of Bancroft at work in his Washington study. From Cleveland on December 29, he wrote to Richard Watson Gilder, editor of the *Century*, urging him to publish the photograph in the magazine.[41] Gilder went Hay one better. He asked Marian Adams for the photograph and Henry Adams for an article on its subject, the aging historian.[42]

Meanwhile, without telling Richardson he would be their architect, Henry and Clover urged his visiting them to *recommend* an architect and see a plan they were drawing. Simultaneously the architect who had designed the Hays' house in Cleveland made a sketch of a Washington house that would suit their needs, and Hay sent Adams the sketch.[43] Thus the matter of retaining Richardson as architect for two adjoining Washington houses was placed wholly in the Adamses' hands.

Hay, Gilder, and King were creatures of the present. As much as Gilder, Hay had a magazine mind. The enormous *Lincoln* that he and Nicolay were writing would appear as instalments in Gilder's *Century*. Without injustice, the work could be described as the longest of all America's magazine articles, perhaps quite readable if sampled now and then in the magazine, but downright unreadable when later republished as ten large volumes.

It had not occurred to Hay that Henry and Clover were creatures of the future. They were makers of intendedly enduring, even permanent, books. Clover's excellent photograph of Bancroft was not an isolated effort. It was one of a sheaf of pictures which, when grown sufficently, could be mounted as a book—privately held, but still a book.

The Adamses had no desire to explain their orientation to Gilder, Hay, or others. As unoffendingly as possible, Clover refused Gilder both her picture of Bancroft and the article by Henry.[44]

Richardson gladly heeded the Adamses' summons. On January 16, 1884, he came to Washington as their guest. For two days, he studied the sketch by the Hays' former architect and the complete plan that Henry had drawn of his and Clover's house. Henry wrote to Hay, "He was quite angelic, and goes in with enthusiasm for all my peculiar idiocies." But Richardson rejected the sketch made for the Hays. He proposed to move their entrance around the corner from H Street to 16th Street.

When he returned to Massachusetts, Richardson was burdened with opposite but interlocked assignments. He would design for the Adamses a superior but inexpensive house along the lines they had fixed for all its floors. He would design for the Hays' approval an outwardly similar but larger, costlier house freely invented by himself. If a shadow fell over the project, it was Richardson's increasing illness. A kidney ailment was causing him to gain weight enormously. That he could live long was doubtful. Yet his high spirits never faltered.

In January 1884, Henry worked through the day on his *Second Jefferson* and afterwards rested by reading. At the moment, he was reading Anthony Trollope's *Autobiography*. He wrote to Hay: "At this season my wife and I stay at home. . . . Trollope has amused me for two evenings. I am clear that you should write autobiography. I mean to do mine. After seeing how coolly and neatly a man like Trollope can destroy the last vestige of heroism in his own life, I object to allowing mine to be murdered by anyone except myself."

Hay had once heard Adams say that a person who causes the birth of a child "incurs a heavier responsibility" than a person who commits a murder. The line had stayed in memory.[45] Henry's new remark—his saying he meant to kill himself in an autobiography— may have affected Hay as not memorable. It could pass for incidental light-comic irony.

Behind the remark was the fully developed idea of *The Education of Henry Adams*. With important exceptions, the future book would be factually accurate with respect to the world in which its protagonist moved and with respect to persons other than Adams. Both in total effect and in innumerable details, it would be fictional and anti-factual with respect to its "Henry Adams." Because the real Henry would be mostly absent and Clover would nowhere appear, the book would amount, among other things, to a comic murder. It would not kill the actual Henry. Instead it would bar him from the stage.

Adams meanwhile was advancing in a *History* which would reveal its author as heroic. His heroism could be said to center in his making historical discoveries—or in his honesty about past events—or in his sustaining a highly readable and deeply suggestive story. For any of these reasons, or for all, he was deserving of praise, not murder.

These were matters that Henry could discuss with Clover but would not raise with Hay or King. Neither friend had a true idea of Henry's historical and literary ambitions. Neither understood his *History*.

Hay had responded to Henry's *Aaron Burr* as a centerpiece. It in fact was peripheral. If the scope of Henry's *History* had been limited to the doings of early Democratic-Republican politicians in the United States, Burr might have come to mind as just the person to figure in the narrative as Satan. As things stood, the scope of the *History* was incomparably larger. It extended throughout the United States and to all the foreign countries with which the Americans of 1800–1817 had dealings. *Three* persons in the work would be outstandingly Satanic. The least was Aaron Burr of New York, who tried to separate the western states from the Union, preferably with British assistance, but without if necessary—a hopeless venture. A worse demon was Timothy Pickering of Massachusetts, who masterminded efforts to separate the New England states from the Union, mainly by creating a confederacy of state legislatures and state officials—a more workable scheme. The worst demon by far was a Corsican ruler in France, Napoleon Bonaparte. As presented in the *History*, he was Satan in human form and Milton's arch-demon returned to print.[46]

In essence, Adams's *History* was an account of a single action: a tide or stream of human doings. A prominent event near the start of the stream was the inauguration of Jefferson as president of the United States on March 4, 1801, and his saying surprisingly to his fellow Americans in his inaugural address, "We are all Republicans, we are all Federalists." But the stream began with a still-earlier event.

On November 9, 1799, Bonaparte seized control of the French government. France and Great Britain were at war. The new ruler of France was in process of losing a French army in Egypt. To offset the debacle in the east, he secretly conceived a stroke of statecraft in the west. The richest possession of France in America, richer than all the rest combined, was the West Indian island of St. Domingo. In 1795, France had extorted from Spain the larger portion of the island. Napoleon's idea was to make the island the center of a western empire. For the present, because of the English war, he could not communicate with his magnificent colony. It chanced too that during the French revolution the slaves on St. Domingo had gained their freedom, as had the slaves on Guadeloupe; and a black general, Toussaint Louverture, was ruling St. Domingo in mere nominal subordination to France. Moreover, St.

Domingo and Guadeloupe depended for supplies on the United States.

In August 1800, Napoleon sent an emissary to Spain to force that country to give back to France a former colony, Louisiana, with a view to the colony's displacing the United States as the supplier of St. Domingo and Guadeloupe. Next, on October 6, 1801, Napoleon made peace with England. Six weeks later, a French army commanded by his brother-in-law, General Leclerc, sailed for St. Domingo. Leclerc carried secret orders by Napoleon to subdue the blacks and mulattoes on St. Domingo, capture Toussaint Louverture and other troublemakers and ship them to France, and return the remaining blacks to slavery.

Leclerc's army dealt successfully with the troublemakers but met with appalling resistance by the mass of blacks. Also his army fell sick with fever. Officers and men died of wounds and fever faster than new victims could be sent from France to take their places. At the same time, blacks on St. Domingo learned that blacks on smaller Guadaloupe were being returned to slavery. Black resistance on St. Domingo, already unimaginable, intensified.

Realizing that Leclerc's army was lost, Napoleon ordered the sale of Louisiana to the United States. The sale would help finance the raising and deployment of new armies. It pointed towards later disasters, first at Moscow, ultimately at Waterloo.

The historian who first took an interest in Napoleon's suppressed secret orders to return the blacks to slavery on St. Domingo and Guadaloupe was an American, "H. Adams." He had found the documents in Paris in 1879–1880. At an unknown time, he wrote an article telling the history of Napoleon's attempted stroke of statecraft and the black response, placed it in the hands of Gabriel Monod, editor of the *Revue Historique*, and arranged its publication in the magazine in French. The French version—H. Adams, *"Napoléon Ier et Saint-Domingue"*—would appear in the issue for April 1884.

The not-yet-published article was one of Adams's important works. He eventually would publish it in English, improved, as "Napoleon I. at St. Domingo." In two languages and in slightly dissimilar versions, the article would relate to his *History of the United States* as both overture and finale. Its central figure was General Leclerc, whose reward for unremitting effort to execute his brother-in-law's orders was a feverish death. Another vivid figure in the article was Toussaint Louverture, who strangely delivered himself to the French—much as Napoleon would deliver himself to the British after Waterloo. The theme of the article, however, was the love of freedom felt in every human being, of every ancestry or color. Its heroes were the masses of nameless leaderless blacks on St. Domingo. Their heroic act was their successfully fighting off the re-enslavers sent from France.[47]

Adams could not publish the article with advantage in the United States in 1884. Its radical tendency would make it more or less unwelcome. Because it would first appear in Paris and in French, it would be unnoticed by Americans. All the same, albeit mutedly, the article would appear. Adams's *History* was no longer silent. Its stirring music was beginning to sound.

C. F. Adams, Jr., read *The Bread-Winners* when it appeared in book form and made, or so he thought, an unprecedented discovery. On January 31, 1884, he wrote to Godkin about the authorship. He said he had no special information, yet he was positive that *The Bread-Winners* was written "by the same hand that wrote the novel 'Democracy.'" The newer book had "the same coarse, half-educated touch" and "Nast-like style."

Charles was proud of his discovery and wanted it published without delay. He asked whether Godkin could have a paragraph written for the *Nation* propounding the idea. "I am very clear in my own mind."[48]

On February 2, Henry Adams received two deliveries. The larger was "a bound copy of the first volume of my History." Next day, writing to Gaskell, he said about the volume: "I have had six copies privately printed as a first edition for my own use. When I am ready, I shall reprint and publish two volumes at once." Knowing Gaskell would wonder whether he would receive a copy, Henry continued: "I admit to thinking the book readable, but to you it would be sadly dull reading. You see, I am writing for a continent of a hundred million people fifty years hence; and I can't stop to think what England will read."

The other delivery was an envelope from Godkin containing a letter he had just received from Charles. The editor had written in its bottom margin: "What shall I say to this?" Henry read the letter, put it in an envelope of his own, and sent it to Hay with a commentary:

> The enclosed . . . is a joke, so far better than any I ever thought this world could produce, that I hardly dare send it. . . . I want to roll on the floor; to howl, kick and sneeze; to weep silent tears of thankfulness to a beneficent providence which has permitted me to see this day. . . .

He asked Hay to return the letter and keep its existence secret. Also he said he would urge Godkin to elicit a note from Charles and publish it "with the writer's initials." (A note was shortly printed, signed "A."[49]) In a postscript, Henry added: "My coarse and half-educated wife has had a fit over her brother-in-law's Nast-like touch."

Part of the joke was Charles's assuming that something thought by him could not previously have occurred to others. In fact, the mistaken theory had been advanced as soon as *The Bread-Winners* began to appear in the *Century*.[50]

A quite separate joke was that *three* novels might soon be puzzling readers. Neither King nor the Hays had been told; but during the coming month, March 1884, Holt would publish *Esther*. The title page would bear a meaningless pseudonym, "Frances Snow Compton." In the sense of penning words on pages, the book was written by Henry, but its being *by* him did not matter. It only mattered that its leading ideas belonged to Clover and she too was represented by a novel.[51]

Without damage to their marriage, Henry and Clover were opposites with respect to faith. Henry could be taken for an agnostic but was not one.[52] He was a believer who had parted company with two religions. Plainly, yet without noise, he had recently said he was neither Jew nor Christian.[53]

Clover was a through and through agnostic. She believed a saying of her invention: "The principles of agnostics are not respected."[54] The hope that her *Esther* might gain a modest following even if not advertised was possibly hers and was not an unreasonable hope. For all that she or Henry knew, American agnostics might discover the book and take it up in their own support, against their church-going attackers.

Later her book would be listed for sale in England as *Esther; or the Agnostics*.[55] The inserted subtitle could seem misleading. In any proper sense of the word, the novel contained only one agnostic, its heroine. Yet, rather dramatically, the subtitle made sense. It accepted the heroine as spokesperson for *all* agnostics.[56]

While buying the corner from Paine, Adams and Hay had to deal with the complication of a Corcoran mortgage on the property. As overseer of the Adamses' investments, Edward Hooper urged Adams and Hay to prepay the mortgage, and they assented. Henry sold his Calumet stock at a $30,000 profit. He simultaneously received his portion of a distribution of capital bequeathed by his Brooks antecedents. With this timely assistance, he paid with cash the full costs of his 44' x 131' lot and the inexpensive Richardson house.

1884 was an election year. President Arthur was looking forward to renomination by the Republicans. Blaine was ostensibly not a candidate, but his supporters were active on his behalf, and their numbers were growing. Wayne and Virginia MacVeagh were visiting the Adamses when possible, and the political alliance between the couples was intact. In Washington in the first week of March, the couples agreed to attend the Republican convention at Chicago on June 3. While there, they would be house guests of Wayne's brother Franklin. Wayne meanwhile predicted to Henry and Clover that Blaine would win the nomination but lose the election. He believed that the Independents siding with the Democrats would be numerous enough to turn the tide.[57]

Without warning, on March 12, the plaster ceiling in the parlor at 1607 H Street crashed to the floor. In the normal course of things, Henry and Clover would have entered the room just minutes later for morning tea. Their narrow escape from injury or death reminded them that old houses had dangers. Their new house seemed a necessity.

Ten days later, Hay left a sick bed in Cleveland to visit Washington. He was needed to join the Adamses in reviewing with Richardson the complete preliminary plans for the adjoining houses. Clover wrote to her father that "the problem of windows & general scale we gave [Richardson] . . . was a difficult one & he has dealt with it like a master." ". . . [Henry and I] do not wish a fine house— only an unusual one & that we certainly shall have. . . ."

Hay stayed with the Adamses till March 25. Before he left, he received a cable from King in Europe asking him to come abroad till June, without Clara, for a bachelors' holiday. With some amazement, Clover saw that Hay meant to go. She listed reasons. ". . . the Cleveland climate is detestable in spring & he far from well or gay—& King is to him like the Sun in heaven. I never imagined such fanatic adoration could exist in this practical age." For the interval preceding his flight to Europe, Hay returned to Cleveland. To insure progress on his house, he sent Adams his power of attorney.

King had proposed that he and Hay take a west-bound steamer to New York on June 10. Adams knew of the plan and wrote to Hay in Cleveland promising that he and Clover would arrive at the Brevoort House on June 20. "Give [King] . . . our love, and tell him we hate writing as much as he does. . . ." To ease Hay's mind entirely, Henry extended a broad assurance. "I will take care of your house and look after it like my own. I am not afraid of responsibility. . . ."

❖ ❖ ❖

On April 19, 1884, the Adamses risked a dinner for twelve at the Andersons' new house and suffered in air kept warm by a central heating system. They learned that the fireplaces designed by Richardson for the house were treated by the Andersons as "for show only." Clover, a devotee of open fires, wrote to her father: "There's no use in having a fine house if you don't know how to live in it. We adjourned to a reception at the Geo. B. Lorings at 10½. It was quite pleasant—& plenty of fresh air. Blaine looked like death. Such a bloodless face I never saw on a man who is not supposed to be ill."

The governor of New York, Grover Cleveland, had come forward as a possible Democratic candidate. Being owner of Pitch Pine Hill, Henry could vote in Massachusetts. Clover advised Dr. Hooper on April 28: "Look out for a *Cleveland* boom soon. We are going to vote for him . . . if they'll have the sense to run him."

MacVeagh shortly assured the Adamses that, if nominated, Cleveland would vanquish Blaine beyond a doubt. The couples dropped their plan to attend the Republican convention. Any influence they could exert would be thrown to the Democrats, starting right away.

Brooks arrived but stayed at Wormley's. Charles too arrived and stayed at Wormley's. The elder brother had long held stock in the Union Pacific railroad. For a year, he had been a director of the corporation, obliged to work in cooperation with Jay Gould, the president. The railroad was in financial straits, and Charles's errand in Washington was to ask a Senate committee to help the corporation.[58]

Ulysses S. Grant, Jr., known as Buck, had married an heiress and become part-owner of a Wall Street brokerage, Grant & Ward. Knowing his father lacked occupation, young Buck had given him a chance to join the brokerage. The ex-president bought a $100,000 interest. The brokerage appeared to prosper, but certain of its executives were securing multiple loans with the same securities. On May 4, 1884, a Sunday, old Grant was told that the firm could not meet its obligations the following morning unless he raised some money. He visited W. H. Vanderbilt and borrowed $150,000 in his own name, but the firm's collapse was not prevented, and other brokerages and several banks went under. Many capitalists, Jay Gould included, lost heavily in the panic. General Grant owed Vanderbilt $150,000 he could not pay.[59]

The Union Pacific railroad was in the west, but its heaquarters was in New York and its financial office in Boston. During the panic in New York, C. F. Adams, Jr., became the man in line to succeed Gould as president of the road. As it happened, transfer of the presidency from Gould to Charles would not occur till June 24.[60]

While in England with King, Hay learned that King had no intention of returning to America. Hay booked passage on the *Brittanic*, to reach New York by June 22.[61] By then the final house plans might be ready.

Senator Cameron's stay abroad had faltered in mid course. Adams wrote to Hay on May 27: "Mrs. Don has come home, which consoles me for much. The society of this village is charming with the mercury at 90°. I am loath to go off to the sea-side, and we mean to hang on till the 20th, and drink Champagne & selzer with you on the 22d."

MacVeagh's prophecies were coming true. Blaine's juggernaut won at Chicago; but a large bloc of Independents—Schurz, Godkin, and C. F. Adams, Jr., among them—dissociated themselves from Blaine. Tempers began to fray. Long-time friends turned suddenly to enemies.

En route to New York, Henry and Clover visited the MacVeaghs in Bryn Mawr. Next, as agreed, they met Hay at the Brevoort. Hay and the Adamses journeyed together to Richardson's office in Brookline near Boston. There they saw and mostly approved the final plans.

The Democratic convention on July 11, likewise held at Chicago, nominated Cleveland, as expected. On the 16th, MacVeagh wrote to Adams returning the *First Jefferson*. He had read the volume twice and said his only objections were merely verbal. He disliked a sentence ended with "on," and he noted that such words as "Monocrats," "Nov-Anglian," and "occlusion" could seem pedantic. "I sought for some real defect as with a lighted candle, but whoever wrote it for you, and I suspect I know, it is extremely well done. . . . Its interest never flags and it often rises above the style of narrative to an eloquence which adorns the subject and is adorned by it. . . . How a man New England born can be of such wide mind and catholic sympathies I do not know."

Adams liked to think negatively about his volume. He replied on July 20, "I know where and why the book fails." He explained that its strength was bounded by his mental limitations; that if another brain could be patched onto his, to give him "scope double and different" from his present range, he would "write four times as good a book." Part in fun, part in earnest, he warned that he was "going to suppress the work." What the public wanted, he said, was such a writer as Blaine. "The public doesn't want me; and it cries for Jim. Have you read the letter of acceptance? I . . . read paragraphs here and there, and just wilted."

MacVeagh knew Henry as well as anyone but Clover. He realized that Henry was perfectly capable of suppressing the *First Jefferson* or even the entire *History*, if not for faults, then for virtues. Writing again on July 22, he said peremptorily: "You will do no such thing as suppress the book. . . ." "It is a great book—of which everybody who cares for you now must be justly proud. . . ." "You ought to be ashamed of yourself that you are not also proud of it. Whether you ever are or not, I am, and your wife is, and my wife is; and we three know all about it. And our order is to publish and at once."

21

DISASTER

The children the Adamses knew best were Edward Hooper's daughters, Ellen, Louisa, Mabel, Fanny, and Mary, fondly known as the monkeys. In the summer of 1884, the nieces as usual were brought by their father to their grandfather's house at Beverly Farms. Since building Pitch Pine Hill, the Adamses had bought added land, including a tract connecting their property with Dr. Hooper's. The nieces knew a path through the woods that led to Aunt Clover and Uncle Henry's house. They liked to go there and especially to play in Uncle Henry's study while he sat at his desk in cool white clothes and wrote his *History*.

On days when the monkeys did not appear, Clover and Henry usually walked to visit them, or, if riding, stopped to see them. The visits fixed themselves in nine-year-old Mabel's memory. She remembered in later life: ". . . [Aunt Clover and Uncle Henry] loved all young small things including dogs, and the dogs played an important part in their daily lives. Three little long-haired terriers were always to be seen tumbling about their feet or trotting after them on their walks."

The nieces studied the couple and noticed their singular happiness. In Mabel's words: "Often in the afternoons, the nieces would watch—almost enviously—the two figures on horseback vanishing into the flickering sunlight of the woods. An impression of oneness of life and mind, of perfect companionship, left an ideal never to be effaced."[1]

Through the summer of 1884, Adams's attention was divided between a project and an anxiety. The project was the *Second Jefferson*, which was advancing on schedule. The anxiety was the Blaine-Cleveland contest, which from its beginning was savage on both sides.

His *History* excepted, Adams was keeping quiet about his writings. On August 9, he received a letter from Hay, sent from Windsor, Vermont, where Hay was visiting Evarts. Hay said, ". . . [Evarts] had just been reading your Randolph and was full of admiration of it—and I made his mouth water for the Burr." Replying, Adams by-passed *John Randolph* and *Aaron Burr* in order to exclaim: "I have just finished with T. Jefferson! He has gone off to Monticello forever, carrying eight years of my life with him."

By "finished," Adams meant that he had completed three writings of the *Second Jefferson* and was ready to give the printer the books not yet supplied. It helps to know that the books were titled:

Book I	*The Florida Negotiation & the Carrying Trade*	8 chapters
Book II	*Burr's Conspiracy*	7 chapters
Book III	*The Berlin Decree: the Affair of the "Chesa-peake:" the Orders in Council, 1806–1807*	8 chapters
Book IV	*The Embargo*	8 chapters
Book V	*Repeal of the Embargo*	8 chapters

In August and September, Adams corrected proofs of the later books.[2] Also, in silence, he decided that Book II, "Burr's Conspiracy," said quite enough concerning Burr and his activities. The decision reduced the biography to waste paper.[3] *Aaron Burr* would be destroyed.[4]

While suppressing his *Burr*, Adams erased his plan to publish half the *History* in 1885 and adopted a plan to publish the entire work in instalments. As rapidly as possible, he would write, rewrite, and privately print the *First Madison* and *Second Madison*.[5] He then would publish the four volumes at six-month intervals.

The new plan was at odds with public events. It presupposed a victory for Cleveland. Such a victory had become impossible. The public had learned that the Democratic candidate when young had fathered an illegitimate child. Cleveland frankly confessed the error and proceeded with his campaign; but, popular attitudes being what they were, his chance of election had disappeared.

In late September, Cleveland's impossible victory became possible, after all. Candidate Blaine and Mrs. Blaine were revealed to have parented a child out of wedlock. On September 21, Adams wrote to Gaskell: "We are here plunged in politics funnier than words can express. Very great issues are involved. . . . But the amusing thing is that no one talks about real interests. . . . We are afraid to discuss them. Instead of this, the press is engaged in a most amusing dispute whether Mr[.] Cleveland had an illegitimate child[,] and did or did not live with more than one mistress; whether Mr[.] Blaine got paid in railway bonds for services as Speaker; and whether Mrs[.] Blaine had a baby three months after her marriage. . . . Society is torn to pieces. Parties are wrecked from top to bottom. . . . Yet, when I am not angry, I can do nothing but laugh."

In the same letter to Gaskell, Adams outlined the new plan for his *History* and revealed a plan of travel. "My history rolls on. I am privately printing my second volume. I hope to finish the whole on or about January 1889 [near the end of Cleveland's hoped-for first term]. We mean then to go round the world. . . ."

Henry failed to mention two aspects of this double plan. When volumes of the *History* began to appear, say in 1889, he and Clover would be on the oceans or in foreign lands and in that sense would be invisible. Yet their going around the world might also make them a subject of comparisons. After two terms as secretary of state, Seward made a trip around the world; and, after two terms in the White House, Ulysses and Julia Grant did the same. The precedents would be remembered.

By summer's end, Henry and Clover felt diminished fear of Blaine. The Republican candidate remained a powerful contender. Yet he had proved a national absurdity, a would-be president whose past mistakes tended always to be exposed and to dim his prospects just when his prospects were brightest. Writing to MacVeagh from Beverly Farms on September 30, Adams said that Americans lacked "a sense of humor." "Some jokes are so colossally perfect . . . that they dazzle and blind our simple natures. Dear Blaine is such a joke. Positively I love him. Never have I dreamed of getting such amusement from a candidate for office."

The Hays did not remotely share Henry and Clover's passionate desire that Blaine be ruined. Hay was active in Ohio as a Blaine supporter and a Republican Party regular.[6]

After an absence of more than two years, King was back in New York. He strongly wanted Blaine to be president. He half-wished to see the Adamses; but he had become a believer in the superiority of Europe; he assumed that Henry and Clover lived in America by choice; and he had learned that both—Clover especially—were boosters of Cleveland.

King traveled to Boston on business and failed to win new backing from Alex Agassiz and Quincy Shaw. He meant to visit the Adamses at Pitch Pine Hill but returned in silence to New York. On

October 6, he wrote to Henry: "How much I long for a chat with you; to find out among other things why you live in America. It has puzzled me much when I have thought of you[,] which was often and often." As if the outcome of the election were sure, he added, ". . . Blaine is going in."

Construction of the Hay and Adams houses in Washington was under way. Starting on October 13, Henry and Clover hurried to Washington on errands relating to the houses. King was in New York at the Brevoort, but they did not stop to visit him. From the capital on Sunday, November 2, Henry wrote to Hay: "I've not seen or heard anything of elections since I've been here. But the woods are lovely and the roads perfect. . . ." He continued: "I want to know how the dear King is. Do you happen to have heard what part of the world he may be in?"

The election took place on Tuesday and was much too close to be funny. Blaine lost by the breath-taking margin of a few votes in a single state, New York. King wrote to Hay: "For Blaine I am truly sorry. . . . The shadows will gather about him thenceforward. . . ."

The thought of shadows applied less well to Blaine than to King himself. His prospects were poor and his feelings negative. Living in Washington seemed to him unthinkable. Passages in his letter showed antipathy to the United States and antipathy to Clover. He said that "a grovelling ignoramus"—Cleveland—had been forced on the country by "the fastidious moralists." He told Hay in exasperation:

> If England becomes a democracy[,] as it will[,] there will always be left the large national reserve of common sense to save them and for centuries they will desire to be led by men of intelligence. Let's go there!
>   Washington will be grotesque enough for the next few years. I wonder how dear Mrs[.] Adams will enjoy her Grover?[7]

The Adamses were as relieved as King was miserable. In consequence of Cleveland's victory, Henry had gained four added years of freedom at the State Department. Yet he thought the election had been harmful to all participants. On November 9, writing to Congressman Abram Hewitt, a leading New York Democrat, he asked whether Hewitt had "suffered under the strain of the election." He said about himself: ". . . it came hard on me. . . . A pachydermatous rhinoceros would break down under a nervous agony so prolonged."[8]

The six privately-printed copies of the *First Jefferson* had been shown to Clover, the Bancrofts, the MacVeaghs, Hay, Charles, and presumably Justin Winsor; but, apart from MacVeagh's reaction, the results are unknown. The copies were later destroyed.[9]

Charles apparently was sent the *First Jefferson* in January 1884. He was interrupted while trying to read it. In his diary, he noted visiting Henry in Washington three times in early May and twice on May 28 and 29. He recorded in Quincy on June 8: "Worked on Henry's book all day. Looked up some letters in the John Adams & J. Q. A. files." He again visited Henry in Washington on June 16. On June 21 and 22, just prior to assuming the presidency of the Union Pacific, he noted having "read Henry's history." "Corrected some of Henry's proof."

During the summer, Henry vanished from the elder brother's diary; but, at Quincy on October 14, Charles recorded, "Read Henry and to town at 8.37 [A.M.]." Thereafter he wrote fifteen entries about reading the *First Jefferson*. Also, during trips to Washington, he wrote:

[Nov. 14]   Breakfasted at Henry's with Mrs. Cameron.
[Nov. 16]   To Henry's.
[Nov. 27]   Dined at Henry's.
[Nov. 28]   Called w. Henry on old Bancroft in the evening.
[Nov. 29]   Breakfasted w. Henry.

He ended on December 28, 1884, "Finished Henry's book." Presumably he returned the copy when next in Washington.

If Charles's jottings were in any way peculiar, the oddness related to Clover. He ate meals at 1607 H Street at least six times during 1884, yet took no written notice of Henry's wife. On the evidence of the diary, Clover did not exist.[10]

The walls of the Hay and Adams houses were completed in the autumn, but the houses remained unroofed. In December 1884 and January 1885, construction was halted by bad weather.

Clover at some point described Richardson's architectural style as "Neo-Agnostic," and word of her opinion got to Hay.[11] Possibly, in secret, she viewed *Esther* and her future house as kindred works.

Esther had been on the market in the United States since the previous spring. The Adamses wished it might be sold as well in England. On January 6, Henry wrote to Holt asking him to reprint it "without change of title-page or hint of authorship" and arrange the sale of the edition in England in a way involving advertisements and the sending of copies to reviewers.

As a result of Henry's plea, a supply of copies would shortly be sent to London and published by Richard Bentley and Son. There did not seem much hope that *Esther* would attract a following in the British Isles; few copies had been sold in America; but a scattering of persons would read it in both places. That perhaps was the initial object that Clover and Henry wished to achieve.[12]

Henry's privately printed *Second Jefferson* was dated "Cambridge/ 1885." When copies reached him is unknown. He may have sent copies at once to MacVeagh and Hay, but no trace survives of his doing so, nor any trace of their responses.[13] He took a copy to Mrs. Bancroft (her responses are lost). He later elicited reactions from her husband.[14]

A natural question was whether Henry asked Brooks to read the *First* and *Second Jefferson*. It appears that he did not. He also avoided asking Lodge to read the volumes.[15]

For Henry, the whole matter of his writing history had been complicated by changes in the lives of Brooks and Charles. Perhaps in part because of his breakdown, Brooks was beginning a new career as a prophetic philosopher. In 1884, following the November election, he was persuaded by Horace Scudder, an editor at Houghton Mifflin and Company, to write a history of Massachusetts. In this way, a path was opened for Brooks to publish, not ordinary history, but history suited to his new philosophy, oracular, fiery, and apocalyptic. Keeping quite clear of Henry and Clover, he would labor to complete a book called *The Emancipation of Massachusetts*. When published in 1886, it would earn him a place among America's unwise geniuses and clamorous savants.[16]

Charles equally had turned to history. In the 1870s, he had been asked to write a history of Weymouth, Massachusetts. He had found the project satisfying and on his own initiative wrote papers on "The Settlement of Boston Bay" and "The Antinomian Controversy." In 1883 at the University Press, he had privately printed the latter works under the title *Episodes in New England History, Vol. I*.[17] And in the winter of 1883–1884, he had written the first draft of a history of Quincy—a 500–page manuscript, till then his longest work.[18]

A factor Henry had to weigh was Charles's incapacity as a reader. The volumes of Henry's *History* could be read with full comprehension at high speed by readers of the first ability but would tend to be closed books to readers of limited intelligence. Wayne and Virginia MacVeagh had the mental powers the *History* presupposed. So did George and Elizabeth Bancroft, especially the latter, at least in Henry's judgment.[19] Hay perhaps came near to possessing the mental minimum. But Henry appears to have found that Charles could not read the *First Jefferson*. He could only read at it. That being the case, Henry postponed asking Charles to read the *Second Jefferson*.[20]

Earlier a resident of Brookline, Edward Hooper had moved to a new winter house in Cambridge. The house was built directly next to the house erected in 1870 for Whitman and Ellen Gurney.

Dr. Hooper continued to live in Boston and Beverly Farms but was suffering badly from angina. On March 5 or 6, 1885, warning reached Clover that her father's condition had worsened. She wrote to him in her usual way, as if nothing had happened. Meanwhile, to facilitate his being cared for, the sufferer was moved to the Gurneys' house in Cambridge. His need of care quickly became continuous.

The change occurred at an unlucky moment. Many details of the Hay and Adams houses remained unsettled, Hay was in New York, and Henry or Clover had to be at hand to deal with questions asked by the contractor or by Richardson. Unluckily too, the Adamses were at low ebb. Henry wrote to Hay on March 7, 1885: "Bunged up by the nastiest cold I have had for years, I write in double straits because my wife may have to go to Boston next week, and possibly I may go with her, or for her."

Added news from Cambridge resulted in the Adamses' journeying to New York on March 11. They put up at the Brevoort. Clover left for Boston in the morning. Henry and Hay called on Mrs. Whitney, who was not at home, and Henry and Richardson spent an hour with St. Gaudens and La Farge. At 11:30 P.M., Henry wrote to Clover from the Brevoort: "Funny world with elements of grotesque. . . . The lunatic preponderates. Pleasant dinner with King and Hay."

Next morning, Adams and Hay took the Limited to Washington. Henry reported to Clover: ". . . we inspected the houses, and I think Hay was a good deal impressed by them. Ours is certainly going to be handsomer than his, unless the roof changes the effect; but the double result will make a sensation."

Clover wrote daily from Cambridge, Henry from Washington, but her letters were later destroyed, presumably by Henry. Her first letter evidently said her father was dying. He wrote back on the 15th, "The report was worse than I expected, and made my reply very uncheerful to the numerous enquiries I met."

Henry's return to Washington had been forced. He and Clover meant to sublet 1607 H Street, and he needed to interview a potential tenant. More urgently, he had to visit Dr. Maynard. His trouble was a damaged tooth so sensitive that he was trying to avoid exposure to cold air.

Hay stayed till March 18, much occupied in conferences with Nicolay about their *Lincoln*. Because Clover planned to stay with her father till the end, perhaps also because she requested it, Henry sent her a picture from their walls. "Your Mantegna goes with this letter."

Clover was sleeping, not at the Gurneys' house, but next door at her brother Edward's. She tended always to lend a pleasing lightness to situations, even if dark. She varied her work as nurse by giving her nieces dancing lessons.[21] Also she bought a ball for Possum and mailed it to him in Washington. Henry told what happened. "Possum's present arrived, and no sooner did he see the address with his name than he began jumping and screaming till I had to reprove him severely. He kept up a wild dance while I opened the package and then seized his ball and retired to the entry to munch it."

In Quincy, Charles learned of Dr. Hooper's condition. He assumed there might not be space for Henry in Cambridge, if he came north, and so offered him a bed at Quincy on President's Hill.[22]

Doctors proverbially were the worst patients other doctors had to treat. Among such patients, Dr. Hooper was possibly the worst of all. He had studied medicine but seldom practiced. He perhaps thought he knew medicine well but necessarily knew it little. The conclusion is impossible to avoid that he intended to treat himself and succeeded. In his case, the principal doctor was the patient.[23]

It needs repeating that Robert Hooper was descended from Marblehead sea kings and bankers and that his deceased wife was a daughter of a Cape Cod sea king and Boston merchant prince. Dr. Hooper's manner was agreeable, but his assumptions were lordly and commanding. Strength of will had been masked by generosity. Since the death of his wife, he had showered kindnesses on his children. In 1885, his kindnesses to Ellen, Edward, and Clover were unforgotten; and it was presupposed by both father and children that they should be as kind to him as he had been to them.

His chief demand was that they not hire trained nurses. He wished to be attended by his children and Gurney, with the sole addition of a practical nurse who had earlier assisted during family illnesses.[24] The demand was one that could have been predicted by readers of Hawthorne's tales. In "The Minister's Black Veil" (earlier mentioned in connection with Clover's covering her face), Hawthorne described the last illness of a New England minister, Mr. Hooper, and emphasized that the person who attended him was "no hired handmaiden of death" but his one-time fiancée, who still loved him, although he had prevented their going forward with an earthly marriage.

The decision not to hire trained nurses could seem natural, even usual, in 1885. Such nurses remained very few. Hospitals likewise were few. General hospitals—as distinct from charity hospitals for the poor—were only struggling into existence.

Ellen, Edward, and Clover did more than accept their father's demand; they later pretended to be its authors. It became accepted doctrine in the Hooper family that Ned and his sisters made the arrangement. In the words of a carefully prepared "Chronology/ Henry Adams" written by Ned's daughter Louisa in the mid 1930s: "With mistaken filial devotion, his [Dr. Hooper's] children wished to do all the day and night nursing themselves. (Professional nurses had barely started in those days.) Marian Adams came to stay with her brother, next door to the Gurneys. She and her sister, her brother[,] and her brother-in-law organized all the nursing turn & turn about."[25]

The nursing arrangement would be injurious to Clover if long continued. Tragically, she was heroic. Other women were considerate and kind, but she was kind in heaping measures. She had fallen in love with Henry after he had undergone extraordinary strain watching at a deathbed. Her kindness at the time had proved her better than a nurse and better than a doctor of medicine. In a more than metaphorical sense, she had returned her future husband from the dead.

Edward Hooper and Whitman Gurney were later alleged to have done their shares of nursing, but Ned was treasurer of Harvard and was also the father of five growing children.[26] Gurney was dean of Harvard and could not lightly shirk his university duties, and his wife Ellen could not easily be asked to absent herself from her husband's side through the nights. For all these reasons, good intentions notwithstanding, it would fall to Clover to take an unequal share of the hardest shifts, between late evening and daybreak.[27]

This is not to say that, in Cambridge in 1885, Clover had any idea that nursing could prevent her father's dying. It is only to say that Dr. Hooper's demand was not the controlling factor in Clover's situation. It was *her* idea that she should extend heroic kindness—

that she should withhold no effort—that she should help without limit and even not sleep.[28]

A step at a time, Henry was becoming very worried. Interruptedly for several months, he had been drafting chapters of his *First Madison*. At 1607 H Street, he tried to write but advanced with little speed. The houses were progressing with irksome slowness. The "interminable winter," as he called it, was the longest in memory. He was daily visiting Dr. Maynard.

On March 20, when he and Clover had been nine nights separated and Hay had gone, Henry received a delivery, a barrel. He wrote to Clover: "I got hammer and chisel, and opened it. I found a white porcelain tea-set; a tray; tea-pot; sugar and cream jug; and five cups and saucers. All are prettily decorated with little bunches of ròses, and each has on it a rose clock-face with hands pointing to five o'clock." (He could have added that, seen from above, the cups and saucers were heart-shaped.[29]) "This comes certainly from Clarence King, who said something to me about a barrel when I was with him in New York."

Henry sent immediate thanks to King. Still, the gift could awaken worry. It was ominous that a tea-set had been made for the Five of Hearts, an attempted club whose full membership had not once met since its sudden inception in New York. It was ominous as well that the members were dispersed in four places; that only Henry was in Washington; and that Clover, the prospective pourer of tea, was continuously in Massachusetts on an errand fraught with risk.

While Henry was opening the barrel, Clover telegraphed from Cambridge asking him to come, preferably soon. She did not say where he would sleep. Answering at 9:15 next morning, March 21, 1885, a Saturday, Henry said Friday had been a "frightful day," windy, dusty, and very cold. He had paid his daily visit to Dr. Maynard. He returned "low in mind," attempted to work, but merely "felt helpless." "This lasted till five o'clock when . . . Richardson walked in. . . . After kiting about the houses, he came back here and had a talk with Edmundson [the contractor]. In the middle of it Alex Agassiz came in, browned and burned in Sandwich Island suns, and swearing energetically at the arctic weather here." At 6:30, Clover's telegram arrived. "After consultation and dinner I decided to take the two-oclock train with [Richardson] . . . on Monday. I can't readily go before . . . for I dread trouble in my teeth, and have much to do here."

That Saturday in the afternoon, obeying a directive of Clover's,

Henry took Richardson to the White House, gained admittance, and, by talking with various persons, elicited an invitation to return in the evening and meet the president. After dining at the Yellow House, Adams and Richardson returned to the executive mansion. Rose Cleveland, the president's sister, was acting as hostess. Henry wrote to Clover from his study on Sunday, March 22:

> . . . Miss Cleveland received us, and took us into the red room where we found the President seated in a melancholy way, with four or five ladies. . . . Richardson strolled off with Miss Cleveland into the greenhouse. I had a good chance to see our new President. . . . We must admit that, like Abraham Lincoln, the Lord made a mighty common-looking man in him. I expected it, and I was satisfied. He was very quiet, and said little; presently Miss Cleveland returned with Richardson who had evidently been coaching her about me, for she . . . invited me to join her; so we sat down on a sofa. . . .
> Miss Cleveland . . . carries an atmosphere of female college about her, thicker than the snow storm outside my window. She listens seriously and asks serious questions. Her commonest expression was that some piece of my idiocy was "a very valuable suggestion". . . . I liked her. . . . When I rose to come away, I explained why you were not with me, and she cordially asked me to bring you. . . .

Ending his Sunday letter, Henry remarked, "As you send for me, I assume you mean me to come to Ned's and not to accept Charles's invitation." The plan to travel with Richardson on Monday still held, and there was time to fit in a letter to Cunliffe. Henry told his friend: ". . . my poor father is a complete wreck, and my mother almost a cripple; while, only within a few weeks my wife's father has broken down, and my wife has gone to Boston to be with him in his last moments. I must follow her tomorrow. I have no idea how long we shall be kept in Boston; but meanwhile our house here needs attention, for the plasterers will soon be at work on it, and the finishing will follow fast."

With regard to himself, Henry spoke in unpromising terms. "My poor history does not get on at all. I have finished and actually printed for my private use two large volumes, 600 pages each; but two more will be needed to complete the work, and I am tired of it. For a month I have hardly touched it, and my interest in it is gone. This is rather hard, as the result of ten years work, with the prospect of five more."

Henry's assumption that he and Clover would reunite in Cambridge and remain together was disappointed. Dr. Hooper's illness was painful and was becoming protracted. It had burdened Ellen, Edward, and Gurney heavily, Clover even more. Henry stayed at

Cambridge for the better part of four days. Writing to Henry Higginson on the last, Friday, March 27, he said he was returning to Washington but would be back in Cambridge "next week." "The poor old Doctor is fading away like a Stoic, without a murmur of complaint. I wish we might all face death as coolly and sensibly; but the process is harsh and slow."[30]

Because he left Boston late on Friday afternoon, Henry had just time enough in New York to sleep. He then ferried to Jersey City, caught a train to Washington, and read till the train reached Wilmington. Thinking he had best stretch his legs, he walked through the cars. In the third car, he was greeted with a hello from King.

King was hurrying to Mexico on mining business. They talked till they reached the capital. On the assumption that he would very shortly be changing trains, King refused an invitation to 1607 H Street. After they parted, he learned he was wrong about his train, took a cab, and paid Henry a cheerful visit.

That night, Henry wrote to Clover about the meeting on the train and King's unplanned appearance. ". . . King walked in. His train did not start till ten. We indulged in a cup of tea, and then went out in the rain to see the houses[,] which he warmly approved. Hay's roof is getting on, but the workmen had gone and we could not see the interiors, so we went to Anderson's and sat half an hour with Madame. . . . Then we had dinner and pleasant talk till half past nine."

The dogs needed baths. Henry said he would pay a Sunday visit to Dr. Maynard. ". . . I shall prepare to start north on Monday and be with you on Tuesday morning." ". . . my only perplexity is to decide whether to bring the camera or not. I wish you would telegraph instructions, but I shall have to decide without them." "Perhaps I shall be with you almost as soon as this letter reaches you. . . ."

Maynard refused to treat Henry further till a definite schedule of appointments could be made. Clover meanwhile telegraphed asking Henry to wait for instructions before he again came north. He replied by letter on Monday afternoon: "I shall hardly wait [for?] your orders, and if I do not start at two tomorrow, I shall probably go to New York by the four o'clock train. I want to see Richardson."

Clover again telegraphed, this time saying *not* to come. The message arrived on Tuesday when Henry was about to get a cab. He wrote: ". . . I have decided to obey your order; but tomorrow I mean to go, no matter what you say. If the news is no worse, I shall stop to sleep in New York, and go on to Boston Thursday. . . . I must take a hand at the nursing, for I see that what I feared has happened, and that the refusal of a trained nurse has made the nursing a very serious matter. You will therefore see me soon after you get this letter."

His second trip to Cambridge did not result in changes relating to trained nurses. The force that prevailed against him was concerted charity. The kindness shown to Dr. Hooper by his three children and Whitman Gurney was shown also to Henry. They told him he was not to be distracted by their problem. He was to attend as usual to things in Washington. Resistance was adamant.[31]

Late on April 6, he left Boston a second time. He did not stop in New York. He boarded a sleeping car at Jersey City and passed a sleepless night en route to Washington. At 9:30 A.M., April 7, he wrote to Clover from 1607 H Street: "The country [near the capital] looks very much like that about Cambridge for absence of spring, but the square is green. . . . I am up to my eyes in unpaid bills, and must go to Maynard at twelve, and tell him to go ahead. . . . The dogs bark as usual, and Possum seems peacefully happy to get me back."

Rebecca Dodge, a young friend in Washington, had written to Henry requesting news. He wrote to her on April 8, 1885: "My wife has been four weeks away, and I bolt forward and back like a brown monkey. . . . They won't take me for a nurse, and I can't live all alone in a big, solitary house when it rains and I can't ride."

Rebecca was sufficiently a friend to justify a candid estimate of Clover's father's condition. Henry said that Dr. Hooper could no longer take nourishment. ". . . I do not know whether his malady is immediately fatal, for the doctors do not even know what it is. . . ."

Henry's attention had shifted from Dr. Hooper's dying to Clover's rest and recovery. He and she had agreed that they should not return to Beverly Farms for the summer but should go to alternative places that were healthful and cool. On April 8, Mac-Veagh visited Henry and suggested a July meeting of the Mac-Veaghs and Adamses in the mountains at White Sulphur Springs, West Virginia. Nothing was decided, but the Adamses had definite preferences. They hoped to spend the first weeks of the hot season in the Appalachians, the last weeks in the Rockies. One reason was the theory of "oxygenation"—that recoveries from strain were assisted by mountain air.[32]

On April 9, Henry searched at the Smithsonian for a sort of

stone they might use in the fireplace of their new house. He found
"a small slab of Mexican onyx of a sea-green translucency so
exquisite as to make my soul yearn." He wrote to Clover about it
on April 10. Using some records he had kept, he went on to
measure the lateness of the spring.

> . . . I came back at three o'clock, and started off for a ride on Prince.
> The day was fine though cool (Therm. 44°), and I took my first three-
> hour spring excursion round by the dog-tooth violets and Riggs's
> farm. A few maples show a faint flush here and there, but not a sign
> of leaf is to be seen, and even the blood-root and hepatica hid
> themselves from my eyes. A few frogs sang in the sun, and birds sang
> in the trees; but no sign of a peach-blossom yet, and not even the
> magnolias and *Pyrus Japonica* have started. In 1878 the magnolias were
> . . . killed by frost on March 25, and in 1882 the frost killed them on
> April 10. . . . Last year the *Pyrus Japonica* was reddening on April 2.

Dr. Hooper had lost consciousness. Clover was writing but did
not say that Henry should come. He replied on April 11: "I wished
you had called me; but perhaps I should be in your way, and in
such circumstances I must depend on your judgment. As I am
pretty confident that the call is very near, I wait the more patiently."

His next letter, sent April 12, indicated that he was waiting at
the cost of mounting fear. "So another day has passed. Uneasy as I
am about you, and unable to do anything here, I go on from hour
to hour and make no engagements at all."

Dr. Hooper died on April 13. Henry went to Cambridge,
attended the funeral, visited Richardson in Boston, and returned
to Washington with Clover, arriving on the 19th. Her absence had
lasted six wintry weeks.

In appearance, both Adamses were well and strong. Henry was
forty-seven, Clover not yet forty-two. During thirteen years of
marriage, neither had experienced a serious illness nor even an
important interval of diminished health, physical or mental. During the same years, they had given themselves the benefits of a
moderate diet and constant exercise in the open air. At first, sure
of Clover's strength and fitness, they planned a trek in the Canadian Rockies. In Washington, they somewhat reconsidered, arranging instead to spend the latter part of the summer camping in
Dakota Territory, near the Yellowstone.[33]

A letter to Clover from Hay required an answer. Replying on
April 24, she said her father had succumbed in a state of "comfort"
and even "gayety." She wrote in the tones of a person whose health

and strength were intact. "Come [to Washington] in May. We stay till well into June. Houses booming. We face *west* after June & shall let [our] Beverly house."[34]

In more candid accents, she wrote two days later to Anne Palmer in Florida: "Please come north *soon*. . . . We came back last Saturday—I tired out in mind and body after six weeks nursing my father, who died of heart disease on the 13th at my sister's in Cambridge. . . . He was unselfish & brave & full of fun until he lost consciousness, & he kept us all up. As he did not fancy hired nurses, we had enough to do all those weeks to keep us sound. No one fills any part of his place to me but Henry[,] so that my connection with New England is fairly severed as far as interest goes."[35]

The Chief had become extremely fragile. Henry was required to go to Quincy, returning on June 10. Uncertainty about his father caused him new anxiety and cast doubt on the wisdom of going west.

Seeking cooler air, Henry and Clover immediately shifted to White Sulphur Springs. They took the horses, intending a gradual tour from one hotel to another. The area was new to them and very beautiful.

On June 12, Clover wrote to Rebecca Dodge urging her to come to the mountains and bring her cousin, Clifford Richardson.[36] On the 16th, the Adamses rode seventeen miles to a hotel at Old Sweet Springs. They were the season's earliest guests.

Henry sent Rebecca instructions about the best train and warned against strenuous efforts. The entertainments he offered were shade and indolence. ". . . we are fit to do nothing but sit in the shade and whistle to the birds." "My belief is that [Clifford] Richardson will do better by taking a week of dense laziness under our oak trees."

Rebecca and Clifford came to Old Sweet Springs, stayed a week, and returned to the capital, leaving the Adamses by themselves.[37] Clover had taken a fine picture of Rebecca outdoors by a field, with trees and hills in the background. She soon developed and printed it.[38]

In exchange for free lodging, Theodore Dwight, the State Department librarian, had agreed to live at 1607 H Street, mind the dogs, guard the pictures, and watch the workmen.[39] On June 28, Adams wrote to say that he and Clover were leaving on horseback for Mountain Lake, Virginia, "two or three days' journey over the mountains." He wanted Dwight to forward all letters to Mountain Lake "till Saturday, 5th July."

At the Yellow House on June 30, Dwight drew "Four diagrams of the original drawings on the walls of Henry Adams['s] study" and keyed the diagrams to a thirty-two item list. His diagrams showed that two pictures held places of honor at the center of the north wall. The larger he identified as Blake's "Nebuchadnezzar." The smaller, hung below, he described as "Lion wounded? Crayon on blue paper by Rubens."

Among nine pictures on the west wall, to the left of the door, he noted a picture that somewhat puzzled him. He listed it as "Death bed? —figures—venerable man in prayer. W. Blake."[40]

His motive in making the diagrams and the list seemed less related to the pictures than to Adams. He evidently had come to think of Adams as a great man or at least a great historian. While there was time, he wanted to make a record of a room the historian had worked in.

In Cambridge while separated from Henry and attending her father, Clover had committed an error of extreme devotion and had overtaxed herself. On July 1, 1885, or just before, in tranquil surroundings at or near Mountain Lake, Virginia, she went mad.[41] Both she and Henry grew suddenly aware that she unquestionably was insane.[42]

From Stayside Station on July 2, Henry countermanded his previous request to Dwight. He simply wrote: "Our movements are so extremely doubtful and uncertain that I think it best to have no more letters forwarded. Will you kindly retain anything that comes to the house. We may be in Washington at very short notice."

From the instant he apprehended Clover's condition, Henry ceased to think in long perspectives and acted "from minute to minute."[43] His first problem was to move Clover and himself to their best retreat. Their house at Beverly Farms had luckily not found a renter. With all possible speed, he effected their return to Washington, gave Dwight new orders, and, with little preparation, left with Clover for New York and Quincy. They went to the Old House, as the only convenient base from which to open Pitch Pine Hill.

Clover had wanted to avoid Beverly Farms as gloomy, on account of her father's absence.[44] Gloomy it was, but secluded. Also help was at hand. Ned was next door. The Gurneys were building a Richardson summer house at Prides Crossing. They too were near.

Clover's insanity was unmistakable. She was depressed and melancholy, could not sleep, and had no appetite. She dwelt continuously and self-disapprovingly on more or less imaginary injuries she said she had done to others in the past. One of her symptoms terrified her. She thought she was not real. As her sister later wrote, "Her constant cry was 'Ellen I'm not real—oh make me real'!"[45]

Two injuries that tormented Clover were unfortunately very real. She had sinned against her marriage. Love, intelligence, and tradition had advised that she must cleave to her mate. Without need or warrant, she instead had left her mate and attended exclusively to her father. While thus separated, she had sinned a second time. She wholly undermined the health of her beloved husband's wife. Her errors might possibly have been retrieved if she could have thought herself forgiven. She however believed that her trespasses were beyond forgiveness.

It might be assumed that, beginning in the Virginia mountains and continuing at Pitch Pine Hill, Henry and Clover were separated by a gulf. One was sane, the other mad. But they were in love; and it may be assumed that they were close, indeed closer than they had ever been, yet both intensely happy and intensely unhappy.

Evidence of love sustained and intensified was that husband and wife did things that needed doing. Clover "kept up her riding during the summer, and a semblance of her daily round with her family in and out of the house."[46] Henry journeyed weekly to see his parents. He and Clover recovered most or all of her letters to her father and a scattering of Dr. Hooper's other papers. Henry had brought materials from Washington to help him limp a distance in his *History*. He tried to write. He began a complete reading of Molière in French. He took an interest in Hooper genealogy and started tracing Clover's unknown progenitors. At the same time, together, through her "terrible summer," he and Clover waited for her insanity to vanish.[47]

Henry's relatives at Quincy were kept in perfect ignorance of her condition.[48] Dwight did not realize that Mrs. Adams was seriously ill.[49] In his letters, Henry only slowly disclosed her being in jeopardy. He advised Gaskell on August 30, "My wife has been out of sorts for some time past, and, until she gets well again, can do nothing." As long as possible, he continued the deceptions.[50]

For all his genius, H. H. Richardson had not understood that Marian Adams, the client who had most wished him to design the Hay and Adams houses, was an agnostic, and that Henry Adams, though a believer, was not a Christian. Similarly Richardson failed to understand the degree to which Clover and Henry were opposed to architectural ornament. During their stop in Washington en route from Virginia to Massachusetts, the Adamses had learned that the workmen would be emplacing stone carvings on their house front, as required by Richardson's plans. Not long after, Dwight ascertained that the largest carving—a device combining a cross and lion—would be installed at a midpoint on the front where it would be most conspicuous. He sent Adams news of the carving.

Henry made no immediate effort to combat the carving. He answered by saying, however, that his interest in the house was "now swallowed up in the cross, which is prophetic of the future."[51] The words seemed heavy with meaning. They possibly indicated that he was troubled by a particular premonition.

The September before, prompted mostly by certain college teachers, a small gathering of male Americans had formed an American Historical Association. Adams had since paid $75.00 for a life membership. The officers scheduled an annual meeting to be held at Saratoga in September 1885. Henry and Clover journeyed from Beverly Farms to attend it. He thought it "a curious congress." He wrote to Dwight on the 13th, "Unless we get more history and less flatulence into our management, we shall not get far towards omniscience. . . ."[52]

The trip to Saratoga served as a test of Henry and Clover's ability to leave the protection of Pitch Pine Hill and venture in other environments. The test was a success. They went back to Beverly Farms and planned to return at their usual time to Washington.[53]

Their future move from 1607 to 1603 H Street would be less a revolution than might appear. The new house was designed to accommodate the furnishings used in the old.

On October 1 or thereabouts, Clover wrote to Margery Talbot, their Washington cook, instructing her to get 1607 in order. Margery had been joined by a capable housekeeper, Maggie Wade. A butler, William Gray, was also in process of being employed.

The Adamses took the 4:30 P.M. train to New York on October 14, intending to proceed to Washington next morning. By coincidence, Charles boarded the train and learned they were in one of the cars.[54] Clover was subjected for a time to his company.[55]

Had they wished to consult a doctor famous for treating the mentally disturbed, Henry and Clover could have stopped in Philadelphia for an appointment with Weir Mitchell. Dr. Mitchell was the country's leading authority on mental illnesses in women, and he earlier had been a welcome visitor at Clover's teas. There however is neither evidence nor likelihood that the Adamses wished to consult him.[56]

They reached Washington without further incident. Dwight was temporarily away. Writing to him on November 4, Henry advised: "We lead a quiet and very retired life at present, as my wife goes nowhere. Every day or two I am at the [State] Department, where I miss you, for I occupy your desk, and need your help."

Clover was not accepting invitations, but she frequently went out. Weather permitting, she and Rebecca Dodge took daily drives. Rebecca apparently divined that Clover's illness was desperate. Yet Rebecca would not say so. Indeed she would deny it. In the words of her own account, written a half-century later:

> . . . the fall after D⁻. Hooper's death, I was continually with her, up to the end. I drove with her; and as the days grew cooler, a little black net bonnet she was wearing seemed too thin, & I got her a black silk one, & some handkerchiefs. She was very sad, & kept smoothing her hair at her brow. I think the trouble was not a nervous breakdown, but the inevitable "change of life." One day he [Henry Adams] came to the door with me, as usual, & said[,] "Oh! you have made Clover laugh," which made me very happy. . . .
>
> So many lovely memories about them both—I love to share them with you. My big collie dog used to go there with me—& one day he went alone, much to their amusement, just at breakfast time.[57]

Any hopes the Adamses may have formed that Clover would improve in the capital were wholly dashed. Her niece Louisa would later summarize: ". . . the building of the new house brought many worries. Insomnia and depression increased alarmingly."[58] Yet, while growing worse, Clover gave even close friends a strong impression of getting better.

Elizabeth Cameron returned to Washington in mid-November but had troubles of her own. Her senator husband had sold their big house and rented another. Their marriage showed signs of serious dysfunction. As sometimes happened in such cases, she had discovered she was pregnant. Her changed condition kept her increasingly in bed.

H. H. Richardson came the day before Thanksgiving and stayed at 1607 as a live-in guest. He knew something of Clover's plight and observed her carefully. He later wrote to Hay: ". . . [I] was with her two days. She was much improved & I told Henry so[,] & while she was hardly enthusiastic about the house she was decidedly interested."[59]

❖ ❖ ❖

Passionate love was not the hallmark of American marriages as usually described. Henry and Clover were passionately in love. They had evidenced the fact since 1870–1871 by maintaining a rigorous protection of their privacy. In late November 1885, their life was divided sharply between public and private aspects. What was new was that the aspects were disconnected and at odds.

Publicly Mr. Adams was going about his work as historian and owner of a virtually completed house. It was common knowledge that he and Mrs. Adams would move by New Year's Day. It was generally known as well that she had been ill and was being careful of her health.

The Adamses called often on Mrs. Cameron. On one occasion, Henry visited alone and told her and her mother that Clover was suffering "nervous prostration" after nursing her father. His explanation was reassuring. He led daughter and mother to believe that, once Clover was stronger, he and Clover would move to their new house."[60]

Aside from their love for each other, the Adamses' best support in Washington was their friendship with Rebecca Dodge. Beginning on December 2, 1885, a Wednesday, Rebecca was not available for drives with Clover. Relatives from California were visiting the Dodges. In Rebecca's words, ". . . I was all tied up until the morning of the 6th."[61]

On Friday evening, December 4, Clover visited Lizzie Cameron and sent her a gorgeous bouquet of Maréchal Niel roses. Visit and gift seemed normal. If outward signs could be trusted, Clover was recovering.[62] The signs, however, were diametrically misleading.[63]

When by themselves, Henry and Clover were truthful to each other to a degree that other persons, had they known of it, might have thought unnecessary, inordinate, or unwise. Truthfulness had placed them in a most difficult position. Possibly earlier but at the latest by November 30, two important changes had occurred. Clover slept well. Also she told Henry she was not alive, could not return to life, and was going to kill herself. If, as seems likely, she asked him whether she had a right to kill herself, he told her that for a long time he had assumed he had a right to kill himself and he could only assume her right was as good as his—but that he infinitely preferred her staying alive and their staying together, whatever her condition.[64]

Had he been different, Henry, without her knowledge, might have arranged to have her committed to an asylum. The course would have required his being an average husband. He could not meet the requirement. Neither he nor Clover would do anything of consequence without the other's previous knowledge, and they together had rejected the alternative of medical supervision, in or out of an institution. Yet Henry did one thing Clover did not know about. He sent a message. He notified Ellen Gurney and Edward Hooper that their sister had fatal intentions and that they should keep themselves in readiness.[65]

The public record of Mrs. Adams's death began with an account in the *Washington Post*, a morning paper, on Monday, December 7, 1885. On its front page, the newspaper said, in part:

Death's Sudden Summons
Mrs. Henry Adams Stricken by Heart
Disease

> Mr. Henry Adams, a son of Charles Francis Adams, of Boston, was leaving his residence, 1607 H Street, for a walk yesterday morning, when he was met at the door by a lady visitor.
> "Is Mrs. Adams feeling well enough to see me," said the lady.
> "Wait one moment and I will see," said Mr. Adams, and he returned to his wife's room. On entering the door, he saw that she had fallen from the chair where she had been sitting, and was stretched on the rug in front of the fire. He ran to her and, finding that she was unconscious, took her in his arms and carried her to a sofa. Then fearing that her sudden illness might be very serious, he hurried to Dr. C. F. Hagner, who resides at the corner of Fourteenth and H streets.
> The doctor was just leaving his house when Mr. Adams came up but went immediately to render all the aid in his power. The first glance, however, on entering the room, revealed to the doctor the true state of affairs. Mrs. Adams was dead, and in the opinion of the physician had probably died instantly from paralysis of the heart.
> Her sudden death was a severe blow to her husband. Mrs. Adams had been an invalid for several months, but had been quite rapidly recovering. Indeed, yesterday morning, she told her husband, in reply to questions regarding her health, that she was better than she had been for a long time. Her appearance certainly indicated as much, and Mr. Adams noticed a marked improvement in his wife['s] condition. The unexpected suddenness of her death made the blow all the more severe.

The *Post* did not name its informants. An evening paper, the *Washington Critic* repeated what the *Post* had said and added that Mr. Adams, seeking his wife's answer, "went upstairs," and, seeing her lying on a rug before the fire, "was horrified." The *Evening Star* also repeated the *Post's* account but asserted that Mrs. Adams was alive when found. ". . . a few minutes after[,] she passed away without a sign of recognition." But no reporters gained admission to the house. None interviewed the husband.

On Tuesday, December 9, the *New York Sun* divulged that Mrs. Adams had committed suicide with poison. "Although she was still warm, they could not revive her. The fumes of the poison and the empty phial that contained it, told plainly enough the cause of death."

In the capital that evening, the *Critic* took up the cry. "The certificate of Coroner Paterson and Dr. Hagner in the case of Mrs. Henry Adams, who died suddenly in this city on Sunday last, is to the effect that she came to her death through an overdose of potassium, administered by herself. A New York Sun correspondent states further that there is no doubt Mrs. Adams intended to take her own life. She was just recovering from a long illness, and had been suffering from mental depression."

Differently on Tuesday, without having seen the accounts in the *Sun* and *Critic*, General Anderson penned a record based in part on Washington gossip. He wrote to his son Lars: "The death of Mrs. Henry Adams was a great shock to us. She and her husband breakfasted at noon on Sunday, and she had gone to her room. At two a lady called to see her, and Henry went to her room and found her, as he supposed, in a swoon before the fire. He placed her on a lounge and summoned a physician who said she had been dead an hour. I called as soon as I heard it, but Henry refused to see anyone. I appreciate his state of mind, but I am sorry he would not let me show my sympathy by my acts."

Anderson's account was in error. It added fictional hours of day, a fictional noonday meal, an apparently fictional physician's estimate that Clover had been dead an hour, and a misleading picture of Henry self-confined to an unnatural isolation. The additions made the husband almost a figure of ridicule. The general concluded: ". . . I can imagine nothing more ghastly than that lonely vigil in the house with his dead wife. Poor fellow! I do not know what he can do."[66]

The *New York Tribune* printed important last details on December 10. ". . . the death certificate issued by the attending physician and the Coroner assigns as the reason paralysis of the heart, superinduced by an overdose of cyanide of potassium, administered by herself without the knowledge of her family. The presence of this deadly poison in the house is explained on the ground that Mrs. Adams, for the last few weeks had been greatly interested in amateur photography and had used the drug in the preparation of her plates."

❖ ❖ ❖

The private record of the Adamses's Sunday is scant but telling. Public accounts notwithstanding, Henry knew that Clover's condition had worsened catastrophically. He did not go for a walk or begin to do so. He visited Dr. Maynard. The dentist, one may believe, did not accept Sunday visits by Washington residents except in emergencies. It thus is a fair assumption that Henry hurried to Maynard because he had to. The problem was pain.

Clover may not have realized that the hour of her death had come till after Henry left the house. She was writing a note to her sister Ellen. She can be presumed to have written a note also to her brother Edward and a last note to Henry. She possibly placed all three envelopes on Henry's desk. She at any rate entrusted all her messages to him.

The notes are not extant, but Ellen quoted hers in letters to close friends. Writing to Godkin on December 30, 1885, she said: "I have been re-reading part of a little note—I may have told you about it— not posted[—]which Henry gave me the day I got there. It is more touching than you can dream. I don't know if a *man* could read it. I hope some distant day Henry may. I should like to quote you a few words about Henry from it. She says[:] 'If I had one single point of character or goodness I would stand on that and grow back to life. Henry is more patient and loving than words can express. God might envy him—he bears and hopes and despairs hour after hour'—'Henry is beyond all words tenderer and better than all of you even.' "[67]

Next day, December 31, Ellen wrote to Elizabeth Cabot, the Adamses' neighbor at Beverly Farms (and sister of deceased Mary Parkman, who in confidence had been told about *Democracy*). She explained: "The shock was largely for you outside. We had been consumed with anxiety, and probably others think if we had only done this or that. I have no such feeling. We did the best we knew how, and we know no better now. I think any other course would have been cruelty. The courage and manliness and wisdom and tenderness, and power of meeting so intense a strain, for days and nights—months and months—at first looking for the cloud to lift within a few months—finally satisfied that it might be years before it did—which Henry Adams went through we only knew—his family were wholly ignorant of it—and we felt it might kill him or worse. The week before Clover's death she struck outsiders—Alex Agassiz & Richardson—who had seen her before—as much better. She slept well, even[;] but we knew Henry thought her not better— on the contrary. He went out to the Dentist's for a short time

Sunday morning and when he returned—she was at peace. God knows how he kept his reason those hours. . . . In her last note to me—never posted—which no one has read—t'would break their heart—she says—'If I had one single point of character or goodness. . . . ' " (The extracts quoted to Mrs. Cabot match those in the letter to Godkin.)[68]

Ellen's private record and the account in the *Washington Post* agreed that Henry left the Yellow House in the morning. He may have left as early as 9:30. Other details in the newspaper about Henry's discovery of Clover's act were doubtless true. He did find Clover unconscious. He did rush for and bring Dr. Hagner.

Yet the newspaper accounts were manifestly part-invented. Some important details remain in doubt. One cannot even be sure where Henry found her. The layout of 1607 H Street was such that she could have had a room of her own on the main floor, facing the back garden and across the center corridor from the dining room.[69] He conceivably found her there. Whatever the actual case, her body was kept in her and Henry's bedroom till removed for the funeral and burial.[70]

Rebecca had been free on Sunday to resume her drives with Clover. Ahead of time, she walked to the Yellow House to say so. ". . . William [Gray] opened the door of 1607, & said 'Mrs. Adams is not at home'—& I said, 'Why, William—' and he said 'Mrs. Adams is dead.' I must have gone right home then & written him [Henry Adams]. . . ."[71]

The note from Rebecca to Adams was hand-delivered. Henry could not immediately answer it. He was sending telegrams to Edward Hooper and the Gurneys to bring about their hurrying to Washington, and he possibly was required to speak with the police or the coroner. Later he sent telegrams to his elder brothers (Brooks perhaps was in Florida), telling the news and urging their attendance at the funeral.[72]

When he at last wrote a message for hand-delivery to Rebecca, night had fallen.[73] His note was limited to four lines. He refused to see her soon. Yet he asked her help.

> Wait till I have recovered my mind. I can see no one now. Tomorrow I *must* be myself; and I can't think yet. Don't let *any one* come near me.

22

ENDURING

Adams did not need to recover his mind, not having lost it, but he needed quickly to learn his best means of endurance. His Sunday telegrams reached Edward Hooper and the Gurneys without delay. They caught the 4:30 train to New York, changed at Jersey City to the night train, and arrived at the Yellow House within twenty-four hours of Clover's death. In Ellen's words, they found Henry "as steady and sweet and thoughtful of us as possible."[1] Evidently by then he knew the course he was going to follow.

Charles was away from home and did not get Henry's telegram till 6:00 P.M. He took the 11:00 P.M. train, arrived at 1607 H Street after 4:00 on Monday afternoon, and found the Gurneys and Hooper there. He dined at Henry's but presumably stayed at Wormley's. On Tuesday he drove with Henry out of town and took a walk with him. Presumably on Tuesday, John appeared, accompanied by George, his younger son.[2]

When news spread that Clover had died, King and Hay were in New York and Richardson was in Brookline. The idea that the Hoopers and the Adamses were Bostonians was so ingrained in people's minds that all three men assumed that Clover would be buried in Massachusetts. They did not understand that she and Henry were Washingtonians and she would properly be buried in the capital.[3]

The funeral was planned for Wednesday noon. Henry, the Gurneys, and Hooper had sent for Edward Hall, a sympathetic Massachusetts clergyman. He conducted the funeral service at 1607 H Street and, in a driving rain, the burial service at Rock Creek Cemetery, the yard of St. Paul's Church. Henry had so managed things that all arrangements had been completed before news that Clover killed herself appeared in the Washington papers. Because suicide was considered criminal, objections could be made to her being buried in a churchyard. If objections *were* made, they postdated the burial ceremony.[4]

Five carriages had been hired, and as many as twenty persons went to the cemetery. The interment was postponed, pending better weather. The coffin was taken to the vault at Oak Hill Cemetery in Georgetown for storage.[5] Their duty done, the visiting Adamses left for Quincy.

Nephew George resembled his father and his Uncle Charles, though not his Uncle Henry, in cultivating roughness. At the Yellow House, perhaps at dinner on Tuesday, George had seen his Uncle Henry tear mourning crepe from his sleeve and throw it on the floor. The nephew thought the action laughably peculiar. In later years, he told his sister Abigail about it as an instance of ludicrous behavior.[6]

C. F. Adams, Jr., likewise saw something he thought peculiar. The receptacle ordered for the burial was not a proper coffin made of wood. It instead was a long willow basket covered with black cloth. Charles later impressed the fact on his daughter Elizabeth as scandalous or at least as macabre or very odd.

Apparently Henry Adams and Edward Hooper had made the funeral arrangements together on Monday afternoon. The willow coffin, traditional in the Sturgis family, signified Henry's wish that Clover keep her native identity and be buried as her blood relations would prefer.[7] Yet the burial plot was intended for Marian Adams *and* Henry Adams. When Henry, Hooper, and the Gurneys went to the cemetery on Saturday for the interment, they saw one burial where eventually there would be a second. A day would come when Clover's grave would be also Henry's.[8]

In the time between the intermitted burial on Wednesday and their leaving for Cambridge on Sunday afternoon, the Gurneys and Hooper saw fresh evidence of Henry's steadiness. To their enjoyment, during an evening or two, he read Shakespeare aloud. He moved books to the study and library of his new house. On Sunday he said he would resume sleeping that night in his and Clover's room.[9]

Adams was mindful of Rebecca Dodge. Possibly at their first meeting after the catastrophe, he gave her a pair of gold bracelets Clover had bought in Egypt and worn constantly as emblems of her marriage. Rebecca accepted the bracelets but valued them so highly that in old age she returned them to a Hooper—Edward Hooper's daughter Louisa—for preservation in the family.[10]

Elizabeth Cameron remained confined and could not visit. Adams wrote to her on December 10: "All Clover's friends have now infinite value for me. I have got to live henceforward on what

I can save from the wreck of her life, and it is lucky for me that she had no friends but the best and truest." At Christmas, as if to repeat the message, he sent Mrs. Cameron a "little trinket"—a piece of jewelry, doubtless valuable—that had been "a favorite of my wife's." He asked, "Will you keep it, and sometimes wear it, to remind you of her?"[11]

The correspondent to whom Adams most fully stated his intentions was Hay. On December 8, answering a telegram from Hay, he said he expected to regain "strength and courage." "I am going to keep straight on, just as we planned it together. . . ." He said too that the Hays could help him by speeding the completion of their house and moving into it; also that Dwight had agreed to live with him.[12]

The phrase "just as we planned it together" was susceptible of variant readings. The Hays could believe that Adams was referring to plans earlier made by two couples, the Adamses and themselves. Or possibly Adams wrote the phrase with King, too, in mind; for after Clover's death he redoubled his efforts to make the three-way friendship of King, Hay, and himself a continuously sustained reality. The essential reading none the less was that Henry and Clover had planned their life together and Henry was going to lead it. The principal basis of his conduct was not that Clover was dead, which was all too true, but that in some form or manner she was living, which, as *he* sensed the facts, was truer and still more serious.

A pressing question was the use best made of the Richardson house within the situation created by her act. The house had been designed to afford its owners three connecting rooms across its third-floor front. Differently, the three rooms across the top-floor front were separate from each other. The center room of the three had no fireplace. As nearly as can be determined, Henry chose it as his bedroom and decided that the narrow bed and other furnishings moved into it would be as starkly simple as might be wanted by a monk. The adjacent room to the east, having a fireplace, would be his upstairs retreat. Off the hall nearest his rooms, there was a large cedar closet meant for linens but also providing space for trunks. He packed a trunk with Clover's most valued clothes and accessories, locked it, and placed it permanently in the cedar closet.[13]

He evidently occupied his rooms by December 31, 1885. Dwight possibly occupied a back bedroom on the floor below. At all events, the third-floor rooms on the front were freed for guests. Thus 1603 H Street, meant originally as a home for a couple, and furnished almost entirely as Henry and Clover had wished it furnished, was turned into a hospitable convenience for trains of relatives and friends. Its chief differences from other hospitable houses would be its spacious stairs, halls, and rooms and its being readied by an owner who so arranged things that he would keep remarkably out of sight.[14]

Designed to have ornate interiors, the Hay house needed many months of work after the Adams house was finished. Henry begged the Hays to use *his* house temporarily, in every way that was convenient. He meanwhile professed to be idly hanging pictures.

He in fact was very busy. An urgent concern was Clover's money. Assisted by John Chipman Gray, his Boston lawyer, he shifted her holdings to the support of her nieces. The arrangement gave the nieces the income till his death and the capital thereafter. He seemed prepared to think he might someday be their guardian. The time was not far distant when he would refer to them as "my children."[15]

His most silent effort was also the most headlong. Apparently beginning early in January 1886, he resumed drafting his *History*. There is no telling how many chapters of the *First Madison* he had written prior to Clover's cataclysm. When privately printed, the volume would run to thirty-nine chapters. He set himself so accelerated a pace that by the end of May 1886 he would write all its unwritten chapters plus the first book of the *Second Madison*, say another eight chapters.[16]

Among his motives for prodigious work, possibly the strongest was his sense of having to swim against a brutal current of bad luck. He was anxious about the Gurneys. Whitman had come for Clover's funeral but was beset by an illness—later referred to as "pernicious anemia"—that could not be diagnosed or treated and caused increasing weakness. Ellen's situation was worsening proportionally.[17]

His own great danger was self-imposed overwork. As a countermeasure, weather permitting, he rode. He had long had a passion for finding the earliest flowers in the woods, noticing the first buds on trees, hearing the promptest frogs. He liked to record their dates. On March 11, 1886, returning from a circuit on Prince or Daisy, he continued a record he had been keeping since 1883. Its entries were written on a page torn from a printed pocket notebook. He wrote a new entry: "1886. March 11. Frogs." Subsequent rides permitted his adding "Hepatica" on March 14; "Magnolia" on April 12; "as last year [i.e. on April 19] Dog-tooth violets";

and "Apples—Dogwood" on April 22. The record he expanded was the one he had consulted when writing to Clover the previous spring. There was no longer a possibility of sending her letters. He could however do loving things. He could continue to ride along their favorite routes. He could go on making entries.

After he had added two entries, on March 25, their friend Mrs. Bancroft died; and, on April 27, when no space was left on the torn-out page, Richardson died of Bright's disease. It chanced that the page on its back bore the printed heading "BRIGHT'S DIS-EASE." Perhaps on that account, Henry twice folded the page and placed it where it would not be lost—evidently in a wallet in his desk. By taking the precaution, he insured the record's survival till he himself had died.[18]

For Henry, Richardson's death in part was Clover's death repeated. At the cost of a thousand miles of travel, he went to Boston for the funeral. He apparently stayed with his parents at their house in Boston. Charles recorded on April 30: ". . . out to Mt. Auburn [Cemetery] with Hooper and Henry. Got in at 2 o'cl. At 4 o'cl at Mt[.] Vernon St[.], and Henry dined with us."

Worthington Chauncey Ford, a young man from Brooklyn, was employed by the State Department as chief of the Bureau of Statistics. Ford was an exceedingly diligent and successful searcher for historical materials relating to America, especially George Washington's letters. He and Henry Adams had formed an acquaintanceship of such a kind that Adams was asked to scan a manuscript, an attempted biography of Noah Webster.[19] The author was Ford's mother, Emily Ellsworth Ford. The manuscript was sent from Brooklyn by the youngest of her sons, Paul Leicester Ford. A hunchback, Paul had talents as a writer. He shared Worthington's campaigns to recover old documents.[20]

That the Ford brothers wanted Adams to see their mother's problematical biography showed knowledge and aspiration. Among persons qualified to judge, Adams's *New England Federalism* and *The Life of Albert Gallatin* had earned him first place on the list of historians of the United States. The Fords had much to gain if admitted to his circle.[21]

Leafing through the Noah Webster manuscript, Adams was surprised to find that Mrs. Ford had amassed and organized an overplus of material. She had then committed the error of forcing practically all the material into a would-be narrative. Rather than grow impatient, Adams reviewed the entire mass. To reward himself, he studied the genealogical materials relating to Webster's in-laws, the Greenleafs, who, he was pleased to learn, were among his own progenitors.

Wanting to help Mrs. Ford, he wrote a guide titled "Memoranda for Biography." He sent it to Paul Ford on March 22, 1886, when returning the manuscript. It said:

Memoranda for Biography.

1. Choose some volume or volumes as the standard and limit of space.
2. In cutting down the material to fit the standard, keep a few rules in mind. Cut out by preference; 1, Whatever has been printed before. 2, Whatever sounds like a repetition. 3, Whatever seems to delay the *story*, for a biography ought to be a story. All didactic matter delays the story, and should be stated, as to its points, briefly and once for all.
3. Concentrate on the qualities or character in which the subject differs from other men. The world wants to know the exceptional, not the usual. Of course this is a process of exaggeration, but biography *is* exaggeration, and has no other literary advantage.
4. Ignore attacks on one's grandfathers. Doubtless they are irritating, but as people will in any case patronize our grandfathers, all we can legitimately do in return is to patronize theirs. If they have none, we must take our revenge by patronizing all the grandfathers there are. We flatter them by direct notice, and encourage a repetition of the offense.
5. Finally, every literary work is good, when it is very good, rather by what is left out than by what is put in. One mistake of *ad*mission mars a book more than a dozen of *o*mission.

The sensitive issue for Adams was biography's "advantage" of "exaggeration." The issue was sensitive because by preference he was the obverse of a biographer, a general historian, and he believed that history's great advantage was its promise to *avoid* exaggeration. Till Clover died, he had thought himself capable of undistorted mirrorings of past realities in a *History of the United States.* Unhappily, the force of Clover's act had made him suspicious and distrustful of his newest judgments. He expected that, with time and good management, he might recover the gift of perfect or near-perfect vision; but his present state of being seemed to him to involve a disturbance of response. His reactions were too dramatic. He could hope to bring his *History* into final form only when they were not.

He meanwhile was reminded that his *History* needed mending with respect to documents. Perhaps by speaking to Worthington, he advised the Ford brothers that his searches for historical materials had failed at particular points. Some weeks later, Paul furnished him copies of letters by William Henry Harrison. In his note of thanks, Adams said to Paul: "No one can ever tell what documents will be of service. One must have everything. Sometimes a mere date is very valuable."[22]

One of Henry's failings had been impatience when shopping. During their transit from Beverly Farms to Washington the previous October, he and Clover had shopped in New York for wallpapers, curtains, rugs, and other items for their almost-finished house. At the time, he had written to Hay: ". . . I feel helpless under this chaos of houses. If I run away, and hide in Japan, can I furnish from there?"[23]

For Henry and Clover, a visit to Japan had been entirely workable. On her mother's side, she had a cousin, William Sturgis Bigelow (known as Sturgis), seven years her junior, who had forsaken his career as a doctor and gone to Japan to become a Buddhist. She appears to have ascertained that she and Henry could depend on Bigelow's assistance if they stopped in Japan during their projected trip around the world.[24]

Shortly after Clover's death, Henry wrote to Bigelow—the letter is lost—inquiring about the possibility of passing the summer of 1886 in Japan, preferably in part near Bigelow's summer house in the mountains at Nikko. Bigelow sent an encouraging reply, also lost.

Hay planned to join Adams in Washington on January 26, 1886, and presumably did. Soon after, he and Adams traveled to New York. (King momentarily was in Massachusetts.) It appears that, while with Hay in New York, Adams contacted John La Farge and offered to pay all expenses if La Farge would accompany him to Japan. For such an artist as La Farge, the offer was impossible to refuse.[25]

On April 25, Adams disclosed his plan for a journey in a letter to Gaskell. ". . . I have decided to get myself quite out of the way. All winter I have never left my house except to ride, or for a short walk; nor seen society except for the old friends who came to see me . . . . Fortunately Washington is a cheery place where people take life gaily, and I have been by no means solitary or deserted. As the summer comes on, I groan at the need of departing; but as there is no choice, I have decided to pass it in Japan. I leave here about June 1, to return in October; and shall amuse myself by two long sea-voyages, which I abhor; and by two months among the Japanese[,] whom I do not in the least pine to see. I can't go to Europe. It is full of ghosts."

To outsiders, even friendly outsiders, Adams's plan to spend a summer in Japan could suggest that he wanted to *flee* a ghost—the ghost of his dead wife. Clover's death had awakened detracting gossip. An opinion widely adopted in Massachusetts attributed her suicide to hereditary insanity in the Sturgis and Hooper families. Echoing what was told him in letters from Cambridge, Henry James had written from London that "poor Mrs. Adams" had "succumbed to hereditary melancholy."[26] James possibly knew or was advised that one of Clover's aunts, Susan Sturgis Bigelow (mother of Sturgis Bigelow), had committed suicide with arsenic in 1853. Recently, too, James may have heard that Ellen Gurney's mental balance was disturbed.[27] The moral tacitly drawn from such particulars was to avoid all Hooper and Sturgis offspring.

Adams knew as much as anyone about recurring troubles in Massachusetts families. His reaction was not detraction and was not avoidance. He would not say so, but his voyage to Japan would be taken *with* Clover and even *towards* her. His initial object would be to visit at Nikko the shrine erected in memory of the greatest man in Japanese experience, the first Tokugawa shogun, Iyeyasu. The shrine was the counterpart of Abu Simbel, carved in Egypt to memorialize Rameses II. With respect to its aiming point, Henry's new journey was a match of his and Clover's wedding journey. His taking it would be an act of devotion. As a mere incidental benefit, the journey would permit his seeing what he understood to be an utmost effort by human builders.[28]

In November 1885, if his tale was true, King had lost the incipient manuscript of his *Aristocracy* and other writings through the carelessness of a chambermaid at a New York hotel.[29] By mail in late February 1886, King tried to interest Adams in joining with him and Hay to write a book of essays on the condition of the United States and its political and social tendencies. He seemed unwilling to realize that Hay was overburdened by his "detested work" on instalments for *Abraham Lincoln/ A History*. Similarly, he neglected to guess that Adams was advancing in the concluding volumes of his *History* with desperate energy.[30]

In March 1886, King stopped in Washington to see Adams. Somewhat impulsively, Adams mentioned that he had written and published a second novel, titled *Esther*. He said too that, wanting to learn whether a book could win an audience without being publicized, he had arranged with Holt that *Esther* not be.[31] He did not give King a copy.

When King had gone, Adams resumed drafting chapters of his *History*. To assist his work, he had acquired a custom-made

Davenport desk with eight banks of drawers—double banks at the user's left and right and matching banks on the desk's other side.[32] Sometime late in May, he put into his desk the manuscripts of all the books of the *First Madison* and Book I of the *Second Madison*. Partly because the work thus stored had cost him an extraordinary effort, he struck a gentleman's agreement with La Farge that when leaving for Japan they would "bring no books, read no books, but come as innocently as we could," the one compromise being La Farge's outdated Japanese grammar.[33]

Before setting out, Adams gave caretaker Dwight written instructions relating to bills, servants' pay, etc.[34] He went to Quincy to see his mother and the Chief, who in different ways were very infirm. Apparently at the same time, he either loaned Charles a copy of the *Second Jefferson* or promised that a copy would shortly reach him.[35]

When Henry started for New York, expecting to join La Farge and start their journey, Charles accompanied him to the station. As president of the Union Pacific, he volunteered that the directors' car would soon be in Albany and could be placed at the travelers' disposal while going west. Henry gladly accepted the offer and proceeded to New York. There his first necessities were to apprise La Farge of their good fortune and jostle him towards readiness for departure.

King had known Adams would pass a day in New York. He had obtained a copy of *Esther* and had made as good an effort to read it as his feelings allowed. His chance of understanding it was partly spoiled by his determination to read it as a *roman à clef*, indeed as one of the simplest sort. It was spoiled altogether by his religious conservatism. He mistook the heroine for Clover. It deeply troubled him that the book was irreligious. It troubled him still more that Esther Dudley—to his mind Clover—was fascinated by Niagara Falls.[36]

Necessarily Marian and Henry Adams were present in every character and action in *Esther*. Henry wrote it and Clover caused it. But Henry had formed the novel's characters by using a particular method. In connection with each, he had begun by drawing on two or three persons he knew as models. As soon as a fictional character began taking form, he let the models recede from consciousness. The models for Esther Dudley can be assumed to have included Anne Palmer. (Clover could not have served, being far too capable and accomplished.) Yet Esther was not Anne. Exclusively and only, Esther was Esther.[37]

In New York on June 4, 1886, perhaps at breakfast, Adams and

King briefly discussed the novel. Adams said King might pass the news of the book to Hay if so inclined, but he explained that his authorship of *Esther* was an even deeper secret than his authorship of *Democracy* and he wanted it to stay so.

King ventured that *Esther* was not properly ended. In his words, "I had the hardihood to say to him that he ought to have made Esther jump into Niagara[,] as that was what she would have done."[38]

Too late Adams realized that King had no tolerance for heretics and lacked the faculty of reading a novel as a novel or fiction as fiction. It was Adams's practice to terminate any discussion that might better not have started. One of his methods was to half-assent in words to a proposition with which he did not agree in fact. When King said Esther would have killed herself, Henry answered, " 'Certainly she would but I could not suggest it.' "[39] Discussion turned to something else.[40]

That same day, June 4, 1886, evidently by prearrangement, Adams went to the studio of Augustus St. Gaudens. He told the sculptor that his and Clover's burial plot was in Rock Creek Cemetery in Washington and that he wanted for the site a human figure in bronze. Just as he and Clover had given Richardson a detailed plan for the house they wanted on Lafayette Square, Adams gave St. Gaudens a complete idea of the desired human figure. A youth, a male model, was present in the studio. Adams asked the model to take a seated position. Seizing an American Indian rug he saw nearby, he wrapped the model in the fabric till shrouded except at the face—and except that the right forearm was visible, held at the elbow by the left hand—and the right forearm was raised so that the hand contacted the head along the jaw. Satisfied, Adams said "I've got it"—or words to the same effect.[41]

To that point, the idea was simple, but Adams made four requests. He asked that the figure not suggest divinity.[42] He wanted the figure so formed as to indicate complete stillness, absence of motion, and especially mental calm and repose.[43] He wished, too, that the figure be male-and-female; that it belong to neither of humanity's divisions but instead to both, with the effect that it would correspond to whomever might chance to see it.[44] In addition, he asked that his providing the exact idea for the figure be kept secret and that St. Gaudens protect the secret by saying that his patron gave him a mere general idea, with full freedom to go on from there.[45]

St. Gaudens was a consummate artist who knew by whom he

was going to be paid. Just as Richardson enthusiastically accepted Henry and Clover's plan for a house, St. Gaudens wholeheartedly welcomed Henry's idea for a figure. He and Adams possibly agreed at the same moment that the necessary stone work would be best designed by Stanford White. But the latter arrangement could wait.[46]

Had there been time and impulse, the sculptor could have asked the patron where he got his idea. A candid answer to the question would have touched on several matters. One was Story's seated figure of Cleopatra near the instant of her suicide. Another was Story's standing figure of Medea, especially the positioning of the arms. A third was the great figures of Abu Simbel, never moving. But sculptural precedents, possibly numerous, were mere lesser origins of the figure.

Adams was a loving grandson who felt himself the male counterpart and continuation of a woman, his father's mother. He was also a loving brother whose elder sister had so died that he wanted to live for both of them; if not, she would die indeed. He still more was a husband who had become himself and his wife—a new change that would never change. Thus the figure to be made by St. Gaudens would represent an existing reality. Admittedly the reality was not what human beings were usually born as. It was however what human beings sometimes turned into.[47]

Initially offered to carry them only to Omaha, the Union Pacific directors' car bore Adams and La Farge all the way to San Francisco. While traveling, Adams read. He had not held himself to the pledge of not bringing books. He was carrying Murray's *Handbook for Travellers in Japan* and some works—it is not clear which—on Buddhism.[48]

After a rough 22–day voyage on the *City of Sydney*, Adams and La Farge were greeted at Yokohama by Bigelow. Adams planned a five-part tour of Japan. They would spend an interval at Yokohama and Tokyo with Bigelow; shift northward to Nikko for an extended stay as neighbors of Bigelow and an American couple, Ernest and Lizzie Fenollosa; return to Yokohama and see at Kamakura the Daibutsu, the huge bronze statue of Buddha; move south by ship to Kobe and thence to a hotel at Kyoto; and while traveling overland from Kyoto to Yokohama—a long journey—see Fuji to advantage, if not hidden by clouds.

From the time he had boarded the directors' car, Adams had written letters recounting his and La Farge's journey in its external aspects. Some of his letters to Hay took the form of instalments and verged on being a journal. Writing from Nikko on July 24, 1886, Henry described the Tokugawa shrine, or rather two shrines together; for the Japanese had also provided a tomb for Iyemitsu, grandson of Iyeyasu. "Nikko is the prettiest part of Japan; here are the great temples of Yeyas (Iyeyasu) and Iye-mitsu, the first and third Shoguns. . . ." "Photographs give no idea of the scale. They show here a gate and there a temple, but they cannot show twenty acres of ground, all ingeniously used to make a single composition. They give no idea of a mountain-flank, with its evergreens a hundred feet high, modelled into a royal posthumous residence and deified abode. I admit to thinking it a bigger work than I should have thought possible for Japs. It is a sort of Egypt in lacquer and greenth."

For Adams, the journey had also an inner history on which outward influences might impinge. Nothing affected his feelings more than the estimates made of Clover by the persons who knew her best. The opinion of her close woman friends was uniform. They thought her a heroine, all the more so for her suicide. Anne Palmer had married on May 25, 1885. Her first child, a girl, was born after Mrs. Adams died. With no hesitation, Anne named her baby Marian.[49]

When still in Washington, Adams had learned that, despite the capital's predictable torridness in June and July, the Camerons meant to stay till after Mrs. Cameron gave birth. He also learned they had no further plans. To fill the void, he told Mrs. Cameron she should go to live at Pitch Pine Hill. She heard his offer but did not respond.[50]

The Camerons wanted a boy. A girl was born on June 25, 1886. (Hay cabled the news to Adams in Japan.) Mrs. Cameron stayed in Washington, infirm but recovering. The name she preferred for her girl was Marian. The senator concurred, but no decision was reached.[51]

For Hay, the birth of the Cameron baby was simultaneous with his learning about a novel. After Adams left New York, King sent Hay a copy of *Esther*. He asked Hay to read it, and, without saying why, urged his trying to guess the identity of "Compton." Hay put the copy aside, but Clara one evening started reading it aloud for their amusement. She paused to say it reminded her of Hay, King, and Adams—and went on reading.

Silently Hay had been thinking that "Compton" was Adams. He wrote King a letter of inquiry and received an account of Henry's disclosures. During additional evenings, Mrs. Hay completed her reading of *Esther* aloud. Hay then repossessed the copy.

". . . I read it again for myself—with feelings of absolute amazement."[52]

From Washington on July 15, Mrs. Cameron wrote to Mrs. Hay about her baby's name. Mrs. Hay read the letter and gave it to her husband. Hay at the time was writing to Adams about several matters, especially *Esther*. Thinking it would interest him, he enclosed Mrs. Cameron's letter with his. Her letter partly concerned a problem of permission. She said: "The little girl who should have been a boy is nearly three weeks old. . . . We wanted to call the baby Marian, but Mr[.] Adams was so far away there was no means of knowing whether he would like it or not, and I dared not give her the name without his permission. So Mr[.] Cameron, to gratify his father, gave her the old-fashioned name of his grandmother,— Martha Cameron—which I like very well, but which has no association as the other would have had."[53]

At Nikko, La Farge was sketching, and Adams at intervals was reading. La Farge wrote on August 2, 1886, ". . . Adams, upstairs in the veranda, is reading in Dante's 'Paradiso,' and can see, when he looks up, the great temple roof of the Buddhist Mangwanji."[54]

Buddhism interested Adams, to a point. Temples in memory of the greatest shoguns interested him much more. With reference to the latter, he wrote on August 4 to John White Field, a Washington friend: ". . . [Nikko] is so well worth seeing that in many ways nothing in Europe rivals it. I should class it very high among the sights of the world. If architecture falls short of perfection, nature steps in to give the perfection wanted; and the result is something quite by itself. Sky, mountains, and trees are exquisite."

Eerily, Adams felt his surroundings as more familiar than strange. Writing to Field, he said the mountain forests at Nikko reminded him of Thun in Switzerland and Bagni di Lucca in Italy.[55] (He had joined Loo at the former in 1859 and saw her die at the latter in 1870.) On August 13, answering a note from Mrs. Cameron, not extant, he said with similar but unhidden pointedness, "The scenery is . . . not unlike that of the Virginia springs. . . ."[56]

During his wanderings, he came upon a temple in the woods called Somentaki. It was abandoned. He returned several times. In addition, he photographed it, made a print, and wrote on the back: "My favorite deserted temple buried in forests and unworried by tourists. I photographed it for the little gate, and the bamboos. Nikko. Aug. 1886."[57] Of the human works he saw in Japan, the buried temple was the most attuned to his wants. He could say he photographed it for its gate and the adjacent bamboos, but for him its value began with its desertion. For a lone visitor, its gate could open to freedom—limitless freedom to being with the absent.[58]

On August 23 at Nikko, two letters reached Adams from Hay in a single envelope. One was a letter from Mrs. Cameron to Mrs. Hay about the choice of a name. The other was a letter from Hay containing comments so extravagant that Adams "hardly knew what I was reading about."

Like King, Hay had read *Esther* as an easily decodable *roman à clef*. He thought—but would not say—that Esther Dudley was Marian Adams. (In his letter, possibly out of fear, he contrived to mention neither the one nor the other.) Yet he had no hesitation in saying that the novel's artist, Wharton, was La Farge.[59]

Hay's reaction could appear to have value. He extended a compliment to the novel that it possibly deserved. "It is the first New York story I have ever read in which there is real human talk and feeling—a grade above that of shop-girls and reporters." But mostly his comments were large-sounding and unspecific. He said Adams's book was "a masterpiece"—"the best thing that has been printed in ten years." He said it shocked him that "a novel so powerful in motive, so vital with wit and brilliancy, so magnificently simple in style, so popular, confound it, so *readable*," had been published two years earlier in New York and neither he nor King had ever heard of it. Yet conspicuously he failed to state what the "motive" was. He detoured around agnosticism. The book seemed both to delight him and get on his nerves.[60]

In itself, Hay's puff of *Esther* was not especially disturbing. Adams answered on August 23: ". . . I do feel pleased that the book has found one friend." He said also that the public "could never understand that such a book might be written in one's heart's blood." And he asked a favor. "Perhaps I made a mistake even to tell King about it; but having told him, I could not leave you out. Now, let it die!"

Positive disturbance entered with the letter by Mrs. Cameron. He confessed to Hay, ". . . Mrs[.] Don's letter has rather upset me. . . ." The cause of the upset was a doubleness of names. Where the Cameron baby might have been nothing more than a daughter of good friends, her being called Marian and then Martha moved her into a relation with Adams that he had not expected. To his mind, a new woman was born who had two names. She would know herself as Martha, but for him she would be both Martha and Marian. The first-suggested name could not be erased.

❖ ❖ ❖

While Adams was weathering his upset, a new letter was in transit. On August 16, Mrs. Cameron had written to him: "I little thought when I said goodbye to you in Washington that my first letter would be written from your own house at Beverly. Do you know that I am here? And do you mind? It was with the greatest hesitancy that I asked about the house, but when I remembered that you had offered it to me early in the summer, I took courage and came."

Mother and child had been ill and weak on arriving but mended very quickly. Mrs. Cameron continued: ". . . I found everything so comfortable and homelike that I felt in an hour's time as if we had always been here. . . . The little baby—I present Martha to you, dear Mr. Adams,—lives out under the pine trees and is growing strong and big, and I lie on the piazza and watch the sea."[61]

One might think from Mrs. Cameron's words that the senator was not a party to the sojourn at Pitch Pine Hill. He was. But events had so entwined that "Mr. Adams" and "Mrs. Cameron"—the name he invariably would use when addressing her—were brought into a close but unusual relation. They no longer were good friends. One had lost a heroic wife, the other a heroic friend. Each could judge the other's hurt. Their situation made possible a mutual attachment, and the attachment had been formed. Its outward sign was an already presented child.[62]

Adams and La Farge left Nikko on August 28, 1886, saw the bronze Buddha at Kamakura (also at Hase a huge gilt figure of Kwannon), proceeded to Kobe and Kyoto, and, in the face of possible cholera, risked the eleven-day journey to Yokohama by land.[63]

On the way, they realized their hope of seeing Fuji to advantage. After midday on September 25, seated on two-wheeled vehicles drawn by runners, they left Kambara and hurried along the beach of Suruga Bay. In La Farge's words: "At the end of the great curve of the gulf stretched the lines of green and purple mountains, which run far off into Idzu, and above them stood Fuji in the sky, very pale and clear, with one enormous band of cloud halfway up its long slope, and melting into infinite distance towards the ocean."

A short while later, where the road passed a promontory, they saw the mountain at closer range. La Farge recorded: "Its cone was of a deep violet color, and as free of snow as though this had been the day of poetic tradition upon which the snow entirely disappears to fall again the following night. No words can recall adequately the simple splendor of the divine mountain. As Adams remarked, it was worth coming to far Japan for this single day."

Finding that their path along the beach was blocked by a river, the Fujikawa, which had flooded and borne off all bridges, they went back a distance and waited for emergency conveyance by a junk and its boatmen. Fuji stood opposite them as before, and La Farge undertook a sketch.[64]

One of Adams's purposes in coming to Japan had been to "gain three or four months of hardening to my difficulties." He perhaps needed hardening. He certainly needed confidence in the rightness of his vision. While La Farge worked at his sketch, Adams in a notebook twice attempted "by the eye" to draw lines repeating the right and left slopes of Fuji. He then held the notebook at arms length towards the mountain and drew new lines "by comparison." As he may have expected, his freely-drawn lines were too steep. Yet in both attempts his errors were slight. He had taken reaction tests and had passed them.[65]

La Farge for many weeks had been studying Adams's abilities. On July 12, when they were first visiting tombs at Tokyo, he and Adams had discussed Japanese architecture. La Farge was astonished. ". . . I do not think that I could grasp a subject in such a clear and dispassionate and masterly way, with natural reference to the past and its implied comparisons, for Adams's historic sense amounts to poetry, and his deductions and remarks always set my mind sailing into new channels." On September 25 near the Fujikawa, La Farge compared his artistic sketch of Fuji with the sloping lines Adams had made in a notebook. He handsomely wrote, "You can have no idea how much closer the clearer mind worked out the true outline of the mountain, which my excitement had heightened at least a couple of thousand feet. . . ."[66]

Though Adams in other respects was his proper self, he was harboring a disorder that promised to re-attack him when he was again in Washington. His disorder was restlessness, the impulse to get up, move about, travel far. The previous June, poised at San Francisco for the voyage to Yokohama, he had written to Dwight, ". . . I should not be tearing about the world, seasick and uncomfortable, if I were able to keep still." At its worst, his restlessness was violent.

La Farge and Adams postponed their return to California, changing to a later ship. The change made them fellow passengers on the *City of Peking* with the Fenollosas. Adams anticipated the voyage with misgivings. He had learned on the westward crossing that the Pacific was not peaceful. As it happened, though the eastward crossing was dark and rough, he seldom was seasick. He almost regretted leaving the ship.

Charles was waiting in San Francisco and offered the travelers free transportation, again in the directors' car. The offer was welcome but unfortunately came together with news that Gurney had died and Clover's sister was widowed.[67]

Whitman's death fixed Henry's itinerary. From San Francisco on October 21, 1886, he wrote to Dwight: "I must go to Boston first to see Ellen Gurney and the children. My brother is to take me round to Southern California. . . . We expect to reach Boston in a fortnight. I shall stay a few days there, and then shall bring the dogs on to you." Because his Washington household had lost Margery Lite, the cook, and her replacement had not proved competent, Adams pressed Dwight to make inquiries and "engage anyone who seems very satisfactory."

The important result of Adams's stay in Japan, or rather the one he was willing to talk about, was interest in going to China. The Hays at last were moving into their Washington house. Though the message was sure to startle him, Adams wrote to Hay on October 21: "I have henceforward a future. As soon as I can get rid of history and the present, I mean to start for China, and stay there." As if China and heaven were neighbor countries much alike, he proposed to avail himself of the similarity. "Five years hence, I expect to enter the celestial kingdom by that road, if not sooner by a shorter one. . . ."

While in Japan, Henry had exchanged letters with Charles. They are missing. In part, they may have concerned Henry's *History*. On September 5 and 6, 1886, Charles had recorded in his diary that he was reading Henry's *Second Jefferson*. The copy was bound as two volumes, interleaved with blank pages to facilitate making corrections and comments.[68] He evidently meant to finish reading the copy but was prevented from continuing by a press of railroad business. Presumably, at San Francisco, he told Henry about the delay.

The route taken by Charles and his guests led from Los Angeles to Albuquerque, Dodge City, Kansas City, Chicago, and Albany. La Farge proceeded alone from Albany to New York. Charles and Henry reached Boston at 7:45 A.M. on November 5 and went at once to Quincy.[69]

At the latest on November 9, Henry left with the dogs for Washington and reoccupied 1603 H Street. Dwight had not found a cook and was away. Mrs. Cameron had returned—to a new address. During the confusions of the past year, her husband had bought a fine old house on the east side of Lafayette Square. It had since been refurbished.

Henry called. Mrs. Cameron was out but shortly sent a note. Next morning, November 12, Henry sent a detailed letter. He said that he received her note but was hastening to dine with Bancroft, that later he called a second time at her house, and that again she was out. The purpose of Mrs. Cameron's note had been to offer a meal to Mr. Adams and Mr. Dwight. Adams explained that his trouble was "not so much one of food as of a sentimental wish to see you again, and hear of your welfare." He thought, too, that she was the only friend he had who would tell him no bad news. "I hope my harvest of thorns is now gathered in, and I can enjoy the few flowers there are."

It was clear in his letter that Adams wanted the closest tie with Mrs. Cameron that their respective situations would permit. He spoke of Martha. The baby was a week shy of six months old. As if her age were sixteen years, he suggested that she might act as her mother's messenger. Mrs. Cameron might want him soon for a particular meal. ". . . you have only to ask Martha to stop and tell me so." He closed by writing: "Very seriously Yrs Henry Adams."[70]

Later in the day, Charles arrived at 1603 H Street, doubtless on railroad business involving Congress. The brothers dined at Henry's club—presumably the Cosmos Club.

Next day, November 13, they lunched at Mrs. Cameron's fine new residence, the Ogle-Tayloe house.[71] The lunch was an early instance of what in time would prove a general rule: meetings of Elizabeth Cameron and Henry Adams would very often occur when they were not by themselves and were accompanied by one or more persons who had small understanding of their altered relation.

The elder Charles Francis Adams's last years were marred by loss of memory, but his demeanor for the most part was mild and pleasant.[72] At 2:06 A.M., on Sunday, November 20, 1886, he died. John took charge of arrangements. Henry was summoned to Boston, arrived on Monday night, and on Wednesday attended the funeral and burial at Quincy.[73] Afterwards, he wrote to Dwight that "everything was as little painful as could be expected." The phrase was superficially assuring, yet left room for pain in almost any amount.

Charles's daughter Mary, known as Molly, was nineteen and sufficiently at loose ends to be invited to spend the winter in Washington. Uncle Henry and Molly left together for the capital on November 28.[74]

La Farge earlier had heard that Henry was ill, not seriously so, but ill enough to be noticed. He had written to him on November 20, ". . . I am so very confident of your having shown all the time appearance of improved health & especially of elasticity and freshness—that I feel sure of your getting over any slight drawback."[75]

The serious threats to Henry's well-being were more of the spirit than the flesh. The death of the Chief carried him back to funerals and burials. In a letter to Gaskell, he said on December 12, "The fact is, I am going crab-wise. . . ." The assertion was lifted from one of Hamlet's speeches. As sources went, the speeches were uncheerful.

The death of C. F. Adams brought forward the question of his importance. As understood by many Americans, his importance had been great. For them, he ranked as the president who *should* have been: the one who ought to have been elected in 1868 and 1872, displacing Grant.

Henry had quietly exerted himself to keep the Chief from attending nominating conventions, becoming a candidate for president, and being elected. These efforts were partly inspired by a conviction that the modern Adamses could best serve as politicians by being not in office. In addition, the efforts were made in self-defense. No worse assignment could have been thrust on Henry than a term of service at the White House as other president. His efforts must have been guided also by a conviction that the Chief, if bundled into the presidency by persons who did not know him and had no idea of his true strengths and limitations, might prove a worse president than Grant, not a better.

Henry's very qualified judgment of his father was a judgment he had expressed in preventive acts. It was being expressed, too, in the gradual building of a myth: the myth that U. S. Minister to England C. F. Adams was a politician of the first rank, superior to England's Prime Minister Palmerston and Foreign Secretary Russell. One aspect of the intended myth was single-handedness. The myth would picture an Adams who virtually alone, without effectual allies or aides, fought with two English dragons simultaneously and came home victorious.[76]

Henry's twofold policy with respect to the Chief—shielding him against being president and mythologizing him as a heroic diplomat—was one of the elements of a difficult subject: that of *Henry's* importance as a politician. It has already been said that, secretly, during his buried first life, the son achieved a political importance not approached by any American his age—an importance relating to peace, war, and the saving of an anti-slavery Union. Here the question, differently, is Henry's political importance in his second life.

It was true that the U. S. mission to England remained highly important after the *Trent* affair, and Henry's sharing the mission with the Chief was no slight addition to his political achievements. But it needs to be remembered that the anti-slavery Unionists did not command sufficient votes to re-elect Lincoln in 1864 *as a Republican*. In 1865, after Lincoln was killed, Henry raised with Evarts and Seward the matter of Negro suffrage: political freedom for the former slaves. Their answer was not to answer!—and the silence had a dismal meaning. The political situation in the United States following the murder of Lincoln was simply impossible. As the party of freedom, the Republicans had expired, and the Democrats were worse. In this impossible situation, Henry went to Washington and elaborated a national program—not the ideal program he might have wanted but the only good one that was possible in an impossible situation.

From that point forward, from 1868 through 1886, his program was carried out with respect to peace with England, carried out with respect to the avoidance of territorial aggrandizement, and partly carried out with respect to civil-service reform, but not with respect to revenue reform and the equalization of wealth. Meanwhile, beginning in 1865, he protected against the mis-casting of his father as a new Adams president; he attempted the promotion of better men in place of Grant; he helped avert the miscasting of Blaine as president; and he, Clover, and the MacVeaghs effected Blaine's dismissal as secretary of state following the murder of Garfield—a murder that promised great advantage to one man only, the indescribable secretary.

Henry achieved these objects for the most part without seeming to have done so. In 1886, other than himself, the MacVeaghs were the only living Americans who could have offered a roughly accurate estimate of his political importance. If asked to summarize what their brother had done as a politician, John and Charles could not have developed a passable summary. They lacked both the information and the inclination requisite to fair judgment. For his

part, Brooks was too absorbed in the problem of his own importance as a philosopher fairly to consider Henry's history and try to
add it up.

Thus, for the present, Henry was free to go on as a historian
as if he had never been a politician and as if he could ever *not* be a
politician. This hard-won freedom should itself be listed as an
extraordinary achievement. Among American politicians who mattered, he was alone in perfecting the ability politically *not* to exist
while he existed. Among the tests of political strength and craft,
that test was a most severe one. He could pass it.

23

GREAT PROGRESS

Thomas Dudley had served as U. S. consul at Liverpool during the Rebellion. More than any other Federal official, he had been responsible for detecting the effort by the Confederate government to acquire a navy and other wartime necessities from British suppliers. The most important suppliers were firms in the Liverpool area.

In December 1886, soon after the death of Charles Francis Adams, Dudley wrote to Henry Adams in Washington asking whether he could furnish a sketch of his father's life, to help Dudley prepare his reminiscences for publication. The request posed questions the sons of C. F. Adams would sometime have to answer. Should their father be made the subject of a biography? If so, which son should write it? If the writer was not to be a son, what records, if any, would the sons withhold from the biographer, and for what reasons?

Dudley had presumed that the son who served as the minister's wartime assistant was the son who could most readily supply a sketch. Henry replied on December 15 that, being a resident of Washington, he was "too far from my father's papers." "Probably my brother Brooks, who was with my father at Geneva, could furnish the material most easily. His address is at 23 Court Street, Boston."

Henry continued by suggesting that Dudley dispense with a sketch and simply write on the strength of his knowledge. He said Dudley knew more about Minister Adams than any other person, was familiar with his papers, and understood the occasions for their being written. He said too that he could himself "furnish only dates and facts" that already were printed. Thus any "critical treatment" would "have to come from some other source."

By claiming he could supply only dates and facts, Henry denied the evident truth that *he* could make the best appraisal of his father as minister. Moreover, he concealed the important fact that, during the war, he had sustained a correspondence with his brother Charles which could be read as a history of the Legation. He also concealed something his letters to his brother had referred to: the astounding truth that he had acted as his father's confidential aide and simultaneously had acted, without his father's knowledge, as the anonymous London correspondent of the *New York Times*. And one may say he *had* to practice concealment. Bound runs of the *Times* were extant, and his despatches had been so printed as to be a fully traceable series. If Dudley or other inquirers learned that he secretly wrote such a series and if its parts were found and studied, the wartime careers of *two* Adamses in England would acquire radically altered configurations.

In 1886, Henry's letters to Charles—those Charles had kept—were resting unnoticed among Charles's papers. If Henry wanted them to stay unnoticed, his best course was to say nothing about them. And silence would be best with respect to his despatches to the *New York Times*. Meanwhile he himself possessed a different body of pertinent data: the early volumes of his diary. The volumes were stored in Boston.[1] Those for 1861 and 1862 possibly told in some valuable form the story of his *Times* correspondence. They perhaps contained the despatches, secretly clipped in London for preservation.[2] But, for the present, he did nothing about the volumes. He let them remain in storage.

Deaths in the years 1881–1886 had cost Edward Hooper his wife, his father, his younger sister, and a brother-in-law. Friends and relatives worried about him and worried more about his surviving sister. The same deaths had cost Ellen Gurney her sister-in-law, father, sister, and husband. Her losses could be viewed as increasing.

For her part, Ellen worried about the husband of her dead sister. On January 10, 1887, she wrote to Godkin: "Henry Adams is pegging at his history. . . . Of course he has no heart for that or anything—but I long for him to get back the habit of work—and to exorcise the demon of restlessness which pursues him. Charles Adams' daughter is with him—and young life—even if at moments fatiguing—is good for him—and Dwight is very satisfactory. . . ."[3]

Saying Henry had no heart for anything, Ellen showed how little she knew him. She really spoke about herself. Henry's case was extremely difficult, but he was steadily contending with old problems and contending also with new ones. Her own case was worse. Without Whitman, she was practically resourceless.

In January 1887, Henry was obliged to deal with a new inquiry about the Chief. Houghton, Mifflin and Company wrote to him about a proposed book on the life and public services of Charles Francis Adams, to be written by John Torrey Morse, Jr., for the American Statesmen Series. As editor of the Series, Morse had previously awarded himself the honor of writing the biographies of John Adams and John Quincy Adams. The Boston firm wished to know whether Morse would be given the necessary assistance. By implication, though not explicitly, the company was asking that Morse be given access to important unpublished records, beginning with the deceased minister's diary.

The letter from Houghton, Mifflin and Company interrupted Henry's work on his *History*. His work had a pattern. He had written each of the Jefferson volumes three times before privately printing it. His current necessity was to complete the second draft of the *First Madison*, preferably before the onset of summer. He wanted no delays. But already his brother John had involved him in exchanges that would eventuate in his writing the inscription for their father's grave.[4] Also Charles was coming to Washington and would stay at 1603 H Street.

Henry sent the Boston publisher two replies. The first is missing and may only have said that an answer would follow. Charles arrived on January 18 and left for Massachusetts on January 20.[5] On the 22nd, Henry assured the publisher that Morse would "receive every assistance"—that, if asked, his brother, John Quincy Adams II, would "make whatever arrangements may be needed."

Later Henry would say *he* was urged to undertake the biography of his father and "obstinately" refused. The presumable date of his refusal was January 18–20, 1887. Its presumable hearer was Charles.[6]

Henry's promise to Houghton, Mifflin could seem to imply his approval of Morse as his father's biographer. Its actual meaning was that Henry relegated the problem of the biography to Charles. It was unthinkable that either John or Charles were approving of Morse. It was unthinkable, too, that Charles would want Morse to see the minister's papers. Instead, the second son would want the papers reserved for himself, to make whatever use of them he would think possible.

Charles had found that work as a railroad president was an empty game affording no satisfactions. He was in search of a historical project that would need his doing, preferably one of great importance. He also seemed anxious to measure himself against Brooks and Henry. When again at Quincy, he took up Brooks's *Emancipation of Massachusetts*, thought it "poor stuff," yet read to the end. He then resumed reading Henry's *Second Jefferson*. Rather than read it by itself, he read it comparatively with John Fiske's *Cosmic Philosophy* and Franklin's *Autobiography*. Reading the three works in rotation took time but gave him "thorough enjoyment."[7]

Henry met with a third vexation. Brooks was distressed because a critic in the *Nation* had misread *The Emancipation of Massachusetts* and readers generally were not understanding it. Henry had read the book and given Brooks an opinion, perhaps in person. Writing from Quincy on March 7, Brooks told him he was "almost the only man" who had grasped the book's implicit message. Thinking a postscript would help, he asked Henry to plant a 10–line note in the *Nation* stating the message. He suggested that the note be unsigned or signed by Dwight. Also he set forth what Henry was to say: that *The Emancipation* was meant "to prove the identity of the laws which control mind and matter."[8]

The worst annoyance was the coming summer. Recently their mother had undergone an attack of illness. She had the help of a companion, Lucy Baxter, but her health was so poor that she needed the presence of one or more of her sons throughout the year. John and Charles had found beachside accommodations away from Quincy to which they and their families were repairing every summer. Brooks usually stayed at the Old House in summer; but, thinking he should learn German, he wished to pass the summer in Vienna. Henry thus was obliged to say he would return to the Old House for the season, from early June through October.[9]

At intervals, Charles had been visiting Washington on business.[10] Because of Mrs. Adams's attack, Henry and Molly had traveled to Boston for a short visit and returned to the capital. Soon after, on April 17, 1887, Charles completed his reading of the *Second Jefferson*. He noted in his diary, ". . . finished Henry's second volume." He entered no comments, positive or negative.

Apart from Adams-family disturbances, Henry's winter and spring had been happy enough. By offering midday "breakfast" and evening dinner to such friends as wished to come, he made his house a social center. He saw a great deal of the Hays, Mrs. Cameron, and Martha, and attended Martha's christening. He found a new English friend in Cecil Spring Rice, a young assistant at the British Legation. Spring Rice learned that guests went unasked to 1603 H Street for meals. He liked the arrangement and frequently appeared.

On schedule in late May, Henry completed the second draft of the *First Madison*. When he left for New York and Quincy a few days later, he took with him Books I-III. He supposed that writing the third draft of three books would fully occupy the summer months.

On June 11, Charles was at home on President's Hill. After dinner, he walked to the Old House and found Henry "settled for the summer."[11] One may assume that, on arriving, he gave Henry the interleaved copy of the *Second Jefferson* with his annotations.

The copy became a doubly revealing document. Apparently in September 1886, before meeting Henry at San Francisco, Charles had written two complaints in the copy. Presumably at Quincy in June 1887, Henry read the complaints and wrote replies:

> [Charles] This chapter is, to my mind, long, obscure and dull. It could be compressed into half the space to advantage. Verbose and inconclusive diplomacy can be spared in history. It will bear boiling down.
>
> [Henry] Nonsense! This is the most important chapter in the book, and readers must not only read, but study it.
>
> [Charles] . . . Jefferson and Madison failed to appreciate their own insignificance. A battle of giants was going on. To the giants America was a peculiarly contemptible pigmy. . . . This Jefferson and Madison failed to realize; consequently they made themselves ridiculous. They did not take in the real facts of the situation.
>
> [Henry] Don't underestimate America. Let the public do that.[12]

While finishing the *Second Jefferson*, Charles had confirmed himself in a number of beliefs: that Henry misunderstood the characters in his narrative, that he was writing a kind of history too heavily weighted with documents, that he was failing to say what the American people *ought* to have done during Jefferson's second administration, and so on. With regard to passages he disapproved, Charles had written:

> This seems to me to be stuff!—So far from rising to a higher level, [Jefferson] . . . descended to the commonplace in thus abandoning the principle of least government. He showed that he was not a really great man by thus yielding to the allurement of power. . . .
>
> The extract from the [annual] message of 1806 is a mass of fallacy and unwisdom.
>
> All this needs to be compressed.
>
> The plan of telling the story by extracts from contemporaneous documents is carried to excess in this chapter. The extracts are long and not peculiarly pointed.

... the course both of courage and safety was for the United States to accept at once the principles of the Berlin decree [by Napoleon] and of the Orders in Council [the retaliatory orders by the British], and resolve itself into a nation of pirates.[13]

Henry's reply to Charles's comments was avoidance of reply.[14] He wrote no rejoinders in the annotated copy except those already quoted. His avoidance showed dissent and awareness of his brother's problem as a would-be reader. Charles could not face, still less like, the evident possibility that Henry's *History* was a great book in the making. He had so responded as to obviate its being one. While mostly failing to see the *Second Jefferson* before his eyes, he had taken it to be a wrong-headed work by Henry that he could readily imagine.

An additional significance could be found in Henry's silence. He wished neither to help nor hinder the careers Brooks and Charles were seeking as historians. He had declined to write the note Brooks urged him to plant in the *Nation*.[15] His invariable attitude towards Charles was that Charles should do as Charles preferred. If that meant giving him abundant opportunity to criticize volumes of the *History*, Henry would give it cheerfully.

The dislike King had formed of Clover was somewhat personal to her, yet mainly reflected a general dislike he was forming of well-placed American women.[16] He perhaps never wished Clover dead, but her suicide restored his chance to have a friendship with Henry of a sort he could fully want. On his side, Henry was glad to have King's friendship on any uninjurious terms, if only he had it.[17]

Though ill-adapted to understanding Adams as a novelist, King could be a discerning judge of Adams as a biographer. Like Henry, he viewed biography and history as humane branches of science that also were fine arts. He knew something of American biography, and he knew many of the persons then attempting to write it.

In the summer of 1887, he took with him to Mexico and California all the volumes of the American Statesmen Series. At New Orleans while returning, he bought a recent addition, an 800–page, two-volume *Henry Clay* by Carl Schurz. By the time he reached New York, he had read many volumes. On July 23, he sent a commentary to Adams in Quincy. Among other things, he said:

... I have done Randolph twice with the keenest pleasure & admiration. . . .
Why you are not nailed to a Virginia tree on the transpotomac end

of the long bridge only a past master in the decline & fall of Virginia could explain. The series of Biographies [is] . . . more an exposition of the minds of the writers than of their victims. The flippancy and perky narrowness of Morse, the pedantic sage inaccuracy of Lodge & the redundant fact and germanic perspective of Schurz are amusing. . . .

Randolph on the contrary is a joy to me page by page, an instruction in human analysis, a model of literary art. . . . You have compressed and minimized the daily details of politics & kept the living man all the time under the focus of your microscope. His big kicks & his petty little wiggles are shown with true clinical skill. The irrita [sic] of public life are seen gradually to affect his ganglia less & less, he stops kicking, he dies! Meantime your demonstrational lecture is full of subtle psychology and overflows with true wit. . . .

If the big history reads like this . . . I should think the dull soul of America would wake up to your genius. . . .

While King's praises were still in the mail, Adams wrote from Quincy to Dwight in Washington arranging that the second draft of Books IV and V of the *First Madison* be sent or brought to him at the Old House. His need for the concluding books was urgent. He was working almost twice as fast as he had expected.[18]

Work at such speed strained eyes and hand. To rest, he rode to Cambridge once a week to spend the day with his Hooper nieces and see Ellen Gurney. At intervals while working, he walked in the rose garden adjacent to the Stone Library, began a study of roses, and grew interested in their cultivation. In the evenings, he memorized the meanings of Chinese characters. He continued speaking of going eventually to China. Also he planned for the coming summer a five-month escape to the Pacific, this time to the Sandwich Islands and distant Fiji.

For lack of evidence, one of his necessary actions during the summer cannot be followed. He recovered his letters to his father, kept a few, and destroyed the rest. It appears, too, that he and Ellen divided Clover's letters to Dr. Hooper, perhaps intending to read and discuss them. Ellen kept half. Henry kept half.[19]

Reviewing letters was indispensable. Henry wished especially to control what future inquirers might learn and write about Clover and himself. One letter was much at issue. Ellen had thought she might sometime show him the last letter Clover wrote to her. She may have let him read it.[20]

His overriding problem day by day was the final draft of the *First Madison*. Mrs. Cameron and Martha were again at Pitch Pine Hill. He did not visit them. He once prevailed on Mrs. Cameron and Rebecca Dodge to join him and his nieces at Cambridge for a brief visit.[21] To his joy, King stopped for an hour at the Old House.

Meanwhile the shadow of illness was everywhere. Martha for a time was very sick at Beverly Farms. King's mental and emotional equilibrium was restored, but his physical ailments were multiplying.[22]

Charles hated railroad work and wanted to escape it. On August 21, 1887, he wrote in his diary: "I am an artist; that is, it is out of the exercise of the artistic qualities that are in me, that I have always got the greatest enjoyment. . . ." He outlined a solemn purpose: ". . . to retire from active railroad management and hereafter to be an artist, even if a poor one."

The fields in which Charles was likeliest to ply his talents were autobiography and grand-scale biography on the order of Nicolay and Hay's *Abraham Lincoln/ A History*. As he would view its possibilities, a biography of his father could fitly be expanded and become a history of the American Civil War in its broadest bearings, both national and international. It might fill several volumes.

He did not immediately quit work as president of the Union Pacific. Perhaps the dimensions of the visionary biography made him hesitate. Besides, he faced a barrier. As preparation, he would have to read all fifty-six years of his father's diary.[23]

As summer waned, two of Henry's nieces, Louisa and Mabel Hooper, came to stay with him for several days at Quincy. They played in the Stone Library while he was working.[24] Responsibility for their visit was possibly Louisa's. She apparently was the first niece to learn that visiting Uncle Henry was very easy. She and the other nieces, both Hoopers and Adamses, needed only to say when they would come.[25]

Temporarily Adams employed a typist. He may have taken the step to relieve or prevent writer's cramp. In late August and September, he dictated the third drafts of Books IV and V to his "caligraphess" and she typed them. By summer's end, all the *First Madison*—three books handwritten and two books typed—was readied for private printing. The volume went to Cambridge, and Henry turned his mind to a vacation.

Literally from the day he learned of Clover's death, King had attempted to get Henry to go with him to Mexico. An opportunity offered in 1887, and they agreed to go. Temporarily in better health, King went to California, where Adams would shortly join him. Adams moved back to Washington, avoided hiring a cook, drafted new chapters for the *Second Madison*, and waited for word from King.[26]

Hay had spent the summer in England, had returned to America, but would be in Cleveland till November. Friendless in the capital, Henry bought a greenhouse on New York Avenue, believing it could be used as an alternative warm place for friends to meet in cold weather. He wrote to Hay: "My gardener Durkin is refitting it, and I shall stock it. I mean to have a Japanese tea-house there, and give Marshall Niels as rewards to beauty."

Floods in Mexico prohibited journeys, and King wrote to Adams that their expedition could not be tried.[27] Adams hired a cook, corrected proofs of his *First Madison*, and drafted more chapters for the *Second Madison*. With Spring Rice, he accompanied a party of English visitors to Mount Vernon. Also, through Spring Rice, he met an English politician, Joseph Chamberlain. Apprised of Henry's habits, Chamberlain several times came to 1603 H Street to dine with him.

By then, Mrs. Cameron, Martha, the Hays, and their four children had returned to Washington. Adams was expecting Edward Hooper, Ellen, Louisa, and Mabel as December guests. Lodge had been elected to Congress and soon would occupy a house on Jefferson Place. The change was welcome because Mrs. Lodge would be a neighbor and Adams had always greatly liked her. He similarly liked her eldest children, Constance Lodge and George Cabot Lodge, especially the latter.[28]

In Cambridge during the evening of November 19, 1887, a Saturday, Ellen Gurney left her house, walked in the dark to a railroad, and stepped in the way of an approaching train. She died of injuries the following day.[29] By unknown means, news of her suicide passed to Adams. One has to assume he went to Boston to attend the funeral, but not a word concerning her death appears in his extant writings.

Well after the funeral, on December 1 in Washington, Adams learned that Edward Hooper was in bed, incapacitated and depressed but waiting quietly to recover. There was a question whether Adams should go and see him. Henry had promised to join his mother for Christmas at Mount Vernon Street in Boston. He decided to break the promise. He wrote to Lucy Baxter on December 19: "I don't want to come on until [Hooper] . . . is better, for fear of exciting and upsetting him, yet I have not an idea whether he is really improving. Anyway I have given up Christmas. . . ." He said he would come instead in January.

In the last days of 1887, Mrs. Cameron brought Martha to 1603 H Street for a usual visit. Adams presumably welcomed them in the library, facing Lafayette Square. During the visit, without saying why, he showed Martha a small red picture of George Washington—a two cent postage stamp. At eighteen months, Martha was inventively talkative. She said the pictured individual was "Dobbitt." Adams then told her he too was Dobbitt! During later visits by mother and daughter, he told Martha that his name was Georgie Dobbitt and that, being too young to pronounce Georgie, he could only say Dordy.[30]

The disclosures took effect. From the time of the visits, Martha addressed him and spoke about him as Dobbitt or Dordy. In seeming imitation of her daughter, Mrs. Cameron frequently addressed him as Dor. Onlookers assumed that the names were affectionately nonsensical, but Mrs. Cameron knew their history. She retained clear memories of the visits and did not forget that Dobbitt and Dordy were encoded forms of Washington and George.[31]

It could be urged that the underlying meaning of Adams's disclosures to Martha was that he had fallen in love with her mother. There is no denying that he was coming to feel an emotion so like love for Elizabeth Cameron that later he would not quibble and would fully suppose he loved her. Yet, probably, the disclosures had a fundamentally different meaning in which his feelings towards Martha's mother were a concomitant, not a decisive, element.

It could be suggested, of course, that Adams showed visiting Martha a picture of George Washington because her name reminded him of Martha Custis, who became Washington's wife, and too because her *other* name— the never-used Marian—put him in mind of his own wife. The suggestion would have the advantage of touching on matters that Adams could be assumed to have been aware of. Yet at best it would account for a part of Adams's action, not the action in its entirety.

Here a broader and more complicated suggestion is offered, not with a view to insisting on its literal truth, but rather to assist reflection about a moment when Adams's behavior was exceptionally revealing, yet also hard to interpret. The suggestion begins with his love for his wife. It must be said that the love Henry Adams felt for Marian Adams became so securely established and strongly developed that any love he could have or seem to have for another woman or the woman's daughter would be a subsection, echo, or phantasmal replacement of that one emotion.[32] But recently, for an unspeakable though evident reason, his love for Clover had been strengthened. Ellen Gurney had killed herself out of love for

her husband and inability to live without him. That much was plain
to see. But, to a knowing observer, her suicide arose in a *three-
person* context and had another cause. She had partly killed herself—or even mostly killed herself—in emulation and praise of her
sister. In a marked degree, the controlling person was Clover.[33]

Assuming that he saw Ellen's suicide in this way, Adams's
conduct when visited by Mrs. Cameron and Martha reflected a new
phase of his marriage. A terrific reminder of Clover had precipitated his choosing among his friends the person to whom he could
speak on a deeply confiding basis. His purpose in so speaking
would be to initiate a relation on which he could permanently
depend. He chose Elizabeth Cameron ahead of Clarence King or
John Hay because of the kind of relation he wanted. He felt a need
for a *witness*, a passive, inactive person who would fully know who
he was and what he was doing, yet be under no pressures or bonds
to show equal candor.[34] Accordingly, he changed the terms on
which he and Elizabeth Cameron knew each other, not by talking
to her, but by having her witness his telling uncomprehending
Martha that he was not Henry Adams, simply, but instead had two
names.

The only account of his conduct appears in a letter written by
Mrs. Cameron to Adams's niece Louisa in 1934.[35] The account is
over-brief and requires the reader to supply indispensable details.
It fails to say that the meetings with Martha and her mother
occurred in Adams's house, in the library, and that Adams drew
Martha's attention to the postage stamp in hopes of setting events
in motion. Its omissions, however, lend increased emphasis to a
detail which to this point has been kept unmentioned.[36] Mrs.
Cameron wrote:

> When Martha was making efforts to talk, she one day put a fat
> forefinger on a postage stamp with the head of George Washington—
> bald and in profile, you remember—and looking at Henry with a
> chortle, said "Dobbitt." That started that name. Later on they had a
> game in which she was the mother and he her little boy Georgie—
> which he was unable to pronounce, & called himself Dordy. . . .
> This is the little history which made the background of so much.
> There was a time when I couldn't have written this. But "Time
> remembered is Grief forgotten." I now live in the past.

The recounted occurrences could be thought of as belonging
to a play. The persons in the play were at ease with each other
although widely different in age. Mr. Adams was born in 1838,
Mrs. Cameron in 1857, and Martha (or Marian) in 1886.[37]

More important than age was a cleavage between two eras.

Adams had the faculty of moving on with the times, indeed of anticipating and adapting to the future; but it none the less was a fact that his character had been formed in the 1840s. He in that sense was the creature of a forgotten time, long anterior to the Civil War.

Adams's being so much older was the key to what he did. The views from his library and study windows were views of Lafayette Square, the White House on its other side, and, rising in the distance behind the White House, the spire of the Washington Monument, then the highest structure in the United States. He had first seen the monument when he was twelve, in 1850. At the time, it was only half-finished. Work had been discontinued, and the monument had a two-part appearance. Half was stonily real. Half was airily missing.

Work on the monument was resumed in the 1880s. The spire was completed in 1885, during the winter before Clover's death. When Adams began his disclosures to Martha and her mother, the monument was an already-accustomed sight. For most persons, its reference was to *one* George Washington, the general and first president. But Adams had formed his idea of the monument when its half-completed condition could suggest both someone who once existed and someone yet to appear; when it could suggest both the Washington that was—a man his grandfather knew—and the Washington that was going to be—his growing self.[38]

To the fourth child and third son of C. F. Adams and Abigail Brooks Adams, names greatly mattered because bound up with his problems of self-recognition and self-development; also of self-concealment, self-disclosure, and recognition by others. There is evidence that from an early moment "Henry Brooks Adams" had secretly wished to take the better name Henry Adams, had secretly weighed the relation between himself and George Washington, and had secretly reached extreme conclusions.[39] He had recognized himself as one of the George Washingtons—as a person belatedly included in the historic assemblage of persons who half-built the American nation.[40] He had still more positively recognized himself as the Washington who would lead in a rebuilding of the United States, or, failing that, would create a basis on which the nation could eventually be rebuilt by others.[41]

These recognitions strengthened with age and trial. When he named himself Dobbitt and Dordy—encoded forms of Washington and George—he was repeating what for him were plain though hidden truths. He felt himself the last great American of the older time.[42] Yet he was laboring to be that American who in the ultimate reckoning would be looked upon as the Union's new founder, the greater Washington.[43] And by his own count, he had two names, Henry in public, George in secret.[44]

It was not lost on Adams that his ideas about himself could appear impermissible, inappropriate, possibly laughable, or less than sane.[45] Yet his ideas were what they were, and he was anxious that in Clover's absence they not remain undeclared. By revealing his ideas to a child, he effected a great change in his life. His secret was no longer a secret. Martha was publicly shouting his other name.

In another sense, the change was no change at all. Martha knew his secret only in an unbroken code.[46] She could call him Dobbitt and Dordy all she pleased. Her piercing cries made no difference. He would go on undisturbed as Henry, Henry Adams, Mr. Adams, and H. A.

A final aspect of the matter was what happened to the chosen witness. Beginning when she learned he was Dobbitt, Elizabeth Cameron took a far more serious view of Henry Adams and the chance he had given her to know him. Whether he might fall in love with her or she with him were ancillary considerations. They both knew him to be the leading person in the country's present and future. On that new footing, they would stay permanently in a close relation that never changed.[47]

As planned, in January 1888, Adams went to Boston and Cambridge to see his mother and Edward Hooper. He found his mother exceedingly weak. Hooper being somewhat improved, he reinvited him to come to Washington, bringing Ellen, Louisa, and Mabel.

Looking ahead to the coming summer, Adams contemplated two hardships he wanted to avoid. The greater was a presidential campaign. The less was another interval at Quincy as guardian of his mother. He wrote to Godkin from Boston, "Next summer I am intending a trip to the Fiji islands where they eat missionaries, and may, if they like, eat me, but at least will not elect a President."

He returned to Washington and worked. Signs increased that, if he wanted to take a vacation, he would have to take it immediately. The best possibility was a tour of the West Indies with King, who supposed himself in good enough health to attempt it.

At weekly intervals, on Sundays, Adams was keeping a diary. How much he had kept a diary since the early 1860s is unknown. He possibly had been keeping one all the while, without significant interruptions. In the earliest entry that survives, that for February

12, 1888, he said the *Second Jefferson* was drafted through Chapter VI of Book II. Charles was at 1603 H Street, in Washington on railroad business. Friends were loyal and Mrs. Cameron very "winning." "Martha Cameron comes for biscuit and books, and howls if she is not allowed to enter the house. My little knot of friends are steady in their allegiance, and Mrs[.] Cameron is more winning than ever; but Clarence King telegraphs that he will be ready to start next Thursday, and I hope a week from today to be in Charleston, on my way to Cuba."

King's doctors changed their verdicts and forbade him to travel. He wrote to Adams: "Now *don't* let me spoil the fun but gather up Hay and put off by easy stages to St. Augustine and then to Tampa & the Islands. . . . Later I will come down to Washington. . . ."[48]

Dwight obtained leave from the State Department and took King's place. Adams and Dwight, accompanied by Hay, went by stages to St. Augustine. Hay turned back. Adams and Dwight proceeded to Narcoosee. Henry later wrote in his journal: "Here we passed a day and saw Anne Palmer, and the baby, whom she named after Clover. A stranger establishment I have seldom seen than theirs, dropped in the middle of a Florida lake, and surrounded by forest and swamp, with a colony of English wanderers two miles away, trying to grow oranges in the sand. Yet Anne is happy and contented and an important personage, with a brick house and comparative wealth. Marian is a quiet child who gives no sign of marked character as Martha Cameron does."

A ship sped Adams and Dwight from Tampa to Havana. As actively as possible, they explored Havana and accessible towns in the western part of Cuba. For lack of ships to take them, they did not go to eastern Cuba or to other islands. Dwight's leave being limited, they returned to Washington. Mrs. Cameron and Martha met their train and took them to the Ogle-Tayloe house for breakfast. The welcome lent a happy ending to a largely frustrated, makeshift journey.[49]

A week at home afforded Adams time to write one chapter. He then vacationed briefly in Virginia with Hay and King, especially enjoying days at Williamsburg and Fredericksburg. Their return coincided with the arrival of spring. Adams recorded on April 8: "I have begun to ride once more. My breakfast table is rarely deserted. Travel has done me good. I have not suffered much from depression, and not at all, of late, from excessive and alarming turns of temper. Not that I am really able to reconcile [myself to?]

life with limitations; but the day-by-day work runs without positive distress."

In Boston, failing Mrs. Adams had suffered her worst attack of illness till that time.[50] The attack had predictable results. Brooks again proposed an interval abroad. Henry recorded on April 15, "Brooks is going to Europe, and I suppose I must go again to Quincy."

The prospect of Henry's reappearing at the Old House lent impetus to a plan that earlier had been mentioned and dropped. The plan was that Dwight should leave the State Department and enter the service of the Adams family, beginning as summer archivist. He was to start work in June. He and Henry would both work in the Stone Library. Henry would proceed with his *History*. Dwight would begin transforming the family's vast accumulation of papers into an organized collection.[51]

Very slowly, St. Gaudens had been advancing towards the creation of the bronze figure for Clover and Henry's grave. The previous September, Adams had sent some photographs to the sculptor at his summer home and studio near Windsor, Vermont. The photographs were partly ones La Farge and Adams had taken in Japan. Others were views of works by Michelangelo. La Farge had helped Adams select both groups of pictures. He was involved because Adams wished to put about an impression that the Rock Creek figure was a work conceived by St. Gaudens after hearing La Farge's expert counsel.[52]

St. Gaudens had welcomed the photographs and was finally at work. Writing to Adams, he said he had "time here to make some sketches." He expected to be in New York after October 1. "If you catch me in[,] I will show you the result of Michael Angelo[,] Budha[,] and St. Gaudens. I think what I will do may not be quite as idiotic as if I had not had these months to chew the cud."[53]

Adams had not visited St. Gaudens's studio in New York. At the suggested time, he had already journeyed from Quincy to Washington. But he, the sculptor, or both at some point asked Stanford White to design the stone work for the figure. White knew from experience that St. Gaudens could be very slow and unconscious of time. On January 9, 1888, he wrote to Adams saying he had prodded St. Gaudens with "a fierce letter" but then had learned to his surprise that the sculptor had done some sketches. Two, White said, were "very stunning."

St. Gaudens and White urged Adams to come to New York to see the sketches. He could not be induced to come. St. Gaudens accordingly photographed the sketches and asked his boy model to have the negatives printed. When he mailed them at last on January 25, he explained that the boy "who posed so finely as Budha before you" had failed to get the prints, as directed. During the delay, St. Gaudens and White had realized on second thought that the figure would be better seated on an unshaped rock. To accommodate the change, a bench that White had designed to face towards the figure had to be redesigned. He at once prepared the necessary plan. St. Gaudens approved the modification and sent it to Adams with the photographs.[54]

Edward Hooper was well enough to come with Ellen, Louisa, and Mabel to Washington, and Adams went to New York to assist them on their journey. While there, on April 22, 1888, he saw La Farge and St. Gaudens, presumably at the sculptor's studio, and "made another step . . . towards my Buddha grave." The step was simple: he approved the sculptor's sketches and White's attendant plan. He recorded, ". . . St[.] Gaudens hopes to play with [the figure] . . . as a pleasure while he labors over the coats and trowsers of statesmen and warriors."

The Hoopers' five-day sojourn in Washington coincided with ideal spring weather. On April 27, a diminutive neighbor paid two visits. Mrs. Cameron was away at Harrisburg, and Martha was seizing chances to see Dobbitt all she pleased. Adams wrote to her mother the following night: "I have to thank you for the kindness of your infant daughter to my nieces. Martha was with them both morning and afternoon yesterday, and made herself charming. She found my horse Daisy rather alarming . . . but she behaved with becoming composure."

By working at every possible moment, Adams had finished drafting Book II of the *Second Madison* and was starting Book III. Mrs. Cameron's absence continued. He wrote in his journal on May 6 that the Hoopers had gone. ". . . I have made love to Martha Cameron and by dint of incessant bribery and attentions have quite won her attachment so that she will come to me from anyone. She adores Del Hay's pigeons! and takes a fearful joy in visiting Daisy in my stable. Her drawer of chocolate drops and ginger-snaps; her dolls and picture books, turn my study into a nursery."

As was natural, Martha's activities made Adams remember his earliest years. Revived memories helped him think to a purpose about *The Education of Henry Adams*. More difficult to write than his *History* and potentially its superior as a work of genius, *The Education* would have to be started sometime. It was auspicious that matters that would appear in its opening chapter were turning up in his letters.[55]

Mrs. Lodge appeared for breakfast. Mrs. Cameron came back from Harrisburg and likewise appeared for breakfast. Adams wrote on May 13: ". . . I am low-minded, though since Cuba I've had hardly any jim-jams. Everyone is going away. I want to go and stay; but have got to repeat the old desperate Quincy effort."

The worst of April and May in Washington was memories of Clover's reaching the Yellow House in 1885 unable to sleep, tired beyond all expectation, and destined for insanity. In April-May of 1888 in the Richardson house, Henry had the comfort of working with easy speed. He was far along in the first draft of the *Second Madison*. He wrote on May 20: "The last month has shown great progress, and I see the day near when I shall at last cut this only tie that still connects me with my time. The Hays have gone north. Spring Rice sails for England tomorrow. I am almost alone except for an occasional visit from Martha or her mother, and I have been been sad, sad, sad. Three years!"

Adams was fifty. On May 27, writing to Cunliffe, he said his effort to finish his *History* would be completed in two years and he then would be "free forever from my duties in life, as men call the occupations they are ashamed to quit, but are sorry to follow." He revealed that he had a plan for his future that projected a new life, perhaps without duties. Although inclined to talk, he also seemed disposed to give only a very minimum account of his intention. He told Sir Robert he would begin afresh in the spring in 1890 by sailing west on the Pacific. ". . . I shall begin a new life, in which the old one can hardly have any sequence. I say that I *shall* do it; but I mean that if I still feel then as I do now, and if nothing prevents, I shall cross the Pacific within two years for an absence which will last as short or long a time as may be."

Mrs. Cameron again wished to spend the latter part of the summer at Pitch Pine Hill.[56] During the earlier part, she would stay at Lochiel, her husband's farm near Harrisburg. She left Washington before Adams and, to his surprise, invited him to visit her and Martha for a day and a night. Thinking the occasion would be his "holiday," he went to the farm on June 6, 1888, happily stayed his permitted twenty-four hours, and with mixed feelings went on to New York, where he would be seeing King and La Farge.

The train that bore him to New York mostly carried, or so he said, German Jews from Chicago. He felt some dislike of Germans, some of Jews, and much of Chicago. In his next letter to Mrs.

Cameron, he mentioned his companions on the train. His doing so was indicative of a quite separate, unrelated irritation. What he truly disliked, indeed hated, was forced return to Massachusetts.

At the Old House on June 10, a Saturday, he judged his mother to be much weakened. His mood approached being suicidal. He recorded in his journal: "A quick and easy end would be a great blessing for her, and would save her much suffering. I might say the same for myself. I would certainly be quite willing to go with her."

On Monday, June 12, 1888, acting as Adams's representative, Dwight visited the office of a New York publisher, Charles Scribner's Sons. He spoke with the present Charles Scribner and Roger Burlingame, a chief editor. The result of the meeting was broad agreement that the firm would publish Adams's *History of the United States*. The terms of the contract would be settled after Dwight and Adams furnished more complete information.

For Adams, Quincy was endurable only because conducive to steady work. He resumed drafting chapters of the *Second Madison*. After a week, he wrote that he had "settled into the deadly routine of last year." He however was cured of "acute depression" and could use his mother's infirmity as an excuse to avoid "social effort." So helped, he advanced in the *Second Madison* to Book III, Chapter VIII.

Rather tardily, he went to Cambridge to see the Hoopers. Niece Louisa—then known both as Noony and Loulie; later only as Loulie—asked him when Martha would be at Beverly Farms. Loulie had noticed in Washington that Martha was to be received, not as a mere neighbor's child, but a valued friend. She had promptly made friends with Martha. Loulie's action was a step towards becoming her uncle's trusted ally.

Without explanation, Mrs. Cameron stopped writing letters to Mr. Adams. She instead sent him Martha's newest photographs. On June 23, as a means of communicating with daughter and mother, Henry addressed a letter to Martha. He told her he had placed her photographs against the books by his desk. "I wish you were here in my library with Possum and Mr[.] Dwight and me and two or three other dogs. I should be much more contented. . . . I have been to Cambridge to see your friend Noony [also Loulie]. . . . She is going to Beverly about July 10, and hopes you will soon be there."

Niece Ellen Hooper seemed predisposed to hay fever. Rather than permit her tendency to worsen, Edward Hooper took all his daughters to a hotel at Bethlehem in the White Mountains near Franconia Notch. She gradually recovered strength.

Mrs. Cameron still supposed she would return to Pitch Pine Hill. Dwight visited the house to be sure it was ready. Adams wrote history ten hours a day, studied Chinese, and relaxed by writing letters. Hay was going to Colorado, a fate Adams wished he could share. Yet he was in some ways content to be where he was. He explained to Hay, ". . . the frenzy of finishing the big book has seized me, until, as the end comes nigh, I hurry off the chapters as though they were letters to you."

The *History* was so near to finished that its form was settled beyond a doubt. He had nine chapters still to draft. When they were written, the work would have the form it had had from the time he began to write it: four volumes each containing five books. Particular books would contain as many as nine chapters. These specifics were pertinent because Adams was about to compel Charles Scribner's Sons to publish the *History* in an altered and somewhat forbidding form.

When they talked in New York, Scribner had asked Dwight to send one of Adams's privately-printed volumes. On July 12, Dwight sent the publisher a copy of the *Second Jefferson*. He also sent a memorandum by Adams and a letter by himself. Describing it in his letter, Dwight said that Adams's memorandum listed "such points as have occurred to him as essential for a discussion of the publication by you."[57] The memorandum itself set forth seven points. All seven were demands. The first and second demands concerned the matter of form. They did not appear offensive. They simply said:

> Eight volumes, five hundred pages each.
>
> Every pair of volumes to make a separate work, with titlepage and index.

Differently, the seventh demand was outrageous—as will be shown. Because the seventh would monopolize attention, the first and second would tend to be overlooked. Their being overlooked was Adams's object. He wanted the *History* published in an altered form, and he was using shock tactics to achieve the object.

The seventh demand concerned the money that might accrue to the author. Adams said he had never received royalties from a publisher in excess of ten percent. He also said that, after sufficient copies of the *History* were sold to create a profit, *half* the profit should be passed to him. He said he "always thought and still thinks the author ought to share equally with the publisher." As he possibly expected, the demand would wait two weeks for an answer.

A "letter" came from Martha—her approximation of hand-writing. With it came a message from Mrs. Cameron that she was growing thin.[58] Henry replied to the mother on July 15 and turned to politics. The Democrats had nominated Cleveland for a second term, and the Republicans had chosen Benjamin Harrison to oppose him. With reference to Harrison, Henry said: ". . . I see or dimly hear that some new political jackanapes is set up for President, and that Congress is likely to be in session for two months yet; but I am still waiting to know when you are to be at Beverly. I shall not see you, but I want to send Martha a wooden pail and shovel to dig in the sand on the beach."

On the same day, Adams wrote to Gaskell. His letters to Gaskell and Cunliffe had become infrequent but, if anything, were gaining in importance. He told Carlo how travel and return to Quincy affected his sense of age. He felt young when he journeyed to new places, old when he had to live at the Old House. 'The worst of a childhood's haunt like this place, where I am, is that it forces on one's mind the passage of time. Once I get to a new place, I feel as young and as lively as at twenty."

Mrs. Cameron could not go to Pitch Pine Hill. Her husband decreed that she stay at fashionable Newport and later at fashionable Lenox in the Berkshires. She sent Adams the news and said she was sorry.

The difference made by the news was more emotional than practical. Henry answered on July 29: ". . . I freely admit that I am very sorry you are not coming to Beverly, and still more sorry that you should be sorry. As for the house, you need not waste a thought upon it. I keep it only to lend to friends, and no friend but you has ever wanted it."

Scribner scarcely wished to deal with a writer who hoped to make off with half the firm's net profit on a book. He however thought well enough of the sample Second Jefferson to offer Adams a royalty of fifteen percent.[59]

The offer elicited a letter by Adams, dated August 1, 1888, which would still be talked about at the firm in the 1940s.[60] He explained to Scribner that his History had required an investment of $80,000 and that on businessmen's principles he would expect an annual return from it of ten percent—$8,000—forever. "As I am not a publisher but an author, and the most unpractical kind of an author, a historian, this business view is mere imagination. In truth the historian gives his work to the public and the publisher. . . . History has always been, for this reason, the most aristocratic of all literary pursuits, because it obliges the historian to be rich as well as educated."

In essence, Adams's letter was very simple. He wished the *History* to be a gift to Scribner and the public. He only refused to admit that Scribner's share in producing the book was greater than his own. "This may be a fad, but I have seen the author squeezed between the public and publisher until he has become absolutely wanting in self-respect, and I hold to preserving the dignity of my profession."

To complete his message, Adams proposed to have things both ways. He foresaw that a sale of 1,500 sets would defray the publisher's costs and that the sale of the *History* could not possibly rise to 2,000 sets. On these assumptions, he asked for a contract stating that, once 2,000 sets were sold, the author would receive "one half the proceeds, after deducting only the charge for printing, binding, and paper." Such a contract would "admit the author to have half the credit, if there is any credit, of the work," yet would guarantee the publisher "all the profits" that could be anticipated. The author would win acceptance of his claim to equality. He in addition would have the comfort of giving his work to the publisher and the public for nothing.

Peculiar though it seemed, Adams's counter-offer proved a basis for cordial negotiation. For bookkeeping reasons, his proposed contract could not be adopted. As a substitute, Scribner suggested that the author get twenty percent after 2,000 copies were sold. Adams agreed; a contract was reached; and author and publisher proceeded with the complex process of readying the *History* for general sale.[61]

An absurdity supplied an ending. In the capital, the contractor refitting Adams's greenhouse so bungled the work as to cause it to collapse. Ward Thoron, an apprentice lawyer in the firm handling Adams's affairs in Washington, sent him a telegram and letter saying what happened and requesting orders. Adams knew what he wanted both in the long run and the short. He answered on August 11, "I intend to rid myself of the whole affair in regular process of time, and under no circumstances shall I build or rebuild the greenhouse or any part of it." Yet he directed that the wreckage be cleared away and the lot be used for a temporary purpose. Expecting to work hard on the *History* through two more intervals in Washington, he asked that the lot be turned into a garden for autumn and spring flowers.[62]

Clover Hooper as a child, about ten years old (ca. 1853). The studio portrait by Southwork & Hawes is the only known photograph of Clover—later Mrs. Henry Adams—fully to show her face. While the picture may suggest the kindly side of her character, it fails to show her vivacity or animation. *Courtesy Louisa Hooper Thoron and Massachusetts Historical Society.*

Henry Adams's private spring diary, 1883–86. He and Clover rode together in the countryside surrounding Washington, eagerly looking for signs of spring, and noting nature's annual rebirth. During the spring of 1885, Henry made use of these notes in a letter to her from Washington, while she attended her dying father in Massachusetts. Following her death in December 1885, Clover could no longer receive letters, but her husband continued to do loving things: ride their favorite routes; share the first woodland blossoms. Adams preserved the record until his death in 1918, when the page was discovered by Aileen Tone. *Author's collection.*

Elizabeth Cameron with her daughter Martha, ca. 1891. The full scope of Adams's imaginative ambitions for the United States was revealed in a baby-talk game with Martha, to which Mrs. Cameron was a witness. Part-jokingly, and with Martha in mind, Adams wrote to Lucy Baxter: "Children are an illusion of the senses. They last in their perfection only a few months, and then, like roses, run to shoots and briars." *Courtesy Mrs. Henry S. Sherman.*

Henry Adams in his top floor Washington workroom, 1891, shortly before leaving for the South Seas. Although friends were invited to the main-floor study and the library at 1603 H Street, Adams considered the top floor private. His friend Elizabeth Cameron thought well of the picture, taken by Adams's then-assistant Theodore Dwight, and acquired it. *Author's collection.*

The Adams Memorial, early 1890s, perhaps photographed by Theodore Dwight. A prized possession of Mrs. Adams's niece, Mabel Hooper La Farge, and highly regarded by Clover's descendents, this photograph later became the property of Mrs. La Farge's sister, Louisa Hooper Thoron. With exceptional clearness, it shows the bronze figure as androgynous: the face is feminine; the right arm is masculine. Adams himself avoided "interpretations" of the sculpture, which he conceived, designed, and presented to the sculptor, Augustus St. Gaudens, for execution on June 4, 1886, with the help of a young male model and an American Indian rug. *Courtesy Louisa Hooper Thoron. Author's collection.*

24

IMMOLATIONS AND ADJUSTMENTS

Adams went briefly to the White Mountains to see his Hooper nieces and their father. When back at Quincy, he took new steps to free himself from his second life and open a path to a third. By mail, he requested a contract from St. Gaudens for the bronze figure and arranged a contract with Stanford White for the stone work.[1] As the same time, he read proofs of the *First Madison* and resumed drafting the *Second Madison*. He recorded on August 26, 1888, that he had finished drafting Book IV. There would be eight more chapters. ". . . of these," he noted, "only four are narrative."[2]

On Sunday, September 9, he wrote a letter to Martha. His letter made explanations. "I love you very much, and think of you a great deal, and want you all the time. I should have run away from here, and looked for you all over the world, long ago, only I've grown too stout for the beautiful clothes I used to wear when I was a young prince in the fairy-stories, and I've lost the feathers out of my hat, and the hat too, and I find that some naughty man has stolen my gold sword and silk-stockings and silver knee-buckles. So I can't come after you. . . ."

Imagination played a part in the lines, but fact may have played a larger. Possibly, in Quincy or Boston, Adams had removed his diplomatic uniform from storage and dumped it in the rubbish. If he did exactly that, he may have seemed intent on nothing more than a throwing out of unwanted clothes. As will appear, however, he was in a mood for sacrifices that mattered.

One of his objects was to immolate and replace a once-existent person. He meant to rid the world of the Henry Adams who in London in 1861–1862 had been a highly-important though concealed unofficial peace commissioner, and later, for six years, an unofficial minister. To this end, he would destroy evidence, and his uniform apparently was the evidence soonest to go. Eventually, by writing *The Education of Henry Adams*, he would replace the immolated Adams with a fictional Adams, an insignificant private secretary.[3]

He meanwhile was advancing rapidly in the *Second Madison*. That same Sunday, September 9, he wrote to Hay: ". . . [I] spin my web with the industry of Anthony Trollope. I can hardly believe my own ears when I say that tomorrow my narrative will be finished. . . ."

In his diary, he similarly noted that on Monday he would reach the end of Chapter IV in Book V—the chapter that "closes my narrative." He would still have to draft four "economical and literary" chapters, but he hoped to complete the task before he returned to Washington.

Without disputing Adams's statement that the narrative portion of his *History* would end with Chapter IV of Book V of the *Second Madison*, one may notice that the *History* could be read in competing ways.[4]

> *Reading 1.* In pretence, the *History* had something of the aspect of an administrative history. It could be read as a history of four U. S. administrations—which it partly is, but which emphatically is *less* than it is.

So read, the work begins with an introduction—6 chapters; continues with a narrative—143 chapters; and ends with a conclusion—4 chapters.[5] Also the work gives wrong impressions. One is that Presidents Jefferson and Madison are and remain its leading persons. Another is that the main action begins with Jefferson's inauguration on March 4, 1801, and ends with Madison's retirement on March 4, 1817.

Currently, in his diary, in letters, and even within his last volume, Adams was treating the *History* as if it were the work just described.[6] On September 16, he said in his diary: "The narrative was finished last Monday. In imitation of Gibbon I walked in the garden among the yellow and red autumn flowers, blazing in sunshine, and meditated. My meditations were too painful to last. The contrast between my beginning and end is something Gibbon never conceived."[7]

It was true that on Monday he had finished the narrative in the sense of completing the chapter in which Madison leaves office. But where, one may ask, does the narrative in the *History* really end?

> *Reading 2.* The work could be read as a history of the Americans and their government, in short a national history—which is much more nearly what the *History* is.

When the work is so read, the American people are the central concern and the entire work becomes the narrative. The "present story"—Adams's phrase—is sustained through all 153 chapters.[8]

Reading 3. The work could be read with close attention to the structure Adams gave it.[9]

So read, the *History* shows itself to be both a national history and a universal history. It is formed in three parts written in different expository modes: an analytical introduction; a sustained, tightly-knit narrative of linked events; and a somewhat discursive conclusion. The parts are *substantive*, as is shown by their contents and by the wordings of their beginnings and endings. Moreover, the parts organize the work's twenty books. The analytical introduction is one book (6 chapters). The tightly-knit narrative is eighteen books (139 chapters). The discursive conclusion is one book (8 chapters). (The parts outlined above under Reading 1 are best noted and then ignored.) [10]

The narrative—the heart of the work—begins with a great event. Its *ostensible* starting point is Jefferson's inauguration in March 1801, but its *substantive* starting point is Napoleon's attempted reenslavement of the blacks in the French West Indies, begun in October 1801 but secretly planned in 1800.[11] Likewise, the narrative ends with a great event: the negotiation of the Treaty of Ghent by Albert Gallatin and others late in 1814, concluding the War of 1812.[12] (Adams by September 10 had long since drafted the narrative's last book: Book IV of the *Second Madison*.) Taken as a whole, the narrative sets forth a still greater event: the uniting of the Americans. Indeed it explains their uniting. It shows why and how it happened.[13]

The narrative is much concerned with individuals. The leading person is Secretary Gallatin. The concluding books make clear that it was Gallatin who pulled the Americans' chestnuts out of the fire in 1813–1814, after his colleagues Presidents Jefferson and Madison, by dint of varied incompetencies, had put the chestnuts into the fire. All the same, Gallatin is not the subject of the work. The subject is an un-united people who rather suddenly unite, form a nation, and exhibit particular, apparently heritable, characteristics. Gallatin is the hero only in the sense that he consistently and decisively abets this swift metamorphosis.[14]

The truly important aspect of the *History* is its largest dimension. The Americans are interesting to Adams because humanity is interesting to Adams. The achievement of the Americans is set forth because indicative of human achievement overall. Thus the ultimate subject is not the Americans when they united; it is humanity at large through all time. In similar fashion, the message of the work is the message that can be learned about humanity in general from what has been learned about the Americans in particular.[15]

These points require notice because Adams was creating false impressions. One false impression was that his interest in the *History* was dying and nearly dead. While saying in his diary on September 9, 1888, that in less than two months he had drafted eight chapters, he had added in the same sentence that he had "nothing else to do." "If I have no satisfactions, I have little interest."

In fact, his interest was unabated. On September 10, after completing the chapter in which Madison leaves office, he took his meditative walk. Yet he quickly curtailed the walk, returned to the Stone Library, and started to draft the four "economical and literary" chapters that were still unwritten. He returned because of interest.

In the same week, he initiated a "long meditated action." On September 16, he recorded, "I have brought from Boston the old volumes of this Diary, and have begun their systematic destruction." He was too intelligent not to sense the irony and virtual contradiction of recording in a diary the destruction of its early volumes. Neither irony nor contradiction stayed him from his intent. New entries told the story.

[September 23]

. . . I have come to the last page of my history. I wish I cared, but I do not care a straw except to feel the thing accomplished. At the same time I am reading my old Diaries, and have already finished and destroyed six years, to the end of my college course. It is fascinating, like living it all over again, but I am horrified to have left such a record so long in existence. My brain reels with the vividness of emotions more than thirty years old.

[September 30]

Steadily working ahead towards my demise. My third volume is at last printed. . . . I have read and destroyed my diary to the autumn of 1861. Nothing in it could be of value to anyone, but even to me the most interesting part was my two closing College years. Much is unpleasant and painful to recall.[16]

[October 7]

> Continue reading old diary, but I hesitate to destroy much of the record since 1862, not that I think it valuable, but that I may want to read it again. Portions are excessively interesting to me; nothing to anyone else.[17]

It may seem that HA felt or should have felt the burning of his early diaries as a moral error, yet deliberately did it. Or it may seem that in the present instance he thought that error was out of the question. He may have believed that, being the author of the diary, he had a right to destroy it when he pleased, with or without recording its destruction, and with or without a reason.

His action was complicated by hidden factors. He had started his diary in 1852 when fourteen, perhaps just after the death of Louisa Catherine Adams. Ever a keen judge of talent, he had known at the time that the Adamses could claim only one survivor whose talents equalled or surpassed the talents of the Adamses of former years. Young he assuredly was, and there was much he did not know, but comparative talent he did know. One accordingly might conjecture that he started the diary with the purpose of speeding his development and taking the fullest, swiftest advantage of his talents that might be possible.

His development bore on the matter of his diary's worth. In 1888, reading and destroying the volumes written in 1852–1862, he found them fascinating. His brain reeled with past-felt emotions. He was most affected by the record of his last two years at college, which notably had included his election by his classmates to speak as their representative before the public on Class Day.[18] He nevertheless burned the volumes, went on reading, and burned more volumes. Having reduced to ashes a continuous record of his first life, concluded in London early in 1862, he found it difficult to go on. He hesitated. He stopped.

His reactions considered, it can be said that the volumes already burned were valuably informative and that their destruction was a calamitous loss.[19] Doubters might insist that the diary's beginning volumes, written in his middle teens, could contain nothing of worth; but the volumes begun after 1855 can be believed to have gained in substance till they approached equality with the best extant writings of his first life, his despatches to the *New York Times*. It can also be believed that, as Adams saw the matter, the great merit of his diaries from early November 1860 through mid-January 1862 was their recording the actions of a mere American private citizen who intervened importantly, albeit secretly, in public affairs, national and international. Obviously, in his eyes, that merit required his burning the pertinent volumes. Moreover, because they shared the merit, he undoubtedly at unknown times destroyed additional papers he controlled that dated from the months when the Union dissolved and the *Trent* affair brought the already-embattled Unionists to the verge of war with England.[20]

It seems likely, however, that Adams destroyed old records not only on account of merit but also with a less ironic motive. He evidently wished to start writing *The Education of Henry Adams.* Because the book would be part-fiction, he possibly felt he could not start the book till disencumbered of physical records; that is, till the diaries and parallel materials ceased being available *even to him.* In that event, the central issue was not something negative—concealment. It instead was something positive—freedom to write.[21]

A last consideration is that Adams in one sense did not destroy the diaries and other records. *He read them.* He transformed them from old words on paper to new elements in the mind—to new resources of the Adams who would be leading his third life. Once considered, this preparatory transmutation seems something he had to do.

Of Adams's closest English friends, Charles Milnes Gaskell was the more narrowly English and Sir Robert Cunliffe the more adapted to broad experience. Cunliffe had informed Adams that he wished to come to the United States for an autumn visit. Adams was "more than delighted" and replied that, among other places, they might visit Mexico.

Sir Robert reached New York while Adams was still tied to Quincy. To bridge the interval, Henry arranged that Cunliffe be entertained by King, Hay, Abram Hewitt, and others.

Adams's besetting problem was the form the *History* would have when published. Scribner had agreed that Wilson's University Press would do the printing. Adams visited the press in late September and indicated that he wanted the published version to have an ideally readable page, preferably elegant. He gave directions concerning the page's desired size, lineation, etc.[22]

On October 8, 1888, free to travel, he met Cunliffe and Hay at Albany and began a long journey. One of his purposes was to acquaint Sir Robert with some of the results of Richardson's genius. Franklin MacVeagh, brother of Wayne MacVeagh and a resident of Chicago, had met the Adamses in Washington when their plans for a Richardson house were in embryo.[23] He had later commissioned

Richardson to design a fine house in Chicago. Advised that Adams and an English friend wished to see the house, MacVeagh and his wife insisted that they be house guests.

King meanwhile had warned Adams to avoid Mexico, suggesting California and especially Yosemite in its place. Charles, still president of the Union Pacific, arranged that Henry again have use of the directors' car.[24] Boarding the car at Chicago, Henry and Cunliffe proceeded to Salt Lake City, detoured through the Utah mountains by narrow-gauge railroad, regained their car at a junction, fitted in a side trip to seldom-visited Shoshone Falls, descended the Columbia River by steamer to Portland, skirted Mount Shasta in fine weather along a new railroad, and at last, shorn of the car, rested for a time at the Palace Hotel and the Union Club in San Francisco. A feature of the journey was absence of servants. Adams wrote to Gaskell, "Fortunately Robert brought no valet, and we carry our own dust, inch-deep . . . in patience, without being obliged to dust a servant too."

As a climax, the friends explored the Yosemite Valley and saw the sequoias. Richardson's successors had designed a campus for Stanford University. Adams and Cunliffe lingered a day to survey it. (Henry wrote to his mother, "The buildings are going to be the prettiest and most artistic in America, or perhaps in Europe; and I was anxious to see them, though they are not quarter finished.") By ordinary trains, they shifted to Santa Barbara ("a sort of Sorrento"), turned east at Los Angeles, and four days later stopped at New Orleans, where they visited the banks of the Mississippi on which General Jackson won the last battle of the War of 1812—recounted in Book IV of the *Second Madison*. They reached Washington in the evening on November 25. Adams soon recorded that they had "travelled in all about nine thousand miles with perfect success." The figure was testimony that travel as he went about it was not a dimension of leisure but a means of learning and an aspect of work.[25]

Sending Adams's demands to Scribner on July 12, Dwight had repeated the first by saying, "You will understand that it is Mr. Adams['s] present purpose to print the four volumes . . . in eight smaller ones; each of his will make two for the public."

In September at Wilson's print shop, Adams had rejected a sample page for the *History* and requested another. He could seem merely to have wished to limit the number of words on a page, but his request had an undeclared purpose. Adoption of the page he specified would *force* the publication of each volume as two volumes.

And once that change was decided irreversibly, he would have a pretext or excuse for concealing from the public the fact that his original volumes were each comprised of *five* books—an odd number impossible to halve.

Scribner was perhaps more a businessman than a bookman; but he had assistants, Roger Burlingame and William Crary Brownell, who were attentive to literary values. The publisher and his aides shortly realized that Adams, by requiring that four volumes be printed as eight, was making it impossible for them to issue his work as he had written it—in books. On November 13, Scribner wrote Adams a letter in which the question of books was avoided or at least did not appear; yet a somewhat parallel question did appear, that of titles.

When privately printed, Adams's *volumes* bore similar but variant titles given in full only on the title-pages. The *books* bore distinctive titles given only in the volumes' tables of contents. *Chapter* titles were sequences of phrases listing the chapter's contents. These too were given only in the tables of contents.[26]

Scribner wanted the chapter titles to appear in the tables of contents *and again in the text*. He offered a general rule: ". . . the Chapters should have some heading. . . ." He also said, "In regard to Chapter-Headings . . . , we feel like suggesting a summary of contents [in the text] . . . as not beneath the dignity, and adding to the lucid presentment, of the subject." He added that, if Adams opposed the suggestion, each chapter could be given a short title indicating its principal subject, and the short titles could be repeated as headings at the tops of each chapter's odd-numbered pages.[27]

Adams found Scribner's letter waiting in Washington when he and Cunliffe arrived from New Orleans. On November 26, he replied concerning chapter titles and simultaneously took up the matter of the work's organization in books. "I think that the reader who has a table of contents at the beginning [listing short titles of chapters] . . . would neither need nor look at chapter- or page-headings [within the text]. If you assent, I propose to drop the arrangement in books, and run [i.e. number] the chapters through the [new, smaller] volume."

The letters of both publisher and author were cordial, yet a sharp contest was in progress. Scribner and his aides wanted "lucid presentment." To that end, they wanted chapter titles throughout the text, and finally got them, though only as page headings. Adams wanted eight small volumes and wanted to "drop the arrangement in books." He was very pertinacious and succeeded in both respects.

It was further determined that the eight volumes would be published in pairs, at intervals. With this plan in mind, Scribner proposed that the chapters be numbered continuously *through each pair*. If adopted, this numbering of chapters would hark back to the work's having been written in four volumes.[28]

Adams vetoed the proposal. ". . . I rather dislike to run chapters through more than one volume. A volume [the smaller new one] seems to me a good division. . . . I feel always a little shock at seeing a volume begin with anything but Chapter I."

Persisting as he did, Adams obtained a format for the public edition which would suppress all the original obtrusive signs that the *History*, as written, was highly organized.[29] The suppression needs notice, for the "arrangement" that Adams meant to drop was not a mere arrangement; it was a structure. Much as Beethoven's symphonies were written in successive substantive movements, the *History* was written in successive substantive parts: a one-book beginning, an eighteen-book continuation, and a one-book conclusion.

Nothing would be gained by painting over Adams's conduct with thin defenses. He had set out to give the public his *History* with key guides to its structure deleted. Later, to make sure the deletion was permanent, he would discard the privately-printed copies of the *First Jefferson* and the manuscripts of the *Second Madison*. Admittedly these measures could not prevent close readers from adducing from internal evidence where the books of his *First Jefferson* and *Second Madison* begin and end. His measures however would absolutely prevent recovery of the titles he had given to the ten books that comprised those volumes. Meanwhile, he treated all his twenty books as if they had no right to anything except to have their existence denied. Indeed he arranged that four be split. If plans held, the eight-volume format would create new Volumes II, IV, VI, and VIII. Each would split a concealed Book III by beginning in its middle.

That Adams stripped the *History* of indicators of its structure does not admit of a doubt. Doubt only enters with regard to his motive.

In the text of the *History*, he mentions Shakespeare and makes allusions to *Othello, Julius Caesar, Hamlet*, and *Macbeth*.[30] Taking cues from these passages, readers might wonder what relation Adams thought there was between his *History* and Shakespeare's plays, which by custom were edited and reprinted as if they were five-act works. On the basis of such wonderings, it perhaps could be theorized that Adams averted the publication of his work as four volumes each containing five books in order not to be mistakenly trumpeted as a writer of volumes redolent of Shakespeare's histories.[31]

A different possible motive was private. It has been noticed that Clover may have suggested that the *History* be given the form of twenty books. It can be theorized that Henry, following her death, was willing to give his work to the public only *without* what she had supplied, its governing structure. In that event, his motive might be described as jealous possessiveness.

A third possible motive involved only Adams. It had been his experience that actions or writings known to be his, and also many of his actions and writings that were anonymous or otherwise *not* known to be his, were met with loud immediate attention. There was every likelihood that his *History* when published would raise a noise. The likelihood was the greater because the *History's* sentences and paragraphs were marvels of clarity, readable in the highest degree.

It is here assumed that all three motives were operative but the third was uppermost. Adams's controlling purpose was postponement of fame. He of course knew that the merits of the *History* would insure its renown. He could anticipate a day when the work's form and substance would receive appropriate scrutiny. He could foresee that literary sleuths would eventually recognize and draw attention to its division into three parts, embracing twenty books. But however much he hoped the *History* would be read, understood, and valued in the long run, he hoped it might be less sold, less read, less understood, less valued in the short run. For the coming years, perhaps till his death, he wanted a discouraged readership, and he arranged to publish the *History* in a form that would get it.

Two devices for discouraging readers would be a carefully crafted reduction of lucidity and a false appearance of tediousness. Adams used both. By arranging the publication of his *History* without its original chapter titles, without its book divisions and book titles, and in as many volumes as possible, he both decreased the work's intelligibility and lent it a false appearance of excessive length and uniform, featureless, arid monotony.[32]

Cunliffe wished to visit Boston. Adams was glad to have a reason for absenting himself from H Street on December 6, 1888—the "haunting anniversary," as he said, of his wife's tragic action.

While with Cunliffe in Massachusetts, Adams gave Wilson the first pages of the *History* for printing. He earlier had hoped to start printing by October 1. What with Sir Robert's arrival and various distractions, he had incurred a long delay.

Molly joined Uncle Henry and Sir Robert on their return trip to the capital. They stopped in New York, and Adams visited St. Gaudens at his studio. The sculptor was attempting the figure and deciding its scale. Adams made clear his preference not to see the statue again until it was cast in bronze and installed at the grave site.[33]

Sir Robert went to Washington with Adams and Molly but soon left for England. Adams waited a few days and wrote to tell him, "Your visit has been a boon to me, and I feel it the more as I settle back upon routine."

Adams's activities were in fact the opposite of routine. He had to send Wilson copy for printing but was learning that the much-rewritten *First Jefferson* no longer satisfied. On December 16, he recorded that he was working "desperately" to prepare additional chapters. He had found that he was having to "rewrite the whole first volume."

It bears repeating that Adams was misrepresenting his *History* and himself as historian. On January 6, 1889, he wrote to Lucy Baxter that he was trying to get his "poor old history" into publishable condition. "As fast as I plaster and white-wash one chapter, those behind and before crumble and tumble. The printers howl for copy, and I must let the poor old asthmatic, rheumatic, astigmatic, but not even dogmatic, prehistoric wreck totter into the world." Being humorously hyperbolic, the passage perhaps was harmless. But there would be other passages, and some would be far from harmless.

Two years later, after reading the *First Madison* in published form, Mrs. Cameron would write to Adams that the later volumes of the *History* seemed more critical than the earlier. On January 2, 1891, he would reply that the *First Madison* had mostly been written within the past "five or six" years and in a changed "frame of mind"—that he had found it difficult to "pretend either sympathy or interest in my subject." "If you compare the tone of my first volume . . . with that of the [last] . . . when it appears, you will feel that the light has gone out."

On February 13, 1891, he would tell her: ". . . [my *History*] belongs to the *me* of 1870; a strangely different being from the *me* of 1890. There are not nine pages . . . that now express anything of my interests or feelings; unless perhaps some of my disillusionments. . . . I care more for one chapter, or any dozen pages of *Esther* than for the whole history, including maps and indexes; so much more, indeed, that I would not let anyone read the story for fear the reader should profane it."[34]

His very strong statements were designed to give impressions that successive portions of the *History*, beginning with the first chapters and ending with the last, belonged to different Henry Adamses ranging from the one of 1870 to the one of 1890; that the parts deteriorated; that they decreasingly expressed the author's feelings; that they were the work of a historian who lost interest in his subject; and that at last his interest fell to zero.

His strong statements are open to still stronger objections. Perhaps the strongest has to do with his saying he lost sympathy with his subject. With respect to any particular subject, sympathy was not the issue. His *History* was not intended to sympathize with Gallatin, Jefferson, Madison, or any other person, party, faction, or interest.[35] Sympathy, however, *was* an issue with respect to humanity at large. The work from start to finish was testimony that his interest in *all* his fellow humans remained exceptionally strong.

Interest had another side. The interest to which he subordinated every other interest was the perfection of the *History* as a work of science and a work of art. His interest in this interest remained at least constant. It possibly intensified.

Because he destroyed the privately-printed copies of the *First Jefferson*, destroyed all manuscripts of the *Second Madison*, and destroyed many related materials, inquirers are barred from fully knowing in what ways and how much he *improved* his great work during the interval when he prepared it for publication. But it is true beyond a doubt that as nearly as possible he made its elements simultaneous. As published, the entire work belongs to a Henry Adams past fifty. If final form is the measure—and can there be any other measure?—every chapter and every sentence should be dated after November 25, 1888, the date he got back from New Orleans.

Because the words "early" and "late," when applied to the volumes of a multi-volume work, can mean earlier or later written or can mean earlier or later in the set, discussion of the *History* was sure at some point to breed a myth that the lower-numbered volumes were comparatively youthful, *and thus were the best.* That particular myth gained currency and, once supported in the 1930s by the publication of Adams's misleading remarks to Mrs. Cameron, turned into a supposed established fact. But it can be said that the beginning chapters are not the best; and, whether they are or not, Adams considerably rewrote the beginning chapters *after* he completed the first writing of the final chapters. Thus the myth is not debatable. It is simply false.

In place of all myths, a single truth needs recognition. Starting late in 1888, Adams dealt with his *History's* 153 chapters as a single act and brought the entire work to a very high level of performance.

He accomplished the feat at a heavy price. His diary indicated strain. He wrote on January 13, 1889: "Horseback every day. Shocking labor over first volume of history[,] which has to be rewritten."

He more comfortably continued on January 20: "Work on the history is easier now I have got into diplomatic affairs [Book III of the *First Jefferson*]." Copy for Scribner's small Volume I was nearly finished.

On January 27, after noting that he had revised 350 of the 580 pages of the *First Jefferson* and sent them to Wilson for printing, he went on to say uncomfortably: ". . . another week or two ought to complete it, and then I can begin rewriting my last volume [the *Second Madison*]. The work is trying; when I quit it, at three o'clock in the afternoon, my nerves are raw, as though I had scraped them."

While Adams and Cunliffe were in the West, on November 6, 1888, the voters had rebuffed Grover Cleveland by a narrow margin and again elected a Republican. The president-to-be was Benjamin Harrison, and the person he wanted to head the State Department was James G. Blaine.

Blaine's return to the department would cause Adams no harm as a writer and none as a politician. He had already mined the department's library and archives sufficiently for his purposes as a writer. Moreover, by repeatedly publishing an anonymous novel, he had done Blaine sufficient injury to be happy about the wounds.

While the Republicans prepared to reinstall themselves in the White House and the executive branch, Adams presented pictures of himself as a fugitive from politics.[36] He wrote to Cunliffe, "To me, politics have been the single uncompensated disappointment of life—pure waste of energy and moral[e]." The picture was largely false, as his third life would show. Yet for the moment it could seem true. Adams had only one evident occupation. He was at work on his *History*.

A compulsory third summer at Quincy seemed more than

likely. The prospect again suggested a winter vacation. On February 7, 1889, he left the capital for the North Carolina coast, planning thereafter to revisit Charleston and inspect Savannah. His companions were Tom Lee and Willy Phillips, two Washington irresponsibles skilled in duck hunting and poker. He later recorded some details of their expedition.[37] They had gone via Baltimore to Fortress Monroe, Norfolk, and Elizabeth City. By chartering a steamer, they went "to Manteo on Roanoke Island, whence we crossed to Body Island Light." "After four days vainly trying for duck, we beat back to Manteo in an open boat, and passed four days investigating Roanoke island and Raleigh's lost colony."

That Adams visited the site of Sir Walter Raleigh's settlement was typical and apparently, as things developed, was indispensable. He had on his conscience his earliest historical publication, "Captain John Smith." He had made many changes in the article since its publication in 1867, but no thorough renovation. Possibly while on Roanoke Island in February 1889, he thought of a new idea concerning Smith's story of being rescued from imminent execution by Pocahontas. It struck him that the lie Smith conceived in old age in London inverted an event in the life of his distinguished predecessor in Virginia. Raleigh was incomparably more famous than Smith. One event had secured his fame everlastingly. Condemned to execution by Queen Elizabeth, he was *not* marvelously spared. As wished, he was beheaded.[38]

Apparently on his return to Washington on March 2, Adams reviewed his essay on Smith and began a drastic revision amounting to a replacement. Soon his work on *one* paper confirmed him in a resolve to publish a *volume* of papers. The volume would be published by Scribner after the *History* and would be titled *Historical Essays*.

Adams's labor on his *Historical Essays* was so quiet it left no trace in his diary or letters till it was finished.[39] As a first step, he sorted his published and unpublished articles and sketches into two divisions. The larger group he would keep out of sight. The few he would publish would give readers, not a full idea of who he was or what he had written, but a view so limited as to be a reductive error.

What with wandering in the West and South, Adams had seen little of Mrs. Cameron. Yet his interest in her had not waned, and if possible his and Martha's mutual interest had grown. He recorded on March 10, 1889, that it was inauguration week and he had closed his doors and worked. A few visitors had appeared, but his "society" was "chiefly little Martha Cameron."

When at his desk in his study, Adams faced west, towards the open door to his library—a door he never closed. Behind him and to his left was a cupboard, built against the study's east wall. Martha one day learned that the cupboard contained a doll's house all her own. Increasingly from that moment, the study had two busy occupants, a man writing and a small girl playing.[40]

Wilson had printed twelve chapters of the new Volume I. Adams was reading proofs and was writing the second draft of the *Second Madison*. His mastery of its contents was such that he was writing backwards, working first on its concluding chapters.

Brooks visited and confirmed that his summer would be spent in Europe. Henry recorded on March 17 that his would be spent in Quincy. His "society" meanwhile consisted of "Martha Cameron and her mother."

Being intimate with Blaine, Hay was "deep in Blaine and Harrison office-distribution." He freely told Adams the inner history of the new administration. The news was funnier than expected. Adams's diary entry for March 31 included a hidden reference to *Democracy*. "President Harrison is amusing me by developing the characteristics peculiar to Indiana politicians. [Adams had given his novel a president from Indiana.] Hay's private account, derived from Blaine, of Harrison's behavior, is convulsing."

To speed the second draft of the *Second Madison*, Adams again hired a typist. For her guidance, he penned changes into the manuscripts of Books I and II. While he continued his rewriting "back from the end," he directed her to start "at the beginning." On April 7, he recorded that work was proceeding rapidly.

The pattern of Adams's friendships was taking an altered form. The change was partly initiated by King. In 1887, under an assumed name and without a license, King had begun a clandestine marriage to Ada Copeland, a black woman in New York. For King, up to a point, the union was serious. While he lived, he would stay faithfully by his mate, except that he would bar her, their children, and her relations and friends from knowing his true name and actual history.[41]

It might seem that Adams did not know what had happened. There is no evidence that he did. But it would have been safe for King to tell Adams his secret and ask that he not repeat it. As King surely knew, the basis of Adams's overall dependability was strict self-government. He could keep secrets because he had control of himself. He certainly would tell no tales he was asked not to tell. Perhaps, because told about Ada, he was more than ever King's faithful friend.[42]

A practical effect of King's marriage was that Adams's opportunities to see him were considerably diminished. By the same token, Adams depended more heavily for company on Hay.

Rumor had it that Harrison might give Hay the English mission. Had he done so, Hay's absence would have created a void in Adams's Washington life too big for anyone to fill. Fortunately for Adams, the mission was given to Robert Lincoln, son of the martyred president.

The elections of 1884 and 1888 had increasingly set Adams the task of maintaining good relations with friends who supported Blaine. As it related to King and Hay, the task was difficult enough. As it related to Theodore Roosevelt and Henry Cabot Lodge, it required two widely different responses. Roosevelt and Lodge had supported Blaine against Cleveland in 1884. While lending their support, they had formed a close personal and political friendship. Adams had met Roosevelt when he was still a youth, in Cairo in 1872.[43] He liked him, liked his wife even better, and felt no wish to quarrel with him about his political predilections, even regarding Blaine. Adams, however, had strong reason to quarrel with Lodge; for Lodge had gone over to Blaine after holding leading positions as an undoubted Independent.

Lodge's attaching himself to Blaine and the Republicans had ended his friendship with Adams, but Lodge did not know it. Neither did his children. Adams's manner towards their father did not seem to change. It remained exactly what it was before.[44]

Among Adams's reasons for going on as if still friendly with Lodge, one undoubtedly was a general principle. He believed in maintaining his political contacts, of course with friends, also with opponents, and even sometimes with enemies. A second reason was growing fondness for Constance and George, Lodge's elder children. The third and strongest was mutual esteem between Adams and Lodge's wife.

Anna Cabot Mills Lodge was herself in a difficult position. Since coming to Washington with her congressman husband, she had grown well-acquainted with John Hay. Also she grew friendly with Mrs. Cameron. All three persons—Mrs. Lodge, Hay, and Mrs. Cameron—were restive in their marriages. Rather quickly, without the knowledge of Mrs. Hay or Congressman Lodge, Hay and Mrs. Lodge formed a romantic attachment. A person well posted on the change was Mrs. Lodge's friend, Mrs. Cameron. In turn, Mrs. Cameron's knowledge gave her a key position in a constellation of four intimates: Mrs. Cameron, Adams, Hay, and Mrs. Lodge.[45]

In the spring of 1889, Senator Cameron decided that he, Mrs. Cameron, and Martha should spend the summer in Scotland. They made an early start. Writing to Cunliffe on April 29, Adams said:

. . . [Mrs. Cameron] sails tomorrow in the "City of New York," for Liverpool, with her husband and little daughter Martha. . . . I have told her to write you a note, and . . . take lunch with you. She is, as you know, my special ally. . . .

The Hays sail on the 15th, I think, and go to London direct. If you are in town, look them up. . . .

All America is on its way to Europe this month, including my brother Brooks[,] who leaves me to nurse my venerable mamma at Quincy till his return. . . .

. . . My mind is absorbed in the amusement of printing my history, which is now well under way, and will burst upon the world this year. The business of printing is like that of chopping straw or sawing wood, monotonous and fatiguing, but it absorbs one's mind. . . .

Adams traveled with Mrs. Cameron and Martha as far as Baltimore and returned to the capital. Mother and daughter proceeded to New York. After sailing, Mrs. Cameron sent a note from Sandy Hook by the pilot boat to *her* "special ally."[46] Adams had made no secret of wanting the company of Mrs. Cameron and Martha. Knowing he suffered in their absence, the Hays and others sympathized and, in his words, "gently soothed" him. To his surprise, he received a note from Mrs. Cameron, sent from her ship. The note made him very happy. Indeed it made him happier than he had been for several years.

On May 2, 1889, he began a strongly worded reply. "The receipt of your note, after I have gone through two melancholy days of rain and sympathy, is like seeing the sun again. I am infinitely grateful to you for writing it, and feel quite as though I were on board."

His letter marked a beginning. When in Japan, he had sent Hay, not mere letters, but extended letters written in instalments. In response to Mrs. Cameron's note, he had started writing *her* a letter that would continue in instalments.

Interrupting a mining journey, King stopped in Washington. On May 5, in the second instalment of his letter, Adams mentioned: ". . . I strolled with Clarence King and noticed that he was quite gray, almost like myself. Strange how suddenly the young turn gray nowadays."

In the third instalment, on May 9, Adams said he had heard

from the Hays (who heard it from Mrs. Lodge) that the Camerons without incident had arrived in Liverpool. He went on to say: "I am glad, and I will close these remarks and drop them into the box as I go to the War Department to rummage old papers. . . . I pass your house sometimes, always with a pang, wondering whether Martha was seasick or homesick, but hoping you have been really getting thorough satisfaction from your ocean, and enjoyment from your summer."

The Hays left for Europe, and Mrs. Lodge took charge of Adams. He began a new letter to Mrs. Cameron on May 15, 1889, saying, "Washington consists of Mrs[.] Cabot Lodge[,] with whom I dine tomorrow." He added on the 19th: "Theodore Roosevelt was at Lodge's. You know the poor wretch has consented to be Civil Service Commissioner and is to be with us in Washington next winter with his sympathetic little wife."

Talking with Roosevelt at the Lodges', Adams had learned that the commissioner was searching for a Washington house. "I told him he could have this if he wanted it; but nobody wants my houses though I offer them freely for nothing." The offer of 1603 H Street was serious and had no strings attached. Adams believed the *History* could be printed by January 1890, and he wished thereafter to be out of the country. The Roosevelts could make use of the house, rent free.

Roosevelt said no. Perhaps ideas that Adams was a supporter of Cleveland and a hopeless Democrat made acceptance difficult, but in any event such a house as Adams's was too enviable in location to be occupied by a junior official in the administration, even temporarily, as a matter of friendship. Yet Adams's offer worked a change. It made the Roosevelts feel they could visit 1603 H Street as valued friends. In consequence, there would soon be a constellation of *six* Washington intimates in which the Roosevelts were included. The leading person in the enlarged constellation would be Adams.[47]

Writing his *History*, Adams had learned a great deal about the evidence he lacked. He reacted by making last efforts to reach for documents. In February, he had written from Savannah to Dwight in Washington asking him to try to obtain a new French work, *Lettres inédites de Talleyrand à Napoleon, 1800–1809*. He needed the letters soon. They related to chapters of the *History* that Wilson was setting in type.

As Adams saw them, the weaknesses of the Madison volumes

related chiefly to the War of 1812. Hence his remark to Mrs. Cameron on May 9 about going to the War Department to rummage papers. One may suppose that his walks to that department were necessary and frequent.

On May 20, he received from his brother John an urgent request to come to Quincy ahead of time. John said their mother was practically insane and that Lucy Baxter needed support. ". . . some sympathetic co-operation must be speedily given Miss Baxter. . . . She was not asked or expected to take charge of an insane person and yet her position for ten days past has been of that character."

Henry had already been in touch with Lucy Baxter, had advanced his arrival eight days, and wished not to hurry it further. He left for New York on June 2, a Sunday, dined with King and La Farge late that evening, and stayed with them through Monday. He wrote to Hay the following Sunday:

> . . . on reaching Quincy last Tuesday I was received by the unexpected announcement that my mother within three days had suddenly sunk into lethargy and was not expected to live through the night. She lived in fact two days, and died at last on Thursday evening at half past ten o'clock. . . .
>
> I shall remain here till the autumn without in any way changing my arrangements. Miss Baxter will continue in charge of the establishment, and Dwight will run his department [the family archives and libraries]. . . .
>
> King seemed fairly well. . . . He has by this time started for Mexico, and will return broken up as usual. . . . Lafarge [sic] was very bright and infantile; quite childlike in his views of men, women and painting.

In his diary that same day, Adams recorded additional details. His sister Mary had told him the news about their mother's lethargy. When he first saw her, his mother was unconscious. During Wednesday and Thursday, he had watched her sinking.

It was of course an accident that Abigail Brooks Adams died at the Old House at a moment when Brooks was in Europe and Henry was back in residence. The accident gave Henry the appearance of being lord of the mansion, chief member of the family, and principal heir. He did not want the appearance and went so far as to say that Lucy Baxter was in charge. Yet the appearance conformed to a fact. He *was* the principal Adams and had been for a very long time.

The truth of his status was implicit in some of his expressions in the June 9 instalment of a letter to Mrs. Cameron. He said: "Apparently I am to be the last of the family to occupy this house which has been our retreat in all times of trouble for just one hundred years. I suppose if two Presidents could come back here to eat out their hearts in disappointment and disgust, one of their unknown descendants can bore himself for a single season to close up the family den. None of us want it, or will take it. We have too many houses already, and no love for this."

Of the houses owned by the Adamses, the house they least wished to keep was the one in Boston at 57 Mount Vernon Street. Henry directed Dwight to initiate the removal of its contents. He seemed to want it sold. He may have wished, too, that the Old House be sold.

Condoling letters began to come. Adams replied with unusual candor. He wrote to Rebecca Dodge, "Even those who cling most to life seem glad at last to leave it. . . ." He seemed to say he was approaching a terminus. He told Eliza Gilman Lippitt, "My mother's death severs . . . the last tie that binds me to my old life, and probably another year will find me fairly at the end."

Mrs. Cameron wrote condolingly from Scotland. A day after getting her letter, Adams saw news in the press of the death of old Simon Cameron. In the circumstances, Senator Cameron, Mrs. Cameron, and Martha would possibly all return, but Adams was not hopeful enough to believe it. He wrote to Mrs. Cameron: ". . . [I] hardly know whether to write to you in England, or to expect your return. On the whole I imagine that, even if your husband should be obliged to come, you will probably wait till September. . . ."

All the Camerons *were* returning. The arrangement was new evidence that Mrs. Cameron wanted Adams's company as often as she could get it. When apprised of her coming, he supposed that mother and daughter might pass some weeks at Pitch Pine Hill. He at once suggested the idea, advising the mother: ". . . I should consider myself under great obligations to anyone who would run the house a month or two. . . . If you will consent to go there, I will offer every inducement, and am not sure but what I would offer to pay a handsome premium." Viewed as a message from a widower to a less-than-happily married woman, the sentences mixed a large amount of practicality with a remarkably small amount of ardor. He and she were dealing with each other on changed, closer terms. Yet his attitude remained quite circumspect and cautious.

With practice, Adams had learned how to write his *History* without waste of energy. Writing from Quincy on June 27, 1889, he said the work was moving "like a limited slow freight train, but will git thar." He was near the midpoint of the third draft of the

Second Madison, and Wilson was close to finishing the fourth of the eight smaller volumes.

Martha wrote to Dordy en route from Scotland, presumably by dictating to her mother. (The letter is missing. It possibly was enclosed with a letter from Mrs. Cameron, also missing.) Following the arrival of Martha's letter, Adams stopped keeping his diary.

Replying, he spoke of houses. "Don't you think you could make me a visit at Quincy . . . ? I have a garden and a pond, and a brook where Possum chases the frogs, and I have Prince and Daisy in the stable, and cows; and you can come and play with me in the library, and have as many dolls and playthings as you want. Then I have a whole house for you at Beverly, and you can go and dig sand on the beach. . . ."

During the next few days, he realized he had to make a fresh effort to obtain British documents. He needed a particular letter from Earl Bathurst to Sir George Prevost; also possible surviving instructions in regard to the invasion of the United States in 1814; similar instructions "given to General Ross about the attack on Washington"; and "the instructions to General Pakenham about the expedition to New Orleans." On July 14, he wrote to Cunliffe asking him to seek the papers at the Record Office.[48]

In a similar document-hunting spirit, he planned an excursion to Canada during which he would visit the national archives at Ottawa. He hoped to take seven guests. He explained to Mrs. Cameron: "I shall carry Dwight, and Mrs[.] Baxter, and perhaps Elsie Adams, Molly's sister, and three of the Hooper children, with their father; a party of eight; and we are to go to Niagara, Ottawa, down the St[.] Lawrence to Montreal and Quebec, and then perhaps up the Saguenay."

He meanwhile was reminded that historians were common in the United States and that their newest books were appearing constantly in bookstores. The reminder took the form of a biography of George Washington by Henry Cabot Lodge and the first volume of *The Winning of the West* by Theodore Roosevelt. Adams looked into copies or at least saw their covers. It then occurred to him with sudden force that volumes of his *History* would be published very shortly. Violently he wrote to Hay:

> . . . I see that both Cabot and Teddy Roosevelt are on the shopcounters in apparent self-satisfaction, which makes me as sick as Possum to reflect that I too can no longer avoid that disgusting and driveling exhibition of fatuous condescension. All books should be posthumous except those that should be buried before death, and they should stay buried.

Holt chose the same moment to write Adams a letter to ask whether he could tell an inquirer whether the author of *Democracy* was an American. Adams consented. "Tell him: Yes!" But Holt had an additional question in mind. He wished something could be done to create a new wave of sales for the novel.

On that score, Adams resisted. He preferred that *Democracy* be treated as a famous mystery of the past. He answered, ". . . I want it to remain forgotten, in order that a certain interest may still attach to it, and that the author may avoid the sort of notoriety which is the curse of authorship as it is of politics."

Mrs. Cameron went with Martha to Newport. Brooks returned from Europe, socialized with fellow Bostonians, and became so taken with Mrs. Lodge's sister Evelyn, known as Daisy, that he proposed immediate marriage and was accepted.

Henry traveled to Canada with his party and, despite confusions, succeeded in visiting the archives in Ottawa. Mrs. Lodge grew fearful that he might not be back in time to attend Brooks and Daisy's wedding. She wrote to him urging haste.

The plan for the trip to Canada had predated the plan for Brooks's wedding, and Henry could not comply. Writing from Ottawa on September 3, he asked Mrs. Lodge to give her sister a message. "Tell her that I will obey her wishes in everything, just as much as though I were present, and that as for loving and honoring I need no church service to make me do it."

On the same day, Adams wrote to Mrs. Cameron. He mentioned that his Canadian trip had been turned around—had begun at the Saguenay River and would end at Niagara Falls. "We expect to reach the Clifton House Thursday, and to start on our return as soon as I have looked at three or four battle-fields."

In the same letter, he named the principal cause that underlay his writing to Mrs. Cameron at all. Without being love, the cause was something very like it. "My only excuse for writing is that I really must imagine you to be somewhere about. My only surviving notion of happiness is the sense that some one, to whom one is attached, is sitting in the next room."

Brooks and Daisy stayed at Pitch Pine Hill immediately following their wedding. After they left, Mrs. Cameron and Martha were free to move in. They soon arrived and enjoyed being back.

Henry had returned from Canada and was again at Quincy. In about two weeks, he would be leaving the Old House. Having come back to the mansion for three last summers, he would be glad of a final departure.

Dwight had received an inquiry from Scribner concerning the publisher's intended announcement about the *History*. Scribner had the impression that much of the value of the work arose from its author's making use of unpublished Adams family papers. Dwight delayed replying till Henry's return and then sent the publisher a corrective letter.

Amazing though it might seem, Scribner until that moment had been given practically nothing by Adams or Dwight in the way of an account of the *History*: what it was, what it was intended to achieve, and what possible buyers might best be told about its author. Necessarily, the letter Dwight sent on September 22, 1889, was written with Adams's full knowledge. The letter said as little as possible about the author. It fixed most strongly, not on the *History*, but on the evidence from which it was drawn. Dwight said: "While Mr. Adams has made use of such of his family papers as related to the period of his work[,] his chief sources of material have been governmental archives at home and in Europe. It is upon this new material from Spain, France[,] England and the U. S. [that] it would be desirable to dwell . . . as the larger part of the foreign documents has never before been consulted, or even opened for consultation, by an historical writer—and the important points of the history were found in those documents."

There matters might have rested; but Dwight, under Adams's guidance, added two sentences which, though helpful to a point, could be read to say that Adams's work was an administrative history much concerned with diplomacy. Dwight said: "Though it is not purely a diplomatic history—diplomacy necessarily plays an enormous part in it[,] as the four administrations he treats were chiefly concerned in foreign affairs[,] which affected our national existence—not alone our prosperity. The story has never before been told."[49]

Mrs. Cameron was free to go to New York with Adams on any train he thought convenient. A series of messages made possible an agreement that she and Martha would join him at the Boston station. He wrote on Tuesday, October 1, 1889, "The tickets are taken." He said he would be waiting for mother and daughter after 9:00 on Thursday morning.

His mood had greatly brightened. "I am eager now to get away and to find myself under your protection again. Don't fail!"

25

NOAH AFLOAT

The trip with Mrs. Cameron and Martha was not less pleasant because Martha said on the way that she did not like her mother's manners.[1] In New York, Adams delivered his companions to Senator Cameron. He proceeded alone to Washington, hired a cook, and set his household in motion. His intentions were settled. He meant to complete his shares of the work of publishing his *History* and his *Historical Essays* by July 1, 1890. Thereafter he would travel.

Uncertainty centered in his having two destinations. Beginning in Japan in 1886, he had talked about going to China. Recently he had been saying he wished to visit the Sandwich Islands and Fiji. The prospective journeys pointed in different directions and corresponded to different aspects of his personal history.

It can be doubted that Fiji was one of the places he most wished to visit. He apparently had been drawn towards the South Seas as a result of reading two books in early youth, the *Voyages* of Captain Cook and Herman Melville's earliest romance, *Typee*. Thanks to Cook, he wished to visit Tahiti. Thanks to Melville, he wished to visit Nuku Hiva in the Marquesas.[2] Originally romantic, his wishes had acquired historical and geological colorings. He wanted to live with Polynesians whose recent forebears had lacked knowledge of metals and written language; and he wanted to study coral reefs, which according to Darwin could be explained by a subsidence of the ocean floor.[3] For both purposes, a convenient stopping place would be Samoa.

When Adams first spoke of going to China, he gave the impression that his object would be to see and collect Chinese art.[4] Yet, for him, China never simply meant China. It chiefly meant Central Asia.

In 1858 in Berlin, Adams had visited Alexander von Humboldt, whose fame rested in part on explorations in Central Asia.

After visiting Humboldt, Henry suggested to Senator Sumner that they drop everything and go to Siberia. Sumner did not respond, but the suggestion had a sequel. At the time, an American from upstate New York, Raphael Pumpelly, was training in Germany at the University of Freiberg with the purpose of becoming a geologist and an expert on mines. He returned to America in 1860, worked first in Arizona, and next was employed as a geologist in Japan. In 1864, he conducted explorations in China. Despite the onset of winter, he then traveled by cart from Peking across the Gobi desert to Siberia, traversed the ice of Lake Baikal by sleigh, hurried by carriage the enormous distance to Nijni Novgorod, the terminus of the railroad in Russia, and proceeded by trains and ships to St. Petersburg, Paris, London, and New York.

Pumpelly's journey around the world became a matter of interest to well-placed persons. He was introduced to Congressman Sam Hooper and met Dr. Robert Hooper. In 1870, by arrangement with Henry Holt, a Yale classmate, he published an account of his journey, *Across America and Asia*; and in 1869–1871 he lived in Cambridge and lectured on ore deposits at Harvard. Other engagements took him away from Massachusetts, but not before he became acquainted with Alex Agassiz, Clover Hooper, and the Adams brothers, Henry and Brooks.[5]

What most recommended Pumpelly to other Americans was an idea of history. He advanced a theory that a certain part of Central Asia, currently desert, might once have been an inland sea; that civilization may have started on its shores; and that all the peoples who spoke languages grouped as Aryan were descendants of early migrants from the area. Fanciful or not, the theory pointed to a particular place as a starting place of civilization, and it elicited strong interest among his acquaintances, Henry Adams included.[6]

In 1879, King chose Pumpelly to prepare a census of mineral industries for the U. S. Geological Survey, directing the work from Newport. Close relations between Pumpelly and Henry and Clover Adams did not begin until 1884, when he twice stayed at 1607 H Street.[7] By then, the Adamses had formed a settled interest in travel and exploration in Central Asia, including all of Turkestan, Tibet, and Mongolia. They actively supported Americans who went to such places.[8]

After Clover's death, Henry searched for persons who would be willing to accompany him on distant travels. In September 1888, he mentioned in passing that Alex Agassiz's son George might be his companion to Fiji and Tibet.[9] In May 1889, thinking he might organize "a sort of Marco Polo caravan," he visited the Russian chargé d'affaires in Washington, Baron Rosen, to inform him that a group of Americans might wish to travel in parts of Central Asia subject to Russian rule. Rosen unencouragingly remarked that the proposed destinations were dirty, but Adams remained attracted by what he called "our Asiatic Mystery." His great dream was to travel from Peking across the Gobi desert to Kashgar in western China.[10]

Thus two journeys—one to Kashgar and another to the South Seas—were outlined in Adams's thoughts. He was unsure which to take first. It would require a good deal of managing to take either. If he took either, he would wish also to try the other.

On October 2, 1889, Charles Scribner and Sons published Adams's *History of the United States of America during the First Administration of Thomas Jefferson*, two volumes, $4.00. The firm sent copies to newspapers and magazines for review. Persons selected to review the volumes faced an unusual problem: their almost unparalleled plenitude. They were clearly a mere first instalment of a longer work. Yet their contents were so many-sided that a reviewer could feel hard-pressed to know what to look at.

Plenitude was conjoined to a blank. The volumes lacked a preface. They afforded no preliminary hint as to the plan of the work, no statement explaining why a *History of the United States* should start with the first administration of the country's third president, nor even a statement saying in what year the narrative would stop.[11]

An all-too-predictable truth emerged in the reviews. It was that Adams would be accorded very divergent sorts of treatment in Boston and New York. Boston's most popular magazine was the *Atlantic Monthly*. The magazine obtained from an anonymous writer, evidently a Bostonian, a review, "Recent Books on American History," appraising three works, including the volumes containing Adams's *First Jefferson*. The review began by saying that books on American history had been "descending upon the country in a flood." Turning to Adams—both his already published volumes and the yet-to-be-published volumes—it greeted his performance with faint praise. It said—falsely—that his *History* was "overmuch expected." ". . . nearly a score of years must have elapsed since it was first whispered abroad that this work was in process of creation; and when a member of the historic Adams family, presumably steeped in fitness for this especial labor, devotes so long a time to incubation[,] the world has a right to anticipate a great production. The anticipation is very nearly fulfilled; Mr. Adams has given us a history which, if the subsequent volumes maintain an equality of merit with the first two, will be almost great."[12]

The mood of the Boston review was languidly appreciative, as if the reviewer could learn little from Adams, having little to learn. A representative passage concerned the Louisiana purchase. The passage said the historian had tried to be light and amusing.

> The most interesting and novel portion of his work relates to the acquisition of Louisiana, and the history of this transaction has never been so exhaustively given. Mr. Adams keeps us long in Europe with Bonaparte, whom he hates and would like to despise, and no short time in St. Domingo with Toussaint Louverture, whom he rather fancies and sketches kindly and well. The scenery is more picturesque than the American stage setting, and we linger not unwillingly to see Napoleon take his perfumed bath before our very eyes, and to hear naughty *bons mots* concerning the Queen of Spain. We forgive Mr. Adams for putting all this into his story, where it does not at all belong, because Jefferson's career certainly needs a little lighting up, or one would get sleepy in its monotonous half-light.

In the same languid spirit, the Boston review charged that Adams was "too obviously possessed by a carping, critical spirit"— that his volumes showed "a certain contradictoriness of temper, which is too often perceptible throughout, as though the truth were now to be told for the first time, and all the blunders of earlier groping and ill-informed writers were to be exposed and swept away." Significantly, the charges had no basis in the volumes, which never carped and never criticized previous writers. The charges were based instead on mistaken gossip much valued in Boston-Cambridge to the effect that Adams was a caustic, contentious person who was nothing if not conceited.

A different attitude was shown by a two-part review in the *New York Sun*, published on November 24 and December 1, 1889. The newspaper assigned Adams's volumes to a writer who, except in one respect, tried to form an opinion from the volumes themselves.[13] The exception was the author's lineage. The reviewer knew that Adams was descended from two presidents and a minister to England. After considering the volumes and the author's parentage, the reviewer offered an opinion.

> It may at first sight seem unreasonable to expect a just estimate of Thomas Jefferson from a great-grandson of John Adams. We should bear in mind, however, that the author of these volumes is also a grandson of John Quincy Adams, who, far from sharing his father's intensely Federalist opinions, showed himself in the matter of the Louisiana purchase a far more consistent and resolute advocate of a strict construction of the Constitution than Jefferson himself. It is in the judicial, impartial, conscientious spirit of John Quincy Adams,

although without a trace of his censorious and waspish temper, that this narrative is penned.

The review in the *New York Sun* was possibly the best-considered judgment of the *History* that would be published in Adams's lifetime. In its first part, without delay, it placed his work among the best American histories. It said that he had begun to publish an addition to historical literature "which will take rank with Bancroft's" and "is likely to long remain without a rival in the field that the author has marked out for survey."

The New York review was quick to say that Adams's work was unprefaced and unexplained. In the absence of positive information, the writer offered an intelligent though erroneous guess. ". . . [Adams] nowhere indicates the point to which he purposes to continue his history, but . . . we opine that it will be carried no further than the close of Monroe's second term. The same delicacy and discretion which forbade him to deal with the Administration of his great-grandfather may also disincline him to discuss his grandfather's."[14]

The chief purpose of the New York review was to afford the *Sun's* readers an ample foretaste of Adams's beginning chapters by quoting extracts. Without knowing that the opening chapters were written as one of the work's many books, the reviewer said they "form, so to speak, the vestibule of this capacious history." The reviewer summed up: ". . . in the extracts here presented, the author's literary competence, his ripeness of culture and fulness of information, his breadth of sympathy and unswerving impartiality, speak for themselves."

The New York review made no attempt to guess the drift that Adams's *History* might show itself to have when all its volumes were published. In its second part, however, it stressed that Adams had freed himself from the curse of *English* history: party bias. "The time has gone by when the purport of English history could be acceptably interpreted by men of undisguised Whig or Tory predilections. Political bias ought to be as misplaced in the outfit of an American historian. The author of this book is neither a Federalist nor a State Rights Democrat. It may fairly be said of him, as was said of his grandfather, John Quincy Adams, that he is both the one and the other. He can take either point of view with equal perspicacity and equal sympathy. . . ."[15]

Also, in its second part, the New York review came to grips with Adams's volumes in a way that showed appreciation of meaning. The review turned to a single strand of Adams's narrative. It said that Adams recounted President Jefferson's failure to carry into practice the strict-constructionist principles he was elected to enforce. Indeed Adams recounted Jefferson's carrying *opposite* principles into practice, in effect continuing and intensifying what Presidents Washington and Adams had started.

The strand selected was one of the most ironic and disturbing in the *History*. It necessarily had imposed strains on Henry Adams when writing the *First Jefferson*. Similarly it imposed strains on the reviewer. The latter said: "It is with extraordinary clearness that Mr. Adams brings out the strange and novel aspects of the political situation at the outset of Jefferson's first term, and it is with equal lucidity that he explains the change which had come over the country by the close of four short years. In the inaugural address, delivered on March 4, 1801, the new President declared, in a spirit rather conciliatory than prophetic, 'We are all Republicans, we are all Federalists.' The prediction was to be fulfilled in a sense which the author [President Jefferson] can hardly have expected. The next Presidential election was to show that nearly all the voters of the United States had become Republicans, in the sense of being willing to vote for Jefferson. But Jefferson himself—to demonstrate this is the capital merit, if not the purpose, of this history—had done more than all Federalists combined to establish Federalist principles."[16]

With some differences, Adams was leading his usual Washington life. Niece Molly came for a second winter. Cecil Spring Rice returned on a temporary mission that led to one less temporary. Theodore and Edith Roosevelt rented a house on Jefferson Place and often visited.[17] Constance Lodge begged a room. Martha Cameron appeared continuously. On November 5, 1889, Adams wrote to Lucy Baxter: "Constance Lodge is with us now, and Martha comes in, two or three times a day. Today she left me her doll Gretchen for me to mend."

Adams was busy. He was finishing the third draft of the *Second Madison*, supplying copy to Wilson as fast as copy could be printed, and rapidly correcting proofs. He also was revising materials for his *Historical Essays*. He in addition was going through his files, finding papers he intended to preserve. Patiently too, but without success, he was casting about for someone to join him on an expedition to "Fiji," as he continued to say, or to "Pekin" and "the desert of Gobi."

He meanwhile imposed a rule that his friends should not speak to him about his *History*. ". . . [I] do not allow the book to be mentioned in my hearing. . . ." Making some pretence of imposing a parallel avoidance on himself, he claimed not to read the reviews. ". . . I never read a newspaper. . . ." But Dwight was there in the house and was *collecting* the reviews. It accordingly can be assumed that Adams heard about the more important ones and knew what they mainly said.

From the review in the *Atlantic*, he would learn only that Boston criticisms of him—doubtless also of Clover—were being repeated by force of habit. From the review in the *New York Sun*, he would learn two things of positive interest. One was that his *History* was being misread in the way he had wished it misread, as an administrative history principally attentive to Presidents Jefferson and Madison. The other was that he was being granted praise he could live with. The *Sun* merely paired him with George Bancroft. Great scientists and great writers—Darwin, Milton, and comparable figures—were not mentioned. That the *History* was an epic was apparently not thought of. In that sense, serious acknowledgment of the *History* had not started, and Adams was the contented, hidden agent who had contrived that it be postponed.

The publication of the *History* in two-volume instalments at half-year spaced intervals necessitated an index for each instalment. In December 1889, Adams and Dwight discovered that the index prepared by the publisher for the second instalment was deficient. Dwight informed Brownell: ". . . the Index prepared for the next pair of volumes . . . is not satisfactory. . . . This causes us to think that in future we must take the matter into our own hands. . . . It will be easier for us to do the entire work than to patch and correct that of your Indexer."[18]

Till then, Adams and Scribner had failed to make plans concerning a necessary feature of the work: a general index. If Adams was to prepare it, the general index would require, as he said, "at least a hundred pages." It happened too that his *Second Madison* was longer than preceding segments of the work. It gave a detailed account of the War of 1812, supported with numerous maps.

These considerations led to a change of plan. Adams informed the publisher on January 12, 1890, that he could not accommodate his "last four years" and the general index in two volumes. "I shall have to make three. . . ."[19] Scribner agreed to the change, and preparations went forward to issue the *History* in nine volumes instead of eight.[20]

In keeping with the changed plan, Adams had to decide which chapters of his *Second Madison* would appear in Volumes VI, VIII, and IX. While so deciding, he wrote letters to the publisher containing last comments on the form of the work. In one comment, he made clear that the work's "conclusion" was made up of *many* chapters.[21] In another, he said the last four chapters could properly be termed an "epilogue."[22]

Here it has been said repeatedly that Adams wrote his *History* in books. Judging from internal evidence, he persisted in this respect to the end. It has been noted too that he destroyed his records relating to any titles he may have affixed to the books of his *Second Madison*. It is not difficult, however, to furnish possible titles.

Book I	*The Campaign of 1813 against Canada*	8 chapters
Book II	*The Campaign in the Southwest: Russian Mediation*	8 chapters
Book III	*Campaigns of 1814*	8 chapters
Book IV	*Last Battles: the Achievement of Peace*	8 chapters
Book V	*The Nation Secured and United*	8 chapters

Apportioning the *Second Madison* between the last three volumes of the Scribner edition, Adams could have made the book divisions clearly visible, though unmentioned. He partly did so. He put sixteen chapters in Volume VII and thus silently created a volume that contained Books I and II. Conversely, he put fourteen chapters in Volume VIII and ten chapters—plus the general index—in volume IX. So doing, he split Book IV and carried its climactic chapters over to the start of a last volume. The overall effect was concealment. As before, readers could be expected not to apprehend that the *History* had a completely developed structure of parts, books, and chapters.[23]

Structure was a precondition of intelligibility. If Adams had permitted its book divisions, titles, and numbers to appear in his *History* when published, the structure would have given the *meaning* of the work all possible accessibility and clearness. He instead made the *History* seem as little structured as possible. In the eyes of its buyers and readers, the nine Scribner volumes would present a remarkably undifferentiated run of text—a long road with few signs.

It none the less was true that the structure of the *History* survived intact.[24] Structure was integrated with content. Structure helped determine the wording of the beginnings and endings of chapters. It thus would be possible in a future age to reprint the *History* in a form that would make its structure visible. Once that happened, Adams would be more easily read, better understood, and much more valued.[25]

Among the sons and daughters Adams knew in Washington, the eldest was his recent live-in guest, Constance Lodge. Emboldened by the marriage of her Aunt Daisy to her host's brother Brooks, she had addressed him as "Uncle Henry." As she used it, "Uncle Henry" seemed meant for wide adoption by members of the younger generation, male and female.[26] Soon the name was used not merely by his Adams nephews and nieces and Clover's Hooper nieces, but also the younger Lodges, possibly all the younger Hays, and even young Roosevelts. When spoken by these young persons, the name was a pointed comment. It expressed their knowing that Adams was easy to approach, sociable, and always kind.[27]

A comment still more pointed was one he himself invented. In the past, he had called himself a modern Noah.[28] Early in 1890, he gave the idea a particular form: that of Noah floating in the ark. He wrote to Cunliffe: ". . . I have a niece staying with me [Molly Adams] who helps to tell me gossip. The doves go out of the ark every night and return with dinners to tell about, but they bring astonishingly little food for Noah at home." He wrote similarly to Lucy Baxter, "I sit in my ark, and send out my doves—Dwight, Hay and Molly—to pick up information at dinners, but the result is hardly one olive-branch."

The image suited the facts of Adams's past, present, and future. His past was drowned by Clover's catastrophe. He was alive and safe, but he had no knowledge of where he would be when the flood subsided, nor much idea of what he might better do.[29]

The image also reflected a current, invisible catastrophe. Adams belonged by origin to an earlier America that he thought deeply interesting. This was the America storied in his *History*. As his *History* passed from his hands to those of anonymous readers, he was losing it and losing the America it contained. He moreover was losing that America without fully knowing what America he would be in when his loss was complete.[30]

In both applications, the image of Noah afloat reflected his being a heavy loser, still alive. It also pictured him much in doubt, with chances of future gain.

On February 8, 1890, Scribner published Volumes III and IV: *History of the United States of America during the Second Administration of Thomas Jefferson*. Adams was making new efforts "to organise my

Gobi expedition" and also was readying for a stay in the South Seas.

Wilson was printing the Scribner edition just slowly enough to be worrisome. Adams informed the publisher on February 14 that he meant to sail from San Francisco "for the east" by July 1 and that the date of his return was "altogether doubtful." "I am for that reason anxious not to be caught at the last moment with half the Index undone. It would be awkward to correct proofsheets at Kashgar or Tahiti."

William W. Rockhill, an acquaintance at the Smithsonian Institution, had recently conducted explorations in Tibet and Mongolia. Adams asked him to dinner. ". . . we talked a little Gobi."

Another acquaintance, Charles W. Stoddard, author of *South Sea Idylls*, joined Adams for breakfast. Possibly they talked Tahiti.[31]

There seemed every prospect that Adams would soon be somewhere on the Pacific, yet his feelings were divided. The voyage he most wanted to take was the voyage back in time to the years when he and Clover were newly married. He especially remembered the summers of 1874 and 1875 at Beverly Farms, when he and Clover had lived in a rented cottage and were building Pitch Pine Hill. He confided to Lucy Baxter, ". . . no amount of Stoicism can prevent one from hankering, not for the future but for the past. . . ."

Adams had the problem of being a man who had such feelings that he could marry only his no-longer-living wife. In the early months of 1890, he was constantly seen with another unavailable person, the young wife of Senator Cameron. Weather permitting, Adams and Mrs. Cameron were riding together on Prince and Daisy. The avowed reason was her wanting to lose some weight. An advantage for both riders was conversation out of earshot. She and Adams had seldom been by themselves, indoors or out. Long frequent rides was their chance, and they were taking the rides without compunction.[32]

In early April, Edward Hooper and his daughters came to 1603 H Street for their usual spring visit. Niece Louisa knew she was not to mention Uncle Henry's *History*, but she had been reading it and she had the temerity to continue reading it in his house without his knowledge by stealing volumes from his study. She temporarily succeeded. Then Uncle Henry noticed that a copy of Volume IV was missing. He found it lying on her bed, stole it back, and restored it to its shelf. Loulie however stole it again and brought on a negotiation the result of which was his permission to do with his writings as she pleased.[33]

The episode indicated that there were persons who would try hard to read Adams's *History* even in the face of discouragements invented by the author. Yet the matter had a dark, second face.

The discouragements Adams devised, all rather simple, were sufficiently effective to insure that sales of the *History* would be limited and many readers would balk if urged to read it.[34] An effective barrier was length in pages. As printed in nine volumes, the work had something of the look of a novel, except that the text, not counting maps or indexes, would fill almost 3,800 pages. Just to turn that many pages would be a labor many readers would shrink from.[35]

Scribner was sensitive to length and anticipated only moderate sales. He readied 1500 copies of Volumes I through VI. The reviews were more enthusiastic than otherwise. Sales continued, and the publisher readied more copies, in small amounts.[36] During the first twelve years of publication, sufficient volumes would be sold to comprise about 2200 full sets.[37]

Quite apart from Adams and Scribner's actions, a condition was in play that would prevent the *History's* meaning from being known. Pertinent evidence was an early review, perhaps the earliest to appear. The review was published in the *New York Times* on October 27, 1889. It concerned Volumes I and II and filled two and a half columns. Much of its space was given to the sale of Louisiana to the United States.

The issues involved need explanation. On November 9, 1799, when Bonaparte seized control of France, Talleyrand had already initiated a policy of rebuilding the French colonial empire. As judged by Adams, Talleyrand, though exceedingly corrupt, was a patriot. His colonial policy was meant to serve the national interest of France. Bonaparte made Talleyrand's policy his own but secretly changed it in such ways as would make it highly military and morally repulsive.[38]

As has been noticed, Bonaparte aimed to wrest control of St. Domingo from its black leaders, deport the principal leaders to France, and restore the remaining blacks to slavery. He also aimed to use Louisiana as a source of food and other supplies for French centers in the West Indies, chiefly St. Domingo and Guadeloupe. He failed. According to Adams, the armies Bonaparte sent to St. Domingo fell prey to yellow fever and to resistance by the black masses so desperate as to include their destruction of their own property and group suicides. In view of the failure, but at a great sacrifice of French national interest, Napoleon sold Louisiana—but not St. Domingo—to a hated democracy, the United States.

The reviewer for the *New York Times* gave an appearance of being greatly taken with the chapters in which Adams told the story of Napoleon's effort, its failure, and his decision to trade a French dependency for an influx of cash. Saying that the chapters were "extremely entertaining," the reviewer passed along some selected scenes. Yet in the process, the reviewer so altered the story that the difference between Talleyrand and Napoleon's policies was smoothed away, Adams was made to seem Napoleon's defender, and every trace of the attempted re-enslavement disappeared! In the crucial passage, the reviewer misleadingly said: "It seems difficult to conceive of Napoleon as a possible ruler of the beneficent and civilizing sort. But in the year 1800 he had still this path open to him, and Mr. Adams shows that the state papers of the time prove that the intention of Napoleon was not European war, but colonial development."[39]

The simplest explanation of this response may perhaps be the best. American reviewers and readers were disposed to welcome whatever Adams might publish that could be felt as agreeable.[40] They would hurry past, un-read, or invert whatever affected them as disagreeable.[41]

The attitudes shown by Adams as a historian were the converse of the attitudes shown by self-comforting reviewers and readers. He did not *create* the events recounted in his amazing narrative. He *found* the events in the evidence. Or, to speak more strictly, by dint of hard study, cold logic, and a tireless imagination, he *reconstructed* the events. That done, he also *accepted* them.

The events formed a story. Or rather, to be precise, the events that Adams reconstructed formed a congeries of stories. What his *History* concerns is a series of interdependent yet separate human efforts, and appropriately he wrote his narrative somewhat as Shakespeare wrote many of his plays: in the form of more-or-less parallel plots.

The plots are clearly defined and for the most part easy to follow. Their result is the swift emergence of a unified United States—a great democracy. Here, however, the issue is not the many plots or their result. It instead is the great event with which the *History* gets into motion. Once again, that event is Bonaparte's frustrated effort in the West Indies.

From the instant he appears in Adams's *History*, Napoleon is Satan. The passage is the opening lines of Book III in the *First Jefferson*. The lines borrow words and phrases from Milton's *Paradise Lost*.[42]

Most picturesque of all figures in modern history, Napoleon Bonaparte, like Milton's Satan on his throne of state, although surrounded
by a group of figures little less striking than himself, sat unapproachable on his bad eminence; or, when he moved, the dusky air felt an
unusual weight. His conduct was often mysterious, and sometimes so
arbitrary as to seem insane; but later years have thrown on it a lurid
illumination.

The passage announced a literary event. Adams's *History*, without ceasing to be scientific, and though in prose, was a Miltonic
epic of a new kind in which God was nowhere evident and Satan
was vividly present and ever-active. The passage was fair warning
that a mysterious ruler—"a freak of nature," as Adams also calls
him—would figure in the *History* as an unsuccessful architect and
executor of events on a tremendous scale.[43] It was warning too that
Adams meant to deal with questions of good and evil.

Napoleon reappears as Satan in the first chapter of Book IV of
the *Second Jefferson*. This time the ascription of devilry is furnished,
not by Adams, but by Lucien, one of Napoleon's brothers. The
occasion is a meeting between Lucien and the emperor in 1807 in
Mantua. They are talking about what part of the empire Lucien
may be given and what parts may go to others in the family. Adams
quotes Lucien's record of the talk:

> "As for you, choose!" As he [the emperor] pronounced these words
> . . . his eyes sparkled with a flash of pride which seemed to me Satanic;
> he struck a great blow with his hand, spread out broadly in the middle
> of the immense map of Europe which was extended on the table by
> the side of which we were standing. "Yes, choose," he said; "you see I
> am not talking in the air. All this is mine, or will soon belong to me; I
> can dispose of it already. Do you want Naples? I will take it from
> Joseph, who, by the bye, does not care for it; he prefers Morfontaine.
> Italy,—the most beautiful jewel in my imperial crown? Eugene is but
> viceroy, and far from despising it he hopes only that I shall give it to
> him, or at least leave it to him if he survives me: he is likely to be
> disappointed in waiting, for I shall live ninety years: I must, for the
> perfect consolidation of my empire. . . ."[44]

The suggestion that Napoleon is Satan remains conspicuous in the
History.[45] And among Adams's reasons for including him, apparently the strongest was that his evil presence would indicate the
ultimate scope of the work and the seriousness of what the work
had to say.

It was Lincoln who said that if slavery was not wrong, nothing
was wrong. It was Henry Adams who disclosed that a European
arch-enslaver attempted re-enslavement of blacks in the Western
Hemisphere and was resisted successfully by the blacks. The theme
was the same in both cases; Adams's *History* was writing at its most

important; his narrative was both a great work of historical science and *the* American epic; and its literary superiorities made the meaning of its initiating books and chapters lightning clear.

Unfortunately, Adams had his fellow Americans to contend with. He and his *History* were one thing; the America of 1889 and 1890 was quite another. As the review in the *New York Times* had evidenced, heroic force, clarity, and openness on Adams's part would not suffice to get reviewers or readers to let his *History* say what it said and mean what it meant. The *History* was not at fault. Admittedly Adams's narrative was unprefaced. Admittedly it was printed on too-numerous pages. Admittedly the titles and numbers of its twenty books were withheld. But its many *stories* were all intact, and all were told extremely well.

Taken together, the stories showed a decisive increase of freedom. His narrative recounted not so much re-enslavement as resistance to re-enslavement; not so much dictatorship and autocracy as resistance to dictatorship and autocracy; not so much government by a few as increasing government by the many. In chapter after chapter, the movement of events was from conservatism to innovation, from bigotry to science, from tyranny to government by consent. If his expression in the narrative was very strong, it was nowhere excessively strong. Instead the problem was that reviewers and readers, while perhaps well-intentioned, were incapable and weak. The writer had been ready to write. By and large, readers were unready to read.[46]

Adams and Lucy Baxter had formed a relation like that of brother and sister. His letters to her were forthright. He told her he had to defend himself against women, herself not excluded. "You all abominate second marriages, yet you all conspire to bring them about. . . . My only precaution is to show a pronounced attachment to married women, so as to preclude any attachment that could cause a rumor of other ties."

He came close to telling her as well that he had to defend himself against his warmest friends. "You need not be surprised to see me yet in the closest intimacy with Mr[.] Blaine, for my only intimate friends—Hay, Mrs[.] Cameron and Mrs[.] Lodge—are also Blaine's nearest intimates, and he is liable at any moment to be brought into very close contact with me. Naturally I don't mind, if he can stand it, but it is droll."

As things developed, Secretary Blaine and Adams were luckily not brought into contact. Instead, Adams enjoyed the Roosevelts. Writing to Miss Baxter on April 13, 1890, he explained: "As luck will have it, Washington is peculiarly pleasant and sympathetic as I quit it. Our little set of Hays, Camerons, Lodges and Roosevelts, never were so intimate and friendly as now, and for the first time in my life I find myself among a set of friends so closely connected as to see each other every day, and even two or three times a day, yet surrounded by so many outside influences and pressures that they are never stagnant or dull."

Adams was telling people he was retiring as a writer. He had written to Holt on March 5 that within the present year he would "retire from authorship." "As an occupation I can recommend it to the rich. It has cost me about a hundred thousand dollars, I calculate, in twenty years, and has given me that amount of amusement."[47]

Had he been willing to speak more truthfully, he would have said he meant to *work* in the future but not publish. He would soon remark to Charles that he hoped by means of travel to fit himself "for ten years more work." Charles might suppose that by "work" Henry could only mean more books. Yet, being the creature he was, Henry was sure to work as both a writer and a politician.

In early May 1890, Adams neared a turning point. Wilson had finished printing the *Historical Essays* and was printing the last volumes of the *History*. Adams was writing the general index and wished to correct the proofs himself. Nothing essential would then be left to do that Scribner, Wilson, and Dwight could not do without him.

Either Adams or Hay—it is not clear which—broached the idea that Hay should go with Adams to Polynesia. It was thought that Mrs. Hay and the children might join Adams's elder brothers and their families for the summer and pass the autumn in Cleveland without John's assistance. Clara quashed the idea and asked John to oversee the building of a summer house they had planned in Sunapee, New Hampshire.[48]

Mrs. Cameron wished to spend part of the summer at Pitch Pine Hill. Brooks believed the house was his in summer, if desired. He preempted it, and Mrs. Cameron had nowhere to go. Also she suffered an injury. Henry wrote to Lucy Baxter: "Mrs[.] Cameron has fallen and hurt herself so as to have been on her back the last ten days; and Martha has become a big, obstreperous girl. . . . Children are an illusion of the senses. They last in their perfection only a few months, and then, like roses, run to shoots and briars."[49]

Edward Hooper had decided to take his daughters abroad, sailing from Boston on June 7. On May 26, Adams advised Miss

Baxter that he would come to Boston to see his nieces onto their steamer. Because the time for his intended travels was near, he was consulting schedules of ships. He continued by telling her his itinerary. ". . . I shall take the train to San Francisco . . . about July 8th or 10th[,] to sail for the Sandwich Islands [on] July 18, and there take, on August 2, the steamer to Samoa. I expect to reach Fiji in September, and shall pause there to consider further movements. Having no plans beyond these, I ask myself no questions."

From the way he talked, Adams seemed to have substituted a voyage alone for the disapproved voyage with Hay. His new scheme, a sketchy one, possibly included eastward voyages from Fiji to Tahiti and Nuku Hiva, a northeast voyage to San Francisco, a pause in Washington, and a difficult journey thereafter to Peking and beyond, again alone.

In a new letter to Miss Baxter on May 29, Adams said he would arrive in Boston with Constance Lodge late on June 3. He said he wanted Mrs. Cameron to take the Gurneys' summer house at Prides Crossing, assuming Hooper had not rented it. His principal news was that La Farge was visiting at 1603 H Street and seemed to have come with a purpose. "I've half an idea that he means to suggest going to Fiji with me."

Traveling a second time with the artist did not strike Adams as ideal. He intimated that La Farge was directionless and stationary. "He and I might wander far and get nowhere."

Some weeks earlier, Adams had alerted Gaskell that he had preserved Gaskell's letters and would be sending him the bundle.[50] It is clear, too, that Adams had assembled a different trove of evidence. It consisted of more than 250 invaluable letters and telegrams written to him and Clover by forty-five persons between December 1861 and the end of 1886. At an unknown date, perhaps during his visit to Boston beginning on June 3, 1890, he gave the collection to the Massachusetts Historical Society, to be kept forever in its archives. The gift was not simply quiet. The collection was misleadingly put away as Theodore Dwight papers.

In Boston, Adams learned that Hooper had already rented the Gurney house. He returned to Washington much concerned about Beverly Farms. Lucy Baxter had rented a house there for the summer, and he wished to keep her posted about arrangements.

On June 22, from Washington, he wrote her a letter so direct that it spoke of "suicide." He said he was "about to put an end to what is left of all the life I ever cared for." He called himself a man who "can give nothing . . . is bankrupt and a fugitive—when his friends imagine him to be rich." What was upsetting him was houses, one in particular. He went on to disclose: "The little cottage on the road below your hill, where the road forks towards the beach, was where I passed the two happiest summers of my life, the constant and haunting memory of which is now driving me to the ends of the earth in the hope of somehow escaping it. I wanted Mrs[.] Cameron to take the cottage this summer [but she] . . . will probably . . . take the El[l]iot Cabot's house next you. . . . Whether she will go at all is a matter of much doubt."

As was expected in late June, Washington grew very warm. Adams and Hay were kept at their desks by the arrival of proofs. Nicolay and Hay were finishing last work on their *Abraham Lincoln*. Simultaneously Adams was finishing last work on his *History* and his *Historical Essays*. In the evenings, he and Hay welcomed opportunities to sit on the balcony of the Camerons' house, overlooking Lafayette Square. They drank icy juleps, against the heat.

A facile writer, Hay had the ability to turn out sonnets at will. He wrote two sonnets that Mrs. Cameron had opportunities to copy. She made copies for Adams, whereupon *he* wrote a sonnet titled "The Capitol by Moonlight." He sent her his, introduced by an undated note.

Adams's sonnet was unimportant. His introductory note was highly important, but in a way that Mrs. Cameron, Hay, and Mrs. Lodge could not possibly appreciate. It began:

> I can't let Hay write verses all by his lone. I too was in Arcadia born— or in Hancock Place, beneath the shadow of the State House dome,— much the same thing I presume. Anyway I send you a sonnet.

The lines involved an error of memory. Adams was born on Hancock *Avenue*, not Place, in a house directly west of the Massachusetts State House. He eventually would discover his error and correct it.

In the instant, all that mattered was that Adams had started his greatest book. He was writing the opening paragraphs of *The Education of Henry Adams*, or at least had found the germ of its opening line. His note to Mrs. Cameron could be called his celebration.[51]

Adams had told Gaskell about his travels. His letter took note of the well-known fact that Robert Louis Stevenson and his wife had moved to Samoa. Henry summarized: ". . . I expect to be a pirate in the South Seas. In thus imitating Robert Louis Stevenson I am inspired by no wish for fame or future literary or political notoriety, or even by motives of health, but merely by a longing to try something new and different." ". . . I mean to take a vacation; but I know not where or how long. Anything may happen,—even my reappearance in Europe. So keep up your spirits,—unless you will join me at Kashgar."

Roughly on July 1, 1890, La Farge wrote to Adams asking the privilege of joining him on his voyage to the South Seas. Adams yielded to the request and anticipated that their partnership in one way would be ironic. He would pay all expenses and would be unaccompanied by a servant. La Farge would have his expenses paid but would bring along his Japanese servant, Awoki—declaredly to assist them both.[52]

Before departing, La Farge would need two weeks or a month to arrange his affairs. Adams also needed time. The proofs of the general index were coming from Wilson very slowly. The Washington temperatures meanwhile rose unbearably. Escape was a pressing matter.

Second thoughts were inclining Adams to make still another change of plans. He was tempted to turn his vacation into a journey around the world. He might go to the Sandwich Islands, Samoa, Tahiti, and other points in the South Seas, thence to Ceylon or India, then to Egypt, France, England, and finally to the United States. He wrote to Charles on July 3, "As I know not where I am going, I am as likely to turn up in Europe as in Asia. . . ."

In different letters, Adams gave different reasons for his journey and also professed a mere wish to try something new. In addition, he denied particular reasons. He said he would not be traveling for his health, nor for the sake of future literary or political notoriety.

The assertions were made by a man whose single actions were sometimes inspired by very numerous motives. If only to assist his being understood as well as he *can* be understood, the motives underlying his impending action should be listed. He would make his journey

   — to lend his second life its proper conclusion. (He said it befitted a man of the world to leave a party before the other guests departed and before the host and hostess were tired.[53])
   — to reduce or interrupt ceaseless remembering of his marriage and especially its strongly amorous aspect. (He remained too young to be a widower with anything approaching reliable contentment.)
   — to learn better what his feelings were about Elizabeth Cameron. (He felt he loved her but was not fully satisfied that he understood his feelings or what he should do about them.)
   — to learn what Mrs. Cameron felt about him. (He had left Clover

Hooper for the west in 1871. The maneuver had helped precipitate their marriage in 1872. A similar maneuver would perhaps result in a settled understanding between himself and the senator's wife.)

– to improve his health. (Finishing the *History* had been a serious strain, so serious that he had lost fourteen pounds.)

– to rid himself of a particular non-physical illness. (He told Gaskell, "My disease is ennui, probably the result of prolonged labor on one work, and of nervous strain.")

– to avert being reached by reporters, interviewers, and critics while publication of the *History* continued and the *Historical Essays* appeared. (He meant that *some* attention be given to his works, but no attention to himself.)

– to get overdue relief from a surfeit of American experience. (He told Charles, "You and I have had our minds fairly soaked with the kerosene of American ideas and interests, until we can neither absorb more, nor even retain what we have. Nausea has set in. . . .")

– to read Homer's *Odyssey* while himself a wanderer. (He would take with him copies in Greek and German, perhaps also in English.[54])

– to do new and different things that he would feel inclined to write about. (In expectation of writing many letters, he would take with him a large supply of paper, ink, and pen points.)

– to meet Polynesians. (If such fancies as Pumpelly's were correct, there was a possibility that the Polynesians were Aryans—descendants of migrants from Central Asia.[55])

– to see a great volcano. (He would visit Mauna Loa on Hawaii.)

– to visit a part of the world which had become a meeting ground of rival empires. (The French, British, and Americans were being challenged in the South Seas by the Germans.)

– to compare notes with Darwin. (The Englishman's outstanding contribution to geology was his theory of coral reefs.[56])

– to explore Tahiti, the island that appeared in Captain Cook's illustrations. (Ever since their first publication, the engravings in Cook's *Voyages* had been powerful incentives to travel.[57])

– to experiment as a painter of watercolors. (He would take with him the requisite brushes, colors, and paper.)

– to set foot, if possible, on hard-to-reach Nuku Hiva. (As shadowed forth in Melville's *Typee*, the island was a setting that encouraged unfettered love.)

Hay completed his work and left the capital. Writing to Adams on July 8, he said he was "low in mind" on account of Henry's imminent "far wanderings."

Writing again on July 12, Hay prophesied: "That pleasant gang which made all the joy of life in easy, irresponsible Washington, will fall to pieces in your absence. You were the only principle of cohesion in it."

Rebecca Dodge had married an engineer and become Mrs. Rae. She and her husband sought relief from Washington's heat by renting a cottage far up the Potomac at Berkeley Springs, near Hagerstown. She invited Adams to join them.

A Harvard classmate of Adams's, Alfred Hartwell, was a resident of the Sandwich Islands. He opportunely came to Washington and stayed with Adams. Somewhat as an exchange, he extended to Adams the use of his house in Honolulu. Also he gave Adams letters of introduction, including one to King Kalakaua.[58]

Adams was waiting for last proofs of the general index. He went for a few days to Berkeley Springs to stay with Rebecca and her husband. Soon after, he visited Mrs. Cameron and Martha at a hotel at Blue Mountain. During some undisturbed evening moments, he and Mrs. Cameron watched a summer moon.

Arrangements had grown definite. Adams and La Farge would leave New York for San Francisco on August 16. Meanwhile Spring Rice had gone for the summer to Magnolia on the Massachusetts North Shore not far from East Point, the Lodges' house at Nahant. From Washington on July 27, Adams wrote teasingly to Spring Rice, ". . . think of me tumbling over cataracts with old-gold naiads in Nukuheva."[59]

Senator Cameron, his wife, and daughter were at Blue Mountain together. Adams went there a second time and returned with them to the capital. Mrs. Cameron would soon be staying at a seaside hotel at Manchester, Massachusetts. There seemed a possibility that Adams, Mrs. Cameron, Hay, and Mrs. Lodge could meet at or near Nahant before Adams left. He finished proofreading the general index, went to Quincy, met Mrs. Cameron at her hotel in Manchester, and stayed as a guest at the Lodges' house at Nahant. Hay, however, was somewhat detained in New Hampshire. The four-person rendezvous may have proved impossible.

It appears that, on joining her in Manchester, Adams went with Mrs. Cameron to Eagle Head, where—assuming this biography is correct—he and Clover had gone in an earlier time.[60] The return to Eagle Head was evidence that Henry felt Clover as attendant in all situations when he and Mrs. Cameron were otherwise by themselves. Really their case was simple. It unchangingly involved three people. Mrs. Cameron was not in the fullest sense a married woman. But Henry in the fullest sense was a married man, and Clover was the married woman.

At the agreed time, Adams appeared in New York. La Farge had difficulty freeing himself but did. When they boarded their train, Adams was more than usually loaded with baggage. He was prepared to stay in the South Seas for as much as two years or as little as a few months.

Even before starting, he began a letter in instalments to Mrs. Cameron. He continued the first instalment on the train and mailed it at Albany. As he wrote, he remembered happily the evenings on the Camerons' balcony and other moments when he and Mrs. Cameron were in close proximity. ". . . I admit to being a trifle homesick. I should like to be going to get my julep, or to watch the moon at Blue Mountain, or to stroll on the beach at Manchester. My only reserve is to hope that my friends are thinking of me as I of them."

26

Taura-atua i Amo

Adams and La Farge, assisted by Awoki, debarked from the *Zealandia* at Honolulu at 10:00 A.M. on August 30, 1890. By mid-evening, they were comfortably installed in Hartwell's house. The house overlooked the city and the Pacific. "While our rooms were made ready we sat on the verandah and smoked. The full moon rose behind us and threw a wonderful light as far as the ocean-horizon. On the terrace were twin palm trees, about fifty feet high, glistening in the moonlight, and their long leaves waving, and, as Stoddard says, 'beckoning' and rustling in the strong gusts, with the human suggestion of distress which the palm alone among trees conveys to me."

On the train to San Francisco, La Farge had started giving Adams painting lessons. Once housed in the Sandwich Islands, they looked for places to paint, especially at a pass five or six miles away where a lava cliff dropped suddenly to sea level. Adams wrote: "The view is one of the finest I ever saw, and quite smashed La Farge. Yet I am amused to think what my original idea was of what the island would be like. I conceived [Oahu] . . . as a forest-clad cluster of volcanoes, with fringing beaches where natives were always swimming. . . . The reality, though beautiful, is quite different. The mountains are like Scotch moors, without woods, presenting an appearance of total bareness. . . . The absence of tropical sensation is curious."

Adams and La Farge sometimes paid calls but mostly painted and loafed. Henry wrote to Mabel Hooper: "The only person I have wanted to see is the King, who is a very droll character and the only amusing one I have heard of; but though we brought a letter of introduction to him, we have not been energetic enough to deliver it, and so we shall probably miss his Majesty, for we go off, day after tomorrow, to another island to see the volcano, and shall be ten days gone, leaving only five days before we sail for Samoa."

Crossing to Hawaii, the largest island, involved reliance on small vessels. When pitched about by a landing boat, Adams became so seasick that La Farge grew frightened. It proved that both men were easily made seasick, but Adams for the present was quicker in recovering.

They visited an active volcano at Kilauea but derived more pleasure from an impromptu overland expedition. On bad horses along bad roads, they rode almost a hundred and fifty miles, passed through unexpectedly beautiful ravines and canyons, stopped uninvited at sugar plantations for meals and bed, and tried to communicate with natives they met who knew no English. Adams all the while learned color from La Farge, whom he described as "a spectacled and animated prism." "He has taught me to feel the subtleness and endless variety of charm in the color and light of every hour in the tropical island's day and night. I get gently intoxicated on the soft violets and strong blues, the masses of purple and the broad bands of orange and green in the sunsets. . . . The outlines of the great mountains, their reddish glow, the infinite variety of greens and the perfectly intemperate shifting blues of the ocean, are a new world to me."

Once back on Oahu, Adams delivered his introduction to the king, with mention of La Farge. Kalakaua asked the Americans to visit him on September 26. In his continuous letters to Mrs. Cameron, Adams wrote: "We went to the little palace at half-past nine in the morning . . . . His Majesty is half Hawaiian, half negro; talks quite admirable English in a charming voice; has admirable manners, and—forgive me just this once more—seems to me a somewhat superior Chester A. Arthur. . . ."

Adams did not expect anything to come of meeting Kalakaua. "I have listened by the hour to the accounts of his varied weaknesses and especially [of?] . . . his sympathies with ancient Hawaii and archaic faiths, such as black pigs and necromancy; but yesterday he sat up straight and talked of Hawaiian archaeology and arts as well as though he had been a professor." It emerged that Kalakaua was interested in all of Polynesia and especially the problem of Tahiti.

In ancient times, because they lacked written language, Polynesian chiefs memorized their islands' histories along skeletons or nets of genealogy. The genealogies were secret. Kalakaua had tried to obtain a history of Tahiti from a great chiefess, Arii Taimai, the hereditary leader of the Tevas, the clan or family who in earlier times ruled most of the island. Her memory reputedly was prodigious. He had asked her to dictate her memories to a secretary and send him the result. He recounted his effort to Adams and La Farge, including the unhappy fact that Arii Taimai refused.

The disclosure changed the aspect of Adams's journey.[1] He had not intended to trouble the natives with inquiries concerning their histories. It was opportunely impressed upon him that irreplaceable histories were being lost as natives died and their memories died with them. His journey did not acquire the added purpose of meeting Arii Taimai and eliciting from her the history that Kalakaua had not obtained. His state of mind was too relaxed to accommodate an added purpose. Yet his thoughts were invaded by an idea too attractive to be ignored.

It happened too that, as a historian, Adams was drawn towards ancient peoples and ancient women. When readying his *Historical Essays*, he had revised his 1876 Lowell Institute lecture on "The Primitive Rights of Women." He placed the lecture first in the book. As revised, it went into detail about the rights held and asserted by two heroines in ancient and early medieval literature, Penelope in Homer's *Odyssey* and Hallgerda in the Icelandic *Njal-saga*.[2] His lecture, one can say, predisposed him to inquire concerning women's rights in ancient Polynesia.

Adams, Mrs. Cameron, Hay, and Mrs. Lodge had given their association a name, "the family."[3] The four persons made a pretence of communicating with one another equally, but in reality they were two pairs, each with their own secrets. The tie between Adams and Mrs. Cameron remained innocent but was becoming problematical. At Manchester, he had given her a copy of *Esther*, with explanations. Apparently, too, he had told her he was in love with her and could not stop it. Writing aboard the *Zealandia* on August 26, he had repeated the assertion. ". . . in the long watches of these nights, as the ship flops slowly from side to side, and the waves pass under with a regular rhythmic rush, not conducive to laughter, I think and think, and go on thinking a great deal, and for my life I can see no way out of it."

She read *Esther* and prepared to start a changed correspondence. She wrote on September 2: "I am almost afraid to begin my first letter. It is harder to write to you now. There is so much that I want to say that all that I can say seems too *banale* to be worth receiving."

Shortly before, Brooks and Daisy Adams had relinquished Pitch Pine Hill. Prior to taking it herself, Mrs. Cameron paid them a visit. She knew that Brooks—in his new career—shared Boston's view of Henry. ". . . I grasped all the courage I own and came over.

. . . Brooks growled at me for an hour principally about you and was too tiresome for words. And [Daisy] . . . really seems to like him. And she echoed his opinions till I hated her and him and their very atmosphere."

Mrs. Cameron re-occupied the house on August 26. ". . . in 24 hours [I] felt as if I had never been away—or rather like a tired traveler who had come *home*. I know now why this has from the first been home to me, the place where I belong, it is the atmosphere of *you* about it which I have always felt but never recognized till now."

Her husband joined her at Pitch Pine Hill. She all the while was attempting to teach herself photography. In a new letter on September 13, she said about her new pursuit: "I have a place all arranged in my mind's eye for my chemicals in Washington. You had much better come home and help me. Donald said last night that he was going to England in April. May he continue to be of that mind!"

On October 5, 1890, the steamship *Alameda* paused on the open ocean near one of the lesser Samoan islands, Tutuila. Adams, La Farge, and Awoki descended from the ship and boarded a small schooner. Its native captain knew only scraps of English. Because of bad weather, he could not head for Apia, the trading port and modern capital of Samoa, sixty miles away on the island of Upolu. He instead steered the schooner to a harbor at Nua, a village on Tutuila.

Adams meant to stay only a month in Samoa, then voyage eastward to Tahiti and Nuku Hiva, beyond which point his plans were undetermined. He and La Farge had no wish to spend the night on the schooner, whose cabin was scarcely large enough to accommodate its bulky captain. They went ashore, entered a large thatched native house, and became guests of the village chief.

White men were rarities in Nua. The arrivals were given food and shelter. To their astonishment, during the evening in the firelight within the house, they witnessed dancers performing the "seated siva." The leading dancer, herself named Siva, was the daughter of the chief. Adams's account of the dance began with La Farge. "I imagine he never approached such an artistic sensation before. For my own part, I gasped with the effect of color, form and motion, and leave description to the fellow that thinks he can do it."

Next day the schooner rounded a promontory of Tutuila and stopped. Two passengers in white coats were brought aboard, also bound for Apia. One was Lieutenant Parker of the U. S. Navy; the other Consul Harold Sewall, a young man from Maine, a Harvard graduate, who, it chanced, had exchanged letters with Adams in 1882.[4]

By the time the schooner reached Apia, Adams and Consul Sewall were firm allies. It was agreed that Adams and La Farge would board at the consulate, an American-style house with enormous verandas, situated in Vaiale, a village a mile from Apia. They would sleep in a nearby frame house affording two rooms and two beds. Also, through the courtesy of a chief, Magogi, they would rent a native guest house, an airy structure in the midst of the village, next to the consulate and the sea.

When Adams and La Farge reached Apia, a new system of government was in the making. Samoa had suffered encroachments, German, British, and American. The Germans had deposed a Samoan king, Malietoa, and prevented the accession of another, Mataafa. The natives had turned for help to the Americans; and the commander of an American frigate, the *Adams*, had ostentatiously befriended them. The evident risk of naval conflict gave rise to international negotiations. In keeping with a treaty signed in Berlin, Samoa was to be ruled by a Swedish chief justice. He was coming but had not arrived.

A particular episode had perfected Samoan-American friendship. In 1889, several German and American warships were wrecked in Apia harbor by a hurricane. Seumano, the chief of Apia, led the natives in heroic rescues of sailors from the wrecks; and in gratitude the U. S. government gave him a large fine whaleboat.

Without delay, Sewall introduced Adams and La Farge to Malietoa, Mataafa, and Seumano. In addition, he put it about that Adams was traveling for pleasure and was a great-grandson of the president after whom the *Adams* was named. The news had strong effects. The natives understood that Adams's forebears were kings and he a nobleman.

Seumano gave a feast in the Americans' honor, at which they saw his adopted daughter Fanua dance the siva. During the performance, she kissed Adams—as a figure in the dance.

For their part, Adams and La Farge installed tables and chairs in the guest house, which would serve them as studio, study, and reception room. Also Adams hired a boat and rowers, to be always in readiness. Meanwhile Mataafa, a resident of Vaiale, often visited the guest house. Adams valued his company and thought him a man of the first ability.

These developments lent Adams a status he felt as comic, advantageous, and requiring that he comport himself as the natives expected and preferred. He wrote to Mrs. Cameron: ". . . I am a great *alí*,—nobleman—because all the natives knew the frigate 'Adams,' and I am the first American who ever visited the country merely for pleasure; so I am bound to look grave and let Sewall do the talking." He later explained that the natives knew him as Atamu or Atamo (pronounced Akamu), which was also the word in their Bibles for Adam.

Robert Louis Stevenson was a world-famous, best-selling author. A victim of disease, he had found that living in Polynesia moderated his symptoms.[5] Wanting to make his home in Samoa, he had bought forest land on high ground and arranged its being partly cleared, preliminary to building a large house. He and his wife were living on the site in a virtual construction shack, without proper facilities.

Sewall conducted Adams and La Farge on a visit to the Stevensons. In what he assumed was the privacy of a letter to Hay, Adams described the Scotsman and his wife as "queer birds." "Stevenson has cut some of his hair; if he had not, I think he would have been positively alarming. He seems never to rest, but perches like a parrot on every available projection, jumping from one to another. . . ."

Adams and La Farge supposed the visit would be their only chance to draw on Stevenson's wide knowledge of Polynesia. The author urged their going as planned to Tahiti and Nuku Hiva, which he said were his ideals among the islands. The meeting, however, was partly awkward. Stevenson had heard of La Farge as a New York decorator, but Adams he could not place.[6] In Adams's words: "He had evidently not the faintest associations with my name, but he knew all about La Farge and became at once very chummy with him. He talked incessantly for more than an hour, and became affectionate—to La Farge—at the close, but his wife would not let him invite us up there to a meal because they had nothing to eat, and I suppose nowhere to eat it, while he could not promise to return our call because it would cost him a day's work."

At Vaiale, La Farge sketched and painted as if being in Samoa were the opportunity of a lifetime. Adams painted. Using a camera he had brought with him, an Eastman Kodak, he took many snapshots, expecting to send the films to Australia for developing and printing. Increasingly he inquired about Samoan history. His principal informants were Mataafa, a near king; To-fai, a chief in the village; his brother Patu, a great warrior; and Papalii, the native chief justice.

Foreign influence had hurt Samoa but not transformed it. Natives vastly outnumbered whites. The ancient cleavage between chiefs and commoners remained in force and disposed the natives to study whites for signs of rank. Adams remarked to Mrs. Lodge: ". . . the natives caught on to me at once as a great man, and Sewall has cultivated the illusion. . . . I am rejoiced to find, for the first time in my life, that my name is worth something to me; but the natives are solid aristocrats to a man, and they evidently know a swell when they see one." Part-seriously, he later mentioned to Rebecca Rae, "The Samoans are aristocrats beyond the dreams of a Washington newspaper correspondent, and detect instantly the shades of difference among whites."

Adams intended to make the most of his presumed nobility. He wrote to Hay: "The consulate is here [in Vaiale] and for many reasons I have found my convenience to require support from our authority. As you know I have always maintained that there was some use in our government, and Consul General Sewall has been worth to us several Presidents and at least one Senate." He stated the result. "We have associated only with the first society—the families of the powerful chiefs. . . ."

A *malanga* was planned—a boat-excursion. Seumano, Sewall, Adams, and La Farge were to visit the largest island, Savaii, historically the native capital. They would go in Seumano's boat, flying the Samoan flag. Baggage would follow in Adams's lesser boat, flying the American. As chief guest, Adams would bring with him a sufficient fund of American gold coins, the presents most liked by native hosts.

Before starting, La Farge suggested their staying an added month at Samoa. Adams so dreaded seasickness that he was himself reluctant to start the voyage to Tahiti. He wrote to Mrs. Lodge: ". . . the further I go, the more I am appalled by the horrors of the journey back. . . ." But no final decision was made.

Adams was closing a letter to Mrs. Cameron. In a last paragraph added on October 23, 1890, he turned to the advisability of their seeing each other in Europe. His lines expressed conflicting feelings. ". . . I flourish and am not only well in health as possible, but well in spirits, greatly amused, and constantly occupied. If your report is equally good, I shall go ahead without anxiety; but I dare not think about next summer, if you go to Europe, for I cannot foresee whether it will be possible for me to get there, and, if I did get there, I cannot help foreseeing that I should have done better not to go. . . . Anyway remember that I belong to you, and am ever yours."

On September 27, Dwight had learned at a Boston bookstore that the third instalment of Adams's *History* had been issued.[7] As its volumes appeared, the *History* was revealing itself to be centrally concerned with large agglomerations of humans: populations, peoples, nations, races.[8] With some exceptions, individuals appeared in it mainly as *representative*, rather than on their own accounts.[9]

The narrative began in a time of peace which turned into a time of war. By the same token, the narrative had to do with peoples under stress: the Spanish in revolt against Napoleon; the Indians attacked by the Americans; the English beset by Napoleon *and* the Americans; the Americans in a second war against Great Britain. Moreover, the narrative showed that Adams was disposed to view the concerns of each embattled people from within, as they themselves perceived them.[10]

Very obviously, and more importantly, Adams's work concerned the *evolution* of nations and especially the full emergence of the Americans, a new nation, distinctive in "intellect" and "character."[11] The matter at issue was thus the making and remaking of humanity.

In Samoa, Adams had opportunities to study a people extremely removed historically from the Americans. During the *malanga*, he and La Farge were welcomed with much ceremony at several villages and towns, including Papalii, the home of the Malietoas. The visitors had with them a half-caste interpreter, Charley, with whose aid they talked readily with their hosts.

Adams formed especially friendly ties with Lauati, the chief of Safotulafai, and his unmarried daughter Fa-auli. On an impulse, he took Fa-auli's measurements. The action had to do with history. To his way of thinking, Samoan reality "surpassed all expectation." "The Samoans are not only interesting, but personally the most attractive race I ever saw." He said about Fa-auli: "She has none of her father, Lauati's, fineness of face, but is grand as a grenadier, and, what is more curious, as she strides across the village green, she does not look broad or heavy, but has a masculine figure with little breadth of hip, and only a broad acre or two of brown back, on which the sunlight plays in oceanic planes of light and shade. I never tire of watching her, especially when she lies stretched at full length on the mats in the dusk, and rolls from one position to another, while La Farge furtively dashes rapid sketches of her on his sketch-book."

Adams was interested but even more was surprised. "The most curious part of our experience here is to find that the natives are so totally different from what I imagined, and yet so like what I ought to have expected." "Family is everything, and a great chief is a feudal lord. . . ." ". . . the chiefs are the handsomest men you can imagine. . . . " "My size is a subject of constant self-reproach. Any man in Samoa would handle me like a baby. When I visit one of their towns, and am formally received by their chiefs in the guest-house, with speeches and a feast, I feel like an impostor. I never know whether I am violating some standard of good manners, so I sit cross-legged on the ground, and look as solemn as a Justice of the Supreme Court. When the giants have dismissed me, and I can sprawl on the mats among the girls, I begin to be happy, and when the handsomest one peels sugar-cane with her teeth, and feeds me with chunks of it, I have nothing more to ask."

Because Consul Sewall was in the party, the *malanga* had an imperialist aspect and could suggest that the Americans wished Samoa were their plaything. Privately, La Farge took the view that the Pacific "should be ours, and it must be."[12] Adams had opposite ideas and tried to make them evident. His sympathies were with the Samoans against all comers. He accepted Samoan ranks and titles as binding upon himself. His attitude worked to his benefit, as well as that of the Samoans. He wrote to Rebecca Rae, "I do not know whether you appreciate the brilliancy of my position, but I assure you I was never treated with so much distinction or lived in such elevated society."

On the *malanga* and thereafter, Adams measured many young Samoan women, studied their characters, and tried persistently to sound their feelings; but as a rule he thought their fathers more arresting. "The chiefs own their own villages and do all entertaining. They give and receive the presents. They are high born, and physically the finest men I have yet met in the world. They are warriors and politicians. Their manners are astonishingly fine, and their rhetoric, either in conversation or oratory, makes me ashamed of my own race."

A thought that recurred in Adams's letters was that being in Samoa was just like being in the *Odyssey*. He wrote to Lucy Baxter: "You can imagine me living in a model archaic world . . . where everything is thousands of years old, yet to me new; and where Christianity is a mere veil which covers a paganism almost as fascinating as that of Greece." "Homer is constantly before me. If you never read the Odyssey, read it now. Get Bryant's translation, and imagine me a companion of Ulysses instead of La Farge. You can see the whole picture."[13]

During a stay at Tahiti in 1888, Stevenson had been moved for his health to Tautira, a village at the southeast end of the island. There he had formed cordial ties with a Teva sub-chief, Ori a Ori. At his own suggestion, Stevenson and Ori exchanged names—a native custom. The name Ori gave Stevenson, Terriitera, was a name of some importance among the Tevas.[14]

While Sewall, Seumano, Adams, and La Farge made their excursion to Savaii, Stevenson learned who Adams was. When they returned, Stevenson appeared at Vaiale and gave Adams letters of introduction to Ori a Ori and Tati Salmon. The latter was a son of Arii Taimai. On his mother's behalf, the son was leader—great chief—of all the Tevas.

Adams appreciated Stevenson's consideration but was not sure that he and La Farge would reach Tahiti. The *Richmond*, the only steamer plying regularly from Samoa to Tahiti, had stopped at Apia. Adams and La Farge had gone aboard and learned that all its staterooms were below decks near the waterline. Disliking the prospect of extreme confinement for some 1300 miles, they postponed their departure for Tahiti.

The *Richmond* would return in mid-December. To help occupy the interval, Adams organized a new *malanga*, a gradual circumnavigation of Upolu. As before, Adams and La Farge would be taken by Seumano in his whaleboat, followed by Adams's craft. Sewall would stay in Vaiale.

The details of the circumnavigation mattered less than certain continuous features of Adams's conduct. He was corresponding with Mrs. Cameron, Hay, Dwight, Lucy Baxter, and Mabel Hooper, while at the same time writing letters to other people. At one point, La Farge noticed that Adams was "absolutely immersed in his writing, a feat of which he is always capable."[15] The artist seemed not to realize that Adams's letters were a sort of book. The main series would all survive, and within a century a large fraction of the total would be published.[16]

During and after the *malangas*, Adams tried hard to enlarge his fund of information concerning the Samoans. The great obstacle in his way was secrecy. Numerous aspects of native history were secrets carefully guarded. He part-penetrated the secrets by establishing such trusting relations with particular chiefs—To-fai, for one—that they would tell him all they knew. He then used the data as a basis for interrogating less-willing chiefs who might have added information.

La Farge witnessed the inquiry with amazement. In his opinion, fathoming the Samoans required that the investigator have "a very receptive, a very acute, and a very truthful mind." He said of Adams: ". . . he is patient beyond belief; he asks over and over the same questions in different shapes and ways of different and many people. . . . But everywhere one comes right against some secret . . . something that cannot be well disentangled from annoyance to the questioned one. For instance, in the question of genealogy, Seumano told us that had he been interrogated some years ago in such a direction he should have struck the questioner down on the spot. Still we have hope, and if any one can manage it, Atamo will. Web after web I have seen him weave around interpreter and explainer. . . . As many times as the spider is brushed away, so many times he returns."[17]

Adams's inquiry led him close to conclusions but no further. He explained to Mrs. Cameron: "I am pretty well convinced that all matters involving their old superstitions, priesthood, and family history, are really secret. . . . Indeed, To-fai made no bones of telling me, at great length, the whole story, and on his information I have in several cases surprised other chiefs into admissions that they did not intend to make. . . . I feel sure that they have a secret priesthood more powerful than the political chiefs, with supernatural powers, invocations, prophecy, charms, and the whole paraphernalia of paganism. I care too little about these matters to make any searching inquiry, so they may keep their secrets for anything I shall do; but I never imagined a race so docile and gentle, yet so obstinately secret."

Because of the impedences, Adams viewed his inquiry as a comical defeat.[18] He complained to Hay about the Samoans, "They've no business to exist unless they mean something, and they won[']t let me know what they mean." Yet on one point that mattered to him, he gained enough ground to change his mind. He concluded that the Samoans were more archaic than he had first supposed. They represented a phase in human development earlier than anything in Homer.[19] Writing to Mabel Hooper, he said about the women: ". . . they never talk, as we understand talking, and if they have what we call minds, they never show it. They show no curiosity about foreign countries, and no imaginations. Their good-nature is endless, and their spirits seem always gay; but they are more childlike than any child you ever saw."

❖ ❖ ❖

A letter from Hay brought news that Sombrerete, a Mexican silver mine on which King was heavily dependent, was in process of liquidation.[20] King's setback made Adams more than ever determined to be a friend. Rather than send mere letters, he resolved to write for King a personal report on Polynesia, geological and ethnological.

Briefly during the second *malanga*, with his future report in mind, Adams stopped to geologize at Nuutele, a small island off Upolu, an ancient crater. Darwin's theory of the coral reefs required a *subsidence* of the ocean floor. At the crater and elsewhere on Upolu, Adams found consistent evidence of *elevation*. In a broad sense, he was a Darwinian. His findings all the same seemed to him a glorious joke. He confided to Mrs. Cameron: ". . . the only thing I have proved is that one Pacific island was first a sea-beach, and then was elevated about five hundred feet, and since very ancient times—say ten thousand years perhaps—has not subsided at all. Indeed a very recent coral bed shows eight or ten feet of elevation. Naturally I feel rather floored about subsidence, but will go at it again with sublime defiance of facts. Darwin must be sustained. . . ."

The fifth anniversary of Clover's death, December 6, 1890, coincided with Henry's arriving at Vao-vai, west of Apia, near the end of the second *malanga*. That evening, he received a letter from Constance Lodge, forwarded by Sewall. With it came a newspaper from Auckland, New Zealand, announcing "a financial panic of the worst kind, and the practical failure of the Barings"—the London bank.

Adams was meeting expenses with drafts on Baring Brothers, and it seemed possible that he and La Farge would be immobilized by lack of funds. They shortly reached the consulate at Vaiale but were uncertain what to do. The *Richmond* returned to Apia as scheduled. Mainly because La Farge asked to stay, Adams consented to a new postponement of their departure for Tahiti.

An American, Dorence Atwater, was traveling from San Francisco to Tahiti and would be leaving on the *Richmond*. He came to the consulate for dinner. To appreciate the meaning of his arrival, one had to know some Teva family history. Arii Taimai married Alexander Salmon, an English Jew no longer living. She bore ten children. Her daughter Marau married the king of Tahiti, Pomare V. (The Pomares reigned by virtue of foreign intervention.) Another daughter, Moetia, married Atwater, then U. S. consul at Papeete, the capital of French Oceania and Tahiti's seaport.

The dinner with Atwater verged on the providential. Adams

wrote to Mrs. Cameron: "Atwater was very friendly and promised to prepare the way for us at Tahiti, especially with his brother-in-law, Tati Salmon, the head of the greatest native family on the island, to whom Stevenson had already given us a letter. Tati Salmon is half London Jew, half hereditary high chief of the Tevas or Tefas; and looks down on the Pomares with lofty contempt, as parvenus. We shall probably put ourselves at once under his protection. . . ."

From letters and newspapers, Adams learned that Baring Brothers was saved from extinction and made the property of a syndicate. His drafts on the bank would accordingly be honored. Simultaneously, he learned that financial pressures in the United States had caused the eviction of Charles from the presidency of the Union Pacific. The president replacing him was Jay Gould.[21]

Sewall was keeping a file of the *New York Tribune* at the consulate. Energetically, Henry studied a long series of back issues. On January 2, 1891, writing to Mrs. Cameron, he said he had studied the newspaper from October through December 16 with "more excitement than I ever expected to feel again on such subjects." ". . . the howls and groans of the unfortunates whom the bears hugged; the awful crash of the Barings, and my own narrow escape from being stranded penniless here; the collapse day by day, and the gradual taking form of the mysterious power that was to profit by it all; the looming up of Jay Gould in the background, and his gentle, innocent-minded comments day-by-day on the situation; the seizure of Pacific Mail; the seizure of Union Pacific; and the unrelaxing severity of the grip that is to restore order by creating chaos;—all this would be a delight if I were twenty years younger, for, if you happen on my new volume of Essays which ought soon to be published, you will see that I wrote the first chapter of this story in an article called the 'Gold Conspiracy.' "[22]

On reflection, Henry wished that he and La Farge had gone with Atwater on the *Richmond*. His mood was changed. He ceased his inquiries about Samoa. He deliberately stopped taking snap-shots, turned against photography, and said he would rather trust to memory.[23] In place of other occupations, he wrote letters and read the first half of a German translation of the Odyssey he had inherited from Clover.[24]

While circumnavigating Upolu, he and La Farge had stayed awhile at Fangaloa, a village situated on a fjord. The chief's daughter, Fasaei, inveigled Adams into learning to use a native outrigger canoe. To his delight, he found it was fast and he could easily manage it.

Fangaloa was astonishingly beautiful. He wrote on leaving, "All our grandeur was no compensation for the charm of what we should never see again." At Vaiale, waiting to start the twice-postponed eastward voyage to Tahiti, he daily went out in a canoe to watch the sunsets. Occupation for occupation, none compared with it. He wrote on January 24, "Out on the reef I am happy."

Wanting to welcome Adams and La Farge, Dorence Atwater and Jacob Doty, the former and current U. S. consuls at Tahiti, boarded the *Richmond* on February 4, 1891, on its arrival at Papeete. Adams and La Farge were glad to be welcomed and asked which hotel was best. Atwater and Doty answered that Tahiti was too poor and little-visited to have hotels.[25] Subsequent inquiries disclosed one available cottage and one available cook. Intending to stay only a week, prior to going to other places on the island, Adams rented the cottage and hired the cook.

Adams viewed his arrival as an occasion for good manners. He arranged that he and La Farge pay their respects to King Pomare. The monarch received them but was a king only in name. He had abdicated in 1880, and the government of Tahiti and the neighboring islands had been entirely assumed by French authorities.

Adams and La Farge also called on Pomare's divorced wife Marau and her sister Manihinihi. Among the daughters of Arii Taimai, Marau alone had not received a European education. She spoke English and French but was thoroughly Polynesian.

The week's stay in Papeete stretched to three weeks. Adams formed a habit of taking evening walks alone. "My favorite stroll is back to the saluting battery, which stands on a shoulder of the central mountains. . . . I can lie down on the decaying parapet, and watch the sunset without society; and what strikes me more and more, with every visit, is the invariable tone of pathos in the scenery."

For him, scenery was inseparable from geology. He was yet to start his report to King on Polynesian geology and ethnology, but his ideas were as good as formed, were his own, and affected how he felt. It seemed to him that the islands of the South Pacific were built up in extremely ancient times by volcanic action; that the lower islands had since been eroded to sea level by ocean waves; that the higher islands, Tahiti for one, were much eroded on their perimeters; and that coral reefs had simply formed on the sites of the erosion. The theory had a certain poetry. He could not look at Tahiti or its reefs without knowing them as old, indeed as very very old.[26]

Adams did all his best writing in prose, yet more or less continuously thought like—or as—a poet. An instance was his experiencing Tahiti as an inscrutable grandmother. While telling about his walks to the saluting battery and his contemplations of the scenery, he explained to Mrs. Cameron: "Lovely as it is, it gets on my nerves at last—this eternal charm of middle-aged melancholy. If I could only paint it, or express it in poetry or prose, or do anything with it, or even shake it out of its exasperating repose, the feeling would be a pleasant one, and I should fall in love with the very wrinkles of my venerable and spiritual Taitian [*sic*] grandmother; but when one has nothing else to look at, one rebels at being forever smiled upon by a grandmother whose complexion is absolutely divine, and whose attitude indicates the highest breeding, while she suggests no end of charm in conversation, yet refuses to do anything but smile in a sort of sad way that may mean much or mean nothing."

Tahiti also reminded him of a grandmother who was easy to understand, Louisa Catherine Adams. In his reveries, the island and his grandmother sometimes became confused. He wrote to Mabel Hooper: ". . . Tahiti is melancholy even when the sun is brightest and the sea blue as glass. I don't mean that the place is gloomy, but just quietly sad, as though it were a very pretty woman who had got through her fun and her troubles, and grown old, and was just amusing herself by looking on. . . . She has retired a long way out of the world, and sees only her particular friends, like me, with the highest introductions; but she dresses well, and her jewels are superb. In private I suspect she is given to crying because she feels so solitary; but when she sees me she always smiles like my venerable grandmother when I was five years old."

Expecting soon to visit Tati Salmon and Arii Taimai at their home at Papara, a considerable distance around the island, Adams—perhaps from Atwater—obtained a commercial photographer's picture of the chiefess with three of her sons and four of her daughters. He sent Mrs. Cameron the photograph and, while identifying other persons, said somewhat disrespectfully: "The fat old lady sitting on the right, is the hereditary chiefess of the Tevas, the grandest dame in Tahiti. She is the widow of Salmon, the London Jew. Behind her stands her eldest son, Taati Salmon, the representative of his mother as chief, and a sort of king in his way, especially since Pomare abdicated."[27]

Tati Salmon came to Papeete and spoke at length with Adams and La Farge. He urged them to visit him and his mother at Papara and then proceed to remote Tautira. There they would pass a month near Ori a Ori in the five-room house that Stevenson had occupied in 1888.

Tati was huge, spoke English more rapidly than Adams, and resembled H. H. Richardson in vitality and power to organize.[28] His attitude towards the visiting Americans was almost brotherly. Yet it was not lost on Adams that the members of the Salmon family were as large as he was small. It was not easy to relate to them. All were "whales."

Completion of the memorial Adams had ordered from St. Gaudens and White had been long delayed, and Adams had grown proportionally impatient. In letters from Samoa, he had asked Dwight and Mrs. Cameron to visit Rock Creek Cemetery and see whether the stone work and bronze figure were in place.

On reaching Tahiti, he received an accumulation of mail including letters from Dwight and Mrs. Cameron reporting a new delay. She wrote rather skeptically: "The foundation is there, also great blocks of granite, and two sections of the bench, all more or less enclosed in boxes. They now promise it for January, Mr[.] Dwight says, but I do not think that they can work here at that season."

Adams's impatience was possibly bound up with an unhappy feeling that his wife could not die till the memorial was completed. He very certainly had a feeling that being in Polynesia would be for him a means of dying. Before departing he had told Mrs. Cameron that he was going out of the world, or, alternatively, to the other side of the world, or to the "Happy Valley" in Dr. Johnson's *Rasselas*.[29] From Samoa, he had sent her some verses he had written about her, Martha, Hay, Mrs. Lodge, and himself. The last stanza said he had died and did not regret it. The stanza seemed serious.[30] If so taken, it suggested that he was in, or near, a posthumous existence.

His newest instalments to Mrs. Cameron reverted to the possibility of her going to Europe. ". . . you have said no more about Europe, and I am almost glad of it, for evidently I cannot get there next summer, however much I might wish it." The instalments also raised the possibility of his neither going to Europe nor returning to America. He said he still envisioned spending the following winter in Peking.[31]

En route from Papeete to Papara, Adams noticed that the road was a reef that had been raised above sea level and was paralleled by a new reef a distance out from shore. The Salmons' house proved to be an old French affair. Built close to the water, it faced a gap in the reef.

Tati welcomed Adams and La Farge and introduced them to his mother. Arii Taimai resembled no other Polynesian they had met. Her language was *old* Tahitian. She obstinately adhered to ancient ways. Adams wrote to Gaskell: "She will sit at none of your vulgar tables, on chairs, but [sits] on mats on the ground, like a true princess; and I, who like lying on mats, was glad to sit by her side and ask her about her ancestors and race. . . . Only one generation separates the old chiefess—who is only sixty-eight—from her pagan temple on the neighboring point, and from human sacrifices of your choice. I was taken to see the remains of the family temple, which were about as extensive as Wenlock Abbey, and I told the old lady that the only unusual part of the visit was the not going as victim. She laughed, but denied that chiefs were ever sacrificed at her temple;—only commoners."[32]

Adams would have liked to stay at Papara, but the Salmons had other engagements, and after three days he and La Farge journeyed with Tati to remote Tautira. Tati introduced them to the local chief, Arié, who spoke French, and to sub-chief Ori a Ori, who knew only Tahitian.[33]

Tautira resembled Vaiale in Samoa but was more beautiful. La Farge resumed his painting. Adams painted and wrote letters. On March 2, 1891, writing to Hay, he remembered the three days at Papara with Arii Taimai. "Every evening at sunset, the mats were laid on the grass by the sea-shore, where the heavy surf rolled in through an opening in the reef, and when I lay down at her side, she told me to ask questions. So I asked all the questions I could imagine, especially about the women of pagan times, and she talked by the hour, bothering her daughter and grandson terribly because they did not understand her old-fashioned . . . words, and scolding them because they did not know their own language."

Doty had gone back to the States, and an acting consul was forwarding the mail to Tautira. On March 3, Adams received a letter from Mrs. Cameron in which she thanked him for a letter and some verses from Samoa. She liked the verses but expostulated with him for having a wrong idea. ". . . the verses I keep by me. They are dear but too sad. You are not dead, but very alive—a living presence by my side in many long hours, and I think, I *have* to think, that you will come back. Oh, how I wish that it may be soon!"[34]

A pattern was emerging in their letters. Mrs. Cameron missed

Adams painfully and wanted to resume the life they had before he left.[35] Although he missed her painfully, he meant to end their former life and could welcome a new one only if it offered two protections. Sensitive in matters of reputation, he wanted not to be the victim of gossip to the effect that he and she were sexual partners. Indeed he wanted to preclude such gossip. Also, being a vigorous male, he wanted not to be the victim of unrequited desires to *be* her sexual partner. The only means he knew to secure both his wants was near-continuous geographical separation.

He wrote to her on March 4: "You will say I am not contented here. True! but I am not in mischief. . . . Do you really think I should improve matters by going home?" He at the same time recognized that she had a voice in their decisions. He did not insist on his own ideas and was willing to yield to hers. He continued: "If you think I ought to come home,—I am willing to accept you as judge,—I will agree to come. Can I say more than that?"

That same day, March 4, he started the geological first-half of his long report to King. Thenceforward for a month, he painted, wrote letters, and canoed. Changing his habits, he wore only native dress. He resumed his reading of the Odyssey in German, in Clover's copy.[36] He at the same time made efforts to arrange conveyance for himself and La Farge to Nuku Hiva on a French warship. The efforts failed.

Soon after reaching Tautira, Adams had learned with dismay that Ori wished to exchange names with him and La Farge. There was no chance of preventing his own exchange. He became Ori a Ori. Ori a Ori became Atamu. Yet Adams contrived to make the exchange conditional. He sent a message to Arii Taimai saying he would accept the name Ori a Ori if *she* approved its being given him.

Several reasons lay at the back of this maneuver. Adams believed that exchanging names was not Ori's idea; that it had originated with someone else. (He first suspected Marau, later Ori's wife.) He knew that in ancient times the names of Polynesian chiefs and sub-chiefs were legal enfeoffments conferring ownership of land. Having that knowledge, he wanted not to participate in a mere modern bandying of words. Also it worried him that his coming to the South Seas could make him appear an imitator of Stevenson, and, worse, that Ori's action might seem *evidence* that he and La Farge were Stevenson imitators.[37] Most of all, he wished to be treated, and treat himself, as the guest, not of Ori a Ori, but of

Arii Taimai and Tati Salmon; and the basis of his preference was affection. He strongly liked both.

He meanwhile was possessed by new conflicting emotions. He wrote to Mrs. Cameron: "I have horrors. No human being ever saw life more lovely than here, and I actually sit, hour after hour, doing nothing but look at the sky and sea, because it is exquisitely lovely and makes me so desperately homesick; and I cannot understand either why it is so beautiful or why it makes me so frantic to escape."[38]

There was only one means of swift escape from Tahiti: aboard the *Richmond* to New Zealand. The prospect did not suit Adams, but he seemed forced to choose it. The steamer would return on April 28, en route to Auckland.

Tati reappeared at Tautira. He invited Adams and La Farge to come to Papara a second time and urged that thereafter, while waiting for the *Richmond*, they stay at a house he owned on Moorea, the island adjacent to Tahiti, twelve miles west of Papeete. They gladly accepted his invitations, which, in addition to being kind, made them his guests for the remainder of their stay.

While still at Tautira, Adams conceived the idea of paying the owners of the *Richmond* "any necessary amount" to convey him and La Farge directly to Fiji. To provide the accommodation, the ship would have to deviate widely from its usual route.

There were reasons for the new idea. Adams had had an excruciating toothache on Samoa. It had stopped, but he had since found he was losing teeth and needed recourse to a first-rate dentist. In addition, a cyst was forming on his shoulder, and he wanted it removed.

Greater reasons were feelings. There were signs in Mrs. Cameron's letters that she wanted urgently to see him. With equal or greater urgency, he wanted to see her. There seemed a chance of their meeting in Paris and London for a month. He then might start other travels, say to India and China.[39]

He had already written to her, ". . . if [La Farge] decides to take the European route [to New York], I shall be strongly tempted to go with him, and vary Polynesia by a little Paris and London. . . ." The statement had been worded as if decisions rested with La Farge, but Adams was paying for their journey and decisions were largely in his hands.[40] It can accordingly be inferred that the statement was upside down. It was Adams who had decided, and he was going to Paris. La Farge had had no say in the decision. Perhaps he was not yet told.

❖ ❖ ❖

Dwight had written to Adams on January 23, partly to report that the concluding three volumes of the *History* had appeared. Adams did not find the news inspiriting. On March 8, he replied: ". . . I thought they were to wait till spring; but I am glad to get the thing done with. I can hardly hear less about it than I have heard, but henceforth I may at least count with security on hearing nothing at all."

Francis Parkman had been reading the volumes as they came out. He interrupted his reading to send Adams a commendation of the *History* as a whole. "One of its cardinal virtues is its candor. You speak what you know, without dressing out the story to suit the million." ". . . never was history more honestly written. . . ."[41]

Wayne MacVeagh took the publication of the last volumes as a signal to read the entire *History* in one effort. He wrote from Philadelphia that he had read "every word" and thought it "a great work in every sense." Rather than go into details, he offered a prophecy. "While you and I decrease[,] it will increase."[42]

The letters from Parkman and MacVeagh reached Adams in Tahiti and so touched his feelings that he saved them. At least in pretence, however, his attitude towards the *History* was negative. Writing to Hay on April 2, he pretended he had received no news concerning his "weary volumes."[43] ". . . I wish to wash them from my mind."

He meanwhile had before him the history or, more to the point, the tragedy of the Tahitians. He wrote to Lucy Baxter about the people of the island: "You can imagine what a wreck they are when you think that a little more than a century ago they numbered two or three hundred thousand, and that barely ten thousand are left, including a large proportion of half-breeds. They were once the gayest people in the world, and now are as quiet and silent as Americans."[44]

He wanted to form in his mind a truthful image of the Tahitians as they were at the time of the first arrivals of white explorers. It was difficult to see in living descendants the lineaments of their predecessors, but he thought he part-succeeded. He remarked to Hay that the Tahitians were "on the whole a more aristocratic race than the Samoans, and . . . the women occasionally show style very unsamoaesque. In Captain Cook's day they must have been stunning; but in long cotton nightgowns they lack something in the way of naked simplicity."

In Adams's opinion, the only living representative of old Tahiti was Arii Taimai, known among the Tevas as *Hinari* or *Hinarii*—

mother of chiefs.[45] He and La Farge went back to Papara and found her in the midst of "a big family party." "There was Hinari . . . sitting on her mats surrounded by small grandchildren. . . ." Three of her daughters were present, including Queen Marau. Two giant girls, a daughter of Tati's and one of Marau's, resembled "pictures from Gulliver's Travels." The setting was as striking as the inhabitants. ". . . [there were] smaller children, dogs, chickens, occasional pigs, horses and domestics; and beyond, hardly a stone's throw away, the surf rolling in miles of foam straight up to our hands. Tati . . . seemed to take us in at a gulp, as easily as if we had been more children."

Adams and La Farge had been summoned to participate in a series of Teva festivities. The contrast between unvisited Tautira and sociable Papara was extreme. "Hinari, Marau and the two sisters were cordial as possible, and we sat down to dinner feeling a little as though we had returned to the world."

When they had been four days at Papara, in the morning on April 6, 1891, Arii Taimai sent word to Adams and La Farge that she wished to see them. Adams's account of what followed concerned both an action and a response. ". . . the old lady with a certain dignity of manner, drawing a chair near mine, sat down and made me a little formal speech in native words, which [Marau] . . . translated. The speech . . . was the proper, traditional and formal act of investiture, and conferred on me the hereditary family name of Taura-atua, with the lands, rights and privileges attached to it. . . . For once, my repose of manner was disturbed beyond concealment."

When done with naming Adams, the great chiefess also conferred a name on La Farge. They did not instantly know it, but the name Adams was given had no superior among the names inherited in the Teva family. Amo, the plot of land to which his name entitled him, was very small in area but very great in meaning. It was the site of the ancient temple—the *marae*—from which subsequent *maraes* in the district of Papara had been derived.[46] He was driven to the plot that afternoon and affirmed his ownership by wresting an orange from a tree.[47]

The name given to La Farge, Teraaitua, was a subsidiary Teva name, also related to little Amo. La Farge later noted that in his eyes his double adoption into the family, first by Ori, then by Arii Taimai, changed the aspect of his surroundings, making them more valued.[48]

A critical aspect of the entire transaction was Adams's losing his repose of manner. Evidently the loss had been brought on by his not expressing in words what was uppermost in his thoughts. He of course responded by saying he appreciated the honor that Arii Taimai had bestowed on him, and Marau had translated what he said; but his words, as far as they went, were a weightless formality. The sufficient reply would be very different.

Like other men, or women, Adams stood permanently in need of appropriate recognition. One may say that his extraordinary threefold life had begun with the smiles constantly shown him by his Adams grandmother when he was a grandson five years old. Similarly one may say that his second life attained the consummation it lacked when a distinguished stranger, leader of another race, judged him the proper beneficiary of the greatest gift it was in her power to give.

What did Arii Taimai see in Henry Adams? She saw her equal and the equal of any of her ancestors back to the time when high priests and great chiefs were capable of prodigies. Adams realized what she saw. Had her judgment been an error, he would have been unmoved and self-controlled. She judged him accurately, and he was overcome.

Oponohu, on Moorea, was the place where Melville stayed before he escaped to America. With five rowers, on April 12, 1891, Adams, La Farge, Awoki, and their cook, Peraudot, crossed to Oponohu in a whaleboat. As they approached, Adams studied the sharp volcanic peaks ahead and thought the scenery the finest he had ever witnessed.

At Tautira, he had said that its mountains had not changed since they rose:—"I feel here immortal longings, for time is always the same."[49] At Oponohu, he added: ". . . I never shall meet another spot so suitable to die in. The world actually vanishes here. Papeete was silent and sleepy; Tautira was so remote that existence became a dream; but Opunohu [sic] is solitude such as neither poetry nor mathematics can express. . . . Nothing has ever changed. The seasons are all summer; the trade-wind has always blown; the ocean has always been infinite about it. Moorea is the oldest spot of earth I ever saw."

At Tati's house on Moorea on April 23, Adams began the ethnological second-half of his report to King. The history of the Polynesians had clarified for him. He thought them descendants of Aryans who migrated to India. In India they became great mariners, in an age of mariners. They were few, and they undertook a new migration. They passed through Java, built ocean-going canoes, risked heavy losses during many voyages, and eventually, by

way of Tonga or Samoa, settled Tahiti and places as remote as
Easter Island and Hawaii. "They consisted of families, each led by
a chief, and the chief was the state. When the chief said: I go,—the
state went. The chief still remains, and still does the same thing.
Today a chief who had reasons for doing it, would start in the same
way, and possibly in the same craft."

Adams supposed the landing at Tahiti had been recent, a
matter of only forty or fifty generations, and he was positive the
arrivals had lost by isolation. "Not for nothing is a people shut up
in islands five or six or seven thousand miles from its nearest equals
in blood and genius. It has deteriorated. Yet the chiefs are still true
nobles—a distinctly higher type than the common people; and in
many respects, the race has preserved a sort of pre-Homeric quality
which tells the story of its origin. Its physical beauty goes with its
refinements and especially its order of intelligence."

The ethnological report ranged widely, was mostly serious,
partly facetious, and ended with matters personal to Adams.
". . . we are trying to charter a steamer to take us to Fiji. I want to
see one black island. . . . Fiji had great influence on Polynesia,
chiefly in cannibalising my poor friends. . . . In my time—as Taura-
atua—I ordered a human sacrifice on any great occasion. . . . I
never ordered very many sacrifices; one or two or three a year
perhaps; but only a great head-chief like me had the right at all.
What I did, when not fighting, was to drink very strong kava which
acted like opium. Chiefs alone did that, and when we had kava, we
dressed in full dress, and forbade the cocks to crow or the dogs to
bark."[50]

When passing through Papeete on the way to Moorea, Adams
had left word that he wished to charter the *Richmond* and go to Fiji.
On April 23 at dusk, a boat reached Oponohu with news that the
Richmond was in port and that the offer to charter the ship had
been refused. There seemed no alternative for Adams and La
Farge but to take passage at once and go to Auckland. They
packed, began the crossing at 3:00 A.M. in beautiful moonlight,
and reached Papeete in eight hours. It further developed that the
ship was crowded to capacity. No berths were available. They could
not go to Auckland.

Condemned to a six-week extension of their stay, Adams and
La Farge moved into Doty's empty consulate. The move had the
advantage that the adjacent cottage was the residence of Arii
Taimai and several of her daughters when in town.

Adams took stock of himself and his situation. On April 27, he wrote to Rebecca Rae: "Tahiti is—queer. To tell you the secret truth, not to be whispered to anyone else, it has done me a deal of good. I am more like a sane idiot than I have known myself to be, in these six years past." Not satisfied with saying that Tahiti was queer, he changed to a second description. "Tahiti is so unreal, so like a totally different planet, that I have been bothered by very little sense of myself. I can sit for hours dozing on the porches, waking up only to a sense of wonderful air and light, and lovely scenery, but thinking of nothing at all." He then erased both descriptions in favor of a third. "Tahiti is not to be described. Don't expect me to do it. I call it an exquisitely successful cemetery. One would like to be buried here."

It bothered him that his attempt to buy direct passage to Fiji had flatly failed. He stirred himself and offered to charter a schooner. The sums he offered rose to $3,000, but every offer was refused.

When she decided to make Adams an important Teva, Arii Taimai had at her command a large array of remembered names. Like many Tahitian names, the one she chose was metaphorical. Taura-atua meant bird perch—hence landing place—of a god.[51] It seemed not to imply that the name's possessor was a god or demigod, but it could easily suggest that the possessor had godlike qualities.

On April 6, 1891, Adams was told that his name had been a Teva name for "many centuries." He was told in addition that a song and some stories survived about a Taura-atua i Amo who lived "some fifteen generations" prior to Arii Taimai. While visiting Amo in the afternoon, he was shown the site where his storied predecessor had a house. The predecessor was a great warrior, had the right to order human sacrifices, and drank strong kava. He was most remembered for having been obliged to leave a mistress he found among the commoners.[52]

Apparently very soon, Adams learned things that immeasurably added to the meaning of his name. There was a great chief of all the Tevas named Taura-atua i Patea. (Arii Taimai was his granddaughter.) He had a brother, Opuhara. In Adams's later words, Taura-atua i Patea "was always a wise and peaceful man who gained his objects by diplomacy, rather than by force."[53] Oppositely, Opuhara was a warrior. Early in the nineteenth century, the Tevas were embroiled in desperate wars with native rivals, and peaceable Taura-atua was replaced as great chief by militant Opuhara. On November 12, 1815, Opuhara was killed in battle; and Taura-atua again became great chief.[54] He lived to what he believed was his eightieth year and died in 1854. From an early age, he was known as Tati.[55] Out of affection and high regard, Arii Taimai referred to him as her "father."[56] Thus, in 1891, in making Henry Adams a new Taura-atua, the hereditary great chiefess of the Tevas not only linked him to untold Tevas of the distant past and to a famous warrior fifteen generations anterior to herself, the lord of Amo; she also linked him to her grandfather, whom she knew as her father, and to Tati, her leading son.

She in addition linked Adams to Tati's second son Taura-atua, a boy of twelve. The son chanced to travel with Adams and La Farge as far as Papeete when they were shifting to Moorea, and Adams had a chance to observe a Tahitian boy who hated going back to school.[57]

A first effect of all the linkages was Adams's ceasing to address his fellow Tevas formally. He easily addressed them by their first names, and they easily reciprocated, using his Tahitian name.[58]

A second effect was an attempted history. One day in conversation, the new Taura-atua remarked to Marau that she "ought to write memoirs, and if she would narrate her life to me, I would take notes and write it out, chapter by chapter." As he described it, her book would begin with family history, going back to ancient times. Provisionally, it would be titled *Memoirs of Marau Taaroa/ Last Queen of Tahiti*. But what the proposer was angling for (as Marau must have guessed) was not *her* memoirs but her mother's. If obtained, the memoirs of Arii Taimai could be expanded into a general history of Tahiti.

Marau consented. On May 10, Adams wrote to Mrs. Cameron: ". . . she took up the idea seriously, and we are to begin work today, assisted by the old chiefess mother, who will have to start us from Captain Cook's time. If I had begun this job when I first arrived, I might have made something of it; but now at best I can only do a fragment."

From that day, Adams was often at the house next door. He continued on May 17: "Whenever Marau comes to town, I get from her a lot of notes, which I understand very little, and she not much; then I write them out; then find they are all wrong; then dispute with her till she becomes energetic and goes as far as the next room to ask her mother."

While working on the memoirs, Adams seemed also to be mentally at work on something else. In his continual letters to Mrs. Cameron, he allowed himself to say things that could hardly be understood. He mentioned wanting "to know all about myself." Cryptically he continued: ". . . myself and I are two different persons; one a mere shadowy possibility in Washington; the other an almost equally thin shadow in unknown or uncertain night." As if to complete a puzzle, he roundly stated, "You are the only person who can tell me what I want to know, and this letter will have to be answered to Paris. . . ."[59]

It emerged that the incipient memoirs could not be written unless Adams first had access to the Teva genealogies. A week later, he told Mrs. Cameron that he had gotten his relatives into "a condition of wild interest in history." "My interest appears to have captured the old lady, who astonished her children by telling me things she would never tell them; and as they had to act as interpreters, they caught the disease one by one, till at length they have all got out their pens and paper, and are hard at work, making out the family genealogy for a thousand years back. . . ."[60]

As before, departure was an unsolved problem. Adams was overtaken by upsetting ideas. "Sometimes I half feel as though I really were Taura-atua i Amo, and never should know more of the world than that the ocean is big and blue." He said he wondered whether he would ever escape, whether Mrs. Cameron would be the same, or he the same, and whether Lafayette Square was where he dreamed it. In his current state of being, he could realize that his "old life" was "still going on" only when the monthly mail ship arrived from San Francisco. "At other times," he said, he was "dead as Adam."

A new hope was that of chartering the *Richmond* as far as Tonga. There a schooner might be hired to take passengers to Fiji. A schooner would be very slow, but there seemed no other means.

Adams and La Farge had long since diverged with respect to Arii Taimai. Adams had written, "La Farge is not in love with her as I am; he takes more to Marau and the girls; but I think the Hinarii is worth them all." On his side, La Farge remarked that Adams was "more Teva than the Tevas." ". . . he has given up painting, and has returned to congenial and accustomed studies. . . ."[61]

While it was true that Adams's work on the genealogy-and-memoirs was a return to accustomed studies, the work also was consistent with his conduct for many months. He had had many purposes in coming to the South Seas, but since leaving Honolulu he had become purposive in a high degree. He had made well-conducted efforts to trace the history of the Samoans and Tahi-

tians; he had satisfied himself that the Polynesians were descendants of migrants from Central Asia; and he was obtaining day by
day the most valuable of Tahiti's genealogies. In separate archipelagoes, he in addition had found evidence disturbing to Darwin's
theory of reefs. In a word, he had transformed an intended
experience of travel into a scientific and historical inquiry.

The *Memoirs of Marau* were not large enough to be called a
book but might possibly grow into one—it was too soon to tell.
Writing as usual to Mrs. Cameron, Adams said on May 31, 1891:
"Positively I have worked. . . . I have written two chapters, making
a very learned disquisition on Tahitian genealogy, mixed up with
legends and love-songs." He had told his relatives that he would
leave the chapters with Marau, who, if willing, was to treat them as
an introduction and add chapters of her own devising. She would
then send him the manuscript, and he would put it into shape for
private printing.

He seemed already to know, however, that the *Memoirs* would
be completed only because he, principally, was going to write them.
He said he had no belief in enterprises "left in Tahiti to the people."
"They finish nothing."

27

THE APOCALYPTIC NEVER

Earlier, in March 1891, the Washington contractor engaged by White and St. Gaudens had completed the stone work at the Adams grave site at Rock Creek Cemetery and emplaced the bronze figure. Mrs. Cameron hastened to see the statue. She wrote to Adams on the 14th: ". . . I think that you will be satisfied and pleased with it. To me it is inexpressibly noble and beautiful. But I am going to try to photograph it for you from various sides to give you a more just idea of it than anything I can say. . . . Many people come to it, and do not understand it. They make no criticisms, but it seems to awe them." Onlookers noticed especially that the memorial bore no inscriptions.

On March 22, St. Gaudens, White, Mrs. Cameron, and Dwight went to the cemetery together, and Mrs. Cameron and Dwight took photographs. She was displeased with hers but sent some to Adams anyway. ". . . I shall try again," she said, "if it ever stops raining. The whole thing grows upon me more and more. It is as big as the conception."

On the 25th, Dwight, Hay, Mrs. Lodge, and Mrs. Cameron visited the figure. Dwight took more pictures. Mrs. Cameron wrote to Adams: "His plates were much better than mine[,] which were disgusting failures. But between the two you may get some idea of the beauty of that work."[1]

Hay tried to approximate in words what he saw in the cemetery. He wrote to Adams: "The work is indescribably noble and imposing. It is, to my mind, St Gaudens' master-piece. It is full of poetry and suggestion. Infinite wisdom, a past without beginning and a future without end, a repose, after limitless experience, a peace to which nothing matters—all are embodied in this austere and beautiful face and form. The architectural portion is also splendid in dignity and simplicity. You have done a great work twice over in this last year. You have published the finest history we have and have caused to be set up the finest monument in America."

Dwight had seen no harm in photographing the statue, any more than Mrs. Cameron. He sent prints of his photographs to St. Gaudens and soon at Quincy or Boston gave prints to Henry's brother Charles.[2]

Interrupting the doings about the memorial, Senator Cameron made a suggestion to his wife that came as a complete surprise. For reasons connected with his Cameron relations, he urged her going to Europe for a six months vacation without him. She wrote to Adams: ". . . how I jumped at it! So Martha, her governess and I, sail together . . . on the Teutonic." It shortly developed that Rachel Cameron, a grown daughter of the senator by his previous marriage, would join the party.[3]

Charles was interested in the bronze figure. He assumed it related narrowly to his deceased sister-in-law and was "Clover's memorial." He studied Dwight's photographs and judged it "awful." To his eyes, the figure seemed a "mendicant, wrapped in a horse-blanket."

On April 29, a Wednesday, Charles had occasion to be in Washington. Clover's cousin, Sturgis Bigelow, was there as well. Next day with Bigelow, he drove to the cemetery, saw the figure, and changed his mind. By accident the following Saturday, May 2, on a train between New York and Boston, he was thrown together with St. Gaudens, whom he had not previously met. They had a chance to talk.

According to Charles, St. Gaudens asked Charles to write immediately to Henry about the memorial. Charles wrote on Sunday and told the story of seeing Dwight's photographs, forming a bad impression, going with Bigelow to see the figure, and accidentally meeting St. Gaudens on the train to Boston. He ventured to reproduce the sculptor's remarks. " 'Yes! I would like to have broken Dwight's head, for sending round those photographs without first submitting them to me. . . . I don't wonder you got the impression you did. . . .' "

Charles continued by telling Henry: "Your original scheme I do not know;—St Gaudens told me that it was the only commission he had ever received based on the entirely correct principle,—that you had simply given him a general idea, leaving him absolutely free as to the way in which he would work the problem out."

These preliminaries permitted Charles to reach the crux of his letter. He began to reveal, yet mostly concealed, a private theory he had newly conceived. He said that St. Gaudens so modeled the figure as to reveal a "history." "It is rest,—complete, sudden[,] priceless rest,—after weariness, trial and suffering;—yet the thing is worked out with a touch so subtle that there is in it nothing obtrusive, nothing to excite curiosity, nothing to send one away with an unpleasant taste in the mouth."[4]

When the *Richmond* returned to Papeete on June 1, 1891, the owner was aboard. He gave Adams the unlooked-for news that the vessel had been permitted by the New Zealand authorities to vary its route. If Adams would pay £400 plus passage, the owner could take Adams, La Farge, and Awoki to Fiji, starting as soon as the ship was ready.

The *Richmond* brought Adams's mail from Samoa, including Mrs. Cameron's March and April letters; a letter from Hay; a letter and photographs from Dwight; and a letter from St. Gaudens regretting that Dwight had taken photographs and enclosing the few he believed "would give a fair impression of what is now in the cemetery."[5]

On the strength of Mrs. Cameron's April letter, Adams assumed she was already in London and might be free to be in Paris when he arrived. He accordingly settled with the owner of the *Richmond* for conveyance to Fiji.

Adams was near to completing a letter to Mrs. Cameron, to go by sailing ship via San Francisco. That same day, June 1, he thanked her for her news about the figure. He said he had letters also from St. Gaudens, Dwight, and Hay, whose description of the statue had given him "a regular old-fashioned fit of tears." Yet *her* letter had told him more than the others and ended his "last anxiety." He explained that, if the figure was "half" what she reported it was, he would be content to be buried under it and "sleep quietly" with Clover.

At Papeete on June 3, Adams and La Farge shared a last meal with Arii Taimai and several children and grandchildren. In a new letter to Mrs. Cameron, to go by steamer via Australia, Adams said: ". . . I cared much less for the gaiety than I did for the parting with the dear old lady, who kissed me on both cheeks . . . and made us a little speech, with such dignity and feeling, that though it was in native, and I did not understand a word of it, I quite broke down. I shall never see her again, but I have learned from her what the archaic woman was."

The only habitable part of Tahiti that Adams and La Farge had not visited was its east coast.[6] That afternoon by carriage, they traveled the coast as far as Hitiaa, "an ideal Tahitian village." Off shore, the *Richmond* was being loaded with oranges. They slept two nights in a native house and went aboard early on June 5. The ship paused three hours at Papeete, and they "again bade good-bye to all our family, with tender parting from the old chiefess." They sailed at 4:00 P.M., onto heavy seas.

When he left Tahiti, Adams had two histories in mind. At parting, Queen Marau said she was "dead bent" on doing her share of the work on the *Memoirs*. Adams's share would include obtaining and studying books relating to the Tahitians. Many would be old and rare. He might most easily obtain them in Sydney, Paris, and London.

Much though Adams pretended that his *History* was a closed chapter in his life, the chapter was not closed. One worry was supplementary documents. He wished to get copies in London of records he lacked concerning the relations between England and the United States in the time of Presidents Washington and John Adams.[7]

A quite different worry was an honor. He had been told by Hay in a letter that he had been elected vice president of the American Historical Association.[8] He may have encountered the same information in American newspapers. Needless to say, his election had been precipitated by the appearance of the *History*.

The honor seemed likely to precipitate a greater honor. Election as vice president of the Association for a given year usually augured election as president in a later year. If so elected, Adams would have to preside and speak at an Annual Meeting and figure before the public as the members' spokesman. To another person, such duties might seem agreeable and easy. For him, they were impossible. He had long since desisted from appearing before audiences. After attending the Association's Annual Meeting in 1885, he had begun a careful avoidance of all professional meetings. He also had done his best to avoid the press. He counted himself a "recluse" and wished to stay one.[9]

What was worse, he and the Association's more typical members differed in their beliefs about history and historians. He thought history a branch of learning and both a science and an art. He thought historians were historians by dint of conducting historical investigations and writing what they learned in prepossessing form. The members of the Association more or less agreed with these propositions, and they had made him vice president because persuaded that his *History* was meritorious and important, but a controlling faction among the members hewed to an additional belief that Adams did not share. They thought historians were historians by dint of holding doctoral degrees in history from accredited institutions and by dint of holding teaching posts in history departments at colleges and universities. By their standard, Adams could never be a historian (he lacked the necessary degree) and was not currently a historian (he held no academic post). This is not to say that any large group among the members felt a wish to quarrel with Adams, or he with them; but he and the typical members so differed in their beliefs that they could talk to each other, if at all, only across a chasm.[10]

A further difference in belief concerned matters for study. By and large, teachers of history in the American colleges and universities thought of history as the study of past politics, including past law. If they felt affinities with teachers in other academic departments, their usual affinities were with those in "political science." From the perspective of the history teachers, Adams's *History of the United States* was administrative history. They saw it as a study of Presidents Jefferson and Madison's politics (including diplomacy), with some attention to Chief Justice Marshall's countervailing law.[11] This reading falsified what Adams's great book was about and neglected what it said; but it responded to false clues Adams himself had set in place; and, still more, it was agreeable to the teachers who were its authors.

It matters that Adams was a student of *peoples* who had published a step-by-step narrative of a single episode in universal history: the doings of the Americans that brought about their transformation from an aspiring but not-yet-united people to a united people, race, or nation possessed of a new, describable character. To the extent that he felt affinities with researchers in the United States not usually thought of as historians, his closest affinities—setting aside Clarence King—were with the ethnologists. The foremost living figure among America's ethnologists was Lewis Henry Morgan, but the person the American ethnologists regarded as the founder of their science was Albert Gallatin. In his later years, he had pioneered serious study of the Indians by concentrating on their languages.[12]

As has been shown, Adams knew Gallatin best as a *maker* of the American people. In the tightly-knit middle part of Adams's *History*, the eighteen-book narrative, Gallatin appears from start to finish. He appears in connection with varied important acts of national business. The most important of these acts is his going to Europe during the War of 1812 in hopes of negotiating a treaty of peace with England. He succeeds, and in consequence the Americans unite and succeed.[13]

An important reality here is parallels. Adams was linked with

Gallatin in that when young, albeit in secret, he too had led in effecting a peace with England. Moreover, at Papara and Papeete, he had learned that in the 1840s, when the Tahitians had been nearly exterminated by imported diseases, wars of their own making, and wars encouraged by European explorers, missionaries, and miscellaneous intruders, mostly British, a young Tahitian great chiefess, Arii Taimai, had studied the British and French comparatively and negotiated a peace uniting the Tahitians and placing them in endurable submission to the French.[14]

The persons named, Albert Gallatin, Henry Adams, and Arii Taimai, might seem a very odd assortment. Yet there was nothing odd about them. Or rather one of their characteristic oddnesses was combining a passion for peace with ability to get it.

When all these matters are considered, it grows clear that Adams's departure from Tahiti was an occasion when he could feel little affinity, if any, with the teachers of history in America's colleges and universities. Equally it was an occasion when the unity of his life and work was unmistakable to him. His early despatches to the *New York Times*, his *Life of Albert Gallatin*, his *History of the United States*, and two works to come, his *Memoirs of Arii Taimai* and *The Education of Henry Adams*, were consistent, related works. Their consistency strongly encouraged going on. As first things to do, he would study the Fijians and inquire concerning books relating to the Tahitians.

The Fiji Islands were a British colony. The British governor, Sir John Thurston, was half-expecting Adams and La Farge. From June 15, 1891, the day they arrived in Suva, the capital, till July 22, when they left for Australia, he made them continuously his guests. Being so welcomed, the guests behaved and dressed as was required in British colonies. Adams often had the feeling he was somewhere in India.

At Government House in Suva, Thurston had a collection of books relating to Polynesia. Adams later wrote to Hay, "While there I read up South Sea literature in his library, and became well posted on it."

Adams and La Farge had chanced to arrive when Sir John was on the point of beginning a march across Viti Levu, the principal island, to choose a site for a sanitarium. A few whites and a large company of native helpers were to pass through Fijian areas seldom entered by whites and inhabited by villagers newly persuaded to cover their ancient beliefs with a veneer of Christianity. Adams and La Farge were invited to join the march. Adams was physically adapted to the effort, La Farge much less so. Both survived it, and along the way they saw more of the Fijians in a near-aboriginal state than they could possibly have anticipated.

It had been one of Adams's hobbies to joke about cannibals, especially Fijian cannibals. On reaching Fiji, he wrote to Mrs. Cameron: "I have always found the cannibal a most insinuating fellow, remarkable for his open and sympathetic expression. His impression of human nature is evidently favorable. . . . Even the Solomon Islanders, who are still, when at home, cannibals of the most gormandising class, and black as night, look like the jolliest, cheeriest and friendliest of human kind. Once among cannibals, I feel that my heart is with them. They may eat me, but they will do it in pure good-fellowship."[15]

The march north across Viti Levu lasted more than two weeks, resembled an expedition by Stanley in Africa, and was climaxed by superb views from high volcanic ridges. Thurston found a site for the sanitarium, and Adams learned more than he had bargained for about the existence the natives had anciently endured.

He was sickened by what he learned. There was perhaps some comfort in finding that the Fijians were superior as artists and built the finest native houses he had seen. He none the less came to think that the ancient Fijians were the "most feelingless, ferocious brutes on earth." He later wrote to Mabel Hooper that they were "an immense population of two or three hundred thousand people" and they appeared "to have had no other steady industry but fighting and eating each other, not once . . . but all the time; so that the men in a mountain village never slept at night, but watched, expecting to be attacked, and every village was fortified with double and treble rows of deep ditches, and walls and palisades so that no one could even find the way in without a guide. The ditches and walls are still there, in many villages. . . ."

The steamer from Fiji to Australia was the *Rockton*. In Adams's words, it was "a comfortable, tolerably steady ship of some fifteen hundred tons." All the way to Sydney, the weather was fine. Yet Adams was "more suddenly and violently seasick than I ever remember to have been since childhood." His sufferings created serious doubts whether he could ever go to China or other places requiring voyages on small or mid-sized ships.[16]

Earlier, by letter, he had suggested to Mrs. Cameron an exchange of telegrams when he reached Sydney. Hers was waiting when he arrived. He sent one in return: "Start Thursday via Batavia." The point of his message was that he could not go to

Europe by the fast route along the south coast of Australia. The risk of seasickness was too great. He instead would have to go to Batavia in Java, change ships, proceed to Singapore and Ceylon, and change again to a ship bound for Marseilles. Luckily a ship that plied the route, the *Jumna*, could be overtaken at a northern port in Australia by means of trains. He was thus sure of speedy progress as far as Java.

The letters passing between Adams and Mrs. Cameron all survived. A passage by Adams, written at Sydney on July 31, was perhaps the most deserving of attention. "I have much to consult you about, and even a few hours talk would be everything. Give me all the margin you can. Hang on [in Paris] till the very end of October, if possible." The passage was forthright and full of urgency, yet disclosed no secrets.

The idea most emphatically expressed by Mrs. Cameron was that she meant to take him with her to America. On reaching Europe, she had written to him: "Of course you understand that if you come here you come home. I'll use force, if necessary, but home you must come."[17]

At Sydney, he was fully aware of her purpose, knew his own, and knew how oppositely they were thinking. He continued in his letter of the 31st: "I cannot go back to America with you, but my going back at all will depend much on my seeing you before you sail."

They disagreed, yet he was determined to tell her his thoughts and feelings. In a new instalment written next day, he explained: ". . . I want no one except you to know anything of my future plans. When the time comes, I want only to say that I am coming back temporarily, for personal reasons, and leave myself free from questions that would require lies. Above all, I want to return quietly and unexpected, so that I mayn't be bothered by Historical Societies and invitations which I should decline. Is this morbid? I don't care if it is. . . . I have no more interest in the world than I had when I came away, and have given it all I have to give."

For a long time, Henry had avoided corresponding with Charles. In explanation, he had written to Lucy Baxter from Tahiti, ". . . I am not fond of family lectures. . . ." He had added that he objected to "family disquisitions."[18]

At Sydney, he received from Charles a rather considerable letter, mostly about St. Gaudens and the Rock Creek figure. In the letter, Charles said he had learned directly from the sculptor that Henry, when ordering the statue, had suggested only a general idea. Charles apparently was very curious about the alleged idea. He seemed to think he had guessed it. He in addition seemed to think he understood what the sculptor had created. He began to divulge an opinion of the figure, yet seemed hesitant to do more than hint what his opinion was. He said: "As I told St[.] Gaudens yesterday, it was a case in which he took all possible chances. . . . Had he failed, the failure would have been awful. The thing could not have remained there. As it is, I am somewhat disposed to fancy it may . . . prove epochal."[19]

On August 3, 1891, from Sydney, Henry thanked Charles for his "kind letter" and admitted having feared—also *continuing* to fear—that he would not like the statue St. Gaudens had produced. He said he could not help "looking forward with a little dread to my own first sight of it, not because I doubt that his artistic rendering of an idea might be better than my conception of the idea, but because the two could hardly be the same, and what is his in it might seem to mix badly with the image that had been in my mind."

The statement was as forthright as Henry could make it. He was open about his fear. He was truthful about the figure's origin. He divulged his having conceived the figure by forming an "image" in his mind. He only concealed his having shown St. Gaudens the image very definitely, with the help of a boy model and an Indian rug.[20]

How deeply Henry saw into his brother's thinking might be a subject for debate, but he certainly knew the general outline of the situation then affecting himself, John, and Charles. John had failed as a politician. Charles had failed as a railroad president, albeit after a struggle. In the sense that his *History* was in the bookstores and was being reviewed, Henry simultaneously had succeeded as an author. He thus could seem to have committed a sort of lese majesty. By birth, he stood third. In terms of worldly success, he stood first.

A further impropriety could be seen in Henry's *Historical Essays*. The volume would not appear till September, but Dwight was acting as supplier of news concerning Henry, and he had gone to Massachusetts and talked with Charles. Doubtless Dwight had told him about the soon-to-be-published volume.[21] As viewed by the public, the *Essays* would seem a harmless collection of nine articles by Henry, mostly old, on varied subjects. Differently, if discussed with Charles, the volume would require analysis. Charles would want to know which of Henry's papers would be included. It happened that four of the nine articles in the *Historical Essays*—

"Captaine John Smith," "The Bank of England Restriction," "The Legal-Tender Act," and "The New York Gold Conspiracy"—had been published twenty years earlier in *Chapters of Erie, and Other Essays*, by Charles F. Adams, Jr., and Henry Adams. The collection issued in 1871 had preserved appearances and given the elder brother greater prominence than the younger. In the new volume of 1891, the younger brother would appear alone.[22]

The issuance of Henry's *Historical Essays* might have been very galling for Charles even if he construed it as nothing worse than Henry's way of declaring his independence. As things stood in the spring of 1891, its publication could be viewed instead as Henry's means of informing the public that Charles did not exist. It could also be felt as Henry's *enjoying* Charles's expulsion from the headship of the Union Pacific—hence as dancing on a brother's grave.

On May 3, 1891, the day he wrote Henry a letter, Charles also wrote secretly and at length about Henry's dead wife. Whenever the spirit moved him, the elder brother was adding entries to what he called his Memorabilia—a private record composed for his own satisfaction and for the instruction of posterity. He had mostly used the record to vent his unhappiness as president of the railroad and his dislikes of persons he dealt with while suffering the trials of corporate management. In this instance, he turned to a different matter. He meant to write all he wished to write about Henry's wife, the memorial in Washington, and its creator, St. Gaudens, then leave the subject "forever." The result was a statement that Henry would never see—a disquisition that ran to more than 1300 words.[23]

In the disquisition, Charles gave an appearance of believing he could speak "correctly" concerning the genesis of the memorial.[24] The account he gave departed from the one he wrote on the same day in his letter to Henry. In the letter, Charles pictured Henry as giving St. Gaudens a general idea known only to Henry and the sculptor. In the disquisition, Charles pretended he *knew* the idea and pictured Henry as giving the sculptor *both the idea and an array of facts*. "Henry's idea was,—rest after pain. He left the sculptor to work the result out,—merely telling him the facts of the case. . . ."[25]

The case Charles meant was Clover's case, which in his view could have been factually described by Henry only as that of a person doomed by heredity to kill herself. Thus, according to Charles in the disquisition, the sculptor had been challenged by Henry to make the statue a representation of a woman who committed suicide by reason of birth and the sculptor had accepted the challenge.

In the elder brother's view, the important factor was not Henry's idea and the "facts" but the sculptor's willing initiative. Charles claimed to have spoken to the sculptor about his willingness. "As I told St Gaudens yesterday, according to all generally accepted ideas, it is a questionable thing to thus accentuate and publicly immortalise in bronze the fact of self-destruction. . . ."[26]

Also, in his secret record, Charles gave an appearance of believing he could speak correctly concerning the finished work. He said the statue was an idealized portrait of a female suicide at the instant when, after death, seated by the grave, she at last feels a burden fall away. "The pain is all over,—the weariness is gone,—the disappointment is felt no more,—every muscle is relaxed, and the tired eye-lids fall on tired eyes."[27]

Concerning the woman he said the statue represented, Charles again gave an appearance of knowing authority. He said Clover "inherited a latent tendency to suicidal mania." "It was in the Sturgis blood. . . ." He alleged, too, that Clover when a child was present when her aunt, Susan Sturgis Bigelow, the mother of Sturgis Bigelow, took a "fatal dose of arsenic."[28] Moreover, he averred that, during her marriage, Clover was troubled by intervals of "excitement and unnatural action" followed by "long" periods of "depression and morbid reaction." He specified that there were three such periods.[29] He dated the last as prior to her suicide. He gave no dates for the asserted others.[30]

The elder brother had the problem of accounting for his knowledge. He explained that, following Clover's suicide, he had gone at once to Washington and that, during "next few days," he and Henry had "talks." ". . . talking freely, and so finding relief, Henry told me the whole story. . . ."[31] Charles stated in addition that Henry at the time was imbued with the mistaken idea that, if he could bring Clover safely through her newest period of reaction, she would again be well. "How this may have been I do not know; his theory was certainly specious."

The disquisition took up other matters, notably a prophecy Charles said he had made that Clover would kill herself.[32] Also the disquisition was consistent. From beginning to end, it cast Charles in the role of the right-minded brother who knew best, gave timely warning, and deserved the chance to explain the hidden aspects of a woman's mysterious history.

There was small possibility that the elder brother's outpouring would be valuable as a history of Marian Hooper Adams or a history of the memorial. When it came to Henry and more especially when it came to Clover, there increasingly had been questions whether Charles intended to help or harm. Writing the entry in his Memorabilia, he convicted himself of intent to harm.[33] He created for future reading by the inheritors of his papers an unfactual screed which, if taken as fact, would perform the function of a retroactive assassination, or rather two assassinations, a greater and a less. It would make of Marian Adams a suicide and almost nothing else. It would make of Henry Adams little better than a loving, ever-patient, devoted fool.[34]

Recent deaths had changed the aspect of Henry's travels. King Kalakaua had died the previous January in San Francisco, reportedly from overeating; and in June, a week after the *Richmond* sailed for Fiji, King Pomare had died at Tahiti, presumably of syphilis.

Pomare's death made a practical difference. Marau was more than ever queen, and Arii Taimai and her heirs were socially and politically unrivaled on the island. In Adams's words, ". . . our family is pretty near all the royalty and nobility that is left."[35]

In Sydney, Adams found books he needed—"a lot of old Travels in Polynesia." The books filled a packing box. He sent the box to Washington in care of Willy Phillips, a South Seas enthusiast.

Adams's reason for not reading the Tahiti books and instead sending them to Phillips was work on another project. While doing things he could share with La Farge and describe in his letters, he was doing something he was concealing even from Mrs. Cameron. With the help of three very different reliances, he was mulling the London chapters of *The Education of Henry Adams*. The reliances were memories of past experiences, imaginative invention, and pertinent books. He earlier had bought and studied biographies of William E. Forster and Earl Russell and found them "shockingly poor." At Sydney, he glanced into a *Memoir of the Life of Laurence Oliphant and of Alice Oliphant, His Wife*, in two volumes. He recoiled and did not buy it. He however bought a two-volume biography of Lord Houghton: *Life, Letters, and Friendships of Richard Monckton Milnes*, by Thomas Wemyss Reid.[36]

Consul Sewall was traveling from Samoa to Java. He joined Adams and La Farge at Sydney and went with them by train to Townsville in northern Australia to catch the *Jumna*. Adams had never heard a good word said about voyages along the route the steamer would follow to Batavia. He was surprised, indeed amazed, when for thousands of miles the steamer glided on seas as smooth as ponds.

Entirely spared from being sick, Adams read both volumes of Reid's *Milnes*. He found them worse than poor. He wrote to Gaskell:

"If Houghton had read his own Life, he would have needed all his own goodnature to bear it without murdering his biographer. . . . I hate to growl, but Lord Houghton was one of the best subjects for biography that our time has produced, and to throw it away like this is to throw away the lighter and gayer part of our age. . . . What annoys me is the want of art; the lack of sharp outline, of moving figures and defined character; the slovenly way in which good material is handled; above all, the constant attitude of defence, almost apology. . . . If Houghton never understood himself, that is no excuse for his biographer's not understanding him."

Adams thought Lord Houghton easy to judge. ". . . as a statesman [he] was a failure; as a poet, he was not in the first rank; as a social centre for the intelligent world he was an unrivaled and unapproachable success. . . ." Reid showed the failures but, Adams said, simply omitted Houghton's triumph. The biographer's non-feasance suggested a conclusion. "The moral seems to be that every man should write his own life, to prevent some other fellow from taking it."[37]

To that point, Henry was frank. He as good as said that the moral was one he was going to act upon; that he would prevent some other fellow from trying to be his biographer. Yet there was one thing he did not say. He did not tell Gaskell he had started *The Education of Henry Adams*, a book that was neither biography nor autobiography and instead was something new.

The precautions taken by Adams in 1889–1891 against his *History's* being noticed could seem gratuitous but were indispensable. One may view him as a fleeing offender. The offense he had committed was unapproachable achievement. When he wrote his *History*, he did more—very much more—than other Americans and other historians. And the question was not simply his relations with Americans and historians. It was his relations with his contemporaries in general.

His offense had two forms, of art and science. In thinking history an art, he was serious. Moreover, he had sufficient abilities to *make* it an art. Using his abilities, he had produced a fully realized epic. It was hardly an accident that, in Samoa and Tahiti, he had read the Odyssey. He had written, in America, a story as vast and compelling as the stories told anciently by Homer and more recently by Milton.

True, Adams's *History* was deficient in gods and demigods. The author claimed no close acquaintance with the Creator or the angels. He confined himself to the actions of human beings, in settings furnished by the planet Earth and all of nature. The limitation, however, did not operate as a limitation. As any impartial reader who undertook to read it would see, the *History* was a marvel of knowledge, scope, completeness, trenchancy, succinctness, irony, energy, and candor. It was full of tragedy and comedy. When read for its leading characters—or, equally, for its wars, crimes, betrayals, recoveries, heroisms, and redemptions—it was as alive as the stories told by Shakespeare. The only trouble was that many excellent readers would hesitate to read it. Also, out of dislike or envy, many poor readers would hurry through it and try to diminish it. It had the aspect of a work that would not be rivaled for centuries. It was both too big and too good.

In thinking history a science, Adams again was serious. The sort of science he had in mind required that the historian be someone impossible, a person narrow and broad. He was that person. In willingness to fix with burning concentration on a limited congeries of events, he resembled Thucydides. In breadth of interest, he exceeded Herodotus. He aspired to discover the end or outcome to which human action was leading. The events of 1800–1817 that he investigated brought into rivalry and conflict peoples representative of widely separate epochs, phases, or moments in humanity's development. He energetically and intelligently looked into the peoples' principal actions and interactions. The better to understand the actions and interactions, he *wrote* them. He discovered their showing a tendency—a direction; and he reached conclusions previously unestablished and unconsidered.

As has been said, the central action of the *History* is the transformation of the Americans from an un-united to a united people. The transformation very nearly does not occur. It is endangered by conspiracies to separate particular Americans (in New England and New York; also in the west) from the incipient federal Union. During the War of 1812, the treasons of the New England Federalists and the incursions of British forces bring the Union to the verge of dissolution. The weakness of the Union is compounded by incompetences of varied kinds in the federal government, first under Jefferson, then under Madison. Weakness increases to such a point that the *capital* is defenseless.

For Americans, reading Adams's narrative can be deeply humiliating. The most Shakespearean aspect of the story is its subjecting the reader to excrucuation. The story is most instructive when it reaches its nadir, the capture of Washington and the burning of the Capitol and the White House. The great point at issue is how—by what means or process—the Americans come together and become a nation. Adams shows that during the war they at times are united by victories. Still more, and paradoxically, he shows that they are united by failures so inexcusable and abysmal as to leave the generality of citizens no recourse but to pull together and feel as one.

The resolution of the *History* is sudden. At the critical moment, when events can turn either way, Gallatin and his fellow negotiators send home from Holland a treaty with England that frees the Americans from war and frees them to join unitedly in the pursuits to which they feel particularly suited, those of peaceful industry.[38] For an American reader, it is thus possible that the narrative, if read to the end, will be pleasing, comforting, reassuring.

The case is more complicated than may appear. Adams did not write for Americans only, nor did he write only as an American. He wrote as a universal historian, for *any* reader who might read him.[39]

All human pursuits had risks. Those incurred by a historian could be great. As a reader of evidence, Adams was swift, frighteningly perspicacious, and still more frighteningly honest. These qualities put him in a position much like that of messengers in ancient Greek plays who had the duty of returning from the oracles of Apollo with godsent news. The messengers could be sure that the news they brought, though indifferent to some hearers, would be horridly disappointing to others and—what might be more perilous—elating to the rest.

After writing his *History*, Adams exhibited the behavior of a bearer of good-and-bad news. On November 24, 1889, following the publication of Scribner's Volumes I and II, he wrote to Gaskell: "I have sent no copies about. If any American should ask if I sent them to you, say Yes,—and that you have read them with much pleasure. The conversation will not go further, and both of us will have made a proper appearance before posterity."

Adams's not sending Gaskell his epic was an omission too sweeping to be excused with jokes. Writing again on April 13, 1890, Henry said straightforwardly that he did not think the *History* "a pleasant book for English reading" and wished not "to send my old friends anything that could annoy them."[40]

English friends were not the only persons for whom an attempted reading of the *History* might become at points deeply annoying. Bad news could be found in the *History* for Virginians; for admirers of Jefferson and Madison; for descendants of the leaders who tried to bring about the separation of New England

and New York from the Union; for adulators of Andrew Jackson; and most especially for idolaters of Napoleon Bonaparte.[41] The English could read it only at the cost of learning more than they might care to learn about the conduct of past English prime ministers, foreign secretaries, ministers to the United States, and naval and military commanders; or about inferior English ships; or about English soldiers killed in the field.

Adams had not written bad news for various categories of potential readers with a purpose of inflicting hurt. The advantage and drawback of being a historian—at least *his* sort of historian—was freedom to say whatever the accumulated evidence left the historian no choice but to understand and reveal. His great narrative was meant simply to say what the evidence made him learn.

At one point in the *History*, he wrote a passage about the English which English readers, should they ever see it, might regard as highly complimentary. He said: "For a thousand years every step in the progress of England had been gained by sheer force of hand and will. In the struggle for existence the English people, favored by situation, had grown into a new human type,— which might be brutal, but was not weak; which had little regard for theory, but an immense and just respect for facts. . . . England had never learned to strike soft in battle. She expected her antagonists to fight; and if they would not fight, she took them to be cowardly or mean."[42]

The passage about the English was valuable partly for standing in contrast with what the *History* said about the Americans. Among the assertions made by Adams in his long narrative, the ones most likely to stir extremely positive or negative responses in a reader were those in which he said that the Americans were a still newer human type, mainly different from the English in that the average American was *more intelligent* than the average Englishman.

Adams waited till the latter part of the concluding chapter of his *History* to set forth the tests which he said left no doubt of this historic increase. His exposition continued page after page. He said in typical sentences: "The conclusion seemed incredible, but it was supported by the results of the naval battles. The Americans showed superiority amounting in some cases to twice the efficiency of their enemies in the use of weapons." "The greater skill of the Americans was not due to special training, for the British service was better trained in gunnery, as in everything else, than the motley [American] armies and fleets that fought at New Orleans and on the Lakes. Critics constantly said that every American had learned from his childhood the use of the rifle, but he certainly had not learned to use cannon in shooting birds or hunting deer, and he knew less than the Englishman about the handling of artillery and muskets."[43]

It must be stressed that Adams, in writing the *History*, had no intention of demeaning one people or commending another. For all that anyone can know, he may have started work on the *History* without expecting, still less believing, that the Americans of 1812–1815 in the opinion of a serious historian would prove to have been more intelligent than the English of those years, once the evidence was gathered and permitted to show its meaning. He was fully as likely as his readers to be surprised by evidence.

When he found out what he found out, Adams had taken the chance of saying it for publication. Had he said it in his twenty books as written (rather than as published), or had he said it in a loudly-touted *History* and talked with reporters about his interesting conclusions, the dangers to himself might have multiplied indefinitely. As things stood in late 1891, his *History* had been published and sold; copies were scattered about; but they existed in such modest numbers and had been given such a faceless, uningratiating appearance that a century might pass before his narrative would find readers wholly disposed to follow its argument to its very striking conclusions, take in all it said, and consider its meaning with an open-mindedness comparable to his own.[44] He accordingly was safe. Who can begrudge his safety?

La Farge had no knowledge of the true nature of Adams's association with Mrs. Cameron. If Adams could manage it, La Farge would continue to have no knowledge. When they arrived in Batavia, Adams appeared to be traveling. In reality, he was hurrying. The fastest conveyance they could take from Batavia to Ceylon was a French steamer. Scheduled to arrive at Columbo on September 7, 1891, it reached port early, in the late evening of the 6th.

As soon as possible, Adams and La Farge left Columbo by train, ascending through superb scenery to Kandy. Adams wrote to Mrs. Cameron: "Ceylon is certainly the most interesting and beautiful island we have seen. . . . In one way, Hawaii is grander; in another, Tahiti is more lovely; but Hawaii is a volcano and Tahiti a dream; while Ceylon is what I supposed Java to be, and it was not:—a combination of rich nature and varied human interest, a true piece of voluptuous creativeness. We have seen nothing to approach the brilliancy of the greens and the luxury of the vegetation; but we have been even more struck by the great beauty of the few girls we have caught a glimpse of; especially their eyes, which have a large, dark, far-off beseeching look, that seems to tell of a coming soul—not Polynesian."[45]

Adams's stated object in coming to Ceylon was to visit Buddha's sacred bo-tree at Anaradhapura. To get there, he and La Farge traveled eighty miles from Kandy by ox-cart, mostly at night. They saw the tree, what there was of it, and sat in its shade for half an hour.

A once-great city boasting large Buddhist temples, Anaradhapura had reverted to jungle. Adams thought the transition merited. "I have hunted for something to admire, but except [by] the bigness, I am left cold. Not a piece of work, big or small, have I seen that has a heart to it. The place was a big bazaar of religion, made for show and profit. . . . I am rather glad the monkeys and jackals own it, for they at least are not religious formalists, and they give a moral and emotion to the empty doorways and broken thresholds."[46]

Unsuccess in leaving Columbo on a fast British steamer and a three-day wait for a slower French one threw Adams a week behind the schedule he had wished to keep. He would not reach Marseilles till October 10.

He and La Farge remained on very good terms but meant to separate in Paris. La Farge wished to visit relatives in Brittany. Adams might see him again in England before he sailed for New York, but Paris would be the terminus of their joint adventure.[47]

In Washington in June 1890, finishing his sonnet "The Capitol by Moonlight," Adams had made two copies, one for himself, one for Mrs. Cameron. After he left on his Pacific odyssey, she somewhere—perhaps not at Beverly Farms—showed her copy to Hay and let him borrow it or copy the copy. In her letters to Adams, perhaps out of a dawning sense of error, she kept silent about her action.[48]

Somewhat as a reaction to Adams's copied or borrowed sonnet, Hay wrote a poem in five stanzas, "Two on the Terrace," which used the same setting, the west terrace of the Capitol in Washington, and used twenty distinctive words that appeared in Henry's lines.[49] Hay then visited Mrs. Cameron at Pitch Pine Hill. He showed her his poem but evidently did not give her a copy. She read it, retained a vivid impression that it pictured Hay and Mrs. Lodge kissing in the Washington moonlight, but said nothing in her letters to Adams either about Hay's writing it or her having read it. Soon her memory of "Two on the Terrace" grew blurred. She mistakenly remembered its five stanzas as a sonnet.[50]

Never loath to appear in print, Hay offered "Two on the Terrace" to *Scribner's Magazine,* and it appeared in the July 1891 issue. Copies of the issue were sent to Australia for general sale. La Farge bought one in Sydney and, on the express train to Brisbane, noticed that it contained a poem by Hay. He gave Adams the magazine "with the remark that John Hay had something in it."[51]

Adams could remember his own writings with accuracy and probably could recite his sonnet almost as easily as his name. He saw at once that Hay's five stanzas, without echoing the meaning of "The Capitol by Moonlight," repeatedly echoed its vocabulary.[52] Adams had not shown Hay *his* copy of the sonnet. He thus *knew* that Mrs. Cameron had lent him hers or let him make a copy.

Several days later, on the *Jumna,* Adams included in a letter to Mrs. Cameron an amused and amusing account of his having seen Hay's "Two on the Terrace" in *Scribner's Magazine.* In the account, he remembered that there had been *four* persons on the Capitol's terrace and that the second male and second female—himself and Mrs. Cameron—had known nothing of any kiss. He went on to inquire: ". . . can John have been shown my own poetic crime on the same topic? I never showed it. If he saw it, as his verses seem to suggest by echo, he got it from lovely female, No. 2."[53]

Adams's letter from the *Jumna* reached Mrs. Cameron in Scotland. She perfectly understood that she had been asked by Adams whether she showed her copy of his sonnet to Hay, but she did not realize that Adams already knew the answer. She did not know enough about writing to understand that the derivation or part-derivation of one work from another was something a writer could establish in an instant. What perhaps was less excusable, she failed to make allowances for the overall strength and accuracy of Adams's intelligence.[54]

In Scotland on September 26, she started a letter to Adams which would be finished in London and Paris, mailed in Paris, and delivered at Marseilles. On the third page, she lied about her copy of Adams's "The Capitol by Moonlight." She said: "John Hay's sonnet amused me immensely. He wrote it almost immediately [that is, in July 1890] for I saw it at Beverly. And he never saw yours unless some one robbed me of it for a night, for I like best to have that and other things just between you and me alone."[55]

It could seem that the matters at issue were small. The sonnet by Adams and the poem by Hay were literary molehills. Her lie about her guardianship of her copy of Adams's sonnet was another molehill. For Adams, however, one matter at issue was important. The episode had turned into a revelation of Mrs. Cameron's limitations. It would end with Adams's seeing at Marseilles that in a situation in which she had every reason to tell the truth, she resorted to dishonest chatter she supposed he could not penetrate.

Her choice was revealing. It showed that what she put first was her being a fashionable lady and a figure in society. Possibly Adams had wanted *not* to know it. Thanks to a helpful series of occurrences and a timely question by himself, he was forced to learn it when only hours removed from being again in her company.

Mrs. Cameron had never liked Paris. She found on returning that she liked it extremely. One reason was not living in a hotel. She had taken a sunny walk-up apartment at No. 12, Rue Bassano, south of the Champs Élysées and three blocks east of the Arc de Triomphe.

It was hardly usual for a married American woman, wife of a senator, to wait in a foreign city for the arrival of an American widower who had traveled 12,000 miles to see her. To Mrs. Cameron, the imminent meeting with Adams was exciting. Far more than her husband, he was the man in her life, the most interesting she had known.[56]

Adams reached Paris at midnight on October 10, 1891. He was thin but fit. During fourteen months of travel, his health had generally improved. Yet he looked older than fifty-three. He had about him an air of arduous experience. He was very bald, and his remaining hair was almost entirely white.

In prospect as felt by him, the meeting with Mrs. Cameron could have many meanings and shades of meaning, but at some point along the way it had partly come to seem an assignation. They had not been lovers. At least for him, their traveling to meet, after so long and distant a separation, had somewhat indicated that they might be.[57]

Neither he nor she kept a record of their meeting, but an outline of what happened can be collected from lines in their subsequent letters to each other and his letters to other people. On reaching Paris, he put up at the Grand Hôtel du Louvre, about a mile from the Rue Bassano. At her apartment, Mrs. Cameron was far from alone. She was attended by older Rachel, young Martha, and Martha's governess. Also she was busy. She knew many people and found it hard to repel their claims on her attention.[58] In consequence, while in Paris, Adams saw "much more" of Rachel and Martha than he saw of her.[59]

Soon Adams, Mrs. Cameron, and her party were in London. He stayed at the Bristol Hotel. She took rooms on No. 5A, Cork

Street, in Piccadilly. She thought her dealings with Adams were going smoothly and were as satisfactory to him as to her. Seeing him had given her the feeling that past times were restored, that they were again together, and that life had returned to normal. The idea that she was sexually attractive presumably crossed her mind, but it seemed not to occur to her that anything should come of her attractiveness other than its continuance. An impression she made on Adams was that her mind was taken up with everything except the acts that her attractiveness might inspire.[60]

Her schedule was definite. On November 4, 1891, she would be sailing from Liverpool on the *Teutonic*. She knew Adams wished to visit Charles Milnes Gaskell and was due in Shropshire that same day. She also knew that in one respect she had failed. Henry would not accompany her to America. He would be staying for many weeks in Europe.[61]

Sometime in the evening of November 3, a short walk distant from her rooms, she was seated in a Hansom cab. Adams evidently had helped her get the cab, had assisted her into it, and was walking away. Then —"across the darkness of Half Moon Street"— he said good-bye.

It was her understanding that they were to meet next morning and *then* say good-bye. She had formed this mistaken understanding despite his telling her earlier in the day, during a meeting in her rooms, that their meeting then and there would count as their parting. In the evening there would be no time for anything but a small last word.

In the cab, with astonishment, she realized that there would be no meeting next morning. They had already parted. Her own good-bye would have to be said at once.

Instantly she was "furious."[62] Their dealings had taken a turn she had not anticipated.

Adams went to Shropshire and was greeted at Wenlock Abbey by Carlo, his wife Catherine, and Mary, their eldest child. On November 5, the grownups and Mary went riding. Daughter Mary had formed advance impressions of the American whose portrait— the Samuel Lawrence—was always on the wall of her father's room. It surprised her that, rather than ride a horse, Mr. Adams elected to ride a Shetland pony, just as she did.[63]

Some seventy years later, when asked about Adams's visit, the same daughter said at once that the visitor was "omniscient." She went on to volunteer that, rather oddly, Mr. Adams had ridden a pony. She also said he was a "kindly cynic."

Asked whether "cynic" was a word she thought entirely suitable, she took it back and explained that what she remembered was not cynicism but irony—"closer to that."

Unprompted, she raised the conversation to another plane. She said with emotion that her father loved Henry Adams, longed for his visits, and suffered when he could not come. She explained too that her father would not have liked America. He had been delighted, however, "to have America come to him."[64]

Adams was happy to be at Wenlock but faced the necessity of announcing a change. That same day before dinner, he wrote a long paragraph that would serve as the first instalment of a letter to Mrs. Cameron. For its length, the paragraph was possibly the most suggestive of all his compositions. It was very strongly worded. His days in Paris and London had brought to mind some lines he had read and memorized in college. Strange, indeed preposterous, the lines appeared in a poem by Elizabeth Barrett Browning, "Lady Geraldine's Courtship." They posed the question:

Know you what it is when Anguish, with apocalyptic *Never*,
   To a Pythian height dilates you, and Despair sublimes
   to Power?[65]

In his paragraph, Adams quoted the lines and self-deprecatingly applied them to his conduct beginning at an unstated time when he was still in America. ". . . an elderly man, when hit over the head by an apocalyptic *Never*, does not sublime to Power, but curls up . . . and . . . does not even squirm; then he tumbles about for a while, seeing the Apocalypse all round him; then he bolts and runs like a mad dog, anywhere,—to Samoa, to Tahiti, to Fiji; then he dashes straight round the world, hoping to get to Paris ahead of the Apocalypse; but hardly has he walked down the Rue Bassano when he sees the Apocalyptic *Never* written up like a hotel sign on No. 12; and when he, at last[,] leaves London, and his cab crosses the end of Cork Street, his last glimpse of No. 5A shows the Apocalyptic *Never* over the front door."

Adams had an aptitude for making himself—in words—merely weak, incapable, blundering, or ridiculous. In this instance, he began with self-diminishment but concluded with strong assertion. Starting his paragraph, he had said he supposed her ship had sailed. Ending it, he spoke in the accents of a man who was conscious of his powers. ". . . now that you are tossing on the ocean, you have time to see the apocalyptic Never which has become yours as well as mine. I have dragged you face to face with it, and cannot now help your seeing it."

Aboard the *Teutonic*, Mrs. Cameron received a going-away present of fruit and butter and assumed mistakenly that it had been sent to her by Adams. She fully recovered from her fury and, when the ship stopped at Queenstown, sent him a note of thanks.[66] It reached him while he was still in Shropshire.

A storm prevented the Gaskells and Adams from doing all they might have wished to do at and near Wenlock Abbey. Adams went for a day to Highbury to visit one of his old-time breakfast guests in Washington, Mary Endicott. She had married Joseph Chamberlain and was well along in the process of becoming an Englishwoman.

All the while, Adams was adding instalments to his letter to Mrs. Cameron. He wrote on November 10 that, despite bad weather, he was "more cheerful" than he had been in the tropics. He felt as if he had "reached harbor."

It occurred to him that he should not mail his letter. One of its features was a pretence that he still loved her and was inveterately moved by base or improper impulses. ". . . the pain is actually mine, not yours; your position is right enough, and easily held; mine is all wrong and impossible; you are Beauty; I am the Beast, and until I turn into somebody else I cannot with propriety lead a life fit for you to associate with."

He was expected to go to Tilliepronie in Scotland to visit Sir John and Lady Clark. Not wanting to go alone, he wrested from Carlo an agreement to accompany him.

At Wenlock on November 12, 1891, he wrote the final instalment of his letter. He said he felt "at home" and as if he were "in hiding." He believed his "source of repose" was the Abbey itself. "An atmosphere of seclusion and peace certainly lingers in these stones. . . ."

To the last, he was not sure he had written precisely the letter that was needed. Yet he was going to mail it. ". . . Kismet! Let fate have its way."[67]

Running through the letter were notes of resolution. It was sufficiently plain that his last problem had been solved. Whatever needed doing for him to become a different person—different enough to associate with Mrs. Cameron, or anyone else, with complete propriety—had been done by the time he walked away from her cab on Half Moon Street during the evening of November

3. He had changed to the extent that her attractiveness could not tempt him. She would not possess him.[68]

Next day, November 13, he and Gaskell went to Crewe and caught the Scotch express. It was pleasant to be together, and there was promise of intelligent, friendly company in going to see the Clarks.

ABBREVIATIONS

ABA   Abigail Brown Brooks Adams(1808–1889)—HA's mother
AHR   American Historical Review
AP   The Adams Papers, Massachusetts Historical Society
AT   Aileen Tone—HA's companion in old age
AUTOBIOGRAPHY   *Charles Francis Adams/ 1835–1915/ An Autobiography*, Bost
   & NY 1916
BA   Brooks Adams (1848–1927)—HA's younger brother
BADV   *Boston Daily Advertiser*
BARRETT   C. Waller Barrett, editor, *The Making of a History/ Letters of Henry
   Adams to Henry Vignaud and Charles Scribner*, Bost 1959; also published
   in MHS *Proceedings*, vol. 71 (1953–1957)
BCOUR   *Boston Daily Courier*
BIP   Bigelow Papers, New York Public Library
BLANCK   Jacob Blanck, "Henry Adams," *Bibliography of American Literature*,
   New Haven 1955, I, 1–11
BOST   Boston, Massachusetts
BRP   John Bright Papers, British Library, London
BPL   Boston Public Library
CAMB   Cambridge, Massachusetts
CATER   Harold Dean Cater; also *Henry Adams and His Friends/ A Collection
   of His Unpublished Letters*, compiled with a Biographical Introduction
   by Harold Dean Cater, Bost 1947
CFA   Charles Francis Adams (1807–1886)—HA's father
CFA2   Charles Francis Adams (1835–1915)—the younger of HA's two
   elder brothers
CFA2P   Charles Francis Adams Papers (1890–1915), MHS
CFA3   Charles Francis Adams (1866–1954)—HA's nephew; son of JQA2
CMG   Charles Milnes Gaskell—close English friend of HA
CP   Richard Cobden Papers, British Library, London
DEGRADATION   Henry Adams, *The Degradation of the Democratic Dogma*, NY
   1919—a posthumous compilation for which Brooks Adams bore sole
   responsibility
DEMOCRACY (1880)   [Henry Adams], *Democracy/ An American Novel*, NY
   1880
DEMOCRACY (LOA)   *Democracy/ An American Novel*, as published in Henry
   Adams, *Novels/ Mont Saint Michel/ The Education*, NY: Library of Amer-
   ica 1983

DP   Theodore Frelinghuysen Dwight Papers, MHS

EASL   Henry Adams a. o., *Essays in Anglo-Saxon Law*, Bost 1876

EC   Elizabeth Sherman Cameron (Mrs. James Donald Cameron)—close friend of MHA and HA

ECP   Elizabeth Cameron Papers, MHS

EDA   Ephraim Douglass Adams—historian associated with CFA2; not related to HA and CFA2

EHA (1907)   [Henry Adams], *The Education of Henry Adams*, privately printed, Wash 1907

EHA (1918)   [Henry Adams], *The Education of Henry Adams*, Bost & NY: Houghton Mifflin Company 1918—intrudingly and damagingly mis-subtitled *An Autobiography*

EHA (LoA)   *The Education of Henry Adams*, as published in Henry Adams, *Novels/ Mont Saint Michel/ The Education*, NY: Library of America 1983

EHG   Ellen Hooper Gurney (Mrs. Ephraim Whitman Gurney—sister of HA's wife

Eppard   Philip Blair Eppard, ed., *The Correspondence of Henry Adams and John Hay, 1881–1892*, Ann Arbor: Univ. Microfilms 1982

ESTHER (1884)   Frances Snow Compton [Henry Adams, under a pseudonym], *Esther/ A Novel*, NY 1884; also facsimile reprint, NY 1938

ESTHER (LoA)   *Esther*, as published in *Novels/ Mont Saint Michel/ The Education*, NY: Library of America 1983

F, I   *Letters of Henry Adams (1858–1891)*, edited by Worthington Chauncey Ford, Bost & NY 1930

F, II   *Letters of Henry Adams (1892–1918)*, edited by Worthington Chauncey Ford, Bost & NY 1938

F   Worthington Chauncey Ford—friend of HA; editor of *EHA* (1918); first editor of HA's letters

FP   Worthington Chauncey Ford Papers, NYPL

FTKP   Faith Thoron Knapp Papers—letters, books, photographs etc. relating to HA and MHA, collected by Mrs. Knapp's parents, Ward Thoron and Louisa Hooper Thoron. Mrs. Thoron gave large portions of the collection to H. She gave some items to MHS.

FWS   Frederick William Seward—son of William Henry Seward; assistant secretary of state

GWA   George Washington Adams (1801–1829)—eldest brother of HA's father

H   Houghton Library, Harvard University

HA   Henry Adams (1838–1918)—christened Henry Brooks Adams; dropped middle name in 1870

HA2   Henry Adams (1875–1951)—HA's nephew; son of CFA2

HA–1   Edward Chalfant, *Both Sides of the Ocean/ A Biography of Henry Adams/ His First Life: 1838–1862*, Hamden CT 1982

HAL   Henry Adams Library, MHS

HA-MICRO (PLUS REEL NUMBER)   *Microfilms of the Henry Adams Papers*, MHS, 1979, 36 reels, edited and compiled by Stephen T. Riley, incorporating papers held by MHS, Harvard University, and Brown University. (The reels containing Harvard materials are cited as HA-micro H. The reel containing Brown materials is cited as HA-micro B.)

HJ   Henry James, Jr.—writer; friend of MHA and HA

HP   John Hay Papers, John Hay Library, Brown University

HUA Harvard University Archives
HUS (SCRIBNER) Henry Adams, *History of the United States* . . . [nine volumes variously titled], NY: Charles Scribner's Sons 1889–1891; last reissued in 1931; also issued in four volumes, NY: Albert & Charles Boni 1930
HUS (LOA) Henry Adams, *History of the United States* . . . [in two volumes], NY: Library of America 1986
JA John Adams (1735–1826)—HA's great-grandfather
JQA John Quincy Adams (1767–1848)—HA's grandfather
JQA2 John Quincy Adams (1833–1894)—HA's eldest brother
JTA James Truslow Adams—HA's first biographer; not related to HA
L, I, II, III *The Letters of Henry Adams*, Volumes I-III [1858–1892], edited by J. C. Levenson, Ernest Samuels, Charles Vandersee, Viola Hopkins Winner, Camb & Lond 1982
L, IV, V, VI *The Letters of Henry Adams*, Volumes IV-VI [1892–1918], edited by J. C. Levenson, Ernest Samuels, Charles Vandersee, Viola Hopkins Winner, Camb & Lond 1988
LAG Henry Adams, *The Life of Albert Gallatin*, Phila 1879; also facsimile reprint, NY: Peter Smith 1943
LAK Louisa Catherine Adams (1831–1870)—HA's elder sister; married Charles Kuhn
LC Library of Congress, Washington DC
LCA Louisa Catherine Johnson (1775–1852)—HA's grandmother; decisively influential in his life
LETTERS TO A NIECE Mabel La Farge, editor, *Letters to a Niece . . . / by Henry Adams*, Bost & NY 1920
LEVENSON J. C. Levenson—chief editor of L, I-VI (see above)
LHT Louisa Hooper—niece of MHA; confidante of HA in his later years; married Ward Thoron
LOND London
LP Henry Cabot Lodge Papers, MHS
LTIMES *The Times* of London
MA Mary Gardner Adams (1846–1928)—younger sister of HA; married Henry Parker Quincy
MBAG Henry Adams, "Albert Gallatin," in *Memorial Biographies of the New England Historic Genealogical Society*, Bost 1880, I, 203–12
MHA Marian (Clover) Hooper Adams (1843–1885)—wife of HA
MHS Massachusetts Historical Society
MORAN Benjamin Moran; also *The Journal of Benjamin Moran/ 1857–1865*, Chicago, 1947, also the unpublished continuation of the journal, LC
NA National Archives, Washington DC
NAR *North American Review*
NEF Henry Adams, compiler, *Documents Relating to New-England Federalism/ 1800–1815*, Bost 1877
NEQ *New England Quarterly*
NY New York City
NYHS New-York Historical Society
NYPL New York Public Library
NYTIMES *New York Times*
NYTRIBUNE *New York Tribune*
OED *Oxford English Dictionary*

OP   Ogden Papers, University College, London
PHILA   Philadelphia
PP   Palmerston Papers, Broadlands Archives
RWH   Robert William Hooper—HA's father-in-law
SKETCHES   *Sketches for the North American Review*, by Henry Adams, edited
    by Edward Chalfant, Hamden CT 1986
SPRREPUB   *Springfield Republican*
WASH   Washington DC
WHS   William Henry Seward—secretary of state

NOTES

The narrative is based on extremely numerous source materials and at points touches on matters that require detailed supplementary attention. It is sometimes self-annotating. In such cases, it simply makes an assertion and names the source on which the assertion depends.

Chapter 1 is based on scattered sources. Its notes need no special explanation. Chapters 2–27 are each based on a compact body of principal sources and a scattering of additional sources. I accordingly have begun the notes for these chapters by listing the chapter's principal sources and then as necessary have cited additional sources. The device is unusual and requires my giving an assurance. If an assertion is neither self-annotating nor supported by a note citing an additional source, the assertion rests on one of the principal sources, which either is specified by the narrative or should not be difficult to trace.

I also have written "comments." Some are long. The pertinence of each will be apparent if it is read in conjunction with the narrative.

The most important sources relating to Henry Adams are the writings he published, privately printed, or preserved; his letters and fragmentary diary entries; his wife's letters; and all the letters to him and to his wife.

The diary entries and many of the letters are helpfully assembled in the *Microfilms of the Henry Adams Papers*, compiled by Stephen T. Riley, and published in 1979. Because the letters as filmed are virtual equivalents of the manuscripts, I have coordinated my notes with the *Microfilms*.

The *Microfilms* unfortunately are accessible in few places. For this reason, I must give a second assurance. Most of the letters by Adams cited in the notes appear in printed form in *The Letters of Henry Adams*, edited by J. C. Levenson and others, and published in six volumes in 1982 and 1988. Similarly, the letters omitted from the volumes appear in a Supplement published in 1989.

1. THE *TRENT* VOLCANO

Letters by and to HA are in HA-micro 2, unless otherwise noted.

1. Moran, 31 Jul 1861.
2. CFA to CFA2, 2 May 1862, AP.
3. Visiting the room in 1962, I inferred that CFA and HA used it as

their study from its matching the room CFA earlier took for his library in Boston. See *Autobiography*, 5. I had visited the Boston library in 1956.

4. CFA to WHS, 13 Apr 1861, AP. As written by HA in CFA's letter book, the "s" in "Secretary" is capitalized. The capital letter possibly is evidence that HA and/or CFA supposed that HA would rank equally with Secretary Wilson, or even above him. The capital "s" also appears in HA to CFA2, 30 Jan 1863.

5. On 14 May 1861, Moran recorded that HA was "about 25 years of age." He was newly twenty-three. He aged rapidly in appearance thereafter. See Chap. 5.

6. Detailed descriptions of HA's physical makeup, voice, manner, etc. were written of him when older but with allowances seem applicable to him when younger. The fullest description is provided by J. Laurence Laughlin, "Some Recollections of Henry Adams," *Scribner's Magazine*, May 1921, 576–85.

7. Defense by HA of his lifelong reliance on secrecy may perhaps be implicit in his explaining to Henry Watkins Anderson, 17 Jul 1916, L, VI, 735, ". . . I wanted room to move."

8. The importance to HA of his relation to LCA is explicit in his letters relating to the vexed problem of her genealogy. See HA to Ford, 2 May 1910, 13 Dec 1910, 28 Jan 1911, & 11 Feb 1911 (w. attachments), FP, explaining (2 May 1910), "The true object of my affections is . . . Louisa Catherine (Mrs. J. Q.). . . ."

9. See HA–1, illustrations, 92–93.

10. The most obtrusive evidence of HA's sense of fusion with LCA is his design for a memorial. The memorial is in Washington, their city of preference. It bears no inscriptions. Its central feature is a human figure in bronze. The figure is androgynous. Whatever else the figure may be taken to represent (mostly obviously the marriage of Henry Adams and Clover Hooper), the figure's design is traceable to experiences of HA's going back to 1873, 1869, 1865, 1860, and still earlier. Of his earliest experiences, one perforce was awareness of the physical resemblance between himself and LCA. The transition from that experience to a design for a figure female-and-male was no great leap. Just the reverse, the transition was stationary.

11. No question about HA is more important than the degree of his precocity as a reader. One would especially like to know at what age he read a two-volume Federalist work of marked anti-Adams tendencies: George Gibbs, *Memoirs of the Administrations of Washington and John Adams, edited from the papers of Oliver Wolcott, secretary of the Treasury*, NY 1846. Such are the *Memoirs* that the gap between what they say and what a young Adams might have wished them to say could very possibly have been the *fons et origo* of many of HA's principal writings, including *Democracy, The Life of Albert Gallatin*, his *History of the United States*, and *The Education of Henry Adams*.

If HA read Gibbs's *Memoirs* when eight or nine, which seems not impossible, the feat could have signaled to JQA and LCA that a gifted grandson was taking the family's political wars upon himself. If he read the *Memoirs* later, when ten, eleven, or twelve, the achievement could still have helped him win a privilege he was granted at an early date, a writing table of his own in CFA's Boston library.

A copy of the *Memoirs* subsequently owned by HA is in HAL. Partly cut, partly uncut, its volumes contains annotations, scorings, and paper slips which show that HA knew the volumes well and could readily find his way about in them.

12. All aspects of HA's plan are evident in his college writings, notably his articles and reviews in the *Harvard Magazine*, papers as Hasty Pudding Alligator, and autobiography in the Class Book.

13. Best titled *A Journey to Italy*, the book (though not presented as a book) has been published. See letters from HA to CFA2 nos. 1–9, starting at Vienna, 5 Apr 1860, ending at Sorrento, 15 Jun [1860], L, I, 110–78.

14. David M. Potter was the first writer to recognize that HA in the winter of 1860–1861 figured as a politician of independent importance. See his *Lincoln and His Party in the Secession Crisis*, New Haven 1942, 234—". . . Gideon Welles, William H. Seward, Henry Adams, Edward Bates, William Pitt Fessenden and other leading Republicans. . . ."

15. A full account appears in HA-1, 190–225, 416–22. HA's BAdv reports have not been reprinted.

16. The earliest published mention of HA's BAdv reports appeared in a little-known pamphlet: James Truslow Adams, "Bibliography of the Writings of Henry Adams," NY: Albert & Charles Boni 1930. The reports are correctly identified, but only by date of publication.

17. *EHA* (1907), 86; (LoA), 812. The words quoted are HA's only revelation of the *place* he first met Raymond. Evidently the *date* of their meeting was 28 or 29 Jan 1861. See HA-1, 220.

18. The NYTimes reprinted HA's sixth BAdv report (excising a minor paragraph and adding numerous italics) on 31 Dec 1860. When HA and Raymond met four weeks later in Washington, the fact that Raymond's newspaper had availed itself of a BAdv report gave HA a possible pretext for divulging his authorship of the reports to Raymond at once, thus initiating their association on a basis of confidence. It seems next to certain that HA took that exact secret course.

The possibility that CFA would be named by Lincoln to serve as minister to England became a subject of published speculation in January 1861. Hence the thought that HA might write anonymously as NYTimes correspondent in London could have been tentatively broached between Raymond and HA in January-February 1861 in Washington.

19. HA, "The Great Secession Winter," MHS *Proceedings*, 43 (1909–1910), 656–87. Reading the article when it first appeared, knowledgeable persons were much impressed by its value. See FWS to CFA2, 3 Jan 1911, FP—"His account . . . is singularly graphic, discriminating and just." And see John Bigelow to CFA2, 5 Jan 1911, FP—". . . it contains much that will be new to every man living that was born since 1850."

20. Levenson and his fellow editors mistakenly date HA's clerkship in late 1860. See L, I, 207n1. HA dates it in mid-March 1861. See *EHA* (1907), 83 & 93; (LoA), 809 & 819.

21. *EHA* (1907), 103; (LoA), 829; CFA to WHS, 13 Apr 1861, AP.

22. The secret of HA's arrangement with Raymond was originally known only to HA, Raymond, and CFA2. Raymond and CFA2 appear to have kept the secret. The person who disclosed it was HA. He did so in 1907, but only in a single, passing, exceedingly understated sentence in *The Education*: "He [Adams] had written pretty frequently to Henry J.

Raymond, and Raymond had used his letters in the *New York Times*." See *EHA* (1907), 103; (LoA), 829.

23. HA's acting without his father's knowledge has been criticized as immoral. See especially Evan John, *Atlantic Impact/ 1861*, NY 1952, 197— ". . . Duplicity could go no farther. . . ." I believe the action was moral, but only according to the little-respected, uncodified morality of youth, which seems forever to be at variance with the more touted and codified moralities of maturity and age.

24. For details concerning CFA2's writing political pieces and his sending them to HA for English publication, see HA–1, 285–86, 309–10, 313–14.

25. In London in September 1861, John Bigelow learned that CFA, after four months as minister to England, still did not know Samuel Lucas, editor of the London *Morning Star* and brother-in-law of Radical leader John Bright. He wrote: "The idea of our Minister not being in relation with the only organ of the only considerable party in England friendly to America in this crisis is marvellous. Ever since I left home my respect for Mr[.] Seward's administration of the State Department has been diminishing. I do not hear of a single first rate appointment he has made. . . . He cannot sink his personal ends in the selections he makes." See Bigelow, Diary, 10 Sep 1861, BiP.

26. From the moment he sent his first despatch, the anonymous London correspondent of the *New York Times* stood in mirror relation with world-famous William Howard Russell, who currently was writing from America to *The Times* of London as "Special Correspondent." The mirror relationship became explicit on 30 Nov 1861, when Raymond printed HA's despatch no. 27 under the heading "From Our Special Correspondent."

Although published in England, Russell's LTimes despatches were widely read in the United States, partly as a result of regular distribution of the newspaper, partly as a result of piracy.

Matchingly, HA's NYTimes despatches were read in the British Isles. See John Witherspoon DuBose, *Life & Times of William Lowndes Yancey*, Birmingham AL 1892, 606—"Libraries, club rooms, hotel rooms, [and] numberless public places [in Europe in 1861–1862] were abundantly supplied with the newspapers of the United States. . . ." "The metropolitan press of the United States were required to publish news especially adapted to European circulation, and large sums of money were s[p]ent by the Union government to distribute those papers [abroad]."

27. For details relating to HA's efforts to publish in the *Atlantic Monthly*, see HA–1, 110–20, 227–28, 244–50, 310–21, 373–74, 448.

28. The only account is HA–1, Chaps. 17–27 and attendant notes.

29. JQA most strongly expressed his estimate by naming his first child George Washington Adams. See HA–1, 35.

30. *Sketches*, 151.

31. Ibid., 159.

32. HA prevailed on CFA to write unsigned notices of Vols. II & III of the *Memoirs of John Quincy Adams* (edited by CFA) for publication in the *North American Review* (edited by HA) in October 1874 and January 1875. The first notice, a remarkable statement, says (471): "The present volume opens to view for the first time the establishment of that policy of friendly

relations between the United States and Russia which was intended to serve, and which has in fact served, as a check to the domination of Great Britain on the Ocean."

33. "Mrs. John Quincy Adams's narrative of a journey . . . ," *Scribner's Magazine*, Oct 1903, 449–63. HA hand-copied the narrative in 1869. See Chap. 9.

34. CFA2, *Charles Francis Adams*, Bost & NY 1900, 7.

35. In MHS *Proceedings*, 45 (1911–1912), 244–45, BA says, ". . . [CFA] took me for long walks and told me stories of his boyhood; how he had travelled in a carriage alone with his mother across Europe from St. Petersburg to Paris, in the winter in 1815 . . . how he had seen Napoleon at a window in the Tuileries during the 'hundred days' . . . ." It seems a fair supposition that HA too was told stories by CFA. The important difference is that HA, being ten years older than BA, was born in time to be told stories also by LCA and JQA.

36. HA took a marked interest in Hawthorne's "Old Esther Dudley," a story in which the leading character—after whom HA named the heroine of his second novel—conducts herself historically.

37. At different points in his writings, HA recorded very high estimates of Washington, Franklin, Gallatin, and Lincoln, possibly ranking them in that order. See *EHA* (1907), 38; (LoA), 763—". . . like the Pole Star . . . [Washington] alone remained steady, in the mind of Henry Adams, to the end." Also see HA's Preface in *EHA*, praising Franklin as a unique "model" of "self-teaching." Further see HA's "Albert Gallatin," *Memorial Biographies of the New England Historic Genealogical Society*, Vol. I (1880), 212—"As a practical statesman he had no equal in his day, and his scattered writings show him to have had no superior as a man of science and study." Finally see HA's Preface to *Letters of John Hay*, privately printed 1908, published NY 1969, viii, praising Lincoln as "the most sympathetic among all Americans."

38. HA to EC, 3 Mar 1901, HA-micro 17.

39. Compare *EHA* (1907), 10; (LoA), 733, ". . . he [HA] was . . . admitted to a sort of familiarity . . . ," with *Autobiography*, 10, "In his library he [JQA] was always at work, or nodding in his chair."

40. For "Toil and Trust," see CFA, Diary, 22 Jan 1865, AP.

41. HA's expectations are shown vividly (and I assume accurately) by an action in *The Education*: the twelve-year-old protagonist's leaving LCA's Washington house before breakfast to inspect the unfinished Washington Monument. See *EHA* (1907), 35–36; (LoA), 759–60.

42. This account of England's response to American developments owes much to the detailed testimony of a knowledgeable English witness, John Formby. See his long letter to CFA2, 31 Jan 1914, CFA2P.

43. HA, *Historical Essays*, NY 1891, 269—"When [C. F.] Adams arrived in London . . . the American Union was universally supposed to be at an end. Not one Englishman in a hundred took a different view. The possibility of a civil war, believed to be necessarily futile, irritated Englishmen against President Lincoln and his supporters."

44. Hope was evidenced by Lord Palmerston's visiting the Confederate steamer *Nashville* at Southampton. Doubt was evidenced by Lord Russell's cautious reaction to the same vessel's remaining in an English port. See Warren F. Spencer, *The Confederate Navy in Europe*, University AL 1983, 28, and references to the *Nashville* affair, *passim*.

45. Of the many accounts, one of the most helpfully detailed is an old one: Frederic Bancroft, *Life of William H. Seward*, NY & Lond 1900, II, 223–34.

46. Richard Henry Dana to CFA2, 12 Apr 1912, CFA2P—". . . the warlike preparations [of England] . . . differentiated the Trent case from all other cases of its kind."

47. Bancroft, *Seward*, II, 231n5. See also Glyndon G. Van Deusen, *Thurlow Weed: Wizard of the Lobby*, Bost 1947, 277.

48. Starting in October or November 1861, HA supplied material to the editors of English periodicals for anonymous use. See *EHA* (1907), 103; (LoA), 829—". . . [HA] had . . . become fairly intimate with the two or three friendly newspapers in London; the *Daily News*; the *Star*; the weekly *Spectator*; and . . . tried to give them news and views . . . ."

Apparently on the basis of good but partly mistaken information, William Yancey, chief Confederate commissioner in London, believed that during the *Trent* affair the *Morning Star* was both the organ of John Bright and Richard Cobden and "the organ of the United States minister." See DuBose, *Yancey*, op. cit., 625. Yancey presumably was not aware that a younger Adams at the U. S. Legation was acting independently of Minister Adams.

HA's one extant letter to Weed, L, I, 273–74, is dated only "Friday night." The letter in no way shows Weed to have known that HA was the London correspondent of the *New York Times*. It shows instead that HA and Weed formed very confidential relations with respect to guiding the *English* press. HA tells Weed that he is disposed to write on a political topic for English publication without his father's knowledge, in fact has drafted a "letter" for anonymous publication. One may assume that the intended vehicle for HA's "letter" was the *Star* and that HA was supplying *written* material to that organ only.

Levenson and his fellow editors date the letter [24 January? 1862]. In my view, this date, or any other Friday subsequent to 3 Jan 1862, is impossible. See Chap. 2, notes 10 & 26.

49. Gladstone later wrote: ". . . we have seen Mr. Lincoln deliver up Mason and Slidell, contrary to expectation here [in England] . . . and to very serious and even authoritative indications of public sentiment [in the United States]." See "Memorandum by Mr. Gladstone on the War in America [for use at a cabinet meeting of 25 Oct 1862]" in Philip Guedalla, ed., *The Palmerston Papers/ Gladstone and Palmerston . . .* , Lond 1928, 242.

50. A helpful English account is Anthony Trollope's. He was near at hand when the decision to return the captives was made. He wrote: "I was in Washington at the time, and it was known there that the contest among the leading Northerners was very sharp. Mr. Sumner and Mr. Seward were, under Mr. Lincoln, the two chiefs of the party. It was understood that Mr. Sumner was opposed to the rendition of the men, and Mr. Seward in favor of it. Mr. Seward's counsels at last prevailed with the President, and England's declaration of war was prevented. I dined with Mr. Seward on the day of the decision, meeting Mr. Sumner at his home, and was told as I left the dining-room what the decision had been. During the afternoon I and others had received intimation through the embassy that we might probably have to leave Washington at an hour's notice. This, I think, was the severest danger that the Northern cause encountered during the war."

See *Autobiography of Anthony Trollope*, NY: George Munro [1883], 129, or, in other editions, Chap. IX.

51. Weed sent frequent letters to WHS. More than one must have arrived by 26 Dec 1861. In their *Abraham Lincoln/ A History*, NY 1890, V, 35, John G. Nicolay and John Hay say that the 25–26 Dec 1861 meetings involved "a reading of the few letters which had been received from Europe." They do not specify all the writers. I am left with the impression that Seward produced none of the letters received from Weed.

52. HA's critically important despatches, nos. 30–34, appeared in the NYTimes on 25, & 30 Dec 1861, 5, 4, & 11 Jan 1862. His presenting himself as an *older* Unionist is boldest and most obtrusive in no. 32.

53. The *James Adger* first put into port in England on 2 Nov 1861 at Falmouth. The warship then moved along the English coast to Southampton. There on November 6, the commander, Captain John B. Marchand, read a report in *The Times* of London that Mason and Slidell had reached Cuba at Cardenas. Next day he visited CFA at the Legation and showed the minister his orders. HA presumably was present, but during the following afternoon he left for Manchester.

During HA's absence, CFA received word from Marchand that he would direct his vessel homeward as soon as it was ready for sea. Early on November 12, the *James Adger* left Southampton, repaired, coaled, and provisioned for the Atlantic crossing.

That same morning, November 12, CFA received a note from Prime Minister Palmerston asking him to come to the latter's London residence between 1:00 and 2:00 P.M. The Union envoy arrived as asked. Palmerston and CFA met for about thirty minutes. (This was the only business meeting the two men would ever have.) Palmerston did the talking. He said that Mason and Slidell were understood to be aboard a British mail ship expected to arrive next day or the day following; that it had been intimated to him that the *James Adger* had been sent to British home waters to intercept the Confederate envoys, even at the cost of committing violence upon the British flag; and that he was "very doubtful" whether such an act "could lead to any good."

CFA interrupted Palmerston to ask what grounds he had for thinking that Captain Marchand of the *James Adger* would venture to commit violence on a *British* vessel. Palmerston could only give as grounds the date of the Union warship's arrival and the fact of its departing from Southampton that very morning. CFA interjected that Captain Marchand had visited him and shown him his orders. The orders required Marchand to search for and if possible seize the Confederate paddle-steamer *Nashville*, on which Mason and Slidell were reported to have sailed from Charleston, presumably with a view to a direct crossing of the Atlantic, ending at a British port. (The orders had been inspired by false stories planted in the Confederate press, saying the envoys had sailed for Europe on the *Nashville*. Marchand had doubted the truth of the stories but had had no choice but to voyage to England as ordered.)

Palmerston and other officers of the British government disbelieved CFA's assurances and thought him dishonest, incompetent, or both.

CFA wrote two accounts of his meeting with Palmerston, the first in his diary on November 12, the second in a despatch to Seward on the 15th. In the first account, he reported Palmerston as having said that the British mail ship thought to be carrying Mason and Slidell was due at a British port on the 13th or 14th. In the second, he reported the prime minister as having vaguely referred to "the period assigned for the approach of the gentleman in the West India steamer."

One presumable reason for this inconsistency is that, during the three-day interval between his meeting with Palmerston and his writing the account to Seward, CFA ascertained that no British mail ship had arrived with Mason and Slidell aboard. A second reason—which may or may not have been brought to CFA's attention—is that a problem existed about the mail ship that Palmerston had said was soon arriving. The problem could be stated in few words. *Which ship was it?*

In 1974, a well-informed historian said the ship was a British vessel plying the St. Thomas-Southampton run. See D. P. Crook, *The North, the South, and the Powers/ 1861–1865*, NY Lond Sydney Toronto, 1974, 121–24. Crook was speaking of the *Seine*, which reached Southampton early on November 13. But there was never a possibility that Mason and Slidell could be aboard the *Seine*. There had not been time enough for the envoys to travel from Cardenas, Cuba, to far-distant St. Thomas and ask for passage.

When I was finishing the first book of this trilogy, I assumed—like Crook—that Palmerston was speaking of an actual ship. Try as I might, I could find no trace of a ship that precisely answered to the prime minister's description, as reported by CFA. At the last minute, I permitted myself to cite news in *The Times* of London that the *Conway* reached Southampton on 16 Nov 1861. See HA–1, 440n13.

This was scholarly desperation. The *Conway* too was an actual ship and had come from the Caribbean area, but I had no basis for believing that it was in any way connected with Palmerston's talk with CFA.

Subsequent investigations produced the following discovery. On 31 Oct 1861, the *New York Herald* published new information just received from Cuba. The information included three items:

> Cardenas, October 17, to the *Prensa de la Habana*: "It seems that Messrs. Mason and Slidell will leave for Havana in a few days, where they will take passage on the English steamer for Europe."
> Colon, October 19, to the *Prensa de la Habana*: ". . . [Mason and Slidell] will go on to Havana, to leave on the first steamer that leaves direct for Europe."
> Havana, October 25, to the *New York Herald*: ". . . [Mason and Slidell] leave . . . in the British steamer of November 7, for Southampton. The British steamer *Trent* arrived . . . from Southampton, with several travellers . . . belonging to the Confederate States . . . ."

Reduced to essentials, the items said that a British steamer, the *Trent*, was plying a direct route between Southampton and Havana; that the steamer would be leaving Havana for Southampton on November 7; and that Mason, Slidell, and their party would be passengers on the voyage.

If usual procedures were followed, this news was no sooner printed in the *New York Herald* than it was telegraphed by Reuters to Halifax, Nova Scotia, to be carried by the Cunard steamer *Arabia* to Liverpool. The news was then telegraphed by Reuters from Liverpool to London, in ample time to be the basis for Palmerston's summoning of CFA.

This reconstruction of events has several important features. It gives the British reason for putting two things together: the departure of the Union warship *James Adger* from Southampton and the supposed approach of a British steamer coming from Havana with Mason and Slidell aboard. It gives the British reason for fearing a Union attack on a British vessel *in British home waters*—meaning a deliberate insult to Great Britain by Secretary Seward, intended to bring on a new war between Great Britain and the United States. And it gives the British reason for an immediate test of Minister Adams, to see how much he knows, and how much he will lie, about the insult-in-the-making.

The case was complicated by ironic particulars. The reports from Cuba published in the *New York Herald* were—by accident—misleading and untrue! To begin with, there was no steamer that regularly plied a direct route between Havana and Southampton or any other British port. The steamer named, the *Trent*, had not arrived from Southampton and would not sail for Southampton on November 7. A subsidiary ship, the *Trent* merely plied a route between St. Thomas and ports in Mexico by way of Havana.

It thus appears that the ship that Palmerston talked about when he spoke with CFA, while believed at the moment by Palmerston to be real and almost due at Southampton, was wholly imaginary.

The ship's being imaginary did not prevent the British from acting (a) as if Mason and Slidell were arriving on a British ship coming directly to British waters; (b) as if the *James Adger* had not returned to America but was hovering near Ireland, to attempt the seizure of the Confederate envoys; and (c) as if *some* Union insult, intended to provoke a war, would almost certainly occur in the immediate future within miles of the British coast.

HA returned from Manchester late on November 13. He learned all that CFA could tell him about the meeting with Palmerston. He learned too that the *James Adger* was returning straight to America.

An adept at checking ship schedules and shipping news, HA possibly was in process of learning what routes and what ships Mason and Slidell could actually take. At all events, he heard—or invented—a story that the British mail ship allegedly bringing the envoys from Cuba was delayed by storms. In addition, he learned that a British frigate, the *Phaeton*, had been sent to watch the supposedly hovering *James Adger*.

HA then cut to the heart of the matter by warning in his next despatch to the *New York Times*, sent on November 16, that the British were braced for an expected Union insult in home waters and that the British navy was keeping watch. The point of the warning was that the British were in earnest and would resent what they thought would be a deliberate provocation.

For documentation and further details, see Edward Chalfant, "A War So Near/ Imagined Steamers in the Trent Affair," *Journal of Confederate History*, VI (1990), 139–59. A corrected copy is at MHS.

54. CFA2 to HA, 3 Dec 1861.
55. HA to CFA2, 11 Apr 1862.
56. HA's letters subsequent to the *Trent* affair repeatedly refer to the possibility that the Union will initiate war with England. See especially HA to FWS, 29 Oct 1862 and 20 Mar 1863, L, I, 314, 337–38.

57. This aspect of the *Trent* affair is best explained in the invaluable but neglected writings of Richard Henry Dana, principally a pamphlet, "The Trent Affair/ An Aftermath," Camb 1912. The pamphlet is an improved version of a paper part-published and part-suppressed in MHS *Proceedings*, 45 (1911–1912), 508–22. Also see Dana's letters to CFA2, 8, 12, 22 Apr & 22 May 1912, CFA2P, and Dana's letter to Ford, 15 May 1912, FP.

58. Touching on American antipathy to England, Lowell explained in a letter to Godkin, 2 May 1869, Godkin Papers, H: ". . . it is not the *Alabama* that is at the bottom of our grudge. It is the *Trent* that we quarrel about. . . . That was like an Eastwind to our old wound & set it atwinge once more. Old wrongs are as sure to come back on our hands as cats. . . . That imperious despatch of Lord John's made all those inherited drops of ill blood as hot as present wrongs."

59. HA's NYTimes despatch no. 30 stands in contrast with a letter from his eldest brother to their father, dated 30 Dec 1861, in which JQA2 declared:

> Mason and Slidell are free and we have suffered the greatest national disgrace that ever we have undergone. . . . You may be sure . . . that we are humiliated to the very bone, that old men with cold blood absolutely tremble with impotent rage. . . . For my own part, I . . . disbelieve in the policy of war or unfriendly feelings . . . but it does seem . . . that this people will be false to itself if they do not lay up in silence, great store of wrath for the treatment we have now received at England's hands. . . . Individually I hope that we shall not make an outcry nor threaten loudly nor brag what we might have done. But, as soon as we can, begin soberly and seriously to prepare for a war with England. . . . I at least would care to impress but one thing on a son of mine and that should be inveterate, undying, immortal hatred of Great Britain. In this I do not feel I am at all exaggerating the general feeling here. . . . I feel most sincerely for your very painful situation, and I wish we were strong enough to withdraw you, but let us patiently and cheerfully bide our time and wait. Then in some awful hour of England we will leap upon her back and tear her. I believe it well known that of all quarrels, the fiercest are family wars, and that no hate can equal the rancour of enraged brothers, but be sure no rancour ever hatched equals the deep and savage animosity which boils in our blood here.

CFA2 discovered JQA2's letter and wrote to Ford, 16 Dec 1911, FP: "It is . . . utterly unfit for publication, being a private letter, which both the writer thereof and his family would now shudder at seeing in print. . . . Nevertheless, I send you a copy. . . ."

The original of JQA2's letter is missing. Extant letters from JQA2 to CFA are in the Homans Collection, supplementary to the Adams Papers, MHS. For whatever reason, letters from JQA2 to CFA dated 1861 are conspicuously absent in this collection.

60. In old age, CFA2 wrote that the "deluge of the Civil War" so submerged his memories of events during the war's earliest phase that he was deprived of all awareness that, at the time, he kept a diary. See *Autobiography*, 83.

61. HA to CFA2, 22 May 1862.

62. That Unionists wanted revenge was taught immediately to HA by a family letter. See note 58, above. Through various channels, news that many Union wanted revenge also reached the English. John Bright accordingly commented to HA, ". . . you Americans . . . mustn't go and get stuffy to England." See HA to CFA2, 16 May 1862.

63. Older Americans most effectual in resolving the *Trent* affair were W. H. Seward and Montgomery Blair in Washington; Thurlow Weed and John Bigelow in Europe. HA was alone in being a *young* effectual American participant.

64. That HA believed he had been an unofficial but effectual peace commissioner is confirmed by his later writing a documentary history of the Treaty of Paris—see *Sketches*, 154–59—and two documentary histories of the Treaty of Ghent—see *LAG*, 493–547, and *HUS* (Scribner), IX, 1–53; (LoA), II, 1185–1219.

65. An instance of Union fury is a passage in a letter by Lt. Col. Francis Channing Barlow (whom HA had known at Harvard), written 28 Dec 1861 to "Edward," Barlow Papers, MHS: "I certainly do *not* approve of giving up Mason and Slidell. I would go to war with the whole of them first. We are lost if we show any cowardice or want of spirit on any point. I also believe that a war with England would bring out a spirit which this war [against the Confederacy] never has."

66. *EHA* (1907) 103; (LoA), 829.

67. That HA did in fact start a new life is shown by his engagement books, 1862–1868, HAL. The books manifestly record a fresh beginning from its first moments in London in January 1862 to the end of a critically important winter in Washington in March 1869. The earliest book is inscribed "H. B. Adams,/ London,/ 1862." Its earliest daily entry appears in the space the book provides for 15 Jan 1862.

There may appear to be two explanations of HA's starting a second life, one centering in the success of his NYTimes despatches, the other in the exposure of his authorship of an article, "A Visit to Manchester" (see Chap. 2). In my opinion, the explanation centering in the despatches is the essential, sufficient explanation, and the explanation centering in the exposure is important but merely additional and supportive.

68. HA's resolution to build at high levels and aspire to still higher levels is most strongly expressed in his *Mont Saint Michel and Chartres*. There it first appears in the opening line: "The Archangel loved heights."

69. This object, part-achieved by the negotiation of the Treaty of Washington in 1871, was wholly achieved by the Geneva arbitration of 1872.

70. The despatches are completely listed only in HA–1. That the list is complete is owing to the fact that the despatches are self-identifying. HA wrote them connectedly, like the chapters of a book; and Raymond published them under headings which in varied ways leave no doubt of their being the work of a single writer.

Of the thirty-five despatches, nos. 1–6, 8, 10–18, 22, 24, 26, & 28–35 appear under the heading "From Our Own Correspondent." No. 27, published 30 Nov 1861, is headed "From Our Special Correspondent"—a different wording with the same meaning.

No. 7, published 15 Jul 1861, follows a despatch by "Malakoff," the

Paris correspondent; and the Paris and London despatches together are headed "Our Foreign Correspondence."

No. 9, published 26 Jul 1861, precedes a despatch by "Malakoff." The two despatches are headed "Our London and Paris Correspondence."

No. 19, published 13 Oct 1861, and no. 20, published 28 Oct 1861, are each headed "Correspondence of the New-York Times." Corroboratively, the same heading also precedes nos. 9 & 25.

No. 21, published 28 Oct 1861, precedes a despatch by "Malakoff." The two despatches are headed "Our Foreign Correspondence."

No. 25, published 18 Nov 1861, is headed "Correspondence of the New-York Times." It is preceded by a despatch from "Malakoff." The two despatches are headed "Our Paris and London Correspondence."

For additional details, see HA–1, 428–47.

71. I am indebted to the newspaper division of the New York Public Library for access to a much-worn run of the NYTimes in 1956–1962 when I first studied the despatches; also for recent permission to check my list of the despatches in HA–1 against a magnificent run whose volumes for 1861–1862 remain as good as new.

2. CONQUERORS

Letters by and to HA are in HA-micro 2, unless otherwise noted.

PRINCIPAL SOURCES

(1) eight letters, HA to CFA2, 15 Mar–6 Jun 1862, including the unsigned fragment [27 Apr 1862].

(2) letter, HA to Palfrey, 20 Mar 1862.

(3) letter, HA to CFA, 15 Apr 1862.

ADDITIONAL SOURCES; COMMENTS

1. One of the barriers in the way of HA's becoming a lawyer was his falling asleep while trying to read Blackstone. See HA to CFA2, 26 Jul 1861—". . . I invariably go to sleep over him. . . ."

2. The CFA-JQA2 correspondence, 1861–1868, AP, Homans Collection, is predicated throughout on the imaginary rule. Father and eldest son can be described as believers in a variant of primogeniture. For HA's adverse opinion of primogeniture, see *Sketches*, 165–66.

3. HA–1, 142–44, 206, 229, 244, 247, 309–10, 399, 413, 426.

4. *Autobiography*, 40–41; MHS *Proceedings*, 43 (1909–1910), 656–87.

5. JTA insightfully suggested that HA accompanied CFA to England as "son, personal secretary, courier, and general handy man." See *The Adams Family*, Bost 1930, 254. The scope of HA's duties can be gleaned from the entries in his engagement books, 1862–1868, HAL, and scattered passages in his letters, May 1861–June 1868, HA-micro 2–3.

6. CFA2 to HA, 23 Aug 1861.

7. CFA2 to HA, 17 Dec 1861.

8. Being equivalent to "I am at liberty to say," Lunt's "we feel at liberty to say" reflects CFA2's permission and also his advice.

9. *The Times* (London), 10 Jan 1862, 6, leader headed " 'To see ourselves as others see us'. . . ."

10. CFA to CFA2, 10 Jan 1862, AP. That CFA extracted a vow from

HA, and that HA willingly and strictly kept it, can be inferred from HA to Palfrey, 20 Mar 1862—". . . my pen is forced to keep away from political matters. . . ."; also HA to Palfrey, 29 May 1863—". . . [it is] forbidden ground to me to appear in print on matter connected with the affairs of the Legation." The inference is supported too by HA to FWS, 14 Feb 1862—". . . [I] dare not appear as a writer, even anonymously, for fear of compromising my father." The inference is again supported by HA's writing to CFA2, 21 Nov 1862, that, following the publication of "A Visit to Manchester" and the response to it by the English press, he avoided "every and any act" that might expose him even to a mere risk of a similar "scorching." Finally, the inference is supported by the apparent fact that HA from 10 Jan 1862 till late 1868 *did* avoid publication on "political matters."

Of course a vow not to publish on political matters would not preclude HA's furnishing news and views to English editors orally. That he was going to do so may be indicated by an entry in his 1862 engagement book in a monthly space provided for January: "Thomas Walker Esqʳ Editor/ Daily News/ Bowerie St. Fleet St. E.C."

11. HA–1, 384–87; HA to CFA2, 22 Jan 1862.

12. An instance of a childhood action of HA's being critically noticed is given in F, II, 472n1. See also the Irish gardener episode in *EHA* (1907), 12; (LoA), 734.

13. On HA's anticipating the possible necessity of suicide, see *EHA* (1907), 103; (LoA), 829–30—". . . Adams thought his 'usefulness' at an end in other respects than in the press. . . ."

It deserves noting that HA thought the better of George Washington Adams because he committed suicide. See HA to CFA2, 21 Dec 1912, HA-micro 27—". . . his drowning himself showed a tragic quality far above the Adams average."

14. *EHA* (1907), 103; (LoA), 829.

15. Moran, 1 Mar 1864—". . . [HA's] place as *private secretary* is that of a menial. His social status rests on the foundation of his being the Minister's son, and if he were introduced [in England] as *private* Secretary he would sink at once."

16. In relation to the possibility of perfect management, see HA's eventual very relevant comment, *HUS* (Scribner), III, 210; (LoA), I, 748: "Gallatin made no mistakes. . . ."

17. Raymond Papers, NYPL.

18. HA's understanding of his mother and her upsets was later expressed in three letters, HA to CFA, 7, 14, 21 Jan 1872, HA-micro 3.

19. CFA to CFA2, 3 Oct 1862, AP.

20. HA's lifelong solicitousness with regard to BA may have been caused by the death of Arthur Adams, which occurred when HA was eight.

21. HA to CFA2, 22 Jan 1862.

22. *EHA* (1907) 49; (LoA), 774; HA–1, 85.

23. HA to CFA2, 14 Feb 1862.

24. HA to CFA2, 5 Oct 1861 & 15 Mar 1862.

25. The complete change in attitude of the Adamses towards Weed, following his arrival in London, is reflected in CFA2 to CFA, 11 Mar 1862, AP—". . . to find you working heart and hand with Weed . . . is something I did not dream to see."

26. The one extant letter from HA to Weed, L, I, 273–74, is dated only "Friday night." The letter concerns the imminent publication of "documents." Also HA speaks in it about a "letter" by himself (not extant) intended for anonymous publication, presumably in a London newspaper, "without the knowledge of my father."

Apparently guided by the second paragraph of HA to FWS, 30 Jan 1862, L, I, 274, Levenson and his fellow editors date HA's Friday night letter [24 January? 1862]. So dated, the letter has some importance, but not much.

In my view, the editors' conjectured date is impossible because CFA asked HA on 10 Jan 1862 to vow not to publish on political matters and HA made the vow and kept it. See note 10, above.

I suggest that the probable date is Friday, 3 Jan 1862, and that the letter relates to a particular matter. By 31 Dec 1861, some of the interchanges between Minister Adams and Foreign Secretary Russell had been published in the U. S. and had reached London, where republication was likely. See Frank Lawrence Owsley, *King Cotton Diplomacy/ Foreign Relations of the Confederate States of America*, rev. ed., Chicago 1959, 82.

I suggest too that the letter is important—that it initiated the confidential relations later manifest between HA and Weed. Last, I suggest that Weed preserved it on that account.

27. HA to CFA2, 10 Jan 1862.

28. HA to CFA2, 22 May 1862—". . . I have a free swing at the Sturgis's place [at Walton]. . . ."; *EHA* (1907), 104; *EHA* (LoA), 831— "During two years of miserable solitude, she [Mrs. Sturgis] was . . . the single source of warmth and light."

29. HA also believed that success in politics could be assured by helpful efforts on the part of politicians' *wives*. In regard to his mother's efforts, see HA to ABA, 13 Feb 1860, HA-micro 1. In regard to Lady Palmerston's efforts, see *EHA* (1907), 115; (LoA) 841–42.

30. Writing to CFA2 on 23 Apr 1863, HA mentions his "shiny black tile." Louisa Hooper Thoron told me repeatedly that his "tile" was an ever-reappearing part of his dress. For its importance, see Chap. 13. Also see the photograph of HA and others, L, III, opp. 33.

31. With regard to the date HA started to save, see his letter to JQA2, 2 Mar 1867, HA-micro 3, mentioning "vows" made "five years" earlier with the "principal object" of becoming "independent."

For a misleading date HA assigned to the start of his re-education, see his letter to CFA2, 23 Oct 1863—"Two years ago [October 1861] I began on history . . . [meaning his first attempt to investigate Smith]."

A date attuned to actualities is early March 1862, when HA began to study financial theories and began sustained investigation of Smith.

32. On his income, see HA to CFA2, [4 Jul 1861]. At the time, his income matched Secretary Wilson's annual salary.

33. On the necessity of earning money as a lawyer, see HA to CFA2, 18 Jan 1859, HA-micro 1.

34. *Autobiography*, 19, saying CFA "failed to discriminate between individuals" and imposed "one rule" with regard to the training of his sons.

35. See especially CFA to CFA2, 17 Apr 1862 & 13 Mar 1863, AP.

36. LCA to HA [Feb 1850?], *Colophon*, Autumn 1938, 489; HA, "Holden Chapel," *Harvard Magazine*, May 1855, 210–15.

37. HA to CFA2, 18 Jan 1859, HA-micro 1.

38. HA, "Reading in College," *Harvard Magazine*, Oct 1857, 317.

39. It is suggested in Chap. 15 that HA when a boy very possibly had opportunities to peruse four volumes owned by JQA and bound as a set. The volumes' covers were lettered *Adams's History of the Republic*. The set embraced JA's *Defence of the Constitution of the Government of the United States* and *Discourses on Davila*. In title and number of volumes, the set anticipated—and conceivably suggested—HA's *History of the United States*, which, as written, though not as published, was a four-volume work. The set was described and offered for sale in Goodspeed's Catalogue 492.

40. In his diary, 16 Sep 1888, L, III, 143, HA links the date he began work as author of his *History of the United States* with the date of his first knowing how Gibbon conceived a history of Rome.

41. HA began to write regularly about himself in 1852, when he began his diary. While at Harvard, in 1856–1857, he wrote a series of comic papers as Hasty Pudding Alligator in which he presented himself in the third person singular—a device he later made the most evident feature of *The Education of Henry Adams*. In 1859 in Europe, he completed (but did not publish) an article on education in the form of two pretended letters about his experiences while attending a Prussian gymnasium. He preserved the manuscript and possibly had it with him in 1860 in Rome when he read the extract from Gibbon's *Memoirs*.

42. For details, see Palfrey to Deane, 11 Nov 1861, Deane Papers, MHS; Deane to Palfrey, 17 Nov 1861, Palfrey Papers, MHS; and Watts to HA, 5 Dec 1861, DP.

43. Twenty-six works by Smith appear in the two-volume *Catalogue of the Valuable Private Library of the late Charles Deane* . . . , Bost: C. F. Libbie & Co. 1898.

44. Moran, 23 Mar 1862.

45. Ibid., 5 Apr 1862.

46. CFA to CFA2, 17 Apr 1862, AP.

47. The move of the Adamses to the house on Park Crescent prefigured HA's real estate coup of the 1880s, his negotiation to buy the non-church corner lot directly facing the White House in Washington.

48. On 23 Aug 1860, HA wrote a letter in French to CFA2. In his *Henry Adams/ The Myth of Failure*, Charlottesville 1980, 66–67, William Dusinberre quotes a translation of a phrase in the letter and says the phrase implies that HA at the time was resorting to prostitutes. It should be noticed, however, that another passage in the same letter confutes that reading. HA states in the passage that, despite felt sexual necessities, he is being well-behaved.

49. HA to BA, 3 Mar 1872, HA-micro 3. When he became twenty-four, in 1872, BA rushed into a scrape in Paris. His action possibly was modeled on HA's, even to the place and the year-of-life at which each had his "first experience."

50. CFA to CFA2, 2 May 1862, AP.

51. Moran, 26 Apr 1862.

52. *EHA* (1907), 101; (LoA), 827; also MA to CFA2, 16 May 1862, AP.

53. Moran, 12 May 1862.

54. CFA to CFA2, 17 Apr 1862, AP.

55. CFA to CFA2, 16 May 1862, AP.

56. Telegram, WHS to CFA, 1 May 1862, AP.

57. Moran, 21 May 1862.

58. Writing in old age to Ford, 4 Dec 1914, FP, CFA2 spun a misleading story relating to unofficial Union diplomats in London.

> . . . privately he [CFA] never . . . hesitated in saying that he was encumbered in the early years of his mission by assistance worse than useless. There was one dreadfully funny incident connected therewith that is worth recording.
>
> [John Lothrop] Motley . . . had a very large social acquaintance in London. . . . He had an aptitude for that sort of work, of which my father was entirely devoid. My father . . . received a letter from Motley . . . telling him that Seward had written him . . . requesting him to go over to London and use his influence socially to aid my father and forward the cause of the Union. Motley appreciated the delicacy of the situation, and wrote to my father, frankly asking what should be done. My father felt considerably annoyed, but after reflecting on the matter, he determined to consult Thurlow Weed, who was then in London. He took an opportunity of doing so after dinner one day, Weed being his guest, and there explained to him, as the best means of reaching Seward, how embarrassing it was for him to have these volunteer diplomats in London, as their presence discredited him, giving the impression that he was not qualified for his work. His influence, therefore, was seriously impaired. Then came in the amusing part of the situation. Weed, whose relations with him were very friendly, listened in silence, and then was obliged to confess that Seward had written to Motley at his (Weed's) suggestion. Weed, however, at once saw the force of my father's objection, and did communicate with Seward, who then put a stop of [sic] his pernicious practice of volunteer diplomatic cooperation.

The story skirts key facts. Motley was in Europe *officially*, as minister to Austria, and Weed himself was the unofficial diplomat who put CFA in the shade in London. Moreover, the story unintendedly grants that Weed, because incomparably closer to Seward than CFA, could alter the Union's diplomatic arrangements in Europe, and did so.

Also see Chap. 3, note 58, and Chap. 7, note 14.

59. CFA to CFA2, 16 May 1862, AP.

60. *EHA* (1907), 117; (LoA), 843.

61. Palmerston to CFA, 11 Jun 1862, PP. The complete correspondence is given in CFA2, *Charles Francis Adams, op. cit.*, 248–60.

A letter from Palmerston to Russell, 14 Jun 1862, PP, contains no suggestion of rape. It simply asserts that Butler's order rendered "respectable women of every class" liable to be "imprisoned with the most abandoned & profligate and degraded of their sex."

Palmerston's suggesting rape found a parallel in something HA heard said by Thackeray. See *EHA* (1907), 113; (LoA), 839—"He [Thackeray] never doubted that the Federals made a business of harrowing the tenderest feelings of women—particularly of women—in order to punish their opponents."

62. *EHA* (1907), 118; (LoA), 844.

63. CFA to Palmerston, 20 Jun 1862, PP.

64. Moran was shown the correspondence after its completion. In his journal, 25 Jun 1862, he said concerning the closing sentence of CFA's third note, "This severe reprimand had its intended effect, and his Lordship has remained silent under it."

65. The American notes are in the Palmerston Papers. The first, 12 Jun 1862, is in CFA's handwriting throughout. The second, 16 Jun 1862, and third, 20 Jun 1862, are in HA's handwriting but signed by CFA. A copy of the third note preserved by the Adamses, AP, likewise is in HA's handwriting. It might therefore be imagined that the son did something in the way of writing or revising the notes, especially the second and third. As it happens, however, no word or phrase in the notes is suggestive of either authorship or revision by HA.

The account of the correspondence with Palmerston later given by HA in *EHA* (1907), 117–18; (LoA), 843–45, describes CFA as "perplexed in the extreme." "Not that Mr. Adams lost his temper, for he never felt such a weight of responsibility, and was never more cool; but he could conceive no other way of protecting his government, not to speak of himself, than to force Lord Russell to interpose." Emphatically this account ascribes to CFA alone the stratagem which the American notes successfully carried out.

66. CFA to WHS, 20 Jun 1862, with attachments, in *Despatches from United States Ministers to Great Britain, 1791–1906*, Microcopy 30, roll 75, NA. The missing first report included Palmerston's first note to CFA and CFA's first note in response. Details are given in HA to FWS, 29 Oct 1862, L, I, 313–14. (The editors' note 1 on 313 says in error that the documents at issue were the *last* notes, not the first.)

67. In 1863, CFA2 declined an increase of rank in the army and wrote to his relatives in London about his action. On 25 Sep 1863, HA responded: "I am glad of your decision; I cannot doubt of its wisdom . . . . Very true it is that promotion is not progress, and you and I have worked out that problem for ourselves at just about the same time, though by rather different paths. My ideas on such subjects have changed in two years more than I could have guessed. . . ."

In my view, the passage reflects HA's history relating to *official* promotion. (Unsuccessfully, he had sought in March 1861 the place of first secretary in London. Also, in March 1861, he had twice refused the place of second secretary in London.) Except in its mention of "progress," the passage is silent concerning a subject of much greater importance: HA's *unofficial* ranks and functions while living and working at the Legation. The silence considered, the passage shows a sharp decline in HA's willingness to confide in CFA2.

3. HOPES FOR US ALL

Letters by and to HA are in HA-micro 2, unless otherwise noted.

PRINCIPAL SOURCES

(1) thirty letters, HA to CFA2, 4 Jul 1862–30 Jul 1863, including the undated fragment beginning "Mr[.] Evarts wants me to go over to Paris. . . ."

(2) letter, HA to WHS, 23 Jan 1863, *Despatches from U. S. Ministers to Great Britain, 1792–1870*, Microcopy 30, roll 78, NA.

(3) letters, HA to Cobden, 22 & 23 Apr 1863, L, I, 342–43, 346–47.
(4) HA, "Report on the Trades Union Meeting [Lond, 26 Mar 1863]," Microcopy 30, roll 78, op. cit., NA; published in Charles I. Glicksberg, "Henry Adams Reports on a Trades Union Meeting," *NEQ*, Dec 1942, 725–28.

ADDITIONAL SOURCES; COMMENTS

1. With regard to the plaque, see CFA to CFA2, 19 Sep 1862, AP.
2. HA–1, 20, 25, 401. Bestowed on the child to make him more a Brooks, the name clearly strengthened his resolve to be an Adams.
3. See principal sources for Chap. 2, above.
4. Before 1870, HA was sometimes formally referred to as Henry Adams, e.g. in letters from Moran to CFA, 10 & 24 Nov 1862, AP; but in his extant papers HA first signs himself as Henry Adams when ending a letter to Henry Lee Higginson, 24 Oct 1870, HA-micro 3. See Chap. 10.
5. HA's feeling that he in a measure was America is most plainly evidenced by his erecting his own memorial in the national capital.
6. The violence of HA's reaction against Robert E. Lee is clear in Jacob E. Cooke, "Chats with Henry Adams," *American Heritage*, Dec 1955, 44. His reaction against Lee can be seen as the obverse of his admiring George Washington.

In HA's *Democracy*, Lee's vacant house in Arlington is contrasted with Washington's still-lived-in Mount Vernon. See Chaps. VI & IX.

A character in the novel, John Carrington, is said to be a relative of a deceased New Yorker, Lightfoot Lee, and is categorized in Chap. II as a Virginian "of the old Washington school." Carrington's war service on the side of his state, Virginia, is treated sympathetically. It thus is clear that HA differentiated several sorts of rebels, several sorts of Virginians, and at least two sorts of Lees. So helped, he could introduce a Carrington into the novel as he might introduce a tragic friend or unfortunate cousin, as distinguished from a traitor.
7. Moran, 29 Jul 1862.
8. Ibid., 30 Jul 1862.
9. Subsequent to the *Trent* Affair, HA sometimes feared that several European powers might jointly intervene in the American conflict, but he seems not to have feared that England would act alone. His belief that England would not act unassisted rested partly on his understanding of the divisions within the Liberal Cabinet. This understanding seems accurately reflected in *EHA* (1907), 134–43; (LoA), 861–72.

A virtually identical understanding is set forth and documented by HA's nephew HA2 in the latter's paper "Why Did Not England Recognize the Confederacy?" MHS *Proceedings*, 66 (1936–1941), 204–22. This able paper is keyed to Gladstone's Newcastle speech.
10. HA's 1862 engagement book, HAL, at the back under July.
11. Jos. L. Chester to HA, 29 Sep 1862; CFA to Palfrey, 19 Sep 1862, AP.
12. CFA2 to HA, 4 Aug 1862, AP.
13. CFA2 to CFA, 22 Aug 1862, AP.
14. Quoted in *EHA* (1907), 135; (LoA), 862. There is no evidence that HA was intimidated by Gladstone, but there *is* evidence that HA deeply hated him for being an active proponent of the Confederacy. The depth of the hatred is vivid in HA's revision of *EHA* (1907), 136. See the Thayer copy, MHS.

15. CFA to CFA2, 24 Oct 1862, AP—"It turned out to be a false alarm. . . . In the meanwhile I lost my house."

16. MA's horse was named by HA (or by MA at his suggestion) in response to mention in CFA2's letters of an English soldier-author, Major Hodson. See CFA2 to ABA, 9 Dec 1862, AP.

17. CFA2 to ABA, 25 Sep 1862, AP.

18. HA self-effacingly attributed the withholding of his article to the advice of an American bookseller in London, Henry Stevens, but not improbably the advice was welcomed because consistent with a decision HA had already made. See HA to Palfrey, 27 Mar, 29 May 1863.

19. In the most famous passage in *The Education*, the young protagonist defies his mother by refusing to go to a country school in Quincy, whereupon he is forcibly escorted to the school by his Adams grandfather. The boy is described as living at his grandparents' residence, the Old House, and thus *not* living at his parents' summer house a short walk distant on President's Hill. See *EHA* (1907), 9–10; (LoA), 731–32.

The passage is treated in this biography as true. Perhaps it is. But there is no guarantee that it is not fiction, down to its last detail. And whether it is fact or fiction is a secondary matter, considering that it is the passage in *The Education* in which HA is most at pains to make a quintessential point. The statement in the passage that the protagonist rebelled when living at the Old House, combined with the statement that he rebelled against his mother (who also is said to be living there at the moment), suggests that *in his wishes HA rightly belonged to his grandmother's household, and equally did not belong to his mother's*.

The point deserves to be heeded. If HA is viewed as always self-identified with LCA and persons closely associated with her, and never self-identified with ABA, much though he honored and helped her, his conduct through life consistently explains itself and makes sense.

20. HA reiterated to the Sewards (also Sumner) the self-protecting lie that, although he was living at the Legation, he took no share in its business. E.g. see HA to FWS, 29 Oct 1862—". . . my position here is just such a one as to get me into trouble if I mix in business."

HA was sometimes more candid. Writing to Palfrey on 27 Mar 1863, he asked that he not be classed as a diplomat and claimed to be only an "independent gentleman." Yet he said in the same breath that he was assumed "to enjoy the confidence of the Minister and occasionally to be employed by him in delicate affairs." "I go into society as Mr[.] Adams, and I look down with calmness from a prodigious height upon the herds of attachés and secretaries that haunt in a mournful manner the St. James's Club. My own field is among English politicians and writers. . . . Politicians nowadays work on public opinion. . . ."

21. HA to CFA2, 12 Feb 1862—"my favorite Englishman." HA partly valued his relations with Bright because the English leader taught him to believe in free trade. Bright was in touch with an American freetrader, Edward Atkinson, of Boston. See Atkinson to Bright, 6 Feb 1862, BrP. Information concerning the start of HA's friendship with Atkinson is lacking; but it seems not improbable that their friendship was set in motion, perhaps very early, in a way involving Bright.

22. Milnes to HA, 17 Jul 1862; same to HA, 25 Nov, 2 Dec 1862.

23. HA to CFA2, 20 Mar 1863. It seems curious that HA misspells Oliphant's name.

24. *EHA* (1907), 118–24; (LoA), 845–51.

25. In his *Monckton Milnes/ The Flight of Youth*, Lond 1951, 141, reacting to HA's *Education*, James Pope-Hennessy says that HA's memory "misled him about the outward circumstances" of his visit to Fryston; that three women and three children were also then at the house.

Memory is not the question. HA had used the words "a very jolly little bachelor party" in the very month of the visit. See HA to CFA2, 26 Dec 1862. It thus appears that HA's descriptions in *The Education* are accurate; that persons were so distributed in the Milnes house that there indeed was what could be called a "bachelor party."

26. The Fryston episode in *The Education* has become a peg on which to hang vaporous theorizing concerning HA. See John Cheever, "Journals of the Seventies and Early Eighties," *New Yorker*, 12 Aug 1991, 46— "Reading Henry Adams on the Civil War [i.e. relevant pages of *EHA*], I find him distastefully enigmatic . . . . Walker Evans once said that he was queer, and this struck me as an idle remark; but his descriptions of Milnes and Swinburne, and the posthumous gossip of the period that is, alas, unknown to me [*sic*], bring the matter up once more. . . . So here is Henry vastly connected in London, quite androgynous, and absolutely incapable of admitting any such condition."

27. HA to Milnes, 28 Dec 1862—"the maniac" (i.e. Swinburne).

28. CFA to CFA2, 5 Dec 1862, AP.

29. That the slaves in the United States could lawfully be emancipated by the federal government under the war power was believed by the Adamses to have been first pointed out to Congress by JQA. See Leonard L. Richards, *The Life and Times of Congressman John Quincy Adams*, NY & Oxford 1986, 112–23; 224–25. Also see BA to Ford, 10 Feb 1918, FP— "Didn't Charles write a paper on J. Q. A's enunciation of the theory of the war power? . . . J. Q. A. certainly did state it, if I remember right, in the House, somewhere about 1840. . . ."

30. It appears that HA was the only Adams other than CFA whom Seward tried to add to the State Department payroll.

31. HA's letter to FWS, 4 Apr 1862, contains an important comment on the *Trent* Affair—L, I, 288: that the Unionists, and more particularly Secretary Seward, "managed to put England in a position from which she is absolutely unable to move."

32. Moran, 18 Apr 1863.

33. Bright to Mrs. Bright, 9 Feb 1863, OP.

34. HA's copies of Lyell's *Antiquity of Man* and Darwin's *Voyage of the Beagle* are in HAL. Neither contains important markings. HA's copy of Darwin's *Origin of Species* is missing. Darwin's name first appears in *EHA* in Chap. XIII. As privately printed by HA, the chapter's heading is simply "1864." This may be good evidence that in later life HA supposed he first read Darwin in 1864. It none the less seems entirely possible that HA read Darwin in 1863, immediately after reading Lyell.

35. *EHA* (1907), 194; (LoA), 925. The passage also explains why HA did not meet Tennyson.

36. HA to CFA2, 13 Feb 1863—describing Mill as "the logician and economist."

37. Two questions, whether HA was introduced to Thackeray and whether he became so known to Thackeray that the writer would remem-

ber him as a Unionist associated with the Legation, are left unanswered by the passage in *The Education* dramatizing Thackeray's Confederate sympathies. See *EHA* (1907), 112–13; (LoA), 838–39. HA's silences on both scores are presumably deliberate.

38. Ministers and secretaries of legation were admitted to the club by virtue of their commissions. HA first appeared at the club through the intercession of his father. See CFA to Palfrey, 25 Mar 1863, AP. These considerations weigh little when compared with HA's election to membership in 1863. The election made him a member by personal right.

39. On his speed, see *EHA* (1907), 413; (LoA), 1151—"the runaway star Groombridge, 1838, commonly called Henry Adams." *EHA* (LoA), 1245, provides details about Stephen Groombridge's discovery of "the swiftest moving of all observed stars."

40. John Bright, *Speeches on Questions of Public Policy*, Lond, 1869, I, 245–65.

41. Seward praised HA's report in a despatch to CFA and thus exacerbated the hurts of Moran, who wrote in his journal, 4 May 1863, that HA's being permitted to attend the meeting and report about it had been an "assault" by CFA on his and Wilson's rights.

42. The assertion rests on writings by Ephraim Douglass Adams, who in this instance may not be an entirely trustworthy authority.

In 1910, or soon after, EDA spoke with HA about a passage in John Spargo, *Karl Marx*, NY 1910, 223–25, containing the lines: "It was he [Marx] who . . . caused the trades unionists of London to take the first step toward raising a protest of the working class against the action of the [British] government, and in favor of Lincoln. . . . Marx called upon one of his lieutenants, George Eccarius, a leading spirit of the London Trades Council, to move in that body for the holding of a great demonstration of the organized workers of London. . . ."

On the basis of that talk with HA, EDA, *without naming Marx*, said in a letter to CFA2, 7 Mar 1914, CFA2P, ". . . your brother Henry . . . told me that he understood at the time of the meeting that the little Socialist group in London was really the starting point of this meeting, and had organized it." (In this letter, EDA confuses the 26 Mar 1863 meeting with the meeting on 29 Jan 1863 in Exeter Hall. But helpfully he points out that CFA wished to keep aloof from the more revolutionary of the English supporters of Lincoln's proclamation, which may explain why HA was the member of the Legation who attended the March meeting.)

Seven years after HA's death, EDA named Marx. See *Great Britain and the American Civil War*, NY 1925, II, 292—". . . [HA,] who attended and reported the meeting . . . then understood and always since believed Marx's to have been the guiding hand in organizing the meeting."

43. Philip S. Foner, *British Labor and the American Civil War*, NY & Lond 1981, 62, quoting Marx's letter to Engels, 9 Apr 1863—". . . I attended the meeting held by Bright at the head of the trade unions."

44. HA's understanding of Europe as in its own way revolutionary, yet of the United States as "the great embodiment of the Revolution," is clearest in his subsequent letter to CFA2, 25 Sep 1863.

45. Warren F. Spencer has held that "England and France did maintain a consistent neutrality towards the belligerents." See his *Confederate Navy in Europe*, op. cit., 215. This contention flies in the face of considered

opinions by Unionists who dealt with the English at first hand in 1861–1865. An example is BA, "The Seizure of the Laird Rams," MHS *Proceedings*, 45 (1911–1912), 243–333. The paper is a powerfully argued statement written with HA's active support and, for the most part, consistent with his views.

46. Moran, 20 & 21 Apr 1863. Walker had been secretary of the treasury under President Polk and was sent abroad in 1863 by the incumbent secretary of the treasury, Salmon P. Chase. See Philip Van Doren Stern, *When the Guns Roared/ World Aspects of the American Civil War*, NY 1976, 202–03. Meeting Walker was one of many steps by which HA in London became linked with the Treasury Department.

47. [Richard Cobden], *Speech of Mr. Cobden on the Foreign Enlistment Act . . . ,*" Lond 1863, 7–9.

48. Moran, 25 Apr 1863.

49. *Speech of Mr. Cobden. . . . ,*" op. cit., 8.

50. On 10–12 Aug 1963, I copied HA's letters to Cobden at the Manuscript Division of what was then the British Museum. At the time, I searched for traces, published or unpublished, of the letters' having been noticed by previous inquirers. I could find none.

51. HA–1, 23, 30–31.

52. CFA2 all his life affected expertise about HA. He however saw little of HA after August 1856 and after 10 Jan 1862 was never fully in his confidence.

53. *EHA* (1907), 177; (LoA), 907. When indexing *EHA* (1907), HA alphabetized his friend's name under M as "Milnes Gaskell, Charles" and under G supplied a cross-reference, "Gaskell (see Milnes)." To HA's best knowledge, the name in effect was Charles Milnes-Gaskell.

54. At Much Wenlock, Shropshire, on 16 Aug 1962, Gaskell's daughter, Mary Ward, told me apropos of HA that her father "loved to have America come to him." She clearly intended to state her father's opinion of HA as briefly and forcefully as possible. Her phrase achieved the object by making HA and America synonyms.

I see no reason to doubt that CMG formed this view of HA in the minutes when they first spoke.

55. Data concerning HA's relations with James Milnes Gaskell and the Wynns is regrettably thin. On the importance of HA's relation with the elder Gaskell, see *EHA* (1907), 178–79; (LoA), 909–10.

56. CFA2 to CFA, 24 May 1863, AP.

57. CFA2 believed he was made "an entire man" by army service. He wanted HA to undergo a parallel metamorphosis. See CFA2 to HA, 5 Apr 1863—"Don't travel,—don't go into society,—rough it for a while among men & you don't know how prodigiously you'll expand."

58. It is evident that CFA was trustful of Weed as his undoubted diplomatic superior. Oppositely, CFA was distrustful of Evarts, even before his arrival, as a threatened diplomatic equal. The evidence is some striking entries in Moran's journal. On 1 May 1863, Moran writes of Evarts as "Mr. Adams' shadow." On 14 Jan 1864, he writes: ". . . [Evarts] is not welcome. Mr. Adams is evidently very sore at his being here. . . . If we want a new Minister, why not recall Mr. Adams, instead of Japanese like, keeping a double?" On 7 Feb 1865, he says: ". . . CFA showed a good deal of feeling at Mr. Evarts' having been sent out here, and there was not a little

bitterness against Evarts personally. . . . Mr. Adams said Mr. Seward had made many mistakes, and sending emissaries to Europe, extra-officially, was one of them." It must be added that Evarts was *officially* the Legation's visiting counsel.

59. The reported animus of CFA against Evarts (see note 58) can be thought of as both unjustified and justified. CFA was wrong if he thought Evarts wished to supplant him as minister, for the lawyer in no way showed such a wish. Yet CFA could rightly think that Evarts was sent abroad to watch him. Part of Evarts's work would of course be legal; but the work he could most readily and silently do was spy—or, in gentler language, notice or observe.

60. *EHA* (1907), 177; (LoA), 907–08.

61. CFA2 to ABA, 12 May 1863, AP; CFA2 to CFA, 8–9 May 1863, AP.

62. CFA2 to JQA2, 19 Jun 1873, AP.

63. One of the lies had alleged the capitulation of McClellan's army during the Seven Days. See HA to CFA2, 19 Jul 1862, and CFA to CFA2, 18 Jul 1862, AP.

64. CFA to CFA2, 19 Jun 1863, AP.

65. HA four times wanted to join the army: in April 1861, in response to Lincoln's call for volunteers; in July 1861, on learning of the Union rout at Bull Run; in September 1862, on learning of the second Union rout at Bull Run; and in July 1863, on learning of Lee's invasion of Pennsylvania.

On each occasion, he felt a different shade of patriotic feeling. He thereafter felt a lingering strange emotion, a need to be once in a battle to witness the combatants in action. See HA to CFA2, 23 Oct 1863—"I have a dreadful and a trembling longing to be in a battle. Coward as I am, I would like once to see in practice that great monstrosity of human nature; men committing suicide by profession."

66. CFA to CFA2, 17 Jul 1863, AP.

4. Extreme Restlessness

Letters by and to HA are in HA-micro 2, unless otherwise noted.

PRINCIPAL SOURCES

(1) letter, HA to CMG, 18 Aug 1863.

(2) eighteen letters, HA to CFA2, 3 Sep 1863–15 Jan 1864. The letters belong to a distinct, but broken, series. According to his 1863 engagement book, HAL, HA sent CFA2 letters on 11 & 18 Sep 1863. They are missing. There also appears to have been a letter dated 8 Jan 1864. It too is missing.

(3) letters, HA to Henry Higginson, 10 Sep, 18 Dec 1863.

(4) three letters, HA to FWS, 20 Nov, 11 Dec, 1863, L, I, 409, 414–15.

(5) three letters, HA to Palfrey, 15 Jan, 15 Apr, 16 Sep 1864.

(6) sixteen letters, HA to CFA2, 15? Apr–11 Nov 1864. The letters belong to the beginning of a new, numbered, but broken series that HA started after CFA2's return to America. HA's 1864 engagement book, HAL, gives numbers and dates of some of the missing letters: No. 3, 22 Apr; No. 15, 15 Jul; No. 18, 9 Sep; No. 20, 23 Sep; No. 23, 14 Oct; & No. 28, 18 Nov 1864.

(7) HA to Evarts, 20 Jul 1864, author's collection.

(8) HA to WHS, 25 Aug 1864, Microcopy 30, reel 83, NA; also L, I, 443–44.

ADDITIONAL SOURCES; COMMENTS

1. HA and BA had previously made a brief trip together to Antwerp. See HA's 1863 engagement book, HAL, 12–15 Apr 1863; also HA to CFA2, 16 Apr 1863.

2. After seeing many other coasts, HA described the west coast of Scotland as "the grandest coast I know." See HA to Hay, 3 Sep 1882, HA-micro 5.

3. The brothers' second escape made up for a walking trip in Cornwall they had planned the year before but had not been permitted to take. One of HA's traits was determination not to be cheated.

4. CFA, Diary, 4 Sep 1863, AP.

5. Moran, 4 Sep 1863.

6. Like HA, CFA judged the *Trent* Affair to have been "the most perilous hazard of the war." See CFA, "The Struggle for Neutrality in America," NY: Charles Scribner & Co. 1871, 8.

7. CFA's note to Russell became famous because soon published. His notes to Palmerston (see Chap. 2) were secret and remained so till 1900. On the merits, the latter seem deserving of greater fame.

8. CFA to Russell, 5 Sep 1863, AP—two states: as drafted by CFA and as copied by HA.

9. Moran, 5 Sep 1863.

10. CFA to CFA2, 2 Oct 1863, AP.

11. Moran, 1–23 Oct 1863.

12. The passage in *EHA* (1907), 27–28; (LoA), 751–52, about the "disappearance of religion" is negatively fictional with respect to HA's continuing to believe in God and to pray. Clear evidences that he did both are his poems and translations of poems. Also relevant is his inscribing in his wife's copy of *Pilgrim's Progress*, FTKP, a line from Tobit: "Mercifully grant that we may grow aged together."

13. HA to CFA2, 9 Jan, 1 May, 10 Jul 1863.

14. See *Democracy* (1880), 182; (LoA), 751–52—". . . there are two officers . . . whose service is real—the President and his Secretary of the Treasury"; also *LAG*, 267—"In governments as in households, he who holds the purse holds the power."

15. Higginson's letters to HA are missing, but their contents can be partly inferred from HA's replies.

16. Records concerning HA's earliest dealings with Hay, Richardson, Henry Higginson, and Alexander Agassiz are extremely meager.

17. Moran, 19 Jan 1864.

18. On 10 Sep 1861, Consul Bigelow met C. F. Adams and "his son attache" at 5 Mansfield Street. See Bigelow, Diary, 10 Sep 1861, BiP. Bigelow and HA presumably corresponded occasionally, but no letters have been found.

19. Moran, 16 Feb 1864; CFA2, Diary, 16 Feb 1864, AP.

20. CFA2, Diary, 17 Feb 1864, AP; transcript, CFA2 to Palfrey, 21 Feb 1864, Cater Collection, MHS—". . . [HA] I find a very aged man. He is more changed than any of the rest of the family, with the exception of

... Brooks. . . . Henry philosophizes, and seeks the society of the profound and had better return to America as soon as my father can spare him;—which won't be for the remainder of his term." Also see CFA2, Memorabilia, 1888–1893, 740ff, AP.

21. CFA2, Memorabilia, 1888–1893, 740ff, AP. When at last presented to Queen Victoria on March 12, CFA2 went "in Cavalry uniform." See Moran, 14 March 1864.

22. Moran, 20–22 & 27 Feb 1864.

23. Ibid., 1 Mar 1864; for "two Legations," 22 May 1863.

24. For details concerning the manning of the Legation in 1861, see HA–1, 231–42. HA's opinion of the process may be clearest in his remark, *EHA* (1907), 97; (LoA), 823: ". . . in the mission attached to Mr. Adams in 1861, the only rag of legitimacy or order was the private secretary. . . ."

25. Moran, 2 Mar 1864.

26. CFA2, Diary, 6–7 Mar 1864. In his letter of 3 Dec 1863, HA had warned CFA2 that he might not be allowed to go to Paris except in the company of their parents, Mary, and Brooks. The chance to go with no Adamses except HA may explain CFA2's saying they started gaily.

27. CFA2, Diary, 10, 25–26 Mar 1864, AP; Moran, 5–26 Mar 1864.

28. See especially David Herbert Donald, *Charles Sumner and the Coming of the Civil War*, Chicago 1960, 377–80.

29. Comments quasi-favorable to European socialism disappear from HA's writings subsequent to this letter to Palfrey.

HA was aware of Bright's rejection of English socialism as "sham-socialism" and possibly was affected by it. See *EHA* (1907), 164; (LoA), 894. He none the less continued to believe that Europe's socialist revolutionaries were important. In 1872, when an editor, he published an outstandingly informative article about them. See Ernst Gryzanowski, "The International Workingmen's Association; its Origins, Doctrines, and Ethics," *NAR*, Apr 1872, 309–76.

30. HA first openly commented on his fear that CFA might be promoted to the Cabinet in his letter to CFA2, 28 Oct 1864—". . . if the Chief is called to Washington to enter a Cabinet . . . then indeed I shall think the devil himself has got hold of us. . . ."

31. That the passage anticipates HA's *History of the United States* seems the more certain if one notices his eventual decision not to send a copy of his *History* to Gaskell. See Chap. 27.

32. HA, 1863 engagement book, HAL.

33. CFA also came to write of the civil war as one of "annihilation." See his letters to CFA2, 17 Jun, 2 Nov 1864, AP.

34. JQA2's tendency to fish for smelts, to the neglect of his work as a lawyer and politician, is a leading theme in a typewritten memoir of him by his daughter Abigail, Mrs. Robert Homans. In 1956, she permitted me to photocopy the memoir for biographical use.

35. Invariably when writing to the Sewards, HA used the language of subordination and thus lent consistency to his and his father's manner towards the elder Seward, but HA's so writing is hardly evidence that he was himself a Seward follower, and his refusals of the secretary's offers of diplomatic commissions strongly show he was not one.

HA's letter to Evarts, 20 Jul 1864, given complete in this chapter, makes an implicit but unmistakable, sharp criticism of the Sewards, father and son, as practicers of nepotism.

36. In 1952 or thereabouts, through the kindness of Mrs. George Grinnell, I became well-acquainted with Effingham Evarts, grandson of William M. Evarts. In 1956, I urgently pressed "Eff" about the possibility that letters from HA might survive among his grandfather's papers. I visited him at his Vermont house (earlier his grandfather's house), prepared to copy such letters. During the visit, I offered to search his grandfather's library, then still in order on its shelves. But Eff told me there were no letters by HA: he had searched and was sure of it.

I thought Effingham an honest man and have not changed my belief. Subsequent to his death, many properties in the house were sold. I have been authoritatively advised that one of the properties was a box of papers and that the papers included letters from HA to William M. Evarts dated 20 Jul 1864, 14 Jul 1865, & 23 Feb 1866.

In 1989, I was advised by a friend, Richard Stone, that the 14 Jul 1865 letter was currently offered for sale by an autograph dealer, Paul C. Richards. I bought it. In 1990, Richards was also able to supply me the 20 Jul 1864 letter, quoted here. I have not seen the 23 Feb 1866 letter, which I assume is privately held.

37. In his 22 Aug 1864 reply, sent from Windsor VT, Evarts tells HA he received his letter "on the 10th inst." Evarts continues: ". . . I have delayed answering you in the expectation of going to Washington, the fountain of truth and light, whence I might hope to transmit you such rays of both as can penetrate the fog of England. I leave here for Boston, New York & Washn today and will write you from there something that may be an answer to the more serious parts of your letter. In the meantime I can only say that, in my judgment, there is no foundation for your hope [etc.]. . . ."

Evarts may have started for Washington that day, as indicated, but I know of no evidence that he wrote thence to HA, as promised. In my judgment, Evarts had already done something else. He had sent HA's letter to Washington for Seward's attention, had received an answer, and, writing to HA from Windsor, knew full well that the answer from Windsor was the only one HA would be accorded.

38. HA, 1863 engagement book, HAL.

39. *EHA* (1907), 179; (LoA), 909.

40. *EHA* (LoA), 909. 1864, the date given in *EHA* (1907), 179, was corrected by HA in the Thayer copy, MHS, to read 1857.

41. Present opinion concerning the house and ruins at Much Wenlock is that they are properly referred to as Wenlock Priory. See Nikolaus Pevsner, *Shropshire*, revised ed., Lond 1974, 27, 207–11.

42. For "congestive asthma," see HA to Palfrey, 16 Sep 1864. Also see Moran, 8 Sep 1864—". . . Miss Adams had an attack last night of congestion of the lungs and came very near dying. This is the second within as many months. She looks consumptive, and unless great care be taken, cannot live long."

43. Moran, 10 Nov 1864.

44. Ibid., 5 Oct–18 Nov 1864, passim.

45. HA to CFA2, 16 Dec 1864.

46. Writing from the office of the National Union Executive Committee, Raymond explained to Simon Cameron, "We must have a radical change in the *spirit* prevailing in Washington or we stand not the ghost of

a chance in November." See Raymond to Cameron, 19 Aug 1864, New York Times Archives.

47. HA evidently planned the march in late October. See HA to CFA2, 28 Oct 1864—". . . I mean to oppose the most effective resistance in my power to any further abode in London at all. . . ."

5. The Charge of a Family

Letters by and to HA are in HA-micro 2, unless otherwise noted.

PRINCIPAL SOURCES

(1) ten letters, HA to CFA2, 25 Nov 1864–14 Jul 1865—Nos. 29–44. The letters belong to a broken series. Nos. 30 & 33, sent on unknown days, are missing. Nos. 36, 37, 40, & 43, dated 13, 20 Jan, 12 Mar, & 12 Jun 1865, are missing also. Their dates are noted in HA's 1865 engagement book, HAL.

(2) fourteen letters, HA to CFA, 4–5 Feb–27 Apr 1865—apparently an unbroken series.

(3) two letters, HA to CMG, 3 Mar & 23 Apr–10 May 1865.

ADDITIONAL SOURCES; COMMENTS

1. CFA2 to HA, 25 Dec 1864, AP.
2. Moran, 28 Nov 1864.
3. HA wrote to CFA2, 6 Jan 1865, "All the rest of the family . . . have been there before, but I was never asked and did not expect to be." Baring's gesture can be read as evidence of English appreciation of HA, quite apart from CFA, at a time when it appeared that HA and CFA would both be leaving England.
4. Moran, 1 Feb 1865.
5. Ibid., 9 Feb 1865; also Jeffry Wert, "Gettysburg . . . ," *Civil War Times Illustrated*, XVII, 4 (Summer 1988), 37–40.
6. Factors indicating that HA wanted to be abroad three years, starting in Italy, are noted in HA–1, 91–101, 124.
7. *Esther* (1884), 108; (LoA), 239. It may seem overreaching to find autobiography in HA's translation, but autobiography is unmistakably present in all his translations of sonnets by Petrarch. This one apparently is the earliest.
8. As presented in HA's letter to CFA2, 2 Mar 1865, the lines are parts of a take-off of ABA by MA which innocent HA is merely repeating. But at many points in his letters before and during the party's journey to Sorrento, HA ascribes to other persons initiatives for which he can fairly be assumed to have been principally or wholly responsible. The take-off is best ascribed to HA.
9. His elders' choosing to return to 5 Upper Portland Place in late December 1864 could have been sign enough to HA that, say what they might, CFA and ABA were disposed to stay in England through another London season; also that CFA would not resign as minister.
10. Moran requested promotion to first secretary, but he wrote, 26 Aug 1864, "Henry Adams has declined the Ass't. Secretaryship and Mr. Adams [CFA] recommends [to Seward] that the new appointee shall be

permanent. If I had known he entertained such an idea, I never would have asked for promotion."

Moran's reaction indicates his believing he had made the discovery that his appointment as first secretary was a mere temporary concession. Clearly he expected that, in March 1865, Seward would make HA first secretary and retain Alward as second secretary.

It should be added that CFA had wanted HA to *accept* the interim second secretaryship. See CFA to CFA2, 25 Aug 1864, AP. And surely Seward had wanted HA to accept it.

The truly serious question was who would have the place of *future first secretary.* At least one person—Seward—was trying to give HA the post. So Moran was quite right in fearing (mistakenly, as things developed) that HA was going to have it.

11. CFA to HA, 20 Mar, 5 Apr, 18 Apr, 14 May 1865.

12. *Autobiography,* 165–67; Edward Chase Kirkland, *Charles Francis Adams, Jr., 1835–1915,* Camb 1965, 30–33.

13. This account of Hay's getting the first secretaryship in Paris draws on HA's account in the unsigned preface to *Letters of John Hay,* op. cit., I, vii-ix. Also see Tyler Dennett, *John Hay/ From Poetry to Politics,* NY 1934, 57.

14. In a letter written at the time, Hay says Seward's offer of the secretaryship was "entirely unsolicited and unexpected." See Hay to Charles Edward Hay, 31 Mar 1865, in Dennett, *John Hay,* op. cit., 57.

If it is true that Hay did not request an appointment and was given the secretaryship by Seward unexpectedly, the case is all the stronger that Seward was thwarted in a design to advance HA and substituted a person more manageable, Major Hay.

15. Details relating to the death of GWA are given in HA–1, 37–38. HA explicitly treated his uncle's death as a suicide in a letter written late in life. See HA to CFA2, 21 Dec 1912, HA-micro 27—"his drowning himself." The letter appears to have irritated its receiver. CFA2 entertained a different idea of the uncle's death. He wrote ten days later: "It was gossiped that he [GWA] had committed suicide, throwing himself from the steamer. There is, however, no evidence of this, and the more natural assumption is that, being restless in the night, he had left the cabin, going up on deck, and accidentally stepped overboard from an unguarded place in the gangway." See CFA2 to Ford, 31 Dec 1912, FP.

The only detailed account of the death of JA2 is Paul C. Nagel, *Descent from Glory/ Four Generations of the John Adams Family,* NY Oxford 1983, 171–73.

16. With regard to HA's naming himself George, see Chap. 23; also HA–1, 50–52.

17. Earlier, in the first paragraph of a letter to CFA2, 3 Sep 1863, HA had outlined two opposite situations. He had said, ". . . I like of all things to be independent. . . ." In contrast, he had said he was placed in the situation which was for him the "most uncomfortable and harrassing [*sic*]": "I am left in charge of your mother, your sister, your youngest brother, a lady's maid, and a drunken foot-man. . . ."

Except that the latter outline omits CFA, the outlines correspond to the alternative courses HA reconsidered in January-March 1865. His saying he found it uncomfortable and even harassing to be in charge of relations (and servants) scarcely meant he would not choose that alternative. A case can be made that he *usually* chose it; that more often than not, and at great cost to his independence, he acted the part of protector of his relations.

18. The address is given in a note accepting a dinner invitation, HA to Mrs. W. W. Story, "Friday eve⁸·" [14 Apr 1865?]. Formerly in my collection, the note is now in other hands.

19. Story's "Cleopatra" and "Medea" are presently exhibited in the American Wing of the Metropolitan Museum of Art, New York.

20. A flat assertion by HA that he will "wait long before trying" marriage appears in his letter about Story's "Medea," 9 Apr 1865. Six months later, in his letter to CFA2, 20 Oct 1865, HA at last says he will marry. He then links marriage with "work." But there is no reason *not* to suppose that the idea of marriage for love, without children, and in the interest of work, was fully developed in his mind when he wrote the earlier letter. He usually had ideas well in advance of the time he told other Adamses he had had them.

21. HA first mentions the *Revue des Deux Mondes* in his letter to CFA2, 30 Jul 1867. There he speaks of the quarterly as if accustomed to reading it. I assume he read it even before April 1865.

22. The telegram is missing. Its contents can be inferred from HA's letter in reply and from Moran, 26 Apr 1865.

23. CFA2 to CFA, 10 Apr 1865, AP; *Autobiography*, 165–67. For the date he was breveted brigadier general, see the genealogical summary *Adams/ Brooks/ Hammond*, CFA2P, Box 27 (a not entirely reliable source).

24. HA's comments relating to the assassination of Lincoln are few and tend to emphasize, not what was lost, but what survived. See, for example, *EHA* (1907), 364; (LoA), 1100—"Three hideous political murders, that would have fattened the Eumenides with horror, have scarcely thrown a shadow on the White House."

HA later took pains to record that Hay wrote nothing whatever about the assassination of Lincoln when it occurred. See *Letters of John Hay*, op. cit., ix–x.

25. See especially HA to FWS, 9 Jan 1863, L, I, 326—". . . remember me to Mr[.] Weed whenever you see him. . . . I would like occasionally to write to Mr[.] Weed, but am shy of giving him trouble."

26. Weed formed impressions of CFA at the start of the *Trent* affair. The elder Adams was then at his worst as minister. See HA–1, 345. Also see Moran, unpublished diaries, LC, 12 Aug 1865—". . . Mr[.] Adams' gloomy views during the Trent affair."

27. CFA and JQA2 showed their assumptions most clearly by continuing to accept nominations for high public office till 1876.

28. In their letters written in late 1864 and early 1865, CFA and HA repeatedly allude to conjectures that the former may replace Seward as secretary of state. CFA's expectation that the place has become his emerges plainly in his supposing, after Lincoln's death and Seward's re-injury, that he is in process of being recalled to Washington.

HA was the observer best positioned to know whether CFA expected to be president. For details concerning his labors to avert his father's becoming president and for details concerning his father's expecting to be elected, see especially Chaps. 10 & 11.

29.   The centrality of deliberate avoidance of political office in HA's

thought and conduct is forcefully but obliquely communicated by the striking passage in *EHA* (1907), 281; (LoA), 1014: "Adams had held no office, and when his friends asked the reason, he could not go into long explanations, but preferred to answer simply that no President had ever invited him to fill one. The reason was good, and was also conveniently true but left open an awkward doubt of his morals or capacity. Why had no President ever cared to employ him? The question needed a volume of intricate explanation."

30. HA's use of the card-game metaphor in April 1865 can be viewed as a step in the development of his greatest book. In the second paragraph of *The Education*, HA's metaphor of American politics as a card game is expanded into a metaphor of American *life* as a card game. The protagonist is said to be a player who holds an unrivaled hand. "Probably no child, born in the year, held better cards than he."

Also see note 32, below.

31. Perhaps the closest HA came to expounding the latter premise is the first paragraph of Chap. VIII of *Democracy*. The paragraph is a speech by the author-narrator. It begins: "Of all titles ever assumed by prince or potentate, the proudest is that of the Roman pontiffs: 'Servus servorum Dei'—'Servant of the servants of God.' "

32. HA's metaphor of a foot race, implicit in his words "you are rapidly being caught up with and will soon be left behind," and again in his words "enormous strides," is fully as notable as his metaphor of a card game—see note 30, above. Since both metaphors appear in the second paragraph of *EHA*, one can seriously wonder whether HA partly formulated the second paragraph in Sorrento or Rome early in 1865.

Convincing evidence exists that HA wrote the opening part of *EHA* in June 1890. See Chap. 25. It thus appears that he was perfectly capable of forming detailed ideas for the book twenty-five years before he carried them into execution.

33. CFA, Diary, 12 Jun 1865, AP.

34. Ibid., 22 Jun 1865; Arthur F. Beringause, *Brooks Adams/ A Biography*, NY 1955, 33–34.

35. HA to CFA2, 26 May 1864, 13 Mar 1863.

36. It is not known when and where HA and Hay first met in Europe. Hay wrote that he would "sail probably in June." See *Letters of John Hay*, op. cit., I, 254. In his preface to the Hay *Letters*, I, x-xi, HA may seem to rely on his memory concerning Hay's mood on reaching Paris. But it seems *not* likely that HA was still in Paris when Hay arrived.

For a recorded early meeting of HA and Hay in London, see Chap. 7.

37. CFA, Diary, 25 Jun 1865, AP.

38. Beringause, *Brooks Adams*, op. cit., 33.

39. Ibid., 35.

40. It deserves mention that HA's death in 1918 gave BA a *second* opportunity to praise HA in his absence. BA made vigorous use of it. See his "Introductory Note" and "The Heritage of Henry Adams" in *Degradation*, v-xiii, 1–122.

41. CFA, Diary, 7 Jun 1865, AP.

42. For details concerning the recovery of this letter, see Chap. 4, note 36.

6. MY REIGN

Letters by and to HA are in HA-micro 2, unless otherwise noted.

PRINCIPAL SOURCES

(1) letter, HA to CFA2, 20 Oct 1865—No. 48. The letter is the last of a numbered, broken series. Nos. 45–47, dated 11 Aug, 8 Sep, & 15 Sep 1865, are missing. Their dates are noted in HA's 1865 engagement book, HAL.

(2) six letters, HA to Palfrey, 4 May 1866–28 Jun 1867, L, I, 506–10, 513, 539–41.

(3) three letters, HA to Norton, 24 Aug 1866–28 Jun 1867, L, I, 510–11, 521–22, 538–39.

(4) eleven letters, HA to CFA2, 10 Nov 1866–22 Jun 1867. The letters belong to a new, unnumbered series. Some letters in the series are known to be missing. The missing letters cannot be dated.

(5) [HA], "Captain John Smith," *NAR*, Jan 1867, 1–29—Article I, unsigned. Norton excised the last paragraph. The paragraph is given in *Sketches*, 218–20.

(6) [HA], "British Finance in 1816," *NAR*, Apr 1867, 354–85—Article II, unsigned.

(7) [HA], "The Bank of England Restriction. 1797–1821." *NAR*, Oct 1867, 393–434—Article III, unsigned.

ADDITIONAL SOURCES; COMMENTS

1. Moran, unpublished journal, 31 Jul 1865, LC.
2. CFA, Diary, 6 Sep 1865, AP.
3. Ibid., 19 Sep 1865; Moran, unpub. journal, 16, 21 Sep 1865, LC.
4. Evarts to HA, 18 Sep 1865. The fact that their father would be staying a long while abroad was kept from JQA2 and CFA2. On going to Europe that autumn, CFA2 learned the truth. See CFA2 to JQA2, 6 Dec 1865, AP—"As to their plans, they are far more vague than we had supposed. Do not be sure . . . they are coming home next Summer . . . . They . . . won't do it, unless Seward is perfectly willing."
5. CFA to HA, 23 May 1865; CFA, Diary, 18 Jun 1865, AP.
6. Use of the cable to send despatches in code raised afresh the matter of Henry's rank. See Moran, unpub. journal, 30 Nov 1866, LC-". . . Henry B. Adams came . . . and got the Cipher. A telegram had arrived by the cable from Washington. Instead of asking me to decipher this, as Mr. Adams was bound to do, he had his son do it . . . ." ". . . the son . . . has no right to know anything about it."
7. The case developed by the Legation can be inferred from *The Case of the United States, to be Laid before the Tribunal of Arbitration, to be convened at Geneva . . .* , Wash: Government Printing Office 1872.
8. The letter raises a hard-to-answer question whether HA two and a half years later helped arrange the publication in the *London Gazette* of CFA's correspondence with Earl Russell about the case.
9. The possibility that the U. S. might initiate war with England is raised also in HA to CFA2, 20 Mar 1863—"Some day [England] . . . will wake up and find itself at war with us. . . ." Also in HA to CFA2, 27 Mar

1863—"We have strength enough already to shake the very crown on the Queen's head if we are compelled to employ it. . . ."

10. HA adds: ". . . this is crowner's quest law; crazy as the British Constitution; and would get England soon into war with every nation on the sea. The question now is whether the Government will mend it."

The passage includes one of HA's many allusions to *Hamlet*. See the Grave-digger's lines, V, I.

11. The letter explicitly speaks of the Union's future "success" and "prosperity."

12. HA's thirty-second *NYTimes* despatch leaves no doubt that in 1861 he wanted not only peace and friendship with England but also steps towards "the unity and brotherhood of nations and races." See HA-1, 362–64.

13. Seward's despatch created unease at the Legation. See Moran, 17 Mar 1865—". . . we received a Despatch from Mr. Seward. . . . It is hostile in the extreme to England, and gives color to the idea so prevalent here that he really wants to quarrel with Great Britain . . . . Mr. Adams . . . says he will withhold it from Lord Russell . . . ."

14. Duberman, *Charles Francis Adams/ 1807–1886*, 323; CFA, Diary, 6 Sep 1865, AP.

15. That the Legation's record after 1865 became a near blank with respect to important diplomatic efforts is clear in all accounts. That the Legation's *social* efforts grew, climaxing in a Fourth of July reception in 1867 attended by 278 guests, is reflected in HA's engagement books, HAL. It is a fair inference that these opposite tendencies became realities in part because HA acted to make them realities.

16. Building his father's reputation to mythic proportions was one of HA's most persistent efforts. The effort is most evident in the pages of *The Education of Henry Adams*. See, for examples, the beginning of Chap. XIII, the first eight paragraphs of Chap. XIV, and especially *EHA* (1907), 168; (LoA), 898—". . . [CFA] gained a position which would have caused his father or grandfather to stare with incredulous envy"; and *EHA* (1907), 183; (LoA), 914—"Minister Adams became, in 1866, almost a historical monument in London; he held a position altogether his own."

17. CFA2 to JQA2, 6 Dec 1865, AP; Paul C. Nagel, *Descent from Glory*, op. cit., 246–47.

18. CFA, *Diary*, 25 Dec 1865, AP. In late 1865, HA was certainly preparing to write "British Finance in 1816," but exactly when he began to write the article is unknown. It also is hard to guess. His habits as a writer are a somewhat closed book.

19. Tyler Dennett, *John Hay*, 162. On p. 94, Dennett lists some of Hay's closer friends and says, ". . . not one of these men, except Adams, and King rarely, ever called Hay by his first name. . . ."

20. Moran, unpub. journal, 20, 23, 24 Feb 1866, LC. Moran later recorded, 4–5 Feb 1867, that HA was permitted by Sir Edward Cust to attend the opening of Parliament "in the distinguished strangers' gallery in his diplomatic uniform." He also recorded, 27 Feb 1867, that CFA, he, and HA went to Court. (They necessarily were in uniform.) He did not specify the order in which he and HA were presented.

21. Ibid., 20, 22 Mar 1866. Moran also noted on the 22nd that his and Alward's work day was 10:00–4:00 and that CFA visited the office

from 12:00–2:00 and sat "like a fool in the little room behind us." CFA apparently discontinued the visits.

A year later, 9 Apr 1867, Moran recorded that nearly all visitors were going to 54 Portland Place, rather than to 147 Great Portland Place. All the same, in his later journals, Moran used "Legation" to mean exclusively the rented office in which he and Alward worked. In July 1867, Hay likewise used "Legation" to mean the office in which he found Moran and Alward. See *Letters of John Hay*, I, 296–98.

Moran and Hay's ideas concerning the whereabouts of the Legation were not shared by the bulk of the Adamses' visitors, who usually assumed that the house at 54 Portland Place was the Legation and that CFA and HA were respectively the minister and the sole official secretary. For an example, see Spencer Hall to HA, 22 Mar 1867, addressing him as "The Secretary to the U. S. Legation."

22. In 1914, having managed to borrow Moran's manuscript journal, CFA2 "sent a few extracts . . . to my brother Henry." He shortly remarked, "Henry manifestly winced over possible criticisms and remarks which might be found therein. . . ." See CFA2 to Ford, 11 Nov 1914, FP.

23. The page of HA's 1866 engagement book for May 15–16 was reproduced in 1936 in Thoron, opp. xiv. Thereafter sight was mostly lost of the fact that the engagement books were in the Henry Adams Library, uncatalogued. In 1988, I requested a search for the books, citing the reproduced page. It developed that the staff at MHS, while starting a new catalogue of HA's library, had recently come upon seven such books. The books are a prime source of data relating to HA in 1862–1869.

24. Soon after MHA's death, HA arrestingly remarked that a "great mass of material is almost as troublesome to a biography as a short allowance." See HA to Paul Leicester Ford, 22 Mar 1886, L, III, 6.

25. Recollections spoken to me by LHT.

26. The best measures of the father's error were the successive suicides of all his children.

Dusinberre infers as "likely" that RWH engaged in a duel in Paris about a woman, Marian Marshall, after whom he later named his second daughter. See *Henry Adams/ The Myth of Failure*, 59 & 231n26. The inference seems justified. In view of Hooper's life as a whole, the duel and the perpetuation of the name were in character.

27. In 1975, Faith Thoron Knapp—MHA's grandniece—kindly showed me MHA's close-cut Worth gown in green velvet; also her gloves and shoes. They confirmed the evidence supplied by available photographs.

28. Col. O. W. Holmes, Jr., joined the Adamses for dinner on 11, 14, & 29 May 1866. See HA's 1866 engagement book, HAL.

Dusinberre says Clover Hooper first met HA in London on May 11, as a consequence of seeking Holmes at the Legation. See his *Henry Adams/ The Myth of Failure*, op. cit., 54–55, 230n2.

A passage later written by James has frequently been construed and quoted as containing very important evidence concerning Clover Hooper. Writing to his brother William, 8 Mar 1870, James said: "As for women I give 'em up. . . . I revolt from their dreary deathly want of—what shall I call it?—Clover Hooper has it—intellectual grace—Minnie Temple has it—moral spontaneity." See *Henry James Letters*, Camb 1974, I, 208. The passage hardly specifies Clover Hooper or Minnie Temple's leading attribute. It instead struggles to define an attribute allegedly not often found in women the possession of which makes Clover Hooper and Minnie Temple exceptions *not* revolting to James.

29. Marian herself noted the gesture. See Clover Hooper to Ellen Gurney, 5 Mar 1872, FTKP.

The tintype published in Thoron, frontispiece, and in L, II, opp. 132, affords almost no impression of Marian's features but shows her face's oval structure. Among the photographs HA made at Wenlock Abbey in 1872, HAL, MHA faces the camera in only one. See L, II, opp. 159. The part showing her face is damaged. Drawing my attention to the fact in 1982, Viola Hopkins Winner suggested, I believe with reason, that the presumable damager was MHA.

30. Transcript of letter, Alice Mason Hooper to Annie M. Hooper, 27 Aug 1865, FTKP—"I have been having the most charming visit from Ellen [Hooper] & Miss Low—they went yesterday morning & in the evening Clover & George Sohier came down."

31. As printed in Thoron, xiv, the tradition lacks essential details. In the 1950s and 1960s, LHT repeatedly told me that RWH spoke with CFA on Derby Day and that RWH wrote to Ellen. Her sister, Ellen Potter, separately added the same details.

HA later said that Brooks was "the first person who ever suggested" the marriage. See HA to BA, 3 Mar 1872, HA-micro 3.

32. The strongest pressures moving HA away from unqualified support of sound money were common sense and practicality. "The Bank of England Restriction," though very supportive of *convertible* paper, includes the following qualification, *NAR*, Oct 1867, 422: "The evils of inconvertible paper are no doubt many, but there are also advantages in the system during times of political trouble; and it is impossible to deny that the violent convulsions of 1815 would have proved too severe a trial for any but the most elastic form of credit."

33. Exactly when HA became consciously a collector of data for his *History* is unknown; but it is reasonable to suppose that the collecting process gained greatly in impetus early in 1863 when he obtained Hammond's letters to Jefferson, and gained fresh impetus thereafter when he successfully assembled the voluminous evidence underlying "British Finance in 1816" and "The Bank of England Restriction."

34. The first mention of Reeve in HA's engagement books is in the 1862 book under May 29: "Evening. Mr. Reeve." According to the 1867 book, Reeve and his wife dined with the Adamses on May 16—when HA had nearly finished "The Bank of England Restriction." Thomson Hankey, governor of the Bank of England, was a guest at the same dinner. He first appears in the engagement books on 15 Apr 1864.

35. Details concerning Deane's annotated private reprint are given in *Catalogue of the Valuable Private Library of . . . Charles Deane*, op. cit., II, items 3272–3275.

36. Details concerning publications by Deane and HA relating to Smith appear in my dissertation, *Henry Adams and History*, Univ. of Pennsylvania, 1954, 1–28—published Ann Arbor: Univ. Microfilms 1975.

37. Cater, 31n1.

38. Russel B. Nye, *George Bancroft*, NY 1944, 230–31.

39. HA to Parkman, 21 Dec 1884, HA-micro 5—". . . as I often tell him, [Bancroft] . . . has written the History of the United States in a dozen volumes without reaching his subject."

40. That irritation could open doors to friendship was an old story to HA. See HA–1, 115–16.

41. The terms HA exacted from Norton in 1866 were the terms he had wanted and almost fully obtained when a contributor to the *New York Times* in 1861–1862.

42. Other than his relevant actions, which are evidence enough, the evidence relating to HA's aspiring to help edit both quarterlies is partly-misleading testimony in *The Education*. The statement "He wanted to win a place on the staff of the *Edinburgh Review* . . ." is keyed misleadingly to 1868, rather than to 1865–1866. See *EHA* (1907), 224; (LoA), 956. A further statement says that access to the *North American Review* "in the fancy of Henry Adams . . . led, in some indistinct future, to playing on a New York daily newspaper." See *EHA* (1907, 203; (LoA), 934. Misleadingly, this statement suggests that HA had *not* played on a New York daily newspaper, and very fully, in 1861–1862.

43. *Autobiography*, 170–71.

44. Ibid. CFA2, apparently quoting the editor, says the article was " 'judiciously edited' " by Norton.

45. The contents of the letters can be inferred from HA's reply. The phrase "thoughts of suicide" is quoted from the reply.

46. In later life, describing his start in railroads, *Autobiography*, 172, CFA2 used the phrase ". . . I began operations. . . ." He thus repeated "operations," a word HA had put before his eyes many years earlier, in 1866.

47. Deane to HA, 6 Jan 1867.

48. So reacting, Froude came close to anticipating the last suggestion Adams would print about Smith. Developed in 1889–1890, the suggestion was that Smith in old age, still feeling rivalry with Raleigh, who had been beheaded in the Tower of London, invented a yarn about how *he* had been condemned and readied for execution in far-off Virginia, only to be rescued at the last instant by a female intercessor. As Adams came to see it, Smith's fabrication merited, not scorn, but detection and understanding. Yet detection would not have occurred in the absence of willingness to see the possibility that Smith was fabricating. Deane had seen the possibility. He and HA then developed successive proofs of fabrication. HA alone arrived at the thesis outlined above, in which Raleigh and Queen Elizabeth I—not to mention the Virgin—take roles alongside Smith and Pocahontas.

49. *Pall Mall Gazette*, 18 Feb 1867.

50. A full account of the abortive National Union effort is given in Patrick W. Riddleberger, *1866/ The Critical Year Revisited*, Carbondale IL 1979, Chap. 9.

51. Abigail Homans, JQA2's daughter, read her father's letters to CFA and wrote a typewritten memoir, op. cit., which includes the following passages by JQA2: ". . . Henry too—a philosopher—takes it for granted that I should have modified my course if I had foreseen the President's. How humiliating it is that with my name I should wait for such trifles as that." "I am fond of a shindy and I like a minority."

52. *Autobiography*, 172.

53. Kirkland, *Charles Frances Adams, Jr.*, 75–76—"In 1871 . . . he had a floating debt of $50,000; a decade later he owed $200,000 'and more'; in the later eighties . . . these sums mounted till he owed well over a million. . . ." "He was not a confident investor. The slightest tremor of misfortune sent him scurrying for comfort and calm to Thayer, Higginson, or other associates in seemingly threatened enterprises."

54. Transcript of letter, William Sturgis Hooper to Caroline Sturgis Tappan, 2 Mar 1857, FTKP. Hooper says Alice's father, Jonathan Mason, is "rather poor than otherwise"; also that the Masons "board at the corner of Beacon & Mount Vernon Street."

55. Ibid.; transcripts of letters, Alice Mason Hooper to Anne Sturgis Hooper, 17 Oct, 19 Dec 1864, & 6 Aug 1865, FTKP.

56. Donald, *Charles Sumner and the Rights of Man*, 269–74.

57. *Letters of John Hay*, I, 258–59. The entry in Hay's diary about Sumner's "eminently characteristic" letter to ABA is the more important because HA decided which letters and diary entries would be included in the privately-printed *Letters*.

58. Donald, *Sumner*, op. cit., 275, gives the Sumners' address as 322 I Street. The house owned by HA's aunt, Mary Catherine Adams, was at 292 I Street. (It was later renumbered 1601 I Street. See HA to Hay, 26 Oct 1884, HA-micro 5—"my old family house.")

59. Donald, *Sumner*, op. cit., 274–77, 289–93.

60. Norman Rich, *Friedrich Von Holstein/ Politics and Diplomacy in the Era of Bismarck and Wilhelm II*, Cambridge: Camb. U. Press 1965, I, 27ff—"On 6 May [1864] Holstein . . . was temporarily attached to the Prussian Embassy in London. . . . He stayed in London till mid-summer 1865." Also see Moran, 3 Mar 1865.

61. Rich, *Holstein*, I, 34–36; Donald, *Sumner*, 293–95.

62. OP; HA's 1867 engagement book, HAL.

63. *NAR*, Oct 1867, 429.

64. Inducing other persons to reconsider his value by quitting their company was a maneuver of HA's which several persons would experience, beginning with his parents in 1858–1860, Norton and Lowell in 1867, and Clover Hooper in the summer of 1871.

7. THE ASCENT OF OLYMPUS

Letters by and to HA are in HA-micro 2–3, unless otherwise noted.

PRINCIPAL SOURCES

(1) ten letters, HA to CFA2, 30 Jul 1867–13 Dec 1868.

(2) ten letters, HA to CMG, 25 Aug 1867–5 Nov 1868.

(3) letter, HA to Norton, 10 Apr 1868, L, I, 569.

(4) three letters, HA to Cunliffe, 16–27 May 1868.

(5) Henry Brooks Adams, "The Principles of Geology," *NAR*, Oct 1868, 465–501.

(6) H. B. A., "The Argument in the Legal Tender Cases," *Nation*, 17 Dec 1868, 501–2.

ADDITIONAL SOURCES; COMMENTS

1. Details concerning the drawing are given in Ernest Scheyer, *The Circle of Henry Adams: Art & Artists*, Detroit 1970, 52–53. Scheyer's book

provides helpful data concerning works bought by HA and MHA but unhelpfully mistakes them for art collectors. They bought solely as *owners*, to enhance the interiors of their homes, intended or actual. Collecting, as usually meant, was far from their minds.

2. HA could not forget that the London *Times* on 9 Jan 1862, while ridiculing "A Visit to Manchester," quoted a passage in which "Mr. H. Adams" said about the welcome extended to visitors in London houses, ". . . the guests shift for themselves, and a stranger had better depart at once as soon as he has looked at the family pictures."

3. Palgrave to HA, 4 Jul 1867; *EHA* (1907), 187–90; (LoA), 918–21; Scheyer, *Circle of Henry Adams*, op. cit., 51–52; HA's 1867 engagement book, HAL—March 28, "Lunch with Mrs. Sturgis at 2, and go to Woolner's studio at 3"; June 24, "10 A.M. With Palgrave to Mr[.] Malcolm's"; and July 1, an equivalent entry.

4. William Blake, *Songs of Innocence and Experience*, Lond: B. M. Pickering 1866. The preface concerns Wordsworth as much as Blake and presumably helped HA towards appreciating the former's works. The volume includes poems drawn from a manuscript owned by the publisher, including "The Mental Traveller" and "Auguries of Innocence." Since the previous owner of the manuscript was Lord Houghton, who bought it c. 1864, HA possibly read the added poems in Blake's handwriting before they were published. See William Blake, *The Pickering Manuscript*, ed. by Charles Ryskamp, NY 1972.

5. [CMG], "The Easter Trip of Two Ochlophobists," *Blackwood's Magazine*, v. 102, 42–59, 188–207. I see no reason not to take Gaskell literally (195) with respect to "Granville's" quoting Rousseau.

6. "Ochlophobists" means persons averse to crowds. The word is cited in the *OED* in relation to CMG's article. He thus stands as the word's originator.

7. *Blackwood's Magazine*, v. 102, 47, 51. Separately, in his letter to HA, 24 Mar 1867, AP, CMG had said that HA was "delightful."

8. Granville's function in "The Easter Trip" is at times straightforwardly satirical. Describing London parties to a young woman Stuart fancies, Granville assures her (195): "If it is a political party . . . you might present two Polar bears and a chimpanzee with perfect safety to your hostess, and she would only ask them to go into the next room, telling them, at the same time, that it was very good of them to come, and that her husband would be delighted to talk to them." Speaking of literary wives in London, Granville explains (196), "They talk about what they don't understand, or else rush into the opposite extreme—"

9. "The Easter Trip" valuably reflects HA when approaching thirty. It says Granville spoke French imperfectly (53), had lost some of his Greek and disliked the language (206), seldom swore (54), was a heavy smoker (49), and could be criticized for fault-finding (196) but claimed in his own defense (196–97), ". . . I am the most good-natured man in the world, only nobody but myself has made the discovery."

A notable passage (200) presents Stuart as having the outlook of Hamlet, Granville that of Horatio.

The spoof is the earliest source linking HA with Austen (Mrs. Bennet in *Pride and Prejudice*) (50), Shelley (198), and Wordsworth (198). It is the earliest evidence that HA sought chances to study prehistoric human bones, saying (199), ". . . we stayed some time [in a museum at Liege] looking over the bones of the cave inhabitants, which were very complete—more so, I thought, than those in the British Museum." And it indicates (199–200) that HA inspected the site of the battle of Waterloo—an experience useful and even indispensable to him as author of his intended *History*.

10. Hay arrived in New York on 1 Feb 1867. See William Roscoe Thayer, *The Life and Letters of John Hay*, Bost & NY, 1915, I, 245. (Thayer's book was written with HA's help and under his influence.)

For an indication that Hay did not travel via London, or at least did not meet HA, see note 17 below.

11. Bigelow, *Retrospections*, III, 597; IV, 6–98, passim.

12. Bigelow's introduction is dated 28 Dec 1867. "Autobiography" had been imposed on Franklin's work for more than a decade. See especially *Benjamin Franklin: his autobiography; with a narrative of his public life and services by Rev. H. Hastings Weld*, NY 1855.

13. Thayer, *Hay*, I, 233–79; II, 16. For his becoming acquainted with Clover Hooper, see Tyler Dennett, ed., *Lincoln and the Civil War in the Diaries and Letters of John Hay*, NY 1988 reprint, 266, 270.

14. *EHA* (1907), 173; (LoA), 903. The episode can be dated. See Bigelow, Diary, 10 Sep 1861, BiP—"Motley has not yet gone to Vienna. He is circulating among his Aristocratic friends in London. . . . He thinks the aristocracy of England the 'perfection of human society,' so says Mr[.] A. They [the Adamses] seemed greatly amused at the pleasure he [Motley] seemed to take in airing his new dignity, among his old friends the nobility."

15. Bigelow, *Retrospections*, III, 634–48; *Letters of Hay*, I, 285– 93; Dennett, *Hay*, 64–65; Oliver Wendell Holmes, *John Lothrop Motley/ A Memoir*, Bost 1879, 129–40; and carbon-copy of transcript, Motley to Sumner, 14 Oct 1867, W. C. Ford Papers, MHS—ending: "This letter . . . is confidential and I particularly request that it not be published. I am especially desirous that [Samuel] Hooper should read it." In the letter, Motley tells Sumner that he was "accused of disgraceful conduct by an unknown person who had never seen me or heard the sound of my voice." But McCrackin, not unknown, had signed his accusation.

16. *Letters of Hay*, I, 295–98; Moran, unpub. journal, 11 Jul 1867, LC; HA's 1867 engagement book, July 12, HAL; CFA, Diary, 13 Jun 1867, AP.

17. HA's 1867 engagement book lists "Major Hay" as a July 16 dinner guest. This is HA's earliest known mention of Hay. It may seem to demote him; for Hay was commissioned a major on 12 Jan 1864, promoted to lieutenant colonel in April 1865, promoted on 31 May 1865 to colonel on "leave of absence without pay," and mustered out as a colonel on 8 Apr 1867, while in Illinois. See Dennett, *Hay*, 35. But HA's listing Hay as a major simply shows that HA was respectful of wartime ranks and less-than-respectful of the brevet ranks showered on Union officers just before and after war's end. On the same principle, for HA, CFA2 was assuredly a colonel but not assuredly a general.

18. HA's 1867 engagement book, HAL. Another traveling politician concerned with questions of public finance was Senator John Sherman of Ohio, a younger brother of General Sherman. The senator visited London and came to the Legation. Moran recorded that "Henry Adams was

present with Senator Sherman" at a reception given by Lord Stanley, then foreign secretary. See unpub. journal, 9 May 1867, LC.

19. Moran had recorded the year before, unpub. journal, 28 Aug, 4 Oct 1866, LC, that ABA was so unwell that CFA thought her illness might be mortal. Moran noted too, 21 Oct 1867, that Charles and Louisa Kuhn were sometimes long separated. Without pointing towards possible divorce, he remarked, ". . . I suspect no one can live long with her."

20. Writing from Rome to CMG on 23 Apr 1865, HA had said he meant "to write a new work on art, which is to smash the Greeks." It seems that Story by that time had come to value HA's opinions of his works. Later, while visiting London, Story said in a note to HA, 28 Oct 1867: ". . . as you expressed so much interest in the statue of Peabody[,] I write to say that I shall be very glad to show you the sketch. . . ." ". . . I shall be delighted to have your criticism."

21. Two incidental personages in HA's novel are the "Grand-Duke and Duchess of Saxe-*Baden*-Hombourg (italics added)." See *Democracy*, (1880), 279; (LoA), 139. It is typical of HA that he planted "Baden" in his book and thus placed and dated his first attempt to draft it.

22. HA had visited Mount Vernon in 1850 and apparently again in 1851. He visited the White House in 1850 and 1861, Seward's house on Lafayette Square in 1861, and the Lee's house in Arlington in 1861.

23. The deadliest feature of *Democracy*, considered as a political weapon, is its suggesting that Ratcliffe's pursuit of the presidency is hopeless. This feature arguably was present in the novel from the outset. A second feature of *Democracy*, HA's averting the marriage of Ratcliffe, a long-time widower, to Madeleine Lee, the young widow, can be viewed as part of the original plot. The underlying theme of both features is attempted dictatorship that fails. Ratcliffe can neither be president at will nor acquire at will the wife he thinks he needs as his future first lady.

In August and September 1867, HA hoped that Sumner might be driven from the Senate—also from a conceivable presidential candidacy— by a rival in Massachusetts, John A. Andrew. The hope was dashed on 30 Oct 1867 by Andrew's death. See HA to CFA2, 16 Nov 1867. By then, however, Sumner had a dangerous new critic to contend with, the un-named author of the Boston letter in the *New York Evening Express*.

24. In his 1867 engagement book, HAL, HA listed "Taylor, G. Car-rington," as a guest at the Legation's July 4 reception.

25. That the baron in *Democracy* is an older man of ministerial rank may reflect, in part, HA's having met Baron Gerolt, the Prussian minister to the U. S., in Washington in 1861; also his having met aged Baron Alexander von Humboldt in Berlin in 1859.

26. *Alice's Adventures in Wonderland* was published late in 1865, was much reviewed, and sold with tolerable rapidity. That the book affected HA is clear, but exactly how early he first read it is unknown. His copy, if he owned one, is not in evidence. Writing to CFA2 on 16 Nov 1867, evidently well after he first read the book, HA made references to it which CFA2 presumably was not in a position to recognize. For example, ". . . he's a hatter" (reflecting Chap. VII).

27. CMG to HA, 27 Dec 1867, and the reply, HA to CMG, 30 Dec 1867, L, I, 563, 564n4, include three expressions meant to be recognized as references to the title-page and opening chapters of Carroll's book:

"adventures"; ". . . Lady Mary has grown, & certainly could not get out of her rabbit-hole. . . ."; and "Grown or not she is too tall for you. . . ." (Gaskell currently was hoping to marry Lady Mary Hervey.)

28. Two passages in Chap. IV of *Alice's Adventures* can be viewed as most arresting to HA: (1) " 'The first thing I've got to do,' said Alice to herself . . . ,' is to grow to my right size . . .' "; and (2) " '. . . I've got to grow up again. Let me see—how *is* it to be managed?' "

29. A passage in Chap. IV of *Alice's Adventures* can be viewed as bearing on HA's original idea for a book about himself and especially on the unsatisfactoriness of the idea as too confining; also on life at the Legation as confining. The passage says: " 'There ought to be a book written about me, that there ought! And when I grow up, I'll write one— but I'm grown up now . . . at least there's no room to grow up any more *here.*' "

30. With one exception, evidence directly linking HA and Franklin's *Memoirs* is conspicuously absent. The exception is the Preface of *The Education*, in which HA says Franklin's narrative offers "a model . . . of self-teaching." HA may have formed this opinion by himself, but it was an opinion often formed. For example, on 28 Aug 1867, Sumner wrote to Bigelow: "I have always thought his [Franklin's] Autobiography the finest specimen of that species of composition that exists. . . . Next to it, but very unlike, is Gibbon's. . . . These two books are educators. . . ." See Bigelow, *Retrospections*, IV, 100.

31. In my view, efforts to trace the genesis of *The Education of Henry Adams* should concentrate on HA's innovative radicalism, yet give attention to outside influences. One such influence evidently was the Mock Turtle's story of having been "a real Turtle" and received "the best of educations" when at school "in the sea." See *Alice's Adventures*, Chap. IX. In HA's masterpiece, the idea is turned around. A *real* Adams tells the story of a *mock* Adams's attempts to acquire a sufficient education while in schools and not in schools.

32. Donald, *Sumner and the Rights of Man*, 294–95, 312–15; Rich, *Baron Holstein*, I, 36.

33. The letter appeared definitively in the *New York Evening Express*, 22 Oct 1867, p. 4, under the headlines: "From Yesterday's Editions. A Part of the following appeared in our 2d and 3d Editions of Yesterday." The letter as first published was reprinted in the *World*, 22 Oct 1967, p. 8, under the headlines: "The Senator Sumner, Baron Holstein Affair. (Correspondence of the New-York Express)."

Reacting to the letter, Bigelow wrote to W. H. Huntington on 4 Nov 1867: "The public press . . . has dreadfully aggravated a situation sufficiently painful when the knowledge of it was confined to the parties immediately concerned. . . . The copperhead class of all shades enjoy this scandal prodigiously and delight in fitting it on to all imaginable hypotheses." See *Retrospections*, IV, 115–16.

34. Because JQA2 was running for governor of Massachusetts as the Democratic candidate, the letter printed in the *Express* and *World* was a matter of concern to CFA and HA. It perhaps can be assumed that HA came upon the letter himself, but it seems likely too that someone in America sent CFA or HA a clipping from the *World*.

A sentence in the letter says about Frederick Holstein and Alice

Sumner, "The Baron attended to the lady in *matinees* and *soirees*, and in other public places, and occasionally escorted her from the Senate, where both had been to hear the Senator speak." In his novel, HA uses but alters the story the sentence tells. Madeleine Lee is persuaded by Carrington to go with him to the Senate in order to hear "the last great speech" to be given by Ratcliffe while a member of that body. See *Democracy* (1880), 22–26; (LoA), 13–15.

35. To his relations and friends, HA in 1867 said much in praise of JQA2, as if he admired his brother's course. Directly to John, however, HA was courteously critical. See HA to JQA2, 2 Mar 1867—"You propose that the world shall swallow J. Q. A. without regard to the state of its stomach."

36. Early in 1868, at least to *his* satisfaction, Moran discovered that CFA expected to be elected president in 1872. See Moran, unpub. journal, 24 Feb 1868, LC. Without receding from the discovery, he added on 12 Mar 1868: "Mr. Adams pretends he does not want the Presidency. I strongly suspect he would not refuse it if he were elected."

In my view, HA can safely be inferred to have discovered CFA's expectation several months earlier, surely before 16 Nov 1867.

37. The last lines of the comment correspond to two passages in *Alice's Adventures*. One is in Chap. II: " 'Who am I, then? Tell me that first, and then, if I like being that person, I'll come up: if not, I'll stay down here till I'm somebody else. . . .' " The other is in Chap. X: " 'You may not have lived much under the sea. . . .' "

The image of an oyster concealing a pearl evidently refers, not to *Democracy*, which HA was at work on and possibly was hoping to publish anonymously in the near future, but to his more distant third book. See note 29, above.

38. HA's account in *EHA* (1907), 195–96; (LoA) 926–927, misdates the tenth edition of Lyell's *Principles* 1866, in place of 1867–1868. For the date of HA's agreement with Lyell, see note 42, below.

39. HA to CFA2, 8 May 1867.

40. CFA, Diary, 4 Jan 1868, AP.

41. Thinking he would return to American sometime prior to the Democratic convention and thinking his best course was "resolute retirement to private life," CFA much regretted the recent permanent withdrawal of the Cunard steamers from Boston and their going only to New York. He generally seemed at a loss. "What I am to do on my return to avoid being mixed up in the chaos, I cannot define." See CFA, Diary, 5, 6 Jan 1868, AP.

42. Writing to CMG on 1 Jan 1868, HA began a concluding passage by saying, ". . . I read nearly all the second volume of Piebald. . . . It is natural, simple, easy; there is a vein of sentiment in it which seems to me quite 'tender'. . . ."

Levenson and his fellow editors note that Robert Frederick Boyle, a friend of Gaskell's, wrote *Piebald, a Novel*, published in 1867. See L, I, 565n5. The information is helpful; but obviously, as used by HA, "Piebald" is (a) a pun on Lyell, (b) a reference to Boyle and his novel, and (c) a humorous conflation.

In consequence, the passage has four values. It dates HA's agreement with Lyell as reached in the last days of 1867. It tells CMG that HA's effort to finish reading Lyell's new edition is easily succeeding. It indicates to CMG that HA's work on Lyell is a secret best referred to in cryptic terms. And it offers an irreverent comment on Lyell's second volume as an expression of tender sentiment of a sort HA had found, with agreeable disappointment, in Boyle's novel.

43. Lyell's note, AP, asks HA to forward the copies to Humphreys in recognition of "the help which he & his surveyors have rendered me." It is undated. I assume that Lyell wrote it after agreeing that HA should review his tenth edition; also that the note and the sets in need of mailing reached HA prior to 5 Jan 1868, when he left for Italy. But it seems equally possible that Lyell came to the Legation carrying the note and the sets, talked with HA, and thus started the conversation that ended in HA's becoming his reviewer. In that case, HA kept Lyell's note in part because it came into his possession on the day he himself suggested a most remarkable arrangement.

44. CFA, Diary, 10 Mar 1868, AP; Duberman, *Charles Francis Adams/ 1807–1886*, 331–32. That HA accompanied CFA to the office is implicit in CFA's diary entry and accounts for the sentence mentioning HA.

45. CFA, Diary, 20, 23, 26 Mar 1868, AP. That CFA could be both nominated and elected was fully believed at the time by well-informed Democrats. One such person was John Fiske, a contributor to the New York *World* and currently in close touch with its editor, Manton Marble. Fiske wrote on 27 Feb 1868: "All the large States are dead certain to go Democratic, except Illinois, which is doubtful. It is thus probable that the Democrats will carry the day. . . . Charles Francis Adams is talked of as Democratic candidate." See *Letters of John Fiske*, edited by Ethel S. Fisk, NY 1940, 172.

46. That HA represented his move to Washington in these terms is first documented by CFA's letter to HA, 10 Mar 1869, AP, saying: "We had last week Professor Lowell and Mr. Godkin to dine with us. The latter expressed much interest in the success of your experiment." I assume CFA said "experiment" because HA had used that term from the moment he first part-disclosed his plan.

47. Nagel, *Descent from Glory*, op. cit., 142, 150–51, 179–80.

48. Bigelow considered moving to Washington but was strongly advised not to by Seward, on the ground that former government officials were not respected or even acknowledged in the capital by current government officials. See Bigelow, *Retrospections*, IV, 42–43.

49. A notable affirmation of HA's preeminence in his family is Mark Twain's lampooning of the Adamses in his story "The £1,000,000 Bank-Note." The story was published in 1893 but relates to Adams realities as they were in 1866–1868. A first-person narrative mainly set in London, the story introduces (but does not name) a U. S. minister to England residing on Portland Place. Slowly it divulges that the narrator, a Californian who has drifted to London from San Francisco, bears a sensitive name. A lesser character speaks the crucial line: ". . . it never occurred to me that *you* could be the Henry Adams referred to."

50. *EHA* (1907), 224; (LoA), 956.

51. Writing to CFA2 on 24 Dec 1867, HA said, "I have a few more articles in view. . . ." "Few" might seem to indicate that his plan was vague, but his execution of the plan shows exact, detailed prevision.

52. *EHA* (1907), 29; (LoA), 752–53; Palgrave to HA, 9 Sep 1868, AP. I assume HA borrowed CFA's set intending to read it on the voyage to New York. HA's own copy of Wordsworth, *Poetical Works*, Lond 1888, HAL, is notable for its date.

53. Lyell to HA, 28, 29 May 1868.

54. Lyell to HA, 10 Jun 1868.

55. The portrait was first reproduced in 1930 as the frontispiece in a special edition of Ford, I, bound in red. So reproduced, it became the basis of a new, attempted drawing of HA used on the jacket of a widely sold reprint, HA, *The Education of Henry Adams*, NY: The Modern Library 1931. For innumerable readers, the latter drawing was the first picture they had seen of HA. Unfortunately, it lent him an appearance suggestive of Robert Louis Stevenson, but not of any Adams.

56. Moran, unpub. journal, 25, 26 Jun 1868, LC. The latter entry contains the parting comment, ". . . in the main he [HA] is a well-meaning and kindly young man."

57. HA appreciated Wordsworth enough to memorize a good many of his lines. See HA, *Letters to a Niece*, Bost & NY, 1920, 4–6.

58. *EHA* (1907), 206–09; (LoA), 937–40; CFA, Diary, 8 Jul 1868, AP.

59. CFA did write to John Bright, 4 Dec 1868, BrP, but only after being sent his newly-published *Speeches*.

60. Palgrave to HA, 9 Sep 1868, AP. Palgrave's mention of Milton may suggest that HA had reported reading Wordsworth's *Prelude*.

61. The interest BA took in the review of Lyell was permanent and close to proprietary. See his account in *Degradation*, 35–36. For this reason, I have assumed that his interest was partly shaped by his being entrusted by HA with the article's delivery.

62. HA to CFA2, 30 Jul 1867.

63. *Autobiography*, 172–73; Gurney to CFA2, 24 May 1868, AP; *EHA* (1907), 210; (LoA), 941.

64. CFA to HA, 7 Apr 1869. HA appears to have made two sets of copies. For his own use, he copied entries from JQA's *undergraduate* diaries, and for CFA's use he copied entries from JQA's *later* diaries. The reason is evident. In addition to planning five articles for the *North American Review* and *Edinburgh Review*, HA was building articles-in-reserve.

He later used the extracts from JQA's undergraduate diaries in an important article: "Harvard College. 1786–87." *NAR*, Jan 1872, 110–147"—the first of his works to be signed "Henry Adams." With reference to another article-in-reserve, see note 84.

65. How HA came to know Atkinson is unclear. One notices that, in his 1864 engagement book, HAL, HA lists "Mr. & Mrs. Atkinson—2 Highbury Park—"as guests at a July 14 reception.

66. Paul C. Nagel, "Reconstruction, Adams Style," *Journal of Southern History*, Feb 1986, 3–7; also L, II, 16n1.

67. CFA, Diary, 12 Oct 1868, AP.

68. On 22 Oct 1868, after HA called on Godkin, the *Nation* passed a lukewarm judgment on HA's "Principles of Geology," newly published in the October *NAR*. Godkin evidently did not write the judgment. It said: "Mr. Henry Brooks Adams talks learnedly and, to our mind, sensibly, though we do not wholly follow him, in his review of the tenth edition of Sir Charles Lyell's 'Principles of Geology.' He shows the inconclusive nature

of the results already attained, but perhaps is a little long in doing it—or lengthy, to use a term somewhat more fully expressive."

For HA's responses to judgments in which Godkin *was* involved, see Chaps. 17 & 19.

69. *EHA* (1907), 212–14; (LoA), 943–45.

70. HA's address was 158 G Street (renumbered as 2017 G Street in 1870). The distance from his rooms to Lafayette Square was short. In *The Education*, he would fictionally say that the protagonist's "bachelor's quarters" were "far out on G Street, towards Georgetown." See *EHA* (1907), 221; (LoA), 953.

71. Robert A. McCaughey, "The Transformation of American Academic Life: Harvard University 1821–1892," *Perspectives in American History*, VIII (1974), 272n21—"Ellen's net worth in 1870 was . . . $175,000."

72. *NAR*, Oct 1868, 476.

73. *EHA* (1907), 221; (LoA), 953.

74. "Visiting List. Washington. 1868." in the front of HA's 1868 engagement book, HAL—"Taylor, Mrs./ [Taylor] Gen. & Mrs. 10 Nov^{r}."

Friendship with Richard Taylor became highly important to HA. The remarkable passage in Chap. III of *EHA* concerning snowball fights in Boston contains a reference to Turenne. This reference is traceable to a passage in what is commonly judged to be the best book written by a Confederate participant in the Civil War, Taylor's *Destruction and Reconstruction*, NY 1879. Taylor's passage (64) recounts "a story of Turenne, the greatest soldier of the Bourbons."

When read together with HA's later passage, Taylor's passage can suggest that HA was involved in snowball fights when very young, not as an appendage to CFA2, but as a leader, perhaps sometimes visibly nervous, but still a leader.

75. CFA to HA, 28 Oct, 4 Nov, 22 Oct 1868, AP.

76. For HA's being patted on the back, see HA to CMG, 5 Nov 1868.

77. HA wrote to Reeve on 8 Nov & 14 Dec 1868, 1 Feb & 5 Mar 1869; also on 9 Mar 1869, sending "letter & proof." See "Letters sent," a chronological list in the back of HA's 1868 engagement book, HAL. The dates indicate that Reeve was replying fairly promptly. Neither the contributor's letters nor the editor's replies have been found. Presumably at a later time HA destroyed the replies.

78. Lyell to HA, 8 Nov 1868; *EHA* (1907), 202; (LoA), 933.

79. On Survey pay scales, see the passage on inflation and its effect on professional persons in HA, "American Finance, 1865–1869," *Edinburgh Review*, Apr 1869, 532.

I assume Emmons began to form his opinion of HA as a geological critic by reading "The Principles of Geology" in 1868. Emmons later said in print that HA was the "most competent critic" of Clarence King's *Systematic Geology*. See Samuel Franklin Emmons, *Biographical Memoir of Clarence King*, Wash: Judd & Detweiler 1907, 4. Emmons does not mention HA by name; but he clearly knows who wrote the anonymous review of King's treatise in the *Nation*, 23 Jan 1879; he has the review at hand; and he goes out of his way to state his high opinion of the author as a geological critic.

80. There are two notes from Gurney to CFA2, 10, 14 Nov 1868, AP. (The replies are missing.) In the second, Gurney says he has "already

written to your brother" about a suggestion the brother made concerning the current number of *NAR*.

Presumably the brother was HA. The current number of *NAR* was the January 1869 issue, then in preparation. What HA had proposed is unknown, need not have been an article, and possibly was a book notice. Evidently HA had made his proposal by stating it in a note or letter to CFA2, as if CFA2 were in charge of Adams family affairs relating to the magazine. Gurney evidently resisted, first by writing to HA in care of general delivery, Washington, and next by asking CFA2 whether HA had a proper address. One may assume that, sometime after November 14, Gurney again wrote to HA and that this second letter afforded a basis for their beginning a direct correspondence, by-passing CFA2.

81. "Letters sent," HA's 1868 engagement book, HAL.

82. For Mrs. Sumner's "unhappy stay in Boston" and the eventual divorce, see Donald, *Charles Sumner and the Rights of Man*, 318–20.

83. HA to Palmer, 21 Nov 1868. HA was closer to Gaskell and Cunliffe than to Palmer, but both Gaskell and Cunliffe had suffered broken engagements. Hence the direction of this significant disclosure.

84. There is more than a possibility that HA in December 1868 was seen visiting the State Department and consulting its library and archives. If he made such visits, they related to an article. According to CFA's reply, 2 Dec 1868, AP, HA in his missing letter no. 7 to CFA, 29 Nov 1868, asked whether CFA had any objection to his preparing "a paper upon the negotiation of 1861 on the Paris Declaration of 1856." CFA replied, "I have none."

HA prepared the paper, no one knows when or where. He published it without explanation in *Historical Essays*, NY 1891, under the title "The Declaration of Paris. 1861." The paper is partly based on CFA's diary, to which HA may not have had access till after his father's death in 1886. An introductory phrase, "In those days . . . ," *Historical Essays*, 252, indicates that the text was given final form not long before the book went to the printer.

85. *EHA* (1907), 217; (LoA), 948. The passage is startlingly fictional in one respect. It places Curtis, not *with* Evarts on the side of the government, but *against* him, "employed to argue against the constitutional power of the government to make an artificial standard of value in time of peace." It thus conceals and suppresses the notable fact that HA publicly challenged the team of Evarts and Curtis on important points of law in a highly important federal case.

86. HA's 1866 engagement book, HAL, April 21, 27, & Schofield's address at the back; "Visiting List" in HA's 1868 engagement book, HAL —"Randall. Mr[.] Secretary & Mrs." and "Schofield. Gen."

87. "Visiting List," op. cit.,—"Chase. Mr[.] Chief Justice & Miss. 8 Nov^r."

88. *EHA* (1907), 214; (LoA), 945–46.

89. *EHA* (1907), 217–18; (LoA), 949.

8. A TIME IN THE CLOUDS

Letters by and to HA are in HA-micro 3, unless otherwise noted.

PRINCIPAL SOURCES

(1) fourteen letters, HA to CFA2, 8 Jan–22 Jun 1869.
(2) letter, HA to Wells, [12 Jan 1869], L, II, 11.
(3) letter, HA to Atkinson, 1 Feb 1869.
(4) two letters, HA to Bright, 3 Feb, 30 May 1869, L, II, 17–18, 33–35.
(5) four letters, HA to CMG, 30 Mar–20 Jun 1869.
(6) [HA], "American Finance, 1865–1869," *Edinburgh Review*, Apr 1869, 504–33.
(7) Henry Brooks Adams, "The Session," *NAR*, Apr 1869, 610–40.

ADDITIONAL SOURCES; COMMENTS

1. CFA to HA, 19 Dec 1868.
2. CFA to HA, 6 Jan 1869.
3. M. A. De Wolfe Howe, *Portrait of an Independent/ Moorfield Storey/ 1845–1929*, Bost & NY 1932, 129.
4. CFA to HA, 9 Dec 1868.
5. *EHA* (1907), 228–29; (LoA), 960–62.
6. *Edinburgh Review*, Apr 1869, 527.
7. HA evidently sent Reeve "American Finance, 1865–1869" on 1 Feb 1869, together with a letter. See "Letters sent" in HA's 1868 engagement book, HAL.

The first Americans to learn that HA meant to contribute something to the *Edinburgh Review* were presumably Wells and McCulloch, in late October 1868. HA told CFA the secret in early January. See CFA to HA, 13 Jan 1869—"In my youth, I wrote my papers over nearly as many times as you do." But HA informed CFA2 only after learning the article had been accepted. See HA to CFA2, 11 Mar 1869.

The article has been neglected and not reprinted but is more informative than HA's other articles of 1869 with regard to his program as it concerned domestic affairs.

8. Reeve at first refused to produce pamphlet copies. See HA to CFA2, 29 Apr 1869.
9. The phrase "matter, thought, and style" echoes and alters the phrase "matter, form, and style" in Milton's sonnet "On the Detraction Which Followed upon My Writing Certain Treatises."
10. The attitude of the author of *Democracy* towards democracy is extremely favorable and is stated explicitly—also figuratively—in the hard-to-read paragraph beginning Chap. VIII. (Here it is quoted complete at the start of Chap. 15.) It should be added that the novel was largely developed in the years when, in HA's view, England was induced by the Union victory in America to liberalize. In "The Session," he referred to the United States and England as "two democracies." See *NAR*, Apr 1869, 639.
11. The best evidence that HA wanted to write a novel—as opposed to a *roman à clef*—is *Democracy's* characters, at least six of whom show abundant aliveness and assert identities quite their own.
12. "Letters sent," in HA's 1868 engagement book, HAL.
13. Storey thought HA was in Washington "to study literature." It bears noting, too, that in January–February 1869 in Washington, when he

was much in their company, HA saw both Storey and Hoar become engaged. See Howe, *Moorfield Storey*, op. cit., 124, 129.

14. An instance of a strong statement by HA is his writing earlier to CFA2 about their father: "I mean to block the movement to put the Governor into the Cabinet. I don't want him there. He would be in my way." See HA to CFA2, 13 Dec 1868. Possibly the statement was worded just strongly enough to preclude CFA2's taking it seriously.

15. CFA to HA, 20 Jan 1869.

16. CFA to HA, 3 Feb 1869.

17. *Edinburgh Review*, Apr 1869, especially 507, 525–26, 533. The same argument appears, with different details, in all of HA's political articles of 1869–1870 through "The New York Gold Conspiracy."

18. *Edinburgh Review*, Apr 1869, 517.

19. HA later wrote that the sentence was one of the "commonplaces" that men of Grant's intellectual calibre would turn to "when at a loss for expression." See *EHA* (1907), 230; (LoA), 962.

20. The only account is in *EHA* (1907), 227–28; (LoA), 959–60. It is simplified, makes no mention of Washburne and Stewart, and pretends that Fish and Boutwell were named on March 5. Yet it seems factual in several respects, notably in saying that HA was at the Capitol when the Cabinet appointments were made public.

21. HA had said a month before—letter to Atkinson, 1 Feb 1869– that rejection of the Alabama treaty would mean "a determination on our part to have, sooner or later, a war with England." Also see HA to Thomas Baring, 2 Feb 1869, L, II, 16—"The bitterness of the old war-feeling is very great; in fact it is greater than ever. . . ."

22. *EHA* (1907), 219; (LoA), 950.

23. HA's most comprehensive summary of Seward's record as secretary of state during the Rebellion is a passage in "The Session," *NAR*, Apr 1869, 629–30: "The foreign policy of Mr. Seward was . . . simple . . . although his expedients were innumerable. His intention was always to avoid war, but always to gain his objects; and he achieved astonishing success."

24. HA's foreign policy did not change and was best judged from his actions as well as his writings. "The Session" affords an excellent introduction to his policy, notably with regard to not seeking additional territory. See *NAR*, Apr 1869, 627—"We have little sympathy with the policy which prompted . . . purchases of new territory. There is a peculiar brilliancy and seductiveness in that vast scheme which . . . grasped in succession three such commanding points as Russian America, St. Thomas, and the Isthmus of Darien; the imagination is dazzled by it; and yet we should be heartily glad to discover any honorable mode of release from the obligations of the St. Thomas Treaty."

25. I have accepted HA's understanding of Seward's expansionist policy as so well-informed as to be practically indubitable. While divulging the policy in "The Session," HA partly attributes it to Americans generally. Yet he makes clear that the country's foreign policy decisions had been made by Seward. See *NAR*, Apr 1869, 611, 626–40.

26. This summary of Sumner's policy rests on HA's actions and writings relating to Sumner subsequent to 4 Mar 1869. See especially *NAR*, Apr 1869, 638—". . . [the Alabama Claims] were to be reserved and used

to lead or force England into a cession of territory." And ibid., 639—
". . . war is always within sight. The Senate practically forces this complication upon the President and the Cabinet."

The summary is not meant to imply that Sumner intended war, but
rather that he expected it; also that his course much increased the
likelihood of war and thus necessitated counteraction by HA and others.

I have accepted HA's understanding of the matter as better informed
than the carefully considered understanding set forth by Sumner's biographer. See Donald, *Charles Sumner and the Rights of Man*, op. cit., Chap. X.

27. There seems to be no reason to disbelieve HA's later statement
that in 1869 he continued to like Sumner and even admire him. See *EHA*
(1907), 219; (LoA), 950.

28. Clarendon to Bright, 22 Mar 1869, BrP.

29. "Letters sent," HA's 1868 engagement book, HAL.

30. William S. McFeely, *Grant/ A Biography*, NY 1981, 293–94—"some
bright lawyer." It is not suggested that HA was the person who drew
Sumner's attention to the forgotten statute, but it is a fact that HA steeped
himself in Treasury history from an early age and was as likely as anyone
to know of the statute.

31. HA to CFA2, 3 Apr 1867.

32. Boutwell was so ignorant of finance that he could not understand
certified checks. See A. Barton Hepburn, *History of the Coinage and Currency
of the United States*, NY 1903, reprinted NY 1968, 329.

33. McFeely, *Grant*, op. cit., 297—". . . Julia Grant saw to it that Julia
Fish's husband became secretary of state." See also Fish to Sumner, 13
Mar 1869, in Edward L. Pierce, *Memoirs and Letters of Charles Sumner*, Bost
1894, IV, 379: ". . . I am going to Washington to undertake duties for
which I have little taste and less fitness. . . . My name was sent to the Senate
without my knowledge."

34. F. C. Barlow to HA, 5 Mar 1869.

35. The arrangement giving the magazine an editor for politics
clearly began with the April 1869 issue. It was evidenced by the delayed
date on which that issue appeared, the issue's contents, the contents of the
magazine's issues thenceforward, and HA's altered relations with Gurney,
Godkin, and other editors. For a later arrangement making CFA2 editor
for politics, see Chapter 10.

36. With regard to things financial and economic, HA and Hodgskin
had very similar interests. See the Hodgskin listings in the *Nation* indexes
compiled by Haskell and the *NAR* indexes compiled by Cushing.

37. Clarendon to Bright, 22 Mar 1869, BrP. The foreign secretary
appears to have depended on Bright for assistance with regard to dealings
with the United States.

38. Bright to HA, 25 Mar 1869. The letter is explicitly a reply. It
begins: "I was very glad to see your handwriting again, & had I known
what to say I should at once have replied to your letter."

39. Bright to his wife, 29 Jun 1862, OP.

40. HA to CFA2, 17 Jul 1863, HA-micro 2.

41. HA to Carl Schurz, 16 May 1871.

42. A remarkable letter written by Badeau to Sumner while serving
as assistant secretary is cordial, yet consistent with HA's intentions with
respect to England and at odds with the intentions of Sumner and Motley.

See Badeau to Sumner, 8 Jul 1869, in the Motley-Fish-Sumner Letters, W. C. Ford Papers, MHS.

43. *NAR*, Apr 1869, 615.

44. Ibid., 639.

45. Sanborn's "Another Adams" is typical of many overconfident assertions made about HA by Massachusetts residents and Harvard graduates, beginning as early as 1856–1858 and continuing till very recent years. Knowing they knew something about HA, such persons sometimes incautiously spoke and wrote as if they knew everything.

46. CFA to HA, 5 May 1869.

47. CFA to HA, 12 May 1869.

48. HA's letter is missing, but certain of its contents can be inferred very readily from the reply, Forster to HA, 24 Jun 1869.

49. The *degree* to which HA was the author of the independence of Canada is an important but special question. All that is intended here is to make clear that he had *some* influence favoring that very important change.

Just as the letter to Bright ends by proposing the independence of Canada, "The Session" ends by suggesting a "large and permanent settlement of our English relations." See *NAR*, Apr 1969, 640—". . . we . . . should induce her [Great Britain] to abandon it [Canada] to itself: so it will be safer from violence than if it were a part of the British Empire."

50. Forster to HA, 24 Jun 1869.

51. *NAR*, Apr 1869, 630–31.

52. If his letters to Forster continue not to be found, it might be inferred that in the second letter HA asked Forster to destroy the letters as dangerous to both their countries; also to Canada.

9. Seasons of Death

Letters by and to HA are in HA-micro 3, unless otherwise noted.

PRINCIPAL SOURCES

(1) fifteen letters, HA to CMG, 11 Jul 1869–8 Jul 1870.

(2) letter, HA to Cunliffe, 13 Sep 1869.

(3) letter, HA to Cox, 8 Nov 1869, L, II, 50–51.

(4) letter, HA to George Caspar Adams, 8 Dec 1869.

(5) letters, HA to Garfield, 30 Dec 1869, 12 May 1870, L, II, 59, 72.

(6) letter, HA to Eliot, 3 Jul 1870, L, II, 72–73.

(7) Henry Brooks Adams, "Civil Service Reform," *NAR*, Oct 1869; also the same reprinted as a pamphlet, Bost: Fields, Osgood & Co. 1869.

(8) Henry Brooks Adams, "The Legal-Tender Act," *NAR*, Apr 1870, 299–327.

(9) Henry Brooks Adams, "The Session" *NAR*, Jul 1870, 29–62 (in a series of annual articles under an unchanging title).

(10) [HA], "The New York Gold Conspiracy," *Westminster Review*, Lond edition, Oct 1870, 411–36; NY edition, Oct 1870, 193–204; and the same as reprinted in Charles F. Adams, Jr., and Henry Adams, *Chapters of Erie, and Other Essays*, Bost 1871, 100–34.

(11) [HA], three unsigned Washington newsletters, as follows:

    (a) "Men and Things in Washington," *Nation*, 25 Nov 1869, 454–56;

(b) "A Peep into the Cabinet Windows," *Nation*, 16 Dec 1869, 531–32;

(c) "The Senate and the Executive," *Nation*, 6 Jan 1870, 5–6.

(12) [HA], eight unsigned editorials (* = new attribution; for substantiation, see note 42 below):

(a) "A Political Nuisance," *Nation*, 27 Jan 1870, 52–54;

(b) "Mr. Dawes—President Grant—General Butler," *Nation*, 10 Feb 1870, 84;

(c) "The Census Imbroglio," *Nation*, 24 Feb 1870, 116–17;

*(d) "A New Party," *Nation*, 10 Mar 1870, 151–52;

*(e) "The Senate and the Chief Justice," *Nation*, 24 Mar 1870, 188–89;

*(f) "The Reopening of the Legal-Tender Case," *Nation*, 7 Apr 1870, 218–19;

*(g) "A Debate on the Tariff," *Nation*, 21 Apr 1870, 250–51;

*(h) "The Revenue Reformers and the Republican Party," *Nation*, 5 May 1870, 283–84.

(13) [HA], an unsigned editorial:

"A Delicate Suggestion," *New York Evening Post*, 2 Feb 1870. (See note 43 below.)

(14) three polemics by HA on a special topic (* = new attribution; for substantiation, see note 72 below):

(a) H. B. A., "The North American Review and the Hon. Elbridge G. Spaulding," *Nation*, 12 May 1870;

*(b) [HA], paragraph signed "Ed. Nation," *Nation*, 26 May 1870, replying to a letter to the editor signed "G. B.," Bost, 16 May 1870 (the letter and HA's reply are headed "The Murderous Assault on Mr. Spaulding.");

*(c) [HA], paragraph signed "Ed. Nation," *Nation*, 30 Jun 1870, replying to a letter to the editor signed "G. B.," Bost, 27 May 1870 (the letter and HA's reply are headed "The Necessity of Legal Tender.").

ADDITIONAL SOURCES; COMMENTS

1. CFA to HA, 24 Mar 1869.

2. HA, *Notes toward a Memoir of Louisa Johnson Adams*, H.

3. HA returned LCA's papers to Quincy, thought "some" were "good" (see L, V, 144), and may have been involved in the eventual publication of one: "Mrs. John Quincy Adams's Narrative of a Journey from St. Petersburg to Paris in February, 1815/ With an Introduction by Her Grandson,/ Brooks Adams," *Scribner's Magazine*, Oct 1903, 449–63.

4. HA, manuscript usually known as "Two Letters on a Prussian Gymnasium," H—published in *AHR*, Oct 1947, 59–74.

5. For example, HA to CFA2, 25 Jun 1863, saying that boating was "a branch of pleasure more than usually innocent, healthy and beneficial, but too much neglected in our education."

6. CFA to HA, 24 Mar 1869.

7. In 1918, when editing the first public edition, Henry Cabot Lodge and Worthington Chauncey Ford, with the support of the publisher, Houghton Mifflin Company, added to HA's title the subtitle *An Autobiography*. It is difficult to find a presentable excuse for this literary atrocity. It

was an evident fact but not a defense that the editors and the publisher thought that adding a subtitle, and precisely that subtitle, might increase sales, profits, and royalties. See the relevant materials in the Lodge Papers, 1918, MHS.

8. That HA found a new form is affirmed by the incessant use of the first three words of his title as the first words of other titles.

HA published a foretaste of the discovered form in 1882: his *John Randolph*, especially its first chapter.

9. NYTimes, 19 Jun 1869, last page, "President Grant's Visit to the City." At this point, the chapter becomes dependent on two sources relating to the gold panic of 1869: *Gold Panic Investigation*, House of Representatives. Report, No. 31. Forty-first Congress, Second Session. Report of the Committee on Banking and Currency . . . [Washington: GPO, 1870]—the bible of the subject, cited hereafter as *Gold Panic*; and Kenneth D. Ackerman, *The Gold Ring/Jim Fisk, Jay Gould, and Black Friday, 1869*, NY 1988—the best and most detailed account published in recent years, cited hereafter as *Gold Ring*. I am indebted to Ackerman for generous assistance relating both to the Congressional report and to unanswered questions raised by his book.

10. It is impossible to understand HA's conduct during the critical period June 1869–July 1870 in the absence of knowing what he was able to learn about Raymond's death.

One can ascertain within reasonable bounds what he learned; but it is necessary first to determine what in fact happened—what he *could* learn; and this is not easy. Among the notable occurrences of 1869, the death of Raymond must have been one of the most poorly reported.

The principal published contemporary account appears within the obituary editorial, "HENRY J. RAYMOND," NYTimes, Saturday, 19 Jun 1869. In its first sentence, the account says that the paper's "founder and editor . . . died suddenly at his residence yesterday morning of an attack of apoplexy." All other details appear in the concluding paragraph.

> Mr. RAYMOND passed the afternoon previous to his death [Thursday, June 17] in Green-Wood, making arrangements for the interment of his son WALTER'S remains, and called at the office of the TIMES about 6 o'clock in the evening. After a few minutes' conversation with the writer of this sketch on matters pertaining to the business of the paper, he returned home. After dinner he sat with his family and some friends who came in until between 9 and 10 o'clock, when he left them to attend a political consultation; and his family saw no more of him until he was discovered, about 2:30 next morning, lying in the hallway unconscious and apparently dying. He had locked the outside door and shut the inner one, and was then apparently stricken with the malady that closed his life. The most eminent medical aid was at once summoned, and the utmost that science and skill could do were done, in vain. He remained unconscious, and died tranquilly about 5 o'clock in the morning.

The *Times* account was unquestionably written by George Jones, the paper's co-founder, publisher, and business manager. On one score, the account could be faulted. It failed to say whether Raymond arrived at the alleged political consultation, and, if so, when he left it.

As will be shown, the whole matter of the consultation was a lie invented to provide a plausible reason why the editor left his house. The presumable inventor was Jones.

The editor's house was at 12 West Ninth Street. The *Times* account was manifestly based in part on information furnished by one or more of his housemates. The account could seem shaped to serve a private purpose. In stopping to say the editor locked his outside door and shut the inner, it could appear to imply that his death was an entirely private matter, to be dealt with by his family and their doctors, and not requiring the presence of the police, still less the coroner. The account did not mention the latter authorities.

An independent account was published that same morning, Saturday, June 19, in the *New York Tribune*. It agreed with the *Times* account with regard to Raymond's Thursday errand at Green-Wood and visit to the *Times* office before going home. It then diverged.

> After tea, he remained in the house till nine o'clock, when he went out, as he said, to take a short walk. As nearly as can be ascertained, he returned home at about 11, and, after locking and bolting the door, was seized by apoplexy, and fell to the floor.
>
> In the early morning at about 3 o'clock, the sickness of one of the children caused several of the family to rise, when the groans and hard breathing of Mr. Raymond were heard. On going to the hall, he was found lying on his face, still breathing, but unconscious and in great agony. He was at once removed to his room, and several physicians were summoned, who pronounced his disease apoplexy. Every effort was made to revive him, but without avail, and about five o'clock this morning [Friday, June 18] death ensued.

On one score, the *Tribune* account could be faulted. It failed to note that the reported two-hour absence would indicate a long walk.

The account offered new details. It was manifestly based in part on information provided by a housemate who saw Raymond lying on the floor of the hall. Because it said the editor not only locked his outside door but bolted it, the account could be said to stress heavily that his death was a private matter, a sudden illness within the home.

It can be assumed that the information in the *Times* and *Tribune* accounts that was supplied by the Raymond household, though inconsistent, was all furnished by Mrs. Raymond or on her behalf by her daughter Mary. As will be shown, the information so supplied was false with respect to the cause of the editor's death, his return to the house, and the discovery of his condition.

The funeral was held on Monday, June 21, and was conducted by Henry Ward Beecher. Evidently on Monday, Jones talked with Beecher about the problem of finding a replacement editor. He asked Beecher to urge John Bigelow to accept the appointment.

Bigelow was still residing at Highland Falls near West Point. He was keeping a diary and readying to write his autobiography. He came to New York for the funeral. In the afternoon, he visited Mrs. Raymond. She told him that three of her husband's relations died of apoplexy. She did *not* tell him the essential truths about what happened.

Bigelow also visited E. D. Morgan and Thurlow Weed. Each advised him that he should be Raymond's successor, and Weed informed him that he "already had sent word to Jones and James B. Taylor [another *Times* business executive] that I was the only and the indispensible [*sic*] man for the place." See Bigelow, Diary, 22 Jun 1869, BiP—cited hereafter as Diary.

On Tuesday, June 22, on the train to Highland Falls, Bigelow and Beecher sat together. (How this may have happened is not made clear in the diary.) Beecher raised the subject of editing and told Bigelow that several persons had been mentioned in talks the day before about a successor to Raymond. Bigelow interjected that Raymond had earlier spoken with him and Mrs. Bigelow about his sometime taking the editorship. Beecher urged Bigelow to put aside his autobiography and accept the appointment.

Later on June 22, Bigelow recorded the foregoing details and added that Raymond was discovered by Mary. (Presumably his source was Mrs. Raymond, during his call on the 21st.) He also recorded that the entry door had been opened for Raymond on his return by a servant who "was in her night clothes & ran as soon as she had turned the key." (Again his presumable source was Mrs. Raymond.)

What Bigelow was most careful to record was news he had learned— evidently in confidence—from Beecher. The news was that Raymond did not leave his house "to attend a political meeting" as reported in the *Times*; that in fact he visited an actress, Rose Eytinge, at her apartment; that he had been trying to free himself from her toils; that she had letters of his which were "her instruments of torture"; that she meant to make him "pay"; that she summoned him on the 17th, on penalty of her visiting his house; and that their meeting was "very stormy."

Bigelow was religious. The tale he recorded having heard was one of sin ending in death. The teller, Beecher, was the foremost minister in the United States. In the circumstances, Bigelow was perhaps disinclined to ask Beecher how he had come by the news, especially the news that the editor's meeting with the actress was very stormy.

Recording Beecher's story, Bigelow showed no disposition to doubt it. He both recorded it and went on to conjecture that Raymond was a victim of lust because he had never learned the efficacy of prayer.

A sceptical reader of the entry in Bigelow's diary might wish to think that Beecher invented every part of his moral tale from thin air. An alternative possibility suggests itself. When he went to the *Times* office at 6:00 P.M. on Thursday, Raymond may have told Jones that he would have to see Rose Eytinge that night at her apartment; that she had summoned him, on pain of visiting his house; that she had letters of his and meant to make him pay; and that he expected their meeting would be very stormy. If Jones passed these details to Beecher when they had their talk about a replacement editor, Beecher—in his mind— could easily have transformed the editor's announced expectation into a certifiable Raymond-Eytinge experience.

It must be added that, in his diary on June 22, apparently by accident, Bigelow misdated Raymond's return to his house as occurring on "Friday night." Also he said that Mary "discovered" her father "about 3 in the mg."—that she "overheard" his "sterturous [*sic*] breathing."

The word "stertorous" needs noting. One perhaps may suppose that Beecher originated the description of Raymond's breathing as "stertorous" and that he chose the word for the sake of its rhetorical impressiveness. In that event, Bigelow merely echoed it—and misspelled it.

On Tuesday, June 22, Weed sent Bigelow a telegram advising him that he was appointed editor of the *Times*. (The telegram is pasted into Bigelow's diary.) Bigelow did not wish to accept the appointment without first buying 10% of the company's stock. He returned to the city, talked again with Weed, and learned that the persons considered for the editorship had included William Evarts, E. L. Godkin, and G. W. Curtis. He later changed his mind and preferred not to buy stock. At last, on Monday, August 2, he started work as editor.

Apparently during the morning of Thursday, August 5, he received from President Grant, then in New York, an invitation to call. Caleb Norvell, the financial editor of the *Times*, later testified: ". . . he [Bigelow] had an interview with the President; probably at Mr. Corbin's house. On the 6th appeared an editorial [in the *Times*] wholly irrespective of any matter of gold." See *Gold Panic*, 275.

The meeting with the president was important to Bigelow. On August 29, he wrote an entry in his diary concerning his first month as editor. He failed to specify where he and Grant met; he did not mention Corbin and did not mention gold; but he was careful to write: "When Genl. Grant passed through on his way from Long Branch, he sent me word that he would [like?] to see me. I went and spent an hour with him. He spoke at length of all the domestic questions of his administration and very well. I wrote an article next day suggested by his array of the promising financial results of his administration."

The importance of the August 6 editorial centered in its special status. Bigelow understood that the *Times* had been asked to speak "semi-officially" for the president. See *Gold Panic*, 279.

Evidently on Monday, August 23, Bigelow was approached by James McHenry, an old friend from England. McHenry offered him an unsigned article and said it was written by a "particular friend of the President." McHenry appears also to have explained that he brought the article "from Mr. Corbin," the president's brother-in-law.

Again Bigelow understood that the *Times* was being asked to speak semi-officially for the president. The article said that publication of Grant's policy with respect to the sale of gold by the Treasury could not be expected earlier than the appearance of his Annual Message in December but meanwhile his policy could be adduced from his "*acts*." The article went on to affirm that the president would bar the sale of gold by the Treasury during the approaching harvest season.

Bigelow accepted the article and had it set in type. An assistant of Norvell's read the article in proof and urged a delay till Norvell could see it. When next in the office, Norvell read it and thought its last paragraph was possibly written with a "sinister purpose to 'bull' gold." On August 25, the newspaper published the article as an editorial, but only in an altered and shortened form, without its last paragraph. As modified, the article still could be read to say that the president would prevent the sale of gold by the Treasury during the harvest. See *Gold Panic*, 275–79.

When he reviewed his work in his diary on August 29, Bigelow did not mention the unsigned article brought by McHenry and published on August 25 in altered form. How soon he realized that the article was *by* Corbin as well as *from* him is not clear, but the interval could not have been long.

The *Times* for "Black Friday," September 24, was issued at the usual early morning hour. It contained an editorial written by Norvell at Bigelow's urging. The editorial said rumors were being spread in the gold market that President Grant, his brother-in-law Abel Corbin, and Secretary Boutwell were participants in a Gould-Fisk "ring" that had cornered gold and created a panic. The rumors were real. As a needful defensive measure, the editorial deemed them "false," even "monstrous."

At the moment, the president and the secretary were in Washington. Abel Corbin was in New York. According to later testimony, the editorial was immediately "telegraphed to Washington"—meaning to Grant. See *Gold Panic*, 279–80. The presumable sender was Corbin.

Later that morning, George Jones and Jim Taylor visited Bigelow at his "room" (presumably meaning his lodgings) and complained to him that he had run up the expenses of the *Times* and was raising the paper to a standard too high for New York. (The complaints were false. He had served the paper too briefly to have done what was charged.) Bigelow defended his work as editor but indicated he might resign.

It seems inescapable that the true reason for Jones and Taylor's visit was a strong message to Jones from Corbin, perhaps delivered in person and buttressed with feigned or actual White House sanction.

Still later on Friday, Bigelow recounted in his diary the visit by Jones and Taylor. He recorded that he was "pretty much discouraged or rather disgusted with newspaper work" and was meditating a withdrawal.

On Monday, Bigelow quit. He asked Jones to strike him from the payroll, effective the previous Friday. See Diary, 24, 27 Sep 1869.

It can be assumed that, in part, Bigelow quit in fear for his life. His experiences in August relating to Grant, McHenry, and Corbin gave him ample cause to believe that at least one of the persons named in Norvell's editorial of September 24—Grant, Boutwell, or Corbin—was a participant in a criminal gold ring. In the circumstances, Bigelow's readiest defense was a quick retreat to Highland Falls.

Beginning at an early date, one of Raymond's assistants, Augustus Maverick, set to work on a full-scale biography of the founder-editor. Maverick included in the biography an account of Raymond's death even briefer than those published in the *Times* and *Tribune*.

Returning to his residence in West Ninth Street at about twelve o'clock on the night of Friday, the 18th of June 1869, an attack of apoplexy prostrated him in a moment. Two hours later, his stertorous breathing attracted the attention of one of his children. The alarmed family, hastening to assist him, found him lying in the hallway, unconscious and apparently dying. He had locked the outside door and closed the inner one. The most eminent medical aid was summoned; but he remained unconscious, and died tranquilly about five o'clock in the morning.

Maverick's account—see *Henry J. Raymond and the New York Press for Thirty Years*, Hartford 1870, 205—partly followed the *Times* account of 1869 but included an error, a notable avoidance, and previously unpublished details. Maverick misdated Raymond's return to his house, moving it from Thursday night, June 17, to Friday night, June 18. He avoided saying that Raymond went out to attend a political consultation. He attached a new hour—about midnight—to Raymond's return; and he asserted that the editor's breathing was stertorous and attracted the notice of one of his children.

In view of the wrong date and the "stertorous," one may be sure that Maverick was permitted to read Bigelow's diary entry of 22 Jun 1869. Presumably Maverick misdated Raymond's death because disconcerted by the entry's contents. He doubtless avoided mentioning a political consultation because he *believed* Beecher's story that Raymond visited Rose Eytinge and because he learned that Jones's statement about a consultation was a lie invented as an attempted concealment.

One may assume that Maverick invented the false new hour—"about twelve o'clock"—for Raymond's return in order to lend the return an appearance of normalcy. He permitted no trace of the Rose Eytinge story to appear in the biography. He doubtless withheld the story partly out of consideration for Mrs. Raymond.

Bigelow in later life completed five volumes of *Retrospections*. He published Volumes I-III in 1909 and died in 1911. Volumes IV and V appeared posthumously in 1913.

Under the heading "FROM MY DIARY," Volume IV contained (289–90) a sensational page-and-a-half account of the death of Raymond. A hasty reader might think the account a faithful printing of what Bigelow had written in his diary on 22 Jun 1869, but a moment's study of the page-and-a-half would indicate that it was a blend of old material taken from his diary and new material drawn from memory. Unfortunately the account was so written that, at important points, a reader could not tell whether it was taken from the one source or the other.

Similarly, a hasty reader might not grasp what deceased Bigelow wished posterity to know. His published account included Beecher's tale of sin, told in fewer words. At first glance, the account could appear to do no more than disclose a scandalous but simple, coherent history: Raymond yielded to lust, became entangled with an actress, and died. But very differently, if read with care, the account would reveal itself to be complex and incoherent. As will be shown, it mixed two sets of signals. One set suggested that Raymond died because he sinned with an actress. A stronger set suggested that he was murdered.

The United States in 1913 and for decades thereafter was evidently inhabited by hasty readers. Bigelow's published account was read as simple, coherent, and more credible than those published by the *Times*, the *Tribune*, and Maverick in 1869–1870. On the basis of the combined accounts, Raymond's death was attributed to "an emotional crisis" that brought on a "cerebral hemorrhage." See the Raymond entry, *DAB*.

1951 was the centennial of the *New York Times*. An editor of the *Times*, Francis Brown, published a popular, undocumented biography, *Raymond of the Times*, NY 1951, in which he gave an account of Raymond's death (331–32) based principally on an uncritical reading of Bigelow's published account of 1913. Simultaneously, a *Times* reporter, Meyer Berger, published a popular, undocumented history, *The Story of the New York Times*, NY 1951. In his account of Raymond's death (30–32), Berger gave an appearance of quoting from Bigelow's original diary entry of 22 Jun 1869. Actually Berger adapted for his own use (and in places misquoted) Bigelow's published account of 1913.

Both Brown and Berger treated the mixed signals in Bigelow's 1913 account as if they were one signal: a pleasingly scandalous story of two celebrities, an editor and an actress.

Bigelow preserved his diary. It stayed in private hands till 1925. It then was given with other papers to the New York Public Library but could be consulted only with permission of the donor, Alice Bigelow. She died in 1932. The Library's processing of the Bigelow Collection was completed in 1963, whereupon the diary became available for unrestricted reading and use. (Data courtesy of manuscript staff, NYPL.)

Bigelow's diary entry for 22 June 1869 begins with the following words:

June 22. 1869. Tuesday.

Henry J. Raymond on his return Friday [actually Thursday]* night to his house from a visit to Rose Eytinge, fell dead† in the Hall of apoplexy. The servant who opened the door was in her night clothes & ran as soon as she had turned the key. What happened there after was not discovered till about 3 in the mg. when his sterturous breathing was overheard by his daughter Mary.

*The correction in brackets is mine.
†Bigelow's "fell dead" is an attempted overall summary.

The account Bigelow prepared for his *Retrospections*, Volume IV, is headed "FROM MY DIARY" and begins:

June 22, 1869. At a late hour last Friday night [June 19]* the body of Henry J. Raymond was brought home in a carriage and thrown on the hall floor of his residence by two men who immediately disappeared.† The servant who opened the door, being in her night clothes, escaped‡ as soon as she had turned the key of the door [to admit the party]§, so that¶ what happened thereafter was not discovered till early in the morning, when Raymond's stertorous breathing was overheard by his daughter Mary.

*The date in brackets is Bigelow's and compounds an error in his diary. Not only did Raymond go out on *Thursday* night; Friday was June *18*.
†Bigelow gives the reader no sign that the opening statement cannot be found in his diary, is new, *replaces* the opening statement in his diary, and in the process deletes the word "apoplexy."
‡Bigelow has changed his original word "ran" to "escaped." The change can be read to say that the servant unlocked the door, saw what the men were doing, and fled in fright, presumably to alert Mrs. Raymond, who—it would follow—came at once to the entrance hall.
§The phrase in brackets is Bigelow's. It can be read to say that the servant not only heard the doorbell but, before going to unlock the door, saw Raymond, his deliverers, and the carriage. (One may conjecture that the servant's room

was on the ground floor in front and that her window afforded a view of the street.)
¶Bigelow inserts two new words: "so that." Also he drops the capital letter in the following "What." By these means, he completes the manufacture of a summary opening passage that is burdened with two opposed meanings: a strong new one, that an atrocity was openly imposed on a household at an early morning hour; and an old one, that Raymond returned alone at an unknown hour, was at once stricken by illness when indoors, and later was discovered by Mary.

The new information Bigelow inserted was manifestly information he fully believed and wished to publish, yet also was afraid to publish. He accordingly arranged that it be published after his death.

Even on those terms, Bigelow remained so afraid that he wrote, not a wholly new account, but a split account that began with the new information, ended with assertions he had recorded in June 1869 after listening to Mrs. Raymond and Beecher, and gave a false appearance of coherence and consistency.

This is not to say that Bigelow ceased to believe that Raymond went to Rose Eytinge's apartment. Bigelow possibly assumed Raymond did. But when he prepared his published account, he used the Raymond-Eytinge story mostly to dilute, complicate, and somewhat gloss over an added, important, very gruesome story that he knew was true beyond a doubt.

The added story very possibly should be believed. It conforms to a classic pattern of terrorist acts: the hostile delivery of dead or wounded human bodies (or severed body parts). Also it does not have the appearance of being anything that Bigelow would invent.

Hoping to make sense of Bigelow's split published account, imaginative readers may wish to suppose that the men reported to have brought Raymond's body and thrown it into his hall were hired by Rose Eytinge for the purpose; that she arranged the delivery of her visitor to his house because she did not want a failing man in her apartment. (In effect, *Times* editor Brown and reporter Berger put this construction on Bigelow's 1913 account.) But the meaning of Bigelow's new opening passage is completed and underscored by two things he was quick to add.

Without concealment, Bigelow wrote the last paragraph of his published account solely on the basis of memory. It begins with a sentence that describes what happened to the *Times* on 17–18 Jun 1869 as a "beheading." The metaphor is very strong. It suggests that someone used an ax, or at least used a murderous weapon, say a club.

Moreover, Bigelow made his account of Raymond's death a mere part of a narrative. On a later page (316), he added the following:

> In consequence of my appointment as editor, one of the most experienced men on the *Times* [he presumably could name the man but does not do so], who was disappointed on not getting the place himself, disappeared, and whatever became of him has never transpired, as far as I know; but he was presumed to have killed himself or to have suffered death at the hands of others or by accident.

In view of the foregoing particulars, one may reach a conclusion. Bigelow learned that Raymond was *not* killed by apoplexy. He learned that his predecessor was dealt an injury to the head severe enough to be fatal;

moreover an injury that well-paid physicians, because requested, would not report to the police, the coroner, or the press.

Subordinate conclusions can also be reached. Bigelow *knew* he did not learn all that happened to Raymond while the editor was away from his house—somewhat as he *knew* he did not learn what happened to the much-experienced *Times* man who disappeared. Very probably, Bigelow did not begin to fear for his safety till after the much-experienced man was reported missing. Almost certainly, Bigelow was not told about the carriage, the two men, and the atrocious delivery till after he quit as editor and till after he assisted Maverick.

Necessarily Bigelow was told about the atrocity by Mrs. Raymond, Mary, or both. They had long known him as a rich gentleman and good friend. They presumably told him because they wanted to tell him and because they thought he could be trusted to keep a secret. While telling him about the arriving body, the servant's alarm, the men's departure, and their own rush in panic for doctors, they must also have told him that they lied in different ways to the *Times* and *Tribune* because terrified, suspicious of outsiders, and in haste about what to say.

Last, one must reach a conclusion about HA's knowledge of what happened to Raymond.

One item of evidence is silence. HA was at pains to avoid the subject. His one reference to it is a sentence in *The Education*. After saying that "Adams" in 1868 needed access "to a New York daily," the narrative continues by saying, "He lost his one chance by the death of Henry J. Raymond." See *EHA* (1907), 212; (LoA), 943.

A second item of evidence is HA's knowledge of a larger phenomenon, the gold panic of 1869, and especially his knowledge of its chronology. This chronology was so important to him that he both knew it and falsified it. (See note 61, below.) As part of the chronology, he knew that Raymond died at the precise moment when it was arranged that Jay Gould, because unable to control the U. S. government by persuasion, should instead control it by purchase. In other words, HA knew that Raymond's death coincided with the springing into action of the principal figure in the gold conspiracy, Abel Corbin.

A third item of evidence is one of HA's deliberate false datings. In his *Education*, as noted above, he treated the death of Raymond as if it stood in the way of "Adams" *in 1868* when he wished to gain access to a New York newspaper. But Raymond's death and the real Henry Adams's wish to get free use of a newspaper were matters belonging to *1869*. It goes without saying that the great event of U. S. history in 1869 was the gold panic. It follows that HA misdated Raymond's death in *The Education* as a means of very conspicuously pretending that the death was *not* linked to the gold panic.

Adams could be sure that this intricate stratagem would someday be noticed. He could be sure because *The Education* contains, not one, but two remarkable sentences involving Raymond. First to appear is the one in which HA both revealed his having been the London correspondent of the *Times* and concealed the importance of the correspondence and its relation to the *Trent* affair. (See Chap. 1, note 22, above.) Second to appear is the sentence in which HA very visibly dragged the editor's death away from its context—1869 and the gold panic. The sentences form a pair. They are matched in sweeping factual deficiency.

The three items of evidence suffice to warrant a conclusion. HA never said—not in anything *written*—that Raymond was murdered; but, beginning as early as the late summer of 1869, he acted as if he knew that Raymond was fatally injured and delivered to his house at the direction of Abel Corbin, the objects being to terrorize and incapacitate the *Times*, and later to make free use of it.

Actually two men's fates were at issue. Assuming he learned of the disappearance of the much-experienced man on the *Times* staff, HA can be assumed to have believed that again the author was Corbin.

It should be stressed, however, that HA could not have learned what he learned all at once. He can be believed to have thought Raymond murdered from the moment he saw the deficient accounts in the *Times* and *Tribune*. He formed his ideas about Corbin's agency only later and by increments, while investigating the gold panic.

11. Kirkland, *Charles Francis Adams, Jr.*, 41–42. Presumably HA, not Gurney, was the editor of CFA2's "A Chapter of Erie" and read and corrected the manuscript and proofs.

12. HA's concern about economic inequity is evident in many of his political writings in 1869–1870 but is expressed strongly and fully in "American Finance, 1865–1869," "The Legal-Tender Act," and "The New York Gold Conspiracy."

13. The last paragraph of "The Session [1869–1870]" can be read as a summary of HA's politics during the preceding twelve months. The summary involves a time-frame reaching forward several "generations."

14. The closing paragraphs of "The Legal-Tender Act" provided the texts of two resolutions for introduction in Congress. The resolutions illustrate HA's strong preference for the simplest possible measures.

15. HA merely says, ". . . I am reading Gibbon. . . ." See HA to CMG, 5 Oct 1869. Since he earlier had read Gibbon's *Memoirs*; since he later wrote as if conversant with the *Decline and Fall*; and since the *Decline and Fall* is a work that readers tend to read either complete or not at all, I have credited HA with reading all of Gibbon's long history.

16. No undetermined dates in HA's history are harder to fix than the date he fell in love with Clover Hooper and the date he started to correspond with her. They presumably did not meet in the summer of 1868. If they met in the summer of 1869, a presumable reason was that Gurney wanted to bring his editorial associate into friendly conjunction with his wife Ellen and her Hooper relations. If, conversely, they did not meet in the summer of 1869, a presumable reason was that Clover stayed continuously with her father in the area of Beverly Farms on the North Shore, while Henry, domiciled with his father at Quincy on the South Shore, never visited north of Boston.

17. Wells was still commissioner of the revenue. (Grant and Boutwell later permitted the office to lapse, effective 30 Jun 1870.) It seems possible that he already knew HA's answer to the question. If he did, his asking the question may have been a means of cryptically signaling to HA that Gould's manipulation of the gold market had resumed.

18. The phrase "phantom gold" is Fisk's. See *Gold Panic*, 181.

19. For Fisk, see *EHA* (1907), 235; (LoA), 967—". . . they paid their

respects in person to the famous Jim Fisk in his Opera House Palace. . . ."
For newspapers, see *EHA* (1907), 212; (LoA), 943. JQA2 gave HA a letter
of introduction to Marble of the *World*, dated 24 Oct 1869. Now in the
Marble Papers, LC, it is accompanied by HA's card, bearing his notation:
"Regrets to lose the opportunity of seeing Mr. Marble."

20. See note 10, above.

21. *Nation*, 21 Oct 1869, in "The Week."

22. CFA to HA, 5 Nov 1869.

23. Evarts to HA, 14 Jul 1869. Evarts had been executor of the estate
of Charles M. Leupp, an early partner of Gould's who committed suicide.
It thus seems possible that Evarts was one of HA's informants concerning
Gould's character and background.

24. Badeau evidently learned while in London that the place he really
wanted was consul-general. The incumbent was leaving office. On 21 Apr
1870, reporting his appointment to the post, the Washington *Star* said
Badeau was successor to "Freeman H. Morse of Maine, formerly a member
of Congress from that State, and a gentleman of much ability."

25. See especially CFA to HA, 19 Apr 1870—". . . I confess I am not
an optimist now. . . ."

26. HA believed that giving meals to officials was a "fair means" in
politics. See "The New York Gold Conspiracy," Lond ed., 422; NY ed.,
198—the sentence beginning, "If he were determined. . . ."

HA is known to have given dinner to Secretary of the Interior Cox.
See HA to CMG, 7 Dec 1869.

27. *EHA* (1907), 37, 91, 213; (LoA), 761, 817, 944–45. 28. Though
the suggestion was never acted upon, it was hardly a secret in Washington
that Mrs. Grant and her husband's associate, Gen. John A. Rawlins, wanted
Congress to give Grant a large annual income for life—also possibly a title,
as the British had done for Arthur Wellesley, the victor at Waterloo.
Wellesley, as everyone knew, was made First Duke of Wellington. See
McFeely, *Grant*, 264–65, 455–hereafter cited as *Grant*.

29. In "The Session [1869–1870]," HA used the simile of a derelict
sea captain, saying (34): "The President may indeed in one respect resem-
ble the commander of an army in peace; but in another and more essential
sense he resembles the commander of a ship at sea. He must have a helm
to grasp, a course to steer, a port to seek; he must sooner or later be
convinced that a perpetual calm is as little to his purpose as a perpetual
hurricane, and that without headway the ship can arrive nowhere. The
President, however, assumed at the outset that it was not his duty to
steer. . . ."

30. *Gold Panic*, 1.

31. Ibid., 20.

32. The young woman can perhaps be identified. HA was a grooms-
man at the wedding of Moorfield Storey and Gertrude Cutt in Washington
on 6 Jan 1870. The *National Republican* reported (same date): "The
bridesmaids were Miss Cutts, sister of the bride; Miss Freeman, daughter
of the late Colonel Freeman; Miss Alden, daughter of Capt. Alden, U.S.N.;
Miss Campbell, Miss Stoughton, Miss McCorkle, Miss Harris, and Miss
Clymer, daughter of Dr. Clymer, of the United States navy."

HA also was an usher at the wedding of Henry Metcalfe and Hattie P.
Nicholl in Washington on 21 Apr 1870. The *Evening Star* of that date

reported that Misses Harris and Clymer were among the bridesmaids. It thus appears that inquiry might best begin with regard to Miss Clymer and Miss Harris and their dates of death.

With regard to a young woman in *Democracy*, see note 46.

33. HA's saying his novel would appear in 1880 was of course a joke. It was also an admission of planning, including *political* planning. He expected the novel to have political uses, and 1880 would be an election year.

It might seem improbable that HA would plan ten years in advance to put a novel to political use. It instead was typical. For his use of the novel in the election of 1880, see Chaps. 14–15.

34. *Gold Panic*, 23ff. Hodgskin's testimony can be viewed as a repetition before the whole committee of a "preliminary text-book" he privately furnished Garfield when the chairman saw him in New York. Hodgskin later summarized his conclusions in an unsigned article. He said the conspiracy was the work of Gould, whom he described as "no vulgar knave, but an adventurer possessing rare faculties for combination." He excused Gen. Butterfield, Corbin, and others as victims of Gould's genius. "The net was cunningly flung out; the Assistant Treasurer of the United States in New York, and a brother-in-law of the President, were securely entangled in it, and even the President himself, though untouched in his integrity, was deluded by cunning sophistry, while open bribes were tendered to confidential officers of his staff and to the members of his family." See "The Erie Ring and American Credit," *Nation*, 5 May 1870. The article is attributed to Hodgskin in Haskell's *Indexes*.

35. Gould testified in the morning, Fisk in the afternoon. They did not bother to coordinate their stories. See *Gold Panic*, 131–83.

Gould proved a dangerous witness. He volunteered information so shocking that the committee was dissuaded from asking him pointed questions. The situation was clear and ironic. Were pointed questions asked, the witness could not be trusted to lie.

As far as it went, Gould's testimony rang true. Perhaps his most notable statement was a passing remark (141): "There are other ways of having things done."

Fisk's testimony was entertaining and in style perfectly candid; but many of the important things he said were at best repetitions of things he had heard said—or liked to believe he heard said—or felt should have been said—by Corbin, Jennie Corbin, or Gould.

The popular estimate of Gould and Fisk was that both were honestly corrupt. See *Gold Ring*, 269—". . . what most people admired about them was their honesty. Fisk and Gould made no bones about their greed and corruption; they paraded it."

36. Corbin was the witness who testified in detail and manifestly lied—for the most part with success. Longer than Gould or Fisk's, his testimony contained inconsistencies and towards the end included an outbreak of defiance. An accomplished actor and talker, he affected the roles of good husband and unhappy old man. See *Gold Panic*, 242–75.

37. Such questions abounded. Gould testified (*Gold Panic*, 157) that William O. Chapin, the Erie company employee who was sent as a messenger to rural Washington, Pennsylvania, carried not only a short letter from Corbin to Grant's secretary, Gen. Porter, and a long letter

from Corbin to Grant, but also a letter from Jennie Corbin to Julia Grant. (If ever written, the third letter could have been sent in the same envelope as the long letter from Corbin to Grant.)

Fisk testified (173–76, 182–83) that he had assurances from Gould, Corbin, and Jennie Corbin that the Grants owned gold on margin, bought for them by Gould. He also testified that Mrs. Grant had been paid $25,000 by check on the basis of that alleged ownership. He said he had learned on 23 Sep 1869 from Gould that Corbin wanted a check for $100,000 and had supposed at the time (175) that Corbin meant to "feed out" added money to "parties in interest"—a phrase which could seem to include the Grants.

Corbin testified (253–55, 271–73) that he consented to Gould's buying $1,500,000 in gold contracts for *Mrs. Corbin* and on the basis of that arrangement obtained $25,000 by check from Gould after the gold price had risen; further, that he then kept the $25,000 in his own account. Also Corbin testified that he bought $250,000 in U. S. bonds for Mrs. Corbin and then offered Mrs. Grant the profit on half the bonds, if a profit was realized, because she was, in a manner of speaking, his sister-in-law. He added that Mrs. Grant refused the offer.

38. Allan Peskin, *Garfield*, Kent OH 1978, 311, 652n12. Because HA—in his own words—was "pulling wires behind the Congressional Committee," it can be assumed that he was told very soon about the accommodation Grant requested via Cox and was very soon told as well about Garfield's willing compliance.

39. "Views of the Minority," *Gold Panic*, 471–72.

40. On February 5, after it was decided that Mrs. Grant and Mrs. Corbin were not to testify, the committee heard a reporter for the *New York Sun*, Ford C. Barksdale, repeat details he had gathered about the conspiracy. Barksdale said he was told that $60,000 worth of paintings and statuary had been sent by the gold ring in New York to the White House in care of Gen. Fred Dent, the brother of Mrs. Grant, who after the inauguration moved into the White House and superintended renovations ordered by Mrs. Grant. Barksdale also said he was told that the "adornments" were put in suitable places in the White House; further, that the president, back from his summer travels, learned the source of the adornments and ordered that they be repacked "in the night" and returned to New York. (The date of the repacking evidently was 23 Sep 1869, the eve of Black Friday.) In addition, Barksdale said he had learned that Fred Dent was a pupil of Corbin's in St. Louis in 1835, when Corbin was a teacher. See *Gold Panic*, 418, 425–27.

The committee ended its work by attempting to learn from various witnesses whether money had been sent from New York to Mrs. Grant in a package. (No package was traced that surely contained a large sum.) This effort by the committee showed diligence and perhaps active suspicion, but suspicion had been warranted from the beginning.

It was common knowledge in the U. S. that the Grants, prior to the general's becoming president, accepted substantial gifts from subscribers. Bostonians gave them a $75,000 library; Philadelphians gave them a furnished house; former neighbors in Galena, Illinois, gave them a house; and New Yorkers more than assisted their purchase of a house in Washington on I Street. The New Yorkers' gift totaled $104,000. ". . . Daniel

Butterfield, Alexander T. Stewart, and their fellow subscribers . . . provided $30,000 for the mortgage. . . . Even more comfortingly, they . . . supplied $54,000 in government bonds and $20,000 in cash." See *Gold Ring*, 56, 67, 76; *Grant*, 232, 236, 245, 253.

The difference between the gifts in earlier years and the alleged $60,000 shipment of adornments in 1869 was that the gifts were publicized and the source of the alleged adornments was secret.

41. Release from teaching was arranged for Gurney but was officially temporary. See *Letters of John Fiske*, op. cit., 194–95.

42. Other than the editorials themselves, the principal evidences that HA wrote editorials for the *Nation* at two-week intervals are letters by HA and Godkin.

HA wrote to CMG, 7 Mar 1870, ". . . I write about two articles a month in the Nation. . . ."

Godkin wrote to Garfield, 11 Jan 1871: "Could you be persuaded to furnish us a Washington letter once a fortnight or thereabouts? We should be glad to pay you well for it, and if you chose to be anonymous to keep your secret carefully. We want something better than can be got from the ordinary newpaper man and since Henry Adams left Washington [we] are at sea." See William M. Armstrong, ed., *The Gilded Age Letters of E. L. Godkin*, Albany 1974, 168.

The editorials here attributed to HA were published fortnightly until his departure for Europe.

The first two editorials—"A Political Nuisance" (27 Jan 1870) and "Mr. Dawes—President Grant—General Butler" (10 Feb 1870)—were attributed to HA by Ernest Samuels in *The Young Henry Adams*, 318. CFA refers to the first editorial in his letter to HA, 2 Feb 1870.

The third editorial—"The Census Imbroglio" (24 Feb 1870)—is attributed to HA in Haskell's Indexes to the *Nation*.

The fourth editorial—"The New Party" (10 Mar 1870)—is echoed by HA in a contemporary letter. See HA to CMG, 28 Mar & 3 Apr 1870—"I have wasted the winter writing for newspapers. . . ." "We are now in the middle of a battle . . . and I . . . have been helping to organize . . . *a new party* [italics added]. . . ." CFA responds to the content of this editorial in his letter to HA, 16 Mar 1870, and again in his letter to HA, 6 Apr 1870.

The fifth editorial—"The Senate and the Chief Justice" (24 Mar 1870)—clearly was written from Washington. It carries forward arguments and themes found in HA's previous contributions to the *Nation*. CFA responds to the content of this editorial in his letter to HA, 6 Apr 1870, and says unencouragingly, "Writing leaders for newspapers is a business scarcely worth pursuing."

The sixth editorial—"The Reopening of the Legal Tender Case" (7 Apr 1870)—explicitly continues the argument HA had made "when treating this same subject two years ago," meaning in his article, "The Argument in the Legal Tender Cases." See *Nation*, 17 Dec 1868.

The seventh editorial—"A Debate on the Tariff" (21 Apr 1870)—is a Swiftian lampoon of a sort HA had the ability to write. It carries forward his arguments in relation to revenue reform.

The eighth editorial—"The Revenue Reformers and the Republican Party" (5 May 1870)—links in content with the fourth and seventh. It is the authoritative paper reflecting the proceedings of the revenue reformers who met in HA's rooms on 20 Apr 1870. Wells apparently presided, as nominal head of the movement. That HA was the actual director could not have been wholly lost on the persons who attended.

43. One editorial contributed by HA to the *Post* was traced and reprinted by the pioneer Henry Adams researcher Charles I. Glicksberg. See "Henry Adams the Journalist," *NEQ*, 21 (Jun 1948), 232–36. Other *Post* editorials presumably can be identified as HA's, but to date no added identifications have been achieved.

44. The assertion is new. I have presented supporting evidence and arguments partly in the text of this chapter, partly in the notes.

The inquiry that resulted in the assertion was sparked by my noticing two conjunctions of interest: HA and Julia Grant were both interested in a sum: $100,000; HA and Julia Grant were both interested in what she called "that dreadful Black Friday." See John Y. Simon, ed., *The Personal Memoirs of Julia Dent Grant*, NY 1975, 182.

That HA had a burning interest in an occurrence involving $100,000 in U. S. bonds cannot be doubted. An occurrence involving $100,000 "in United States Coupon Bonds" is the central occurrence around which the action of his *Democracy* came to turn. The occurrence is recounted in the novel in three versions which so contradict each other that no two can be true. Yet the amount—$100,000—and the form—U. S. bonds—remain constant in the versions. See *Democracy*, Chaps. XII-XIII. (In early editions, the chapters are misnumbered XIII-XIV.)

In 1894, long after Black Friday, but when her memory of that day was still strong, Julia Dent Grant negotiated to sell her autobiography. A publisher offered $25,000. She demanded $100,000—which the publisher declined to give. See *Personal Memoirs*, 23.

Obviously the repeated figure, $100,000, might be coincidental and meaningless. It ceases to be meaningless when the principal sources relating to the gold panic are read with that sum continuously in mind.

For HA's invention of the name "Julia Schneidekoupon," see note 75.

45. The significant figure, $100,000, reappears in an article: Adam Badeau, "The Mystery of Grant," *Cosmopolitan*, Feb 1896, 190.

McFeely says Badeau "was on Grant's army staff in 1869 and after the inaugural moved into the White House, living there until he won a consulship." See *Grant*, 498. Although mistaken with respect to two of Badeau's places of residence before becoming consul-general in England, McFeely's statement can be assumed to be right in suggesting that, on returning to Washington from service as assistant secretary in London, Badeau resumed living in the White House for a few days—prior to renting rooms below HA's on G Street.

46. The items in HA's experience in January-February 1870 which became materials for *Democracy* are many. One example is the visit of England's Prince Arthur to Washington. See HA to CMG, 20 Jan 1870. The corresponding portion of the novel is a visit to Washington by a European princess. See *Democracy*, Chap. XI.

A more instructive example is the rich bridesmaid HA said he was attentive to in Washington, knowing she was fatally ill. *Democracy* contains a Washington girl, Victoria Dare, who is not rich and not ill. Especially see Chap. VI. The wide differences between Victoria Dare and the dying bridesmaid helps to illustrate HA's determination to make *Democracy* an actual novel—and not a *roman à clef*.

47. HA later attributed the article to "Francis A. Walker and Henry Adams." See *Chapters of Erie*, table of contents; and *Historical Essays*, 279n— also *EHA* (1907) 241–42, (LoA), 973–74. The attribution should be set aside as a fiction needlessly generous to Walker. There is nothing in the article that does not fit perfectly in the ordered sequence of HA's writings in the winter of 1869–1870. And HA alone was capable of the article's savage use of heavy rhetorical weapons.

48. *Gold Panic*, 475. Cox and Jones's claim to "reticence" was partly a cover. They *had* an opinion. Their minority report (461ff) supports a specific serious accusation (468): "Unconsciously, or consciously, the President in his letters to Mr. Boutwell worked in unison with the conspirators."

49. The *Nation* also said, 3 Mar 1870, ". . . Mrs. Grant declined to have gold bought for her. . . ." The statement reflected belief in the testimony of Grant's secretary, Gen. Porter. See note 67.

50. In saying his language would be "libelous," HA did not mean it would be false. He meant it could be used by Erie lawyers as a pretext for an unfounded legal attack under British law. He was right to anticipate legal attack. See *Chapters of Erie*, 132–33n.

51. The passage stands in contrast with a passage in *The Education* saying that "he"—the protagonist—knew only what the committee printed, which was "all that was to be known." See *EHA* (1907), 235; (LoA), 967— "At first he feared that Congress would suppress the scandal, but the Congressional Investigation was ordered, and took place. He soon knew *all that was to be known*; the material for his essay was furnished by the government [italics added]."

Differently, the passage written in 1870 can suggest that HA knew *more* than the committee—even much more. Judging from available evidence, the statement written in 1870 is reliable, and the statement in *The Education* is false and misleading. The difference between the statements illustrates the mostly fictional character of HA's best and most famous book.

52. CFA to HA, 23 Feb, 9 Mar 1870.

53. *Nation*, 7 Apr 1870, 218.

54. That HA knew the article was exceedingly dangerous is shown by his writing an added, different account of the panic, to be published, signed, in the July 1870 *North American*. The added account would serve as cover while the authorship of the main account remained unknown. He said in the added account: ". . . one may sometimes almost seem to see the mechanical process by which a new idea eats its way into Grant's unconscious mind. . . . This faculty for assimilation of ideas . . . under ordinary circumstances . . . gives elasticity, freedom from inveterate prejudices, and capacity for progress. . . . But when used by Jay Gould and Abel Rathbone Corbin with the skill of New York stockbrokers for illegitimate objects, the result is the more disastrous is proportion to the energy of execution for which the President is remarkable." See "The Session [1869–1870]," 32–33. Reduced to its essentials, the passage says that Gould and Corbin *persuaded* Grant and he gave an energetic order. This was a grave charge— but conveniently *not* true.

HA's main account, written for publication in England, unsigned, said that Grant *could not be persuaded; therefore persuasion had to be purchased, and shortly was.* This charge was more than grave. Once understood, it would be devastating. And HA fully believed it true.

55. HA's acquaintance with the details of the gold conspiracy was wide and deep and was based not only on printed materials but also on private testimony, beginning with what he could learn from Badeau, Mrs. John, Evarts, Sumner, Hodgskin, and many others. When writing "The New York Gold Conspiracy," he deliberately *omitted* very important details. Most important were details relating to Abel Corbin, Jennie Grant Corbin, Julia Dent Grant, and Fred Dent. He avoided mentioning that both Julia and Fred Dent were pupils of Corbin's when in high school in St. Louis; that Corbin made a fortune in Washington by working doubly as a clerk of the House of Representatives and a broker in bribes; that his hallmark as a bribe-broker was audacity so headlong that he was exposed and had to retire; that his profits permitted him to buy a fine house on I Street; that in 1866 he sold the house to General Grant and became a private investor in New York; that on 4 Mar 1869 he attended President Grant's inaugural festivities in the Treasury building (supervised by Fred Dent); that Corbin's wife Elizabeth died the following month; that he instantly courted and married Grant's sister Jennie; that Grant meanwhile sold the I Street house to the mayor of Washington; that Mrs. Grant abrogated the contract as not providing a sufficient return; and that A. T. Stewart and other subscribers purchased the house from the president at a price more to her liking. See *Gold Ring*, 50, 53–58; *Grant*, 289, 303.

If included by HA in his article, certain parts of the above data could easily have led the Grants to believe themselves betrayed to the writer by Badeau. As things developed, Badeau remained on good enough terms with the Grants to complete his *Military History of Ulysses S. Grant* (the second and third volumes were published in 1881) and assist Grant in relation to the writing of his *Personal Memoirs* (published in two volumes in 1885–1886). See *Grant*, 497–99.

56. The charge that Gould, when unable to persuade Grant, *purchased* the persuasion of Grant, is HA's. Broadly stated, it appears in "The New York Gold Conspiracy." See Lond ed., 421; NY ed., 197, paragraphs beginning "In the operation of. . . . "

The broad charge is one thing; the details are another. The argument that HA knew the price of purchase to be $100,000 in U. S. bonds and knew the purchased persuader to be Mrs. Grant originates in study of *Democracy.* Just as an inquirer can see HA transfer items from his experience in Washington in January-February 1870 to his novel, so too an inquirer can look at the central occurrence in *Democracy*, a transfer of $100,000 in U. S. bonds, and infer that learning of such a transfer of bonds was part of HA's experience early in 1870.

More narrowly, one may infer that HA early in 1870 learned there had been such a transfer from Gould to Mrs. Grant in June 1869.

Such an inference at the outset is necessarily wholly tentative. Whether it deserves credence depends on study of evidence. Minimally it depends on study of all this chapter's "principal sources," plus *Democracy*, plus the House committee's report, plus related monographs and biographies, as a test of two propositions: (a) that a transfer of $100,000 in U. S. bonds from Gould to Mrs. Grant occurred very soon after 15 Jun 1869, either at one remove through Corbin, or at two removes from Corbin to Jennie

Corbin and from her to Julia Grant; (b) that, roughly on 1 Feb 1870, HA learned convincingly about the transfer, either in outline or in fairly complete detail.

I have found both propositions to be everywhere supported and nowhere undermined by the above-listed evidence, which, though compendious and complicated, is startlingly meaningful and sharply clear.

The most pointed item of evidence is HA's inventing a name, "Julia Schneidekoupon." See note 75.

57. The quotation follows the original text. See Lond ed. 422; NY ed., 198. As revised by HA for his *Historical Essays*, NY 1891, the passage is simplified and reads (337): ". . . Gould must control the government, whether by fair means or foul, by persuasion or by purchase."

58. Demonstrably, HA concluded that the master spirit of the gold conspiracy, so far as it had one, was Abel Corbin; that the main ring was Corbin's; and that its members came to include Corbin, Julia Grant, Jennie Corbin, and up to a certain hour Grant himself—but only as an uncomprehending and instructed complier.

HA's strategy in "The New York Gold Conspiracy" was to start and end the narrative *as if* the main ring were Gould's and only allow his true opinion to become explicit in the narrative's middle pages.

The great difference between "The New York Conspiracy" as published in the *Westminster Review* in October 1870 and as reprinted in *Chapters of Erie* in 1871 is that the original printing does not contain, and the revised printing does contain, a one-sentence paragraph about Corbin, saying: "Mr. Corbin was right; throughout all these transactions his insight into Mr. Gould's character was marvellous." See *Chapters of Erie*, 125. It is conceivable that the paragraph was part of HA's manuscript but was deleted by the British editor in 1870 and restored by HA in 1871. Equally it is conceivable that HA thought he could not safely include the paragraph till he had tested the waters—till the article had been published once and elicited responses.

When published *without* the paragraph, the article said the conspiracy was a New York affair, yet hinted that perhaps it was not—hinted that there were three separate main actors, Gould, Corbin, and Fisk—and hinted that Corbin required the closest attention. When re-issued *with* the paragraph, the article said there were swindlers in New York beyond a doubt; yet in addition it emphasized that the one marvel to be found in the conspiracy was the perspicacity of mysterious Corbin.

The article in its later form, *with* the paragraph, if taken seriously by students of American history, would increase awareness that the great American artists in corruption were not New Yorkers—not in HA's opinion. They instead were persons like Corbin, schooled in their art in Washington, under the shadow of the Capitol.

59. HA understood Fisk to be very important in the conspiracy only later, and then mainly because Chapin, the messenger who carried letters to Washington, Pennsylvania, was chosen by Fisk, knew Fisk, acted under Fisk's orders, and telegraphed to Fisk after delivering the letters and eliciting a response from Grant. See note 64.

60. Fisk testified that, on 16 June 1869, Gould traveled with him and Grant by rail from Fall River to Boston. See *Gold Panic*, 172. In fact, Gould left the boat at Fall River early on the 16th, telegraphed to his brokers in New York, and at once returned by train to New York. See *Gold Ring*, 72.

61. Gould told the House committee that his purchases for Corbin included both gold contracts and "governments," meaning U. S. bonds. This moment in the testimony was critical. *Gould offered the committee a chance to ask him whether he ever gave U. S. bonds to Corbin to be given by him to Mrs. Grant, either directly or through Mrs. Corbin, the president's sister.* The committee did not take the chance. See *Gold Panic*, 157, 159.

There is a comparably critical turn in "The New York Gold Conspiracy." HA says that Grant in June 1869 "accepted an invitation to Mr. Fisk's theatre" and "sat in Mr. Fisk's private box." Also HA sets forth a chronology, stating that Grant went to New York "on 15th of June 1869," sat in Fisk's box that evening, and dined next evening on Fisk's steamboat with Fisk, Gould, Cyrus Field, and others. See Lond ed., 423–24; NY ed., 198, paragraph starting "The first requisite . . . ." But HA's chronology is untrue.

The evidence is clear that the Grants went to New York on the 13th; Grant dined on the steamboat *Providence* on the 16th; he started his return from Boston on the 17th; and, on the 18th, "The President and family accompanied his brother in law and wife to the Fifth avenue Theatre. . . ." See *Gold Ring*, 73–74 & 299; "President Grant's Visit to the City," NY Times, 19 Jun 1869, 8.

To explain the mistaken dates in HA's account, it might be imagined that he bungled while reconstructing the chronology of the panic. He, however, was good at dates. A far more credible explanation is that *he knew the date of the theatre episode but falsified it, lest the meaning of the episode be too evident.* That the Grants appeared in Fisk's box on 18 Jun 1869 with the Corbins was consistent with Mrs. Grant's being the persuader Gould had to purchase; consistent with her having been purchased within the past two days; and consistent with her having become a willing, active, effective member of *Corbin's* ring.

One must remember, too, that 17 & 18 Jun 1869 were important days in HA's personal history. They included the night and morning when Henry J. Raymond was disabled, became unconscious, and died. One can assume that HA saw and did not forget the issue of the *New York Times* for 19 Jun 1869. The issue was printed with black borders. On its editorial page, it announced the death of the newspaper's owner-editor and principal founder.

If HA consulted a Washington file of the *Times* while writing the "New York Gold Conspiracy," and if he paid special heed to the issues just before, during, and after Gould's unsuccessful effort to *persuade* the President, he necessarily consulted the black-bordered issue of June 19. On its last page, the issue reported the attendance of the Grants and Corbins at the Fifth Avenue Theatre.

62. McFeely describes the summer wanderings of the Grants away from the White House to Long Branch, New Jersey, and thence on visits and travels continuing till they arrived at Mrs. Grant's cousin's house in Washington, Pennsylvania. He calls them mostly results of "Julia's plans." See *Grant*, 303–04, 325, 330.

63. The phrase "unsuspicious President" is HA's. See Lond. ed, 424; NY ed., 199. HA applies the phrase to Grant as he was on the day, 2 Sep 1869, when he sent his order to Boutwell not to sell gold in excess of uniform monthly amounts. HA then extends its application past the

moment on 19 Sep 1869 when Chapin obtained a reply from Grant and departed. HA's wording thus makes Grant—till the still later moment on September 19 when he at last grew suspicious—an assistant in the conspiracy, a helper who was told what to do and was doing it. Also HA's wording indicates that Grant was in a conspiracy but did not know it. See note 66.

64. Messenger Chapin arrived at Washington, Pennsylvania, in the morning on 19 Sep 1869. His employer, Fisk, testified before the House committee on 22 Jan 1870. Chapin testified five days later (by which time he possibly had been coached). See *Gold Panic*, 168–83, 231–33.

Fisk testified that Chapin was admitted to a room in Mrs. Grant's cousin's house; Grant was outside the house but came in; and Chapin gave him a sealed letter. Fisk continued (174): ". . . [the president] read it, and said . . . , 'You wait a few minutes.' General Grant went out, and in a few minutes returned and said, 'All right.' Chapin drove to the nearest telegraph office, according to instructions, and we got a telegram about 1 o'clock [P.M.], 'Delivered. All right.' "

Chapin testified that he carried two sealed letters, one from Corbin to Grant's secretary, Porter, the other from Corbin to Grant. He said he handed Porter his letter and handed the president his when he came in. Chapin would *not* testify that Grant said "All right." He said he could not remember the *words* of his telegram, only its substance, which was that "the letter or letters were delivered all right." He continued, "It was in one sentence. . . ." Under questioning, he clung to his story. "I meant to say that he had received the letters [*sic*] and read them all right."

HA had to educe a meaning from Fisk and Chapin's conflicting testimonies. He wrote in his article (Lond ed., 428; NY ed., 201):

> . . . the President . . . entered the room and took his brother-in-law's despatch. He then left the room, and after some ten or fifteen minutes' absence returned. The messenger, tired of waiting, then asked, 'Is it all right?' 'All right," replied the President; and the messenger hastened to the nearest telegraph station, and sent word to Fisk, 'Delivered; all right.' "

One might assume that HA accepted Fisk's account and rejected Chapin's. The case, however, was not simple.

HA was accustomed to the use of ciphers. Gould had earlier testified (167) that government telegrams relating to gold sales were "sent in cipher." In later testimony, Gould's broker, Henry N. Smith, said (439) he received a message from Corbin saying "Will see Mr. Gould about Jersey City railroad" in which " 'Jersey City railroad' " was "a cipher." "It means the sub-treasury."

Fisk's testimony ran to fifteen and a half printed pages. He used the expression "all right" eleven times, the word "all" an additional thirty-two times, the word "right" an additional seventeen times, and the expression "all-important" once.

As well as anyone, HA could see that Fisk's testimony was evidence that "all right" was code. He could see, too, that Fisk's testimony explained what "all right" was code for. Chairman Garfield asked Fisk whether he had received any messages from Assistant Treasurer Butterfield at the Sub-Treasury during Black Friday. Fisk answered (181): ". . . only what was brought by my man, who kept going backward and forward. . . . Butterfield would send back word, everything is all right; no news from Washington. . . ."

It can be concluded that HA understood that "all right" was a Fisk code for "no news from Washington." Moreover, HA understood that Grant was provided the code by one of the letters carried by Chapin. Further, HA understood that Chapin was instructed by Fisk to ask Grant "Is it all right?" Finally, HA understood that Chapin was instructed to wait as long as necessary for the answer and to telegraph the answer to Fisk as soon as possible.

HA accordingly can be said to have believed that Chapin gave Grant a sealed envelope; Grant left the room for as many as fifteen minutes and returned; Chapin felt the wait had been long; he asked Grant the required question and the president said "all right" in reply; Chapin's telegram to Fisk consisted of the words "delivered" and "all right"— the punctuation did not matter; the telegram was clear to Fisk, Gould, and Corbin; and it meant there would be no news from Washington—that Grant was not changing the order to Boutwell, and the Treasury would not sell gold.

Gen. Porter also gave an account of what happened between Chapin and Grant. See *Gold Panic*, 444–49. HA accepted one detail in Porter's account: Grant assumed that Chapin was a local U. S. postman.

The result was a paragraph in "The New York Gold Conspiracy." It says that Grant learned from Porter after Chapin left that Chapin was a special messenger from New York and the letters he brought were urgent, *whereupon Grant spoke with his wife*. "The President's suspicions were at once excited; and the same evening, at his request, Mrs. Grant wrote a hurried note to Mrs. Corbin, telling her how greatly the president was distressed at the rumor that Mr. Corbin was speculating in Wall Street, and how much he hoped that Mr. Corbin would 'instantly disconnect himself with anything of that sort.' " See Lond. ed., 429; NY ed., 201, paragraph beginning "The messenger . . . ."

65. Kimber disappeared. He was one of several potentially important witnesses who for one reason or another did not testify before the House committee. See *Gold Ring*, 272–73.

66. See note 64, above.

67. The testimony which most permitted Americans to say that the president and his wife were blameless and had no part in the conspiracy was that of Grant's secretary, Horace Porter, given near the end of the hearings, on 10 Feb 1870. Gen. Porter was under strong pressures to clear the Grants. He gave an account of the exchange between Chapin and Grant which banished the expression "all right." Two sentences mattered most. ". . . the President returned [to the room], and this gentleman [Chapin] arose, hesitated a moment, and said, 'Any reply?' or 'Anything further?' The President said, 'No answer,' and the messenger started off, got into a buggy, and drove away." Porter also testified that he "frequently" heard Mrs. Grant state that no gold was bought for her. Porter in no way alluded to U. S. bonds. See *Gold Panic*, 444–49.

68. HA said about Corbin's asking Gould for a check for $100,000, "A proposition more impudent than this could scarcely be imagined." See Lond ed., 429; NY ed., 201, paragraph starting "Mr. Corbin proposed. . . ." The paragraph continues in a manner not easy to follow. It appears to say that Corbin, making the demand, was trying to *blackmail*

Gould. It thus also suggests that Gould had done something Corbin knew about that was very wrong—something that could suggest a particular amount to be extorted. The amount that Corbin thought suitable in the circumstances was $100,000.

69. *EHA* (1907), 269; (LoA), 1002.

70. *Nation*, "The Week," 28 Apr 1870. For the place of the meeting, see Wells to HA, 14 Apr 1870—"I have notified our friends that we will have our first meeting at your rooms on Tuesday eve. Please pass the word. . . . I think we shall have a good crowd, though Atkinson will disappoint us."

71. *Nation*, 24 Feb 1870, 116.

72. HA's savage article, "The Legal-Tender Act," drew a published reply from its chief victim, Congressman Spaulding of New York.

HA furnished the *Nation* a counter-reply, still more savage, signed "H. B. A." Godkin published this polemic on 12 May 1870 under the title "The North American Review and the Hon. Elbridge G. Spaulding."

HA's new attack on Spaulding was read in Boston by Gamaliel Bradford, one of the contributors to the January 1870 *North American*. Bradford felt so sorry for Spaulding and so disagreed with HA that he wrote a letter to the editor of the *Nation*, signed "G. B.," taking issue with HA about the merits of the Legal-Tender Act.

This new dispute was not between Bradford and Godkin. It was between Bradford and HA. Godkin accordingly sent Bradford's letter to HA in Washington. On May 17 or 18, just before he sailed for Europe, HA wrote a paragraph replying to Bradford and sent both Bradford's letter and the paragraph to Godkin.

Godkin published the letter and the paragraph under the heading "The Murderous Assault on Mr. Spaulding." In the process, he signed HA's paragraph "Ed. Nation," as if he, Godkin, had written it. This was a standard procedure for editors. When an editor or contributor wanted readers not to know who wrote a particular contribution, the editor would claim the authorship.

Bradford understood that his answerer was Adams, not Godkin, and he had more things he wished to say about legal tender. So he wrote a second letter to the editor of the *Nation*, signed "G. B." Godkin sped the second letter to HA in London. HA received it, wrote another paragraph replying to Bradford, and sent the papers to Godkin.

Godkin published the new communications on 30 Jun 1870 under the heading "The Necessity of Legal Tender." He signed HA's paragraph "Ed. Nation." and inserted a sentence: "The publication of 'G. B.'s' letter has, we are sorry to say, been delayed."

The importance of the rejoinders by HA is that they permit readers to hear him debate with a friendly colleague, Bradford, about difficult points of economics.

Also the rejoinders complete a published but never assembled book by HA on public finance, the first chapter of which is "British Finance in 1816." The book is not a small one. It remains pertinent to the financial perils of the United States.

73. The ally HA thought the most capable by far was McCulloch, but the ex-secretary did not have a political following and could not become a national leader. See *EHA* (1907), 215–16; (LoA), 946–47.

74. HA's account in *The Education* of Badeau's acquisition of a consul-generalship involves a statement which may seem to be an explicit denial of something said in this chapter: that one of HA's presumable informants concerning a transfer of bonds was Badeau. The statement says: "Loyal to Grant, and still more to Mrs. Grant, who acted as his patroness, he [Badeau] said nothing, even when far gone, that was offensive about either. . . ." See *EHA* (1907), 229; (LoA), 961. (The expression "far gone" may indicate extreme indulgence in drink.) But, if carefully reconsidered, the statement may *affirm* HA's having learned from loyal Badeau precisely the things Badeau was most *not* to say.

75. HA received the news of Hartman Kuhn's death in January 1870. He subsequently learned from CFA that the details of Kuhn's death—reported to CFA in a letter from LAK—had been "fearful." See HA to CMG, 30 Jan 1870; CFA to HA, 26 Jan, 1 Mar 1870.

The death of Hartman Kuhn was later reflected in *Democracy*, as part of the shifting of material from life to fiction. Also HA's relations with Kuhn bear on the question of HA's interest in particular persons of Jewish descent. This interest is apparent both in *Democracy* and "The New York Gold Conspiracy." The persons involved were Palgrave, Charles and Hartman Kuhn, August Belmont, and Gould. Since HA usually was as serious about genealogy as he was about history, one may suppose he believed he had good information about the genealogies of the Palgraves, Kuhns, Belmonts, and Goulds.

HA's best friend in 1870 was Gaskell. Gaskell's brother-in-law, Francis Turner Palgrave, was a son of Sir Francis Palgrave, who was born a Jew and whose name was originally Cohen. See *EHA* (1907), 185; (LoA), 916.

In 1870, HA had *one* brother-in-law, Charles Kuhn. HA later wrote to Gaskell: "It is rather curious that you and I should each have a brother-in-law evidently of the same lineage and name (Cohen = Kuhn)." See HA to CMG, 9 Sep 1883, HA-micro 5; L, II, 511.

HA's brother JQA2 had highly important political dealings with August Belmont, who was reportedly Jewish by ancestry.

In "The New York Gold Conspiracy," HA said that Gould was "small and slight in person, dark, sallow, reticent, and stealthy, with a trace of Jewish origin." See Lond ed., 414; NY ed., 194, paragraph beginning "Personally Mr. Fisk. . . ."

Two characters in *Democracy* are a brother and sister, Hartbeest and Julia Schneidekoupon, who are happy Philadelphians of Jewish ancestry and proud to say so. They are rich, likable, and at home in Washington society. Hartbeest Schneidekoupon is never killed. He thus resembles Victoria Dare—see notes 32 & 46 above. Julia Schneidekoupon bears a name which, translated, means Julia the coupon clipper. For the relevance of the name to both *Democracy* and "The New York Gold Conspiracy," see note 44 and 56, above.

It might be thought that "The New York Gold Conspiracy" is evidence that HA thought Gould a Jew and for that reason disliked or even hated him. The article instead is evidence that HA understood Gould to be slightly Jewish by ancestry, more ambitious and more ingenious but not more dishonest than other Wall Street capitalists, speculators, and swindlers, and a victim in the gold conspiracy, as well as a villain. In the article, HA quoted Fisk's great line: "I knew that somebody had run a saw right into us. . . ." See Lond. ed, 433; NY ed., 203. By "us," Fisk meant Gould and himself. By "somebody," Fisk meant a member or members of Corbin's ring. Clearly agreeing with Fisk, HA showed that the persons who at last ran a saw into Fisk and Gould were the Grants and Corbins. This is not to say that HA *liked* either Gould or Fisk, nor is it to say that he *hated* the one or the other. It is only to say that, if there were persons in the gold conspiracy whom HA hated, by far the likeliest candidates were Corbin, Mrs. Grant, and Grant.

Apparently on the basis of information new to him, HA later came to think of Gould as not Jewish in the slightest. The evidence is an intricate series of words in *The Education*: ". . . neither Jay Gould nor any other astute American mind—still less the complex Jew,—could ever have accustomed itself to the incredible and inexplicable lapses of Grant's intelligence. . . ." The words appear in a cluster of three chapters (XVI–XVIII) which begins by speaking of Indians, Americans, and Jewish immigrants arriving from Poland. Fair reading of the chapters leads to a definite conclusion: the words say that Grant's lapses of intelligence were so incredible and inexplicable that they could not be adapted to or anticipated by astute Americans like Gould, still less by Jews in America, who were "complex" because of two national affiliations, and who individually might be more astute than astute uncomplex Gould, who was an American only. See *EHA* (1907), 237; (LoA), 969.

76. When he came to write his *Education*, HA chose to say that the article was read and rejected by Reeve. The shift is one of many that help make the book what it largely is, a work of fiction. See *EHA*, (1907), 249; (LoA), 981.

77. It is unclear whether HA, leaving London for Italy, took with him the manuscript of his rejected article. (He might have entrusted it to Gaskell or Palgrave.) If he had it with him, he could alter it prior to its going to Froude.

78. CFA to HA, 13 Jun 1870.

79. Nagel, *Descent from Glory*, op. cit., 256–58.

80. *EHA*, (1907), 250; (LoA), 982.

10. BOTANY BAY

Letters by and to HA are in HA-micro 3, unless otherwise noted.

PRINCIPAL SOURCES

(1) twelve letters, HA to CMG, 13 Jul–19 & 24 Dec 1870.

(2) letter, HA to Higginson, 24 Oct 1870, L, II, 83 (the earliest extant letter HA signed "Henry Adams").

(3) letter, HA to Wells, 25 Oct 1870, L, II, 85 (also signed "Henry Adams").

(4) letter, HA to Whitney, 25 Oct 1870, L, II, 85 (also signed "Henry Adams").

(5) letter, HA to Schurz, 27 Oct 1870, L, II, 86.

(6) six letters, HA to Cox, 31 Oct–8 Dec 1870, L, II, 86–94.

(7) Henry Brooks Adams, "The Session," *NAR*, Jul 1870, 29–62 (in a series of annual articles under an unchanging title).

(8) the same, reprinted in the *Chicago Times*, 5 Aug 1870. The head-

lines are: " 'THE SESSION.'/ A Terrible Arraignment of the Radical Party. The Political Condition of the United States. Grant's Character—The Defects of His 'Unconscious Mind'—No Policy. Secretary Boutwell Dissected—His Absolute Deficiency. The Questions of Reconstruction and Finance—Foreign Policy. A Gloomy View of the Future—No Constitution—No Responsibility."

The introductory sentences are: "The *North American Review*, for July, contains the following article from the pen of Henry Brooks Adams. It is a scathing arraignment of the course of the radical party on matters of vital interest to the country, and will repay a careful perusal."

The article fills eight and a half columns and is adapted for newspaper use by the addition of captions within the text, the printing of 52 paragraphs as 36, and the conversion of 78 words to italics.

Crucially one word is changed. The opening phrase of HA's fourth paragraph, "The two great theories . . . ," is changed to read "The three great theories. . . ." The change, a bold one, indicates that the editor of the *Chicago Times* had Copperhead or secessionist sympathies and wanted to give HA the appearance of accommodating secessionist theories concerning the rights of states under the Constitution.

(9) the same, as incompletely reprinted in *The World* (New York), 8 Aug 1870. The headlines are: "A RADICAL INDICTMENT./ The Administration—Its Corruptions and Shortcomings. Its Weakness and Stolidity. Thorough Analysis of Grant and Boutwell's Mental Calibre. No Policy — No Ability. A Graphic Review of our Recent Political History."

The introductory sentence is: "The following article from the pen of Henry Brooks Adams appeared in the *North American Review* for July."

The article is adapted for newspaper use by the addition of captions within the text and the deletion of slightly less than a quarter of the text.

(10) source no. 9 reprinted as a pamphlet by the National Democratic Executive Resident Committee, Washington, D. C., n. d. An exclamation point is added, making the first heading read "A RADICAL INDICTMENT!" The text is printed in pages rather than columns. A phrase is added to the introductory sentence to make it read: "The following article from the pen of HENRY BROOKS ADAMS, a prominent Republican, appeared in the *North American Review* for July."

For campaign purposes, the Committee reprinted the pamphlet in 1872. See JTA, *Henry Adams*, 218. The reprint is differently titled and is dated.

(11) [HA], "The New York Gold Conspiracy," *Westminster Review*, Lond edition, Oct 1870, 411–36; NY edition, Oct 1870, 193–204.

ADDITIONAL SOURCES; COMMENTS

1. While fictional at innumerable points with respect to HA's personal history, *The Education of Henry Adams* appears to be painstakingly factual concerning some of that history's most critical moments. In a remarkable passage, the protagonist is pictured at Lake Geneva in 1870, gazing at Mount Blanc and seeing it as "a chaos of anarchic and purposeless forces." The passage may seem to say that HA reacted to the death of his sister Louisa by ceasing to be a religious believer. See *EHA* (1907), 251–52; (LoA) 983–84.

The passage is perhaps best studied in conjunction with the undated pair of sonnets by HA titled "Illusion./ I." and "Illusion./ II." See HA-micro, end of reel 7. The sonnets invoke the beauty of the Alps. They indicate that HA was a believer, but of an unusual sort. They represent him as believing that illusions are very valuable, even indispensable; that commonly they are lost; and that sometimes they are lost through over-reaching efforts to learn what lies behind them.

Read together, *The Education* and the sonnets may possibly indicate that HA in 1870 found himself a believer without beliefs—a person who had had a religion, no longer had it, yet believed that a religion, far from being a mere benefit, was an outright necessity.

2. Motley's eventual letter to HA, 11 Dec 1870, is a model of aggrieved loquacity.

3. Palgrave to HA, 12, 30 Aug 1870. HA's Mantegna is not among the art works noted in Scheyer, *The Circle of Henry Adams*, op. cit.

4. Froude to HA, 7 Aug 1870. Froude said in addition, "Your stand against these commercial bandits deserves braver support—but I cannot help myself." He seemed unaware that the article concerned President Grant fully as much as Gould and Fisk. He seemed unconscious too of the importance of Corbin.

5. CFA2, Diary, 22 Aug, 2, 15 Sep 1870, AP; also ABA to HA, 19 Jul 1870—"those days too awful to dwell on."

6. John Spencer Clark, *The Life and Letters of John Fiske*, Bost & NY, 1917, I, 349–77; *Letters of John Fiske*, op. cit., 378–79.

7. *Gilded Age Letters of E. L. Godkin*, op. cit., 149–57.

8. CFA to HA, 11 Jul 1870.

9. CFA2, Diary, 21 Sep 1870, AP. In an exceptionally detailed passage, *The Education* says that CFA2 told HA the following things: that Washington was not a respectable place to live; that he and HA should start "further joint operations in a new field"; that HA "had done at Washington all he could possibly do; that his position there had wanted solidity; that he was, after all, an adventurer; that a few years in Cambridge would give him personal weight; that his chief function was not to be that of teacher, but that of editing the *North American Review* which was to be coupled with the Professorship, and would lead to the daily press." See *EHA* (1907), 254–57; (LoA), 987–90.

The account possibly reports with perfect accuracy the opinions expressed by CFA2 to HA between his arrival in Quincy on 15 Sep 1870 and the evening of the 21st. Taken at face value, the reported opinions might pass for friendly and candid. It is evident, however, that HA on returning was not only attemptedly advised but also attemptedly subjected to punishment. As felt by CFA2, perhaps somewhat unconsciously, HA's offense in Washington was his having succeeded beyond his station as third son, with the result that CFA2 wanted HA's energies redirected while redirection was possible.

10. ABA, Diary, 21 Sep 1870, AP. ABA's attention to her son's not being paid as editor may suggest that better information is needed concerning sums given to Harvard by CFA while HA edited the *North American* and served as a member of the Harvard faculty. If money was given by CFA and if the sums equalled or outran his son's salary, HA's editor-and-professorship would have the aspect of an appointment financed by his parents.

11. CFA2, Diary, 22 Nov 1870, AP, comparing the "conference" that day in New York with the meeting in Washington "last Spring."

12. In addition to reprinting HA's "Session," the *Chicago Times* published long editorials, "Our Peaceful Revolution" and "The Political Situation," agreeing with HA's views concerning the Legal-Tender Act and the usurpation of power by Congress. See the issues for 5, 6 Aug 1870.

13. "The Session" as incompletely reprinted in the *World* and "The Session" as incompletely reprinted by the National Democratic Committee very closely matched. See principal sources 9 & 10, above. Perhaps all the printing was done by Marble's newspaper.

14. It is not suggested that JQA2 and CFA2 were responsible for the headlines and the introductory sentence printed by the *World* to introduce HA's article, nor the slightly different headings and introductory sentence printed by the National Democratic Committee. See principal sources 9 and 10, above. It *is* suggested that they sent the article to the *Chicago Times*, encouraged Manton Marble to reprint it in the *World*, and encouraged the Democratic National Committee to reprint it as a campaign pamphlet.

The main heading used by the *World* introduced the word "radical." In American political parlance at the time, "radical" could mean (a) fundamental or (b) having to do with Charles Sumner, Thaddeus Stevens, and their political adherents. It more commonly meant the latter.

HA had called himself a radical when in England but since returning to America had not done so, apparently because Sumner and Stevens had effectively monopolized the term and also, presumably, because in his view they had subverted it.

By using the headline "A RADICAL INDICTMENT," the *World* initiated a serious disservice to HA. The headline line said both that HA's "Session" was fundamental and that it was written by one of Sumner's allies. This is not to say that Manton Marble *believed* that HA was allied with Sumner. It is only to say that Marble may have had some slight impression that HA was allied with Sumner and that Marble wished to *paint* him as allied with Sumner.

The National Democratic Committee changed the heading to read "A RADICAL INDICTMENT!" and added a statement that HA was "a prominent Republican." See principal source 10, above.

The exclamation point and the explanatory phrase intensified the already-present suggestion that HA was a Republican in the Sumner camp. Readers, however, would fix on the salient fact that HA's article was being printed *by the Democrats*. On that basis, they would conclude that, contrary claims notwithstanding, HA was a prominent *Democrat*.

The neatness of this trick should be noticed. Under the cover of mere verbal indicators alleging him to be a radical Republican in Sumner's camp, editor Marble and the National Democratic Committee safely, easily, and permanently fixed on HA the reputation of being as much a Democrat as his eldest brother. See note 15.

15. In *The Education*, HA described the printing of "The Session" by the Democrats as irreversibly damaging to its author. See *EHA* (1907), 254; (LoA), 986—"He was henceforth in opposition, do what he might; and a Massachusetts Democrat, say what he pleased. . . ."

16. Levenson and his fellow editors assert, L, II, 79: ". . . [HA] pursued power of a more obvious sort by helping to organize the Liberal

Republican movement. All four of Charles Francis Adams' sons acted vigorously on the assumption that they might be helping to elect their father president in 1872."

The assertion is erroneous. It inverts HA's wishes concerning a possible presidency for CFA; it conflates HA with his brothers; and it conflates the organization of the revenue reformers, which was very much HA's work, with the organization of the Liberal Republican movement, which HA kept track of, once said he wished to assist, in fact did not assist, and eventually foiled. See Chaps. 11–12.

17. HA to Norton, 13 Jan 1871, L, II, 96—"They determined to try me [as editor] for one year. If I can make the Review pay for itself, it will go on. If not, it must die."

18. ABA, Diary, 21 Sep 1870, AP.

19. See especially HA to Norton, 13 Jan 1871, L, II, 97—". . . I took [the professorship] . . . to relieve Gurney's difficulty."

The suggestion that HA met with Gurney on Sunday rests mainly on the phrase "at twenty-four hours' notice" in *EHA* (1907), 256; (LoA), 988. I take the phrase to mean that HA received on Saturday from Gurney an insistent request that he come to Gurney's house on Sunday; that HA complied; and that on Sunday, on a basis of friendship and affection, HA and Gurney arrived at the understanding which HA's Monday talk with Eliot would only serve to rubber-stamp.

20. The account of HA's interchange with Eliot in *EHA* (1907), 255; (LoA), 987–88, differs from his account to Gaskell, 29 Sep 1870, mainly in indicating that HA came close to telling the president that the appointment of a teacher in medieval history seemed to him unnecessary.

21. *College Records*, II, 243, HUA.

22. *EHA* (1907), 260; (LoA), 993. Read by itself, the second paragraph of the chapter may seem to indicate that BA was already living in Wadsworth on the second floor; but the first two paragraphs, if read together, indicate that the impulse to try for space in "the old President's House on Harvard Square" originated with HA, after seeing Eliot.

23. ABA, Diary, 26 Sep 1871, AP.

24. *Henry James Letters*, op. cit., I, 247.

25. BA understood that he lived in Wadsworth, not separately, but "with" HA. See *Degradation*, 6. The rent was deducted from HA's pay. It was originally $300 but was changed to $400. See *College Records*, op. cit., II, 258 & 334. Presumably the increase reflected HA's taking added space for BA; and, by *giving* BA the space, HA got around a College rule against students living with faculty in faculty quarters.

26. Lest Cox mistakenly gather that he was a Democrat or a Republican, HA later told him (letter of 11 Nov 1870), ". . . I do not consider myself a member of either party."

27. The pamphlet bears neither place nor date. The quoted phrases appear on 2–4, 9, 11, & 13.

It seems likely that Howe formed his impressions of HA's 1870 "Session" mostly from the article as printed in the *Chicago Times*. See principal source 8. If he did, Howe was led to think that HA himself—not just the *Chicago Times*—had Copperhead or secessionist leanings! That mistaken idea would help explain Howe's reacting with all possible energy and venom.

28. CFA2, Diary, 16, 23 Oct 1870, AP.

29. Lodge, *Early Memories*, NY 1913, 147, 186, 274.

30. *Records of ye Hasty Pudding Club*, first term, 1857–1858, HUA, referring to HA as "Old 'Brooks.' "

31. On 1 Nov 1875 at the home of Faith Thoron Knapp, its owner, I saw the English copper plate from which HA's bookplates were printed. An incomplete identification of the engraver hammered into the back of the copper plate says "Engraver/ to Her Majesty/ 287/ Regent St."

32. Timothy O. Howe, *Political History./ The Republican Party Defended./ A Reviewer Reviewed*, 1–4, 9.

33. Ibid., 1.

34. In 1956, searching the Stone Library for books and papers relating to HA, I found a copy of Howe's pamphlet buried among other pamphlets in a drawer. Free of marks and apparently never opened or read, the copy presumably was put in the library only as a record.

35. HA preserved two fragmentary undated clippings from an unidentified periodical. See HA-micro 3, following HA to CMG, 29 Sep 1870. The clippings concern his 1870 "Session." One of the clippings bears a legend in HA's handwriting: "Both these [clippings] are from the same paper." The clipping names "Mr[.] Henry Adams" as author of "The Session." The other clipping is the one that calls HA "Harry" and repeatedly confuses him with Brooks.

36. The meaning of the sentence is doubtful. It can be read (a) as continuing what HA just said to Gaskell about an aunt having died; (b) as introducing a new subject that is pursued in the sentence that follows; (c) as noticed by HA to be ambiguous but permitted by him to stand uncorrected; and (d) as originally meant to indicate that his aunt left him money but on second thought qualified by a succeeding sentence to which Gaskell might think it an introduction.

37. Letter to myself from the deputy register of wills, Superior Court, D. C., 24 Mar 1989.

38. Though his choices to become an editor and a teacher were free actions for which he knew himself to be responsible, HA clearly felt that the choices also were forced, the first by his family and the second by Harvard. An important consequence was lasting resentment. An instance is HA's outburst: "The College chose to make me Professor of History—I don't know why, for I knew no more history than my neighbors. And it pitchforked me into mediaeval history, of which I knew nothing." See HA to Lodge, 2 Jan 1873.

39. CFA2, Diary, 10 October 1870, AP; HA to Norton, 13 Jan 1871, L, II, 97. In his diary entry, CFA2 refers to the *North American* as "our organ." The phrase belongs to a pattern of evidence indicating that CFA2 at HA's insistence joined HA as one of *two* unpaid saviors of the magazine.

40. HA's letter to Motley is missing but its content and date can be gleaned from Motley's reply, 11 Dec 1870.

41. Moran, II, 833.

42. The invitation was one of long standing and permitted CFA to choose his date. It was construed by CFA as a means of reaching a very large audience. See CFA to HA, 26 Jan 1869 and especially CFA to HA, 29 Dec 1869—"An invitation has already been given to me to communicate to the public whenever I please. . . ."

By the time the date for his address was set, CFA's New York supporters were very eager to support him.

43. Mary W. H. Schuyler to CFA, 6 Nov [1870], AP.

44. It can be inferred that CFA relayed Mrs. Schuyler's message to ABA and that she passed it on to HA. The evidence that she did so is the presence in *Democracy* of a Washington hostess named Mrs. Schuyler Clinton, wife of a senator from New York. (Her guests include an aspirant to the presidency, Senator Ratcliffe.) See *Democracy*, Chap. II.

45. In *The Education*, HA asserted that both "The Session [1869–1870]" and "The New York Gold Conspiracy" were "instantly pirated on a great scale." See *EHA* (1907), 255; (LoA), 986. The statement appears to be flatly false. No piratical reprinting of "The New York Gold Conspiracy" has been discovered. The substantial reprintings of the new "Session" were manifestly initiated by HA's elder brothers; hence not pirated, unless CFA2 and JQA2 were the pirates.

It seems probable that HA knew perfectly well that neither article was pirated. Conceivably he wrote his fictional account of piratings in part with the purpose of concealing his elder brothers' conduct with regard to "The Session," which was hardly to their credit.

46. CFA2, Diary, 21 Nov 1870, AP.

47. It may seem incredible that HA's authorship of "The New York Gold Conspiracy" remained unknown in late November 1870 to CFA2, Wells, Hodgskin, Godkin, and every other American. It may seem incredible too that HA's authorship was not suspected from the moment the article appeared. But HA not only *had* secrets; he had the ability to write in a way that would *keep* secrets. Even in this extraordinary case, he could be confident that his authorship would remain unapparent until it was attested by him or by an editor or publisher.

48. CFA2, Diary, 22, 23 Nov 1870, AP; *Gilded Age Letters of E. L. Godkin*, 163.

49. The *public* dinner held on 28 Nov 1870 was much advertised and became the subject of a partly hostile, five-column report in the *New York Tribune* the following morning. The letters sent by CFA2 and JQA2 are quoted in the report.

That the *Tribune* gave so much space to the dinner possibly indicated worry. Horace Greeley, the newspaper's owner-editor, was himself a presidential hopeful. He thus had personal reason to wonder what JQA2 and CFA2 might be trying to promote.

50. For HA's principal effort to organize some of the country's self-styled reformers as a junto, see Chap. 14.

51. The address was shortly published as a pamphlet: CFA, *The Struggle for Neutrality in America*, NY: Charles Scribner & Co. 1871. The quoted phrase appears on p. 8.

52. Robert Carlton Clark, "The Diplomatic Mission of Sir John Rose, 1871," *Pacific Northwest Quarterly*, XXVII (1936), 234–38.

53. The changed life that HA was living in Cambridge had a very practical meaning for Godkin. In a letter dated 1 Dec 1870, the editor asked Senator Schurz to supply the *Nation* "a fortnightly letter from Washington during the Session, giving not a recital of events, but the comments on them of a well-informed and intelligent observer." In effect, Godkin asked the senator to send anonymous newsletters resembling those

HA had begun supplying the previous December. Schurz declined. Godkin appealed next to Congressman Garfield. (See Chap. 9, note 42, above.) Garfield too declined. See *Gilded Age Letters of E. L. Godkin*, 159, 168.

It is no small comment on HA that he thus preceded—and was not succeeded by—a leading senator and a leading congressman, each older than himself.

11. ENGAGED AND DISENGAGED

Letters by and to HA are in HA-micro 3, unless otherwise noted.

PRINCIPAL SOURCES

(1) four letters, Clover Hooper to Eleanor Whiteside, [10 Jan] 1871 – 8 Mar 1872, Shattuck Papers, MHS.

(2) letter, HA to Norton, 13 Jan 1871, L, II, 96–98.

(3) letter, HA to Wells, 17 Jan 1871, L, II, 98.

(4) letter, HA to Cunliffe, 6 & 13 Mar 1871.

(5) eight letters, HA to CMG, 27 Mar–13 Nov 1871.

(6) three letters, HA to CFA, 7, 14, 21 Jan 1872.

(7) letter, Clover Hooper to Ellen Gurney, 5 Mar 1872, FTKP.

(8) HA, "Oh, litle bird . . ."—a sonnet translated from Petrarch, found only as published in HA, *Esther* (1884), 114; (LoA), 242.

(9) HA, "Eagle Head"—original sonnet found only in the letter HA to EC, 22–23 Aug 1890, HA-micro 7; published in L, III, 264.

(10) Charles F. Adams, jr., and Henry Adams, *Chapters of Erie and Other Essays*, Bost 1871.

(11) [HA], "Two Historical Essayists"—an article in two parts: "No. 1.—Mr. Froude."; "No. 2.—Mr. Freeman."—*Nation*, 14, 21 Dec 1871. (A new attribution. For confirmation of HA's authorship, see note 64, below.)

(12) Henry Adams, "Harvard College. 1786–87." *NAR*, Jan 1872, 110–47; also in *Sketches*, 3–38.

(13) [HA], "Freeman's Historical Essays," *NAR*, Jan 1872, 193–96; also in *Sketches*, 39–43.

(14) [HA] "Maine's Village Communities," *NAR*, Jan 1872, 196–99; also in *Sketches*, 44–48.

ADDITIONAL SOURCES; COMMENTS

1. Conceivably, through the agency of Ellen Gurney, HA was the guest of her uncle, Congressman Hooper. If that occurred, HA for the first time slept in a house within steps of Lafayette Square.

2. See *EHA* (1907), 240; (LoA), 972—"Adams repeated the story to Godkin, who made much play with it in the *Nation*, till it was denied."

When first printing HA's news on 19 Jan 1871, the *Nation* shielded him by pretending the news was old. The words used were: "A story has long been current, and is tolerable well authenticated, that antipathy to and distrust of Mr. Motley were first roused in the President's breast by seeing that he parted his hair in the middle. . . ."

3. Why Fish and HA met is unknown, but two things indicate that the meeting took an important turn. One was its timing. The other was its being given the cover of a repeatable story that possibly was true and was distractingly entertaining.

4. J. C. Bancroft Davis, *Mr. Fish and the Alabama Claims*, Bost 1893, 59.

5. Sometime in the 1930s, Ward and Louisa Hooper Thoron transcribed Clover's letters to Eleanor (principal source 1). Mrs. Thoron drew my attention to the letters in 1956 and permitted me to copy her and her husband's transcriptions, with her informative annotations.

6. My account of Henry's relations with Clover in this chapter rests mainly but not solely on my datings and readings of the sonnets listed as principal sources 8 & 9. While arriving at my dates and readings, I considered other conceivable dates and readings, to each of which there seemed to be fatal objections based on evidence. My final dates and readings are offered partly because I have found no evidence that can fairly be considered contrary, partly because the narrative that becomes possible when the dates and readings are followed is in my judgment eminently credible.

7. That Henry and Clover were meeting in a way that would lead to marriage was kept so secret that the news of their formal engagement came as a complete surprise to Brooks, the Adams to whom Henry at the time was closest.

8. HA's later attachments to women can be explained as continuations and consequences of his passionate attachment to his wife, which itself owed some of its character to three losses—of Louisa Johnson Adams, Louisa Adams Kuhn, and Mary Hellen Adams.

9. The suggestion that Clover's psychology was greatly influenced by the psychology of medicine and medical nursing is mostly based on evidence relating to her conduct in 1885 from the time her father became fatally ill until both he and she were dead. See Chap. 21.

10. The best photographs of HA taken prior to 1877 can be said to show such steadiness and the asserted trace of defiance.

11. The poems of Ellen Sturgis Hooper so mattered in the Hooper family that her grandchildren were continuing to quote them in the 1950s and 1960s. The one most quoted to me by Louisa Hooper Thoron was the one beginning "I slept and dreamed that life was Beauty,—/ I woke, and found that life was Duty."

12. It may be asked, to what degree do the HA's translations from Petrarch reflect and express HA's experiences as well as Petrarch's? I discussed this question many times with Louisa Hooper Thoron. Partly raised by her Aunt Clover and Uncle Henry, LHT knew her uncle very well. While still young, she became a Henry Adams researcher. When I met her in 1952, she was as positive as I was in concluding that HA's translations from Petrarch are autobiographical and have meanings that are referential and hard, rather than free-floating or "poetical." We only differed about particular datings and readings. My date for "Oh, little bird . . ." was new to her. On reflection, she agreed with it.

13. Principal source 8. It may seem that "bitter years" in the penultimate line is a typographical error, since "better" would simplify the sense. (HA may himself have seen advantages in "better." Another of his translations from Petrarch, beginning "From impious Babylon . . . ," contains the phrase "better hours." See HA-micro, end of 7, or F, II, 62n.) But Petrarch's *amari* requires "bitter"; and the sense of the line, though not simple, fits the experiences of both Henry and Clover.

14. Some years after Henry and Clover married, the poems of Ellen Sturgis Hooper were privately printed. HA and MHA appear to have been parties to the printing, but details are lacking.

15. When Clover first saw the translation is not indicated by any evidence so far found. I assume that he *postponed* showing it to her and that he showed it to her only well after their formal engagement.

16. The pamphlet is dated "Republican Office, Springfield, Mass., January 28, 1871."

17. I have tried not to give too detailed an account. The full truth was that controversy was set in motion, first by HA's anonymous article, next by criticisms of Field by the *New York Times*, then by a report to the *Springfield Republican*, and last by the latter paper's editorial. See editorial, "Mr. David Dudley Field," NYTimes, 7 Dec 1870; report by "Carlfried" headed "From New York," SprRepub, 7 Dec 1870; and editorial paragraph starting "Now that a first-class British review . . . ," SprRepub, 8 Dec 1870.

18. HA himself understood that the Fields-Bowles controversy was sparked by his anonymous criticisms of Field's professional conduct in "The New York Gold Conspiracy." See *Chapters of Erie*, 132n.

19. "Note," *Westminster Review*, Apr 1871, NY edition, 281–82. The Note prints counsel Field's objection and a prefatory statement: "The writer of the article which we published last October on 'The New York Gold Conspiracy' is not now in England: we therefore publish the following letter without those comments which had he seen it he would have added, and which he will probably supply for publication in our next Number."

20. The July 1871 *Westminster Review*, NY edition, 151, ends with an editor's comment titled "The New York Gold Conspiracy." Although signed *"Editor of the Westminster Review*," the comment unmistakably was written for editor Chapman by HA. See note 22, below.

21. Barlow's letters appeared in the *New York Tribune* on 7, 8, 9 Mar 1871. Each letter was printed under the heading "Facts for Mr. Field." A reply by Field appeared in the *Tribune* on 13 Mar 1871 under the heading "Mr. Field Answers." But Field replied, not to Barlow's letters, but instead to an eight-point summary which the *Tribune* had presented in an editorial. Barlow took advantage of this evasion and sent the *Tribune* a huge added letter. Printed on 24 Mar 1871 under the heading "More Facts for Mr. Field," the added letter filled an entire page. Barlow reprinted all these materials and others in a pamphlet, *Facts for Mr. David Dudley Field. . . . Supplement to Field's and Bowles' Correspondence*, Albany 1871.

Also see the editorial, "Mr. Field winces and scolds . . . ," SprRepub, 9 Mar 1871.

22. In the comment he supplied Chapman for the July 1871 *Westminster*, HA says in part: ". . . we have found no occasion to modify or retract any of the statements made in that article. . . . If English readers are interested in following up the subject they will find the case as against Mr. Field stated in a series of letters, published in March last by Mr. F. C. Barlow, in the *New York Tribune*, and lately republished with Mr. Field's reply, in pamphlet form; and also in articles of the *North American Review* for April. But the charges brought against Mr. Field now go far beyond anything we suggested, and their justice or propriety are matters for the American bar to determine."

Field was later saved from disbarment through the mediation of Evarts. See Chester L. Barrows, *William M. Evarts/ Lawyer, Diplomat, Statesman*, Chapel Hill NC 1941, 193.

23. The Brown and Harvard dinners were reported at length in the *New York Tribune*, 22, 23 Feb 1871. HA does not appear in the reports.

24. SprRepub, 24 Feb 1871. After reporting an explosion of rumors, the correspondent, "Carlfried," pulled back, saying, ". . . I am disposed to doubt such reports on principle, and place little credit on those in this case." In later paragraphs, "Carlfried" said that David Dudley Field was under attack within the New York bar association; that early action by the association could not be expected; and that charges against Field were likely to be referred to "a higher tribunal—that of public opinion."

25. HA, 1866 engagement book, entry of June 19, HAL; Moran, II, 1173, 1396. HA listed Dudley Field (the son) in his 1867 engagement book as attending the legation's July 4 reception.

26. The possibility of libel suits in England or America relating to HA's "New York Gold Conspiracy" was diminished and then eliminated by the article's being merged after March 1871 with bewildering complications arising in New York concerning corporate, legal, judicial, and political matters. For complications related to Gould, McHenry, and Barlow, see Maury Klein, *The Life and Legend of Jay Gould*, Baltimore 1986, 118.

27. I assume that, as editor of the principal magazine from which the essays would be drawn, HA negotiated the contract; and I further assume that he did so just after his February visit to New York; but direct evidence concerning the negotiation is lacking.

28. By presenting HA as less important than CFA2, also as less a man of affairs, *Chapters of Erie* anticipated two of the principal fictions that would appear in his *Education*.

29. That Gould was hurt irreparably by the article is attested in all well-informed commentaries. Appreciation of the venality of Julia and Ulysses Grant has been hesitant during the past 120 years, the article considered, but it promises to grow. Partly thanks to the article, Corbin was crushed by notoriety in 1870–1871, but his notoriety may be expected to increase when the article is better understood. It bears repeating that HA inserted a one-sentence paragraph in "The New York Gold Conspiracy" when reprinting it in *Chapters of Erie*. The insertion concerned Corbin and was designed to help attentive readers separate the strands of HA's argument and follow with greater ease the strands relating to the Corbins and Grants. See Chap. 9, note 58, above.

30. See especially CFA2, *Lee at Appomattox and Other Papers*, Bost & NY 1902, 116–47; Donald, *Charles Sumner and the Rights of Man*, 480–97; and William Lewis Morton, *The Critical Years/ The Union of British North America/ 1857–1873* (The Canadian Centenary Series, vol. 12), 212–62—a superb account, which in passing quotes HA.

31. Schurz's replies to HA's letters of 25 Apr–24 May 1871, L, II, 107–11, are missing. HA's last letter seems to have drawn from Schurz a definite reply that he could not write the article.

HA's next step is uncertain. He possibly waited for several months and then asked CFA2 to contribute a political review not unlike his own 1870 "Session." See CFA2, Diary, 22 Feb 1872, AP: ". . . resolved to start my N. American article, but on examination found that I didn't have the courage,—so went over to Cambridge & found that Henry had enough without me & so let me off."

There is no doubt that, when it came to political nerve, JQA2 and CFA2 claimed to have it and HA had it. Of the three elder sons, only HA wrought important results in politics.

32. Thurman Wilkins, *Clarence King/ A Biography*, NY 1958, 150, 395.

33. King's success as a teller of tales is a recurring motif in the varied accounts of him in the Century Club volume of *Clarence King Memoirs*, NY & Lond, 1904. The account by W. C. Brownell says (223) that King's truly exceptional quality was his ever-active imagination. "At moments assuredly it held him quite enthralled within an almost hypnotic control. . . . But for the most part he was on terms of complete understanding with it and checked and tested its suggestions with the sagacity that gave its pronounced scientific turn to his mind."

34. Wilkins, *Clarence King*, op. cit., 141.

35. Clover wrote to Eleanor Whiteside, 5 Mar 1871, that her father was "much absorbed in the Beverly house." She went on to say, "The sea and pine woods are so lovely there even now that I can hardly wait till the middle of May to get there." The sentence might be taken to indicate that Clover would cheerfully forgo the company of persons she was seeing in Boston if she could have sea and pine woods in their places, But wild shores and pine woods had freer uses for unmarried women than Boston parlors, and the sentence could well have a romantic meaning.

36. HA to BA, 3 Mar 1872. HA dates BA's making the suggestion, saying, ". . . in our walks last Spring you discussed it." For a further reference to BA's suggestion, see note 71, below.

37. Palgrave to HA, 6 Jul 1871.

38. HA quickly grew fearful that King's mountaineering sketches would diminish him in the eyes of the public and work against his receiving proper credit for his work in science. See HA, *Sketches*, 65.

39. HA's letter to Emmons, 3 Jul 1871, L, II, 113–14, is clearly the last letter of an exchange the earlier parts of which are missing.

40. Whitney had directed the California State Geological Survey and was currently a professor of geology at Harvard.

41. See Weston J. Naef, *Era of Exploration/ The Rise of Landscape Photography in the American West, 1860–1885*, Bost 1975, passim.

42. In his letter to Gaskell, 27 Mar 1871, HA said, L, II, 103, "I wish I had a good historical collection of cathedrals in photograph." For his interest in taking an ideal view of Abu Simbel, see Chap. 12.

43. Duberman, *Charles Francis Adams*, op. cit., 342.

44. HA wrote to MHA, 14 Mar 1885, HA-micro 5, ". . . it is now thirteen years since my last letter to you. . . ." His statement fails to suggest the date of his *first* letter. It however confirms that there were letters, and it can be taken to suggest that prior to 27 Feb 1872 he and Clover exchanged many letters.

45. Ten months later, HA openly played on the clever/Clover resemblance. See his letter to Brooks, 3 Mar 1872, saying, ". . . the devil and all his imps couldn't resist the fascination of a clever woman who chooses to be loved."

46. HA had experienced separation as a test of love. When a collegian, he was much in the company of Caroline Bigelow. He separated

from her by going to Europe and confirmed to himself how little feeling there had been between them. In the present instance, tests were dispensable, but he apparently did not realize it.

47. Principal source 9. That "Eagle Head" dates from the early summer of 1871 is evident, once the possibility is considered.

Among HA's sonnets, "Eagle Head" appears to be the one he was least willing to publicize. He did not preserve a copy among his papers. He instead encapsulated a copy within a private letter sent to a person he at the time of sending wholly trusted.

48. HA's reasons for wanting to buy land and build a house at Beverly Farms were numerous, one being the North Shore's comparative coolness in summer. A reason that might be overlooked was association of the North Shore with his and Clover's first physical union—an occurrence that apparently long antedated their wedding and exceeded it in importance.

49. "Eagle Head" appears to be the only work in which HA brought together his experience of being with his dying sister and his experience of complete involvement with his future wife.

For details concerning LAK's carriage driving and her injuries during her accident, see Nagel, *Descent from Glory*, op. cit., 257–58. For a fictitious account of her being "thrown from a cab," see *EHA*, (1907), 250; (LoA), 982.

50. It should be noted that Henry and Clover did not hesitate to live together for a time at her father's house at Beverly Farms in advance of their wedding. See Chap. 12.

51. *EHA* (1907), 271; (LoA), 1004. HA's account in *EHA* of his adventure in the West in 1871 remains the principal source of data concerning a crucially important experience. The account harmonizes with his talk titled "King." See note 55.

52. Confusion about the meaning of the phrase was ended by David H. Dickason in his article "Henry Adams and Clarence King/ The Record of a Friendship," *NEQ*, Jun 1944, 230–32.

53. *Clarence King Memoirs*, op. cit., 136–39.

54. In his *Clarence King*, 150, Thurman Wilkins supplied new details (e. g. concerning Evans) but permitted himself to state that the mule "brought a frail rider, somewhat taller than a dwarf, with an auburn goatee and a beautifully drooping moustache, a rare and intensely polished young man in whom some truculent senator could fancy the semblance of a begonia. It was Henry Adams."

This pretended description of HA, one of the most mistaken and demeaning ever published, might be used to illustrate how the easily obtainable facts of HA's exhaustless energy, physical toughness, and adequate size were in some minds erased and reversed by the misleading Samuel Lawrence drawing (first published in 1930) and the even more misleading drawing on the jacket of the Modern Library edition of *The Education* (published in 1931 and for many years thereafter). But even those mistaken and error-creating images did not exhibit the goatee invented by Wilkins for *his* enfeebled "Henry Adams."

55. HA wrote a talk, titled "King," for an intended King Memorial Meeting at the Century Club. He took as his theme "How I first knew King" but continued by saying, ". . . when I come to think about it, I fear that the motive would cut too deep into King's life, not to mention my

own; and . . . the odor of youth and the pine forests is a little sacred, like the incense of the mass. We had ideals then, ambitions, and a few passions. . . . They were as fresh and exciting as the air of the Rocky Mountains, and the smell of the camp-fires in which we talked till the night grew tired of us."

The passage evokes, not Estes Park in Colorado, but the Uintah range in Utah. It can be taken to indicate that HA "knew King" only when he and the geologist were able to talk at length, without interruptions. See *Clarence King Memoirs*, 159–61.

56. The wide difference between Lyell's uniformitarianism and King's modified catatrophism is too often studied with reference only to King's short paper, "Catastrophism and Evolution," *American Naturalist*, XI (1877), 449–70. HA first saw the difference when looking at geological formations in Utah. Some slight idea of what he saw is suggested by a sentence in King's *Systematic Geology*, Wash 1878, 533: "The great Archæan precipices brought to light in Uintah and Wahsatch ranges are absolutely unparalleled in the topography of to-day."

57. Wilkins, *Clarence King*, 153–56.

58. See HA to CMG, 27 Mar 1871, on his reading Ruskin, Fergusson, and Viollet le Duc.

59. Ernest Samuels, *The Young Henry Adams*, Camb 1948, 340.

60. L, II, 120.

61. Moran, II, 833.

62. Her usual signature when married would be Marian Adams.

63. King, *Systematic Geology*, op. cit., xi—"The method of this volume is historical. It is an attempt to read the geology of the Middle Cordilleras, and to present the leading outlines of one of the most impressive sections of the earth's surface-film."

64. The article is not listed in Haskell's *Nation* indexes. HA's authorship is wholly established (a) by his beginning his next notice of Freeman with a parallel first sentence and (b) by his *signing* his last Freeman notice "H. A." See *Sketches*, 40, 77, 84.

65. J. C. Hooker to CFA, Naples, 26 Jan 1872, AP.

66. His teaching principles centered in the needs of students and took note of the failings of teachers. He said that students were entitled to "complete social equality." ". . . no instructor can well be allowed to forget the fact, which, nevertheless, is extremely apt to be forgotten in practice, that the teacher exists for the sake of the scholars, not the scholars for the sake of the teacher." He said too that teaching had ill effects on most persons who tried it. ". . . the habit of instruction and the incessant consciousness of authority tends to develop extremely disagreeable traits in human character, especially wherever character naturally inclines towards selfishness. . . ." See *NAR*, Jan 1872, 139, 116, 137; or *Sketches*, 30, 28, 10.

67. Barlow by then was attorney general of the state of New York. His pamphlet, *Facts for Mr. David Dudley Field*, was published in Albany by Weed, Parsons & Co. It thus seems possible that HA went to Albany to confer with Barlow—or conceivably with Weed. For the most part, however, his errand in Albany is an unsolved mystery.

68. "A Chapter of Erie," *Pall Mall Gazette*, 10 Jan 1872, 11.

69. My suggestion that Henry secretly visited Clover's father is based

partly on the social norms of the time, partly on HA's overall record of respecting Dr. Hooper's rights, and partly on HA's having waited till both fathers were in Boston.

My idea that HA may have requested a letter from Dr. Hooper is based on HA's understanding of the uses of documents and on there being an interval between Sunday afternoon or evening and Tuesday afternoon, when HA would first be able to visit Clover. In the interval, Dr. Hooper could easily send a letter.

70. Faculty records, HUA.

71. In her letter to her sister, principal source 7, Clover gives the impression that HA's attentions to her began only a few weeks before they became engaged. She says, "*This winter*, when the very cold weather came, the sun began to warm me . . . [italics added]."

In his letter to his brother Brooks, 3 Mar 1872, Henry dates the courtship as having begun in May 1871. He says, ". . . I have had the design ever since last May and have driven it very steadily."

The accounts conflict. Each is an evident fiction adapted to the sensibilities of the sibling to whom it was written. Clover's letter assures Ellen that romantic secrets were kept from her only briefly. Henry's letter assures Brooks that his springtime advice the year before had an effect:— "You are partly responsible. . . ."

Neither fiction stands in the way of this chapter's suggesting that the secret meetings of Clover and Henry actually began much earlier, in November 1870.

72. HA's letter to BA, 3 Mar 1872, contained two sentences that require special notice: "I know better than anyone the risks I run. But I have weighed them carefully and accept them."

The factors considered by HA and Clover did *not* include a fear that Clover would someday kill herself. If the suicide of her Aunt Susan in 1852 is evidence that they should have had that fear, then three cases of self-destruction in the Adams family in the period 1829–1870 is evidence that they should have feared still more that HA would someday kill himself. They evidently had neither fear.

There was of course a risk that *Clover* could best judge: the risk that by marrying she would destroy her father's happiness. Doubtless HA weighed this risk, but not as a first consideration. The great risk he had to keep in mind—a risk *he* could best judge—was the risk that Clover would be exposed to if she married a person as deeply involved in politico-economic wars as he was. It had been bad enough that Lincoln was murdered and Seward slashed with a knife. It similarly had been bad that Raymond, for reasons only too easy to learn or infer, was placed dying in the hall of his house. It would be worse if a woman was attacked because of a man's activities.

12. ABU SIMBEL

Letters by and to HA are in HA-micro 3, unless otherwise noted.

PRINCIPAL SOURCES

(1) letter, HA to BA, 3 Mar 1872.
(2) letter, Clover Hooper to Ellen Gurney, 5 Mar 1872, FTKP.

(3) letters, Clover Hooper to Eleanor Shattuck, 8 Mar, 24 Jun 1872, Shattuck Papers, MHS.

(4) eight letters, HA to CMG, 26 Mar 1872–4–18 Mar 1873.

(5) letter, HA to Reid, 15 May 1872, L, II, 136.

(6) letters, HA to Lodge, 2 Jun 1872, 2 Jan 1873.

(7) 26 letters, MHA to her father, sister, and brother, 28 Jun 1872–11 Mar 1873, FTKP and Thoron, 13–84.

(8) three letters, HA to RWH, 28–29 Jun–10 Nov 1872.

(9) letter, HA to Cunliffe, 25 Jul 1872.

(10) letter, HA to Bancroft, 16 Sep 1872.

(11) letter, MHA to Samuel Gray Ward, 10 Mar [1873], H.

(12) [HA], "Taylor's Faust," *Sketches*, 49–61.

(13) [HA], "Howells's Their Wedding Journey," *NAR*, Apr 1872, 444–45; also in *Sketches*, 62–63.

(14) [HA], "King's Mountaineering in the Sierra Nevada," *NAR*, Apr 1872, 445–48; also in *Sketches*, 64–68.

(15) [HA] "Holland's Recollections of Past Life," *NAR*, Apr 1872, 448–50; also in *Sketches*, 69–72.

ADDITIONAL SOURCES; COMMENTS

1. HA informed ABA of his engagement on 29 Feb 1872. She told the news that night to CFA, who recorded that it "filled me with surprise." He later added that he had long thought HA "peculiarly well adapted to domestic happiness." "The young lady has not been much known to us, but she has all the reputation among her friends which could be desired at the outset." See CFA, Diary, 29 Feb, 2 Mar 1872, AP.

2. HA's going and returning are recorded in CFA, Diary, 7, 9 Mar 1872, AP.

3. CFA to BA, 13 Mar 1872, AP.

4. BA to CFA, 31 Mar 1872, AP.

5. CFA2, Diary, 16 Mar, 6 Apr 1872, AP; CFA2 to CFA, 30 Apr 1872, AP.

6. In Boston on 3 May 1891, CFA2 wrote a long entry in his Memorabilia, 1888–1893, 279–87, AP. In a portion that is relevant here, CFA2 claimed to recall a "brutal prophecy" he made in the "autumn of 1871" — an "awful speech" which "no man could ever forget." He said he had not known at the time that HA, through E. W. Gurney, who had married Ellen Hooper, was "intimate" with Clover Hooper. He continued:

> One day we [CFA2 and HA] were driving with my mother—my father was then at Geneva,—and she suddenly said,—"Henry, I do wish you would marry Clover Hooper!["]—taken by surprise and suspecting nothing, I exclaimed,—"Heavens!—no! they're all crazy as coots. She'll kill herself, just like her Aunt!"

> . . . Henry denied all idea of ever marrying &c—but he was . . . engaged to Clover at the time! A fortnight later, the engagement was announced.

In my judgment, the alleged episode is specious. A glaring sign of unreliability is the mistaken chronology. A glaring sign of dishonesty is CFA2's pretence that after twenty years he can recall conversations verbatim. (For further comments, see Chap. 27, note 32.) Some of the alleged particulars might be believable if voiced by CFA2 in a letter to HA. He wrote to HA on the same day, HA-micro 9, so opportunity was not lacking. But CFA2 alleged them in his private Memorabilia, where HA could be expected never to see them.

The story perhaps has value to this extent: it recounts something CFA2 so much wished had happened that in 1891 he wrote it out for posterity in a private record as having occurred. Understood as false, the alleged episode reveals more about CFA2 than might be anticipated. In its lines, he awards himself the role of family seer whose accurate foreknowledge is tragically and accidentally uttered too late to have a saving effect; he silently excuses his own family, the Adamses; and he violently libels two other families, the Sturgises and the Hoopers. In addition, he fails to acknowledge the presence of self-destruction in the Adams family, fails to include his own consideration of suicide in 1866, and creates a chance for himself to voice the hideous canard that all Hoopers and Sturgises were suicidally insane—a canard which was as false in 1891 as it would have been had he said it in 1871.

CFA2's entry should be read together with his letter to Ford, 31 Dec 1912, CFA2P, offering an explanation of the death of George Washington Adams. CFA2 alleges that the death, far from being a suicide, was an accidental drowning caused by the absence of a guard rail on the steamer *Benjamin Franklin*. But contemporary evidence says otherwise.

7. During the winter of 1966–1967, Harold Dean Cater started work on a corrected edition of *Henry Adams and His Friends/ A Collection of His Unpublished Letters* (1947), to be issued by the Octagon Press. His work brought him into renewed contact with Louisa Hooper Thoron and Aileen Tone, the two persons still living who had been closest to HA. On 6 Jan 1967, Mrs. Thoron spoke with Cater by phone. Next day she suggested I call him. I did and, during a long interchange (he and I had recently been brought together by Miss Tone), Cater told me that in the 1940s he and Wilhelmina Harris, the caretaker of the Old House at Quincy, came upon a letter in a desk or similar piece of furniture in the house, thought its contents were such that they had no choice but to give it to HA2, and after doing so never again saw the letter. As Cater described it at the start of his account, the letter was written by CFA2 *to* HA and told him not to marry into the Hooper family. As he described it later in his account, the letter was written by CFA2 *about* HA to another member of the family (Cater did not specify which) and suggested that several Adamses should join to prevent HA's intended marriage. He added that he avoided mentioning it in the Biographical Introduction of *Henry Adams and His Friends* so as not to hurt the feelings of Louisa Hooper Thoron and Mabel Hooper La Farge.

Because I previously had had occasion to doubt the truth of an assertion by Cater (see note 47, below), I did not mention to him that he had told me contradictory stories about a letter. Neither did I mention that Mrs. La Farge died three years before his book came out. I merely recorded what he had told me, contradictions included.

My present opinion is that a letter by CFA2 roughly of the sort he described should be looked for but that the probability of its having existed is zero. The evidence against its existing seems definitive. The principal word CFA2 used in 1872 to describe HA's engagement (he used it also to describe

HA's wedding) was "peculiar." See CFA2 to CFA, 28 Jun 1872, AP. Far from indicating that the engagement was seen by CFA2 as a mistake in need of reversal by him or by several Adamses together, CFA2's "peculiar" indicates that he saw the engagement as a social oddity he wished to view with unconcerned detachment and, at most, mild annoyance.

8. Mention of Pumpelly does not appear in HA's writings till 1877. That HA had become acquainted with La Farge is evidenced by a line in Palgrave's letter to HA, 9 Nov 1871.

9. The novel was published in 1872. How and when the copy came into Clover's hands is not known. In his *Clover*, 136–37, Friedrich says HA gave Clover the copy on 27 Feb 1872 but cites no evidence. His statement might be called a natural inference, but it has no support.

10. "Jay Gould Surrenders," NYTribune, 13 Mar 1872.

11. CFA wrote an extraordinary account of his dealings in Washington with Fish (whom he had not previously met), Grant ("a short insignificant looking person"), and the Cabinet. See CFA, Diary, 23 Feb 1872, AP. CFA says in the account that the place of secretary of state should have been awarded to him in 1869, not to Fish, yet says he was lucky to escape the assignment. ". . . the country ought to have called me to that place under any ordinary circumstances—and yet could anything have been more fortunate for me than to have been spared the trial of educating such an ignoramus!"

12. CFA, Diary, 18 Mar 1872, AP.

13. *Sketches*, 49, 223–24.

14. The letter from Wells to Atkinson is missing. (It was shown to CFA by CFA2 but conceivably passed first from Atkinson to HA, from him to CFA2, and at fourth hand to CFA.) CFA understood the letter to say that his sons should be sent to Cincinnati and there should give "pledges to advance my nomination." He seems also to have understood that the sons were *to pledge Cabinet places in exchange for added convention votes*; that is, the sons were to engage in the sort of trading that won the Republican nomination for Lincoln at Chicago in 1860. See CFA, Diary, 16 Apr 1872, AP.

Wells can be presumed to have intended no such trades. He needed a means whereby CFA could accept the nomination. Because CFA would be on the ocean when the convention met, the means had to be either acceptance in advance by letter or spoken pledges by deputies he sent to the convention. Wells was accorded neither.

15. The letter from Wells to CFA was apparently destroyed. CFA described it as giving assurance that Trumbull was willing to be CFA's running mate; also as requesting that CFA "put in the hands of somebody authority to act for me." See CFA, Diary, 18 Apr 1872, AP.

16. The letter can be rightly estimated only on the basis of its entire text. As printed in the *Springfield Republican*, it said:

Boston, April 18, 1872.

My Dear Mr[.] Wells:—
    I have received your letter, and will answer it frankly. I do not want the nomination, and could only be induced to consider it by the circumstances under which it might possibly be made. If the call upon me were an unequivocal one, based upon confidence in my character earned in public life, and a belief that I would carry out in practice

the principles which I professed, then, indeed, would come a test of my courage in an emergency. But, if I am to be negotiated for and have assurances given that I am honest, you will be so kind as to draw me out of that crowd.

With regard to what I understand to be the declaration of principles which has been made, it would be ridiculous in me to stand haggling over them. With a single exception of ambiguity, I see nothing which any honest republican or democrat would not accept. Indeed, I should wonder at any one who denied them. The difficulty is not in the profession. It lies, everywhere, only in the manner in which they are carried into practice.

If I have succeeded in making myself understood, you will perceive that I can give no authority to any one to act or to speak for me in the premises. I never had a moment's belief that, when it came to the point, any one so entirely isolated as I am from all political association of any kind could be made acceptable as a candidate for public office. But I am so unlucky as to value that independence more highly than the elevation which is brought by a sacrifice of it. This is not inconsistent with the sense of grateful recognition of the very flattering estimates made of my services in many and high quarters. But I cannot consent to peddle with them for power.

If the good people who meet at Cincinnati really believe that they need such an anomalous being as I am (which I do not), they must express it in a manner to convince me of it, or all their labor will be thrown away. I am, with great respect,

Yours,   Charles Francis Adams.

David A. Wells, Esq., Norwich, Ct.

17. Describing the Cincinnati convention as a "trap" (letter to CFA, 13 Oct 1872), HA said that what made it so was the presence and the power of the Greeley managers. HA could equally have said that what made it a trap was the strong likelihood that Grant could not be beaten. Most of all, HA could have called it a trap for himself. If CFA had won the presidential nomination at Cincinnati, HA would have had little choice but to attempt to help his father win the Democratic nomination at Baltimore, help get him try to defeat Grant at the polls, and, in the unlikely event of victory, help him try to enjoy a creditable term in the White House. To HA, each of these prospective tasks was in the highest degree repugnant.

18. CFA2, Diary, 23–24 Apr 1872, AP; CFA2 to CFA, 30 Apr 1872, AP.

19. CFA2, Diary, 24–26 Apr 1872, AP. CFA2 and Godkin may have seen CFA's letter as published in the *New York Times* on 25 Apr 1872. There it was set as one paragraph. Wells was misprinted "Welles."

The Niblo's Garden advertisement in the *Times* for April 24 bills "The Great Dramatic Picture, Black Friday," lists the actors playing the roles of Rob King, Dash Hoffman, Sam Simms, Violet Spearheart, and Rosa Budd, but offers no further clue as to the character of the drama.

20. See Schurz to Godkin, 23 Nov 1872, Godkin Papers, H—"The disaster might easily have been prevented, had not our friends, probably you and I among the rest, considered the nomination of Mr. Adams certain until the last ballot was taken."

Duberman, *Charles Francis Adams*, 363–64, gives details concerning the intended casting of 27 Illinois votes for CFA, most of them shifts from Trumbull, following the sixth ballot.

21. "Greeley Nominated!" NYTimes, 4 May 1872, provides a detailed account of the building of Greeley support, naming names. The account is signed "E. C."

22. CFA2 was to attend the convention but was directed by CFA not to attend in consequence of the letter from Wells to Atkinson suggesting that CFA send his sons as a council. See CFA, Diary, 16 Apr 1872, AP— ". . . my sons will not go. . . ."

Later, speaking in public and mentioning the reversal of his plan to attend, CFA2 explained the reversal in such a way as not to disclose the receipt of the letters from Wells or their effects. See "Cincinnati and Louisville," BAdv, 1 Oct 1872.

23. CFA2, Diary, 3–4 May 1872, AP. The second son's disgust was the greater because he was an extreme freetrader and Greeley was an outspoken protectionist.

24. CFA, Diary, 4 May 1872, AP.

25. CFA to HA, 22 May 1872.

26. While communicating Conkling's offer to CFA in Boston, Barlow disclaimed all part in it other than its transmission. CFA said in answer that he could begin considering to accept a nomination by the Stalwarts only after such a nomination was voted by their convention, with no encouragement at all from him. Barlow remarked that such an attitude had no precedent in American politics. CFA, however, cited one—that of George Washington. Perhaps better than any other evidence, the riposte indicates the altitude from which CFA tried to speak down to political suitors in 1872. See CFA, Diary, 16 Apr 1872, AP.

Duberman, in his *Charles Francis Adams*, 500–01n16, says that CFA responded to Conkling's offer and Wells's letter "in exactly the same manner." While true in the sense that CFA used similar words, the statement can be objected to as false because the elder Adams's similar responses were uttered in dissimilar contexts. The Stalwart Republicans would not give CFA the vice-presidential nomination unless he accepted it in advance. A very large number of the Liberal Republicans *would* give him the presidential nomination without his accepting it in advance and later came within seconds of achieving that exact object. CFA was not a political innocent. He could and did see the difference. His response through Barlow to Conkling was thus an outright refusal. Differently, the letter to Wells did not in CFA's mind preclude his getting the Liberal Republican nomination. On the contrary, in his view, it put his candidacy on a proper footing.

27. The Straight-out Democrats met on 3 Sep 1872. For JQA2's letter of acceptance, see BAdv, 1 Oct 1872, 4.

28. An instance of HA's assigning a medieval subject to one of his students (George Edward Woodberry) is given in John Erskine, *The Memory of Certain Persons*, Phila & NY 1947, 156.

29. The quotations are from HA's earliest publication concerning Sohm: [HA], "*Die altdeutsche Reichs- und Gerichtsverfassung.* 1. Band." Nation, 27 Aug 1874. Haskell's *Index* attributes the notice to HA.

30. The portrait of JQA evidently was the one by Gilbert Stuart and

Thomas Sully. See Andrew Oliver, *Portraits of John Quincy Adams and His Wife*, Camb 1970, 130.

31. J. Laurence Laughlin, "Some Recollections of Henry Adams," *Scribner's Magazine*, May 1921, 576–79.

32. CFA2, Diary, 3 Jun 1872, AP. At the time, CFA2 was readying to give a political oration at Quincy on 4 Jul 1872.

33. *Nation*, 26 Jan 1871; ibid., 3 Aug 1871.

34. Mildred Howells, ed., *Life in Letters of William Dean Howells*, Garden City NY 1928, I, 172.

35. On 24 Oct 1872, the *Nation* reported that Thomas Sargeant Perry "will have charge of the [*North American*] *Review* in the absence of Mr. Lowell and Mr. Henry Adams."

36. The suggestion that CFA2 was the never-divulged author of "The Political Campaign of 1872" is mine. See *Sketches*, 239. Confirmation of his authorship may be found by comparing the article in content with a speech CFA2 gave at Quincy on 30 Sep 1872. The latter was published in BAdv, 1 Oct 1872, under the heading "Cincinnati and Louisville."

CFA2's authorship may have been guessed by, or confidentially told to, the *Nation*. On 24 Oct 1872, after saying that "The Political Campaign of 1872" was "the article which will attract most attention in the October *North American*," Godkin's weekly dilated on its contents respectfully at exceptional length.

37. CFA2, Diary, 27 Jun 1872, AP; CFA2 to CFA, 28 Jun 1872, AP.

38. CFA2 to CFA, 28 Jun 1872, AP.

39. CFA2's attitude concerning a present is clearest in his writing to CFA, 12 Jul 1872, AP: ". . . if Brooks hasn't done anything, ask him to hold on and consult Henry,—I know Henry prefers that,—and then do the very handsome thing and go halves with me. I don't at all care what or how much I give,—it only comes once."

40. CFA2, Diary, 8 Jul 1872, AP.

41. Henry and Clover so conducted their travels in 1872–1873 that she went to many places he earlier had visited or lived in. She thus came a long way towards overtaking him in knowledge of Europe.

42. The phrase is drawn from a letter written by MHA while on a later journey. On 2 Nov 1879, she wrote to her father from Madrid, Thoron, 195: "The country to the south of us is flooded and it will be folly to move until this spell is broken. We made the fatal mistake of going to Venice seven years ago in such weather, and my impression of it is such that nothing would make me willing to go back . . . ."

43. Lodge's account includes HA's first reply. See Lodge, *Early Memories*, 225–40.

44. In old age, to the delight of his niece, Louisa Hooper, HA took a photograph of himself in her presence. In the photograph, his hands are together and are blurred. See L, V, frontispiece. In the 1950s and 1960s, telling me about his action, LHT explained that HA moved his hands while actuating a mechanism that permitted the tripping of the shutter from a distance.

In the photograph of HA taken on the *Isis* at Christmastime in 1872–1873 and again in the photographs taken at Wenlock Abbey in 1873, HA's hands are together. In view of this repeating phenomenon, I conclude that *he* —not MHA—took the photograph of him aboard the *Isis*.

45. The photograph of Abu Simbel by HA reproduced in Thoron, opp. 70, can fairly be called a standard view, taken from an easy-to-find location. Thus it cannot be the photograph he described to Gaskell.

46. Information given to me by Aileen Tone.

47. In 1930 and 1936, sufficient letters by HA and MHA were published to provide an unbroken account of their wedding journey. See Ford, I, and Thoron. The account nowhere suggested a serious impairment of the health of HA or MHA during the journey. Other evidence then available nowhere indicated a serious impairment. Neither did any evidence indicate so much as a suspicion of a serious impairment.

In my judgment, the same condition obtains at the present time. With a single exception that is not an exception—a statement made in 1947—*there is no evidence of a serious impairment during the journey.*

On the fiftieth page of the "Biographical Introduction" at the front of *Henry Adams and His Friends* (1947), Harold Dean Cater turned to an important matter: the breakdown experienced by MHA *in 1885* prior to her committing suicide. He said:

> . . . she was not herself. A kind of nervous collapse had set in, accompanied by depression. Of this condition Henry had always been apprehensive, ever since there had been a severe strain from it on the Nile in 1872, caused by boredom from the sun, the flat landscape, and the unpredictable winds.

In support of the closing sentence, Cater supplied note 110, cxiv:

> Confidential source. There is an interesting letter from Mrs. Adams to Mrs. Samuel Ward, in the Houghton Library at Harvard University, which may confirm it.

The evidence available to me indicates that, when he thus alleged a severe strain experienced by MHA on the Nile in 1872, Cater published a fabrication for which he himself was principally accountable. With luck, the "severe strain" he alleged could have been looked into in 1947 by additional researchers; the "confidential source" on which he claimed to depend could perhaps have been brought forward; and the "source," if a living person, could have been asked to give details and supporting evidence. No inquiry was made. Just the opposite, beginning in 1955, the "severe strain" was re-alleged by a parade of other writers. Thus what began as a one-man affair turned into an affair for which many persons are accountable.

The allegation and the re-allegations are best treated separately.

Cater's note 110 was grossly in error in saying that a letter from MHA to Mrs. Samuel Ward might confirm the alleged severe strain. The letter is to *Mr.* Samuel Ward and is one of two letters by MHA containing matched passages saying that she and HA *improved* in health on the Nile. (See the quotations in the text to which this note relates.)

I became suspicious that the alleged severe strain was a fabrication in 1966 while completing a chronological study of the evidence then available to me for use in writing this book. On 21 Nov 1966, I wrote to Louisa Hooper Thoron asking her help with regard to what I thought a fabrication. I said, ". . . I believe there is no foundation whatever for the 'severe strain' in Egypt idea." ". . . [Cater's] statement is incredible and ridiculous on its face; for no one who has read the letters Mrs. Adams wrote while in

Egypt would think of saying anything about 'boredom from the sun, the flat landscape, and the unpredictable winds.' The phrase is obviously written in the language of someone who imagines Egypt as one sort of place, while Mrs. Adams's letters show it to have been a very different one. There is also the objection that Mrs. Adams's letters (and her husband's) indicate no serious strains for her in Egypt, and indicate on the contrary that their plan of going there for health, relaxation, and renewal was a complete success." In the same letter, I asked Mrs. Thoron to make inquiries about the claimed "confidential source." Especially I asked her to ascertain whether the "source" was an intimate friend of hers, Abigail Adams Homans.

Mrs. Thoron had independently concluded that the alleged severe strain was an "error" (one of her euphemisms for fabrication). She phoned me on 22 Nov & 1 Dec 1966. In the interval between the calls, she made energetic inquiries in the Boston area. She learned to her satisfaction that Mrs. Homans was not the claimed "source." Her effort only slightly settled for her who was.

On the phone, she volunteered two items of Hooper-family data. One item concerned Ellen Hooper Potter, her elder sister. Mrs. Thoron explained that, near the start of Cater's interviews with persons who had dealings with HA and MHA, she herself said in passing that Ellen had "not reacted well" to Egypt when she and Ellen were "on the Nile" in 1904; that Ellen was "upset by the dust." She conjectured that her remark "may have encouraged" Cater to form impressions and get into conversations the end result of which was an "error" relating to their Aunt Clover. (The quoted words are Mrs. Thoron's.)

The other item concerned her younger sister, Mabel Hooper La Farge, who lived till 1944, and who had separate talks with Cater when he was starting his interviews. Mrs. Thoron wished me to know that Mabel "embroidered"—"had too much imagination, although she believed in her own tales." Without stressing the point, she said there was a possibility that something "embroidered" by Mabel, something that was false but imagined, believed, and told as fact, had a share in the development of Cater's eventual "error" concerning their Aunt Clover.

Mrs. Thoron did not believe that Cater was referring to her sister Mabel when he used the phrase "confidential source." On the contrary, she was inclined to think that the "source" was a person still living in the Boston area in 1947 and, too, in 1966. Also she had become distrustful of Cater, as I had. Rightly or wrongly, we joined in preferring that questions about the "source" not be put directly to him.

What she and I were left with was a shared belief that fabrication occurred in the period 1942–1947, more or less as follows:

– Louisa Hooper Thoron remarked to Cater that Ellen Hooper Potter "did not react well" "on the Nile"—was "upset by the dust";
– reminded by Cater of Ellen's reaction, Mabel Hooper La Farge *possibly* embroidered in his hearing;
– a person not-to-be-identified became what Cater would call a "source" and talked with him about matters relating to "the Nile";
– during or after Cater's talks with the "source," Ellen and 1904 were phased out; Marian Hooper Adams and 1872 were phased in;

– "did not react well" was phased out; "a severe strain" was phased in;
– "upset" was phased out; and a "condition"—"nervous collapse . . . accompanied by depression"—was phased in;
– "by the dust" was phased out; and "caused by boredom from the sun, the flat landscape, and the unpredictable winds" was phased in;
– as a capstone or climax, another idea appeared: that HA during about twelve years of marriage was "apprehensive" that MHA would undergo a *second* "severe strain."

To me, it also seemed that Cater, when writing his "Biographical Introduction," so confusingly worded his sentences that many readers would honestly not be sure that his allegation was: namely that MHA when on the Nile in 1872 experienced a severe strain from a condition (a kind of nervous collapse accompanied by depression) caused by boredom from the sun, the flat landscape, and the unpredictable winds.

On 10 May 1967, when he submitted suggested corrections to Octagon Press for a reissue of his book, Cater showed no disposition to withdraw or alter his allegation. Neither did he disclose the "confidential source" he claimed in note 110. (I have his list of corrections.) To the best of my knowledge, his claimed "source" has not since been identified.

The principal writers who have re-alleged Cater's allegation are:

Elizabeth Stevenson (*Henry Adams*, 1955, 110–12);
J. C. Levenson (*Mind and Art of Henry Adams*, 1957, 197);
Jack Shepherd (*Adams Chronicles*, 1975, 394);
Otto Friedrich (*Clover*, 1979, 162–65);
William Dusinberre (*Henry Adams/ Myth of Failure*, 1980, 61–71);
Eugenia Kaledin (*Education of Mrs. Henry Adams*, 1981, 124–26);
Levenson/Samuels/Vandersee/Winner (*Letters of Henry Adams*, 1982, II, 80, 644n2); and
Paul C. Nagel (*Descent from Glory*, 1983, 264–67).

The writers fall into two groups: those whose main concern is HA and those whose main concern is MHA. Friedrich and Kaledin form the MHA group. The others form the HA group.

The relevant passages by the writers are fully as remarkable for what they do *not* say as for what they *do* say. Every writer in the HA group avoids mentioning or citing Cater while re-alleging a severe strain experienced by MHA on the Nile. The writers in the MHA group do mention Cater while re-alleging a severe strain but avoid citing the pages in his book where his allegation and note 110 appear.

Friedrich excepted, the writers avoid quoting or repeating Cater's phrase "caused by boredom from the sun, the flat landscape, and the unpredictable winds." They instead pick and choose among its terms. Without acknowledgment, Stevenson appropriates "the flat landscape" but recasts the phrase as "the limited variety of the river." Without acknowledgment, Levenson and Nagel appropriate "boredom" but drop "from the sun." Levenson alleges plain "boredom." Nagel intensifies the allegation, introducing "her enemy, boredom." All the writers ignore Cater's "by the unpredictable winds."

Friedrich excepted, the writers do not quote or repeat Cater's "severe strain."

Without acknowledgment, Stevenson, Shepherd, Dusinberre, Kaledin, and Nagel appropriate Cater's "depression." Shepherd intensifies the allegation, introducing "a deep depression." Dusinberre conflates two of Cater's terms and alleges "severe depression."

Friedrich excepted, the writers do not quote Cater's "A kind of nervous collapse." Without acknowledgment, Kaledin appropriates the phrase and recasts it as "some sort of nervous collapse." Without acknowledgment, Nagel appropriates "nervous collapse," intensifies the allegation, and introduces "serious nervous collapse."

The writers are far from liking the allegation that MHA, in 1872, suffered a collapse of *nerves*. Stevenson instead alleges a "downward spiral of her *emotions* [italics added]" and Levenson alleges that "Her high *spirits* faltered, then collapsed [italics added]."

Disposed to hedge, yet also intensify, Friedrich says, "Clover apparently suffered an attack of profound depression, which may have brought her to *the edge of a nervous breakdown* [italics added]." He turns to a variant allegation made by another writer (Francis Russell) that MHA suffered " 'a brief neurasthenic collapse.' " He continues by saying, ". . . there is no documentary evidence for such a clinical statement, and it is quite possible, as often happens with attacks of madness, that there was nothing sudden, no specific symptoms that a psychiatrist could identify with any confidence. Clover's letters reveal nothing, nor do Henry's. . . ." By these means, Friedrich introduces the very hedged but very strong allegation that MHA may have been attacked by madness without exhibiting symptoms and that her condition may thus have been imperceptible to her; also to her husband.

Without acknowledgment, Levenson/Samuels/Vandersee/Winner fasten on Friedrich's phrase "to the edge of a nervous breakdown," phase out "to the edge of" and "nervous," phase in "psychological," and state as an established fact that MHA while on the Nile suffered a "psychological breakdown."

All the writers present an appearance of knowing *the time* when the alleged severe strain occurred. Yet not one reveals that, of the 88 days HA and MHA were aboard the *Isis* and afloat on the Nile, 27 fell in 1872 and 61 fell in 1873. Moreover, none attaches dates to the alleged severe strain.

Stevenson alleges that, after arriving in Egypt, MHA became "painfully irresolute," "cast down," and "lacking in enthusiasm"; that her mood was one of "apathy" and "slow, dull care"; that she grew "distrustful of self"; that she suffered a dire feeling of "isolation" that grew more dire as wife and husband approached their farthest point into Africa; and that there at last was a "near tragedy," presumably meaning that MHA verged on committing suicide.

This cascade of allegations might seem to affirm both a date and a place, but Stevenson's version of Nile geography is imaginary. In her account, the temple of Abu Simbel is one of several "lost monuments" the travelers passed *en route to* their farthest point "into Africa." Creative geography goes hand in hand with omitted dates. The "near tragedy" is merely alleged to have occurred towards the *latter* part of the couple's journey up the river.

Levenson ventures a date-without-dates. He alleges that a collapse of spirits occurred during "a two-and-a-half-week gap in Mrs. Adams' letters." According to the letters, however, Levenson's alleged gap does not exist. There is a 16–day interval from 5 to 21 Dec 1872 between two of MHA's letters *to her father*. But she says that during the interval she has written *to her brother's wife*.

One may add that Levenson's fallacious gap occurred during the *earlier* part of the couple's journey up the river. Levenson and Stevenson are thus at loggerheads when gesturing towards, but not giving, dates.

Shepherd specifies *the place*. With the air of a writer referring to a known event, he says, "Neither [HA nor MHA] mentioned [in their letters] that during their visit to the Temple of Karnak on the Nile, Marian had suffered from a deep depression." He cites no evidence in support of this very firm allegation; he does not explain that MHA was within visiting distance of the temple of Karnak both on the way up the Nile and on the way down; and he fails to say that available evidence is wholly silent concerning her ever being at the temple, much less being deeply depressed there. (The evidence does show that *HA* photographed the temple in late February 1873 while descending the river.)

Friedrich is swayed enough by Shepherd's unsupported allegation of a place to say, "At about this point, perhaps at Karnak, something important seems to have happened." Dusinberre treats the Karnak suggestion as better dropped. Without acknowledgment, Kaledin reverts to Levenson's fallacious "two-and-a-half week gap" and changes it to a fallacious "two weeks" during which MHA "ceased writing letters." Nagel suggests neither place nor date.

Thus, after 28 years of re-allegation (1955–1983), Cater's successors end without having a credible time or a credible place to offer.

Beginning in 1960 or soon after, matters were complicated by new testimony, or rather old testimony at last made accessible. Qualified visitors to the Massachusetts Historical Society were permitted to read and copy a private record—an entry written by CFA2 on 3 May 1891 in his Memorabilia, 1888–1893.

CFA2's entry concerns himself, HA, MHA, and other persons. It is long and complicated.

I take CFA2's 1891 entry and Cater's 1947 allegation to be different in motive. I believe that Cater was guilty of a fabrication that was not knowingly harmful but instead was mere attempted "scholarship." Differently, in my judgment, CFA2's entry can be shown to have been written with intent to harm. (See Chap. 27.) It can be added that his effort to harm is in process of failing. It is failing because the entry consists in part of fabrications. For an instance of fabrication, see note 6, above.

Here two assertions made in CFA2's entry are relevant. One is his allegation that MHA suffered from a "hereditary," "organic" "tendency to suicidal mania." The other is his claim that he was told by HA in December 1885 that MHA underwent *three* intervals of impairment, the last being fatal.

At first sight, these 1891 assertions by CFA2 may seem to confirm part or most of Cater's 1947 allegation. Studied seriously, the assertions instead reveal themselves as *not* supportive. Cater alleges two intervals of impairment, dating both. CFA2's assertions allege *three* intervals and fails to date the first and second.

Shepherd, Friedrich, Dusinberre, Kaledin, Levenson/Samuels/Vandersee/Winner, and Nagel were all more or less apprised of CFA2's 1891 entry before they published their re-allegations that MHA suffered a severe strain while on the Nile.

The writer most strongly affected is Dusinberre. By conflating things said by CFA2 and Cater, he establishes for himself that the first interval of impairment that CFA2 alleges and the "severe strain" that Cater alleges are one and the same; also that the alleged first interval thus has a date, the one alleged by Cater, "1872." Wanting a date for the second interval, Dusinberre finds what to him seems a likely moment, and says, broadly, what he thinks it is.

Dusinberre's energetic example considered, subsequent writers might be expected to articulate detailed accounts of *three* intervals of impairment for MHA. Such accounts are made to seem the more imminent by Dusinberre's saying that MHA's alleged third interval in 1885, ending in suicide, is "*less* well-documented [italics added]" than what he takes to be the first interval, on the Nile. But in fact the subsequent writers do not offer accounts of three intervals. Interest in three simply stops. With respect to what happened on the Nile, the allegations offered by Kaledin and Nagel repeat with minor changes the allegations made by writers prior to Dusinberre.

One reason for failure to produce a detailed account of what happened on the Nile is the admitted peculiarity of the evidence. Stevenson and Levenson acknowledge that evidence of MHA's having undergone a severe strain is sparse. Levenson reports that "no word" of evidence to support an alleged severe strain in 1872 can be found in HA's letters. Stevenson says there is "no witness except her [MHA's] own words in her letters."

Friedrich voices louder warnings. He raises the possibility that the alleged strain in 1872 is a "story"—indeed a story of new vintage. He says, "The origin of the story about Clover's breakdown on her honeymoon seems to lie in Harold Dean Cater's *Henry Adams and His Friends* . . . published in 1947." He quotes Cater's allegation in full; also he adverts to Cater's note; and he states that the allegation has small support at best. Finally, as if half-disbelieving his own very hedged but very strong allegation of a possible attack of madness without symptoms (hence imperceptible), he half-confidently says, ". . . although we lack the basic details of Clover's breakdown, her letters home do seem to reverberate with a certain ill-defined unhappiness."

Of course the difference between madness and a certain ill-defined unhappiness is a large difference—indeed a contradiction.

In my opinion, a fabrication does not gain truth and credibility if many writers in succession play follow-the-leader, repeat the fabrication, and declare the existence of a consensus. Kaledin declares the existence of a consensus. She says, "It is generally accepted that Clover . . . experienced some sort of nervous collapse. . . ."

Kaledin further says *there always was a consensus.* ". . . Cater's interviews with friends of Henry Adams suggest that there can be little doubt of such an illness. . . ." With these words, she initiates a new fabrication. She pretends that "friends" of Adams voiced a consensus about an illness when interviewed by Cater. But which friends? She does not list them—and no wonder. Cater names no such friends.

What *is* offered as evidence by most of the repeaters of Cater's allegation is excerpts from MHA's contemporary letters.

Stevenson tries to show that MHA experienced a "downward spiral of her emotions" by quoting first one and next a battery of seven excerpts from MHA's letters "torn out of context." (The phrase is Stevenson's.) Levenson, Friedrich, Dusinberre, Kaledin, and Nagel quote the same or similar excerpts from letters by MHA.

The excerpts fall into two groups. One group supports the following conclusions: that MHA liked America; that she liked New England's seasons; that she missed New England's autumn foliage; that she missed her father and other relations; and that, when in Egypt, she sometimes missed her father strongly and felt very far from home. But the excerpts in this group do *not* support nor even nearly support such conclusions as that MHA when in Egypt fell into "apathy" or felt a dire sense of "isolation" (Stevenson); suffered "a devastating homesickness for her father" (Levenson); "languished" (Dusinberre); was thrown into "momentary despair" (Kaledin); or experienced the Nile journey as an "ordeal" (Nagel). The accounts of unrelieved and near-disastrous suffering offered by Stevenson, Levenson, Dusinberre, Kaledin, and Nagel are each consistent in a novelistic way, but each is out of harmony with MHA's letters taken whole and also out of harmony with the very excerpts produced to enrich the imagined "misery" (Stevenson).

The other group of excerpts consists of passages taken by the writers from MHA's letters as evidence of what they allege is "abnormal self-abasement" (Stevenson), "self-reproach" (Levenson), and "self-loathing" (Nagel)."

It is helpful to see one such passage in context. Writing to her father from the *Isis* on 3 Jan 1873, MHA says, Thoron 66:

> We lunched among the ruins of the Memnonium and wandered about, trying to imagine how it looked when we were three thousand years younger than we are now. We took [photographed?] the two colossi on our way back, and to me they far surpass anything else. They look like monuments to patience, as if time could have no effect on them. But it is useless to try and tell you how it all looks. *I never seem to get impressions that are worth anything, and feel as if I were blind and deaf and dumb too* [italics added; the line is quoted by Stevenson, Friedrich, Dusinberre, and Kaledin]. The fields are green and filled with sweet flowers and it is hard to imagine that you have snow and ice.

In the passage, as should be clear, MHA does not merely reproach herself. She *deprecates* herself, and strongly.

MHA's self-deprecation is a problem, yet not a problem that is hard to solve, nor a problem that anyone writing about her for publication would have any excuse not to solve. For the solution is given outright by the evidence. Two letters are especially pertinent. One is a letter Clover wrote to her father from Venice on 20 Oct 1872; the other a letter she wrote nine years earlier, on 11 Oct 1863, to her six-year-old niece, Mabel Chapin.

In the letter to her father, Thoron, 51, Clover points to a solution of the problem. She tells him that a letter she has received from her sister Ellen, said by Ellen within the letter to be "stupid," is in fact informative and "delightful."

In the letter to her niece, FTKP, Clover says she is unable to *print* a letter properly. On the first page, she says:

> I wish I could print as well as my brother Ned does. I think you and Hermie will laugh when you see this. *It looks just as if a fly had dipped his legs into the ink-stand and scrabbled all over the paper* [italics added]."

On the second page, she pens a sketch of her dog Scalawag on his back asleep with his feet in the air. Next to Scalawag she pens a sketch of a four-footed fly. She signs the letter by drawing a clover.

What matters is that the printing, although original in style, is neat, uniform, and wholly legible, and the drawings are clear and deft. For what is shown by the strong self-deprecation in Clover's letters, early and late; also by the strong self-deprecation in the letters of her sister Ellen; also by the strong self-deprecation in the letters of their niece Louisa Hooper Thoron, is that self-deprecation was a Hooper trait, a Hooper indulgence, a Hooper pleasure, and above all a Hooper means of effectual self-discipline and self-improvement.

There remains a letter by HA to Anna Ward, written on 22 Dec 1885, less than three weeks after MHA's suicide. Speaking both for himself and MHA (almost as if MHA is living), HA says, L, II, 644:

> Clover was always warmly attached to you. She has much regretted to have seen you so little. . . . You were closely associated with the heaviest trials and keenest pleasures of our life.

The first writer to quote this letter as evidence is Kaledin. She quotes the words beginning with "closely" and ending with "life."

Levenson/Samuels/Vandersee/Winner publish the letter and gloss it, saying with attempted authority, L, II, 644n2:

> The Wards and the Adamses were frequently together in the winter of 1872–73, when both couples were traveling on the Nile. The "heaviest trials" apparently refers to Marian Adams' breakdown at that time.

The gloss shows inattention to evidence and ignorance of evidence. It should be noticed that HA says "trials"—plural—and the "trials" are assertedly shared by husband and wife. It should be noticed also that a list of heavy trials experienced by HA and MHA in 1872–1873, complete with dates and places, is given in the writings of two authorities who were there. These authorities were HA and MHA.

If their evidence is a guide, the probable worst trial was Clover's "real terror" at 114 Beacon Street in Boston on February 27, 1872, when leaving the ice-world she had to escape. (Anna Ward was close enough to MHA when on the Nile to be told what a break-out from a New England ice-world was like.) The probable next-worst trial was the deluge of rain that fell on the Adamses (also the Wards) during October 1872 in Italy. The probable third-worst trial—and *not* a bad one—was the hard, cold north wind the Adamses and Wards experienced below Luxor in the period 16–28 Feb 1873 while descending the Nile.

Notice should be taken of the probable third-worst, the one that was not very bad. Writing to her father on 20 Feb 1873, MHA reports that she and HA have just visited Samuel and Anna Ward. She says:

> We made a long call on the *Lotus* and vote the Nile in such weather a *trial* [italics added].

It would be typical of MHA if "Nile" and "trial" originated with her, for they rhyme and the rhyme is funny, enjoyable, and memorable. And it is typical of MHA and HA that an enjoyably funny rhyme which they shared with the Wards in 1873 was remembered and echoed by HA in 1885 when writing to Anna Ward on his own and MHA's behalf.

One might suppose that biographers, editors, and critics writing about MHA would show awareness of her sense of humor. Unfortunately, her humorous touches can be so unexpected and so much in her individual style that commentators of poor or indifferent ability as readers cannot hear her voice, catch her inflection, know her meaning is funny, or enjoy what she says.

Should anyone wish to persist in alleging that MHA had a breakdown of nerves, emotions, spirits, or psychology during the Nile journey, the persister can claim no support in HA's "heaviest trials" and none in MHA's saying that the Nile weather on certain days was voted by two couples to be a "trial." Indeed the persister can find support *nowhere* in presently available evidence, Cater's exceptionable words excepted.

What is more important, any persister will persist against a current of testimony by MHA. Her last testimony is the strongest. In a letter to her father from Naples on 16 Mar 1873, she says, Thoron, 86:

> . . . Isis . . . protected us so lovingly for three months.

The words make clear that, among the several phases of her and her husband's wedding journey till that March day, she thought the happiest and best was the phase on the Nile. That is *her* summary. There is neither reason nor evidence to dispute it.

13. By an Atom

Letters by and to HA are in HA-micro 3 or 4, unless otherwise noted.

PRINCIPAL SOURCES

(1) twenty-six letters, HA to CMG, 4 Mar 1873–24 May 1875.
(2) twelve letters, MHA to RWH, 11 Mar–23 Jul 1873, Thoron, 80–134.
(3) three letters, MHA to CMG, 18 May 1873, Ford, I, 248–49; 17 May 1874, 29 Mar 1875, AP.
(4) nine letters, HA to Lodge, 11 Jun 1873–30 Dec 1874.
(5) letter, HA to Garfield, 13 Dec 1873, L, II, 185.

(6) letter, HA to Bowles, 23 Apr 1874, L, II, 191–92.

(7) letter, HA to Cunliffe, 6 Jul 1874.

(8) letter, HA to James Freeman Clarke, 20 Nov 1874.

(9) letters, HA to Schurz, 26 Dec 1874, 12 Apr 1875, L, II, 214–15, 222.

(10) letters, HA to Wells, 16, 20 Apr 1875, L, II, 222–23.

(11) an unsigned book notice, [HA], "[Sohm's] *Die altdeutsche Reichs- und Gerichtsverfassung.* I. Band." *Nation*, 27 Aug 1874. (Attributed to HA in Haskell's *Index of Contributors*.)

(12) an initialed book notice, H. A., "Freeman's History of the Norman Conquest," *NAR*, Jan 1874, 176–81; and eleven unsigned book notices by HA in *NAR* issues, as follows:

"Coulanges's Ancient City," Apr 1874, 390–97;

"Saturday Review Sketches and Essays," Apr 1874, 401–05;

"Sohm's Procedure de la Lex Salica," Apr 1874, 416–25;

"Stubbs's Constitutional History of England," Jul 1874, 233–44;

"Kitchin's History of France," Oct 1874, 442–47;

"Parkman's Old Regime in Canada," Jan 1875, 175–85;

"Von Holst's Administration of Andrew Jackson," Jan 1875, 179–85;

"The Quincy Memoirs and Speeches," Jan 1875, 235–36;

"Bancroft's History of the United States," Apr 1875, 424–32;

"Maine's Early History of Institutions," Apr 1875, 432–38;

"Palgrave's Poems," Apr, 1875, 438–44.

(The notices appear in *Sketches*, 77–174.)

(13) [HA], *The Radical Club. A Poem, respectfully dedicated to the Infinite. By an Atom.*—as published in the *Boston Times*, 8 May 1875. (Attributed to HA by LHT in August 1950; here attributed to HA largely on the basis of data furnished by LHT, 1955–1962.)

ADDITIONAL SOURCES; COMMENTS

1. Available evidence uniformly attests that HA and MHA when married confided in one another unfailingly.

2. MHA to RWH, 7 Aug 1872, Thoron, 24.

3. It can be assumed also that HA was especially affected by a third passage in *Middlemarch*. In Chap. 56, noting that Middlemarch (the community) belongs to a "hundred" (a division of a county), Eliot touches upon the subject HA assigned himself as a researcher studying medieval England.

4. MHA's copy of *Middlemarch* is missing. Her copy of *Pilgrim's Progress*, Lond 1875, FTKP, is a facsimile of the first edition.

5. *Henry James Letters*, I, 360.

6. The death of LAK elicited two statements from CFA. In the earlier, he tells how he reacted at Quincy after reading the cable from Florence saying his eldest child had died. "I rushed out, and wandered in the most solitary portion of my pastures, endeavoring to collect my faculties." See CFA to HA, 18 Jul 1870. In the later, he says that, in Florence, Charles Kuhn proposed taking him and BA for a drive; that the carriage stopped at the iron gate of a cemetery; and that he was told his daughter Louisa was buried therein. Recording the episode— Diary, 4 Jan 1872, AP—CFA avoids saying whether he left the carriage and visited her grave. He evokes the gloomy day, the wintry street, and flowers

killed by frost. He especially dwells on her being buried in "solitude." "This was said to have been her desire, and I had no right to draw in question her decision. But it all contributes to my inclination to get out of Florence."

7. CFA2 to his wife, 27–28 Mar 1872, AP.

8. For titles, see Cushing's *Index of Writers*; also *Sketches*, 75, 102–12, 250.

9. LHT to myself, 26 Jun 1952—"Aunt Ellen married at 30 years old, in '68. Hers was a very lover-like marriage though she had kept refusing E. W. G. . . . . She was supposed to have been broken-hearted over some man who was killed in the war."

10. CFA2's dissemblings concerning HA and MHA apparently began more or less at the moment he learned of their having the use of Gaskell's Park Lane house. Paul C. Nagel says concerning this period, ". . . when Charles was in London while Henry and Clover were also in town, he carefully avoided them." See *Descent from Glory*, 266. The statement might seem correct, for CFA2's writings can convey an impression of avoidance. See for example CFA2 to CFA, 1 Jun 1873, AP. But the statement is in error. CFA2 unquestionably stayed two days with HA and MHA at 28 Norfolk Street and shared one of their dinners.

11. Lowell to MHA, [22] Jun 1873, HA-micro 4; Lowell to HA, 27 Jun 1873. The letter dated June 27 is in rhyme.

12. Henry James, Jr., had earlier written the notable words "the genius of my beloved country—in the person of Miss Hooper." See HJ to Grace Norton, 20 May 1870, *Henry James Letters*, I, 240.

13. The photograph appears in L, II, 158.

14. CFA to HA, 29 Apr 1873.

15. Wilkins, *Clarence King*, 179, 205.

16. Perry, *Life and Letters of Henry Lee Higginson*, op. cit., 283. The financial histories of Henry Higginson and Henry and Marian Adams appear to have taken parallel courses, but how much the Adamses were assisted by Higginson as a stock broker is unclear. Every summer in 1870–1875, Henry and Ida Higginson rented a cottage at Beverly Farms. See ibid., 275.

17. Nagel, *Descent from Glory*, 268.

18. Edward Hooper managed several financial interests. His daughter Louisa remembered, "My father looked out for the Sturgis & Hooper trusts which gave Cousin Bel [daughter of Alice Sumner] . . . lots more money (through 'Uncle Sam H.') than my grandfather Robert H. had." Source: LHT to Helen P. Chalfant, 9 Aug 1963.

19. On 24 Oct 1872, the *Nation* reported that Thomas Sargeant Perry "will have charge of the *Review* in the absence of Mr. Lowell and Mr. Henry Adams." The choice of Perry was Howells's doing. See *Life in Letters of William Dean Howells*, op. cit., I, 172.

20. In his *Early Memories*, 240–41, Lodge erroneously recalls that HA told him he had just been made editor of *NAR*. The evidence is clear that HA's editorship never lapsed; it merely went into abeyance. Perry brought out six issues.

21. Young, Emerton, and McVane later taught courses in medieval history at Harvard that HA had introduced, and Lodge later inherited the course HA introduced in American colonial history. See Stewart Mitchell,

"Henry Adams and Some of His Students," MHS *Proceedings*, 66 (1936–1941), 296; also Lindsay Swift, "A Course in History at Harvard College in the Seventies," MHS *Proceedings*, 52 (1918–1919), 71.

22. HA attended faculty meetings on 23 Sep, 13, 25 Oct, 24 Nov, 15 Dec 1873; 12, 19 Jan 1874. See Faculty Records, 1873–1874, HUA.

23. Gail Hamilton, *Biography of James G. Blaine*, Norwich CT 1895, 276–77, 286.

24. Donald says HA and MHA stayed with Sumner. See *Charles Sumner and the Rights of Man*, 583. In fact, they stayed with Hooper and only visited Sumner.

25. HA to Cunliffe, 6 Mar 1871. In 1872, the Friday Club became "The Club," meeting on the second Tuesday of each month at Parker's in Boston. As listed on 10 Apr 1872, there were fourteen members other than HA: J. M. Crafts, John Fiske, John Chipman Gray, Jr., Charles E. Grinnell, Charles Hale, Oliver Wendell Holmes, Jr., Henry James, Jr., William James, John Torrey Morse, Jr., Thomas Sergeant Perry, J. C. Ropes, Arthur G. Sedgwick, Moorfield Storey, and W. P. Walley. See Sheldon M. Novick, *Honorable Justice/ The Life of Oliver Wendell Holmes*, Bost 1989, 433n44. Of the fourteen members, HA is known to have had important dealings with all but Crafts, Sedgwick, and Walley.

26. Mrs. John T. Sargent, ed., *Sketches and Reminiscences of the Radical Club* . . . , Bost 1880, especially "Origins of The Club." The volume provides samples of the papers and discussions but fails to date them. There seems a possibility that Ellen and Clover Hooper attended occasional early meetings or were even early members.

27. Lilian Whiting, *Louise Chandler Moulton/ Poet and Friend*, Bost 1910, 58.

28. L, II, 449.

29. The historian of early England praised by HA as "much the greatest" was Sir Francis Palgrave. See *EHA* (1907), 185; (LoA), 916. Palgrave was Jewish by parentage but became a convert to Christianity. At the front of *Essays in Anglo-Saxon Law*, Bost 1876, HA and his students cite "TURNER, SHARON. The History of the Anglo-Saxons. London, 1852." Turner was the preeminent collector of Anglo-Saxon manuscripts in England. He was Jewish. The evidence is clear that HA, as a historian of England, felt affinities with the elder Palgrave, and possibly Turner, and aspired to rival them in industry and disinterestedness.

For the thread that he was following, see Chap. 14.

30. *Sketches*, xi–xii, 222–50.

31. HA persuaded CFA to write anonymous notices of two books CFA himself had edited, Vols. II & III of the *Memoirs of John Quincy Adams*. See CFA, Diary, 3, 5 Sep, 5–13 Dec, 1874, AP; also *NAR*, Oct 1874, 472–76, Jan 1875, 231–35. CFA's notices can fairly be described as excellent introductions to the volumes. His authorship was later withheld from Cushing. In his indexes, the notices are by-passed.

32. *Sketches*, ix–xi.

33. Two maps, FTKP, are relevant. One, c. 10″ × 15″, shows added tracts bought by HA at Beverly Farms. It bears sellers' names in HA's hand and notes in an unidentified hand. The other, c. 24" × 30", is dated 28 Jan 1886. It shows tracts bought by HA at Beverly Farms in the period 1875–1884 and in an unidentified hand gives the sellers' names. The

maps agree in indicating that HA bought lots from Preston and Perry in 1875, J. Elliot Cabot in 1878, and T. K. Lothrop in 1884; but neither map indicates the dimensions of any lot.

According to *Valuations and Assessments of the Town of Beverly*, 1886, HA owned a house, a stable, and 22 acres of land. The assessments totaled $24,400.

34. "Advertising versus Death," *Index*, 19 Nov 1874. The article says a Boston newspaper had suggested that "R. W. L." might be the Rev. Rowland Connor. The suggestion seems not to have carried conviction.

35. All but Samuel Longfellow and Wasson are pilloried by HA in *The Radical Club*. Why Longfellow escaped is unclear. Wasson had HA's respect. When the obituary by "R. W. L." appeared in the *Tribune*, HA was publishing Wasson's "The Modern Type of Oppression," *NAR*, Oct 1874, Art. I. A sophisticated analysis, Wasson's article bears reading in connection with HA's radicalism and his interest in the contrasting political outlooks of Washington and Jefferson.

36. That HA read the obituary is most evidenced by his achieving the object "R. W. L." only part-accomplished, the murder of the club. For evidence that MHA read the obituary, see Chap. 14.

37. Samuels, *The Young Henry Adams*, op. cit., 245–46, 340–41.

38. Thomas Wentworth Higginson, "The Boston Radical Club," *Index*, 19 Nov 1874.

39. According to Frank Luther Mott, *A History of American Magazines/1865–1885*, Camb MA 1957, 78, Abbot, then a minister, started *The Index* in 1870 in Toledo at the suggestion and with the aid of "Petroleum V. Nasby" (David R. Locke). He moved it to Boston in 1873.

40. T. W. Higginson, "Boston Radical Club," op. cit. His rejoinder asks a pointed question and gives a weakly defensive answer. "Why is it that this particular Club attracts such exceptional attention? It certainly does not invite remark; it meets at a private house; the members present cards at the door; professional reporters are excluded. All authentic reports are written by members of the Club, and sometimes even these have been prohibited. The Club . . . has no work for which advertising is essential. It is simply a modest, private gathering, converted by public attention into an affair of general interest."

41. That HA favored equality across the board was evident in his current writings. In *Sketches*, see No. 1 for equality for students as against teachers and administrators. See No. 9 for equality for mothers and children as against fathers and for equality for the living as against ancestors conceived as gods. See Nos. 13 & 18 for equality for younger as against older sons.

While favoring *equal* rights, HA very possibly did not favor *identical* rights for men, women, children, the aged, etc. He may instead have favored *appropriate* rights.

Theodore Tilton and Victoria Woodhull were principal celebrities in the great sensation of 1874–1875, the trial of Henry Ward Beecher for adultery. HA evidently thought Beecher not innocent. See L, II, 204, 205n1. Evarts defended Beecher and won a split verdict.

42. The party was to be "small and as informal as may be." See principal source 8. If she was the only woman, MHA presumably was in the library when Garrison displayed his photographs and gave his lecture.

But if there were other women and if after dinner they moved to the parlor while the men went up a flight to the library, MHA missed his laughable performance. If she missed it, the deprivation might account for the arrangement that led to the arrival of the Adamses and Ellen Gurney at a meeting of the Radical Club.

43. The decisive evidence that HA, MHA, and EHG attended the 18 Jan 1875 meeting is HA's poem *The Radical Club*. See notes 52, 53, 55, 58, & 60–64.

44. HA's *The Radical Club* was preceded not only by Nasby's definition and the obituary by "R. W. L." but also by a comical episode five years earlier involving Clarence King.

On 31 Dec 1870, King was taken by James T. Fields to a meeting of the Saturday Club at Parker's in Boston. Oliver Wendell Holmes, Ralph Waldo Emerson, and Henry Wadsworth Longfellow were present. It was disclosed that King knew Bret Harte. ". . . Longfellow . . . asked [King] if he [Harte] were a 'gen i us.'—'Why, Mr. Longfellow,' said King, 'I didn't know there was a three-syllabled genius in the country outside of Massachusetts." Upon which the gloom of offended Saturn fell upon the company, and even Dr. Holmes didn't dare to laugh . . . ." See Wilkins, *Clarence King*, 140; M. A. DeWolfe Howe, *John Jay Chapman and His Letters*, Bost 1937, 122.

45. Schurz to Godkin, 20 May 1872, Godkin Papers, H—". . . although I am willing to take any risk to aid a good cause, I feel also that the fiasco at Cincinnati has seriously injured my influence . . . ."

46. Writing to LHT on 24 Sep 1957, Lamar's biographer, Wirt Armistead Cate, said that Lamar's acquaintance with HA was made "by 1875." (I have Cate's original letter.) Because HA and MHA during 1875 were in Washington only in February, I have dated the start of the friendship in that month.

47. Garraty, John A., *Henry Cabot Lodge*, NY 1953, 41.

48. NYTribune, 28 Apr 1875. The newspaper reported that Schurz, Parke Godwin, Wells, CFA2, and Murat Halstead gave speeches; CFA2, Wells, and Reid were seated with Evarts; and HA was seated away from Evarts. Reportedly, in his speech, CFA2 described the persons present as belonging to "the new party of Independents" and said that Schurz was "our leader." Explaining the logic of having a party of the center, he said the Independents had the power to act in ways "unpleasant" or "destructive" to the Democrats or Republicans; hence could affect the conduct of the major parties. He did not use the key term "junto."

49. HA's hostility to Blaine may have been strengthened by Blaine's seductively inducing BA and Lodge to dine with him at his house on 15th Street and having them sit with him in the House of Representatives at the speaker's table. See Garraty, *Henry Cabot Lodge*, 41.

50. HA to CFA, 21 Jan 1872. In CFA's ears, HA's words would point back to the Civil War and the *Trent* Affair. For HA, the words in addition would point back to the *New York Times*.

It is striking that, when he started a battle in Boston in 1875, HA used as his vehicle a newspaper similarly named, the *Boston Times*.

51. I have followed the list of leading Boston newspapers given in *The Radical Club*, by a Chip. See note 52.

52. The discovery that HA wrote *The Radical Club*, by an Atom, was

made by Louisa Hooper Thoron. I am indebted to her for telling me about her discovery, for sharing with me her ideas concerning problems relating to the poem, and for her voluntarily supplying me relevant documents in quantity.

To the best of my knowledge, the first *published* attribution of the poem to HA appears in this chapter. My attribution agrees with LHT's but is my responsibility. It rests on a larger array of evidence than was available to her.

I want to emphasize that my suggestions relating to the poem and the evidence concerning it depart from hers in many particulars.

Presently available evidence permits a step-by-step reconstruction of the roles taken by HA, MHA, and other persons while the poem was in the making, went through five main printings, and remained a matter of burning interest.

The central documents on which I have relied while developing the reconstruction are five annotated copies of the poem, plus a counter-poem, *The Radical Club*, by a Chip.

Copy A. *The Radical Club*, by an Atom, FTKP. Broadside edition, undated. In the handwriting of MHA, the copy bears eight attempted identifications of persons who appear in the poem. The identifications end on reaching Mr. Fairman. They evidently are superseded by the identifications on Copy B.

LHT found Copies A & B in late August 1950 among odds and ends of MHA's papers which had come into her possession in 1918 when the Adamses' house at Beverly Farms was sold. She did not consider Copy A useful. I consider it very useful.

Copy B. Same, H. Broadside edition, undated. In the handwriting of MHA, the copy bears various annotations, including thirteen attempted identifications of persons who appear in the poem; also three notable large question marks.

When found by LHT, the copy was folded and yellowed. LHT considered it all-important. She gave it to H in November 1950.

Copy C. Same, MHS. Broadside edition, undated. In the handwriting of Ellen Hooper Gurney, the copy bears fourteen attempted identifications of persons who appear in the poem; also the words "for Mrs. Curtis."

The copy was given to MHS by Mrs. Robert S. Russell. See MHS *Proceedings*, 52 (1919), 117–18.

Mrs. Russell was the daughter of Mrs. George W. Curtis (born Anna Shaw). Mrs. Curtis was a relation of the Hooper sisters on the Sturgis side. See Thoron, 467.

Copy D. Same, MHS. Pamphlet edition, Bost 1876. In this edition, a signature, "Sherwood Bonner," is printed at the end of the poem. In an unidentified handwriting (#1), the copy bears on the title page an attribution, "Mrs. McDowell," and on pp. 6–13 fourteen attempted identifications of persons who appear in the poem. In an unidentified handwriting (#2), the copy bears on the front cover the legend "Mrs. L. C./ June 5, 1912." In an unidentified handwriting (#3), the copy bears on the title page the insert "Katherine" and on the verso an attribution, "By Mrs. Katharine [*sic*] McDowell." In an unidentified handwriting (#4), the copy bears on the verso an attribution, "Katherine Sherwood (Bonner) MacDowell [*sic*]/ (1849–1883)"; also in To the Reader a mistaken correction of "8th" to "9."

Mrs. Lucien Carr gave the copy to MHS in 1912. See MHS *Proceedings*, 45 (1911–1912), 628.

In substance, though not in details of form, the fourteen identifications of persons in Copy D in handwriting #1 match the fourteen identifications that appear in Copy C. I accordingly infer that handwriting #1 in Copy D is that of Anna Shaw Curtis, for whom Copy C was annotated.

Copy E. Same, NYPL. Pamphlet edition, Bost 1876. Lacks outer covers. In an unidentified handwriting (#1), the copy bears on pp. 6–13 twelve attempted identifications of persons in the poem. In an unidentified handwriting (#2), the copy bears on the title page an attribution, "Sherwood Bonner/ Mrs. Kate Sherwood (Bonner) McDowell."

Handwriting #1 in Copy E closely resembles handwriting #1 in Copy D but is not the same.

Handwriting #2 in Copy E matches handwriting #3 in Copy D.

Counter-poem. *The Radical Club./ A Poem/ respectfully dedicated to/ An Atom.* By a Chip. Bost 1876. Pamphlet, BPL.

When she found Copies A & B, LHT had no previous knowledge of the poem. The copies she found belonged to the broadside edition, which bears the attribution "by an Atom" but omits the mock-signature "D. Scribe." At the top of Copy B, LHT saw in MHA's handwriting an attribution, "By 'Sherwood Bonner'—of New—Orleans—La." Three things sufficed to alert LHT immediately that the poem was not by "Sherwood Bonner" and certainly was by HA. The three things were the attribution "by an Atom," the poem's text, and the mimicry of Poe. See note 57.

I do not suggest that the combination of factors that revealed the poem's authorship to LHT should be convincing to other minds. On the contrary, I think the argument that HA was the author is most conveniently started with the name Ziegel in the poem's twenty-third stanza. This is an approach LHT herself came to favor and went a long way to develop. See note 62, below. But I think it worth knowing that one Bostonian, LHT, finding Copy B, instantly knew HA to be the author despite the absence of the mock-signature "D. Scribe" and in the face of a contrary attribution she knew was in the handwriting of MHA.

53. After four months' research relating to *The Radical Club*, by an Atom, LHT wrote a detailed statement, "L. H. Thoron's Belief/ that the Author of the Poem/ The Radical Club/ is now uncovered!" She later gave me the original typescript, dated by her in ink 16 Dec 1950.

Her typed statement says, among other things: "H. A. knew Poe's 'Raven' by heart. When we were young girls, he recommended it to us for its music—its eerie build-up—its telling words. He read it aloud to us then with his wonderful voice. He used to say snatches of it aloud to himself—with expression."

54. That the preamble is drawn from a reconsidered editorial is

partly shown by an error. The preamble wrongly says the poem appears "in another column." It appears in the same column.

Newspaper editors routinely used the phrase "in another column" when speaking in editorials concerning items printed elsewhere in their issues. I think it follows that the preamble was drafted as part of an intended editorial.

55. HA later alluded to his authorship of the poem. The protagonist in his "Prayer to The Virgin of Chartres" identifies himself as "the dead Atom." See especially the text of the "Prayer" as written by HA in the notebook titled "The Yellow Ribbon," HAL.

56. Different editions of the poem are differently punctuated. As quoted in this chapter, the stanzas conform to the broadside edition, which MHA and EHG annotated, and which in my view is the definitive, last edition. See Chap. 14.

57. The phrase in parentheses evidently alludes to the obituary by "R. W. L."

58. The genius of *The Radical Club*, by an Atom, is partly to be found in its easy introduction of 19 persons in 24 stanzas.

The persons are: (1) a host, Mr. Pompous; (2) the reader of the meeting's paper, Mr. Wiseman; (3) a hostess [presumably Mrs. Pompous]; (4) a Colonel cold and smiling; (5) a British Lion; (6) a lady fair and faded; (7) an ancient Concord bookworm; (8) a kindred spirit; (9) a matron made for kisses; (10) a charmer noted as a dress-reformer; (11) a member, Mr. Fairman: (12) a maid with eyes as bright as Phœbus and hair dark as Erebus; (13) a tall, red-faced bishop; (14) a Kindergarten mother; (15) another *magnum corpus*; (16) a rarely gifted mortal; (17) Look-sharp; (18) Wriggle; and (19) Ziegel.

The attempted identifications of the persons that appear in Copies A to E (see note 53, above) were ventured many months after the 18 Jan 1875 meeting the poem describes. (For the dates of the attempted identifications, see Chap. 14.) So allowances must be made for failures of memory caused by the passage of time.

On their faces, Copies A, B, C, and E are annotated by persons who were present at the meeting. Copy D is the reverse. In my view, the copies establish that 14 of the 19 persons who appear in the poem represent *actual participants* who took active roles at the meeting. Keyed to the list above, the actual participants were: (1) Rev. John Turner Sargent—Mr. Pompous; (2) John Weiss—Mr. Wiseman; (3) Mrs. Sargent —hostess; (4) Thomas Wentworth Higginson—Colonel cold and smiling; (5) Charles Bradlaugh—British Lion; (6) Mrs. Julia Ward Howe—lady fair and faded (7) A. Bronson Alcott—Concord bookworm; (8) Dr. Cyrus A. Bartol—kindred spirit; (9) Mrs. Louise Chandler Moulton—matron made for kisses; (11) Francis Ellingwood Abbot—Mr. Fairman; (12) Miss Abby May—maid with eyes as bright as Phœbus and hair dark as Erebus; (13) Julius Ferrette—tall red-faced bishop; (14) Miss Elizabeth P. Peabody—Kindergarten mother; (15) Mrs. Edna D. Cheney—another *magnum corpus*; and (16) Christopher P. Cranch—rarely gifted mortal. Of the 14 identifications, five are supported by all four copies, three by three, three by two, and three (Mrs. Sargent, Charles Bradlaugh, Abby May) by only one. Concerning the identification of Abby May, see note 60.

According to p. 14 of *The Radical Club*, by a Chip, the Atom's poem includes more than one fictional participant. The Chip, however, names only one: the charmer noted as a dress-reformer, listed as (10) above. I believe the charmer is HA's *lone* fictional participant.

Next to the sixteenth and seventeenth stanzas (those that introduce the charmer), Copies A through E bear five different legends: "Abby May"; "forgotten/ [ditto mark] eheu!"; "Mrs. Crane"; "Miss Crane"; and "Miss Phelps." In my view, the last three legends are guesses based chiefly on the wrong assumption that the charmer was actual. The first two legends are by MHA. I suggest that, when annotating Copy A, MHA identified the charmer as Abby May because (a) she had forgotten that the charmer was fiction and (b) she was in the process of remembering one of the fiction's sources. This source was a report by Mrs. Moulton, "Boston./ Literary Notes./ 'Dress Reform' . . . ," NYTribune, 5 Dec 1874, about a book by a dress-reformer, Abba Gould Woolson. I further suggest that, when she annotated Copy B, MHA had recovered awareness that the charmer is fiction *but wished not to record her being fiction*. Hence, pretending the charmer was actual, MHA wrote in the margin "forgotten" and "eheu!" Read together, the two expressions could mean *better forgotten*!

59. The fictional charmer is the only woman in the poem represented by two stanzas.

60. It may be conjectured that a second fictional participant appears in the poem: a maid with eyes bright as Phœbus, and hair dark as Erebus, listed as (12) above. She appears in the nineteenth stanza and is represented as supportive of Mr. Fairman.

Next to the nineteenth stanza, Copies A, C, & D are blank. Copy B bears a question mark. But Copy E bears an identification, "Abby May." In my opinion, the bright-eyed, dark-haired maid *is* Abby May and she was an active actual participant, as listed above. The identification in Copy E is tersely definite. It appears to reflect the annotator's positive knowledge. I see no reason to doubt it.

I suggest that, when annotating Copy C, Ellen Gurney likewise knew that the bright-eyed, dark-haired maid was Abby May but wished not to show her knowledge and so left the margin blank. (The blank in Copy D merely duplicates the blank left by Ellen on Copy C.)

I further suggest that MHA, when annotating Copy A, got as far as Mr. Fairman and the supportive maid, knew the maid was Abby May, realized she had erred in previously identifying the charmer as Abby May, and stopped annotating Copy A.

Finally I suggest that MHA, when annotating Copy B, knew in advance what she would write concerning Mr. Fairman and the supportive maid. She identified the former as "Rev. Francis Abbott" and wrote beside the latter a question mark featuring an enlarged black dot. In my opinion, the question-mark-with-enlarged-dot does *not* indicate uncertainty. It indicates knowledge and disapprobation.

As has been noted, the description of the maid includes the phrase "dark as Erebus." HA had used this phrase in a letter in 1872. (It is quoted in Chap. 12.) As re-used in *The Radical Club*, by an Atom, the phrase "dark as Erebus" can indicate that the maid, though suggestive of heaven ("with eyes as bright as Phœbus"), may be hellish, having fallen. Other words in the stanza support this reading.

Its terms considered, the nineteenth stanza is detracting. It can only have been designed to breed troubles for—and between—Francis Elling-wood Abbot, Miss Abby May, and the leaders of the club.

61. Unquestionably the counter-poem, *The Radical Club*, by a Chip (see note 52), is the authorized reply of club to the Atom.

The Chip takes several attitudes towards the Atom. First the Chip minimizes the Atom as "shallow" (p. 8). Quoting the words *"magnum corpus"* applied by the Atom to Miss Peabody and Mrs. Cheney, the Chip deflects them as one of the Atom's "sneers" (p. 8). Next the Chip reprehends the Atom as "strange" (pp. 9, 13–15). Finally the Chip reacts to the Atom's likening Miss Peabody to a hen and says the representation of her as "clucking" is "monstrous" (p. 22).

The word "monstrous" is very strong. It evidently was meant. It appears to be the word felt by the club's leaders to be best applied to the Atom's poem as a whole.

62. That Ziegel is a comic equivalent of HA is, in my view, impossible to doubt (see note 63).

That Look-sharp and Wriggle are grouped with Ziegel suggests that they are comic equivalents of Ellen Gurney and MHA.

Copies E, C, D, & A are blank with respect to Look-sharp, Wriggle, and Ziegel. I read the blanks in Copy E as positive indications that the annotator did not know the three persons' identities. I believe that Ellen Gurney, when annotating Copy C, did know all three identities but meant *not* to hint them, still less record them. To my mind, the blanks in Copy D are mere carryovers from the blanks in Copy C.

In my opinion, Clover stopped annotating Copy A well before she reached Look-sharp, Wriggle, and Ziegel.

When annotating Copy B, Clover wrote question marks side-by-side next to Look-sharp and Wriggle and wrote nothing at all next to Ziegel. By these means, she lent Copy B an appearance of indicating (a) that Look-sharp and Wriggle seemed to her a pair, (b) that she could not identify either member of the pair, and (c) that, after writing an entry next to every one of the preceding eighteen persons, she had nothing whatever to offer in relation to Ziegel. From Clover's point of view, these marginal responses, *if shown to Ziegel*, might be the most amusing possible, and the most reassuring. See Chap. 14, note 35.

63. No copy of the poem that I have seen bears an attempted identification of the "young conceited Ziegel."

That conceited Ziegel is a comic representation of HA is indicated conclusively, in my opinion, by pertinent though miscellaneous data.

The derogation "conceited" was affixed to HA when an undergraduate. It was repeated insistently in Boston-Cambridge both while he lived and after he died (e.g., Winslow Warren to Ford, 18 Oct 1918, FP—". . . I consider the 'Education of Henry Adams' as a monumental piece of conceit. . . .") When a Harvard senior, HA had defiantly *agreed* that he was conceited and did so in print in the undergraduate magazine. See HA–1, 84. In 1875, he could easily have believed that his old tactic was well-remembered.

"Ziegel" is German for tile. As used in the poem, "Ziegel" translates the London slang term "tile." HA habitually used the term to designate the London-supplied black top hats he invariably wore in colder months as part of his more formal dress.

It was generally known in Boston-Cambridge that, as a teacher of medieval history and law at Harvard, HA was depending heavily on the best and latest German authorities. *Any* German appellation would thus point towards Professor Adams.

"Ziegel" in German comes close in sound to "Zekle" (Ezekiel) in New England dialect. The name "Zekle" was familiar to Bostonians. It appeared in a favorite poem, "Courtin'," by James Russell Lowell, in the *Biglow Papers*. The pertinent lines are:

> Zekle crep' up quite unbeknown
> An' peeked in thru the winder. . . .

HA knew that one of his anonymous contributions to the *Nation* had been given the title "A Peep into the Cabinet Windows." See Chap. 9.

Ziegel, understood as Ezekiel, was suggestive of both HA and MHA. The Blake drawing of Ezekiel given to them by Palgrave as a wedding present was hanging on a wall of their house at 91 Marlborough Street.

The Book of Ezekiel contained a pertinent line. Ezekiel prophesied (King James Version—26:7): ". . . thus saith the Lord God; Behold, I will bring upon Tyrus Nebuchadrezzar [*sic*] king of Babylon, a king of kings. . . ." In 1875, at least in pictured form, the king of Babylon was eating grass in Boston. The Blake color print depicting him was the most assertively displayed picture at the Adamses' house. It hung in the library near HA's desk. It was part of the setting in which Garrison had given his unscheduled lecture.

HA can be presumed to have read *The Marriage of Heaven and Hell*, by William Blake, as etched by him c. 1793. The book contains a "Memorable Fancy" beginning, "The Prophets Isaiah and Ezekiel dined with me, and I asked them how they dared so roundly to assert that God spake to them. . . ." A compelling argument can be made that, when HA and Forster were joined for dinner by Garrison and, after dinner, were subjected by Garrison to a lecture, HA was reminded of Blake's "Memorable Fancy" and saw a ridiculous contrast between his and Forster's being instructed by Garrison and Blake's instructive colloquy with Isaiah and Ezekiel. The argument hinges partly on unforgettable dinners, each involving three notable persons.

The argument hinges also on the words "the infinite." Blake says:

> Isaiah answer'd: 'I saw no God, nor heard any, in a finite organical perception, but my senses discover'd the infinite in everything, and . . . I cared not for consequences but wrote.'

Moreover, according to Blake, Ezekiel after dinner said much the same, telling his host that he was moved by " 'the desire of raising other men into a perception of the infinite.' "

Necessarily, discovery that HA was the Atom is of a piece with discovery of his reasons for dedicating his poem respectfully to the "Infinite." One of his reasons, perhaps *the* reason, was his sense of solidarity with greater prophets: Blake, Ezekiel, and Isaiah.

64. MHA knew herself as "Wriggle who would make an angel giggle." Late in 1877, almost three years after they attended the meeting of the Radical Club in Boston, MHA and HA attended a club meeting in the

capital. Her account of the experience echoes *The Radical Club*, by an Atom. "Last night we had an experience such as rarely falls to mortals & then only to 'gifted ones.' We went to a 'literary club[,]' a 'Washington' literary club. Pickwick pales beside it. I thought I had seen fools. . . . The Miss[es] Evarts & I got into such a hopeless state of giggling in a corner that death would have been a welcome release." See MHA to RWH, 2 Dec 1877, AP.

MHA's account repeats two words in *The Radical Club*, by a Chip. The words she puts within quotation marks—" 'gifted ones' "—are taken from the counter-poem, p. 25.

14. DOCTOR BARBARICUS

Letters by and to HA are in HA-micro 4, unless otherwise noted.

PRINCIPAL SOURCES

(1) six letters, HA to Morgan, 14 May 1875–3 Jun 1876, L, II, 224ff.

(2) twenty-four letters, HA to Lodge, 19 May 1875–30 Jun 1876.

(3) four letters, HA to CMG, 24 May 1875–14 Jun 1876.

(4) letters, HA to Cunliffe, 31 Aug 1875, 5 Mar 1876.

(5) eight letters, HA to Gilman, 3 Nov 1875–15 Jan 1876, Cater, 73, 85–86; L, II, 243–46; and Cater Collection, MHS.

(6) letters, HA to Schurz, 14 Feb, 6 Mar 1876, L, II, 249–52, 261.

(7) letter, HA to Walker, 29 Feb 1876, L, II, 259–60.

(8) letter, HA to Wells, 20 Mar 1876, L, II, 262.

(9) letter, HA to Harvard U. Academic Council, L, II, 270–71.

(10) four unsigned book notices by HA in *NAR* issues, as follows: "Green's Short History of the English People," Jul 1875, 216–24; "Tennyson's Queen Mary," Oct 1875, 422–29; "Walker's Statistical Atlas of the United States," Oct 1875, 437–42 (tentative attribution—see *Sketches*, 225–26); "Palfrey's History of New England," Oct 1875, 473–80. (The notices appear in *Sketches*, 175–211.)

(11) [HA], *The Radical Club. A Poem, respectfully dedicated to the Infinite. By an Atom.*"—as published in the *Boston Times*, 8 May 1875. (For the attribution to HA, see Chap. 13.)

(12) same, as pirated in the *Index*, 3 Jun 1875.

(13) same, as reprinted in the *Boston Times*, 2 Jan 1876.

(14) same, reprinted as a pamphlet, Bost: The Times Publishing Company 1876. (The poem bears at the end a printed signature, "Sherwood Bonner.")

(15) same, reprinted as a broadside, n.p., n.d. (For a conjectural date and other details, see note 35, below.)

(16) HA a. o., *Essays in Anglo-Saxon Law*, Bost 1876.

ADDITIONAL SOURCES; COMMENTS

1. MHA's brother and sister (also their cousin Anna Shaw Curtis) acquired roles relating to the publication and/or annotation of the poem. See note 35, below.

2. Abbot's reprinting *The Radical Club* greatly extended the poem's readership. The *Index* was the weekly newspaper of the Free Religious Association, a national body whose president was HA's cousin Octavius B.

Frothingham and whose vice-presidents included Lydia Maria Child, George W. Curtis, Ralph Waldo Emerson, Lucretia Mott, Robert Dale Owen, and other notables. The paper was widely distributed among Unitarians.

3. Prefatory note in the published version, Bost 1876.

4. In 1874, a week after the *New York Tribune* published the letter by "R. W. L." saying the Radical Club was dead, MHA had written to Lodge about "a piece of wholesome criticism" by T. Wentworth Higginson published in the *Index*. Higginson had alleged that the *Nation* and the *North American Review* were "conducted on the principle 'wherever you see a heart[,] hit it.' " See MHA to Lodge, 14 Oct 1874, LP. Judging from her letter, MHA either read the *Index* often or tended to hear about its contents as they related to HA and herself.

Since Col. T. W. Higginson thought the *North American* an aggressive attacker of "hearts" (presumably meaning persons of feeling; hence of inspiration and Christian faith), and since Higginson can be assumed to have known that HA was the chief editor of the *North American*, it is inescapable that HA from the outset was a suspect as the Atom.

5. On 12 Oct 1879, writing to her father from Paris, MHA asked that two copies of *The Radical Club* be sent to her. See Thoron, 188; also note 35, below. Seven months later, writing from London, she told him how she and HA passed Bank Holiday. Her letter involved a use of "atoms" that possibly had multiple references. She said: ". . . bank holiday . . . is a perpetually returning festival here & very gloomy to all but bank officials. H & I took each other by the hand & proceeded to [the] S. Kens^n Museum. . . . Went on . . . to an aesthetic tea. . . . Knowles of the '19th Century' defending Tennyson's de Profundis[,] which six women declared utterly incomprehensible—then they discussed 'atoms' & [ate] . . . very thin bread & butter." See MHA to RWH, 23 May 1880, AP.

6. The earliest publication about MHA is a Bostonian commentary of the 1930s: Katharine Simonds, "The Tragedy of Mrs. Henry Adams," *NEQ*, Dec 1936, 564–82. Simonds quotes Eleanor Whiteside (572) as having remarked about MHA after her death, ". . . she had a reputation for saying bitter things and of unsparingly using her powers of sarcasm whenever an opportunity presented itself." Simonds agrees with the remark.

It should be noted that Mrs. Whiteside was out of touch with MHA for many years; also that Whiteside and Simonds fail to say who gave MHA the alleged reputation; and, in addition, Simonds avoids the good question whether MHA was sarcastic or humorous.

A second Bostonian commentary quickly followed: Charles Knowles Bolton's review of the *Letters of Mrs. Henry Adams*, *NEQ*, Mar 1937, 140–41. Bolton ascribes to MHA a sort of "partisanship"—a "lack of urbanity, some might call it." He says her letters offer "nothing but a narrow stream of partisan prejudice." He especially regrets that her judgments of persons, when published, were not offset in footnotes by "some sage comment of Mr. Rhodes, or [by] Mr. Gamaliel Bradford's estimate of the person described."

Bolton's position—that MHA was a woman whose opinions were better superseded by the wise opinions of older Bostonians—is precisely the position taken by the Chip with respect to "*Atoms*" in 1875–1876.

7. For convenience, see *Sketches* Nos. 2–3, 8–9, 11–15, 17–18, 20, and 22–23. (No. 22 may help account for the opening paragraphs of HA's *History of the United States*.)

8. Much of the idea of history that HA formed in 1872–1875 is outlined in *Sketches*, Index of Subjects, 259–61, "History, a survey of."

9. HA would have wanted in any case to give only a limited time to English history, but as things happened he had reason to hurry. He was racing with Sohm to be first in print with discoveries relating to Germanic institutions as perpetuated by the Anglo-Saxons. Hence his note, *Essays in Anglo-Saxon Law*, 22n: "The appearance of the second volume of this most brilliant work [Sohm's *Altdeutsche Reichs- und Gerichtsverfassung*] will be expected with the greatest interest as it is to contain an account of the Anglo-Saxon constitution."

10. In *Essays in Anglo-Saxon Law*, 151n, Young uses the expression "students of comparative history." The expression possibly was the one that HA and his helpers thought most accurately delineated their momentary specialization.

11. Laughlin, "Some Recollections of Henry Adams," op. cit., 579–80.

12. L, VI, 326. Presumably letters passed between HA and Young, but no letters have been found. Their non-appearance may be connected in some way with Young's death. He committed suicide in March 1888, reportedly on account of overwork as a Harvard history professor. See Novick, *Honorable Justice, Life of . . . Holmes*, op. cit., 183.

HA's notice, "Maine's Early History of Institutions," *NAR*, Apr 1875 (or *Sketches*, No. 18), reads most clearly and suggestively if read together with Young's "The Anglo-Saxon Family Law" in *Essays in Anglo-Saxon Law*. In HA's notice, the Germans are described as *politically* democratic and not subject to patriarchs. In Young's essay, the Germans and Anglo-Saxons are described as *familially* democratic and not subject to patriarchs. Admittedly, in Young's essay, 143, Anglo-Saxon women are found to be dependents *by law*. None the less, Adams's notice and Young's essay concern nations and families remarkable for practical equality, or at least near-equality, between free grown men and women.

Young's findings about barbarian marriage and how it differed from Roman and feudal marriage, as stated in his essay, are very apt if read as commentaries on the marriage Henry Adams and Clover Hooper did make and on the sorts of marriage they did not make.

14. Democracy among the Germans and democracy among the American Indians are brought together in Young's notes in *Essays in Anglo-Saxon Law*, 151–52, relating to Lewis Henry Morgan's writings.

15. By late 1874, HA came permanently to conceive of history in terms of conservatism and innovation, and similarly in terms of stasis and motion. His ideas concerning human beings as *conservative* are especially called into use in his unsigned notice of Parkman's *Old Regime in Canada*, *NAR*, Jan 1875 (also *Sketches*, 133–38) and in his "Anglo-Saxon Courts of Law." The notice and the essay concern people shifted to new homes (French emigrants to Canada, Saxon emigrants to Kent) who, having arrived, tenaciously persist in inherited habits.

In 1875, while finishing his study of the Anglo-Saxons, HA was overtaken by suspicion that the Germans did not wander into Europe in "historic" times but had lived there from "archaic" times. Writing to William Dwight Whitney, 25 Dec 1875, L, II, 245, he asked whether the "latest philologists" believed the Germans came into Europe later than the Greek and Romans. He asked too whether "any of these races were ever technically speaking nomadic." He said he was developing his own conclusions but wanted to know "the latest fashions in philology." His letter implied that he, the latest *historian*, had formed conclusion opposite to those of the philologists and believed the Germans to have been fixed occupants of Europe from an extremely early time.

16. Because HA's ideas about medieval Europe changed in 1872–1875, because the change was mainly caused by exhaustive study of evidence not looked at exhaustively by other inquirers, and because his newer ideas were clearer, more interesting, and incomparably more revolutionary than the ideas they replaced, attention should be directed to his *last* writings of the time about medieval Europe. They are his notice, "Maine's Early History of Institutions," *NAR*, Apr 1875 (or *Sketches*, No. 18), and his essay, "The Anglo-Saxon Courts of Law."

17. Undue notice has been given to HA's slaps at Freeman (e.g., Oscar Cargill, "The mediaevalism of Henry Adams," in *Essays in Honor of Carleton Brown*, NY 1940). They are insignificant compared with his fully-considered differences with Maine.

18. All of HA's historical writings in the *Nation* and the *North American* between January 1872 and April 1875 are written on the unconcealed assumption that he can become—and in later sketches has become—a historian superior to any of the other living historians in the English-speaking countries. His assertion of superiority becomes still more aggressive in *Essays in Anglo-Saxon Law*. There *he leaves it to a student*, Ernest Young, to refute Sir Henry Maine's idea that the German family was patriarchal. See *Essays*, 148–52.

Persons inclined to doubt HA's entitlement to the rank he claimed as a historian in 1875 should not form settled judgments without first inspecting a notebook at the Houghton Library containing 254 pages of his notes on Anglo-Saxon laws. The notes advance from the laws of Aethelbert in Kent (550–616 A.D.) to those of Edward the Confessor; they end with translations of charters and other originals; and they are spectacular evidence of systematic, intelligent work.

19. On Green, see HA to Parkman, 11 Dec 1884, L, II, 563.

20. That HA's "The Anglo-Saxon Courts of Law" could disturb persons imbued with received opinions concerning England's history and institutions is vividly apparent in an American review of *Essays in Anglo-Saxon Law* by a Boston Anglophile, Oliver Wendell Holmes, Jr., HA's friend and Harvard colleague. With more emotion than accuracy, Holmes wrote that the "five essays [*sic*]" in the book are "remarkable in the first place for their entire and almost polemical renunciation of English models." See *American Law Review*, Jan 1877, 327.

21. My relations with Aileen Tone and Louisa Hooper Thoron were guided by an irritated response Miss Tone voiced on the telephone in 1952 before I first saw her. She said in effect that she would grant *no more interviews*.

I and my wife became intimate friends of Miss Tone in large measure because we allowed none of our meetings with her to degenerate into interviews. This precaution permitted my learning more from her about HA in the give-and-take of friendship than would have been possible during interviews, however well conducted.

When introduced by Miss Tone to Mrs. Thoron, I hewed to the policy of not asking questions. This permitted my forming a relationship with Mrs. Thoron which was both a friendship and a partnership in research. The partnership involved surprises. During a visit to Boston in 1955, I was invited by her to go for a walk in the neighborhood of her apartment. As we walked, she turned to one of our chief problems, the suicides of her Aunt Clover and Aunt Ellen. She stopped on the sidewalk and offered the sweeping comment, "My family did not know what to do about death."

She then led me to a spot adjacent to a house and showed me a window from which, she said, *her father* had leapt in 1901, attempting suicide. She explained that clothes lines in the yard broke his fall; also that he was taken to McLean Hospital, partly recovered, but died of pneumonia, a complication incident to his injuries.

While we were walking back to her apartment, she turned to a different subject. She told me that when young she undertook to learn why her aunts were childless. She said she persistently asked questions and eventually got the answer. As she talked, I interjected some remarks about birth control and a book I had noticed in the Henry Adams Library, MHS: *Clinical Notes on Uterine Surgery*.

She was eager to speak. Yet it was also apparent that sexual matters were very difficult for her to talk about. She said her aunts *concertedly* succeeded in not having children and did so with the help of "something from the East." She worded the phrase in response to my mention of birth control and the medical text. Her word "East" was spoken in the context of talks we had been having about her Sturgis and Hooper ancestors engaged in the China trade; also talks we had been having about the residence of William Sturgis Bigelow in Japan.

It was clear she knew more but had reached the limit of her effort to impart information. The subject had to be dropped. Because our walk had centered in her showing me the window from which her father tried to kill himself, I assumed that her father was her informant—that it was their brother who had known and said how Ellen and Clover avoided conception.

22. On bases of slender or nonexistent evidence, commentators have insisted that MHA *wanted* children, and they have done so without so much as entertaining the possibility that MHA and EHG did *not* want children. Examples are Simonds, "The Tragedy of Mrs. Adams," op. cit., 570, 577; and Kaledin, *The Education of Mrs. Henry Adams*, op. cit., 145–46.

23. Evidence abounds that HA wished to end his editorship creditably. He thought his Centennial Issue fairly creditable. Writing to Gilman, 18 Jan 1876, he praised its articles as "all good, some excellent." The very political October 1876 issue that permitted HA to end his editorship affected him as still more creditable.

24. HA to William D. Whitney, 15 Oct 1874, L, II, 209. The issues HA edited possibly deserved much more attention than they received. A specimen of their interest is a notice in the July 1875 issue reviewing the newly-issued second volume of Nietzsche's *Unzeitgemasse Betrachtungen* (often translated as *Thoughts out of Season*).

25. Nervous uncertainty about the name best used to designate the club shows even in the title of Mrs. Sargent's eventual book, *Sketches and Reminiscences of the Radical Club of Chestnut Street, Boston*, op. cit., 1880. Also see the dedication: "To/ The Living and the Dead/ of/ The Chestnut Street Club/ This Book is Dedicated/ by M. E. S."

26. Mrs. Moulton remained in Europe for two years. Thereafter she made London her second home and the center of all her summer social and literary activities. For winter purposes, she and her husband moved from Beacon Hill to a house in Boston's South End. See Whiting, *Louise Chandler Moulton*, op. cit., Chaps. IV–V.

27. The chief biographies of Bonner are a pamphlet, Alexander L. Bondurant, *Sherwood Bonner/ Her Life and Place in the Literature of the South*, "reprinted from the *Publication of the Mississippi Historical Society for 1899*, 42–68; and Hubert Horton McAlexander, *The Prodigal Daughter/ A Biography of Sherwood Bonner*, Baton Rouge & Lond, 1981. Both are very informative at some points, unhelpful or misleading at others.

Bondurant (51) passes over in silence the question how Mrs. McDowell got the money to go to Europe. McAlexander says (87–88) she went to Europe as the "traveling companion" of Mrs. Moulton, almost implying she was a paid companion. He adds (89) that Henry Wadsworth Longfellow "evidently" sent her money and her father "evidently" did also. In a different vein, he says (95) that her "funds" originally seemed sufficient for "eight months of travel." He nowhere firmly says where the funds came from, and he seems not to know.

28. McAlexander, *Prodigal Daughter*, op. cit., 90.

29. The *Boston Times*, 2 Jan 1876.

30. The innocent believers in Sherwood Bonner's authorship of "The Radical Club" include her biographers.

Handicapped severely by lack of evidence, Bondurant mistakenly says (52) that Bonner wrote the poem after her return from Europe. By then— October 1876—it had been published in full at least four times.

McAlexander mistakenly says (68–70) that the poem, though published anonymously, was attributed to Bonner from the moment of its first appearance. (He cites no supporting data and can be taken to be airing unconfessedly a mere gap-filling supposition.)

Seeming not to suspect that he has involved himself in an intricate subject, McAlexander shows carelessness in relation to key documents. He misreports (70, 71n) the title of the counter-poem by a Chip. He says (70n) that "the copy" of the Atom's poem at MHS is a pamphlet copy annotated by "Ellen Sturgis Gurney," whereas there is more than one copy at MHS; one is annotated by Ellen *Hooper* Gurney; and it is not a pamphlet but a broadside.

He also says (222): "Every major Boston library has the pamphlet among its holdings, and in the 1950s, Mrs. Ward Thoron, born a Hooper and the niece of Mrs. Henry Adams, made sure that the copies in both the Massachusetts Historical Society and Widener Library were fully annotated for the benefit of posterity." The sentence is thick with errors. Most notably, it misreports as annotations by LHT on a pamphlet copy in Widener Library what in fact are annotations by MHA on a broadside copy in Houghton Library.

31. The advertisement in the *Boston Times*, 5 Mar 1876, does not

specify that the poem is reprinted as a pamphlet, but the pamphlet is the only printing by the *Times* that attests authorship by Sherwood Bonner. Her name does not appear on the cover or title page; it appears only at the end of the poem and there supplants "D. Scribe." A note is subtended: "The AUTHOR of this Poem is now travelling in Europe, in company with Louise Chandler Moulton, and is writing a series of entertaining letters to the *Boston Sunday Times.*"

32. An important feature of the pamphlet version is the opening words of the preface, titled "To The Reader." The words are: "The following Poem was *written for* and first appeared in the columns of the Boston Sunday Times . . . [italics added]." "Written for" can suggest (a) that the *Boston Times* commissioned the poem, (b) that the *Times* was singled out by the contributor as the poem's most suitable vehicle, or (c) that the *Times* was singled out by a contributor who paid the editor to publish the poem. The third meaning deserves consideration. It is hard to escape the conjecture that the *Times* was paid at every stage to publish and re-publish the poem. See note 35.

33. Sherwood Bonner, "Julia Ward Howe," *Cottage Hearth*, Apr 1875, 85–86.

34. McAlexander, *Prodigal Daughter*, op. cit., 81–86.

35. Louisa Hooper Thoron theorized that HA and MHA through an intermediary, Senator Lamar of Mississippi, gave Bonner the money for a trip to Europe as correspondent of the *Boston Times* on condition she accept a false ascription of *The Radical Club* to herself. Mrs. Thoron saw the supposed arrangement as in part a charity. She also saw it as creditable to Sherwood Bonner. In her words—letter, LHT to myself, 24 Sep 1955: "I believe Bonner's memory augmented both as an authoress and as a strong, game character by having listened to friendly persuasion in accepting 'authorship' of that poem."

That a Hooper niece would offer the theory seems to me a possible indication that the supposed arrangement in fact was made. If a niece could easily imagine the scheme in the 1950s, could not her Aunt Clover have conceived or at least helped execute the scheme in 1875?

I subscribe to the main component of the theory. I believe that HA and MHA secretly, through an intermediary, financed a trip to Europe for a needy Southern writer on condition that the writer accept ascription to herself of a poem she did not write. But I doubt that charity had much share in the arrangement. It seems to me that what happened was more a trading of benefits.

I see no grounds for supposing that the intermediary was Lamar. On the contrary, I believe it was necessary he *not* be the intermediary.

I view Bonner's accepting the bargain as understandable and, because steadfastly kept by her, positively defensible. I view HA and MHA's effecting the arrangement as forgivable—but for a reason I did not learn till assisted in the 1980s by data printed by McAlexander in his biography of Bonner.

It long seemed that a most difficult problem relating to the Atom's poem was that of dating its undated broadside edition. According to McAlexander, *Prodigal Daughter*, 30n, 70, 70n, 182n, Bonner's missing scrapbook was reported in 1930 to contain a statement that the *Boston*

Times reprinted the poem *in 1877*. By combining this shred of testimony with others equally small, and by adding some conjectures, it is possible to outline a history of the poem which, if not upset by contrary evidence, might (a) account for the existence of the broadside edition; (b) date the broadside within a short period; (c) specify the earliest possible dates of the annotations on the five copies of the poem I rely upon in this biography and list as principal documents for Chap. 13, and (d) explain certain things MHA wrote when annotating Copy B.

This inferred history of the poem incorporates large amounts of fact and is logically compelling, with the result that it tends when presented to seem virtual fact throughout. But it is partly conjecture all the same and will have to be scrapped if adverse evidence appears.

One starts with nine propositions. HA and MHA restricted knowledge of the authorship of *The Radical Club* within the smallest possible circle of persons. Their intermediary in the affair of *The Radical Club* was MHA's brother (who in turn could engage *his* intermediaries, if necessary). Through Edward Hooper (and possible unknown helpers chosen by him), HA and MHA paid the editor of the *Boston Times* to publish an anonymous printing of the Atom's poem on 8 May 1875. In the fall of 1875, HA and MHA decided to transfer the authorship to another person. They had first learned about Sherwood Bonner from Lamar in Washington, and they subsequently learned more from Boston-Cambridge informants. Through Hooper, HA and MHA paid the editor of the *Boston Times* to publish, first, an anonymous reprinting of the poem on 2 Jan 1876 and, second, a pamphlet edition signed "Sherwood Bonner" in March 1876. Through Hooper, HA and MHA gave Bonner money sufficient for an eight-month trip to Europe, on condition that she accept false ascriptions of the poem to herself in the *Boston Times* and in a pamphlet edition of the poem published separately, and on the further condition that she arrange with the editor of the *Times* to serve the paper as a paid traveling correspondent. The rate paid to Bonner by the *Times* was $10.00 per letter (McAlexander, 89). Bonner arranged to send travel letters also to a paper in Tennessee, the *Memphis Avalanche* (ibid.).

The foregoing outline raises an evident problem. Why did HA and MHA renew the attack on the Radical Club after it changed its name?

A possible motive was defensive. Knowing or sensing they were in danger of public charges that they were the authors of the poem and the perpetrators of its publication in the *Boston Times*, HA and MHA pre-empted the field of public announcement. Before the erstwhile club could make charges, they arranged that a culprit (conveniently gone to Europe) was named in the *Boston Times* as the author of the poem; and, to make the identification stick, they arranged the sale of the poem in pamphlet form with a printed signature, "Sherwood Bonner."

A second possible motive was aggressive. HA and MHA were politicians, armed with the experience of politicians. When the club changed its name, they did not think the club was dead. They knew that political victory was commonly illusion; that it could turn to defeat in the space of a month or a new election. They had not forgotten the letter by "R. W. L." in the *New York Tribune* in October 1874. The letter had said that the Radical Club was dead, and humorously it had added that the club *might be sleeping*. The exact expression was " 'Not dead but sleepeth.' " (In a similar vein, MHA would later write to her father about the defeat of Gen. Benjamin Butler in an election for governor in Massachusetts: "So old Ben—is dead for a year! Not dead but sleeping I fear." See MHA to RWH, 11 Nov 1883, AP.) The politicians' ideal being victory that lasts, HA and MHA struck the erstwhile Radical Club a new blow. The blow was prepared for with the 2 Jan 1876 reprinting of the poem in the *Boston Times*. The blow itself was the false news in the *Boston Times* on 17 Feb 1876 that the Radical Club had been killed the previous May by a pleasant young woman from the South who was currently sending entertaining letters to the *Times* from Europe.

The blow succeeded. The leaders of the club tried to strike back. They issued a printed version of a counter-poem by a Chip indicating knowledge of, but disbelief in, Bonner's authorship (see note 36). But the gesture was weak, and the club did not return to its proud original name.

The affair of the Atom's poem doubtless afforded HA and MHA a great many satisfactions. It afforded Sherwood Bonner the satisfaction of going to London, Paris, Rome, Florence, Venice, and back to Paris, before returning to Massachusetts; also the satisfaction of furnishing letters to the *Boston Times* and *Memphis Avalanche*. Bonner regained her position as Longfellow's secretary in Cambridge. She so successfully avoided conceding the untruth of the ascription of the Atom's poem to herself that Louise Chandler Moulton believed in her authorship—except that Mrs. Moulton attributed the poem jointly to Bonner and an elderly Bostonian male (not Longfellow) with whom she could be sexually linked in false gossip. See McAlexander, 155–57.

In December 1876, Bonner was forced by marital and other problems to return to the South. She stayed many months. Writing to Longfellow from Mississippi on 31 Aug 1877 (Longfellow Collection, H), she said: "I have lost that slight taste for Bohemianism, that you have gently regretted from time to time; I could even find it in my heart to wish that I had not written the 'Radical Club.' I want no more enemies; but only friends among those who are strong and good. If Mrs[.] Julia Ward Howe were not so brilliant and busy a woman I should hope to gain her friendship. She has been very lovely to me; and no one ever fascinated me more. Do you know if she has returned from Europe?"

On 26 Mar 1877, the Rev. J. T. Sargent died. In the absence of its host, the Chestnut Street Club could anticipate nothing better for itself than feeble last meetings. I conjecture that *at this time*, in April–May 1877, HA and MHA arranged the last printing of the Atom's poem, an anonymous broadside. This dating conforms to data reported in 1930 to be in Bonner's scrapbook: that there was an 1877 printing.

HA and MHA's principal motive for printing the broadside was evidently simple. *They wanted to re-attach the poem to the Atom.*

Edward Hooper arranged the printing of the broadsides. They are 23 × 37 cm. sheets, well-printed but cheap to produce per copy. They bear no place of publication, publisher, or date. If inserted in the *Boston Times* when readied for distribution, copies could be delivered gratis to all the newspaper's subscribers and buyers at modest cost.

So delivered, the broadside would function for some receivers as an informative letter. Its distinguishing peculiarity is that the poem, signed as usual at the start with the words "BY AN ATOM," is signed at the end neither by "D. Scribe" nor by "Sherwood Bonner."

Assuming that the broadsides were distributed in April–May 1877, this change conveyed a twofold message: that the poem, after all, was *not* by Sherwood Bonner; and that it was what it always had been, a poem by an "Atom."

The broadside could function too as a letter to Bonner. When she saw a copy, she would see that her name did not appear; moreover that ascription of the poem to her had ceased in such a way that the ascription to her—a temporary one—was *publicly* counteracted.

For HA and MHA, the broadside could offer a sense that the affair was well ended. Yet for them it remained extremely dangerous.

Before explaining *how* dangerous, it is necessary to establish the earliest possible dates of the annotations written by MHA and her sister Ellen on Copies A, B, and C of *The Radical Club*; also the dates of the principal annotations on Copies D and E (see Chap. 13, note 57).

Copy A, a broadside copy, and Copy B, a broadside copy, both annotated by MHA, could have been annotated as early as April–May 1877, provided the conjectured date of the broadside is correct.

Copy C, a broadside copy annotated by Ellen Gurney for Anna Shaw Curtis, could have been annotated as early as April–May 1877, on the same proviso.

Copy D, a pamphlet copy presumably annotated by Anna Shaw Curtis—merely replicating the annotations on Copy C—could have been annotated as early as April–May 1877, on the same proviso.

Copy E, a pamphlet copy, principal annotator unidentified, could have been annotated as soon as March 1876, when the pamphlet edition was published.

These datings lend importance to Copy E, as possibly annotated more than a year sooner than the others, and within fourteen months after the meeting of the Radical Club that the Atom's poem concerns. Also the datings warn that MHA's annotations on Copies A and B were possibly written twenty-seven or more months after the meeting and after many intervening occurrences.

Louisa Hooper Thoron advanced a sub-theory that MHA annotated Copy B *for her father*. Specifically she theorized that Dr. Hooper already knew the secret of the poem's true authorship, that MHA annotated a broadside copy mainly to give him details concerning the persons who appear in the poem, and that while so doing she wrote on the copy some allusions to the arrangement making Bonner the putative author.

LHT also theorized that Copy B remained at Dr. Hooper's house in Beverly Farms till his death in the spring of 1885, and that it was then moved with other papers to the Adamses' nearby house. (Papers in the Adamses' house were moved in 1918 to the Thorons' house in nearby Danvers, and eventually Copy B was found among them.)

I subscribe to two parts of Mrs. Thoron's sub-theory: (1) that MHA annotated Copy B for her father and (2) that Copy B survived by the process conjectured, or by its practical equivalent.

LHT's idea that Dr. Hooper knew the true authorship of the poem when MHA annotated Copy B seems to me an unexamined assumption at odds with the evidence. MHA's annotations on Copy B are many. Those that matter for present purposes are the following legends, in the positions indicated.

[in the top margin]   By "Sherwood Bonner"—of New Orleans—La
see L. Q. C. Lamar—
her dear friend
1876—[to the left of the poem's title]

late   [in the left margin, identifying the host, "Mr. Pompous"]
Rev John
T. Sargent
11 Chestnut
Street

[in the bottom margin]   Printed in Boston Sunday
Post
Reprinted by F. E. Abbott in the
"Index"

The left-margin legend dates the annotations as subsequent to Sargent's death. Other legends correctly name the year—1876—in which the poem was advertised and published as by Bonner and correctly say that Lamar was her friend. All the legends could have been written in April–May 1877, the conjectured date of the broadside edition. But there are a number of complications.

There is a wrong spelling. "Abbott" should be Abbot.

There is a wrong word. MHA confuses the *Boston Sunday Times* (which repeatedly printed the poem) with the *Boston Post* (which she and HA had inconclusively negotiated to purchase in 1876).

There is a wrong place. Bonner did not come from New Orleans. She and Lamar both came from Holly Springs, Mississippi. (The misstatement possibly is evidence that MHA and HA never met Bonner, only knew *about* her, and, by chance, formed a wrong idea of her place of origin.)

There is also a lie. No satisfactory explanation of the opening words "By 'Sherwood Bonner'" is possible except that explanation which says that MHA: (a) agreed with HA that the authorship of *The Radical Club*, by an Atom, was to be a truly secret secret, to be kept forever; (b) faced the problem of a father who by some means had learned that his son Edward had caused the poem to be reprinted and had copies; (c) had the problem that the edition Edward printed was the best, last edition which says—and says only—that the author is "An Atom"; and (d) agreed with HA that it was still too soon for *any* older person, even Dr. Hooper, to be told the authorship.

On the basis of the evidence, I have to conclude that MHA so annotated a broadside for her father that he would *believe* the poem was by Sherwood Bonner. If that happened, Dr. Hooper would not worry that it might be the work of his younger daughter and/or his younger daughter's ingenious husband.

LHT originated the suggestion that the authorship of *The Radical Club* was meant to be a truly secret secret. When she wrote her paper

outlining her ideas—"L. H. Thoron's Belief that the Author of the Poem
The Radical Club is now uncovered!"—she began it by saying, "The Atom
did not mean to be found out."

The suggestion seems true enough, and quite important; but, as tends
to happen even in cases of secret secrets, qualifying suggestions are
necessary. I suggest that persons who *knew*, were *told*, or *learned* the secret
(see lists below) did things or wrote things that sooner or later would let
the secret out. I further suggest that Dr. Hooper learned sometime in
1877–1879 that Edward had reprinted the poem, perhaps learned more
by 1880 (see note 5, above), and may have been told the rest sometime
before he died in 1885.

Evidence supports the 1877–1879 portion of this last suggestion. In
Paris in 1879, MHA came upon a book she liked, Fromentin's *Maitres
d'Autrefois*. She regarded it as "a running commentary" on the contents of
the Louvre. A two-part fancy occurred to her. She imagined her brother
Edward might read Fromentin's book if her sister Ellen left a copy open
in his Harvard office or if Ellen scattered "its leaves tract-wise in State
Street"—i.e., in Boston's financial district. She wrote her fancy in a letter
to her father and added: "Oh, by the way, I want him or you to mail me
two copies of that 'Radical Club' poem he had reprinted. I want it for two
people on this side. Don't forget, please." See MHA to RWH, 12 Oct 1879,
Thoron, 188.

MHA's letter establishes that Edward Hooper had the poem reprinted
in a broadside edition whose "leaves" could be scattered in State Street. The
letter also establishes that Dr. Hooper did *not* know the true authorship of
the Atom's poem. In 1879, he still knew only that Edward had had "that
'Radical Club' poem" reprinted and possessed a supply of copies. Finally
the letter supports the thesis that MHA, prior to October 1879, lied to her
father by writing on Copy B, "By 'Sherwood Bonner.' "

The above considerations, admittedly complicated, join in pointing
towards simple questions.

Who originally knew the authorship of *The Radical Club*?
The only possible answers appear to be:
- Henry Adams—who wrote it;
- Marian Hooper Adams—who from the start shared the project in
all its ramifications.
Who was *told* the authorship of the poem, and when?
The answers appear to be:
- Edward Hooper; by April–May 1875—so he could arrange its
publication, three reprintings, and the false ascription to Sherwood
Bonner;
- Ellen Hooper Gurney; by April–May 1875—because she attended
the meeting the poem described and because she was Clover and
Edward's sister;
- possibly Dr. Robert Hooper, but not till after 12 Oct 1879, if ever,
and then because he already knew a part of the secret and because
he was the father of three persons who knew the entire secret.
Who by other means *learned* the approximate authorship of the poem,
and how did they learn it?
The important answer is:

– sundry leaders of the Radical Club, through a combination of thorough knowledge of Boston and sound inference after study of the Atom's poem.

Who did *not* learn the secret?

The evidence supports a list that includes three key persons:

– Louise Chandler Moulton—who is known to have been misled;
– the editor of the *Boston Times*—who could enjoy his profits more easily if he was kept from knowing the secret;
– Anna Shaw Curtis—for whom Ellen Gurney annotated a copy of the broadside, but in such a way as to impart no hint of the poem's true authorship;
– Sherwood Bonner—who presumably was shielded by HA and MHA from knowing the identity of the Atom.

Does the history of the poem have a hero or heroine?

– It appears that Sherwood Bonner firmly adhered to a pledge *not* to reveal that she did not write the poem. Keeping silent, she successfully shielded a person unknown to her. She thus placed in her debt all persons who might care about the Atom.

36. The authorship of *The Radical Club*, by a Chip, is unknown. Conjecturable authors include Cyrus A. Bartol, C. P. Cranch, and Samuel Longfellow, especially the last, who had incurred the dishonor of being by-passed by the Atom.

Responsibility for the publication of the Chip's poem is a different matter. It must have rested on the club's leaders, without whose permission the counter-poem would surely not have appeared in print.

Being a club publication, the counter-poem should be read as a position paper. It need not be read as a poem. It hardly is one.

37. The account of HA's attempted junto in this chapter rests in part on recovered evidence of unusual importance. See note 46, below.

38. The dedication seems a mere instance of HA's courtesy but may reflect assistance given by Eliot to the researchers of which no record has yet been found.

39. A few months later, Lodge was *told* by HA that he might well become a senator. See HA to Lodge, 31 Jul 1876, L, II, 283, 284n2.

At what date HA first *thought* Lodge would rise to that eminence is an open question. My guess is that HA—often an uncanny anticipator of political developments—foreknew Lodge's becoming a senator from the time of Sumner's death.

40. Lodge learned HA's ideas concerning the major parties and in addition was able to express them. In a remarkable letter addressed to "My dear Roger," 15 Jul 1878, FP, he said: ". . . as long as you tie yourself to the apron-string of one party you will never effect anything. . . . You proclaim your intention of sticking by the party at all events[;] and as long as you do that the party managers, and they are quite right, laugh at you and use you and do not care a rap what you say or desire. I have no faith in reform inside the church. It is true to get anything done in politics you must work through the medium of the great parties, but you must be prepared to use one against the other[,] and then you may do something and make them bid up instead of down. No other way can the young reformers be aught but a laughing stock."

41. As originally planned, the articles would review the nation's achievements in politics, law, economy, literature, religion, and science. The categories may be important, as indicating an approach to history which HA at the time thought attractive, but later minimized. It may be relevant that HA later jokingly wrote that he was carrying "about six" burdens of history. See HA to Morse, 9 Apr 1881.

42. The quoted passage is from HA to CMG, 9 Feb 1876. Also see Garraty, *Henry Cabot Lodge*, op. cit., 43.

43. Garraty, *Lodge*, 43–44.

44. An idea underlying HA's tactic was that by sending out an ideally-timed letter the Independents could exert a saving influence *without revealing their weakness in numbers*. Put in military terms, the problem was one of gaining advantage in a three-way war. The suggested tactic is as follows. An army of not-yet-visible size announces loudly a future attack so that it might be *feared* as an army of large size. The fear might then cause a desired retreat by one of the other armies.

45. CFA2 was ill when Schurz first wrote. HA in consequence was able to act with an entirely free hand.

46. The Henry Adams Papers, 1891–1918, were opened to scholars in 1955. While reading the papers that summer at the Massachusetts Historical Society, I was given permission to attempt a quick examination of the thousands of books in the Henry Adams Library. I chanced to notice that a possibly important letter from Carl Schurz to HA, 24 Feb 1876, was inserted in HA's copy of Schurz's *Henry Clay*, Bost 1887. During a return visit in 1985, I asked to see the *Henry Clay*, thinking the letter might still be in the book and thus lost to use. The letter was still there and was even more important than I originally supposed.

A considerable meaning may inhere in HA's having inserted *that* letter in *that* book. Perhaps he had in mind two pairs: John Quincy Adams and Henry Clay in earlier times; Henry Adams and Carl Schurz in 1876.

47. Schurz to HA, 24 Feb 1876, op. cit. Schurz misstates what HA proposed. As if HA proposed a meeting of the Independents following *both* the major party conventions, Schurz speaks of a meeting after the party "conventions." What is more important, Schurz entirely fails to acknowledge what HA emphasized: the advantage that could be gained by issuance of a Independent circular letter at a very particular time, a week before the Republicans would meet.

48. HA to Lodge, 4 Sep 1876.

49. Lodge Papers, MHS.

50. Schurz asked Lodge whether he and Brooks Adams could come to New York to help him execute "that part of our plan that admits of no more delay." See Schurz to Lodge, 20 Mar 1876, LP. BA assisted as wished. See Claude Moore Fuess, *Carl Schurz*, NY 1932, 221.

Beringause, *Brooks Adams*, 57–59, says mistakenly that HA issued the call and otherwise gives a misleading account.

51. Schurz's imperviousness to political realities was evidenced by his writing that it was "quite probable" that the Republicans would nominate Bristow. He added, "Blaine seems no longer in the way." See Schurz to Lodge, 18 Apr 1876, LP.

52. Details about the children's illnesses and deaths appear in CFA2,

Diary, 10–13 Apr 1876, AP; and Nagel, *Descent from Glory*, 243–44.

53. Garraty, *Henry Cabot Lodge*, 46–47.

54. "The Reform Campaign," NYTribune, 17 May 1876.

55. The 1876 conference of Independents can be described as a renewal by Schurz of the pattern of political behavior he had set for himself and others at the 1872 Liberal Republican convention in Cincinnati and at a Fifth Avenue Conference of disappointed C. F. Adams enthusiasts held soon after in New York. By hewing to this pattern, he proved he had a great talent, but of a negative order. In both 1872 and 1876 under his guidance, potentially *large* political combinations were quickly reduced to nullity.

56. Schurz to Lodge, 17 May 1876, LP—". . . you disappeared all of a sudden." In his letter, Schurz calls the Conference a "success."

57. It goes without saying that HA's survey of early English and German history was a survey of "origins" of the United States. (In this respect, it paralleled King's survey of the Cordilleras, Darwin's survey of pigeons, and the survey of progenitors in Genesis.) But it should not be supposed that HA thought that origins were *explanations*. He thought them more-or-less ascertainable facts well worth knowing.

For HA's explanation of the coming into existence of the United States, one must go to his *History*. Among his historical works, that book alone gives an intended full explanation.

58. *EHA* (1907), 321; (LoA), 1056.

59. Under common law, Blaine owned the literary rights relating to the Mulligan letters. Under American law, the physical letters were Mulligan's property. Blaine's seizing them was theft.

60. Blaine had two sons, Emmons and Walker. On 4 Jun 1876, the eve of his speech, he characteristically wrote to Emmons: "I have been very anxious to hear from you to know how you were enduring, like a good son, the fiery ordeal through which your father is passing. Its fierceness no one but himself can know. . . . The defeat in the convention is as the small dust of the balance to him, though no one knows better than himself the prize for which he was contending. But the thought which takes the manhood out of him is that you and Walker, who are just entering life, may, perhaps, be forced to see, not only all your proud and happy anticipations disappointed, but yourselves put on the defensive. . . ." See Hamilton, *Biography of Blaine*, op. cit., 390. The passage is partly notable for Blaine's shifting from "I" to "himself," "him," and "he." Though replete with Biblical touches, his use of the third person is much in the style of Shakespeare's Julius Caesar. It is gratuitous, political, and falsely important.

Blaine's use of the third person contrasts with HA's writing in the third person about a largely fictional "Henry Adams" in *The Education of Henry Adams*. HA's use of the third person is literary and indispensable. It is the door permitting him as author to move with easy freedom between useful fact and useful fiction.

61. Once Mulligan produced the letters, HA wished Blaine *were* the Republican nominee. Presumably he reasoned that, if required to run for president immediately after stealing the letters, the speaker would suffer complete destruction.

Blaine was equally a calculator. Even before giving his speech in the

House, he anticipated not being nominated at the Republican convention. See his letter to his son Emmons in note 60.

62. Garraty, *Henry Cabot Lodge*, 47–48.

63. Young's commencement paper and his argument concerning patriarchs in his doctoral essay, "The Anglo-Saxon Family Law," were noted with approval by William Francis Allen in his review of *Essays in Anglo-Saxon Law*, *NAR*, Mar 1877, 329–30.

15. Biographer of Gallatin

Letters by and to HA are in HA-micro 4, unless otherwise noted.

PRINCIPAL SOURCES

(1) ten letters, HA to Lodge, 16 Jul 1876–29 Jun 1877.

(2) letters, HA to Trescot, 9 Aug, 1 Sep 1876, L, II, 286, 290.

(3) four letters, HA to CMG, 8 Sep 1876–22 Aug 1877.

(4) letters, HA to Morgan, 16 Oct 1876, L, II, 311–13; 14 Jul 1877, Cater, 80.

(5) letter, HA to Holmes, 5 Dec 1876, L, II, 299–301.

(6) letter, HA to FWS, 4 May 1877, in *Miscellaneous Letters of the Department of State*, Microcopy 179, roll 485, NA.

(7) letter, HA to Albert R. Gallatin, 14 Oct 1877, L, II, 323–25; also the enclosed expense account, Gallatin Papers, NYHS.

(8) [HA], *Democracy/ An American Novel*, NY 1880—cited hereafter as *Democracy* (1880).

(9) Henry Adams, *Democracy/ An American Novel*, NY 1925—cited hereafter as *Democracy* (1925).

(10) *Democracy* as printed in Henry Adams, *Novels/ Mont Saint Michel/ The Education*, NY: Library of America 1983—cited hereafter as *Democracy* (LoA).

(11) HA a. o., *Essays in Anglo-Saxon Law*, Bost: Little, Brown & Co. 1876; also Lond: Macmillan & Co. 1876—cited hereafter as *EASL*.

(12) [HA], "Lodge's Cabot," *Nation*, 5 Jul 1877, 12–13. (Attributed to HA in Haskell's *Index of Contributors*.)

(13) [HA], paragraph relating to King's "Catastrophism and Evolution," *Nation*, 30 Aug 1877, 137. (Attributed to HA in Haskell's *Index of Contributors*.)

ADDITIONAL SOURCES; COMMENTS

1. *Democracy* (1880) is the only original text. There are no manuscripts.

2. HA effected the attribution of the book to himself on 22 Jul 1915 by silently not resisting Thayer's proposal to attribute *Democracy* to him in *The Life and Letters of John Hay*. For details, see Charles Downer Hazen, *Letters of William Roscoe Thayer*, Bost & NY 1926, 250, and L, VI, 701. For the attribution, see Thayer, *Hay*, II, 58–59.

It was known among publishers that Thayer wrote his *Hay* with HA's active assistance. On 1 Apr 1918, five days after HA's death, Henry Holt & Co. issued a news release beginning, "That Henry Adams was the author of DEMOCRACY was a well kept secret for over a generation and was only lately revealed in 'The Life of John Hay.' " See the enclosure titled

"Literary Note/ THE LITERARY OUT-PUT OF HENRY ADAMS" accompanying the typed copy of Holt to BA, 1 Apr 1918, LP. Holt's news release documents the importance of Thayer's disclosure. Later Holt stated publicly that Thayer's disclosure was the first "authoritative utterance." See *Democracy* (1925), vi.

In 1929, notice was taken of the fact that *Democracy* had been published in Germany in 1907 as HA's work. See Stephen Gwynn, ed., *The Letters and Friendships of Sir Cecil Spring Rice/ A Record*, Bost & NY 1929, 59n1. The 1907 attribution was correct but had no authority.

3. GWA, *An Oration delivered at Quincy, on the fifth of July, 1824*, Bost 1824.

4. Barrows, *William M. Evarts*, op. cit., 292–94.

5. *Sketches*, 240–42.

6. Ibid., 232–34. New-found evidence indicates that Sarah B. Wister wrote "Lathrop's Study of Hawthorne." See Wister to Lodge, 13 Nov, 2 Dec 1875, LP. The actual writer of "Frothingham's Transcendentalism" remains unidentified. A natural guess is James Russell Lowell.

7. *Sketches*, 236–40.

8. How much HA wanted CFA2 not to be told the authorship of *Democracy* can be gathered from his not permitting its disclosure until after CFA2 had died. How little Lodge could guess the authorship is shown in Chap. 18, note 17.

9. The date suggested here for HA's completion of *Democracy* is the first to be supported by evidence and argument. What is more important, it is the first that conforms to the date intimated by HA. See HA to EC, 23 Aug 1901, L, V, 282—"my five-and-twenty-year old sins." Also see HA to Thayer, 22 Jul 1915, L, VI, 701, in which HA, responding to Thayer's assertion that he wrote *Democracy*, mentions the "Mulligan letters" (disclosed 31 May 1876).

In his published writings concerning *Democracy*, Holt made no effort to date the book's composition. Reviewing *Democracy* (1925), Laurence Stallings asserted, "Adams wrote his work shortly after Rutherford B. Hayes had defeated Samuel J. Tilden in a manner not convenient to mention. . . ." See unidentified clipping, "The First Reader/ Aesthete, 1879 Model," FP, Box 49. Stallings's date, c. summer of 1877, is an unadmitted guess clothed in the language of established fact. Subsequent writers (e.g. Elizabeth Stevenson, Ernest Samuels, and J. C. Levenson) have offered dates in 1878–1879 that similarly are unadmitted guesses.

10. *Democracy* (1880) contains errors and a repetition which indicate that HA wrote successive drafts, finished the concluding chapters of the last draft in a rush, and did not reread the last draft with a view to correcting it. There are two gross errors.

Chaps. XII and XIII are misnumbered XIII and XIV. (The error may indicate that a previous draft had fourteen chapters.)

On p. 306, Mrs. Lee walks from a ballroom on the grounds of the British legation to a room inside the legation. On p. 311, though she has not again moved, she is said to be "in a ball-room." (The error can be taken to indicate that in a previous draft she stayed in the ballroom on the grounds.)

There is a glaring repetition. A sentence on p. 195—"Every step he had taken he had taken with her approval."—is all but repeated by a sentence on p. 197—"She herself had approved every step she had seen him take." The repetition is one of a sort that HA occasionally fell into (e.g., the repetition in *EHA*, Chap. XIII, concerning ladies noticed in London to be well-dressed). I believe HA would have eliminated the repetition had he noticed it. On that basis, I infer that he did not attempt, or did not complete, a final editing.

11. HA showed an interest in the Centennial in several ways known to Lodge. He insisted that there be a Centennial Issue of the *North American* in January 1876. With Clover and others, he visited the Centennial Exhibition in Philadelphia in early September 1876. He made the October 1876 *North American* a conspicuous document in the centennial election. And he flatteringly told Lodge (letter, 23 Aug 1876) that the last paragraph of Lodge's article in that issue would count as *his*—HA's—"Centennial Oration."

All four actions indicated to Lodge that HA's interest in the Centennial was of a kind that might be considered ordinary and usual. The same actions served to conceal an interest in the Centennial that was quite unusual and involved the writing of an ambitious novel.

12. In July–September 1876, CFA2 was keenly aware that Blaine, although corrupt, might soon be secretary of state. He argued in "The 'Independents' in the Canvass" that Hayes, if elected, would *not* give places in his Cabinet to Grant's current secretary of war, Don Cameron, son of Simon Cameron (who again was senator from Pennsylvania), and Grant's secretary of interior, Zachary Chandler (who also was campaign manager for Hayes). Both secretaries were viewed as egregiously corrupt. CFA2 continued: "Having disposed of them, who is to be his Secretary of State? If usage is to be observed, it must be Mr. Blaine." See *NAR*, Oct 1876, 448.

13. For the quoted phrase, see *Democracy* (1880), 331; (LoA), 164.

14. HA's inventing the name Julia Schneidekoupon for use in *Democracy* is of a piece with his calling himself Ziegel in *The Radical Club*. Each name makes use of German to point towards a person whose identity, once realized, is very meaningful.

15. For HA's having known Sumner as corrupt, see *EHA*, Chap. III.

16. Fictional Silas P. Ratcliffe is preceded in HA's writings by so-called John Ratcliffe, the second president of Virginia. See [HA], "Captain John Smith," *NAR*, Jan 1867, 18—"Ratcliffe, whose real name was Sicklemore, was really a poor creature, if the evidence in regard to him can be believed."

17. Readers were the likelier to remember Lincoln's 1861 appointment of Simon Cameron as secretary of war because Cameron was again a senator and his son, James Donald Cameron, was currently secretary of war. See note 12, above.

18. Hooper's Washington address is listed in the editions of the *Congressional Directory* that were issued while he served.

19. Thoron, 170.

20. That the Adamses wanted to rent 1501 H Street comports with their living in other Hooper residences and their building a cottage at Beverly Farms. Their conduct perhaps should bring to mind a sentence in HA's "Primitive Rights of Women": "In some [American Indian] tribes the husband seemed to belong to the wife even more than the wife to the husband." See *Historical Essays*, 10.

21. Fifty-two students, more than a tenth of the undergraduates, completed History VI. See HA's grade book, 1873–1877, HAL.

22. HA's phrase "a trifling disagreement" may seem ironic understatement. It seems likely, however, that the publisher's objection to the issue was minimal. HA did not quit till the next week. His quitting seems to have come as an unexpected, last-minute surprise and may have involved his using a slight objection by the publisher as a weighty pretext. Whatever the details, HA threw off the editorship at a time convenient to him and on a basis largely of his making.

23. A long-standing myth asserts that HA was the Prometheus who brought graduate seminars from the German universities to the United States. Possibly the myth originated at the moment HA arranged that Young, Lodge, and Laughlin be doctoral candidates and that their meetings with him be called a seminar. Of course the arrangement could seem imported from Germany, but there is not the slightest evidence that HA knew anything about German graduate seminars or desired their emulation. The evidence indicates something quite opposite. His historical research team at Harvard resembled the geological exploring parties of the Fortieth Parallel Survey in the mountains of the American West. The relation of leader to associates was not hierarchical but democratic. The inspiration was American, not European.

24. HA to Macmillan & Co., 21 Oct 1876, L, II, 298.

25. See Maine to HA, 26 Dec 1876; CMG to HA, 14 Dec 1876; Palgrave to HA, 9 Feb 1877; HA to Gilman, 26 Oct 1876, L, II, 299.

HA had previously sent Maine his own essay, "The Anglo-Saxon Courts of Law." In response, Maine vaguely assured HA (letter of 26 Dec 1876) that his essay "appears to me to have very great value." He expressed astonishment that American students, unlike English students, could and would read German books. He professed interest in Sohm's work and said his opinion of it was "not quite" the same as HA's. For the most part, he seemed disposed to avoid discussion.

Whether HA sent copies to Thévenin and to Sohm is not known and is beyond the scope of this biography, as requiring access to French and German collections.

26. Holmes's unsigned notice of EASL in the American Law Review, Jan 1877, 327–31, is a document of some importance. It gives the impression that the reviewer is thoroughly conversant with German books on medieval law. This impression needs counteracting. According to one of Holmes's biographers, ". . . [Holmes] did not read German. . . ." See Novick, Honorable Justice, 152. (Asked to review the statement, Novick helpfully modified it, saying in a letter to myself, 23 Sep 1989, that Holmes "did not read German with any ease.") When his limited German is taken into account, Holmes's notice shows itself to be dependent on the book it reviews and on notices relating to medieval law written earlier for the North American by HA, Lodge, Thévenin, and Allen.

Three added points should be made. Holmes says about EASL, ". . . such monographs as these prepare the ground for a truly philosophical history of the law. . . ." He enters into a niggling argument whether a change in the manor courts was sudden (HA) or gradual (Holmes). He bypasses the main concern of HA's essay, the presence of democracy in England from the earliest times. The points considered, it can be suggested that HA's "Anglo-Saxon Courts of Law" disturbed Holmes because unsupportive of Holmes's own "philosophical history of the law." It disturbed Holmes too by seeming an incursion by HA from history into law. And it disturbed Holmes in his capacity as a friend and upholder of England's aristocracy.

Holmes's notice contains a protest, 330: ". . . there is a limit to historical explanation. . . . Some things . . . receive more light from an analysis of human nature." The protest imputes that HA and his students are not analysts of human nature. The imputation is refuted by the essays Holmes reviews.

27. Allen was more a professor and less a lawyer than Holmes or Maine. His notice of *EASL* is ungrudging, explanatory, and admiring. See "Essays in Anglo-Saxon Law," *NAR*, Mar 1877, 328–30.

An unsigned British notice of *EASL* in *Law Magazine and Review*, 1877–1878, 120–23, is remarkable for saying that HA and his associates "are perfectly independent, alike of each other, and of the English and Continental historians whose works they chiefly quote."

28. The full text is given in *Sketches*, xi.

29. There was a hidden reason for secrecy. A precisely parallel unsigned political article by CFA2 had appeared in the October 1872 *North American*. See *Sketches*, 226, 239.

CFA2, in his egoistic 13 Oct 1876 diary entry, AP, assumes that the difference of opinion leading to HA's retirement as editor narrowly concerned Article V. But it seems likely that the difference of opinion was provoked by *all* the articles in the issue.

The Trescot article was a historical satisfaction for HA. Trescot, being competent, was the man the Confederate government might better have sent to England in 1861, rather than Mason.

30. CFA2, Diary, 13, 23 Oct 1876, AP.

31. Bancroft read all the articles and supposed the publisher was forced by leading Bostonians to quarrel with the editors. He wrote to Lodge to say it was ironic that the editors brought out "a number that the world likes to read," whereupon "good society compels the publisher to break with them." See Bancroft to Lodge, 21 Nov 1876, LP.

32. *Sketches*, xi, 242.

33. CMG to HA, 14 Dec 1876, AP, and Palgrave to HA, 9 Feb 1877, indicate that HA had written to them and to Cunliffe.

34. CFA2, Diary, post-election entries, *passim*, AP.

35. L, II, 282, 288, 296, & 298. It seems likely that all four addressees were going to vote for Hayes.

36. HA's remarkable paper "The Primitive Rights of Women," published in his *Historical Essays* (1891), is described (1n) as a "Revision of a lecture delivered at the Lowell Institute, Dec. 9, 1876." The paper cites works published as late as 1886 (2n). The date of HA's revision was possibly still later.

Its date of revision notwithstanding, the paper suits December 1876 in substance and documents HA's rejection of law as the key to history. The paper is partly comic. HA shows strong disrespect towards lawmakers and makers of baseless theories of law and the history of law. He reduces to absurdity European historico-legal theories that women were subjected in early times, and he ridicules attempts by Roman writers of law and medieval writers of church doctrine to bring about the subjection of women. Seriously he asserts that women, whatever their rights in theory or law, have been capable of asserting their rights in fact. He takes the position that women have all the rights of men, plus a right to protection when endangered. As evidence of women's freedom, he cites the conduct of the heroines in Homer's *Odyssey* and the Icelandic *Njalsaga*. Also he draws on facts of American Indian practice.

37. HA to CMG, 14 Apr 1877—"again in New York."

38. See Chap. 2, note 39, above.

39. *EHA* (1907), 25; (LoA), 748–49.

40. A myth exists that HA "concluded that, for a brief time under King Alfred, the Saxon 'hundred' had served as the basis for a confederate state based on republican principles." See Dorothy Ross, "Historical Consciousness in Nineteenth-Century America," *AHR*, Oct 1984, 922, citing, not *EASL* itself, but a reading thereof by Levenson.

HA's thesis concerned nothing brief. It concerned the lingering of the hundred in England as a basis of political and judicial organization from the fifth century A.D. to 1876.

41. *NAR*, Oct 1876, 361.

42. For detailed evidence and argument that HA did not co-author the article, still less write the concluding paragraph, see *Sketches*, 240–42.

43. L, II, 218.

44. HA to Lodge, 22 Feb 1880, HA-micro 4, L, II, 393, remembering HJ "in Marlborough Street"; HA to EC, 1 Mar 1916, HA-micro 30, L, VI, 724, remembering HJ in the seventies.

45. Novick, *Honorable Justice*, op. cit., 133, 142–46. At HA's suggestion, CMG invited the Holmeses to Wenlock for three days. The host found Fanny "very bright and cheery" and Wendell "so simple & unaffected in manner, as to make him very popular, I should think." See CMG to MHA, 26 Oct 1874, AP.

46. In September 1876, the Adamses had been halted by a carriage breakdown while driving to visit the Holmeses at their farmhouse in Mattapoisett. See L, II, 296. The Adamses' non-arrival was curiously fitting, for HA at the moment was beginning to distance himself from law and from Holmes.

47. See Ford to HA, 21 Nov 1912, HA-micro 27—"Will you have any objection to permitting the Historical MSS. Commission of the American Historical Association to print the letters of Elbridge Gerry to John Adams, or those of William Vans Murray to John Quincy Adams? I should, of course, do the editing myself. . . ." Also HA to Ford, 23 Nov 1912, FP— "By all means! All the more because I recollect, as a boy, copying these letters for some one, and getting paid for it."

When printed, the Murray letters ran to more than 400 pages. See W. C. Ford, ed., *Letters of William Vans Murray to John Quincy Adams, 1797–1803*, Wash 1914—reprinted from AHA *Annual Report*, 1912, 314–717.

48. The copy of Gibbs's *Memoirs* in the Henry Adams Library appears to be a copy HA acquired late and for special uses. Only partly cut, it is cut in a way that indicates familiarity with the contents.

49. The notice, reprinted in *Sketches*, 150–59, includes HA's own history of Franklin's negotiation of the Treaty of Paris in 1782.

50. The titles are adduced from the earliest surviving source, the second and third volumes of HA's *History* as privately printed.

51. See HA's comments regarding *"state," "United States,"* "race," and "nation" in *EASL*, 3–4. Also see *Sketches*, 259n1, about confusions of terms in HA's historical writings, 1872–1875.

52. HA preserved a notebook headed "Manners and Customs" and dated "Aug. 1877." HAL. On the second to last page, it contains paragraphs by him possibly written in that month. If written then or soon after, the paragraphs afford a glimpse of his ruminations when his *History* was planned but not yet started. The paragraphs say:

> One great nationality is not necessarily a better means of aiding human development than several smaller nationalities would be. All human development hitherto has been due to the intense struggle of existence between numerous nationalities. China may be an exception.
>
> U. S. History from 1801, ending in the War of 1812[,] fixed the nation in its groove of national development. Did it effect more? Did it prove Americans to possess new powers, or faculties greater than those of previous peoples? Had they shown great political genius, either for civil or military administration? Broader grasp, keener vision, loftier motives, or more economical methods than their predecessors?

53. HA's best formulation of his purpose was not written till 1907 but was already true of his conduct in 1876. He wrote: "All I have sought has been the direction, or tendency, or history, of the human mind, not as religion or science, but as fact,—as a whole or stream,—and this with no view of its relation to me or my benefit." See HA to Clara Hay, 15 May 1907, HA-micro Brown, or *L*, VI, 67.

54. [HA], "Green's Short History of the English People," *NAR*, Jul 1875, 216–24; also in *Sketches*, 175–84.

55. Strictly speaking, King's Survey did not concern a single area. For geological reasons, it concerned five contiguous map areas not in perfect alignment. They totaled about one hundred miles by a thousand. See maps in the Atlas of the Report.

56. HA to FWS, 4 May 1877 (principal source 6) is the only evidence of HA's talking with Evarts and does not give a date.

57. HJ to HA, 13 Jan [1877].

58. Woolner to HA, 4 Mar, 29 Apr 1877; HJ to HA, 13 Jan, 5 May, 31 May, 5 Jun [1877].

While trying to bring about a visit by HJ to Wenlock, HA wrote to CMG, 22 Jun 1877: ". . . I like him though I don't read his books." The statement should be taken with two grains of salt. Clover can be assumed to have read James's books; and Henry's statement may indicate that he scanned James's *Roderick Hudson* and *The American*, thought them slight, and wished not to express his opinion to anyone but Clover.

59. Woolner to HA, 29 Apr 1877.

60. CFA, Diary, 12 Apr 1877, AP. ABA's illnesses were evidently multiple. Writing to CMG, 14 Apr 1877, HA said the immediate problem was "rheumatism."

61. CFA, Diary, 14 Apr 1877, AP. His train arrived at 5:45 P.M.

62. How HA got the Gallatin papers in one of the completest myster-

ies his biographers have to face. The conjecture outlined here owes its details to (a) the depth of concealment; (b) HA's having spoken with Evarts; (c) Evarts's close relations with Weed; (d) HA's saying he hobnobbed with the leaders of both parties; (e) Albert R. Gallatin's later writing to HA that he "had not been able to find anyone competent to write his [Albert Gallatin'] history and with whom I was willing to trust his papers"; and (f) HA's saying in a letter to Tilden, 24 Jan 1883, L, II, 491, ". . . I sent you my *Life of Gallatin* in consequence of the assistance which you rendered me in regard to it."

The letter from A. R. Gallatin to HA, 27 May 1880, is enclosed in HA's second copy of *LAG*, dated 1880, HAL.

63. See letters, HA to Stevens, 8, 12 Jul 1877, L, II, 310–11. The letters indicate that Stevens had at most a minor role in HA's becoming Gallatin's biographer and editor. HA conceals from Stevens the fact that Albert R. Gallatin had been searching for a *biographer* (see note 62). Misleadingly he gives Stevens the impression that the biography is a mere possible future option.

64. See HA to Justin Winsor, 6 Jun 1881, L, II, 428, suggesting the making of "a strong box, with stout hinges, iron handles, and a double lock." HA continues, "I handled all the Gallatin papers in this way for years, sending them forward and back between here and New York and Washington, without the smallest loss."

The Gallatin papers were bulky. According to his next biographer, Gallatin "collected some twenty thousand personal and family papers and documents." See Raymond Walters, Jr., *Albert Gallatin/Jeffersonian Financier and Diplomat*, NY 1957, vi.

65. CFA, Diary, 16 Apr 1877, AP. Nothing in the diary indicates that CFA had any share in, or as yet was even told of, HA's getting the Gallatin papers. It must be noted, however, that CFA held an opinion of Gallatin little different from the one HA would reach while acting as his biographer and editor. In 1841, CFA had written: "He [Gallatin] is one of the very few remaining among us, under whose hand the giant energies of the infant republic were moulded into form. And . . . he has, for certain peculiarities of mind which go to produce the character of a statesman, no equals among the generations that succeed his own. In him, there is very little of the merely brilliant . . . . But [he has] the talent of going to the bottom of all questions of public policy. . . ." See CFA, "Northeastern Boundary," *NAR*, Apr 1841, 428–29.

Further, CFA wanted Gallatin rescued from oblivion. In 1871, he had said in public: "Time . . . obliterates . . . the ephemeral reputations raised amid the conflicts of mere partisan politics. . . . From such a doom Albert Gallatin merits to be excepted. . . ." See CFA, *The Struggle for Neutrality in America*, op. cit., 42.

66. Various causes have made Gallatin little known to present-day Americans. One cause is lack of books. The only powerful book devoted to Gallatin exclusively is HA's *Life of Albert Gallatin*. It is a rare book, both in the original edition, Phila: Lippincott 1879, and in the facsimile edition, NY: Peter Smith 1943.

67. Letters, HA to Samuel F. Haven, William S. Lincoln, Hugh Blair Grigsby, William Wirt Henry, and Elizabeth Susan Quincy, L, II, 305–25.

68. Expense account, HA to Gallatin—see principal source 7.

69. MHA to RWH, 25 Nov 1877, AP, saying she and HA waited "from May till August" for a "decision."

70. HA specified 1827 because Gallatin held federal office till 1827. In that year, he retired as minister to England.

71. The resignation perhaps was verbal; no letter has been found.

72. *Letters of Fiske*, op. cit., 366.

73. There is no evidence that Whitman and Ellen Gurney, Edward and Fanny Hooper, or Dr. Robert Hooper were given the least idea in 1876 or later that HA wrote *Democracy*. Similarly there is no evidence that HA or MHA gave the forenamed persons advance notice that HA would not remain at Harvard past the spring semester of 1877, or definite word that he would not consider returning to the Harvard faculty.

74. Author's collection. The copy is signed, dated, and corrected by Lodge.

75. The complete talk was immediately published. See "Catastrophism./ Clarence King's Address at Yale./ A Blow at the British Philosophy of Uniformity and Slow Evolution./ The Grand Geologic Record of the American Continent," NYTribune, 27 Jun 1877, 2–3.

76. Lodge, *Early Memories*, 321.

77. Writing to President Eliot, 2 Mar 1877, L, II, 301–02, HA urged that he and Lodge be permitted to teach courses in U. S. history during the academic year 1877–1878 from opposed points of view. He said in defense of the proposal: "His [Lodge's] views being federalist and conservative, have as good a right to expression in the college as mine[,] which tend to democracy and radicalism. The clash of opinions can hardly fail to stimulate inquiry among the students."

Submitting the proposal, HA tried to achieve two objects the proposal did not specify. He tried to make possible his either leaving Harvard or staying for one more year (if unable to move to Washington). He tried to make possible Lodge's becoming sole teacher of U. S. history if he himself left the faculty.

The Harvard corporation "gladly gave its consent" to HA's proposal, and Lodge remained a faculty member till 1879. See Samuel Eliot Morison, *The Development of Harvard University*, Camb MA, 1930, 156.

Though HA soon left Harvard, the "clash of opinions" he recommended shortly occurred in print, in the form of Lodge's *Cabot* opposed by HA's *Documents Relating to New-England Federalism. 1800–1815.*

78. CFA to HA, 6 Jul 1877.

79. CFA to HA, 14 Jul 1877; CFA, Diary, 20 Jul 1877, AP. In the former, CFA says, ". . . I am a little surprised that you contemplate printing the last address to the thirteen signers." In the latter, he records searching "to find in my father's letter books his famous onslaught on the Massachusetts Federalists, but in vain."

The "onslaught" was in the Stone Library, but CFA had forgotten its whereabouts. (He was suffering memory lapses.) In diary entries for August 6–8, he recorded HA and MHA's visit, saying, ". . . Henry and his wife came in to look up some historical points, which I could not readily hit upon, and he found them." The "points" HA found must have included the onslaught, for soon CFA was reading it.

80. Palgrave to HA, 25 Aug 1877.

81. See note 69, above.

82. HA sent the paragraph to the *Nation* by way of Emmons. See HA to Emmons, 11 Aug 1877, L, II, 313–14. One may assume that, if King was within reach, Emmons showed King the manuscript for correction.

83. In the same letter, CFA urged HA to exercise "great moderation of tone" when publishing JQA's "Reply."

16. An Entirely New Career

Letters by and to HA are in HA-micro 4, unless otherwise noted.

PRINCIPAL SOURCES

   (1) six letters, HA to CMG, 15 Nov 1877–21 May 1879.

   (2) forty-nine letters, MHA to RWH, 15 Nov 1877–11 May 1879, AP.

   (3) eight letters, HA to Lodge, 2 Dec 1877–1 Feb 1879.

   (4) letter, HA to Gallatin, 24 Dec 1877, L, II, 330–31.

   (5) letters, HA to Bancroft, 7 Jun 1878, 25 Apr 1879.

   (6) letter, HA to Cunliffe, 7 Aug 1878.

   (7) five letters, Taylor to MHA, 4? Jan–23 Mar 1879, HA-micro 4.

   (8) letters, HA to Mary Parkman, 20 Feb, 26 May 1879, L, II, 353–54, 360.

   (9) HA, editor, *Documents Relating to New-England Federalism/ 1800–1815*, Bost 1877; cited hereafter as *NEF*. (As spelled in the page headings, the title is *New England Federalism*.)

   (10) [HA], "King's Systematic Geology," *Nation*, 23 Jan 1879, 73–74. (Attributed to HA in Haskell's *Index of Contributors*.)

   (11) HA, editor, *The Writings of Albert Gallatin*, Phila 1879, 3v.

   (12) HA, *The Life of Albert Gallatin*, Phila 1879 (or facsimile reprint, NY 1943); cited hereafter as *LAG*.

   (13) HA, "Albert Gallatin," in *Memorial Biographies of the New England Historic Genealogical Society*, Bost 1880, I, 203–12; cited hereafter as *MBAG*.

   (14) Frances Snow Compton [pseudonym for HA], *Esther*, NY 1884; cited hereafter as *Esther* (1884).

   (15) HA, *Esther*, as reprinted in Henry Adams, *Novels/ Mont Saint Michel/ The Education*, NY: Library of America 1983; cited hereafter as *Esther* (LoA).

ADDITIONAL SOURCES; COMMENTS

   1. When and how HA gained access to records held by executive departments other than the State Department has not been determined, but he had long been acquainted with Secretary of the Treasury John Sherman and thus knew three of the seven members of Hayes's Cabinet.

   2. In the 1950s, recalling her experiences when she began to live with HA in 1912, Aileen Tone told me that to her surprise the Library of Congress wagon came regularly to bring and recover books requested by HA, and that, on making inquiries, she learned he had "always" been given the service. I have assumed that the beginning of "always" was sometime in 1877–1878.

   3. References to *Alice in Wonderland* also appear in MHA to RWH, 18 Nov 1877, AP, and HA to Walker, 17 Feb 1878, L, II, 335.

   4. Little, Brown & Co. to Ford, 17 Jul 1913, FP.

   5. Little, Brown could reasonably assume that the books were com-

panion volumes, for the books have documents in common. That they were not companion volumes would become apparent only to persons willing to read them carefully and consider their implications.

HA obtained copies of letters by Timothy Pickering and attendant papers owned by MHS. See bound volume titled *Timothy Pickering MSS*, HAL. He must have lent Lodge the volume, for some of the letters it contains appeared first in Lodge's *Cabot* and again in his own *NEF*.

6. HA sent a copy to Herbert Baxter Adams (no relation), a young history fellow at Johns Hopkins University, newly created in Baltimore. See HA to Adams, 24 Dec 1877, L, II, 330.

HA's influence on the study of history at Johns Hopkins apparently had two main aspects. One related to appointments. Offered a chance to be the university's inaugural professor of history, he had advised President Gilman on 1 Dec 1877, "... I do not care to become again a Professor on any terms. . . ." He then urged that the position be filled soon and suggested candidates. See letters, HA to Gilman, 12 Nov 1877–21 Jan 1879, L, II, 325–28, 334, 250–51, and Cater Collection, MHS.

The other aspect related to *Essays in Anglo-Saxon Law*. The book evidently was accepted by Gilman, H. B. Adams, and others at Johns Hopkins as a historian's bible. In part for that reason, the book continued to sell. Little, Brown reprinted it in 1905.

7. Though it may not seem so at first, the statement is ironic. A manifest object of the volume is to stop controversy by being incontrovertible. It thus sets out to do on a larger scale in 1877 what JQA had hoped to do in 1829.

CFA had urged HA to avoid controversy when publishing the *Reply*. Yet on seeing what Henry published, he welcomed the volume in a similarly ironic spirit, writing to him on 23 Dec 1877 that *NEF* "will at any rate do as a permanent settlement of the controversy."

8. *NEF* links with many of HA's works. Read as a commentary on history, it is as much *A Letter to American Teachers of History* as the book Adams would send to teachers in 1910 under that title. The lines in the Preface of *NEF* that concern JQA's recollection in 1829 of an operatic refrain—"O Richard! O mon roi!/ L'univers t'abandonne."—tie the volume to *Mont Saint Michel and Chartres*. For a link with *The Education*, see note 48, below.

9. [Lodge], "New England Federalism," *Nation*, 3 Jan 1878. The notice shows Lodge at his critical best and lawyerly worst. He tries to defend the Federalists implicated in designs for disunion in 1804–1815 by resorting to hair-splitting and pettifoggery.

Apropos of lawyers, CFA wrote to HA on 13 Feb 1878: "I have met with several persons[,] chiefly lawyers[,] who have read your volume, and speak of it [JQA's *Reply*] . . . as on the whole the most powerful of your grandfather's production. They ask me why he suppressed it, and why you suppressed the severity upon Otis. I tell them what is true[,] that the two Everetts to whom he sent the manuscript were chiefly responsible for the first and you for the last. They did not approve of your proceeding, and not much of the other."

10. Without even faintly suggesting the fact, HA made his *NEF* a vehicle for materials essential to an understanding of himself. The best early essay about him is "The Heritage of Henry Adams," by BA, in

Degradation, 1919. The essay may seem to err in linking HA with George Washington and with JQA's proposed program of internal improvements, but *NEF* supports these linkings and apparently was the basis on which BA first thought of them.

BA would have understood his brother still better if he had noticed HA's interest in *Gallatin's* program of improvements, which antedated JQA's by a half-generation. See *LAG*, 350–52, and especially *MBAG*, 208 —". . . [Gallatin] prepared a very grand system of internal improvements. . . . The only portion of this scheme ever carried into effect was the famous Cumberland Road."

11. The documents referred to in this summary all appear in *NEF*.

12. Much of the power of the *Reply* resides in the corroborative evidence JQA obtained after writing the clarification. But the literally crushing power of the *Reply* as printed in *NEF* largely arises from the fact that it as good as predicts the further corroborative evidence that HA found, then used to perfect the book.

13. HA could well have mentioned the death of George Washington Adams in the Preface to *NEF*, yet the Preface avoids the subject. A possible reason was stated or potential objections by CFA to public references to his brother's death.

A stronger reason involves HA's calling himself George. See Chap. 23. If he assumed from an early date that he was a replacement for his father's lost eldest brother, as apparently he did, HA had a motive for treating George's death as a subject requiring exceptional caution.

14. The phrase is drawn from JQA, Diary, 31 Mar 1829, AP.

15. HA surely had a copy of the *Reply*—the one he used as part of the MS. of *NEF*. The copy is not in evidence. If he made the copy himself at an early age, he may have been anxious to destroy it, after *NEF* was printed and published, as too revealing of his personal history.

CFA appears to have read HA's copy against the original. In his letter to HA, 17 Sep 1877, he speaks of "a few errors in the *copy* that need correcting [italics added]."

16. The Preface of *NEF* says that both Plumer and Lodge "had the free use of this paper in manuscript." The phrase might be understood to say that CFA loaned Plumer and Lodge the *Reply* for long periods; but CFA's diary entry for 20 Jul 1877, AP, shows that he knew the MS. was in the Stone Library (though momentarily he could not find it).

Once one assumes that Lodge was lent a copy of the MS. and that HA owned the copy, HA's superior knowledge of the *Reply* is accounted for, CFA's diary entry makes sense, and Lodge can have seen the paper without disturbance of the original at the Stone Library.

17. For "this political drama," see *NEF*, 273.

18. "*1800–1815*," the dates given on the cover and title page of *NEF*, are wrong dates if intended by HA to bracket the documents that appear in the volume; for their dates are 1804–1829. "*1800–1815*" are wrong dates if intended by HA to bracket the interval referred to by JQA in his *Reply*, for JQA has much to say about events in 1799 relating to peace with France. But "*1800–1815*" are right dates if meant to refer to Jefferson's first election as president and to the arrival in the U. S. of the news of the Treaty of Ghent. According to HA (and previously JQA), these two events were the beginning and the completion of the New England Federalists' ruin.

19. The *Reply* ranges more widely than might be expected. To give four examples, it considers in detail: (a) the attempt by Hamilton and others in 1799 to establish a military dictatorship under Hamilton; (b) John Adams's successful thwarting of this attempt by sending a mission to France; (c) Jefferson's effort to bring about numerous removals of Federalists from office (thus anticipating "Jacksonian democracy"); and (d) Jefferson and Madison's violation of the natural rights of the Louisianans after purchasing Louisiana from Napoleon.

20. *NEF*, 249 (Pope); 275 (Milton); 61, 110, 215, 307, 320, 328 (*Hamlet*); 114, 130, 143, 217 (*Othello*); 166 (*Macbeth*); 284 (*Measure for Measure*); 280 (*As You Like It*); 280 (*A Midsummer Night's Dream*).

21. In 1913, Ford advised HA that he meant to reprint JQA's *Reply*. HA warned in answer, 29 Nov 1913, FP: "You will have to fill up some small gaps in the N. E. Federalism from the MS. My grandfather was a bad writer, and I tried to leave out some of his stuff."

22. The cuts are indicated: *NEF*, 213, 226, 263, & 300.

23. When HA started assembling material for *NEF*, he lacked the materials published in Virginia newspapers. Such newspapers were not to be found in Massachusetts. For his efforts to get the *Richmond Enquirer*, see his letter to Grigsby, 20 Aug 1877, L, II, 315.

24. In his letter to HA responding to *NEF*, 22 Dec 1877, Bancroft more than accepts the Adams-family estimate of Timothy Pickering as a traitor, corroborates the Adams-family estimate of Theophilus Parsons as a nullifier, accepts the Adams-family argument that Alexander Hamilton and others intended a military dictatorship headed by Hamilton, and agrees with the Adams-family belief that President John Adams's frustration of that particular design accounted for Hamilton's "bitter hostility" (Bancroft's phrase) to Adams. Bancroft adds that, in his opinion, Washington meant to uphold Adams's administration and "remained true to that intention to the last."

25. A measure of the *political* aspect of HA's return to Washington was the violence of CFA2's reactions against Clover and King, HA's main partners in his return. The violence is best seen in the pages about them in CFA2's Memorabilia, 1888–1893, AP.

Similarly violent was CFA2's eventual outright dismissal of *NEF* even as a contribution to history. On 27 Nov 1911, Ford wrote enthusiastically to CFA2 about "a knock-out blow"—meaning JQA's *Reply* as published by HA with supporting materials in 1877. CFA2 answered: "As to that 'knock-out blow' to which you refer, I make little account of it. The use my brother Henry may have made of this material forty years ago seems to me quite obsolete now. . . . The volume . . . is, I fancy, not often consulted. Certainly it is not a 'classic'." See CFA2 to Ford, 28 Nov 1911, FP.

26. HA to William Wirt Henry, 15 Sep 1877, L, II, 320.

27. For example, HA to Grigsby, 30 May 1878, L, II, 339—"I have unearthed much private correspondence of that time, including masses of John Randolph's and [Nathaniel] Bacon's letters. . . ."

28. At Harvard in 1876–1877, the students taking History VI tended to suppose that Adams had read everything relating to U. S. history, but there was much he had not read. In connection with the course, he acquired *The Works of John C. Calhoun*, six volumes, HAL. On May 1, 1877, he read for the first time Calhoun's celebrated *Disquisition on Government*

and wrote marginal comments. Calhoun ventured that government "is of Divine ordination." HA wrote in the margin, "Surely this is wretched stuff." Calhoun said, "In earlier stages of society, numbers and individual prowess constituted the principal elements of power." HA countered: "Prove it! The elements were always complicated. Even numbers and prowess were not simple elements but results of conditions and intelligence was the most active factor of all." Calhoun shared the common idea that "barbarous nations" had overpowered "the civilized." HA would have none of it. "Quite untrue. Civilization was never overpowered but by its own diseases."

At the end of the *Disquisition*, HA wrote two short paragraphs in the margins. In the first he said: "I am bitterly disappointed. This work reads to me like the crude vagary of a South Carolina planter, half-educated and half-trained. I never in my life was more surprised than with this exhibition of Calhoun's famous intellectual power." In the second, he sketched a proof that Calhoun's mind was "wretchedly sophistical." He initialed the paragraphs and apparently read no more.

29. After ceasing to be president in 1829, JQA wrote two long works. His *Reply to the Appeal of the Massachusetts Federalists*, written in Washington, concerned union and disunion. His *Parties in the United States*, written in Quincy, concerned the political parties that existed in the Union from its inception to the time of writing. He did not publish it. The original draft and a fair copy were kept at Quincy. Another copy escaped the family's control. See JQA, *Parties in the United States*, ed. by Charles True Adams (no relation), NY 1941.

It is tempting to believe that, while locating JQA's *Reply* in the Stone Library in August 1877, HA found the fair copy of JQA's *Parties in the United States*, borrowed it with CFA's permission, and kept it at hand while writing *The Life of Albert Gallatin*.

At the time, HA was troubled by the question whether historians of the United States would learn anything of consequence by studying the country's parties and more particularly by studying the opposition between two party leaders, Hamilton and Jefferson. He was partly inclined to think these matters suited to historical beginners. Writing to Grigsby, 9 Oct 1877, L, II, 322, he said: "Dear old Jefferson! Never was there a more delightful ground for people to argue about! We discuss him . . . as though he were alive. . . . He is supremely useful still (he and Hamilton) as a sort of bone for students of history to mumble, preparatory to getting their teeth."

Apparently, during the winter of 1877–1878, HA decided to re-study parties and related isssues. He made *The Life of Albert Gallatin* not only a biography but also a record of a historian's struggle to achieve a credible analysis of the Union's parties in the period 1789–1812 and a credible account of the movement of American politics through short- term cycles. The subjects were intricate, and the struggle did not lead to a settled result.

The *Life*, as printed, hesitates between a two-party theory and four-party theory of American history. It also gravitates towards a center-party theory. HA's two-party and four-party theories (two extreme and two moderate) are much in evidence in Book II. His center-party theory appears in Book II but is more evident in Book III. Two archetypal centrists are Gallatin and J. Q. Adams.

Book II and Book III are each given to a twelve-year phase. Thus *LAG* anticipates the passage in HA's *HUS* (Scribner), VI, 123; (LoA), II, 380, beginning, "Experience seemed to show that a period of about twelve years measured the beat of the pendulum." (The passage is quoted with appreciation in Arthur M. Schlesinger, Jr., *The Cycles of American History*, Bost 1986, 23.)

Without denying either their seriousness or their value, one may say that HA's unsettled party theories and his cycle theory, as set forth in *LAG*, or even in *HUS*, are comparatively incidental and inessential among his ideas relating to the United States. A negative lesson of both books is that HA, having already backed away from law as the key to history, also backed away from parties.

30. Another of HA's inessential ideas is the notion that the Treasury Department is the controlling organ of government in the United States. The idea appears in Chap. VII of *Democracy*. It is affirmed at the beginning of Book III of *LAG* but dropped when Gallation goes abroad as peace commissioner. It is practically invisible in *HUS*.

31. HA says in the *Life*, 26, "His [Gallatin's] story must be told as far as possible in his own words. . . ." With this imperative as its excuse, the biography quotes a very large number of letters by and to Gallatin and between other persons.

32. The letters written during the winter of 1877–1878 by MHA to RWH and by CFA to HA mostly survive; but HA's letters to CFA, RWH's letters to MHA, and the letters that HA and MHA exchanged with other relatives that winter are all missing.

33. CFA to HA, 18 & 29 Jan 1878.

34. In his letter to Hay (early 1877?) beginning "Of course you have . . . ," HP, King says he will write " 'the great American novel' " — putting the phrase within quotation marks.

35. See note 41, below.

36. See note 47, below.

37. Writing to her father on 31 Mar 1878, MHA mentions HA's saying it was twenty-seven years since he was last at Mount Vernon. This is the only evidence of a visit by HA *in 1851*. (The visit recounted in Chap. III of *EHA* is dated 1850.)

Because Chap. VI of *Democracy* recounts an excursion by a party to Mount Vernon and because HA reportedly said he had not been there since 1851, it may be imagined that Chap. VI must have been written after HA and MHA went there with friends on 1 Apr 1878. But HA was capable of writing the chapter without returning to Mount Vernon. Moreover, the published chapter has more the air of fancy than of fact.

38. In his Introduction to HA's *History* as reprinted by Albert & Charles Boni, NY 1930, Henry Steele Commager remarked metaphorically, "It is not too much to say that Henry Adams at Monticello is the most pregnant, the most profound problem in American history." When he made the remark, Commager had no way of knowing that HA was once at Monticello in the company of one of Jefferson's great-granddaughters. It can be added that, far from being a problem, HA's being at Monticello — whether metaphorically or literally—was an instance of his seldom-failing ability to go where he needed to go, often under the best possible auspices.

39. HA to Theodore Dwight, 17 Jun 1878.

40. Wilkins, *Clarence King*, 199–201, 399.

41. Taylor begins his book by saying, "The history of the United States, as yet unwritten, will show the causes of the 'Civil War' to have been in existence during the Colonial era. . . ." The words involve an allusion to HA's not-yet-written *History* as anticipated by Taylor. He very quickly goes on to say: "The first serious difficulty of the Federal Government arose from the attempt to lay an excise on distilled spirits. The second arose from the hostility of New England traders to the policy of the Government in the war of 1812, by which their special interests were menaced; and there is now evidence to prove that, but for the unexpected peace, an attempt to disrupt the Union would then have been made."

Taken together, the quoted statements allude to the secession of the South in 1861–1865, the Whiskey Rebellion in western Pennsylvania in 1794, and the rebellion intended by the New England Federalists in 1814–1815 (a rebellion snuffed out by the news of the Treaty of Ghent).

A history of the Whiskey Rebellion and Gallatin's leading role in defusing it would appear in Book II of HA's *Life of Albert Gallatin* when published.

HA's *New England Federalism* is the evidence Taylor means when alluding to a later "attempt to disrupt the Union."

Taylor's never-resting wit considered, there is more than a possibility that his "New England traders" involves a pun on "traitors."

42. In the Gallatin entry in the *DAB* (1931), David H. Muzzey reported that Gallatin's papers "have not yet been made available." In the Preface to his *Albert Gallatin*, NY 1957, Raymond Walters, Jr., said that the Gallatin family authorized the cataloguing and opening of the papers c. 1947. "It was my good fortune to be the first person in almost seventy years to use the collection in its entirety."

43. HA was not paid for the review. See HA entry in *The Nation—Ledger/ 1873–1881* in the *Nation* Records, NYPL. I infer that HA offered Godkin the review gratis and Godkin welcomed the offer.

Writing to RWH on 15 Jan 1879, MHA said that King began a visit at 1501 H Street on the 10th. I assume HA wrote the review after King's arrival and did not consider it finished till King approved it.

44. The arrival of Charles Trevelyan necessarily brought to mind his brother, George Otto Trevelyan, whom the Adamses also knew. The Trevelyans were nephews of Lord Macaulay. Two years earlier, George had published Macaulay's biography. At the time, Palgrave assumed that HA had read it and remarked in a letter to HA, 9 Feb 1877, "What more comic than the seriousness with which he takes his uncle to task for not esteeming a Carlyle or a Ruskin as highly as his nephew does!" HA's copy of the biography is in HAL. Mention of the biography appears in the Preface to *Mont Saint Michel and Chartres*.

45. Writing to him on 28 Nov 1881, L, II, 413, HA reminded Godkin that he had told him about *Democracy* at a moment when he, HA, "had almost decided not to print" it. Late January 1879, when Godkin visited the Adamses in Washington, seems a moment that fits HA's description.

There is no direct evidence indicating when HA told the secret of his authorship of *Democracy* to King. In the same letter to Godkin, HA speaks of King as "my other confidant." (In fact, apart from MHA, there were four early confidants: Mrs. Parkman, King, Godkin, and Taylor; but by

November 1881 Taylor and Mrs. Parkman were dead, so in that sense HA's phrase can be correct.) It is hard to imagine that HA confided in Godkin sooner than in King. For reasons of caution, it is still harder to imagine that he confided in them together. I accordingly infer that he told King the secret first and told him as early as January 10, 1879, when he arrived for a visit.

46. The best evidence that HA read Taylor's *Destruction and Reconstruction* in January 1879, prior to its being published, is HA's permitting Taylor to read the manuscript of *Democracy*. In turn, the evidence that Taylor read *Democracy* is a letter to MHA. See note 47.

It seems next to certain that in 1876, when completing *Democracy*, HA had written with Taylor somewhat in mind. A leading character in the novel, John Carrington, a Virginian and a veteran of the Rebellion, had been preceded in HA's writings by a July 4 entry in his 1867 engagement book, HAL: "G. Carrington *Taylor* [italics added]."

47. Of the letters by Taylor to MHA (principal source 7), the most important is that dated 3 Feb 1879, a Monday. The circumstances in which it was written were apparently as follows. Taylor's "Presidential Aspirants" had appeared in New York in the *World* on Saturday. On Sunday, Taylor learned that MHA had already clipped "Presidential Aspirants" and sent it to her father with instructions to show it to Mrs. Parkman so she could guess who wrote it. Taylor meanwhile had obtained a copy of an editorial in a Boston newspaper criticizing an article he had contributed to the February 1879 *North American* titled "A Statesman of the Colonial Era." Also Taylor had read—or was near to finishing— the MS. of HA's *Democracy*. On Monday, he sent MHA the Boston editorial and a two-page letter. His letter began:

> At a meet of Her Majesty's buck-hounds appeared the great artist—the late lamented Poole. Carefully arrayed in immaculate hunting garb[,] he superciliously regarded the vulgar crowd, then addressed the noble master of the hunt—'Good morning, my Lord. Good morning, Poole. Very mixed attendance, my Lord. Ah! True, my good Poole; but you see we can't all be tailers.'

This ostensibly simple passage was crowded with meanings that the Adamses were sure to catch. To begin with, Poole was HA's London tailor. By making Poole a "great artist," Taylor has played on Chap. XI of *Democracy*, in which Worth, the Paris dressmaker, ranks above all other persons in the western world as "the great genius of the nineteenth century." In my view, the Worth-Poole linkage is sufficient evidence that Taylor had read or was still reading *Democracy*.

By saying, ". . . we can't all be tailers," Taylor suggests both that we can't all be Taylors and we can't all be Adamses, meaning in both cases that we can't all be presidents, and meaning too that he and HA *are* presidents: the rank inheres in the names.

"Tailers" suggests tailors but was then in use as a word meaning followers, persons who wait in a queue, or game fish who flash their tails above the water. "Tailor" and the various senses of "tailer" each lend an added meaning to the passage. Needless to say, the meanings comically move off in widely different directions.

The passage ending with "tailers" leads directly to a sentence beginning "We can't all be Bostonians. . . ." Mock-seriously, Taylor goes on to suggest that Bostonians, MHA and HA perforce included, are superior to "your crushed friend/ R. Taylor."

48. It has already been noted—Chap. 7, note 69—that Chap. III of HA's *Education* draws upon Taylor's *Destruction and Reconstruction*.

There are very strong links between a principal sentence in the Preface of HA's *Education* and writings by HA, CFA, and Taylor published in 1877–1880. The sentence reads:

> The tailor's object, in this volume, is to fit young men, in Universities or elsewhere, to be men of the world, equipped for any emergency; and the garment offered to them is meant to show the faults of the patchwork fitted on their fathers.

The sentence is a recasting of the closing sentence in the Preface of *NEF*, which says about HA's purpose as editor, ". . . his *object* has been . . . to stimulate, if possible, a new generation in our *universities* or *elsewhere* . . . [italics added]."

Also the sentence draws upon CFA's short biography of JQA written in parallel with HA's short biography of Gallatin. CFA's work contains the statement: ". . . President Washington . . . marked the writer [JQA] as a person fit for confidence *in any emergency* . . . [italics added]." See *Memorial Biographies of the New England Historic Genealogical Society*, I (1880), 114.

Finally, the sentence begins with a metaphor of the author, HA, as a tailor. This metaphor echoes Carlyle's *Sartor Resartus*. It echoes a pun in the fable included by Richard Taylor in his letter to MHA, 3 Feb 1879 (see note 47, above)—a fable climaxed by the statements " '. . . we can't all be tailers,' " and "We can't all be Bostonians. . . ." In addition, it harks back to Taylor's "Presidential Aspirants," for in his article Taylor makes comic use of Carlyle's Professor Dryasdust.

It seems possible that Taylor had an inkling that HA was going to write a book called *The Education of Henry Adams*. Taylor begins his "Presidential Aspirants" with a comic evocation of a school for underprivileged boys in Boston.

49. "Presidential Aspirants" appears to reflect detailed knowledge of HA's personal history. One of the article's funniest aspects concerns the sons to whom the "wise man" is addressing his words. The reader has to believe that the sons, rather than keep their father's article secret, as they have been enjoined by him to do, have given it to the *World*, a Democratic newspaper in New York. So doing, the sons have reenacted JQA2 and CFA2's giving HA's 1869–1870 "Session" to the *World* in 1870.

The reenactment is part of a comic, yet serious reconstruction of HA's place in the Adams family. In Taylor's article, the wise man—the son and grandson of aspirants to the presidency—is the last and greatest figure in a political dynasty. He also is HA, except that the Adams family is so changed that CFA does not exist, HA is the only son of JQA, and JQA2 and CFA2 are HA's unworthy, disobedient *sons*.

50. I have repeated the gist of Taylor's lampoon of Blaine but have omitted its laughable complexities. In the course of the representation, Taylor draws a comic parallel between the senator and Clive of India and another between the senator and an applicant for a clerkship on an Ohio River steamboat.

51. It seems sufficiently obvious that HA's *Esther* was written in response to Eliot's *Middlemarch* and Hawthorne's *Scarlet Letter*. In Eliot's novel, with tragic consequences, the heroine marries a clergyman unsuited to be her husband. In Hawthorne's, the heroine suffers the tragic consequences of having trusted and loved a clergyman who is not her husband. In *Esther*, the heroine saves herself from tragic consequences by refusing to go through with a marriage to a clergyman.

Of the three heroines, HA's Esther Dudley may be the slightest, but she has the merit of giving her story a self-respecting, distinctive, and anti-tragic close.

It is typical of HA that he masked his interest in Hawthorne's most famous character, Hester Prynne, by naming his heroine after Hawthorne's inconspicuous Esther Dudley. The mask successfully *conceals*. "Esther" and "Hester" are differently pronounced and look unalike. Yet it also successfully *reveals*. "Hester" is a variant form of "Esther." It uses the same letters, albeit in a different order.

It may be added that in *The Scarlet Letter* Hester Prynne does not enter churches. Also, for varying reasons, she at intervals stands on a scaffold, meaning a platform. HA presumably knew that MHA had told her father she needed "a platform to stand on."

52. *Esther* (1884), 19; (LoA), 195.

53. *Esther* (1884), 289, 297; (LoA), 429, 332.

54. On 25 Dec 1911, HA told Louisa Hooper that he was the author of *Democracy* and that he wrote and published a second novel, *Esther*. LHT wrote to me about the experience on 17 Feb 1956. According to her letter, HA told her, in part, that the church under construction in *Esther* is Boston's Trinity Church, moved to New York.

When LHT wrote her letter, two ideas were being bruited in publications: that MHA did not know HA wrote the novel, and that the heroine is MHA. With respect to the first idea, she said, ". . . I don't see how it is tenable that H. A. wrote it except in his own house with Aunt Clover there and seeing him do it all the time." With respect to the second idea, she said that, of the models HA drew upon when creating the heroine, one certainly was Anne Palmer.

For further statements made by LHT in her letter, see Chap. 22, note 37, below.

55. HA to Barlow, 17 Apr 1879, L, II, 357. Making an allusion that Barlow very probably would catch, HA adds, ". . . those of us who have no *political aspirations*, will, I suspect, remember him better than some others [italics added]."

56. HA's short biography of Gallatin says as little as possible about political parties and concentrates instead on personal and political specifics. The following passage is representative: "Mr. Madison, on assuming the presidency in March, 1809, wished to make Mr. Gallatin his Secretary of State, but was compelled to abandon this plan by opposition in the Senate, led by William B. Giles of Virginia, Michael Leib of Pennsylvania, and Samuel Smith of Maryland. During the next four years the government was distracted by this personal opposition, to which the Vice-President, George Clinton, also belonged, and with which Mr. Robert Smith, brother of the Senator, and Secretary of State, was in sympathy. All, or nearly all, Mr. Madison's and Mr. Gallatin's schemes were defeated

by this Senatorial faction, which held a balance of power. The War of 1812 was probably due to the paralysis of government caused by this personal hostility, of which Mr. Gallatin was the chief victim." See *MBAG*, 208–09.

57. *MBAG*, 212. In the biographies, HA did not say that Gallatin was a "great man"—not in so many words. The avoidance lends importance to HA's letters to, and meeting with, John Russell Bartlett, who had published *Reminiscences of Albert Gallatin* in 1849. He wrote to Bartlett: "The comments of a great man on his own career—especially on his own faults and character—are invaluable to a biographer. A word,—sometimes even a look or a moment of mere silence,—may tell more than all the printed volumes." See HA to Bartlett, 4, 12 Nov 1878, L, II, 346–48; also HA to same, 12 May 1879, HA-micro 4.

58. *MBAG*, 211.

59. In his *Garrulities of an Octagenarian Editor*, Bost & NY 1923, 136, Holt recalled: "In the spring of '79 Henry sent me the manuscript of *Democracy*, under a pledge of dead secrecy. I read it myself and accepted it at once."

I assume that HA, to avoid reliance on the mail, sent the MS. to Holt after reaching New York.

A week later, HA wrote to Mrs. Parkman, L, II, 360, "D——y is d———d." I take his line to mean "*Democracy* is delivered."

60. *Democracy* (1880) is manifestly unedited by the publisher. I infer that HA asked Holt to print it exactly as he wrote it.

In his *Garrulities*, op. cit., 137, Holt says mistakenly that his firm "must have rushed" *Democracy* into print in 1879. There in fact was no rush. There instead was a long wait. In its earliest-published state, *Democracy* included a front paste down dated 31 Mar 1880. See Blanck, 3.

One of HA's favorite days was April Fool's Day. I infer that he asked Holt to publish *Democracy* on that day. Holt as good as did so. For Holt's own use of April Fool's Day, see Chap. 15, note 2, above.

61. There was time before the Adamses sailed for Holt to send his acceptance.

62. CFA, Diary, 20 May 1879, AP. It is not known what alleged statements by MHA were at issue. With one exception (CFA to HA, 4 Dec 1878), all the letters that passed between HA and his Adams relations during the winter of 1878–1879 are missing. Nothing in the letters MHA wrote to her father during the winter indicates awareness of the problem HA later raised with his father at Quincy. The only Adams recorded by MHA to have visited that winter in Washington was CFA2.

63. CFA, Diary, 22–23, 25 May 1879, AP.

17. A Checkered Ocean

Letters by and to HA are in HA-micro 4, unless otherwise noted.

PRINCIPAL SOURCES

(1) seven letters, HA to CMG, 8 Jun–20 Dec 1879.

(2) twelve letters, MHA to RWH, 8 Jun–28 Dec 1879, Thoron, 139–224.

(3) nine letters, HA to Cunliffe, 15 Jun 1879–20 Apr 1880. The fragment written by HA at Gibraltar is misdated 21 Nov 1879 in L, II,

380–81. The correct date, 22 Nov 1879, is given by the fragment, once it is read together with HA to CMG, 21 Nov 1879 and MHA to RWH, 19 Nov 1879, AP.

(4) letter, HA to Salisbury, 3 Jul 1879, L, II, 364.

(5) letter, HA to Currie, 11 Jul 1879, L, II, 364.

(6) six letters, HA to Lodge, 31 Aug 1879–3 May 1880.

(7) letter, HA to Grigsby, 1 Sep 1879, L, II, 370–71.

(8) nine letters, HA to Lowell, 13 Sep 1879–3 May 1880.

(9) eight letters, HA to Henry Vignaud, 29 Nov 1879–24 Mar 1880, L, II, 384, 390, 394–97. The letter dated only "Tuesday" by HA is misdated "[Dec. 1879]" in L, II, 384. It was written on 6 Jan 1880. See MHA to RWH, 11 Jan [1880] (misdated 1879), AP.

(10) letter, HA to Godkin, 25 Dec 1879, L, II, 387–88.

(11) twenty-six letters, MHA to RWH, 4 Jan–27–28 Jun 1880, AP.

ADDITIONAL SOURCES; COMMENTS

1. Transcript of J. B. Lippincott's account with Albert R. Gallatin, made by Cater for LHT, given later by her to me. The account says the firm sent HA the *Writings* on 6 Jun 1879 but does not say he was sent the *Life*. Of his two copies of *LAG* in HAL, the copy published in 1879 is defective; its table of contents is inverted. (It contains his list of errors.) I infer it was an advance copy sent to him by Lippincott off the record. His other copy belongs to an 1880 printing.

2. Notebook headed "Foreign Office,/ Diplomatic Correspondence./ America. 1800–1815." and signed "Henry Adams/ July, 1879," HAL. HA overwrote the closing number in "1801" to make the year "1800."

3. Lippincott's account with Albert R. Gallatin, op. cit.

4. CFA2, Diary, 19, 22 July 1879, AP. Searching the Old House in 1957, I found CFA2's copy of *LAG* in a trunk that was shipped to Quincy in 1912 containing materials from HA's Paris library. The trunk still contained such materials. It seemed a strange place to find the copy, which cannot easily be conceived ever to have been included among HA's Paris properties. CFA2's marks are marginal scorings, cross references, and a note (636) citing an opinion of Gallatin expressed by CFA in 1841 (see Chap. 15, note 65, above).

5. RWH clipped the BAdv review and sent it to MHA. See her letter to him, 10 Aug 1879. HA preserved it; see his notebooks, HAL. The review says that, because of a "dryness and hardness in his own method," HA fails to make Gallatin "an object of interest to the reader."

6. CFA, Diary, 25 Jul 1879, AP—". . . I devoted my time partly to [HA's] Gallatin. Tried my hand at a sketch of the substance but did not satisfy myself."

7. Henry Cabot Lodge, "Albert Gallatin," *International Review*, Sep 1879, 250–66; the same reissued as a signed pamphlet, *Albert Gallatin*, NY: Chas. Scribner's Sons 1879; [John Torrey Morse, Jr.], "Albert Gallatin," *Atlantic Monthly*, Oct 1879, 513–21. For Morse's authorship, see the bound volume titled *Magazine Articles*, Morse Papers, MHS.

8. CFA2, Diary, 1, 3 Aug 1879, AP.

9. [CFA2], "Albert Gallatin./ I." *Nation*, 21 Aug 1879, 128–29, and "Albert Gallatin./ II." 28 Aug 1879, 144–45.

There is no evidence that either CFA or CFA2 knew in the summer of

1879 that HA was contemplating a history of the United States in the time of Presidents Jefferson and Madison. The respectively patient and impatient responses of CFA and CFA2 to HA's *LAG* were apparently written in the absence of information on that point.

CFA2 viewed Gallatin as interesting in three ways: as a convert to Rousseau's "wilderness ideal," as secretary of the treasury during the administrations of Jefferson and Madison, and as a failure. His second instalment said:

> As a minister of finance [Gallatin] . . . cannot be ranked lower than the first class. He was great enough to be perfectly simple. . . . He administered the Treasury of the United States as it has never been administered before or since. . . . By systematic frugality and spending less than the revenue, he proposed to pay off the public debt, and then the surplus was [either] to be remitted . . . or applied to great projects of internal improvement.

To that point, the passage only repeated ideas expressed by HA in the *Life*. But CFA2 went on to say that Gallatin was wrong-headed from the beginning, could only fail, and did fail—the national debt was not entirely paid off. "The curious part of it is that he both failed and was wrong; he wholly overestimated what was humanly practical under our political conditions. Yet neither at the time nor since has any one ever doubted that he was a great man; in its very massive simplicity his handiwork bears the stamp of greatness."

CFA2 took Gallatin's biographer to be a gifted *historian* who inexcusably had botched a *biography*. The evidence he evinced of HA's talent as a historian was a 250–page stretch of the *Life*—pp. 300–550. He said in the second instalment, ". . . it would not be easy to find anything superior to it in the many recent volumes devoted to American, or, for that matter, to other history."

As if HA agreed with him that Gallatin was a failure (he did not), CFA2 said in relation to pp. 300–550, ". . . it is the story of his failure that Mr. Adams tells, and he tells it with great spirit and ability, interspersed at times with a controlled eloquence which is made doubly attractive by its admirable taste."

10. As his article made clear, CFA2 wanted from HA the biography of Gallatin that he himself would have written in HA's place, if given the chance. That there were good reasons why HA, Albert R. Gallatin, and J. B. Lippincott and Company had not produced a biography conforming to *his* prescription was a possibility CFA2 evidently did not think of or thrust aside.

11. For Gallatin's outburst about his tailor, see *LAG*, 266. When he used the outburst to start his article, CFA2 could not have known that ideas about tailors had already been strongly impressed on HA's mind both by Gallatin and by General Taylor. See Chap. 16, notes 47. Conceivably Taylor had himself been moved to invent his fable about Poole by reading the relevant page of *LAG* in manuscript or in proof.

12. Seeking material for the Biographical Introduction for *Henry Adams and His Friends* (1947), Cater had an experience best summarized in his own words (cxiii–cxiv):

There is a story told rather widely that Henry Adams got Wendell Phillips Garrison, then book review editor of the *Nation*, to let him review a book that was just published by his brother, Charles Francis. . . . Just what book was involved . . . is not clear, and some people seem to have heard the story in reverse order: Charles Francis reviewed Henry's book. One version of it is that when Charles Francis read the review of his book, he considered it so hostile that he complained in a letter to Edwin L. Godkin and asked for the name of the reviewer, and said, "You have let loose an ignoramus on me." Godkin wrote to Henry and asked if he should divulge his name to his brother. Henry replied: "For God's sake, no; not by any means." The story is not only interesting, but curious, because it has been persistently handed down to the present time without any origin for it except that the present teller of the tale [Cater gives no name] got it from someone else who got it direct from Godkin or Garrison.

Cater also says: "Oswald Garrison Villard, nephew of Garrison, and connected with the *Nation* since before 1897, never heard the story; nor did Frank Jewett Mather, who was sub-editor of the *Nation* from 1900 to 1905. Freda Kirchwey, the present editor, never heard it. But other members of the past and present staff claim to have heard it, in varying versions."

Cater's account has important implications. It indicates: (a) a story concerning an anonymous book review was put into circulation, not by Garrison, not by Godkin, not by HA, but by CFA2, sometimes in forms that made HA the guilty party in a transaction in which CFA2 was himself the culprit; (b) the story involved a fabrication concerning Garrison, making him, not Godkin, the editor who permitted publication of the review of Henry's book; (c) the story was sensed by early hearers to be tainted, with the result that Cater would not or could not name his sources and avoided saying whether he was told the story by one or more informants; (d) Cater gave considerable credence to a false story the grounds of which he was at a loss to understand; and (e) he was willing to repeat as "interesting" and "curious" a fabricated representation of HA as the inventor of an unsigned attack on one of his elder brothers.

13. Macdonough's review is recorded as "not used" in *The Nation-Ledger/ 1873–1881* in the *Nation* Records, NYPL. In his *Index of Contributors* and *Index of Titles*, Haskell erroneously attributes CFA2's article to Macdonough.

14. Perry, *Life and Letters of Henry Lee Higginson*, op. cit., 263–64, 272–73.

15. The population of Massachusetts being what it was, persons born and raised in Boston and its environs in HA and MHA's generation formed impressions of Jews only after traveling to other places. Henry Higginson, for example, wrote from Vienna in 1858, ". . . I never saw a Jew before coming here. . . ." See Perry, *Higginson*, op. cit., 125. Similarly HA and MHA first formed impressions of Jews when abroad.

The hostess who most often entertained HA and MHA in London in 1879 and 1880 was Lady Goldsmid. Disraeli was prime minister. MHA liked Lady Goldsmid and disliked Disraeli in roughly equal measures. She associated the prime minister with aristocracy, conservatism, and political expediency. When the Tory government fell, she wrote, 4 Apr 1880: "We have been amused, surprised & interested in the huge spring tide of liberalism which has risen over the land this week. . . . As for Dizzy, that Jew bagman with his quack medicines, it's nice to see him ordered off the premises. . . . If England doesn't get a thirst for ideas & freedom, sandwiched as she is between two big republics like France and America[,] it will be in spite of natural laws."

MHA also wrote, 25 Apr 1880: ". . . dined . . . with Lʸ Goldsmid[,] who is a mother in Israel to us. There is a theory now that England is so much in the hands of the Jews that the English are the twelve [sic] lost tribes. Probably Dizzie spread the notion."

16. In 1879–1880, though well adjusted to the English and happy in the company of English radicals, the Adamses gravitated towards friends who shared with them the condition of being less-than-fully English. Lady Goldsmid, Mrs. J. R. Green (Alice Stopford), and Lady Clark (Charlotte Coltman)—respectively Jewish, Irish, and Scottish—were examples.

A principal cause that impelled HA and MHA away from English company was English women. Through HJ, the Adamses met elderly Mrs. Duncan Stewart. Thinking her a personification of London at its best, MHA wrote, 10 Aug 1879: "Mrs. Stewart is a good instance of how little money decides even in this money-loving land. Having a secure social position and a great love of society, she goes everywhere and knows everyone; poor as a rat and living in two wee rooms over a tailor's shop in an unfashionable street. She has none of the heavy attributes of the average English female, being an Irishwoman."

At a dinner in London on 11 Jun 1880, HA was pleased to meet the Scottish wife of Sir Theodore Martin, the biographer of Prince Albert. After mentioning HA's experience, MHA wrote, 13 Jun 1880: "Scotch people are so much brighter & lighter in hand than the English—especially the women. They seem like a different race."

17. HA to Parkman, 21 Dec 1884, HA-micro 5.

18. *Saturday Review*, 26 Jul 1879. Like the critic in the *Saturday Review*, Lodge and Morse in their notices of *LAG* (see note 7, above) commend Hamilton strongly.

19. MHA to RWH, 22 Dec 1878, AP.

20. MHA to RWH, 9 Feb 1879, AP.

21. Alice's daughter Isabel was soon to marry a member of the Scottish gentry, Edward Balfour.

22. Rouen has three great Gothic churches. I assume the Adamses visited all three, but MHA only mentions their being at the church of St. Ouen.

23. Duberman, *James Russell Lowell*, 291, 295–98.

24. Lowell to HA, 21 Sep 1879.

25. Lowell to HA, 4 Oct 1879.

26. MHA's phrase "pastures new" is the closing phrase of Milton's "Lycidas" and the best evidence of her acquaintance with his work.

27. HJ to his brother William, 15 Jun 1879, James Papers, H; HJ to Boott, 28 Jun [1879], and HJ to his father, 11 Oct [1879], *Henry James Letters*, II, 246, 258. 28. While calling attention to expressions in HA's letters and works that can be read or misread as derogations of the Jews, critics have mostly avoided calling attention to HA's expressions concerning the Jews that can be read as neutral or commendatory. His saying that

the Spanish inhabitants of Madrid were "faded Jews" has been little noticed. The phrase may indicate that HA when first in Madrid had impressions that the Jews who lived in Spain in the fifteenth century were colorful and/or strong—hence were imitated by the Spaniards, with results evident in the Spaniards after a lapse of four centuries.

29. Taking HA to be a descendant of Adam, MHA not only jokes; she links her husband with the Adam of the Bible and the Adam of *Paradise Lost*, and herself with the Eves. Also she allies HA and herself with humanity at large, rather than a supposed or actual subdivision.

This passing action is harmonious with HA's belief that the proper identification of a great writer is with all humanity.

30. MHA wrote from Granada that Tetuan was reportedly "more fascinating by far than Cairo."

She partly wished to visit Tetuan for reasons involving her relations. Her cousin William Sturgis Bigelow had visited Tetuan and stayed at the hotel she and HA would stay at. Also her father owned a sketch by Fortuny presumed to have been made somewhere on the route between Ceuta and Tetuan. See Thoron, 202, 207–08.

31. HA's "checquered" was not an unknown spelling; see *OED*. One may suppose that HA, seeing the checker board at Tetuan, was reminded of the checkered land in which Alice finds herself in Lewis Carroll's *Through the Looking Glass* (1871). He then imaginatively replaced the checkered board and checkered land with a checkered ocean—a useful image. Among other things, the image could suggest a single humanity set off as many nations, races, etc.

32. The Moorish, Jewish, and Spanish names HA invented can all be pronounced to contain the name Adam. They accordingly can be read as evidence that HA believed that there is one—and only one—humanity.

It is possibly worth reflection that only the Jewish name contains the name Adams. A hard-to-answer question is whether HA envisaged the Jews as more a nation or a family. For him, many consequences might follow if the Jews and the Adamses equally were families.

33. See principal source 3 with respect to the fragment's date.

34. The mythic and literary parallels and part-parallels at work in HA and MHA's remarks concerning their journeys to and from Tetuan via Ceuta appear to have been important to them and rather numerous. Of the literary works they had in mind, two presumably were *Othello* and *The Merchant of Venice*.

35. In his *James Russell Lowell*, Bost 1966, 308–09, Martin Duberman presents HA's remark as if it were a foundation stone of an edifice of anti-Semitism. ". . . Lowell, and most of his friends, were incapable of the harsher anti-Semitism which seized upon such New England aristocrats of the next generation as Brooks and Henry Adams and such patricians of New England ancestry as John Jay Chapman . . . . Though the Adams brothers and Chapman . . . had their share of admiration for certain 'Jewish qualities,' it gave way, especially as they grew older, to a dislike more virulent than anything known in Lowell's generation. Thus Henry Adams, as early as the 1870's, could write while traveling in Spain, 'I have now seen enough of Jews and Moors to entertain more liberal views in regard to the Inquisition, and to feel that, though the ignorant may murmur, the Spaniards saw and pursued a noble aim.' "

Duberman shows prejudice in supposing HA to be a New England aristocrat. HA was all his days an American democrat. The difference was a real difference, not to be overlooked.

Duberman takes HA's sentence to say only that HA is becoming *less* tolerant and less tolerant *only of Jews* (he elides the Moors). But the sentence is clear. It says that HA is *correcting an intolerance*, and it is part of an important body of evidence that HA went to Spain prejudicially somewhat disliking the Spanish and left Spain much more fair-minded about the Spanish.

Attestations by Duberman and others notwithstanding, HA through the years with which this book is concerned was neither a pro- nor anti-Semite. (It is sometimes alleged that the attitude he took towards the Gans family, a family he had dealings with in Dresden in 1860, is evidence that in youth he was pro-Jewish. His letters of the time state clearly that, to the extent he was supportive of the Gans daughters, it was because he saw them as young *Americans* mistreated by Germans when staying in Germany. The daughters' being Jewish was known to him but did not occasion his support.)

That expressions in HA's letters and works in the period 1855–1891 can strike readers as indicating that he was averse to Jews or sympathetic to Jews is true; but throughout the period he was (except in one way) relatively so little concerned about Jews that there was no question of his becoming an anti-Semite or the converse. The exception was that knowledge of the Bible disposed him *for* the Jews of ancient times.

36. The marquis was part American. His grandfather, while minister to the U. S., married a daughter of Governor McKean of Pennsylvania.

37. CFA2, Diary, 3 Nov 1879, AP. Also see CFA2 to Godkin, 30 Oct 1880, Godkin Papers, H.

38. See especially the letter written by R. R. Hitt, U. S. chargé d'affaires in Paris, to naval minister Jaurégilberry, 29 Oct 1879, in Max I. Baym, "Henry Adams and Henry Vignaud," *NEQ*, Sep 1944, 444. Hitt says in part: "Monsieur Adams appartient à une famille illustre dans notre histoire nationale; c'est un homme d'un grand mérite dont le dernier ouvrage sur 'Albert Gallatin" a obtenu un légitime succès."

39. The date is given in HA's letter to Vignaud marked "Tuesday." See principal source 8.

40. By then, HA and MHA had learned that they had outraced Tennyson, who likewise wanted No. 22. They possibly learned as well that, in 1784, Palmerston was born at No. 20, next door.

41. Lowell to HA, 4 Feb 1880.

42. Badeau, Hoppin, Lowell, and similarly interested persons may be presumed not to have known that a recently published biography of Motley by Oliver Wendell Holmes, Sr., owed its existence in a large measure to help privately given by HA. See O. W. Holmes, Sr., to HA, 16 Mar; 6, 10, 27 Apr 1878; 31 May, 21 Jun 1879.

43. William Jones Hoppin, *Journal of a Residence in London from January 1st to June 22d 1880*, H, entries of 7, 15, & 22 Feb 1880.

44. The article presumably was "Napoléon Ier et Saint-Domingue," published in *Revue Historique*, Janvier-Avril 1884, 92–130, signed "H. Adams." HA conceivably attempted an article on the subject while at work on the Jefferson and Madison papers in Washington early in 1879. He

however could not have fully decided the article's ultimate line of argument till December 1879–January 1880 in Paris, for the documents the finished article relies upon are mostly papers he was then reading in the Archives de la Marine.

How soon he drafted the article in final form is unknown. How the text (apart from the documents) came to be in French is unknown also. One supposes there was a translator; but HA might have written the text in the best French he could summon, with the purpose of prevailing on Monod, editor of the *Review Historique*, to correct his errors.

45. HA's letter to Vignaud, 20 Mar 1880, L, II, 396, illustrates how strongly HA preferred diplomacy conducted through private channels and how strongly he preferred not to involve Secretary Evarts in official correspondence with the French authorities.

46. Lowell to HA, 25 Mar 1880.

47. The review of *Democracy* is a paragraph within an unsigned article, "Recent Novels," *Nation*, 22 Apr 1880, 311–13. The article concerns eight novels, *Democracy* being fifth. The notices of the first seven are attributed in Haskell's *Indexes* to William Crary Brownell.

48. CFA2 to HA, 4 Jun 1880.

49. Judging from the successive states of the first edition of *Democracy* as described in Blanck, 3–4, the publisher had to deal with unexpectedly large orders.

50. Spencer Walpole to HA, 8, 11 Jun 1880.

51. The copies are in two volumes of transcripts titled *British State Papers* that HA later gave to the Library of Congress. The volumes include materials dated 1798–1814. HA notes on the first page that the papers he is copying are "Perceval MSS lent by Mr. Spencer Walpole. June, 1880."

When studying the volumes in the 1960s, I was told by Mrs. Eaton of the LC staff that HA's transcripts of British papers cannot be superseded because they are "sometimes from unexpected sources."

52. That the house was being renovated and would be occupied by an Adams could be viewed as symbolic. Before the Rebellion, the house was occupied by Senator John Slidell—later famous for being removed from the British mail ship *Trent*. See *An American Democrat/ The Recollections of Perry Belmont*, NY 1940, 116.

18. Some Good Influence

Letters by and to HA are in HA-micro 4 or 5, unless otherwise noted.

PRINCIPAL SOURCES

(1) eleven letters, MHA to RWH, 27 Jun–12 Sep 1880, AP.

(2) four letters, HA to Vignaud, 1 Jul 1880–26 Jan 1881.

(3) five letters, HA to Lodge, 9 Jul 1880–21 Nov 1881.

(4) seven letters, HA to CMG, 12 Aug 1880–9 Jul 1881.

(5) letter, HA to Cunliffe, 11 Sep 1880.

(6) forty-six letters, MHA to RWH, 31 Oct 1880–18 Dec 1881, Thoron, 228–314.

(7) ten letters, HA to Godkin, 22 Nov 1880–13 Dec 1881, L, II, 410–11, 413, 433–37, 440, 446–47.

(8) five letters, HA to Winsor, 25 Nov 1880–16 Oct [1881], L, II, 412, 428, 438–39, 441.

(9) letter, HA to Curtis, 3 Feb 1881, L, II, 418.

(10) letters, HA to Hay, [undated]–27 Mar 1881, L, II, 423–24.

(11) letters, HA to Morse, 9, 27 Apr 1881.

(12) letter, HA to Walker, 6 Jun 1881, L, II, 427.

(13) three letters, HA to MacVeagh, 9, 18 Jul, 25 Sep 1881, L, II, 430–32, 436–37.

ADDITIONAL SOURCES; COMMENTS

1. See bound volume, *Spanish State Papers. Casa Yrugo. 1801–1807.*, given by HA to the State Department, now in LC, Manuscript Division.

2. According to MHA's letter to RWH, 28 Jun 1880, the papers contained new evidence relating to John Henry, the British agent in Boston. The importance of the agent to HA is readily traceable through his *New England Federalism*, Lodge's review thereof, and HA's *History*.

3. I have found no corroborative evidence that would lend weight to HA's passing mention of a three-volume *History* or a six-volume *History*. In his letter to Sir John Clark, 6 Mar 1881, L, II, 420–22, he anticipates a five-volume *History*, for which, again, I have found no corroborative evidence.

4. HJ to MHA, 9 Sep [1880], HA-micro 4.

5. HA's strongly wanting the oil painting and/or the sketch by the French artist G. Washington bears comparison with his strongly reacting to an English book, *Bad English Exposed: A Series of Criticisms on the Errors and Inconsistencies of Lindley Murray and Other Grammarians*, by G. Washington Moon. In 1957, Thomas Boylston Adams, the owner, showed me HA's copy of the book and kindly permitted me to photocopy its annotated pages. The copy belongs to the 7th ed., Lond 1881, and possibly was obtained in that year; but HA's numerous marginal notes and textual corrections are signed and dated "October, 1883." He wrote on the front flyleaf, "Will the proof-reader please glance at the marginal notes." The notes show HA to be extremely serious about good English and confident of the rightness of his opinions in that connection. He repeatedly quotes the Bible and Shakespeare to put Moon in the wrong. He ends by characterizing the book (227) as "The work of one of the smallest cockney critics yet born to spoil our language."

6. On 16 Nov 1966, Aileen Tone told me that, while living with HA at 1603 H Street, she visited 1607 and found that its principal floor was arranged as four large square high-ceilinged rooms off a center hall leading straight from the front entrance to the garden. In her letter to RWH of 19 Dec 1880, MHA speaks of thirteen-foot ceilings.

7. CFA, Diary, 14, 16, 21, 23 Oct 1880, AP.

8. MHA to Godkin, n.d., appended to HA to Godkin, 28 Nov 1880, L, II, 413. If he bragged only to the Gurneys and it was they who told RWH, Godkin could have felt his error was slight.

9. Inferred from CFA2 to Godkin, 30 Oct 1880, Godkin Papers, H.

10. CFA2's saying he "laughed consumedly" bears noting. MHA says "she laughed consumedly" in her letter to RWH, 21 Dec 1879 (quoted in Chap. 17). HA says "We laughed consumedly" in his letter to Godkin, 22 Nov 1880 (quoted in the present chapter). With regard to the expression as used by HA, Levenson and his fellow editors say, II, 411n1, that "laughed consumedly" appears in Farquhar's *The Beaux-Stratagem*. Their

note is scholarly but fails to deal with the difficulty at issue: why MHA, CFA2, and HA successively used an expression so unusual within a twelve-month period.

11. In her article " 'The Man Around the Corner': An Episode in the Career of Henry Adams," *NEQ*, Sep 1950, 401–03, Evelyn Page quoted parts of CFA2's letter to Godkin and commented, "It can only be surmised in what spirit of jocularity, triumph, or brotherly righteousness he signed himself Charles Francis Adams, Jr." Her word "jocularity" apparently served as a cue to other writers to assume that CFA2 and Godkin understood the article on *LAG* as a practical joke. As if the point were settled, Levenson and his fellow editors note, II, 411n2, "Since HA declined to take offense, Godkin and CFA2 were left with their practical joke dead on their hands." But there is no evidence that Godkin thought the article either a joke or a practical joke. It perhaps can be claimed that CFA2 thought it a practical joke; but the claim, if made, should specify the person CFA2 most intended to annoy and why. The editors avoid supplying these essentials.

Page excused CFA2's article as having taught HA not to write heavy biographies. The excuse is groundless. There is no evidence that the article affected HA's subsequent biographies, whether in length, form, style, or anything else.

12. Earlier, after seeing Gail Hamilton at a reception given by Mrs. Beale, MHA had written to RWH, 27 Jan 1878, AP: "Gail looks like a caricature of a scarecrow—both eyes squinting madly—mouth like a dying sculpin—hair like Medusa." The description might seem mere gossipy detraction were it not that mention of snake-haired Medusa brings it to a serious close.

13. HA eventually formed a poor opinion of Dwight. See L, V, 581. How early he became aware of Dwight's worse qualities is unclear.

14. See note 10, above.

15. Godkin's replies are missing, but their gist can be inferred from HA and MHA's letters. He appears to have offered the defense of minimal sin. They were glad to accept it.

16. Dwight lived in Washington before, during, and after 1607 H Street was renovated. He drew "Four diagrams of the original drawings on the walls of Henry Adams['s] study in [the] Yellow House" and at some point dated the diagrams "summer of 1885?" See notebook headed "T. F. Dwight./ Washington. Nov. 29, 1877.," MHS. His words indicate that the phrase the "Yellow House" was in habitual use. I infer that the phrase came into use shortly after the house was repainted.

17. From March–April 1880, when it was published, till October 1915, when HA through Thayer revealed his authorship, *Democracy* was most notable in three ways. Possession of an opinion of the book was viewed as an expected accomplishment among educated Americans, with the result that the book was read and sometimes reread. The notion that the book contained actual persons under pseudonyms was unquestioningly accepted, but the list of persons supposedly to be found in it was not settled. The mystery of the authorship gave rise to many conjectures, none convincing, and to an eventual condition of general bafflement.

Two readers who did not know the authorship were Theodore Roosevelt and Henry Cabot Lodge. On 2 Sep 1905, Roosevelt wrote to Lodge:

"The other day I was reading *Democracy*, that novel which made a great furore among the educated incompetents and the pessimists generally about twenty-five years ago. It had a superficial and rotten cleverness, but it was essentially false, essentially mean and base, and it is amusing to read it now and see how completely events have given it the lie."

Lodge replied on 7 Sep 1905: "I have not read *Democracy* for years, but I remember when it came out it impressed me as very clever, probably more clever than I should think it today, and also extremely sordid. . . . Events have shown singularly how worthless it really was as a study of our political society." See F, II, 480n3, quoting *Correspondence of Theodore Roosevelt and Henry Cabot Lodge*, II, 189, 191.

After 27 Mar 1918, when HA died, Senator Lodge bore himself as an authority on HA's life and work. Writing to Holt on 6 Apr 1918, LP, Lodge said in passing, "Mr. Adams was undoubtedly the author of *Democracy*, as I have known for a great many years. . . ." In view of his letter to Roosevelt, quoted above, Lodge's claim to have known the secret of the authorship for "a great many years" can be dismissed as false.

Lodge also claimed to know that HA's novel was a *roman à clef* and claimed he knew the names of the chief persons who appeared in it. In 1919, Worthington Ford was serving as editor of the Massachusetts Historical Society (a multi-purpose position). He wrote to Lodge asking him to have his secretary "copy the real names in the novel Democracy" and send them to Boston. In his letter, Ford said he supposed "Carrington might be James Lowndes" but added that the novel antedated his experience of Washington. See Ford to Lodge, 9 Oct 1919, LP.

Lodge had a house on Lafayette Square. He replied to Ford from his Senate office on 11 Oct 1919, FP: "Carrington in 'Democracy' was undoubtedly James Lowndes. I will take your letter home and try to remember to take the list of names from my wife's copy, which Henry Adams gave her and in which the names are written in in John Hay's handwriting." But Lodge did not send the names. When he died, on 9 Nov 1924, his promise to send them remained unkept.

In July 1925, Henry Holt reprinted *Democracy*, adding a "Publisher's Foreword." An octagenarian, Holt was aware that his memory was faulty. He thought too that his records were strangely few. He said in his Foreword that he was unable to find early letters from HA he supposed had once been in his files. Yet he stated in positive tones: "Adams' reasons for keeping the authorship secret were not so much that he feared knowledge of it might visit unpopularity on him . . . but because some of the characters were carefully drawn from prominent living persons who were his friends, and some of these he touched humorously and ironically." Holt stopped there. He named no prominent living persons. Neither did he say who told him how HA carefully drew the characters.

Three months later, Ford wrote to Lodge's son John Ellerton Lodge about the copy of *Democracy* allegedly given by HA to John's mother and annotated by Hay. John Lodge did not own the books his father had kept in the Washington house. They were the property of a new Henry Cabot Lodge, grandson of the senator. But John either assumed or believed that the alleged copy of *Democracy* was still among those books. Also he understood that the books had been moved to Massachusetts. He replied on 20 Oct 1925, FP: "All the books my father had in Washington now

belong to my nephew, and among them was Henry Adams' 'Democracy,'
which, together with the rest, is in one of many packing boxes at the
storage warehouse in Lynn. My nephew himself is at present doing
newspaper work in Washington, and although I have no doubt that he
would gladly let you have the list of characters which my father promised
you, I fear that circumstances are not very favorable to your receiving it at
any near . . . date. However, I'll speak to my nephew about it."

The great bulk of Ford's papers are in the New York Public Library.
They contain no evidence that the alleged copy of *Democracy* was found or
that he heard more about it. Between 1919 and the present, innumerable
books that belonged to Senator Lodge have come onto the market. As
nearly as I can determine, they have not included a copy of *Democracy*, still
less a copy of the sort he described to Ford. In my view, Lodge's 1919
statement about the alleged annotated copy can be taken to be a second
instance of empty bragging.

In 1929, a two-volume compendium was published in Boston and
New York: *The Letters and Friendships of Sir Cecil Spring Rice/ A Record*, edited
by Steven Gwynn. The compendium contains a letter, I, 80–81, written by
Spring Rice on 15 Dec 1887 in which he claims to know the identities of
the four persons who appear in *Democracy* as Carrington, Victoria Dare, a
foreign diplomat, and Mrs. Lee. He does not give their names. However,
Gwynn supplies a footnote, I, 80n2: "Carrington was Mr. James Lowndes;
Victoria Dare was Miss Emily Beale; the diplomat, Aristarchi Bey; and
Mrs. Lightfoot Lee was Mrs. Lawrence." Gwynn cites no source for the
offered particulars. Both the claims in Spring Rice's letter and the particulars added by Gwynn appear to have been based on mere available
gossip, especially Washington gossip.

Ford's papers include a half sheet of paper bearing, among other
things, the following array of words:

Characters in Democracy:
    Mrs. Bigelow Lawrence.
    Miss Fanny Chapman.
    Miss Emily Beale.
    James Lowndes, a Washington lawyer.
    James G. Blaine.

The half sheet is undated and unattached to any other paper. Everything
written on the half sheet appears to have been written by Ford, using the
typewriter he used in 1925 and for some years thereafter. The source of
the listed names is in no way given or hinted.

In 1930, in a footnote in his edition of *Letters of Henry Adams* (*1858–
1891*), 336n1, Ford quoted Holt's 1925 statement that *Democracy* contained
prominent living persons. Ford added a sentence of his own: "The principal characters represented were Mrs. Bigelow Lawrence and her sister,
Miss Fanny Chapman, Miss Emily Beale, James Lowndes, and James G.
Blaine." In this instance, too, Ford did not name a source. He said nothing
about a copy of *Democracy* given by HA to Mrs. Lodge and annotated by
Hay. He merely printed a list as if it had a basis. One may assume he wrote
the list himself, drawing on accumulated gossip.

Taking cues from Spring Rice's 1887 letter, Holt's 1925 Foreword,
Gwynn's 1929 footnote, and Ford's 1930 footnote, subsequent writers have

evidently felt free to believe: (a) that sufficient authority exists to permit all concerned to categorize Adams's novel as a *roman à clef*; (b) that Ford's list of five "principal characters" can properly be repeated without acknowledgement as belonging, not to the realm of gossip, but instead to the realm of established fact; and (c) that Ford's list, being skeletal, can properly be extended and embellished—also freely amended and altered. My judgment is that this belief is totally unwarranted.

There is evidence that HA, when writing and rewriting *Democracy*, had the problem of getting away from actual persons (Charles Sumner, Alice Mason Hooper, and Baron Holstein) and successfully establishing imaginary persons. The novel itself is decisive and overwhelming evidence that its characters are types and that HA inventively developed the more important characters till they became fully realized fictions. There accordingly can be no assumption that HA or MHA could offer Hay or anyone else a key to the "real names in the novel Democracy."

There is no question that MHA, in banter with friends, did on occasion speak comically of *Democracy* as containing actual persons. See Thoron, 339. But there is no corroborative evidence that HA or MHA gave Hay a list of "real names." Neither is there evidence that Hay could read *Democracy* better than Emily Beale or Gail Hamilton or Harriet Loring or Theodore Roosevelt or any of the countless other persons in the United States and Europe who excitedly misread it in the 1880s. There is no corroborative evidence that HA or MHA told Holt that *Democracy* is a *roman à clef*. The statement by Holt in 1925 that HA carefully drew some of the characters from prominent living persons who were his friends is manifestly a worse trick of mistaken memory than his statement in 1921 that the novel was published in 1879. See his *Garrulities of an Octagenarian Editor*, 127, 136–37.

In sum, the structure of received opinion concerning *Democracy* rests mostly on vaporous, nonexistent, and false foundations.

18. In keeping with the three-part belief outlined in note 17, above, numerous writers—most notably Harold Dean Cater (*Henry Adams and His Friends*, 1947); Elizabeth Stevenson (*Henry Adams*, 1955); J. C. Levenson (*Mind and Art of Henry Adams*, 1957); Ernest Samuels (*Henry Adams/ The Middle Years*, 1958); and William Dusinberre (*Henry Adams/ The Myth of Failure*, 1980)—have variously repeated, extended, and embellished Ford's list of five names. While naming actual persons as present in *Democracy*, Cater, Stevenson, Levenson, Samuels, and Dusinberre fail to cite Ford's list, although it is their principal source.

Cater states as fact (lxx) that "Loundes [*sic*] . . . is Carrington." He adds a sixth person, saying (128n1) that Aristarchi Bey is "the diplomat in Adams's Democracy"—Baron Jacobi. He fails to say that his source for the sixth person is Gwynn's 1929 note, which itself failed to state a source.

On the claimed ground that "Miss Beale recognized herself" in the character, Stevenson (171) says Emily Beale is "Vicky Dare [*sic*]." She fails to mention that this linkage had appeared in Gwynn's unsupported note; moreover, she cites no evidence that Miss Beale saw herself in that particular role.

Levenson (91) says that James G. Blaine was "the unwitting model for Ratcliffe." Samuels (93) states that the "elegant" Mrs. Bigelow Lawrence is Madeleine Lee. Similarly, in his Introduction to *Democracy and Esther/ Two*

Novels by Henry Adams, NY 1961, he states that the "ravishing" Fanny Chapman is Sybil Ross.

With one exception, the same six actual persons and their alleged fictional representations recur, without acknowledgement to Gwynn or Ford, in what might appear to be a definitive statement on *Democracy*, the introductory note in the Library of America reprint (1983), 1229. The note was written by Ernest and Jayne N. Samuels. The exception is that Lowndes is not permitted to be Carrington. He is required to give way to Senator Lucius Q. C. Lamar.

The scrubbing of Lowndes is part of a process begun by Stevenson. She and the other writers listed above, Cater excepted, both assert that *Democracy* is a *roman à clef* and fudge the term to make it mean that HA did not represent *persons* in the novel; he represented sides, traits, temperaments, tastes of persons—or even an idea held by a person. By having the matter several ways, the writers free themselves to see Ratcliffe as Blaine, Roscoe Conkling, and Dr. Hooper; Mrs. Lee as Mrs. Lawrence, MHA, and HA; Carrington as Lowndes, Lamar, Richard Taylor, William H. Trescot, and HA; Nathan Gore as John Lothrop Motley, James Russell Lowell, and HA, etc. They also free themselves to list and de-list actual persons without limit and proceed to do so.

Fudging pervades the Samuelses' note in the Library of America reprint. The note can be read to say, deny, or avoid saying that *Democracy* is a *roman à clef*. It thus may come as an ironic relief that the note in closing announces definitely, without supporting evidence, that Perry Belmont is the actual person—the "affluent resident of New York City"—who appears in the novel as Hartbeest Schneidekoupon.

19. In *Hamlet*, Polonius distinguished two sorts of plays, heavy and light. The distinction can be applied to *Democracy*, which HA did what he could to lighten, in part for the sake of lightness, and in part to disguise the novel's considerable weight.

The lightness of *Democracy* is such that it can seem a throwaway. Its characters can have an appearance of being borrowed by the "poor novelist"—the author-narrator's phrase—from somebody else's plays. Lightness inheres as well in the author-narrator's economical humor (e.g.—"There was nothing very encouraging in all this, but it was better than New York.").

That *Democracy* is heavy shows most obviously in its scale. The action takes place in a dozen settings in Washington and thereabouts, including Mount Vernon, the Lee house in Arlington, and the British legation. The plot is expansively theatrical. Adapted to the stage, it would require fifteen male actors, six with talent; eight female actors, four with talent; and a little girl. Of the twenty-four highly visible characters, seventeen are American, seven are foreign. There are additional characters who are only glimpsed or mentioned, including an unnamed secretary of state, the president's private secretary, several newspaper correspondents, dozens of office seekers, and the whole Pennsylvania delegation, "ready for biz."

The overall effect is at once American, cosmopolitan, and large. The author-narrator heightens the effect by never saying "I."

20. Misreading of *Democracy* can be expected to diminish when it is generally recognized that HA wrote *The Radical Club*. In his novel, as completed and published, HA reversed the strategy he had used in the

poem. The poem was a *satire à clef*. With one exception, its fully-described characters were representations of actual persons. Thus the poem was a mostly soluble puzzle—a card game with one joker.

Democracy is different. Its characters are both well-considered types and distinct fictional individuals based partly on imagination and partly on a very large experience of human beings, living, historical, fictional, and mythical. Each character can bring to mind an indefinite numbers of actual persons without being those persons. Thus, for persons capable of accepting it for the novel that it is, *Democracy* can function as instructive comedy, intelligent and far-reaching; but for persons unable or unwilling to recognize its being a novel, it may continue to function cruelly as a pseudo *roman à clef*, a fool's paradise of false leads.

21. Madeleine Lee is a heroine in that she undertakes an action, a winter's residence in Washington, which other persons would not think of. In addition, she comes to understand her own motives. But she also is comic in the weighty sense that, when visiting the engine room of American democracy and trying to understand the engines, as she says she wishes to do, she is given chances to learn the secrets of their workings from Mrs. Baker and Secretary Ratcliffe but bars Mrs. Baker from further visits to her house and flees the secretary forever.

22. A politician who officially can get only so far and no farther was a type of no small interest for HA, his father being a reason. When perfecting *Democracy* in the summer of 1876, HA could hope that Blaine's high point as a politician would be an unsuccessful effort to enter the Cabinet, or perhaps a second unsuccessful effort to become a presidential candidate; but he so shaped the novel that it could hurtfully affect *any* effort by Blaine to become a secretary, remain a secretary, or become president.

Without claiming that the publication of *Democracy* importantly eroded Blaine's presidential chances in the election of 1880, one can note that the high point of Ratcliffe's career, his appointment as secretary of the treasury, necessarily served many readers of the novel in 1881 as a statement that Blaine had reached his high point when made secretary of state by Garfield. Similarly, in 1882–1884, Ratcliffe's fading prospects at the end of *Democracy* would serve many readers as a prophecy that Blaine would never be president.

23. *Democracy* contains three stories involving $100,000 in the form of U. S. bonds. (It is not a coincidence that the same amount in U. S. bonds figures centrally in the history of the Gold Panic of 1869, as understood by HA. See Chap. 9, especially note 44.)

The first story alleges that Samuel Baker gave $100,000 in bonds directly to Senator Ratcliffe as a bribe to secure the passage of a measure desired by a steamship company. Learned by Carrington from Mrs. Baker and from her husband's since-destroyed papers, the story rests ultimately on the credibility of dead Mr. Baker.

The second story alleges that, if the alleged bonds were given by Baker to anyone, they were given to a member of the national committee of the country's dominant political party; that Ratcliffe, then a young politician, knew nothing of such a payment; that all he did was change his stand with respect to a steamship measure when ordered to do so by his party superiors.

The first and second stories conflict. Both cannot be true. The second story rests on the credibility of Ratcliffe.

A third story is introduced hypothetically and last by the author-narrator. It supposes that Ratcliffe's subalterns, under orders from him to bribe the Illinois legislature sufficiently to secure his election to the U. S. Senate, contracted large debts in their own names. When the subalterns asked Ratcliffe for money to pay their debts, he suggested that $100,000 could be extorted from a certain steamship company if he would bottle up a measure in committee. Thanks to this stratagem, the subalterns got the money to pay the debts.

The point of the third story is that the originators of corruption are *politicians*. The story is said by the author-narrator to be the sort of story the subalterns would favor. The fact that the author-narrator superadds it lends the third story superior weight.

It is not difficult to imagine a fourth story that merges the first story with the third but leaves the problem that Baker said he gave the bonds to Ratcliffe but Ratliffe in *his* story says no bonds came to him. To get around the problem, one can suppose that Baker did indeed give the bonds to Ratcliffe; that the national committee never got a cent; and that Ratcliffe is highly dishonest—first, in having bought his election by the Illinois legislature with money he fastidiously obliged others to borrow and helped them recoup; second, in lying to Madeleine Lee concerning every aspect of the case that matters.

The main point about the fourth story is that it must be generated by the reader. It is nowhere stated or suggested in the novel.

24. Of the important characters in *Democracy*, Mrs. Baker has been the least noticed by commentators, yet is the most mysterious and possibly the ablest. The author-narrator recounts her visit to Mrs. Lee but does not explain why it occurs. The reader is left free to imagine either that Mrs. Baker comes of her own accord, without coaching by Carrington, or the converse. Moreover, the scene may be a trap. The reader is given no protection against the possibility that Mrs. Baker comes with good motives! If the reader is as quick as Mrs. Lee to form a derogatory judgment of Mrs. Baker, the question may arise whether the reader shares with Mrs. Lee a tendency to rush impulsively into errors.

25. Fictional John Carrington in *Democracy* is preceded in HA's writings by the entry "Taylor, G. Carrington, Langham Hotel" in the front of his 1867 engagement book, HAL. The Langham Hotel was much frequented by Americans. It is curious that the entry links two names that become important to HA: Carrington and Taylor.

HA may have developed the character of Carrington in part because arrested by a reference in Hugh A. Garland, *The Life of John Randolph of Roanoke*, NY 1850, I, 126: ". . . Mr. Carrington, a confidential friend of [George] Washington."

One should notice too the unexplained reference to a "Mr. Henry Carrington" in HA's *Randolph*, Chap. X. (For data concerning the Virginia Carringtons, Henry included, see William Cabell Bruce, *John Randolph of Roanoke/ 1773–1833*, NY & Lond 1922.)

26. Baron Jacobi is one of several characters in *Democracy* who perform more than one function. He is a comic type, a European condemned to live in the United States. He is the chorus of the drama. Since at the end

he canes Ratcliffe, he is a dispenser of comic justice, avenging Mrs. Lee. (He also avenges Mrs. Sumner.)

27. Being a Massachusetts historian, Nathan Gore is as much a type as a Kentucky colonel or a Nevada prospector. Perhaps somewhat incongruously, he in addition is the lone male character who is a convinced and convincing democrat. It is typical of the novel as comedy that he is rejected when seeking office in the world's leading democracy.

28. I have assumed that MHA's list of reputed authors of *Democracy* was true to the best of her knowledge, as far she carried it. (The list does not include HA.) For another account of King's being cut by Blaine and Gail Hamilton, see Wilkins, *Clarence King*, 258.

29. The principal grounds that Blaine and Gail Hamilton had for thinking Ratcliffe in *Democracy* a representation of Blaine was the novel's description of Ratcliffe as a statesman so capable that the new administration is managed by him from the moment he is assured admission to the Cabinet. HA presents Ratcliffe as extremely capable. He thought Blaine more capable than his rivals. But it was Blaine, not HA, that confused the one with the other.

30. Blaine's effort to choose Garfield's other Cabinet members is outlined in Justus D. Doenecke, *The Presidencies of James A. Garfield & Chester A. Arthur*, Lawrence: Univ. Press of Kansas 1981, 30–36.

31. There are passages in *Democracy* that could be read by Blaine and Gail Hamilton as descriptive of his expected, wished-for dominance of President Garfield and the Cabinet. See Chap. VII. Moreover, the novel could be read as *knowing* that he, Blaine, would again try to be president.

32. Evidently Blaine and Gail Hamilton changed their minds about the authorship. See Chap. 19.

33. Linking Taylor and King, MHA wrote to RWH, 23 Jan 1881: "We all miss General Taylor sadly and no one takes his place. We look for Mr. King daily; he is overdue . . . but he bloweth where he listeth and official traces cannot keep him in the shafts."

34. In August 1955, Elizabeth Cameron's nephew Henry S. Sherman invited me to visit him in Cleveland at his expense—a kindness not untypical of persons who help biographers. During my visit, he told me he discovered that his aunt had falsified her age. He explained that, in her teens, she fell in love with Joe Russell, a New York lawyer, and wished to marry him; that she decided not to do so at the urging of her elder brother Henry, who warned that Russell was a drinker; that she lied about her age because she wished to treat the two years she was in love with Russell as no longer extant; and that she changed her birth year as recorded in the family Bible.

Mr. Sherman also told me that his aunt contracted her loveless marriage to Senator Cameron, which followed soon, without knowing that Cameron was a Bourbon drinker, a heavy one. He said too that in the 1890s, when he was about fifteen, he mentioned Russell to his mother in his aunt's presence and saw that his aunt was so distressed as to be nearly overcome. Finally, he said that later, when he discovered his aunt's true age, he mentioned her fib to her, and she admitted it.

The strongly-worded account of young Elizabeth's "abortive love affair" and it "disastrous consequences" in Arlene Boucher Tehan, *Henry Adams in Love*, NY 1983, 19–20, chimes very well with what I was told by Sherman in 1955.

35. Curtis may or may not have noticed that HA is echoing Macbeth's " 'If it were done, when 'tis done, then 'twere well it were done quickly," spoken in a soliloquy preliminary to killing Duncan.

36. Ellen Gurney, Edward Hooper, and Marian Adams inherited ideas relating to fatal illness, death, and burial from seafaring antecedents. One effect of this inheritance was the burial of Fanny Hooper in a coffin of a kind made at sea by sailors. The coffins were woven of wicker and covered with muslin or duck.

Beginning in 1959, for reasons relating to the burial of MHA in 1885, Louisa Hooper Thoron and Ellen Hooper Potter compared memories of the burial of their mother in 1881. Their memories agreed. On 26 Feb 1967, Mrs. Thoron told me that their mother was buried in just such a coffin, covered additionally for the occasion "with alamanda flowers on their vines with their leaves." For the connection of these memories with the burial of MHA, see Chap. 22.

37. Garland, *Randolph*, op. cit., II, 154; HA, *Randolph*, Chap. II.

38. Evidence abounds that HA, beginning in 1848 at the latest, attuned his life to the successive four-year administrations of the U. S. government. It was thus a foregone conclusion that the volumes of his *History of the United States* would be keyed to four-year intervals corresponding to successive administrations.

The best external evidence that his *History* required the mental completion of *seven* volumes recounting the nation's experience through *seven* administrations is the array of British papers he eventually gave to the State Department, now at the Manuscript Division, LC. See especially the *British State Papers, 1789–1801*. These papers are themselves a virtual British history of the United States during the administrations of Washington and John Adams. (They fill eight volumes. The first three volumes contain the Hammond papers, 1789–1795, that HA obtained from the State Department in 1863 and lent to Cobden.)

39. Because HA later destroyed his *Aaron Burr*, it is tempting to suppose that the biography contained sensational information that does not appear in his *History* and is lost. For developments bearing on this possibility see Chaps. 19–21.

40. HA's remarks concerning his plans especially reward notice when accompanied with dates. He says in his letter to Lodge, 29 Oct 1881, "After fifty, I mean to devote myself to frivolity and friends." He would turn fifty-one on 16 Feb 1889.

41. When a nonagenarian, Morse consented to talk to the members of the Massachusetts Historical Society on his editorship. His talk was published as "Incidents Connected with the American Statesmen Series," MHS *Proceedings*, v. 64 (1931), 370–88.

With regard to HA, the talk is so contrary to fact at some points as to be dubious at all others. Specifically, Morse claims (385ff) never to have heard of HA's *Aaron Burr*. Apart from MHA, he appears to have been the *first* person to have heard of it.

42. In 1875, when HA was editing the *North American*, Houghton proposed that payments to contributors be eliminated or at least reduced from the current low figure to a lower. See L, II, 224.

43. The later rejection of HA's *Aaron Burr* by Houghton for the American Statesmen Series on the ground that Burr was not a statesman

appears to have been an attempted offset to the earlier, similarly captious judgment by Morse that Randolph *was* a statesman—hence could be the subject of a biography in the series.

44. It may not need noting that MHA, amusedly, is invoking the garden of Eden and the forcible expulsion of Adam and Eve therefrom.

45. The suggestion by modern writers that Victoria Dare was Emily Beale might possibly agree with Miss Beale's idea (though there is no evidence attesting which role in *Democracy* she thought she had), but the suggestion by-passes two matters that need attention: HA's powers of invention and his having known young Washington women long prior to 1876, in good time to help him complete the novel.

46. Emily Beale was later accused of having co-authored the novel. In reaction, she said at the Adamses' dinner table that *Democracy* was " 'a horrid, nasty, vulgar book, written by a newspaper man not in good society.' " See Thoron, 306, 339. Emily's second response concerning *Democracy* can be thought as sensible as her first.

47. Essential details concerning Guiteau and his writings appear in James W. Clarke, *American Assassins/ The Darker Side of Politics*, Princeton 1982, 198–222.

48. Defenders of Blaine could urge that his walking within inches of flying bullets proved there was no connection between him and the assailant; that is, none relating to the attack. Differently, HA came to believe there *was* a connection between the secretary and the assailant relating to the attack. See note 63, below.

49. A measure of HA and MHA's improved relations with Godkin is HA's review of his own *Randolph* in Godkin's weekly. See Chap. 19.

50. One possible means was sheer political persuasion. According to HA's letter to Lodge, 16 Nov 1881, MacVeagh subsequent to Garfield's death conducted "an heroic and desperate as well as prolonged struggle to drag President Arthur into the assertion of reform principles," but "utterly and hopelessly failed."

51. Patricia O'Toole, in *The Five of Hearts/ An Intimate Portrait of Henry Adams and His Friends/ 1880–1918*, NY 1990, xv–xvii, dates the creation of the club during the winter of 1880–1881. She gives what may appear to be factual details concerning daily teas, frequent dinners, etc. Her account is bogus and can be classed with such accounts as those touched upon in note 55, below. It does not mend matters that O'Toole later says, 68–69, "Apart from a few stray remarks in Clover's letters to her father, the quintet who came to call themselves the Five of Hearts *left no records of their gatherings* [italics added]. . . ." It scarcely avails to give a history of gatherings and add sixty-odd pages later that records to support it are lacking. It happens, too, that there are no "stray remarks" by MHA during that winter indicating the formation of a club.

A similarly serious offence is O'Toole's treatment of a record that *was* kept. She attempts to paper over MHA's weekly letters recounting her and HA's actual doings. The attempt can be seen as a serious infringement of a dead woman's rights.

52. Edward L. Pierce, *Memoirs and Letters of Charles Sumner*, Bost 1877, I, 161, 229; II, 3, 156, 321.

53. Hay to MHA, 5 Nov 1881—"I had . . . paper made for . . . The Club and send a sample . . ."

54. The Hays were told the simple fact that HA wrote *Democracy*. They evidently were not advised concerning two matters of comparable importance: when the novel was written and how it was to be read.

55. The creation of the Five of Hearts affords an instance of HA's getting a desired response from onlookers interested in his actions. A year and a half later, on 20 Apr 1883, he would write to Hay:

> Several times within the last fortnight I have been told a story that you and King (sometimes one, sometimes both,) had heard the Manuscript of "Democracy" read in a house in Washington, had been asked to write a chapter, and so on with variations (such as that King had written the account of Worth's clothes in that veracious work), and finally, what was more important, that you both said the house in question was mine.
>
> In each case this story seems to have come from Tom Appleton [of Boston]. I have in all cases, emphatically, and in your names, denounced it as one of Tom Appleton's lies. . . .

The leading feature of the false story was its tending to say that *Democracy* had three authors: Adams, Hay, and King.

After HA's death, William Roscoe Thayer published an article, "Henry Adams, Central Figure in a Literary Discovery," *Boston Evening Transcript*, 10 Aug 1918, which, in part, seemed to offer an authoritative account of the writing of *Democracy*. The account in fact was false from start to finish. Thayer said:

> There were many guesses as to its authorship, but all finally narrowed down to Henry Adams, John Hay and Clarence King. Each of these gentlemen vigorously denied the allegation, and they had a device behind which they could screen themselves. Mr. and Mrs. Adams, Mr. and Mrs. Hay and Clarence King formed a most intimate little circle which they called the 'Five of Hearts,' and before this group Henry Adams read his 'Democracy' chapter by chapter. They all fell to and criticized it and they agreed to regard it as their joint production to the extent that no one individual could claim to have written every word of it.

Thayer's account is valuable partly for showing that a false story attributed to Appleton in 1883 was still current in Boston and its environs, albeit in a modified form, thirty-five years later.

The false story invented by Appleton (or whomever), repeated and modified by other tellers, and eventually printed as fact by Thayer can be said to have created the exact impression that HA (and MHA), beginning in late October 1881, hoped might be formed in many minds: the impression that *Democracy* was the work of all five Hearts.

The false story persisted. In 1947, it reappeared in a still more elaborate form in Cater, xliv. Cater named no sources. He presented the tale as fact, yet in such a way as to introduce the word "legend."

In 1957, as fact and without indicating a source, Levenson repeated a portion of the story in *Mind and Art of Henry Adams*, 97.

56. Subsequent letters by HA, MHA, Hay, and King can be adduced to show that the Adamses were not the leading Hearts or that all Hearts were equal. But the two concerns around which the Five of Hearts

continued to center were *Democracy* and residence in Washington. These concerns lent the Adamses a definite primacy.

57. Because no copies of the privately-printed first volume of HA's *History* survive, I have had to infer the title of the first volume from the parallel titles of the second and third volumes, as privately printed. The titles are suggestive of more volumes than HA wrote. Especially they raise the question, where is Adams's *History of the United States of America during the First Administration of George Washington—1789–1793*? In other words, they imply a series that could only have begun at the beginning.

58. Robert Brent Mosher, *Executive Register of the United States 1789–1902*, Wash 1905, 244.

59. Clarke in his *American Assassins*, op. cit., 207–09, treats the writings as insane and delusory. He does not consider the possibility that the writings were prepared and the letters carried to establish a cover story and a defense. The most notable feature of the writings was success in eliciting belief. On their evidence, it was usually supposed that Guiteau *was* a Stalwart.

60. Clarke, 210–11, dismisses the plea of divine intervention as insane. The plea, however, was partly grounded in experience. Guiteau in youth had been six years a member of the Oneida Community. He had dealt directly with its founder, John Humphrey Noyes. At first hand, he had seen that Noyes's claims of having experienced the Lord's will were credited as true within and outside the Community by persons who by usual standards were sane. Guiteau thus knew that a claim of divine intervention could be credited in the United States, and he could hopefully suppose that his claim might be granted a degree of credit.

61. During an unknown day or days, Grinnell attended the trial, presumably in his capacity as editor of the *American Law Review*. See his editorial note in the issue for January 1882, 50–55.

62. MHA told her father she was horrified by *two* persons, Guiteau and Corkhill. See her letter to RWH, 31 Jan 1882, Thoron 339: ". . . Corkhill,—the beast,—whom many of us would like to see flanking Guiteau on the gallows."

Presumably she was *more* horrified by a different pair, Guiteau and Blaine, but she would not say in her letters what she thought Blaine's part in the case had been.

63. Later, in 1882 in Ireland, an English official, HA's long-time friend Frederick Cavendish, would be killed while walking in a Dublin park with another English official, the *intended* victim; and HA would react by making a remark: "Strange that people always murder the wrong man." See HA to Cunliffe, 29 May 1882, L, II, 457.

Since Garfield and Blaine too walked together, it might appear that HA believed Guiteau killed President Garfield by mistake and intended to murder Secretary Blaine. But such a reading is impossible. It was believed by practically everyone, Cunliffe and HA included, that Guiteau meant to murder the man he did murder.

One thus is driven to an alternative reading. The reading is that HA believed that Blaine, although not ticketed by Guiteau for murder, *deserved to be murdered*.

Later HA wrote a pertinent sentence: "Thackeray and Balzac never invented anything so lurid as Garfield, Guiteau and Blaine, but even they are surpassed by Brady and Dorsey, and Arthur is a creature for whose skin the romancist ought to go with a carving knife." See HA to Hay, 4 Mar 1883, L, II, 493.

The sentence has a violent beginning. The beginning is violent because it lists Garfield, Guiteau, and Blaine in sequence as a murder victim, the victim's murderer, and a ———?

Interestingly, the violent beginning is counteracted with a two-part false climax. Evidently HA saw that his sentence's beginning too fully expressed one of his most secretly held and most deeply felt opinions. As a cure, he could have torn up his letter. He instead drowned his sentence's too-expressive beginning with extravagant and less-than-believable added words.

An attentive reader is left with the question, What role did HA think Blaine had in the murder of Garfield? On the basis of presently available evidence, only one answer is possible. HA thought Blaine the man under whose guidance unstable Guiteau decided which man to murder.

64. MHA's line evidently draws on the proverbial idea that "The road to hell is paved with good intentions." Presumably it draws also on the line "The paths of glory lead but to the grave" in Gray's "Elegy in a Country Churchyard." It seems possible too that MHA had read in Blake's *Marriage of Heaven and Hell* the proverb "The road of excess leads to the palace of wisdom."

19. The Authors of *Democracy*

Letters by and to HA are in HA-micro 5, unless otherwise noted.

PRINCIPAL SOURCES

(1) forty-six letters, MHA to RWH, 25 Dec 1881–31 Dec 1882, Thoron, 314–412.

(2) letters, HA to Parkman, 23 Jan, 20 Feb 1882.

(3) six letters, HA to CMG, 29 Jan–3 Dec 1882.

(4) three letters, HA to Lodge, 31 Jan–31 Oct 1882.

(5) three letters, HA to Morse, 2 Mar–19 Nov 1882.

(6) nine letters, HA to Hay, 30 Apr 1882–7 Jan 1883.

(7) three letters, HA to Cunliffe, 29 May–12 Nov 1882.

(8) five letters, HA to Holt, 21 Sep–16 Oct 1882, Cater, 122–24.

(9) [HA], "*John Randolph.* By Henry Adams. [American Statesmen.] Boston: Houghton, Mifflin & Co. 1882.," *Nation,* 14 Dec 1882, 514. For the attribution to HA, see note 75, below.

ADDITIONAL SOURCES; COMMENTS

1. Thoron, 277, 295. Also see *Letters and Journals of General Nicholas Longworth Anderson,* NY 1942, 254—". . . do you not think Cincinnati is a better place to visit than to live in?"

2. Thoron, 295.

3. HA-micro 4. HJ visited Washington in January 1882, April 1883, and January 1905. Three texts are especially relevant: a work in the form of fictional letters, "The Point of View," *Century Magazine,* Dec 1882; a story, "Pandora," *New York Sun,* 1 & 8 Jun 1884; and an essay, "Washington," *NAR,* May & Jun 1906. Notes pertaining to "The Point of View" and

"Pandora" appear in F. O. Matthiessen & Kenneth B. Murdock, eds., *The Notebooks of Henry James*, NY 1947 (hereafter *Notebooks*).

On 18 Mar 1879, more than a year before the publication of *Democracy*, HJ recorded (*Notebooks*, 15) the possibility of producing "an alternation of letters, written from an aristocratic, and a democratic, point of view." "The Point of View" corresponds to that outline.

On 17 May 1883, after *Democracy* had been widely sold in the United States and Europe, HJ recorded (*Notebooks*, 51): " 'The self-made girl' —a very good subject for a short story." On 29 Jan 1884, HJ wrote a paragraph (*Notebooks*, 56) involving mention of his story "Four Meetings," his short novel *Daisy Miller*, and the proposed story in which he would "do the 'self-made girl.' " He said of the proposed story: "It must take place in New York. Perhaps Washington would do. This would give me a chance to *do* Washington, so far as I know it, and work in my few notes. . . . I might even *do* Henry Adams and his wife. . . ."

Soon after, HJ wrote "Pandora," a story about a self-made girl. The title character, Pandora Day, has a name which shares a sound both with the name of HJ's earlier character Daisy Miller (referred to by name in "Pandora") and the name of the American girl who figures prominently in Chap. VI of *Democracy*, Victoria Dare. Also "Pandora" includes a picnic excursion from Washington to Mount Vernon noticeably similar to the excursion to Mount Vernon in Chap. VI of *Democracy*. (HJ's "Washington" introduces the reader to the capital by way of a stop at Mount Vernon. I have found no evidence that HJ visited Mount Vernon. In the absence of evidence of his making a visit, it seems possible that, while writing the Mount Vernon portions of "Pandora" and "Washington," he drew on Chap. VI of *Democracy*.)

The character in "Pandora" second in importance to Pandora Day is a German secretary of legation in Washington, Count Vogelstein. It accordingly can be inferred that HJ read *Democracy* with attention and became convinced that it bore upon the scandal in the late 1860s involving Charles Sumner, his wife, and Baron Friedrich von Holstein. (HJ knew the baron. See Fred Kaplan, *Henry James*, NY 1992, 165.)

In 1947, editors Matthiessen and Murdock stated authoritatively (*Notebooks*, 56–57) that two characters in "Pandora," Mr. and Mrs. Alfred Bonnycastle, are "the Adams family" (i.e. HA and MHA). Likewise, in 1963, Leon Edel averred that "the Henry Adamses" appear in "Pandora" and "are named . . . Bonnycastle." See Edel, *Henry James/ The Middle Years/ 1884–1894*, Lond 1963, 58. Received opinion since 1963 has reiterated these pronouncements.

In this instance, received opinion is mistaken. HJ's stories differ widely in quality. "Pandora" is one of the flatter failures, derivative, strained, prolix, and vapid. Neither HA nor MHA can be found in its pages. If Mrs. Bonnycastle is MHA, as alleged, the story convicts HJ of failing totally to mimic MHA's voice or approximate her turn of mind. If Mr. Bonnycastle is HA, as alleged, the story is evidence that HJ had no idea what HA was like. Bonnycastle is given the story's most notable line: ". . . let us have some fun—let us invite the President." (In later versions, HJ amended it to read, ". . . let us be vulgar and have some fun—let us invite the President.") The line may possibly indicate that HJ aspired to the sort of flippancy the line represents; but no similar flippancy, or *any* flippancy, can be found in HA's writings or actions of any date.

Reconsidered with ordinary care, "Pandora" suggests that HJ very slightly tried to "*do* Henry Adams and his wife" but backed away from the attempt and instead did something else. This conclusion involves no scolding of HJ. It represents him as sufficiently intelligent to know he could not perform a task he had thought he might set himself. In place of HA and MHA, he invented the Bonnycastles, fictions somewhat reflective of his own traits and qualities.

4. "Familiarly" does not appear in "Pandora," but Washington is said to have "a society in which familiarity reigned," and "familiar" twice appears with regard to a tour guide at Mount Vernon.

5. HJ to MHA, 6 Nov 1881, HA-micro 4. Presumably both sender and receiver were aware of the similarity of "clever" to "Clover."

6. Some details of this episode are drawn from Leon Edel, *Henry James/ The Conquest of London/ 1870–1883*, Lond 1962, 451–64.

7. See note 3, above.

8. In my view, comparison of two letters, MHA to HJ, 15 Nov 1881 and HA to Godkin, 13 [Dec] 1881, leaves no alternative to the conclusions offered here about HJ's question and Godkin's response.

9. HJ to HA, 20 Dec 1881.

10. In his new letter to HA, 27 Dec 1881, HJ says that, after four months of travel, involvements with relations, etc., his "desire for a quiet corner of my own" has become "*ferocious.*" HA and MHA could thus suppose that HJ was coming to Washington partly to write.

11. HJ to Clark, 8 Jan 1882, *Henry James Letters*, II, 366; HJ to Godkin, 15 Jan [1882], Godkin Papers, H; HA to CMG, 29 Jan 1882; and HJ to Mrs. Gardner, 23 Jan [1882], *Henry James Letters*, II, 373.

In the letter to Clark, HJ goes on to say, "One excellent reason for their [the Adamses'] liking Washington better than London is that they are, vulgarly speaking, 'someone' here, and that they are nothing in your complicated Kingdom."

The Clarks were not likely to agree that HA and MHA were nothing in the U. K. Contemporary letters to the Adamses by English friends extended them a status as longed-for visitors that was much at variance with HJ's negative estimate.

12. When writing "Pandora" in 1884, HJ knew that HA had published a biography of Randolph and was writing a history involving Jefferson and Madison. HJ so shaped "Pandora" that Pandora Day has a brother and that Count Vogelstein, when he first sees Pandora Day, is reading a Tauchnitz copy of *Daisy Miller*. Moreover, HJ assumed that readers of "Pandora" would have read *Daisy Miller* and would remember that Daisy, its heroine, has a brother, Randolph Miller.

These preconditions permitted a shuffling of names. In "Pandora," the narrator says, ". . . there was, for Vogelstein . . . an analogy between young Mr. Day and a certain small brother—a candy-loving Madison, Hamilton, or Jefferson—who, in the Tauchnitz volume, was attributed to that unfortunate maid [Daisy Miller]." In the next sentence, the narrator less complexly miscalls Randolph Miller "the little Madison." See *New York Sun*, 1 Jun 1884, 2.

In "Pandora," HJ nowhere concedes that the first name of Daisy Miller's brother is Randolph. The avoidance is skittish, as if HJ wished to approach HA but also wished not to.

13. In a letter to HA, 21 Mar 1914, *Henry James Letters*, IV, 706, HJ said: "I still find my consciousness interesting—under *cultivation* of the interest. Cultivate it *with* me, dear Henry—that's what I hoped to make you do; to cultivate yours for all that it has in common with mine." As I understand the passage, HJ recalls an early moment when, in person, he urged HA to become a writer more like himself. I suggest that the place-and-time when HJ was likeliest to urge HA's taking such a course was Washington, January 1882.

14. HJ to Godkin, 15 Jan [1882], op. cit.—". . . Guiteau . . . appears never to be spoken of here."

15. MHA to RWH, 17 Jan 1882—saying about Betsy when nursing family members who were ill, ". . . her ghoulish whispers make my flesh creep as I remember them."

16. *Henry James Letters*, II, 366.

17. For MHA's view of Wilde, see Thoron, 328, 338–39, 342. The Adamses thought the London production of *Patience* "convulsing" but were rather bored by the production in New York. They saw the latter with the Hays and King on 26 Oct 1881, following the second dinner of the five friends at Delmonico's. See Thoron, 293.

18. HA was usually supportive of new administrations. Not leaving his card when Arthur became president (see letter to CMG, 30 Apr–2 May 1882), he guarded against the risk of encountering Blaine if invited by Arthur to the White House. HA and MHA had reason not to mention this precaution to HJ. HJ was far from being their political ally.

19. Doenecke, *Presidencies of Garfield & Arthur*, op. cit., 78.

20. Edel, *Conquest of London*, op. cit., 463–64.

21. HJ to Godkin, 22 Jan [1882], Godkin Papers, H.

22. In "Pandora," HJ's narrator says that in Washington "functionaries engaged . . . to usher in guests and wait at supper" had "a complexion which served as a livery." See *New York Sun*, 8 Jun 1884, 2.

Thinking another wording better, HJ in later printings substituted "that rich racial hue which of itself served as a livery."

23. When living at 1501 H Street, the Adamses tried to recruit white servants, with poor results. When living at 1607 H Street, they apparently depended on black servants from the beginning and as a rule found them helpful and skilled.

24. According to Edel, *Conquest of London*, 460, HJ started "The Point of View" while in Washington.

25. HJ to his mother, [29 Jan 1882], *Henry James Letters*, II, 375–76.

26. Edel, *Conquest of London*, 464; Thoron, 336.

27. Beringause, *Brooks Adams*, 70–73.

28. See note 32, below.

29. HA's letter to MacVeagh, 26 May 1882, concerns his preferring not to investigate a woman—not identified—in Pennsylvania. Because the letter was written five weeks prior to the execution of Guiteau and because the assassination of Garfield became a central concern for HA and Mac-Veagh, the letter can be imagined to relate to Guiteau's act. See Warner B. Berthoff & David Bonnell Green, "Henry Adams and Wayne MacVeagh," *Pennsylvania Magazine of History & Biography*, Oct 1956, 497.

30. The account of King's physical illnesses in Wilkins, *Clarence King*, Chaps. XVI-XX, seems more detailed and candid than the account of King's misjudgments—a more difficult subject.

31. In 1888, Ward Thoron, a legal apprentice, acted as caretaker of HA's house and assisted him with regard to business details. It is possible that in 1888–1890 HA told Thoron rather fully what he thought of Blaine. Such a course by HA would lend weight and interest to the many Blaine-related materials excerpted from the *Nation* that Thoron reprinted in 1936 as notes and appendices in the *Letters of Mrs. Henry Adams*. None of the materials are indexed by Haskell as by HA. Yet it would be easy to believe that some of the materials bear HA's impress. See especially the paragraph in the *Letters*, 556–57.

32. Levenson and his associates say the manuscript HA refers to is "Probably the life of Aaron Burr." See L, II, 452n1. What HA delivered to Morse, however, was the manuscript of *John Randolph*. Also the existence of an already-written *Aaron Burr* appears to have come as a complete surprise to Morse the following October, when he had to deal with HA's offer of the book for publication.

33. Mrs. Proctor to HA, 15 Aug 1882, HA-micro 5. Her letter is evidence that the tendency of English readers to attribute *Democracy* to MHA originated as early as 1880 and certainly by 1881.

34. Thoron, 357n2. It is clear that Mrs. Green and HJ discussed *Democracy* before he returned to America.

35. MHA reported that King was "sewer-poisoned." See MHA to RWH, 19 Feb 1882.

36. In her letter to RWH, 12 Mar 1882, MHA treats the offer of the mission to Costa Rica simply as an action by Frelinghuysen and almost as something she could favor. "I wish we wanted it, it would be so new and fresh. . . ." One may doubt that her lines to her father revealed her full opinion. See note 37.

37. HA's sentence is best read with the following considerations in mind. In 1880, Gail Hamilton and Blaine supposed that *Democracy* was written by King. At some point in 1881–1882, they began to attribute the novel to MHA. In the novel, Secretary Ratcliffe wants to remove Carrington from Washington and secretly contrives to have the government offer him a mission to Mexico that he cannot refuse. In life, Secretary Frelinghuysen offered HA a mission to Costa Rica which if accepted would have removed HA and MHA from Washington. Thus HA and MHA *had* to wonder (a) whether the offer of the mission, though extended by Frelinghuysen, was suggested by ex-Secretary Blaine and Gail Hamilton, (b) whether the offer was a humorless attempted repetition of Ratcliffe's maneuver, and (c) whether its purpose was to exile the writer of *Democracy*. Assuming HA and MHA did so wonder, HA's word "conspiracy" is entirely pertinent.

38. Details concerning MHA's purchase appear in a series of letters from MHA to Theodore Dwight, January-February 1882, HA-micro 5, as well as in her concurrent letters to RWH.

39. Testimony printed by the *Nation*; reprinted in Thoron, 377n1.

40. Macmillan advertised the edition as "just ready," *Athenaeum*, 27 May 1882, and prominently re-advertised the edition as "now ready" either as one volume or as two volumes, clothbound, *Athenaeum*, 24 June 1882. A Macmillan notice, LTimes, 27 Jun 1882, lists the one-volume form, clothbound, and a paperbound edition.

HA acquired a one-volume copy, clothbound, and signed his name on the title page. It is the only copy of the novel in HAL in English.

41. I know of no evidence that the reprinting of *Democracy* by publishers in Europe was arranged by Henry Holt and Co. The Macmillan edition was freshly set in type, in 280 pages, as compared with Holt's 374. So was the Ward, Lock edition. See note 54, below.

42. Wilkins, *King*, op. cit., 283–87.

43. The letter from HJ to MHA is missing. Her letter to RWH, 14 May 1882, continues, "Am I then vulgar, dreary, and impossible to live with?" Considering that she was an interested reader of HJ's writings, her question can be taken to reflect HJ's published complaints about the U. S. and, too, his complaints to MHA and HA in conversation.

44. Edel, *Conquest of London*, 475–76.

45. Wilkins, *King*, 284–87.

46. *John Randolph*, published 21 Oct 1882, was quickly reissued in corrected form, dated 1883. See Blanck, I, 4. Even corrected, the book contained distracting blemishes. For example, in Chap. XII, Randolph is said to have passed "near a year in England" and also is said to have remained in England "about eighteen months." In the same chapter, he is described as "lolling against the railing" in the Senate chamber. A page later, he again is "Lolling against the rail." The faults are not many, but they are there.

47. Morse's opinion of the *Randolph* is reflected in a letter to him by Richard Grant White, 7 Dec 1882, Morse Papers, MHS, saying about the biography, ". . . I think with you that it is . . . very clever. . . ."

48. HA to CMG, 3 Feb 1884, confirms that there were six copies of the *First Jefferson*. In his letter to Scribner, 12 Jul 1888, Barrett, 16, Dwight speaks of the "privately printed edition of six" and says there were six copies each of the first three volumes. He goes on to say that the fourth volume was not privately printed.

49. HA's letters to Cunliffe, 9 Jul & 12 Nov 1882, say, "History grinds on . . ." and "I have to write history. . . ." His letter to Gaskell, 3 Dec 1882, says, "The result of four months by the sea-side was only a certain amount of manuscript, and a small volume [*John Randolph*]. . . ." HA nowhere states how far he advanced in the *History*.

50. Reviews appeared in *Blackwood's*, 31 May 1882; *Pall Mall Gazette*, 15 June 1882; *Athenaeum*, 24 Jun 1882; *Edinburgh Review*, Jul 1882; *Saturday Review*, 8 Jul 1882; and *Westminster Review*, Oct 1882. A review by Mary A. Ward, "Democracy: An American Novel," *Fortnightly Review*, 1 Jul 1882, 78–93, links the novel to a passage in HA's "Civil Service Reform" and says, ". . . *Democracy*, whether Mr. Adams had a hand in it or not, represents . . . an attempt to strike the popular imagination and to overcome the sluggishness of the public mind."

An unsigned review, *Academy*, 1 Jul 1882, 5, concludes: "The literary worksmanship as a whole reminds us of Mr. Henry James; but the new writer's method is more direct and less tantalisingly elaborate than that of the author of *Washington Square*, suggesting occasionally the homelier, because less aggressively analytic, manner of Mr. Anthony Trollope. Cleverness is not the most valuable quality in art, but it is always interesting; and *Democracy* is certainly the cleverest novel which has appeared for some time."

51. King to Hay, 15 Aug 1882, HP; Hay to HA, 17 Aug 1882.

52. King's delusory "woman from Boston" in *Democracy* (letter to Hay,

15 Aug 1882, HP) may relate to the scene in Chap. VIII in which Mrs. Lee—a New Yorker—decides that Mrs. Baker should never re-enter her house. One part of King's delusion is the mistaken idea that Mrs. Lee is MHA. See Chap. 22, note 38, below. But far more strongly the delusion appears to indicate sensitivity concerning what King felt were unfair or dismissive judgments expressed about him by Bostonians, starting with Alexander Agassiz and Quincy Shaw. In his letter to Hay, 24 Aug 1882, HP, King likens *Democracy* to "those clever bits of advocacy at the bar by which a bright lawyer so groups admitted facts as to produce a wrong conclusion." Again, it appears, the real problem for King is not a flaw in *Democracy* but what he was feeling as unfair ideas expressed about him by Bostonians.

The delusory elements in the letters are obvious but seem to have been invisible to King. Out of friendship, Hay may have wanted not to see them, and in that sense they may have been invisible to him also.

53. King to Hay, undated letter beginning "I am quite too low in my mind . . . ," [Dec 1882?], and King to Hay, 8 Mar [1883], HP.

54. JTA, *Henry Adams*, 221, lists an edition of *Democracy* published by "Ward, Lock & Co., London (1882), 186 pp." Entries in the British Library Catalogue under Henry Adams and *Democracy* agree with JTA's listing. The copy sent by Hay conceivably belonged to this edition.

55. At an unknown date, evidently not earlier than the spring of 1882 and possibly as late as the winter of 1901–1902, HA confided to BA that he wrote *Democracy*. Also, in a letter dated 11 Jul 1905, he told BA, "The wholesale piracy of *Democracy* was the single real triumph of my life." See L, V, 414, 691. The phrase "wholesale piracy" seems at least part-true but possibly too strong. Exactly how much *Democracy* was pirated, and by which publishers, is still to be established.

56. Dennett, *Hay*, 107, 115; Wilkins, *King*, 288; George Monteiro, *Henry James and John Hay/ The Record of a Friendship*, Providence 1975, 39–40, 156; Hay to HA, 16 Aug, 17 Sep 1882.

57. Dennett, *Hay*, 115n1.

58. Howells and Warner had facts on their side. DeForest had written two political novels set in Washington, *Honest John Vane*, New Haven 1875, and *Playing the Mischief*, NY 1875.

59. After not hearing from King for more than three months, the Adamses obtained an indirect account of him from his friend James T. Gardiner, based on letters by King to his mother. See L, II, 468.

60. CFA2 was one of the persons asked by HA to read and criticize privately printed volumes of his *History*. In the absence of evidence to the contrary, one may assume that HA asked CFA2 for this assistance during one or another of their meetings in September 1882.

61. Perhaps Holt would have avoided advertising the cheap edition even without urging by HA. The avoidance did not spoil the sales. See JTA, *Henry Adams*, 221—"In 1882 a cheap edition [of *Democracy*, published by Holt,] went through five printings."

62. Saying his *Randolph* will appear in obituaries of himself, HA may mean it will be remembered as good or remembered as bad, but in either case he means it will be remembered—which is no small boast.

63. Hay to HA, 22 Oct 1882.

64. See especially William Wirt Henry, "The Rescue of Captain John

Smith by Pocahontas," *Potter's American Monthly*, Jul 1875, 523–28, & Aug 1875, 591–97.

65. HA preserved a Virginian attack on Morse as editor and himself as author of *John Randolph*. See Daniel B. Lucas, *John Randolph of Roanoke; His Convictions and Their Influence on his Public Career*, NY 1884, HAL. The attack is interesting for saying (12) that HA's book is not history, not satire, and not biography. Though meant as derogation, the judgment possibly involved a dawning sense that the book belongs to a new genre.

66. CFA2, Diary, 12 Nov 1882, AP.

67. How the French translation came into existence and how HA came to know about it in advance are at present complete mysteries. HA preserved a copy of the 2nd ed. marked by himself, "From John Hay, February, 1883"; also a copy of the 1st ed. marked by himself, "Bought on the Quai Mal[a]quais, August 26, 1908. fr. 1.25." Both are in HAL. (HA also acquired a Swedish translation. His copy is in HAL.)

68. JTA, *Henry Adams*, 221, notes a "Tauchnitz edition, Leipzig, 1882." The history of the edition has not been traced.

69. The remarks MHA said she pled guilty to are represented by HJ in the Cockerel letter in the following terms: ". . . [the English] talk about things we have settled ages ago. . . . In England they were talking about the Hares and Rabbits Bill, about the extension of the County Franchise, about the Dissenters' Burials, about the Deceased Wife's Sister, about the abolition of the House of Lords, about Heaven knows what ridiculous little measure for the propping up of their ridiculous little country." See Henry James, Jr., "The Point of View," *Century*, Dec 1882, 266. Being derisory rather than funny, the lines are remote from MHA in style, however much the list of items may originally have been hers.

70. Edel, *Conquest of London*, 488.

71. The attribution of the review of *John Randolph* in the *Nation* to HA is my own. Arguments and evidence in its support are given in note 75, below.

72. King to Hay, undated letter [Dec 1882?], op. cit., HP.

73. The comments in the *National Republican*, 19 Dec 1882, appear in a column of Washington society news. The passage is remarkable for placing Gail Hamilton and Blaine first in a list of alleged authors of *Democracy* and for masking the gibe under a pretense of amused but accurate reporting. The passage reads: "The anonymous novel 'Democracy' is a fruitful theme of parlor conversation in this early season, and the guessers present a long list of possible perpetrators of that brilliant satire upon Washington life and manners. The list include[s] Gail Hamilton and Mr. Blaine in an Erckmann-Chatrian partnership affair, Mr. John Hay, Mr. Clarence King, Mr. William Vance, Mr. Adam (of the British Legation), Mrs. Mary Clemmer, Miss Hattie Loring, Mrs. Harriet Prescott Spofford, Grace Greenwood (Mrs. Lippincott), and about all the other gifted literary people who have lived here within ten years. Unfortunately for the settlement of the vexed question, each and all of these people resent and deny the flattering suspicion of authorship, and the clever writer remains a sphynx." The newspaper's Washington readers might notice the similarity of "clever" to "Clover."

74. Hay repelled the suggestion that King was mentally disturbed. In his reply to HA, 22 Jan 1883, he wrote: "I am sorry to hear what you say

the Boston men say ab^t King. He was working like a Turk for their interests all the time he was in Paris. That he did not succeed was owing to the stars in their courses. The vacillation, and treachery[,] of Frenchmen in business matters, small and great, is not conceivable to square and serious men like Agassiz, Shaw & Co. King is simply the same King you know."

75. Attribution of the *Randolph* review to HA first appeared in my *Henry Adams and History*, Ann Arbor: Univ. Microfilms (pub. no. 8539), 131–34. It is supported by evidence and argument in three areas.

The first area is appropriate action. An unsigned review of HA's *Randolph* written by HA himself was an appropriate consequence of Godkin's mistaken acceptance and publication of CFA2's unsigned article on HA's *Life of Albert Gallatin*. Godkin's error cried for correction. HA's review is the correction.

The second category is appropriate language. The *Randolph* review is written throughout, not in the language of judgment natural to a critic of a book, but in the language of inside knowledge and authoritative declaration appropriate only to the author of the book.

The third category is particular terms. The review uses terms that can also be found in writings by HA and MHA that are close to it in date. For example, the metaphor of literature as dissection had appeared in HA to Holmes, 3 Nov 1881, L, II, 443, and would appear again in HA to Holmes, 4 Jan 1885, L, II, 566. The happy family in Barnum's circus appears in MHA's letters to RWH, 3 Feb 1878, AP, and 18 Nov 1883, AP. Strikingly, in her letter to RWH, 6 Jan 1884, AP, MHA speaks of both "literary vivesection" and Barnum. Examples can be multiplied.

76. That HA wrote *John Randolph* as a Unionist and a Northerner did not mean that he thought himself incapable of writing unbiased United States history. Nor did it mean that he set out to disparage Randolph. A leading quality of the *Randolph* is forthrightness, and the evident basis for the forthrightness is HA's confidence is his fairness. He says, for example (Chap. VIII): "The story of Randolph's famous quarrel with his party [the Jeffersonian Republicans] has now been told in a spirit as friendly to him as his friends can require or expect,—has been told, so far as possible, in his own words, and shall be left to be judged on its merits."

It should be noticed that HA's copy of Garland's *John Randolph of Roanoke*, HAL, belongs to the 13th ed., NY 1860. Possibly HA acquired the copy in the winter of 1860–1861 in Washington. His many marks in the copy are undated and perhaps were made in 1881, but it seems possible that he studied the book repeatedly and did so for the first time before or during the Rebellion.

77. Although he claimed to be indifferent to the reception of his *Randolph*, HA took pains to record its remarkable success. He twice-yearly tallied the sales and royalties. See his account in HA-micro 5, October 1882. His first entries are those for 1 Feb 1883, the last for 31 Jul 1911. The entries say that 19,388 copies were sold and that the royalties totaled $2,077.32.

78. HA's notice of *John Randolph* is possible most valuable for the attention it gives to the terms "cadaver" and "lay figure." A lay figure is a jointed dummy of wood on which an artist hangs costumes preliminary to painting them. By saying that the author of the *Randolph* does not "hang historical drapery" on a lay figure but instead dissects a cadaver, HA points

towards two possible sorts of books within the new genre he discovered, the education. The sorts are the imaginative (or fictional) and the critical (or non-fictional). The already-published *John Randolph* is critical. It reveals for examination the ideas held by an actual person when alive. Hence the metaphor of a cadaver and its dissection. The not-yet-written *Education of Henry Adams* would be imaginative. For purposes of study, the book would drape a narrative on a dummy: a fictional person, a Henry Adams who never lived.

In the Preface of *The Education* when written, HA would introduce the metaphor of a dummy, except that the term used would be "manikin." Needless to say, that term and "lay figure" are interchangeable.

The cadaver vs. lay figure polarity is admittedly harsh. It none the less is clear and helpful.

20. A Great Book

Letters by and to HA & MHA are in HA-micro 5, unless otherwise noted.

PRINCIPAL SOURCES

(1) twenty-two letters, MHA to RWH, 7 Jan–27 May 1883, Thoron, 412–52.

(2) five letters, HA to CMG, 21 Jan 1883–18 May 1884.

(3) thirty-one letters, HA to Hay, 4 Mar 1883–3 Jul 1884.

(4) note, HA to MHA, 10 Apr 1883.

(5) letter, HA to Lowell, 15 May 1883, L, II, 501.

(6) three letters, HA to EC, 18 May–25 Dec 1883.

(7) thirty-eight letters, MHA to RWH, 23 Oct 1883–8 Jun 1884, AP.

(8) letters, MacVeagh to HA, 16, 22 Jul 1884.

(9) letter, HA to MacVeagh, 20 Jul 1884, L, II, 545–46.

(10) HA, "Napoléon Ier et Saint-Domingue," *Revue Historique*, Apr 1884, 92–130.

(11) HA, "Napoleon I. at St. Domingo," in *Historical Essays*, NY 1891, 122–77.

ADDITIONAL SOURCES; COMMENTS

1. HA to Gilman, 2 Mar 1883, L, II, 492–93.

2. Ibid. HA says in the letter that he "always" writes his biographical and historical works twice. Yet also he says he will write his *First Jefferson* three times. "I . . . am going next summer to put a twice-written volume of history into type, in order to rewrite it before publication."

3. The titles of the first and fourth volumes are adduced from the privately-printed copies of the second and third volumes, HAL.

4. The inference that the *History* was written as twenty books rests on varied but decisive evidence. No manuscripts of the *History* survive. HA privately printed his *First Jefferson* but recovered and destroyed all six copies. He privately printed his *Second Jefferson* and *First Madison*, recovered copies, and kept some. He did not privately print his *Second Madison*. As is shown by the copies, the *Second Jefferson* consists of five numbered and titled books. The same is true of the *First Madison*. One assumes that the same was also true of the *First Jefferson* and the *Second Madison*; and, though the books' numbers and titles are omitted in the *History* as pub-

lished, the book divisions are easily found with the help of internal evidence.

5. I am inclined to believe HA did not so much invent the twenty-part form as find it in the occurrences the *History* recounts. Occurrences and form coordinate with little or no sign of strain.

6. Thoron, 405, 410, 412. One of the Adamses' Washington acquaintances knew George Sand. In the autumn of 1882, HA and MHA befriended a German, an employee at the Smithsonian, Dr. D. E. Bessels, of Heidelberg. He helped Clover arrange to have her Reynolds portraits cleaned. On January 7, 1883, he called for tea. Clover wrote: ". . . to save him a lonely restaurant dinner, we asked him to share ours. He told me . . . about George Sand, whom he knew through his brother, who is married to a relative of Alfred de Musset. He dined with [her] . . . in Paris in 1867 and then passed two days at her chateau at Nohant . . . ; [he] says . . . the dining room opened with folding doors on to a terrace, where Chopin dragged his piano and played to the stars; the Chopin piano still stood there." See Ibid., 341, 348, 351, 414–15.

7. That HA titled the five books of the *First Jefferson* is adduced from the book titles that appear in the privately printed copies of the *Second Jefferson* and *First Madison*, HAL.

8. The titles in the list are my own suggestions and, in my view, suit the books' contents.

Book I of the *First Jefferson* has been much reprinted in paperback as Henry Adams, *The United States in 1800*, Ithaca NY 1955. In a Prefatory Note in the paperback, Dexter Perkins shows no awareness that the *History* took the form of short books, that the six chapters reissued are a book, or that the book is one of twenty. He says the six chapters are "essays on social history." Also he or the publisher invented for the chapters an inert title, *The United States in 1800*.

On the grounds that HA's *History* throughout is narrative, not discussion, and is national, not "social," I suggest a different title, "1800: the Americans Not United." This title suits both the contents of Book I and the contents of the *History* as a whole, which does not end until the Americans *are* united.

9. In Cleveland on 18 Aug 1956, Henry S. Sherman, Mrs. Cameron's nephew and executor, told me that his aunt had a very good mind, that her mental power came to him as a surprise, and that her mental power did not seem to go along with other parts of her nature.

10. MHA to Mrs. Hay, 16 Feb 1883, AP.

11. Hay to HA, 13 Feb 1883.

12. HJ to MHA, 28 Feb 1883.

13. Tragedy visible in Washington had been a subject of many of HA's works other than *Democracy*, notably "The Great Secession Winter of 1860–61," "The New York Gold Conspiracy," *New England Federalism*, *The Life of Albert Gallatin*, and *John Randolph*. None had been a failure with respect to the subject. And a greater success impended.

14. Eppard, 121n2, alleges a link between matters taken up by HA in this letter to Hay and matters that later appeared in the novel *Conspiracy* by Adam Badeau.

A topic that might better reward investigation is the influence of HA's *Democracy* on two works by Badeau: *Conspiracy/ A Cuban Romance*, NY 1885, and *Aristocracy in England*, NY 1886.

15. It is natural to suppose that the five-book form of the volumes of the *History* was affected in one degree or another by the printing of Shakespeare's *tragedies* as five-act works. (*Henry IV* excepted, HA paid small attention to Shakespeare's histories.) The supposition is not corroborated by any evidence that I know of, but it would seem unwise to thrust the supposition aside as untrue or unimportant.

16. The third book clearly begins with the chapter titled "The Spanish Court." For further details, see note 46, below.

17. See especially Woolner to MHA, 6 Aug 1883, HA-micro 5, saying he has completed a book-length poem, *Silenus*, and telling her, ". . . one of my griefs is that you say you do not much care for poetry. . . ."

18. MHA to RWH, 27 Mar 1881, Thoron, 279—"Have just begun Gibbon's *History*, a bone which will take months to gnaw."

19. Although they contain a comment that the *Burr* was "much better" than the *Randolph*, Thoron, 405, MHA's writings contain no comparable judgments of the *History* or portions thereof. I take her silence to indicate, not ignorance, but knowledge. This inference is supported by MacVeagh's letters to HA reacting to the *First Jefferson* (quoted in this chapter).

20. The photograph was first published in Thoron, facing 414.

21. Hay to HA, 19 Mar 1883.

22. HA commonly took liberties with the spelling of names beginning with Mc or Mac; hence his misspelling of MacVeagh.

HA's statements to Hay and Lowell that he adored Mrs. Cameron and had fallen in love with her were qualifiedly true (and would be understood by Hay and Lowell as qualifiedly true), the qualification being that *HA and MHA together* adored and fell in love with EC. Similarly for several years, HA and MHA together adored and loved Anne Palmer. In each instance, they can be said to have exhibited behavior commonly found in childless married couples who have young friends.

In her *Henry Adams in Love*, 69, 96, Arlene Tehan quotes—actually misquotes—HA's 1883 statement to Lowell as if it was unqualified. She also misquotes without its date and as if written in 1886 a letter HA wrote to EC in November 1891. She thus falsifies the chronology of HA's later romantic attachment to EC and especially the date of its inception. It began well after 1886 and long after the death of MHA.

23. Dennett, *John Hay*, 133–36.

24. My assertion that HA had the *First Jefferson* privately printed by the University Press has for support only the fact that he had the next two volumes of the *History* printed by that firm.

25. In his *Garrulities of an Octogenarian Editor*, op. cit., 138–39, Holt dates HA's offer of *Esther* after MHA's death. Also he says HA made the offer by letter—a letter not kept in the firm's main files, and somehow lost. Holt was mistaken on the first count, and I assume he was mistaken also on the second. I assume there was no letter, only a visit; I have given the visit the time and place that would most suit HA and MHA's convenience; and I have assumed that the use of an unsuggestive pseudonym was agreed upon immediately.

The rest of Holt's account in the *Garrulities* is credible in the main and agrees with contemporary records. He says that HA's handwriting was "recognizable as far as it could be seen." He further says: ". . . I haven't told of Adams's experiment with his second novel. He wanted to test how much the success of a book depends on pushing—how far a book can make its own publicity. He didn't want *Esther* advertised, or, I think, tho it hardly seems possible, even any copies sent to the press. . . . The result was *nil*. But who can tell if it would have been enough to pay for the advertising if any had been done. There are many respectable books that don't [repay the publisher the cost of advertising?], and *Esther* was not *Democracy*."

26. MHA to EC, 26 Jul 1883, AP.

27. A document that evidently relates to HA's owning a typewriter is the large volume of typewritten copies of *Timothy Pickering MSS*, signed "Henry Adams[.] Washington. D. C.," HAL.

A later relevant document is a letter from HA to Holt written at Pitch Pine Hill on 29 Sep 1882, Cater, 123. In the letter, HA says concerning copied notices of *Democracy* that he is enclosing to the publisher, "My machine has not been in use for years[,] which accounts for the bad printing. . . ."

To my mind, the documents leave little doubt that HA owned the typewriter used by the typist who copied the Pickering papers and that, when his typewriter was no longer needed for that purpose, he moved it to Pitch Pine Hill.

28. The photograph appears in L, II, facing 497, and is dated 13 Aug 1883.

29. Dennett, *John Hay*, 110–15.

30. The details concerning Osgood, as well as Houghton, appear in HA's reply to Morse. The trigger actuating Osgood and Houghton was undoubtedly the lively sales of the assumedly-similar *John Randolph*.

31. HA to Holt, 9 Nov [1883], L, II, 516, 517n3.

32. Hay to Robert Lincoln, 27 Jan 1884, in *Letters of John Hay*, II, 87.

33. HA to Mrs. Bancroft, [Nov? 1883].

34. In her letter to RWH, 16 Dec 1883, AP, MHA says, "Hay offered him [Anderson] 85–90—& finally $100,000 which he refused & also refused to 'name a price'—"

35. Hay to HA (telegram), 4 Dec 1883.

36. MHA to EC, 11 Jan 1884, AP—"I who have always been utterly opposed to building [meaning in Boston or Washington, but not in Beverly Farms] am the one who jumped first. I like to change my mind all of a sudden."

37. MHA to Mrs. Hay, 6 Dec [1883], Eppard, 180–81, telling her that in the new house the southwest room will be a "large library," the northwest room a "large dining room," and the southeast room a "large study," 18′ × 20′. The same and other specifics appear in MHA to RWH, 16 Dec 1883 and 30 Mar 1884, AP, and MHA to EC, 11 Jan 1884, AP. Most notably, MHA says there will be eleven foot ceilings and the library, 22′ × 27′, will take the place of a parlor.

38. MHA to Mrs. Hay, 6 Dec [1883], op. cit. The effort by MHA to set aside sufficient space for a house for King may be the strongest evidence there is that HA and MHA wished to bring themselves, the Hays, *and King* into permanent close association.

39. Hay to HA (telegram), 7 Dec 1883. Why Hay vetoed space for King is unclear.

40. Hay to HA, 7 Dec [1883].

41. Hay to Gilder, 29 Dec 1884, in *Letters of John Hay*, II, 86–87.

42. Gilder's request for the photograph and article was more or less simultaneous for the Adamses with vexations relating to the visit of Matthew Arnold to the United States and his expecting rich citizens to house him and docile audiences to pay for his lectures. Invited by Bancroft to a dinner for Arnold on 23 Dec 1883, HA attempted to escape and failed. See HA to Bancroft, [20 Dec 1883], [26 Dec 1883], L, II, 523–26.

Both HA and MHA felt the arrivals of British authors as something less than a blessing. She wrote to RWH, 6 Jan 1884, AP: "I shall have to give up reading if I see any more authors. I cannot read anything of Arnold until I forget him. I've never enjoyed Browning since knowing him. By & by Herodotus will be all that is left if this importation of foreign writers keeps on. P. T. Barnum will be sure to hire Tennyson."

Writing again to RWH on 13 Jan 1884, AP, she continued: "P. T. Barnum . . . has lately bought a snow white elephant in Siam. I fully expect that for a sum not exceeding his usual bait he will induce Lord Tennyson to come over & ride the white elephant in his hippodrome."

43. Hay to HA, 30 Dec [1883].

44. Writing to RWH on 6 Jan 1884, AP, MHA said: "I've just written [to Gilder] to decline & telling him Mr[.] Adams does not fancy the prevailing literary vivisection. The way in which Howells butters Harry James & Harry James Daudet & Daudet some one else is not pleasant. The mutual admiration game is about played out. . . ."

45. Hay to HA, 20 Dec [1884], Eppard, 282.

46. The key passage concerning Napoleon appears in the *First Jefferson* at the start of Chap. XIII, "The Spanish Court." (The full passage is quoted here in Chap. 25.) Mainly the passage says:

> . . . Napoleon Bonaparte, like Milton's Satan on his throne of state, although surrounded by a group of figures little less striking than himself, sat unapproachable on his bad eminence; or, when he moved, the dusky air felt an unusual weight. His conduct was often mysterious, and sometime so arbitrary as to seem insane; but later years have thrown on it a lurid illumination.

The chief meaning of the passage is that Napoleon *is* Satan. A lesser meaning is that Napoleon *resembles* Satan as found in Milton's *Paradise Lost*. To establish the latter meaning, HA echoes Milton's expressions in *P.L.*, I, 59–63, 225–27, 589–99, and II, 1–6.

47. The article's most striking line concerns leaders and masses and is thoroughly radical. As it appears in the version in English, *Historical Essays*, 175, the line is: "The idea that leaders were everything and masses without leaders were nothing, was a military view of society which led Napoleon into all his worst miscalculations."

48. CFA2 to Godkin, 31 Jan 1884, AP.

49. As published in the *Nation*, 21 Jan 1884, 165, under "Correspondence," CFA2's paragraph is a letter to the editor signed "A.," dated "Boston, February 8," and headed "The 'Breadwinners' and 'Democracy.'" It shows how little CFA2 could see, or permit himself to see, that *Democracy* was written by the elder of his younger brothers. He says: "I am by no means an admirer of either book; yet in both there is the same

strong, coarse, Nast-like drawing of . . . characters in social and political life. . . . The work is crude, and there are few fine touches to it. It is always provokingly near the verge of being very good, and yet distinctly never is very good. In 'Democracy,' as in the 'Breadwinners,' we feel conscious of the same keen, observant eye, working through a hand which is quite lacking in training, and which also, either naturally or from indolence, is unequal to a sustained effort. I fancy it would be safe to guess that the author had worked on a newspaper. He certainly has seen a good deal of politicians, and was never a man of business. That he was once in the army is plain. Who he is, I have not the remotest idea."

50. With his letter to HA, [3 Aug 1883], Hay enclosed an unidentified newspaper clipping which says in part: "The prevailing opinion in New York is that the Washington novel 'Democracy'—the authorship of which is the best kept secret of recent years—and 'The Bread Winners' are by one and the same hand." See Eppard, 140–41.

51. I am indebted to the ethnologist Martin Anthony Brunor for his reaction. An expert on Polynesia, Brunor had read Adams's principal writings and published letters, but not *Esther*. I chanced to visit him just when he finished reading a copy I had lent him. His first words were, "He didn't write it!" He said the leading ideas were not HA's.

52. CFA2 assumed HA was an agnostic or at least assumed his *History* was agnostic. In copy 5 of HA's privately printed *First Madison*, HAL, the elder brother wrote, opposite 426, "Isn't 'Divine Providence' a little out of place in agnostic historical composition?"

For evidence that HA was a believer, though not a church-goer or church member, see note 53.

53. HA wrote to Hay, 8 Apr 1883: "Do you mean that King will return with you? Believe it Jew—or Gentile! Not this old Heart!" Eppard helpfully explains, 126n1, "Adams is making a play on a line from Horace, 'Credat Judaeus Apella': 'Let Apella the Jew (i.e. a credulous person) believe it (I won't).'" Levenson and his fellow editors parrot Eppard's note, saying, L, II, 498n2: "An allusion to Horace, *Credat Judaeus Apella, non ego* . . . meaning "Let Apella the Jew believe it, not I.")

Hay replied to HA, 24 Jan 1884: ". . . [King] starts once more for this happy land today. Credat Judaeus Rothschildus." Eppard remarks, 218n1, "Hay has modernized the quote from Horace . . . by substituting a modern Jew, Rothschild, for Apella."

It should be noticed that in their reactions Hay, Eppard, and the editors of the *Letters* ignore HA's dissociating himself from both Jews and Christians. It might be urged that HA's remark is merely joking, but the remark itself forbids such dismissal. The implicit play on HA's name as a variant of Adam and the glaring play on the return of a King must be taken as indicating (a) that HA was both joking and in earnest and (b) that he had come to see himself jokingly as pre-Jewish/pre-Christian and seriously as post-Jewish/post-Christian.

To state the case simply, HA remained a believer while ceasing to believe much or most that Jews and Christians believed.

54. Thoron, 354.

55. The publishers of *Esther* appear to have understood the book. In the *Athenaeum*, 25 Jul 1885, 101, Richard Bentley & Sons advertised "New Works/ now to be had. . . ." In small type, the advertisement named "other

popular six-shilling novels also ready." One novel so named was "Esther; or the Agnostics. By Francis [*sic*] Compton." Whether Holt or Bentley ever sold copies bearing a title page on which the subtitle *or the Agnostics* appeared is not clear and perhaps should be doubted, but Bentley's advertisement is itself important. It not only offers the book; it *reads* it; and the reading conforms to what the novel has to say.

56. Practically all modern commentators on *Esther* have read the novel anti-chronologically and in the dark light of MHA's eventual suicide. Such readings, in my opinion, are egregiously mistaken, as well as lugubrious. *Esther* yields its meaning only to readers not misguided by irrelevant knowledge and to readers willing to realize that the book was written in a cheerful household by a happily married person for another happily married person with every intention that it be published at a convenient time in an appropriate manner.

Being an agnostic book produced in a still believing or professedly believing age, the novel is not tragic but bold. It is all the bolder because the heroine is not swayed from her irreligious opinions by the death of her father, whom she loves, or by the loss of a fiancé she loves but must turn away.

57. The Republican and Democratic conventions were both scheduled to meet in Chicago. HA's letters do not specify which Chicago convention the Adamses and MacVeaghs were to attend. I assume HA meant the Republican. I further assume that the MacVeaghs and Adamses preferred that Blaine be nominated, then beaten in November—preferred it as the surest means of wholly ruining his prospect of ever being president.

58. Kirkland, *Charles Francis Adams, Jr.*, 81–92.

59. McFeely, *Grant*, 489–94; Klein, *Life and Legend of Jay Gould*, 326–32. HA's interest in the "financial squeeze" (his phrase) centered in Gould. He wrote to Hay, 27 May 1884—"Jay Gould has had a hard time of it, and even Vanderbilt has laid down more millions than I should care to throw away. . . ."

60. Kirkland, *Charles Francis Adams, Jr.*, 91–92, makes clear that CFA2 routinely consulted Gould about the corporation's affairs after becoming its president.

61. Hay to HA, 12 May 1884.

21. DISASTER

Letters by and to HA are in HA-micro 5 or 6, unless otherwise noted.

PRINCIPAL SOURCES

(1) twenty-eight letters, HA to Hay, 27 Jul 1884–22 Nov 1885.

(2) seven letters, HA to CMG, 21 Sep 1884–8 Nov 1885.

(3) letter, HA to MacVeagh, 30 Sep 1884, L, II, 551.

(4) four letters, HA to Holt, 6 Jan–13 Nov 1885, Cater, 136–38, 157.

(5) three letters, MHA to RWH, 18 Jan–8 Mar 1885, AP.

(6) twenty-one letters, HA to MHA, 14 Mar–12 Apr 1885.

(7) letters, HA to Cunliffe, 22 Mar, 29 Nov 1885.

(8) three letters, HA to Field, 4 Jun–20 Sep 1885, L, II, 614–15, 621, 627–28.

(9) letters, HA to Rebecca Dodge, 16 Jun and [6 Dec 1885], L, II, 615–16, 640.

(10) twelve letters, HA to Dwight, 28 Jun–4 Nov 1885. The letter of 2 Jul 1885 is not in HA-micro 6 but is given in Cater, 151.

(11) HA, *History of the United States of America during the Second Administration of Thomas Jefferson/ 1805–1809*, privately printed, Camb 1885. (For details concerning copies, see note 13, below.)

ADDITIONAL SOURCES; COMMENTS

1. Mabel La Farge, *Letters to a Niece*, 7–8. Impressions that HA and MHA were happily married were formed by Adamses as well as Hoopers. See BA, *Degradation*, 6—". . . he and his wife moved to Washington, where they lived contentedly until her death. . . ." Also CFA3 to Aileen Tone, 17 Jan 1947, H (LHT provided me a copy)—". . . this picture [Cater's *Henry Adams and His Friends*] lays to rest for all time any thought that the relations between Uncle Henry and his wife were not perfect. We [his relatives] knew better. . . ."

2. The privately-printed *Second Jefferson* displayed its book and chapter titles only in the table of contents. Presumably HA intended that this format be used when the volume was published.

An earlier great American historical work which was divided into titled books each containing titled chapters was Prescott's *Conquest of Mexico*. In that work, book titles and chapter titles were given in the table of contents and again in the text—which many readers may have considered helpful. It is impossible to believe that HA did not look at Prescott's book and consider the merits of the format.

As in Prescott's work, each of the chapter titles in HA's privately printed *Second Jefferson* names several topics (set off with dashes). Thus the table of contents functions as a subject index of the volume.

3. HA had great abilities as a collector of elusive evidence. An example is a note he inserted in his copy of *John Randolph*, 1883, 21, HAL: "He [Randolph] was secretly married to Hester Mensgrewe [spelling unclear], the daughter of his boarding-house mistress. authority Joseph Bryan." In view of the example, one may imagine that HA's *Aaron Burr* contained information that was lost to posterity because he destroyed the manuscript. The main considerations, however, were not tidbits concerning Burr or his contemporaries but the near- and long-term fates of HA's *History*. HA's possibly helped the *History* by destroying a biographical weed he had planted and grown beside it.

4. Writing to EC on 25 Dec 1898, HA-micro 15, HA referred to Burr as an "overrated scoundrel." This may have been his opinion from the beginning. His having the opinion would not prevent him from thinking that Burr was an "ideal scamp," partly meaning suitable for biographical demolition. It could even encourage that idea.

5. In my view, HA's planning to write the rest of his *History* without pausing to publish the Jefferson volumes can be attributed wholly to fear of losing access to the State Department archives; that is, to fear of Blaine's becoming secretary of state in 1889—which in fact occurred when Benjamin Harrison took office as president.

6. Hay to Howells, 16 Sep 1884, in *Letters of John Hay*, II, 88–89.

7. King to Hay, 5 Nov [1884], HP.

8. L, II, 555.

9. HA's *Education* states that its protagonist, as author of the *History*

of the United States, had "but three serious readers:—Abram Hewitt, Wayne McVeagh and Hay." See *EHA* (1907), 286 (LoA), 1019. No evidence has been found that Hewitt saw any volume of the *History* as privately printed. No evidence has been found that MacVeagh read privately-printed volumes other than the *First Jefferson*, and none has been found that Hay was lent privately-printed volumes and read them. But HA did not key his statement to the privately-printed volumes.

I assume Hay did read the first three volumes as privately printed. I doubt that MacVeagh saw any privately printed volume beyond the *First Jefferson*. I assume HA listed Hewitt as a serious reader on the basis of reactions voiced by him after the *History* was published.

10. Though small, CFA2's 1884 pocket diary, AP, was not so diminutive as to forbid mention of MHA.

11. Hay to HA, 27 Apr 1885—"Her definition of Richardson's style as Neo-Agnostic assists one in comprehending his serene and tranquil wickedness. We are in his awful hands. . . ."

12. HA's rather elaborate proposals to Holt concerning the New York and London editions of *Esther* had the effect of securing the circulation of hundreds of copies in North America and hundreds more in Europe without risk of the book's becoming a subject of immediate intrusive curiosity. It can be inferred that this modest circulation was the Adamses' short-term object and that HA mostly concealed the object from Holt because it ran contrary to the publisher's natural desire to sell many copies soon.

13. The copies of the privately printed *Second Jefferson* were numbered. Copy 1 was used as the copy text during Scribner's printing of *HUS* for publication and is not extant. Copies 2–6 were in HA's Washington library when he died and were included in the Henry Adams Library, MHS, when formed. Notes by George Bancroft appear in copies 2 and 4. Notes by CFA2 appear in copy 5 on interleaved blank pages. Copy 6 was sold by MHS in 1949 to Seven Gables Bookshop. Presumably it contained no notes. Copy 3 was sold by MHS in 1949 to Parkman D. Howe. It contains unimportant notes by HA and a minor deletion.

14. Bancroft's notes reflect one reading of the volume conducted for unknown reasons in two copies. See note 13, above. The notes apparently were meant to supplement more general opinions expressed to HA verbally. In copy 2, Bancroft writes (173), "Burr was a vagabond." In answer to HA's statement that the chances of success for Burr's conspiracy were "not yet desperate," Bancroft writes (193), "Chances of success had never existed." Elsewhere in copy 2, Bancroft sharply disagrees with HA concerning James Wilkinson and Andrew Jackson. In copy 4, he objects to statements by HA as unclear, "too strong in expression," and "Very much too strongly expressed."

15. Without citing evidence, Levenson and his fellow editors state that HA "probably" asked Lodge to read the privately printed *First* and *Second Jefferson*. See L, II, 508n1. As nearly as I can learn, the statement is groundless. At the times when he wanted the volumes read, HA was remarkably out of touch with Lodge.

16. BA thought of his book as philosophy as well as history. See BA, *The Emancipation of Massachusetts*, Bost & NY 1919, Preface to New Edition, 3.

17. See Mrs. Wendell Garrett, "The Published Writings of Charles Francis Adams, II . . . ," MHS *Proceedings*, v. 72, 238–93, especially items 55, 63, 167, & 177. CFA2 had the copies of his *Episodes* printed with wide margins to assist readers in noting errors and additional sources.

18. Kirkland, *Charles Francis Adams, Jr.*, 203.

19. In his letter to MHA, 11 Apr [1885], HA says: ". . . I took in my new volume of history to Mrs[.] Bancroft . . . who was very entertaining, and is by long odds the most intelligent woman in Washington." HA and MHA certainly thought Mrs. Bancroft intelligent. HA's concluding words none the less may involve a private joke between him and MHA.

20. With regard to CFA2's annotations in copy 5 of the privately printed *Second Jefferson* and HA's responses thereto, see Chap. 22.

21. Quotation from a letter, LHT to Cater (date not given), Cater, cxiv, note 108.

22. In his letter to MHA, 17 Mar 1885, HA says: "Charles telegraphs me to come to stay with him when I come on. What are your orders in the matter?" Though he did not stay with them, HA dined with Charles and Minnie at Quincy. See CFA2, Diary, 4 Apr 1885, AP.

23. In 1956, responding to an account I had written of the events leading up to the death of MHA, Louisa Hooper Thoron sent me three pages of "Tentative Remarks." She said about RWH and psychiatric work: "I can't help doubting that he knew anything of this beyond native wisdom, sympathy with suffering & a certain open-mindedness about best current practise of the day. . . . Care of the eyes was his special interest—Mass*tts* Eye and Ear Infirmary one of his babies. . . . You are right that he was high up on the board of the Worcester Insane Asylum and was one of its most useful visitors but . . . I think his [psychiatric] practise there . . . was non-existent."

24. LHT gave me the data about the practical nurse in her "Tentative Remarks." Her source was her own memory. She was eleven when her grandfather died. She lived in the adjoining house.

25. LHT, "Chronology/Henry Adams" [c. 1934], 8. The "Chronology" is a handwritten, 29–page document written by a witness of MHA in Cambridge during RWH's last illness and in Beverly Farms during MHA's last summer of life. It is based in part on family memories, including those of Edward Hooper and Ellen Gurney. LHT gave me a photocopy on 11 Aug 1967.

LHT was a most loyal Hooper, sensitive to the stigma that attaches to any family in which one or more suicides have occurred; and she was also an indefatigable, astute researcher, honest to the last degree. Her entries in the "Chronology" are valuable records of what she was prepared to say defensively as a Hooper, but still more they summarize what she learned as a researcher. She says in ink (9), ". . . on December sixth [1885] she [MHA] died at 1607 H. Street, over-dose of sleeping medicine." Presumably at a later date, she corrects the passage and writes "poison" in pencil in the margin next to "sleeping medicine." Family defensiveness, in short, yielded to a wish to tell the truth.

The entries relating to MHA reveal that LHT was especially sensitive about three matters: the nursing arrangements that undermined her aunt's health, her aunt's subsequent insanity (the touchiest of the three), and her aunt's still-later suicide.

The principal documents concerning the nursing arrangements are two letters: HA to MHA, 31 Mar 1885, mentioning "the refusal of a trained nurse," and MHA to Anne Palmer, 26 Apr 1885, saying that RWH "did not fancy hired nurses" (both quoted in this chapter). In my opinion, the letters indicate that RWH's children hired a trained nurse but RWH rejected the arrangement. I assume that blame for the ruinous, substitute nursing arrangement that followed was shifted to RWH's children gradually, during a considerable period of years.

LHT's attribution of the new nursing arrangement to RWH's children appears in her "Chronology" under a page heading "The Storm Gathered and Broke." When she wrote this attribution, LHT did not have access to the first letter named above and may not yet have become the owner of the second. She however may have known all along that RWH rejected a trained nurse. A chance thus exists that she knowingly attempted to shield her grandfather from possible imputations that he was the author of MHA's disaster. Also see note 26.

26. In a letter she furnished Cater sometime in the mid 1940s, LHT says, "Aunt Clover stayed for that month in our spare room, she and my father, my aunt and uncle Gurney, dividing up the twenty-four hours, each with their turn of watching." See Cater, cxiv, note 108. And in 1956 in her "Tentative Remarks," op. cit., she states specifically that "E. W. G. & E. W. H. shared the night watches."

Making the latter statement, LHT represents the men as sharing the night watches equally with the women, or at least she comes very close to making that representation. Read at face value, the statement protects her father and uncle from possible imputations that they were the authors of MHA's disaster. Also see note 25, above.

27. In view of the severity of the hurt incurred by MHA, one may infer that Edward Hooper and Whitman Gurney fully intended to take an equal share in the night watches, and Ellen Gurney did also, but that, much more often than was planned, the actual night watcher was MHA.

Although nominally it contradicts this reading of the case, LHT's defense of her father and uncle—see note 26—may support it.

28. There can be no question that, of the relations who nursed RWH, MHA alone was given to strong and even extreme efforts guided by generous impulses. Her sister, brother, and brother-in-law, by comparison, were workaday Americans, not disposed to heroism.

29. A photograph of pieces of the set appears in O'Toole, *The Five of Hearts*, op. cit., 69.

30. L, II, 592.

31. Another weighty factor in HA's leaving again for Washington was an idea shared by RWH, MHA, and HA: that owners of houses under construction *had* to oversee the work. Clover had written to Eleanor Whiteside, 5 Feb [1871], Shattuck Papers, MHS, ". . . [RWH] couldn't possibly be away this spring as the house [RWH's summer house in Beverly Farms] will need constant overlooking in its finishing stages." The same imperative was in full force in 1885, with the difference that HA had the construction of two houses to oversee and, in addition, had promised Hay that he would carefully superintend the work.

32. See HA to Hay, 8 Apr 1883—"Oxygenation is mostly cure for all that is curable."

33. HA to Raphael Pumpelly, 21 May 1885, L, II, 612.

34. Eppard, 305.

35. My transcription from the original letter, made with the permission of LHT, who was then its owner. (She later gave it to MHS.)

It is conceivable that the idea of searching for documents relating to her Aunt Clover's disaster was implanted in niece Louisa's mind by a remark HA made to her in a letter: "Compared with your grandfather, Doctor Hooper, your father's end was easy." See HA to Louisa Hooper, 6 Jul 1901, L, V, 261,

36. Cater, 150n1, reports the existence, date, and content of MHA's letter to Rebecca Dodge but does not provide the text. Clearly the arrival of Rebecca and her cousin was advanced at their suggestion, and they came, stayed, and departed before 27 or 28 Jun 1885.

37. Rebecca Dodge Rae to LHT, 8 Apr [1930s?]. LHT found the letter among her papers in May 1966 and sent it to me to photocopy. She later gave the letter to H.

38. MHA's photograph of Rebecca Dodge is reproduced in Shepherd, *The Adams Chronicles*, 400. She is mis-identified as "Rebecca Lodge."

39. LHT, "Chronology/ Henry Adams," op. cit., 8—"With kindness which was to them habitual, they [HA and MHA] invited Theodore Dwight, then Librarian of the State Department, to save himself rent by spending the summer at 1607 H. Street. Dwight in return could watch the building of the new house, & report to them."

40. Notebook signed "T. F. Dwight./ Washington, Nov. 29, 1877." MHS. The list is dated "June 30, '85." I believe Dwight made the diagrams and the list in conjunction on the same day. The diagrams bear a later query by Dwight, ". . . summer of 1885?"

Blake's lesser picture—"Death of Ezechiel's Wife"—can give the impression that, among the figures around the wife on her death bed, the one prominently shown at the right is *the wife's father*. This figure may not be precisely venerable, as reported by Dwight, but assuredly is male and far advanced in age.

41. Review of all her extant papers makes clear that MHA experienced minor physical ailments and had interests and held opinions that might be thought unusual, but also makes clear that her slipping into insanity when forty-two could rightly have come to her and her husband as a surprise.

She had suffered from hay fever, periodic headaches, colds (including some bad ones), trouble with a nerve in a tooth, and trouble with a ringing ear—that is all. She loved fresh air and recoiled from overheated rooms. She knew her father thought her "delicate." Yet she considered her husband her "sensitive half." She was rugged enough to like riding at a canter. She believed that riding cured colds.

She viewed the lore of the medical profession as mostly nonsense. Her favorite restorative was sleep. She liked to be in bed by midnight. Forty seemed to her the age at which one begins the "home stretch," and she said on the basis of experience that "Sleep to the aged is better than flattery."

Her way of doing things was non-stop inventive. She believed one should "make all one can out of life and live up to one's finger ends." She hated tedium and considered the Théâtre Français in Paris "duller than

King's Chapel" in Boston. Yet she also was content in the belief that life is long. She looked forward to being seventy but hoped for "heart disease or lightning when my time comes." Disagreeing with the Episcopalians, she emphatically favored *sudden* death. She thought of death as peaceful sleep and release from suffering. She loved Arlington cemetery for containing 15,000 quiet sleepers and "no unsightly iron flummery & granite."

Her definition of mental health was not thinking of oneself. Insanity she thought of as pure suffering, unlikely to end while the victim's life continued. She was shocked that William Hunt "put an end to his wild, restless, unhappy life," yet felt that his suicide "saved him years of insanity, which his temperament pointed to." Similarly she wrote: "So poor Mrs. Parker has ended her struggling life at last—how did it happen—not in a tragic way I hope—like her sister. It will be a sad loss in many ways and yet a relief too."

She cannot be said to have believed in the distinct and separate immortality of individual souls. She was fascinated, however, by a ghostly painting of the face of a dead woman.

42. The Hays' son Adelbert died on 23 Jun 1901 at Yale, reportedly in a most unusual manner. During the very late hours of a night of frightful heat, he sought cool air by sitting on a third-story window ledge but while so sitting fell asleep and dropped helplessly to his death. For an account by his father, see John Hay to Henry White, 30 Jun 1901, in *Letters of John Hay*, III, 212–14.

In a letter to Mrs. Hay, 25 Jul 1901, written on the occasion of Adelbert's death, and, too, in explanation of his not having written sooner, HA said, L, V, 266: "My deepest regret was . . . that I could not be with you; for I remembered the awful horror of solitude, for the hours before friends could reach one, in the first instants of prostration, and I thought that perhaps my knowledge of suffering might make me more useful than another friend could be. For that, I was too far away. For writing, I knew you would be overwhelmed with letters. . . . I was afraid even of doing harm; for the one idea that was uppermost in my mind was that when I was *suddenly* struck, sixteen years ago, I never did get up again . . . [italics added]."

The passage should be read as shaped by HA's experience, yet tailored to the needs of Mrs. Hay. It may seem to reflect a single sudden shock: HA's finding MHA dead or unconscious and dying on 6 Dec 1885 in their rented house in Washington. And there seems no reason to remove his description "sudden" from that shock. But in view of the date of HA's letter and the date and reported manner of Adelbert Hay's death, the passage indicates that HA suffered a sudden shock *in June-July 1885*. That is the view adopted here: that HA suffered *two* sudden shocks. His first was finding in June-July 1885 that MHA was suddenly insane, and his second was finding in December 1885 that she had suddenly gone ahead with her intended suicide.

43. HA to Hay, 23 Aug 1886, L, III, 34—"Today, and for more than a year past, I have been and am living with not a thought but from minute to minute. . . ." The passage leaves no doubt that Clover's insanity antedated the previous August 23, and it lends strength to the thesis that it began suddenly in Virginia in the interval 29 Jun–1 Jul 1885.

44. Writing to CMG on 18 Jun 1885, HA explained, "My wife did not

care to pass her long summer months at Beverly, which was a gloomy spot to her after her father's death. So we cast about for a refuge."

45. Knowledge of MHA's symptoms rests on a sequence of plainly worded documents. HA's 29 Nov 1885 letter to Cunliffe (see note 50, below), in addition to indicating general poor health, specifies loss of appetite. Ellen Gurney's letter to Elizabeth Cabot, 31 Dec 1885 (a transcript is quoted near the end of this chapter), specifies MHA's tending towards extreme and needless apology and her conviction that she was unreal. Ellen says in part: "You can't imagine what she was this summer. She took Whitman and me to her heart as never before. She was tender and humble—and appealing—when no human help could do anything. Sorry for every reckless word or act—wholly forgotten by all save her."

LHT's "Chronology/ Henry Adams," op. cit., 8–9, says that in April 1885 the Adamses "returned to Washington, M. A. very sad, run down in health & suffering from insomnia." LHT adds that during the summer at Beverly Farms Hill, MHA's health "showed serious undermining." "She missed her father dreadfully. . . ." (In the margins, LHT names as her sources "Unpublished letters" and "Family memories.")

What has gone unnoticed is the importance of insomnia in the middle and final stages of MHA's catastrophe. Sensitivity to this element in the case may may help to explain the false account of MHA's suicide that LHT gave (and later corrected) in her "Chronology." (See note 25.) I suggest that, in saying that MHA killed herself with an "over-dose of sleeping medicine," LHT not only reached for a false explanation that could make the death seem an accident, and not only reached for a false explanation that could create a picture of easy death; she also responded to an important fact she had learned at Beverly Farms in 1885 about her aunt's disaster: MHA had one problem perhaps greater than any other, desperate and worsening inability to sleep.

46. LHT, "Chronology/ Henry Adams," op. cit., 9.

47. Gurney to Godkin, 11 Dec 1885, Godkin Papers, H—"It has been a terrible summer as you know for poor Clover[,] and one can scarcely wish her otherwise than at rest, though we had hoped that the worst was over."

48. In his Memorabilia, 1888–1893 (see note 55, below), CFA2 says he knew "only" that MHA had "not been well." Because this understatement of MHA's condition matches the sort of news that HA and the Hoopers put about in the process of not informing relatives and friends that MHA was insane, it can be inferred that HA told all his Adams relations—not just CFA2—that MHA was temporarily "not well." The inference is supported also by the letter, Ellen Gurney to Elizabeth Cabot, quoted near the end of this chapter.

49. Dwight's letters to HA are missing. HA's letters to Dwight nowhere indicate that the recipient knew MHA's true condition.

50. In his 29 Nov 1885 letter to Cunliffe, written either just before or at the moment when MHA's condition took its decisive turn for the worse, HA wrote, "My wife . . . has been, as it were, a good deal off her feed this summer, and shows no such fancy for mending as I should wish. . . ." In view of its date, the passage can be said to be HA's extremest understatement of MHA's condition so far found.

51. In his 4 Nov 1885 letter to Dwight, HA says that Richardson

"toned down the worst carvings"; but it is not known whether the cross-and-lion was toned down, nor is it known whether the modification, if there was one, resulted from a protest by HA to Richardson by letter or by means of a visit to his Brookline office.

52. A division showed itself at Saratoga between the teachers and some historians most concerned about finding, editing, and publishing documents. HA sided with the latter and had the comfort of learning that a speaker at the conference, Eugene Schuyler, made no bones about the deepness of the rift. See HA's letter to John White Field, 20 Sep 1885— "Luckily for my nervous system[,] Eugene Schuyler has so much less self-control than I, that he relieved my feelings by showing no concealment of his." ". . . wisdom liveth not among the learned."

HA did not attend the concluding evening session on Thursday, 10 Sep 1885, during which Schuyler read a paper on "Materials for American History in Foreign Archives." Schuyler said in his paper, "It is important to us as a nation that a full catalogue should be made of all such papers, and that the most important should not only be copied but printed." See *Papers of the American Historical Association*, NY & Lond 1886, I, 461.

53. MHA's last surviving letter, written to "Dearest" Rebecca Dodge, 22 Sep [1885], appears in Cater, 153–54. With about equal convincingness, it can be read to show that MHA on that date was more sane than insane or the converse. For whatever reason, MHA fails to tell Rebecca when she and HA will arrive in Washington.

54. CFA2, Diary, 14 Oct 1885, AP—"4.30 train to New York. . . . Henry and Clover on train." ". . . took midnight train to Washington."

No added mentions of HA or MHA appear in the diary before December 6.

55. In his Memorabilia, 1888–1893, AP, in a long entry dated 3 May 1891 that mixes accuracy, inaccuracy, and, in my view, malicious invention, CFA2 secretly described the "last time" he saw MHA. "It was in the cars between here and New York. They,—Henry and she,—were on their way to Washington, a few days before her death. I . . . went to where they were sitting and tried to talk with her. . . . She sat there pale and care-worn, never smiling, hardly making an effort to answer me, the very picture of physical weakness and mental depression. As she was then, she had been for a long time. Her mind dwelt on nothing but self-destruction. . . ." (For further consideration of this entry and especially its features which do not warrant belief, see Chap. 27.)

56. MHA to RWH, 11 Mar 1883, Thoron, 428—saying that her "only new acquaintance" during the week was "Dr. Weir Mitchell of Philadelphia, whom I've long wished to know. He was brought to tea, and was very bright and full of talk. . . ." Also see MHA to RWH, 22 Apr 1883, Thoron, 442—". . . a nice long chat with Dr. Mitchell after dinner. He is very full of fun, always comes in to tea now when he is in town."

That Mitchell was interested in cases somewhat resembling MHA's can be seen in his description of a case, albeit less severe: "A woman . . . undergoes a season of trial or encounters some prolonged strain. She may have undertaken the hard task of nursing a relative, and have gone through this severe duty with the addition of emotional excitement, swayed by hopes and fears, and forgetful of self and what everyone needs in the way of air and food and change when attempting this most trying task."

". . . the woman grows pale and thin, eats little, or if she eats does not profit by it. Everything wearies her,—to sew, to write, to read, to walk— and by and by the sofa or the bed is her only comfort." See S. Weir Mitchell, M. D., *Fat and Blood: An Essay on the Treatment of Certain Forms of Neurasthenia and Hysteria*, 4th ed., Phila 1885, 38.

57. Rebecca (Dodge) Rae to LHT, 8 Apr [1930s?], op. cit.

58. LHT, "Chronology/ Henry Adams," op. cit., 9, citing "Family memories."

59. Richardson to Hay, 8 Dec 1885, HP.

60. Eliza Williams Sherman to Mary Sherman Miles, 21 Dec 1885, L, II, 641n1. For details concerning EC's pregnancy, see Tehan, *Henry Adams in Love*, 85.

61. Rebecca (Dodge) Rae to LHT, 8 Apr [1930s?], op. cit.

62. Eliza Sherman to Mary Miles, 21 Dec 1885, op. cit.

63. HA wrote to EC, 3 Aug 1895, HA-micro 12: "You are, as I told you last spring, walking into nervous collapse. Most women do so as they approach middle life. My own existence went to pieces on the same rocks. . . . I suppose the physicians would order complete rest and quiet amusement. They can do no more, yet in my experience neither rest nor amusement nor absence of care nor the devotion of husband and family nor medical assistance nor friendship nor wealth, stayed perceptibly the exhaustion of nervous energy which was the only real difficulty I had to deal with. All I could do was wholly useless though I knew that my life depended on it."

To Mrs. Cameron and to readers unaccustomed to HA's conduct when speaking or writing to persons in difficulty, the passage could seem a most valuable, literal, trustworthy description of a nervous collapse undergone by MHA in 1885. Instead, as I see it, the passage is keyed to the nervous collapse HA says EC is walking into. What is more important, the passage may be evidence that, by agreement between MHA and HA in 1885, EC was *never to be told* the kind of illness MHA fell prey to in that year, still less its degree. Though a good friend, Mrs. Cameron was not so intimate a friend of the Adamses in 1885 that they would let her know or want her to guess that Clover was insane and near the end. They presented her false pictures, and HA later went on presenting her false pictures.

The friend the Adamses trusted in Washington in the late months of 1885 was Rebecca Dodge. They communicated their true problem to her mostly by combining silence with daily routines suited to Clover's unfolding catastrophe. They did not talk; they acted. Judging from the course they took, their opinion of Rebecca was extremely high.

64. Transcript of a letter and envelope, Ellen Gurney to Elizabeth (Mrs. J. Elliot) Cabot, 31 Dec [1885], FTKP (quoted near the end of this chapter). LHT permitted me to make a Contoura copy of the transcript in 1957. She at the time was withholding her aunt's letter from other inquirers. She did not tell me who made the transcript.

Among the relevant portions of the letter, the portion most relevant here is "She slept well, even[;] but we knew Henry thought her not better— on the contrary."

65. *Ibid.* The portions of the letter most relevant here are "The shock was largely for you outside . . ." and ". . . *we knew* Henry thought her not better . . . [italics added]."

66. Anderson, *Letters and Journals*, 252.

67. Ellen Gurney to Godkin, 30 Dec 1885, Godkin Papers, H. In connection with this letter, LHT told me that Ellen Gurney and Marian Adams closed all their letters with sealing wax. The bearing of the comment should be obvious. That Mrs. Gurney received via HA a last sealed note written to her by MHA, *did not show it to HA on the spot, and meant not to show it to him till a later time,* can be understood to indicate that MHA also wrote a sealed note to her brother and a sealed note to her husband—that sister, brother, and husband each received a sufficient sealed message intended solely for the receiver. In short, MHA left three sealed notes.

68. Ellen Gurney to Elizabeth Cabot, 31 Dec [1885], op. cit. A wrong idea may be imparted by the expression "little note." Ellen Gurney applies this expression to the letter Clover had written her, but in the opening sentence of the letter she is writing to Lizzie Cabot she says she is starting "a little note" when in fact she is starting a letter of approximately 800 words.

In view of Mrs. Gurney's describing a letter as a note, there is more than a possibility that MHA's last communications to her sister, brother, and husband were actually letters.

69. 1607 H Street had four principal rooms on the main floor. No evidence is available about the assigned use of the fourth room.

70. Ellen Gurney to Elizabeth Cabot, 31 Dec [1885], op. cit.

71. Rebecca (Dodge) Rae to LHT, 8 Apr [1930s?], op. cit.

72. For details concerning the telegrams, see Chap. 22.

73. Below his signature, HA writes "Sunday night." The envelope indicates hand-delivery to "Miss Rebecca Dodge/ Jefferson Place."

In 1938, Rebecca Dodge Rae gave the note and envelope to Louisa Hooper Thoron. They unfortunately became misplaced. LHT found them in 1966, retained photocopies, gave me copies for use in this book, and gave the originals to H.

22. Enduring

Letters by and to HA are in HA-micro 6, unless otherwise noted.

PRINCIPAL SOURCES

(1) eleven letters, HA to Hay, 8 Dec 1885–21 Oct 1886.

(2) four letters, HA to EC, [10 Dec 1885]-[12 Nov 1886]. (Concerning dates of HA's undated letters to EC, see note 70, below.)

(3) letters, HA to P. L. Ford, 22 Mar, 18 May 1886, L, III, 6–7, 18.

(4) HA, "Memoranda for Biography," Misc. Personal Papers/Henry Adams, NYPL (enclosed with HA to P. L. Ford, 22 Mar 1886).

(5) letter, HA to Emily Ford, 30 Mar 1886, L, III, 7.

(6) nine letters, HA to Dwight, 11 Jun–24 Nov 1886.

(7) letters, HA to CMG, 25 Apr, 12 Dec 1886.

(8) letter, HA to Cunliffe, 21 Jul 1886.

(9) HA, a record of signs of spring, 1883–1886, author's collection. (For details, see note 18, below.)

ADDITIONAL SOURCES; COMMENTS

1. Transcript of letter, Ellen Hooper to Elizabeth Cabot, 31 Dec 1885, FTKP.

2. CFA2, Diary, 6–9 Dec 1885, AP. CFA2 notes that JQA2 and George went to the cemetery on Wednesday but does not say when they reached Washington.

3. Richardson to Hay, 9 Dec 1885, HP; Hay to HA, 9 Dec 1885; King to HA, 10 Dec [1885].

4. The Rock Creek Cemetery record names "Paral' Heart" as the cause of MHA's death. The aged rector of the parish controlling the cemetery, Dr. Buck, doubtless learned that the recorded cause of death was untrue and that the true cause was suicide by poisoning. He later took a negative view of HA's installing a memorial on the burial plot. See Thoron, 457n1.

5. Photograph of the record of Oak Hill Cemetery, FTKP, and copies in my possession of a letter, John P. Gawler to G. d'Andelot Belin (Louisa Hooper Thoron's lawyer), 4 Apr 1962, recapitulating expenses billed to Edward Hooper by Joseph Gawler, funeral director, 9 & 12 Dec 1885, and a memorandum by Belin, "Information concerning Mrs. Henry Adams (Marian Adams)," summarizing the records of the cemeteries.

6. Ernest Samuels states in his *Henry Adams/ The Middle Years*, op. cit., 281: "At dinner [on Monday, 7 Dec 1885], moved by a sudden impulse, he [HA] startled the family by coming down wearing a bright red tie and tore off the mourning crepe from his arm and threw it under the table. His wife would have understood the gesture, for as a Sturgis she scorned such tokens of mourning." Samuels cites (469n32) "Mrs. Robert Homans, in an interview with the author in March 1954."

Louisa Hooper Thoron and Mrs. Homans (JQA2's daughter Abigail) were friends from youth. LHT read the statement by Samuels and could not believe its second sentence, because to her knowledge HA and MHA wore mourning continuously during the months from RWH's death to MHA's. On 25 Nov 1958, she wrote to me: "I asked her [Mrs. Homans] about her contribution to the red tie affair. Her answer was her brothers who had gone on for the funeral told her H. A. ripped the mourning band off his sleeve & threw it on the floor. She seemed not to know anything about the red tie. . . . She kept repeating H. A. *threw* the band on the floor. Her brothers told her this & *laughed* about it. (It must have been years afterwards when they told her as she was only 5 when Aunt Clover died!) I must pursue this with her. The red tie may or may not (?) be pure after-invention! George, her brother, was a professional humorist. . . . The story does not offend me . . . but I'm really believing . . . that somebody's fiction grew to be added!"

Late in 1966, I urged LHT to question Mrs. Homans again about the red tie and especially to ask whether her father, JQA2, told her about HA's alleged conduct. After a delay, on 11 Mar 1967, LHT assured me by phone that Mrs. Homans, asked anew, evinced no knowledge whatever of a red tie but did remember "something about a mourning band."

In my opinion, HA's removing and throwing down a mourning band can be fact, but the date of his action was probably Tuesday, not Monday. The red tie detail lacks substantiation. So does the suggestion that Mrs. Homans's other brother, CFA3, attended the funeral.

7. In June 1960, Aileen Tone told me MHA was "buried in a willow basket." She said she had not imparted the fact to other persons; also that she learned it sometime in 1913–1918 from CFA2's daughter Elizabeth, who earlier learned it from her father as scandalous or macabre or odd. AT had thought the information shocking; hence her silence. (At the time, I was unaware that willow and wicker are synonyms.)

AT shortly visited Louisa Hooper Thoron in Boston and gave her the same information. LHT wrote to me on 27 Aug 1960: "She told me something about Aunt Clover that I'd never heard before! that M.A. was buried not in a coffin but in a long wicker basket, and I recognized it at once as the William Sturgis tradition for burying their loved family! My mother was buried in such a basket. . . ."

On 18 Nov 1966, after jogging her memory, AT told me she "probably" learned about the basket in March 1918, when she and Elizabeth Adams together made the funeral arrangements for HA.

The letter from Gawler to Belin (note 5, above) states that Edward Hooper was billed on 9 Dec 1885 for "a black cloth casket."

8. For "final interment," see Gurney to Godkin, 11 Dec 1885, Godkin Papers, H. The interment was effected in good weather. See Ellen Gurney to Elizabeth Cabot, 31 Jan 1886, op. cit.—"She is laid on a *sunny* slope in a most peaceful churchyard . . . [italics added]."

9. Ellen Gurney to Elizabeth Cabot, op. cit.; also Gurney to Godkin, op. cit.—"Henry was a good deal shaken. . . . Now he has recovered in a measure his tone, and is setting his face steadily towards the future. . . ."

10. Louisa Hooper Thoron's written comment accompanying her gift to H of the note, HA to Rebecca Dodge, [6 Dec 1885]—". . . [the note was] kept preciously by Mrs Rae until a year or two before she died and then turned over to Louisa Thoron with the pair of Egyptian gold bracelets worn by Marian Adams from the time of her honeymoon in Egypt until her death."

11. The weight of evidence indicates that the closest friends of MHA in her last months, in order of decreasing intimacy, were Rebecca Dodge, Anne Palmer Fell (married to Nelson Fell in 1885), and Elizabeth Cameron. HA's correspondence with Anne Fell is missing.

12. No implication is intended that HA's condition at the time was less than critical. He ended his letter to Hay: "I shall come out all right from this—what shall I call it—Hell!" In a subsequent letter to Hay, 11 Jun [1886], he said, ". . . had it not been for you and yours, I should probably by this time have settled my little account with the Hotel Company Unlimited, and cleared for a new chance."

13. In 1938, Louisa Hooper Thoron obtained from Coolidge Shepley Bulfinch & Abbott, Architects, reduced photostats of drawings made by Richardson and his assistants when designing the Adams house. In 1956, LHT permitted me to make Contoura copies. During two occasions in 1956 and 1966, I studied the copies with Aileen Tone and obtained from her all the details she could furnish concerning the house and HA's use of it when she lived with him in 1912–1918.

AT was definite about HA's occupying the two top-floor rooms and about the placement of the trunk in the closet. She did not say how long HA had occupied his rooms or how long the trunk was so placed, but she said that HA's habits as user of the house seemed habits of very long standing.

A letter from HA to Holt, 8 March [1886], Cater, 158–59, may relate to HA's use of the trunk. Evidently Holt had written to HA concerning newspaper criticisms of *Esther* or a lack thereof. HA replied, in part: "When the only chapter of one's story for which one cares is closed forever, locked up, and put away, to be kept, as a sort of open secret, between oneself and eternity, one does not think much of newspapers."

One of the items placed in the trunk was MHA's green velvet Worth gown. It seems fair to assume that HA associated the gown with the green dress worn by Petrarch's Laura. One may also assume that HA's decision to preserve the gown went hand in hand with his turning again to Italian poetry, including Dante's.

MHA's varied possessions later became the property of LHT and then the property of her daughter, Faith Thoron Knapp. The green gown is among them. It leaves no doubt that MHA was small and curvaceous.

14. 1603 H Street was a slightly smaller house than 1607. By designing it to contain few rooms, each large and approached via broad stairways and wide halls, the Adamses and Richardson made 1603 pleasingly spacious.

15. HA to John Chipman Gray, 25 Jan 1886, L, III, 4. Further details appear in Samuels, *Henry Adams/ The Middle Years*, 240, 469n32. For "my children," see HA to Lucy Baxter, 15 Nov 1887, L, III, 92–93.

16. The principal record of HA's progress in the Madison volumes is his letter to Dwight, 24 Jul 1887. It indicates a long gap of time since HA put Book I of the *Second Madison* in a drawer of his desk.

Direct but very fragmentary evidence of HA's progress is a piece of paper, FTKP, bearing in HA's handwriting the words "Correspondence of our Legation at Paris in 1811–12./ Henry Adams/ 26 April. 1886."

17. L, III, 11, 20, 43n1.

18. Principal source 9. Aileen Tone found the record in her New York apartment in 1965 while cleaning out a drawer. She recognized it as likely to have biographical value and on 14 Jul 1965 made me a gift of it. She at first could not remember how she came to have it. On reflection, she told me she found it in a wallet in HA's desk just after his death—which itself occurred in spring. She said too that her inclination to keep the record was strengthened by her having accompanied HA on spring walks in the Washington woods during which he energetically searched for arbutus and other flowers.

The small ruled page, taken from a pocket diary or notebook printed for use in 1883, bore advance calendars for April 1885 and April 1886 at the top of the page. Evidently in 1883, HA crossed out "1885" and "1886" in ink at the tops of the advance calendars and wrote "1883" in the upper margin. (As things developed, the advance calendars later gained direct relevance.)

The reverse side bears fragmentary printed matter advertising medical and pharmaceutical services. The page is headed "Our Field of Success." A main heading, "KIDNEY DISEASES," is printed at the top left. To its right is a lesser heading: "BRIGHT'S DISEASE, DIABETES."

HA's entries on the ruled side bear reading in tandem with a famous passage at the start of Chap. XVIII of *The Education* about the "delicate grace and passionate depravity" of spring in Washington. The passage mentions "the dogwood and the judas-tree, the azalea and the laurel."

(The words are echoed in the line "In depraved May, dogwood and chestnut, flowering judas" in T. S. Eliot's poem "Gerontion.")

19. The early letters HA exchanged with W. C. Ford, if any, are not extant. I tend to think that Ford started the friendship between himself and HA. The idea is not supported by any particular document that I know of but is supported, in my opinion, by Ford's papers, NYPL, considered as a body.

20. For details, see L. H. Butterfield, "Worthington Chauncey Ford, Editor," *MHS Proceedings*, vols. 83–84 (1971), 46–82.

21. HA had received extraordinary letters of appreciation concerning his *NEF* and *LAG*. As examples, see Bancroft to HA, 22 Dec 1877; Tilden to HA, 22 Mar 1878; Parkman to HA, 12 Nov 1879; and Tilden to HA, 12 Jan 1883 (HA-micro 4). In the last, Tilden speaks of "the great services which you have rendered to the history of our country." "I consider your Life of Albert Gallatin as the most valuable contribution which has been made to this department of our literature. I agree with your very high estimate of Mr. Gallatin as a practical statesman."

22. Paul Ford's sending the Harrison letters can be read as added evidence of HA's rapid progress in the Madison volumes.

The date HA received the letters indicates too that the conjectural date, [1887], attached by Levenson and his fellow editors to HA's letter to J. R. Soley, L, III, 51, should be superseded by some such date as [April-May 1886?].

23. HA to Hay, 1 Oct 1885.

24. The influences tending to make the Adamses think of visiting Japan had included personal acquaintance with Jushii Kuki, the Japanese minister in Washington. When in Japan, however, HA made very minimum use of the letters of introduction furnished him by the minister.

25. King to HA, [c. 20] Feb 1886. Also CFA2, 1886 Diary, AP—[NY, Feb. 15] "met Henry at Knickerbocker"; [NY, Feb. 16] "Dined w. Henry & the Hays at Brunswick"; and [Wash, Feb. 17] "Took 3'ocl train to Wash. Henry and the Hays on the train."

Judging from CFA2's last entry, the Hays were the first persons to use the third-floor front rooms at 1603 H Street.

26. HJ to Godkin, 6 Feb [1886], *Henry James Letters*, III, 187; HJ to Elizabeth Boott, 7 Jan [1886], ibid., III, 107.

27. Data about Ellen Gurney's medical history is conspicuously absent in HA's extant papers. Kaledin's account in *The Education of Mrs. Henry Adams*, op. cit., 240, 277n62, is unhelpfully elliptical.

28. It is hard to escape the supposition that HA and MHA read and were much affected by Isabella L. Bird's *Unbeaten Tracks in Japan/ An Account of Travels in the Interior/ Including Visits to the Aborigines of Yezo and the Shrines of Nikko*, NY 1880.

29. King to Hay, Monday 30 [Nov 1885], HP—". . . I have suffered a horrid loss at the Brunswick. All my MSS.—including what little I had done on the English novel. . . . So far as I can judge they were flung to the waste paper by an unreflecting chamber maid."

30. King to HA, [c. 20] Feb 1886; Hay to HA, 19 Jan [1886].

31. King to Hay, "Brunswick as usual" [5? Jun 1886], HP—"I send you a novel I have just read, called 'Esther.' It has given me a strange, painful interest and I await with some palpitations to hear what you say of

it and who you conclude wrote it. It ought to be immediately evident who
Compton is but such things after all are harder to guess than they seem."
The letter's approximate date can be adduced from the line, "Henry and
Lafarge [*sic*] went off in high spirits. . . ."
32. Remark by Aileen Tone to myself, 24 Nov 1966, correcting the
partly erroneous description given in Cater, lxiv.
33. John La Farge, *An Artist's Letters from Japan*, NY 1897, 17.
34. The instructions are in HA-micro 6, beginning of 1886. They are
given in full in Cater, 162n.
35. CFA2, 1886 Diary, AP—[Quincy, May 31] "Henry came up at 10
o'cl [A.M.], having just got in from Washington. Old house in the evening";
[Quincy, June 3] "Henry started for Japan."
No entry explains how or when CFA2 received the *Second Jefferson*. His
only entries about reading it appear under September 5 & 6.
36. King to Hay [5? Jun 1886], op. cit.; King to Hay, 4 Jul [1886],
HP—"I think it far more compact and vivid than Dem., but one of the
most painful things imaginable."
37. Subsequent to King, Hay, and Mrs. Cameron, the first person to
whom HA disclosed his authorship of *Esther* was Louisa Hooper. Talking
with her on Christmas Day 1911 aboard the *Olympic*, HA said he wrote a
"best seller," the novel *Democracy*, and also wrote a "better" novel, *Esther*,
that purposely was not advertised.
LHT first told me of HA's disclosures in 1955. During later discussions, and in letters, she further recalled that HA on the *Olympic* told her
how he developed *Esther* and especially how he developed the novel's
heroine. Summarized, the method she said he described was one of
working *away from* data given him by first-hand experience.
On 17 Feb 1956, wanting to contradict Elizabeth Stevenson's assertions
in her *Henry Adams/ A Biography* that Esther Dudley is Marian Adams, LHT
wrote to me about HA's "drawing the heroine" of *Esther* "from two or
three people." She offered her opinion that Anne Palmer was one of the
three. Anne, she said, was "intrepid, attractive, vivacious." Anne's mother
was "a strict Episcopalian." Her father was living. LHT continued:

Both M. A. & H. A. were devoted to her. She spoke their language.
They met her first at the Schurzes' in Washington, it seems, in '78
when she must have been about 18, and ran across her in Europe in
'79–80 where she was travelling with her parents.
Not that Uncle Henry named any names that Christmas Day 1911,
but what he said was as if he wanted to tell me it is a composite
heroine—two or 3 in one, and he left me with the impression that it
was 3 rather than 2. Definitely he said he took the theme from the
building of Trinity Church & placed it in New York. He was in his
narrative vein, & I was electrified at being told. I could not look at
him because of emotion. I was on his bed in his big stateroom looking
at the ceiling, he was on the sofa between the port-holes, the sun
streaming into the cabin, books on books piled up near the sofa.

The account HA gave to his niece appears to have been valuable but
incomplete. HA failed to say that the method he used when inventing a
heroine for *Esther* was the method he used when inventing most or all of

its principal characters. He also failed to say he drew from actual persons only as a means of getting started.

I attribute the phrase "composite heroine" to LHT, not HA. The phrase can suggest that HA disassembled three persons and made a new, fictional person of selected parts. Such a procedure, however, would not produce Esther Dudley. As she appears in the novel, she is a coherent fiction, all of a piece. Manifestly HA ceased concerning himself about actual persons and instead exclusively attended to his emergent fictional person. That he did the same when creating the other characters is similarly manifest.

The ironic upshot of HA's reported disclosure is that the persons he drew from are immaterial. What *is* material is the fictive persons.

38. King to Hay, 4 Jul [1886], op. cit. King simply started by assuming that MHA was Madeleine Lee in *Democracy* and Esther Dudley in *Esther*. On that assumption, he told Hay that HA *regretted*—my emphasis—"having exposed his wife's religious experiences and[,] as it were[,] made of her a clinical subject vis a vis of religion[,] as in Democracy he had shown her in contact with politics."

That King had such notions becomes unsurprising when one considers that his tendency as a story-teller was always to talk or write autobiography, in or out of disguise. Hay had the same tendency. Neither showed aptitude for developing fictional characters.

39. Ibid. The answer by HA that King reports was one of assent followed instantly by strong, veiled dissent (presumably followed also by silence or a change of subject). That King understood the answer seems more than doubtful.

40. HA must have noticed King's newer attitudes towards MHA. In his letter to HA brought on by MHA's death, 10 Dec [1885], op. cit., King had said, "I had confidently expected that you would have passed through New York en route to lay the form of your wife near Boston and that I should meet you. . . ." He made no other reference to MHA. The avoidance could have easily suggested to HA a fully matured dislike of MHA (or her ideas), active disapproval of her suicide (reported two days earlier in the *New York Sun*), or both.

41. From the time I first knew her in 1952, Aileen Tone told me HA told her he gave St. Gaudens the complete design for the Adams Memorial. After one such occasion, I made the following note:

Nov. 18, 1966 NY

Aileen Tone told me today on the phone the story she has told me many times:—

Adams told her that at St. Gaudens' studio, finding St. Gaudens at work on a figure, and using a beautiful Italian boy as a model, he took an American Indian rug that was there in the studio, wrapped it around the boy, who had taken a pose (she said, by *chance*), and said to St. Gaudens in effect, "There you are."

I pursued the subject with AT next day. She repeated the story, only varying to say that in his account, as she recalled, HA flung the rug "over the boy's head" and said in effect, "'I've got it.'"

AT's account has a modicum of confirmation. St. Gaudens's letters to

HA, 5, 27 Nov 1888, HA-micro 7, contain references to the boy who posed for HA in 1886.

Two comments must be made about AT's revelation. She seemed fully to realize that HA made her a vehicle for disclosing some of his deepest, best-kept secrets. She seemed *not* fully to realize that HA's disclosure to her about his designing the figure at Rock Creek Cemetery was in one sense complete—he claimed *full* authorship of the idea for the figure—but in another sense was incomplete—he did not itemize to her the stipulations he must have given St. Gaudens before, during, or after his demonstration involving the model and the rug. (With regard to the stipulations, see notes 42–45, below.)

A further comment is necessary. AT seemed not fully to realize, or had forgotten, that HA, in telling her that he designed the figure, was in part reacting to accounts of the development of the figure published soon after she became a resident of his house.

The accounts had appeared in *The Reminiscences of Augustus Saint-Gaudens, Edited and Amplified by Homer Saint-Gaudens*, NY 1913. One of the accounts was given by the sculptor. In his *Reminiscences* (I, 354), the elder St. Gaudens wrote just one sentence that concerns the figure. It reads: "Following the 'Chapin' on the scaffolding was the figure in Rock Creek Cemetery which I modeled for Mr. Henry Adams."

The sentence could seem to convey very little but may convey almost too much. The sculptor says he "modeled" the figure, evidently meaning both that he made it and that he gave it its precise form. In addition, he says he modeled it "for" HA, surely meaning that HA would be the figure's owner but possibly meaning too that HA was the figure's designer—that HA gave the sculptor an exact idea for the figure that needed only to be carried artfully into execution.

Homer Saint-Gaudens was a child when the figure was commissioned and completed. Rather than allow his father's account to stand without comment, he devised an account of his own. He did so without so much as suspecting that the patron designed the figure, that the patron required that his doing so be kept secret permanently, and the sculptor consented to keep the secret.

The account Homer Saint-Gaudens devised was not mistaken merely here and there. Its last words presumably excepted, it was mistaken as a whole and in every part. He tried to bolster the account with illustrations—photographs of sketches in clay by his father that he said were sketches for the "Adams Monument." The illustrations were themselves for the most part misleading. He wrote (I, 356, 359):

At the date Mr. Adams gave Saint-Gaudens the commission he felt in sympathy with the religious attitudes of the East. Yet he did not cast his desires for the figure in any definite mold. Rather, when he first discussed the matter, he explained that Mr. La Farge understood his ideas on this subject and that, accordingly, my father would do well, in his work, not to seek in any books for inspiration, but to talk with the painter and to have about him such objects as photographs of Michelangelo's frescoes in the Sistine Chapel. As a result of this advice, in the beginning of his attempt to grasp Mr. Adams' wishes, my father first sought to embody a philosophic calm, a peaceful acceptance of death and whatever lay in the future. Therefore he turned his attention to a number of large photographs and drawings of Buddhas. Of course he himself could not model a Buddha. But from the conception of 'Nirvana' so produced, his thought broadened out in sympathy with Mr. Adams', becoming more inclusive and universal, until he conceived the present figure which he occasionally explained as both sexless and passionless, a figure for which there posed sometimes a man, sometimes a woman.

The account reveals that Homer Saint-Gaudens did not know the date when the figure was commissioned and assumed a date much later than the actual one. The actual date is documented. HA wrote that he saw Augustus St. Gaudens in New York on 4 Jun 1886, and he dated the commission "nearly five years" prior to 10 Feb 1891. See HA to Hay, 11 Jun [1886], and HA to Dwight, 10 Feb 1891, HA-micro 8.

The illustrations supplied by Homer Saint-Gaudens include a sketch in clay by his father of Socrates seated and holding a cup. (The cup presumably is filled with hemlock, and Socrates is at the point of killing himself.) The son's belief that this sketch had anything to do with the figure is perhaps the most vivid proof that he was descanting on a subject with which he had little acquaintance.

The illustrations included two other sketches in clay: a seated figure of a woman, framed by a cape or other drapery, with her arms crossed in her lap; and a seated figure, framed by drapery, with arms positioned somewhat as the arms appear in the Adams Memorial, but reversed, so that the *left* arm is raised. How these sketches may relate to the Adams Memorial is for biographers and critics of the sculptor to settle; but, as they appear in the photographs published by Homer Saint-Gaudens in 1913, the figure with crossed arms can seem irrelevant to the Adams Memorial, and the sketch of a figure with the left arm raised can seem possibly relevant. It suggests an experiment by the sculptor relating to the question *which arm* was to be raised.

How a need for such an experiment might arise is readily conjectured. One may imagine that HA suggested the *right* arm, most people being right-handed (HA among them), and that he and St. Gaudens then agreed that both arms should be tried. In that event, the sculptor made, then disregarded, a minimal sketch with the left arm raised.

42. A striking quality of the figure when seen in place is its being contrary to much sculpture of the 19th century in not suggesting the divine and suggesting only the human. It seems to me legitimate to infer that this feature was a leading element of HA's design from the beginning—that HA explicitly asked on 4 Jun 1886 that all suggestion of divinity be somehow obviated.

Then or later, Augustus St. Gaudens supplied the means. He made the figure smaller than life—at five-sixths scale. Photographs tend not to suggest the figure's well-calculated smallness, which, it can be argued, is half the secret of the figure's great success in the eyes of those who go to see it.

43. In a scrapbook, now in the Saint Gaudens Collection, Dartmouth College Library, the sculptor noted in ink, "Adams/ Buhda/ Mental Repose/ Calm/ reflect [sic]"—but stopped in mid-word. Also he faintly sketched in ink a seated human figure. (The arms in the sketch are not positioned as the arms of the Adams Memorial would be positioned.) He then returned

to the word "Calm," added "reflection" to its right and so continued writing as to complete the phrase "Calm reflection/ in contrast with/ violence or/ force of nature." (His notes appear by permission of the Dartmouth College Library.)

In my view, the sculptor's interrupted note, sketch, and renewed note were begun on 4 Jun 1886 during HA's visit and completed moments later, after HA demonstrated what he wanted with the help of the boy model and an American Indian rug. HA undoubtedly wanted a figure in repose, physical and mental. He could well have used (among others) the phrases "mental repose" and "calm reflection." Also, to reinforce his meaning, he could have spoken about statues of Buddha.

St. Gaudens later mentioned "Budha" when writing to HA about the figure. See his letters to HA, 11 Sep 1887, [25 Jan 1888]. The sculptor's reverting to the word is, in my view, evidence enough that stillness, repose, and calm, both mental and physical, were stipulated by HA at the outset as an effect that the sculptor was to try for.

44. Casual visitors to the Adams Memorial commonly mistake the figure for female and do not suspect it is both female and male. In a letter to Theodore Roosevelt, 16 Dec 1908, L, VI, 198, HA urged the president to "do St[.] Gaudens the justice to remark that his expression [in the bronze figure] was a little higher than sex can give." ". . . he wanted to exclude sex and sink it in the idea of humanity. The figure is sexless." It must be added that HA was not writing to explain the figure. That was something he could be counted upon not to do. He instead was writing to counteract Roosevelt's having declared in public that the figure was "a strange, shrouded, sitting woman." See L, VI, 198n2. In this context, HA's "sexless" means *not a woman*.

In 1913, Homer Saint-Gaudens published his own view that the figure is "sexless and passionless." (See note 41.) Objection can be made to "sexless" as used by the sculptor's son on the ground that the son's term reduces *doubled* sexuality to none at all.

In my view, the testimonies first to be borne in mind are HA's reportedly having himself proposed the idea for the figure with the help of a *boy* model and the sculptor's reportedly having made the figure while using as a model "sometimes a man, sometimes a woman" (see note 41). These reports, I suggest, combine to warrant my inferring that HA asked on 4 Jun 1886 for a figure representing both sexes.

The ultimate evidence is the figure as finished. That the figure represents both sexes may in time become widely recognized. After second looks, observant visitors may agree especially that femininity is more apparent in the face of the figure, masculinity more apparent in the figure's right forearm.

45. In 1891, CFA2 saw the figure—newly emplaced at the gravesite in Rock Creek Cemetery—and almost immediately encountered Augustus St. Gaudens on a train. CFA2 then wrote to HA and received a reply. For details concerning this interchange, see Chap. 27.

46. Both HA and St. Gaudens appear to have lacked a good idea for a foundation on which the bronze figure could rest. For White's idea, see Chap. 23.

47. It is not suggested that the wanted figure was to be in any degree a representation of HA. It was in one way the reverse. The calm that HA

wanted the figure to have and that St. Gaudens succeeded in giving it was at a far remove from the restlessness HA was suffering when he gave the sculptor the commission.

48. HA's "Murray" was first identified in Eppard, 363, 367n.

49. L, III, 94n3.

50. EC to HA, 16 Aug [1886].

51. EC to Clara Hay, 15 Jul 1886, DP; the letter is given in full in Eppard, 371.

52. Hay to HA, 18 Jul 1886; the letter is given in full in Eppard, 368–70.

53. EC to Clara Hay, 15 Jul 1885, op. cit.

54. La Farge, *Artist's Letters*, op. cit., 125. Wherever necessary when quoting La Farge, I silently change his "A——" to "Adams."

55. HA to Field, 4 Aug 1886, L, III, 26—"My life here is not very different from what it might be at the Baths of Lucca or at Thun."

56. HA's letter to Hay, 22 Aug 1886, includes a relevant passage: "Fenollosa is unwell; La Farge is hard at work; but Mrs[.] Fenollosa, Bigelow, and I, started to visit Yumoto, the Saratoga, or White Sulphur, of Japan. Yumoto lies just fourteen miles above us among the mountains, and with one of my saddle-horses I could easily go there and return on the same day. . . ." The passage, I suggest, is good evidence that HA was remembering his and MHA's rides from White Sulphur Springs to Old Sweet Springs and to or towards Mountain Lake—ending in MHA's mental breakdown.

57. The photograph of Somentaki appears in L, III, 32.

58. In a notebook he kept in Japan, HAL, HA copied eight lines of poetry in French, beginning (112): *"Beatrix Donato fut le doux nom de celle/ Dont la forme terrestre eut ces divines contours. . . ."* On an unnumbered later page, he translated Dante's *Paradiso*, xiii, 76–78, to say, in part, "Nature is always imperfect like the artist."

59. Hay to HA, 18 Jul 1886. The paper is Five of Hearts stationery, and the letter begins, "I just now found this sheet of paper in my desk and can use it in no other way than this." In view of the letter's containing Hay's account of his experiences relating to *Esther*, his use of the stationery can perhaps be viewed as his means of saying he has understood Esther Dudley to be Marian Adams. The means, if that it is, can be looked upon as undeclarative, even evasive.

60. Ibid. Hay's commendation of *Esther* is presumably sincere, but it raises questions. Was Hay familiar with Henry James's *Washington Square*? The novel had appeared in book form in 1881 and was surely a New York story. Is one to suppose that Hay remembered it but thought HA's *Esther* incomparably superior? The questions are hard to answer.

61. EC to HA, 16 Aug 1886, op. cit. For some readers, the letter may indicate that one of EC's traits was a tendency to incite amorous arousal in men without letting herself realize what she was doing or how far she was carrying the incitement.

62. In my view, no evidence concerning the relation between HA and EC is more telling than the names they used when addressing each other, whether in person or in writing. Tehan's representation of HA and EC as respectively "Adams" and "Lizzie," or "La Dona" or "Mrs. Don," as if he ever addressed her by any name except Mrs. Cameron, is, I believe, seriously misleading. See *Henry Adams in Love*, op. cit., Chaps. 8–18.

The mode of address between HA and Mrs. Cameron was familiar, easy, yet always *formal*. Aileen Tone and Louisa Hooper Thoron gave me emphatic testimony on the point, based on experiences of being present when HA and EC met.

63. With regard to the travelers' seeing the figure of Kwannon, see La Farge, *Artist's Letters*, op. cit., 228, 234.

La Farge understood Kwannon to be female (as opposed to androgynous). He speaks (234) of "the form of K'wan-on, carved by early art, leaning her cheek on long fingers."

64. La Farge, *Artist's Letters*, 265–66.

65. HA's pocket notebook kept in Japan, op. cit. His first note reads "Temples called mountains/ Why?" On the unnumbered page bearing his first drawing of Fuji, he notes, "Fuji above the clouds, from the Fujikawa. 25 Sept. 1886. Four attempts to give the slope gentle as it is." A later page bears a second set of lines and HA's note, "True slope of Fuji as compared on the spot from Fujikawa, 25 Sept. 1886."

HA's dates next to his drawings conflict with the date, 26 Sep 1886, that La Farge gave for their seeing Fuji. See *Artist's Letters*, 265ff. Perhaps HA kept his Japanese records without regard to the change imposed on him when passing the international date line; and La Farge, preferring his own way, did the opposite.

It may be relevant that Letter I of Bird's *Unbeaten Tracks in Japan* (see note 28, above) is illustrated in part with an engraving of Fuji so misdrawn as to lend the mountain a resemblance to the Matterhorn. She says in a footnote, 2n1: "This is an altogether exceptional aspect of Fujisan, under exceptional atmospheric conditions. The mountain usually looks broader and lower. . . ."

66. La Farge, *Artist's Letters*, op. cit., 25, 269.

67. In addition to HA's relevant letters, see CFA2, Diary, 20 Oct 1886, AP.

68. HA, *History of the United States . . . during the Second Administration of Thomas Jefferson . . .* , Camb 1885, HAL, copy 5.

69. CFA2, Diary, entries for 23 Oct–5 Nov 1886, AP.

70. Of the four letters from HA to EC that underlie this chapter, HA failed to date two. Levenson and his fellow editors conjecture 19 Nov 1886 to be the date of the "Friday morning" letter beginning "Your note reached me. . . ." See L, III, 46. The conjecture is incorrect. In view of CFA2's 12 & 13 Nov 1886 diary entries, the date is 12 Nov 1886.

71. CFA2, Diary, 12 & 13 Nov 1886, AP.

72. HA to LHT, 30 Apr 1901, L, V, 246—"My father lost his mind at seventy [i.e. in 1877]. . . ."

73. CFA2, Diary, 21–23 Nov 1886, AP.

74. Ibid., 28 Nov 1886.

75. The slight illness did not immediately abate. In a letter to HA, 10 Dec 1886, La Farge remarked, "Hay says you are none so well[,] which I hope is nothing but this beastly weather."

76. The most influential works relating to Charles Francis Adams as minister are CFA2, *Charles Francis Adams*, Boston & NY 1900; HA, *The Education of Henry Adams*, privately printed, Wash 1907; and EDA, *Great Britain and the American Civil War*, NY & Lond 1925. The biography by CFA2 omits HA and Moran and minimizes the efforts of Weed and Evarts.

HA's *Education* fictionally shifts Weed's mission from 1861–1862 to 1863, slightly mentions Evarts's coming to London, and makes HA and Moran the merest of secretaries. EDA's history omits Evarts and Moran, concedes no importance to Weed or HA, treats CFA as an undoubted hero, and climaxes in his note to Russell about the Laird rams. All the books help build the myth that HA wanted built. All suggest single-handedness.

23. GREAT PROGRESS

Letters by and to HA (also diary entries by HA) are in HA-micro 6, unless otherwise noted.

PRINCIPAL SOURCES

(1) letter, HA to Dudley, 15 Dec 1886, L, III, 50.

(2) two letters, HA to Cunliffe, 17 Jan 1887, 27 May 1888.

(3) letter, HA to Houghton, Mifflin & Co., 22 Jan 1887, L, III, 53.

(4) letter, HA to Hay, [28 Feb 1887], Eppard, 403; eighteen letters, HA to same, 17 Apr 1887–8? Aug 1888; letters, HA to same, ? Dec 1887 & 4 Mar 1888, HA-micro B.

(5) thirty-five dated letters and undated letters more or less possible to date, HA to EC, 10 Mar 1887–29 Jul 1888, plus a dozen undated letters and notes to EC that appear to belong to the same interval but cannot be dated.

(6) sixteen letters, HA to Dwight, 10 Apr 1887–14 Jun 1888.

(7) four letters, HA to CMG, 8 May 1887–15 Jul 1888.

(8) six letters, HA to Lucy Baxter, 5 Nov 1887–29 Apr 1888, L, III, 90–94, 98, 100–01, 110–11.

(9) seventeen entries, HA, Diary, 2 Feb–5 Aug 1888.

(10) memorandum, HA to Scribner, 12 Jul 1888, and letter, HA to Scribner, 1 Aug 1888, L, III, 125–26, 130–32.

(11) HA, *History of the United States of America during the Second Administration of Thomas Jefferson*, privately printed, Camb 1885.

ADDITIONAL SOURCES; COMMENTS

1. In his diary, 16 Sep 1888, HA says only that he brought the volumes to Quincy "from Boston." They perhaps had been kept in a locked box or trunk at 57 Mount Vernon Street.

2. In connection with his brother's work as biographer of their father, HA wrote to CFA2, 2 Feb 1896, HA-micro 12: "I have not a line of writing or a slip of paper, letter, memorandum or note relating to that time. If you have my letters, you have the only record that exists, as far as I know, of my residence in England. When you have done with them, if you do not want them, please return them to me." His sentences require several comments.

In 1896, he surely knew he had written letters from England to persons other than CFA2, but his sentences are silent about such letters.

In 1896, he had materials of the sort his first sentence says he does not possess. At the time of his death in 1918, his library contained a scattering of materials relating to his life in England in 1861–1868, notably all his engagement books.

His supposition that his letters to CFA2 were in his brother's possession was certainly true, but CFA2 seems to have left the letters unlocated and unread. Evidence in the Ford Papers, NYPL, indicates that Ford got possession of the letters in 1918–1919 by gaining the permission of Mrs. C. F. Adams, Jr., to search for and find them.

3. Godkin Papers, H. Ellen's letter is evidence that she and HA were corresponding, but all the letters they exchanged are missing.

4. JQA2 to HA, 12, 21 Jan, 26 Sep 1887; CFA2 to HA, 21 Feb 1887.

5. CFA2, Diary, 18–20 Dec 1887, AP.

6. HA to EC, 5 Mar 1900, HA-micro 16—"I've been trying to read my brother Charles's Life of our father, and it makes me sick. Now I understand why I refused so obstinately to do it myself."

Editing this letter in the 1920s or 1930s, Ford silently omitted the words "and it makes me sick," possibly out of respect for CFA2. See F, II, 271.

7. CFA2, Diary, 21, 29, 30 Jan, 6, 22, 27 Feb, 13 Mar, 3 Apr 1887, AP.

8. BA to HA, 7, 8 Mar 1887, HA-micro H. BA would continue to believe that the same laws controlled mind and matter; he would come to believe that HA shared his belief; and the latter persuasion would underlie his publishing HA's "The Rule of Phase Applied to History" and *A Letter to American Teachers of History* in 1919 in *The Degradation of the Democratic Dogma*.

The extent to which BA misinformed himself about HA in this connection will be shown in the final volume of this biography.

9. See especially BA to HA, 8, 11, 22, 25 Mar 1887, HA-micro H.

10. CFA2, Diary, 12, 13 Feb, 1, 12 Mar, 12 Apr 1887, AP.

11. Ibid., 11 Jun 1887.

12. Principal source 11, copy 5, HAL, opposite 15 & 50.

13. Ibid., opposite 227, 257, 460, & 538.

14. HA revised the paragraph that elicited from CFA2 the comments beginning "This seems to me to be stuff!" Compare ibid., 227, with *HUS* (Scribner), III, 345; (LoA), I, 840–41. But it is not clear whether he did so because of CFA2's remark, his own views, or comments by others.

15. BA to HA, 11 Mar 1887, HA-micro H. For further details relating to BA's unhappiness about his book, see Beringause, *Brooks Adams*, 90–93.

16. One of King's strong statements about well-placed American women would appear in a letter to Hay, 12 Aug [1888], HP—"Henry Adams wants to go to Fiji this autumn & with that tragic way he has of jesting, whets my appetite for the voyage with the promise that we shall drink our enemies' blood from their empty skulls. He does not seem to know that enemies are impossible to me among archaic peoples, & that if a sudden and mad thirst for blood-drinking ever should overtake me I should as a matter of choice begin with the American damme du monde, like the Doña [Mrs. Cameron], where liquor sanguine would be thin & cool enough for an August beverage."

17. HA's choosing not to ask King to read the *First* and *Second Jefferson* as privately printed was evidently inspired, not by alienation from King, but by knowledge that King was dragged down by physical ailments and overburdened with work.

18. King's letter was sent Saturday, 23 Jul 1887, and presumably reached HA on Monday. HA's letter to Dwight was dated Sunday.

19. After the Adams Papers were opened to scholars in 1955, Louisa

Hooper Thoron learned to her surprise that roughly as many letters from her Aunt Clover to her grandfather were in that collection as were in the collection she and her husband, Ward Thoron, had held from an early time. How a near-perfect set of MHA's letters to RWH had come to be divided into two sets of odd batches remained a mystery to LHT.

To my mind, the division of the batches between the Hoopers and an Adams owner, necessarily HA, can be taken to indicate (a) that Ellen Gurney and HA in the summer of 1887 made a *temporary* division of Clover's letters to Dr. Hooper for reading purposes; (b) that, following Ellen's suicide, the division became a permanent one; (c) that HA secreted his portion in the Adams Papers to insure its preservation; and (d) that by gradual steps Ellen's portion passed into the protective hands of her niece Louisa.

20. An important mystery concerns the collection and destruction of the vast bulk of MHA's letters to her brother and sister. It seems probable that the person who collected and mostly destroyed them was HA. The supposition is strengthened by the disappearance of all letters whatsoever between HA and Whitman Gurney.

A still more important mystery may be *when*—if ever—HA read MHA's letters to her sister. If HA in the summer of 1887 asked Ellen to let him read the letters she had received from Clover, Ellen may have lent him every one, including the last. If that happened, HA gained full knowledge of what was said in a letter by Clover that may have been a contributing cause of Ellen's suicide on November 19.

21. HA tried to arrange a one-day trip with EC to North Easton, Massachusetts, to see, first, the remarkable buildings Richardson designed for the Ames family, with sculpture by St. Gaudens and tiling by Tiffany, and, second, a stained glass window by La Farge at a nearby church. It is not clear whether HA and EC made the trip. See HA to Hay, 28 Jun 1887, & HA to EC, [16 Sep 1887], L, III, 66–67, 79.

22. King to HA, 10 Sep, 20 Oct 1887; King to Clara Hay, 30 Dec 1887, HP.

23. I assume that CFA2's decision to write his father's biography followed very shortly after HA's refusal in late January 1887. As it happened, CFA2 both wrote a biography of CFA for the American Statesmen Series (published in 1900) and attempted a much longer biography of CFA—his magnum opus. His work on the biographies was spasmodic and interrupted. The Dana family prevailed on him to write a biography of Richard Henry Dana (published in 1890).

CFA2 later said he completed a draft of his magnum opus in 1890, but the year may be an error. Available accounts of his effort do not agree concerning dates. See *Autobiography*, 206, and compare ibid., 200, with Kirkland, *Charles Francis Adams, Jr.*, 206.

24. Writing to me on 24 Aug 1952, Louisa Hooper Thoron said, ". . . I hope particularly to visit the Library of the Old House . . . that Library where my sister Mabel & I played as children. . . ."

25. On 19 Jan 1965, Louisa Hooper Thoron visited Abigail Adams Homans and sent me a report of their conversation. ". . . [A] tit-bit that interested me was her saying that it was Papa—my father [Edward Hooper]—who put her up to writing to Uncle Henry saying might she go on [to Washington]. . . . That was a propos to my saying what arguments I

used to have with Elsie [Elizabeth Adams, daughter of CFA2] about why didn't she ask herself to 1603 as Mabel & I did, so blatantly & freely for ourselves. Hitty [Mrs. Homans] said her father [JQA2] & her Uncle Charles w^d never even have thought of getting their daughters to write and propose themselves! It was up to H. A. to do the writing! That was always Elsie's argument. When she finally gave in and tried it, she got round to proposing herself 'for a week' but . . . went on keeping it [the visit] for some time beyond!"

26. King to HA, 10 Dec [1885].

27. King to HA, 20 Oct 1887.

28. Lodge's biographer says that HA took so strong an interest in the Lodges' son George, born in 1873, that he "practically adopted him as his own son." See John A. Garraty, *Henry Cabot Lodge*, 192.

Garraty does not say when the alleged virtual adoption began; but one may assume that HA and MHA from an early time shared an interest in the Lodges' eldest children, Constance and George; and one may further assume that HA's special interest in George began in 1887 or 1888.

29. The only modern account of Ellen's death that provides factual details is that in Friedrich, *Clover*, 332–34.

30. EC to LHT, 18 Feb 1934, FTKP.

31. "Dobbitt" became a fixture early in 1888. Writing to Martha in care of EC, HA said on February 3 that "Mr[.] Dobbitt" was pleased to accept Martha's "very kind invitation" and was sending her flowers for her table. Soon Martha's grandmother wrote about her: "She at 19 months old talks like a child three years old—repeats verses and verses of Mother Goose. She is the most graceful little thing I ever saw. . . . Mr. Henry Adams is perfectly devoted to her. He says she has all the accomplishments of a fashionable flirt. The child is devoted to him and calls him Dobbitt and often worries to go and see Dobbitt and when she goes he takes her all over the house—and gets down on all fours and plays with her—and this pleases her immensely." See Eliza Williams Sherman to Mary Miles, 19 Feb 1888, ECP.

It seems possible that HA added the Dordy before or on his fiftieth birthday, 16 Feb 1888. He was in Washington that day and departed with Dwight and Hay the day after. See HA to Lucy Baxter, 16 Feb 1888, L, III, 100–01.

When she adopted "Dor" as a name for HA, EC could appear to use a convenient abbreviation of her daughter's often-repeated Dordy. In EC's ears, however, Dor may have suggested *d'or* in French; hence a man—or heart—of gold. A more serious possibility is that EC learned HA's trick of encoding names and invented Dor as *her* form of George. If that happened, HA was called George by EC a great many times, during three decades of his life.

32. Efforts by commentators to construe HA's relations with EC in 1888–1891 as an attempted sexual involvement or as realized adultery disregard those of HA's letters which show him to be highly aware that his relations with EC *parody* adulterous approaches.

EC and HA had many protections against adultery. One was her consistent ranking of love as less important to her than social position and closeness to persons holding political office. Another was her strait-laced view of her marital duties. The most complete was HA's marriage, which survived his wife's suicide intact in the sense that he acted thereafter as both himself and his wife's representative. The outward sign of his attitude was his always wearing black in winter.

33. It is not suggested that Marian Adams and Ellen Gurney committed suicide for identical reasons—far from it. But MHA's last letter to her sister (presumably destroyed, and known in part only because quoted by Mrs. Gurney in her own letters) may have contained a statement that she—MHA—was committing suicide out of love for her husband. In that event, her agency in Ellen's suicide was possibly maximal or even decisive, although entirely unintended.

34. When in Japan in 1886, HA wrote letters to Hay that approached being a diary. After leaving Washington in 1890 for the South Seas, HA would write letters to EC (usually in instalments) which *were* his diary in a new form. He would go on writing to EC when practicable as long as he lived. For twenty-eight years by this means, he made her the witness of his life. But what is suggested here is that HA initiated EC's being his witness, not by means of letters in 1890, but *in person* much earlier, at the end of 1887 and the beginning of 1888.

That HA wanted and expected EC to take a rather passive, inactive role was clear between them and led to an extreme disparity between their letters. *His* letters unite to form a large-scale, highly interesting, powerful narrative. *Her* letters were designedly different. Describing them in a letter to Ford on March 16, 1920, FP, she said: "The letters are merely bulletins of welfare, announcement[s] of plans, trivial gossip (which he loved)—quite superficial and uninteresting. . . . I had complications in life to meet, and he understood—it was tacitly agreed that we should never go beneath the surface. So they [her letters] are damningly superficial and trivial."

35. EC to LHT, 18 Feb 1934, op. cit., FTKP.

36. The disclosure that HA invented a game in which he pretended to Martha that she was his mother requires a four-part commentary.

Martha could not know it, but the game paralleled the history of Louisa Catherine Adams, who in 1801 permitted her husband to name their first child after George Washington.

The game also reversed the conduct of Abigail Brooks Adams, who in 1838 named her third son after her deceased brother Henry Brooks and by so doing gave him a defective name he would have to alter.

By making Martha a mother and by empowering her to name her child, the game created a new George Washington, born, it would appear, in late 1886 and not able to pronounce his name correctly at the time of the game, say in February 1888.

The new George Washington in the game was assigned such an age that his conception was dated approximately at the moment of Clover's death.

37. Martha was accustomed to men of fifty. Her father and HA were contemporaries.

38. *EHA* (1907), 36; (LoA), 760—". . . he was chiefly attracted by an unfinished square marble shaft, half-a-mile below, and he walked down to inspect it before breakfast."

While *The Education* presents a mostly fictional "Henry Adams" in its later chapters, the first three chapters appear to be autobiographically factual in a high degree. The statement that Henry Adams when first in the capital was chiefly attracted by the Washington Monument speaks for itself and, in addition, requires biographers to infer the conclusions that Henry's inspecting the monument led him to form at the time and during subsequent times.

39. The conclusions offered in this and the next two paragraphs are based on study of the whole range of HA's known actions and writings in combination with intensive study of the following categories of relevant special evidence:

— evidence relating to HA's awareness of the names given to him and his siblings by their parents; also his awareness of names given to his antecedents on his father's side.
— evidence relating to HA's awareness of George Washington, Mount Vernon, and the Washington Monument.
— evidence relating to HA's awareness of George Gibbs, the historian of the administrations of Washington and John Adams.
— evidence relating to HA's awareness of his deceased uncle, George Washington Adams; also of other persons whose names involved the words George Washington or the first name George.
— evidence relating to HA's awareness of General Grant as a heralded new George Washington and as a failure in the role.
— telltale confusions-of-names fallen into, discovered, and corrected by HA when writing *The Education* (the confusions evidently arose in part because his memory was overcrowded with persons meaningful to him who bore similar and/or related names, one being George).
— BA's long introduction to *The Degradation of the Democratic Dogma*, in which he linked HA to George Washington.

40. Much of the power of HA's *New England Federalism, The Life of Albert Gallatin, John Randolph*, and *History of the United States* arises from his assuming that his extraordinary acquisition of evidence and his extraordinary ability to read the evidence makes him as good as a party to the events those works concern. An insight into HA's experience while gaining that command of evidence is offered by his reaction in 1877 to the accidental death of Frances Gallatin Stevens, daughter of Albert Gallatin. Mixing tenses in a suggestive manner, he wrote to her brother, Albert R. Gallatin, 24 Dec 1877, L, II, 331: "To me your sister was still the child whom I am watching with your father and mother here in Washington nearly eighty years ago." He went on to say he was as shocked by her death as if he had known her from birth.

41. The evocations of George Washington that appear in HA's first printed essay, "Holden Chapel," published in 1855 when he was a Harvard freshman, show that he strongly identified with George Washington, yet did not confuse himself with him.

HA's scattered references to George Washington Adams show that he identified with his uncle (and even, to his cost, participated vicariously in George's suicide), yet did not confuse himself with him.

HA's reactions for and against Grant as the country's supposed new Washington and failed new Washington can be read as having less to do with Grant than with HA's problem of being himself the new Washington, either by being a politician or by being a writer on the basis of whose writings a new American politics could be established.

HA's idea of the American Union was much like his early experience of the Washington Monument. He saw the Union as unfinished. Albeit in a preliminary and in places defective form, he forthrightly stated this idea in *The Life of Albert Gallatin*, 492: ". . . one fact stands out in strong relief on the pages of American history. Except those theories of government which are popularly represented by the names of Hamilton and Jefferson, no solution of the great problems of American politics has ever been offered to the American people. Since the day [in 1813] when foreign violence and domestic faction prostrated Mr. Gallatin and his two friends [Madison and Jefferson], no statesman has ever appeared with the strength to bend their bow,—to finish their uncompleted task." (The metaphor of the bow draws on the bow of Ulysses in Book XXI of the *Odyssey*. Notably, the hard-to-bend bow is also invoked in the last sentence of Milton's *Of Education*.)

In my opinion, had he cared to rewrite the above-quoted statement in his *Gallatin* for inclusion in his *History*, HA would have retained the metaphor of a task and the wait for a workman strong enough to perform it. But the *History* dispensed with any such statement, for the good reason that the statement is implicit in every line of the work.

It needs to be recognized that HA did not write his *History* on the assumption that knowledge was an end in itself. Neither did he write it on the assumption that a high place among the American historians was an object worth his trying to achieve. He instead wrote it on the assumption that full understanding of the Union's half-construction in the period 1775–1815 was a precondition that had to be met before full redevelopment of the Union could begin. In short, the new Washington he came to think necessary could not be a great president or general. He could only be a great learner and a great writer.

42. The narrating voice in the *History* is a voice that speaks not only as if the narrator fully understands the events described, and not only as if the narrator is one of the great Americans the narrative involves, but also as if command of the evidence gives the narrator an effective rank superior to that of Jefferson, also that of Madison, but not that of Gallatin, who emerges as the story's hero.

43. The suggestion is that HA's labor, while both scientific and artistic, was mostly programmatic. In an American spirit, it corresponded to the lines by Blake in his *Milton*:

> I will not cease from Mental Fight,
> Nor shall my Sword sleep in my hand:
> Till we have built Jerusalem,
> In Englands green & pleasant Land.

44. One of the purposes of the third volume of this biography will be to continue the story of his having two names through its dramatic last phase, his breakdown in 1912, following the sinking of the *Titanic*—on which he had expected to travel.

45. HA was himself the first to make fun of his preoccupation with George Washington. His laughter is evident in Chapter VI of *Democracy*, with its talk of persons who want to *be* George Washington.

46. I have encountered no evidence that Martha was ever told that Dordy Dobbitt was a coded form of George Washington. On the contrary, there is evidence that HA wished Martha to think he had many names. Hence his writing to her from the South Seas as Captain Gulliver.

47. Writing to Ford on March 2, 1919, FP, EC described HA as "a great man" who late in life was "unrecognized and almost unknown." In connection with HA's secret and public lives (also his poem "Buddha and Brahma," written in 1891), EC wrote to Ford on October 12, 1930, FP, ". . . he *did* lead two lives, and the veil was seldom lifted."

48. King to HA, 13 Feb [1888]. HA and King were to have started for Cuba on HA's fiftieth birthday.

49. On 7 Mar 1888 while in Cuba, HA had sent EC a letter, L, III, 102–05, that lampooned him and her as a romantic Spanish gentleman and a demanding Spanish lady. The letter made clear that both parties in their "romance" were conscious of its saving unworkability.

50. BA to HA, 5 Apr 1888, HA-micro H.

51. The hiring of Dwight was proposed by CFA2 in his letter to HA, 21 Feb 1887.

52. Although La Farge was given an appearance of being a virtual co-designer of the bronze figure, St. Gaudens' letters to HA make clear that the essential transactions were all conducted directly between HA and himself.

53. St. Gaudens to HA, 11 Sep 1887.

54. St. Gaudens to HA, 25 Jan 1888.

55. Having learned of Martha's illness at Beverly Farms, HA had written to EC on 11 Sep 1887, L, III, 77: "Tell Martha that I know all about it, and distinctly remember my sufferings at her early age. Perhaps she won't believe it, but you must assure her that I never hesitate to tell a lie." Clearly his reference was to his having had scarlet fever in childhood. His lie was his saying that his and Martha's ages when stricken with illness (respectively about twenty-seven months and fifteen months) were the same. His scarlet fever would appear prominently in the first chapter of *The Education.*

Having learned of Hay's determination to live in summer at Sunapee, New Hampshire, HA wrote to him on 3 Jun 1888, L, III, 118: ". . . I too was in Arcadia born, and know from long experience how insoluble the Arcadian problem of summer is; but if the children like it, all is well, for summer was made for children. . . ." The passage can be viewed as a near outline of the first chapter of *The Education.*

56. HA knew of an early report that EC would not return to Beverly Farms. Her plans appear to have changed repeatedly. See L, III, 113.

57. Barrett, 16.

58. EC's message perhaps had a meaning that HA would know.

59. Barrett, 19n4.

60. In 1947, I visited the Scribner office on Fifth Avenue in New York and was cordially received by an elderly Charles Scribner. He regaled me with a story about a letter in the firm's possession in which HA said a historian had to be rich as well as educated. I also was told about the letter by one of Mr. Scribner's assistants. Both tellers of the tale seemed to believe that HA had a lot of gall.

61. Barrett, 19n4.

62. HA to Thoron, 11 Aug [1888], L, III, 134.

24. IMMOLATIONS AND ADJUSTMENTS

Letters by and to HA (also diary entries by HA) are in HA-micro 6 or 7, unless otherwise noted.

PRINCIPAL SOURCES

(1) thirty-one entries, HA, Diary, 12 Aug 1888–7 Jul 1889.

(2) twenty-nine dated letters and letters more or less possible to date, HA to EC, 19 Aug 1888–1 Oct [1889]. (The letter of 16 Aug [1889] is misdated 1888 in HA-micro 6 and in L, VI, 795.)

(3) twelve letters, HA to Hay, 19 Aug 1888–14 Sep 1889.

(4) seven letters, HA to Scribner, 19 Aug [1888]–20 Sep 1889, L, III, 136, 140–41, 156–58, 161, 163, 200.

(5) two letters, HA to Martha Cameron, 9 Sep 1888, 14 July 1889, L, III, 137–38, 186–87.

(6) seven letters, HA to Cunliffe, 10 Sep 1888–14 Jul 1889.

(7) two letters, HA to CMG, 28 Oct 1888, 21 Apr 1889.

(8) ten letters, HA to Dwight, 4 Nov 1888–26 Feb 1889.

(9) letter, HA to ABA, 14 Nov 1888, L, III, 154–55.

(10) two letters, HA to Rebecca Dodge, 16 Jun, 7 Sep 1889, L, III, 181, 197.

(11) two letters, HA to Anna Lodge, 18 Jun, [3 Sep] 1889, L, III, 182–83, 195.

(12) two letters, HA to Holt, 3, 8 Aug 1889, Cater, 186–87.

ADDITIONAL SOURCES; COMMENTS

1. St. Gaudens to HA, 9, 11 Oct 1888; Stanford White to HA, 13, 28 Aug & 2 Oct 1888; also HA, Diary, 2, 16, 30 Sep 1888.

2. The *Second Madison* differed from the preceding volumes in one particular: its books were alike. Each was made up of eight chapters.

3. When written, *The Education* would (a) impose a fictional Henry Adams on its readers, (b) make the imposition so transparent that attentive readers would know that fiction was fiction, and (c) supply essential clues concerning the actual Henry Adams (e.g. the clue that he wrote the London despatches to the *New York Times*). Thus the book would both propound a fiction and offer means to its being dispelled.

How early HA hit upon this strategy is unknown. I have assumed that he started with one purpose only: propounding the fiction.

4. Because HA in January 1890 would make comments to Scribner about the length and character of the work's conclusion, last details concerning the structure of the *History* are given in Chap. 25.

5. In his letters to Scribner, HA said he considered part of the *History* an "Introduction." He described it as "eight chapters" (letters to Scribner, 26 Nov, 19 Dec 1888), said too that his "first seven or eight chapters are wholly introductory" (letter to Scribner, 19 Dec 1888), but then so published the opening of the *History* that there is general agreement that the first *six* chapters form the introduction. This juggling of "eight" and "seven or eight" where it could seem HA should have said "six" can perhaps be attributed to anxiety on his part not to tell Scribner that the introduction— Book I of the *First Jefferson*—was a settled, six-chapter unit. But another

possibility is that HA had written an eight-chapter Book I, disliked it, and was in process of eliminating two chapters.

It may be relevant that the opening chapters of the *History* underwent very considerable revision even in the galleys. See Dwight to Chas. Scribner's Sons, 16 Apr 1889, Barrett, 27—". . . correction of the press in the first volume will be found in excess of that required for the others."

6. The *History* can seem to label itself "the story of Jefferson and Madison." The pertinent lines are: "Readers might judge for themselves what share the individual possessed in creating or shaping the nation; but whether it was small or great, the nation could be understood only by studying the individual. For that reason, in *the story of Jefferson and Madison* individuals retained their old interest as types of character, if not as sources of power [italics added]." See *HUS* (Scribner), IX, 226; (LoA), II, 1335. The phrase, however, is at odds with the vast bulk of the narrative, which concerns an un-united people that becomes united.

Similarly, the *History* can seem to specify where its narrative ends. The fifth-to-last chapter, "Retirement of Madison," contains the words "Readers who have followed the history here closed. . . ." See *HUS* (Scribner), X, 135; (LoA), II, 1273. The words, however, appear well after the narrative close cited below in note 12. Also they are contradicted by the later words "present story" cited below in note 8.

7. HA is referring to the passage in Gibbon's *Memoirs* beginning: "It was on the day, or rather night, of the 27th of June 1787, between the hours of eleven and twelve, that I wrote the last lines of the last page [of *The Decline and Fall*], in a summerhouse in my garden. After laying down my pen, I took several turns in a *berceau*, or covered walk of acacias, which command a prospect of the country, the lake, and the mountains."

It bears repeating that, in *his* historical masterwork, HA was still four chapters short of writing the last lines of the last page.

8. That the narrative in the *History* is coextensive with the text is indicated in the third-to-last chapter by the words "With this phase of his influence [that of William Ellery Channing] the present story has nothing to do." See *HUS* (Scribner), IX, 182; (LoA), II, 1305.

9. The *parts* are substantive and essential, like the *books*. By comparison, the *volumes* are mere external conveniences.

10. On the basis of internal evidence offered by the first published edition, the book divisions of HA's destroyed, privately-printed *First Jefferson* have been set forth in Chap. 20. Once noticed, the divisions become very obvious.

On the same basis, the book divisions of the *Second Madison* (never privately-printed) are likewise very obvious, once seen as falling at eight-chapter intervals. (That Book V is made up of eight chapters is confirmed by the entries in HA, Diary, 9 & 16 Sep 1888.)

Possible titles for the books of the *First Jefferson* have been suggested in Chap. 20. Possible titles for the books of the *Second Madison* are suggested in Chap. 25.

11. The key passage begins: "That the recovery of colonial power was the first of all Bonaparte's objects was proved not only by its being the motive of his earliest and most secret diplomatic step, but by the additional evidence that every other decisive event in the next three years of his career was subordinated to it. Berthier hastened to Madrid and consumed

the month of September, 1800, in negotiations. . . ." See *HUS* (Scribner), I, 368; (LoA), I, 248–49.

Mention of West Indian slavery first appears in the later sentence: "To him [Leclerc], October 23, [1801,] Napoleon entrusted the command of an immense expedition already ordered to collect at Brest, to destroy the power of Toussaint Louverture and re-establish slavery in the Island of St. Domingo." See *HUS* (Scribner), I, 378; (LoA), I, 255.

12. That a narrative has ended is made clear by the sentence that concludes the ninth-to-last chapter of the *History*, "The Treaty of Ghent": "Perhaps at the moment the Americans were the chief losers; but they gained their greatest triumph in referring all their disputes [with the British] to be settled by time, the final negotiator, whose decision they could safely trust."

That the narrative has already given way to a conclusion is made clear, too, by the sentence ending the eighth-to-last chapter, "Close of Hostilities": "These combats and cruises, with the last ravages of the privateers, closed the war on the ocean as it had long ceased on land; and meanwhile the people of the United States had turned their energies to undertakings of a wholly different character."

13. In his *History*, HA makes a remark which can give an impression that in his view historians are under no obligation to *explain* events and need only *recount* them. He says: "The quarrel between law and history is old, and its source lies deep. . . . The lawyer is required to give facts the mould of a theory; the historian need only state facts in their sequence." See *HUS* (Scribner), III, 45; (LoA), I, 632.

A line in *The Education* can give a different impression: that a rigorous stating of facts in their sequence may serve an important purpose. The line reads: "He [Adams] had even published a dozen volumes of American history for no other purpose than to satisfy himself whether, by the severest process of stating, with the least possible comment, such facts as seemed sure, in such order as seemed rigorously consequent, he could fix for a familiar moment a necessary sequence of human movement." See *EHA* (1907), 334; (LoA), 1069.

In practical fact, HA's *History* affects the reader as explanatory. The fairest test is the 18–book narrative at the center of the work. Just as the events of a dramatic masterpiece, say Shakespeare's *Macbeth*, explain themselves by interrelation as they occur on the stage, so the many events that appear in HA's narrative—a long, complicated sequence—explain themselves by interrelation as they occur on the page. Much of the satisfaction of reading the narrative arises from confidence that, if the reader took the trouble to list the events that the historian recounts and study the list, the events would show themselves to have the qualities of a plot: they not only are told; they also move; and *why* they move is self-explanatory.

Not surprisingly, HA's *History* is conducted with the help of a theory of human action and a vocabulary of explanatory terms. For a discussion of the theory and the principal terms in the vocabulary, see Chalfant, *Henry Adams and History*, op. cit., Chap. 7.

14. Readers of HA's *History* have been reluctant to recognize, and perhaps even *afraid* to recognize, that it concerns the emergence of a new sort of human being, the American; that it ends by describing the "American Character"; and that it treats this "character" as heritable and even in a measure fixed—resistant to change.

This aspect of the *History* may have the appearance of being controversial. It certainly is central. What most interested Adams about human beings was their *historical* evolution. He made it his business to find out and say what that evolution produced.

15. No reading of the *History* can be satisfactory that fails to account for its most remarkable passage, the eleventh paragraph of the final chapter, ending with the lines: "In a democratic ocean science could see something ultimate. Man could go no further. The atom might move, but the general equilibrium could not change." See *HUS* (Scribner), IX, 225; (LoA), II, 1335.

16. HA's very strong statement that nothing in his diary to the autumn of 1861 "could have value to anyone" can be set aside as mere rhetorical disparagement. It is helpfully contradicted by the remainder of the sentence in which it appears.

17. It can be assumed that HA's strong statement that nothing in his diary since "since 1862" could be interesting to anyone but himself was inspired by the diary's being *too interesting*, both to him and to potential others.

18. John Quincy Adams kept a diary while a student at Harvard. When preparing JQA's diaries for publication, CFA excluded the Harvard volumes, perhaps thinking them valueless because youthful and immature.

HA reacted differently. In 1872, in his "Harvard College 1786–87," *NAR*, Jan 1872, 110–47; *Sketches*, 3–38, he published numerous extracts from his grandfather's undergraduate diaries and offered a comment on such diaries generally: ". . . students' diaries are apt to be so feeble productions that the writers, if they ever think to read them in later years, commonly put them in the fire. Yet feeble as they are, they represent the most important part of any educational system [the student], and their place can by no means be taken by mere reminiscences, no matter how entertaining or extensive the latter may be."

His 1872 reaction considered, it is a paradox that HA burned his own undergraduate diary *in toto*. And the paradox is more extreme than might appear. The experiences of the grandfather and the grandson when students at Harvard were in important ways very different. The grandfather did not emerge as the leader of his class. The grandson did.

19. One may suppose that HA's diaries more or less faithfully reflected his achievements. As it happened, his achievements during the three and a half years following his graduation from Harvard had no parallel in the previous experience of the Adamses and were in several ways unparalleled in American experience altogether. Admittedly, he was young. One notices, however, that his *New York Times* despatches were written as if he were a man in his fifties or thereabouts. He could carry off the imposture because, for his age, he was very mature. Once can thus assume that if they erred, his diary entries, at least in the period December 1860–January 1862, erred on the side of strength and importance, not triviality or unimportance.

If he saw his burning the diaries as a necessary wrong, he may soon have wished to replace what he burned with something better. It may be that, after the act, he did not merely *want* to write his *Education*; he *had* to write it; and rather than a book merely good, he had to write a book he could think actually great.

20. Conspicuously absent in HA's extant papers are letters, notes, or memoranda written to him by Weed, Bright, and comparable persons at the time of—and relating to—the *Trent* affair.

21. Because his *Education* would be most fictional in relation to him, factual data about him was precisely the sort of thing he would want not to have on record when trying to write it.

22. In his diary, 23 Dec 1888, HA says the "new page" is "that of Froude's cabinet edition," but the detailed request he made to Wilson concerning the model is not in evidence.

23. MHA to RWH, 13 Apr 1884, AP.

24. King to HA, 6 Oct [1888].

25. The journey with Cunliffe was HA's third experience of traveling in the West and riding western railroads. He would later continue his travels until he traversed the greater part of the country's western rail system.

26. Barrett, 16.

27. The shape given to the Scribner edition was a compromise between suggestions made by author and publisher. Lesser details are documented by the volumes and by the relevant letters in Barrett.

Compromise bred good feelings, and relations between author and publisher improved. King wrote to HA, 3 Aug [1889]: "From Brownell I learn how your History comes on. I wish I could hope ever [to] have one reader so thoroughly an admirer as B. is of you and your work."

28. The letters written by Scribner and his aides to HA and Dwight indicate that the publisher's aides understood the structure of the *History* and were disposed to make it visible to the reader. Their efforts were thwarted, not because of a failure of understanding or will, but because HA got ahead of them with his first demand.

29. The format also would somewhat blur for the reader the fact that the work was written in four volumes.

30. For HA's alluding to "Shakespeare's tragic invention," see *HUS* (Scribner), IV, 120; (LoA), I, 1010. For *Othello* (Iago), see *HUS* (Scribner), IV, 333; (LoA), I, 1155–56. For *Julius Caesar*, see *HUS* (Scribner), V, 122; (LoA), II, 88. For *Hamlet* (Polonius), see *HUS* (Scribner), VI, 273; (LoA), II, 481. For *Macbeth* (the witches), see *HUS* (Scribner), VI, 423–24; (LoA), II, 590.

31. It would be an error to associate HA's *History* with Shakespeare's histories. The Shakespearean element in HA's *History* is linked to the tragedies.

32. Scribner's edition, fully printed and bound, would fill almost twelve inches of shelf space. This fact alone would tend to discourage many readers.

33. HA, Diary, 10 Dec 1888. Combing the St. Gaudens papers in the Manuscript Division of the Library of Congress, Cater found a clipping from the Washington *Star*, 17 Jan 1910, "that describes an interview given by John La Farge to Gustav Kobbe." He published a passage from the clipping in *Henry Adams and His Friends*, cxviii-cxix. La Farge's words, quoted by the newspaper, have the appearance of an authoritative account of a three-person meeting late in 1886 between HA, St. Gaudens, and La Farge during which the sculptor was commissioned to create the Rock Creek figure.

I think the account is highly untrustworthy. The evidence against it begins with its dating *in 1886* HA's agreement with the sculptor not to see the figure till completed. HA's diary ties the agreement to his (and perhaps Cunliffe's) meeting with the sculptor in December 1888.

34. These lines by HA to EC, especially those of 13 Feb 1891, are freighted with meanings not related to the *History*. They express HA's undiminished love for his wife; hence the outburst concerning *Esther*. They express his attachment to EC, to whom he had disclosed his authorship of *Esther*. And they express how strongly he wished to put his second life behind him and begin a third. Hence his displacement of the *History* to 1870, a year when it remained a mere decided intention. In addition, the lines are representative of things HA would say to dissuade relatives and friends, EC included, from discussing his writings in his presence or in letters addressed to him.

The truly important dates relating to the *History* were October 1881, when HA started to draft the work, and November 1888, when he began the writing-and-revision that would give it its final form.

35. Although the work evinces no intention to sympathize with or create admiration for particular persons, it in fact shows marked sympathy for persons both capable and blameless, notably the American inventor John Fitch, the Canadian governor and soldier Isaac Brock, and the Indian revolutionary Tecumthe. In the course of the narrative, all three die tragic deaths. The American diplomat William Pinkney, a very capable but not tragic figure, is treated with comparable sympathy.

36. Adams ceased drawing upon the State Department's archive of documents, but he continued to borrow books from its library. See HA to Frederic Bancroft, [6 Mar 1890], L, III, 226.

37. Amusingly, HA informed EC (letter, 23 Feb 1889) that his companions obliged him "to learn euchre and poker, by means of which they took away all my money, leaving me no resource but to follow them as long as they would pay my expenses."

The passage stands in contrast with the passage about Washington's more typical politicians (also about a fictional young Henry Adams) that ends Chap. XIX of *The Education*: "They [the politicians] knew not how to amuse themselves. . . . Work, whiskey and cards were life. The atmosphere of political Washington was theirs,—or was supposed by the outside world to be in their control,—and this was the reason why the outside world judged that Washington was fatal even for a young man of thirty-two, who had passed through the whole variety of temptations, in every capital of Europe, for a dozen years; who never played cards, and who loathed whiskey."

The actual young Adams drank whiskey and champagne and engaged Seward in a game of whist. The occurrence of the game is attested, comically enough, by another passage in *The Education*, in Chap. XVI.

38. For details concerning HA's revisions of "Captain John Smith," see Chalfant, *Henry Adams and History*, op. cit., 1–28. In its last and subtlest form, HA's essay has never been answered.

39. HA's first mention of his *Historical Essays* postdates Wilson's sending him proofs. See HA to Scribner, 3 May 1890, L, III, 236–37.

40. Aileen Tone gave me details concerning HA's use of his desk, his ever-open study door, and the cupboard containing Martha's doll's house.

I have assumed that HA purchased the doll's house prior to 15 Mar 1889 but know of no evidence bearing on the point.

41. Wilkins, *Clarence King*, 317–22. Wilkins gives the impression that HA knew about King's secret marriage but offers no evidence to support the impression. O'Toole, *Five of Hearts*, 188, furnishes Ada's last name.

42. King was strongly sympathetic to persons he thought of as non-white and as belonging to old, ancient, or archaic cultures and races. He possibly realized that J. Q. Adams and C. F. Adams had been anti-slavery agitators, not because they liked blacks, but because they believed that the slaves, being human, were entitled to release from slavery and to possession of civil rights. And King presumably realized that HA (unlike some of the other living Adamses) *was* somewhat partial to blacks. It thus can be supposed that King would of course tell HA about his marriage and do so with the hope that HA would view the union with sympathy and understanding.

43. Edmund Morris, *The Rise of Theodore Roosevelt*, NY 1979, 66–67; Thoron, 62, 67. HA and MHA were wanted as friends by the *elder* Roosevelts. See MHA to RWH, 17 Feb 1884, AP—"Our kind friends the Theodore Roosevelts have had a tragic double death—mother & daughter on the same day. We met them in Cairo in 1872. Mr[.] and Mrs[.] Roosevelt [were] young & gay & rich & full of life. They were overwhelmingly hospitable to us in New York if we let them know we were there."

44. Lodge's belief that his friendship with HA remained intact is stated very pronouncedly in a letter to Ford, 27 Mar 1918, FP. There he says that HA's death was "a terrible loss to me, for he has been one of the most intimate friends I had for 40 years. . . ."

HA's success in maintaining an appearance of friendship with Lodge depended heavily on his manners. Constance Lodge later said about him, "He had the most delightful manners you ever beheld." She noted their "grace," "finish," "humor," and "an underlying philosophic quality." See Garraty, *Henry Cabot Lodge*, 100.

45. With the exception of one letter (16 Aug [1886]), all of EC's notes and letters to HA prior to 2 Sep 1890 are missing. Her letters to him beginning on that date show knowledge of the relation between Hay and Mrs. Lodge. I think it reasonable to assume that the relation dated from the moment when Hay and Mrs. Lodge became winter neighbors and that EC knew of the relation from the time it started.

46. The note is missing. I infer that, among other things, she said she wished HA had come with her and sailed on the ship.

47. Roosevelt would form extremely happy associations with 1603 H Street. A vivid outburst of his about his experiences in the house will appear in the third book of this biography.

48. HA's appeal to Cunliffe led to an arrangement with a copyist in London, Miss Byrne, who supplied HA papers which he considered "most valuable" and which he said completed his "series of MSS. quotations in a most satisfactory manner." See HA's letters to Cunliffe, 20 Oct, 10 Nov 1889, 4 Jan 1890.

49. Barrett, 37.

25. Noah Afloat

Letters by and to HA are in HA-micro 7, unless otherwise noted.

PRINCIPAL SOURCES

(1) approximately twenty-seven letters and notes, HA to EC, many undated. Known dates and conjecturable dates range from 5? Oct 1889–16 Aug 1890.

(2) thirteen letters, HA to Dwight, 8 Oct 1889–[Jun] 1890.

(3) fourteen letters, HA to Lucy Baxter, 10 Oct 89–22 Jun 1890, L, III, 202–52 passim.

(4) seven letters, HA to Hay, 18 Oct 1889–22 Jun 1890.

(5) five letters, HA to Cunliffe, 20 Oct 1889–16 May 1890.

(6) sixteen letters, HA to Scribner, 23 Oct 1889–7 May 1890, L, III, 205, 211, 216–38 passim.

(7) three letters, HA to CMG, 24 Nov 1889–4 Jul 1890.

(8) letter, HA to Holt, 5 Mar 1890, L, III, 225.

(9) letters, HA to Spring Rice, 27 Jul, 4 Aug 1890.

(10) HA, *History of the United States of America during the First Administration of Thomas Jefferson*, 2 vols, NY 1889.

(11) HA, *History of the United States of America during the Second Administration of Thomas Jefferson*, 2 vols, NY 1890.

ADDITIONAL SOURCES; COMMENTS

1. EC to HA, 8–11 Oct 1890, HA-micro 8.

2. On reaching Tahiti, HA wrote to EC, 6 Feb 1891, HA-micro 8, that the island's name had for him "a perfume of its own, made up of utterly inconsequent associations; essence of the South Seas mixed with imaginations of at least forty years ago; Herman Melville and Captain Cook head and heels with the French opéra and Pierre Loti." The passage can be taken to indicate that HA read Cook's *Voyages* in early youth and almost certainly indicates that he read Melville's *Typee* (1846) and *Omoo* (1847) when they were still recent books.

His copy of the English edition of *Typee*, Lond 1846, and his copy of Melville's *Mardi*, NY 1855, are in HAL.

3. His copy of Darwin's *Voyage of the Beagle*, Lond 1860, is in HAL.

4. HA to Hay, 9 Sep 1886, HA-micro 6—". . . if I want good things, I must buy Chinese [not Japanese]. In porcelain there is no comparison; in embroidery, none; in kakimonos, not much. The Chinese is always out of sight ahead, as in cloisonné, and, I think, even in bronze, though bronze is *the* Japanese metal."

5. Raphael Pumpelly, *Reminiscences*, NY 1918, 480ff, 551–53, 592–96, 700. He explains (553) that his Harvard appointment was made possible by a "Sturgis-Hooper endowment."

6. Ibid., 434–35; 698–702.

7. Ibid., 618, 624; MHA to RWH, 30 Mar 1884, AP—". . . we made him [Pumpelly] transfer himself from Wormley's to us[.] This morning I photographed him. . . ." (The photograph is reproduced in *Reminiscences*, opp. 210.) Also MHA to RWH, 6 Apr 1884, AP—"We had a nice visit from Mr[.] Pumpelly of nearly a week—he is a quiet charming guest. . . . He is coming back on the 15th . . . & will stay here again."

8. See especially MHA to RWH, 10 Feb 1884, AP—"Didn't you read & enjoy ["]Tent Life in Siberia" by George Kennan?—if not, get it—he is giving a course of lectures in Boston now at the Lowell Institute & is

staying at Young's Hotel; he is a friend of our friends Dr[.] Bessels & Theodore Dwight here. Won't you call on him & give him the run of the Athenaeum?"

9. HA to EC, [27 Sep 1888], L, III, 146.

10. HA to EC, 15, 19 May 1889. The journey HA had in mind somewhat anticipated expeditions conducted by Pumpelly in 1903 and 1904. During the 1904 expedition, several of Pumpelly's associates crossed the passes leading from Russian to Chinese Turkestan and reached Kashgar from the west. See *Reminiscences*, map opp. 698.

11. The review in the *New York Times*, 27 Oct 1889, speaks of "Mr. Henry Adams's history of the Administrations of Jefferson and Madison" and says "six" volumes are to follow the two already published. It thus might seem that Scribner furnished this information to all reviewers. But, other evidence considered, it seems better to assume that the reviewer for the *Times* obtained the data by making positive inquiry at the Scribner office.

12. This report that word of HA's projected work circulated as early as 1870 is exaggerated and irresponsible. His intended *History* remained a nearly complete secret till the spring of 1877.

13. The articles in the *Sun* bear the initials "M. W. H." I have not been able to identify the writer.

14. In the unsigned review in the *Nation*, 12 Dec 1889, 480–82, the writer began: "Mr. Adams enters at once upon the historical task set before him . . . without a word of formal preface. . . . Nor was it needful that he should make any such sign. . . . To those who are familiar with his former writings it is enough to say that prefatory hints of the most significant kind as to the author's *manière de voir* may be found in his excellent biography of Albert Gallatin, in his careful edition of Gallatin's works, in his vivid sketch of John Randolph, and in his study of 'New England Federalism.' "

This suggestion that HA's former works are a suitable, sufficient preface to the *History* misleadingly implies that lesser works can be guides to a greater. A better suggestion is that Adams's text *is* prefaced in the sense that, subtly and along the way, it contains remarks that might usually be found in a preface.

15. HA's freedom from party bias was attested by a reviewer who knew him at first hand. See Worthington Chauncey Ford's notice of HA's first and second instalments in *Political Science Quarterly*, Sep 1890, 541–44, especially the line: ". . . [Adams's] judgement is excellent; the thread of the narrative is never broken; there is no padding with digressions—no striving after effect; and he shows a complete mastery of his subject,—a mastery all the more noticeable from the absence of partisanship."

16. In the second instalment of the *History*, which of course was not yet available to the *Sun's* reviewer, HA would make an important statement concerning Jefferson's ideas: that, when president, Jefferson shifted, albeit with important exceptions, from his own ideas to those of Gallatin. "So it happened that Jefferson gave up his Virginia dogmas, and adopted Gallatin's ideas." See *HUS* (Scribner), III, 18; (LoA), I, 614. The main exceptions were that Jefferson clung to his unworkable idea of "peaceable coercion" of foreign nations and vainly tried by various means to obtain West Florida.

17. Morris, *Rise of Theodore Roosevelt*, op. cit., 412.

18. Dwight to Brownell, 6 Dec 1889, Barrett, 41.

19. In his letters to Scribner, HA all along had treated ease of handling as a leading issue. He eventually said, 30 Jan 1890, "I like light volumes. . . ."

20. By suggesting that more words be printed on a page, or by suggesting the use of thin paper, HA could have brought about the publication of the work as four reasonably light, easy-to-hold volumes.

The four-volume edition published in New York by Albert and Charles Boni in 1930 was printed on thin but perfectly serviceable stock. Each volume weighs roughly the same—a pound and a half—as each of Scribner's nine. Its four volumes together are less thick than Vols. I-V of the Scribner edition and are thinner than Vols. I-IV of Bancroft's *History of the United States* in the Centenary Edition, Bost 1879.

21. In his letter to Scribner, 12 Jan 1890, HA proposed to end Vol. VIII with the chapter on the battle of New Orleans and said the arrangement would make Vol. IX a small one, containing the "mere conclusion and winding up of the story." By this rather cavalier accounting, the conclusion of the work fills *ten* chapters. It is manifest, however, that the tightly-knit narrative in the *History* is ended in the chapters "The Meeting at Ghent" and "The Treaty of Ghent." They *follow* the chapter titled "The Battle of New Orleans." Thus, HA's remark notwithstanding, the *History* has an *eight*-chapter conclusion. Four of the eight chapters can be described as an indispensable postscript. HA called the remaining four an epilogue. See note 22.

22. In his letter of 12 Jan 1890, HA told Scribner there would be "four chapters in the nature of an epilogue." Without saying so, he thus raised the possibility that the opening six chapters of the *History* can best be described as a "prologue."

23. The Scribner edition of the *History* gives a wrong impression of HA's abilities as a writer of beginnings and endings. Volumes II, IV, VI, and IX begin with mere chapter beginnings. Volumes I, III, V, & VIII end with mere chapter endings. The resulting general effect is one of apparent tedium. The text is made to seem unresounding.

In fact, HA knew very well how to write appropriate beginnings and endings for parts, books, and chapters—hence also for his original volumes. He wrote such beginnings and endings for each part. He wrote them for every book. And he retained them while arranging that the work be so published that the presence of the parts and books not be indicated.

The book divisions in the *Second Jefferson* and *First Madison* are displayed in surviving copies of the volumes as privately printed. The book divisions in his *First Jefferson* and *Second Madison* have to be searched for in the Scribner edition. They are readily found with the help of HA's appropriately-written beginnings and endings.

Once its part and book divisions are known and the text is read as structured, the *History* has resoundingness aplenty and its literary superiorities become very evident.

24. In his *Henry Adams/ The Middle Years*, op. cit., 340–41, Ernest Samuels says that the structuring of historical narratives in volumes, books, and chapters had become old-fashioned in England and the United States by the time HA published his *History*. He says too that Scribner may have

originated the idea of "dropping the too pat division of the original draft into four sections of five books apiece." And he says that HA's "neat plan of five 'books' for each administration . . . imposed a coherence on events that was frequently arbitrary." But clearly the dropping of the books was originated by HA in his initial communication to Scribner. Also, if the structure of the *History* in books was too pat or neat and imposed a coherence that was frequently arbitrary, Samuels adduces no evidence of its being so, or doing so.

The essential point is that *the books were not dropped.* Instead their presence in the work was simply kept unstated (their titles and numbers were expunged). Also the work was so reordered as to make their presence more invisible than visible.

Once the continued presence of the books is recognized, the *History* becomes accommodating. It offers the reader a long narrative in comprehensible small units, each devoted to a distinct subject or cluster of subjects, and each effecting a clear advance of the action.

25. HA's *History* is appreciably more readable when its structure is indicated in one's copy. Persons interested in its twenty books can locate their beginnings with the help of the table on page 872.

26. Louisa Hooper Thoron told me in 1955 that HA "was named 'Uncle Henry' by Constance Lodge, and Bay [her brother George], because Bay and Constance were nephew and niece of Mrs. Brooks Adams." Somewhat differently, I have assumed that Constance alone introduced the name, late in 1889, when HA's live-in guest.

27. HA's nephews and nieces, actual and additional, sometimes attempted to describe him. An instance is a comment in a memorandum, *re Henry Adams/ Mens Sana in Corpore Sano*, written by Louisa Hooper Thoron in 1934 for Ralph Adams Cram, FTKP: "Adams-y with a big difference! A richer vintage. A lighter handed social manner."

Mrs. Thoron offered details. "In all the times I have been with H.A.[,] . . . I have never heard him or seen him wound anybody of any age or station in life, nor have I heard him make a sneering remark. His irony, often gentle, was as original as he was himself! It had many facets. It could be merry and witty; it could be fanciful; it could be shrewdly penetrating; it could be a polite game enjoyed by the players as politeness; on very, very rare occasion[s] there could be one flash of anger! Whatever form the conversation took[,] there was a mute invitation to see over, under & around the mulberry bush, to build up interests & tastes, to explore the Cosmos, come down again & laugh with human nature, see through the knocks & go on."

28. HA to CMG, 5 Nov 1872, HA-micro 3—"a modern Noah."

29. According to Louisa Hooper Thoron, *Chronology/ Henry Adams*, op. cit., 24, the Adamses' dog Boojum died not long after MHA, presumably early in 1886. Thereafter HA owned two dogs and two horses. The fact may itself have put him in mind of Noah, but he was inclined in any case to think of himself as Noah because extremely sympathetic to animals, whether real or imaginary.

30. In a letter to William D. Shipman, 11 Feb 1890, L, III, 222, HA said apropos of his *History* that a book "once given to the public ceases to belong to the writer." There is no reason to suppose that he was not in earnest, or that losing the *History* to its readers was for him an inconsiderable event.

The Books	SCRIBNER*		LIBRARY OF AMERICA†	
	Volume	Page	Volume	Page
First Jefferson				
(suggested titles)				
I 1800: the Americans Not United	1	1	1	5
II The Jeffersonian Revolution	1	185	1	126
III Napoleon and Toussaint Louverture: the Sale of Louisiana	1	334	1	227
IV Centralization	2	74	2	352
V Quarrels with Spain and England	2	245	2	467
Second Jefferson				
(Adams's titles)				
I The Florida Negotiation and the Carrying Trade	3	1	1	603
II Burr's Conspiracy	3	197	1	739
III The Berlin Decree: the Affair of the "Chesapeake:" the Orders in Council. 1806–1807	3	370	1	858
IV The Embargo	4	105	2	1000
V Repeal of the Embargo	4	290	2	1127
First Madison				
(Adams's titles)				
I Erskine's Arrangements	5	1	1	7
II Contract with France	5	176	1	125
III Approach of War	5	358	1	249
IV Declaration of War	6	113	2	374
V Campaign of 1812	6	289	2	492
Second Madison				
(suggested titles)				
I The Campaign of 1813 against Canada	7	1	1	621
II The Campaign in the Southwest: Russian Mediation	7	206	1	764
III The Campaign of 1814	8	1	2	907
IV Last Battles: the Achievement of Peace	8	239	2	1076
V The Nation Secured and United	9	54	3	1220

*The Scribner volume and page numbers apply also to the Albert and Charles Boni edition, except that their volumes are called "books."
†*The Library of America* edition recasts the work in two parts, a Jefferson part and a Madison, in two bindings. Together the two parts contain nine "volumes."

31. For Stoddard, see L, III, 230, and the letter, HA to Stoddard, 29 Jul 1890, L, III, 257. For Rockhill, see three letters, HA to Rockhill, 11 Mar, [29 May], 10 Jul 1890 (the first two appear in L, III, 228, 241). HA had known Rockhill earlier. See MHA to RWH, 17 Feb 1884, AP, listing "Mr[.] & Mrs[.] Rockhill" among the guests expected for dinner.

32. EC to HA, 13 Sep 1890, HA-micro 8—"Martha is so brown and well and happy. We are both growing horribly fat, but she does not mind, and I do. But I can ride it off later as I did last year,—only alone this time."

33. LHT repeatedly told me the amusing story of her reading the *History* in HA's house, but she never dated the episode. I remember her once saying the volume HA found on her bed was Vol. IV. This chimes with the date I have adopted. Knowing her character and the strength of her attachment to HA, I would in any case date the episode in April 1890. She was sixteen, and copies of four Scribner volumes were in HA's study, to be had for the taking.

34. With respect to structure and sales, HA's *History* stands in contrast with Prescott's *Conquest of Mexico*. Prescott's volumes were structured in numbered and titled books, each made up of numbered and titled chapters. 4,000 sets were sold in four months. See *The Literary Memoranda of William Hickling Prescott*, Norman OK, II, 118.

HA wrote his *History* in a nearly identical form but wished *not* to sell in comparable amounts. Deleting all book numbers and book titles evidently helped him secure his object.

35. A New York magazine, reviewing the second instalment of the *History*, pointed to a particular page and said it could "compel rereading and yield keen enjoyment to lovers of the grand manner in literature." It added, ". . . such pages in the history are numerous." See *The Critic*, 5 Apr 1890, 164.

On the recommended page, HA describes the Yankee privateers of the War of 1812. See *HUS* (Scribner), IV, 75; (LoA), I, 979.

When reviewing the third instalment, the same magazine less encouragingly said that the *History* had the aspect of a "library." See *The Critic*, 8 Nov 1890, 229.

36. In his notes on the texts in the Library of America edition, Earl Harbert incompletely reports the number of copies of the *History* that were printed in the early years and gives no clear idea of the number sold. See *HUS* (LoA), I, 1303–04; II, 1429, 1431.

37. I am indebted to William Jordy for permission to copy and use notes he made when permitted to see the Scribner files. According to Jordy's notes, Scribner by May 1898 printed 2500 copies of Vols. I & II. In November 1901, 44 copies remained unsold. The print runs and sales for Vols. III-VI were somewhat smaller. Scribner printed 2300 copies of Vols. VII-IX in December 1890. In March 1902, 106 copies remained unsold. Thus not more than 2194 complete sets could be assembled from the volumes that were sold by March 1902.

I have seen no figures beyond that date, but sales continued in sufficient amounts to warrant Scribner's reissuing the work in 1921 and 1931. Also, by arrangement with Scribner, Boni in New York reissued the work in 1930.

It should be noticed that sales of HA's *History* were far smaller than

those of his *Randolph*. According to Houghton Mifflin's reports to HA—
see AP, reel 597—more than 19,388 copies of the *Randolph* were sold
between 1882 and 31 Jul 1911.

It is difficult to escape the conclusion that sales of the *History* would
have been much larger if HA had pursued in the period 1888–1891 an
advertising and publishing strategy comparable to the one he had in mind
in 1881 when he wrote *John Randolph* and *Aaron Burr* as "outriders" for
the great work that was to follow.

38. HA's *fullest* description of Napoleon's character is the first. See
HUS (Scribner), I, 334–35; (LoA), I, 227. His *tersest* description of Napoleon's conduct is the repeated word "violence." He also speaks of Napoleon's "artillery politics" and "revolution without ideas." See *HUS* (Scribner), II, 310; (LoA), I, 511. In a later part of the narrative, he ascribes to
Napoleon a "mixture of feline qualities,—energy, astuteness, secrecy, and
rapidity,—combined with ignorance of other natures than his own." "Politics were to him a [military] campaign, and if his opponents had not the
sense to divine his movements and motives, the disgrace and disaster were
none of his." See *HUS* (Scribner), V, 257, 259; (LoA), II, 182–83. The
accumulated expressions are all consistent with Napoleon's being a mere
human being but are consistent also with his being Satan and in many
respects a Miltonic Satan.

39. The reviewer for the *Times* read HA's volumes closely enough to
be able to say, "Yellow fever and the courage of the negro laborers in the
end vanquished the French arms." But the word "laborers" does not make
clear, still less acknowledge, that the blacks were free (they had gained
their freedom during the French Revolution); and the review nowhere
discloses that the blacks resisted courageously because their re-enslavement was intended and they knew it.

40. While telling the story of Napoleon's sale of Louisiana to the
United States, HA remarks that the Americans—the beneficiaries of the
sale—wanted *not* to know that blacks in the West Indies were the ultimate
authors of the windfall. ". . . the prejudice of race alone blinded the
American people to the debt they owed to the desperate courage of five
hundred thousand Haytian negroes who would not be enslaved." See *HUS*
(Scribner), II, 21; (LoA), I, 316.

There is no possibility that the reviewer for the *Times* did not see what
HA said about re-enslavement. The text is too plain-spoken to be mis-
seen. To use HA's words, there however is every possibility that the reviewer
was guided decisively by "prejudice of race."

41. Evidence abounds that the American reading public at the time
liked history when presented as a light pleasure and varicolored diversion.
Some reviewers responded to comic aspects of Adams's *History* at the cost
of ignoring other aspects. *Harper's Magazine* (May 1890), 968, in a brief
notice of the second instalment, dwelt on "the famous conspiracy of Aaron
Burr." "The clear light which the historian throws upon this plot to
dismember the Union gives an oft-told tale the charm of novelty, and must
set it before most readers for the first time, we fancy, with all its amazing
suggestions of opéra bouffe."

This reaction fails to reflect the balance in the *History* between the
comic and un-comic. In a serious vein, HA calls Burr "the Mephistopheles
of politics." See *HUS* (Scribner), II, 171; (LoA), I, 416. Still more seriously,

he discloses attempts by New Englanders, most notably Timothy Pickering, to dismember the Union.

Treasons and betrayals are prevalent in the *History*. Chronologically, they first appear with Bonaparte's seizure of France in 1799.

42. *HUS* (Scribner), I, 334; (LoA) I, 227. The corresponding lines in *Paradise Lost* are the first ten lines of Book II.

43. *HUS* (Scribner), I, 336; (LoA) I, 228—"a freak of nature such as the world had seen too rarely to comprehend." Also see *HUS* (Scribner), II, 13; (LoA), I, 311—". . . Bonaparte was not a man like other men, and his action could never be calculated in advance."

44. *HUS* (Scribner), IV, 124–25; (LoA) I, 1013. Also see Matthew 4: 8–10; Luke 4: 5–8; and Milton, *Paradise Regained*, III, 251ff.

45. For the New Englanders' reacting to Napoleon as anti-Christ and John Randolph's likening bargains with Napoleon to bargains with the devil, see *HUS* (Scribner), V, 344–45; (LoA), 238–39. (The chapter — "Contract with France"—concludes Book II.) For Napoleon's schemes of world dominion, see *HUS* (Scribner), IV, 302–04, 315–16; (LoA) I, 1135–36, 1144. (The chapter—"The Dos de Maio"—begins Book V.)

46. Napoleon's attempted re-enslavement of West Indian blacks was a test of American readers and reviewers they evidently were likely to fail. Five examples are especially pertinent.

A detailed response to the first published instalment of HA's *History* is the anonymous review in the *Nation*, 12 Dec 1889, 480–83. The reviewer fills two columns with comments relating to Napoleon's unsuccess in St. Domingo without once mentioning attempted re-enslavement.

The earliest edition of HA's *History* printed with an introduction by another writer is the Boni edition, NY 1930. In his 12–page "Introduction," Henry Steele Commager finds space to mention the Louisiana Purchase but none to mention Napoleon or attempted re-enslavement.

The earliest abridgment of HA's *History* is HA, *The Formative Years*, condensed and edited by Herbert Agar, Bost 1947. In his "Introduction," Agar says: "Napoleon took Louisiana from Spain in order to re-create the French Empire of North America. His campaign was planned, his armies ready, but he could do nothing unless he held the strategic island of St. Domingo. The Negroes of that island wasted two French armies, and there seemed no reason why they might not waste a third. So Napoleon turned eastward . . . and tossed Lousiana to America for a few million dollars." Agar immediately continues: "Somehow, in the Adams book, these narrow escapes do not seem like accidents; they seem part of a plan which is related to the meaning of history." But Agar avoids saying *why* the blacks on St. Domingo wasted two French armies, and he says nothing about attempted re-enslavement.

A comparable publication is HA, *History of the United States . . .* , abridged and with an introduction by George Dangerfield and Otey M. Scruggs, Englewood Cliffs NJ, 1963. In their "Introduction," Dangerfield and Scruggs remark that the Louisiana Treaty "imparted a vigorous impulse" to the development of American nationalism, but they make no mention of Napoleon in connection with the West Indies and they say nothing about attempted re-enslavement.

A last case is HA, *History of the United States . . .* abridged and edited by Ernest Samuels, Chicago & Lond, 1967. In his 13–page "Introduction,"

Samuels is silent about Napoleon's West Indian enterprise and silent about attempted re-enslavement.

The five examples would have small interest if the matter by-passed was a detail. But the attempt to re-enslave the blacks on St. Domingo occupies a place in Adams's *History* comparable to the murder of Duncan in *Macbeth*. It is a pivotal atrocity. Readers who keep clear of it lose the ability to follow the general course of the action.

47. When he wrote this letter to Holt mentioning $100,000, HA had just read the proofs of "The New York Gold Conspiracy," as printed for inclusion in his *Historical Essays*. The sum accordingly is a joke intelligible only to its teller. HA equates himself with Julia Grant, except that he *pays* $100,000, commits the felony of telling the truth about the U. S. A., and escapes with a proportionate fund of amusement.

The letter is valuable evidence. Fully understood, it links a sum, $100,000, not to *Democracy*, but to "The New York Gold Conspiracy."

48. Hay to HA, 30 Jul, 6 Aug 1890.

49. HA's striking use of the word "illusion" might conceivably be thought a clue to the date of the undated and unexplained pair of sonnets, presumably written by HA, titled "Illusion. I." and "Illusion. II." See end of HA-micro 7. Supposing HA to be the author, and judging from what they say, the sonnets appear to have been written, not in 1890, but much earlier, while MHA was alive.

50. One may conjecture that, when he arranged to return Gaskell's letters, HA also arranged to return Cunliffe's, but extant letters to Cunliffe do not mention the subject.

51. EC copied an untitled sonnet and a sonnet titled "Estrella." (See the materials addressed by Hay to EC, ECP.) At the bottom of her copy of "Estrella," EC wrote: "Washington. June 1890. J. H." She added the same information to her copy of the untitled sonnet.

The sonnets were later published in *Complete Poems of John Hay*, op. cit. There the untitled sonnet is headed "Night in Venice." Both sonnets involve night sky and stars. "Night in Venice" also involves the light of a "young moon . . . on dome, and tower, and palace wall."

Similarly HA's sonnet, "The Capitol by Moonlight," involves night sky, the planet Mars, the Capitol's "dome" seen in moonlight, and an "obelisk" (the Washington Monument). It clearly is related to Hay's "Night in Venice" and must be the sonnet HA refers to in his note.

HA's note is dated only "Wednesday." The probable date of both the note and HA's sonnet is late June or early July 1890.

52. For La Farge's letter to HA concerning the use of Awoki's services, see James L. Yarnell, "John La Farge and Henry Adams in the South Seas," *American Art Journal*, XX, 1 (1988), 103n7.

53. HA to Lucy Baxter, 13 Apr 1890, L, III, 233.

54. For HA's reading the Odyssey, see Chap. 26.

55. For HA's saying the Tahitians were Aryans, see Chap. 26.

56. HA's annotated copy of Francis Darwin, *The Life and Letters of Charles Darwin*, NY 1888, HAL, seems pertinent to his journey, except that it is not clear when HA read the copy.

57. HA evidently owned a set of Cook's *Voyages*. He cites its volumes in his *Memoirs of Marau Taaroa/ Last Queen of Tahiti*, n. p. 1893, and *Memoirs of Arii Taimai*, Paris 1903. The set, however, is conspicuously absent from HAL.

58. Later, when convenient, Hartwell made use of 1603 H Street. See EC to HA, 27 Jan–21 Feb 1891, HA-micro 8.

59. HA's spelling, "Nukuheva," repeats Melville's in *Typee*.

60. HA sent his sonnet "Eagle Head" to EC with his letter from San Francisco, 22–23 Aug 1890, HA-micro 8. It might be imagined that the sonnet was newly written and directly concerned his relation with EC; but HA's language—"You have not seen my sonnet on Eagle Head. I will write it out for you on the opposite page."—indicates that the sonnet had existed for some time.

In my opinion, the sonnet matches the decisive stage of the mutual courtship of HA and his future wife. See Chap. 11. Hence HA's sending the only extant copy to EC reflects his wanting her to have some idea of his and Clover's history.

It would be typical of HA if he took EC to Eagle Head without telling her he had been there with Clover, and without telling her he had written a sonnet, then later sent her the sonnet, unexplained, for her to fathom, if she could.

26. Taura-atua i Amo

Letters by and to HA are in HA-micro 7–9, unless otherwise noted.

PRINCIPAL SOURCES

(1) fifteen letters, HA to EC, [18 Aug 1890]–31 May 1891.

(2) three letters, HA to Mabel Hooper, 20 Aug 1890, 4 Mar, 6 May 1891, Cater, 195–97, 240–42, 245–47; three letters, HA to same, 10 Sep, 2 & 24 Nov 1890, L, III, 273–75, 319–22, 349–51; letters, HA to same, 19 Jan, 9 Feb 1891, HA-micro 8; letter, HA to same, 6 Apr 1891, partly printed in *Letters to a Niece*, 46–50.

(3) eleven letters, HA to Dwight, 10 Sep 1890–11 May 1891.

(4) six letters, HA to Hay, 15 Sep 1890–8 Feb 1891, HA-micro B; three letters, HA to same, 2–4 Mar–8 May 1891.

(5) five letters, HA to Lucy Baxter, 27 Sep [1890]–2 Apr 1891, L, III, 283–85, 323–27, 396–99, 443–44, 454–56; letter, HA to same (typed copy), 24 Dec 1890, HA-micro 8.

(6) letter, HA to Anna Lodge, 21 Oct 1890, L, III, 305–08.

(7) letters, HA to Rebecca Rae, 8 Nov 1890, 27 Apr 1891, Cater, 209–12, 242–44.

(8) letters, HA to Phillips, 13 Dec 1890, 7 May 1891, L, III, 367–70.

(9) letter, HA to Hooper, 27 Dec 1890, Cater, 230–33.

(10) letter, HA to Thoron, 8 Feb 1891, L, III, 413–15.

(11) letter, HA to CMG, 1 Mar 1891.

(12) letters, HA to King, 3 Mar, 22 Apr 1891.

(13) letter, HA to Arthur Adams, 9 May 1891, L, III, 474–76.

(14) HA, *History of the United States of America during the First Administration of James Madison*, 2 vols, NY 1890.

(15) HA, *History of the United States of America during the Second Administration of James Madison*, 3 vols, NY 1891.

ADDITIONAL SOURCES; COMMENTS

1. In his extant writings, HA says nothing about Kalakaua's effort to elicit Arii Taimai's recollections and her refusal. In my opinion, this is one of his louder silences.

In an article, "Tahitian Literature/ The Teva Poets: Notes on a Poetic Family in Tahiti," La Farge wrote concerning Arii Taimai: "The old lady Hinaarii is the chiefess representing the great line of the Teva, alongside of which the Pomares—the kings [of Tahiti] through the foreigner—are new people. Some years ago King Kalakaua of Hawaii had wished to obtain the traditions and genealogies of her family; but the old lady had never been favorable." See Charles Dudley Warner, ed., *Library of the World's Best Literature*, v. 36 (1897), 14393.

More concisely, in his *Reminiscences of the South Seas*, Garden City 1912, 345, La Farge wrote, "Some years ago King Kalakaua of Hawaii had wished to obtain the traditions and genealogies; but the old lady had never been favourable. . . ."

La Farge's statements are helpful but remarkably incomplete. They fail to specify when and from whom he learned that Kalakaua so wished, and when and from whom he learned that Arii Taimai was unfavorable. I infer that HA and La Farge learned the story of Kalakaua's effort and the chiefess's refusal from Kalakaua. The principal basis of the inference is HA's *conduct*. As I see it, his conduct in Samoa and later on Tahiti and Moorea is indicative of (a) his having learned the story from Kalakaua at Honolulu, (b) his incrementally so reacting as to give the king's story a remarkable continuation, and (c) his asking La Farge to be discreet. Of course, HA may also have been told about Kalakaua's effort by Stevenson or Atwater at Samoa. But these are minor possibilities. What affected HA was disclosure by Kalakaua.

2. HA did not preserve his lecture as given in 1876. The revised version, titled "The Primitive Rights of Women," is partly based on materials published as late as 1886. Like "Captaine John Smith" as last revised, it is best read as new writing by HA, essentially subsequent to his *History of the United States*.

3. For example, EC to HA, 10 Jan 1891—"Our little 'family' has disbanded. . . ."

4. For "white coats," see La Farge, *Reminiscences*, op. cit., 94. For Sewall and HA's exchange of letters, see L, II, 453.

5. HA supposed that Stevenson's illness was tuberculosis, but he was assured by a doctor on Samoa that it was asthma. See L, III, 372.

6. Hay wrote amusedly to HA, 30 Dec [1890]: "Now I will have to tell you . . . of Stevenson's account of your visit to him. Your account of that historical meeting is a gem of description. . . . *His* is no less perfect and characteristic. He writes to Ned Burlingame[:] 'Two Americans called on me yesterday. One, an artist named Lafarge [*sic*], said he knew you. The name of the other I do not recall.' Bear up under this, like a man, in the interest of science. It completes the portrait of the shabby parrot."

After learning more about HA, and after visiting him and La Farge on 24 Nov 1890, Stevenson wrote: ". . . went over in the evening to the American consulate; present Consul-General Sewall, Lieut. Parker and Mrs. Parker, Lafarge, the American decorator, Adams an American historian; we talked late. . . ." See Sidney Colvin, ed., *The Works of Robert Louis Stevenson*, NY 1923, vol. 22, 301.

7. Barrett, 57–59.

8. HA's *History* begins with a sentence that may seem merely informative but in fact states the subject of the work. The sentence says, "Accord-

ing to the census of 1800, the United States of America contained 5,308,483 persons."

9. An instance is the British leader George Canning. HA explains: "Of him and his qualities much will be said hereafter, when his rise to power shall have made him a more prominent figure; here need be noticed only the forces which sought assertion through him, and the nature of the passions which he was peculiarly qualified to express." See *HUS* (Scribner), II, 417; (LoA), I, 585.

10. It is not surprising that HA in his *History* was able to set forth English concerns as understood by the English. What might be surprising is his ability to set forth Indian concerns as understood by Indians. Relevant passages in the *History* are easily consulted with the help of HA's index entries under "Indians" and those relating to Tecumthe, the Indians' most representative figure.

11. HA's *History* makes use of a vocabulary designed to facilitate historical reasoning and explanation. An important passage involving such terms appears in his last chapter. ". . . history had its scientific as well as its human side, and in American history the scientific interest was greater than the human. Elsewhere the student could study under better conditions the evolution of the individual, but nowhere could he study so well the evolution of a race. The interest of such a subject exceeded that of any other branch of science, for it brought mankind within sight of its own end." See *HUS* (Scribner), IX, 224–25; (LoA), II, 1334. The passage is partly remarkable for suggesting that history will end—that humanity has a destination and will arrive. Still more remarkably, it assigns its author a status. It places him on a basis of parity with and even superiority to Darwin.

12. La Farge, *Reminiscences*, 278.

13. On 4 Dec 1890, HA offered EC a different picture: "As usual I felt like Odysseus. . . ." See HA to EC, 27 Nov–11 Dec 1890.

14. Joseph W. Ellison, in his *Tusitala of the South Seas*, NY 1953, 33, says that Ori spoke French. "Stevenson and Ori soon became warm friends. . . . Since both spoke French[,] they were able to carry on long conversations." But HA reported oppositely. See note 33, below.

15. La Farge, *Reminiscences*, 235.

16. HA's letters from the Sandwich Islands and the South Seas are voluminous, overlapping in content, and written as if intended to be parts of an immense scrapbook, suitable for reading even if parts are lost. In 1920 in her *Letters to a Niece*, Mabel La Farge published a sampling of the letters to herself. In 1930 in *Letters of Henry Adams (1858–1891)*, Ford published a hundred pages of the letters to Mrs. Cameron and Mrs. Lodge. In 1947, in *Henry Adams and His Friends*, Cater published fifty pages of the letters to Hay, Dwight, Mabel Hooper, Edward Hooper, and Rebecca Rae. In 1974 a large sampling of the letters appeared as a separate volume—translated into French. See Henry Adams, *Lettres des Mers du Sud*, edited and translated by Evelyne de Chazeaux, Paris 1974. In 1982 in *The Letters of Henry Adams*, vols. I-III, Levenson and his fellow editors published a large sampling, including letters to Lucy Baxter, William Phillips, Ward Thoron, King, HA's nephew Arthur Adams, and Martha Cameron. Some of the letters are yet to be printed, and conjecturable letters (e.g., to Constance Lodge) may be missing. Were all the letters published in a body,

the effect, already great, might be enhanced, especially because HA was telling different stories to different readers. However, some series, notably the letters to Lucy Baxter, grow more intelligible and much more valuable when read in isolation.

17. La Farge, *Reminiscences*, 242–43.

18. HA's inquiry was important negatively. He could learn nothing of the Samoans' history more than three centuries back. He found no ancient artefacts. See HA to Phillips, 13 Dec 1890, L, III, 369—". . . no one has ever seen a very old [Samoan] stone-implement, to know it as such. I have made no end of inquiries, all over the islands, without discovering a trace of older civilisation. Even their traditions hardly go back to their Tongan war, some three hundred years ago."

19. For HA's most detailed assertion that the Samoans he visited were more ancient than Homer's characters, see the passage beginning "Homer's women—Penelope, Helen, Nausicaa . . ." in his letter to King, 22 Apr 1891, L, III, 467.

20. Hay to HA, 9 Oct 1890.

21. HA's information was partly furnished by EC's letter to him, 17–24 Nov 1890—"I suppose some one else will tell you of the virtual failure of Baring Bros. which caused a panic on Wall St. Rothchilds and the Bank of England came to the relief of Barings, and a syndicate now controls it. As for Wall St[.], it went through its worst period since Black Friday, and Gould came out in control of Northern Pacific and the papers say of U. P. [Union Pacific]. . . . And they also say that your brother is to resign."

22. It possibly is significant that HA drops the "New York" from the title of "The New York Gold Conspiracy." The deletion shifts attention away from Gould and Fisk and towards Corbin and the Grants.

In the same letter, HA goes on to identify a "second" chapter: CFA2's presidency of the Union Pacific and its "foredoomed failure." He moreover says a "last" chapter is "close at hand." He adds: ". . . Gould . . . is certainly a great man, worth writing about. If I thought I should be alive twentyfive [*sic*] years hence, . . . I should prepare to continue my history, and show where American democracy was coming out."

23. HA's revolt against photography had been building for some time. On 21 Oct 1890, when first using his Kodak on Samoa, HA wrote to Mrs. Lodge: ". . . the photograph takes all the fun out of the tropics. Especially it vulgarises the women, whose charm is chiefly their size and proportions, their lines, the freedom of their movement, the color of their skin, and their good-natured smile." On 24 Jan 1891, writing to EC about the colors of Samoan sunsets, he said: ". . . I have thrown aside my Kodak and my water-colors, and trust to memory." From Tahiti on 13 Feb 1891, he explained to EC: ". . . I hate photographs abstractly, because they have given me more ideas perversely and immoveably wrong, than I ever should get by imagination. They are almost as bad as an ordinary book of travels." See L, III, 307, 388, 408.

24. In passages written to EC on 9 & 18 Jan 1891 and in his letter to Lucy Baxter, 18 Jan 1891, HA says he is reading, studying, and annotating Homer. See L, III, 382, 387, & 396. He does not say whether he is reading Homer in Greek or in translation.

He had with him a German translation, *Homers Odysee*, Leipzig 1872–1873, in two volumes, inherited from MHA, FTKP. Later, at Tahiti, he read the second volume and noted on pp. 1 & 163 that he began reading at Tautira on March 16 and finished at Papeete on May 7. It thus seems a fair assumption that he read the first volume while at Samoa.

25. HA's detailed account to EC, 6 Feb 1891, L, III, 402, is supplemented by another in La Farge, *Reminiscences*, 302.

26. The geological portion of HA's report to King, 3 Mar 1891, L, III, 435–42, makes clear that HA formed his theory of the reefs at Samoa and only confirmed it at Tahiti.

27. The photograph is reproduced in L, III, opp. 420, and in Chazeaux, ed., Henry Adams, *Lettres des Mers du Sud*, op. cit., illus. 20.

28. HA said about his host: "Tati ought to be King or Governor, but is too shrewd to want such honors, and duties. He is powerful enough as he is." See HA to Lucy Baxter, 5 Mar 1891.

29. Writing to him, 27 Nov 1890, EC describes HA as "out there in infinity." She goes on to say: "I used to wonder when I was a child and read fairy tales, where the prince came to the end of the world and went down on the other side[,] what he found there. And I find myself in the same curiously real and unreal state of curiosity about you. Are you really out of the world? And what do you find there? And *is* there such a place?" She resumes: "It *is* the other side of the world, isn't it? And your brain will scarcely hold all that you see and hear in that strange other existence." See EC to HA, 17–27 Nov 1890.

In her next letter, she asks, "Are you in the Happy Valley?" See EC to HA, 2–5 Dec 1890.

To my mind, it is a practical certainty that portions of the quoted sentences by EC echo things HA had said to her while with her in America and, too, are intended by EC to be recognized by him as echoing.

30. The verses accompany HA's letter to EC, 8–25 Nov 1890, and are dated "Apia. November 25, 1890. 4:00, A.M." The last stanza reads:

> Death is not hard when once you feel its measure;
> One learns to know that Paradise is gain;
> One bids farewell to all that gave one pleasure;
> One bids farewell to all that gave one pain.

31. Writing later to EC, 16 Mar 1891, L, III, 446, HA mentions "the desert of Gobi" and says, "Motion alone amuses. . . . ."

32. The ruined medieval church at Wenlock was large—just under 350 feet long. See Nikolaus Pevsner, *Shropshire*, op. cit., 208. The pyramid erected by the Tevas in the *marae* of Mahaiatea was likewise large. Captain Cook measured it and found it 267 feet long. See HA, *Memoirs of Arii Taimai*, Paris 1901, 68. Considering that the exterior of the Teva pyramid was formed of shaped stone blocks made by workers without metal tools, the greater wonder was the Tahitian.

33. Writing to Hay on 2 Mar 1891, L, III, 433, HA said: "Here at Tautira we are quite alone in a remote native village. We cannot even find an interpreter to make conversation possible. Ori, Stevenson's adopted brother, a big native and properly the chief here, can speak no word of a foreign language. Arié, the actual chief, speaks French, but is not interesting." I see no reason to doubt HA concerning Ori and accordingly suppose that Stevenson conversed with Ori only through a translator, possibly Arié. See note 14 above.

34. EC to HA, 10–23 Jan 1891.

35. The principal outburst by EC to HA about her wanting him to return appears in her letter of 27 Jan–16 Feb 1891:—"I dared not write to you yesterday. It was one of those days when I felt that you must come back. . . . Even Martha felt it in sympathy for she talked of you all day, and at tea wanted you 'so bad!' I do miss you more and more and have horrible revolts now and then when I think how the days are passing by, and our lives drawing near their end, and all these months are wasted, lost. It isn't life without you. And yet not for worlds would I bid you return if you must return to restlessness and unhappiness. . . . I think that these last days of revolt have been made worse by your last letter which was unhappy, restless, dissatisfied, whatever you choose to call it. If I could feel you were happy over there, I would be happy here,—or calm at least. I must not write in this way, I know. I thought that there was no danger when I began. If you let me unsettle you I shall never forgive myself."

36. See note 24, above.

37. HA's anxiety not to seem an imitator of Stevenson was possibly intensified by the latter's being another of Scribner's authors.

38. HA had written to Hay from Samoa, 4 Jan 1891, L, III, 391, "I begin to understand why Melville wanted to escape from Typee. . . ."

39. HA had told King, 3 Mar 1891, L, III, 442, ". . . I shall probably get through the Pacific this summer, and begin on Asia." As his plans changed, HA retained the idea of going to China (also to India) but revised the anticipated date of his journey.

40. Even earlier, on 4 Mar 1891, L, III, 423, HA had written to EC: "I have repeatedly offered . . . to take the next steamer to Auckland, and go straight to Paris. . . ." The message, when received and read, may have intensified EC's desire to get to Europe; but equally it may have seemed to her unserious.

41. Parkman to HA, 28 Jan 1891.

42. MacVeagh to HA, 14 Feb 1891.

43. HA had in fact heard *some* things concerning his *History*, but he may not yet have received the letters from Parkman and MacVeagh.

44. The population of ancient Tahiti was a famous problem, and HA's earlier remarks about it varied. Writing to Hay, 8 May 1891, he said: "Here once dwelt a population which may have numbered fifty thousand people; or a hundred thousand for all I know. . . ."

Eventually HA would take pains to show that the Tahitian population in 1774 was "between one hundred and fifty thousand and two hundred thousand at the least," and was reduced to "only about five thousand in 1803." See *Memoirs of Arii Taimai*, op. cit., 2–6, 136.

45. The translation is La Farge's. See his "Tahitian Literature," op. cit., 14392.

46. HA, *Memoirs of Arii Taimai*, 16—". . . the original Marae in the territory now known as Papara was on the small subdistrict called Amo, a mile from the sea and close under the mountains. The Marae of Amo was called Taputuarai; from this Marae a stone was taken to found the Marae of Tooarai near the shore; and close to the Marae of Tooarai, almost within the same enclosure, Purea and Amo built for their son Teriirere the great stone pyramid at which . . . Captain Cook and Sir Joseph Banks wondered, on the point of Mahaiatea."

47. HA wrote to EC, 8 Apr 1891, L, III, 453–54, "I took investiture of my duchy in the shape of an orange."

48. La Farge, *Reminiscences*, 329—"The place has now for us an increased charm; a still more subtle influence envelops me when I think that this is the home of Amo and Oberea [Purea], who first met Wallis and Cook; and as I look from the violet beds . . . to the solemn hills of dark green crowned with cloud, I wonder if somewhere there may be the hidden tomb of Oberea, now my ancestress. . . ."

49. To Dwight, 8 Mar 1891, parodying Shakespeare's Cleopatra (*Ant. & Cleo.*, V, ii, 280–81)—". . . I have immortal longings in me."

50. Between them, HA and La Farge heard Tahitian stories in which, at the direction of great Teva chiefs and chiefesses, dogs were not to bark, cocks were not to crow, and the ocean was not to storm. See HA, *Memoirs of Arii Taimai*, 44 "'Not even the cocks may crow or the ocean storm.' " Also see ibid., 170—"The natives still show the cave where Marama drank kava and no sound was permitted; not even the crowing of a cock, that his repose should not be disturbed."

51. I am indebted to the ethnologist Martin Anthony Brunor for the translation. For HA's translation, see note 57, below.

52. For "many centuries," see HA, *Memoirs of Arii Taimai*, 36. For the words of a traditional song involving Taura-atua and his mistress, see ibid, 36–38. In his *Reminiscences*, 321, La Farge repeats a fragment of a story: "Here [in Amo] lived Tauraatua, sixteen generations back, simply and frugally, refusing to change his habits with increased power, and contented with cheap fare. Here . . . he drank *kava* . . . and once, while lying under its influence (dead drunk, as it were), came near being surprised by the enemy." La Farge's "sixteen generations," counting back from himself, is equivalent to HA's "Some fifteen generations ago" if HA is counting back within the Teva family, starting from Arii Taimai. See HA to EC, 16 Mar–8 Apr 1891, L, III, 453.

53. *Memoirs of Arii Taimai*, 149.

54. Ibid., 71. The *Memoirs* can be viewed as a well-calculated counterpoise to HA's *History of the United States*. In the *Memoirs*, Taura-atua i Patea and Opuhara are the central characters. Opuhara's death marks the end of what HA says (148) were "the dark ages" of the Tevas' history—"between 1800 and 1815."

55. HA, *Memoirs of Arii Taimai*, 38 (genealogical Table II), 148. Taura-atua i Patea is mentioned as Tati in connection with events of 1807 and reappears by that name thereafter. See 152, 154, 157–160.

56. Ibid., 60—"My father Tati. . . ." Also see HA, *Memoires d'Arii Taimai*, Paris 1964, 162, index entry beginning "Tati de son vrai nom Taura Atua i Patea." In the entry, the editor notes, "Ariitaimai [*sic*] le nomme son père alors qu'il est son grand-père."

57. HA wrote to EC, 13 Apr 1891, L, III, 456: ". . . [we] were driven to Papeete by Johnny and Taura. Taura is Tati's second son . . . . Taura and I have the same name, Taura-atua—God-perch; Japanese Toro; lighting-place or resting-place of a God, I am told. Taura was going back to school, and being twelve years old, had the sentiments of his age on the subject; while Johnny, another boy, who was charged with the equipage, bore the assurance of a thrashing if Taura should escape. The adventures of Taura and Johnny diverted us greatly, for Johnny succeeded only by the aid of

two aunts and several cousins in at last penning Taura in the Frères' prison. . . ."

Watching twelve-year-old Taura may appear to have been the experience that moved HA to write the most famous passage in *The Education*, the account in the first chapter of a very young Henry Adams being forcibly taken to school by his Adams grandfather. It may be more likely, however, that HA took note of Taura's imprisonment because the first chapter of *The Education* was already mostly drafted.

58. Writing to Hay, 8 May 1891, HA says that because of "our very formal adoption," the Salmon family has "become ours." "Of the Salmon ancestry we know little, though the Salmons are assumed to be good Jews or Bohemians in England; but we are proud of our Polynesian blood, which is the highest possible. . . ." He continues: "As Taura-atua I associate with the Papara family, and find it a convenient excuse for getting rid of formalities like Mrs[.] and Miss. The natives never use such stupidities. . . . I too have learned to say Tati and Marau when I speak to them, and I expect them to address me as Taura-atua."

59. In this instance, HA's saying he is two different persons may most relate to separate elements in his experience which the quoted passages successfully confuse.

One element is his work on *The Education of Henry Adams*. This work is requiring him to invent a fictional Henry Adams to be paraded serio-comically in the book in place of the actual.

The other element is his relation with EC. The relation involves two divergent Henry Adamses: he who will exist if his anticipated meeting with EC in Europe merely takes up the threads of their past life in America, and he who will exist if their relation, beginning when they meet, is radically transformed. HA ends by suggesting that which one he will be depends entirely on EC.

60. Later, in his *Memoirs of Arii Taimai*, 162, HA would say on the Tahitians' behalf, ". . . we have no history apart from genealogy."

In his *Reminiscences*, 344–45, La Farge suggests that the Tahitians at the moment were making public their genealogies because pressed to do so by the French government, as a step towards securing claims to land. HA's contemporary writings are silent on this score, and there seems more than a possibility that La Farge's *Reminiscences* as they relate to Tahiti pretend to be written at the time but are in fact the product of a later assembling of materials diverse in date, without much regard to their chronology.

61. La Farge, *Reminiscences*, 344, 351. HA had learned to paint partly in order to illustrate Melville's *Typee* for EC. See HA to EC, 3–14 May 1891, L, III, 474—". . . I shall not visit Nukuheva, where I hoped to sketch for you the scenes of Melville's book. . . ." As things developed, he produced a number of respectable watercolors, mainly Tahitian scenes. (Examples are reproduced in L, III, following 400.) Also he learned at first hand the difficulties of painting and—what perhaps is more important—developed strong feelings and opinions about the adequacy of oils and watercolors when employed as a medium to suggest such a place as Tahiti. His feelings and opinions appear in a passage in his letter to Thoron, principal source 10, saying in part: "These skies and seas and mountains are not to be caught by throwing paint on their tails with ever

so accurate an aim. The painter is only maddened by their evanescence when he tries to fix them."

The passage goes a long way to explain why HA in his later years grew less interested in painting and more interested in stained glass.

27. THE APOCALYPTIC NEVER

Letters by and to HA are in HA-micro 9, unless otherwise noted.

PRINCIPAL SOURCES

(1) ten letters, HA to EC, 17 May–12 Nov 1891.

(2) letters, HA to Dwight, 2 Jun, 3 Aug 1891.

(3) three letters, HA to Hay, 21 Jun–21 Aug 1891; letter, HA to same, 14 Nov 1891, HA-micro B.

(4) four letters, HA to Mabel Hooper, 21 Jun, 30 & 30 Sep, 8 Oct 1891, as printed in *Letters to a Niece*, 51–68; letter, HA to same, 1 Aug 1891, Cater, 248–50.

(5) letters, HA to Lucy Baxter, 23 Jun, 2 Aug 1891; letter, HA to same, 30 Sep 1891, L, III, 549–52;

(6) letter, HA to St. Gaudens, 23 Jun 1891, L, III, 496.

(7) letter, HA to Thoron, 7 Jul 1891, FTKP.

(8) letter, HA to CFA2, 3 Aug 1891.

(9) letter, HA to Lodge, 4 Aug 1891.

(10) letters, HA to CMG, 17 Aug, 27 Oct, [29 Oct] 1891.

(11) letter, HA to Phillips, 8 Oct 1891, L, III, 552–55.

(12) HA, *History of the United States of America . . .* , 9 vols, NY 1889–1891.

(13) HA, *Historical Essays*, NY 1891.

ADDITIONAL SOURCES; COMMENTS

1. EC to HA, 9–28 Mar 1891, HA-micro 8 & 9.

2. In his Memorabilia, 1888–1893, 279, AP, CFA2 says Dwight brought him prints. In his letter to HA, 6 Apr [1891], St. Gaudens says he received prints from Dwight but does not mention a visit.

3. EC to HA, 9–24 Apr 1891.

4. CFA2 to HA, 3 May 1891.

5. St. Gaudens to HA, 6 Apr [1891].

6. HA's seizing a last opportunity to complete his circuit of the island can be understood as indicating how seriously he intended to complete a history of the Tevas and of the Tahitians generally.

7. HA shortly obtained the records. He later gave them to the Library of Congress.

8. Hay to HA, 10 Jan 1891, HA-micro 8.

9. HA soon wrote to CMG, 17 Aug 1891: "I have been so long a recluse, that a party of mixed acquaintances would be a trial that I am a little afraid to attempt. Total strangers I mind less, for I can turn my back and go home if I like. I can't talk. Nothing is more fatiguing."

10. The prevailing attitude of the Association towards HA is perhaps best indicated by the issue of *AHR* headed "The American Historical Association: the First Hundred Years, 1884–1984," Oct 1984. In the portion of the issue relating to the Association's presidents, HA is listed as

having been president (1020) but is otherwise not mentioned. In the portion relating to the Association's metamorphosis from learned society to professional organization, HA appears in a note (945–46n42) as a non-professional historian but is otherwise not mentioned. In the article by Dorothy Ross, "Historical Consciousness in Nineteenth Century America," HA is said to have "studied abroad" (921), apparently meaning—errone-ously—that he studied history in Europe as a graduate student. He is mentioned too as having been hired by Harvard to teach medieval history (922), as having plunged "with his students into the study of Anglo-Saxon law" (922) and having published unspecified "work" in 1876 (923); but his appointment at Harvard is misdated as having occurred in 1872; and it is not mentioned that the students with whom he studied Anglo-Saxon law were doctoral candidates who completed their dissertations under his supervision and received their degrees. The issue nowhere mentions his *History of the United States*.

11. Godkin reportedly "used only professional historians [i.e. profes-sors] to review historical works." See *AHR*, Oct 1984, 954. His magazine reviewed the successive instalments of HA's *History*. See *Nation*, 12 Dec 1889, 480–83, & 19 Dec 1889, 504–06; 8 May 1890, 376–78, & 15 May 1890, 395–97; 20 Nov 1890, 405–07, & 27 Nov 1890, 424–26; 16 Apr 1891, 322–23, & 23 Apr 1891, 344–45. The reviews appear to be the work of one writer, as yet unidentified. Judging from internal evidence, they were written by a teacher of history, political science, or both. They are very detailed, disputatious, and quick to instruct; they are narrowly politi-cal; and they have no special value.

12. HA, "Albert Gallatin," *Memorial Biographies of the New England Historical Genealogical Society*, Bost 1880, I, 211—"His ethnological papers on the American Indians and their languages, published in 1836, 1845, and 1848, may be said to have created that branch of science."

13. Part of HA's achievement was recognized in an AHA publication. See George Matthew Dutcher, "Tendencies and Opportunities in Napo-leonic Studies," *Annual Report of the American Historical Association for the Year 1914*, I, 190: "Irving and Prescott and Motley did reveal some of the glories of European history to American readers, but it remained for Henry Adams to grasp and to demonstrate the inextricable and indissolu-ble relationship of American with European history. For this reason, if for no other, his *History of the United States* . . . is the most notable contribution yet made by any American to the study of the Napoleonic period, though Americans and Europeans have alike failed to give Mr. Adams his proper meed of credit."

14. As finished, HA's *Memoirs of Arii Taimai* would end with an account of her peacemaking achievement dictated by herself. I assume that HA first learned of her action while in her company on Tahiti.

15. Apparently on the same day, 16 Jun 1891, HA wrote a letter to Martha Cameron, L, III, 493, partly about the "people that eat little girls." Martha reportedly liked the letter. See EC to HA, 8 Sep 1891—"Martha quotes your letter from Fiji incessantly. It made a great impression upon her."

16. To reduce seasickness when aboard the *Richmond*, HA had passed his nights in a chair on deck. Despite the precaution, his sufferings between Tahiti and Fiji had approached being dangerous.

17. EC to HA, 21 May–13 Jun [1891].

18. HA to Lucy Baxter, 5 Mar 1891, L, III, 443.

19. CFA2 to HA, 3 May 1891.

20. HA's letter to CFA2, 3 Aug 1891, has not received due attention as a source concerning the genesis of the figure. In its use of the word "image," the letter contradicts the fiction that HA gave St. Gaudens only a "general idea."

The "general idea" fiction can safely be attributed solely to HA. The fiction was typical of HA's fictions in being generous. It lent St. Gaudens all possible credit for the figure and reserved for HA only a nebulous remainder.

The sum of the matter is that HA conceived a usable image for a statue, showed the sculptor the image with the help of a model, and devised the fiction he and the sculptor were to use to prevent him, HA, from getting credit for conceiving the image.

21. Dwight was watching for the publication of HA's *Historical Essays* and wrote to the publisher the moment he knew the volume had appeared. See Dwight to Brownell, 2 Oct 1891, Barrett, 61.

22. The volume is important partly for including a previously unpublished essay, "The Declaration of Paris." HA formed a desire to write such an essay at the start of his second life. See HA to F. W. Seward, 14 Feb 1862, L, I, 283. For further details, see Chap. 7, note 84, above. The essay indicates that CFA and HA, wanting to understand Palmerston and Russell and learn better how to deal with them, studied the history of the relations between the United States and England as thoroughly as the resources available to them permitted. The essay accordingly can serve in part as an antechamber to HA's *History*.

23. CFA2, Memorabilia, 1888–1893, 279–87, AP.

24. Ibid. CFA2 uses the word "correctly" with all possibly emphasis. He says the story of the mysterious figure in Washington will necessarily be told. He adds, "Let it be told correctly."

25. Ibid. CFA2 makes no claim to have learned this different account from HA or St. Gaudens. He presents it as *logically necessary*. It is consistent with what *he* believes is the true meaning of the figure. And he indicates it was he that discovered the meaning.

26. Ibid. Domineering by habit, CFA2 was less likely to learn meaning from evidence than to invent and impose meaning as suited him. His account of the genesis of the figure is rather obviously a free invention and unchecked imposition. His claimed remarks to St. Gaudens may also be invention and imposition. They may never have been made.

27. Ibid. CFA2 nowhere shows awareness that the figure is androgynous. He speaks of "the woman, sitting there on the boulder at the grave." The point he most forcefully insists upon is that the figure is post-suicide Clover idealized, with a face and form not her own.

28. Ibid. MHA's biographer Eugenia Kaledin accepts as fact CFA2's assertion that Clover Hooper when a child witnessed her aunt's suicide. See *The Education of Mrs. Henry Adams*, 34, 163. In my view, acceptance of the statement is highly incautious. CFA2 does not say from whom or when he acquired this alleged item of data. One is forced to assume that the item is part of the "whole story" CFA2 says he learned from HA following MHA's death. Thus the credibility of the item depends on the credibility

of CFA2's claim to have heard the "whole story." For the credibility of that, see notes 29–34.

29. Ibid. CFA2's assertion that MHA at "long intervals" underwent three periods of excitement and unnatural action, each followed by a long period of depression and morbid reaction, has no support in other surviving evidence relating to MHA. If the assertion none the less tempts belief, the reason may lie in its meeting the requirements for the invention of myth, especially the requirement that fateful things be said to come in threes.

For data about a false allegation that MHA suffered a "nervous collapse" while on her wedding journey, see Chap. 12, note 47, above.

30. Ibid. CFA2 dates two events in MHA's life. Both dates are mistaken. He says MHA was engaged to HA in the "autumn" of 1871—an error of many weeks. He says MHA's father died in the "Spring of 84, I think"—an error of a year. The errors may be unimportant in themselves, but they assume considerable importance when it is remembered that CFA2 avers in his entry that what he tells is told "correctly."

31. Ibid. There is no direct, explicit evidence to support CFA2's claim that, for a "few days" after MHA's death, he and HA had "talks" by themselves during which HA found "relief" by "talking freely" and telling the "whole story" of the occurrences leading to MHA's suicide. Moreover, the balance of evidence is strongly *against* the occurrence of the alleged talks.

CFA2 says he learned of MHA's death the day it occurred and went to Washington "that night." The statement is mistaken. According to his diary, he reached Washington the next afternoon, 7 Dec 1885, at 4:00 P.M.

CFA2 appears to have stayed at a hotel, presumably Wormley's. According to his diary, he dined "with Henry" on the 7th and "with him and the Gurneys" on the 8th. It appears from other evidence that the persons at dinner on the 7th also included Edward Hooper and the Gurneys and that on the 8th the same persons were present, plus JQA2 and his son George.

CFA2 did not stay in Washington a "few days." He stayed two days. According to his diary, he left on 9 Dec 1885 at 4:00 P.M.

In his diary entry for the 8th, CFA2 says: "Drove with Henry out of town and took a walk with him." In view of his diary entries concerning the dinners, this entry cannot with certainty be construed to mean the brothers drove or walked without companions. But assuming they did drive and walk unaccompanied, there is still the question whether HA told CFA2 "the whole story" and thus found "relief."

Other evidence concerning the events of 6–9 Dec 1886 makes clear that the persons with whom HA was willing to talk freely were Clover's sister, brother, and brother-in-law. They were invited first, arrived first, and stayed with HA at 1607 H Street. If HA needed to find relief by talking, they were constantly available.

The idea that CFA2 became HA's confidant early on 8 Dec 1885, when they began a drive out of town, and ceased to be his confidant later in the day when they completed a walk within the city, strains credulity in both its parts. As other evidence makes clear, HA had ceased to confide in any deep way with CFA2 beginning in 1863 when he, HA, formed a friendship with Gaskell. HA's not deeply confiding in CFA2 continued till the latter died, in 1915. That there was a one-day exception is conceivable. It is also extremely improbable.

CFA2 says that one thing HA told him during their "talks" was that he, HA, expected MHA to recover. Considering that HA warned Clover's relations that she was not better, just the opposite, this small part of CFA2's Memorabilia entry may be evidence that HA treated CFA2 during his visit as an outsider, never to be told her actual history.

32. Ibid. MHA's biographer Otto Friedrich accepts as fact CFA2's assertion that he prophesied Clover Hooper's suicide. See *Clover*, 138. In my view, acceptance of the assertion as it stands is impossible and acceptance of the assertion in a modified form would compound a fiction with new fictions devised by the acceptor.

CFA2's assertion involves eight elements: CFA was at Geneva; in her husband's absence, ABA was driving with CFA2 and HA; ABA said she wished HA would marry Clover Hooper; CFA2 interjected that all the Sturgis descendants were crazy and Clover would commit suicide like her aunt; HA looked annoyed and said he had no intention of marrying; his denial notwithstanding, HA was then secretly engaged to Clover; the drive occurred in the autumn of 1871; and HA's engagement to Clover was announced two weeks later.

The asserted elements fail to coordinate with the known facts concerning the engagement. Henry and Clover became secretly engaged on 27 Feb 1872 and delayed announcing the engagement to his elder brothers and to the public till 9 & 10 Mar 1872. At the time, CFA was in Boston. ABA had his company, and she had no known reason to drive without her husband and with two of her sons.

It should be noted also that, of the three persons who figure in CFA2's assertion as participants, ABA was two years dead when the assertion was written; HA was not told it was being written; and CFA2 could write whatever he pleased without fear of being contradicted.

33. While there is strong reason to say that CFA2's entry in his Memorabilia is so worded from start to finish as to do serious and not-easily-counteracted harm to MHA and HA, there is equal reason to infer that CFA2 was only slightly aware, or not at all aware, that his words would be destructive in effect and were malicious in motive.

The motive most evident in his entry is self-congratulation. The entry shows him always aware of what he takes to be his own informed intelligence and perfect or near-perfect insight.

34. If value is to be found in CFA2's entry, it may lie in its phrases concerning HA and MHA as a "well-matched pair" who "lived very happily" and in its phrases concerning MHA's success as a wife. There may be value also in CFA2's saying twice in the entry that HA "never" spoke to him concerning MHA's history.

35. HA to EC, 1–12 Dec 1891, L, III, 577.

36. HA's copies of the Forster, Russell, and Milnes biographies are in HAL.

37. In his letter to CMG, HA also says: ". . . I know not one good picture of the society [of Great Britain] of the middle of our century. Perhaps George Trevelyan's Macaulay is the best." The biography of Macaulay reappears in HA's Preface to *Mont Saint Michel and Chartres*.

38. There were five American commissioners trying to bring the British to terms, but HA's narrative shows that Gallatin's share in their effort was disproportionately large and very possibly decisive.

39. Writing about the last instalment of the *History*, an anonymous reviewer wondered whether Adams had been "brought up as a naval officer or shipbuilder." See "Through Four Administrations," *The Critic*, 28 Feb 1891, 106. Far from foolish, the query was grounded in masterly passages in the narrative relating to ships, especially fighting ships, and their murderous engagements. Similar queries could be devised, equally grounded in pages of the *History*. One could ask whether HA had begun as an army officer, a geographer or cartographer, a financier, statistician, diplomat, newspaper editor, congressman, traveler, inventor, judge, projector of canals, architect, even minister of religion.

Such imaginable queries would help point to one of HA's strengths. He possessed that order of genius that permits a person to enter and achieve considerable competence in numerous specializations, yet not suffer limitations while gaining the competences achieved. He widened his learning and by so doing grew less limited. It perhaps was this strength that most suited him for work as a universal historian.

40. Both letters to CMG are in HA-micro 7.

41. HA's *History* is usually not simple. It presents accounts of Jefferson, Madison, and even Jackson that at points speak strongly in their favor. Napoleon emerges as a destroyer of France, the world, and himself, but also as a destroyer of extraordinary ability. Burr very quickly reduces his western conspiracy to collapse. Yet he stays in memory, if only as a faint approximation of a Napoleon. Pickering is simpler. Uniformly, his designs lack interest and fail.

42. *HUS* (Scribner), IV, 74; (LoA), I, 978.

43. *HUS* (Scribner), IX, 233–35; (LoA), II, 1340–41.

44. HA's principal discoveries as a historian can all be found in *History*, openly expressed in terms that competent readers should find easy to follow. Here *one* discovery—that the Americans were more intelligent than the English (and generally that human intelligence was markedly increasing)—has been brought forward; but there are others.

The finding that HA himself treats as most important is that democracy is the end towards which human action is tending. See *HUS* (Scribner), IX, 224–25; (LoA), II, 1334–35.

45. The passage is representative of many passages in HA's writings which show him always at work upon, and when possible improving, a comprehensive idea of the origin of human beings, their migrations, and their development of new attributes and capacities—for example, the development or near-development of a "soul." Details of this idea could be gleaned from his writings and pulled together.

What chiefly matters is that he presents an *epitome* of universal history in one work. His *History of the United States* brings within a single narrative human actions that, in type, are (a) very old, (b) currently the rule, and (c) indicative of the future.

46. On shipboard on the Indian Ocean between Ceylon and the Red Sea, HA wrote a 251–line poem, "Buddha and Brahma." See pencil MS. in HAL; also *Yale Review*, Oct 1915, 82–89. The idea set forth by the principal speaker in the poem is that all things whatsoever begin and end "in one sole Thought/ Of Purity in Silence."

Readers may differ concerning the relative weight this idea should be given among the ideas brought forward by HA in his varied writings, but it may stand against the idea that it is conveyed in verse. HA *was* a poet, but as a rule he showed little poetic ability when versifying. When he meant what he said, he would find ways to say it memorably, but almost always in what passes for mere excellent American prose.

47. For La Farge's experiences after their parting, see his three November 1891 letters to HA from Finisterre and London, HA-micro 9.

48. The conclusive evidence that she showed the copy to Hay is Hay's poem. See note 49.

49. Sixteen words in HA's "The Capitol by Moonlight"—beneath, Capitol, dome, dreaming, eyes, light, moonlight, night, obelisk, peace, stars, still, strong, terrace, warm, and white—reappear in Hay's "Two on the Terrace." Four others—gleams, slumbers, sobs, and throbs—reappear as gleaming, slumber, sobbing, and throbbing.

50. EC to HA, 26 Sep–7 Oct 1891.

51. HA to EC, 12–22 Aug 1891.

52. The octet of the sonnet suggests a building, the Capitol, that is drugged and asleep. In contrast, the sestet suggests a memorial, the Washington Monument, that is awake and aspiring. The mood of the sonnet is elusive. It can appear to range from the elegiac to the ironic. Consensus about the sonnet's meaning might be hard to reach.

53. *Ibid.* In his account, HA shows not a trace of being upset or angry. But he directly asks what happened.

54. When confronted by HA's question, EC apparently had at hand neither her copy of HA's sonnet nor any copy of Hay's poem. Lacking the texts, she had double reason to take the safest course, which in this instance was surely to tell the truth, even at the cost of writing at considerable length.

55. The letter—EC to HA, 26 Sep–7 Oct 1891—is incomplete. The last page or pages are missing.

The precise wording of EC's lie may indicate what happened. She *failed* to keep HA's sonnet just between the two of them. She instead told Hay about it and let him borrow or copy it. He wrote *his* poem immediately and brought it for her to see. It amused her immensely.

56. See especially EC to HA, 10 Aug [1891]—"To think that you are coming, are on your way! That I shall see you, shall take you home. I can scarce realize it tho' I walk on air in consequence."

57. HA's word for possible adultery between himself and EC is "mischief." In his decisive letter to her, 5–12 Nov 1891, he says that, being much the older, he would be solely responsible for any "mischief" the two of them could get into.

58. HA to Rebecca Dodge Rae, 5 Dec 1891, L, III, 582—"Mrs[.] Cameron is no good. She has too much to do, and lets everybody make use of her, which pleases no one because of course each person objects to other persons having any rights that deserve respect."

59. Ibid. Writing to Hay on 14 Nov 1891, HA listed less personal aspects of his stay: "I haunted the theatres, operas and concerts. . . . Réjane was admirable in the Cigale; I went twice to see her. . . . The plays were very indecent, but not more so than formerly, and they were certainly funny. I did some real laughing, and enjoyed it."

60. The best evidence of the impression she gave him is the contrast he draws between "Beauty" and "the Beast" in his letter to her, 5–12 Nov 1891.

61. EC may have tried to prevail on HA to do two things: return at once to America and make an open bid for political power. The pertinent evidence is the statement in his letter to her, 5–12 Nov 1891: ". . . an elderly man . . . does not sublime to Power. . . ."

62. EC to HA, Thursday [5 Nov 1891]. In his letter to her, 5–12 Nov 1891, HA says the moment on Half Moon Street was like their whole time together in Paris and London in being "unsatisfactory."

63. As if the choice were Gaskell's, HA mentioned to Hay in his letter of 14 Nov 1891, L, III, 369, that "Gaskell mounted me on a poney." But on 14 Aug 1962, when I spoke with her, Mrs. Mary Ward, Gaskell's daughter, said oppositely that HA made the choice.

HA commonly placed himself on a footing of equality with children, not by treating them as adults, nor merely by addressing them in plain language, but instead by the harder process of becoming something of a child himself. In this instance, trying to deal with an English child, his tactic created, not pleasure, but surprise.

64. Persons who met HA commonly tried to take his measure with the help of whatever word or idea first came to mind and did not think more accurately till prompted to do so by an outside stimulus. An apposite case is that of Henry James. When Hay gave him a typescript of letters HA sent him from the South Seas, James replied, "What a power of baring oneself—hitherto unsuspected. . . ." See *HJ Letters*, III, 343. It is striking that James had not earlier credited Adams with the power.

65. It seems more than possible that Elizabeth Barrett Browning's poem was at hand in Gaskell's Wenlock library.

66. EC to HA, Thursday [5 Nov 1891].

67. HA himself pointed to his letter as the dividing point between his second life and an attempted third. Referring to it when he next wrote to EC, he called the letter his "last, or first." See HA to EC, 14–18 Nov 1891, L, III, 564.

68. HA wished others to know he was making a new beginning. In his letter to Mrs. Lodge, 25 Nov 1891, L, III, 575, he said, ". . . [I] am going in for a new Avatar."

INDEX

The index embraces the text and supplementary and explanatory materials in the notes. It excludes the preface, the acknowledgments, and (with some exceptions) the lists of principal sources in the notes, mere citations of lesser sources in the notes, and matters in the notes subsequent to the end-date of the text: November 13, 1891.

Abu Simbel, 259–60, 276–77, 512, 515, 731, 741, 744

Adam, 52, 596, 616, 800, 813, 830

Adams, Abigail (daughter of JQA2; later Mrs. Robert Homans), 506, 671, 681, 742, 842, 855–56

Adams, Abigail Smith (wife of JA; great-grandmother of HA), 193

Adams, Abigail Brooks (mother of HA): heiress, 80; accompanies husband to Washington & London, 7–8; politician's helpful wife, 660; visits Continent, 32–34, 66–67, 88–94, 96–97, 99, 101, 105, 136, 145–46; in English society, 34; travels in British Isles, 45, 65–67, 84–85, 110; London's horrors, 68; part-resides away from London, 48, 68–69, 86–89, 113–14; anticipates retirement, 66–67; learns of Sumner's engagement, 128, 682; restored to Boston & Quincy, 146, 236, 245–46, 250–51, 406, 443; new visit to Europe, 254, 260, 262–64; illnesses, 254, 344–45, 491, 529, 540, 543, 782; thought insane, 565; dies, 565–66

as mother: has seven children, 5; names HA & BA, 42, 97, 221–22, 664; HA related less to her than to Adams grandmother, 665; helped by HA, 21, 23; led by HA to Sorrento, 66–67, 88, 91–95; parodied by HA, 93–94, 673; protected & deceived by HA, 98–100, 106–110, 674–75; treats elder daughter's last days as too awful to dwell on, 213, 722; records changes in HA's life, 213–15, 217–18; question of her financing HA's editor-professorship, 722; told of HA's engagement, 257, 735; recorded as saying HA was cleverest son, 226; acquires HA as summer guardian, 529, 538, 540, 561, 565. *See also* 3, 7–8, 27,

31, 36–37, 45–48, 51–52, 73–74, 79, 82, 106, 128, 136, 139, 148, 213–15, 375, 378, 537

Adams, Arthur (younger brother of HA), 5, 659

Adams, Arthur G. (nephew of HA; son of JQA2), 877, 879

Adams, Brooks (christened Peter Chardon Brooks; youngest brother of HA): seventh child, 5; schooled in England, 24, 106; visits Continent, 33–34, 88–94, 96–97, 99, 101, 105, 136, 670; travels in British Isles, 45, 65–67, 85–86, 670; prepares for Harvard, 106; law student, 218, 283; friends with Lodge, 221; writer, 222, 291–92, 486, 529, 531; secretary to CFA at Geneva, 250–54, 272; gets into scrape in Paris, 254, 504, 661; Independent, 292, 296–97, 318; petted by Blaine in Washington, 754; attends ABA in New York, 344–45; suffers breakdown, 435–36; becomes prophetic historian & philosopher/ publishes apocalyptic book, 486, 835; spends summers in Europe, 529, 540, 561, 565; courtship & marriage, 568

as brother & brother-in-law: allied with HA, 21, 24, 57, 64, 79, 82, 146; shares London quarters with HA, 24; protected by HA, 98–100, 659, 674–75; admires & loves HA/ eager to praise him, 106, 271, 676; suggests HA marry Clover Hooper, 117, 245, 680, 731; delivers HA's "Principles of Geology," 146, 689; given space in HA's rooms at Harvard, 218, 221–22, 724; his & HA's names confused, 223, 725; taken aback by HA's engagement, 257–58, 728; invited to Egypt by HA & MHA, 283; guest of HA & MHA in Washington, 440, 478; following breakdown avoids HA, 524–

893

of mail), 73–75, 114, 678 (court dress & appearances at Buckingham Palace & Parliament), 87, 114–15, 679 (two Legations), 110 (opening despatches), 677 (using ciphers); privately rages against English & French governments for partiality to Confederacy, 55, 667–68; lends Hammond papers to Cobden/ floats idea of pecuniary compensation to U. S. for British violations of neutrality in American War, 35, 51–52, 55–57, 101; forms three-way friendship with Gaskell & Cunliffe, 57–58, 61, 93, 134, 136–37, 140, 668; finds mentor in Palgrave, 58, 133–34; drops idea of being lawyer/ revives it, 58, 77; forms tie with lawyer Evarts, 59–60; sees & feels effects of Confederate lies, 13–14, 62, 78, 669; tells English about Gettysburg & Vicksburg, 64; appreciates Seward's wartime diplomacy, 666; feels peaceful & quiet as a giant, 65; studies middle ages/ wishes he were an abbot, 66, 71; rejoices at rout of Confederate envoy from England, 67–69; as Legation detective investigates thieving butler, 67; raised a Christian/ believer but a church-avoider, 69, 670; known in family as philosopher/ has settled views of universe & animated beings, 69–70, 670; anticipates continued association with State Dept., 70–71; prepares for association with Treasury Dept., 71, 96, 670; worried by incomplete Union success on battlefield, 72, 78–79; dreads 1864 as election year, 72; makes arrangement with Bigelow/ presented to Napoleon III, 55, 59–60, 73, 670; newly exasperated/ compelled in 1861 to counteract CFA's failure to arrange appointment of needed aides, 73–74, 671; long friendly with Sumner/ raises question of his being minister, 76; sees enmity between European socialism & American democracy, 76, 671; faces conscription as aide if CFA becomes secretary of state or president, 77, 671, 675; writes cryptically about future book, 78, 671 (see also HA, *Writings: History* . . .); thinks well of Grant as supreme commander, 77–79; smokes cigarettes at Strawberry Hill, 79; conspires with MA & BA to return family to America, 79; recognizes Civil War as annihilation at will of Confederate victims, 79 (*see also* battles: *American Civil War*, Gettysburg through fall of Richmond); foresees impossibility of Lincoln's reelection as Republican, 79–80; CFA a follower/ HA a leader, 81, 671; writes to Evarts (& Seward) seeking assurance CFA can leave English mission/ text of letter/ Evarts's reply, 81–85, 671–72; with CFA recommends Moran's promotion, 84, 673–74; for second time refuses appointment as assistant secretary, 84–85; surprised by fall of Atlanta & by Sherman's ability, 85–86; invited to Wenlock Abbey, 86–87; learns of Lincoln's victory as National Unionist, 88; plans journey to Italy as device to effect CFA's retirement, 88–89, 95, 673; attempts message to Seward, 90; leads ABA, MA & BA

via Avignon to Sorrento, 90–93; encounters Gettysburg veteran, 91; fears death & prays, 92–93 (see also HA, *Writings*: "For my lost life . . ."); parodies mother/ advises father, 93–95, 673; journey forces re-manning of Legation as HA prefers, 90, 95–96; Seward turns to Hay as alternative protégé, 97, 674; HA praises Lincoln/ learns Treasury headed by McCulloch, 96; values Story's statue of knife-bearing Medea, 99, 101, 136, 675, 685; plans great life/ is already leading it, 99–100, 142; mentions Richmond has fallen/ prompts demurral by McClellan, 99–101; advised Lincoln is murdered, Seward reinjured & CFA waiting recall, 101, 675; tells CFA staying in London is necessary, 101; leads ABA, MA & BA back to Folkestone, 96–97, 99–101, 105; learns CFA2 was first Union soldier to enter Richmond, 102; HA an experimental Adams/ father & eldest brother expectant Adamses, 102–04, 675–76; says he has become more radical, 104–05; adulated by BA, 106, 676; describes CFA, 105–06; sends new letter to Evarts & Seward/ full text/ letter deceptive/ elicits desired reply, 106–11, 677; puts question of Negro suffrage to Evarts & Seward, 107, 524; shares in developing Alabama Claims/ seeks peace & friendship with England (despite contrary indications), 111–13, 677–78; works to reduce Legation's diplomatic efforts & increase its social, 113, 678; finds smaller house for Legation, 114–15, 679; propagates myth of CFA as great American, 112–13, 677–78, 852–53; welcomes future wife as Legation visitor, 115–17 (see also *marriage*); gathers historical evidence, see HA, *Writings: History* . . . ; writes two-part report/ gains acceptance at Treasury, see HA, *Writings*: "British Finance . . ." & "Bank of England . . ."; intends his writings to originate events, 110; seeks extraordinary access to *North American Review* & *Edinburgh Review*, 119, 122, 681; becomes privileged contributor to *North American*, 119–22, 681 (see also HA, *Writings*: "Captain John Smith"); seizes chance to interest Bancroft, 120–21, 124; joined by CFA2 as contributor to *North American*, see Charles Francis Adams, Jr., *joint ventures* . . . ; elicits validation of Smith article by Froude, 124, 681; uses expression "better in darkness," 124; views political strife in Washington as chance to make money/ deprived by CFA2 of intended gains, 125–28; predicts Franco-Prussian war, 127; announces retirement from *North American*, 131, 682; wishes he could guide Lowell through London, 131–32; improves as writer, 131–32; buys pictures in London as means of having Washington house, 133–34, 682–83; appears as Englishman in parody by Gaskell, 134, 683; recognizes fellow spirits in Shakespeare, Milton, Blake, Rousseau, Wordsworth, Shelley & Austen, 134, 683–84, 689; interested in prehistoric humans, 683–84; meets Congressmen Blaine, Gar-

Adams, Henry (*continued*):
  (Mrs. Lippincott), Harriet Spofford, William Vance & Mr. Adam of the British Legation, 411–12, 432, 438–39, 441–42, 445–46, 451–53, 811, 813, 823; book centers satirically on egoistic desire for place, position & office, 411; Blaine (with Gail Hamilton) construes book's Ratcliffe as representation of Blaine, 411–12, 811; book temporarily fails in its political purpose/ Blaine named secretary of state by Garfield/ HA & MHA set on their heels, 412; Blaine & Gail Hamilton drop idea of King's authorship, 412, 811; HA ceases research in State Department's archives/ with MacVeagh tries to effect Blaine's removal, 413–15; Emily Beale says *she* is represented in *Democracy*, 418–19; HA & MHA disclose authorship to Hays & organize club, the Five of Hearts, with King as fifth member, 424, 813–15; Hays not told deeper secret of not-yet-published novel (see *Esther*), 424; formation of club gives rise to desired suspicion that members wrote *Democracy* cooperatively, 424, 814; Blaine replaced as secretary of state, 427–28; James imitates *Democracy's* heroine, 431–35, 820; asks whether MHA is author, 432, 818; treats HA as historian & urges his becoming writer more like James, 433, 819; Blaine investigated by Congress for Peruvian involvements when secretary, 435–37; HA expects that Blaine is blown up forever, 436; only three copies of *Democracy* circulating in England/ author said to be MHA, 438, 820; Alice Green reports James looked severe & grave about it, 438; HA offered mission to Costa Rica as means of exiling supposed author MHA/ offer an attempted imitation of maneuver in book, 439, 820; HA renews use of book to hurt Blaine/ arranges English editions, 441, 820–21; King misreads *Democracy* when mentally disturbed under pressure of dealings with Boston magnates, 441, 445, 453, 819, 821–24, 847; HA receives inquiries from England whether MHA is author, 441; HA denies her authorship to Cunliffe/ says book is forgotten, 442; book treated in Ohio press as written by Hay, 442; HA & Hay join in exchanges involving Hay as undoubted author, 442; Blaine investigation fails/ Congress does not understand testimony, 443; book much reviewed in English periodicals, 444, 821; Hay & King criticize it as supportive of English prejudices, 444–45; King proposes a counter-novel, *Monarchy*, or *Aristocracy*, & claims to be about to start it or to have started it, 445, 452, 460, 512, 790, 845; *Democracy* pirated in England in six-penny edition, 445, 822; Hay writes & publishes an anonymous novel, *The Bread-Winners*, 445, 460, 464, 467; Howells tells James, Hay & King that he & Warner have realized that *Democracy* is work of DeForest, 445–46, 822; King suspends relations with HA & MHA, 446, 822; Hay rereads *Democ-*

racy & tells HA it is best thing of sort ever done, 449; HA arranges 25-cent American editions, 447, 822; book published in France in translation/ also in Tauchnitz edition in English, 451, 823; book selling not by copies but by editions, 451; Blaine reported to have said that MHA has acknowledged authorship, 452; Blaine & Gail Hamilton themselves head published list of alleged authors, 452; book a European sensation, 459–60; Hay sends HA copy in French & says book is read by Prince of Wales, 459–60; James reports book is talked about by Gladstone, 460; HA & MHA visit house described in *Bread-Winners*, 468; CFA2 propounds unintended joke/ publishes his theory of common authorship of *Democracy* & *Bread-Winners*, 475–76, 829–30; Blaine wins 1884 nomination/ HA's fear of him diminishing, 479–80, 483; Blaine narrowly defeated in election/ Cleveland president/ HA gains four added years at State Department archives, 484; King avoids HA & MHA, 483–84; Blaine made secretary of state in 1889/ HA's interests not affected, 559; HA amused by Harrison's behaving like president from Indiana created for *Democracy*, 559; Holt proposes new edition, 568; secret of authorship not dispelled till 1915, 325, 776–77. *See also* 670 (Treasury), 817 ("Pandora" & "Washington"), 859 (*being* George Washington)

Education of Henry Adams, The (prototype of new literary genre/ begun 1890/ privately printed 1907/ published 1918): vaguely conceived, 18–19, 28–29, 648, 661; better conceived with help of Gibbon's *Memoirs*, 661; reconsidered with help of *Alice in Wonderland*/ real HA will recount education of mock or fictional HA, 138, 676, 685–87; relation to Franklin's *Memoirs*, 134–35, 686; reflects HA's discovery of new literary genre, the education, 182, 696–97; plan for book possibly known to Taylor, 693; HA reads Trollope's *Autobiography*/ has plan for *anti-autobiographical* education, 472; book's threefold strategy, 861; ideas relevant to future book appear in HA's letters, 541–42; as prerequisite to writing *Education* HA reads & destroys early volumes of diary, 541–42; finds opening words & starts to write, 586, 676, 884; reads bad but relevant biography of Milnes, 629–30; *Education* consistent with HA's other writings, 623; book builds myth concerning CFA, 678, 852–53; key episode makes quintessential point about HA, 665; important passages misleadingly present HA's *New York Times* despatches & misleadingly date death of Raymond, 705–06; phrase misstates HA's knowledge of gold conspiracy, 712; work atrociously mis-subtitled *An Autobiography* when posthumously published, 696–97. *See also* 664 (Gladstone), 666 (meeting at Fryston), 666 (Darwin), 666 (Tennyson), 666–67 (Thackeray), 667 (Groombridge), 668 (Gaskells), 670